HALIFAX TOWN
THE COMPLETE RECORD
1911 - 2011

HALIFAX TOWN

THE COMPLETE RECORD

INCLUDES FC HALIFAX TOWN 2008-11

1911 - 2011

JOHNNY MEYNELL

First published in Great Britain in 2011 by The Derby Books Publishing Company Limited, 3 The Parker Centre, Derby, DE21 4SZ.

© Johnny Meynell, 2011

All Rights Reserved. No part of this publication may be reproduced, stored in a retrieval system, or transmitted in any form, or by any means, electronic, mechanical, photocopying, recording or otherwise without the prior permission in writing of the copyright holders, nor be otherwise circulated in any form or binding or cover other than in which it is published and without a similar condition being imposed on the subsequent publisher.

ISBN 978-1-78091-321-6

Printed and bound in the UK by Copytech (UK) Ltd Peterborough

Contents

Forewords	6
Introduction	8
Halifax Town History	10
Halifax Town Grounds	168
50 Matches to Remember	182
101 Halifax Town Greats	254
Halifax Town Managers	346
League Seasons	402
Against League Clubs	596
Against Conference Clubs	598
Abandoned Matches	600
Players of the Year	602
Sendings Off	602
Internationals	606
Halifax Town on TV	607
Chairmen	608
Secretaries	609
Minor Cups	610
Friendlies	632
Halifax Town Players 1911–2008	642
FC Halifax Town Players 2008–11	682

Forewords

I must admit to being somewhat overawed when Johnny Meynell asked if I would say a few words as a 'foreword' to this excellent account of 100 years of football in Halifax.

How great it is to be talking about football in the Town reaching such a milestone, as the history describes the numerous highs and far too many lows of days gone by. No matter, as football engenders a whole raft of experiences, played out in public, at all the different levels and yet we all come back for more. As custodians of the current football scene in Halifax I and my two fellow directors, Bobby Ham and Stuart Peacock, are honoured to be trying to put a smile back on the faces of the Halifax footballing fans, not just the older ones but involving many new fans as well.

In many ways, we cannot afford to look back as we have to ensure that what happens going forward leaves a positive legacy. For fans who have witnessed a greater or lesser part of the history described in this book, it is interesting to remember what has taken place before, to enjoy all that is good and to hope the less favourable parts are never to return. What is happening now must be enjoyed and enhanced for the future.

To be able to enjoy the future, we have been delighted that the genuine fans of Halifax Town AFC have rallied round and in true 'Dunkirk' spirit, fought tooth and nail for what they love, their football club, now FC Halifax Town. People have given their time freely to help get the club up and running again, without these genuine fans you have no future, no club. Yes, the fan base has to keep growing and it is important that we create a genuine pride in the youngsters, to ensure their first club is FC Halifax Town and not some Premiership team 40 or 50 miles away. Of course, watch these great players on the television or go see them play occasionally, but first and foremost enjoy the drama and camaraderie of supporting your local team, identify with your local football heroes and enjoy the sheer passion that is required, to be a true 'Shayman'.

Any successful football club aspires to play at the highest possible level, but it has to be within achievable resources whether these are location, financial, potential fan base, facility etc. Above all, it has to be enjoyed! Yes, FC Halifax Town reformed in the fourth tier of non-League football, and some venues have provided real challenges. Despite this, the fans have really enjoyed the experience of visiting new towns, new grounds, local travelling and moments of real fun and joy. In the three seasons of the new club, there have already been some great highlights, stunning goals, progress on and off the field and great games with that special atmosphere and drama. Oh yes, the drama, no one who was there will ever forget Garforth!

A constant in all this time for both clubs, has been the Shay Stadium and it is with great credit to Calderdale Council that the new East Stand has been completed. The town of Halifax desperately needed a venue with a modern outlook, a hub for community development in the area and now there is a facility of which local people can be proud. A venue which can be used for weddings, parties, business meetings, conferences and allows the whole area to benefit from such footfall.

No one must underestimate how important professional sport is to the Town. It is vital that the name of FC Halifax Town not only survives the next 100 years but progresses through success, as it brings profile to the whole Town and Calderdale in general. Press, television and radio are such powerful mediums and sport is paramount for all these media and so it is vital that everyone sees a positive outlook for HALIFAX.

Congratulations to Johnny Meynell in bringing this book together, a real feat. We can only wonder what the next 100 years will bring. It is amazing how all this information has been collated and we say, devour the past but please, please take part in the future. With YOU, the future is bright.

Come on the Shaymen!

David Bosomworth
Chairman, FC Halifax Town, May 2011

It gives me great pleasure to write a Foreword for the centenary edition of the Halifax Town Football Club History, of which I'm told is a work of art, so thanks Mr Meynell, I am honoured.

Halifax Town is a fantastic club who I first fell in love with during the early 1980s as a boy watching an FA Cup tie against Notts Forest. I was there supporting my uncle Russell Black, and I loved every minute of the game. Even at that age I knew that The Shay is where I wanted to play. During my time we had some fantastic moments, like beating Rushden 2–0 in front of a full house, winning the League in 1997–98 and the night of Manchester United coming to town…

Managers we had plenty…A special thank you must go to Jim McAlliog who gave me my debut at Old Trafford which I, and I'm sure all you wonderful supporters, will never forget! And also to George Mulhall who made us all believe we were the best. There have been some amazing players over the years such as Stevie 'goal machine' Norris, Rick Holden, Lee Richardson, Kieran O'Regan and Super Geoff! They were all great guys on and off the field. The supporters and people involved with the club were magnificent to me in my time and I would like to take this opportunity to say a big thank you to you all you made my career so much more enjoyable. The club has a brilliant manager and committee behind them at the moment, so let's hope Neil and the boys keep up the good work and take FC Halifax Town back into the Football League where they belong. I certainly wish them all the best.

This book will remind us all of some fantastic people who have graced The Shay and some great memories of the good old days. I hope it brings a smile to every supporters face, I know it will to mine.

Aye o Shaymem, Shaymen aye o…

Jamie Paterson
Australia, June 2011

When Johnny Meynell contacted me asking if I'd be willing to contribute a few words for his exciting book about the history of Halifax Town, I said I would be only too delighted. Halifax, were, after all, the club which gave me my start in League management, and they hold a special place in my affections.

Football has given me some marvellous memories, many of them chronicled in this book. Who can forget that incredible season of 1972–73, my first in charge, when we won our last four League games to avoid relegation to the Fourth Division? But stop up we did – on goal average. I can still see Alan Waddle rising to head home the decisive goal at Walsall in our last match. After that we competed well at Halifax despite existing on meagre attendances. But we had some good pros in our team such as David Ford, David Pugh and Dave Gwyther and we finished in the top half of the table. We even finished higher than Huddersfield!

I spent a good 20 years away from the club, managing at Bradford City and Bolton in between, but returned under John Bird to oversee the youth team. When I was asked to take over the running of the first team little did I realise what a roller-coaster of a ride it would be. With Kieran O'Regan assisting me, Halifax avoided relegation from the Conference by winning their last game against Stevenage in 1997. But I knew how I wanted the team to play and brought in players, quality ones at that, to fit the system. We won the Conference in style, with Thackeray and Bradshaw roving up the wings, Kevin Hulme marauding in the midfield, wee Jamie Paterson weaving his magic, and Geoff Horsfield firing the bullets. What a team! I sensed we were on to something when we won 3–0 at Telford early on in the season, and the players never let me down. The day we clinched the title at Kidderminster was one of my proudest days in football, and I shall never forget it.

Hopefully, the good times are returning to the club. They are certainly on the crest of a wave at the moment under Neil Aspin, and long may it continue. The supporters deserve success as much as anyone after suffering hardship for so long.

I shall enjoy reminiscing my times with Halifax when I sit down to flick through the pages of this book, as I'm sure you will, too. I'm certain it will also jog my memory of things I'd forgotten. It is a credit to the writer, and I hope it is a success. I'm sure it will be.

It's great to look back, but it's also great to move forward. Long live Halifax Town!

George Mulhall
June 2011

Introduction

It was in September 1972 that my father took me to watch Halifax Town for the first time, a game that saw Chesterfield come out 1–0 winners. It was one of three matches I saw during that season, the last being the final home game with Bournemouth which, happily, Town won 2–0. The Shaymen were then embroiled in a relegation battle which they would survive by winning their last match at Walsall three days later, but being only nine years of age, little did I understand or appreciate the circumstances at the time. I would, of course, come to get used to similar scenarios over the coming years. As generations before me had.

Not for Halifax Town an endless tale of silverware and success. More a fight against the odds, where survival has often been deemed a triumph in its own right. But for those who helped form the town's club back in 1911, none of the traumas that followed could have been foreseen, such was the excitement back then. Halifax Town have had their moments, of course, however fleeting, and many great players, either past stars or those of the future, have worn the club's colours. But with low crowds and usually with no money, for most of the time the club's existence was one of struggle. Nevertheless, for those who embraced it, as I came to do, Halifax Town became a way of life.

My own interest in the club extended itself to its history from an early age. Having initially kept my own statistics taken from old *Shoot!* magazines and *Rothmans Football Yearbooks*, I have since trawled through back copies of the *Halifax Courier*, where reports of matches and news of Halifax Town's affairs were brought to us expertly by the likes of Tom T. Dickinson (Pioneer) and Bill Carter. The Saturday *Green Final* editions, which would hit the streets within an hour of the match finishing, provide in depth coverage in much the same way that FC Halifax Town's media team do today, though it has to be said, not quite as instant! All this information has helped build up a profile of the club and its players, and at long last, this labour of love has manifested itself into the volume you have in your hands.

The timing of this club history is not accidental. The 100th anniversary of the formation of Halifax Town is an anniversary that deserves to be recognised. This publication thus encompasses the full 97 years of the original club, and comes up to date following the formation of FC Halifax Town in 2008. Fittingly, it also coincides nicely with the success brought about by back-to-back promotions.

Though very much a solo project, the author is indebted to numerous people and organisations who have kindly helped with its production. Firstly, I must thank Derby Books Publishing Company, and in particular, Alex Morton, for backing me on the project. The FC Halifax Town chairman David Bosomworth has also lent his support and has kindly written up the Foreword, and the efforts of the Halifax Town Supporters' Club through Kit Walton and Andy Gilchrist, who gave up their time to promote the book, have been greatly appreciated.

Many photographs appear within the book's pages, and for the use of these I must thank the *Halifax Courier*, who have supplied the majority. For many years Keith Middleton acted as the club photographer, and he has allowed me to use as many photographs as I desired. Vicky Senior, Kelly Gilchrist, Steve Gee and Masahide Tomikoshi have also given permission for the use of photographs from their own collections.

INTRODUCTION

My thanks go to both George Mulhall and Jamie Paterson, both Halifax Town legends in their own right, for also contributing the Forewords, and to Jack Haymer for his sterling work. Other former players and managers also gave up their time to offer information about their time with the club, and in particular I would like to thank Peter Wragg, John Carroll, Mick Rathbone, Alex South, George Holt and Lee Richardson. Secretaries past and present have also been of useful assistance, so may I thank Richard Groves and Angie Firth for their help, and to Hayley Horne, who has provided the more recent necessary information.

Most of my research has been done using the facilities at the Halifax Central Library, though I must also thank the staff at Bradford Library and Huddersfield Library, Peter Holm at the National Football Museum at Preston, and David Hanson at the Halifax Courier Library.

There are others who have willingly or unwittingly offered information, without whom my job would have been so much more difficult, so I would like to acknowledge the contributions of the following: Savvy Aslam (Port Vale), Phil Ashworth Sam Barnes, Keith Barraclough, Roger Bottomley, Gavin Butler, Roy Carter (WRCFA), Richard Catton, Phil Chadwick (Witton Albion), Barry Chapman, Tim Clapham, Luke Couchman, Stuart Deans (Partick Thistle), Simon Denton, Fergus Desmond, Ian Ellis, Craig Ellison, Ben Fawkes, Andy Gallon, Bob Gething, Michael Harker (Doncaster Rovers), Alan Jackson, Mick Jowett, Andrew Kirkham, Nick Maden, Ian Nannestad, Dai Owen, Glyn Owen, David & Jill Pickles, George Probets, Jack Ramsden, James Riley, Jez Sayle, Gordon Shirlaw, Andrew Smith, Pete Smith, Terry Sunderland, Ned Vaught (Bath City), Nigel & Janet Walker and Brian Whelan (Drogheda United).

Not least, my eternal thanks must go to my long-suffering, but understanding wife Yvonne, who has found herself undertaking more household chores than she would care for while I've been compiling this book. Without whom…

Johnny Meynell
Halifax, June 2011

Halifax Town History

Formation and Pre-League Days

Although Association Football had been played in Halifax towards the latter end of the 19th century, it was not until 1911 that a motion was set in place to form a town's club. By then, many people were casting an envious eye over their near neighbours who had formed their own, with the West Riding of Yorkshire home to five Football League clubs. The city of Bradford was lucky in that it had two, with Bradford City and the Park Avenue outfit, formed in 1895, elected members of the Football League in 1903 and 1908 respectively. Leeds City were elected in 1905, and with the popularity of the sport ever increasing Huddersfield Town was elected to the League in 1910, two years after they had been formed.

The pioneer behind Halifax Town was a certain Ernest Albert Jones, who, using the nom-de-plume 'Old Sport', wrote to the *Halifax Courier* suggesting the formation of a town's club. His letter, which was published on 20 April 1911 and invited public opinion, read as follows:

'With the growth of the Association game in the neighbouring towns of Bradford, Leeds and Huddersfield, it has become a source of wonderment why the local enthusiasts of the dribbling code are so backward in establishing a town club in Halifax, with some pretensions to class. Probably there has been, and is, an undercurrent feeling of sympathy with those grand exponents of the sister code who have from time to time written the name of Halifax on the scroll of fame, and all honour to them. Neither is it the purpose of this letter or the wish of the writer to see the grand game pass out of existence. It is simply to state a plain fact, which put briefly is that a large number of people leave Halifax on Saturday afternoons during the season, to watch first-class soccer either at Valley-parade or at Park-avenue. There are many

'Old Sport's' letter which appeared in the *Halifax Courier* on 20 April 1911, the catalyst for the formation of Halifax Town AFC.

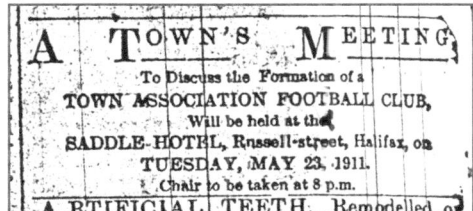

An advert informing readers of the first public meeting to discuss the formation of a town's club, which appeared in the *Halifax Courier* on 16 May 1911.

that think, and with a good show of reason, that an earnest attempt to establish a town club would tend towards keeping these people and their money in Halifax. Is it too much to appeal to some wealthy sportsmen to financially back a carefully-conceived scheme to establish a good Midland League team? It would not cost a great deal, and the nucleus of a fairly strong side would not be hard to find in Halifax.

'I therefore beg to suggest, sir, as a preliminary, that the "Courier" should invite all its readers interested in soccer to send in a post-card stating if they would appreciate and support a town club if formed, the answer to be yes or no, with no name or address, the latter, of course, not for publication. This course would in all probability give a definite reply to the query – "Is Halifax Ripe for Soccer."'

Reaction to Jones's invited referendum was in the main favourable – there were some objections from a faction of rugby supporters – and a week after his original letter, Jones wrote again to the *Courier* and predicted, 'If a team was built up on gradually progressive lines with a sound enthusiastic executive behind it, the club would naturally consolidate itself.'

On Tuesday, 23 May 1911, the concert room of the Saddle Hotel, Rawson Street, was host to a packed public meeting, chaired by Edmund Braginton in his role as honourable treasurer of the Halifax & District Football Association, where many important issues were discussed, such as finance, which League to play in, and where to play. Joe McClelland proposed three schemes by which the club could be run, and at the close, Ernest Jones proposed that 'this meeting of townsmen of Halifax heartily approves the establishment of a town's Association football club.' Halifax Town was thus formed as a public limited company with a capital of £1,000 in £1 shares, and when Charles Deantry seconded the motion, and this resolution was carried. Braginton asked for a show of hands of those willing to become guarantors of £1, and altogether a total of fifty men came forward.

A second public meeting held at the Lecture Theatre of the Halifax Literary and Philosophical Society, Harrison Road, on 8 June 1911, before which Dr Howie Muir accepted the position as the club's first chairman. By the end of this meeting, no one was left in any doubt that the formation of Halifax Town – the name proposed – was virtually a reality. Muir said that the club was very close to being a body, adding, 'We want you to feel that this is your baby, and you must all feel that you have got a strong personal interest in this club. We

The Saddle Hotel, venue for the first public meeting to discuss the formation of the club. This popular public house was originally opened in 1819 and rebuilt and incorporated into the present Halifax Borough Market in 1896. Situated on the corner of Market Street and Russell Street, the Saddle Hotel remained virtually unchanged until its controversial demolition in 1966.

feel that you must leave to your directors the formation of the club, and what food is going to be supplied to your baby. We think in a while this baby of yours will grow healthy and strong, and enter a vigorous manhood, that in time it will occupy a position like that of our neighbours, Bradford City.'

Following this second meeting, more positive moves were made with the drawing up of the first board of directors, comprising Muir, Braginton, William R. Black, Walter Tweedy, H.A. Brown, William Corner Stansfield, Egerton Denison, and later Richard Edgar Horsfall. The new club took up the lease on a Corporation ground at Sandhall Lane, Highroad Well, and 19 June 1911, the *Halifax Courier* reported that at a meeting held over the weekend, Halifax Town had been accepted into the Yorkshire Combination.

Joe McClelland, hitherto secretary of the Halifax & District Football Association, took on the mantel of the club's first secretary-manager, and using his contacts, he assembled his first squad, a job perhaps not as hard as it seemed as many players were literally queuing up to play for the club once an advertisement had been placed in the local press. Some, he said, were 'men of note in the footballing world.'

Among these were half-back Charlie Morgan, goalkeeper Horace Finch, who had made three appearances for Bradford in their Southern League days, popular local sportsmen Joe Chadbourne, Jock Nixon, and George 'Judd' Wild, who hailed from Sowerby Bridge. Several practice matches were held and the side geared itself up for the first match in the Yorkshire Combination, a tough opener at reigning champions Bradford City Reserves at Valley Parade on 9 September 1911.

McClelland was forced to draft in Clem Garforth at centre-half for his only Town appearance before a career in Rugby League beckoned, but having put selection difficulties behind them, the side almost pulled off a shock victory, taking a two-goal half-time lead courtesy through Bill Redding's brace, only for the side to run out of steam and lose 6–2, the match a personal triumph for City's John Young who scored five. And there was no joy either when Halifax Town hosted their first match at Sandhall the following week. In front of a 3,000 strong crowd, Johnson's goal from a free-kick gave visitors Scarborough both points, and Town's first victory was reserved for their third match, a 2–1 success over Knaresborough in the Bradford Hospitals Charity Cup.

Town went on to reach the semi-final of that competition and also hit form in the League, winning 11 of 12 matches up to the turn of the year, topping the table following victory at Stourton United on 30 December 1911, running up a 7–0 away success at York City on the way. Featuring at centre-forward for six matches was future Olympic gold medallist and music hall entertainer Harry Walden, who scored eight goals before being snapped up by Bradford City.

Town could not maintain their form in the League throughout the second half of the season, winning only three of their final nine games, but they did take advantage of a dispirited Heckmondwike side which turned up at Sandhall with only ten men. Skipper Chadbourne racked up a personal tally of five goals as Heckmondwike were swept aside 8–1.

Halifax Town eventually finished seventh, though they may have finished higher but for their involvement in the West Riding Junior Cup, which seemed to take precedence over the scrap for League points. The side went on to reach the Final, though it took seven games – two replays were needed to see off the challenge of Knaresborough alone in round five – to get there. In readiness for the Final, Joe McClelland sent out a virtual reserve side for the

THE HISTORY OF HALIFAX TOWN

Halifax Town players and officials on the occasion of the first match on 9 September 1911 against Bradford City Reserves at Valley Parade. Back row (from left to right): Joe Midgley (trainer), Bert Firth, Harry Street, Clem Garforth, W. Midgley (director), Harry Finch, George Houldsworth, Charlie Morgan, Joe McClelland (secretary-manager). Front row: Jock Nixon, Andy McGill, Joe Chadbourne, Bill Redding, George Wild.

League match at West Vale Ramblers for which Town were later fined, but the rest did little good for the players, who came a cropper when they met Cup holders Mirfield United at the Dewsbury and Savile Ground on 13 April 1912. The resilience the players had shown to see off the strong challenge of Barnoldswick United in the semi-final suddenly deserted them and their feeble efforts enabled Mirfield to retain the Cup, with the otherwise dependable goalkeeper Charlie Sutcliffe culpable, allowing Moon's soft long range effort in the second half to go straight in after Mirfield had held a one goal advantage at the break.

Halifax Town would enjoy even greater Cup success during **1912–13**, a season which saw them take their place in the stronger Midland Counties League, having being elected on 8 June 1912. New players arrived in the form of Harry Farren, who joined his brother Fred to form the full-back partnership, halfback Tom McGovern, centre-half Ted Wagstaffe and forwards Tommy Simons, Tom McAllister and Jimmy Whyte, while several weeks into the season, McClelland signed up the celebrated Leicestershire cricketer Aubrey Sharp. But the biggest capture was undoubtedly that of former England international winger Fred Pentland, from Middlesbrough, and it was he who scored the side's first goal in their opening Midland League match at Sandhall on 7 September 1912, though Town lost the game to Doncaster Rovers. Town's first win in the League came in their third match over Grimsby Town Reserves but while they adapted to life in the Midland League, it was in the FA Cup that they hit the headlines.

Town began their exploits with a 4–2 win at Horsforth, and their Cup run through the qualifying rounds included victory in a tense affair against Hebden Bridge at Calder Holmes, and replayed successes over Nelson and Walsall to set themselves up with a first round home tie with reigning Southern League champions Queen's Park Rangers. But when their opponents offered £200 plus half the gate receipts, Town agreed to switch the tie to Rangers' Park Royal ground, and though by doing so they greatly reduced their chances of further progression, a shock result looked on the cards as firstly Percy Roscoe saw his third minute corner kick sail straight in, then on the half-hour, Pentland, a former Rangers player, lobbed the advancing 'keeper to give Town a 2–0 lead. But the home side rallied, levelled the scores before the break through Revill and Birch, then ran away with the game with further goals by Whyman and Ovens to win the tie 4–2. But the money from the Cup hadn't made Halifax Town a rich club, and on 3 February 1913, Dr Muir launched a Shilling Fund in the *Courier*, appealing for £500.

In the League, Town experienced mixed fortunes as well as the odd selection difficulty. McClelland had been forced to play himself (not for the last time) for a game at Grimsby Town Reserves on 25 January when Tom McAllister missed his train connection, but more permanent replacements were needed when, as a result of the tight financial position, Fred Pentland was sold to Southern League Stoke City on 4 February for a substantial fee. Inevitably Town struggled without him and a disappointing run included defeats within the space of ten days by bottom club Denaby United. But they wrapped up the campaign in fine style defeating Rotherham Town 6–1, despite the sending-off of Jock Nixon for retaliation, the first Halifax Town player to receive his marching orders.

The FA Cup was the main feature of the **1913–14 season**, too. Once again the side battled through the early stages of the qualifying rounds before losing at Norwich City's quaint Rosary Street ground in the fourth qualifying round, though in the first they had set a club record by defeating local rivals West Vale Ramblers 12–0. The Ramblers had actually surrendered home advantage for the sum of £12 10s, and lived to regret it. George Whitehead was the game's outstanding player on the left wing, and though he was not a scorer, he was the instigator of many of Town's goals, with six being scored in each half. Judd Wild led the way with four, while Tommy Blackburn also scored a hat-trick. 'Keeper Bob Suter may as well have taken the day off, for he never touched the ball directly from any West Vale player.

Whitehead had arrived at the club in the close season from Barnoldswick Town and Suter was signed from Goole Town as replacement for York City-bound Sutcliffe, but he became all things and more to Halifax Town over a career spanning 20 years. Other new faces included full-back Tom Splitt, who had crossed the Pennines from Burnley, Boothtown lad Clem Longbottom, Billy Martin, and centre-half Jack Hughes, formerly of Newcastle United.

Halifax Town made a promising start to their League programme, but despite their second decent run in the FA Cup, club finances were still a cause for concern. So once the side had exited the Cup there followed an exodus of players, with forward Joe Linford, who had only been at the club for two months, Longbottom, Judd Wild and Jack Hughes all joining Bradford City within a few weeks, leading to accusations of Halifax Town acting as a nursery for the Valley Parade outfit. Offsetting these departures were the signings of Tom Beevers, Billy McCreadie, centre-half Joe Wishart, Harry Adams, Tom Hauxby, Frank Cannon, Tommy Birtwhistle, and perhaps most pleasingly, Fred Pentland, who returned in December after a disappointing stint at Stoke.

Town fell away in the second half of the season but made up for it by lifting silverware with the winning of the Bradford Hospitals Charity Cup, having reached the Final by disposing of a stubborn Heckmondwike in a semi-final replay thanks to Cannon's early goal and heroics performed by Suter. But victory came at a price. Pentland was injured early on and was forced to miss the Final against Scarborough scheduled just two days later.

Bradford Hospitals Charity Cup-winners, having defeated Scarborough 5–0 at Bootham Crescent, York. Back row (from left to right): Joe McClelland (secretary-manager), William Black (chairman), Billy Martin, Tom Birtwhistle, Bob Suter, Arthur Brearley, Joe Wishart, Joe Firth (director), unknown director, Bright Heyhirst (trainer). Middle row: Harry Adams, Frank Cannon, Tom Splitt, Tom Beevers, Jim Child. Front row: Billy McCreadie, Percy Roscoe.

The match was played at York City's Holgate Road ground but Town proved too strong and ran out 5–0 winners, with left-winger Percy Roscoe the game's outstanding player. He netted a second half hat-trick, running the length of the field for one of his goals, while another was a cross which sailed straight in, thus adding to the first half-goals by Adams and Cannon.

The **1914–15** season kicked off under the shadow of the First World War, and Town, like all clubs, were handicapped once players were signed up to help with the war effort. But Joe McClelland put together a side which at one point looked capable of lifting the title. Judd Wild returned from an unhappy spell at Bradford City to link up with Jack Scrutton, former Middlesbrough forward Fred Kirby, and the robust Dick Armitage, and Town strung together an unbeaten run of fourteen matches to go level at the top with Leeds City Reserves. In fact, had the home game with Worksop Town on 31 October been completed, Town would have opened a clear lead. Only eight minutes remained when the referee abandoned the game due to fading light with Halifax leading 3–1. 'I could not do myself justice,' he said, but this was scant consolation to the home side, who pointed fingers at the official after he himself had arrived at Sandhall six minutes late.

Inevitably the side suffered when players were called up to for military duty, though it was a ten-man Town side which secured a 2–1 victory at Goole Town on 30 January, with McClelland forced to turn out again following the non-appearance of Nixon, Armitage and Scrutton. Further selection problems had earlier seen Arthur Brearley forced to act as emergency 'keeper for the match with Sheffield Wednesday Reserves, while Town's season degenerated, having struggled to recover from their ill-fated trip to play Grimsby Town Reserves on 13 February.

The Town players and officials had set off by train from Halifax at 9.30am, and were then forced to walk the mile to Blundell Park with the winter weather at its worst. Arriving at the ground soaked to the skin, the players stripped in changing rooms devoid of any heating, and after the referee gave the game the go-ahead on a quagmire-like pitch, they played the first half into driving wind and rain. By the interval, Grimsby had run up a five-goal lead, but the drama was reserved for the half-time dressing room. With some of the Halifax players in no fit state to continue, the side refused to take the field for the second half and amid pandemonium, the game never restarted.

Despite a club official claiming that *'half the side were not in a fit condition to go on'*, the merciless Midland League Committee ordered the game to be replayed, but when they returned to Grimsby for the last match of the season, Town fared little better. They arrived at the ground with only eight players, so McClelland signed on two players, Dixon and Robinson, prior to kick-off and Town played the first 30 minutes with only 10 men before another player, Lumb, was recruited and took his place on the left-wing. Up against it from the start, defeat was inevitable and Grimsby cantered to an ironic 5–0 win.

With war still raging across Europe it was wisely decided to suspend all Leagues until hostilities had ceased. The Midland Counties League called a halt at their AGM in Sheffield on 31 July 1915 but they did sanction the hastily organised Midland Combination, of which Halifax Town were one of nine clubs to take part. The League was run on strictly amateur lines, with no trophy or medals for winners, but even so, with Halifax Town being able to call upon the services of the likes of Suter, Birtwhistle, Parton, Hibbert, Wild, Longbottom and Roscoe, they did quite well, remaining unbeaten throughout **1915–16** and dropping only one point from their seven games at Sandhall. Three successive victories during November elevated them to second place but heavy defeats at Chesterfield and Sheffield United Reserves during December saw their title hopes disappear. Indeed, it was poor away form which cost them, having failed to win at all on their travels and gaining only two points.

It was a constant struggle to keep things going at Sandhall, though of course difficulties were not exclusive to Halifax Town. Occasionally some players came straight to the ground having just worked for 26 hours. Twice their home fixture with Worksop Town was postponed, and in the end it was never played, nor was the return with the same team.

Numerous friendlies with regimental sides complimented the Midland Combination fixtures, which were concluded with a sorry 7–2 defeat at Doncaster Rovers, and though Town were in favour of playing another season in the Midland Combination, on 22 July 1916, at a meeting in Sheffield, competition was abandoned due to a lack of clubs willing to compete. When Town's application to join the Midland section of the Football League was not accepted the decision to close the club down was virtually made for them. At their own AGM on 18 August it was decided that, rather than play games at irregular intervals, activities should be suspended for the forthcoming season. Town thus ceased football at Sandhall, with the last game played there, as things transpired, being the 2–1 defeat of the Royal Engineers on 26 March 1916.

Halifax Town reformed after the war following a public meeting at the Saddle Hotel on 5 June 1919, but not without problems. The most pressing concern was that of finding a new home after neighbouring machine tool makers Asquith's had expanded their premises to help with the war effort and partially built over the Sandhall Lane playing area. The club was forced to take up the lease of a ground at Exley, though it was far from an ideal base as there was no access to it other than by foot, and the ground, situated on what was in essence a clifftop, was greatly exposed. But as Joe McClelland explained, 'It is a case of leaving the club dormant for another season or playing at Exley. Every effort had been made to get a ground elsewhere.' Money was needed to prepare the new ground and at the close of the meeting, seven directors pledged to give £10 each towards the £500 needed.

Many familiar players returned, with the line-up for the first game at Mexborough being made up of old players with the exception of left-back Bill Livingstone. Town now discarded their black-and-white-striped shirts for all-royal blue, but though they lost 3–0 at Mexborough, the following week they turned round a half-time deficit against Scunthorpe United to triumph 2–1 in what was their first ever game at Exley. But even with the additions of players such as Ted Lowe and winger Ernie Smith, the side was inconsistent. Nevertheless, McClelland was willing to pitch in local lads such as John Mulroy and Sam Robinson, as well as popular sprint champion John Pagan, though after only two games he switched codes and joined Halifax RLFC.

All told, an astonishing fifty-one players were used that season, but none was more controversial than that of Alec Turnbull. He made a scoring debut in a 4–2 defeat at Sheffield United Reserves on 29 November, but having been found employment at Campbell's Gas Company on Hopwood Lane and crossing a picket line where union members were protesting against the firm employing unskilled ex-servicemen, his was an unpopular selection and he never played again, either through politics or lack of ability.

The side was, however, bolstered by the arrivals of half-backs Brook and Slater, and at centre-forward Maurice Wellock, who had been plucked from Bradford City's reserve side. Later, left-back Jack Scull and centre-half Harold Heath also joined the club and helped Town climb to eighth place. However, the side contrived to lose their last five matches, and finished with a 6–1 drubbing at the hands of Hull City Reserves, an unhappy debut for trialist 'keeper Baker.

It hardly mattered, for by now, the club was switching attentions to the Football League. On 15 May 1919, McClelland Muir had represented the club at a meeting of northern clubs at Sheffield where they listened to proposals to form a third division comprising clubs from both northern and southern regions. But at the their AGM in June, the Football League decided to form a new Third Division made up entirely of the 22 clubs of the Southern League's first division. They agreed, however, to consider the formation of a northern section should there be enough suitable clubs, and would meet in February of the following year when a final decision would be made.

With Exley wholly unsuitable to host League football, moves were made to find a new ground, and approaches were made to the Town Clerk with a view to acquiring The Shay Estate which was currently in use as a Corporation rubbish tip. A public meeting was held on 9 July 1920 in which Dr Muir asked for public money to start the scheme, and with the *Halifax Courier* launching a fund which realised almost £400, the club took up the lease of The Shay on 4 August 1919 at a cost of £10 for the first year, £75 for the second and £100 for the third and subsequent years and work subsequently began on its conversion into a football ground.

In the mean time, the **1920–21** season so many new players join Halifax Town, among them Ernie Whiteside, Arthur Rogers, Harry Clark, John 'Darkie' Jones, David Anderson

The Halifax Town side which played at Exley in 1920–21. Back row (from left to right): John Jones, Joe McClelland (secretary-manager), Tom Birtwhistle, Bob Suter, Ernie Whiteside, Arthur Rogers, Joe Firth (director), Jack Scull. Front row: Ernie Smith, David Anderson, Tommy Stott, Tom Jenkinson, Sam Robinson.

and the free-scoring pair of Tommy Stott and Tom Jenkinson. Town made a flying start, winning their first two Midland League games and moving through the early rounds of the FA Cup at the expense of Rowntrees, of the York and District League, Liversedge and Allerton Bywater before Jenkinson's penalty saw off the challenge of Harrogate, who arrived at Exley in dribs and drabs and forced a delayed kick-off. Making the most of the time available, Dr Muir made an appeal to the crowd for £600 in subscriptions to help with the conversion of The Shay estate into a football ground, and skipper Whiteside laid down the first £1.

Town negotiated a tricky tie at Calverley, for whom Ernie Dixon scored his side's two goals in a 4–2 defeat, though hopes of progressing to the first round proper were dashed at Castleford Town and they returned to League action with lots of ground to make up. Jeffery took over in goal from Bob Suter and made his debut in the 2–0 home defeat by Rotherham County Reserves on 30 October, but this proved to be the last defeat suffered by the side at Exley as the ground became something of a fortress. The 4–0 win over Barnsley Reserves on 11 December heralded the start of an amazing run which saw them win every one of their last twelve League matches there, including the defeat of champions-elect Lincoln City Reserves on 16 April. Points, however, were hard to come by away from home, and consequently Town remained no more than a mid-table outfit.

Not that the club was too concerned. With the formation of a northern section of the Third Division by now a virtual formality, Joe McClelland and Dr Muir attended a special meeting of the Football League on 7 March, 1921 where the issue was of how many clubs to elect and which ones. Fourteen were elected *en bloc* based purely on their facilities and while Halifax Town were not among them, with The Shay conversion well under way, they were viewed favourably and they were elected themselves with 25 votes to become founder members of the Third Division Northern Section, Yorkshire's sole representative.

Joe McClelland wasted little time in team strengthening, signing Scottish duo goalkeeper Jimmy Haldane and inside-forward Jock Jamieson, and winger Johnny Whalley and they helped Town extend their winning streak at Exley to 13 games in the semi-final of West Riding Senior Cup, where, following a draw at Bradford's Park Avenue, Whalley's goal in front of a 4,000 record Exley crowd put Town into the Final for the first time, despite being forced to play the last 35 minutes with only 10 men following the dismissal of Jack Scull. But Town lost the Final 4–1 to a much stronger Bradford City side at Valley Parade, though the players and officials enjoyed a post-match reception and dinner at the Great Northern Victoria Hotel, Bradford, with the West Riding Commission.

Joe McClelland and the Early League Days

During the close season, activity continued preparing The Shay ground, while the directors recruited players for the forthcoming League season. Key signings proved to be full-backs Bill Hawley and Percy Mackrill, half-backs Fretwell Hall, Horace Howson and Sam Challinor, and forwards Fred Dent, Ernest Pinkney, John Woods and Sid Hetherington. Disappointingly, however, the first set of Football League fixtures did not present Halifax Town with a home game on the opening day. Instead, they were forced to play their first Division Three North match at Feethams, home of Darlington. Nor was there a fairytale start. Darlington, much-fancied, took the lead in the very first minute through Hooper's header, and despite a spirited performance by the Shaymen, the game slipped away from them with six minutes remaining when Dickson convert a penalty for hands by Hawley.

But such were the fixtures in those early days that Town had the chance to exact swift revenge, as the football programme gave sides back-to-back fixtures. Seven days later, on 3 September 1921, Darlington thus provided the opposition for the first match at The Shay,

A poem written by 'J.A.E.', which appeared in the *Halifax Courier* in June 1921 after the Football League fixtures informed the newspaper's readers that Darlington would provide the opposition for the first match at The Shay.

> *'Darlington, we wait your coming,*
> *Coming to the Shay.*
> *And a brass band will be drumming,*
> *On that festal day.*
> *Thousands will be there to greet ye,*
> *Hung'ring for the fray,*
> *All fondly hoping Town will beat you,*
> *Coming to the Shay.*
> *Fighters keen tho' you are 'Quakers',*
> *Coming to the Shay.*
> *You will find us far from 'Shakers'*
> *Find our 'Nay' is 'Nay'.*
> *So don't expect to find us martyrs,*
> *Though the game we'll play.*
> *You're likelier far to prove us Tartars,*
> *Coming to the Shay.*

The Halifax Town team and players before the first match with Darlington at The Shay, 3 September 1921. Back row (from left to right): Edmund Braginton (director), Bob Suter (trainer), Joe McClelland (secretary-manager), Percy Mackrill, Bill Hawley, Cecil Phipps, Fretwell Hall, Jimmy Haldane, John Woods, David Anderson, Joe Firth (director), Dr Howie Muir (chairman). Front row: Ernest Pinkney, Sid Hetherington, Sam Challinor, Fred Dent, Johnny Whalley. The Shaymen won the game 5–1.

where a crowd of over ten thousand turned out to see Town overrun their opponents and triumph 5–1. Woods had the honour of scoring the first goal, while near the end, Edmunds's consolation goal at least gave him the distinction of being the first visiting player to score at The Shay.

Action from the first match at The Shay.

Halifax Town would not score five goals again until they played out an incredible draw with Crewe Alexandra in their last match, by which time the euphoria which had surrounded the thrashing of Darlington had long since waned. The supporters had to wait a further two months before seeing Town win their second match, the home success over Hartlepools United ending a run of five consecutive defeats which had seen them slip to 19th in the table.

McClelland tinkered with the side in attempt to buck a worrying trend. The ageing Judd Wild was drafted in, as were full-backs Harry Linley and Alex 'Sandie' Watson, formerly of Bradford. But injuries hampered efforts to pull clear of trouble. Ted Humpish, a trialist inside-forward who arrived at the Shay in January, was rendered a passenger after only 15 minutes of the 3–2 win over Barrow and sat out the next three matches, though he was somewhat luckier than Sid Hetherington, who, with only three minutes remaining of Town's 3–1 defeat at Durham City, suffered a fractured leg after being hacked down by Musgrove when through on goal, and his football career was over.

Towards the end of March, Yorkshire and England cricketer Abe Waddington arrived as goalkeeper, bringing confidence to Town's rearguard. The side made a bold bid to escape the clutches of re-election, but despite concluding their fixtures with the astonishing 5–5 draw with Crewe and climbing out of the bottom two, Tranmere's 4–0 victory over Nelson meant that a draw in their return match at the Park Grounds would see them leap above the Shaymen. And so it proved. Tranmere duly drew 0–0 at Nelson to go above Town on goal average – goals scored divided by goals conceded – and not for the last time were they condemned after they had finished their own programme.

Halifax Town retained their League status by polling more votes, 42 – just two short of the maximum – than the other four candidates at the Football League's AGM on 29 May and by the time the new season began, the supporters were having to get used to new names, such as goalkeeper Herbert Bown, Cyril Treasure, the experienced Sam Blackham, half-backs Jack Lees Ellis Hall (brother of Fretwell) and Tom Langford. The forward line was strengthened by the signings of Lol Burkinshaw, Matt Ellson, Dick Crawshaw and Cliff Price, while McClelland took Ernest Dixon from Bradford City, the same dashing young centre-forward who had so impressed him when playing for Calverley against Town in the FA Cup two seasons earlier.

The side would later be strengthened by the signing of Nelson's rugged half-back Bob Wild and Town maintained their early season promise in the League – they lay fourth following a 2–2 draw with leaders Nelson on Christmas Day – and reached their second West Riding Senior Cup Final by defeating FA Cup holders Huddersfield Town at The Shay. But hopes of lifting the Cup were dashed when opponents Leeds United won the toss to host the Final, and though Town pushed them all the way, the game was settled by the only goal scored by Poyntz.

The Shaymen also progressed through the qualifying rounds of the FA Cup, too, making up for their non-admission into the competition the year before when, controversially, they had been refused entry based on the non-accessibility of the Exley ground, despite the fact that a move to The Shay was well under way. Town moved to the first round proper after seeing off Rotherham Town, Accrington Stanley – after a replay – and Midland League side Mansfield Town, but missing an injured Ernie Dixon, they went down 3–1 at South Shields.

While the income from the Cup run was welcome, it did not solve Halifax Town's worrying financial problems and just five days after the defeat at South Shields, Dr Muir told shareholders at a meeting held at the Mechanics Hall that the club was £1,500 in debt.

Halifax Town players and officials 1922–23. Back row (from left to right): Abe Waddington, Bob Suter (trainer), Joe McClelland (secretary-manager), Tom Langford, Sid Hetherington, Fred Dent, George Vallis, James Hardaker, George Feather, Herbert Bown, Jock Jamieson, Bob Simms, Fretwell Hall, Maurice Wellock. Middle row: Jack Lees, Horace Howson, Matt Ellson, Cyril Treasure, John Ballantyne, Bob Wild, Sam Downey, George Parkin, A. Booth (assistant trainer), Trevor Noble (assistant secretary). Front row: Lol Burkinshaw, Ernie Dixon, Cliff Price, Johnny Whalley, Ellis Hall, Dick Crawshaw, George Wild, Eugene O'Doherty, Sam Blackham, Percy Mackrill.

He called for more shares to be sold – 170 more were taken out on the night – and in an effort to ease the crisis, Dick Crawshaw moved to Nelson.

More players would in all probability have left the club had the side not being do so well in the League – they were lying sixth towards the end of March – but all hopes of promotion disappeared long before the season's close, though a seventh-place finish was still commendable enough. Town wrapped up the season with victory over Stalybridge Celtic, a game in which 'keeper Bown scored a penalty following an earlier miss by Dixon, which, had he scored, would have seen him reach the 20-mark for the season. Nevertheless, Dixon had proved a useful acquisition, as too had Jack Lees, converted by McClelland from half-back to full-back, a position he would fill with authority for many seasons to come.

Among the exodus of players from The Shay during the close season was that of the popular Maurice Wellock, though his departure was offset somewhat by the signing of Huddersfield Town centre-half Fred 'Tiny' Fayers, who arrived initially as player-coach. Another important capture was that of inside-forward Jimmy Moore, and with Ben Wheelhouse and George Parkin ready to step up from the reserves, things augured well. Parkin would form a formidable halfback line with Bob Wild and Ellis Hall, a feature of the side that hit the national headlines with their amazing achievements in the FA Cup.

Town showed inconsistent form during **1923–24**, however, slipping as low as 20th at one point, but capable of lifting their game occasionally, as in their 2–2 draw with relegated Wolves at The Shay on 6 October. But struggling in the League they may have been, Jackie Foster's winner against Wigan Borough gave Town the lift they needed for the following week's fifth qualifying round match in the FA Cup at non-League Peterborough & Fletton United. Foster again netted the only goal, and so began Town's epic run in the Cup. Moore's goal and a penalty save from Bown helped see off Rotherham County saw move Town into the first round where they then played three titanic battles with Northampton Town, the

THE HISTORY OF HALIFAX TOWN

Halifax Town players and officials prior to the first home match of the 1923–24 season. Back row (from left to right): Ernie Dixon, Joe Firth (director), Cliff Price, Jimmy Moore, Bob Suter (trainer), Ellis Hall, Herbert Bown, Percy Oldacre, Bob Wild, Dr Howie Muir (chairman), Joe McClelland (secretary-manager). Front row: Harry Featherstone, Frank Newman, Fred Fayers, Johnny Whalley, Jack Lees.

issue being settled at Sheffield United's Bramall Lane, where the Shaymen ran out 4–2 winners and Wild played the game of his life.

Town thus moved into the second round for the first time and travelled to Maine Road, new home of First Division Manchester City, but far from overawed, they came from behind to lead and only a lack of composure prevented them from winning. The sides replayed at The Shay four days later go when the town of Halifax came to a standstill as factories and warehouses closed down for the day to allow workers the chance to watch what was then the biggest game in Town's history. But the then Shay record crowd of 21,590 saw Dixon miss another penalty and after the game ended goalless, the First Division side made no mistake in the third match at neutral Old Trafford, running out 3–0 winners.

All the while, there was an upturn in League form, with Town moving up to sixth in the New Year, but once out of the FA Cup, the directors began to break up the team with leading scorer Dixon and Wheelhouse sold to Burnley on 11 March, followed by Parkin the very next day. The

Matchday programme for the second-round FA Cup tie at Manchester City's Maine Road, 2 February 1924.

club netted a reputed £2,100, money which the directors claimed was too good to turn down, but unsurprisingly, without such key players, results suffered, though who could have foreseen the then record 7–0 loss at Doncaster Rovers on 22 March? Joe McClelland signed Joe Lees to strengthen the attack, but the side was a shadow of its former glories and won only two of the last 11 matches.

The close season saw the further break up of the famous 'Cup team' but McClelland assembled another fine team. Harry Fryer came in to replace Bown, and centre-half Alf Dark was joined in the half-back line by Andy Martin, while up front, the supporters were soon raving at the exploits of Arthur Seabrook, Jack King and Billy Howson.

Halifax Town's sparkling new strip of blue shirts with gold shoulders – this replaced the blue and white striped shirts worn by the team since January 1921 – was matched by the performance in the 3–1 victory over Lincoln City on the opening day of the **1924–25** season and there was promotion talk, albeit premature, after Town lost only one game from their opening five. A disappointing run throughout October and November, however, saw them slip to 18th and in a bid to reverse the trend, new players arrived, notably the experienced half-back Donald Duckett from Bradford City in December. There was also the re-signing of Ernie Dixon from Burnley just two days before Christmas, and he continued where he had left off, hitting a hat-trick – including two goals in a minute – in the 3–1 win at Chesterfield, and on the back of a four-match unbeaten run, the side elevated itself into the top 10.

But while the team seemed to be heading in the right direction, chairman Dr Muir was concerned at the poor attendances Halifax Town had been getting, and on 23 February he felt compelled to write to the *Halifax Courier*. Under the heading, 'Biggest crisis in the club's existence', his letter read as follows:

The position now reached is one that demands an answer to the query: Does Halifax wish football at the Shay to continue and progress? If so, will the public support it and place the club on a firm and sound basis?

A sum of £500 is necessary before March 1st, as a minimum. Before March 16 it is absolutely necessary, to avoid other eventualities, that £2,000 should be subscribed. Providing the result in support is not adequate enough to relieve the necessities the club, the directors will have no option but to accept the offers for the transfer of players.

I, personally, am convinced that given the present team to build around, with adequate and loyal support, we are on the road to progress and promotion and financial stability, the haven we all desire.

Two days later at a public meeting at the Victoria Hall, Muir told the supporters that without more support the board could not guarantee a good team. One way to resolve the issue, he felt, was for them to buy more shares in the club, and on the night £108 was raised, and later a 'Save The Players Fund' was set up, which realised over £300.

Halifax hoped for a bigger than average gate for the afternoon visit of Crewe on 12 March. The Halifax Corporation had designated the day a public holiday for the visit of Princess Mary, who was due to open the Linford Moore Kitchenman Ward at the Infirmary. In the end, though, only around 3,000 turned up to see the 2–2 draw, but pleasingly, with the side having moved up to eighth, over 11,000 were present for the match with leaders Darlington which was also drawn. And there was another above average crowd for the final match when 9,000 watched the derby with Bradford, though after a fine end of season run-in, Town couldn't finish on a high note as the visitors triumphed 3–1.

But while the club made had been making great strides on the pitch, off it there was disharmony. At their AGM on the eve of the new season there were dramatic scenes when, with the club £7,217 in the red, T.G. Rushworth, president of the Life Members and Shareholders Association of the club, requested that all the directors resign 'en bloc' and be replaced by a committee of five to run the club for a period of three months. Though the resolution was not carried, it was a clear indication of the growing unrest, with some supporters feeling an impetus of new ideas was needed to take the club forward. However, to help improve the income stream, during the summer the Social Section had purchased a new pavilion from the YMCA and erected it at The Shay, with all monies from social events being kept by the club.

New players for the **1925–26** season included goalkeeper Jimmy 'Jack' Newton, fullback Ernie Gadsden and half-back Sandy McGinn, and forwards George Kennie and Alec Smeaton, a player who arrived as a right-winger but established himself as an inside-forward. The new season saw a change in the offside rule, where now only two players were needed to be between the attacker and goalline, and trainer Bob Suter was quick to counter this, deploying Alf Dark as the stopper. Up front, Dixon revelled in the extra freedom afforded him and went on to become the first Town player to net over 20 League goals in a season, four of which came in Town's 5–1 demolition of Rotherham United. The arrival of right-winger Sid Waites from Newark Town gave the side more attacking options and an unbeaten run of eight matches saw Town climb to fifth in November. Victory in the snow at Ashington was considered the best of the season, and when flu victim Dixon was forced to sit out two games over Christmas, Billy Howson took his place and hit a hat-trick in the 5–0 win over Walsall.

Perhaps the most thrilling game of that season came at Park Avenue on 16 January. Town were lying fifth, while Bradford held a four-point lead over Nelson at the top of the table, and not surprisingly the game attracted a great deal of attention. The attendance of

Physical jerks. Bob Suter keeps his eyes on the players as they prepare for an FA Cup tie with Rotherham United, November 1925. Don Duckett and George Kennie are on the left.

22,180 was a then record for a Third Division North fixture, and in an incident-packed game, Town came out the moral victors, despite the 2–2 scoreline, having ended with 10 men following the 80th minute dismissal of 'keeper Jack Newton for retaliation and Martin donning his jersey.

Newton later received a two-match ban, which gave the chance for the supporters to assess the credentials of young reserve Lewis Barber, who had arrived as a trialist the previous October from Broomhill WMC. Ironically, when called upon for Town's game with Accrington on 13 February, Barber was himself nursing a split hand sustained while playing for the reserves, but he performed well enough in a 1–1 draw, and again a week later in a 2–0 defeat at Durham. Newton duly returned to the side the following week, but the fans had not seen the last of Barber.

Joe McClelland gave opportunities for other players in the end of season run-in which saw a dip in Town's form. Left-back Alec Campbell, who had been at the club since September, came into the side, as did newly signed forwards Willie Cotton and John Low, but failing to find any real consistency, and with little to play for, the Shaymen won only two of their remaining seven matches and finished fifth.

For a while, it looked as if Town would better this during **1926–27**. They got off to a super start by defeating Stockport County 4–1, a scoreline which would remain Town's best opening day success for over 60 years, and they kept up their title challenge until the end of February.

Naturally, there had been changes in the playing personnel. Left-winger Johnny Whalley, having been at the club since the Exley days, retired, and his place was initially taken by Joe McCafferty, though Andy Martin, who made a successful transition from left half-back, would succeed him before the season's close. Billy Smith arrived from Rochdale, while the

The Halifax Town side that came close to capturing the Division Three North title in 1926–27. Back row (from left to right): Jack Lees, Lewis Barber, Ernie Gadsden. Middle row: Joe McClelland (secretary-manager), Don Duckett, Alf Dark, Alec Smeaton, Bob Suter (trainer). Front row: Sid Waites, Arthur Seabrook, Ernie Dixon, Billy Smith, Andy Martin.

club also welcomed back Herbert Housley and, in September, full-back Ben Wheelhouse, who returned to the club via Denaby United. New goalkeeper Jerry Best began the season in the side, though in October he would be ousted by Lewis Barber.

Town played some intriguing matches, not least the victory over Bradford at The Shay on 23 October in front of a then club record 18,866 for a League match, and they kept up the pressure on leaders Stoke City, who held a four point lead over a cluster of clubs. The eagerly-awaited Shay clash with Stoke came on 18 December, by which time Halifax Town had suffered a slump in form and the ensuing 2–2 draw suited the visitors more.

Still, that game was part of a 13-match unbeaten run which picked up its pace in the New Year with a record six successive victories, thanks in no small part to the goalscoring form of Dixon and Arthur Seabrook. Seabrook's late winner at Walsall on 2 February, in fact, moved Town up to second place, four points behind Stoke and with a game in hand. But their unbeaten run, and thus their title ambitions, floundered at Lincoln City, when a flu epidemic in the run-up to the match hampered preparations.

Halifax Town slipped temporarily to fourth, but they continued in their pursuit of Stoke, though their failure to gain even a point at 10-man Bradford, who lost Gerry Fell with a shoulder injury, meant Stoke stretched their lead, and all promotion hopes disappeared with a 2–0 defeat at Chesterfield on 26 March, the game being a personal tragedy for 'keeper Barber who uncharacteristically gifted the home side both goals.

Town slipped out of the promotion frame but they did at least surpass the 50-point mark for the first time, and Dixon set a club record when he took his seasonal tally in the League to 23. The fans also marvelled at the performances of young Ernest 'Tim' Coleman, who broke into the side in January and would prove to be one of the club's hottest properties. Town wrapped up their fixtures at newly-crowned champions Stoke, who cantered to a 5–1 win before being presented with the Championship trophy. It was the closest that Halifax Town ever got to it.

These two illustrations form part of Gallagher's 1927–28 cigarette collection. Above, centre-forward Ernie Dixon is flanked by Bradford's George McLean and Ken McDonald at Park Avenue and below, Dixon in action at Stockport's Edgeley Park.

Upon the season's close, Halifax Town released a total of seven players. 'We might be making a mistake, but we cannot keep more than the number retained,' said McClelland, indicating that, despite a successful season, the club was still in a perilous financial position. They had started the season operating £7,992 in the red and clearly money needed to come from somewhere. With Lewis Barber the club's biggest asset, it came as no real surprise when he moved to Manchester City for £1,200 that June.

Former England 'keeper Fred Fox came as Barber's initial replacement, though he would lose his place in turn to Jack Pennington, while other prominent newcomers for the **1927–28** season included half-backs Dan Brannigan, Hugh Hubbert and Webster Swift, and forwards Tom Bell and Norman Proctor, and these players helped take the Shaymen to the top of the table for the first time. In fact, by mid-October, the side had moved three points clear following some scintillating performances, both collectively and individually. They went top following the 3–1 defeat of Lincoln City on 24 September, a game which came in the middle of a club record five-match winning run. The 6–1 defeat of Ashington not only saw Town set a new club record victory, the game also witnessed what was probably the fastest-ever Halifax Town goal, scored by Proctor and timed at just 10 seconds. And a new Shay record gate for a League game was set when 19,935 turned out to see Town come from behind to win 2–1 in their first League encounter with Bradford City, following the Bantams' relegation the previous season.

Town's fine run ended at Stockport County, and the side quickly lost touch with the pace-setters, winning only one more League game before the turn of the year. Off-field disharmony may have accounted in part for this, with skipper Donald Duckett at loggerheads with the board over the team's formation and demanding to leave the club, though the board's decision to sell him just two days before an important FA Cup tie with Hartlepools United was questionable, even more so that the directors should let him sign for leaders and fierce rivals Bradford. The board, as expected, came under fire, and though the team responded in positive fashion by defeating Hartlepools 3–0, in the League the side's chances of promotion had long been diminished.

A run of six games without a win through February and March culminated in a 6–2 defeat in a quagmire at Barrow on 24 March but Town responded two days later by defeating Southport, though by then the fans had given up on the side, with a paltry 1,792 turning out, and their poor end of season form saw them win only one of their last eight games to leave them 12th. McClelland, however, was quick to point out injuries to key players such as Lees, Gadsden and Wheelhouse, plus the controversial sale of Duckett – his Bradford side went on to capture the title – all factors which he felt had contributed to Town's slide. Long spells without a home game hadn't helped, either, and McClelland felt that morale had suffered. However, he was heartened by the emergence of the likes of Coleman and Arthur Groves, players who, like Lewis Barber before them, were jewels in McClelland's side, and in Clifford Binns, who appeared in goal for the last game of the season at Wrexham, he had discovered another.

Sadly, Town were never in a position to hold on to such players, and therefore struggled to make the progress and deliver success the supporters were desperate for, and with the club feeling it necessary to release many players, Martin, Gadsden, Seabrook, Smeaton, Housley and skipper Alf Dark among them, it was clear that they were on a downward spiral.

Indeed, there were raised eyebrows when McClelland signed a 43-year-old goalkeeper in Howard Matthews from Port Vale, though he would keep the first-team position warm for Binns, whose learning curve would be spent in the reserves. Former Huddersfield Town forward Sam Taylor was a well-known signing, and others included centre-half Fred McLachlan, left-back Frank Thompson, half-backs Ted Lowson and Tom Stockdale, and a contingent from West Brom, inside-forward Sid Glidden and wingers George Hickman and Jackie Beynon. But signings such as these came at a heavy cost, and only success on the field would ease the ever-tightening financial burden attached to the club.

Yet Town made a stuttering start, not winning until their fifth match and managed to remain in the top half of the table only thanks to a succession of draws. Still, with no side running away with things, victory over Southport on 17 November moved the side up to ninth and left them just four points behind leaders Wrexham, a side the Shaymen had earlier held to a 2–2 draw in a pulsating game at the Racecourse Ground. But any faint hopes of a promotion charge diminished with the sale of both Groves and Coleman within the space of two months. Groves had come to the fore in December, and following a superlative performance against Tranmere Rovers on Boxing Day, was sold to Blackburn Rovers on New Year's Eve.

There were suggestions that Town were turning a corner when Dixon hit a rich vein of form, but the supporters were dealt another blow with the sale of Coleman to Grimsby Town on 27 February 1929. Town netted £1,250, money which the club considered vital, but that didn't stop a section of supporters voicing their anger, this letter from 'Disgusted' published in the *Halifax Courier* on 2 March, three days after Coleman's departure, being typical of the attitude of many of the supporters; *'Could not the Shay Estate be utilised for something better than a nursery for First and Second Division clubs? I notice with regret the departure of Tim Coleman, and the likelihood of other players leaving the club. Are we to spend our time on Saturday afternoons watching the Colemans, Barbers and Parkins being made for other clubs? I think our motto should be forward, not backward.'*

Halifax Town did indeed seem to be going backwards. In fact, only three more games out of 14 played were won before the close of the season, and only a draw with Rochdale ended a run of four successive defeats. McClelland introduced more new faces, such as wingers George Hickman and Cliff Foster, and 17-year-old inside-forward Sedley Cooper. Then there was the unscheduled re-appearance of goalkeeper Bob Suter.

When Matthews and Binns both reported injured, McClelland had something of a goalkeeping crisis as the side prepared to face South Shields. But cometh the hour, cometh the man, and seven years after appearing in the first team, trainer Suter, took his place between the sticks. Town lost the game 2–0, but Suter was still required to play in the next two games, a thrilling 3–3 draw with Huddersfield Town at The Shay in the West Riding Senior Cup the following Monday and another 2–0 reversal at Darlington two days later. By then Suter was aged 48 years and 288 days old, and became (and remains) the oldest player to play for Halifax Town.

Matthews returned to the side and Town reached the Final of the West Riding Senior Cup following a replay with Huddersfield, meeting First Division Leeds United at Valley Parade. But Leeds boss Dick Ray fielded an almost full-strength side, and two goals in each half courtesy of Duggan and Keetley gave United a 4–0 win and the Cup.

It would be another nine years before Halifax Town would reach the Final of that competition again, though in fairness, apart from the issue of local pride attached to it, the West Riding Senior Cup was hardly high on the list of priorities. Of more concern, in fact, was the very survival of the club itself. For on 25 June 1929, Halifax Town were referred to the Emergency Committee of the of the West Riding County Football Association, who were concerned enough at the financial difficulties which had arisen between the club and the bank. The overdraught now stood at around £1,500, but 10 of the guarantors stated they wished to be relieved of their responsibility and this meant new agreements had to be drawn up.

Bob Suter puts two players through stretching exercises, while Ernie Dixon skips to it, August 1929.

A shock departure from the club in the close season was that of Suter, who terminated his engagement in a manner which suggested all was not well, though he was not the only long-standing member to leave these shores. Before the season was out, Dr Muir would relinquish the chairmanship, and 12 months hence, manager Joe McClelland would stand down, too. The sale of record marksman Ernie Dixon to Huddersfield Town shortly into the **1929–30** season was another blow, though the £1,000 the club received went a long way to ensuring monies owed to players were paid.

With Dixon gone, the board experimented with the forward line, even trying full-back Ben Wheelhouse there, with varying degrees of success. The supporters were by now getting used to new faces such as Bernard Foster, centre-half Dick Strang, Harry Childs, Bob Schofield, Joe Roberts, and a young goalkeeper Edmund Rotherforth from non-League Pontefract Town, while in Manchester United veteran Ted Partridge, it was hoped that he could help bring on promising youngsters such as Sam Julian and 17-year-old winger Edward 'Charlie' Davies.

But it was a difficult season. Without a win in their first five matches, Town sank to the foot of the table, and remained in and around the re-election zone throughout the first half of the campaign while the future of the club came under threat. A public meeting of around 1,000 at the Shay Social Pavilion on 30 October revealed the seriousness of the situation, with Muir revealing that the Halifax Corporation had been one of the first creditors to take action against them, while two days earlier the Sheriff had taken residency at The Shay to oversee the execution of a writ by a creditor who was owed £250. In total, £5,480 14s 10½d was owed to creditors, while adding to the club's woes was a letter read out by Muir from

Charles Sutcliffe, vice-president of the Football League, which stressed that Halifax Town could not take membership of the League for granted;

'If Halifax wants League football it must pay for it…If hereafter, I can help you out in any way, please command me, but unless the Halifax public say "We will not see you through your troubles," I have no time to waste flogging a dead horse.'

An S.O.S. (Soccer On Shay) Appeal Fund was launched and this dramatic period in the club's history saw Muir, Braginton and Calvert all resign from the board on 4 November, leaving Halifax Town in the hands of directors Norman Crawshaw and William Blair, though things looked a little rosier for the club with the formation of a new eight-man board following an extraordinary meeting at The Shay Pavilion on 20 December 1929, with Blair becoming chairman, David Brook as vice-chairman, and with elected directors being Crawshaw, William Parker, J.R. Whiteley, Clarence Holden, G.H. Stead and David Cockroft, a representative of the Social Section. The Corporation also agreed to reduce the rent the club was paying provided an initial £250 was found, and Town survived, helped by the sale of young 'keeper Cliff Binns to Blackburn Rovers for £1500, a record for a Third Division 'keeper.

While the team hovered around the re-election zone and in light of Binns' transfer, Joe McClelland took the unusual step of recalling Howard Matthews, having released him at the end of the previous term. His second game ended in a 7–1 mauling at Accrington, highlighting Town's shortcomings, the position made worse when Partridge, Roberts and Hubbert severed their ties with the club. New players arrived in the shape of 'keeper Jim Wilson and much travelled striker Ken McDonald, but not helped by losing six matches on the bounce, Town found themselves needing to win their last game against Chesterfield and hope that Rotherham lost their last three if they were to avoid the re-election places. Town duly beat the Spireites 3–2 in a thrilling game, but at the same time, the Millers' 1–0 defeat of Doncaster condemned Town to re-election along with bottom-placed Barrow.

A disastrous season did not end there, either. On 3 May a motor-coach carrying Town players to meet Hull City Reserves at Goole collided with a private car at Monk Fryston. Several players were seriously injured; Sam Julian suffered head and internal injuries, Tommy Stockdale sustained a broken collar bone, while Tom Bell, Dick Strang and assistant trainer Clem Reid were treated at Pontefract Infirmary for leg injuries. On the same day, it was announced that only six professionals had been kept on by the club. 'I must confess,' wrote Pioneer of the *Halifax Courier*, 'that Halifax Town's retained list leaves me very despondent.'

He was not the only one, for it was with a heavy heart that Joe McClelland resigned his position as manager with effect from 1 July. He did so knowing

Trainer John Percy, with Norman Proctor and Ben Wheelhouse, greets new signing Dick Strang as Halifax Town return to training in August 1930.

Town had been re-elected with an impressive 40 votes at the League's AGM on 2 June, but he had become tired and frustrated at the lack of support and funds that had hampered his ambitions to make the club successful.

The Alex Raisbeck Years

On 28 June 1930, the former Liverpool and Scotland international centre-half Alex Raisbeck was appointed as Halifax Town's second manager, having worked previously at Hamilton Academical and more recently Bristol City. He arrived at The Shay well aware of the size of the task ahead of him but he rebuilt the side with the likes of goalkeeper Bernard Bilcliff, John McFarlane, Jim Barrie, Billy Hopkins, Bob Graham and left-winger Frank Betteridge, though the two most notable captures were those with Manchester United connections; Albert Pape, who had formerly been with Fulham, and David Bain, one of his former charges at Bristol City.

Raisbeck got off to a good start with successive victories over Hartlepools United and Gateshead, who had taken over the mantle of South Shields, to spark a mood of optimism. Town moved up to ninth but the new Town boss hit his first real crisis in November when Town crashed 7–0 at Chesterfield – a new record defeat – and having to rally his players for the visit of Barrow on 22 November after several had witnessed a serious accident on Skircoat Road, where the mother of Town's assistant secretary, Trevor Noble, was knocked down by a car. One player, Bob Graham, fainted and was so affected that he felt unable to play.

Getting among the goals was Pape, but he was forced to sit out the side's FA Cup second round match at his former club Fulham through illness. Town had won through at the expense of non-League Mansfield Town side courtesy of Sedley Cooper's late angled drive in a replay at Field Mill, but there were no such thrills at Craven Cottage, where Fulham, from the Third Division's Southern Section, cantered to a 4–0 victory.

Out of the Cup, Town concentrated on League affairs but sunk to new lows. They suffered a record home defeat when they were humiliated 5–1 by Carlisle, and two days after playing out a 1–1 draw on Christmas Day with Hull City, collapsed alarmingly in the return at Boothferry Park. Hull inflicted on the Shaymen a new record defeat by running out 10–0 winners, with Simeon Raleigh leading the rout with five goals. It was a result which

Director David Cockroft shows off a cake sent to the club by a well-wisher, March 1931. Players Bernard Bilcliff (left), Fred McLachlan and Dick Strang cannot wait for him to cut it.

prompted Tom Dickinson of the *Halifax Courier* to write, 'From first to last Halifax Town were a beaten collection of ragged units,' and shell-shocked, the side lost their next four matches and slipped into the re-election zone.

Moral in the camp was not helped by the announcement in January of chairman William Blair's decision to stand down to concentrate on new business affairs in the Midlands. This at a time when Town were averting probable suspension by the West Riding Football Association after initially failing to produce receipts of a home match and entering into urgent talks with the club's guarantors, calling on 100 loyal supporters to loan the club £5 each year for the next five years.

Meantime, Raisbeck managed to improve things with the re-introduction of McLachlan to allow Bain to move to the forward line and the promotion from the reserves of wingers Charlie Davies and Frank Betteridge. Though Town failed to put together a consistent run of form, re-election was staved off with victory at Rochdale with two games still to play.

Halifax Town's financial woes, however, continued into the close season, though eased slightly by the sale of Sedley Cooper to Sheffield Wednesday in June. But the club was still in a perilous position, as David Brook, who succeeded Blair as chairman at the end of July 1931, quickly realised. Things were so bad that on 28 October 1931 he called a special meeting 'to consider a matter of vital importance' and revealed that, with the club losing £35 a week, an extra 2,500–3,000 supporters were needed if they were to balance the books. But for the sale of Cooper, Halifax Town would surely have gone the same way as Wigan Borough, who, just four days prior to Town's crisis meeting, had been forced to resign from the League with mounting debts.

Wigan, in fact, had been one of the few teams Halifax Town had beaten during those first two months of the **1931–32** season, though the points they gained from that victory were naturally wiped off their record. Town's winning goal there had been scored by Ted Crawford, one of several newcomers to the club, the most prominent being that of Billy Mays.

With things looking bleak for the club, it was to the FA Cup they pinned their hopes on survival, thus their first round tie at Midland League Newark Town was viewed as one the Shaymen simply dared not lose. Amid mounting tension, Mays' goal secured Town a draw after Hill had given the home side a fourth-minute lead, and they scraped through in The Shay replay. They then accounted for 10-man Accrington – their 'keeper Jack Bell had been sent off for querying a free-kick – in front of 11,648 paying customers, and an even bigger gate saw the Shaymen exit at the hands of Bournemouth, though the receipts were more than welcome.

Halifax Town 1931–32. Back row (from left to right): John Percy (trainer), Alex Raisbeck (secretary-manager), Ben Wheelhouse, Bernard Bilcliff, Charles Helliwell, John Walsh (director), Albert Hanks. Middle row: Tom Donaldson, John McFarlane, Ted Crawford, Joe Johnson, Frank Betteridge, Dick Strang. Front row: Ted Read, Joe McGrae.

Town soon came back down to earth from their Cup exploits. Just seven days later they crashed 9–1 at Lincoln City, with free-scoring Frank Keetley returning to their side and helping himself to six second-half goals. It was yet another embarrassment for the Shaymen, who ironically had been the first side to beat the Imps back in September.

Results would improve – Town scored four in three successive matches towards the end of February – but with poor attendances chairman Brook was still a worried man, evinced by his letter to the *Halifax Courier* on 28 March 1932 in which he urged supporters to take up more shares to 'judiciously acquire and develop that successful team which we are so desirous of seeing, and which would create enthusiasm for good clean sport.' Another public meeting was held in the Shay Pavilion on 1 April where Brook and his directors threatened to hand in their resignations unless the supporters raised £1,000 before the end of the season.

The club issued a Shares Appeal and terminated the contracts of Bain, McGrae and Hopkins, but the uncertainty affected the rest of the players and only two of the last 10 matches were won. Town finished a lowly 17th, but safety had long since been assured since Wigan's resignation and Rochdale having been cast well adrift for months.

The real success story of the season had been the form of 21-goal Ted Crawford, but he, like others before him, was sold to ease the cash crisis. His transfer to Liverpool was pushed through with immediacy following David Brook's announcement at a shareholders' meeting on 20 May 1932 that £700 was needed to pay wage arrears amounting to £90 and the club had faced yet again possible suspension. He also sounded a cautionary note, adding that 'if we are going to be £1,000 behind nothing at the end of the season, or if we are going to transfer any more players, I am going to say I don't think it is worth while carrying on.'

Strang and long-serving Wheelhouse also departed, and Raisbeck's new look side featured well-known goalkeeper Watty Shirlaw, half-backs Oliver Thompson and Albert Cooke, and Ted Craig and the unknown Bill Chambers, signed from non-League Darlaston. Maurice Wellock also returned, as did trainer Bob Suter after a two-year absence.

Town recovered from a heavy opening day defeat at Accrington to move up to sixth, but when they began to lose their way, Raisbeck signed the former Irish international full-back Hughie Flack, and in November, old favourite George Parkin just in time for Town's venture into the FA Cup. Stirring up memories of the Cup run nine seasons earlier, the Shaymen exceeded all expectations, accounting for Lancashire

Halifax Town take on Chester in the fourth-round FA Cup replay at The Shay, 2 February 1933. Fred Brown (second left) challenges for the ball, supported by Charlie Davies (right).

THE HISTORY OF HALIFAX TOWN

A long-distance view of Halifax Town's FA Cup tie with Luton Town showing the pitch at The Shay covered in snow, 18 February 1933.

Combination champions Darwen, North Eastern League side Workington and Doncaster Rovers, before finally overcoming Chester in round four. Town had forced a draw at Sealand Road and memorably won The Shay replay on a Thursday afternoon in front of 14,000. Bob Suter Jnr was forced to stand in for injured Shirlaw, and Davies netted an extra-time winner to send Town into the fifth round for the first time.

It was then that Alex Raisbeck went out and signed arguably Town's greatest-ever player, the former England international winger Fred Tunstall from Sheffield United. His first appearance against Gateshead helped swell the gate to 7,477, but in the run up to the fifth-round meeting with Luton Town in the FA Cup he and his new colleagues experienced heavy defeats at Walsall and Stockport County.

Luton were only a Third Division South outfit and Town had every chance of progressing to the quarter-finals, but their hopes disappeared with the blizzard, so fierce at one point that the referee was forced to take the players off the field for 25 minutes. The

Former England international winger Fred Tunstall (right) shakes hands with Maurice Wellock following his signing from Sheffield United, 4 February 1933.

visitors, with the elements in their favour in the first half, scored through Tommy Tait and added a second after the break, and it was they who went through to meet Everton.

Tunstall went on to woo the crowds, but the Shaymen failed to capture the form that had served them well in the Cup. Manager Raisbeck, though, had found a useful goalscorer in Chambers. He finished with 20 League goals but would score more prolifically the following term.

Halifax Town began the **1933–34** season with a new chairman, Charles Mattock succeeding David Brook at the club's AGM on 23 June 1933, and a balance sheet which was one of the best the club had ever produced. The steady improvement under Raisbeck continued, for having kept most of his players, the side reached the third round of the Cup, though the season would mostly be remembered for an aberration at Stockport in January.

Chambers and Tunstall scored prolifically early on and Town moved up to fifth following victory over Walsall on 7 October, and the side was strengthened further with the arrival of Arthur Mercer from Chester in November. It was an exciting period for the club, for as well as going well in the League, the side progressed to the third round of the FA Cup following an exciting 3–2 success over Barnsley at The Shay and replay victory at Hartlepools where Cooke slammed home an extra-time winner in the fading light.

Town's reward was an away tie at Second Division Bolton Wanderers scheduled for 13 January 1934 but by the time that game came around, they had slipped slightly in the League after losing heavily at Barrow and Hartlepools, and there was concern over goalkeeper Shirlaw. In an earlier victory at Rochdale he had received a thigh injury but had continued to turn out for the club. Now, as they prepared for the trip to Stockport on 6 January he was declared unfit and reserve Stanley Milton was drafted in.

Milton apart, it was an almost full-strength side which took to the field at Edgeley Park, and though Stockport were lying second, Town were only three places below them and there was no reason to expect anything untoward, even when Joe Hill gave the home side a two-goal half-time lead. But in the second half, Town collapsed alarmingly and County ran in 11 goals for an unthinkable 13–0 victory and forcing Tom Dickinson to quip in his report for the *Halifax Courier*: 'What was this – a football match or a whist drive?'

The result, which catapulted both Stockport and Halifax into the record books, was doubtless a fluke, and certainly at Bolton a week later the players showed much more spirit. Tunstall gave Town an 18th-minute lead, but the turning point appeared to be his second half shot which hit the post. Bolton survived and eventually took control to run out 3–1 winners.

League-leaders Chesterfield felt the backlash from the Stockport debacle as Town ran out 5–0 winners on a frost-bound pitch, with Chambers netting a hat-trick. He later scored three goals in a 6–2 win against Southport before going even better when he became the first Town player to net five goals in a game when Hartlepools were beaten by a similar scoreline on 7 April. Town wrapped up their fixtures with a 4–2 victory over Rochdale where Chambers started the scoring to take his tally for the season to 30 – the first Town player to reach such a total.

Bill Chambers's scoring feats had not gone unnoticed, yet his record £2,600 sale to First Division Bolton Wanderers on 6 July 1934 provoked an angry backlash from the supporters. After all, only two weeks earlier chairman Charles Mattock had told the club's members at the AGM, 'We have stopped going backwards, we have just started to go the other way, and the outlook is encouraging.'

The Halifax Town squad that embarked upon the epic 1934–35 campaign. Back row (from left to right): Bill Allsop, Stanley Milton, Watty Shirlaw, Jock Taylor, Bill Banner, Syd Brobbins. Standing: Maurice Wellock (trainer), Gordon Presgrave, Arthur Mercer, Sid Helliwell, Bert Cooke, Frank Betteridge, Charlie Davies, Ted Craig, .. Hall, Alex Raisbeck (secretary-manager). Seated: Albert Valentine, George Millington, Dan Ferguson, Swaine, Fred Tunstall. Front row: Billy Atherton, Jim Hollingworth, S. Jackson.

Chambers's sale, however inevitable, left Raisbeck seeking a replacement, but he found one in Macclesfield Town centre-forward Albert Valentine, a player who had just scored 83 goals in the County Cheshire League. He was not the only newcomer, of course, with Raisbeck also snapping up outside-left Billy Atherton and inside-left Wilf Feeney, as well as Port Vale full-back Bill Allsop, a player who would go on to give Town great service over 16 seasons.

The football played by the Shaymen in the early part of **1934–35** gave real hope of promotion as they mingled with the front runners. By December, thanks to an unbeaten run of eight matches, which included seven victories, they had opened up a six-point gap with Tranmere Rovers at the top of the table, and with the side riding high, chairman Mattock made clear his and the club's intentions. 'We are out for promotion,' he proclaimed, then to prove it, he sanctioned the signing of crafty inside-forward Tom Barkas from Bradford City on 14 December 1934, at no little cost.

Barkas made his debut against Doncaster Rovers, menacingly placed in third, in a game ultimately abandoned because of fog. Town were trailing at the time, but who was to say, given their fine run of results, that they would not have turned the game around and thus altered potentially the outcome of the Championship? More damaging, perhaps, was the 2–0 home defeat by Chesterfield on Christmas Day when some questionable decisions by Nottingham referee G. Jones saw Town's unbeaten home record go.

That was the first of three consecutive defeats which put a serious dent in Town's promotion aspirations, and worse was to follow when they lost a must-win game at home to leaders Tranmere on 9 February 1935. Still, Town kept up their pursuit and moved to within three points, helped by a five-goal haul by Valentine in the 6–2 victory over New Brighton. But the team to watch were Doncaster, who hit a rich vein of form, went top at the end of March and opened up an unassailable lead. The Shaymen virtually conceded the title in defeat at Stockport on 13 April, and though they notched home wins over Crewe and Hartlepools, Doncaster were crowned champions on 27 April. When they hosted Raisbeck's side on 2 May, the Rovers players ran out to *See The Conquering Hero Comes* played by a local band, although Valentine put a dampener on their celebrations five minutes from time when he fired home the game's only goal, his 33rd of the campaign, and two days later, Betteridge's strike ensured that Town not only completed a League double over the new champions, but also moved above Chester to claim the runners'-up spot.

During the close season, Alex Raisbeck announced his battlecry: 'We want promotion. It is what we are here for. We are not here to mess about in the Third Division if we can get out of it. We want to go up with a credit balance and if we can reduce our liabilities next year as well as we have this year, then we are ready for the Second Division.' But despite bringing in a crop of new players such as goalkeeper Cliff Owen, full-back Idris Williams, half-backs Alf Pope and Jack Coode, and Clem Smith, a prolific goalscorer with non-League South Kirkby Colliery, the side soon found themselves off the pace, their cause not helped by injuries to key players, with Valentine, Tunstall, Feeney, Pope and Davies all spending at least some of the time on the sidelines.

The Shaymen managed to remain in the top half of the table throughout the first three months of the **1935–36** season, lying eighth at the end of October, five points adrift of second placed Lincoln, but a poor run during December and January saw them slip as low as 18th. Inconsistent in the League, however, Town did at least raise their game in the FA Cup, for after a comfortable 4–0 victory over Rochdale in the first round, they played three pulsating games with Hartlepools, though ultimately they were to bow out to their north-eastern rivals at neutral St James's Park, home of Newcastle United.

When Clem Smith broke down in training in November, Raisbeck secured the services of Billy Merry from Manchester United and handed debuts to Bill Joyce, a Hebden Bridge youth, and Joe Mills, but the side began to falter alarmingly. Even Cup conquerors Hartlepools managed to win at The Shay for the first time and the supporters quickly began to lose confidence in the side which had become a battered remnant of an already weakened team, with eight players on the injury list.

Valentine's four-goal haul at Oldham Athletic was one of few highlights in the second half of the season as the fans voted with their feet. Only 3,690 turned up for the visit of York City – almost 2,000 fewer than for the corresponding fixture the previous season – forcing the directors to issue a rallying call once more. But the transfer of star winger Charlie Davies to promotion-chasing Chesterfield on 13 March hardly lifted the spirits. Though the fee was not a large one the directors had felt compelled to sell one of their brightest stars to help compensate for lack of revenue through the turnstiles. Davies would help his new club to the Championship, though Chesterfield would be grateful to the Shaymen who sprang a surprise by completing the double over title rivals Tranmere during the Easter period.

Town ended an injury-ravaged campaign in 17th place, and though Valentine, by scoring in the final match, a 2–1 defeat at Walsall, reached 30 League goals for the second season running, manager Alex Raisbeck felt he had taken the side as far as he could. When Chester boss Charles Hewitt left to take over at Millwall, Raisbeck came out on top of a large number of applicants for the vacant position at Sealand Road and on 12 May 1936 the Halifax Town directors agreed to release him from his contract and set about seeking a successor.

Jimmy Thomson and the War Years

Raisbeck remained at The Shay until his successor was found, overseeing the signings of half-backs John Molloy, George Brown, and outside-left Jimmy Murphy, players it was hoped would help offset the departing Frank Betteridge, Bert Cooke, Jack Coode and Fred Tunstall, who left to take over as player-manager at Boston United.

On 15 June 1936, the board appointed as Halifax Town's new secretary-manager the former Coventry City and Bury full-back Jimmy Thomson, who, upon his arrival, said, 'I am sure that given a fair chance and a fair share of good fortune they would soon be able to see Halifax Town take up its correct position in the football world as one of the leading Yorkshire clubs.' In readiness for his first season in charge, he also signed up the veteran half-back Albert Watson, winger Ralph Evans, as well as forward Gladney Robinson and goalkeeper Tom Collier after both had impressed in the pre-season trial matches.

Town made an encouraging start, and with Valentine in free-scoring form, they moved to within one point of Chester at the top. But this was not form they could maintain, and by mid-October, they were well off the pace. Missing the influential Barkas for two months with appendicitis, Town suffered some embarrassing losses, not least the 6–0 drubbing at

New manager Jimmy Thomson meets his players: Tom Barkas, Bill Allsop, Sam Chedgzoy, Alf Pope, Idris Williams, Ted Craig and George Brown, August 1936.

Rotherham United, where a local pressman went on record as saying, 'I don't see how, with all the good will in the world, it is possible to make out a case for Halifax at all. I've never seen a more one-sided match,' and a week later Town slipped out of the FA Cup at the hands of Darlington.

The side was ever-changing, as Thomson introduced half-back Wyn Thomas and winger Ted Widdowfield, but it was the eagerly awaited return of Barkas which perhaps inspired Town when they defeated leaders Chester three days after playing a 1–1 draw at Sealand Road. Clem Smith grabbed the game's only goal in what was regarded as Town's best victory of the season, shading even the 6–1 demolition of Carlisle in their very next match.

That victory over Carlisle was one of several high-scoring matches involving the Shaymen; seven days later they went down 5–3 at York City, and then there was the amazing Good Friday victory by the same score at Rochdale, played in wintry conditions, where Ernest 'Budgie' Hoyland, recently signed from the Rawmarsh Firbeck club, grabbed two goals within the first nine minutes to open his account.

Full-back Harold Jackson was another player who came into the side, making his debut in Town's surprise victory over promotion-chasing Hull on 6 February following the sudden departure of left-back Alf Pope to Hearts three days earlier, yet that victory, however commendable, was only the forerunner to a five-match winless streak, ended ironically by the high-scoring affair at Rochdale. Top scorer Valentine failed to get his name on the scoresheet at Spotland, but he quickly put things to right the very next day, scoring all Town's goals in the 4–1 win over Rotherham. The Shaymen went on to complete a happy Easter programme by doing the double over Rochdale, and by losing just two of their last 10 matches, climbed from 13th to finish seventh.

Valentine ended with 27 League goals to his name, but that did not stop manager Thomson putting him on the transfer-list and selling him to Stockport for just £250. But that wasn't the only shock. Keen to stamp his authority at the club, he also saw fit to terminate the employment of trainer Maurice Wellock and replacing him with Harold Taylor.

Valentine's initial replacement came in the form of the expensive Les Copeland from Chelsea, and he, along with Cliff Birks, Hugh Campbell and Steve Griffiths, made his debut against Alex Raisbeck's' Chester, for whom Clem Smith featured in the forward line. The game ended 1–1 but the point from that game was the only one Town gained from their opening six matches of the **1937–38** campaign and a 3–2 home defeat by Rochdale in the last of those saw them sitting bottom of the table. 'Keeper Tom Collier, who had come into the side after Owen had suffered a back injury, was on the losing side in each of his first three games, but with Owen restored Town recorded their first victory at the seventh attempt over Hull City.

Thomson endeavoured to blood new players, and the likes of Adam Dawson, Andy Pritchard, Gordon Rose and Harry Scott all made their debuts during the first half of the season. Another player, Horace Green, was also handed his first team start in a West Riding Senior Cup tie against a strong Second Division Leeds United side at Elland Road, and he would hold down a regular place in the side that season. Town climbed the table, but bowed out of the FA Cup in the first round, having seemingly done the hard work when gaining a draw at York City, Reg Baines running through to score the game's only goal for the Minstermen in The Shay replay.

THE HISTORY OF HALIFAX TOWN

Halifax Town 1937–38. Back row (from left to right): Harold Taylor (trainer), Harold Jackson, Cliff Birks, Andy Pritchard, Cliff Owen, Hugh Campbell, Wyn Thomas, Les Copeland. Front row: Ted Widdowfield, Steve Griffiths, Bill Allsop, Ted Craig, Tom Barkas.

Perhaps the most memorable match of the season came at Accrington Stanley on 15 January. In treacherous conditions, the home side ran up a three-goal lead before Widdowfield pulled a goal back five minutes before the interval. With the wind at their backs in the second half, Widdowfield scored twice more to level the scores, then ran fully fifty yards through the mud for a breathtaking solo winner five minutes from time. Widdowfield was Town's hero at Hull City two weeks later, too, when he scored a late winner as Town confounded the football prophets, but making the last of just 30 appearances in that game was Hoyland, Town's flying winger, who joined Blackpool two days later.

Halifax Town attack the Bradford City goal in front of over 13,000 at The Shay on 9 October 1937. The visitors won 2–0.

Hugh Campbell came into the side, but only three League games were won from their final 13 matches, though there were some highlights, including Sammy Clark's first Town goal in the 2–0 home win over New Brighton on 26 February, a vicious 45–yard free-kick from near the touchline, and a 2–1 victory over promotion-chasing Oldham Athletic, a game which saw new 'keeper Charlie Briggs make his debut. Re-election was never a serious issue, though, and victory over Lincoln on Easter Monday mathematically ensured Town's safety with three games still to play.

The lack of a potent goalscorer had hampered Town, and would continue to do so in the Final of the West Riding Senior Cup, which they had reached after overcoming plucky Yorkshire League side Goole Town. Goole hosted the Final but the Shaymen were left to rue several missed chances early on and opponents Selby Town ran out 2–0 winners.

While the close season saw the departures of directors Clifford Heaton and William Parker, replaced in turn by Cyril Adams and H. Button, manager Jimmy Thomson saw no reason to make wholesale changes to his squad, for while 'keeper Owen was allowed to leave having lost his place to Briggs and Copeland retired from the professional ranks, the only major additions were those of wingers Stan Wood and Jabez Foulkes, and in September, of Alex Graham, whose arrival increased speculation that Town were about to offload star player Tom Barkas. Town's skipper had been linked with Newcastle, though Thomson was quick to refute such speculation, especially as his side made a poor start to the **1938–39** season and he needed to keep his star player. Though Town won their opening game, they wouldn't taste victory again until October when Barkas showed his worth to the team. He laid on the first minute winner for young debutant Fred Mason in the match with Barrow, then scored with a thumping header against Rochdale on 15 October before grabbing the only goal in a rare away victory at Rotherham United.

The fact that Barkas remained at The Shay, however, was probably more to do with the side's involvement in the FA Cup, where Town memorably reached the third round for the third time. Goalless draws in the League at home against Doncaster and Crewe did nothing to suggest a goal fest when Rochdale arrived at The Shay for the first round match, but in an amazing game Town came from twice being behind to win 7–3, with Widdowfield, making the successful transition from the wing to centre-forward, scoring four.

If that game was memorable, so too was the second-round affair with Mansfield Town, who at first glance offered innocuous opposition. But incredibly the tie lasted 450 minutes before being settled by Bungay's unfortunate own-goal for the Shaymen with just 3½ minutes of extra-time in a third replay at Old Trafford. First Division Birmingham City awaited Town in round three, and though relegation-bound, they ran out 2–0 winners with goals either side of the interval from Jennings and Phillips.

The money Town netted from their Cup run compensated somewhat for the failure to sell Barkas, though who knows how they would have fared had he gone. Already without long term causalities Clark and Brookes, manager Thomson also lost Graham for several weeks after he suffered a dislocated shoulder against Darlington in January, and for the League meeting at Rochdale the Town boss had to throw in young goalkeeper Ernie Ferneyhough after Briggs suffered a bout of quinsy. At the beginning of the season, two games between Town and Rochdale in the Jubilee Fund had produced an amazing eleven goals, and the FA Cup match a further 10. Now Ferneyhough found himself playing in yet another astonishing game with their rivals from over the Pennines, but one in which the

Halifax Town drew 3–3 with Everton in Ted Craig's Benefit Match on 29 April 1939. Standing: Keenan (Everton), Steve Griffiths, Harry Hutton, Davies (Everton), Morton (Everton), Charlie Briggs, Mr Pickering (Everton), Cunliffe (Everton), Bell (Everton), David Cockroft, Horace Green, Lindley (Everton), A. Barber (Everton), Harold Jackson, E. Barber (Everton), Lambert (Everton), Bill Allsop, Stan Wood, Mr W. Adams, Harold Taylor (trainer). Front row: Ted Widdowfield, Gee (Everton), Ted Craig, Jones (Everton), Jake Ruecroft, Tom Barkas.

Shaymen held out for a 5–4 victory. This result came in the middle of a 10-match unbeaten run which culminated in the 5–1 destruction of Carlisle United on 25 March, and further wins over Hartlepools United and Hull City enabled Town to finish a commendable 12th.

The **1939–40** season got under way with war looming, but with new players Walter Bruce, Jack France, Sam Doran and the powerful centre-forward Reg Baines in the side, Town made a promising start. Having achieved two wins and a draw from their first three games, they were lying second behind Accrington Stanley when war was declared on 3 September, whereupon the Football and Scottish League programmes were immediately cancelled and all contracts between clubs and their professional players suspended.

Two days later, however, plans were drawn up to form a wartime League in West Yorkshire and Lancashire composed of clubs in neutral and reception areas, and on 2 October 82 clubs agreed to take part in regional competitions, with Halifax Town included in the North-East Division. The Football League allowed participating players to be paid 30s, while also sanctioning the use of guest players who were stationed locally. For Town, the North East League meant competing against bigger clubs, while for the spectators came the opportunity to view big-name players, not only in the oppositions' sides, but also their own.

While many players were immediately called up for war action, Jimmy Thomson was fortunate that he could initially call on the services of Horace Green, Jake Ruecroft, Tom Barkas and Stan Wood, and for the duration of the war years, full-back Bill Allsop.

Town had engaged themselves with friendlies with Leeds United, Bradford, Sheffield United, Oldham Athletic and Barnsley to extend their unbeaten start to eight games, but once the North East League began there was an immediate downturn in form. Town crashed 5–1 in the first match at Bradford City, and continued to struggle, their 4–1 home

Halifax Town players back in training, August 1939.

reversal with York City on 18 November particularly galling. Included in Town's line-up for that match was their first guest player, Huddersfield Town's Johnny Mahon, but the following week he scored the winner against the club that officially employed him as the Shaymen pulled off a shock 2–1 victory at Leeds Road over a Terriers side containing six internationals.

Town came up against well known players such as Middlesbrough's George Camsell, and Albert Stubbins, who inspired Newcastle United to a 4–3 win at The Shay, and while they struggled in the League, this difficult time was compounded by the winter blast which left them without a home game for two months. It was not until 2 March that Town returned to action, Stan Wood scoring a pile-driver to earn Town a point in a 2–2 draw with Bradford City.

Thomson had called upon Burnley goalkeeper Ted Adams for that match, and the following week Huddersfield Town's international 'keeper Hugh Turner took his place in the side for the visit of Hartlepools United, along with former crowd favourite Charlie Davies, who, after having made his availability known to the Town boss via the *Courier's* Tom Dickinson, went on to play five games. Turner stayed a little longer and featured in some memorable games, notably the 1–1 draw with a Wilf Mannion-inspired Middlesbrough on 6 April, and the match with Leeds United on 25 May, where Town came from two goals down to win 3–2.

By then, Town had already bowed out of the Wartime Cup at Hartlepools but responded by racking up their best victory of the season when defeating Stockport County 4–0 at The Shay. But this game was only a friendly and was watched by a meagre crowd, prompting the directors to review their policy of playing such games. 'The substitute programme for normal League games has been a complete fiasco. It has failed entirely to recapture public interest,' they stated. Town's League programme itself was wound up as late as 29 May when they travelled to Newcastle United, but with five guest players in the side they were humbled 6–1.

Changes to the structures of the regional Leagues were introduced for the **1940–41** season, with the Football League decreeing that north and south groups would be used, but with this resulting in clubs not playing each and every other, the League placings were determined by average points.

Thomson called upon the likes of Freddie Hogg, who had starred against them for an Army X1 in a friendly, Vic Orton, Tom Chester and goalkeeper Ted Rayner, who was on the books of Scarborough. Alf Pope, now engaged in the RAF, also made a welcome return, appearing in the side for the opening fixture in the North Regional League against Hull and scoring both goals in the 4–2 defeat. Town didn't win until their fourth match but overall Thomson was pleased with their performances, especially the 1–1 draw against a Huddersfield Town side which included eight regular first-teamers.

The best result came against Bradford City, a handsome 5–1 victory which compensated somewhat for the hike in entrance admission tax forcing up the amount the supporters had to pay at the turnstiles. Success here heralded something of a purple patch for the side, with further victories being gained against York City, Hull City and Oldham Athletic, although probably the most exciting game was that at Bury's Gigg Lane on Christmas Day. Having been allowed to draft in Bury youngster Frank Pollard after Jake Ruecroft missed his train connection, the Shaymen played out a 5–5 draw after going three goals up within 15 minutes, the first – and so far last – time that Town had played in such a high-scoring draw since 1922.

Among the best matches during the second half of the campaign were the derbies with Huddersfield in the West Riding Senior Cup. Town lost the first leg 2–1 at The Shay, but reversed the scoreline at Leeds Road the following week in a game which went to extra-time. Thomson won the toss for choice of ground for the third match but his side failed to take advantage and it was the Terriers who ran out 4–1 winners. Nevertheless, Widdowfield's goal in that match meant he had scored for the seventh successive game, a record that would never be broken by any Town player.

Halifax Town, December 1940. Back row (from left to right): Horace Green, Bill Allsop, Harold Jackson, Ted Raynor, Jake Ruecroft, Ted Craig. Front row: George Wardle, Fred Hogg, Tom Barkas, Ted Widdowfield, Stan Wood.

Town gained revenge over Huddersfield in the League by triumphing 4–0 on 8 March but their biggest win that season was reserved for Doncaster a month later. With Barkas at his best, the Shaymen took a two-goal lead before running in a further six goals after the break to win 8–1. Both Widdowfield and Wardle netted hat-tricks, while Wood and Hogg chipped in with a goal apiece. Town lost only one of their last 10 League matches – they slipped up at Burnley – and ended the campaign with a 4–2 home victory over Middlesbrough and there was little doubting that having had so many regular players available to them had contributed to a fine season where the side finished seventh out of 36 teams.

Despite Town's standing in the League, chairman Charles Mattock was not guaranteeing the immediate future of the club. Addressing the members at the club's AGM on July 25 1941, he said, 'We have come through very well indeed under the adverse conditions. The future, however, is in the lap of the gods, and of course, everything depends upon the war situation.'

Halifax Town went into the new campaign without the services of Ted Widdowfield, by now stationed in Scotland, and would soon lose those of Tom Barkas. They also found themselves playing under a newly organised set up of two separate Leagues run over each half of the season.

Town kicked off their **1941–42** campaign with a 1–1 draw against Burnley, a match which saw the last appearance for some time of Barkas, who joined up with the RAF. But his departure was offset by the arrival of Coventry City inside-left Bobby Davidson and Sam Hanna, an England international short-stop baseball player. Davidson played a major role in Town's defeat of Rochdale in his first game but that would be their last victory for eight matches. Still, the supporters were treated to some eventful games, not least the encounter with Preston, for whom future England star Tom Finney shone on the wing. While Andy McLaren scored the game's only goal for the visitors, there were misfortunes for his Scottish teammates Jim Dougal and Bill Shankly. Dougal put wide a penalty while right-half Shankly ended up at outside-left having sustained a knee injury, though he was not the only player on the receiving end. Town 'keeper George Greaves broke a bone in his right hand and Harold Jackson replaced him in goal after half-time.

Thomson recruited Bradford 'keeper Jim Nicholls, but he conceded 15 goals in his first two matches, including a 9–1 mauling at Blackpool. England international winger Stanley Matthews gave Bill Allsop a real chasing and his appearance at The Shay seven days later helped swell the gate to over 6,000.

Northern Ireland international inside-forward Peter Doherty, Manchester City's recent record signing, played in the 2–2 draw at The Shay while guesting for Grimsby in a War Cup tournament where League points were also on offer, and though Town crashed out of the competition at Barnsley, they fared better in the Combined Counties Cup, going on to reach the Final, but not before playing out one of the most unusual matches after being paired with Huddersfield in the knockout stages. Having drawn 1–1 at Leeds Road, the aggregate scores were level at in the return leg at The Shay, but long before FIFA sanctioned the Golden Goal in the mid-Nineties, Town progressed only after two hours and 16 minutes of football when Geoff Kershaw grabbed a sudden-death winner. Town also needed extra-time to see off Chesterfield to reach the two-legged Final, where they faced York City, but the Minstermen won their home leg 2–0 and ran up three goals in the first half at The Shay to leave Town with a mountain to climb. But to their credit,

Second leg of the Combined Counties Cup Final at The Shay, 30 May 1942. Ferguson, the York City goalkeeper, baulks Davies. Town won the match 4–3, but it was not enough to overturn a two-goal deficit from the first leg.

Thomson's side gave it their all and came close, rallying to lead 4–3 but finding a fifth goal a bridge too far.

During the season, the supporters had rallied to the club's appeal for coupons to secure outfits for the players and Jimmy Thomson was in the happy position of having sufficient to buy two complete new strips. He was also pleased that most of the regular players were still available to him for the **1942–43** season, with only Johnny Wardle having moved out of the area. Having a settled side paid dividends and Town more than held their own through the First Competition, their success built on impressive home form, with Bobby Davidson, Bradford's Tom McGarry and Alan Niblo, a Scottish amateur, boosting the side. They may have struggled on their travels, but defeat at The Shay was not experienced until 14 November, though this came at the hands of lowly Doncaster Rovers, whom they had beaten at Belle Vue the week before. Helping Rovers to a 2–1 victory at The Shay was Rob Wilson, on the books of Airdrie, but the following week he turned out and scored for Town in a 2–1 win over Huddersfield Town in a heated affair.

Halifax Town's best win during the First Competition was the 5–1 success over Leeds United on 12 December, and they completed their fixtures with draws home and away with Burnley. They then immediately began their series of matches in the War Cup against Bradford City, a match ultimately abandoned due to bad light after 67 minutes with the scores level at 1–1 but a result allowed to stand. Town qualified for the knockout stages and played two entertaining games with Chesterfield, only to rue missed chances in the first leg at The Shay and take a slender 2–1 advantage to Saltergate. A week later, Bicknell's 75th-minute goal took the game into extra-time, where, in a scenario resembling the Huddersfield Town game the previous season, the tie was settled by Booker in the 111th minute.

There were no dramas in the Combined Counties Cup, where Halifax Town bowed out to Huddersfield. Having won the home leg buy a single goal, the Terriers went on to win The Shay return 2–0, despite Halifax's hopes being raised by the return of Widdowfield. The Shaymen finished a lowly 35th from 54 competing clubs, but despite this the board of directors looked back on the previous season with a degree of satisfaction, having kept expenditure down to the minimum and with support on the increase.

At their AGM on 27 July chairman Charles Mattock welcomed onto the board Councillor Walter Beecham and Dr Donald McKay, and the club went into a new campaign full of optimism. But though early season results were not good, the side did end the season on a high by the lifting of silverware in April. While Town were to lose the services of Hogg and Davidson during **1943–44,** they were able to call on the services of Lincoln's Jimmy Grummett and Partick's Jock Wallace, who scored prolifically. Other players to feature included goalkeeper Jack Bell, Henry Topping and Bill Jones, while fleeting first-team run-outs were given to 16-year-old Sowerby Bridge youth Trevor Hitchen and Halifax-born Jack Barrett for the Christmas Day trip to Burnley which concluded the first Championship fixtures.

Two days later Halifax Town took on Manchester United in the group stages of the Football League War Cup but, with United's Old Trafford ground out of action following its bombing after a German raid in March 1941, the match was staged at neighbouring Maine Road. Nevertheless, Town found United in irresistible mood, and in front of 15,000 spectators, Stan Pearson notched a hat-trick in a 6–2 win. But the following week, in what was United's first appearance at The Shay, many people felt they were lucky to escape with a 1–1 draw after Town had dominated for long periods.

Town's failure to qualify for the knockout stages of the War Cup owed much to the loss of several key players but they enjoyed success in the Combined Counties Cup, qualifying for the knockout phase by disposing of Bradford City and Huddersfield Town, before putting out York City and Leeds United in the knockouts to reach the two-legged Final with Huddersfield. The Shaymen, who now included in their ranks 'keeper George Rymer and half-back Richard Woffinden, both of Barnsley, and skipper Tom Barkas, who had returned

Combined Counties Cup-winners 1943–44. Standing (from left to right): Jimmy Thomson (manager), David Cockroft (director), Bill Allsop, Albert Flatley, Richard Woffinden, John Walsh (director), George Rymer, Charles Mattock (chairman), Henry Topping, Walter Beecham (director), Joe Taylor, Jimmy Grummett, Clem Reid (assistant trainer). Front row: Eddie Fleetwood, Billy Jones, Tom Barkas, Horace Green, Jake Ruecroft.

to the club at the beginning of March, went on to lift the Cup, but did so the hard way, pulling off an impressive 4–1 victory in the first leg at Leeds Road and just doing enough in the return at The Shay. With the match tied at 2–2 with eight minutes remaining, Huddersfield rallied to score twice through Bert Price, leaving Halifax Town hanging on nervously for the final whistle.

With no sign to the end of the war, football carried on in the same regional basis throughout **1944–45**, though curiously, Halifax and Hull were the only Yorkshire sides in their North Section group. They did quite well, fortunate still to be able to call upon the services for all or most of the season of Allsop, Barkas, Green and Jake Ruecroft, as well as guests Woffinden, Grummett and Clem Smith, putting together a run of eight unbeaten matches, including five consecutive victories, with Widdowfield back in form and among the goals.

Town's best performances, however, came in the War Cup. They disposed of Huddersfield after holding out for a goalless draw at Leeds Road before running amok at The Shay and bringing an end the Terriers' 13–match unbeaten run. Widdowfield netted a hat-trick in the 4–2 victory, and for the Shay supporters, there was even more in store. On 6 January, Manchester City arrived in Town and were denied victory by Wood's 78th minute equaliser, but at Maine Road a week later it was the Shaymen who turned the tables. Trailing 2–0 after 47 minutes, they hit back through Eric Worthington and Flatley, before Widdowfield rounded off a real team move to grab the winner.

Town went on to qualify for the knockout stages thanks to a 1–0 victory over Manchester United courtesy of a goal by Rotherham's Wally Ardron, but exited the competition at the hands of Chesterfield, but not before a pulsating encounter at Saltergate. Having drawn 1–1 at The Shay, the second leg at Saltergate went into extra-time of two 10-minute halves but in atrocious conditions, skipper Barkas lost the toss for choice of ends and forced to play into the driving wind and rain in the first period, Town fell behind to Davie's goal four minutes in, and three minutes later Milburn's penalty effectively killed off the tie. Two days later, Town went down 4–1 at Crewe, but this defeat was merely the prelude to the worst defeat of the season when they were humiliated 7–0 by Sheffield Wednesday at Hillsborough.

The end of the war in Europe was celebrated by VE Day on 8 May 1945, but with many players still in the forces the FA was unwilling to sanction the return of normal football. Jimmy Thomson said, 'We are carrying on as we did during the war. It is still a transitional period [but] I hope to have available most of the nucleus of last season's regular players.'

It was a memorable **1945–46** season, nevertheless, for not only was there the welcome return of the FA Cup competition, but Town also found themselves vying for the title in the North East Region consisting of 10 clubs.

Early performances were disappointing, however, but the inclusions of East Fife centre-forward David Millar, Louis Gordon and George Oliver, plus the return of goalkeeper Charlie Briggs, helped Town turn the corner during October. They secured a double over Darlington, though neither game was anything but straightforward. At Feethams, Town kicked off with only 10 men while awaiting the arrivals of Briggs and Barkas, both held up on the train from Newcastle, and Millar in goal, and seven days later they won an extra-ordinary game 6–5, with Clem Smith netting a haul of four goals, which included a hat-trick in the space of nine minutes. Darlington's Clarke also scored four goals, yet still found himself on the losing side.

Smith scored a successive hat-trick the following week in the 6–2 victory over Lincoln as Town moved up to fifth place and looking dark horses for the title. But momentum was lost with the return of the FA Cup, which, for one season only was played on a two-legged basis up the Final. Town won their first match at The Shay over York City courtesy of Gordon's solitary goal, and were holding out for extra-time at Bootham Crescent when trailing 3–2, only for Scott to head home York's fourth goal and give them an aggregate 4–3 win.

Town returned to League action with victory over Hartlepools and moved to within two points of leaders Darlington, but hopes of the Championship disappeared when Ardon scored all Rotherham's goals in a 4–1 win at The Shay on Christmas Day and a further two in the game at Millmoor as the home side triumphed, leaving Thomson's side to finish a disappointing sixth.

Town took their faltering form into the North East Cup, failing to qualify from the group stages after losing three of their opening four matches. They needed to win at Hartlepools to stand a chance of progressing but hanging on to the lead given them by Heptonstall-born Jimmy Moncrieff, Town were ultimately undone when Moses lobbed Briggs with no more than twenty seconds remaining. Other results went against the Shaymen and they promptly missed out.

A North East Second Championship was formed for the Northern Section clubs failing to qualify, though Town managed to win only one of their seven matches. But Thomson did at least use the competition to blood new players such as Eric Binns, Arthur Killarney, Eric Turner and Fred England as he geared himself up for the return of the Football League programme.

Jimmy Thomson's task of putting together a strong squad for the forthcoming return to League football was made harder when Barkas elected to join Rochdale and Widdowfield and Briggs also moved on. But he could still draw on useful players such as Rayner, Reg Elvy, Green, Allsop, France, Ruecroft, Jackson and Jack Morefield. He also signed up the Scottish pair of Pat Quinn and Sammy Waters, as well as the former Sunderland amateur Dave Mycock, who had been playing locally in the Halifax & District Wartime League. Thomson was optimistic of Town's chances, but his hopes sadly were never realised. The **1946–47** fixtures were a replication of those from the aborted 1939–40 season, but whereas Town were unbeaten in their first three games back then, there was no such repeat this time around and by the time they won their first match at the sixth time of asking, they were already at the wrong end of the table. Sensing trouble, the board stated that they were 'looking for new players of the right standard' to help improve things, and in came Ken Drake and the experienced Des Collins but there was little improvement. At the turn of the year, Town's position was a desperate one, lying next to bottom.

At least the FA Cup brought some brief respite from League worries and the side moved into the second round after overcoming a gutsy Barrow side in a Shay replay which went into extra-time. Town then played out a 1–1 draw with Stockport in a game marred by thick fog but lost the replay at Edgeley Park, Ruecroft gifting County a penalty by catching the ball in his own area after seeing the linesman flagging for offside.

Town's form in the League, however, continued to give cause for concern after a depressing run of eleven games without a victory included a then club record eight consecutive defeats and left them stranded at the foot of the table. Yet this sequence was broken in sensational and totally unexpected fashion when runaway leaders Doncaster arrived at The Shay on 25 January. Rovers had lost only once all season and were unbeaten away from home, yet with new signing Stan Fisher making his debut, Town pulled off one of the shocks of the season with a 4–2 win.

Victory hardly galvanised the side, and Town would win only a further three matches before the season's close. Their cause was not helped by the terrible winter which gripped the nation throughout February and March, as heavy snow brought Britain to a standstill. At The Shay at one point, three feet of snow lay in places across the pitch and in all five scheduled games involving Town were postponed over this period. With so many games affected, the League extended its fixtures so that the programme did not conclude until the first Saturday in June.

This only to served to prolong the agony for the Shaymen, who were condemned to re-election with four games still to play when Accrington's victory over New Brighton on 10 May put them out of reach. Town still had the chance of overhauling Southport, who had completed their fixtures, but in the end they lost their last three matches and finished for the first time in their history bottom of the division.

For the Town boss Jimmy Thomson, it had been one season too many and he chose now to end his eleven year old association with the club. On 13 June 1947 he resigned his position saying, 'It has been a hard struggle at The Shay for several years, in fact for most of the time I have been in charge. But I am parting with the club on the best of terms.'

POST WAR

On 26 June 1947, the former Manchester United goalkeeper Jack Breedon was installed as the club's fourth manager. Shortly there would also be a new chairman, too, for on 11 July, Charles Mattock relinquished his position and was replaced by Arthur Carter, who, after seeing Town re-elected, said at the club's AGM, 'This is our last chance. A number of clubs are knocking at the door of the Third Division and are organising themselves. I shudder to think what will happen if we have to apply again.'

Breedon acknowledged his job was going to be a tough one, and with stalwarts Allsop and Ruecroft leaving the club, new faces were inevitable. Into the club came half-back Norman Dingwall, inside-left Hubert Cockroft, winger Jack Ormondy and centre-forward Donald Stretton, but the side could not have made a worse start, losing the opening three matches of the **1947–48** campaign, and though the signing of Oliver Burns inspired them to their first win, it proved a false dawn. After 13 matches, Town were bottom of the table with only Oldham for company. Breedon tried all sorts to find a successful formula. Half-back Dave McCormick and left-winger Frank Williams were promoted from the reserves, and right-back Dick Threlfall was signed, while no fewer than five players were tried at centre-forward, including half-back Ken Drake for the game at Accrington on 4 October.

An ever-changing team which soon featured Freddie Fogg, a wartime favourite, Charlie Lewis and Stan Scrimshaw, pulled off a surprise victory over leaders Rotherham United on 8 November and a mini-revival enabled Town to briefly move out of the bottom of the table. But they would not win again until March, by which time the situation looked forlorn.

By then, further players had been signed; Wilf Booth, Hull City half-back Jim 'Smiler' Mills and forward Maurice Priestley, who netted the game's only goal at Crewe as Town

Bradford City goalkeeper Matt Middleton punches clear to repel this Halifax Town attack in the Shay meeting of the two sides, 29 March 1948.

ended a depressing run of 17 League and Cup games without a win. The signing of the former Scotland international Hugh O'Donnell from Rochdale gave the side a further boost, and by winning a second successive match for the first time, Town moved off the bottom of the table. But by gaining only one point from their Easter fixtures, their chances of avoiding re-election looked remote. A goalless draw with Hartlepools United, who were the nearest team above the Shaymen but four points better off, did their chances no good, and when 'Pools triumphed over Rochdale the following week while the Shaymen slipped to a 3–0 defeat at Gateshead, a successive re-election bid looked a formality, and indeed was confirmed seven days later with two games still to play following a 1–1 draw with Darlington.

Prior to the last game, a 5–1 drubbing by Oldham at The Shay, Breedon had been forced to deny 'in the proper quarters' propaganda doing the rounds, allegedly by non-League clubs, that Town were not wishing to seek re-election due to their poor support. A begging letter sent out by Arthur Carter, in fact, not only poured scorn at such suggestions, but seemingly did the trick when Town were voted back into the League on 8 June 1948, polling a near maximum 47 votes.

But amid the understandable elation of the Halifax Town directors came a note of caution from the chairman. At their AGM on 18 August, Arthur Carter reported, 'We have spent all our money to fulfil our summer commitments and if it had not been for the FA Cup Pool Fund, the club would have been in debt.' Any extra income therefore would prove to be a godsend to the club, so the news that speedway promoter Bruce Booth was planning to bring the sport to The Shay was a welcome one, though it would be another year before the first meeting was hosted there.

Jack Breedon's close season signings included half-backs Eddie Hodgkinson and Billy Morgan, and centre-forward Dennis Howsam, while returning after a spell helping out at Scarborough was trainer Harold Taylor, who brought with him his son Derek, a player who would make brief first-team appearances. But once the **1948–49** season kicked off, results followed an all-too-familiar pattern with the side managing just two victories from the opening 10 games.

Full-back Ted Breaks was promoted from the reserves, and further additions to the playing staff were those of half-back George Gilmour, winger Ted Maguire and the

> **HALIFAX**  **TOWN**
>
> Club Colours:
> BLUE & WHITE SHIRTS
> WHITE KNICKERS
>
> Members of
> FOOTBALL LEAGUE Div. III
> YORKSHIRE LEAGUE
>
> ## ASSOCIATION FOOTBALL CLUB, LIMITED,
>
> TELEPHONE
> 3 4 2 3
>
> Shay Grounds,
> Halifax,
>
> SECRETARY-MANAGER
> J. BREEDON
>
> May 25 1948
>
> To the Chairman and Directors.
>
> Dear Sirs,
>
> As Chairman of Halifax Town I shall be greatly obliged if you will read the following and give our club your support.
>
> No doubt you are aware that we are in the unfortunate position of having to apply for re-instatement in Division Three Northern Section, having finished next to the bottom this season.
>
> We were established thirty years ago and have had many difficulties to overcome, but we have managed successfully so far.
>
> We are as well placed financially as most clubs in the Third Division, and have this season had better gates than at any time in the club's history, and, in passing, have paid more in 20% share of gates than the majority of clubs have paid to us.
>
> The ground is one of the best in the Northern Section. We are faced with the same problem confronting every club— defered repairs—and this is receiving our earnest attention.
>
> To lose our League status which we value so much, would mean losing many of our old friends who have stood by us in trouble and are still standing by us.
>
> Therefore I ask for your full support and backing at the Annual Meeting, so that we may obtain a substantial majority towards that which we seek, i.e., to remain in our present company. For I am confident that with the proposals we have in hand our position will be greatly improved next season.
>
> Yours faithfully,
>
> A B Carter
> Chairman.

Arthur Carter's begging letter, dated 25 May 1948, sent out to Football League clubs as he strove for Halifax Town's re-election. Letters such as these were regularly typed up by former and future Halifax Town chairmen.

experienced former Scotland international Jim Dougal. Back-to-back victories over Gateshead and Hartlepools made Town's League position look a little healthier, and their luck seemed to be in when drawn at home in the first round of the FA Cup against non-League Scunthorpe United. But the tie was fraught even before the scheduled meeting on

Legendary Hull City 'keeper Billy Bly thwarts Town centre-forward Roy Crossley in the match at The Shay 18 September 1948. Billy Morgan (number 10) watches on.

27 November, with the frost-covered ground and deep fog causing its postponement. The sides tried again the following Saturday but there were no goals in the first 90 minutes, nor in an unprecedented period of extra-time. The sides reconvened two days later at Scunthorpe's Old Show Ground, but it was the home side who broke the deadlock and won the tie through Barker's free-kick with just five minutes remaining.

In the League, Town continued to frustrate, although they were hopeful of avoiding a third successive re-election bid with Southport and Bradford City becoming detached. However, there was dismay when skipper Horace Green was sold to Lincoln just two days before an important match with high-flying Hull and he was sorely missed and Town crashed to a 6–0 defeat, their worst of the season. A run of nine matches soon followed, and despite the additions of centre-forward Alf Whittingham and inside-left Eddie Murphy, Town were sucked back into the re-election dogfight. But they hit form just when it mattered, a 3–1 Easter Monday victory over Oldham Athletic proving to be the platform for revival. Dougal's header clinched victory at Chester and Roy Crossley planted both ball and 'keeper in the back of the net for the winner as Town came from behind to defeat bottom club Southport 3–2, thus ensuring safety with two games remaining.

The first speedway meeting at The Shay had seen the Halifax Dukes lose to Yarmouth 45–37 on 6 April 1949, but the creation of the track had necessitated the narrowing of the pitch by three yards. Many Town supporters now moaned that they were left further from the action, but with the club lying £8,902 in the red, the directors now welcomed the extra revenue speedway would bring in, worth about £1,400 each year.

New players came to the club in the form of centre-half George Hinsley, forward Billy Dale, and goalkeeper Pat Egglestone, who would make his debut sooner than expected after the side conceded 14 goals from their opening three matches of the **1949–50** season. He came in for a confidence-rocked Ted Rayner and results gradually improved. Local League player Dave McCormick also appeared in the side and performed well enough for Breedon to allow Scrimshaw to join Shrewsbury, but soon results went against the Shaymen and by the turn of the year they found themselves 19th, with only Chester, Accrington Stanley and York City beneath them, separated only by two points.

Centre-forward Walter Bennett arrived from Doncaster, the player evidently having no qualms about leaving a club that was fighting for the title for one deep in trouble, while another local player, John Core, proved to be one of the finds of the season as he scored some important goals, including the winner in an eventful game at Bradford City where Egglestone suffered concussion in conceding a penalty and was temporarily replaced in goal by McCormick – a sign of things to come.

Town's destiny was shaped towards the end of February and throughout March, with the side enduring a run of five consecutive defeats, the nadir being the 4–1 hiding handed to them on 4 March by bottom club Accrington. Town sank to the foot of the table following the home defeat to Lincoln, and re-election looked a certainty, though the fight to escape went to the last day. Four clubs were involved: Town, Bradford City, Wrexham and York, but only victory for the Shaymen over visitors Oldham would guarantee safety. On a rain-soaked pitch they looked to have secured it as they led with just two minutes remaining, but Bert Wadsworth popped up with a goal to break Town's hearts, and Bradford City's 5–2 victory over Accrington Stanley, together with Wrexham's draw at Rochdale, meant that both these clubs overhauled the Shaymen, who were thus condemned to their third re-election application in four seasons. But this time they need not have worried. At their AGM on 3 June 1950, the Football League agreed to extend both Third Division sections by two clubs, and thus the re-election of Town and the other three teams became a formality.

Jack Breedon introduced a new playing strip of maroon shirts with light-blue sleeves to 'change the psychological outlook' for the **1950–51** season but results followed an all-too familiar pattern. With new players brought in such Walkden-based 'keeper Eddie Toze, full-back Frank Westlake and left-winger George Glaister, it took Town until their fourth game before gaining their first point, and their fifth before registering their first goal. In what appeared to be an act of desperation, the deputy mayor, Alderman John Burdock addressed the crowd at half-time during the home game with Barrow to lend his support to a 'Climb the League' campaign and a public meeting at The Shay on 30 August was organised where an appeal was made for £2,000 for new players.

Town won their first match at the eighth attempt but continued to struggle and fared no better in the FA Cup. Despite being drawn at home to North Eastern League side Ashington in the first round, the visitors rose to the occasion and took a two-goal lead through Gibson and Simpson before the Shaymen rallied. Goals from Glaister and Core looked to have reprieved Breedon's side, but the visitors then broke away for Scott to score what proved to be the winner, and for the second year running Town had fallen to non-League opposition.

Defeat here spelled the end for manager Jack Breedon, for five days later, on 30 November, he resigned, claiming, 'I decided to leave before the Cup-tie, but kept it back from everyone because of the effect it might have had on the players. I have tried to do the right thing by the club. It has been continued depression and desperate struggle all the time since [I took over] and I believe it is better to part with the club now, although my contract

Jackie Moss about to shoot in the match against Carlisle United at The Shay on 28 April 1951.

has still to run until 31 July. It is not fair for a new manager to have to take over a struggling club in June.'

Breedon, however, agreed to stop on until a successor had been appointed but results continued to be poor. 'Keeper Ted Elliott arrived from Chester – he immediately displaced Rayner – and in January, the directors dipped into the Climb the League fund and money raised by the Halifax Town Social Section, totalling £1,500, to pay a new record fee to bring Leeds United reserve centre-forward Des Frost to The Shay, along with his teammate Jackie Moss. Frost seemed to be the centre-forward the club had been lacking and he netted all his side's goals in the 4–1 win over Lincoln City on 3 February, a match that had been preceded by a minute's silence following the death of club president and former chairman Charles Mattock.

Full-back Jimmy Lea, signed from Hull City, became the latest recruit, and he took his place in the side that claimed a 2–2 draw with Bradford on 3 March 1951, a match watched by the former Northwich Victoria manager Billy Wootton who, two days later, was installed as Breedon's successor. He strengthened his side with the signing of York City half-back Les Horton and Town scrambled to safety. Helped in no small way by Frost's second hat-trick for the club in the 4–0 win over fellow strugglers Southport, the Shaymen heaped pressure on Accrington, who needed to win both of their last two matches to stand a chance of overhauling Town. When they lost at Tranmere midweek, their own re-election became a necessity, and it was a relieved Halifax Town side that completed its fixtures with a goalless draw at waterlogged York City.

At the end of another disappointing season, the players did at least provide some cheer when they signed off with a friendly against Waterford United on 12 May, one of a series of matches played by clubs to celebrate the Festival of Britain. With Wootton handing starts to Liverpool trialist Tom Hughes and outside-left Derek Priestley, who had slipped quietly into The Shay the previous October, Town ran up a record Shay score as they triumphed

11–2. Hughes netted a brace, as did Jackie Moss, but they were outdone by Fred Dale and Priestley, who both scored hat-tricks, while Dave Mycock also got his name on the score sheet.

A whole host of new players arrived for the **1951–52** season, among them Bob Tomlinson, centre-halves Jack Bickerstaffe and Donald Hunter, and half-back Cyril Coyne. There was also the arrival of a new 'keeper in Alf Taylor, whose competition would come from an unlikely source, Dave McCormick, converted in the reserves from centre-half to goalkeeper. But the squad was made up of only nine full-timers, with the rest being part-time professionals, a situation which did not auger well, and so things proved. Despite registering their first opening day success since the war, Town soon found themselves rooted at the bottom of the table yet again.

Town defeated newly-elected Workington on the opening day, but the fans would have to savour Frost's sensational 30-yarder which set Town on the way to a 3–0 victory over Grimsby Town in their fifth match, for it would prove to be their last win until the beginning of November. The Mariners, in fact, would go on to inflict on Town their worst defeat of the season, bettering the 6–1 hidings handed out in the space of eight days by Bradford and Hartlepools United.

Jimmy Lee became the latest star player to leave The Shay, moving to Chelsea in a record £2,500 deal and though Wootton used some of that money to bring Eric Williams to the club from Manchester City, results did not improve. Town slipped to 23rd but whether their sorry plight and the criticism that came with it had taken its toll on Arthur Carter, nobody can be certain, but on 21 November, the Halifax Town chairman was dead, the result of a

Halifax Town 1951–52. Back row; Dr Donald Mackay, Des Frost, Dave Mycock, Ted Breaks, Bert Taylor, Les Horton, Jimmy Lee. Front row: Billy Dale, Billy Morgan, Eddie Murphy, Jackie Moss, Tom Hindle.

Halifax Town and Halifax RLFC players pose for the camera prior to Dave Mycock's Benefit Match, 1 May 1952.

massive heart attack. It was a shock to everyone, not least the players, who, in the wake of Carter's passing away, crashed to a 3–0 FA Cup defeat at Wrexham.

Cyril Adams took on the mantle of chairman and the club immediately signed schemer Gerry Henry from Leeds United and he in turn was appointed as player-coach, taking charge of the team in Wootton's absence. But such a move did not have any immediate effect, and when Grimsby exacted revenge for their earlier Shay defeat by hammering Town 8–1 on 29 December, Wootton's side found themselves bottom of the table.

Something needed to change, and as things turned out Wootton took charge for the last time for the home derby match with Bradford on 26 January, a game ultimately abandoned, for while a nation mourned the passing of King George V1, Wootton tendered his resignation on 6 February 1952. Henry immediately assumed control and the push to escape from the re-election zone began in earnest with a goalless draw in the rearranged game with Bradford on 10 March. His steadying influence, plus the arrival of giant 'keeper John Savage from Hull City, helped Town lift themselves off the bottom to 21st, and though four consecutive defeats in the run up to Easter meant their position was still worrying, by winning their last three matches, Town finished 20th and thus staved off re-election.

The FA Cup competition was the main feature of Town's **1952–53** season, when the side reached the fifth round for the second time. If that was an achievement in itself, then the manner in which they got there was even more astounding, as the Shaymen put out not one First Division side, but two, a feat virtually unheard of for a side of such low standing.

Of course, there was no sign of the glories to come when the side kicked off that season. Retaining 13 professionals, manager Gerry Henry added to his squad left-back Albert Cox, centre-half Edgar Packard, inside-forwards Andy Geddes and Harry Darbyshire, and

Halifax Town's famous Cup team of 1952–53. Back row (left to right): Jim Mulvaney, Andy Geddes, Des Frost, Dave McCormick, Roy Lorenson, Jack Bickerstaffe, Jackie Moss. Front row: Harry Darbyshire, George Holt, Eric Williams, Eddie Murphy, Derek Priestley, Jimmy Moncrieff.

outside-right Bert Wilkinson, while ready to treat them in his own inimitable manner was new trainer Allan Ure, later to be dubbed 'the man with the magic fingers'.

Dispensing with maroon shirts, which clearly had not had much effect, in favour of the plainer all-blue, Halifax Town began their League programme with defeat at Workington, but on a Shay pitch now widened following the decision by speedway promoter Bruce Booth to discontinue the sport at The Shay – temporarily, at least – the opening two home games were won, and with Town losing only one of their first eight matches they gave an indication of better times ahead. At one point, they moved up to sixth but by the time of the FA Cup, their form had suffered something of a slump.

In light of their ensuing glories, however, it seems almost bizarre that they should have needed two games to see off the part-timers of Ashton United in the first round, for they just scraped through after a replay at a freezing Hurst Cross ground. Even the 4–2 victory over Southport in round two was made harder than it should have been – Town almost let slip a three-goal lead – but nevertheless they moved into the third round and were rewarded with a home tie with First Division Cardiff. But an injured wrist sustained by 'keeper Savage in an earlier derby match at Bradford put him out of action for six weeks and thus opened the door for McCormick, who suddenly became involved in Town's most memorable Cup run.

Though Cardiff were perhaps not the biggest crowd-pullers, crash barriers were erected at The Shay and a crowd limit set of 35,000. But on the day, perhaps it was as well that many Bluebirds fans stayed away, for their side was no match for the Shaymen, who ran out 3–1 winners. Priestley's early goal inspired the team, while at the other end, McCormick was in

Matchday programme for the FA Cup tie with First Division Cardiff City at The Shay, 10 January 1953. Halifax Town won 3–1.

fine form. In round four, Town were paired at home with another Division One side in Stoke City, but few could have expected another shock victory given Town's run of form leading up to the game. The Shaymen failed to win any of the intervening matches in the League, and while they were drawing the last of these at York City, Stoke, despite struggling in the First Division, were winning handsomely 5–1 against leaders West Brom. But come the day of the game, the ground record was shattered, with 35,621 cramming into The Shay, and in a dramatic match Priestley was on hand to net the game's only goal just before half-time.

Into round five and Town were handed yet another home tie against Arthur Rowe's powerful Tottenham Hotspur, whose side included England internationals Alf Ramsey and Ted Ditchburn, the crafty Eddie Baily and the authoritative skipper Bill Nicholson. The tie itself, scheduled for Valentine's Day, was actually in doubt until the morning of the match after heavy snow during the week had covered the pitch. At one point over 50 volunteers and seven wagons had been brought in to shift the piles of snow, and though more followed, with conditions soft underneath,

Halifax Town's FA Cup tie with Tottenham Hotspur, scheduled for the 14 February 1953, was in doubt following heavy snow the previous day. Here, volunteers and one of seven motor wagons maintain a shuttle service in a bid to make the Shay pitch playable.

referee Overton gave the game the go-ahead after volunteers had again helped to clear the pitch, with the markings inked in blue dye. Cup fever once again gripped the town and the gate record was broken once more, with 36,885 packed into the ground. The conditions proved to be a leveller and Town were well in with a chance up to half-time, but their hearts sank when Les Bennett found the roof of the net after 56 minutes and further goals from Len Duquemin and a second from Bennett gave the First Division giants a 3–0 win.

Thereafter, Town struggled to raise their game in the League, crashing 5–1 at Barrow in their first post-Cup match, and injuries to key players hampered their end of season run in. The FA Cup became but a distant memory with only 3,296 turning out for the visit of Chester towards the end of March but though they slipped to 17th, re-election was never an issue and the side rallied to finish 14th.

While work got under way with the construction of a new stand on the Shaw Syke side of the ground during the summer of 1953, Gerry Henry began assembling his squad for the **1953–54** season, bringing in half-back Les Horsman, and forwards Graham Wood, Tommy Bell and the former England B international winger Walter Rickett. But it would be another frustrating season with Town still seeking their first win after five games.

Things improved slightly in September, but a winless streak of eight games, including five straight defeats, saw the side hurtling towards the foot of the table, that despite the credible performances of goalkeeper John Savage. But they were soon to be without their giant custodian, for on 17 November 1953, he was sold to First Division Manchester City, thus giving the opportunity once more to McCormick. But by the end of November things were looking desperate, and if Town were pinning their hopes on another epic FA Cup run as a welcome distraction, they were in for a rude awakening. Cheshire League side Rhyl Athletic held the Shaymen to a goalless draw at The Shay in the first round, and two days later sensationally overturned a two-goal deficit to force extra-time, and took a 4–2 lead through Valentine and Hanlon. Town's recent signing Ray Haddington pulled one back but it was too little, too late and after the heroics of the previous season, the boot was now on the other foot.

Town's first win in 11 League and Cup matches came over fellow strugglers Workington but with only two further victories before the end of January, things looked bleak. A run of three consecutive victories during February, including the shock defeat of promotion-chasing Barnsley at Oakwell, made Town's position look a little healthier but it was not form they could maintain, despite the arrivals of forwards Alf Clarke and Bill Shadbolt. Gerry Henry found himself facing mounting criticism, particularly after Town suffered a torrid time over Easter, crashing 5–0 at Carlisle United and losing all heart when slipping to a 3–0 defeat at home to Scunthorpe United. When they met York City in their penultimate match, they knew that only victory would keep alive their hopes of escaping the re-election zone, but the Minstermen broke away for a late winner after Town had clawed back a two-goal deficit, and the Shaymen's fate was sealed; only a draw in their last match with Tranmere Rovers enabled them to stay above Chester.

While a world record 102,569 had turned up at Odsal to watch the Rugby League Challenge Cup Final replay between Halifax and Warrington on 5 May 1954, it was to Town's poor attendances that certain non-League clubs, primarily Wigan Athletic and Peterborough United, pointed as they stated their own case for Football League membership. But Town survived yet again, if only by polling 28 votes, the lowest number they had ever received, while Wigan pulled in just 18 and Peterborough one less.

Harry Hooper and the Golden Age

At the club's AGM on 22 July, chairman Cyril Adams made his retirement speech; tired of the constant struggles, he had decided to stand down, and a newly-constituted board saw Jim Mitchell (who would be elected chairman), Dick Blackburn, Cyril Thornber and Jack Rushworth being co-opted onto it, along with Vivian Booth, who began a second term.

Blackburn gave a rousing rally call: 'Let us forget the past. Let pessimism die away. Let us have the will to make Halifax Town go and get up the League ladder.' But his words had little effect, at least in the short term. Despite new signings in the tough-tackling duo of George Griffiths and Sid 'Skinner' Normanton, centre-half Tom Waring, winger Joe Dubois, inside-forward Ian Crawford and 'keeper Walter Scott, Town collected only three points from their first eight matches of the **1954–55** season and were still seeking their first win. Henry was left looking for a potent striker, but found him in former Liverpool reserve Bill Watkinson. He scored twice against Barrow on his second appearance as Town registered their first win at the 10th attempt, but soon they found themselves cast three points adrift of Crewe at the bottom.

With a game against third-placed Gateshead looming on 16 October, manager Gerry Henry decided to resign, bemoaning the club's lack of success – excluding the FA Cup run two seasons earlier – as his reason for leaving, so while the directors set about advertising for his successor, in the short term they upgraded Bobby Browne, who had arrived in the summer as coach to the first team. Browne's tenure would last just four games, but he began in style as Town pulled off a shock 4–0 win over Gateshead, and the points gained in further victory over Chesterfield and a goalless draw at Crewe took them above Barrow at the bottom, if only on goal average.

But by then, Town had pulled off a major coup with the signing from Sunderland for a four-figure fee of Willie Watson as player-manager. A well-known sports figure and dual international at football and cricket, Watson included himself in the side for the next home game with Carlisle United and inspired his teammates to a famous 5–3 win in which he also scored. A suddenly confident Town won their next four League matches, including the 3–1 triumph over League leaders Scunthorpe United on 18 December, and climbed to 15th after extending their unbeaten run to nine games.

The Shaymen would enjoy another good run in the New Year following Watson's signings in March of goalkeeper Arthur Johnson and left-sided defender Stan Lonsdale. Jackie Sharp was also given a run-out after impressing in the reserves, as was Eric Newton, who weighed in with some important goals as Town put together an eight-match unbeaten run towards the end of the season. Watkinson took his tally to 15, a handsome return, as was Town's finishing position of 14th; with re-election looking a certainty back in November, Watson had transformed Town's fortunes, and it would be some time before the club would go cap-in-hand to the Football League again.

After Town's encouraging end of season run-in, manager Willie Watson felt the need to bring in only a couple of players, inside-forwards Clive Baker and Joe Dubois, before heading off to South Africa with the touring England Test team. Les Horsman, promoted to player-coach, was left in charge of the side until his return but saw Town make a dreadful start, failing to win any of the first six matches of the **1955–56** season. Watson was back for

Halifax Town 1955-56. Back row (from left to right): Brian Atkinson, John Harris, Harry Mills, Roy Lorenson, George Griffiths, Conway Smith, Allan Jre (trainer). Front row: George Hutchinson, Andy McCall, Harry Darbyshire, Johnny Kelly, Stan Lonsdale.

the visit of Crewe on 10 September and inspired his side to their first win and gradually they managed to pick up points, if only at home. Away form was a problem, though occasionally there were mitigating circumstances. At Mansfield, Alf Clarke was forced to take his place between the sticks when Arthur Johnson missed his train from Liverpool.

Having gained only two points from nine away matches, it was a nervous Shay camp that trekked to Midland League side Goole Town for the first-round match in the FA Cup. But with recent signings centre-half John Harris and the tough forward Tom Capel in the side, Town came from behind to win the tie 2–1. But the Shaymen couldn't negotiate Burton Albion in round two. The Birmingham & District League side held out for a goalless draw on a rain-soaked Shay pitch, and Town's away-day blues continued when they slipped to a single-goal defeat in front of a record 5,217 at Burton's Lloyd's Ground, courtesy of Barker's 17th-minute penalty.

Town's shock Cup defeat was all the more alarming given that, just seven days prior to the home tie, they had run up a record Shay score when defeating Bradford 6–0 with Clive Baker grabbing his first hat-trick for the club. The Shaymen would later put five past Oldham on Boxing Day before banishing their away-day jinx with maximum points from the return with the Latics the following day. Showing new confidence, they continued to impress and by mid-January had climbed the table to 13th.

A new 'keeper arrived in Harry Mills, but having seen his side slip into old habits and lose five games on the bounce to leave them 20th, and with a new cricket season on the horizon, Watson announced his decision to stand down as player-manager. 'I have definitely finished playing football,' he said upon his departure, but having brought in innovative coach Bill Burnikell on 7 February to replace Horsman, the club had a ready replacement. Burnikell took over and the team responded with an unbeaten four-match run which took them to safety, though his first defeat at the hands of Scunthorpe at The Shay was watched by a paltry 2,839, an attendance doubtless affected by Halifax RLFC's involvement in the Rugby League Challenge Cup Final at Wembley on the same day.

Burnikell, whose title remained as first-team coach, began planning for the **1956–57** season by signing several players who would leave an indelible mark at The Shay, not least that of inside-forward Conway Smith from Queen's Park Rangers. There was also the exciting prospect of the former Scotland international winger Johnny Kelly, as well as inside-forward Andy McCall, full-back Phil Roscoe, the robust half-back Brian Atkinson and his Sheffield United team-mate Barry Fowler, and George Hutchinson. These players arrived at a new-look Shay, which now had a new stand and changing rooms on the Shay Hill side of the ground, officially opened by the Mayor, Alderman Frank Swire, JP prior to the opening match with Hull City which fittingly Town won 1–0.

Opening day victory, however, did not result in an immediate challenge for the top placings, and Town soon found themselves near the foot of the table. Heavy defeats at the hands of Scunthorpe and Derby left them languishing in 19th place, so the directors allowed Burnikell to move into the transfer market to bring Liverpool reserve centre-half Alex South to the club. South would be a cornerstone of the side for many seasons and he made a pleasing debut, scoring in a 3–1 defeat at Southport, but he soon saw just how much work there was to do at the club when Town crashed 4–0 at early pacesetters Accrington Stanley in their next match.

At a board meeting on 24 October there were changes at the top when Harry Taylor succeeded Jim Mitchell as chairman, an. Town then spring a surprise by pulling off victory at leaders Hartlepools courtesy of Hutchinson's astonishing goal from an acute angle, but results such as this proved to be the exception rather than the rule and with the Shaymen slipping out of the FA Cup at the hands of Oldham, Burnikell inevitably paid the price for failure. Five days after the home defeat by Chesterfield on 1 December the board terminated

Arthur Johnson being hampered by Stockport County's Holden in this Shay encounter on 30 March 1957. Brian Atkinson and George Griffiths await the outcome.

his employment with the club, citing lack of success and their own determination to provide a higher standard of football. Burnikell retorted that he had turned down coaching positions to see the job through at The Shay and that 'seven managers cannot all be wrong.'

There was, however, to be no immediate successor to Burnikell, as the directors put themselves in the unique position of running the team themselves, playing affairs being overseen by Harry Taylor, director Vivian Booth and trainer Allan Ure. Yet between them, they managed to turn things around. A run of seven straight defeats was ended with a shock 4–2 success over handily-placed Workington on 22 December, and Town's revival ran well into the New Year. The most memorable success was doubtless that on 9 February over a second-placed Derby County side, albeit one depleted by injuries. The game was no less tense but Darbyshire's 55th-minute opportunist strike eventually swung the game in Town's favour. The Shaymen went on to extend an unbeaten run to seven games, including five straight victories, and continued to defy the odds by finishing 11th, pulling off further victories over title contenders Hartlepools and Stockport on the way, and being unbeaten in their final five matches.

Changes were to be made regarding the structure of the Football League when, at their AGM on 1 June 1957, it was decided to replace the regionalised bottom divisions with Divisions Three and Four, with the top 12 from the Northern and Southern sections making up the newly-formed Third Division, and the remaining clubs comprising the Fourth. Halifax Town were fortunate to have such a good crop of players – only forwards Jim McQuade, Cedric Thomas and John Mulholland were initially added to it – and the club went into the **1957–58** season still under the tutelage of Messrs Booth, Taylor and Ure, with no immediate moves to appoint a new manager.

Early season results proved to be a mixed bag, beginning with an entertaining 4–4 draw at Workington and handsome home victories over Gateshead and Oldham Athletic. Against these, however, were heavy defeats, such as at Hull City, and in consecutive games at

Conway Smith fires into the roof of the net for Halifax Town's first goal in their 3–1 victory over Southport at The Shay, 30 November 1957.

Rochdale and Darlington. Town had been forced to field a depleted side at Darlington through injury, illness and suspension, and keen to avoid defeat against bottom side Crewe three days later the directors tried unsuccessfully to have the match postponed. Town, however, won the game 2–0 and continued to compete in the top half of the table.

Off the field, however, there were unexpected ramifications following on from Town's Easter Monday home defeat by Gateshead the previous season. On 7 October the FA acted upon the report of match referee Percy Rhodes, taking a dim view of director Vivian Booth's comments made to him following the game and consequently banned him *sine-die*. In protest, fellow director Jack Rushworth resigned from the board and the club was resigned to finding a new team manager.

From almost 40 applicants, Harry Hooper, a former player with Sheffield United, who was then coaching at West Ham United, was appointed on 27 October, and he proved to be a figure who would lead Halifax Town into one of their most successful post-war periods. He kept the side moving in the right direction with the signing of strikers Alan Blackburn (from West Ham) and Mick Priest, and for a time, automatic promotion became a distinct possibility. The side won six out of nine matches throughout February and March, pulling off an impressive 4–2 win at Oldham Athletic in the first of those, and with South quelling the threat of 30-goal South African front man Alf Ackerman, Town swept to a 5–0 win over Carlisle. By the end of March, the Shaymen had moved up to 10th, yet were just four points behind fourth-placed Bradford City, but such form was not maintained and the side fell away, although they did manage to cement a place in the new Division Three by finishing seventh after winning 3–0 at Barrow in their penultimate fixture and wrapping up with a 4–1 victory over Rochdale.

The Halifax Town side that qualified for the newly-created Third Division at the end of the 1957–58 season. Back row (from left to right): Hugh Ferguson, George Griffiths, Arthur Johnson, Alex South, John Mulholland, Brian Atkinson. Front row: Barry Fowler, Conway Smith, Clive Baker, Jim McQuade, Jackie Sharp.

Preparing to meet the challenge of the largely unknown, yet fancied southern sides during **1958–59**, Hooper brought in the likes of full-backs Paddy Stanley and George Fagan, and forwards Alan Turner and Gordon Rose, and offset the departure of skipper George Griffiths by signing the experienced half-back Peter Tilley from Bury. Off-field, there was also the appointment of a new secretary in Norman Howe, who would be full of ideas of how to run the club.

The Shaymen initially did well in the new Third Division, recording a 3–2 opening day success at Chesterfield courtesy of a Priest hat-trick, and enjoyed early season victories over Southampton and Swindon. They also completed the double over Newport, with debutant Illingworth youth Kevin Verity paving the way for the 2–0 success under the Somerton Park floodlights with the first goal. But despite these results, Town flirted briefly with the relegation zone after defeat at Brentford towards the end of September left them lying 22nd, though relying on home form, they climbed to 13th following victory over Doncaster Rovers on 8 November.

Town may have had the wobbles when drawn at Southport in the first round of the FA Cup, but by producing a fine display they triumphed 2–0, only to be humbled 3–0 on Darlington's frozen Feetham's pitch in round two after the sides had drawn at The Shay. Town's performance at Darlington touched rock bottom, but in the League they hit a purple patch in the New Year, losing only one of eight matches and featuring in some highly entertaining encounters. At Notts County on 3 January, they held a 3–0 half-time lead before settling for a point in a 4–4 draw, and for the first time since the opening day, they moved into the top 10 following home victory over Southend United courtesy of a Conway Smith penalty. Town recorded their highest victory of the season when defeating Doncaster 5–1 at The Shay on 28 March 1958, before Hooper's side came of age with successive draws against FA Cup semi-finalists Norwich City and at champions-elect Plymouth Argyle, who found 'keeper Johnson in superb form. A flurry of goals towards the end of the campaign, including a hat-trick on the final day against Colchester United by emergency striker Tilley, saw Town win five of their last eight matches to finish a commendable ninth, and there was more glory to come in the West Riding Senior Cup.

The Shaymen lifted the Cup for the first time, for having defeated a Leeds side containing Jack Charlton and Don Revie 3–0 in a semi-final replay, they met Bradford City in the Final at Valley Parade on 8 May. There, Stan Lonsdale scored the game's only goal after just three minutes, while the match proved to be particularly memorable for Paddy Stanley, who dislocated his nose in the seventh minute, returned after treatment as nuisance value on the left wing, only to be sent off in the 67th minute after tangling with City's centre-half Jeff Nundy.

At the club's AGM on 7 August 1959, chairman Taylor welcomed back to the board Vivian Booth and Jack Rushworth, two men he felt were vital to the running of the club, while also claiming that the current crop of players could obtain promotion for Halifax Town. 'We have been in office five years – we now have a team that we think can reach the Second Division and we shall go all out for it, regardless of the financial position,' he said.

For a while, that dream looked a distinct possibility. With newcomers Doug Fletcher, Tommy Holmes and full-back Geoff Hudson added to the squad, Town went unbeaten through their first five matches of **1959–60** and joined the early pacesetters, taking their turn enjoying top spot on three separate occasions during September and October, while

Halifax Town 1959–60. Back row (from left to right): Stan Lonsdale, Frank Large, Phil Roscoe, Arthur Johnson, Roy Lorenson, Eric Harrison. Front row: Doug Fletcher, Conway Smith, Peter Tilley, Andy McCall, Alan Blackburn.

vying with QPR, Southampton and Norwich. Home defeat by Shrewsbury Town had people questioning their credentials, but they seemed to silence any doubters by moving back to first place when defeating Bradford City 4–0 in their next game on 10 October, with Conway Smith's brace taking his tally for the season to 12 goals.

But the bubble soon burst. In what was the game of the day a week later, first versus third, Town were handed a lesson by QPR at Loftus Road and lost 3–0, the first game of a winless run that stretched to 10 matches and culminated in the embarrassing 7–0 loss at Port Vale on 28 December, by which time the side had slid as far as 17th.

There was to be little respite in the FA Cup, either, for despite pulling off a fine 4–3 victory at Gateshead, where Roscoe scored an astonishing free-kick from inside his own half, Town went out in the second round at Workington, and in an attempt to buck faltering League form, Hooper signed the enigmatic George Whitelaw to the club from QPR on 27 November. A footballing entertainer by nature, it could be said that his antics were often worth the admission money alone, although he did not enjoy the happiest of starts, sent-off on his debut as Town crashed 5–1 at Newport. Whitelaw was considered to be the centre-forward Town had been lacking, but it was not until the New Year that the supporters began to see any dividends.

Town's poor run of form was ended with the 4–2 success over Mansfield on 2 January and the second half of the season bore witness to some scintillating performances. Barnsley were put to the sword 5–0 at The Shay, with the fast-emerging Frank Large scoring a hat-trick, and there were exciting victories against foes Bradford City and QPR. But Town reserved their best performance for the away match at Accrington on 9 April where, boosted by Whitelaw's early goal, they ran out 5–0 winners to set their record League victory away from home, inflicting their heaviest defeat of the season on the home side, as well as ending a 14-year wait for success at Peel Park.

Town climbed into the top half of the table once more and thanks to impressive home record, eventually finished 14th, with Large, having moved up front from the half-back line, topping the goalscoring charts with 17 League goals. He was certainly one of the finds of the season, as was local goalkeeper Peter Downsborough, who was handed his debut in the final match of the season at Bournemouth. So much promise did he show that manager Hooper was happy to let Arthur Johnson leave the club, although it was another Halifax-born 'keeper, David Knowles, who initially benefited from Johnson's departure.

A significant off-field move during the close season was the creation of the Halifax Town Supporters Club, an idea of Harry Hooper's, who saw its value solely in raising funds for the club. He merged his own 'New Players Fund', set up during the season and which had realised just over £2,000, with the Social Section to form the Supporters' Club and, over the years, this social group would greatly benefit the club.

Happy with his squad, Hooper deemed it necessary to make only one significant signing, that of Crystal Palace winger Gerry Priestley, and the football produced by the side during the first half of **1960–61** was as good as anything the supporters had seen in a good while. Among early season highlights were a thrilling 2–1 victory over neighbours Bradford City and a stormy encounter at Port Vale, where the Shaymen ran out 3–2 but left with a

Halifax Town 1960–61. Back row (from left to right): Alan Blackburn, Frank Large, Roy Lorenson, Phil Roscoe, Peter Downsborough, Alex South, George Whitelaw, Eric Harrison. George Fagan, Paddy Stanley. Front row: David Knowles, Gerry Priestley, Geoff Hudson, Peter Tilley, Harry Taylor (chairman), Harry Hooper (manager), Tommy Holmes, Peter Fexley..

police escort after rough tactics, particularly by Lorenson on Brian Jackson, had led to the home supporters pelting the Town players with stones and orange peel, smashing their dressing room window and stoning the team bus. Still, victory at Vale Park was Town's fourth in a row, and moved them temporarily up to second place.

There was some distraction to League progress with the launch of the League Cup, the brainchild of Football League secretary Alan Hardaker, and although the competition initially received a lukewarm response from many of the top clubs, over the years it would grow in stature. Town were given a bye in the first round, while their second-round match at First Division Nottingham Forest proved to below-key affair, with only 4,445 turning out for the 3pm kick-off on a Thursday afternoon and seeing the home side run out 2–0 winners.

Town confounded their doubters by maintaining consistent form in the League, although they bowed out of the FA Cup after a 5–1 rout of Hartlepools by losing a second-round replay to Crewe. On Christmas Eve they served up possibly their best performance of the season by beating Southend 6–2 at The Shay, but nobody then could have foreseen that it would be three months before the Shaymen won again.

During January, Town, like all other clubs, were faced with the unprecedented move of players going on strike in support of the movement against the retain-and-transfer system. The strike, led by Jimmy Hill, chairman of the PFA, was due to begin on 21 January, with Town's game at Tranmere set to be affected. Chairman Harry Taylor was prepared to play local amateurs, but in the event, the strike was called off, though Town, with a full-strength team, proceeded to lose 6–2 at Prenton Park, conceding the first goal within 17 seconds of kick-off..

New faces had come in the form of Willie Sinclair and Roy Evans, and in March forward John Allan joined from Bradford, his signing seen of some importance following the sad departure of crowd favourite George Whitelaw to Carlisle United on 3 February, a move which did at least net Town around £5,000.

Their 13–match winless streak was ended with a 1–0 home success over Reading on 25 March, and the side rallied to finish ninth, though the players often found themselves in the wars. Losing heavily at QPR on 15 April, Town played out a 1–1 draw at The Shay two days later with only 10 fit men after Hudson sustained a nasty ankle injury following an over-the-top tackle by Mark Lazarus and in the last match, new striker Rodney Green was patched up by trainer Ure after breaking his nose and dislocating a finger as Town claimed their first double of the season when winning 2–1 at Bournemouth.

Large, who had led the way with 18 League goals, continued to score goals the following term, too, helping Town make a good start to the **1961–62** season, remaining unbeaten in their first five matches. But with the first-team squad now made up of only 12 full-time professionals, they were always going to be hard-pressed to stay there. Among new signings were winger Brian Redfearn and forwards Mike Burgess and Graham Barnett, while in October, Ken Smith arrived after a spell playing in Canada to help bolster the attack as the side began to struggle.

While the team slipped down the table, excitement was maintained by off-field activity with the installation of floodlights at The Shay and the board's audacious attempt to lure firstly League and FA Cup double-winners Tottenham Hotspur, then European giants Real Madrid, to provide the opposition at the official switch on. While Spurs quickly turned down Town's offer due to their own European commitments, the chance of Real Madrid

Don't go without Mackintosh's Rolo

Soft, smooth toffee in rich milk chocolate cups

[JOHN MACKINTOSH & SONS LTD., HALIFAX

First Aid facilities Provided by the St. John Ambulance Brigade

HALIFAX Blue Shirt with White V-Neck White Shorts

KNOWLES

RIGHT   2   3   LEFT
STANLEY   ROSCOE

4   5   6
TILLEY or HARRISON   SOUTH   BURGESS

7   8   9   10   11
PRIESTLEY   BARNETT   SMITH (K)   LARGE   REDFEARN

Referee:
A. E. ELLIS
(Halifax)

Linesmen:
F. Ellis
Red Flag
J. Jack
Yellow Flag

11   10   9   8   7
STANKOVIC   JOSIC   SKOBLAR   BOROZAN   MLADENOVIC

6   5   4
ANTIC   SIJAKOVIC   MARIC

LEFT   3   2   RIGHT
POPOV   GAVRIC

KRIVOKUCA

BELGRADE

The Records played at this match are supplied by Teal & Shaw Ltd., George St., Hx.

DON'T MISS THE BEST!

'COURIER' GREEN FINAL

for Racing, Football, Rugby, News and Pictures

The team line ups from the match programme when Halifax Town met OFK Belgrade for the big switch on of the new floodlights on 16 November 1961.

Halifax Town 1961–62. Back row (from left to right): Alex South, Paddy Stanley, Peter Downsborough, Phil Roscoe, George Fagan. Front row: Gerry Priestley, Graham Barnett, Peter Tilley, Mike Burgess, Frank Large, Brian Redfearn.

coming to The Shay remained a realistic one, but hopes disappeared when the Town board felt they could not guarantee meeting their financial terms, and on 25 October the *Halifax Courier* proclaimed, 'It's all off!' Foreign opposition was provided, however, by Yugoslavian semi-professional side OFK Belgrade, who included seven full internationals, and Football League secretary Alan Hardaker performed the official switch on 16 November before the sides played out a 1–1 draw in front of 10,005 spectators.

A culmination of bad weather and poor results saw Town slide down the table, and with crowds dwindling, Harry Taylor rounded on the Halifax public to support the club. The board elected to try Friday night football, but with less than 3,000 turning up for the visit of Reading, the trial was a costly one. Another costly disappointment occurred when Hooper ordered nearly two tons of sand to help with clearing the pitch of snow for the visit of Bradford City on 10 March, only for the referee to call off the game.

The Shaymen found themselves embroiled in a relegation battle following a run of eight games without a win, their confidence rocked by a 6–0 mauling at Swindon on 16 April, but victory over Lincoln the following week eased matters, and relegation was eventually staved off as Town avoided the drop by four points. But with attendances dipping below 2,000 – only 1,557 had turned up for the visit of Southend United on 21 February – troubled times lay ahead.

The season did, however, at least end on a high note when Town lifted the West Riding Senior Cup for the second time on 7 May when Conway Smith, on his last appearance for the club, headed the game's only goal after 25 minutes as Bradford were beaten on their own Park Avenue ground. But by then manager Harry Hooper had already left the club, accepting the invitation to take over at Lancashire Combination side Nelson and Town went into the summer seeking a new manager.

Fourth Division Days 1963–69

With no money in the kitty, chairman Taylor stressed that the way forward was for the club to start producing their own players if they were to survive. Yet set against this was the board's decision to scrap their junior team, which had been playing in the Huddersfield Red Triangle League.

In July, the former Huddersfield Town half-back Don McEvoy arrived under the working title of first-team coach, while the full-time running of the club was put in the hands of secretary Norman Howe. But Howe was to witness many comings and goings, as Johnny Bruce, the reserve coach, and Ted Breaks, who had been acting as first-team trainer following the retirement of Allan Ure in January, followed Hooper out of The Shay. In place of Breaks came Harry Hubbick, one of the game's real characters, who had been acting in a similar capacity at Accrington Stanley, but made redundant when they were forced to resign from the League in March 1962 amid mounting debts. Yet who was to say the same thing could not happen to Halifax Town? They announced a loss of £3,800 during the season, and the sale of Frank Large to QPR on 26 June 1962 for a club record £7,500 was a virtual necessity.

The summer had seen the board strengthened by the arrivals of Sid Hitchen and Tom Scott, and new players included forwards Bill Holden and Barry Tait, while shortly into the season crafty inside-forward Willie Carlin, plucked from Liverpool's reserves, joined the club. But Town soon began to struggle during **1962–63**, shipping five goals at QPR and seven at Northampton, and when the Cobblers completed an early season double with a 3–1 victory at The Shay, Town found themselves in the bottom four. The side's response was to pull off one of the most sensational victories ever seen when they entertained sixth-placed Swindon on 29 September. With 20 minutes remaining, the visitors held a 3–0 lead,

Halifax Town won 1–0 at Brighton on 2 February 1963 during the Big Freeze. Here, goalkeeper Peter Downsborough makes the save, while Alex South (left) tries to keep his footing in the snow.

only for Town to rally late on through Tait's hat-trick and Redfearn's sensational injury time winner, and this victory sparked something of a revival as Town pulled themselves out of the bottom four, if only temporarily.

The season was interrupted by what became known as the Big Freeze when an Arctic blast gripped the country in December and lasted well into the New Year. The football fixtures were decimated and Town went without a home game for fully three months, suffering financially as a result. But secretary Norman Howe did come up with a novel money-making scheme by turning the frozen Shay pitch into an ice rink and on 2 March 1963, when Town should have been hosting Millwall, the gates were opened to the public for skating. The venture proved so successful that it was carried over till the following day and the club profited to the tune of around £100.

Despite no football action at The Shay, Town did manage a couple of matches away from home, one of them being a solitary-goal victory over relegation rivals Brighton on 3 February, a game which featured on the BBC's *Saturday Sport* highlights programme later that evening. But soon the Football League programme returned to normal and Town, with full-back Malcolm Russell promoted to the team, at last staged their first game in a long while when they entertained Colchester on 15 March. But the game ended in victory for the visitors, and worse was to come with heavy home defeats by Port Vale and Bristol City, and although Town were involved in some high-scoring matches, such as the 5–4 defeat at Coventry and a 4–4 home draw with Bradford, they found themselves deep in trouble after going 10 games without a win. Even the arrival of winger Dennis Fidler did not solve their problems, and relegation to the Fourth Division was confirmed with four games still to play when the side picked up only one point from an otherwise creditable draw with Division Two-bound Swindon on 4 May.

With Halifax Town now in the Fourth Division for the first time, the supporters hoped for a swift promotion push, though coach McEvoy was not prepared to forecast it at a heated AGM on 9 August 1963, despite chairman Harry Taylor's warning that, 'Unless there is an improvement we shall come to a sticky end.'

The club elected to use a mix of full and part-time players which included new players in full-back Walter Bingley, half-back David Jackson, forwards Alan Arnell and Frank Bartlett and the quick-silver winger Archie Taylor. Frank Twist also arrived from Bury in exchange for goalkeeper Knowles, in turn forcing McEvoy to bring Hull City reserve Mick Granger to The Shay, but he, like Knowles, would play second fiddle to Downsborough. Town's first game in the Fourth Division during **1963–64** saw them gain a useful point from a goalless draw at Barrow, which was followed by an impressive 5–1 victory over Torquay United. But the side played too many drawn matches and, having won only two games by mid-October, they slipped to 17th. With striker Barry Tait having obtained a move to Crewe, Town looked anything but promotion contenders.

Failing to impress in the League, at least the side enjoyed a run in the League Cup, accounting for Chesterfield, Rochdale and Walsall to move into the fourth round of the competition for the only time where they prepared to entertain Second Division Norwich City. In the run up to the game, however, McEvoy was forced to call up 17-year-old Steve Wilkinson for the League game at Doncaster Rovers due to injuries to Downsborough and Granger, and with no improvement in their condition, he kept his place in the side for the Cup tie with Norwich, only to be on the receiving end of a hiding as the Canaries cantered to

Willie Carlin shows typical aggression in this race for the ball.

a 7–1 win. Granger had suffered a broken finger in an earlier FA Cup tie at Workington, but as was the norm in those days, he 'retired' to the forward line, while Dave Worthington donned the 'keeper's jersey. Town were well-beaten that day, but trailing 4–0 with five minutes remaining, it was Granger who drove home Carlin's crossfield pass for a consolation goal.

In the League, Town continued to under-achieve and heavy defeats towards the turn of the year suggested a second half struggle, particularly when they dropped into the re-election zone following a 4–0 drubbing at Lincoln on 8 February. But who was to know then that that would be Town's last defeat for two months? Buoyed by a goalless draw at leaders Gillingham, the Shaymen went on to enjoy a run of 11 unbeaten matches, their run including a record breaking seven consecutive victories which transformed their season and carried them from 21st to ninth. Town's win at Workington was actually the first on their travels in 17 matches and amid the impressive run, Westlake's header in the 3–2 victory over Rochdale meant he had scored in five consecutive matches, while an unlikely scorer in the 2–1 victory over Bradford was Bingley, a 45-yard free-kick that sailed over the head of 'keeper Hardie.

As the season went into its final weeks, the football world was rocked by the story that appeared in *The People* which reported that several players, internationals Tony Kay and Peter Swan of Sheffield Wednesday among them, had tried to fix matches, while the ringleader appeared to be Mansfield's Jimmy Gauld. Also implicated was Town's Bingley, allegations against him referring to his time with Swindon and York. Gauld, Kay, Swan, and Owls teammate David Laine were later jailed, although Bingley felt that he had no case to answer. He gave an interview to *The People*, then asked the PFA to help clear his name. He said, 'I am completely innocent of all the allegations,' and club secretary Norman Howe concurred, 'The board have interviewed Bingley concerning the allegations, and in the view of the answers from him, the directors are not taking any action.' Indeed, when the **1964–65** season got under way, he was still with Halifax Town.

Missing, though, was coach Don McEvoy who, on 14 July 1964, agreed to take over at Barrow, taking with him Dave Worthington and stalwart Eric Harrison. Clive Baker took

Halifax Town 1964–65. Back row (from left to right): Malcolm Russell, David Jackson, Peter Downsborough, Walter Bingley, Alex South, Archie Taylor. Front row: Dennis Fidler, Frank Twist, Willie Carlin, Brian Westlake, Bryan Frear.

over as second-team trainer, while on 3 August chairman Taylor was happy to announce the return as manager of Willie Watson. But he was rejoining a club whose first policy was simply that of keeping the club going. 'If we cannot do that, there shall be no need for a policy,' Taylor said at the club's AGM.

The Shaymen's opening day 5–2 defeat at Tranmere Rovers was perhaps an indication of the kind of season that was in store for them, although they did respond by defeating Darlington 4–0 in their first home match. The side now featured close season signings Stan Howard and Bryan Frear, while the early weeks of the season had also seen the unscheduled appearance of local League Stainland Athletic goalkeeper John Wray with Downsborough laid low with a virus and Granger nursing a wrist injury.

Town enjoyed a three-match winning run in October, but their 2–0 victory over Newport County turned out to be their last until the beginning of January and they quickly became re-election fodder. Matters weren't helped by the sale of Carlin to Carlisle and a sequence of 11 League matches without a victory, which included a run of six consecutive defeats. Nor was there any respite in the FA Cup for despite being paired with Lancashire Combination side South Liverpool, Town could not make their home advantage count, and the ensuing 2–2 draw only served to highlight the side's shortcomings. They prepared for the replay, but only after chairman Taylor had announced that Town couldn't strengthen the team because there simply wasn't enough money available. 'We have spent £3,800 to clear outstanding accounts. The bank will not allow us to use more than £2,000 of the money on new men, and that is the maximum figure,' he said. And with moral in the camp low, the side never recovered in the replay with South Liverpool once South had headed into his own net and they slipped to an embarrassing 4–2 defeat.

Hampered by injury to South, Watson gave an extended run out to Bob Worthington, and added Bernard Goodall, Graham Wooler and young Jeff Lee to the side. But things continued to look bleak, though Town's depressing sequence was ended when Fidler drove home the ball for the winner against Southport on 2 January. But only two further games were won before the season's close and with Keith Bambridge proving to be the only major addition to the side, the side became locked in a re-election battle with Bradford City and Barrow. When they succumbed to a 4–0 defeat at Notts County in their penultimate fixture their fate was sealed, though prior to the Football League's AGM on 29 May, Sid Hitchen, who had succeeded Harry Taylor as chairman the previous month, went on record as saying that if Town were not re-elected 'it will be one of the biggest shocks in the game.'

Halifax Town 1965–66. Back row (from left to right): Mike Clarke, Jim Smith, John Brier, Bob Raynor, Bill Atkins, Archie Taylor, Keith Bambridge. Front row: Dennis Fidler, Brian Westlake, Eric McMillan, Malcolm Russell, Jeff Lee.

In the event Halifax Town comfortably pulled in 41 votes and retained their League status but the **1965–66** season proved to one beset by financial crises, partly caused by the directors' own decision to move away from the norm and stage Friday evening matches. When the team slipped once more into the re-election zone, resulting in attendances dropping alarmingly, the board elected to review their decision, and the New Year saw them switch five Friday night matches back to Saturday.

Watson had introduced new players to the side, with the signings of the left-back Mick Clarke, half-backs Jim Smith and Eric McMillan, forward Mick Balmer and goalkeeper Bob Raynor, who initially succeeded Downsborough after he was involved in a swap deal with Swindon's lanky centre-forward Bill Atkins. Several weeks into the campaign, Watson also paid Newcastle United £1,250 for young defender John Pickering, a player who would be a fixture in the Town side over the next nine years.

A season of struggle, though, had begun with the side failing to win any of the first nine matches in the League and suffering an early exit at the hands of Bradford in the League Cup. But those early fixtures did bear witness to a little piece of club history when Bambridge replaced Jeff Lee at Stockport to become the first substitute used by Halifax Town in a League game. Town slipped to 23rd but the arrival of 'keeper Malcolm White coincided with an upturn in fortunes in the League, for without the distraction of the FA Cup after a first-round defeat at Southport, Town recorded their biggest win of the season in their 4–0 defeat of Hartlepools, and an entertaining 4–4 draw with Newport County on New Year's Eve extended an unbeaten sequence to five.

The FA Cup defeat, though, had already forced the board to hold crisis talks, and on 22 February 1966, just three weeks after they had announced their plans to build a £20,000

There were fears that Halifax Town's match with Luton Town on 16 May 1966, which concluded their League programme, could have been their last ever. Here, centre-forward Graham Wooler beats Moore (number six) to the ball, while Eric McMillan (right) looks on.

social centre at The Shay, the following headline appeared in the *Halifax Courier*: 'Shay Directors' Ultimatum: More support – or Town quit League'. The directors claimed the club was losing between £150–200 a week and felt compelled to issue a statement to highlight the gravity of the situation: '*The position is now very serious indeed. The question we are compelled to ask is: "Do the people of Halifax want a Football League club or not?" It must be answered one way or another for the simple reason that, unless we get considerably increased support through the gates, from the sales of shares or from the club pool between now and the end of the season, we shall be unable to carry on.*'

The Mayor of Halifax, Harry Ludlum launched a 'Save Halifax Town Fund' on 8 March in the hope of raising £25,000, and though it fell well short – by the end of May the figure stood at £10,847 – it did give hope for the future of the club. The players, too, responded by putting money worries to the back of their minds and climbing the table to 14th. Attendances rose, but nowhere near the 17,000 that turned up for their game at Doncaster, though the board were thankful for their share of the gate receipts, amounting to £400, such was the arrangement in those days. They were also comforted by the regular income stream provided by the re-formed Halifax Dukes speedway club, who returned to The Shay and held their first home meeting in April 1966.

But with the future uncertain Willie Watson's decision to take over the vacant manager's position at Bradford City at the beginning of April was understandable. Vic Metcalfe, formerly at Huddersfield Town and having been acting as youth-team trainer at The Shay since November 1964, stepped up to become 'technical director' and oversee the first team, but he immediately saw the side plunge back into the re-election mire. A 2–0 victory over Port Vale in their penultimate fixture pulled them clear and the season was wrapped up in fine style with a 3–0 win over Luton Town, a game which had been billed as Town's last-ever. However, the headline in the *Halifax Courier* on 24 May 1966 brought cheer to the supporters: 'Town Staying in Football League' though Hitchen stressed that, '*Now is the time for maximum effort from everyone interested in Halifax Town's future. We are not thinking in terms of 12 months or two years. That would be pointless. The aim is to plan ambitiously, but sensibly and to bring into action various action committees capable of translating our hopes into reality.*'

The board was immediately strengthened with the addition of Alan Maden, although his elevation to chairman on 20 September 1966 following the sudden resignation of Hitchen probably came sooner than expected, while Metcalfe was given the perfect fillip with his own promotion to full-time manager, and among his new signings were centre-half Ray Holt, utility player Dick Lee and Barry Holmes, a player who would have a lengthy career with the Shaymen.

With a nation still rejoicing at England's World Cup triumph at the end of July, Town sadly began the **1966–67** season in an all-too familiar fashion. Without a win from their opening seven League matches, they were also dumped out of the League Cup by Darlington, forcing Metcalfe to strengthen the side with the signings of forward John Parks and full-back Norman Bocell from Crewe, though it wasn't until the arrival of Barry Hutchinson in November that Town's fortunes changed for the better. He scored a brace in a 5–2 success over Notts County, a result that galvanised the team, and with Atkins also in fine goalscoring form, Town went on to record five consecutive League victories, hitting form just in time for the FA Cup, having drawn Doncaster Rovers at home in the first round.

Halifax Town would enjoy a memorable journey to the third round, beginning with a 2–2 draw with Rovers at The Shay, then winning the replay in extra-time at Belle Vue, but only after finding themselves a goal down within three minutes. The Shaymen then negotiated a tricky tie at non-League Bishop Auckland, holding out for a goalless draw in freezing conditions before winning The Shay replay by a record 7–0 scoreline, running in six goals in the last half-hour. Town also belied their lowlier status when paired at home with Second Division Bristol City forcing a draw before losing 4– at Ashton Gate.

Town's run in the Cup had not been detrimental to progress in the League, even if their unbeaten home record went in surprising fashion on Boxing Day when they lost 4–1 to lowly Barrow. Successive victories over Tranmere and Bradford City and a series of draws saw the Shaymen climb to 13th in the table, with Hutchinson in fine goalscoring form. But they were soon to lose the services in March – temporarily at least – of Bill Atkins, who moved to Stockport in a player-exchange deal that saw Dave Shawcross move to Halifax. As fates would decree, the two clubs then met each other at The Shay just two days later, with Atkins's new side taking the points in a 1–0 win.

Also slipping into The Shay was Huddersfield Town reserve Bob Wallace, and Town enjoyed their end-of-season run-in, losing just three of

This spectacular shot shows goalkeeper Malcolm White making a flying save to prevent Chesterfield from scoring in the encounter at The Shay on 15 October 1966.

Les Massie signs for Halifax Town from Darlington, watched by manager Vic Metcalfe (standing) and secretary Alan Vidler, 29 June 1967.

the last 12 games to finish 12th, which was satisfying enough, as was their triumph in the Final of the West Riding Senior Cup on 18 May, when Bradford City were beaten 3–0 at The Shay.

During the close season, skipper McMillan and crowd favourite Hutchinson moved on, but Metcalfe made some astute signings, bringing in the Notts County pairing of full-back Ivan Hampton and winger Tony Flower and inside-forward Les Massie, who arrived from Darlington but well-known in these parts from his own time with Huddersfield. The side made a satisfying, if unspectacular, start – the 5–0 destruction of a poor Bradford side in the League Cup aside – to the **1967–68** season, and gave indication of better times ahead. They even pushed First Division Sunderland all the way in the second round of the League Cup before losing 3–2, while three consecutive victories during October had the supporters eyeing the top end of the table for once. When the side showed a slump in form the directors backed Metcalfe by sanctioning the record £5,000 transfer of striker Hugh Ryden from Chester on 3 November 1967, yet just 10 days later, the Town manager had resigned following a board meeting, claiming, 'I don't think the team has done badly and we have made a useful start this time, but I was not prepared to have interference on the playing side. That is what it would have amounted to after last night's meeting and that is why I have resigned.'

The Halifax Town squad at the start of 1967–68 season. Back row (from left to right): Harry Hubbick (trainer), Jim Smith, Ian Blyth, Ray Holt, Norman Bodell, Ivan Hampton, Malcolm Russell, David Shawcross, John Pickering, Vic Metcalfe (manager). Front row: Archie Taylor, Tony Flower, Les Massie, John Parks, Bob Wallace, Phil McCarthy.

THE HISTORY OF HALIFAX TOWN

On 16 November, the abrasive Alan Ball Snr, father of the World Cup-winner of the same name, was installed as Metcalfe's successor, but he would find no easy fix to Town's stuttering League form. In fact, his only victory before the turn of the year was an enthralling 3–2 success over Crewe in the first round of the FA Cup, while home defeat by Port Vale on 30 December extended their run without a win in the League to an incredible 13 games to leave them lying in 18th place.

The Shaymen's fortunes changed with the FA Cup second-round victory over Scunthorpe United on 6 January and with the arrival of Bolton's reserve 'keeper Alex Smith. Malcolm White's days were numbered, as too were Archie Taylor's, who made way for Phil McCarthy. Smith took his place in the side for the visit of Lincoln, a game won courtesy of Shawcross' goal, and suddenly Town looked like a different side, with their new-found form carrying them as high as 11th following victory at York City on 13 April.

The side, in fact, suffered just two defeats during that period, one of which was the 4–2 third-round FA Cup defeat by Second Division Birmingham City at The Shay, although Town were far from disgraced. But if there was one game that epitomised the fighting spirit that Ball was instilling into his side, it was the defeat of League leaders Bradford City at Valley Parade in front of 9,498. The all-important goal was a typical finish from Massie, whipping the ball into the net, and he edged closer to the top of the scoring charts.

Having defeated Scunthorpe United in the second round, the Halifax Town players tune in for the FA Cup third-round draw, where they learn that they have pulled Birmingham City, 8 January 1968. Across the front (from left): Malcolm White, Malcolm Russell, Phil McCarthy, Hugh Ryden, Les Massie, Brian Moncaster, Jeff Lee, Ian Blyth, Tony Flower and Graham Wooler. Lined up at the back; David Shawcross, Norman Bodell, John Pickering, Terry Reeves and Jim Smith.

Towards the end of the season Ball added to the squad Elf Morris, John Sneddon and Fulham's former Manchester United forward Mark Pearson, although he would be sidelines for almost a year. Les Massie's 25th League goal of the season was enough to complete a double over Bradford in the final home game and he ended the campaign as the division's joint top scorer with Port Vale's Roy Chapman. Massie would be crucial to Ball's ambitions, but the Town boss wasn't resting on his laurels and the close season saw him further improve his squad.

Before any new players came to The Shay, the board were forced to appoint a new secretary following the sudden death of Alan Vidler in May 1968. Breaking with tradition, the directors chose a woman, Pauline Hicks, as his successor, and she became the only female secretary in the whole of the Football League. Among the players she found herself registering for the **1968–69** season were current and former internationals Mick Meagan (Eire) and striker Ian Lawther (Northern Ireland), and there was also the arrival of Burnley reserve full-back Mick Buxton. But despite these additions, Town's start was not good as they lost both of their opening two League matches as well as slumping to a 3–0 home defeat by Hull City in the League Cup.

The match with Hull saw the last appearance of Malcolm Russell as he left for Southport, while joining the club after impressing on trial was centre-half Chris Nicholl from non-League Witton Albion, and he cemented a place in the side which, despite the odd aberration, moved into the top half of the table. By going through October unbeaten with four wins and a draw Town climbed to seventh, although as they moved into November the main focus of attention switched to the FA Cup.

The start of what was another memorable Cup run began with a 3–1 victory at non-League Bilston and continued with extra-time replay success at Crewe in the second round. By the time of the third-round match with Swansea, Ball had been forced to sign full-back

The squad that began the successful 1968–69 campaign. Back row (from left to right): David Shawcross, Chris Nicholl, Ivan Hampton, Alex Smith, Malcolm Russell, John Pickering, Mick Buxton. Front row: Ray Holt, Les Massie, Hugh Ryden, Mick Meagan, Tony Flower, Mark Pearson, Bob Wallace, Elf Morris.

in Andy Burgin following a broken leg suffered by the unfortunate Buxton, but the Shaymen progressed on the back of a hard-earned 1–0 win and moved into round four where they were rewarded with an away tie at First Division Stoke City. The Potters boasted England goalkeeper Gordon Banks, George Eastham and the Republic of Ireland striker Terry Conroy in their ranks, and though the home side took an 80th minute lead courtesy of Peter Dobing's goal, the Shaymen, spurred on by 4,000 travelling supporters, equalised three minutes later through Massie and then spurned two late chances to win the tie. The ensuing replay at The Shay drew the crowds, but in the end Stoke won the match 3–0 with a goal from Harry Burrows and a brace from Conroy.

Town returned to League action, and although at first glance their five successive draws did not look too impressive, they were the forerunner to the promotion push that took off with the 2–1 home win over Colchester United on 4 March and gathered momentum. Bolstered by the arrival of Lammie Robertson, Town extended an unbeaten run in the League to 17 matches and joined the promotion race which involved as many as 10 clubs, although it was the Shaymen who had the most hectic programme.

Ball's side moved to fifth thanks to a 2–0 win over Brentford, and while defeat in their next match at Rochdale boosted the Dale's own promotion hopes, it did not seriously dent their own, and by the time the sides met for the return at The Shay on 8 May in what was their penultimate fixture, Town knew that victory would be enough. The match captured enough imagination to swell the gate to 17,186, and in a tense affair, it was Massie who scored the all-important goal, heading home McCarthy's cross after 76 minutes and wild celebrations followed. A goalless draw in their last match at Bradford meant the Shaymen ended the season as runners-up to Doncaster and as a reward for success, the directors treated the players to an end-of-season tour of Europe, a marginally successful one at that, but remembered mostly for the antics of Pearson, who walked out without permission, and Hampton, who was ordered home by Ball after claiming he was bored.

Third Division Rise and Fall

Bolton midfielder Dave Lennard became the first of Ball's two close-season signings, with the other being his former England international team-mate Freddie Hill, a terrific coup. Town began life in back in the Third Division with a win over Shrewsbury at The Shay but a shock omission from the side was Massie, shortly to join neighbours Bradford. Another early season departure was that of Nicholl, who, after impressing against Luton, joined the Kenilworth Road side the very following day for a club record £30,000.

Town also received a decent payout in the League Cup competition, where, following the defeat of Barnsley in the first round, they were rewarded with an attractive tie at First Division West Ham, who, of course, included in their side the England World Cup-winning triumvirate of skipper Bobby Moore, Martin Peters and hat-trick hero Geoff Hurst. West Ham's centre-forward netted three goals in this game, too, as the Hammers ran out 4–2 winners, but Town were still in the hunt until Hurst scored his second having halved the Hammers' 2–0 lead through Ian Lawther.

George Kirby had arrived as coach on 18 August, but the Shaymen began to slip alarmingly down the table after claiming only six points from their opening seven matches

Halifax Town players and officials celebrate clinching promotion following victory over Rochdale at The Shay on 8 May 1969.

and were about to be humbled by a Johnny Haynes-inspired Fulham at The Shay on 16 September. He pulled the strings as the Cottagers ran amok and scored eight times without replay to inflict on Town their heaviest-ever home defeat, with Steve Earle grabbing five goals for himself.

Town's recovery began with a 1–1 draw at home against Doncaster Rovers, and a five match unbeaten run perhaps showed the side's true character. Ball took on loan Aston Villa

The Halifax Town team that began life back in the Third Division in 1969–70. Back row (from left to right): Freddie Hill, Les Massie, Dave Verity, Bob Wallace, Tony Flower, Dave Lennard, Alex Smith, Ian Lawther, Dave Shawcross, John Pickering. Front row: Jeff Lee, Hugh Ryden, Lammie Robertson, Phil McCarthy, Andy Burgin, Mick Buxton.

centre-half Fred Turnbull and Manchester United reserve 'keeper John Connaughton, and at the end of October bolstered the attack by signing former fans' favourite Bill Atkins in a £9,000 deal from Portsmouth. He scored his scored his first goal upon his return in a draw with Chester in the FA Cup, a tie that the Shaymen ultimately lost in a replay, but his goals in the League helped Town to climb into the top 10. Progress, however, would be hindered by the loss of Hill, who would not play again after breaking three toes in a friendly with Sunderland reserves on 19 January.

Without him, Ball made full use of the loan transfer system, bringing in former Wales international Roy Vernon and Barnsley's Peter Graham, while an extended run-out was given to defender Dave Verity, the younger brother of Kevin. But having moved up to eighth place following the exciting 4–2 victory over Rotherham United on 3 March and the hard-earned 1–1 draw at Tranmere Rovers that followed, Town stuttered alarmingly, winning only one of their final 13 matches. They crashed 5–0 in the Easter Monday clash at Rochdale, and the crowds had long since drifted away by the time they completed their programme with a single-goal home defeat to Walsall, the attendance for that match dipping below 2,000 for the first time that term.

Off the field, a season of transition had seen the departures of secretary Pauline Hicks, succeeded by Michael Cosway, while Alan Ball elected to take the vacant managerial position at Preston. Chairman Alan Maden described his departure on 14 May 1970 as 'a body blow', but so too was that of Freddie Hill, who returned to the First Division when he made a £12,000 move to Manchester City.

Coach George Kirby was unveiled as Ball's successor, and he immediately promised a fresh approach, saying, 'Now we shall try to progress, play more attacking football and to give the supporters entertainment.' In that, Kirby would not fall short, and the colourful season Town delivered during **1970–71** was matched by the new strip of tangerine shirts and light-blue shorts the players wore as the club moved away from the essentially traditional blue-and-white strip that the side had worn since 1952.

Other than the signing of Barry White as cover for 'keeper Alex Smith, Kirby made only one other addition, that of Arthur Cox as trainer following the defection of Harry Hubbick to Preston, a move which stoked up the rivalry between the two clubs, who, by a quirk of fate, met each other on the season's opening day. The match ended in a 1–1 draw, a satisfying start for Kirby's side, as was their form during the early part of the campaign. Victory over Plymouth on 22 September saw them sitting fourth and Preston, who had gone top, were beaten 2–1 in an early season return thanks to two Atkins free-kicks.

Following an exciting 3–2 victory over Bradford City in the League Cup, Town pushed Brian Clough's Derby all the way in the second round before bowing out 3–1, but Kirby returned to the Baseball Ground in November to sign centre-half Tony Rhodes, claiming he was vital to future plans. 'We are planning for promotion as soon as possible, and Rhodes is coming to help that aim,' he said.

The biggest match at The Shay was the visit of relegated Aston Villa, but Town proved their worth by winning 2–1 and they later enjoyed comfortable successes over Port Vale and Doncaster, but set against these was the shock Boxing Day 4–1 home reversal by Rochdale, followed by the departure of coach Arthur Cox – to Preston, of course. Brian Green replaced him for a short time but by the time he too left for a coaching role in Kuwait the following February, Town's season was in full swing. They embarked upon an unbeaten run

The Halifax Town team that came close to Second Division football in 1970–71. Back row (left to right): Mick Buxton, Dave Verity, Ian Lawther, Phil McCarthy, John Pickering, Bill Atkins. Front row: Alex Smith, Dave Chadwick, Bob Wallace, Dave Lennard, Andy Burgin, Keith Brierley.

that transformed their season and made Kirby's seemingly bold prediction of promotion a more realistic one. By winning four consecutive matches in January, the Shaymen moved among the leaders and two wins and two draws throughout February saw George Kirby named as Bell's Third Division Manager of the Month.

A week after Lawther's goal won a feisty derby match at Bradford City, Town laid to rest the ghost of the previous season's drubbing by Fulham by coming from behind to win 2–1 at The Shay, then managed a draw at rivals Aston Villa in front of a 33,522 crowd. But Preston and Fulham were forcing the pace and Town could ill-afford any slip ups, and sadly, their promotion aspirations floundered at Torquay where the breaks went against them.

Kirby put on a brave face and though his side won their penultimate match 4–1 over Barnsley, Preston, the only side that the Shaymen could have caught, claimed both points in the all-important top-of-the-table clash at Fulham, and their dream was over.

While Town also lost in the Final of the West Riding Senior Cup to a strong Leeds side, their hard luck story did not end there. The 1970–71 season had seen the creation of the Ford Sporting League, where points were awarded for

Alan Maden (right) greets Fulham chairman Tommy Trinder, the well-known comedian, prior to The Shay clash, 6 March 1971. The last laugh was on the visitors, as Town won 2–1.

Manchester United's George Best tries to bamboozle Barry Holmes (number-12 shirt) in the Watney Cup match, 31 July 1971.

fair play. Going into the final weeks, Town were very much in contention for the honour, but the bookings handed out to Wallace and McCarthy – the only ones the side received all season – in the derby match at Bradford City cost them dearly. With the table being based on only the first 42 matches of the season, Town ultimately finished second to Oldham and missed out on the £10,000 prize money on offer.

There was, however, compensation at the start of the following season in the form of the Watney Invitation Cup, a competition designed for the highest scorers in each of the four divisions not qualifying for Europe or gaining promotion. Halifax Town, by scoring 74 goals, qualified from the Third Division and were handed the plum home tie against a star-studded Manchester United side, who included in their ranks household names such as Bobby Charlton, Denis Law and George Best. All three players

Denis Law finds that Tony Rhodes and John Pickering are never too far away.

Manager Ray Henderson waits to greet George Mulhall on his first day as Halifax Town coach, 18 October 1971.

turned out in the match on 31 July 1971, but it was the Shaymen who pulled off a major shock by winning 2–1 in front of 19,965 and the BBC *Match of the Day* cameras. Town, however, lost their semi-final to Division One West Brom, whose rough-house tactics helped them to a 2–0 win courtesy of Colin Suggett's two goals.

But that game turned out to by George Kirby's last in charge, for some time at least. The following week he left to take over at Watford and, indeed, it was all change at The Shay. On 28 June chairman Alan Maden had resigned from the board, frustrated by the demands of the bank and the Corporation, and while Nottingham-based businessman Arthur Smith succeeded him, in turn Ray Henderson, formerly coach at Hull City and Reading, came in to replace Kirby on 10 August, just four days before the start of the **1971–72** League season.

Henderson, though, must have been encouraged by Town's start, for as well as home victories over York and leaders Bournemouth, and away at Barnsley, they also progressed to the second round of the League Cup at the expense of Rochdale following a replay, and gave First Division Newcastle United – Malcolm Macdonald et al – a run for their money at St James's Park.

But the gradual break-up of the side was detrimental to League progress. Lennard was the first to go, making a record £30,500 move to Blackpool at the beginning of October, and while Henderson signed Ipswich's Frank Brogan to compensate, the player was unlucky to fracture an ankle in only his third match. Pressure mounted on the new Town boss when Town slipped up at non-League Wigan in the first round of the FA Cup, but Henderson tried to appease the supporters with the signings of striker Terry Shanahan and midfielder Fred Kemp, who joined in a record £13,500 deal from Blackpool, both players making their debuts in a 3–1 victory over Walsall on 4 December. But the side would win only one more game before the end of January, albeit a memorable derby win over Bradford City, and dropped as low as 19th.

When Town's game at Shrewsbury on 16 February was called off because of power cuts, the board and manager took the unprecedented move of meeting up with the fans to discuss where the side was going wrong, but this had little impact. True, Town beat Wrexham 4–1 in their next match, but with Chadwick moving to Bournemouth the following week, the side was far the worse far it. On 4 March, Brighton strolled to a 5–0 win at The Shay, leading Bill Carter to quip sarcastically in that evening's Green Final edition of the *Halifax Courier*, 'Here, Brighton! Have a couple of points...' and Town slipped back towards the relegation zone. But helped by three consecutive victories towards the end of March, they secured safety following a goalless draw with Shrewsbury, with just two games remaining.

It had been mightily close, though, and the directors felt that matters needed addressing. On 16 May, four days after Henderson sent out his team for the West Riding Senior Cup Final with recent FA Cup winners Leeds at Elland Road, he was sacked, and while Arthur Smith defended the board's decision, reckoning they felt 'a new man at the helm would be in the best interests of the club to carry out the progressive plans scheduled for the 1972–73 season,' Henderson slipped out of The Shay, claiming, 'I have not been given a fair chance. 36 weeks can hardly be considered as a fair opportunity.'

On 27 June 1972 the board elected to promote from within once more and appointed coach George Mulhall, who had arrived at the club the previous October, as Henderson's successor. He initially brought in only one new player, that of Johnny Quinn, although Ken Hale, who arrived as trainer, would end up getting his boots out when the threadbare squad was sorely tested.

Yet Town, sporting a new all-white kit with tangerine-and-blue trim, made a terrific start to the **1972–73** season, defeating Brentford and Bristol Rovers, and though home defeats by Bury, in the League Cup, and Chesterfield may have been of some concern, when they won at Scunthorpe in their seventh, the Shaymen headed the table. But incredibly, the 1–0 victory at Rotherham two weeks later would prove to be their last in the League until January. Injuries and illness had a serious effect, and never was Town's paucity in numbers more evident than when Mulhall succeeded in getting their game at York scheduled for 15 December postponed after five of his players went down with flu, nor when trainer Ken Hale was forced to register as a player to give Mulhall more options.

While Town slid down the table, there were problems, too, off the field. On 16 November chairman Arthur Smith and director Arthur Mitchell were voted off the board following a shareholders' meeting after coming under fire over the late publication of the club's accounts, and new chairman Percy Albon's first act was to urge business to rally round the club after the *Halifax Courier* led with the headline 'Halifax Town in Financial Difficulties' on 1 December. In turn, the board drew up a four-point appeal to business firms to buy shares in the club, become guarantors at the bank, loan the club money and/or join the board.

Despite Town's precarious League position, Mulhall threw in some surprises, not least the quick-fire sale of Atkins to Rochdale on the morning of an FA Cup tie with Scunthorpe. Later, Lammie Robertson headed for Brighton in return for former Burnley and Northern Ireland international striker Willie Irvine, and a winless streak in the League which had stretched to 15 games was finally ended with single-goal victory over Scunthorpe on 27 January. But by the end of the following month, The Iron were the only club below them as relegation stared the Shaymen in the face. With Hale now filling the left-back berth, Mulhall also signed striker John Wilkie, but who could have foreseen the irony of crowd-pleaser Trevor Womble's loan move from Rotherham on 8 March? Particularly when he scored one of the goals in a 2–2 draw with Blackburn Rovers a month later.

By then, Town's position had improved, even if the 3–2 victory over Brentford was watched by just 970, the Halifax folk evidently giving up on the side. Mulhall was not, however, despite seeing his side slip to defeat at Bolton on 16 April, a result that left them with little margin for error. The Shaymen had four games remaining in which to save themselves, although they were fortunate that the first three were at home, and inroads were made with wins over Charlton and Southend before a 2–0 success over Bournemouth on the last Saturday of the season. With Rotherham having lost their last three games and suddenly sucked into the relegation mire, Town knew that a win in their last match would send the Millers down on goal average, and on 1 May all roads led to Fellows Park, home of Walsall, for Town's do-or-die fixture. When Alan Waddle rose to head home Quinn's centre in the 35th minute, it was a goal that proved decisive. Town hung on for victory and climbed above Rotherham and sent them down by 0.02 of a goal.

There were no relegation worries for Mulhall's side during **1973–74**, for against the odds, the side punched above their weight and found themselves competing, for the most part, in the top half of the table. But given the signings he made, perhaps this was no surprise. While Jeff Lee ended a nine-year association with the club by moving to Peterborough, into The Shay came winger Alan Jones, midfielders David Ford and David Pugh, and Swansea's big centre-forward Dave Gwyther.

Town gave early evidence of their capabilities by more than matching their illustrious opponents in the Final of the West Riding Senior Cup, held over from the previous season, against a strong Leeds side, yet made a slow start in the League and dropped as low as 20th on the back of some poor results. But form improved, and by the end of October they had moved up to 12th. They'd also enjoyed entertaining First Division opposition in the League Cup when Wolves, whose side included familiar names such as Derek Dougan and John Richards, arrived for a League Cup tie on 8 October. They ran out 3–0 winners, though Town's Kemp was left to rue a 51st-minute penalty miss with the visitors holding a single-goal lead. Town, however, welcomed the 8,222 gate that the match attracted and the income it brought for just 10 days later chairman Percy Albon revealed at the club's AGM that the

Halifax Town 1973–74. Back row (left to right): George Mulhall (manager), Johnny Quinn, Dave Gwyther, John Pickering, Barry White, Alex Smith, Tony Rhodes, Willie Irvine, Ken Hale, Brian Hendy (trainer). Front row: David Pugh, Andy Burgin, David Ford, John Wilkie, Terry Shanahan, Fred Kemp, Gerry McDonald.

THE HISTORY OF HALIFAX TOWN

Dave Gwyther scores the second goal of his headed hat-trick as Halifax Town defeat Frickley Colliery in the first round of the FA Cup at The Shay, 24 November 1973.

club had been threatened with closure having received a letter from a firm which was owed £1,000 and needed paying within 48 hours.

With the familiar Dave Worthington reappearing in the side when on a month's loan from Grimsby Town, the players maintained form in the League and gave the fans some real cheer in the FA Cup with the 6–1 defeat of Frickley Colliery, though interest in the competition was ended in the next round when Oldham won 1–0 at The Shay. That game kicked off at 1.45pm to avoid the need to use of floodlights as the country was thrown into a power crisis resulting in a three-day week and Town became one of several clubs who elected to play League games on a Sunday, with Southport providing the opposition of for the first of those on 27 January. The match, which ended 1–1, was watched by 4,178, a figure that was above average, as were the games with Walsall a week later and Cambridge United on 10 March.

Finding themselves in the Third Division for the first time were Huddersfield Town, and they would triumph 4–0 at Leeds Road in the first-ever League meeting between the sides on Boxing Day, but the return, fittingly the 1,000th League match at The Shay, on 2 March ended goalless, although it was far from a dull encounter. After the Football League had agreed to postpone Town's match at Bournemouth on 30 March when the club had reported only 10 fit players, two of which were goalkeepers, manager Mulhall went back to Huddersfield for striker David Smith to help his small squad. He scored the first of five goals for the club from the penalty spot in the home match with Grimsby, but Town's 2–1 defeat turned out to be their last. Unbeaten in their last eight matches, a sequence that included six draws, Town wrapped up their fixtures with a 2–1 victory over promoted York City, and finished the season a commendable ninth.

While Smith declined the offer of making a permanent move to The Shay, another player who had played his last game for the club was John Pickering. A fixture in the side since 1965, and with a club record 367 appearances behind him, he left for Barnsley, while Mulhall also lost right-hand man Ken Hale, who left to take over as manager of Hartlepool. In turn, he promoted Quinn to player-coach, while offsetting the further departure of Fred Kemp with the signings of former Wales Under-23

Halifax Town emblem, designed by director John Crowther and adopted by the club in January 1974.

Halifax Town 1974–75. Back row (left to right): Mark Harrold, Dave Gwyther, Barry White, Alex Smith, Tony Rhodes, Fred Kemp, Terry Shanahan, Brian Hendy (trainer). Front row: Steve Downes, Johnny Quinn, Paul Luckett, Alan Jones, David Pugh, David Ford, Andy Burgin, Steve Mackay.

international left-full back John Collins, Paul Luckett, midfielder Ray McHale and strikers Steve Downes and Ricky Moir, while the loan signing of Oxford United centre-half Nick Lowe became a necessity due to an early season injury crisis.

Mulhall reckoned 'Town could be a force to be reckoned with' during **1974–75**, and was happy with his side's start, which included the 3–1 defeat of big spenders Crystal Palace, whose manager Malcolm Allison was quick to criticise, claiming, 'They [Halifax Town] shouldn't be in the Football League. Their facilities are a disgrace. In fact, they are non-existent.'

Town enjoyed their visit to First Division Stoke City in the second round of the League Cup, though perhaps not the 3–0 scoreline they were on the receiving end, with Terry Conroy, a survivor from the FA Cup tie five years earlier, grabbing a hat-trick, but soon Mulhall was having misgivings about his team. On 18 September, the day after he had handed Mark Harrold his League debut, the first coloured player to play for Halifax Town for the 3–1 home defeat by Chesterfield, he resigned, claiming, 'Halifax Town is not for me and they would perhaps be better with a new face as manager.'

Johnny Quinn stepped up initially in a caretaker capacity, and though Town lost at Blackburn in his first game in charge, he was appointed Mulhall's full-time

Halifax Town reserve goalkeeper Barry White, who made four outfield appearances to help out an injury crisis during 1974–75.

successor following a board meeting on 23 September. As fate would have it, he then found himself with only 12 fit players, and was compelled to thrust reserve goalkeeper Barry White into a defensive role for the match at Peterborough for the first of four outfield appearances.

Quinn appointed Syd Farrimond, on the staff at Tranmere Rovers, as coach and made the signings of the Chesterfield pair centre-back Albert Phelan and midfielder Ray McHale, while Terry Shanahan made the opposite journey back to Chesterfield. Quinn then signed Derby midfielder Kenny Blair, but he would not taste success in the League until his seventh match in charge, a 3–1 victory over Southend United, a win much-needed after Town had slipped towards the relegation zone. Slowly, the side began to climb up the table, winning three League matches in November, among them a memorable 2–1 success at Huddersfield.

But Quinn came under fire following FA Cup defeat at Stafford, Town undone when Jim Sargeant let fly from 20 yards with just 44 seconds left on the clock. Town responded with a 3–2 victory over Bournemouth but it would be a while before they won again as they became embroiled in another relegation fight. Bad weather in January that put paid to several matches did not help their cause, and before they knew where they were, Town were lying 22nd.

The signings of full-back Alex Smith from Colchester United, and loan striker Bobby Campbell (Aston Villa) saw an upturn in form, although it was another loan player, Bobby Scaife (Middlesbrough) who scored the goal of the game, an unforgettable 30-yarder, when defeating Huddersfield 2–1 on 22 February to complete a welcome League double. Encouraging results, such as the 1–1 draw at fifth-placed Crystal Palace and victories over Peterborough and Bournemouth made for a healthier picture, though the Shaymen continued to look over their shoulder and didn't totally guarantee their safety from relegation until the 1–0 defeat of Walsall at The Shay in the penultimate match.

The board of directors had stumped up cash in January to keep the club, but they would not be able to help Town's own spiral to the Fourth Division during **1975–76**. Some might argue that they contributed to the club's downfall by the sacking of manager Johnny Quinn in February and the re-installation of Alan Ball Snr, for the change did not pay off, and Town found themselves finishing bottom and returning to the Fourth Division after seven years.

That scenario looked highly improbable, however, when Quinn's side made an impressive start to the season and moved among the early season pacesetters. With new signings such as young goalkeeper Terry Gennoe, defender Tommy Veitch and striker Derek Bell, they also saw off the immediate challenge of Hartlepool in the League

Steve Downes lifts the ball over Millwall 'keeper Ray Goddard to reduce the arrears as the Shaymen slip to a 2–1 defeat on the season's opening day, 16 August 1975.

Cup, the first time that the first round was played over two legs, to set them up with a home tie with another First Division side in Sheffield United. The Blades themselves would be relegated that season, but had enough armoury in the side to win 4–2, with chief tormentor being Colin Guthrie, who scored a hat-trick.

Town had gone into that game lying third in the table and they maintained their early challenge with a succession of draws before laying promoted Chester to the sword with an impressive 5–2 victory on 27 September. Town went fourth but two months later they were more concerned with the other end of the table. Home form became a major concern and by the turn of the year the side was lying 16th.

Yet Town came good in the FA Cup, moving to the third round with a comfortable 3–1 home victory over non-League Altrincham and exacting revenge over Stafford after the previous year's shock defeat. Bobby Robson's Ipswich Town awaited them in the third round, but class told. Their side included internationals Allan Hunter, Mick Mills, and David Johnson, but it was squad member Mick Lambert who did the damage with a hat-trick in Ipswich's 3–1 win.

Town returned to League action badly needing points, though when freezing weather pity paid to two home games, Quinn kept his players active by including 10 regular first-teamers in a reserve match at Doncaster (which they lost 2–1). As things transpired, that would be the last time he would take charge of a Town team. Those glancing through the Sunday papers of 1 February 1975 may have been shocked to read of the directors' consideration of a change of manager and the *Halifax Courier* added fuel to the rumours with their headline the following day, 'Shock move for Alan Ball stuns Quinn'. When asked, the Town boss claimed, 'You know more about it than me. The first I knew was when I read

Halifax Town 1975–76. Back row (left to right): Johnny Quinn (manager), Syd Farrimond (trainer), David Pugh, Paul Luckett, Geoff Harris, Derek Bell, Steve Cox, Terry Gennoe, Dave Gwyther, Albert Phelan, Alex Smith (full-back), Steve Downes, Mark Harrold, Tony Rhodes. Front row: Brian Hendy (trainer), Alan Jones, David Ford, John Crowther (director), Harry Taylor (vice-chairman), Jack Turner (director), Ray McHale, John Collins, Kenny Blair, Alex Smith.

it in the press,' but that evening the board sat to discuss his position, and the following day Alan Ball Snr was back at The Shay as manager.

Johnny Quinn's sacking, and in particular, the manner of it, prompted an angry backlash from the supporters. 'They could not have sacked a nicer guy,' said one. The board, however, were concerned with results, though Ball's return did not lead to an upturn in fortunes. Losing his first game, ironically at Preston, the side he had left Halifax for nearly six years earlier, Town slipped into the relegation zone for the first time and though Ball was adamant he could save the club from the drop, his wholesale changes to the side did not have the desired effect. While top scorer Gwyther moved to Rotherham United into the club came a succession of players such as midfield hardman Jimmy McGill, strikers Mickey Bullock and George Jones and right-back Bobby Flavell, as well as John Overton, on loan from Aston Villa. But it was all to no avail. Town found themselves bottom by the time they hosted Sheffield Wednesday on 2 March, and though they pulled off one of the shocks of the season by winning 2–1 at leaders Hereford, victory failed to galvanise the side. Only two more wins were recorded before the season's close but with a number of clubs involved in the dogfight, Town's expected relegation was not confirmed until their penultimate match, a 12th home defeat at the hands of Aldershot. With Town confined to bottom place, only 856 bothered to turn out for the last match, a 1–1 draw with Colchester United, and though no one realised it at the time, that would prove to be Halifax Town's last ever in the third tier of English football.

Re-Election Woes 1976–81

Alan Ball had every confidence that Halifax Town could bounce back at the first attempt, despite losing the services of skipper Rhodes and Collins, who left pre-season, and McHale and Alan Jones shortly into the 1976–77 campaign. Instead, he would rely on new signings such as central-defenders Dave Rylands and Jack Trainer, midfield schemer Jimmy Lawson, Johnny Johnston and forward Bobby Hoy, while plucked from non-League London football club was young goalkeeper Mick Leonard.

League Cup defeat by Darlington after a third match gave an indication of a season of struggle, and indeed Town made no easy transition to Fourth Division life. They did not record their first victory until the seventh match, and with crowds quickly drifting away, slipped into the re-election zone following the home defeat to Scunthorpe United on 9 October.

New players arrived in the form of forwards Joe Carroll, defender Lee Bradley and on-loan midfielder Jim McCann, as well as the Chester defensive pairing of Tony Loska and Chris Dunleavy at the end of October. Dunleavy made an instant impact with a sixth-minute headed goal that set Town on their way to a record-equaling 6–0 win over Doncaster on 2 November, and it seemed for a time as if they had turned a corner, the goalless draw with Huddersfield on 27 December completing a seven-match unbeaten run and keeping them four points clear of the re-election zone.

Improved form had come at the right time, for in the FA Cup, Town survived a third successive tie with Stafford Rangers before winning The Shay replay, and then pulled off a giant-killing act of sorts when Third Division Preston were beaten 1–0. But they lost in the third round to Division Two side Luton in front of a welcome 5,519 Shay crowd, with a goal from former Manchester United winger John Aston separating the sides.

The Halifax Town side that began the 1976–77 season back in the Fourth Division. Back row (left to right): Bobby Flavell, Albert Phelan, Mick Leonard, George Jones, Mickey Bullock, Noel O'Brien, Johnny Johnston. Front row: Derek Bell, Ray McHale, Alan Jones, Bobby Hoy, Geoff Harris, Jimmy Lawson.

Town by then had slipped into their old ways, with the defeat to Luton coming in the middle of another winless streak that had stretched to eight games and had the Shaymen looking over their shoulders. But that run was ended emphatically with the 6–1 rout of Workington on 5 February, though their position remained precarious.

Ball had been particularly unfortunate with long-term injuries to Hoy and Rylands, and when the side travelled to Doncaster on 12 April 1977, he found himself without a goalkeeper when Leonard failed a pre-match fitness and was confined to the sidelines along with Gennoe. A dash by trainer Brian Hendy to the home of Roman Chmilowskyj at the 11th hour saw the young 'keeper arrive at the Belle Vue ground just 40 minutes before kick-off for his only League start, but he was unable to prevent Town slipping to a 3–0 defeat.

The Shaymen savoured the derby victory over Bradford City four days later, for it proved to be their last win of the season, and a series of poor results meant that the threat of a re-election place loomed larger. Still, Town went into their last game with their fate still in their own hands, knowing that victory over Southport, who were already condemned, would ensure their safety. But they could only manage a 1–1 draw, and Bobby Flavell's 47th-minute penalty miss ultimately proved costly. Had he scored it, doubtless Newport's one outstanding game would have been rendered meaningless, but by defeating Workington three days later, the Welsh side jumped over Town, and thus condemned them to an eighth re-election bid just 12 months after being relegated.

Halifax Town, in fact, finished top of the voting with 44 votes, but they were perhaps fortunate that among the other clubs going cap in hand to the Football League were the footballing outposts of Workington, whose fourth successive re-election bid ended in failure. They lost their place to Southern League Wimbledon, who, by chance, prepared for their first League match of the **1977–78** season with the Shaymen.

Wimbledon begin life as a Football League club by entertaining Halifax Town on 20 August 1977. Their captain Dave Donaldson (right) shakes hands with Town skipper Chris Dunleavy before the entertaining 3–3 draw.

Town went into that game on the back of inglorious League Cup defeat at the hands of Rochdale, but with the experienced Steve Smith arriving to add to the earlier signings of defender Terry Alcock and winger Tommy Horsfall, they played their part in an entertaining 3–3 draw, twice taking the lead but in the end indebted to Bell, who netted a late equaliser to deny Wimbledon opening day victory.

Town scored three in their next match, too, when defeating Hartlepool, giving hope of a better times, but soon enough, results followed an all too familiar pattern and at the beginning of October they had dropped once more into the re-election zone. Ball was finding the going tough but he bought time when on-loan Wayne Powell scored the winning goal in a 2–1 victory at Southport to end a winless run that had stretched to 11 games, though the three consecutive defeats that followed saw Town lying next to bottom on goal difference from Rochdale. The *Halifax Courier* dated 14 November 1977 reported that 'Ball is walking on thin ice' but that quote had come from the manager himself on the day the board, now headed by demolition contractor Andrew Delaney following Percy Albon's decision to stand down, sat to decide his future. Citing 'lack of satisfactory results' as the reason, the decision to sack Ball was a unanimous one and the board immediately appointed Jimmy Lawson as caretaker player-manager. Much-improved performances followed, such as his first game in charge, a West Riding Senior Cup tie at Huddersfield that saw Town lose on penalties, and the 2–1 defeat of Aldershot, and Lawson was offered the manager's job on a permanent basis on 29 November, despite having just seen his side tumble out of the FA Cup with defeat at Chesterfield.

Lawson appointed striker Mickey Bullock as coach, then saw his side continue their improvement in the League, taking an unbeaten run of eight matches into the New Year and moving out of the danger zone and up to 17th. But with bad weather forcing the postponements of five scheduled matches, plus a heavy defeat suffered at the hands of Southend United on 17 February 1978, Town found themselves worryingly just one point off the re-election zone and without their 'keeper Terry Gennoe, for despite conceding five goals at Roots Hall, he moved to Lawrie McMenemy's Southampton £35,000 four days later.

Jack Trainer heads home Town's first goal in the 2–2 draw at Huddersfield Town, 4 March 1978.

Earlier young Roly Gregoire had made a surprising £5,000 move to Sunderland, and despite the club revealing at their AGM back in December that they had made a loss of £36,000 during 1976–77, money was made available to Lawson for new players. Having already secured Huddersfield winger Francis Firth on a free transfer, the club paid £10,000 for his team mate Bob Mountford, then brought in defender Peter Burke to The Shay. Ex-Huddersfield full-back Geoff Hutt also put pen to paper following a spell in Holland, although his debut would be delayed until the following season.

The new signings paid dividends as the side put together a seven-match unbeaten sequence to move high as 14th following a 3–1 win over Newport on 8 April to seemingly banish re-election worries. But with a cluster of clubs in trouble, Town's own safety was not ensured until their penultimate match that concluded their Shay programme, a physical encounter with champions-elect Watford. Bell scored a memorable overhead kick to earn

After player-manager Jimmy Lawson killed the ball on his chest, slipped his marker and beat two defenders, he then fired home past Newport County 'keeper Turner for a wonder goal at The Shay, 8 April 1978.

THE HISTORY OF HALIFAX TOWN

The Halifax Town squad assemble prior to the ill-fated 1978–79 season. Back row (left to right): Nigel Brown (assistant trainer), Lee Bradley, Jon Nixon, Geoff Hutt, Mick Leonard, Gary Hanson, Kevin Johnson, Francis Firth, Joe Carroll, Mick Kennedy, Brian Hendy (trainer). Front row Derek Bell, Peter Burke, Steve Smith, Mickey Bullock (player-coach), Jimmy Lawson (player-manager), Jack Trainer, Johnny Johnston, Tony Loska, Chris Dunleavy.

Town the point they needed, and although defeat in their final match at promotion-bound Swansea City meant that the Shaymen finished a lowly 20th, they were still four points clear of the re-election zone.

In an effort to brighten things up during **1978–79**, Lawson introduced an all-white playing strip. 'A touch of the Real Madrids?' pondered the *Halifax Courier*, but sadly the colour of the playing strip was about as far as the comparisons went with the Spanish footballing giants.

When Bobby Flavell moved to Chesterfield for £25,000, Lawson used all that money to bring Huddersfield's ball-playing wizard Kevin Johnson to The Shay. But despite performing admirably over two legs over Walsall, Town slipped out of the League Cup and suffered a 4–2 defeat at Barnsley when they began their League programme. Victory over Stockport seven days later at least seemed to redress the balance, but, unbelievably, the supporters would be waiting seven long months before the next win.

Lawson's side sunk to the foot of the table, and the supporters began staying away. Only 985 turned up for the visit of Crewe on 30 September, causing the *Courier* to lead with the cruel headline accompanying a shot of the sparse terracing of 'Spot The Crowd'. A point in that game, plus another from a draw at Rochdale lifted the Shaymen up one rung, but it was temporary respite, for when they collapsed

One fan responds in prose to Jimmy Lawson's belief that his side will get out of trouble, *Halifax Courier*, 25 October 1978.

Shaymen's plight spurs poetic reader to write

Rockhaven, Burnley Road,
Sowerby Bridge
"The Shaymen are good enough to get us out of trouble." (Mr Lawson, "Evening Courier," October 14)

As rare as the sun on a cloudy day.
As rare as sorrow when life seems quite gay,
As rare as a bike on a motor way
Is a goal scored by one of the men from the Shay.

For shooting's a talent they seem to hide —
Their efforts are always too high or too wide.
And scoring a goal they cannot abide,
Unless it's a goal for the opposite side.

"The Shaymen are trying — they huff and they puff,"
The papers all say. So it seems to me bluff
When the players are finding the going so tough.
And the manager says, "The team's good enough."

W. HELLIWELL

Port Vale defenders cannot prevent Bill Bentley turning the ball into his own net and Halifax Town are on the way to their second victory of the season, 24 February 1979. Town players Jack Trainer (5) and Bob Mountford are both on hand to make sure.

3–0 at home to Port Vale on 14 October, they found themselves bottom once more, a position they would occupy until the closing weeks of the season.

Towards the end of October, Derek Bell moved to Barnsley for £30,000, money which Town were in no position to turn down, and while Mick Prendergast arrived at The Shay on loan as part of the deal, Lawson also added Huddersfield players centre-half Arnie Sidebottom and striker Bobby Campbell to his squad, thus bringing the number of ex-Terriers on the books to eight and leading some to call the Shaymen 'Huddersfield Old Boys'. But with no improvement in results, the board's decision to sack Lawson on 30 October surprised no one.

In an unusual scenario, Lawson was kept on the books as a player while the board turned to another former manager in the hope that he might transform the club's fortunes. On 3 November George Kirby, after success in Iceland, returned to The Shay, and though performances improved, helped by the promotion of young Mick Kennedy to the side, that second win proved elusive.

The home defeat by Wigan on 16 November was significant, if only because it proved to be the last match played at The Shay until March. The 1978–79 season was one hit hard by

Winter of discontent. The bulldozers are called in to help clear the pitch of snow, 30 January 1979. Halifax Town were without a home game for three months during 1978–79.

Halifax Town lift themselves off the bottom of the Fourth Division table thanks to this headed Kevin Johnson goal that proved enough to beat Hereford United at The Shay. 9 May 1979.

a terrible winter, with snow, ice and sub-zero temperatures forcing the postponement of 13 scheduled and rearranged Shay matches. With Town finding the going hard on their travels, defeat at Northampton Town on 30 December left the side stranded at the foot of the table, with a re-election bid looking a formality even at this early stage.

The winter almost crippled the club, which was forced to survive on little income other than that from the recently formed Shaymaker Lottery. But the Shaymen returned to action on 10 February at fellow strugglers Crewe, though the 1–0 defeat left their position as unenviable as ever. Two weeks later, however, they began to make slight inroads on the clubs directly above them thanks to Port Vale's Bill Bentley, whose own-goal gave Town only their second win of the season, though it came at a price. Goalkeeper Leonard suffered a nasty facial injury and manager Kirby was forced to take on loan Preston's John Kilner, though he quickly played his part in the downfall of high-flying Portsmouth seven days later in what was Town's first home match since the enforced Winter break.

Results such as these, however, were few and far between, and although Town would win away against Stockport and triumph over another promotion-seeking side in Wimbledon, their own fate was sealed when they lost 1–0 at champions-elect Reading on 28 April. Their only hope of salvaging some pride was in attempting to lift themselves off the bottom, but Kirby would have to do so without Sidebottom, who left to concentrate on county cricket with Yorkshire, and Campbell, sacked for what was described as 'conduct in breach of club rules'. Still, they moved above Crewe, who had gone into free fall, on goal difference courtesy of Johnson's headed goal which was enough to beat Hereford on 9 May, Town's third game in six days as they crammed in their fixtures, and the Shaymen managed to keep off the bottom, though they ensured the issue went to the wire by losing their final two home matches to Hartlepool and Scunthorpe.

Halifax Town had every right to be nervous about their re-election application on 1 June 1979, but they survived despite polling the fewest votes of the four clubs applying. A relieved secretary David Holland said, 'We see this as a fresh start,' and the directors immediately made £45,000 available to George Kirby for team strengthening. He spent wisely, signing young Aston Villa defender David Evans, Bristol Rovers' midfield dynamo Paul Hendrie and centre-half Dave Harris, while the experienced utility player Tony Geidmintis also joined the club, as did teenage centre-back Malcolm Goodman and local lad Andy Whiteley.

There were encouraging signs at the beginning of **1979–80** when Town pushed Shrewsbury all the way before bowing out over two legs in the first round of the League Cup, but they made a stuttering start to their League programme. However, the 3–1 victory over Crewe on 1 September heralded an upturn in the side's fortunes as they went through

Halifax Town 1979–80. Back row (left to right): Tony Geidminits, Andy Stafford, Peter Burke, Mick Leonard, Dave Harris, Bob Mountford, David Evans. Front row: Geoff Hutt, Paul Hendrie, Mick Kennedy, Kevin Johnson, Chris Dunleavy, Francis Firth.

the whole of the month unbeaten, thus landing manager Kirby the Fourth Division's Manager of the Month award, his second with the club after winning it back in February 1971. But his achievement this time around was far from straightforward. Goalkeeper Leonard's £35,000 sale to Notts County forced him to re-sign Kilner on a permanent deal, but when his registration failed to reach the Football League headquarters in time the Town boss was forced to throw in local amateur John Hough for his one and only League start for the match with Hereford. Later, Town came from behind to beat Hartlepool 2–1 after losing Johnson with a broken leg following a crude challenge from Bob Newton.

Kirby took on loan Everton reserve striker John Thomas, then watched his side beat Newport County 2–1 in a thriller, with Kilner saving an injury time penalty, to move up to fifth. Later, Walsall, the last undefeated side in the League, were beaten by the same score and such was the interest in Town's upsurge that over 7,000 turned out for the top of the table clash with Bradford City. But Town lost the game and a sequence of inconsistent results followed. However, they reserved their best form for the FA Cup, seeing off non-League Scarborough before playing three pulsating matches with Walsall in round two, the issue decided with extra-time goals from Burke and John Smith, signed in early November, in a replay hastily arranged at The Shay on Christmas Eve, and Town won the right to host First Division Manchester City.

This was an exciting period for the Shaymen, for two days after the Cup defeat of Walsall, they pulled off a magnificent 2–1 Boxing Day victory over title-chasing Huddersfield. Watched by 10,061, this proved to be the last time a five-figure gate would witness a League match at The Shay, though there were more for the visit of Manchester City, of course, despite the game being in doubt until the morning of the match. Thawing snow and ice had left The Shay pitch in a treacherous state, but with club officials and volunteers working tirelessly to mop up the water, referee Michael Lowe gave the game the

Paul Hendrie slides the ball past 'keeper Joe Corrigan to give Halifax Town a memorable third-round win in the FA Cup over Manchester City.

Pitch inspection by Manchester City assistant-manager Tony Book, referee Michael Lowe and Halifax Town secretary Mike Walker on the morning of the FA Cup clash with the First Division side, 5 January 1980.

go-ahead, and with the conditions proving to be great leveller, Town won the match unforgettably courtesy of Hendrie's 75th-minute goal.

Cup exploits were soon overshadowed by internal wranglings which led to the resignations of directors Jack Turner and Robert Hanson, and the players themselves came down to earth with defeat in their next match at bottom side Crewe. That was the only game Town played prior to the FA Cup fourth-round match at struggling First Division Bolton Wanderers, and though they were cheered on by around 6,000 travelling supporters and giving a good account of themselves at Burnden Park, the Shaymen fell to goals by Roy Greaves and, late on, Neil Whatmore.

Halifax Town players celebrate in the bath after defeating Manchester City. From left: John Smith, Francis Firth, Andy Stafford, Paul Hendrie, Mick Kennedy, John Kilner, Geoff Hutt, David Evans, Dave Harris, Bob Mountford.

Halifax Town's 1979–80 FA Cup run comes to end at Bolton Wanderers. With his side leading 1–0, Neil Whatmore (left) doubles Bolton's lead one minute from time when the ball goes in off his knee. Watching in horror is Chris Dunleavy (centre), while the flailing arms of 'keeper John Kilner cannot prevent the ball crossing the line.

Thereafter, Town struggled towards the end of the season. Kirby pitched into the side young strikers Vernon Allatt and Carl Dryhurst, both plucked from non-League football, but it was teenager midfielder Mick Kennedy, growing in stature, who scored the only goal when Town won their last match of the season, a swirling 30-yarder to beat Aldershot. But with Newport and Huddersfield both putting five goals past the Shaymen, and home form giving cause for concern, Town failed to win any of their last nine matches and finished 18th, although re-election had never seriously been an issue.

Kennedy was soon on his way, making a record £50,000 move to Huddersfield, and George Kirby, who had always reckoned his side would be gearing up for a promotion drive during **1980–81**, signed the experienced defenders Tommy O'Neil, Clive Nattress and Ken

Halifax Town 1980–81. Back row (from left to right): Mickey Bullock (coach), Carl Dryhurst, Francis Firth, Steve Ward, Bobby Mimms, Andy Stafford, John Kilner, Clive Nattress, Dave Harris, Malcolm Goodman, George Kirby (manager). Front row: Ken Burton, Chris Dunleavy, Andy Whiteley, David Evans, Kevin Johnson, Vernon Allatt, Paul Hendrie.

Burton, as well as the versatile youngster Steve Ward. But his ambitions floundered, despite the odd bright performance by his team, particularly the scintillating 4–2 defeat of Bury which somewhat compensated for their earlier League Cup exit by the same club. When Town lost 4–1 at Wigan Athletic on 1 October, Town found themselves bottom of the table.

Kirby reacted by making the double signing of strikers Jimmy McIlwraith and Tommy Graham, and though they immediately helped Town to a 3–1 defeat of York, a 5–1 home defeat by Southend followed, leading to Kirby admit, 'We are now on a survival course.'

The situation would get worse. Banking on a decent run in the FA Cup, Town lost at Hull, and only 987 turned out for the visit of Bournemouth. Matters were not helped by off-field activity that had seen the departure of chairman Delaney on 26 August. John Crowther had taken over from him, but he resigned in November following the breakdown of talks with the rugby club with a view to a ground-share, which, had he got his way, would have seen Town playing home games at Thrum Hall. Elland businessman John Goldthorpe, who had joined the board the previous March, succeeded Crowther as chairman, but his own short time in office would see the club thwarting Scarborough chairman Don Robinson's attempt to sabotage the Shaymen's League status with an audacious £80,000 offer – the total cost of Town's shares – to take over the club, seemingly intent on shifting Halifax Town to their own Seamer Road ground and running a reserve side in the Alliance Premier.

Halifax Town had strengthened their own position, however, when millionaire deer park owner Sam Rorke joined the board and on 19 January 1981 he was installed as the club's fourth chairman in the space of five months, and there was the welcome return of John Crowther as vice-chairman, with responsibility for public relations.

Changes to the team had seen Hartlepool centre-half Billy Ayre arrive on New Year's Day in a deal involving Kevin Johnson, and the arrival of 'keeper Ian Turner on loan from Walsall. A 2–0 win over Stockport on 24 January lifted the mood at The Shay, though Town's position remained a worrying one. Midfielder Brian Chambers joined the club and the side enjoyed back to-to-back wins over Crewe and Hereford, where Allatt's scored an astonishing goal from fully 40 yards. But three consecutive defeats made a bottom-four finish all but inevitable, and despite winning 2–0 over Rochdale on Easter Monday and claiming victory over Aldershot in their last match, the Shaymen prepared themselves for their third re-election bid in five years.

Financial Woes: 1981–87

Nobody was more surprised than vice-chairman John Crowther when Halifax Town polled 41 votes at the Football League's AGM on 5 June 1981. 'I can't believe it,' exclaimed Crowther, and it was a relieved contingent that returned home. The club had published their blueprint for the future of The Shay, which they hoped to buy from the Council for £75,000, with long-term plans including an all-seater stadium, and this may have helped their cause. It would not, however, help George Kirby's. On 29 June 1981 he was sacked after earlier refusing to resign at the suggestion of Sam Rorke.

On 13 July, coach Mickey Bullock was unveiled as the surprise choice as manager and he immediately appointed Billy Ayre as coach, then brought in midfielder Glyn Chamberlain and full-back Everton Carr, while goalkeeper Bobby Mimms and Paul Kendall, having completed apprenticeships, were offered full-time contracts, though his biggest signing was that of young Huddersfield striker Bobby Davison for £20,000.

While Bullock was trying to improve the team, chairman Sam Rorke set about improving the facilities in and around The Shay ground. New £50,000 floodlights were installed and the old Shay Club was demolished and replaced by a function suite originally called Chimes, with the drive-in and car park tarmacced.

Changes off the field, but sadly not on it, despite the Football League introducing three points for a win during **1981–82**. Bullock's side played some attractive early season football, but as well as being knocked out of the League Cup by Preston over two legs, they did not record victory in the League until their ninth match and following a 3–2 defeat at Hartlepool on 26 September, an angry Bullock reacted by placing Kilner, Firth, Allatt and McIlwraith on the transfer-list, then watched his side crash 7–1 at Blackpool.

A shell-shocked Kilner, who had gaffed in a previous match with Tranmere when he placed the ball down for what he wrongly thought was a free-kick for offside, only for Owen Brown to nip in and score, was replaced by Nottingham Forest's Lee Smelt and Town defeated Bury for their first win of the season that heralded a mini-revival. But a second home victory over Mansfield on 21 November came at a price when full-back O'Neil broke his leg.

The money shelled out for Smelt had been funded by the surprise sale of Mimms to Rotherham, a real bonus given that he had yet to make a first-team appearance, and Bullock boosted his side with the signing of Derby midfielder Steve Spooner. He made his debut in a 2–0 defeat at Wigan on 5 December, although this game turned out to be Town's last for

Halifax Town 1981–82. Back row (from left to right): Alan Sutton (physio), Billy Ayre, Francis Firth, Vernon Allatt, John Kilner, Bobby Mimms, Andy Whiteley, Bobby Davison, Brian Hendy (trainer). Front row: David Evans, Steve Ward, Tommy Graham, Paul Hendrie, Tommy O'Neil, Jimmy McIlwraith, Mickey Bullock (manager), Glyn Chamberlain, Everton Carr. On ground: Paul Kendall, Simon Bullock, Malcolm Goodman.

Steve Ward nips in to push the ball beyond Sheffield United 'keeper Keith for Town's second goal, and Town's fightback from two goals down at Bramall Lane on 2 January 1982 is complete.

a month as heavy snow caused a major disruption to the football programme. An enforced break was the last thing that the club needed; they were desperate for revenue, as once again attention switched to their sorry financial plight, and the subsequent off-field activities grabbed national headlines.

The balance sheet for the year ending 31 March 1981 showed a loss of £34,062, leaving the club almost £112,000 in the red and Sam Rorke was concerned enough to call a public meeting at the Civic Theatre on 11 January 1982 to ask the people of Calderdale whether they really wanted a Football League club. Almost 2,000 people packed the theatre to hear Rorke reveal the extent of the club's debts and make a plea to the businessmen of Calderdale and the supporters to find £100,000 within six weeks. But by the end of February only £13,845 had been realised and with the situation looking desperate, Rorke called a press conference on 1 March where, with manager Bullock and John Crowther at his side, he announced that the club was up for sale. Teary-eyed, he told reporters, 'There is no point in trying to keep going a football club which the people of Halifax don't want.'

But overnight Rorke had a change of heart. The following day, he announced his battle cry: 'We fight on!' He felt that if the wage bill could be curbed by one-third, then, providing that the club could see out the present season, there was hope that they could start the following season with a clean slate, though all this came hard on McIlwraith's revelation in *The Sun* that he was earning £350 a week.

Meanwhile, Town had very much returned to action on the field. On 2 January a Ward brace earned them a 2–2 draw at high-flying Sheffield United, and a Davison strike ended a personal nine-match barren spell for when he scored the winner at Rochdale. In a bid to increase attendances, the club once again experimented with Friday night football, with Town playing out a 2–2 draw with Port Vale in front of an above-average crowd. Amazingly, this result was the first of seven successive draws that the side experienced, a run that temporarily took them to 18th, although their position could have been much healthier had they not been guilty of giving away so many last-minute goals as at Tranmere on 9 February, and in the 3–3 draw with Darlington a month later when David Speedie denied them all three points by scoring with the last kick of the match.

Town secured their biggest win of the season, a 4–1 home success over Stockport, but the jitters returned over the Easter period when they conceded five against both Sheffield United and Bradford City and sank to 23rd with only Crewe below them. But a six-match unbeaten run enabled them to climb out of the bottom four, and though they lost heavily at York with two games still to play, Rochdale's defeat by Hull City the following day meant that safety was assured and Town finished 20th, three points clear of the re-election zone.

Bobby Davison cracks in the second goal in the 4–1 victory over Stockport County at The Shay, 2 April 1982, Town's biggest victory of the season.

On 2 June 1982 Sam Rorke stood down as chairman and was succeeded by Jack Turner, who had returned to the board, while Tom McLean and David Sharpe, both of Macdee fitted kitchen manufacturers, became the club's first sponsors. Meanwhile, Mickey Bullock signed up striker Dave Staniforth as player-coach, Martin Nuttall, defenders Keith Nobbs, Tony Smith and Mick Wood, and midfielder Jimmy Hallybone.

The signs looked promising when Town performed well in a newly-devised competition, the Football League Group Cup, where Bobby Davison continued to find the net, and in the Final of the West Riding Senior Cup against Leeds at Elland Road, where they lost 3–2 after extra-time. They went on to make a sound start once the **1982–83** League season began, too, climbing to fifth following Davison's last-gasp winner at Swindon Town in their fourth match, as well pushing Second Division Derby all the way in the League Cup, sponsored for the first time by the Milk Marketing Board. Staniforth netted a last-minute winner in the first leg at The Shay to give Town a 2–1 lead, and the Shaymen forced extra-time at the Baseball Ground with the aggregate scores tied at 4–4, only to concede two goals and lose 5–2 on the night.

After the heroics against Derby, however, Town came off the rails and a run of 10 matches without victory saw them slide down the table. After 15 matches the Shaymen languished in 22nd place, but incredibly they then pulled off a resounding, if unexpected, 4–2 win at high-

Bobby Davison nets Town's first goal of their epic Milk Cup tie at Derby County, 15 September 1982.

Halifax Town 1982–83. Back row (from left to right): Everton Carr, Keith Nobbs, Tony Smith, Malcolm Goodman, David Pearce, Mark Greenway. Middle row: Alan Sutton (physio), Jimmy Hallybone, David Evans, Martin Nuttall, Lee Smelt, Mick Wood, Steve Ward, Paul Kendall, Brian Hendy (trainer). Front row: Bobby Davison, Steve Spooner, Mick Bullock (manager), Dave Staniforth, Paul Hendrie.

flying Wimbledon, where Davison plundered his first League hat-trick. Yet, typically, just seven days later Town were beaten 1–0 by non-League North Shields in the FA Cup at The Shay, their goal a speculative 30-yarder from Bede McCaffrey five minutes after half-time. Town were in desperate need of a good Cup run, so without a hefty source of income they looked for it via other means, hence Davison's move to Derby for a club record £98,000 on 1 December, money without which, according to Bullock, the club would have folded.

Without Davison, it seemed that Town would continue to struggle, and a 2–1 home defeat by Tranmere Rovers, watched by a meagre 912, was just about as low as things could get. But things began to look rosier over the festive period. Town held leaders Hull to a 1–1 draw at Boothferry Park, then swept Scunthorpe away 3–1 at The Shay. This victory was the prelude to a remarkable set of results which began with a 3–0 defeat of Torquay as further home victories over Colchester and Northampton, together with wins at Hartlepool and Mansfield, lifted Town up to 10th, and a welcome crowd of 4,021 turned out for the visit of promotion-chasing Bury on 5 February to see Evans head home the only goal to secure a sixth successive win.

Town's run ended at Chester and only five further games were won before the season's close. Injuries did not help Bullock's cause and to ease the situation he took on loan David Wilkes (Barnsley) and Glen Skivington (Derby), as well as capturing Bradford City's Barry Gallagher on a free transfer. Town wound up their fixtures with a home match with Stockport, where Staniforth's 16th goal of the season secured all three points and ensured Town an 11th-place finish, a position that looked incredibly unlikely back in December.

During the close season Bullock couped around £11,000 from the sales of Allatt and Spooner to Rochdale and Chesterfield respectively, and his new signings included forward

Stewart Mell, who made the opposite journey to Spooner, and the experienced Jeff Cook. The build up to the **1983–84** campaign included an impressive 2–0 victory over a full-strength Leeds side in the West Riding Senior Cup, which for the first time was based on a round-robin format, and they carried this form into the League campaign, with a 3–2 win at Swindon an early-season highlight. Town lost only one of their first seven matches, and despite blips at Wrexham and Bristol City at the beginning of October, three of the next four matches were won, and having taken former England Under-23 international Joe Gallagher on loan from Burnley, his namesake Barry headed the only goal to beat Aldershot on 29 October, and a quarter of the way into the season Town lay 12th.

Town began to hit problems, however, during November. Kieran Vesey of the Town's Northern Intermediate side was called up for the match with Tranmere which the Shaymen lost 2–1, and two weeks later the side crumbled to a shock 3–2 home defeat to Whitby Town in the FA Cup, despite having taken a two-goal lead shortly after half-time. While the fans called for the manager's head, Bullock responded by signing combative midfielder Alan Little and took Birmingham striker Steve Cooper on loan to add some zest to the forward line, but an immediate upturn in Town's form was not forthcoming. The Shaymen sank to 21st position following six consecutive defeats, and only a late Cook goal stopped the rot in a 1–1 draw at fellow strugglers Rochdale on 27 December. On New Years' Eve, however, Little's penalty earned Town their first victory in 10 matches over promotion-chasing Blackpool to briefly lift them out of the danger zone.

A succession of gritty, if unspectacular, performances further lifted Town up to 17th, but their inability to beat sides like Chester, who came to the Shay with only two victories under their belt, highlighted Town's shortcomings. The fans were already voting with their feet,

Halifax Town players and officials 1983–84. Back row (from left to right): Steve Thornber, Barry Gallagher, Mick Wood, Neil Hanson, Lee Smelt, Tony Smith, Paul Kendall, Martin Nuttall, Mark Greenway. Middle row: Alan Sutton (physio), Steve Ward, David Evans, Stewart Mell, Paul Hendrie, Mickey Bullock (manager), Dave Staniforth, Jeff Cook, Keith Nobbs, Gerry Brook (youth coach). Front row: George Fairburn (kit man), Anne Pettifor (assistant secretary), Colin Wood (director), Tom McLean (director), Tom Dawson (director), John Crowther (vice-chairman), Jack Turner (chairman), Peter Dawson (director), Roger Newby (director), Tom Sharpe (director), Dr David Lord (director), Carol Bell (secretary), Tony Thwaites (commercial manager).

Steve Ward pounces to score Town's first goal in the FA Cup first-round match with Whitby Town at The Shay, 19 November 1983. The Shaymen took a two-goal lead, but the non-League visitors hit back to win 3-2.

and only 911 saw Steve Thornber, a member of the Northern Intermediate side, come off the bench to score a 25-yarder with his first touch to salvage a point in a 2-2 draw. A series of disastrous results, such as the 6-1 defeat at Crewe, then worse, a 7-1 mauling at Mansfield, with hapless Vesey between the posts once again, dragged Town into the mire once more. Injuries to Hendrie and Staniforth did not help Town's run-in, but three days after a 4-1 defeat at top side York City, Bullock's side responded with an Easter Monday demolition of Rochdale. Town's 5-0 victory was not only their highest win for seven years, the game was also a personal triumph for Barry Gallagher, who netted four goals, the first Town player to do so since Des Frost in 1951.

Town moved out of the re-election zone by impressively winning their last two home games over Chesterfield and Colchester, and then asked questions of Wrexham, who needed to take seven points from their last three matches to overhaul them. But incredibly, they duly performed their rescue act, trouncing Tranmere in their last match to condemn the Shaymen to re-election on goal difference.

John Crowther, who had succeeded Jack Turner as chairman in April, was optimistic about Town's future, stating, 'I do not anticipate anything going wrong with our application this time, because I feel that clubs generally are sympathetic to the struggling financial position we all find ourselves in,' a feeling that was justified when Town polled a maximum 52 votes to secure their Football League membership for at least another year.

Though pleased with the outcome, manager Bullock had already been forced to curb the wage bill for **1984-85** and top players such as Evans, Staniforth and Smelt were all released while Hendrie also moved to Stockport for £1,500. In their place Bullock assembled a largely inexperienced squad, signing youthful centre-half Alan Knill, midfielder Chris Moyses and strikers Simon Lowe and Paul Sanderson, though he did manage to bring in full-back Cec Podd, record appearance maker at Bradford City, and the former Republic of Ireland goalkeeper Paddy Roche, as well as Billy Ayre, who, after two seasons at Mansfield, returned to take up a position as player-coach.

Halifax Town enjoy the high life on their visit to White Hart Lane for the second leg of the Milk Cup tie with Spurs, 9 October 1984.

Garth Crooks steels in to poke the ball past 'keeper Paddy Roche for Spurs' third goal in their 5–1 win.

Town made a disastrous start to the season winning only two of their opening 10 matches, and the supporters' interest was only maintained by aggregate victory in the Milk Cup over Chesterfield. Their reward was a money-spinning tie with Tottenham Hotspur, who arrived at The Shay for the first leg on 26 September as First Division leaders. Town performed well, but Spurs, with internationals Ray Clemence, Steve Perryman and Gary Mabbutt in their side, ran out 5–1 winners in front of the BBC *Sportsnight* cameras. Garth Crooks scored a hat-trick to add to two goals by Mark Falco, and he was among the scorers in the return leg at White Hart Lane as Spurs cantered to a 4–0 win a fortnight later. Town bowed out as expected, but these two matches netted the club over £30,000.

Bullock was not given any time to spend the money. After a fourth successive League defeat at the hands of Darlington on 19 October, he inevitably paid the price, when, three days later, he was sacked, although Bullock claimed he had been made a scapegoat. 'I am disgusted. I have been held responsible for what has happened when other people ought to be taking a share of the blame,' he claimed.

Billy Ayre took over control of the team, and having stated that he wanted the job on a permanent basis, did his chances no harm with a 3–1 victory at Colchester. But after beating

Halifax Town 1984–85. Back row (from left to right): Alan Sutton (physio), Simon Lowe, Billy Ayre, Paul Kendall, Paddy Roche, Alan Knill, Alan Little, Barry Gallagher, Mickey Bullock (manager). Front row: Glen Alzepedi, Chris Moyses, Steve Thornber, Mark Greenway, Dean Martin, Garry Watson, Jeff Cook.

After a successful period as caretaker manager, Billy Ayre (left) welcomes the newly-appointed manager Mick Jones, 10 November 1984.

Mansfield to move off the bottom, the directors unveiled the new manager as the former Bradford City and Derby County coach Mick Jones, though was more than happy to have Ayre as his right-hand man.

Jones' first game in charge saw his side avoid the potential banana skin by defeating non-League Goole Town in the FA Cup and the side travelled to near neighbours Burnley in round two for the first peacetime meeting. Town lost unluckily 3–1, but once they returned to League action, they struggled and by the turn of the year were once again re-election fodder.

A run of six games without a win was ended with a surprise 4–1 victory over League-leaders Bury on 12 January on a snowbound pitch, with Lowe grabbing a hat-trick. But victories in the second half of the season became sporadic as Town won only four of their next 18 matches, although it was against the odds that they should win at Wrexham with young 'keeper Robert Hunt being forced into action for his League debut just two weeks after the Welsh side had won at The Shay.

Hunt, however, had earlier helped Town pull off one of the more amazing results of the season in the Freight Rover Cup. Jones elected to field juniors such as Dean Martin, John Francis and Paul Fleming for the first-round, first-leg match with Darlington, and the youngsters helped the side to a shock 4–1 win. With a slightly more experienced side for the second leg, however, Town were overrun and crashed 7–1 at Feethams.

And there was no joy for Town when they revisited Feethams for a League match the following week. They fell behind in the first minute, then lost through injury defender Kendall and 'keeper Roche. With the side 2–0 down at the break, Alan Little donned the goalkeeping jersey for the second half which Town played out with only eight men following the dismissals of Knill and Podd, although, remarkably, there was no further scoring.

Supporters invade the pitch following Town's victory over Swindon Town in their last match on 10 May 1985, wrongly believing that a re-election bid had been staved off.

With his side ever-faltering, Jones brought in centre-half Steve Brooks and the experienced former Leeds United striker David McNiven, but four consecutive home defeats saw them sink to 23rd. Just when all hope of avoiding a second successive re-election application had gone, however, the side suddenly hit form, winning three of their last four matches, wrapping up their fixtures on the road with a fine 3–0 victory at Stockport before defeating Swindon in their last match. Sanderson's hooked volley, which sealed victory, proved a fitting finale and Town hauled themselves out of the bottom four. But the following day, Southend defeated bottom club Torquay to move above the Shaymen on goal difference, and a 12th re-election bid duly beckoned.

Halifax Town survived once more, polling 48 votes, the lowest total of the four League clubs, while Enfield, the Gola League champions, managed only eight, though not for much longer could Town rely on the 'old pals' act'. At the end of the **1985–86** season the Football League decided to introduce automatic relegation and promotion between the Fourth Division's bottom club and the winners of the Gola League.

One wonders how Halifax Town might have fared had they had to apply a third consecutive season, although such a scenario initially looked unlikely after Jones's side made a competent start with his acquisitions of full-back Phil Brown, winger Gary Nicholson, the experienced midfielder Billy Kellock, and nippy inside-forward Dave Longhurst. That was despite the club announcing debts of £193,000, something of a headache after the club were set to lose the income from the Halifax Dukes speedway club, who elected to switch to Bradford's Odsal Stadium after objecting to an increase in rates at The Shay. Town were also hit by restrictions following the Bradford City fire disaster the previous May when new regulations necessitated expensive ground improvements, and while a Ground Improvement Fund was launched on 14 July 1985, attendances at the first three matches at The Shay had been affected when all standing areas were closed off. In fact, the first-leg Milk Cup tie with Hull, where Town played well for a 1–1 draw, was watched by just 890 spectators.

Town attempted to entice the fans with Friday night football once more, and three victories from their opening six League games suggested better times ahead. But soon

Halifax Town 1985–86. Back row (from left to right): Mick Jones (manager), Cec Podd, Steve Ward, Robert Hunt, Alan Knill, Paddy Roche, Paul Kendall, Billy Ayre (assistant manager), Alan Sutton (physio). Front row: Phil Brown, Gary Nicholson, Billy Kellock, Barry Gallagher, Simon Lowe, David Longhurst, Steve Thornber, Adrian Shaw.

enough the jitters returned as Town went 13 League matches without a win while also losing at home to Scunthorpe in the FA Cup. By the turn of the year the Shaymen were lying 22nd and looking doomed to re-election.

Fortunes began to change in the New Year, however, following a glut of victories, which began with three hard-earned points from a 1–0 win over Crewe, although most satisfying, perhaps, was the victory at Preston on 11 January. Manager Jones had set off two days earlier to walk the 54 miles solo as a charity fundraiser and he arrived at Deepdale in time to see Kellock head the only goal of the match. Further victories at the beginning of February, with new signing Barry Diamond in the side, saw Town rise to 16th, only for progress to be halted for a month due to a bout of ice and snow.

One game that did go ahead at The Shay, although in farcical conditions, was a Freight Rover Cup group match with Lincoln on Shrove Tuesday, a fixture already rendered meaningless after both sides had earlier lost to Scunthorpe, meaning that neither could qualify. Under obligation to play the match, the clubs hastily arranged to play it on a Tuesday afternoon in front of a paltry crowd officially recorded as 150, though a rough headcount by *Halifax Courier* reporter Graham Marsden suggested a more accurate 122 watched the sides play out a 1–1 draw on a blanket of snow.

Using some of the money from his sponsored walk, Mick Jones signed centre-back Mick Galloway from Mansfield, and

Billy Kellock rises to head home the only goal in the game at Preston North End on 11 January 1986.

Town hit a purple patch by recording four consecutive victories throughout March, a run which saw them put five goals past Wrexham and triumph 3–1 at Burnley in arguably their best performance of the season, capped by a spectacular solo goal by Longhurst. Jones was in the running for the division's managerial award, but missed out after Town lost at Rochdale. The Shaymen then failed to win only one of their next eight fixtures and sailed too close to the wind for comfort as the threat of a re-election application became all too real. The issue went to the final day, with Town level on points with 21st-placed Exeter, who thankfully had completed their fixtures. Going into their last game with Mansfield, the Shaymen needed to avoid defeat by a three-goal margin to be safe, and though they trailed 2–0, Longhurst popped up with a goal to relieve the tension and they survived.

Avoiding re-election was viewed as some sort of success but hardly comparable with Town's Rugby League counterparts who clinched the First Division Championship in 1985–86. But further discussions with them regarding sharing the Thrum Hall ground had led to Town chairman John Crowther resigning in April following a personal attack on him by a fellow director, and the club then pinned hopes on John Madeley, owner of successful DIY chain, took over the chairmanship on 11 June 1986 with rich promises.

The **1986–87** season saw the introduction of automatic relegation and promotion between the Fourth Division and the newly-named GM Vauxhall Conference, and for a while the Shaymen looked odds on to become the first team to be relegated. For despite an early goal from Russell Black, who had arrived in the summer with centre-back Dave Robinson, that proved enough to beat Aldershot on the opening day, an horrendous run of seven consecutive defeats saw them anchored at the foot of the table.

Jones had been forced to pitch in young 'keeper Phil Whitehead for the match at Burnley, and at 16 years and 284 days, he became the club's youngest-ever player. He was

Halifax Town 1986–87. Back row (from left to right): Wayne Allison, Phil Sharpe, Dave Robinson, Paddy Roche, Phil Whitehead, Alan Knill, Jimmy Willis, Paul Sanderson. Middle row: Billy Ayre (assistant manager), Mick Jones (manager), Lee Richardson, Billy Barr, Tony Pearson, Bobby Barr, Mick Galloway, Phil Brown, Adrian Shaw, Dean Martin, Gerry Brook (youth coach), Alan Sutton (physio). Front row: Paul Fleming, Craig Newell, Nigel Foster, Gary Nicholson, John Madeley (chairman), David Longhurst, Steve Thornber, Barry Diamond, Russell Black.

Neil Matthews scores the first goal in Town's 2–1 victory at Wolverhampton Wanderers, 21 October 1986.

joined in the side by left-winger Rick Holden, and the later addition of Mick Matthews helped the side recover from a 6–3 home defeat by Northampton to move off the bottom with victory over Swansea. The revival continued with namesake Neil Matthews arriving on loan, and Town pulled off a famous win at Wolves, though less than a week later, on 28 October 1986, the *Halifax Courier* was reporting that the club was close to collapse.

With Town £425,396 in the red, John Madeley called in accountants Peat, Marwick and Mitchell to look at the books, only to be told they had been operating illegally, and with the debt described by Tony Richmond as 'quite a disastrous deficiency', the situation looked bleaker than ever, so much so that the game with Exeter on 4 November was labelled as potentially Town's last ever. While creditors agreed to hang on for their money, the club's electricity supply, cut off briefly because of an unpaid bill, was reconnected just in time for the first of three exciting FA Cup clashes with Bolton, though Town ultimately bowed out 3–1 in a second replay at The Shay.

Town's financial predicament became ever more critical, and a number of plans were drawn up to help the ailing club. One came from a London-based property firm which wanted to build on The Shay and find a new ground for the club, while a similar scheme was suggested by an Edinburgh property company headed by Michael Knighton which offered to build a £3 million sports complex in exchange for The Shay ground. Then, in December, Elland-based Marshall Construction agreed to help with running costs in the hope of landing a deal which would see them build a new ground for the club while turning The Shay into a supermarket for Gateway Foods.

On 12 December, Madeley called a public meeting at the Civic Theatre at which Calderdale Council Chief Executive Michael Ellison, Chief Legal Officer Gerry Norrie, and councillors Ron Thrower and Michael Taylor were present, and while there was no clear vision in sight, the main outcome of the evening was the launch of the Save Halifax Association Lifeline (SHAL), fronted by local Football League referee Trevor Simpson and lifelong supporters Colin Richardson and Jack Haymer, with the five-year plan to construct a sports centre at The Shay, paid for by fans, who would pay monthly amounts into the fund, but in the end, money raised by the SHAL scheme simply went to meet running costs.

With the club's uncertain future manager Mick Jones resigned on 18 December to link up with Noel Cantwell at Peterborough, and so it was to Billy Ayre that the board turned in the hope of inspiring the team, which, despite the crisis, went on a run of six unbeaten

Dave Longhurst (on left) fires home at Leyton Orient and Town are heading for a 3–1 win, 3 January 1987.

matches to climb as high as 11th. But the side hit another rut and with finances worsening, the match with Torquay was once again viewed as the last-ever after the *Halifax Courier* announced 'Shay on the brink', with the club being given four days to find a way forward when Marshall's pulled out of their deal to save the club.

All hope seemed lost, until the evening of 8 April 1987 when Calderdale Council made a massive u-turn following a meeting to discuss the future of Halifax Town. They came up with a survival plan that involved the Council giving Town up to £210,000, buying back the lease of The Shay, taking control of the club until the start of the following season and sacking the present board of directors. The rescue package, the mastermind of Labour councillor David Helliwell, was subject to creditors agreeing to wipe off almost £200,000 in debts, and to that end, much credit had to go to Jack Haymer and Trevor Simpson, who successfully lobbied all parties. This enabled Halifax Town to be put on its soundest footing since formation in 1911, although there were those non-football supporters who begrudged what was now being perceived as 'soccer on the rates'.

While the council set about taking up a 76 per cent stake of the club's shares, an advisory committee was set up to run the club, and with the immediate future secure, eyes turned back to matters on the field where manager Billy Ayre elected to field a number of promising players from the Under-19 Northern Intermediate side such as midfielder Dean Martin and striker Wayne Allison, as well as introducing exciting left-back Frankie Harrison, and Town picked up enough points to ensure that they kept out of the relegation issue.

The traumas endured during the season were all in stark contrast to the highs experienced by Halifax RLFC who, on 2 May 1987, beat St Helens at Wembley to win the Challenge Cup. But Halifax Town could claim their own success story during 1986–87 when the Northern Intermediate side clinched their League title. Several of the players, of course, had already made their senior bows, but the likes of others such as Lee Richardson, Billy and Bobby Barr and the Willis brothers, Jimmy and Paul, would all prove to be the lifeblood of the club.

THE HISTORY OF HALIFAX TOWN

Struggles and Relegation

Part of the deal that saw the club's takeover by Calderdale Council was the sacking of all the club's directors, save for Mazeley himself, but soon he would be gone too. On 18 August 1987 he stormed out of a meeting with councillors following criticism from David Helliwell about the make-up of the new proposed advisory committee, and the following day, he resigned. Helliwell declared, 'Good riddance to him', the advisory committee took shape and Rod Thomas, as chairman, and Jack Haymer made up a temporary two-man board.

Town went into the new season running all administrative affairs from Old Crossleyans Rugby Union Club after being granted use of The Shay on matchdays only and, following the dismissal of groundsman Norman Southernwood, who had been employed by the club for 11 years, putting up with a pitch which deteriorated so badly that for most of the **1987–88** season it had to be covered in sand. Billy Ayre would also have to get used to being without star forward Dave Longhurst, who made a £40,000 move to Northampton and centre-half Alan Knill, who joined Swansea on the eve of the season.

Town made a promising start and created a piece of football history when, with the Football League allowing the use of two substitutes for the first time, Neil Matthews and Wayne Allison both came off the bench to score their side's goals in the 2–2 draw with Darlington on the opening day. However, there were repercussions when it was discovered that Matthews' registration form following his permanent signing from Grimsby hadn't been sent to the Football League HQ, and in November Halifax Town were fined £500 and had one point deducted for what was universally termed 'fielding an ineligible player'.

After bowing out of the Littlewood's Cup after aggregate defeat to York, the Shaymen claimed their first win of the campaign with 2–1 success amid a thunder storm at Wolves in their second League match, and found themselves fourth following a 2–1 victory over Tranmere on 18 September. But while home form continued to impress Town stuttered on their travels, and by the time the FA Cup came round they had slipped to 12th in the table.

Halifax Town 1987–88. Back row (from left to right): Billy Ayre (manager), Wayne Allison, Phil Sharpe, Stewart Ferebee, Jimmy Willis, Paddy Roche, Dave Robinson, Mick Matthews, Rick Holden, Frankie Harrison, Gerry Brook (youth coach). Front row: Paul Fleming, Billy Barr, Russell Black, Steve Thornber, Lee Richardson, Phil Brown, Mick Galloway, Adrian Shaw, Mick Matthews, Dean Martin, Tony Fearson.

Nevertheless, Town negotiated a tricky tie against Northern League side Billingham Synthonia in a match played at Hartlepool, despite the earlier loss of broken-leg victim Harrison and having sold Galloway to Hearts for £60,000 just three days before the match. Town won 4–2, then saw off Grimsby after a replay to move into the third round, where they faced First Division Nottingham Forest. But the heavily sanded Shay pitch did not deter the Forest players, among whom were internationals Stuart Pearce, Des Walker and Neil Webb, and Brian Clough's side ran out comfortable 4–0 winners.

During the second half of the season, Town proved to be inconsistent, a trait never more in evidence than when, in consecutive matches, they slipped to defeat against a Newport side anchored at the bottom and heading out of business, before coming from behind to beat leaders Wolves at The Shay. A run of eight games without a win through February and March saw them slip as low as 20th, but by then the main focus of attention had switched to the Sherpa Van Trophy where Town's run had the supporters dreaming of a trip to Wembley.

Town topped their qualifying group which had included Grimsby and Scunthorpe and progressed to the northern semi-finals at the expense of Chesterfield and Darlington. Standing between them and a place in the Northern Final were Burnley who had home advantage, but around 1,000 Town fans travelled over the Pennines to help make up the gate of 10,222. They witnessed a thrilling contest, but one that remained goalless, even after extra-time, and the tie was ultimately settled on penalties when sadly, Town 'keeper Paddy Roche, entrusted with the side's fourth kick, crashed his shot against the bar, and it was the Clarets who went through.

Making his debut in that game was Peter Duffield, a loan signing from Sheffield United, and he contributed an impressive seven goals before the season's close. But making one of his last appearances was winger Holden who left for Watford in a £150,000 deal on 23 March. Defender Paul Kendall returned to the club, but as the side struggled the crowds deserted them. Only 866 turned out for the visit of Hartlepool, but with no threat of relegation manager Billy Ayre could at least afford to give extended run-outs to local lad Lee Richardson and former Liverpool trainee Terry McPhillips.

The 1988 close season saw the addition to the board of Douglas Moody, while property developer Jim Brown set up a working committee whose primary aim was to make money for the club and make it viable. Meantime, there were changes in the playing personnel too, with skipper Phil Brown moving to Bolton, while Steve Thornber joined former teammate Knill at Swansea. But Billy Ayre made a number of significant acquisitions, including defenders John Bramhall, Phil Horner, Chris Hedworth and David Logan, and following a pre-season friendly with Harrogate Town, striker Andy Watson.

Town's start to the **1988–89** season was encouraging, despite the first-round knockout in the Littlewoods Cup by Scarborough, who went through on the away goals rule after two drawn matches. Still, Ayre had been buoyed by the 2–0 success in the opening League game at Torquay United, only to see his side slip to 2–1 defeat at the hands of Burnley in their first home match. A scorer from off the bench was McPhillips, but he would command a regular starting berth by scoring prolifically during the first half of that season, although his hat-trick in a 3–3 draw with Carlisle was not necessarily the major talking point. Manager Ayre had fielded a weakened side for that match after taking disciplinary measures against both Neil and Mick Matthews and David Logan for misdemeanours prior to the 4–1 defeat at Exeter City, but while Logan and Mick Matthews soon departed, Neil Matthews returned to

THE HISTORY OF HALIFAX TOWN

Halifax Town 1988–89. Back row (from left to right): Frankie Harrison, Chris Hedworth, John Bramhall, Paddy Roche, Phil Whitehead, Alan Whitehead, Dave Robinson, Bobby Barr. Middle row: Colin Blain, David Logan, Phil Horner, Billy Barr, Neil Matthews, Terry McPhillips, Andy Watson, Gerry Brook (youth coach). Front row: Paul Fleming, Wayne Allison, Paul Willis, Billy Ayre (manager), Mick Matthews, Dean Martin, Lee Richardson.

the side to form a four-pronged attack that scored a glut of goals throughout October, with McPhillips its talisman.

In successive home matches, Town scored four against Wrexham and Rochdale, and at Doncaster they had the game as good as won by the 14th minute after they raced into a four-goal lead. Peterborough, now managed by Mick Jones, were then blitzed by five second-half goals as the 'The Great Halifax Town Gold Rush', the term used by the *Halifax Courier*, showed no signs of abating.

McPhillips popped up with a late winner to see off the challenge of York in the first round of the FA Cup, but had to sit out through injury the second-round match at Altrincham, which Town won 3–0. But hoping for a big-name club in round three, the Shaymen were disappointed to have to travel to Conference side Kettering, where they secured a draw, only to be undone in The Shay replay, bowing out 3–2 after having led 2–1.

In the League, there was one last hurrah for the side when they put five goals past Scunthorpe on 2 January 1989, for thereafter Town struggled, winning only four of the last 23 matches, though matters were not helped by the sale of midfielder Lee Richardson to Watford for £175,000 on 9 February. Chris Pullan arrived on loan from Vicarage Road as part of the deal and Billy Ayre also signed up Lee's older brother Nick Richardson, as well as giving a run-out to local League player Graham Broadbent. Was there ever a more popular scorer that season than Broadbent when he grabbed the second goal in a 2–0 victory over Doncaster on 3 March which bucked a trend of six winless matches? How unfortunate, though, was he when he made his long awaited first start for the club in the match at Colchester, being forced into action as a makeshift goalkeeper after early injury to Roche?

Billy Barr arrives to net the only goal of Town's game with Darlington on 27 March 1989, Town's last victory of the 1988–89 season.

Town's slide down the table had been tempered somewhat by another run in the Sherpa Van Trophy. Once again Town topped their group, which included Scunthorpe and Huddersfield, and cruised past Darlington in the first round. With interest gathering, a home draw with Blackpool drew a welcome 3,289 crowd but Town underperformed and the Tangerines went safely through 2–0.

Victory over relegation-bound Darlington on Easter Monday courtesy of Billy Barr's strike was the last recorded by the Shaymen that term as the side stuttered towards the finishing line. Their depressing sequence of matches without victory to the end of the season stretched to 10 matches, but though they finished a lowly 21st the campaign had at least been a triumph for Terry McPhillips who, by scoring a brace in the final game against Hereford, took his tally to 25 League and Cup goals.

During the season, there had been changes at boardroom level. In February, Douglas Moody, who had taken over the chairmanship from Rod Thomas the previous November, resigned the position himself and his successor Jim Brown welcomed onto the board Barry Dawson and Pam Burton, who became the first female director. Mrs Burton was a headmistress, and linked to schools was the new Football in the Community scheme, formed on 13 June 1989, to which former Scotland star Jim McCalliog was appointed chief coach.

A new board and fresh ideas suggested better times ahead, but sadly they did not manifest themselves in results on the field. Yet the **1989–90** season started so well with a record 4–0 opening-day success over Hartlepool. Scorer of the last goal was Ian Juryeff, a club-record £40,000 signing from Leyton Orient, a deal funded by the monies received from the £100,000 sale of Dave Robinson to Peterborough and the record £250,000 sale of Wayne Allison to Watford. Juryeff was not the only newcomer to the side, of course. Others included Mitch Cook, midfielders Derek Hall and Brian Butler, and goalkeeper David Brown, who now vied for a first-team spot with the emerging Phil Whitehead.

Town moved up to third early on and also progressed to the second round of the Littlewoods Cup by virtue of a three-goal haul against Carlisle. Rewarded in that competition with a two-legged affair with Middlesbrough in round two, Town failed to halt Bernie Slavin, their main goal threat, and when they crashed 4–0 at Ayresome Park in the first leg the tie was all but over.

Town also faltered alarmingly in the League and there were real fears about their prospects in the FA Cup, too, when they were drawn at Stafford, foes from the mid-Seventies, in the first round. The Shaymen won 3–2 but only after two late headed Horner goals had saved their blushes, and respite proved to be temporary as they then crashed 3–0 at Darlington, by now of the Conference, and the Shaymen braced themselves for a long, hard winter.

A disagreement between manager Billy Ayre and Juryeff ended with the striker joining Hereford, who shelled out their own club-record £50,000 to secure him and in January centre-half Bramhall also left for Scunthorpe, but new players arrived in the form of Dominic Naylor and striker Tony Fyfe, as well as an old favourite in Tommy Graham. Both Fyfe and Graham made their debuts in a 4–2 success over Wrexham which checked a run of five games without a win and had seen them drop as low as 21st, and the subsequent run of five unbeaten matches eased the pressure on Billy Ayre.

As did the run in the newly-named Leyland DAF Cup, a competition which Town had come to enjoy. The Shaymen topped their group courtesy of a 3–0 win over Lincoln, and progress to the northern semi-final saw them involved in some exciting matches. After playing out a 1–1 draw with York at The Shay, Town went through 7–6 on penalties – teenager Craig Fleming scored the decisive kick – and extra-time was needed, too, before they saw off the challenge of Stockport. But with the supporters feeling a trip to Wembley was within their grasp, Town came a cropper at Doncaster, where they succumbed to a 3–0 defeat.

Having sold Whitehead to Barnsley for £60,000, four successive defeats in the League heaped pressure on manager Billy Ayre, and the knives were already out when Town

Halifax Town 1989–90. Back row (from left to right): Terry McPhillips, Phil Horner, Billy Barr, Dean Martin, Shaun Smith, Neil Matthews, Andy Watson. Middle row: Graham Broadbent, Ian Juryeff, Chris Hedworth, David Brown, Phil Whitehead, Nick Richardson, Mitch Cook, John Bramhall. Front row: Derek Hall, Paul Fleming, Gerry Brook (youth coach), Billy Ayre (manager), Frankie Harrison (reserve coach), Toby Paterson, Brian Butler.

Moments after Jim McCalliog is installed as permanent successor to Billy Ayre, Town win 2–0 at Rochdale on 31 March 1990. Here, Terry McPhillips fires in the first goal.

prepared to entertain Lincoln on 20 March. When the Imps secured a 1–0 win, Ayre's time was up, leaving the club by 'mutual agreement', though chairman Jim Brown admitted the timing had been bad given that the transfer deadline had just past, while adding, 'We are in a dogfight, but it is one we must win'.

Immediately, the club turned to Jim McCalliog, head of the Football in the Community programme, to look after the team, initially on a caretaker basis, but after better performances, he was given the job full-time prior to the match at Rochdale on 31 March. Town responded with a fine 2–0 win and with teenage centre-back Craig Fleming promoted to the side, recovery continued, most memorably at Doncaster on 21 April. There, Town trailed 3–0 at half-time, but incredibly, they turned the tables in the second half, clawing

Sporting their new Argentina-style kit, Halifax Town gear up for the 1990–91 season. Back row (from left to right): Billy Barr, Paul Donnelly, Tony Gregory, Dominic Naylor, Brian Butler, Derek Hall, Paul Fleming, Terry McPhillips. Middle row: Mark Hans (kitman), Phil Horner, Tony Fyfe, Nick Richardson, Jonathan Gould, David Brown, Chris Hedworth, Mitch Cook, David Evans, Ray Swires (physio). Front row: Dean Martin, Tommy Graham, Paul Futcher, Brian Taylor (assistant manager), Jim McCalliog (manager), Graham Broadbent, Shaun Smith, Craig Fleming.

back the three-goal deficit before scoring the winner through Butler four minutes from time. Victory left Town needing just a point from their remaining three matches to ensure safety and they duly claimed it in a sterile goalless draw with Burnley at The Shay to finish 23rd, with just relegated Colchester, six points adrift, below them.

McCalliog appointed Brian Taylor as his right-hand man, and with strikers Neil Matthews and Andy Watson sold on, signed up the former England Under-23 international Paul Futcher, midfielder Tony Gregory, and trialist 'keeper Jonathan Gould, while returning to the fold was former Town favourite David Evans. Wearing new Argentina-style light-blue-and-white-striped shirts, McCalliog's side played some attractive football at the start of **1990–91** but made their worst-ever start, and after eight League games they were still seeking their first League goal and consequently had sunk to the foot of the table.

Town, however, did manage to win some silverware in the form of the Yorkshire and Humberside Cup, where having finished top of their group, qualified for the Final against Rotherham at their Millmoor ground on 11 September. There, Town surrendered a two-goal lead but took the Cup thanks to substitute Broadbent's winner seven minutes from the end of extra-time.

While still seeking their first League goal, it was somewhat remarkable that, as well as winning a trophy, Town had not only managed to dispose of Lincoln in the first round of the Rumbelows Cup, but also netted in both legs of their second-round tie with giants Manchester United. The Reds fielded familiar names such as 'keeper Jim Leighton, Neil Webb, Paul Ince, Brian McClair and Mark Hughes but in front of an all-ticket 7,500 capacity crowd at The Shay, they were pushed all the way before scoring two late goals through McClair and Webb for a 3–1 win which made the outcome of the tie became something of a formality. United won the second leg 2–1, though Gregory could be pleased with his goal for Town, while a young Jamie Paterson made an impression on his debut as a second-half substitute.

On the grandest stage of all, Halifax Town perform admirably against Manchester United at Old Trafford in the second-round, second-leg Rumbelows Cup tie, 10 October 1990. Here, Billy Barr has his shot charged down by United 'keeper Les Sealey, watched by United defenders Gary Pallister, Steve Bruce and Viv Anderson, while Town's Lee Richardson hopes in vain for a slip up.

During September, McCalliog sold Horner and Hedworth to Blackpool then brought back Juryeff from Hereford for £50,000 – he thus beat the club record he had set – but that first League goal still proved elusive. It finally came in the their ninth match with a 3–0 victory at Carlisle, where Barr took the honours as the player who broke the side's duck. Another scorer was Steve Norris, who had earlier arrived from Carlisle in a player-exchange deal involving Fyfe, and he would prove to be a sensation, going on to net 30 League goals for Town.

Town played some extra-ordinary games that season, one being the 5–3 win over Blackpool, with debutant 'keeper Gould in the side, after they had trailed 2–0 early on, and having being rooted to the foot of the table since their fifth match they moved up two places following a 2–0 home win over Rochdale four days before Christmas. But it was only temporary respite; failure to win any of their next 11 matches saw them slump to the bottom once more.

In the New Year, the commanding Futcher moved to Grimsby, while new arrivals included Shaun Gore, on loan from Fulham, and striker Graham Cooper to add to the earlier arrival of Mark Ellis. But it was Norris who grabbed the limelight with his goalscoring feats, for despite Town's sorry position he went on to equal the club record during February and March of scoring in five consecutive League matches. On 2 March, he netted a hat-trick in the 5–2 defeat of Walsall, an extra-ordinary game which ended a run of five straight defeats, where the Shaymen found themselves two goals down after just three minutes, lost 'keeper Gould with an horrendous facial injury forcing Graham in goal, then turned the tables in the second half.

Town found themselves five points adrift at the bottom, but were safe in the knowledge that no team would be relegated this term after the Football League had decided upon a reshuffle. Still, Town clawed back the deficit by putting together a five-match unbeaten run, among which was a crazy 4–4 draw at Scunthorpe and moved off the bottom following a 2–0 win over Wrexham on 26 March courtesy of two more goals by Norris to climb above the Welsh side and Aldershot to 22nd, where they would remain.

On 3 June 1991, Calderdale Council, no longer wanting to be burdened by shares in a football club that was running at a loss, sold out to Jim Brown and the owners of Aquarius Bathrooms, David Greenwood and Bob Asprey for just £1,000. And with the club's immediate future secure, McCalliog got on with team building having seen teenage centre-back sensation Craig Fleming move to Oldham for £80,000, brother Paul opting for Mansfield, and the popular Butler joining Northwich. In their place came utility player Greg Abbott, defenders Alan Kamara and Steve Richards and young central-defender Chris Lucketti.

Town lost their opening **1991–92** League game to Northampton, then played two crazy games with Second Division Tranmere in the Rumbelows Cup. The Shaymen led 3–1 at home before losing 4–3, then took the game into extra-time at Prenton Park after leading 3–2. But Tranmere scored twice to go through Jim Steel and Republic of Ireland international John Aldridge to go through 8–6 on aggregate.

There was, however, to be no such goal fest in the League, and with only one solitary victory from seven matches the Shaymen found themselves at the wrong end of the table once more. Despite having strengthened the side with the signing of defender Russell Bradley, McCalliog's days were numbered and on 2 October, the club confirmed his

Halifax Town 1991-92. Back row (from left to right): Paul Donnelly, Mark Ellis, Tony Gregory, Neil Griffiths, Ian Hutchinson, Jamie Paterson. Middle row: Steve Norris, Tommy Graham, Nick Richardson, Jonathan Gould, Nick Brown, Steve Richards, Chris Lucketti, Billy Barr. Front row: Kevin Megson, Greg Abbot, Alan Kamara, Brian Taylor (assistant manager), Jim McCalliog (manager), Ian Juryeff, Graham Cooper, David Evans.

sacking, citing Town's inability to win at home as the main reason, the 3-1 defeat by Mansfield five days earlier meaning they had failed to record victory from six Shay matches.

The club turned to John McGrath as his successor, viewing him as a potential saviour after he had turned round the fortunes at Port Vale and Preston. He brought with him Oshor Williams as his assistant but McGrath would find life at The Shay hard going. Things started promisingly enough, however, when he delivered the first home win in his third match, a 2-0 success over Chesterfield, and further home successes over Scarborough and Wrexham, who were beaten in a 4-3 thriller – in front of only 881 spectators, it might be added – moved the Shaymen up to 14th.

The demons returned, however, in the FA Cup when drawn at non-League Witton. Only a speculative 30-yard lob from the recently signed Ronnie Hildersley salvaged a draw, but Town were found wanting in The Shay replay. Goalless after 90 minutes, extra-time goals from Karl Thomas and Andy Grimshaw gave Witton a 2-0 lead and Richardson's reply eight minutes from time proved too little, too late.

In need of team strengthening, McGrath had brought in 'keeper Lee Bracey and in December paid Northampton £30,000 for left-back Paul Wilson, but there was a downturn in League form in the New Year as Town went eight matches without a win. So all the more surprising, then, was McGrath's decision to sell top scorer Norris to Chesterfield for a knockdown £33,000 on 26 February, and while results continued to give cause for concern, centre-half Steve Richards was allowed to leave the following month. McGrath signed former Wales international centre-back Dudley Lewis and made the temporary signings of Kevin Donovan and Jason Hardy, and while there was the odd highlight, such as the 3-2 defeat of Carlisle, and even better, the 3-1 success over promotion hopefuls Barnet, Town struggled to the season's close. Still, they were comforted by the fact that there would be no

Former Liverpool legend Jimmy Case signs for Town watched by manager Jim McGrath and secretary Angie Harrison, August 1992.

relegation for a second successive term following the demise of Aldershot, who amid mounting debts, resigned from the League on 25 March.

During **1992–93**, McGrath pinned his hopes on players he had previously worked with, such as forwards Ian Thompstone, John Thomas and Nigel Greenwood. He also pulled off what appeared the masterstroke signing of former Liverpool midfield legend Jimmy Case, while also signing soccer nomad Howard Gayle and Mick Matthews, who was returning to the club, on the eve of the season. Two weeks into it, he also brought in Leicester's ball-playing midfielder Jason Peake.

Town found themselves in the Third Division following the restructuring of the Football League after the creation of the Premier League, and there seemed nothing to worry about unduly when they won their opening League match 3–2 in the sunshine at Rochdale, nor in the aggregate defeat in the Coca-Cola Cup to Hartlepool. But after five games, they found themselves bottom of the table, though made good their recovery, winning sensationally 5–2 win at Northampton, and with back-to-back wins over Walsall and Gillingham, they moved up to 10th. But dark clouds were gathering, and once chairman Jim Brown had revealed on 6 October that the club was £100,000 in the red and a month away from possible closure, the die was cast.

With a crisis meeting looming, the Shaymen travelled to Northern Premier League side Marine for a first-round FA Cup tie. Defeat was unthinkable, but the side sunk to new

Halifax Town 1992–93. Back row (from left to right): Paul Wilson, Ian Juryeff, Nigel Greenwood, Chris Lucketti, Nick Richardson, Lee Bracey, Ian Thompstone, Russell Bradley, Neil Griffiths, Steve Circuit, Billy Barr. Front row: Jamie Paterson, John Thomas, Kevin Megson, Alan Kamara, Mick Rathbone (physio), Jimmy Case, David German, Jason Hardy, Ronnie Hildersley.

THE HISTORY OF HALIFAX TOWN

Jamie Paterson attempts to lob Northampton Town 'keeper Barry Richardson in this match at The Shay, 16 January 1993.

depths and the resulting 4–1 defeat at Rossett Park represented one of the darkest days in the club's history.

Two days later the board met to contemplate the future, and elected to review things in the New Year. But, by then, McGrath had gone. Following a home defeat by Barnet on 5 December, he resigned his position, claiming, 'A fresh person at the helm might just help solve some of their problems.' And though Oshor Williams fancied taking over, the board turned instead to physio Mick Rathbone to oversee first-team affairs.

The popular Rathbone, who had arrived in the close season, got off to a bad start with a 5–0 defeat at Huddersfield Town in the Autoglass Trophy. But he was encouraged by the point gained from a 1–1 draw at promotion-chasing York on 29 December, and more so with the 3–0 win at Darlington, where new recruit Dave Ridings bagged a brace, as he did the following week in the home game with Northampton, a result that extended an unbeaten run to four games to lift the Shaymen to 17th. But the side suffered with the sale of Wilson to Burnley and the 2–1 victory over Lincoln on 16 February proved to be Town's last at home. Jimmy Case was offloaded to Wrexham, but the biggest shock was the sale of top scorer Thompstone to Scunthorpe on transfer deadline day.

When Town's position became ever more critical and relegation to the Conference looking more threatening, the *Halifax Courier* launched a 'Staying Alive League Lifeline' campaign and drummed up support, giving away discount entry tickets for the home game with Shrewsbury on 20 March. This contributed to a bumper gate of 3,872, a carnival atmosphere ensued, Barr scored a thunderbolt, but the side had to settle for a point. Rathbone sought new players and brought in winger Peter Craven, though the arrival of Nigerian striker Godfrey Obebo bordered more on the desperate. The end-of-season run-in saw Town pull off wins on their travels at Doncaster and Bury, but it was home form that was troublesome, manifested by the 4–0 home defeat by Walsall which saw Town drop to the bottom of the table with only two games to go.

The first of these was a six-pointer at Gillingham, won 2–0 by the home side despite the Shaymen's dominance, and Town's League future came down to the last day. But only

Dave Ridings pulls this close-range effort agonisingly wide, and Halifax Town lose their League status following last-day defeat to Hereford United at The Shay, 8 May 1993.

victory over Hereford would suffice, and that provided Northampton, the only side they could overhaul, lost their match at Shrewsbury. Such was the magnitude of importance, a crowd of 7,451, made up of the loyal, the casual and the curious, swelled the ground to cheer on Rathbone's side, but in the end the goal scored by former Town player Derek Hall which gave Hereford victory proved academic. Northampton came back from two goals down to win 3–2 at Gay Meadow, and Town's fate was sealed.

Manager Mick Rathbone feels the pain of relegation.

Halifax Town players and officials prior to the first season in the Conference. Back row (from left to right): Jamie Paterson, Mick Rathbone (physio), Colin Lambert, Elfyn Edwards, Jason Peake, Billy Barr, Jason Hardy. David German. Middle row: Peter Craven, Nigel Greenwood, Chris Lucketti, Lee Bracey, Martin Filson, Nick Brown, Steve Hook, Dave Ridings, Steve Circuit. Front row: Peter Wragg (manager), John Rawson (director), John Stockwell (director), Brian Boulton (vice-chairman), Jim Brown (chairman), David Greenwood (director), Adie Hall (director), Chris Holland (director), Nick Beaumont (commercial manager).

CONFERENCE DAYS

Following their relegation, Halifax Town clung to the faint hope of a reprieve by the Football League due to the financial difficulties experienced by Barnet, but in the end were forced to accept their fate lay in the GM Vauxhall Conference. They elected to remain full-time and appointed Peter Wragg, a personality who knew the Conference well, as manager. But with Bradley, Bracey and Lucketti all seeking pastures anew, he was forced to assemble a new squad, so in came defenders Elfyn Edwards and Martin Filson, and midfielder Colin Lambert, while Shaun Constable, who impressed during the qualifiers of the Yorkshire and Humberside Cup, was also added to the squad.

Despite encouraging pre-season signs, the Shaymen struggled to adapt to the rigours of Conference life. An encouraging 1,810 had watched the season's opener at The Shay with Kettering on 21 August, but after four games they found themselves lying in 17th place. Yet despite their failings in the League, Town triumphed in the Final of the Yorkshire and Humberside Cup on 7 September, winning a dramatic game against Bradford City in their own back yard. Wragg included a pair of new strikers in Steve Saunders and Dave Hanson, and having seen his side surrender a two-goal lead, second half goals from Saunders and Paterson gave them a 4–2 win and the retention of the Cup they had won three years earlier and not played for since.

But Wragg's side was soon brought back down to earth. Four days later they crashed 5–0 at Runcorn, and a goalless draw with Witton in their next game saw them lying 21st. But

Town score their first goal in the Conference at Southport, 24 August 1993. Chris Lucketti (right) glances home this header to spark a fightback which will earn Town a point in a 2–2 draw.

they responded in style with a 6–2 away win at Woking, then scored a further six in their next match against Telford at The Shay. League form remained patchy, however, but a 3–0 success over Bromsgrove, with new signing Craig Boardman in the side, set them up nicely for the visit of West Brom in the first round of the FA Cup.

It was a match the Sky Sports cameras chose to screen live, an exciting contest that saw goals from Peake and Saunders give Town a two-goal cushion they would hold until nine minutes from time. Andy Hunt's headed goal for the visitors ensured a nervy finish for the Shaymen but they held out for a memorable win. Sadly, they found Stockport, and their giant centre-forward Kevin Francis, a different proposition, and Town were humbled 5–1 at Edgeley Park in round two.

In the New Year, Wragg's side ventured into the FA Trophy for the first time, and having seen off Emley in the first round, they overcame Spennymoor on their sloping pitch in the next to extend an unbeaten run to eight games. But this was not enough to save Wragg's job. The following day he was summoned to The Shay by chairman Jim Brown and told his services were no longer required. Brown later admitted that the decision to sack Wragg had been made before the Spennymoor game, adding that 'the situation is that we have won just seven of our 25 Conference games and we have never been higher than 10th in the table and we [the directors] are not happy with that.'

Twenty-four hours later, the former Newcastle defender John Bird, having managed at both Hartlepool and York, was unveiled as Wragg's successor, but he did not get off to the best of starts, seeing his new side throw away the lead at Telford before losing 3–2, then watching Town bow out of the FA Trophy at the hands of Runcorn in a Shay replay, his first game in charge at home.

Bird rang the changes, bringing in players such as left-back Steve Prindiville, centre-half Alex Jones, who arrived in a swap deal which saw midfielder Jason Peake move to Rochdale, and with one eye on the following season, gave run outs to several trialists such as Nigel Smith, Pat O'Toole and a certain Geoff Horsfield, who arrived from Scarborough. But it was an uninspiring end of season run-in, though Town did at least move up the table, with Paterson's 13th goal of the season which gave them victory over Slough in the last match ensuring a 13th-place finish.

The expected exodus of players during the close season included that of Billy Barr to Crewe, but there was no shortage of new players as Bird began building for what was his planned promotion push. Into the club came midfielders Kevin Langley, Lee Fowler, and Grant Leitch, speedy winger Andy Kiwomya, forwards Andy Flounders and Gary

Worthington, son of former player Dave, as well as lanky striker Dave Lancaster, whose £10,000 signing from Rochdale was part-funded by £2,000 from the Supporters' Club who, under chairman Derek Newiss, had launched a 'Sign A Striker Appeal' the previous summer.

There were some sparkling early season performances during **1994–95**, including a 4–2 win over Woking and a 6–0 hiding handed out to Stafford, and having brought in former Shay favourites Dean Martin, on loan from Scunthorpe United, and full-back Paul Fleming, the side put together an impressive run which saw them climb to fifth. Despite going well, however, the board were concerned at the low attendances, with the match with Runcorn on 10 December watched by a meagre 733.

Town's involvement in the FA Cup provided a welcome financial boost and by seeing off Lancaster in the fourth qualifying round, they then played out two titanic battles with Runcorn, winning a replay 3–1 after extra-time at their temporary home at Witton's Wincham Park. This set up a home tie with Third Division Mansfield Town and though it ended goalless, Town were unlucky to lose the replay, taking the lead, but ultimately falling to Paul Holland's last-minute winner.

In mid-November, controversy reared its head when the Yorkshire Rider bus company submitted plans for a supermarket on The Shay and their adjacent bus depot land. Simultaneously, Town chairman Jim Brown threatened to quit if the council failed to approve plans for Shay improvements after Football League regulations meant the winners of the Conference would only be promoted if their ground met new stringent criteria. This then fuelled a debate regarding the future of The Shay, and when in January the council backed Halifax RLFC's own plans for a super stadium at Thrum Hall, the Town board sat

Halifax Town 1994–95. Back row (from left to right): Mick Rathbone (physio), David German, Ryan Gray, Lee Fowler, David Higgins, George Mulhall (youth-team manager). Middle row: Dave Hanson, Darren Heyes, Colin Lambert, Grant Leitch, Steve Hook, Richard Wilmot, Dave Lancaster. Front row: Jamie Paterson, Andy Kiwomya, Steve Prindiville, John Bird (manager), Alex Jones, Andy Flounders, Craig Boardman.

down with their rugby counterparts to try to dive the plans to fruition with a view to a ground-share. However, when the council then voted against selling The Shay to Yorkshire Rider on 24 February, Brown promptly resigned from the Town board three days later.

All the while, Town put their title hopes back on track in the New Year and, having signed centre-back Mick Trotter, they came from behind to complete a double over Gateshead on a frost-bound Shay pitch, then recorded successive 4–0 home wins over Dover and Woking. They moved up to fourth, but this good run of form made all the more baffling their exit from the FA Trophy at the hands of Unibond First Division North side Bamber Bridge.

But no sooner had John Stockwell taken over as chairman on 6 March than Town were preparing for a make-or-break home game with leaders Macclesfield. Sammy McIlroy's side arrived fully 18 points clear of the Shaymen, but with Town having two games in hand they were not ruling out a late challenge. But when Darren Lyons popped up to head the game's only goal after 42 minutes, Town gave up the ghost.

Nevertheless, they climbed to third but did so against a backdrop of real uncertainty when, on 15 March, the club announced total debts of £175,000, with £100,000 owed to the Inland Revenue. With Jamie Paterson having already left the club in December, big money earners such as Lancaster and Kiwomya were also offloaded, and there was the releasing of the likeable Mick Rathbone, a move that John Bird described as 'the hardest decision I have ever had to make'. Stockwell then announced that unless a backer could be found, the club would fold at the end of the season, and while a 'Fighting Fund' was set up, on 2 May around 250 supporters rolled up at Arden Road Social Club to help try and secure the club's future. With the Inland Revenue clamouring for an initial £30,000, incredibly half that sum was raised on the night to match a similar amount already in the bank, and the target was met. Still, with Bird now relying on the likes of Simon Johnson and Elliot Beddard, Town went ahead with the last home fixture with Kidderminster on 29 April being billed as potentially the club's last ever at The Shay, and hoards of supporters made the trip to Runcorn for the final match to witness a Dave Hanson hat-trick secure a 3–0 win. Town finished the season in eighth but headed into the close season with the future in doubt.

During the summer Stockwell kept the club going after the Conference agreed to waive a £75,000 bond and by entering into a Compulsory Voluntary Arrangement (CVA) at the

'There'll always be the Shaymen,' sing the supporters following the game with Kidderminster Harriers which is billed as Town's last-ever match at The Shay, 29 April 1995.

end of May. But to ensure they did not fall further into debt, manager John Bird was forced to operate on a shoestring budget and thus relied on local players such as Karl Cochrane, John Hendrick, Michael Midwood and Glen Lee. But there were also the welcome additions of the versatile Jon Brown, centre-half Paul Stoneman and full-back Simon Thompson, though the biggest capture was that of West Brom's former Brighton and Republic of Ireland international midfielder Kieran O'Regan. Similarly significant, as things turned out, was the appointment in June of George Mulhall as youth-team coach, though the club's transition from full-time to part-time posed its own problems.

With no real expectation on the shoulders of the players, the 3–0 defeat at Hednesford on the opening day of the 1995–96 season was hard to take, though Bird did have the unexpected fillip of victory in the next match over the champions Macclesfield, who had been denied Football League entry on the same basis of having an unsuitable ground. Pressed into action in that game was former Oldham trainee 'keeper Andy Woods after Darren Heyes had been stuck in traffic, while other players to appear during the first half of the season included loanees centre-back Chris Timons, striker Lee Ludlow and the experienced pair of defender Paul Smith and front man Gary Brook. The side rose to seventh following victory at Runcorn on 7 October, though they bemoaned their FA Cup exit at the hands of the same opposition two weeks later when the referee, who also sent off two Town players, ruled that Worthington's scrambled effort that would have earned a draw had not crossed the line. But key departures hindered progress, with Prindiville, Worthington and Thompson all leaving for Dagenham in mid-December, with only left-back Richard Annan coming in.

Town moved up to 10th and began the New Year promisingly enough with a goalless draw Southport, who also provided the opposition in the first round FA Trophy at The Shay. Cochrane's diving header sealed a 2–0 win, but Bromsgrove were surprise victors in

Halifax Town's cut-price 1995–96 squad. Back row (from left to right): Willie Griffiths, Andrew Hemmingway, Chris Horsfall, Damian Place, Paul Hand. Middle row: Darren Heyes, Danny Megson, Noel Horner, Lee Ludlow, Michael Midwood, Paul Stoneman, Mick Trotter, Gary Worthington, Elliot Beddard, Andy Woods. Front row: Alan Russell-Cox (physio), Simon Johnson, Lee Wilson, Simon Thompson, John Bird (manager), Jon Brown, Steve Prindiville, Kieran O'Regan, George Mulhall (assistant manager).

the second round. Sadly, that defeat seemed to have a profound effect on the players and the rot set in. Failing to win their next five matches, the fans began drifting away with only 509 turning out for the visit of Stalybridge on 5 March 1996, and Town had slipped to 13th by the time they travelled to Macclesfield, where they proved no match and succumbed to an embarrassing 7–0 defeat.

Manager Bird was hoping such a result was a one-off, but sadly, hard on a morale-boosting victory at Morecambe, Town crashed 6–1 at Kidderminster and he knew the game was up. After talks with chairman John Stockwell on 20 March 1996, he departed from the club, explaining, 'I have never been the type to walk away from things, but given the problems the club has had over the season, it might help.'

As a stop-gap measure, the board asked George Mulhall, who had been acting as Bird's assistant since the departure of Rathbone, to take charge of the side, and with skipper Kieran O'Regan assisting him, he steadied the ship, taking the side through an unbeaten run of five matches. But while Stockwell had said he was in no rush to appoint a permanent successor to Bird, despite having in O'Regan a willing taker, following the 1–1 draw at Telford United on 13 April, the Town chairman introduced the new manager to the players in the dressing room; former Runcorn boss John Carroll. He brought with him former Burnley defender Billy Rodaway as his assistant and took charge for the last two matches, the last of which was a 1–0 victory at Bromsgrove which ensured a 15th-place finish.

Carroll's side which began the **1996–97** season included defender Andy Lee and midfielder Ian McInerney, as well as Paul Mudd who was tied to a permanent deal following a loan spell. Gary Worthington returned to The Shay, as did another former player, Bobby Davison, now aged 37, rejoining a club he had left nearly 14 years earlier. The directors also dipped into their pockets to sign Stafford striker Mick Norbury for £10,000.

Chairman John Stockwell's claim that Town would finish in the top four seemed a little bold, particularly when Town crashed 6–0 in the season's opener at Stevenage. Pride was

Halifax Town 1996–97. Back row (left to right): Noel Horner, Willie Griffiths, Damian Place, Gareth Hamlet, Michael Midwood, Mark Cameron, Paul Hand, Andy Lee. Middle row: Alan Russell-Cox (physio), Billy Rodaway (assistant manager), Paul Stoneman, Mick Norbury, Mick Trotter, Chris Horsfall, Andy Woods, Karl Cochrane, Jon Brown, Gary Worthington, George Mulhall (youth team manager),Tommy Gildert (fitness conditioner). Front row: Paul Mudd, Bobby Davison, Paul Kerr, John Carroll (manager), Gary Brook, Kieran O'Regan, Ian McInerney.

salvaged when they held Altrincham to a point in their next match, and there was jubilation in the 4–1 stroll over Slough, but doubts crept in when the Shaymen just about clung on for a 3–2 victory at North West Counties Second Division side Oldham Town in the first qualifying round of the FA Cup. The 4–1 debacle at home to Bishop Auckland in the next round was perhaps a disaster waiting to happen, with the final whistle being the cue for a mass protest against the management and the board by the supporters.

But matters were only worsened in the League when the Shaymen sank towards the relegation zone, with fingers being pointed at either John Carroll, the board, or both. Still, the beleaguered Town boss did have his sympathisers when Town crashed 4–0 at home to Woking following an inept refereeing display by Michael Ryan, who saw fit to send off two Town players, for what appeared to be minor offences.

Carroll made additions to his squad, including that of Macclesfield's hardman midfielder Kevin Hulme, but defeat to Harrogate Railway in the West Riding County Cup on 4 November represented a new low. However embarrassing it may have been, nothing could legislate, however, for Harrogate 'keeper Mark Fenton's bizarre winner when his long punt downfield caught out Town substitute 'keeper Woods, with the ball bouncing over his head and into the net.

Success in the West Riding's senior equivalent at least offered some respite, for in what was a one-off Final with Bradford City at The Shay on 10 December, Norbury's goal cancelled out the lead given the Bantams by Craig Midgley, and it was left to Worthington to slot home the winning goal and give Town the West Riding Senior Cup they had last lifted in 1967.

Christmas came and went with things still looking bleak for the Shaymen, despite Carroll's additions of Witton striker Geoff Horsfield, defender Paul Cox and winger Darren Lyons. The side turned their attention to the FA Trophy competition but despite moving into the second round thanks to Brook's headed goal at Stalybridge, they came a cropper at Gloucester, losing 3–0. Carroll knew the clock was ticking, and seven days later, when struggling Bath came out on top 5–4 in a topsy-turvy game at The Shay to record their first away win of the season, the Town board acted. Hours after the final whistle, Carroll and Rodaway left the club 'by mutual consent' following a 45–minute meeting with the directors.

John Stockwell now once again asked George Mulhall and Kieran O'Regan to take control of first-team matters, adding, 'The crowd have been screaming for this for a long time and now I hope they get behind the team.' They pressed Norbury into an unfamiliar centre-half role and guided the side to three consecutive victories which in the final shake up proved crucial. Despite adding defender Jamie Murphy to the side, Town's Conference future went to the last day after a run of eight games without a win saw them hurtle towards the drop-zone. However, inspired by the 3–3 draw with champions-elect Macclesfield in the penultimate match, Town went into the last game with Stevenage knowing only victory would ensure survival. Fates were at least in their own hands, but they were hanging on nervously to a 3–2 lead when news came through that Bath, the only side who could overhaul them, had overturned a two-goal deficit at home to Northwich to lead in their game. A Stevenage equaliser at The Shay could have proved disastrous, and it was not until substitute Horsfield fired home Town's fourth goal in injury time that their own celebration party could begin.

HALIFAX TOWN: THE COMPLETE RECORD

Halifax Town's 1997–98 Conference winning squad. Back row (from left to right): Michael Midwood, Paul Stoneman, Lee Martin, Brian Kilcline, Andy Woods, Craig Boardman, Geoff Horsfield. Middle row: Noel Horner, Jamie Murphy, Darren Lyons, Michael Rosser, Jon Brown, Andy Thackeray, Mark Bradshaw. Front row: Alan Russell-Cox (physio), Paul Hand, Damian Place, Willie Griffiths, Kevin Hulme, George Mulhall (manager), Jamie Paterson, Gary Brook, Kieran O'Regan, Tommy Gildert (fitness conditioner).

After surviving relegation, the bookies offered Halifax Town odds of 66–1 for the **1997–98** Conference title, but they had reckoned without the wily George Mulhall who made some astute signings, not least that of centre-back Peter Jackson. Two new full-backs arrived in the form of Andy Thackeray and Mark Bradshaw, while there was also the return of the popular midfielder Jamie Paterson, while 'keeper Lee Martin came in to replace Woods.

A shock departure prior to the start of the season was that of Norbury, sold to Hednesford, but Mulhall had seen the potential of Horsfield, and he would score prolifically, beginning with a goal in the opening day victory at Hayes. Town came through their first three matches, all away, unscathed and romped to the top of the table in style following a 3–1 victory over Yeovil on 5 September, though it was an earlier 3–0 victory at Telford which made Mulhall realise just how good the side was.

While setting the pace in the

Geoff Horsfield and George Mulhall pick up their respective awards from the *Mail on Sunday* for performances during September 1997. Horsfield's 11 goals earned him the Scorer of the Month trophy, while Mulhall, who guided Town to seven straight wins, was Manager of the Month.

Defender Peter Jackson, who played a pivotal role in the early months of Town's Conference winning season before he answered the call to take over as manager at Huddersfield Town.

Conference, Town also breezed through the early qualifying rounds of the FA Cup, before suffering defeat at Gainsborough Trinity. This represented something of a crisis, particularly as Jackson had left for Huddersfield as manager, but Mulhall responded by signing former Coventry stopper Brian Kilcline as his replacement. Town, however, were knocked off the top following draws at Morecambe and a 4–0 defeat at Cheltenham but by dropping only two points from their next six matches, reclaimed pole position following victory at Stalybridge on 15 November, and they never seriously looked likely to surrender it, even allowing for a slight wobble over the Festive period. But having taken Cardiff striker Tony Philliskirk on loan from Cardiff, Town went into the New Year seven points clear of Cheltenham and eyeing a return to the Football League.

However, this would not be possible unless improvements were made to The Shay ground. But with Calderdale Council having given the green light to its upgrade in September 1996, and with a ground share scheme involving the rugby club on the horizon, Blakedell Construction began work on Phase One of the ground development – the terracing on the Hunger Hill side, renamed the North Terrace – on 5 January 1998, though this soon turned out to be a race against time with the deadline set for 31 March.

On the pitch, the players got on with the job in hand, extending an unbeaten run to six matches in the Conference, brushing aside their defeat by Slough in an FA Trophy replay. By the time they travelled to Rushden on 7 February, Town had stretched their lead at the top to 10 points, and though they collapsed heavily at Nene Park, once again they responded in style, winning at both Dover and Yeovil, and victory over Farnborough at home edged them nearer the title. The 5–1 rout of Morecambe on 17 March then set them up for the return with Rushden four days later, and spurred on by a 3,951 crowd, Brian Talbot's side were blown away, the 2–0 scoreline not reflecting Town's superiority in the game that day.

Coming in for that match following injury to 'keeper Martin for what proved to be his only appearance was Stoke goalkeeper Phil Morgan, but when he was recalled Mulhall went to Airdrie to capture Andy Rhodes, and the former Oldham 'keeper played his part in the final assault. As, too, did Dave Hanson, who returned to The Shay from Leyton Orient.

On 2 April, after inspecting the North Terrace, Football League officials deemed it suitable, with the capacity being raised from just under 4,000 to 7,400 and Chris Whalley of the Football League ground-grading committee commenting, 'This is clearly a forward-looking club and we will welcome them into the League.' All Town had to do now was tie up the loose ends, and after coming from behind to defeat Southport on Easter Monday courtesy of sub Hanson's two late goals following the dismissal of O'Regan, Town knew victory at Kidderminster five days later would mean the Conference title, and with it promotion, was theirs.

Job done! Manager George Mulhall leads the charge from the bench upon the final whistle at Kidderminster.

The task was duly completed, with Rhodes saving an early penalty before goals from Horsfield and Paterson sealed a 2–0 win in front of a travelling army 1,500-strong to ensure Town's five-year League exile was over. It hardly mattered that they failed to win any of their last three matches., but they did at least keep their unbeaten home record in tact by drawing with Cheltenham, and Horsfield's headed goal in the unexpected 6–2 last-day defeat at Welling meant he finished as the Conference's top scorer with 30 goals.

Return To League Struggles

Sadly, at the moment of their greatest triumph there was discord. Dave Worthington, more recently employed as reserve-team manager, boycotted the open-top parade through the town on the way to a civic reception, while the bus itself was decked out in 'Nationwide Building Society' banners announcing the club's new sponsors for the forthcoming season, thus upsetting director Chris Holland, whose company was still the current sponsors. He resigned from the board but was soon back as chairman on 8 June following the sudden resignation of John Stockwell.

Andy May arrived to take up the position coach of the reserve and youth teams, though there were reservations about the appointment of Peter Butler as coach, with Holland claiming he had not been signed by Mulhall but by Jim Brown, his brother-in-law, now back on the board following a period as club president. Clearly there was disharmony, evinced by Mulhall's sudden decision to step down just four days before the start of the **1998–99** campaign. He was set to take up the position of Director of Football 12 months hence, but now the managerial position was immediately thrust upon Kieran O'Regan, who in turn made May his assistant. On the eve of the first game the *Halifax Courier* led with the headline 'Rift Rocks Big Return' with Holland explaining, 'The board is united behind the manager and we believe that Peter Butler still has a part to play at the club.' Less than a week later, however, Holland had stood down with Jim Brown taking the helm for a second period.

During the close season 'keeper Tim Carter and centre-half Mark Sertori had arrived, but O'Regan was forced to go into his first game at Peterborough without three would-be regulars, and handed debuts to other newcomers in Richard Lucas, Steve Murphy and striker Ian Duerden. The side put politics behind them to pull off a fine 2–0 victory at London Road in searing heat, with Hanson walking the ball into the net for Town's first goal, and seven days later, League football returned to The Shay, Horsfield netting the game's only goal in victory over title-favourites Brentford. After four games, Town briefly went top while progressing to the second round of the Worthington Cup at the expense of Second Division Wrexham following a penalty shoot-out at The Shay after both sides had won their respective away legs 2–0.

Town bowed out to Bradford City in round two but maintained their challenge at the top end of the table. But they did so without top scorer Horsfield, who, having become one of the hottest properties, moved to Kevin Keegan's Fulham on 12 October for a record

The Halifax Town 1998–99 squad which started life back in the Football League. Back row (from left to right): Steve Thorrber (youth coach), Alan Russell-Cox (physio), Gareth Hamlet, Paul Stoneman, Lee Martin, Damian Place, Jon Brown, Geoff Horsfield, Mark Sertori. Middle row: Kevin Hulme, Dave Hanson, Mark Bradshaw, Chris Newton, Mark Carter, James Stansfield, Richard Lucas, Ian Duerden, Andy Thackeray. Front row: George Mulhall (Director of Football), Mark Hitchen (director), Mo Choucri (director), Andy May (assistant manager), Chris Holland (chairman), Kieran O'Regan (player-manager), Adie Hall (director), David Cairns (director), Tommy Gildert (fitness conditioner).

Paul Stoneman glances this header just wide in the FA Cup first-round match with Manchester City at Maine Road, 13 November 1998.

£300,000. Without him, however, Town pulled off some notable victories, with the 4–0 success at Scunthorpe the best of the lot. At Carlisle, they won despite Hulme having to take over in goal following injury to Carter, and the Shaymen rallied to go top following a stormy encounter with Chester on 10 November, a game in which Hulme was sent off with Chris Priest after a mass brawl which had involved 20 players. He was later suspended by the club for the next game, a televised first-round FA Cup tie at Manchester City, but was sorely missed as Town went down 3–0.

With striker Marc Williams now in the side and Steve Guinan arriving on loan, the Shaymen returned to League action and remained top of the Third Division going into December, but they never recovered once they had lost at bottom club Scarborough, enduring a run of seven games without a win and falling off the pace. Williams's brace in a 2–0 victory over Plymouth on 23 January stopped the rot but he was soon sold to York, while O'Regan brought in forwards Lee Power and Justin Jackson. But inconsistent results saw Town drop further down the table and where once a Play-off place had seemed the least the fans could expect, now even that was under threat, a fact not gone unnoticed by chairman Jim Brown.

The Shaymen had slipped to 11th place when they prepared for their Easter Monday clash with Rochdale and the ensuing goalless draw left them three points off the Play-offs, though such a situation could hardly be described as critical. Thus, the dismissal of O'Regan, and with him his assistant Andy May, on 6 April came out of the blue. Brown later claimed he had been sacked following a poor run of results and the decision 'had to be made in the best interests of the club,' though fans were angered by these actions.

In turn, Dave Worthington, stepped into the breach, and to his credit he steered the Shaymen back into Play-off contention. But Town shot themselves in the foot by losing at home to lowly Scarborough, and they travelled to Exeter for the final match knowing that only victory would be good enough for a Play-off place, and then only if Swansea slipped up. Thackeray gave Town an early lead to raise hopes, but the Grecians hit back to win 2–1 and the Shaymen ended the season in 10th position, five points behind the Swans in seventh place.

Dave Worthington was always ever intended as a stop-gap, and on 2 June 1999 Scunthorpe coach Mark Lillis took up his duties as Town's new manager. He inherited a side which now included record £150,000 striker Chris Tate, signed from Scarborough, and the Clarke twins Matthew and Chris, dual signings from Wolves. Lillis added centre-back Graham Mitchell, left-back Mark Jules, midfielder Steve Gaughan, and forward Robbie Painter to his squad but began the **1999–00** campaign without a recognised goalkeeper and

THE HISTORY OF HALIFAX TOWN

Robert Herbert who, at 16 years and 13 days, became Halifax Town's youngest-ever player when he came on as substitute in the 65th minute of the home game with Brighton on 11 September 1999.

was forced into taking West Brom's reserve Chris Adamson on loan until the arrival of Lee Butler from Dunfermline in September.

In a season that would be overshadowed by political intrigue and uncertainty, Lillis had to contend with the early season departures of Jackson, Sertori and Hulme, but shrugged off opening day defeat to Darlington, coupled with the heavy aggregate defeat to West Brom in the Worthington Cup, to see his side string together three successive victories to go ninth. The 2–1 home success over Brighton on 11 September also saw Robert Herbert, at 16 years and 13 days, become the youngest ever Town player when he replaced Chris Newton after 65 minutes.

On the back of fine home wins over Carlisle and Peterborough, the Shaymen rose to third to give the supporters hope of a promotion challenge, but it proved a false dawn, for by the beginning of January they had dropped to 10th, as well slipping out of the FA Cup when, having won at Doncaster in round one, they lost a Shay replay to Reading having secured a draw at their impressive Majedski Stadium. But manager Lillis was certain off-field activities were not helping matters. At the bequest of director David Greenwood, the major shareholder, at a board meeting on 28 October, fellow directors David Cairns, Mark

Halifax Town 1999–2000. Back row (from left to right): James Stansfield, Chris Tate, Graham Mitchell, Matthew Clarke, Tony Parks (coach), Mark Sertori, Jamie Murphy, Paul Stoneman, Chris Clarke. Middle row: Steve Thornber (youth coach), Kevin Hulme, Matt Russell, Robbie Painter, Steve Gaughan, Tommy Gildert (fitness conditioner), Martin Ayscough, Ian Richards, Stephen Murphy, Mark Bradshaw, Charlie Fallas (kitman). Front row: Gary Worthington (youth coach), Jamie Paterson, Mark Jules, Richard Lucas, Peter Butler (assistant manager), Mark Lillis (manager), Lee Power, Justin Jackson, Chris Newton, Alan Russell-Cox (physio).

Hitchen, Mo Choucri and Adie Hall were all forced to quit to allow for potential new investors to come on board. One of the interested parties, Jim Willis, brother-in-law of entertainer Cilla Black, indeed, reckoned a £1 million takeover would be completed by Christmas, while a six-man consortium headed by local businessmen Les Lawson and Peter Siddall also declared its interest, though in the end, nothing came to fruition, and chairman Jim Brown, now the sole board member, was forced to go to the local press to explain the situation.

The decision to allow record signing Chris Tate to rejoin Scarborough in mid-December coincided with the arrivals of full-back Chris Wilder and winger Alan Reilly, while loan signings came in the form of striker Rodney Rowe, Jon Cullen and Lee Potter, and suddenly the side seemed rejuvenated. With Lincoln having been beaten 3–0 on Boxing Day, closely followed by victory at Barnet, Town memorably claimed victory at leaders Rotherham courtesy of Potter's diving header to move back into Play-off contention. Hopes were raised, but not, however, realised as the Shaymen went on to record only three more victories before the season's close.

This was all the more disappointing given the additions to the board of local businessmen Bob Walker, Doug Tait and Ray Crabtree on 22 February, and to the squad of players such as Ian Fitzpatrick and Craig Middleton. City). Town slid down the table, though matters were not helped by in-discipline which saw Peter Butler and Scunthorpe's on loan forward Darryn Stamp dismissed in the 2–1 defeat at Brighton, and worse, three players – Stoneman, Reilly and Middleton – receiving marching orders in the penultimate game at York. Lillis had signed strikers Steve Kerrigan and on loan Gary Jones in an attempt to improve things, and the poor run of form was ended with a stunning, if totally unexpected, 4–3 victory at Northampton on 8 April, where Kerrigan popped up with a dramatic last-minute winner, as he would do several weeks later to sink his former club Shrewsbury. The Shaymen wrapped up a disappointing season with home defeat to Macclesfield and ended the season in 18th.

While Town favourite Jamie Paterson left the club, new players seen during **2000–01** included experienced midfielder Steve Thompson and forward Gerry Harrison, as well as Ian Richards, Steve Hawe and Steve Morgan, along with Gary Jones, who was a secured in a permanent deal. Director Ray Crabtree outlined the main objective being the Play-offs, but Town were never seriously in contention, for when they threw away leads at Carlisle in the opener and at home against Lincoln, they set a precedence for a season of struggle. Town quickly became relegation fodder, and found little respite in the Worthington Cup, tumbling out at the first hurdle, albeit in slightly surreal circumstances, staging a second leg against Tranmere at 'home' at Bradford City's Valley Parade when development work at The Shay, which included a new East Stand, had left them without floodlights.

Without a win from the first six League matches, pressure on manager Lillis had reached fever pitch by the time the side travelled to Mansfield on 9 September 2000. The Shaymen were humiliated 5–1 and sank to the foot of the table and three days later, Lillis was sacked. The board sought a successor, but in the interim, Peter Butler and coach Tony Parks held the fort, claiming the first victory at Torquay and with the signs encouraging Butler threw his name into the ring. But on 3 October, he was overlooked when the board unveiled their new man: former Everton and England midfielder Paul Bracewell, who had been latterly been manager at Fulham. But his appointment was accompanied by two shock moves.

THE HISTORY OF HALIFAX TOWN

Halifax Town 2000–01. Back row (from left to right): Lee Potter, Mark Bradshaw, Steven Underwood, James Stansfield, Gary Jones, Craig Middleton, Paul Stoneman, Chris Wilder, Steve Thompson. Middle row: Tommy Gildert (fitness conditioner), Sarah Scott (physio), Grant Holt, Michael Ord, Matthew Clarke, Lee Butler, Steve Thornber (youth coach), Tony Parks (coach), Chris Clarke, Steve Kerrigan, Charlie Fallas (kitman), Dave Worthington (chief scout). Front row: Alan Reilly, Ian Richards, Mark Jules, Peter Butler (assistant manager), Graham Mitchell, Mark Lillis (manager), Ian Fitzpatrick, Robbie Painter, Steve Gaughan.

Firstly, Jim Brown stood down as chairman – he would remain on the board until breaking ties the following April – while Butler, who had never endeared himself to the vast majority of fans, left the club with immediate effect.

Bracewell claimed the job represented a 'massive test' and several weeks into it brought in Richie Barker as his assistant. But the new Town boss lost his first five games in charge, a sequence that ensured he made the worst start by a new Halifax Town manager. He dipped into the loan system, bringing in winger Neil Wainwright, Peter Murphy and Middlesbrough's classy defender Stuart Parnaby, and saw his side win for the first time with a 3–1 success over Exeter City on 4 November. Town crept away from the foot of the table and went on a mini-run of four successive League wins during December and January which made their League position look healthier. Sadly, however, they could not enjoy as decent a run in the FA Cup as Unibond North Premier side Gateshead proved full value for their 2–0 win at The Shay.

Town, however, did enjoy victory at Wrexham in the LDV Trophy and put up an almighty fight against Stoke in the second round at home before eventually losing 3–2. Bracewell bemoaned his players' lack of a killer touch but still, he must have been pleased that his side held out at Rochdale four days later, when Kerrigan's spectacular overhead kick gave the Shaymen the points and moved them up to 19th, 10 points clear of bottom club Carlisle.

But the side slipped into their old ways and were soon fighting a relegation battle once more. Bracewell brought in further loan players such as winger Rob Matthews and forward Leon Mike, but progress was hampered by a long-term injury to 'keeper Lee Butler. Craig Mawson arrived, but in only his second game, Town lost 4–3 at home to Scunthorpe, and three days later, Carlisle jumped over the Shaymen to leave them bottom of the table.

To help with Town's fight against relegation, Bracewell then signed the vastly experienced midfielder Neil Redfearn, son of former Town winger Brian, from Wigan, while his full-back

Supporters rush onto the pitch at the end of the match at Lincoln City on 30 April 2001 after Craig Middleton's late goal had earned Town a crucial point in their bid to escape the clutches of relegation.

teammate Peter Mitchell and young Sunderland forward Michael Proctor became the latest loan players to join the club, and Proctor went on to grab the third goal in victory over Barnet, a result which in the long run would prove crucial. The Bees were one of five clubs involved in the dogfight to escape the clutches of relegation, though Town did own their chances the world of good with another 3–0 success over Macclesfield.

When Middleton grabbed a last-gasp equaliser at Lincoln, Town were left needing just a point from their final two matches to be safe, the first of which was the final home match with Brighton. Still, they were perhaps fortunate on several fronts. Two clubs below them, Torquay and Barnet had to play each other on the season's final day, and Brighton, who had already made two trips to Halifax only for the games to be postponed, arrived on 3 May having already clinched the Championship. In front of 3,979, the ensuing goalless draw suited the Shaymen, and by losing at Chesterfield in their final match, they avoided the drop by two points.

Halifax Town gambled during **2001–02** with the expensive signings of Paul Harsley, Craig Midgley and Andy Woodward, though there were those who were sceptical about the signing of injury-ridden Dominic Ludden, who arrived having been released by Preston. Before the season began, Bracewell also tied up deals with Steve Swales and Jamie Wood, and his side took encouraging pre-season form into the first game at Lincoln which ended with a 2–1 success. But the euphoria soon died down and when the Shaymen succumbed to home defeat by Oxford on August Bank Holiday Monday, the fifth match of the season, Bracewell had seen enough and resigned two days later.

Chairman Walker claimed Bracewell's resignation was a 'short, sharp shock' but tuned to Neil Redfearn and Tony Parks to look after the first team. They fared well, taking the side to 10th at one point, and were keen to make the positions permanent. But talks stalled and ultimately broke down over the length of contract, leaving Walker left with no option but to look elsewhere, and on 12 October, former Town player Alan Little was named as the new manager.

There was glory in defeat in his first game in charge, an LDV Vans Trophy match at Huddersfield which the Shaymen lost on penalties after a goalless draw, though there was little else to get worked up about as they extended a winless streak in the League to seven matches and dropped to bottom of the table. Their best performances, however, seemed reserved for the FA Cup, for having overcome Conference side Farnborough, the Shaymen were unlucky not to beat Second Division Stoke City in the second-round match at The Shay. Herbert missed a great chance late on and Stoke took advantage in the replay by winning 3–0.

Little claimed his first League win at the seventh attempt with 2–0 victory over Torquay on 24 November and brought in the battling Steve Bushell but he wouldn't taste success again until January. Often Town were simply outclassed, as in the 6–1 defeat at Oxford, while other times they were just unlucky. Injury to goalkeeper Lee Butler, who announced his wish to retire due to injury, meant a call up for rookie Peter Crookes for the home game with Shrewsbury on 15 December, but after conceding a penalty he was sent off and Butler, helping out on the bench, was quickly back in action, though Town lost the match 2–1.

Little signed up Scarborough 'keeper Barry Richardson until the end of the season, but Town's struggle continued, the 3–0 victory over Lincoln on 19 January hardly the prelude to better things. Town soon became marooned at the foot of the table, though just how much this situation affected Little is unsure, but on 4 March he was in hospital, diagnosed with a ruptured appendix. He would not return to The Shay as manager again, released from the club on 9 April.

With Little indisposed, chairman Bob Walker turned once more to Neil Redfearn, but with only 10 games to go and the side 10 points adrift, it was a forlorn task. Redfearn brought in Dave Worthington to assist him, and Town enjoyed back-to-back victories over Kidderminster and Cheltenham, but relegation to the Conference was confirmed with the

Halifax Town's squad that began the ill-fated 2001–02 campaign. Back row (from left to right): Jamie Wood, Alan Reilly Midgley, Andy Woodward, Chris Clarke, Gary Jones, Graham Mitchell, Paul Stoneman, Craig Middleton. Middle row: Gareth Liversidge (kitman), Dominic Ludden, Steve Swales, Lee Butler, Craig Mawson, Peter Crookes, Robert Herbert, Paul Harsley, Tony Parks (coach). Front row: Mark Jules, Ian Fitzpatrick, Neil Redfearn, Richie Barker (assistant manager), Paul Bracewell (manager), Steve Oleksewycz, Peter Wright, Craig Midgley.

Ian Fitzpatrick scores what turns out to be Town's last-ever goal in the Football League as Town slip to 4–2 home defeat by Rushden & Diamonds, 20 April 2002 in the final match of the season.

5–0 defeat at Darlington on Easter Monday. Town enjoyed a fine 4–2 success at Torquay in their penultimate game but lost by the same score to Rushden in what proved to be the last-ever League match at The Shay, with Redfearn having the ignominy of being sent off and forced to see out the game wearing a hard-hat from the building site which was the unfinished East Stand.

While relegation was a massive blow, perhaps of more concern was the future of the club itself. On 14 February, Halifax Town had been put up for sale by Bob Walker, who claimed the wage bill, around £1.2 million, was crippling the club. The sale of centre-back Chris Clarke to Blackpool for £120,000 helped in the short term, but with a view to the bigger picture, the newly formed Halifax Town Supporters' Trust was launched at North Bridge Leisure Centre on 24 February, with the aim being to raise enough money to secure shares and gain membership of the board. But such actions all come too late, as events were about to catch up with the club.

On 6 April 2002 the Inland Revenue demanded an instant payment of £107,000 of a £220,000 tax bill, but 10 days later, with debts amounting to £900,000, Halifax Town took the difficult decision to go into administration, with Peter O'Hara, of O'Hara Insolvency Practitioners, Birstall, overseeing the running of the club. He pledged to work with Bob Walker, but soon the chairman was gone, resigning on 17 May, quickly followed by Neil Redfearn, who claimed O'Hara had refused to sanction a contract for him. Halifax Town headed into the summer looking for a buyer for the club that now had Doug Tait as chairman of a four-man board also made up of Ray Crabtree, Adie Hall and David Cairns, the latter two both having returned the previous November.

WILDER YEARS

There were only two parties interested in taking over Halifax Town. One was from Gameplan International, agents for capitol investors on behalf of businessman Michael Lloyd, while the other was from the more credible consortium led by current directors Cairns and Hall, whose offer was the only one put forward by a set deadline. After terms of the CVA had been accepted on 31 July 2002, the consortium was given the green light to take Halifax Town forward.

The consortium, which now made up the board of directors, in fact, was nine-strong, and featured not only Cairns and Hall, who became chairman and vice-chairman respectively, but also Martin Fox, Ray Moreland, Roy Jackson, Phil Jewitt, Richard Harrison, Bob Bland and Tony Charlton. Solicitor Chris Haddock became another voice in the boardroom, too, when he was elected as the Supporters' Trust representative.

THE HISTORY OF HALIFAX TOWN

Halifax Town 2002–03, preparing to take on the Conference once again. Back row (from left to right): Ian Helliwell (assistant fitness conditioner), Robert Herbert, Paul Stoneman, Adam Quinn, Tom Morgan, Lee Butler (assistant manager), Ryan Poole, Phil Haigh, Steve Kerrigan, Nicky Heinemann, Bobby Barr (youth coach). Middle row: Alan Jackson (physio), Andy Farrell, Steve Bushell, Craig Midgley, Phil Clarkson, Craig Smith, Alistair Asher, Stuart Elliott, Gary Birchall, Sean McAuley, Ian Fitzpatrick, Neil Grayston, Tommy Gildert (fitness conditioner). Front row: Martin Fox (director), Phil Jewitt, (director), Bob Bland (director), Adie Hall (vice chairman), Chris Wilder (manager), David Cairns (chairman), Ray Moreland (director), Tony Charlton (director), Richard Harrison (director).

While Peter O'Hara ran the club through the summer, the consortium got on with appointing a new manager, and turned to former Town player Chris Wilder having been impressed at the job he had done at Alfreton. He took up his position on 2 July and quickly targeted stability, bringing with him Lee Butler – he not only became assistant manager, but also first choice goalkeeper – and Sean McAuley as coach.

Invited back to the club by Wilder were Steve Bushell, Craig Midgley, Steve Kerrigan, Ian Fitzpatrick and Paul Stoneman, joining YTS players Andy Farrell and Robert Herbert, while the initial squad of players also included full-backs Alistair Asher and Neil Grayston, centre-backs Phil Haigh and Adam Quinn, midfielders Stuart Elliott and Phil Clarkson, and the dreadlocked striker Simon Parke. But though Wilder had ambition for the club, during the six years he remained at the club he would find himself handicapped by the terms of the CVA – around £4,000 per month – which O'Hara had negotiated with the creditors.

Sheffield United winger Ryan Mallon arrived on loan in time for the opening game with Telford on 17 August and Town made the best possible start, Kerrigan's 27th-minute headed goal setting them on the way to a 2–0 win. But three successive defeats followed, culminating in the calamitous 5–0 hiding inflicted on them by Northwich at The Shay which left Town lying 20th in the table. Results steadily improved, however, as Wilder tinkered with the side, bringing in experienced centre-backs Shaun Garnett and Mark Monington, lively forward Brian Quailey and left-back Kevin Sandwith, and a run of nine unbeaten matches saw the Shaymen climb to sixth and looking good for the Play-offs which the Conference had by now introduced.

Despite progress in the Conference, there was no joy in the FA Cup, Town bowing out at the first time of asking at Burton in the fourth qualifying round, but they would enjoy a mini-run in the FA Trophy. Having defeated Doncaster 2–1 in the Conference back in September, they went even better when the two sides met on 14 January. Lewis Killeen,

Messrs. Harrison, Hall, Moreland, Jewitt, Cairns, Haddock, Groves, Byrnes, Wilder, Walton, Bland, Charlton on the platform when the Supporters' Trust held a public crisis meeting at the Victoria Theatre, 18 March 2003.

having arrived on loan from Sheffield United once Mallon had returned to Bramall Lane, scored a brace as Town ran out 4–1 winners, and they progressed to the third round at the expense of Grays before losing at Farnborough.

On the back of an impressive six-match winning streak, Town rose to third in the Conference by the end of January, having gone through the whole of that month unbeaten. But when Wilder was named Conference Manager of the Month, typically Town struggled and recorded only three further victories before the season's close.

As well as the constraints put on the club by the CVA, manager Wilder was hampered further when the FA slapped a transfer embargo on the club for still being in administration. When O'Hara also claimed that there was an 'acute cash shortage', the players deferred bonuses owed to them and, after the club revealed on 6 March that it owed £204,466 in football debts which were not part of the CVA, the Supporters' Trust rallied round, organising a public meeting at the Victoria Theatre on 18 March where all club officials took to the platform. On the night, over £20,000 was raised by supporters, and when further pledges saw the total reach £30,000 Town finally came out of administration on 28 March once £97,000 owed to them by the Football League was released.

Four consecutive defeats put a dent in Play-off ambitions, though Town pushed leaders Yeovil all the way at The Shay, taking an early two-goal lead through Parke's headed goals, only to lose to an injury-time winner. Desperate to get back on track, Town were denied three points by Woking's Scott Canham on 29 March after taking an 87th-minute lead through Midgley, and their chances of making the Play-offs disappeared with defeat at Margate in their next game. Town beat Hereford and Kettering as the season petered out and finished their first season back in the Conference in eighth place.

No sooner had the season finished than Wilder was at work assembling his squad for the **2003–04** campaign, immediately snapping up Farnborough's defender-cum-striker Christian Lee and tricky midfielder Lee Elam, then signing up permanently both Mallon and Killeen. Joining them were full-back Darren Hockenhull, midfielders Danny Hudson and Jon Cullen, back for a second spell, and Chester's on-loan striker Dave Cameron, but Wilder went into the new season with Bradford City 'keeper Clint Davies in the side on loan to fill the gap vacated by Lee Butler, whose decision to rejoin Alfreton meant a step up for McAuley to assistant manager.

The Shaymen provided the opposition at St James' Park for relegated Exeter's first game in the Conference, earning a point and enjoying a four-match unbeaten start to the season. But thereafter, performances became patchy, though the 5–3 defeat of Northwich on 6

Halifax Town 2003–04. Back row (from left to right): Adam Quinn, Simon Parke, Ryan Poole, Shaun Garnett, Clint Davies, Christian Lee, Mark Monington. Middle row: Tommy Gildert (fitness conditioner), Michael Senior, Kevin Sandwith, Jon Cullen, Darren Hockenhull, Andy Farrell, Ryan Hindley, Alan Jackson (physio). Front row: Danny Hudson, Craig Midgley, Lewis Killeen, Paul Stoneman (youth-team manager), Chris Wilder (manager), Sean McAuley (assistant manager), Steve Bushell, Lee Elam, Ryan Mallon.

September was entertaining enough. Northwich would gain revenge the following month when they hosted the Shaymen in the first round of the FA Cup, though both names went into the hat for the second-round draw, but only because the game was held over until the Sunday after the draw had been made on Saturday teatime.

In the Conference, Town remained mid-table fodder despite Wilder's efforts to strengthen the side. 'Keeper Mark Cartwright arrived in September, and further additions came in the form of full-back Adam Yates, on loan from Crewe, and forward Jake Sagare, an American teenager from Portland Timbers. Centre-backs James Dudgeon and Jamie McCombe also arrived on loan to offset the departure of Garnett and injury to Monington, but they had the misfortune to be part of the side which crashed 7–1 at Hereford.

Wilder added midfielder Val Owen to the side, but in a difficult period, with crowds drifting away, new chairman Ray Moreland, who had succeeded David Cairns on 17 November, issued a challenge to the supporters in much the same vein as his predecessors had done. A hearty 2,136 thus turned out for the visit of Scarborough on 26 December, but they witnessed a farcical match which gave a new meaning to Boxing Day when two players from each side were sent off following a mass brawl 10 minutes before half-time. Victory in that game, however, moved the Shaymen up to 10th, but as far as the Conference was concerned, that would be as good as it got. The point from the goalless draw with Shrewsbury on 24 January 2004, in fact, proved to be the last they would gain until April as defeat followed defeat.

At least there was the distraction of the LDV Vans Trophy, where, in a throwback to the heady nights of the late 1980s, Town reached the Northern semi-finals having disposed of Third Division York and Lincoln, as well as Conference rivals Scarborough. Barring their way to the Northern Final were Division Two side Blackpool, but despite putting in an heroic performance and twice taking the lead through Killeen and Owen, Scott Taylor

Val Owen is hidden by teammates Steve Bushell, Craig Midgley and Kevin Sandwith after restoring Town's lead in the LDV Vans Northern area semi-final at Blackpool, 20 January 2004. But it was the home side who ran out 3–2 winners.

edged the home side in front after 54 minutes, and Town could not find an equaliser despite their efforts.

The real drama, however, was reserved for the FA Trophy, when having won against the odds at Conference leaders Chester, the Shaymen were paired at home with Staines. The game was eventually played on 10 February after heavy rain had twice put paid to the tie, only for Staines to force a replay which was squeezed in with the fifth round due to be played just two days later. In dramatic fashion, Town forced extra-time after trailing 2–0 and scored a winner through a Midgley penalty, though feelings were running high and upon the final whistle Town's celebrations were cut short when boss Chris Wilder was laid unconscious by a blow allegedly struck by Kezie Ibe. (A subsequent court-case for assault in February 2005, however, cleared Ibe of any wrong doing, though many felt this verdict was clearly unjust).

The Town players had little left in the tank for the fifth-round meeting with Maidenhead and consequently slipped to a 2–0 home defeat, a result that heralded a run of 10 successive defeats which left them 19th in the table, just one place and four points above the drop zone. Defender Denny Ingram and strikers Colin Little and Jonny Allan were brought in and the danger was finally averted, though in truth, the season could not end quickly enough for Wilder, whose job since the beginning of March had been made harder following the resignation of chairman Ray Moreland.

Still, there was a Cup of cheer when the Shaymen lifted the West Riding County Cup under the guidance of Paul Stoneman. Run-outs were given to youngsters such as 'keeper Chris Parry, Pete Naylor, Ryan Toulson, Matt Maslak and Mark Mierswinksi, en route to the Final at WRCFA HQ on 14 April at Woodlesford, Leeds, where Town triumphed 2–1 over Farsley Celtic, despite being handicapped by the dismissal of Michael Senior before the break.

Ray Moreland cut his ties with the club at the end of July 2004, though it would not be the last the supporters would hear of him, but the five remaining directors were soon joined by quantity surveyor Geoff Ralph who assumed the role of chairman on 20 August. Meantime, his batteries recharged, Wilder recruited for **2004–05**, bringing in former Liverpool trainee 'keeper Ian Dunbavin, full-back Matt Doughty, midfielder Martin Foster, striker Ryan Sugden and winger Dean Howell, and Town challenged for a coveted Play-off

THE HISTORY OF HALIFAX TOWN

Halifax Town 2004–05. Back row (from left to right): Tommy Gildert (fitness conditioner), Mark Monington, Ryan Sugden, Craig Parry, Paul Stoneman, Ian Dunbavin, Christian Lee, Adam Quinn, Ian Helliwell (assistant fitness conditioner). Middle row: Alan Russell-Cox (physio), Ryan Mallon, Darren Hockenhull, Karl Munroe, Denny Ingram, Scott Willis, Dean Howell, Steve Haslam, Michael Senior, Gary Thompson (assistant physio). Front row: Matt Doughty, Lewis Killeen, Chris Wilder (manager), Steve Bushell, Sean McAuley (assistant manager), Craig Midgley, Martin Foster.

spot once more in a Conference that had been restructured with the creation of feeder divisions North and South.

Town made a stuttering start, however, losing at newcomers Tamworth as well as having Steve Haslam dismissed on the opening day, and in their third game, letting slip a two-goal half-time lead before going down 3–2 to Barnet. But they moved up to fourth on the back of five unbeaten matches where only two points were dropped and an unlikely goal hero in their ranks; centre-back Mark Monington, who netted in four consecutive games. Jason Blunt and Darren Mansaram strengthened the side, as did Henry McStay, on loan from Leeds, and victory over Farnborough on 16 October saw them lying third. Wilder then hailed his side's 1–0 win at fellow-promotion hopefuls Farnborough as the pick of the bunch, all the while his side putting together a club record of scoring in 25 consecutive matches in all competitions from the start of the season.

That run included games in the FA Cup, of course, though Town were indebted to Midgley's injury-time equaliser in the fourth qualifying round match with Leek at The Shay that earned them a 2–2 draw, and Bushell's extra-time winner in the replay. Victory over

Alex Meechan (left) heads home Town's second goal in the 2–0 home win over York City, 14 March 2005, and Halifax Town maintain their Play-off challenge – for the time being at least.

Third Division Cambridge was more emphatic, with Neil Ross, one of three new player to arrive at the club within the space of seven days following the arrivals of Alex Meechan and Canadian Gordon Chin, the scorer of the last goal in a 3–1 win. He also scored in the second-round game with Chester, though Town were second best and bowed out 3–1.

The Shaymen's scoring spree ended in a goalless draw at Forest Green on 18 December, but they remained Play-off candidates, for after viewing defeat to Northwich in the FA Trophy as a blessing in disguise, they lost only one of 10 matches through January and into March and moved up to second. Wilder brought in defender Greg Young for ankle-victim Doughty, but the later arrival of forward John Grant had an adverse effect on the side, though it would be cruel to lay the blame for the side's demise solely at his feet. Others were culpable, none more so than 'keeper Dunbavin who, in a televised match at Carlisle on 28 March, literally handed the game to the opposition. With the score goalless late on, he walked out of his area with the ball after misreading the referee's gesture to 'play on' as one for being beckoned towards him, thus in the process conceding the needless of free-kicks for hand-ball. Carlisle took it quickly with Dunbavin out of goal and Magno Vieira rolled the ball into an empty net.

Town may have trounced Leigh RMI 5–1 in their next match, but it was the run of four consecutive defeats that followed which saw them drop out of the Play-off race, their cause not helped by a broken leg suffered by skipper Bushell in the 3–1 reversal at Barnet. With other clubs picking up points, Town fell away and not even the 3–0 victory over Woking on the last day proved enough as the Shaymen finished eighth once more, nine points off a Play-off spot.

Disappointment also spilled over in the Final of the West Riding County Cup. Defending the trophy they had won 12 months earlier, Town's mix of youngsters and experienced players put in a poor performance against Guiseley and fell to Mark Stuart's penalty spot in first half injury time.

Making his last start in that match in what had been his testimonial season was Paul Stoneman, for having been given charge of the Under-19s at the beginning of that season, he now moved on while Chris Wilder set about improving his squad for the **2005–06** campaign. To that end, he was successful, but in a season which began at Morecambe and ended at Leicester, there was to be further disappointment.

The close season also saw the surprise departure of assistant manager Sean McAuley to concentrate on his academic qualifications (and later employment at Sheffield Wednesday) but Wilder immediately turned to Bradford City veteran Wayne Jacobs as his replacement, while also welcoming back for third spell Lee Butler as goalkeeping coach. Butler would act as cover for Ian Dunbavin, but Dunbavin's career would be curtailed in November when Wilder felt compelled to release him following his conviction for a driving offence.

Other players new to the club who would play a big part in what was a memorable season were midfielder Tyrone Thompson, winger Justin Bowler, and the Bradford City pair of Danny Forrest and Jake Wright, both on loan, while Wilder sought experience in defender Peter Atherton and the well-travelled midfielder Gary Brabin. Brabin's time would be cut short through injury, though he stayed just long enough time to blast home a rocket free-kick which proved enough to defeat Burton in the first home match following defeat at Morecambe in the season's opener.

The Shaymen's involvement in the hunt for the Play-off places was due in most part to their terrific home form. In the opening months of the campaign, York City, Tamworth,

THE HISTORY OF HALIFAX TOWN

Halifax Town's squad which reached the 2005–06 Play-off Final. Back row (from left to right): Mark Monington, Ryan Sugden, Ian Dunbavin, Greg Young, Lee Butler (coach), Darren Mansaram, Adam Quinn. Middle row: Alan Russell-Cox (physio), Ryan Toulson, Darren Hockenhull, Denny Ingram, Ian Helliwell (assistant fitness conditioner), Steve Haslam, John Grant, Jason Blunt, Tommy Gildert (fitness conditioner). Front row: Matt Doughty, Lewis Killeen, Wayne Jacobs (assistant manager), Steve Bushell, Chris Wilder, Craig Midgley, Martin Foster.

Hereford United, Altrincham and Cambridge United all left empty-handed, as did Bury in the LDV Vans Trophy as the Shaymen turned on the style and romped to a 6–1 victory.

Farsley Celtic, too, proved no match in the fourth qualifying round of the FA Cup but by the time of the first round tie with Rushden & Diamonds, Lee Butler found himself back in the side until the arrival of Birmingham's on loan Adam Legzdins. Town were unlucky not to beat Rushden, and only bowed out on penalties in the replay at Nene Park after playing out a goalless draw.

In the meantime, stealing a march on their rivals in the Conference were Accrington Stanley, who hit top spot at the beginning of December and managed to stay there. But the difference between success and failure proved to be a fine line; in two intriguing clashes between the sides over the festive period the points were shared, though the Shaymen looked the better side. The 1–1 draw at the Crown Ground was the first of four matches Town played without victory, a run which effectively ruled them out of the Championship race, though they were still very much contenders for the Play-offs, vying with Hereford, Stevenage, York City, Grays and Morecambe. Town would rise to the challenge, even if the New Year saw manager Wilder tested to the full.

Ingram's sale to Scarborough in January saw Peter Atherton come into the side, and when 'keeper Legzdins returned to Birmingham, Wilder signed Jon Kennedy. Other players, too, would feature with good effect. Steve Bushell, now free from injury, returned, and when on-loan winger Rory Prendergast declined to commit himself to the cause, Wilder made the signing of Derby's Brian Smikle until the end of the season.

An impressive run of six unbeaten matches took Town to second in the table by the end of February, and they continued to pick up points, finally securing a Play-off place with

John Grant flicks the ball home to give Town a 2–1 lead in the Play-off Final. There were only 17 minutes of the scheduled 90 to play.

victory over Gravesend in their penultimate match at The Shay, a result that preserved their unbeaten home record, only for that to go in surprise fashion when mid-table Canvey Island pulled off a 2–0 win on the last day. Still, Wilder was quick to shrug off the disappointment, claiming his side now had 'bigger fish to fry'.

How true. By finishing fourth, Town were forced to meet Grays in the Play-off semi-finals, and both games proved to be crackers. At The Shay, a fantastic crowd of 3,848 saw goals from Bushell, Sugden and Killeen give Town a dream 3–0 half-time lead only for the visitors to reduce the deficit to one goal. Then, four days later at Grays, Foster's early goal put Town in the driving seat, but the home side hit back with two goals in as many minutes and the tie swung in their favour, only for it to swing back Town's way when Killeen was upended in the box. Foster calmly tucked away the resultant penalty and Town held out to meet Hereford, aggregate winners over Morecambe, in the Play-off Final at the Walkers Stadium, Leicester, on 20 May.

The dream of a return to the Football League was very much a reality, and the match captured the imagination of the town. Around 6,000 supporters ventured to Leicester, but they were to return disappointed after seeing their side lose out despite twice being in front. Killeen's wonder strike after 26 minutes may have been the best goal of the game, and substitute Grant's flicked goal just 17 minutes from time perhaps should have been the winner, but Guy Ipoua's equaliser took the game to extra-time, and Ryan Green's instinctive curling shot into the top corner proved decisive. Town were resigned to at least one more season in the Conference but sadly, they would never go as close to a return to the Football League ever again.

While a lack of commercial activity hampered Town's progress during **2006–07**, chairman Geoff Ralph pinned his hopes on a new initiative launched by the Supporters'

Trust, the 'Shay 500 Scheme', where supporters were urged to buy up £500 worth of shares in the hope of speeding up the paying off of the CVA, the outstanding amount standing at £120,000 at the beginning of April 2006. Sadly, not enough people took up the offer, and Town's debts began to spiral out of control.

Manager Chris Wilder was forced to rebuild and brought back Craig Mawson, as well as signing striker Andy Campbell and a current international New Zealand forward, Shane Smeltz. Dutch player Gus Uhlenbeek also arrived, while Danny Forrest and Jake Wright made their moves permanent. A later addition to the squad was winger Steve Torpey, who had impressed in a pre-season friendly when playing for FC United of Manchester, but even he appeared in the side before Tom Kearney who joined up with his teammates after taking a holiday. The season would also see Nicky Gray and Ryan Toulson feature, but it was one in which proved to be a hangover from the Play-off Final defeat.

Wilder, handicapped by the CVA, was forced to wheel and deal with loan transfers while his side spent much of the season battling at the wrong end of the table, having begun with defeat at newly-relegated Oxford, and only one of their opening nine matches was won, a 2–1 success on the road at Cambridge. Ironically, Wilder considered a move to Cambridge after he felt Ralph had renegaded on promises made to him, but after further talks with his chairman, he stayed at The Shay.

By the end of September, Town had slipped into the relegation zone, and though they managed to climb to mid-table on the back of important home wins over Dagenham, Stevenage, Tamworth and Woking, clearly the side needed strengthening. Wilder used the loan system once more to bring in the Barnsley pair of defender Rob Atkinson and striker

Halifax Town 2006–07. Back row (from left to right): Shane Smeltz, Mark Roberts, Craig Mawson, Ryan Sugden, Lee Butler (coach), Adam Quinn, Greg Young. Middle row: Ryan Toulson, Danny Forrest, Andy Campbell, Alan Russell-Cox (physio), Steve Haslam, Jake Wright, Steve Torpey. Front row: Gus Uhlenbeek, Lewis Killeen, Martin Foster, Chris Wilder (manager), Wayne Jacobs (assistant manager), Chris Senior, Matt Doughty, Tyrone Thompson.

Steve Torpey keeps his head to fire home the only goal in the crucial relegation clash with Cambridge United at The Shay, 7 April 2007.

Nathan Joynes, and a 4–1 win over St Alban's City in December lifted the Shaymen up to 12th, but they would never go any higher.

A run in the FA Trophy was compensation of sorts for the poor League form and early exit at the hands of Burton in the FA Cup at the end of October. Having seen off the challenge of local rivals Farsley Celtic, Town returned to Oxford for a second round match, where Smeltz scored a late equaliser to earn the Shaymen a replay. Three days later they put on possibly their finest show that term to secure a 2–1 win, and while the third round triumph over Redditch was a little easier, Town's run ended shambolically at Kidderminster.

While the players had to take collective responsibility for their defeat at Aggborough, just who was to blame for the side's earlier exit in the West Riding County Cup nobody could be quite sure. They racked up a record 14 goals against Pontefract Collieries, though scorer of the 11th was young debutant Simon Rawnsley, a player who had earlier turned out in the competition – and scored – for Bradford PA, and was thus technically ineligible. Town were thrown out of the competition for fielding a Cup-tied player, so whether the 14–3 result could be ratified as a club record scores nobody could be too sure, either.

Wilder took on loan further players such as defender Neil Trotman, German Under-19 international Felix Bastians and Ryan Cresswell, and while Foster left for Oxford, the Town boss signed up Chris Billy from Carlisle United, Darryn Stamp and experienced defender Greg Strong. But a troubled season was to be plunged further into crisis, for while the Shaymen embarked on a run of six winless matches which saw them slip into the relegation zone once more, chairman Geoff Ralph elected to quit as chairman on 16 March.

At the beginning of the season he had pleaded for additional help to run the club, and in October, Adie Hall, Bob Bland and Richard Harrison had all quit board to allow for potential new investors to come on board. A consortium of businessmen, whose identity at this point remained a secret, had in fact being pumping money into the club, but when takeover talks with them stalled, Ralph stood down. But the consortium now became key players in the running of the club and continued to put money into the club to facilitate the running of it, but they also needed the supporters' help. On 26 March, the Supporters' Trust held a public meeting at the Jumpin' Jaks nightclub, where accountant Chris Yewdell, speaking on behalf of the businessmen, announced that they were willing to devote £200,000 to make the club debt free providing fans could raise around half the £30,000 monthly wage bill. The *Halifax Courier* announced the following day that Halifax Town was 'in new hands today' but by the close season negotiations between Ralph and the consortium were still ongoing.

The day-to-day running of the club had been put in the hands of secretary Angie Firth, while on the field, the players addressed the precariousness of the side's League position, comforted only by the fact that they had games in hand over Tamworth, Grays and Cambridge, the clubs immediately above them. They secured a crucial 1–0 success over Cambridge and relegation worries were finally allayed following victories over Aldershot, and in their last two home matches, against Crawley and Stevenage. The Shaymen lifted themselves to what seemed a respectable 16th, a position which somehow belied the struggle they had endured.

The three businessmen were finally revealed by the *Halifax Courier* as David Bosomworth, owner of Sandal BMW, ex-footballer Bobby Ham, and Stuart Peacock, of Caterleisure, Bradford, but they were clamouring for the total repayment of a loan made to Ralph – the former Town chairman claimed it had been a loan to the club underwritten by himself – while also seeking to get hold of a 75 per cent stake in the club which would give them overall control. But the fans wondered whether the club would see out the **2007–08** season after it had been handed a tax bill – thought to be around £100,000 – but on 31 October, having earlier been granted an extension in the Royal Courts of Justice the High

The Halifax Town squad which began the ill-fated 2007–08 season. Back row (from left to right): Darryn Stamp, Adam Quinn, Rob Scott, Adam Legzdins, Lee Butler, Craig Mawson, Nick Gray, Greg Young, Cortez Belle. Middle row: Alan Russell-Cox (physio), Daryl Taylor, Andy Campbell, Jon Shaw, Danny Forrest, Ryan Toulson, Jake Wright, Anthony Griffith, Ian Helliwell (fitness conditioner). Front row: Alex Bailey, Lewis Killeen, Tom Kearney, Chris Wilder (manager), Peter Atherton (assistant manager), Steve Bushell, Matt Doughty, Steve Torpey.

Court, the consortium reached an agreement with the Inland Revenue and sufficient funds were transferred.

By this time, of course, the Shaymen had kicked off their season in what was now the newly christened Blue Square Premier. Peter Atherton had been promoted to assistant manager in succession to Wayne Jacobs, while Wilder's squad now included the likes of Antony Griffith, Rob Scott, Cortez Belle, loanee Daryl Taylor and Steve Bushell, who returned for a second spell. They were also fortunate to have signed Jon Shaw from Burton, a striker whose goals would, on the face of it at least, prove crucial.

But the Shaymen made a poor start, failing to win any of their opening four matches, though a later Campbell hat-trick in the defeat of Droylsden heralded the start of a five-match unbeaten run which saw them move up to 11th. But soon Wilder's resolve would be tested to the limit as the side slid down the table, the cause not helped by a succession of dismissals, and there was also the embarrassing 4–0 home defeat by Burton in the second round of the FA Cup to deal with.

Wilder had brought back goalkeeper Adam Legzdins to give competition to Mawson, and the addition of Barnsley loanee Simon Heslop would be one of the major successes of the season. But the side struggled to find any consistent form, and remained at best a mid-table outfit. Not that the fans were ready to accept that. They rounded on Wilder following a dire 3–0 defeat by Exeter City on a rain-sodden Shay pitch, and more vehemently when the side succumbed to a similar scoreline in the Boxing Day derby at Farsley Celtic on Boxing Day.

Town would gain swift revenge on Farsley in The Shay return on 2 January, though that would be their last League victory until the beginning of March. But at least the FA Trophy offered some respite. A Shaw penalty and a screamer from Heslop helped see off Leamington in the first round, and after Shaw had grabbed two more goals to earn a replay at Bishop's Stortford, Town cantered to a 4–1 victory in the Shay replay. Perhaps this was their year, but alas, the run ended in the third round, that despite a home draw with Rushden & Diamonds.

Rushden also prevented the Shaymen from appearing in the Final of a new competition created and sponsored by Irish television company, Setanta. Town did well to reach the northern area Final, only for then to suffer single-goal defeat at Nene Park. They also found themselves thrown out of the County Cup once more for naming no less than five ineligible players – in this case all the substitutes – against Ossett Albion, with the competition rules stating that loan players were not permitted to play in the County Cups.

Town's side was indeed ever-changing, as new names continually appeared on the team sheet. Craig Nelthorpe scored in successive drawn away matches at Northwich and Rushden, and winger Mark Whitehouse earned Town a point with a memorable debut solo goal against York. The likes of Simon Ainge, Tom Harban, Tom Clarke, Gareth Davies and Santos Gaia all appeared in the side, with a varying degree of success and a five-match unbeaten run during March to lift them to 17th and seemingly clear of trouble. But suddenly, through no fault of their own, the players found themselves embroiled in yet another relegation battle.

Halifax Town's decision to enter into administration once more on 26 March, a move sparked by a winding-up order served by former chairman Ray Moreland, saw them immediately deducted 10 points, as per FA rules, and plunged from relative safety to 20th, level on 33 points with 21st-placed Farsley Celtic. Now, new questions were being asked of the side, with each game bringing new pressures. At times it looked as if they had given up the ghost; the 6–1 defeat inflicted on them by Kidderminster Harriers on 8 April was the worst at

THE HISTORY OF HALIFAX TOWN

The *Halifax Courier*, which provided the platform for Ernest Jones's letter which heralded the birth of Halifax Town in April 1911, now proclaims the end of the club.

home since Fulham won 8–0 in September 1969 and left them third from bottom. On the other hand, the 4–0 victory at Crawley Town in their penultimate match was as unexpected as it was magnificent, and it meant that going into the final game, the chance of avoiding relegation was at least in their own hands.

Stevenage Borough – who else? – provided the opposition for that game, with the Shaymen knowing that all they had to do was avoid defeat to condemn Altrincham. But in front of a supportive 2,229 crowd, Town lost 2–1, though when the news came through that Altrincham had only drawn at Weymouth, Town appeared to have survived the drop. But in the event, Shaw's penalty would be the last-ever goal scored by a Halifax Town player. The supporters may have rejoiced but many were doing so without looking at the bigger issue and its implications, for the future of the club was about to be played out behind closed doors, with catastrophic results.

With Halifax Town in debt to the tune of £2.1 million, administrator Rob Sadler, for Begbies Traynor, offered the club's creditors 2½ p in the £1 at a meeting on 7 May, but that had had to be abandoned when the major creditors demanded a minimum of 10p. Two days later, on Friday 9 May 2008, Halifax Town were, in the words of the *Halifax Courier*, 'handed their death sentence' when creditors refused to accept a deal to save the club. Sadler emerged from almost five hours of negotiations in offices in Leeds claiming a deal had been impossible, with the final straw being the insurmountable £814,000 owed to the Inland Revenue. After a history of 97 years, liquidation of the club now became the only course of action.

FC HALIFAX TOWN

Halifax Town's expulsion from the Blue Square Premier was announced on 15 May 2008, and though the consortium which had been running the club for over 18 months appealed against this decision, after much deliberation, during which time members of the Halifax Town Supporters' Trust devised a back-up plan, David Bosomworth reluctantly accepted a place in the eighth tier of English football, the Unibond First Division North under the name of FC Halifax Town.

Nevertheless, the board, as they could now officially call themselves, set about running the club in a professional

FC Halifax Town club crest.

Jim Vince's hastily put together squad for the 2008–09 season. Back row (from left to right): Dorryl Proffit, Lincoln Adams, Phil Senior, Craig Mawson, Craig Ellison, Ross Clegg, Steve Payne. Middle row: Jonny Smith, Gavin Rothery, Craig Smith, Ben Jones, Alan Russell-Cox (physio), Justin Walker, Kris King, Luke Hinsley, Tony Barras. Front row: Matt Woolley, Ashley Stott, Adam Morning, Jim Vince (manager), Nigel Jemson (assistant manager), Tom Harban, Ryan Sugden, Junior Brown.

manner, and to that end, the appointment of lifelong supporter Pete Stajic as Commercial Executive was a sound one, and while community and commercial groups were also set up, Kelly Gilchrist and Adam Cheshire became an integral part of the club's media team.

Just as important, of course, was the issue of finding a manager, and on 1 July 2008, the former Witton boss Jim Vince was appointed with a brief to get the club out of the Unibond First Division North, if not at the first attempt, then certainly the second. To aid him, Vince brought in the former Nottingham Forest striker Nigel Jemson, who had been recently been player-manager at Ilkeston, and together, they hurriedly assembled an initial squad of players. But by now, FC Halifax Town were playing catch up with all the other clubs, and Vince was quick to stress that the team which started the season would not be the one that ended it, but for now it was simply a case of getting one out on the pitch.

Several players were familiar. Goalkeeper Craig Mawson was initially happy to remain at The Shay, though after just one game he would move in a swap deal which saw another former Town 'keeper Jon Kennedy arrive from Droylsden. There were others connected with the old club who would appear fleetingly, such as Neil Ross and Tom Harban, but the major signings included defenders Steve Payne, Tony Barras and Lincoln Adams, midfielders Justin Walker and Jonny Smith, and forwards Ashley Stott and Junior Brown, while shortly into the campaign Scott Phelan arrived to compensate for the loss of Ross Clegg, whose career was cruelly ended with injury sustained in Town's third match at Lancaster.

On 16 August 2008, an encouraging crowd of 1,549 saw FC Halifax Town entertain Bamber Bridge on the season's opening day, but there was to be no fairytale start. Goalless at half-time, the visitors took advantage of weary Halifax legs and scampered to a 3–0 win. Town responded by winning at Trafford in mid-week – the first goal for FC Halifax Town was scored by Payne – but after five games the side was lying 17th in the table.

Victory over Warrington Town on 16 September kick-started their season and in the next game a poor Salford side were hammered 7–1 as the new club set up its own scoring record, with the last goal scored by veteran Jemson, who had been coaxed back into playing. But trailing by two goals with eight minutes to go at Garforth, the side had to dig deep to secure a draw, only then to go on and win their next seven matches, a run that coincided with the arrival quick-silver striker Colin Daniel on loan from Crewe. Vince added to the squad midfielders Damien Allen and the pint-sized Tom Baker and Town hit top spot on 8 November with victory at Woodley Sports.

The ever-changing side saw the introduction of full-back Cavelle Coo and centre-half Danny Meadowcroft to offset the loss of injured skipper Payne, whose leadership qualities were sorely missed. Still, the fans were treated to the occasional thriller, such the 3–3 draw with Newcastle Blue Star at The Shay, where Danny Ellis's injury-time header secured a point. Richie Sutton and Paul Collins became the latest players to make their debuts in that game, though the result saw Town slip to third. But a 4–1 win at Radcliffe Borough on 20 December took the Shaymen back into first place where they would remain until February, if only by virtue of having played more games than their rivals after their exits from both FA Cup and FA Trophy at the hands of Nantwich and Harrogate Railway respectively while their rivals still maintained Cup interests.

The Shaymen returned to Harrogate Railway on New Year's Day for their League match, but the 2–0 defeat, and the manner of it, suggested a difficult second half of the season. And so it proved. A run of three consecutive victories at the end of January might have temporarily put their title ambitions back on track, with victory over Garforth Town on 24 January sending them eight points clear, but the threat lingered from Durham. They were nine points behind in third place, but with an incredible nine games in hand, and surely title favourites.

The Shaymen buckled at a crucial time, despite being unlucky not to win their key match on Durham's artificial pitch on 7 March. They had to settle for a point in what was one of their finest displays of the season but were unable to raise their game thereafter. Vince had by now added to the side the experienced former Wales international midfielder Paul Evans and winger Mark Peers, while front runner David Brown also arrived, though his return of just one goal highlighted Town's short-comings.

The dawn of a new era. FC Halifax Town take on Bamber Bridge in their first match in the Unibond First Division North at The Shay on 16 August 2008. Here, striker Ashley Stott takes on Jamie Nay and Glenn Steel.

When the side lost at Skelmersdale on 4 April Town slipped to sixth, and though still in the mix for a Play-off place, a return of 10 points from their previous 10 matches was the form of a struggling team. Concerned at the side's downward turn, the board felt action needed to be taken and three days later, Jim Vince was dismissed, with an accompanying club statement reading, 'Despite taking in to account the start to the season and the difficult injury list, it is felt that with the quality of playing squad, additional resources and facilities, we should have been more able to achieve a more consistent level of cohesive performance, cutting edge and ultimately, results.'

There was also a suggestion of dressing room disharmony, though it was to his assistant Nigel Jemson, the alleged chief protagonist, that the board turned in the hope of salvaging the season. He had just four games left but failed to inspire the team. His first game in charge proved to be a real baptism of fire, as Town drew 2–2 at Ossett Albion in a match refereed perplexingly by James Hermuzzi who saw fit to send off two players from each side and brandish 14 yellow cards. But if the result there did not necessarily spell the end of Town's Play-off chances, the home defeat to rivals Curzon Ashton in their next match did more harm than good, and after gaining draws in their final two matches with Trafford and Chorley, they finished a disappointing eighth.

Nigel Jemson may have had designs on becoming the permanent manager, but he was overlooked in favour of the former Leeds and Port Vale defender Neil Aspin, who took up his position on 29 April 2009 just three days after quitting Harrogate Town, where he had been in charge for five years.

Aspin immediately raided his old club to bring in several players he knew would serve him well, among them 'keeper Jonathan Hedge, defender Aaron Hardy, and attackers Nick Gray and Richard Marshall. Aspin's quest to build his own squad also saw the arrivals of Ryan Crossley, Danny Lowe Dan Codman, Paul Sykes, and centre-forward James Dean from Bury. Centre-back James Riley, too, was ready to stake his claim, having being unfortunate enough to break his leg the previous term after just two senior outings.

Aspin, who appointed former Liverpool and Chester player Trevor Storton as his right-hand man, would deliver for the supporters an unforgettable **2009–10** season, his side having served notice of their intentions by making a start that was hitherto unknown. Kicking off with an impressive 3–0 victory at Colwyn Bay, Town went unbeaten in their first 10 League matches, dropping their only two points and marching to the top of the table.

Doubtless Town would have kept pace with the early leaders had they not been involved in so many competitions but at times they found it hard to stop winning, even when fringe players came in for the minor Cup competitions, such as the West Riding County Cup and President's Cup, while League progress was also stalled through the side's involvement in both FA Cup and FA Trophy.

Town began their FA Cup exploits as early as 29 August with a record 6–0 win at Brandon United, and progressed through four rounds before bowing out gallantly at home against Wrexham, recently relegated from the Football League, undone by a long-range effort in injury time by Wes Baynes. And in the FA Trophy, they saw off the challenges of Trafford, the quaint-sounding Romulus, and Shepshed Charterhouse before losing 3–1 at neighbours Guiseley.

The defeat in the FA Cup to Wrexham had come just two weeks after Town had suffered their first loss in the League at Prescot Cables, and draws at Skelmersdale and Leigh suggested a mini-crisis, but the Shaymen responded by running up their highest League

The Halifax Town squad in readiness for the Championship-winning 2009–10 season. Back row (from left to right): Dan Codman, Nicky Gray, James Riley, Phil Senior, Jonathan Hedge, Steve Payne, Paul Sykes. Sam Jerome. Middle row: Trevor Storton (assistant manager), James Dean, Mark Whitehouse, Luke Smith, Neil Ross, Ross Clegg, Alan Russell-Cox (physio), Kevin Gillespie (fitness conditioner). Front row: Richard Marshall, Aaron Hardy, Danny Lowe, Ryan Crossley, Neil Aspin (manager), Tom Baker, Scott Phelan, Mark Peers, Mark Hotte.

victory of the season, defeating Salford City 6–1. A burst of icy weather intervened, and when Town picked up their League programme, they found themselves lying fourth, five points behind leaders Lancaster and Colwyn Bay.

To help Town in the quest for the Championship, Aspin made good use of the loan transfer system, bringing in Harry Winter from Northwich, but when he was recalled, the Town boss then made the further temporary signings of strikers Michael Wilde and Lee Gregory, and both made telling contributions. At the beginning of February, the Shaymen were nine points adrift of Lancaster and with only two games in hand but a run of five consecutive victories put pressure on the Giant Axe side and left them with little margin for error. But Town were left having to cram in 11 matches in 26 days after their home fixture with Radcliffe, scheduled for 23 March was postponed shortly before kick-off. Still, Town managed to keep up their hot pursuit of Lancaster and the quest for the title developed into a two-horse race, with the sides set to meet at The Shay on 10 April, a game quite rightly viewed as the potential Championship decider.

That as it may be, the psychological advantage swung in favour of Town four days before that scheduled meeting. For while Lancaster were winning at Rossendale, Town were trailing 3–1 deep into injury time at Garforth. Had the scores stayed that way, Lancaster would have held a probable unassailable lead going into the game at The Shay, but incredibly, the Shaymen turned the game on its head, levelling the scores before Marshall got his foot to Hedge's long clearance and lifted the ball over Garforth's 16-year-old substitute 'keeper Tom Taylor for a spectacular winner.

Instead of a five-point lead at the top, a downcast Lancaster side arrived at The Shay just two points clear, and had no answer to a fully charged up Town side which was spurred on by an unexpectedly large 3,152 crowd. Gregory swept them in front after just four minutes and the Shaymen cantered to a 4–0 win to leap over Lancaster, the title now seemingly theirs to lose. They showed no sign of faltering, cruising to a 5–0 win at Curzon Ashton just

The players mingled with the fans to pose with the Unibond First Division North Championship trophy following their final match with Skelmersdale United on 24 April 2010.

two days later and all but wrapped the title up with a 4–2 victory at Ossett Albion with two games still to play. The home draw with Clitheroe in their penultimate match – Tom Baker's stunning equaliser was technically the goal which clinched the title – thus confirmed what the fans had been chanting for some time; Halifax Town were Unibond Division One North champions.

Richard Marshall's goal in the final match with Skelmersdale took the side's League tally to an incredible 108, and the point from the 1–1 draw was their magical 100th. Lancaster, who to their credit had regrouped and were ready to pounce should Town slip up, finished just four points behind, but cruelly, would be denied promotion when they were beaten at home by Colwyn Bay in the Play-off Final.

But for the competition of Lancaster, Town would had wrapped up the title weeks, if not months, earlier. But despite the obvious strengths of the side, manager Aspin wasn't resting on his laurels and he set about further improving the squad. Already in need of two centre-backs following the retirements of Payne and Crossley, Aspin signed Mark Bower, who would form a terrific partnership with Liam Hogan, while also new to the club were forward Danny Holland, and wide players Scott Metcalfe, Nathan Taylor and speed-merchant Jamie Vardy. Harry Winter also returned, but his season would be hit by injury

Despite the new additions, the Shaymen made an indifferent start to life in the newly named Evo-Stik Premier in **2010–11**, gaining only four points from their opening four matches. Clearly missing centre-forward James Dean, who had picked up a knee injury in a meaningless Chairman's Cup match at the end of the previous season, he returned to lend his weight to the attack before finally being forced to rest up in March. Though by then, Town were well on course for a successive Championship.

The Halifax Town squad which clinched the Evo-Stik Premier League title in 2010–11. Back row (from left to right): Sanchez Heffernan, Matt Plummer, Nicky Gray, James Riley, Liam Hogan, Nathan Taylor, Karl Lineghan (goalkeeping coach). Middle row: Steve Bradbury (physio), James Dean, Danny Holland, Phil Senior, Ian Helliwell, Jonathan Hedge, Mark Bower, Harry Winter, Kevin Gillespie (fitness conditioner). Front row: Richard Marshall, Scott Metcalfe, Jamie Vardy, Danny Lowe, Neil Aspin (manager), Aaron Hardy, Tom Baker, Simon Garner, Scott Phelan.

Town hit form, winning their first match at Mickleover Sports on 4 September, going top on 2 October following a 2–0 win at Ashton and extending to 13 matches their run of games without defeat, including 10 consecutive victories. When Dean netted both goals in a 2–1 win at Matlock on 16 November, Town found themselves six points clear of Colwyn Bay, with games in hand.

The Shaymen suffered a shock 2–0 reversal at home to North Ferriby – Aspin's first defeat at The Shay – and then endured an unwanted break as an icy grip took hold and forced the postponement of several games. But they returned to action by winning the clash of the heavyweight clubs – at least in terms of fan base – by defeating FC United at Gigg Lane, then coming from behind to win the return, with Lee Gregory having returned, on New Year's Day in emphatic style. During the second half of the season, they pressed on relentlessly in their quest for the title, at times proving no match for the opposition. Ossett Town were left dazed after losing 8–1 at The Shay, and on 22 February the Shaymen won 6–0 at Nantwich having earlier won at Marine by the same score. And though without Dean, they had another potent scorer in Vardy, who, in tricky matches with Chasetown (at home) and Kendal, scored consecutive hat-tricks in vital wins.

The victory over Kendal came hard on the sad news that assistant manager Trevor Storton finally succumbed to his battle with cancer, but he continued to be in the thoughts of the players as they pressed on in unrelenting fashion, stringing together another lengthy unbeaten sequence. Town duly wrapped up the title with a 2–0 victory at Retford on 9 April, with five games still to play, and still had enough left in the tank to score five on their travels at Whitby, and while they chased the magical 100-point mark for a second season running, performances tailed off and draws from the final two matches left them two points short, but still a massive 19 points clear of second-placed Colwyn Bay.

The players were presented with the Evo-Stik trophy following the final home game with Mickleover, and Neil Aspin began to contemplate his squad for the challenge of the Blue Square North in 2011–12, just one League below that from which the original club had been expelled three years earlier. The initial aim of the new club was to gain what was perceived as their rightful place in the Blue Square Premier, and given Aspin's exemplary record, who is to say the club will not make it by the end of 2011–12?

FC Halifax Town in the striking green away strip on the day they clinched the Evo-Stik Premier title at Retford United, 9 April 2011.

Halifax Town Grounds

SANDHALL LANE

The Sandhall Lane ground was a logical choice as the home for the newly established Halifax Town club, having in its favour two key elements; its availability, and, amid the steep terrain of the surrounding areas, an unusually flat playing area. It was where the club would play their home matches until 1916 and, but for the local implementations caused by World War One where, in all likelihood, they would have remained until moving to The Shay.

The land at Highroad Well, on the junction of Sand Hall Lane (its original and proper spelling) and Gibbet Street, was converted into a football pitch by the Halifax Corporation and leased to the Halifax & District Association Football League on 26 February 1910 in order that they could stage official and representative Cup Finals. With the formation of Halifax Town, new secretary-manager Joe McClelland negotiated with the Halifax Corporation to take over the ground at balance-sheet value, pointing out that the field had become something of a burden for the Association.

According to the *Halifax Courier* dated 9 June 1911, Halifax Town acquired the Sandhall Lane ground after the Ground Committee agreed to hand over the running of it without making a profit from the transfer, insisting all they wanted from Halifax Town was what they had already spent on it, and in turn, the Corporation leased the ground to the new club.

Sandhall Lane was used for the first time for the first of two practice 'trial' matches on 9 August 1911, with the Stripes defeating the Reds 3–1 (the teams being made up from local clubs) in front of a crowd of around 300, and the first Yorkshire Combination match staged there saw Town fall to single-goal defeat at the hands of Scarborough on 16 September before a 2,000 gate.

Initially, there were no dressing rooms; for the first few games the players changed at the nearby Golden Lion Hotel and accessed the ground along Bob Lane. But when the Improvement Committee passed plans for a grandstand on the Sandhall Lane side of the ground, work began on its construction on 1 October 1911 at a cost of between £60–70. Designed by architects Medley Hall & Son, and built by H. Bancroft & Son (joiners), the wooden structure consisted of 13 tiers of seats with accommodation on each for 39 people, making it capable of holding around 500 spectators. The centre portion was sectioned off for the directors, but there was no cover. Dressing rooms were built underneath the seats, seemingly shared by both sets of teams, until a separate structure for the visitors was erected towards the end of the club's second season and used for the first time in 1913–14.

The grandstand was opened on 14 October 1911 when Town hosted Fryston Colliery, but with their election to the Midland Combination League in June 1912, the directors sought better provision for the spectators. The grandstand was moved back several yards and a banking of ashes was laid around the ground, making it possible to stand six to eight deep with the assurance of dry feet and a good view. The Working Men's Committee worked hard on the ground during the close season and the pitch looked in excellent condition for the start of the 1912–13 season. This committee was also responsible for manning the turnstiles of the two new entrance gates, and to check for unseemly behaviour and any tendency to bad language!

The first match played at Sandhall in the Midland League saw visitors Doncaster Rovers triumph 2–1 on 7 September 1912. Despite alterations around the pitch, the playing area remained unaltered, though by the time Knaresborough turned up for a FA Cup match on 2 November, it had been widened by nine yards. Further improvements to the pitch took place during the 1913 close season; concerned at how the goalmouth at the Highroad Well end of the ground resembled a quagmire when it rained, the Working Men's Committee dug up turf and inserted a layer of gravel for adequate drainage.

In July 1914 work began on the building of a covered stand from the gateway to the old stand capable of accommodating 2,000, and plans were put in place for the cover to run the length of the field, though with the outbreak of World War One, these were never completed.

To suggest that the Sandhall Lane ground was a homely place would be misleading. With its elevated position at Highroad Well, it was subject to the elements and became a particularly hostile place in winter. Nevertheless, Halifax Town remained there throughout their first five years, and it was only the hardship caused by the war, rather than the ground's location, which forced the closure of the club.

As things turned out, the last game played at Sandhall by Halifax Town was a friendly with the Royal Engineers on 26 March 1916, won 2–1 by the 'Sandhallites', though nobody then realised that they would not be returning. But no sooner had the club vacated the ground than neighbours Asquith Tool Makers found it necessary to expand their premises to help with the war effort and consequently built over the playing area. When hostilities ceased, Halifax Town were forced to find somewhere else to play.

EXLEY

It was to Exley, then home of local side Salterhebble FC, that Halifax Town relocated upon re-formation in 1919, though such a move was not one borne out of choice, for a more inhospitable place they could not have found. Existing in what was nothing more than an open field, the site presented other problems, as Tom T. Dickinson highlighted in his 1938 publication *Milestones*, when he claimed that Exley 'was not only difficult of access but in wet weather, was generally ankle deep in clay, and in mild weather was frightfully bleak.'

The Exley ground lay two miles out of town on the south side, but situated on the top of a hill at the bottom of Park Lane, there was no tram route to it. The nearest stopping off point was at the Punch Bowl Inn at the bottom of Salterhebble, meaning an arduous climb up the cobbled Exley Bank for players and spectators alike. But having hit snags in tying to obtain the cricket field at Thrum Hall – unsurprisingly the rugby section had objected – and Spring Hall, the field at Exley was better than nothing if the club was to reform then, rather than waiting another year. Comforted by the thought that the club could attract supporters from neighbouring West Vale, Elland, Norwood and Sowerby Bridge districts, they took out a lease on the ground from Halifax Corporation.

Prior to Halifax Town being the star attraction, the Exley district had been famed for hosting the zoological gardens and amusement park on the fields which rose up from the Huddersfield Road thoroughfare. There, animals, such as elephants and tigers could be found, though the scheme was short lived. Having opened in 1909, the zoo was forced to close down in 1916 when the war reduced the number of visitors and made it difficult to obtain food for the animals. The amusements closed the following year. The land on which the zoo was situated is now occupied by Siddal RLFC.

Funded in part by £10 donations from seven directors, Halifax Town improved the Exley ground to the tune of around £500 to bring it up to Midland League standards, and it was first put to use by the club for the staging of the first of two trial matches on 23 August 1919. When the fixtures came out, Halifax Town were forced to travel for their first match, but having suffered a 3–0 defeat, happily got off to a winning start at Exley when a Judd Wild penalty and a goal from Fred Kirby gave them a 2–1 victory over Scunthorpe United on 13 September 1919 in front of a football-starved three thousand. But gates such as these would not be maintained, the access to the ground proving a burden for the out-of-towners, despite the directors' efforts with the Tramways Committee to provide special transport to Salterhebble.

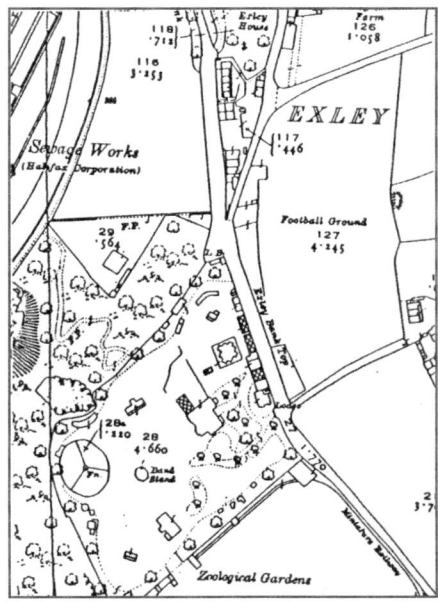

The site of the football ground at Exley prior to Halifax Town's arrival. The map also shows the existence of the zoological gardens.

Shortly into the season, the directors resolved to push on with improvements to the ground and set about erecting a long covered stand which was set to be used for the first time for the match with Rotherham Town on 15 November 1919, only for the match to be postponed due to snow. In the event, these facilities, which included a new refreshments area, were used for the first time the following week, only for Town to slip to a 4–0 defeat at the hands of Chesterfield Municipal.

By the start of the 1920–21 season, the northern clubs were keeping a watchful eye on the progress of the new Third Division, formed by clubs based in the south, and with interest high in creating a northern equivalent, moves were made to find a home which would be deemed suitable to host Football League matches. So while Halifax Town continued to play their home games at Exley, all efforts were put into converting the Shay Estate into a football arena.

Halifax Town thus played their final Midland League match at Exley on 23 April 1919, defeating Sheffield Wednesday Reserves, though the last game played there was an exciting West Riding Senior Cup semi-final replay with Bradford, who must have wondered to where they had just come, which attracted a record Exley gate of 4,000 paying receipts of £139. Johnny Whalley's goal gave Town victory, putting them into the Final and extending a winning run at Exley to 13 matches.

Following Halifax Town's election to the Football League in March 1921, the club geared itself to moving to The Shay, though the legacy of Exley lived on, denied entry into the FA Cup competition for 1921–22 having being assessed on the unsuitability of what was to become their former ground It would seem, then, that Exley reverted to accommodating local amateur clubs, though not for long. When the Halifax Corporation linked Exley to neighbouring Siddal, they began their housing programme in the 1930s, and today Exley Gardens stands on the site of what was Halifax Town's second home.

THE SHAY

The history of The Shay has been as chequered and eventful as that of Halifax Town. Often the cause of much controversy and political intrigue, the fact that it has remained home to the football club for almost 90 years is an achievement in itself.

The name 'Shay' is derived from the old English word 'shaw', meaning a little wood, thicket or grove. The two words are used interchangeably in ancient references to the site. In its earliest existence, the area which became known as 'The Shay' would have been no more than open fields with the first recording of a living dwelling being recorded in the Halifax Manor Court Rolls of 1462, when on 6 July it stated that the wealthy William Brodley 'surrendered the reversion, after his death, of two closes, with buildings thereon, lying on the west of Saghe Loyne, in Halifax, to the use of John, son of the said William Brodley and his heirs, and Margaret, his wife, daughter of Thomas Fournes.' When Brodley died, The Shay Estate descended to his daughter Grace Hely in 1580 and in turn to her husband, John Booth, with the precise transaction recorded as 6 October 1587 when Booth became owner of 'Shaw and Nether Shaw'. The following year John Booth arranged for a small dam to be constructed within the Shay Estate so as to provide enough water for his needs, but by 1604 Booth had surrendered ownership of 'Over and Nether Shaw' to Simon Bynnes of Broadbottom.

Subsequently, The Shay Estate passed into the Stead family in the 17th century, then the Caygills following the marriage of Martha Stead to John Caygill in 1705. In the will of her father, dated 9 September 1735, she was left Upper Shaw and Lower Shaw Syke, while the remainder of the estate was left to her son John Caygill Jnr, and it was he who commissioned John Carr to the building of The Shay mansion around 1770.

Caygill Jnr married Jane Selwin and they had one child, a daughter also named Jane, but commonly referred to as Jenny. Caygill became one of the wealthiest men in Halifax and was the owner of numerous houses in the town as well as a house, warehouse, barn, garden and shops at The Shay Estate. He also contributed to Halifax's lasting heritage, having contributed for the erection of two landmark buildings, The Square, constructed around 1758, and the Piece Hall, built as a trading centre for wool and woollen products and opened on New Year's Day 1779.

Jenny Caygill became sole heiress to her father's estates, including The Shay, and upon her marriage to Sir James Ibbetson, the ownership of The Shay thus passed into the Ibbetson family. They advertised The Shay grounds for letting and in the Halifax Journal dated 18 April 1807, the mansion was described as thus:

'The elegant mansion house…beautifully situated on the south side of the town of Halifax, with a convenient terrace on the south and east fronts; reclining grass banks, shrubbery, serpentine, and other walks to a considerable extent, adorned with plantations and a pleasure garden; well stocked with wall and standard fruit trees; a hothouse and greenhouse with vines, exotic and other plants, etc; besides two kitchen gardens in excellent condition; the whole bounded by a rich meadow forms a lawn of nine acres or thereabouts.' The advertisement also gave details of the mansion itself. On the ground floor was a dining hall 29ft by 23ft and 13ft high, breakfast room, parlour, housekeeper's room, butler's pantry, servants' hall, a large kitchen and gallery 'fitted with every modern improvement for cooking on the steam principle', a spacious passage 12ft 6in wide and 44ft long, an elegant staircase with a double flight of stone steps. There was a landing 13ft wide and a spacious gallery on the second floor, while the drawing room and the five lodging rooms, with dressing rooms adjoining, were on the same scale as the rooms below. The doors were of solid mahogany and it was evidently well fitted for its purposes.'

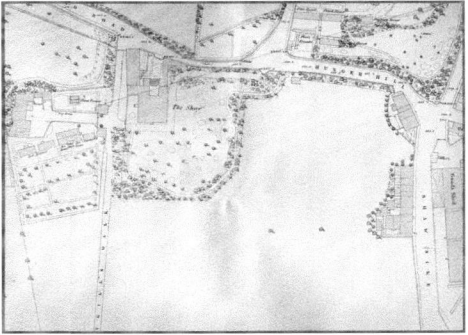

Map showing the site of The Shay mansion house.

The Shay mansion.

Jeremiah Rawson took over the tenancy of The Shay, while subsequent Census returns have indicated the mansion was in turn occupied by William Haigh, magistrate and landed proprietor (1841), Henry McCrea, textile manufacturer and future Mayor (1861), Joseph Wood, worsted spinner (1871), William Dyer (1891) and William Boocock (1901).

Things changed when plans were drawn up in the 1890s to develop the pleasant Caygill's Walk, which ran along the top of The Shay, into what is now the busy Skircoat Road. A beck ran down from Well Head Field to Shaw Syke, and this was covered in when this part of the estate was filled up with countless loads of earth in order to make the present road level. Some of the buildings on The Shay Estate were demolished, though The Shay mansion, bought by the Halifax Corporation on 8 August 1889, remained intact. But this dramatic period in The Shay's history continued when, on 29 August 1891, Skircoat Road was opened for traffic for the first time, and by 1903, with The Shay mansion no longer being used for residential purposes, Halifax Corporation saw fit to demolish it the following year.

What was left of The Shay Estate then became the object of many schemes. On 9 November 1898 a proposal had been put forward to build a goods depot there, and on 31 May 1902 an agreement was signed by the Midland Railway Company for the purchase of The Shay Estate, having sought powers to construct a loop line at Low Moor, Bradford, and to run a part of the Lancashire and Yorkshire line to Halifax. However, shortly after this, due to lack of funding, the proposals were shelved, though work had actually commenced on a tunnel which ran under the newly constructed Skircoat Road, and this is still in evidence today. The only purpose for which it was used, however, was as an air-raid shelter during World War Two.

Between 1908 and 1910 there were proposals to build a slaughterhouse on The Shay, but these plans, having come under fire from locals, were eventually scrapped. There was talk then of converting the estate into playing fields, though despite this being a nice idea, nothing became of it and the land ended up as a Corporation rubbish tip, though part of the estate was used by the local Territorial Army for trench digging and shooting practice during World War One. It was believed that during this period, a stray bullet killed the horse of Romany travellers who had set up camp on the site for a short time, and before departing, the horse's owner, an elderly lady called Vadoma, put on the land what was known as the 'Shay Curse', bringing bad luck to anyone who owned or occupied this land over 100 years. Just how true this tale may be is uncertain but nevertheless, The Shay was exorcised by Canon Arthur Smith in 1983 when, in an act of desperation, manager Mickey Bullock and the directors attempted to rid the club of the bad luck which they felt had dogged the club.

Steps to convert The Shay into a football ground were taken with the Football League's proposal to form the Third Division (Northern Section). The Halifax Town directors met with the Halifax Corporation's Improvements Committee with a view to taking up a lease on The Shay Estate, and on 4 August 1920 this recommendation was put to the committee: 'That the council be recommended to let for a period of seven years a portion of The Shay Estate to the Halifax Town AFC Ltd., subject to a formal lease to be prepared by the town clerk on the following terms and conditions: That a rental of £10 to be paid for the first year, £75 for the second year and £100 for each successive year.' The recommendation was passed and the *Halifax Courier* set up a fund to help with the preparation of the ground, and though it fell well short of the targeted £2,000 – only £391 15s 3d was raised – work began on 16 October 1920 following the delivery of timber. An appeal was made in the evening's *Courier* for volunteers and they, along with players and directors, worked round the clock to get the ground ready, with the first grass sods being laid on 7 December 1920.

The Shay, September 1920, with the mansion house now demolished and work continuing on transforming the area into a football ground.

On 30 July 1921, the *Courier* reported that, 'Banking round the sides holds 20,000 and tipping of late has been used to form a road from the top entrance near the Arcadian Pavilion [on the site of the former Shay mansion] where the ground dropped steeply. This has now been flattened for a more gradual slope. A hut for the use of the directors, secretary and home and away changing rooms is rapidly nearing completion.' What became the club offices and changing rooms was, in fact, a disused army hut which was situated in a corner of the ground on the Skircoat Road side towards what was then known as the tram-garage end of the ground, and used by the club until the mid-1950s.

Following Halifax Town's election to the newly created Third Division North, the first game at The Shay saw Darlington beaten 5–1 on 5 September 1921, despite the ground being far from finished. There was then no covered accommodation for the spectators, though the erection of the grandstand, 120ft long on the Skircoat Road side of the ground would not take long. This was completed, with a cover and 22 rows of seats, in readiness for the match with Hartlepools United on 5 November 1921, and spectators were allowed to sit on wooden benches.

It was in July 1927 that an extension to this stand was added. Stretching 140ft towards the Hunger Hill side of the ground, this stand was constructed using forty tons of steel and there was a refreshment buffet running across the back of it. This new 'Skircoat Stand' funded by money raised from the club's Social Section, was used for the first time when Town played their first home match of the new season against Barrow on 29 August 1927.

On 3 October 1931 a new members' entrance at the top of Hunger Hill was used for first time for game with Darlington, an addition to the existing

Laying the first grass sods on 7 December 1920 are, from left, chairman Dr Howie Muir, secretary-manager Joe McClelland and directors Edgar Denison and Joe Firth.

HALIFAX TOWN GROUNDS

Trainer Maurice Wellock plans the terracing of the south terrace under the watchful eye of groundsman Freddie during the 1936 close season.

members' entrance on Skircoat Road, and used primarily for those who had trouble using steps. The following month, the club opened up a new section of the covered stand for schilling spectators, though there was at this point no terracing. This was constructed three years later and completed by 20 November 1934, with accommodation for 7,000. Over the years, this stand would be labelled the 'Skircoat Shed' and would remain standing-only until August 2000 when seats were installed.

Further developments to The Shay over the years saw the creation of banking at the back of the goal of the north stand of the ground, later to be known as the Trinity Garage End, and terracing was constructed at this end in the summer of 1936. But it was not until September 1950 that the centre section was concreted.

The FA Cup run of 1952–53, and the visit of First Division sides Cardiff City and Stoke City saw further changes, with the erection of crash barriers for safety reasons, and in July 1953 work began on the construction of a small stand on the Shaw Hill side, initially 100ft long, giving cover to between 1,000 and 1,500 spectators and built by members of the Social Section. Two years later, work began on new dressing rooms and club offices which were built onto this structure, later named the Patrons' Stand with the addition of seating, with a section used for the directors. Coinciding with these developments was the club's decision to erect a 3ft 6in concrete fencing for the surround of the pitch to replace the old wooden one which had been put up in 1949 for speedway. At a cost of £1,000 the dressing rooms (which included a Turkish bath), club offices and new fencing were all in place for the start of the new season and on 8 August 1956 the public was allowed into The Shay to view the improvements. The Shay would remain pretty much in this state for many years, the major changes being made to the pitch when the speedway track was laid for a second time in 1965, and the construction of social amenities.

Over the years, Halifax Town made several bids to buy The Shay ground from the Corporation or Council, and though they were turned down on each occasion, in 1965 they

The Shay as it looked in February 1953 when Halifax Town prepared to take on Tottenham Hotspur in the fifth round of the FA Cup – before the snow came.

Birds-eye view of The Shay in the late 1960s.

did manage to extend the terms of the lease, due to expire in 1972, to 1993. But in 1982, these terms were extended further when chairman Sam Rorke managed to negotiate a 99-year lease.

When Halifax Town found itself on the verge of bankruptcy in December 1986, Calderdale Council, under the leadership of David Helliwell, put forward a rescue package on 8 April 1987 that included buying back The Shay's lease, and while different schemes had been put forward to build the club a new stadium, in the end they remained at The Shay and paid rent to the Council for use of the ground on matchdays only.

It was under Sam Rorke that changes were made to the appearance of The Shay. Following disturbances during a pre-season friendly with Huddersfield in August 1981, he erected a 9ft concrete wall around the perimeter of the estate. He had also tarmacced the large car park, which for so long had looked very uninviting and built a new social club, though initially it opened as a restaurant, Chimes. Following the takeover by the Council, further improvements were

Taken around the same time, this view of the north terrace (Trinity Garage End) in glorious colour.

made with new seats being obtained for the Skircoat Stand from the Old Show Ground, former home of Scunthorpe United, a new five-side court built at the Shaw Hill side of the ground to help bring in extra revenue, while a slight modification to the ground's name saw it rechristened 'The Shay: Calderdale Sports Stadium' at the bequest of Councillor Graeme Fish.

On 15 June 1991, Calderdale Council sold its shares in the club to a consortium headed by local businessman Jim Brown, who became club chairman, and he was instrumental in the instigation of work on the north terrace (Trinity Bus Garage End) during 1997–98 that enabled Town to reclaim League status. On 5 January 1998 Blakedell Construction began the work, transforming what was then a bank of overgrown weeds into concreted terracing, and this was given its blessing by Football League officials on 2 April 1998. The north terrace, which could hold 1,020 spectators, was initially used by home fans, but since 2003 they have been housed at the opposite end with the completion of the south terrace and its bar facilities. The south terrace is capable of holding 3,211.

HALIFAX TOWN GROUNDS

In February 1999 the management of The Shay was given to the Halifax Stadium Development Company, and following the completion of Halifax Town's last match of the season with Macclesfield Town on 6 May 2000, the bulldozers moved in to demolish the Patrons' Stand in readiness for the construction of the new East Stand, initially funded by a £1.8 million grant to the football club from the Football Foundation. ER Construction Ltd began the work, but by April 2001, both Halifax Town and Halifax Blue Sox, who had moved to The Shay in April 1998, were needing to find £130,000 between them to release a further £400,000 of funds. When a new grant was agreed the following September work recommenced, only to come to a standstill once more in December 2001 when the project ran out of funds.

With no money materialising from the sale of the rugby club's Thrum Hall ground, which was taken over by supermarket giants Asda, the East Stand remained in its unfinished state, and with only changing rooms in use, the half-built stand remained an eyesore for over eight years.

There were further complications when the Halifax Stadium Development Company went into liquidation, and a new not-for-profit body called Shay Stadium Trust took over the running of The Shay on 23 August 2003 and acquired a 10-year lease. But within seven years, that organisation, too, was forced to be wound up, and in July 2008 The Shay fell back into the hands of Calderdale Council. In December 2005 the Council then decided to sell The Shay, but such was the outcry from both football and rugby fans that the councillors made a swift u-turn. But it was not until the appointment of Owen Williams as the Council's chief executive in January 2008 that things started to happen, and the following October work recommenced transforming the East Stand at a cost to the Council of around £4.5 million. But this involved virtually starting again. The roof was ripped off to allow crane access and the stand was then refitted along with 3,500 seats. New changing rooms, toilets, a control room, offices and shops were also created beneath the stand, as were a banqueting suite capable of holding around 250, six hospitality boxes and press rooms. The work was undertaken by Hall Construction Services Ltd, a firm already involved in five major sports stadium developments including the Leigh Village Stadium in Lancashire and a new stadium for Shrewsbury Town FC.

With EMC having successfully tendered the catering contract, FC Halifax Town made full use of new East Stand and facilities for the first time on 23 March 2010, though the occasion proved to be something of a damp squib as heavy rain prior to kick-off with Radcliffe Borough meant the game had to be postponed. In the event, the club used the new facilities for the first time when they entertained Chorley on 2 April.

On 23 March 2011 it was announced that since the opening of the East Stand, The Shay had lost over £100,000 in its first year of operation, though the same month, The Shay was touted as a possible venue for the 2013 Rugby League World Cup.

The East Stand complete and ready for use.

CAPACITY AND GROUND RECORDS

The figure of 10,143 that witnessed the first match at The Shay against Darlington on 3 September 1921 was broken two weeks later when 10,547 watched the match with Rochdale. Before official figures were made available, an estimated 18,000 saw the visit of Nelson on Christmas Day 1922, but the League record was broken twice when 18,866 watched the match with Bradford on 23 October 1926, and 19,935 turned out for Town's game with Bradford City on 10 September 1927. The ground capacity was by then around 30,000, with the record being the 22,023 that saw the FA Cup second-round replay with Manchester City on 6 February 1924. That figure was broken when 29,235 were present for the fifth-round FA Cup meeting of Luton Town nine years later. However, 35,621 crammed into The Shay for the FA Cup fourth-round match with Stoke City on 31 January 1953, only for that figure to be bettered, and a club record set, when 36,885 watched the fifth-round match with Tottenham Hotspur two weeks later.

The Shay's capacity, which had been raised to 38,000 for the visit of Stoke City, was reduced to 23,000 by 1977 on Home Office instructions, and by 1979 had fallen as low as 15,000. After safety work was carried out, the capacity was raised once more to 16,500 for the visit of Manchester City for a FA Cup third-round tie in 1980. However, the Popplewell Report into ground safety, which was published in January 1986 following the fire at Bradford City's Valley Parade the previous in May, meant that for a short time from the start of the 1985–86 season all standing areas at The Shay were closed and it became a seating-only stadium, with the capacity reduced to just 1,777. Once safety work was carried out, it was raised to 3,600, and increased further to 4,021 for the visit of Nottingham Forest for a third-round FA Cup tie on 9 January 1988. By 1991, following more work to the ground, the capacity was increased to 8,049.

Strict Health and Safety rules have meant that capacity of The Shay has since been reduced, even allowing for the opening of the north and south terraces in 1998. Though it was raised to 9,000, by 2002 the limit was set at 6,561. With the opening of the East Stand, the old Skircoat Stand was made redundant, and The Shay's capacity at the time of writing is 7,721.

PITCH MEASUREMENTS

The Shay pitch originally measured 130 x 80 yards. The creation of the speedway track meant it a reduction in size and in 1980 the pitch measured 110 x 70 yards and was the smallest in the Football League. The building of the East Stand saw the pitch moved towards the Skircoat Road side of the ground, and in 2011 its measurements were 112 x 73 yards.

FLOODLIGHTS

On 16 October 1961, work began on the erection of four floodlight pylons at The Shay to bring Halifax Town in line with many other clubs. The dream of chairman Harry Taylor and Supporters' Club chairman Keith Holloway, the directors had given up hope of them being installed due to a shortage of guarantors and the bank's reluctance to lend them the money, until at the 11th hour an anonymous benefactor stepped forward to pay for them at a cost of £17,000. The four 100ft pylons were installed by the General Electricity Company, and each consisted of 36 lights. Real Madrid were invited to play at the official switch-on, but after Halifax Town could not guarantee meeting their demands, Yugoslav side OFK Belgrade provided the opposition on 16 November 1961, though the lights had actually been switched on the previous Saturday during the second half of Town's home game with Peterborough United.

In the 1981 close season, chairman Sam Rorke replaced the floodlights at a cost of £50,000 and these were switched on in a pre-season friendly with Cliftonville on 10 August 1981. The floodlight pylons themselves were later replaced in August 2000 as part of re-development work which included the construction of the East Stand – later aborted – seats being installed in the Skircoat Stand and the re-laying of the pitch.

SOCIAL CLUB

The Halifax Corporation gave the go ahead for Halifax Town to build a social club alongside the Patrons' Stand in February 1966 and The Shay Social Club thus opened on 18 April 1967.

At the suggestion of chairman Sam Rorke, the Social Club was demolished in 1981 to make way for a restaurant, initially called Chimes. But the restaurant floundered and reopened the following year as a members' bar with catering facilities and renamed the Halifax Sporting Club. Following the Council takeover in 1987, it reopened as The Mill House Bistro, before changing its name to the New Halifax Sporting Club, and finally the Weavers. Available for private functions, it was used on matchdays by Halifax Town for both pre and post-match hospitality. The Weavers was demolished in 2010 to make way car-parking for the new East Stand.

THE SHAY AND OTHER SPORTS

Since 1998, Rugby League has been staged at The Shay following Halifax RLFC's move from Thrum Hall. They played their first match of Super League's third season on 10 April 1998, defeating Huddersfield 30–6. But the rugby club previously used The Shay to stage a home game with Widnes on 22 January 1986 after high winds had damaged the floodlights at Thrum Hall, and 6,368 saw Halifax lose 15–8. On 8 February 1949, work began on the construction of a track for speedway. Its total length was 402 yards and nearly 3,000 cubic yards of earth was moved to accommodate it, with the football pitch narrowed and both sets of goalposts moved three yards into the playing area. The Halifax Dukes held their first meeting on 6 April 1949, with Yarmouth Bloaters. But the venture was not an initial success and amid low gates promoter Bruce Booth announced on 31 March 1952 the end of speedway. Booth had tried to boost

Alterations are made to the speedway track, February 1971.

The Shay plays hosts to Rugby League as Halifax take on Widnes, 22 January 1986.

the coffers by staging a one-off meeting of midget car racing on 10 November 1951, a venture watched by 15,000 spectators, three times higher than the average speedway gate. But speedway returned following approaches made to Halifax Town by Middlesbrough promoter Reg Fearman in November 1962. Negotiations lasted two years, but at the beginning of 1965 work began on constructing the speedway track and the sport returned on 11 April 1966 when the Dukes beat Belle Vue 45–33 in a challenge match. To accommodate the track this time, however, the four corners of the playing pitch had to be cut, and the four portable sections were fitted in place for matchdays. After the Football League had instructed Halifax Town to make them permanent in October 1970, work began re-designing the speedway track. Second time around proved more successful, however, for speedway and the sport remained a regular feature until the Halifax Dukes elected to move to Odsal Stadium after a row over money with the football club in 1986. On 6 June 1966 stunt riders from Canada performed at The Shay, charging 10s admission. For two years prior to World War Two, baseball, too, was staged at The Shay. The team was set up by John Rigby and over 4,000 witnessed their first victory over Leeds in 1938. In that first season, the Halifax team excelled and in a victory over Bolton at The Shay, Sam Hanna, who would later turn out for Halifax Town, set an English baseball record by hitting a hat-trick of home runs. Halifax went on to become Major League champions and on 16 July 1938 a combined Halifax/Leeds side drew 5–5 with a United States side at The Shay in front of 3,000 spectators. On 5 August 1939 they reached the pinnacle of success, beating Rochdale Greys 9–5 at The Shay in the Final of the National Baseball Association Challenge Cup. On 13 July 1931 The Shay played host to boxing and wrestling for the first time, with the bill featuring a wrestling contest, in which Halifax RLFC forward Shirley Crabtree beat the accomplished 'Bash' Oakley from Chesterfield. The chief attraction, however, was the heavyweight boxing contest between Halifax's Arthur Evans and Bill Hudson (Wakefield), won on points by Evans. Over the years, both sports have been

The competitors about to take part in target golf at The Shay, 14 June 1967. Winner Walter Lees is fourth from the left.

held at The Shay. On 29 December 1966, England international Jack Charlton opened a golf driving range at the Trinity Garage end. The range was available at lunch times, afternoons and evenings when there was a demand, and though it was initially supervised by Town player Eric McMillan, professional instruction was provided by Michael Booth following his appointment in April 1967. Target golf, of the lines of archery, where targets were laid out on the pitch, was held at The Shay on 14 June 1967 and the competition was won by Walter Lees from Shipley. It was hoped the driving range would bring in £100 a week, and though it paid its way, it was felt not enough to keep it going and with around 200 balls being lost each week, the driving range closed down in December 1967. But the most innovative use of The Shay was that of ice skating, the brainchild of Halifax Town secretary Norman Howe during the Big Freeze of 1963. He felt the scheme would bring in much needed revenue for the cash-strapped club and with the pitch completely frozen over, the club opened its gates to the public on 2 March 1963 and hundreds of people turned up with skates, adults paying 2s 6d and children 1s 6d, £64 was taken on the first day and skating was carried over to the following day, and all in all, almost £100 was raised. While not connected to sport, The Shay was also the site of a Sunday market on the site of what became the five-a-side football court. It opened on 8 March 1970 and became a popular haunt for many years until it was forced to close down in October 1976 because of alleged harassment by Calderdale Council officials implementing the Shops Act.

Skating on the frozen Shay pitch, 2 March 1963.

50 Matches to Remember

Match to Remember 1   9 September 1911

Bradford City Reserves 6   Halifax Town 2

Yorkshire Combination

There was, of course, no more a historical match for Halifax Town than the first one ever played. Nor, it has to be said, was there a harder one. The Yorkshire Combination fixtures that contrived to send the Magpies, the nickname given the team because of their black-and-white-striped shirts, to Valley Parade to face the reserves of Bradford City were cruel for a new club. City's second strip were no ordinary outfit at this level, for not only were they the reigning champions, they had managed to claim the title by remaining unbeaten throughout the season. The chances of Town pulling off victory? Pretty slim.

For all Joe McClelland's meticulous planning in assembling his first squad, he was forced into making hurried arrangements to include at centre-half Clem Garforth, a player who would never feature for the club again but make a name for himself as a rugby player at Thrum Hall. But despite this, and the huge task facing them, by half-time in the match, Town were on the verge of pulling off a sensational win, having run in two goals without reply.

Covering the game for the *Halifax Courier*, as he would do until moving to the *Yorkshire Post* in February 1941, was reporter Tom T. Dickinson, known to all as Pioneer, and he noted Bill Redding's opener as 'worth going miles to see'. Street pushed the ball out to Jock Nixon who whipped it past full-back Pat Cassidy before serving Joe Chadbourne. The Town centre-forward, who had been elected skipper in the changing rooms before the match, gave a swift pass to Redding, who lashed the ball into the net in an instant, giving goalkeeper Martin Spendiff no chance. And as if not satisfied with having one goal to his name, Redding then went on the grab a second just two minutes later, following a mistake by the City goalkeeper.

The two-goal lead which Town carried into half-time put them in dreamland, of course, though it was always going to be a tall order to hang on to it. City came out for the second half fired up and had soon wiped out the deficit before turning the screw in the last 20 minutes, showing little mercy to the Town players who physically wilted as the game went on. In that period, the home side scored four more, with chief tormentor John Young finishing the game with five goals to his name.

Despite the scoreline, Town could take credit in defeat. According to Pioneer, Chadbourne had led the line well and he had been ably supported, at least in the first half, by Redding and

Joe Chadbourne, centre-forward and elected skipper before the first match at Bradford City Reserves.

Andy McGill. Nixon on the left-wing was 'outstanding'. But the side would lose their first home game to Scarborough seven days later before finding a winning formula. They would lead the table, briefly, towards the end of December before fading. For their part, Bradford City's second string would canter to the title once more, though no one was surprised.
Bradford City: Spendiff, Boccock, Farren, Hampton, Peart, Graham, Bartlett, Fox, Young, Connolly, Seymour.
Halifax Town: Finch, Firth, Houldsworth, Street, Garforth, Morgan, Nixon, McGill, Chadbourne, Redding, Wild.

Match to Remember 2   *11 October 1913*
Halifax Town 12   West Vale Ramblers 0
FA Cup first qualifying round

After enjoying a run to the first round proper of the FA Cup in 1912–13, Town were at it again the following term, just falling short at Norwich City in the final qualifying round. On the way they saw off Rothwell, Mirfield United and Rotherham County, but not before they had run up a record haul over local rivals West Vale Ramblers.

The two clubs had met in the Yorkshire Combination two seasons earlier, of course, and the Town supporters had not forgotten how West Vale had spoiled a run of six successive victories by winning 2–1 at Sandhall Lane in November 1911, before going onto complete the double the following April. But Town had moved on since then and were establishing themselves in the Midland Counties League by the time the sides were paired for this first qualifying round FA Cup tie. They were clear favourites, particularly as Ramblers had agreed to surrender home advantage. 'It could be the making of our club,' said their secretary William Joy, happy to accept Town's offer of £12 10s to stage the game at Sandhall Lane.

On the eve of the match, Joy also went on record as saying, 'I anticipate [Halifax Town] will beat us, but not by so big a margin as many people suppose'. No one is quite sure whether the twelve goals Halifax Town ran in that day was close to Joy's predicted scoreline or not, but the game as a contest was over long before half-time and did much to emphasise the fall and rise of the two clubs.

West Vale, in fact, were outclassed almost from the kick-off, so much so that Town goalkeeper Bob Suter may as well have had a day off. The visitors made the mistake of holding the ball too long in midfield, allowing Harry Farren, Tom Splitt and Jack Hughes to nip their moves in the bud.

On the left-wing, George Whitehead was provider of most of the goals, though he was not to get his name on the scoresheet. Leading the way was pint-sized inside-forward Judd Wild, who claimed four, scoring his first after 10 minutes with a lovely left-footed shot after Town had carried the ball the length of the field. Clem Longbottom grabbed the second with a shot which shook the net, and a minute later Whitehead crossed for Wild to get his second before Hughes made it 4–0 from 20 yards. Longbottom was the creator of the fifth, zig-zagging his way three-quarters of the field in a fashion which had made him the idol of the crowd before passing for Wild to complete his hat-trick in front of goal, then made it 6–0 himself just before half-time.

There was no respite for the Ramblers after the break. Tom Blackburn scored with a skilful shot having been set up by Billy Martin, then got his second for 8–0. Percy Roscoe baffled goalkeeper Worsnop with a long-range effort having raced down the wing, and Hughes headed in Whitehead's cross to take the tally into double figures before Wild and Blackburn scored their fourth and third goals respectively to complete the rout, while near the end Suter added his own touch of entertainment for the supporters whose interest in the game had long since waned by dribbling the ball out of his own box.

Halifax Town: Suter, Farren, Splitt, Martin, Hughes, Child, Roscoe, Wild, Blackburn, Longbottom, Whitehead.

West Vale Ramblers: Worsnup, Wheater, Atkins, C. Sutcliffe, King, Normanton, T. Sutcliffe, Oates, Hey, J. Shepherd, E. Shepherd.

Referee: Sgt Hammond (Bradford)

Match to Remember 3   3 September 1921
Halifax Town 5   Darlington 1
Division Three North

Despite the excitement generated by the club's election to the Football League in 1921, Halifax Town's first season in the Northern Section of the Third Division was one of few highs. This fixture with Darlington, which was the first match ever staged at The Shay, was in all honesty, about as good as things got.

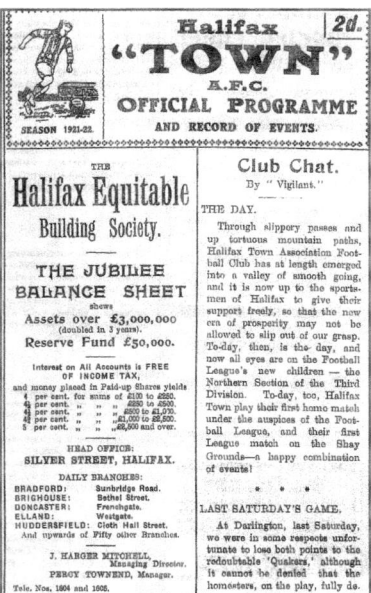

Seven days earlier Town had lost their first match in the League at Darlington, but with the schedule in those far-flung days giving clubs back-to-back fixtures, they were given swift opportunity to exact revenge. They did it in style, but sadly such performances that season were a rarity.

Still the supporters were not to know that, and there was much optimism prior to kick-off which manifested itself with a gate of over 10,000 packing The Shay to witness this historic match, one which gave most of the home fans a chance to see for the first time the new players such as Percy Mackrill, Sam Challinor, Ernie Pinkney, Sid Hetherington, John Woods and Fred Dent. They would not go away disappointed as Town overran their opponents,

Match programme for Halifax Town's first match at The Shay versus Darlington.

nerves settled once Woods had scored the first goal after 15 minutes, a beautiful shot following a cross from Ernie Pinkney. Dent's goal two minutes later, after neat interplay with Woods, put the Shaymen firmly in control and though Darlington rallied, Town's defence, marshalled by skipper Challinor, stood firm and just before half-time Dent added his second goal, a lovely header from Pinkney's right-wing cross.

There was no let up on Town's part after the break. Pinkney, who was proving to be a real thorn in Darlington's side, got away down the right flank, sent the ball over to Whalley on the opposite flank, and his lobbed cross into the box was met by the head of Hetherington. Another Town raid saw Darlington goalkeeper John Ward save from Dent, but Woods returned the ball in an instant to give the Shaymen a 5–0 lead.

A defensive slip-up near the end allowed Bill Edmunds to score a consolation for Darlington and thus become the first visiting player to score at The Shay, but that could not take the gloss off a magnificent Town performance. After the match, one supporter was heard to say, 'I've seen more football this afternoon than in all Town's matches before,' and he no doubt felt, like the rest, that Halifax Town would enjoy a successful season. Sadly, there would be disappointment, for while Darlington would go on to finish runners-up to Stockport County – this Shay defeat was in fact their heaviest that season – Town would soon be fighting a re-election battle they would eventually lose, this victory over Darlington and the euphoria that surrounded it becoming but a distant memory.

Halifax Town: Haldane, Hawley, Mackrill, Hall, Challinor, Anderson, Pinkney, Hetherington, Woods, Dent, Whalley.

Darlington: Ward, Greaves, Barbour, Dickson, Sutcliffe, Malcolm, Dolphin, Hooper, Edmunds, Westenholme, Winslip.

Referee: J. Josephs
Attendance: 10,143

Match to Remember 4   29 April 1922
Halifax Town 5   Crewe Alexandra 5
Division Three North

Halifax Town would not hit as many goals again in that first League season until their last match when they shared 10 goals with Crewe Alexandra, a game which, as the scoreline suggests, was above typical end-of season quality. Victory for the Shaymen would have given them an outside chance of escaping the clutches of the re-election zone, but even so, to play their part in such a goal fest was still a turn up for the books. As it was for Crewe, who had moved up to seventh having not conceded a goal from their last two outings, while the game itself proved to be triumph for Town's Johnny Whalley and Crewe's Alf Winterburn, who both grabbed a hat-trick, yet neither ended up a winner.

The scoring spree began in the fifth minute when Crewe won a corner. Tom Macintyre swung it over and when the ball fell at the feet of Winterburn he hit a rising shot which gave Town goalkeeper Abe Waddington no chance. Shortly afterwards, the same player missed an open goal but the visitors still ran in the second goal following Town's Harry Linley's miskick which enabled an unmarked Stan Rowlands to score. Town hit back through Whalley, latching on to Fred Dent's pass, and despite the close attentions of a defender, he dribbled through and shot home, the ball hitting a defender on the way.

After having a penalty appeal turned down, Crewe restored their two-goal advantage with Rowlands' second which Waddington perhaps should have dealt with, but Town were soon on the attack at the other end, and Dent reduced the deficit from just inside the area. The spectators hardly had time to catch their breath, and before half-time they were witnessing Dent racing half the length of the field before being denied by a fly-kick from goalkeeper Dick Scott. Half-time came and the visitors held their one-goal advantage.

But within seconds of the second period, the scores were level. John Woods kicked-off, sent the ball to Dent and he dribbled through and timed a lovely pass for Whalley, who despite being challenged by Charlie Chorlton, sped away and beat the visiting goalkeeper in the corner.

Another heroic effort by Whalley led to the Shaymen taking the lead for the first time. From the centre of the field, he kicked the ball through and set off in pursuit. Goodwin got to it first but before his back-pass had reached Scott, Whalley had got to the ball and hooked it in – a spectacular finish.

Town's joy turned to despair, however, when Billy Caulfield equalised from close range but the Shaymen began to take command of the game and restored their lead once more through Dent, who, despite carrying a knock from a hefty collision, scored from a narrow angle after Scott had only partially saved Judd Wild's long-range effort. Town perhaps could have seen the game out, but hampered by further injury to Percy Mackrill, they allowed Crewe to score their fifth off a free-kick routine. Moss gave to Winterburn and he fired home from a shot from outside the box for which Waddington, possibly unsighted, never moved.

Still, there was time for the Shaymen to launch one more attack, and having been awarded a free-kick themselves, Maurice Wellock was unlucky to see his shot graze the bar.
Halifax Town: Waddington, Wellock, Mackrill, Howson, Linley, Hall, Pinkney, Wild, Woods, Dent, Whalley.
Crewe Alexandra: Scott, Goodwin, Chorlton, Moss, Perry, Turner, Hassall, Winterburn, Rowlands, Caulfield, McIntyre.
Referee: J.G. Forsham
Halifax Town would feature in another such high-scoring draw on just one further occasion when they shared 10 goals with Bury in a wartime fixture on Christmas Day, 1940.

Match to Remember 5 2 February 1924
Manchester City 2   Halifax Town 2
FA Cup second round

Not for nothing was Joe McClelland's side of 1923–24 termed 'the Cup team'. The defeats of Peterborough & Fletton United and Rotherham County in the early rounds may have been straight forward enough, but it was the gutsy performances the side showed in seeing off

A section of the crowd at Maine Road for the Manchester City v Halifax Town FA Cup tie.

Northampton Town in the first round which made people take notice. The tie ran to three games and was only settled after extra-time at Sheffield United's neutral Bramall Lane. But that was just the appetiser. For Halifax Town's reward in the second round was a trip to Maine Road, new home of First Division Manchester City, and the ensuing battles the sides played out gripped the town. In the event, Halifax Town were unfortunate not to win.

At the time of the first game, the Shaymen occupied 10th position in the Third Division North, and though Manchester City were only a mid-table side themselves – they were 13th – they included in their ranks the bespectacled goalkeeper Jim Mitchell, Alex Hamill and Frank Roberts, and were, perhaps rightly so, expected to settle the tie at the first time of asking. But they figured without the resolve of this Halifax Town side.

Rarely do lower League clubs get the chance to put one over their higher division opponents, but in this case Halifax Town were presented with not one but two golden opportunities. The tie, like that with Northampton, ran to three games, and but for a little more composure in either of the first two matches, Town could have found themselves in the third round.

The crowd of 30,970 was the biggest some of the Town players had played in front of, but still, they were about to give City the fright of their lives, even though it was the home side who scored first. Luck was with City when Billy Murphy's 25th-minute shot came back in the wind – it turned out to be perfect pass to Roberts 10 yards out and he dashed in and gave Town goalkeeper Herbert Bown no chance. At this point Town were being overrun, and Horace Barnes, Jack Warner and Roberts again all went close, but having seen out the half with no further damage, it was the Town players who came out after the interval and took the game to their more illustrious opponents.

Just two minutes in, and they fashioned a grand equaliser. Bown punted the ball upfield, Ernie Dixon knocked it on for Johnny Whalley on the left-wing, and after beating two men, he centred for Jackie Foster. He laid the ball off to Jimmy Moore, and his glorious first-time effort screamed past Mitchell.

For a while, Town outplayed City, and it came as little surprise when they took the lead. Fingers may have been pointed at Mitchell when he fisted the ball out from Whalley's corner, but credit must be given to the cool way in which Ellis Hall lobbed the ball over a cluster of players and Mitchell into an unguarded net from outside the box. Suddenly, Halifax Town held a 2–1 advantage and the players were in wonderland.

But not for long. Just 60 seconds later, in fact, and City were back on level terms. Breaking down the left flank, Barnes saw his effort crash against the bar only for Hamill to fire the rebound goalwards. Ellis Hall, in an attempt to stop the ball crossing the line, got his hands to it, but after a moment's hesitancy the referee gave a goal.

The game swung in favour of City from that point, but Town held out and a replay was deemed necessary four days later.

Manchester City: Mitchell, Cookson, Allen, Sharp, Hamill, Pringle, Morris, Warner, Roberts, Barnes, Murphy.
Halifax Town: Bown, Lees, Wheelhouse, Wild, Hall, Parkin, Foster, Housley, Dixon, Moore, Whalley.
Referee: H. Clayton (Derby)
Attendance: 30,970

Match to Remember 6   *6 February 1924*
Halifax Town 0   Manchester City 0
FA Cup second round replay

The replay the following Wednesday brought the town of Halifax to a standstill. Shops, factories and warehouses all closed down so the workers could attend the match, scheduled for a 2.30pm kick-off. Not to mention the hundreds of children who skipped school to bolster the crowd to a record 21,590, which paid receipts of £1,213, another Shay record.

Town took to the field having made just one enforced change from the first match, Matt Ellson stepping in for winger Johnny Whalley who had sustained a thigh muscle injury at Maine Road. City, for their part, remained unchanged, and Derby referee Clayton resumed his duties. In the 41st minute he handed the Shaymen the perfect opportunity to take the lead.

City had forced the issue up to that point and created three good openings, but when Town's Jackie Foster raced into the box at the other end, he was checked by Charlie Pringle, handling the ball in the process. Intentional or not, the referee pointed immediately to the spot and awarded Town a penalty and Ernie Dixon stepped up to take it.

Dixon would be top scorer in seven consecutive seasons at The Shay, scoring a record 136 goals in all competitions. But it was the one that got away for which, cruelly, he would long be remembered, though it has to be said, his nerves were tested to the limit by City's bespectacled goalkeeper Jim Mitchell, who paraded up and down his area and wiped his glasses to delay the taking of the kick, a procedure he had made into an art form.

Whether his antics affected Dixon or not, the Town marksman's spot-kick was a poor one;

50 MATCHES TO REMEMBER

he shot straight at the City goalkeeper, who made a comfortable save, and Town's best chance to cause an upset had gone.

Earlier though, Town had had another penalty appeal turned down when Herbert Housley was kicked from behind with just the goalkeeper to beat, and having created another opportunity, Jimmy Moore delayed his shot too long before the City cover was back.

The visitors, who had three decent chances in the first half, had most of the possession after the break but came up against a resolute Town defence. The sides played out the 90 minutes with neither making the breakthrough, and extra-time was fought between two flagging teams. Dixon's unhappy afternoon was complete when he was laid out cold following a challenge and he completed the match out on the wing.

Manchester City would not let the Shaymen off the hook in the third meeting, staged at Manchester United's 'neutral' Old Trafford, running out 3–0 winners, although it was felt that their first goal came against the run of play. Nevertheless, it was City who went through to meet Brighton in round three, while just weeks later, Town manager Joe McClelland was allowing his 'Cup team' to be broken up to raise money for his cash-strapped club.

Halifax Town: Bown, Lees, Wheelhouse, Wild, E. Hall, Parkin, Foster, Housley, Dixon, Moore, Ellson.

Manchester City: Mitchell, Cookson, Allen, Sharp, Allen, Pringle, Morris, Warner, Roberts, Barnes, Murphy.

Referee: H. Clayton (Derby)
Attendance: 21,590

Match to Remember 7   *18 December 1926*
Halifax Town 2   Stoke City 2
Division Three North

It was in 1926–27 that Halifax Town made their first serious assault on the Third Division North title. Having lost only three of their opening 16 fixtures, the side was handily placed in eighth, eight points behind leaders Stoke City but with two games in hand. The Potters, under Tom Mather, had just been relegated from the Second Division and were making great strides themselves towards an instant return. Having won 13 of their opening 18 matches, they led the table by six points, though they arrived at The Shay on the back of a shock FA Cup defeat by Rhyl Athletic. Still, this match was a serious ask of the Shaymen's credentials as to whether they were or not real title contenders.

The game drew the crowds, with the 10,000 gate the highest of the season, but as expected, it was the visitors who forced the pace early on, with Town's agile goalkeeper Lewis Barber making a full-

Herbert Housley, the scorer of Town's first goal in the draw with Stoke City.

length save from Charlie Hallam. It was from a Town attack, though, that they broke the deadlock in the 38th minute. Joe McCafferty's corner was cleared out, and Hallam raced away with defenders out of position. Jack Lees failed to check him and when Hallam delivered the cross, Walter Bussey forced the ball home following a goalmouth scramble after Len Armitage's initial shot had been charged down.

Stoke held the lead until the break, but they were on the back foot in the second half as the Shaymen pressed, forcing a succession of corners, having two penalty appeals turned down, and Dixon seeing his header cleared off the line. But after 62 minutes, their pressure told when Dixon and Herbert Housley led the race for Willie Smith's through ball, and while Dixon resisted the challenge of Billy Spencer, Housley drove in from close range.

The game ebbed and flowed, but it was Stoke who regained the lead following a corner. Though Barber fisted it away, Armitage tricked Duckett on the edge of the box before firing home a splendid shot which gave the Town goalkeeper no chance. The visitors then had the chance to wrap up the game, but Barber, who, indeed, had been the busier goalkeeper, dived at the feet of Charlie Wilson.

To the joy of the home supporters, Town were back on level terms with just six minutes remaining when Smith converted Sid Waites's cross to set up a grandstand finish, and it was the Shaymen who came closest to winning it when centre-half Alf Dark's header from Waites' corner just cleared the bar.

The point probably suited Stoke better. They maintained their stranglehold at the top of table, while Halifax Town would pick up the challenge in the second half of the season, moving to within four points of the Potters at the beginning of March. But Stoke proved they were the division's outstanding side, and while the Shaymen's challenge faded, they clinched the title long before the season's close and were presented with the trophy when they entertained Joe McClelland's side in their last match of the season.

Halifax Town: Barber, Lees, Wheelhouse, Willis, Dark, Duckett, Waites, Housley, Dixon, Smith, McCafferty.
Stoke City: Dixon, McGrory, Spencer, Sellars, Williamson, Eastwood, Armitage, Bussey, Wilson, Davies, Hallam.
Referee: H. Hopkinson (Rochdale)
Attendance: 10,965

Match to Remember 8   10 September 1927
Halifax Town 2   Bradford City 1
Division Three North

Among the most eagerly awaited clashes at The Shay during those early Third Division North days were the Yorkshire derbies, particularly those involving clubs from the old West Riding. Huddersfield Town, one of the giants of the game, Leeds United and the two Bradford clubs were all regular opponents of Halifax Town in the local Senior Cup competition, but it was in the League where the rivalry would be fiercest.

By the end of the 1926–27 season, Halifax Town and Bradford had become well acquainted with each other since the Park Avenue club's relegation five years earlier. But as they embarked on a new season, the Shaymen were now anticipating the visit of 'the other' club from the city nine miles up the road.

Bradford City, FA Cup-winners in 1911 and a First Division club as recently as 1922, had been experiencing leaner years of late, and their fall from grace was completed with their own relegation from the Second Division. But they were still a top attraction and when Joe McClelland's side prepared to face them in the season's opening weeks, the game took on the mantel of epic proportions. So much so that a record Shay gate was expected and indeed, the 19,935 figure not only topped the previous record for a League game here, set when Town entertained Nelson in December 1922, it would remain Town's largest-ever in the League.

Following entertainment by the lady pipers from the Palace Theatre and the Lee Mount Brass Band, the spectators that day were then treated to an intriguing football encounter as well. The game was given added spice with Town skipper Don Duckett facing his old club, as was leading scorer Ernie Dixon, who enjoyed netting against his former colleagues to cancel out Ralph Burkinshaw's goal. Yet Burkinshaw's goal in the 20th minute had come very much against the run of play as Town dominated, with City goalkeeper Jock Ewart being forced into making two magnificent saves, the first down by the post from Herbert Housley's screw shot, and the second at full length from the same player following a corner.

At the other end, however, Ewart's counterpart Fred Fox's first meaningful contribution gifted City their goal. When Eddie Harvey delivered a corner, Fox, in attempting to fist out, skied the ball to leave Burkinshaw the chance of an easy goal. It was a lead the Bantams scarcely deserved but one they took into the break with them, despite continuing Town pressure.

The Shaymen bombarded the City goal in the second half but found Ewart in exceptional form but in the 78th minute they finally made the breakthrough. Norman Proctor's pass rebounded off a defender into the path of Dixon, and Town's lethal centre-forward hammered the ball into the net. Now Town went all out for the winner, and with just minutes remaining, they got it. The architect was the inspirational Duckett, who ventured forward, but though his pass across goal appeared to be going out of play, Andy Martin retrieved the ball and sent across to Arthur Seabrook who diverted it over the line before Ewart could react.

Town were denied a penalty late on when Dixon, having raced almost half the length of the field, saw his cross handled by Sam Russell, but it hardly mattered. Moments later the referee's whistle signalled the end of the match and victory for Town, which, on the second half performance alone, they richly deserved.

Halifax Town: Fox, Lees, Gacsden, Duckett, Dark, Hubbert, Seabrook, Proctor, Dixon, Housley, Martin.
Bradford City: Ewart, Russell, Watson, Lloyd, Bancroft, Campbell, Harvey, Moore, Burkinshaw, Cairns, Scriven.
Referee: N. Shuker (Worksop)
Attendance: 19,935

Match to Remember 9   28 February 1931
Newark Town 1   Halifax Town 1
FA Cup first round

There can be fewer games where the future of the club depended solely on one match, but this was to be one of those. When Alex Raisbeck's Halifax Town side travelled to Newark Town for this first round FA Cup tie, they did so with chairman David Brook having stressed how tight the financial situation was at The Shay. Money was, therefore, urgently required and a run in the Cup was not so much viewed as a welcome relief, but more an absolute necessity. Quite simply put, this was a game Town could not afford to lose.

There was obvious pressure, then, on the shoulders of skipper Dick Strang and his teammates when they took to the Muskham Ground, and this intensified when the home side took the lead after only four minutes' play, Hill's shot from 20 yards taking a deflection off Strang, who was returning to the Town side after a lay-off of over two months.

For a time, the Shaymen were on the rocks, with goalkeeper Bernard Bilcliff looking particularly nervous, but gradually the players settled down and five minutes before the break they equalised. Strang was the creator, his long kick down the middle sending Billy Mays away and he kept a cool head to dribble through and beat Newark goalkeeper Streets with a neat finish. Town's cause by then had been helped by injury to the Newark left winger Jeff McLean, who returned to the action after receiving treatment but was far less effective than before.

Nevertheless, the second half was a tense affair with both sides carving out openings. But the longer the game went on, the more the home side fancied their chances and they began bombarding the Town penalty area with high balls. Town found themselves literally fighting for their lives, with Strang proving a tower of strength at the back, and the side was indebted to him as time and time again he rose to repel the home side's constant attacks. On the sidelines, Ben Wheelhouse, out through illness, epitomised the tension felt by the Town players by taking a cigarette and chewing on it as he watched on. With nerves almost at breaking point, the Shaymen held out and prepared to take Newark back to The Shay for a replay four days later.

On more familiar territory, Town defeated the non-Leaguers 2–1 before putting out Accrington Stanley in round two to set themselves up for a third-round match with Bournemouth. In front of a welcome 18,000 spectators, Town losy 3–0, but four sets of receipts from the Cup ties, plus the sale of Ted Crawford the following May, ensured the club's immediate future. Had Town been defeated at Newark, the consequences could have been so different.

Newark Town: Streets, Pearson, Yorke, B. Stanniland, Bennett, C. Stanniland, Richardson, Hill, Burgeon, Kays, McLean.
Halifax Town: Bilcliff, Barrie, Graham, Read, Strang, McGrae, Davies, Mays, Crawford, Johnson, Betteridge.
Referee: J.R. Morrey (Leicester)
Attendance: 2,525

Match to Remember 10   *18 February 1933*

Halifax Town 0   Luton Town 2

FA Cup fifth round

Halifax Town have only reached the fifth round of the FA Cup on two occasions, but while the side of 1952–53 made headlines, at least locally, for disposing of two First Division sides en route, two decades earlier the Shaymen gave the supporters a season to remember, and in particular, this FA Cup tie with Luton Town.

It would be true to say that Town's passage to the fifth round was easier than that of their counterparts 20 years hence, given that they avoided meeting clubs from the top two tiers. Darwen and Workington were both non-League outfits, and Doncaster Rovers and Chester were from Town's own Division, though a replay was necessary to overcome the challenge of the latter in the fourth round. And while many hoped for a big name club in the fifth round, the visit of Luton at least represented the Shaymen's greatest opportunity of making it through to the last eight. The Hatters were a Third Division South side, and lying only 16th, though they arrived at The Shay with the fillip of a 4–0 win over Exeter City behind them.

The sense of occasion drew the crowds and The Shay's record crowd was smashed, with the home support confident of victory. But skipper Olly Thompson may have done well to heed the warnings of a snowstorm 20 minutes before kick-off which covered the pitch, for having won the toss, he elected to play into the wind which blew from one end of the ground to the other, perhaps hoping that his side could hold the visitors and press home the advantage in the second half with the elements in their favour. It was a decision, however, which cruelly backfired.

Braving the elements. The blizzard at its most ferocious during the Luton Town Cup tie.

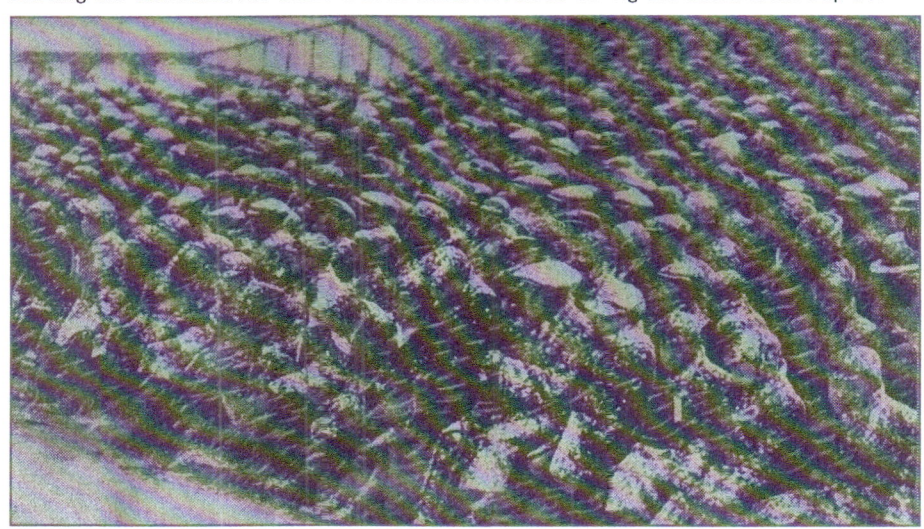

Luton attacked from the start, with Tom Alderson and Arthur Nelson both going close, and as the snow returned, they took the lead after 19 minutes. By this time, Town were playing into blizzard-like conditions, and Luton took full advantage. When the prolific Tommy Tait received the ball just inside Town's penalty area, his shot took a defection off George Parkin, and goalkeeper Watty Shirlaw was well beaten.

That goal apart, the first half would be forever remembered by the halting of the match after 27 minutes. For, by then, the snowstorm was at its worst and the referee had little option but to take the players off the pitch and wait until the conditions improved. The elements were as bad as any The Shay had witnessed, but for the spectators, there was nowhere to hide and they were forced to brave the elements – most of them were not under cover – and wait until the blizzard eased off. After 13 minutes the snowstorm relented and work began then on clearing the pitch, and after a full 25-minute interlude, play was resumed, with Town holding out for the remainder of the half.

But all hope of rescuing the game seemed to disappear with Luton's second goal, scored nine minutes after the break. Town were in trouble the moment Thompson and Hugh Flack blundered in midfield, and though Ted Craig behind them appeared to have Andy Rennie covered, he was muscled out of it and as Rennie ran on, he put in a cross-shot which Shirlaw failed to hold. The ball ran loose and Nelson, following up, knocked it into the empty net.

There was still plenty of time for the Shaymen to save the game, but they lacked ideas as Luton defended resolutely. The Hatters saw the game out and went through to meet eventual Cup winners Everton – Dixie Dean and all – where they would lose 6–0. But for Thompson's decision to play into the elements in the first half at The Shay, who knows, perhaps Town would have had the honour.

Halifax Town: Shirlaw, Flack, Barrie, Thompson, Craig, Parkin, Davies, Brown, Chambers, Wellock, Tunstall.
Luton Town: Harford, Kingham, Mackey, Kean, McGinnigle, Fraser, Nelson, Tait, Rennie, Alderson, Roberts.
Referee: A.H. Kinscott (Long Eaton)
Attendance: 29,235

Match to Remember 11 *6 January 1934*
Stockport County 13   Halifax Town 0
Division Three North

There seemed nothing untoward when Halifax Town travelled to Edgeley Park for their Third Division North fixture with Stockport County at the beginning of January 1934. County may have been lying second in the table, but Alex Raisbeck's Town side were fifth themselves, only four points behind. Besides, the Shaymen had defeated Stockport 4–2 at The Shay back in September, with Fred Tunstall notching all Town's goals. 'Tunny' played in this game, too, as did the likes of Ted Craig, Charlie Davies, Arthur Mercer and Fred Brown, thus pouring scorn on the suggestion that, in light of the impending scoreline,

50 MATCHES TO REMEMBER

The unfortunate Stan Milton, who conceded a record 13 goals on his League debut at Stockport County.

Town must have been seriously understrength. Though it has to be said, they travelled without centre-forward Bill Chambers – and with something of a goalkeeper crisis.

A thigh injury picked up by Watty Shirlaw in the New Year's Day fixture with Hartlepools United now sidelined him, so in turn Raisbeck turned to 20-year-old amateur goalkeeper Stan Milton, a player he predicted had a great future. Milton had shown great promise in the reserves and Raisbeck had no reservations in handing him his League debut. Milton, in fact, had a decent first half and did as much as anyone to keep the score down as the Stockport forwards, playing with the wind at their backs, overran the Town defence. By half-time, Town perhaps felt they were still in the hunt after trailing by only two goals, both scored by Joe Hill, the first a shot on the run after just eight minutes and the second, four minutes later from close range following a corner. Milton made several important saves in the first half, not least that from Alf Lythgoe when he was clean through, to suggest that Halifax Town, indeed, had a star in the making. Opinions may have changed after the final whistle, however.

Lythgoe got his name on the scoresheet four minutes after the interval when he outpaced Ted Craig, at which point the Shaymen physically collapsed. Nothing seemed to be going right for them, and they even found referee Brown in uncharitable mood. A minute later, he overruled Town's appeals that the ball had crossed the goalline before Jabez Foulkes pulled the ball back when Hill scored his third goal, and after only a further two minutes, he awarded Stockport County a penalty for John Johnman's seemingly innocuous challenge on Jimmy Stevenson.

A suspiciously looking offside Foulkes crashed in the sixth in the 57th minute, and a mistake by a shell-shocked Milton less than 60 seconds – he tried to keep in play a shot that was going wide – handed the chance for Percy Downes to make it 7–0.

And still County kept coming. Stevenson scored his second in the 61st minute before Downes scored from near the dead ball line. In the 66th minute, Milton failed to hold Downes's centre and Downes followed up to take the tally into double figures. Lythgoe headed in his second before further goals from Stevenson and Downes, with his fourth in the very last minute, completed the rout.

While the supporters may have been embarrassed by such a scoreline, at least there was the lighter side provided by Hugh Flack when asked (as the 10th went in) by Dan Ferguson, 'How many's that?' Back came the reply, 'Sure I don't know but I think we're losing.' Stockport duly entered the record books for racking up a record score for a League match – it has since been equalled by Newcastle United over Newport County in October 1946 but never bettered – as did Milton, the most goals conceded by a goalkeeper on his debut.

Meanwhile, the theorists had a field day trying to account for what had gone on at Edgeley Park. Some reckoned the players had the minds on the following week's big FA Cup tie and Bolton Wanderers, others simply saw the result as a fluke. But on a historic day, at

least reports of the game were kept off the back pages of the newspapers, which preferred to cover the death of the legendary former Huddersfield Town and Arsenal manager Hebert Chapman, who died on the same morning.
Stockport County: McGann, Vincent, Jenkinson, Robinson, Stevens, L. Jones, Foulkes, Hill, Lythgoe, Stevenson, Downes.
Halifax Town: Milton, Flack, Johnman, Ferguson, Craig, Cooke, Davies, Mercer, Brown, Wellock, Tunstall.
Referee: J.S. Brown (Blackburn)
Attendance: 7,807

Match to Remember 12   9 March 1935
Halifax Town 6   New Brighton 2
Third Division North

Halifax Town achieved their highest-ever League placing in 1934–35 when they finished runners-up to Doncaster Rovers in the Third Division North, but going into the final two months of the season they were one of five sides still in the running for the title. Here, they showed their capabilities with this resounding victory over New Brighton, with centre-forward Albert Valentine at his swashbuckling best, leading the charge by scoring a nap hand.

Town went into this game on the back of a chasing they themselves had suffered at the hands of fellow promotion hopefuls Chester, where they lost 5–0, but quickly began to put this defeat behind them by taking the lead after just nine minutes. Manager Alex Raisbeck had moved to strengthen his side with the signing of inside-left Tom Barkas from Bradford City the previous December, and it was he who arrived in the box to turn home the ball after Valentine's shot from a narrow angle had been parried by goalkeeper Charlie Bird. Twelve minutes later Town doubled their lead with Valentine's powerful drive into the top of the net, a rip-roaring goal.

The third goal came in the 27th minute when Ted Craig, breaking from defence, sent Valentine through to score from 18 yards. There was no holding back the Shaymen, and Gordon Presgrave took the lead in their fourth goal scored after 34 minutes. Following a clever passing move involving Tom Feeney and Barkas, Presgrave dribbled through to set up Valentine who hooked the ball over the line. Two minutes before half-time, Town went five goals up with Valentine's hat-trick, shooting home from 20 yards after another quick break by Barkas and Feeney.

By the interval New Brighton were a beaten side, but to their credit and with nothing to lose, they looked more assertive after the break, though it was Town who scored next after 57 minutes. Presgrave forced a corner and placed the kick perfectly for Valentine to claim his fifth of the match, only the second player to achieve such a feat in a League game after his predecessor Bill Chambers had managed it against Hartlepools United just 11 months earlier.

Towards the end, Town relaxed and allowed New Brighton to score two goals they just about deserved. Beckett and Davis both hit the bar before Miller and Davis reduced the arrears in the last five minutes.

The victory moved Town up to fifth, six points behind leaders Tranmere Rovers, though Doncaster were menacingly placed in second. Tranmere would falter leaving the way for Doncaster to go clear, and Town would finish as runners-up by defeating the newly crowned champions both away and at home in their last two matches.

Halifax Town: Shirlaw, Allsop, Banner, Millington, Craig, Cooke, Presgrave, Feeney, Valentine, Barkas, Tunstall.

New Brighton: Bird, L. Carr, Ratcliffe, Salmon, Amery, Smedley, Lawrence, Butler, Davis, Miller, Beckett.

Referee: J.E. Williams (Bolton)
Attendance: 4,673

Match to Remember 13   26 November 1938
Halifax Town 7   Rochdale 3
FA Cup first round

Was there ever a more enthralling performance by the Shaymen on home soil than this 7–3 victory over local rivals Rochdale? It was game which years later *Halifax Courier* chief sports writer Bill Carter would single out, and one that would not easily be forgotten by those who saw it. Jimmy Thomson's side not only ran riot in a whirlwind second half, they racked up what was then a record Shay score, a total equalled but never bettered at senior level.

There was nothing to suggest such a goal fest, although the sides had produced 11 goals between them in two pre-season Jubilee Fund matches. The League encounter at The Shay in October had been a keenly contested affair, and settled 2–1 in favour of Thomson's side thanks to Tom Barkas's winner just eight minutes from time.

For the FA Cup match, the scoring began as early as the first minute when Rochdale's Jimmy Wynn followed up a through pass, skipped around Harold Jackson and slipped the ball into the net as goalkeeper Charlie Briggs advanced. But the Shaymen's response was swift, for just five minutes had elapsed before Ted Widdowfield scored when Jabez Foulkes returned the ball from the right after player-manager Ted Goodier had headed out Griffiths original cross.

After 17 minutes, the visitors restored their lead when Wynn robbed Ted Craig of the ball on the edge of the Town penalty area. He supplied Joe Duff, who scored at the second attempt. On the half-hour, Jackson, with a penalty awarded following Henry Roberts's challenge on Foulkes, brought Town back level and a minute before the interval the Shaymen went in front for the first time with Stan Wood's header off Foulkes's cross.

Jabez Foulkes, who starred on the wing during Town's 7–3 FA Cup win over Rochdale.

Within five minutes of the second half, Rochdale had made it 3–3 courtesy of Goodier's shot when Town failed to clear Reg Kilsby's corner. But the game swung once more in favour of the Shaymen with a sensational goal scored by Wood on the hour mark. Barkas raced away down the right and though his long crossfield pass flashed across goal, Wood arrived at the far post to head home from an almost impossible angle for what *Courier* reporter Tom Dickinson described as 'a miraculous goal'. It gave Town a new lease of life, and they then completely overwhelmed Goodier's side, with Widdowfield the chief tormentor. He went on to score a second-half hat-trick, beginning with two goals in the space of a minute which killed off the tie. In the 64th minute he headed home Barkas's free-kick, then when Wood had broken through, he ran in to belt home his low centre. Rochdale had no answer, and four minutes from time, Widdowfield grabbed his third of the half and fourth in total when he headed in Foulkes's cross.

The second-round draw two days later paired Town with the winners of the drawn match between Workington and Mansfield Town. It was the Stags who went through, but after producing such an emphatic scoreline at The Shay here, who would have guessed then that it would take the Shaymen four matches to see off the challenge of Mansfield?

Halifax Town: Briggs, Allsop, Jackson, Green, Craig, Ruecroft, Foulkes, Griffiths, Widdowfield, Barkas, Wood.
Rochdale: Doyle, Baird, Roberts, Goodfellow, Goodier, Reeve, Kilsby, Duff, Wynn, Prest, Mee.
Referee: E.E.A. Evans (Liverpool)
Attendance: 10,921

Match to Remember 14   21 December 1938
Halifax Town 2   Mansfield Town 1
FA Cup second round, third replay

Rochdale may have been defeated thanks to the second-half blitz by the Shaymen, but the FA Cup second-round affair with Third Division Southern Section Mansfield Town was anything but straightforward. These were the days long before penalty kicks decided the issue should scores be level after a replay; ties were settled in open play by extra-time and by as many replays as were needed. In November 1971, Oxford City and Alvechurch needed six matches before their fourth qualifying tie was resolved; prior to that, Halifax Town's tie here was settled after a fourth match by Mansfield's Bungay's goal – in Halifax's favour.

The original tie was played at The Shay on 10 December, but after a terrific struggle, the score ended 1–1. The replay at Field Mill four days later was even more of a titanic battle, each side scoring in extra-time as the sides drew 3–3, and a third match, staged at neutral – this was also the norm – Belle Vue, Doncaster ended goalless, again after an extra 30 minutes had been played. So the sides lined up once more two days later in front of the sparsely populated Old Trafford ground, home of Manchester United, on a Wednesday afternoon, a game played on a bone hard ground and in driving snow.

The few spectators did not have to wait long for the first goal. It came after just three minutes courtesy of Jabez Foulkes's cross and Ted Widdowfield's terrific header. But it would not prove decisive. In the 31st minute, the Stags equalised through Alf Somerfield's close range effort which owed much to the work done by Charlie Gardiner, who beat Harold Jackson and drew Ted Craig before slipping the ball across for his colleague.

Two cautious sides played out the second half without any further scoring, and so once more, extra-time was deemed necessary. But it was not until the 117th minute that the crucial winning goal was scored. The architect was Stan Wood, who had swapped places with Tommy Barkas, a passenger following injury, who found himself down the inside-left channel to the left of the area. He dodged a defender then fired across a shot which was swerving away from goal – until that is, Reg Bungay swung his right foot to clear but only ended up slicing the ball up and into the roof of the net behind him.

It was a most unfortunate own-goal by the Mansfield left-back, and one that left his side with little time in which to respond. In fact, it was Town who came closest to scoring again in the last minute when they broke following a desperate Mansfield attack, with Widdowfield seeing his effort scooped off the line by goalkeeper Dan Black. However, it proved to be the last incident of a mammoth FA Cup tie, and it was the Shaymen who went through to meet Birmingham City at St Andrew's, where, despite a courageous performance, they bowed out, losing 2–0.

Halifax Town: Briggs, Allsop, Jackson, Green, Ruecroft, Foulkes, Griffiths, Widdowfield, Barkas, Wood.
Mansfield Town: Black, Stimpson, Bungay, Paterson, Barke, Speed, Bell, Gardiner, Somerfield, Dutton, Wilson.
Referee: H. Hartles (Runcorn)
Attendance: 1,219

Reg Bungay's own-goal caused confusion when news reports came through. Press agencies believed he must have scored for his own team and most people were initially led to believe that it was the Stags who had won the match.

Match to Remember 15   *6 May 1944*
Halifax Town 2   Huddersfield Town 4
Combined Counties Cup Final

The war years put a strain on the whole of the country, but football did its level best to carry on as normal. Halifax Town could call on several players on a regular basis, such as Bill Allsop and Horace Green, as well as using a number of guests, as all clubs did. How exciting it must have been to see internationals lining up in the Town team, as well as those who turned out for the opposition, household names such as Stanley Matthews and Tom Finney, who were among the many famous faces to appear at The Shay.

While it was an austere period, Halifax Town did provide their own supporters with some cheer by winning silverware in the form of the Combined Counties Cup. Here was a strange mix; a Cup competition played over two legs, the results of which also counted for

League points. Town, by seeing off York City and Leeds United in the knockout stages, found themselves in the Final, pitted against Huddersfield Town, whom they had already beaten in an earlier group stage!

The first leg of the Final was staged at Huddersfield's Leeds Road, and helped by an early goal gifted to them by Don Clegg, the Shaymen ran out shock 4–1 winners, a scoreline which stood them in good stead for the second leg a week later. Or so one would have thought, for the return match proved to be one of the most exciting seen at The Shay, and for the home supporters, certainly one of the most nail-biting.

Jimmy Glazzard's goal following poor defensive play by the Shaymen gave Huddersfield a deserved half-time lead to leave them trailing on aggregate by two goals, but when George Taylor headed a simple equaliser for the Shaymen following Tom Barkas's accurate pull-back it seemed the home side were back fully in control. And even when Henry Baird next scored for Huddersfield, a header from a corner in the 76th minute, Town's replay was swift when Bill Jones made it 2–2 six minutes later, following up after Clegg had fumbled Taylor's cross, to keep intact their three-goal cushion.

But in a thrilling finish, Huddersfield rallied and scored through Bert Price, and with their tails up and sensing the Cup was not lost, they came at the Shaymen once more, with Price grabbing his second to give the Terriers a 4–2 lead. Suddenly, Town's aggregate lead looked pregnable, but with the home fans baying for the final whistle, they just about held out. Skipper Tom Barkas was presented with the Cup by the Mayor, councillor T. Greenwood, JP, while George Myers, the president of the West Riding County Football Association, claimed he was pleased at the success of Halifax Town if only for the sake of chairman Charles Mattock who he reckoned had done so much for the club and football in general.

It was Town's first silverware since the winning of the Bradford Hospitals Cup 30 years earlier, but for the players, no medals, just three war savings certificates. There was still a war on.
Halifax Town: Rymer, Allsop, Topping, Green, J. Ruecroft, Woffinden, Flatley, Fleetwood, Jones, Barkas, Taylor.
Huddersfield Town: Clegg, Bailey, Battye, Willingham, Birch, Boot, Isaac, Glazzard, Price, Baird, Smith.
Attendance: 5,537

Match to Remember 16　　　　　　　　*18 January 1947*
Halifax Town 4   Doncaster Rovers 2
Division Three North

When Halifax Town prepared to face Doncaster Rovers for this Third Division North fixture in January 1947, even the most ardent of Shay supporters would not have given much hope of their team's chances. A quick glance at the League table made for unpleasant viewing, with Town lying bottom, level on points with Southport, having undergone one of the worst sequence of results in their history. Without a win in the League since 2 November – a total of 11 matches – Jimmy Thomson's side had also recently conceded six goals on the travels at Oldham and Rotherham, and their poor sequence of results had included a then club record eight consecutive League defeats.

Doncaster Rovers, on the other hand, were flying. Five points clear at the top of the table, they were sweeping all before them, with the prolific Clarrie Jordan having scored 23 goals for himself. They arrived at The Shay with nothing to fear, particularly as they were unbeaten away from home in all 11 matches.

Even when they fell behind after only two minutes, Rovers felt no need to panic. Still, the goal was a pleasing one from Town's point of view, especially for debutant Stan Fisher, signed by manager Jimmy Thomson the day before. Keen to make an instant impression, he made a telling contribution when his shot was saved by Archie Ferguson, only for Bernard Massey to follow up, with the ball being deflected over the line by Ernie Swallow.

The visitors responded by taking the game to Town, but squandered an early chance to get back on level terms when Thompson saw his penalty kick, awarded when Horace Green brought down Jordan, beaten out by Ted Rayner. However, there was nothing the Town goalkeeper could do with Ralph Maddison's surprise rising shot which made the score 1–1 after 25 minutes.

It seemed that normal order had been restored five minutes into the second half when Rovers took the lead when Maddison centred for Paul Todd to score with an instant shot. But an error by Ferguson let the Shaymen back into the match just seven minutes later. Fred England's high pot-shot should have made for a routine catch for the Rovers goalkeeper, but he was deceived by the flight of the ball and allowed it to drop behind him and into the net.

Spurred by this somewhat fortuitous strike, Town stunned the visitors with another goal a minute later with Sammy Waters's spectacular snap shot from a narrow angle following Massey's cross, and from then on in, the supporters were kept on edge as Town defended resolutely to keep Doncaster out. Green cleared off the line and Rayner did well to keep out a ground shot from Jordan before denying the same player with a fine one-handed save.

Town survived the onslaught, then gave themselves daylight with 10 minutes remaining with the goal of the game, scored by Waters, who worked into the middle of the field and beat Ferguson with a low drive into the far corner of the net for his second. Town were in dreamland, and though Maddison's header against the bar momentarily had them worried, they were not to be denied and held out for what was undoubtedly one of the shock results of the season.

If only it could have been the springboard to better things, but the fact was that Town would lose their next five matches and would win again until the beginning of April. Rovers, on the other hand, quickly put this defeat behind them, trouncing Carlisle United 9–2 the following week in what was the first of nine successive victories. They would suffer only one further defeat before the season's close and in racking up 123 goals would go on to win the title by a country mile.

Halifax Town: Rayner, Allsop, Green, France, Ruecroft, Mycock, Jowett, Massey, Fisher, England, Hazeldine.
Doncaster Rovers: Ferguson, Swallow, Corbett, Stirland, Bycroft, McFarlane, Kirkaldie, Thompson, Jordan, Todd, Maddison.
Referee: P. Snape (Manchester)
Attendance: 8,814

Match to Remember 17　　　　　　　　10 January 1953
Halifax Town 3   Cardiff City 1
FA Cup third round

When people talk about famous FA Cup upsets, they tend to pick out the usual crop; Walsall's defeat of mighty Arsenal in 1932–33, Colchester United's 3–2 win over Leeds United in 1970–71 and non-League Hereford United's shock replay victory over Newcastle United the following season to name but a few. But rarely – if ever – mentioned in the same breath are those achieved by the vintage Halifax Town side of 1952–53, when they overcame not one, but two First Division clubs on the way to the fifth round.

It was indeed a remarkable feat by Gerry Henry's side, though it has to be said, they were enjoying better fortunes this term in the League, and by the time of this third-round tie with Cardiff City, were lying seventh in the Third Division North. Yet they were perhaps a shade fortunate to have progressed beyond even the first round in the FA Cup, having needed a replay to see off the challenge of Lancashire Combination side Ashton United and being made to work hard for victory in round two by Southport, despite the 4–2 scoreline.

Cardiff City, while not one of the game's giant clubs, had just returned to the top flight under Cyril Spiers after an absence of 23 years, but lying 18th were fighting a relegation battle. Not noted travellers, they found themselves making the trip to back to Yorkshire only a week after losing at Sheffield Wednesday.

Naturally, a larger than average crowd was expected at The Shay, and in readiness for the game crash barriers were erected and the capacity raised to 35,000. However, the attendance figure fell short of that by some way, with the Cardiff supporters seemingly not 'up for t'cup', as the Welsh club returned most of the 500 tickets allocated them. Perhaps many Bluebirds fans were foreboded; perhaps others felt the game would be a formality.

Having being entertained by the Moderna Brass Band before kick-off, the supporters settled down to watch a rip-roaring performance by the Shaymen which belied their lowlier status. Quicker to the ball, they forced the issue and created a number of chances, notably George Holt's shot which hit the post, and it seemed only a matter of time before they took the lead. The goal duly came in the 22nd minute with Holt the creator, opening up to Derek Priestley, who drove home a fast shot which left Cardiff the 'keeper Ron Howells helpless.

Cardiff awoke from their slumber and created chances of their own, their best of the half coming six minutes before the break following a free-kick awarded just outside the box. Billy Baker took it but Ken Chisholm's header was just wide. They shuffled their pack after the break with Wilf Grant switching to centre-forward and two minutes in he had the ball in the net, only to be ruled offside. Still, the warning signs were there for the Shaymen, and they managed to keep their goal in tact thanks to a superb save from McCormick who denied Chisholm from point blank range. Town's reserve 'keeper, in the side due to injury to John Savage, also made telling saves from Grant and Derrick Sullivan.

Having survived Cardiff's onslaught, Town fashioned for themselves a second goal after 62 minutes, with Alan Hampson, back in the side following a knee injury, setting up Eddie

FA Cup giant-killers 1952–53. From left to right: Derek Priestley, Andy Geddes, Eric Williams, John Savage, Des Frost, Jackie Moss, Jack Bickerstaffe.

Murphy, who hit a first time rising shot that looked a goal all the way.

At this point, Cardiff did not look too deterred, but while they sought to retrieve the game, they found Edgar Packard a tower of strength in the Town rearguard, and behind him, McCormick was having the game of his life. But their hearts sank when Town grabbed a third with eight minutes remaining courtesy of Jimmy Moncrieff, who, having taken a return pass from Priestley, got the better of Stan Montgomery and gave Howells no chance from close range.

Cardiff managed a reply from Baker two minutes later, a stunning drive from almost 30 yards, but it was no more than a consolation. Town, in fact, had the ball in the net once more through Holt, though his effort was ruled out for an earlier infringement. Moments later, the final whistle signalled the cue for a mass invasion of home supporters, who mobbed their heroes and looked forward to another possible big draw in round four.

Halifax Town: McCormick, Williams, Cox, Geddes, Packard, Moss, Hampson, Holt, Moncrieff, Murphy, Priestley.
Cardiff City: Howells, Sullivan, Sherwood, Baker, Montgomery, Blair, Nugent, Grant, Chisholm, Mansell, Edwards.
Referee: F.L. Overton (Derby)
Attendance: 23,162

Match to Remember 18   31 January 1953
Halifax Town 1   Stoke City 0
FA Cup fourth round

By its very nature, the fourth round tie with Stoke City was bigger than the match with Cardiff, yet Town clearly fancied their chances. When manager Gerry Henry sent George Holt on a spying mission the week before, his report suggested that with the right attitude and application, the Shaymen could spring yet another shock despite witnessing an emphatic 5–1 win for Stoke over League-leaders West Bromwich Albion. Holt would prove correct with his prediction.

Stoke City had moved into the fourth round themselves courtesy of a narrow 2–1 victory over Wrexham, but they were a side, like Cardiff, struggling in the First Division. Not only that, but their resounding win over West Brom had come at a price with injury to goalkeeper Dennis Herod forcing manager Frank Taylor, in his first season in charge, to throw in Frank Elliott for his first-team debut having being signed the previous Tuesday from Swansea Town. For the Shaymen, manager Gerry Henry made only one change from the side which had defeated Cardiff, with Des Frost coming into at an unaccustomed outside-right position in place of injured Alan Hampson.

Once again, the town of Halifax was gripped in Cup fever, and the ground record was smashed when 35,621 squeezed into The Shay. They witnessed a classic Cup match, but one spoilt somewhat by a strong breeze which blew from one end of the ground to the other. When Stoke won the toss, they elected to play with the elements in their favour and had most of the early play, forcing a succession of corners and going close with efforts from Harry Oscroft and Don Whiston, while Frank Bowyer's shot tested Dave McCormick.

But Town did offer a warning to the Potters when Eddie Murphy collected a ball on the run and shot narrowly wide, and three minutes before the interval, they scored the vital goal. A classic it certainly was not, but Derek Priestley's strike from almost on the goalline would prove decisive. The architect was Jackie Moss, who did well to lift a high centre across from the by-line and, though Elliott got his hands to Jimmy Moncrieff's header, he could only knock the ball down, and in a brief goalmouth scramble, Priestley drove the ball home.

Before the break, Town almost scored again following a free-kick, and the confidence instilled into the players served them well in the second half as they swung the ball around. There were a series of exciting exchanges, though it was Town who came closest to scoring next. Andy Geddes brought out a good save from Elliot, Priestley's cross worried the Stoke goalkeeper, while Eddie Murphy saw his corner hit the bar. At the other end, however, Town were indebted to McCormick who made a great full-length save to deny Oscroft, the closest the visitors came to getting back on level terms.

Town held out for another sensational victory, and amid scenes which greeted those following the upset of Cardiff, hundreds of supporters ran on the pitch upon the final whistle to chair the Town players off the pitch. Manager Gerry Henry was full of praise for his players, saying, 'Give the lads credit for their team work and confidence, in themselves. We shall be in there trying and fighting next time.'

Halifax Town: McCormick, Williams, Cox, Geddes, Packard, Moss, Frost, Holt, Moncrieff, Murphy, Priestley.
Stoke City: Elliott, Doyle, McCue, Mountford, Thomson, Sellars, Malkin, Bowyer, Whiston, Martin, Oscroft.
Referee: T.W. Glendenning (Sunderland)
Attendance: 35,621

Match to Remember 19   *14 February 1953*
Halifax Town 0   Tottenham Hotspur 3
FA Cup fifth round

Despite being handed a fifth successive home tie, Halifax Town's glorious 1952–53 FA Cup run ended at the hand of Tottenham Hotspur, though in that there was no shame. After all, Spurs were, along with Manchester United, Arsenal and Wolverhampton Wanderers, one of the major forces in the game at the time, having been League champions as recently as

1950–51 when their famous push-and-run style of play, instilled by manager Arthur Rowe, took their rivals by surprise and saw them romp to the title just a year after winning the Second Division Championship.

Spurs may not have been enjoying the best of fortunes this term, but they were still a force to be reckoned with, their side containing six England internationals in goalkeeper Ted Ditchburn, skipper Bill Nicholson, left-back Arthur Willis, inside-forward Eddie Baily, outside-left Les Medley and current right full-back incumbent Alf 'The General' Ramsey.

The interest in the game was intense, so much so that the threat of a strike by the amateur players of the Halifax & District AFL caused the cancellation of that weekend's local programme, though it is unlikely that it would have gone ahead anyway after a fall of heavy snow, which now posed a great threat to the match at The Shay. Two days before the game, there was a four inch covering over the pitch and on the eve of the game, another flurry caused further problems. Work began on clearing the pitch – the lines were eventually marked out in thick blue dye – and just before 10.30am an official announcement that the game was definitely on brought a rapidly increasing flow of supporters to the ground to help shift the piles of snow. By kick-off the gate had been swelled to 36,885, not only a Shay record but also the biggest gate for any sporting event in Halifax, never to be broken.

Gerry Henry's side showed a couple of changes from the side which defeated Stoke, with Harry Darbyshire taking the place of inside-forward George Holt, who had suffered an eye injury in the previous week's victory over Grimsby, and Alan Hampson coming in at outside-right to allow Des Frost to lead the line after flu victim Jimmy Moncrieff had been ruled out.

Spurs manager Arthur Rowe had been quoted in the run-up to the match that, 'We shall treat Halifax Town as if they are the League champions,' and the first half was an evenly contested affair with both goalkeepers busy, though neither having to make telling saves. The Shaymen tried to play an open game, but with the blanket of snow a handicap, it was the visitors who perhaps just shaded things, with the corner count six to two in their favour.

In the second period, Len Duquemin served a warning to Town when he brought a good save out of McCormick, then minutes later Baily blazed over the bar when it seemed easier to hit the target. But Spurs began to turn the screw and after 56 minutes they broke the deadlock. Baily transferred the ball inside to Les Bennett and from 10 yards he found the roof of the net. There was little hiding Spurs' relief, but the goal did not necessarily break Town's resolve. Des Frost nearly equalised with a shot on the run which produced a magnificent save from Ditchburn, but thereafter it was the visitors who took control. Len Bennett released Duquemin, who calmly stroked the ball past McCormick

Action from the Town v Spurs fifth-round FA Cup tie. Here, England 'keeper Ted Ditchburn gathers the ball, while Harry Clarke fends off Town centre-forward Des Frost.

for their second goal in the 62nd minute, and the same player was unlucky to have another effort ruled out a minute later after Medley had strayed offside.

Spurs, however, were not to be denied their third, and nine minutes from the end Bennett compounded Town's misery when he dashed in to net from close range after McCormick had failed to hold Sonny Walters's shot. There, Town's hopes ended, but they could take pride in putting up such a gallant fight.

Spurs would see off Second Division Birmingham City at the third attempt in the next round before bowing out to eventual Cup winners Blackpool in the semi-finals. Meanwhile, Halifax Town were left to concentrate on League affairs in front of more regular crowds, for while the huge attendance for the Tottenham game had brought record receipts of £4,889, their next home fixture with Wrexham drew a crowd of just over 6,000.

Halifax Town: McCormick, Williams, Cox, Geddes, Packard, Moss, Hampson, Darbyshire, Frost, Murphy, Priestley.
Tottenham Hotspur: Ditchburn, Ramsey, Willis, Nicholson, Clarke, Brittan, Walters, Bennett, Duquemin, Baily, Medley.
Referee: F.L. Overton (Derby)
Attendance: 36,885

Match to Remember 20   3 December 1955
Halifax Town 6   Bradford 0
Division Three North

Prior to the start of World War Two, the most goals Halifax Town had scored in a League game was six, a feat achieved on three occasions, in 6–2 wins over Southport, Hartlepool United and New Brighton. Apart from a similar result against Lincoln City during the war, the Shaymen had not managed to score as many goals again until the 1955–56 season. That they managed it when they did, following three successive defeats, was a surprise, though nevertheless a welcome one, made all the more sweeter as it came over local rival Bradford.

Both sides were struggling that term, with Town's 2–1 defeat at Rochdale on Boxing Day leaving them 22nd, and Bradford just two places higher despite impressive home wins over Stockport County and Wrexham in their two matches which preceded this Shay encounter.

Managerless following the departure of former Town supremo Jack Breedon back in October, the visitors found the Shaymen in irresistible form and were on the back foot almost from the kick-off, and a goal down after 13 minutes. Town left-back Bert Ferguson made a raid down the left flank which took him to the by-line, from where he pulled the ball back to leave Clive Baker with what appeared an easy chance. However, he missed his kick only for Alan Hampson, following up, to bang the ball into the net.

Baker made amends in the 23rd minute, arriving to power home a shot beyond goalkeeper Brian Taylor which went in off the far post before the best goal of the game was scored three minutes later by Bill Watkinson, who took the ball from George Griffiths and weaved his way into the box before hitting it into the corner of the net.

Town continued to press, and Capel saw his shot cleared off the line by Geoff Hudson and Taylor was forced to save a close range effort from Watkinson, but these chances only served to act as a warning to the visitors, and a minute before the break, Bradford conceded their fourth. Capel was the orchestrator, carving out a lovely opening and slipping a through pass for Baker, who lofted the ball into the roof of the net for his second goal.

Bradford showed some sign of improvement after the break, but it was the Shaymen who looked the more dangerous. Tommy Bell saw his free-kick diverted over the bar by Jeff Suddards and in the 69th minute Town went five goals up when Baker completed his hat-trick following Lonsdale's corner, forcing the ball home through a ruck of players. And there was time for a sixth, scored by Hampson after 76 minutes, when he took advantage of a wilting Bradford defence to hammer home Lonsdale's left-wing cross.

Bradford had the chance to gain a consolation but Colin Whitaker fired over the bar from a free-kick, while Town went close to adding a seventh, Capel's solo run being ended by a hasty challenge by Frank Hindle.

This result went into the record books as Town's best in the League and would be matched only by Alan Ball's side in November 1976 with victory over Doncaster Rovers.

Halifax Town: Johnson, Griffiths, Ferguson, Watson, Harris, Bell, Hampson, Baker, Watkinson, Capel, Lonsdale.

Bradford: Taylor, Suddards, Hudson, Pickard, Hindle, Roberts, Brickley, Ward, Redfearn, Brocklehurst, Whitaker.

Referee: L. Howley (Middlesbrough)
Attendance: 8,421

Match to Remember 21   *8 September 1958*
Halifax Town 2   Southampton 0
Division Three

The creation of Divisions Three and Four in 1958, which replaced the two regionalised divisions, placed a bigger burden on many of the poorer clubs who now had to make longer journeys for away trips. But for the players and spectators it was a novel and exciting time, given as it did, the chance for the northern sides to pit their wits against their southern counterparts on a regular basis.

Having qualified for the new Third Division, Harry Hooper's side initially did quite well and competed well against the more affluent clubs on the back of important wins such as this against a much-fancied Southampton side with plenty of resources, as one would expect from a club which regularly drew five figure gates at The Dell.

This game was set for a Monday evening and a 6.15pm kick-off, but Town went into it looking for their first victory since the opening day when a Mick Priest hat-trick had given them a 3–2 success at Chesterfield. Since then they had gathered only one further point from a home draw with Notts County and had slipped to defeat at the hands of Bournemouth in their last match at The Shay. For their part, Southampton had failed to build on their sensational 6–1 opening day victory at Mansfield Town, but nevertheless, had suffered only one defeat from their first five matches. The Shaymen would have to be on their guard.

Hooper's instructions to his side revolved around his keenness to attack, and with his side playing towards the Hunger Hill end in the first half, the Shaymen could have been a goal up within minutes of the kick off when Gordon Rose's drive was saved by goalkeeper John Christie, and Stan Lonsdale saw his header diverted by the head of Ron Davies. But they made the breakthrough in the 18th minute when Rose delivered an angled cross and Priest dived to power a bullet-like header past Christie.

That proved to be the only goal of the first half, and for a 15 minute period in the second half Southampton found themselves down to 10 men as left-back Tom Traynor had to go off to receive attention after clashing with Town's Andy McCall. But despite the numerical advantage, the Shaymen failed to capitalise, and though clearly the better side even after Traynor had returned to the field, they did not score their second goal until two minutes from time. Goalscorer Priest turned provider, making the opening for Conway Smith, who sent a low ball past Cheshire.

Victory gave Town the confidence to inflict on Swindon Town their first away defeat in twelve away matches in their next match while a rampant Southampton were putting six past Hull City, before the sides met for the return at The Dell the following Wednesday, where the Shaymen's earlier 2–0 victory was put into perspective as the Saints ran out 5–1 winners in front of 16,493.

Halifax Town: Johnson, Roscoe, Lonsdale, Tilley, South, Lorenson, McCall, Smith, Blackburn, Priest, Rose.
Southampton: Cheshire, Davies, Traynor, Birch, Page, Stevens, Paine, Mulgrew, Livesey, Hoskins, Sydenham.
Referee: H.V.A. Stott (Boston)
Attendance: 6,288

Match to Remember 22   16 November 1961
Halifax Town 1   OFK Belgrade 1
Friendly

It may only have been a friendly, but the occasion, if not the opposition, made it a match to remember. For this was the game in which Halifax Town's new floodlights, funded by a mystery benefactor, were officially switched on just before kick-off by Alan Hardaker, secretary of the Football League.

OFK Belgrade were the first Continental opponents hosted by the Shaymen, but had the Town directors got their way then Real Madrid would have had that honour. Inspired by successful events which had seen then League champions Burnley provide the opposition when Oldham Athletic switched on their lights, and the Czech national side turning out against Bradford at the switch-on of the lights at Park Avenue, their bid to

Gerry Priestley, who had a fine match against OFK Belgrade but had the misfortune to miss a penalty.

attract the Spanish giants floundered due to the inability to guarantee sufficient funds, so they turned instead to one of the leading Yugoslav sides. OFK promised to come for much less money than Real Madrid and the admission price for the game thus became far less than the directors had budgeted for.

The erection of the four floodlight pylons began on 16 October 1961 and took three weeks to complete, and though the club looked forward to the official switch-on, the lights had first been in use for the visit of Peterborough United five days before Belgrade were due, a game won 2–1 by the Shaymen.

OFK Belgrade, previously known as Belgrade Sports Club, were four times Yugoslavian champions and three times winners of the national Cup, but were at the time of this game living in the shadows of the Red Star and Partizan clubs. Nevertheless, they included in their ranks six internationals, the most famous being Sava Antic, the skipper who had won a gold medal at the 1960 Olympic Games in Rome. Their party were met by a delegation of club officials, including manager Harry Hooper and chairman Harry Taylor, at Halifax Railway Station before enjoying a tour of the Mackintosh sweet factory.

The match, a scheduled 7.30pm kick-off, was an entertaining affair, the tone set by the awarding of a penalty for Town early on when Gavric brought down Ken Smith. But Gerry Priestley saw his spot kick saved by Srboljub Krivokuca, the only blot on a fine performance by Town's flying winger.

The visitors then took advantage by taking the lead after 17 minutes, outside-right Samardic making the most of Phil Roscoe's mis-kicked clearance from Popov's forward pass. But eight minutes later, Town were back on level terms with a brilliantly taken goal by Frank Large following a short chip by Brian Redfearn

But there, the scoring ended, and while it was generally felt that Town had shaded the first half, Belgrade, who had the technically better players, controlled things after the break, though it was a half which did not live up to the excitement of the first. Peter Tilley struggled through the match when clearly not fit and the *Halifax Courier* reporter Jack Dunnill had every right to question why manager Harry Hooper never involved substitute Mike Burgess.

Halifax Town: Knowles, Stanley, Roscoe, Tilley, South, Harrison, Priestley, Barnett, Smith, Large, Redfearn.
OFK Belgrade: Krivokuca, Milovanic, Gavric, Popov, Sijakovic, Antic, Samardic, Mildsev, Mladenovic, Cebiaac, Skoblar.
Referee: A.E. Ellis (Halifax)
Attendance: 10,005

A second friendly with Continental opposition was set for The Shay on 6 December 1961, only for the match to be postponed due to a fall of six inches of snow.

Match to Remember 23 29 September 1962
Halifax Town 4   Swindon Town 3
Division Three

In a season that ended in relegation to the Third Division, there were not many highs for the Shaymen during 1962–63. But long after this victory over Swindon Town, the fans would still be talking about it. And not without good reason. With just 20 minutes remaining the Shaymen looked to be heading for their third home defeat as the visitors held a three-goal lead, only to hit back in spectacular fashion to turn the game on its head.

That Town should beat Swindon at all, let along in such a remarkable manner, was welcome enough. By winning only three of their opening twelve matches, they were lying 23rd at kick-off time, with Swindon sixth and laying claim to a promotion spot, having extended an unbeaten run to seven matches with a 3–0 win over Wrexham. They were, indeed, a useful side, among their ranks the likes of John Trollope, Bobby Woodruff, Ernie Hunt – later of donkey-kick goal fame with Coventry City – and a young Mike Summerbee, a winger who would enjoy legendary status with Manchester City and win eight England caps.

Swindon dominated the first half, taking the lead after only 10 minutes when the Town defence stood still while Cliff Jackson calmly headed home Keith Morgan's free-kick. Twelve minutes later, they doubled their lead through Hunt's penalty, awarded when Town 'keeper David Knowles brought down Jack Smith following an error by the usually dependable Alex South. And by half-time, they had scored a third through Smith and at this point Swindon looked as if they would stroll to an easy two points, having outplayed Town in every department.

Town coach Don McEvoy changed things around at half-time by switching Mike Burgess to centre-forward in place of the unhappy John Brier, and with the visitors seemingly happy to sit back on their lead, Barry Tait and Willie Carlin began to exploit the extra space afforded them in midfield.

Still, with 20 minutes to go, the game looked a lost cause for the Shaymen, and indeed, some supporters were making for the exits. Then suddenly, Swindon cracked. Carlin gave Barry Tait the chance to go through with a lovely weighted pass and the inside-forward made no mistake. A mere consolation? Or was there more to follow?

There were 10 minutes left on the clock when Town further reduced the arrears, Brian Redfearn and Burgess combining to cause panic in the Swindon defence, and there was Tait to slip the ball home. With time running out, the Shaymen now threw everything at the visitors in the hope of salvaging a game that had been surely lost, and with two minutes left Tait made a name for himself by scoring his and Town's third goal following good approach work by Dave Worthington, Brier and Redfearn.

With Town having grasped the nettle and Swindon clearly rocked, the home side now went in search of a winner, and with the referee looking at his watch, they got it. Redfearn and Burgess won a midfield scramble for the ball, then suddenly Redfearn was galloping away towards the Swindon goal, hammering an angled drive in one movement past the hapless goalkeeper Mike Turner for a sensational winner. As the ball hit the back of the net there were amazing scenes as the players mobbed Redfearn and supporters danced with delight on the terraces, and seconds later, the referee's final whistle signalled the end of the match, and maximum points for the Shaymen.

To their credit, Bert Head's Swindon side put this game behind them to defeat Bristol Rovers in their next game and continued in their quest for promotion, which they would attain as runners-up to Northampton Town, while the Shaymen's fortunes were in total contrast. Victory here did not inspire the side, and they would win only a further five matches before the close of the season, one which was disrupted by the bitter winter which prevented Town playing at home for three months. They hit bottom spot at the beginning of April and remained there, with relegation confirmed with five matches still to play.

Halifax Town: Knowles, Stredder, Roscoe, Burgess, South, Harrison, Worthington, Tait, Brier, Carlin, Redfearn.
Swindon Town: Turner, Wollen, Trollope, Morgan, Owen, Woodruff, Summerbee, Hunt, Smith, Jackson, D'Arcy.
Referee: K. Howkey (Middlesbrough)
Attendance: 3,123

Match to Remember 24   21 March 1964
Halifax Town 2   Bradford 1
Division Four

When Halifax Town lost 4–0 at Lincoln City on 8 February 1964 it was a result that was in keeping with their recent form. It was their third consecutive defeat and with only one win from their last 11 League outings Don McEvoy's side were left 21st in the table and looking certain re-election candidates. Nor did the goalless home draw with Gillingham which followed it suggest a transformation in fortunes was in the offing. However, a record six consecutive wins later, which surpassed the run of five straight wins of 1956–57, and the picture looked completely different. Town had moved up 12th and were looking to extend their winning streak. What better, then, than a local derby in which to attempt to make it an unprecedented seven wins on the bounce?

Not that it would be easy. Such matches rarely are, and nothing had separated the sides at Park Avenue back in November when they played out a scintillating 4–4 draw. Bradford were themselves struggling then, but their own recent good form which had seen them too pull clear of the re-election zone now made for an intriguing encounter.

The Town board elected for a 6.30pm kick-off so as no to clash with Halifax RLFC's home game with Hull Kingston Rovers, but overnight rain which had removed the last of lying snow had left the pitch a mess and threatened to force a cancellation. The groundstaff worked hard to make it playable and referee Harper gave the game the go-ahead late on, though conditions were very trying.

The Shaymen did indeed extend their winning streak, but the game was not without incident or controversy, though there was no sign of the fireworks to come as the first half drew to a close. But then the game was lit up by an astonishing goal from full-back Walt Bingley, whose 41st minute free-kick 45 yards out, caught Bradford goalkeeper John Hardie too far off his line and the ball whistled past him into the net.

Three minutes into the second half, the Park Avenue outfit levelled the scores when a long cross from Geoff Thomas was headed home by Jim Fryatt. But their relief was short-lived, for just five minutes later, Gerry Lightowler was sent off for a crude tackle on the edge of the area on Archie Taylor, and it was compounded less than 60 seconds later when Bingley and Taylor combined down the right flank for the latter to cross to the near post where Brian Westlake headed home the would-be winner.

In the 59th minute, the Shaymen had the opportunity to extend their lead when Dennis Fidler was fouled in the box, but though he dusted himself down, Town's left-winger put his penalty over the bar, a miss which led to an exciting finish as Bradford pushed for an equaliser. In the closing stages, Town were indebted to 'keeper Peter Downsborough who pulled off two reflex saves from Ron Bird and Kevin Hector and they held out for a memorable victory.

Town's winning run came to an end with a 1–1 draw at Hartlepool United in their next match, though two further victories that followed improved still their League position before they suffered a shock 2–0 home reversal to Doncaster Rovers. But their run of seven successive League wins would remain a club record, threatened only by Mickey Bullock's side of 1982–83 which strung together six straight wins.

Halifax Town: Downsborough, Bingley, Roscoe, Jackson, South, Harrison, Taylor, Bartlett, Westlake, Carlin, Fidler.
Bradford: Hardie, Thomas, Lightowler, Cook, McCalman, Flynn, Hector, Fryatt, Atkinson, Spratt, Bird.
Referee: R. Harper (Sheffield)
Attendance: 4,924

Match to Remember 25 *10 January 1967*
Halifax Town 7   Bishop Auckland 0
FA Cup second round replay

History shows that smaller clubs, generally, only get one real shot at overcoming bigger opposition – Town's well-earned draws with Stoke City in January 1969 and December 2001 being the prelude to resounding replay defeats readily spring to mind – and so it was in the FA Cup competition of 1966–67 when Halifax Town took on Bishop Auckland. Fortunately, for once, it was the Shaymen who handed out a lesson in finishing as they rattled in seven goals to match the tally run up by their 1938 predecessors, though, by not conceding a goal, the result went into the record books as Halifax Town's biggest win at The Shay in a major competition.

50 MATCHES TO REMEMBER

Town had moved into the second round of the FA Cup following a memorable extra-time victory over Doncaster Rovers at Belle Vue, and of course, had they defeated Bishop Auckland in the original tie, such a result here would never have happened. As it was, the Shaymen held out for a goalless draw on their snowbound pitch and brought the Northern League side back to The Shay for the replay three days later.

No matter that Bishop Auckland were a team of part-timers. This match captured the public's imagination, so much so that the Halifax Corporation Passenger Transport Department ran special buses to the ground from Brighouse, Illingworth, Wheatley and Siddal, and the gate figure of 14,297 had only been bettered once since the defeat to Spurs in 1953.

This Bishop Auckland side was one managed and coached by a certain Lawrie McMenemy, who, nine years later, would lead Southampton to a shock FA Cup Final victory over Tommy Docherty's exciting Manchester United team. If the winning of the Cup then was the highlight of his time in football, then this 7–0 hammering by Halifax Town was surely one of his lowest.

Not that Town had things all their own way. The visitors, in fact, had caused Town a few anxious moments early in the first half as Bill Roughley's shot hit the outside angle of the bar and post, and before Barry Hutchinson had turned in Bill Atkins' centre into the net in the 36th minute, Jim Smith had been forced to clear the ball off the line after goalkeeper Malcolm White had been beaten by a bullet header from Tommy O'Connor.

With half an hour remaining of this match that Hutchinson goal was the only one that separated the sides, but Bishop Auckland soon began to tire, their exertions over four matches in overcoming Blyth Spartans in the previous round taking their toll. Once the Shaymen, who were playing in an unfamiliar all-tangerine strip they had worn for the first time at Bishop Auckland, had doubled their lead courtesy of Hutchinson's second, smashing a left-wing cross from Phil McCarthy cross on the hour, the floodgates opened.

Atkins climbed to head home in the 67th minute after Jeff Lee and McCarthy had combined down the left flank, and a fourth goal arrived two minutes later when Atkins released speed merchant Archie Taylor, who made no mistake. With the tie as good as over, Town just kept coming. Parks scored the fifth off another Lee-McCarthy move in the 72nd minute, Taylor scored his second, a header off another McCarthy cross 10 minutes later, and there was still time for Parks to slide in for his second after goalkeeper Kirkbride had saved from Hutchinson when it seemed the ball was going out for a corner.

Town manager Vic Metcalfe was full of praise for his side's efforts, saying, '[They] have done everything I have asked from them and they want to thank the crowd for the encouragement they gave. It was magnificent.'

As was Town's performance in the third-round tie with Bristol City. They would bow out of the competition, but not before taking the Second Division side to a replay at Ashton Gate after The Shay game, played in front of another handsome 15,591, had ended 1–1.

Barry Hutchinson, who grabbed two goals in the 7–0 win over Bishop Auckland.

213

Halifax Town: White, Russell, Bodell, Smith, Holt, J. Lee, Taylor, Hutchinson, Parks, Atkins, McCarthy.
Bishop Auckland: Kirkbride, Thursby, M. Barker, B. Storey, Siddle, K. Storey, McClelland, O'Connor, Brown, Roughley, Connor.
Referee: J.A. Warburton (Manchester)
Attendance: 14,297

Match to Remember 26   25 January 1969
Stoke City 1   Halifax Town 1
FA Cup fourth round

Bill Carter of the *Halifax Courier* described Town's performance in this game as their 'greatest display in years' and those who witnessed it would not want to argue. For though a Fourth Division side, albeit one heading for the Third, the Shaymen more than matched their illustrious First Division counterparts, so much so that many Town supporters came away from the Victoria Ground wondering why their team had not actually won.

Town's route to the fourth round had seen them fend off the challenges of Bilston, Crewe Alexandra – after a replay – and Swansea Town, and Stoke City now represented attractive opposition. Though not the biggest name in English football, they were a useful side, having been promoted to the First Division in 1963 and in the throws of their golden period under manager Tony Waddington, one which would see them reach the FA Cup semi-finals in 1971 and win the League Cup the following year, their first major honour.

Included in their ranks were a couple of star players. In goal was England international and World Cup winner Gordon Banks, soon to be hailed as the best in the world, while in the forward line was George Eastham, with 19 England caps to his name but famed for taking on the Football League in 1961 over 'freedom of contract' when he sought a move from Newcastle United to Arsenal.

Stoke had progressed to the fourth round having negotiated a tricky tie at Fourth Division York City and they now prepared to meet the Shaymen for the first time since the FA Cup fourth round meeting of 1953. Town won that day, and went mightily close to winning this.

Spurred on by a massive following of around 1,500 supporters, they more than matched their First Division opponents, with young centre-half Chris Nicholl, the game's outstanding player, in no way overawed at playing in front of a 30,000 gate.

In a keenly contested match, most of the action in the first period, as expected, took place in Town's half, with Alex Smith the far busier of the two goalkeepers. He was in great form, however, proving his worth by making a memorable save from Harry Burrows, tipping his 25–yard shot over the bar and showing a safe pair of hands. But when he was beaten by Eastham's effort from close range, Nicholl appeared from nowhere to snuff out the danger. Nicholl, in fact, came closest to scoring for Town at the

50 MATCHES TO REMEMBER

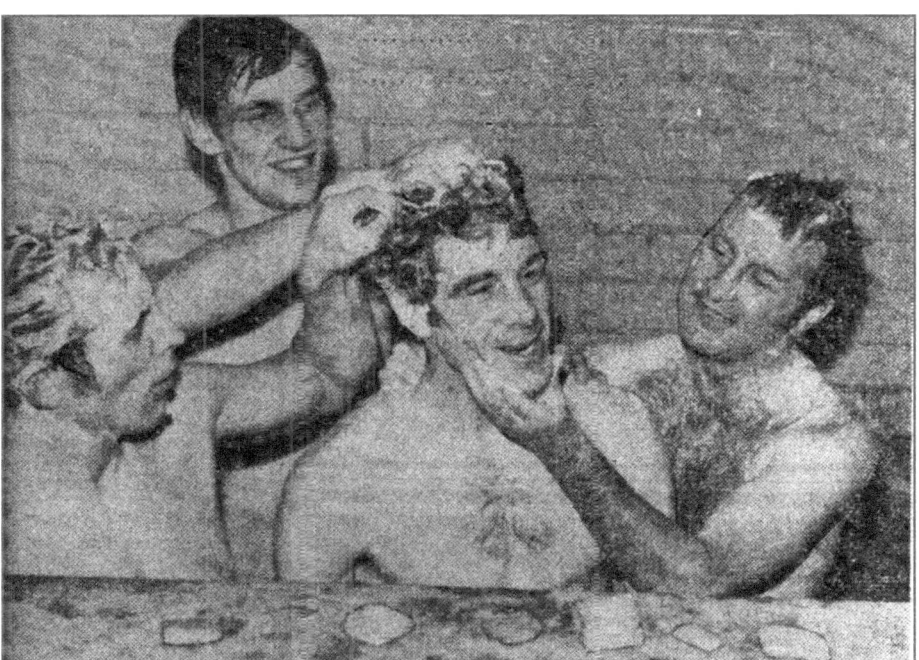

Getting scrubbed up for the Stoke City FA Cup tie are (from left) Ian Lawther, Chris Nicholl, Les Massie and Mark Pearson.

other end, forcing Banks to tip over his header, and shooting just wide following Phil McCarthy's corner in the 36th minute.

In the second half, Stoke full-back John Marsh twice tried his luck from distance as it seemed that would be the only way to breach the determined Town defence. But when Stoke skipper Peter Dobing headed home from close range following a corner with 10 minutes left, it looked as if Town's efforts had been in vain. That was until Nicholl back-headed McCarthy's long throw for Les Massie to score a typical poacher's goal with Banks isolated. There were seven minutes remaining, but still enough time for Town to fashion two more opportunities as they now sought a winner and deem a replay unnecessary. Firstly, Ian Lawther headed the ball over the bar off Tony Flower's cross, probably the better of the two late chances, and with time running out, Massie found himself with an opening on the left, only for Banks to thwart his shot across goal.

Three days later in the replay at The Shay, Terry Conroy's second half brace added to the goal scored by Burrows' in the first period gave Stoke a 3–0 win and a trip to Chelsea in round five, though there was a feeling that it so easily could – and perhaps should – have been Town.

Stoke City: Banks, Marsh, Elder, Skeels, Bloor, Bernard, Eastham, Herd, Conroy, Dobing, Burrows.
Halifax Town: Smith, Burgin, Meagan, Pickering, Nicholl, Wallace, Flower, Massie, Lawther, Shawcross, McCarthy.
Referee: R. Tinkler (Boston)
Attendance: 30,109

Match to Remember 27   8 May 1969
Halifax Town 1   Rochdale 0
Division Four

Halifax Town's 4–0 home defeat to York City on 11 January 1969, which left them sitting 11th in the Fourth Division table, did not give any inclination as to the impending glories that the club would achieve four months later. But by stringing together an unbeaten run of 17 matches in the League, Alan Ball's super-fit side put themselves on the fringes of the promotion race. The goalless draw at Colchester United in the last of those left the Shaymen lying sixth, but at that stage they were one of nine clubs which harboured hopes of a top-four finish, though Doncaster Rovers were clear favourites for the title having opened up a five-point lead at the top.

Town's unbeaten run ended at Exeter City, and they would also slip to defeat less than a week later at Rochdale, whose own victory in that match strengthened their promotion ambitions. However, the Shaymen had chance to exact revenge over their rivals from over the Pennines just two weeks later, and having gained three points from their two intervening matches with Aldershot and York City, they went into the match knowing that victory at The Shay would ensure promotion for the first time in the club's history.

A frozen pitch had caused this original fixture to be postponed in mid-March, but now with

Les Massie (left) about to head home the only goal against Rochdale which clinched promotion from the Fourth Division.

both sides in with a chance of going up, interest in the game was intense, with over 17,000 cramming into The Shay to watch a nerve-tangling match, refereed superbly by top official John Hunting of Leicester.

Rochdale were dogged opponents, determined to thwart the Shaymen who, nevertheless, contrived a couple of decent chances in the first half. Les Massie struck a post following a melee after Bob Wallace had delayed his shot off an Ian Lawther cross, and Lawther himself went close with a header and a shot which Rochdale goalkeeper Chris Harker tipped over the bar. Chris Nicholl, too, who would have his nose broken for his pains during the match, headed wide from Dave Shawcross's free-kick. For the visitors, Jenkins fired a 25 yarder just wide.

The Shaymen continued to do most of the pressing in the second half, with Shawcross going close with a header which just cleared the bar. But the goal which defined a season came in the 76th minute courtesy of Les Massie, his 15th of the campaign. Phil McCarthy flung over a cross which asked questions of goalkeeper Harker, but he elected not to come for the ball, and as it dropped beyond the far post, Lammie Robertson moved to meet it. But though he failed to make contact, Massie was lurking behind him, and with an angled header that sped between Harker and the near post, he scored the goal that returned Halifax Town to the Third Division after an absence of six years.

Upon the final whistle hundreds of supporters invaded the pitch, and many were still outside the players' entrance celebrating after their heroes had made for home. And in a season which had also seen the heroic performance at Stoke, Bill Carter of the *Halifax Courier* now described victory over Rochdale as 'probably the most memorable night in the club's history.' Though typically the last word went to manager Alan Ball, who said, 'When I took over in November 1967 and predicted that we should eventually win promotion, people laughed. I know that. But we have done so in a season and half since that time.'

Town would finish the season as runners-up to Doncaster – as in 1934–35 – while Rochdale would go up in third place and Bradford City in fourth.

Halifax Town: Smith, Burgin, Meagan, Pickering, Nicholl, Wallace, Robertson, Massie, Lawther, Shawcross, McCarthy.
Rochdale: Harker, Smith, Ryder, Leech, Parry, Ashworth, Whitehead, Rudd (Buck 82 mins), Melledew, Jenkins, Butler.
Referee: J. Hunting (Leicester)
Attendance: 17,186

Match to Remember 28 16 September 1969
Halifax Town 0   Fulham 8

Division Three

'When this Fulham side really gets going, someone is going to get such a hiding.' So said Halifax Town boss Alan Ball Snr as his side prepared for this eagerly awaited clash with the Cottagers.

While the Shaymen were gaining promotion from the Fourth Division, Fulham were sliding out of the Second Division only a year after dropping out of the First. A shadow of their former glories, they were, however, still a top drawer, particularly as their side still contained the mercurial talents of the legendary Johnny Haynes, winner of 56 England caps, and whose appearance, it might be argued, was worth the admission fee itself. When the fixtures came out, the visit of Fulham was the one most Town supporters would have looked out for.

Alan Ball may have had a point, though Fulham had made only an average start to Third Division life, winning just three of their opening seven matches. At kick-off time, they were lying 12th, but only one point better off than the Shaymen, though however much of a threat they appeared to be, no one could have predicted this result.

Haynes may have been the star attraction, but it was Steve Earle who made the headlines, helping himself to five goals and thus shooting himself into the record books with the highest individual tally away from home. His first goal came after 13 minutes when he tucked away Stan Horne's pass, though the Town players felt particularly aggrieved that Dave Shawcross's attempted pass out of defence had rebounded off the referee.

The Shaymen may have felt unlucky to go behind in such a manner, and in fairness they put it behind them to carve out a few decent opportunities, though letting themselves down with poor finishing. The same could not be said be of Fulham, whose second goal came on the half-hour through Barry Lloyd. If Town thought they still had a chance in the game, a minute later their task became a daunting one when Earle chased down the middle to score Fulham's third. When Republic of Ireland international Jimmy Conway made it 4–0 from the penalty spot after he had been upended by Andy Burgin, it became a hopeless one.

A minute after the interval, Earle completed his hat-trick, charging into the box to steer home a long pass, and on the hour Conway was on hand to grab his second and Fulham's sixth. But still they were not finished. Less than 60 seconds later, Earle headed home Les Barrett's cross before completing his nap-hand in the 67th minute when he broke into the box to fire home.

With the job more than done, Johnny Haynes left the fray after 80 minutes, by which time many Town fans were leaving the ground. They had seen enough, their team having written themselves into the record books once more for all the wrong reasons.

Halifax Town: Smith, Wallace, Burgin, Lennard, Pickering, Robertson, Flower, Hill, Lawther, Shawcross, McCarthy.

Fulham: Seymour, Brown, Callaghan, Horne, Matthewson, Richardson, Conway, Lloyd, Earle, Haynes (Roberts), Barrett.

Referee: D. Laing (Penwortham, Preston)
Attendance: 5,809

Match to Remember 29 13 March 1971
Aston Villa 1   Halifax Town 1
Division Three

It said much about the calibre of George Kirby's side of 1970–71 that they could compete in the Third Division against clubs with far better pedigrees. Preston North and Fulham both set the pace that season, but Town, operating on gates that averaged less than 4,000, showed their capabilities by defeating both at The Shay, the victory over Fulham on 6 March 1971, itself a contender for Match of the Season, suggesting Town could, indeed, make a late bid for one of the two promotion places.

Their biggest challenge was still to come. Also among the frontrunners that term were Aston Villa, a huge club with a tradition not worthy of the position they now found themselves. Six times League champions, they had been a First Division club as recently as 1967 but their fall from grace had seen them relegated from Division Two in 1969–70. Still, Vic Crowe's side was expected to make an immediate challenge, and indeed, they had led the table just a month earlier.

To further illustrate the size of the task facing Kirby's side, only two weeks earlier Villa had lost to two late Martin Chivers goals in the Final of the League Cup at Wembley against Tottenham Hotspur, having defeated Manchester United over two legs in the semi-final to get there. Villa included in their side the warhorse centre-forward Andy Lochhead, and recently signed Geoff Bowder, yet it is worth stating they were fully aware of the threat posed by the Shaymen; back in November they too had fallen 2–1 at The Shay, with Town's chief destroyer being Birmingham-born centre-forward Bill Atkins.

At kick-off time, Town were lying third, just one point behind Preston and Fulham but having played more games, while Villa had one point fewer, and unsurprisingly this crucial four-pointer attracted a massive gate, the 33,522 figure made up of near enough 1,000 from Halifax, around 340 of whom travelled on the British Rail 'specials'. Town boss George Kirby was forced into making a couple of changes from the side which had beaten Fulham the previous Saturday, with Mick Buxton coming in for injured Andy Burgin, and Dave Verity, recalled from a loan spell at Drogheda, taking the place of ankle victim Phil McCarthy.

As expected, Villa dominated the game but found the Town rearguard in resolute form, with John Pickering and Tony Rhodes outstanding. But they made the breakthrough after 31 minutes when goalkeeper Alex Smith misjudged Chico Hamilton's right-wing corner and centre-half Fred Turnbull, a player who had been on loan at The Shay the previous season, was on hand to put the ball over the line.

Town, proving that they possessed flair for the major occasions, had the better of the exchanges in the second half, and in the 62nd minute they fashioned an equaliser scored by Dave Chadwick, who controlled Ian Lawther's pass, isolated two defenders and slipped a low accurate shot into the right hand corner of the net.

Bill Atkins then went close for the Shaymen, but they found themselves under the cosh in the closing stages as Villa piled on the pressure. Smith dived to keep out substitute Bruce Rioch's effort and was then forced to smother a Willie Anderson cross. And in injury time, there was a heart-stopping moment when Jeff Lee checked Hamilton in the box, only for the ref to award an indirect free-kick.

In the grand scheme of things, the 1–1 draw was a point well-earned by Town, but with Preston and Fulham both winning on

Former Northern Ireland international forward Ian Lawther, who played a crucial role when Town gained a draw at Aston Villa.

the same day it left them still playing catch-up, while Villa would fall off the pace. They would regroup the following year and win the title, and in 1980–81, 10 seasons after this mammoth fixture, would be crowned League champions while Halifax Town were being forced to apply for re-election for the third time in five years.

Aston Villa: Dunn, Bradley, Aitken, Godfrey (Rioch 50 mins), Turnbull, Tiler, McMahon, Vowden, Lochhead, Hamilton, Anderson.

Halifax Town: Smith, Lee, Buxton, Wallace, Pickering, Rhodes, Chadwick, Atkins, Lawther, Lennard, Verity.

Referee: P. Oliver (Leigh-on-Sea)
Attendance: 33,522

Match to Remember 30 *31 July 1971*
Halifax Town 2   Manchester United 1
Watney Cup first round

Sponsorship came to British soccer in the early 1970s with the advent of mini-competitions such as the Watney Invitation Cup and the Texaco Cup. The Watney Cup, as it was more simply known, had been inaugurated in 1970 and was open to the two highest scoring teams in each of the four divisions which neither qualified for Europe or gained promotion.

In 1970–71 Halifax Town had qualified for it by finishing third and scoring 74 goals – the highest total in the Third Division – along with Wrexham, who had scored 72 but finished

England legend Bobby Charlton evades this tackle from Jeff Lee, but it was the Shaymen who came out on top in this Watney Cup tie against First Division Manchester United.

ninth. Their reward was a first-round home tie with Manchester United, who themselves had finished eighth in the First Division.

It was true that United were not the force they once were, but their side still included a host of famous names, such as Bobby Charlton, the then holder of a record 106 England international caps, Scotland international striker Denis Law, and the mercurial George Best, perhaps the most famous name in world football. In an attempt to revive the former glories – United had been European Cup-winners only three years earlier – the board had appointed former Leicester City boss Frank O'Farrell as manager and this was his first competitive game in charge.

Unsurprisingly, the game captured the imagination of the supporters, with the gate of 19,965 one that has never since been bettered for any match at The Shay. It naturally included a sizeable following of Reds' supporters, many of which reaped havoc in the town centre both before and after the match. Also in attendance were the BBC television cameras, ready to capture the action for the return of *Match of the Day* that evening, with commentary provided by Barry Davies.

With an experimental 35-yard offside law in place, the game itself was made more interesting when the Shaymen took the lead after only three minutes. Attacking the bus garage end, Dave Lennard was upended on the right flank by Dave Sadler and Dave Chadwick's flighted free-kick was met by the head of Bill Atkins, moving from the left, and he glanced the ball beyond goalkeeper Alex Stepney and in at the far post.

United responded with a trademark overhead kick from Law but squandered their best chance of levelling the scores in the 25th minute when Willie Morgan saw his penalty-kick, awarded for handball, well saved by Alex Smith, who dived to his left to hold the ball. And Morgan's woe was compounded less than a minute later when Town were awarded a penalty of their own following Sadler's rash challenge on Lammie Robertson, and Bob Wallace tucked home the kick, though Stepney got his hand to the ball.

Stepney, in fact, was the busier goalkeeper, and he prevented Town from going further ahead when he charged down Atkins's effort from 12 yards. But in the second half, United showed more determination and created several openings. Alan Gowling headed just over the bar and Law put in a swerving 20-yarder which just cleared the post.

O'Farrell sent on substitutes Brian Kidd – the fans were demanding his presence – and Francis Burns in an effort to salvage the game, and with eight minutes remaining they reduced the arrears with the game's third penalty, awarded for John Pickering's challenge on George Best, though many reckoned the Irish genius 'took a dive'. Best dusted himself down and tucked his penalty away before being congratulated by hoards of youngsters who ran on to the pitch.

His goal was not quite enough to save United, though it set up a grandstand finish, but the Shaymen hung on for what was one of their greatest triumphs.

Town would lose at home to a rough West Bromwich Albion side in the semi-final and before the week was out, would also see manager George Kirby head for Watford. United, however, seemingly put this defeat behind them to storm to the top of the First Division by losing only one of their opening 14 matches before burning up in the second half of the campaign and finishing a disappointing eighth once more, with George Best then announcing his first 'retirement' from the game.

Halifax Town: Smith, Burgin, Lee, Wallace, Pickering, Rhodes, Chadwick, Atkins, Robertson, Lennard, Holmes.

Manchester United: Stepney, Fitzpatrick, Dunne, Crerand (Burns 77 mins), James, Sadler, Morgan, Gowling (Kidd 65), Charlton, Law, Best.
Referee: K.H. Burns (Stourbridge)
Attendance: 19,965

Match to Remember 31   1 May 1973
Walsall 0   Halifax Town 1
Division Three

With four games left of the 1972–73 season, Halifax Town's position looked hopeless. Lying next to bottom of the Third Division, they were five points from safety – only two points for a win in those days, remember? – and relegation looked a nigh-on certainty. This was not what George Mulhall had intended in his first season in football management, but he believed that where there was life, there was hope.

The situation that presented itself was that for the Shaymen to survive the drop, they needed to win each of their final four matches – the first three at home, the last one at Walsall, a rearranged game after the original fixture had been postponed because of a waterlogged pitch in February. It was a tall order for any side, let alone one that had won back-to-back victories only twice all season. And all the while they had to rely on other results going their way.

They began making inroads with a resounding 3–0 win over Charlton Athletic, their biggest victory of the season on the penultimate Saturday, and clung on for victory in midweek against Southend United. Mulhall had likened the run-in to the Grand National, and with an outside chance of surviving, the fans had turned out in force for the visit of Bournemouth on the last Saturday fixture. Town's subsequent 2–0 win meant that suddenly the great escape was more than a distinct possibility.

The team that the Shaymen had their eyes on were Rotherham United, whose demise had been quite remarkable. Mid-table for much of the season, they had dropped to the fringes of the relegation zone but suddenly, by winning three consecutive matches they climbed 11th to seemingly banish any such fears. However, by losing their last three games they finished on 41 points and left themselves within grasp – should Town win at Walsall.

On the day of the match, Mulhall told the *Halifax Courier*'s Bill Carter, 'Town will continue as a Division Three club next season.' It was a bold prediction but one he backed up by adding, 'I am confident, and so are the players, that we can get a result and by that I mean a win.' But the only thing in their favour was that Bill Moore's Walsall side had nothing to play for, having secured their

Alan Waddle, whose headed goal in the final match at Walsall ensured Town avoided relegation.

own safety with a couple of matches to spare. Professional pride, however, would prevent them from simply handing Town the points.

Around 1,000 supporters made the trek to the Midlands for this nail-biter, but they must have felt fates were against when Terry Shanahan put the ball in the net early on only to see his effort ruled out for an infringement on James Inger, Walsall's teenage amateur goalkeeper. But they were in ecstasy when lanky Alan Waddle scored a legitimate goal in the 35th minute. It stemmed from an untidy clearance by Walsall's Stan Bennett which was pounced upon by Fred Kemp, and the ball was rapidly transferred to Jeff Lee, and in turn, to Johnny Quinn on the left flank. His high centre lured Inger, but he committed himself too soon and Waddle rose to head the ball downwards into the corner of the net.

Town's nerves were tested in the second half and hearts were in mouths when Chris Jones found himself with only goalkeeper Alex Smith to beat, but his strong low shot went wide. But in the final half-hour, with the defence holding firm, Smith was only tested once, tipping substitute Brian Caswell's upward shot over the bar.

Against the odds, the Shaymen completed their Houdini-act, but for Rotherham, it was a cruel way to be relegated. Goal average had decided the issue, with Town's more favourable, 0.81 to their 0.79, meaning the Shaymen had stopped up by 0.02 of a goal. While the visiting supporters celebrated, in the dressing room Mulhall and his players observed two minutes' silence for Jim McAneraney's side, but relegation would mean the Millers' boss would lose his job, he, no doubt, regretting his decision to allow Trevor Womble to join Halifax Town on loan. Womble scored two goals in Town's colours, and they ultimately made a telling difference.

Alan Waddle's goal, despite being only his third of the season, was probably the most important one he would ever score, but it turned out to be his last significant contribution in Town's colours. During the summer, legendary Liverpool boss Bill Shankly took him to Anfield in a record deal, where his next goal was the winner in a Merseyside derby.

Walsall: Inger, Gregg, Atthey, Fenman, Robinson, Harrison, Birch, Shinton, Jones, Bennett, B. Taylor (Caswell 46 mins).
Halifax Town: Smith, Burgin, Lee, Hale, Pickering, Rhodes, Wilkie, Shanahan, Waddle, Kemp, Quinn.
Referee: F.E. Bassett (Swindon)
Attendance: 3,989

Match to Remember 32   27 January 1974
Halifax Town 1   Southport 1
Division Three

There was nothing remarkable about the nature of this game. It was, on the face of it, a mundane clash between a Halifax Town team comfortably placed in mid-table but well off the promotion pace, and a Southport side fighting a relegation battle they would ultimately lose. But what made this game different from any previous game the Shaymen

Southport 'keeper Alan Taylor punches clear from Dave Gwyther (left) in the first-ever match played at The Shay on a Sunday.

had played was that it was the first they had staged on a Sunday.

The energy crisis of 1973 led Prime Minister Edward Heath to set about reducing electricity consumption and thus conserve coal stocks. On 13 December 1973 he introduced the 'Three-Day Work Order' (more commonly known as the Three Day Week) which came into force at midnight on 31 December. To avoid the necessity of the use of floodlights, and/or avoid power cuts, the Football Association ordered all games to be played early, with most clubs kicking off at 2.00pm on Saturday afternoons. But in late December, the FA sanctioned Sunday football for the first time, and on 4 January four FA Cup ties were played, with Cambridge United's meeting with Oldham Athletic (who had knocked the Shaymen out of the competition) being the first to kick off.

The Halifax Town board toyed with the idea of Sunday soccer and at a meeting on 14 January 1974 they decided to give it a go, hoping the novelty would also attract a larger that average gate. Their next scheduled weekend game against Southport would be put back a day with a 2.30pm start, but this decision was one which upset Halifax RLFC, who were set to entertain New Hunslet at Thrum Hall the same afternoon. Their secretary Bill Hughes was not amused as he moaned, understandably, 'If there is any honour between the clubs Town should keep to Saturday. We arranged our fixture to avoid a clash. It is up to Town to reorganise that. After all, we were in first.'

His words fell on deaf ears and both clubs went ahead with their respective home matches, with Town coming out on top in the viewing stakes when 4,178 – this compared favourably with the season's average 2,921 – poured through the turnstiles, while the match at Thrum Hall attracted 1,302. But one key figure who missed The Shay game was the former Town boss Alan Ball Snr, now in temporary charge at Southport, after he failed to link up with the team bus on the way. But in the event he missed a quite lifeless match which seemed for long enough to be heading for a goalless draw.

The deadlock, however, was broken in the 74th minute when Dave Gwyther, who was returning from suspension, turned the ball home after Southport 'keeper Alan Taylor failed to keep out Johnny Quinn's cross. But it was a lead the Shaymen held for just five minutes, for when Alex Russell collected the ball on halfway near the left, he went on a run before supplying Jim Fryatt clear on the right, and he coolly pushed the ball past the advancing Alex Smith for a goal which would earn his side a point.

Halifax Town: Smith, Burgin, Quinn, Hale, Pickering, Rhodes, Ford, Shanahan, Kemp, Gwyther, Pugh.

Southport: Taylor, Sibbald, Ryder, Noble, Philpotts, Scott, Wright, Russell, Fryatt, Provan (Molyneux 46 mins), Coleman.
Referee: D.W. Civil (Birmingham)
Attendance: 4,178

Halifax Town staged two further Sunday games against Walsall and Cambridge United that term, also watched by above average attendances, but it would be a further 20 seasons before another Sunday matched was played at The Shay, a first-round FA Cup tie with West Bromwich Albion.

Match to Remember 33   17 March 1976
Hereford United 1   Halifax Town 2
Division Three

Halifax Town and Hereford United were heading in opposite directions when they met for this Third Division clash in March 1976. The Shaymen's alarming slide down the table had led to the dismissal of manager Johnny Quinn, but even his successor Alan Ball Snr could not buck the trend in his second spell in charge. Relegation beckoned and Town travelled to Edgar Street more in hope than expectation to face John Sillett's Hereford side which was three points clear at the top of the table from Crystal Palace and with two games in hand. Victory for the Bulls over this struggling Town side, which had won only one of its last eleven matches and still smarting from their latest home defeat to Swindon Town four days earlier, would seem a formality, particularly as the Shaymen now arrived bottom of the pile following Colchester United's 2–0 victory over Aldershot the night before. That Town should turn the tables was nothing more than remarkable.

The biggest surprise, however, was that the margin of victory was not greater than it was; 4–1 would have been a greater reflection, so well did the Shaymen play that evening. On a soggy pitch, they soaked up all the pressure Hereford threw at them – Tony Rhodes and Albert Phelan kept a watchful eye on 27–goal marksman Dixie McNeil – in the first half, as well as carving out three great chances. In the 20th minute George Jones shot high over the bar, and he, along with Mickey Bullock, was guilty of wasting further opportunities presented to them.

The fact that they should take the lead in the 63rd minute surprised no one, though, a lovely executed goal begun with full-back Bobby Flavell's overlapping run down the right. He played a wall-pass with Alan Jones before delivering a telling cross which was met with some aplomb by George Jones, who volleyed in one of the goals of the season. Just two minutes later, Town's centre-forward, playing surely his finest match for the Shaymen, went close again only to see his header crash back off the bar.

It seemed, however, that Town would pay for their missed chances when the home side forced an equaliser after 82 minutes. Roy Carter crossed from the left, John Galley headed the ball down and Jimmy Lindsay's shot, slightly mis-hit, skewed in the air and fell invitingly back into the path of Galley who scooped the ball home. Encouraged by this, Hereford pressed once more, and only a reflex save from Alex Smith denied another effort from Galley.

On loan John Overton ghosted in for the injury-time winner in Town's surprising victory at leaders Hereford United.

But the Shaymen would not be denied, more grateful than Hereford for the seven minutes of injury-time which referee John Hough elected to add on. Alan Jones broke down the right, played the ball into namesake George who put in an angled shot which may have been drifting wide, but there was John Overton, on loan from Aston Villa, ghosting in to force the ball home for a deserved winner.

Hereford United: Charlton, Emery, Richards, Layton, Galley, Lindsay, Paine (McCafferty 57 mins), Tyler, Davey, McNeil, Carter.
Halifax Town: Smith, Flavell, Collins, McGill, Rhodes, Phelan, A. Jones, McHale, Bullock, G. Jones, Overton.
Referee: J.D. Hough (Manchester)
Attendance: 7,395

Match to Remember 34   3 March 1979
Halifax Town 2   Portsmouth 0
Division Four

The cruel winter of 1978–79 hit Halifax Town harder than most clubs. Struggling to survive at the best of times on meagre gates and stranded at the foot of the Fourth Division, going into March the club had been without a home game for three months as snow several feet deep had covered the Shay pitch. This fixture with Portsmouth had also been in doubt, with referee Owen only passing the pitch fit on the day before the game, but once he had given it the go-ahead, Town boss George Kirby was hopeful of a decent crowd for several reasons. The Halifax supporters had been starved of soccer, Portsmouth were attractive opposition, and Town had won their second game of the season at Port Vale only seven days earlier to hint at something of a revival.

Portsmouth were a big-name club, though they had recently fallen on hard times with their relegation the previous term under manager Jimmy Dickinson, who, as a Pompey player, had racked up a club record 764 League appearances and won 48 England caps, and was a link to the halcyon days when they were League champions in 1949 and 1950. But they were handily placed in the Fourth Division when they arrived at The Shay, having led the table in January but having slipped to fourth place following the previous week's home defeat to Grimsby Town. Still, they must have felt that a trip to the League's bottom club was the perfect tonic to get their promotion ambitions back on track.

50 MATCHES TO REMEMBER

Portsmouth 'keeper Peter Mellor can only watch as a free-kick from Kevin Johnson (out of picture) is deflected off the defensive wall and into the top corner for Town's first goal in this 2–0 win.

How wrong they were as Town belied their lowly League position to take a grip of the game, once they had survived Portsmouth's initial raids which saw Jeff Heffernan heading over the bar and putting the ball wide after Foster's header had rebounded off the bar. But soon, the action transferred to the other end of the pitch where Town were unlucky not to make the breakthrough before they did when Franny Firth unleashed a 25-yard shot that thudded against the bar.

Town took the lead after 29 minutes when Foster fouled Kevin Johnson just outside the box. Town's diminutive striker took the kick, struck it well towards the left hand, but the trajectory of the ball altered dramatically when it took a wicked deflection off Peter Ellis in the Portsmouth wall and flew into the net at the opposite corner with goalkeeper Peter Mellor stranded. Officially classed as an own-goal, Johnson, however, would not be denied his name on the scoresheet. Six minutes later he tucked home a left-foot shot at an angle and 23 yards out following neat interplay between Steve Smith and Firth.

In the second half, the Shaymen worked hard to deny the visitors the space, and when they were breached, Derek Showers, unmarked eight yards out, volleyed into the sidenetting, the visitors' best chance. Portsmouth began pumping high balls into the box, but these were dealt comfortably by the central defensive partnership of Jack Trainer and Peter Burke, while behind them goalkeeper John Kilner, on loan from Preston following injury to Mick Leonard in the win at Port Vale, showed a safe pair of hands.

As frustration got the better of them, the visitors resorted to rough-arm tactics which had George Kirby remonstrating with the referee, but his side hung on to record a famous win and made further inroads on the teams above them. Portsmouth, on the other hand, would fade from the promotion scene and finish a disappointing seventh.

Halifax Town: Kilner, Bradley, Dunleavy, Smith, Trainer, Burke, Firth, Kennedy, Mountford, Loska, Johnson.
Portsmouth: Mellor, Ellis, Wilson, Denyer, Foster, Davey, Heffernan, Lathan, Showers (Garwood 58 mins), Barnard, Pullar.
Referee: G.P. Owen (Menai Bridge, Anglesey)
Attendance: 1,741

Match to Remember 35   26 December 1979
Halifax Town 2   Huddersfield Town 1
Division Four

For four seasons in the late 1970s, Halifax Town and neighbours Huddersfield Town were Fourth Division rivals. The Terriers would climb out of the League's basement with a swagger in 1979–80, clinching the title having scored 101 goals. Five of those had come in a 5–0 win over Halifax Town at Easter, a result which may have been some sort of revenge after suffering this Boxing Day defeat before a bumper gate at The Shay.

After several years in the doldrums, the Shaymen had been experiencing better fortunes this time around, having risen to fifth in October. Going into December, their League form may have dipped, but the spectators' interest had intensified with their exploits in the FA Cup, where a second round victory over Walsall in a second replay on Christmas Eve in front of 6,530 had given them the right to host First Division Manchester City in the third round, a game destined to be one of the biggest in Town's history.

In what was a hectic period for the Shaymen, just two days after that game the players were forced to pick themselves up to do battle with Huddersfield who, under former Shayman Mick Buxton, were making a strong bid for the Fourth Division title. With it also being a local derby, little wonder then that the game attracted the biggest crowd seen at The Shay for 10 years, with the 10,061 attendance being significant as it proved to be the last time a five-figure gate was recorded for a League game here.

It was a classic contest, with the Shay players keen not to let the Terriers into their stride, and to that end Mick Kennedy, Paul Hendrie and John Smith were successful. Though with the game played in driving rain, perhaps key to Halifax's success, was the winning of the toss by skipper Dave Evans, and his decision to play with the elements at their back in the first half in the hope of taking an advantage into the break.

The Shaymen had their chances in the first period, with Smith heading into the arms of Andy Rankin the goalkeeper, once signed by George Kirby from Everton when he was Watford manager, and winger Andy Stafford trying his luck from 25 yards. But they finally made the breakthrough five minutes before the interval when Stafford delivered an inswinging corner from the right, Huddersfield centre-back Dave Sutton only partially headed it clear, and Kennedy needed no second invitation as the ball fell in his path, driving home a precise left-footed half-volley.

Huddersfield had had their chances, too, with Peter Fletcher going closest with a shot that hit the outside of the post when faced by Kilner, and their second half challenge was not unexpected. But when they managed an equaliser, it was not a Huddersfield player who scored it, rather the unlucky Chris Dunleavy, who inadvertently turned Steve Kindon's low cross from the right by-line into his own net after 71 minutes. The former Wolves striker had just been signed from Burnley, and having replaced Robins three minutes earlier, his cross was, in fact, his first touch of the ball.

While the momentum momentarily swung in the visitors' favour, the goal evoked a response from the Shaymen and within six minutes of Dunleavy's own-goal, they were back

Mick Kennedy (white shirt, arms raised) wheels away after scoring the opener in Town's victory over neighbours Huddersfield Town.

in front. Again, Stafford delivered a corner, Smith flicked it on and Peter Burke threw himself into a mass of bodies to head the ball in.

Now questions were asked of the Huddersfield side, but they found the Halifax defence in resilient mood. Only once did it come close to being breached when Dave Cowling met a cross from the left, but he saw his effort just clear the crossbar.

Halifax Town held out for one of their most memorable of derby victories and looked forward to the visit of Malcolm Allison's Manchester City 10 days hence. Mick Buxton's side would quickly put this defeat behind them and clinch the Fourth Division title two points clear of Walsall.

Halifax Town: Kilner, Dunleavy, Hutt, Evans, Harris, Hendrie, Firth, Kennedy, Burke, Smith, Stafford.
Huddersfield Town: Rankin, Brown, Robinson, Stanton, Sutton, Hanvey, Laverick, Hart, Fletcher, Robins (Kindon 68 mins), Cowling.
Referee: J. Worrall (Warrington)
Attendance: 10,061

Match to Remember 36   5 January 1980
Halifax Town 1   Manchester City 0
FA Cup third round

Having endured several lean years over recent times, Halifax Town were experiencing better fortunes during 1979–80. Challenging in the top half for a change and with some notable victories behind them, the crowds had been returning to The Shay. It was a nice time for all connected with the club. There were also the side's achievements in the FA Cup which had people talking.

John Kilner makes one of several spectacular saves in Town's shock FA Cup victory over Manchester City.

Asked to display their mettle in the second round when paired with a strong Walsall outfit, the Shaymen had finally managed to overcome the Saddlers after three exhausting matches to set up a home tie against First Division Manchester City. With manager George Kirby at the helm when Town defeated their neighbours United in 1971, he now turned his attentions to the blue half of Manchester.

Manchester City were a top draw, of course, a club with a fine tradition and history, but a shadow of the side which had lifted silverware in their golden period with the likes of Lee, Bell and Summerbee among their ranks in the late 1960s and early 1970s. Their coach, however, was a link to that era. Malcolm Allison had returned to Maine Road in January 1979 in an attempt to restore former glories but he had spent a fortune, with midfielder Steve Daley from Wolves costing £1,450,000 alone. Despite that, Allison was struggling to make an impact and City were lying 15th when they travelled to Halifax.

Whether the game at The Shay should or should not have gone ahead that day is a matter of debate. In today's footballing climate, the referee would not have given it a second thought before calling it off but back then folk were made of sterner stuff. The thawing of a week's frost had left the pitch in a waterlogged state but so keen for the game to go ahead were the Halifax Town staff that every effort was made to make the pitch playable. With Yorkshire Television covering the game for their highlights programme the following day – The Shay's modest floodlights necessitated a 2.00pm kick-off to accommodate their cameras – officials and volunteers thus used whatever they could to rid the pitch of water; forks, rollers, even towels, to try and ensure the game went ahead. After a mid-morning inspection, referee Michael Lowe gave the game the thumbs up.

There is no doubt that the conditions proved a great leveller. Perhaps, too, was the part played by celebrated hypnotist Romark, whom George Kirby had called in the day before the game to give his players the belief that they could topple City. Romark was only too keen to assist as he sought retribution, so the story goes, after Allison had rejected his offers of help when manager at Crystal Palace in the 1970s.

But perhaps too much has been made of Romark, for the outstanding performer on the day was Town goalkeeper John Kilner, the only player not put under his spell. He made two superb first-half saves from Bobby Shinton's snap-shot and a vicious volley from Mick Robinson, then in the 65th minute he blocked Shinton's scooped effort.

Not that City had it all their own way. Giant England international goalkeeper Joe Corrigan, another link to the glory days, had to be alert to palm away Andy Stafford's inswinging corner onto the bar, then right on half-time he did well to get down and turn aside Town skipper Dave Evans's stinging drive. Paul Hendrie had the City defence worried twice early on, and the busy Town midfielder must have thought his chance had gone. But he would not be denied.

With 15 minutes remaining and on a pitch that had churned up considerably, Town won a throw-in on the left. Mick Kennedy found Bob Mountford down the line, he played the ball back to Stafford, who delivered a cross which found John Smith on the edge of the box. Smith played the ball first time and Hendrie, who had manoeuvred himself goal side of Colin Viljoen, another ex-England international, swept a low shot past the smothering body of Corrigan and into the far corner. It was a goal George Kirby, speaking on that evening's *Match of the Day* programme described as one England superstar Kevin Keegan would have been proud of, and it was one that rightly propelled Hendrie into the national spotlight, as well as into Halifax folklore.

There was still time for City to fashion an equaliser, of course, but though they threw everything they could at the Town goal, Kirby's team stood firm and held out for a monumental victory, one which grabbed the attention of the national media. The club enjoyed being in the spotlight until they travelled to meet another First Division side in Bolton Wanderers in the fourth round, but despite being spurred on by around 6,000 travelling supporters, Town lost 2–0, though they were far from disgraced. In time folk would forget much about that defeat, but the victory that got them there would live long in the memory.

Halifax Town: Kilner, Dunleavy, Hutt, Evans, Harris, Hendrie, Firth, Kennedy, Mountford, Smith, Stafford.
Manchester City: Corrigan, Ranson, Power, Reid, Caton, Bennett, Henry, Daley, Robinson, Viljoen, Shinton,
Referee: M. Lowe (Sheffield)
Attendance: 12, 599

Match to Remember 37　　　　　*13 November 1982*
Wimbledon 2   Halifax Town 4
Division Four

Halifax Town were Wimbledon's first-ever opponents in the Football League in August 1977. The sides drew 3–3 in a Fourth Division fixture following the election of the Dons, formerly of the Southern League, in place of Workington. By the time the Shaymen visited Plough Lane for this meeting, Wimbledon had experienced two promotions and two relegations and would go up a third time at the end of this campaign. With Town struggling at the wrong end of the table, nobody saw this result coming.

Mickey Bullock's side were in desperate need of a change of fortune. Without a win of any kind since Bobby Davison's last gasp effort claimed all three points at Swindon on 11 September, 12 games ago, Town had slipped into the re-election zone while Dave Bassett's Wimbledon side were making great strides for the Championship, though they went into this game on the back of two defeats, a crumb of comfort for Bullock. Perhaps Wimbledon reckoned such a fixture against the Shaymen gave them the perfect opportunity to get back on track, but with Town employing a sweeper system, they found them hard to break down and were hindered with the

Vernon Allatt, a scorer in the 4–2 win at Wimbledon.

loss of top scorer John Leslie after half an hour. They also found Town sharpshooter Davison at his most lethal.

He opened the scoring in the 42nd minute, a first time strike after Vernon Allatt and Paul Hendrie had combined to set him up, and doubled Town's lead seven minutes after the break when Hendrie sent him clear. Allatt claimed his first goal, upon his return to the club after an unsuccessful spell with Bolton Wanderers, two minutes later following some slack defending by the home side, who, 3–0 down, suddenly awoke from their slumber and attempted to make a game of it. Wayne Entwhistle's goal in the 56th minute, however, only served to offer the home fans false hope, for in the 68th minute Davison completed his hat-trick – it was his first in the League – when he finished off a Steve Spooner-inspired move with a first-time shot.

Wimbledon did make the scoreline slightly more respectable when Dean Thomas scored a 79th minute penalty following a handling offence by Malcolm Goodman, but by then many of the home supporters were already heading home.

A victory such as this was indeed rare for the Shaymen. The last time they had managed it was back in February 1964 when they defeated Workington by a similar score. Davison's hat-trick was the first by a Town player in the League since Terry Shanahan achieved the feat against Brentford over 10 years earlier, and the first away from home since John Parks scored all Town's goals in a 3–1 win at Hartlepool in April 1967. But the victory at Plough Lane was not the start of a great revival – that would start in earnest in January – for just seven days later they came crashing down to earth with a shock 1–0 home defeat by non-League North Shields in the FA Cup.

Wimbledon for their part would put this defeat behind them and go on to win the title by eight points from Hull City, but not without victory over Halifax Town. The sides would draw 1–1 at The Shay in May.

Wimbledon: Beasant, Peters, Thomas, Dibble, Tagg, Morris, Belfield, Entwhistle, Leslie (Gage 30 mins), Downes, Hodges.

Halifax Town: Smelt, Nobbs, Wood, Evans, Smith, Hendrie, Staniforth, Davison, Allatt, Spooner, Goodman.

Referee: K. Barratt (Coventry)
Attendance: 2,104

Match to Remember 38   22 March 1986
Burnley 1   Halifax Town 3
Division Four

Despite their close proximity to each other, Halifax Town and Burnley did not come into contact with each other for a competitive fixture until the mid-1980s. The two sides had

Dave Longhurst completes his magnificent solo run to score Town's third goal in their win against Burnley at Turf Moor.

met during the war years, but the first peacetime meeting was not until 1984–85 when they clashed at Turf Moor for a second round FA Cup tie, a match won by the Clarets.

Burnley were then a Third Division club, but an ailing one, lying £800,000 in the red and about to be relegated. They began 1985–86 in the Fourth Division along with Halifax Town and though, generally, they would have the better of things between the two clubs over the next few years, they came out second best in their exchanges during their first season in the League's basement division. The Shaymen were denied home victory in October when Neil Grewcock's 86th minute strike earned them a point they did not deserve from a 2–2 draw, but when they travelled to Turf Moor the following March, they put on their best performance of the season and made sure there was no slip up.

Star of the show was undoubtedly Town's young striker Dave Longhurst, who capped a virtuoso display by scoring a brilliant solo goal which rounded off this emphatic 3–1 victory. It came in the 80th minute, but long before then he had run ragged a home defence that included former Leeds United stars Peter Hampton and Kevin Hird, having a hand in Town's first two goals and showing why his manager Mick Jones rated him so highly.

Despite his performance, it was Burnley who took the lead in the 13th minute when Hampton fired in a shot from 25 yards which dipped over goalkeeper Paddy Roche, who was caught off his line. But five minutes later the Shaymen were level and destined not to look back. Longhurst nipped in between two defenders on the left and cut into the box to set up Gary Nicholson.

Burnley were unlucky to lose leading goalscorer Alan Taylor with a head injury after 21 minutes, and five minutes later they were behind, with Longhurst playing a major part in the goal. He controlled Paul Sanderson's corner at the near post before turning and firing in a shot which Burnley goalkeeper Joe Neenan could not hold. The ball ran loose and Simon Lowe was on hand to turn it over the line.

For the most part, the Burnley players looked a demoralised lot, affected, it seemed, by troubles behind the scenes, and helpless to prevent Longhurst scoring his breathtaking solo goal. Beating two players in the air, he controlled the ball just inside the centre-circle, then set off on his run. Defenders were alerted to the danger but too late to prevent it. Longhurst homed in on goal, drew Neenan, waltzed round him and planted the ball into the roof of the net. It was without a moment to savour, and reckoned by those who saw it to be one of the best goals ever scored by a Halifax Town player.

Victory here was revenge of sorts for their FA Cup defeat by the same scoreline the previous season, though this, probably, was not on the players' minds. They were more concerned, as was Mick Jones, that they had kept an impressive run going – they could now

claim six victories from seven matches – which moved them out of the bottom four and ultimately to safety.
Burnley: Neenan, Hird, Hampton, Malley, Overson, Heggarty, Grewcock, Deakin, Taylor (Devine 21 mins), Lawrence, Hoskin.
Halifax Town: Roche, Brown, Fleming, Shaw, Knill, Galloway, Sanderson, Kellock, Lowe, Longhurst, Sanderson.
Referee: M.G. Peck (Kendal)
Attendance: 3,321

Match to Remember 39   8 March 1988
Burnley 0   Halifax Town 0
Sherpa Van Trophy, Northern semi-final

The competition for the two lower tier division clubs that began life as the Football League Group Cup in 1981 and which now exists as the Johnstone's Paint Trophy, has had many other guises in between. In 1987–88 it began its two-year life as the Sherpa Van Trophy, but then, as now, there was little interest in the competition until its later stages when the Wembley Final was in sight.

That season, Town were enjoying a decent run under manager Billy Ayre and had qualified for the knockout stages having topped Grimsby Town and Scunthorpe United in their group. Further victories over Chesterfield and Darlington saw them progress to the northern semi-final, where they were handed this mouth-watering tie with Burnley at Turf Moor, scene of their famous League victory almost two years earlier.

Brian Miller's Clarets had themselves reached this far by seeing off Tranmere Rovers and Rochdale in the group stages followed by victories over Chester and Bury, and with home advantage, they were favourites on the night. But spurred on by around 1,000 travelling supporters, the Shaymen played their part in a classic, where no quarter was asked or given.

Town settled into the game quickly and carved out a couple of half-chances for Peter Duffield, making his debut on loan from Sheffield United, and Lee Richardson, while at the other end Town goalkeeper Paddy Roche saved a header from Steve Davis. Burnley had to reshuffle their pack following injuries to both defender Steve Gardner and Neil Grewcock in the first half, though early in the second half, Town's tigerish midfielder Steve Thornber also became a casualty. He

Rick Holden goes close in the Sherpa Van Trophy northern semi-final at Burnley.

was replaced by Terry McPhillips, and there was a certain irony, given the dramatic ending to the match, of the number of strikers Town had on the pitch when Paul Fleming also had to be withdrawn and replaced by Neil Matthews.

Burnley created a number of chances as they held sway midway through the second period, with Paul Comstive firing just wide, and George Oghani hitting a free-kick just over the bar. But as the game wore on, the Shaymen gained the upper hand, and with five minutes remaining came closest to breaking the deadlock when Rick Holden released Duffield and arrived in the box to meet Duffield's cross to the near post, only to see his header beat goalkeeper Chris Pearce but rebound back off the bar.

The game went to extra-time, but there were still no goals despite the Shaymen's domination, and in the end a pulsating game came down to the lottery of the penalty shoot-out, and it was there that Town's Wembley dream ended. With Burnley's Ray Deakin, Shaun McGrory, Ian Britton and Oghani all scoring with their kicks, and Phil Brown, Dean Martin and Mick Matthews netting for the Shaymen, the Clarets led 4–3, to leave much depending on Town's fourth penalty taker. But though forwards Wayne Allison, Duffield, Matthews, Holden and McPhillips were available, Ayre entrusted goalkeeper Roche with it, confident that he would tuck it away as he regularly did in training. But to the anguish of all connected with the club, Roche sent his right-foot kick onto the bar and Burnley's Paul Comstive duly stepped up to score and send them through.

The *Halifax Courier* reporter John Kenealy was scathing of Ayre's decision to allow Roche to take such a crucial kick, as were many of the supporters, but for Roche, a popular player, it was something he had to live with as Town saw their best chance of reaching Wembley disappear. For Burnley, however, they would reach the twin towers following their northern Final over Preston North End, only to lose 2–0 to Wolves, whose goals were scored by the prolific pairing of Steve Bull and Andy Mutch.

Burnley: Pearce, Daniel, Deakin, Britton, Davis, Gardner (McGrory 13 mins), Farrell, Oghani, Taylor, Comstive, Grewcock (Hoskin 42).
Halifax Town: Roche, Brown, Barr, M. Matthews, P. Fleming (N. Matthews 65), Richardson, Martin, Thornber (McPhillips 48), Duffield, Allison, Holden.
Referee: G. Alpin (Kendal)
Attendance: 10,222

Match to Remember 40   21 April 1990
Doncaster Rovers 3   Halifax Town 4
Division Four

This game drew obvious comparisons with the victory over Swindon Town in 1962. True, the four goals scored by Town that day to complete an amazing fightback were condensed into the last 20 minutes while here at Belle Vue, Town had a full 45 in which to turn around a 3–0 deficit. But given Town's League position and current form, it was still an extraordinary achievement.

Action from Town's game at Doncaster Rovers, where the Shaymen overturned a three-goal deficit to win 4–3. Graham Broadbent is the Town player on the ground.

As in 1962–63, Town were fighting a relegation battle, this time to the Vauxhall Conference, and at kick-off time were lying 21st, only five points better off than bottom club Colchester United. Just a month earlier they had replaced manager Billy Ayre with former Scotland international Jim McCalliog in the hope of saving Town, but he would have to find words of wisdom at half-time in this game. Doncaster, for their part, were only one place and three points better off than the Shaymen, so points were precious for them, too. But when they took a three goal lead after just 26 minutes they were looking odds on favourites to win the match.

Billy Bremner's side took the lead after just five minutes when they sprang Town's offside trap and Lee Turnbull finished in style from 25 yards. In the 21st minute, scorer turned provider when Turnbull rounded Town goalkeeper David Brown and crossed for John Muir to score a simple header, and five minutes later it was 3–0 to the home side when David Harle unselfishly set up Neil Grayson. Town had been outplayed and by the end of the half had mustered just one effort on goal, a shot from Andy Watson which hit the post.

During the interval, McCalliog found himself rallying his troops, urging them to keep playing football and whatever words of motivation he could find. Within two minutes of the restart, the fightback was under way. Mitch Cook began it with a curling free-kick that Rovers goalkeeper Mark Samways dropped over the goal-line. Fortuitous, maybe, but Town were not for dwelling on it. In the 66th minute, Billy Barr cut in from the right, beat a couple of defenders and fired home from inside the box. A minute later, McCalliog switched Barr for striker Nick Richardson and with nine minutes to go, the Town substitute levelled the scores, reacting to Neil Matthews's flick on from Brian Butler's corner.

With Doncaster having to cope with the loss of injured defender Rufus Brevett, Town grabbed a sensational winner with four minutes remaining. Mitch Cook delivered the ball from the left and Butler latched onto it on the right-hand side, hammering an unstoppable shot which flew past Samways. The comeback was complete and the small band of travelling supporters went delirious.

As well as making the headlines for the manner of their victory, Town also moved above Rovers on goal difference and all but allayed fears of relegation, with Colchester, who lost at Torquay on the same day, now cast eight points adrift.

Doncaster Rovers: Samways, Brockie, Brevett (Gaughan 77 mins), Harle, Ashurst, Douglas, Muir, Grayson (Adams 67), Turnbull, Jones, Noteman.

Halifax Town: Brown, P. Fleming, Cook, Martin, C. Fleming, Graham, Barr (Richardson 67), Butler, Matthews, Watson, Hall (Broadbent 79).

Referee: I. Hendrick (Preston)

Attendance: 2,212

Match to Remember 41 *13 October 1990*
Carlisle United 0   Halifax Town 3
Division Four

How bizarre that Halifax Town should have managed two goals over both legs of a Rumbelows Cup tie with First Division giants Manchester United and score three goals in the Final of the Yorkshire and Humberside Cup, yet failed to find the target in any of their opening EIGHT League games. By any stretch of the imagination, it was an unprecedented scenario. Not surprisingly did manager Jim McCalliog find his team bottom of the table, but he was insistent that fortunes would change.

In an effort to improve the situation, however, he had traded centre-forward Tony Fyfe for Carlisle's Steve Norris, but Norris had made his debut in the eighth goalless game, a 1–0 defeat at Northampton Town. Now fates decreed he should line up against his former colleagues at Brunton Park, and unsurprisingly he was the focus of attention.

Norris did get on the scoresheet, but the player who made a name for himself as scorer of Town's first League goal of the 1990–91 season was Halifax-born Billy Barr. He struck from 20 yards in the 10th minute after Ian Juryeff had laid the ball back to him to end the side's goal famine which had stretched to 13 hours and 18 minutes since Neil Matthews had scored in the 2–1 home defeat by Stockport County on the last day of the previous season.

The goal inspired confidence, and moments later Paul Futcher tried his luck from 30 yards only to be denied by a spectacular save from Carlisle goalkeeper Jason Priestley. But after 18 minutes Town doubled their lead, Norris latching on to Juryeff's cross to beat defender Colin Methven and tuck the ball under Priestley. And before half-time, Town were in dreamland having scored a third through Tommy Graham in the 37th minute when he arrived at the back post to crash home the ball after Norris had flicked on Barr's cross.

Carlisle, whose line-up featured familiar names in former Ipswich Town striker Eric Gates and ex-York City centre-forward Keith Walwyn, often the scourge of Town defences, threw everything at the Shaymen in the second half, introducing attacking midfielder Gordon Owen, on loan from Blackpool, for centre-back Paul Fitzpatrick, but Paul Proudlock, Walwyn and Owen were all guilty of missing the target. Tony Fyfe appeared as

Billy Barr fires home Town's opening goal in the 3–0 win at Carlisle, Town's first League goal of the season in their ninth match.

a 62nd minute substitute and set up Gates, but Town goalkeeper David Brown, a virtual spectator in the first half, made his only telling save, keeping out his shot with his legs.

Town, in fact, did not muster their first chance of the second half until the 71st minute when Norris was checked by Methven, but they were almost grateful to Carlisle centre-back Simon Jeffels, who dived full length to head Juryeff's cross goalwards, the ball rebounding off the underside of the bar and out. Towards the end, Brown did well to save from Derek Walsh, and the last incident of note was Owen's 25–yarder which rattled a post and ran to safety.

As expected, Town's victory made headlines, and BBC Radio Five were keen to get hold of Billy Barr for his thoughts, and though the win did not take Town off the bottom, he saw no reason why they could not start pushing up the table. The Shaymen, however, would continue to struggle under McCalliog, despite the efforts of 30-goal Norris.

Carlisle United: Priestley, Miller, Edwards, Jeffels, Methven, Fitzpatrick (Owen 46 mins), Walsh, Shepherd, Walwyn (Fyfe 62), Gates, Proudlock.
Halifax Town: Brown, P. Fleming, Barr, Evans, C. Fleming, Futcher, Gregory, Norris, Juryeff, Graham, Butler.
Referee: K. Lupton (Stockton)
Attendance: 3,697

Match to Remember 42   2 March 1991
Halifax Town 5   Walsall 2
Division Four

The 18–month period which Jim McCalliog spent in charge at The Shay was not one fondly remembered by the supporters, as Town struggled near the foot of the table for most of that time. Though in and among there were some eye-raising results, such as this

Bloodied Jonathan Gould leaves the field as Tommy Graham (in background) prepares to take over in goal in the astonishing 5-2 victory over Walsall.

incident-packed game against Walsall, one that, if not quite matching the drama of the game at Doncaster Rovers the previous season, certainly ran it close, although the scoreline did not even tell half the story.

Town went into this game bottom of the Fourth Division and on the back of a winless streak that stretched to eleven matches, the last coming in a 5-1 mauling at Maidstone United. When Walsall, relegated the previous season but comfortably placed in mid-table under new manager Kenny Hibbitt, ran up a two-goal lead after just three minutes at The Shay, it looked as if Town would be on the end of another hiding.

The Shaymen, in fact, had gone behind to a penalty conceded after just 15 seconds when skipper Dave Evans felled Rod McDonald. Willy Naughton tucked the spot-kick away, and before Town had time to gather themselves, the visitors had scored again, Chris Marsh thundering an unstoppable header past goalkeeper Jonathan Gould from Naughton's left wing cross.

After 37 minutes, Town next found themselves without a goalkeeper, Jonathan Gould suffering a horrific facial injury following a collision with Kenny Mower which would keep him out of action for a month. He was led from the field while Tommy Graham donned his goalkeeper's jersey for the remainder of the match, with the game, even at this early stage, looking a lost cause. But Steve Norris's penalty two minutes before the break, awarded after he had been upended by Colin Methven's clumsy challenge in a race for the ball, raised the Shaymen's spirits and in the second half they came out fighting.

Rookie goalkeeper Graham was rarely troubled as Town laid siege on the Walsall goal and the game turned with two goals in as many minutes. In the 61st minute, Nick Richardson broke from midfield, found Ian Juryeff on the right and his dangerous cross was headed home by Norris for a quite stunning goal. Another well-worked goal ended with Billy Barr heading Paul Fleming's cross goalwards for Juryeff to dive and lift his shot over Walsall goalkeeper Ron Green.

To help stem the tide, Walsall made a couple of changes, but the next goal fell to the Shaymen after 71 minutes, Juryeff showing persistence after he had lost the ball to win it back and crack a rising shot into the net. Walsall showed signs of staging a comeback when Peter Skipper hit a dipping 25 yard shot that troubled Graham, but he did well to make the save and nonchalantly polished his fingernails on his green shirt. He was clearly enjoying himself, and with five minutes remaining, Town wrapped up an astonishing game with their fifth goal, a second Norris penalty after he had been ankle-tapped by goalkeeper Green.

Halifax Town: Gould (Ellis 44 mins), P. Fleming, Barr, Evans, C. Fleming, Gore, Richardson, Norris, Juryeff, Graham, Martin.

Walsall: Green, Hutchings, Mower (Littlejohn 64), Methven, Smith, Skipper, Grealish, Ntamark, Marsh, McDonald, Naughton (Cecere 64).
Referee: W. Burns (Scarborough)
Attendance: 1,464

Match to Remember 43   *8 May 1993*
Halifax Town 0   Hereford United 1
Division Three

The introduction of automatic relegation and promotion between the basement division's bottom club and the winners of the Conference from the start of the 1986–87 season probably extended Halifax Town's League status longer than it possibly would have done had the re-election system still been in use. Now, the team finishing bottom of the table could no longer count on the votes of friends and neighbours, but Halifax Town had not needed to contend themselves with that as there always seemed to be someone slightly worse off than them. Until that is, the 1992–93 season, when fates finally caught up with the club.

Going into the season's final weeks, the Shaymen were one of three clubs fighting to avoid the drop, but when they lost 2–0 at fellow strugglers Gillingham in their penultimate match, three became two as the Gills pulled themselves clear, while Town, bottom of the pile, were left two points adrift of Northampton Town. The situation was a desperate one, and put simply, left them needing to win their last match and hope that Northampton failed in theirs at Shrewsbury Town.

Not helping Town's cause, however, was the fact that their last game was at The Shay, where they had won only three times all season, the last victory being against Lincoln City back in February. But their opponents were only Hereford United, a side which too had flirted briefly with relegation until several weeks earlier. They had nothing to play for as such, though player-manager Greg Downs insisted that they would treat the game as any other. With so much at stake,

Derek Hall scores the only goal of the game for Hereford United in the final match of the season as the Shaymen lose their League status.

the game attracted a bumper crowd of 7,451 and kick-off was delayed by 10 minutes. Most were behind the Shaymen and manager Mick Rathbone knew his players would give it their all.

There were few chances in the first half, though Dave Ridings spurned the most clearcut, latching on to Jamie Paterson's pass across goal but putting the ball wide from close range following a last-ditch tackle by Gareth Davies. Billy Barr also tried his luck from 20 yards, though in truth Bulls' goalkeeper Alan Judge was rarely troubled, and in fact it was Town's Lee Bracey who made the most telling save, tipping over a stinging drive from Owen Pickard.

The sides trooped in at half-time with the game goalless, but when news came through that Northampton were losing their match at Shrewsbury, it seemed all Town had to do was score a goal, and the fans tried their level best to lift the players. But dreams of a great escape diminished after 61 minutes when Derek Hall, a former Town player, sidefooted home Darren Rowbotham's pass for what turned out to be the game's only goal.

His strike broke Town's hearts and the tide swung in favour of Northampton, who by now were making good their own escape by turning the score round at Gay Meadow, taking a 3–2 lead. All hope seemed lost for the Shaymen and the atmosphere changed dramatically. But to their credit, the players still went looking for a goal, and chances came and went. A cross-cum-shot from Peter Craven hit the bar, Jason Hardy skewed a shot wide and substitute Nigel Greenwood was denied by Judge from point blank range. But it was all to no avail.

There was a muted reaction on the terraces when the final whistle sounded to confirm Town's relegation, but as the players made for the tunnel, fans swarmed onto the pitch, Halifax-born skipper Billy Barr carried shoulder high, in tears, as were many of the supporters. They chanted defiantly, 'We'll be back,' though did anybody really believe it? Chairman Jim Brown addressed the crowd and said every effort would be made to make an instant return, while Rathbone played testimony to his players, calling them 'a great bunch of guys' and adding, 'If they can come through an experience like this they have great futures ahead of them.'

After 72 years of League football, though, Halifax Town's immediate future would be spent in the GM Vauxhall Conference.

Halifax Town: Bracey, German (Greenwood 62 mins), Barr, Hardy, Lucketti, Bradley, Peake, Ridings, Megson, Paterson, Craven.
Hereford United: Judge, Downs, Anderson, Davies, Abrahams, Morris, Hall, Pickard, Rowbotham, Jones, Nicholson.
Referee: J. Winter (Middlesbrough)
Attendance: 7,451

Match to Remember 44   *13 November 1993*
Halifax Town 2   West Bromwich Albion 1
FA Cup first round

Halifax Town may have struggled to make an impression in their first season in the Conference under Peter Wragg, but they did manage to serve up one of the club's finest FA

Cup victories when they took on West Bromwich Albion in the first round. The moment the draw was made there was the potential for an upset, and rightly the Sky Sports TV cameras elected to screen this tie live on a Sunday afternoon.

The Baggies were a team with a fine Cup tradition, having won the competition on six occasions, the most recent triumph coming in 1968 when a Jeff Astle goal was enough to beat Everton. Second Division Play-off winners the previous May, they were struggling a little in the League, but in Keith Burkinshaw, who had taken over in June, they had a manager who also knew what it took to win the FA Cup, having led Tottenham Hotspur to back-to-back success in the early 1980s. But here he found his side competing at this stage of the competition for the first time since 1924, and about to be humbled.

Exactly a year earlier, Town had produced possibly one of their worst-ever performances in the competition when they were embarrassed 4–1 by non-League Marine. Now they would experience happier times in front of a watching nation.

Though most pundits predicted an easy ride for the Baggies, Town were far from overawed and created the first clearcut opportunity when Steve Saunders' instant strike was headed off the line by Bernard McNally, and just two minutes later they opened the scoring through Jason Peake who, collecting the ball outside the box following a corner, danced through the Baggies defence to slot home past goalkeeper Tony Lange.

Town goalkeeper Darren Heyes had had to make some fine saves during the course of the first half, notably a volley from Elland-born Kevin Donovan, a player on loan at The Shay two seasons earlier, but in the 37th minute, following a West Brom corner, Peake turned defence into attack and a sweeping move saw Jamie Paterson play in Saunders, who drew Lange before gliding the ball into the far corner. Colin Lambert went close moments

Dave Ridings gets in a shot during Town's 2–1 win over West Brom in the FA Cup.

later, but right on half-time Town were indebted to full-back Peter Craven for protecting that two-goal lead when he cleared Kwame Ampadu's effort of the goalline.

After the interval, the visitors came back strongly, with Darren Heyes being forced to save at the feet of Donovan, Lee Ashcroft and Kieran O'Regan pulling efforts wide and Bob Taylor heading over the bar from eight yards. But something had to give and with nine minutes remaining, Albion halved the deficit. Ashcroft's right-wing cross was too deep but O'Regan retrieved the ball and returned it into the box for Andy Hunt to head home under the challenge from Elfyn Edwards, receiving two broken teeth for his pains.

West Brom sensed they could now save the game and Edwards had to make a superb block to deny Hunt twelve yards out, and after winning a succession of corners, McNally blazed over the bar.

The added three minutes of injury time seemed to last forever for the Shaymen, but the referee's whistle signalled the end of the match and a famous win, perhaps not in the same League as the victories over Cardiff and Stoke in 1952–53, or that over Manchester City 14 seasons earlier, but still big enough to earn the club headlines. They would bow out 5–1 at Stockport County in the second round, but nobody could deny them glory that got them there.

Halifax Town: Heyes, German, Craven, Edwards, Boardman, Barr, Peake, Lambert, Paterson (Constable 85 mins), Saunders.

West Bromwich Albion: Lange, Coldicott, Ampadu (Reid 77), McNally, O'Regan, Burgess, Hunt, Hamilton, Taylor, Ashcroft, Donovan (Mellon 61).

Referee: A. Flood (Stockport)
Attendance: 4,250

Match to Remember 45   3 May 1997
Halifax Town 4   Stevenage Borough 2
GM Vauxhall Conference

Four years after dropping into the Conference Halifax Town were on the verge of relegation once more. And but for a change of manager in February, they may have already been condemned before the last game of the season. John Carroll had left the club and for the second time the managerial team of George Mulhall and Kieran O'Regan had assumed control, immediately leading the team to three successive victories which would prove crucial in the long run.

Since then, however, Town had won only one of their next 12 matches and had slipped back into the relegation mire. But they had at least shown the fighting spirit they would need in their penultimate match with champions-elect Macclesfield Town, clawing back a two-goal deficit late on to earn a 3–3 draw and thus deny them the chance to wrap up the title. But, however heroic their performance may have been that evening, the situation for the Shaymen had not altered greatly, and they were still left teetering on the brink.

The Shaymen, however, had one thing in their favour. Though they were fighting with Bath City to avoid the last relegation spot, survival was at least in their own hands. But only just. With one point separating themselves from Bath, only victory for the Shaymen would guarantee safety and ensure the Romans' relegation regardless of the result in their last game.

On the face of it, however, Town had a harder task than Bath, for while the Romans were entertaining Northwich Victoria, the Shaymen's opponents were third-placed Stevenage Borough, a side which had beaten Town on the season's opening day. Such a match was not for the faint-hearted, particularly after Paul Stoneman turned a Robbie Mutchell cross into his own net after 20 minutes. But urged on by an anxious Shay crowd, Town responded with a goal from Mick Norbury seven minutes later, capitalising on Darren Lyons's corner.

When Barry Hayles waltzed through the defence in the 39th minute to restore the visitors' lead, Town were not unduly worried. News had filtered through that Bath were losing 2–0 in their match, so if the scores remained that way, Town would be safe. Things looked even better, though, for Town, when Norbury converted Paul Mudd's cross four minutes before the break and at half-time at The Shay the scores stood at 2–2.

But events were about to take a dramatic twist. Town went in front for the first time in the 56th minute through a somewhat fortuitously awarded indirect free-kick six yards out after the referee had deemed Dean Hooper's touch to former Town goalkeeper Richard Wilmot a back-pass. Lyons nudged the ball to Mick Norbury, who slammed it home for his hat-trick, never a timelier one scored. But then news came through that Bath had overturned the score in their game and were now leading 3–2. A Stevenage equaliser at The Shay would mean only one thing; relegation for Town, and they suddenly began living on their nerves and lost their way.

George Mulhall and his players celebrate after pulling off a 4–2 victory over Stevenage to preserve their Conference status.

Stevenage's Mark Smith indeed could have sealed Town's fate had he not blazed over from six yards after Town goalkeeper Andy Woods had fumbled a corner, but with the Town fans baying for the final whistle, substitute Geoff Horsfield latched onto Mudd's through ball and fired home from 18 yards. The home supporters surged onto the pitch to celebrate, and moments later they were back when the referee's whistle sounded not only the end of the match, but Halifax Town's safety.

Halifax Town: Woods, Brown, Mudd, Martin, Stoneman, Murphy, Lyons, Hulme (Horner 14 mins), Norbury, Brook (Horsfield 80), O'Regan.

Stevenage Borough: Wilmot, Kirby (Cretton 46), Mitchell, Sodje, Barrowcliff, Hooper, Mison, Crawshaw, Trebble (Browne 83), Hayles

Referee: M.J. Jones (Chester)

Attendance: 1,191

Match to Remember 46 *18 April 1998*
Kidderminster Harriers 0   Halifax Town 2
GM Vauxhall Conference

Almost a year after avoiding the drop with that dramatic last day victory over Stevenage, Halifax Town were incredibly on the verge of lifting the Conference title, having swept all before them. Manager George Mulhall had transformed the side with the additions of players such as goalkeeper Lee Martin, full-backs Andy Thackeray and Mark Bradshaw, and having sold striker Mick Norbury in the close season, had put his faith in Geoff Horsfield. Jamie Paterson returned to the club following stints at Falkirk and Scunthorpe United, and after Peter Jackson had taken the managerial position at Huddersfield Town, Mulhall had signed the experienced centre-back Brian Kilcline, without a club, as his replacement. They had teamed up with existing players such as Kevin Hulme, to whom Mulhall had given the captain's armband to help cool his temperament, and Kieran O'Regan and the football they served up was as entertaining as any Town team had displayed before. Going into April, the Shaymen were clear favourites for the title.

Not that Mulhall was taking anything for granted. On Easter Monday his side had been staring defeat in the face in their home fixture with Southport, having had O'Regan sent off and trailing 3–2 with just eight minutes remaining. But substitute Dave Hanson's two goals, which turned the match, now left Town needing two points to clinch the Championship and in turn reclaim their Football League status after an absence of five years. If the Shaymen won at Kidderminster the following Saturday, with three games still to play, the job would be completed.

How could they possibly have failed anyway? Around 1,500 expectant Town supporters made the trip to Aggborough, and with Kidderminster secretary Roger Barlow publicly stating that 'Town won't win the title here,' he'd waved the proverbial red flag.

There were obvious tensions and Kidderminster dominated the early stages, and it looked as if Town were not going to have things all their own way when the home side were

Geoff Horsfield fires home Town's first goal in the win at Kidderminster Harriers on the way to clinching the Conference title.

awarded a penalty after 22 minutes when Kilcline upended Mike Bignall. But goalkeeper Andy Rhodes, who had arrived at the club at the end of March due to injury to Lee Martin, was equal to Ian Arnold's spot-kick and made the save. There were other anxious moments for Town; Rhodes was forced into action again to keep out Kilcline's defensive header which seemed destined for the bottom corner, then blocked an effort from Paul Webb.

Gradually, Town played their way into the game, and three minutes before the interval they got the goal the fans had been waiting for. Kidderminster's Martin Weir made the hash of what should have been a straightforward routine goal-kick, his return pass proving too strong for goalkeeper Darren Steadman, and as he struggled to control the ball, Geoff Horsfield nipped in, rounded a defender and fired into the roof of the net.

After half-time, Kidderminster saw plenty of the ball but the best chances fell to the Shaymen. They were desperate for a second goal to ease the nerves and 10 minutes from time, they got it. Fittingly, it was delivered by Jamie Paterson, the only member of the side that had been relegated five years earlier, cutting in from the left and unleashing a stunning 25 yard shot with his 'wrong' right foot that beat the goalkeeper at his near post.

The goal reduced Paterson to tears, while the Town fans behind the goal at the other end went delirious and 10 minutes later, the referee's whistle signalled the end of the match. The supporters celebrated Championship success on the pitch and called for manager George Mulhall, who duly appeared by the tunnel, his delight clear for all to see. Town's return to the Football League evidently meant as much to him as it did the fans, as he would later claim, 'This is the biggest moment in football for me.'

Kidderminster Harriers: Steadman, Willetts, Prindiville, Weir, Pope, Yates, Webb, Davies, Bignall, Arnold, Deakin.
Halifax Town: Rhodes, Thackeray, Bradshaw, Murphy, Kilcline, Stoneman, Paterson, Hulme, O'Regan Horsfield, Brown.
Referee: P. Walton (West Haddon)
Attendance: 3,151

Match to Remember 47   8 August 1998
Peterborough United 0   Halifax Town 2
Division Three

Halifax Town made a triumphant return to the Football League with this resounding 2–0 victory at Peterborough United on the season's opening day. It was truly a joyous occasion, but such a result was made all the more remarkable given Town's build up to the game.

After seeing the side through several friendlies, George Mulhall seemed set to lead the Shaymen into the new season, but just four days before this game he stood down to allow Kieran O'Regan to take over the reins. But if O'Regan's sudden step-up to management came in less than ideal circumstances, then he was also soon confronted with a selection headache as he found himself going into the match without would-be regulars Jamie Murphy, Jamie Paterson and Peter Butler, all out through injury, and centre-half Mark Sertori, who, like O'Regan himself, was suspended. The new Town boss, therefore, was forced to draft in Steve Murphy, Richard Lucas and Ian Duerden, all of whom were on month-to-month contracts, to form a midfield trio. And though O'Regan wanted to include the experienced central-defender

Jon Brown challenges Peterborough's Scott Houghton in Town's first match back in the League.

Vince Overson, his registration was not cleared in time, just to add to his dilemma, and youngsters Damian Place and James Stansfield found themselves on the bench.

Cheered on by around 600 travelling supporters in baking sunshine the Shaymen deployed a sweeper system which served them well, with Jon Brown and Kevin Hulme featuring in a defensive back five, denying the home side the time to settle and restricting them to but a small handful of chances. In fact, the one that former Northern Ireland Jimmy Quinn missed early on, when he peeled away at the far post only to put his shot wide, was the best of the lot. But he was not alone in passing up golden opportunities. For the Shaymen, Geoff Horsfield found himself in the clear from Duerden's pass on the half-hour, only to drag his left-foot shot wide.

The honour of the first goal upon return to the Football League fell to Dave Hanson three minutes after the interval, a comic-book goal if ever there was one. In shepherding the ball back to his goalkeeper, central-defender Mark Bodley somehow fell over and in the ensuing tangle with Mark Tyler, the ball fell to Hanson, who had never given up the chase, and he had the simple task of walking the ball into the empty net.

It did not matter how the goal had been contrived, but the Shaymen grew in confidence, creating a succession of chances before Horsfield made amends for his first half miss with a goal all of his own making in the 75th minute. Forty yards from goal, he was faced with three defenders, but he battled his way into the area before unleashing a powerful shot which Tyler had little chance with.

The home supporters began rounding on their larger than life manager Barry Fry, and but for Duerden's effort in the last minute which was deflected wide by Bodley, Town could have won by more. It was a dream start for the Shaymen, and one which gained national attention, with O'Regan quickly being rounded up for interview with BBC Five Live. They would build on it, of course, because they were then a quality side and would head the table for a short time in November, but the loss of striker Geoff Horsfield was one they would never be able to replace. In time, this victory at London Road would serve as a timely reminder at just how good things were back then.

Peterborough United: Tyler, Scott, McMenamin, Castle, Bodley, Edwards, Farrell (Gill 46 mins), Payne (Hooper 68), Carruthers (Grazioli 79), Quinn, Houghton.
Halifax Town: Martin, Thackeray, Bradshaw, Lucas, Stoneman, S. Murphy, Duerden, Hulme, Hanson, Horsfield, Brown.
Referee: E. Lomas (Manchester)
Attendance: 5,746

Match to Remember 48   20 April 2002
Halifax Town 2   Rushden & Diamonds 4
Division Three

Though Brian Talbot's Rushden side, in their first season in the League after winning the Conference, arrived at The Shay on the season's last day needing a win to secure their place

Paul Harsley's penalty gives Town the lead against Rushden in what proved to be their last-ever Football League match.

in the Play-offs, for the Shaymen the fixture had a run-of-the-mill look about it. For them, relegation back to the Conference had been confirmed three matches earlier and now it was simply a case of winding up their programme. But the match would prove to be a highly significant one, if only because it was their last-ever in the Football League.

The supporters had long since given up on the team but nevertheless an above average 2,699 turned out for the match, many probably with a sense of occasion. Sadly, though, Town could not even go out with a bang – or even with 11 men on the pitch.

It had been a traumatic season, one which had seen the club with four different managerial teams and gone into administration, not to mention their relegation. Neil Redfearn, who had been joint caretaker manager with Tony Parks following the departure of Paul Bracewell and the appointment of Alan Little found himself back in the hotseat for the final 10 matches after Little had been taken ill and now sent out his charges for one final time.

A penalty from Paul Harsley, the season's one outstanding player, had given the Shaymen a lead they would hold until the interval, suggesting they were capable of a winning finale. It came after 22 minutes when Ian Fitzpatrick went down under a clumsy challenge from Andy Tillson, and Harsley tucked his kick away to goalkeeper, Billy Turley's right.

Harsley might have added another goal before half-time, though Andy Burgess' rising shot which cleared the bar was one that sounded a note of caution to the Shaymen, and one they should have heeded. For the game changed in the space of four minutes at the start of the second half, beginning with Onandi Lowe's glancing header home from Paul Underwood's left-wing cross after just 54 seconds. It was Lowe who then grabbed his 17th goal of the season when he headed in a centre from a Burgess cross.

Any realistic hope Town had of turning the game disappeared with the dismissal of a frustrated Neil Redfearn, who, having already been booked, kicked out at Stuart Wardley in the 54th minute, leaving referee Pike with no alternative but to show him a red card, even though Wardley had been the transgressor.

Town adopted a 3–3–3 formation, but it was to no avail as Rushden increased their lead after 62 minutes, Wardley scoring from close range, and the result was put totally beyond the Shaymen when Paul Hall converted Garry Butterworth's pass with a powerful shot from 10 yards in the 76th minute.

To their credit Town kept plugging away. Andy Farrell had hit the bar before Hall's goal, and four minutes from time Ian Fitzpatrick grabbed a salvo, a tap in following good work involving Steve Bushell, Craig Smith and Craig Midgley, who delivered the ball, with Fitzpatrick scoring against Rushden's substitute goalkeeper Tony Pennock, who had replaced Turley eight minutes earlier.

There was still enough time for a further dismissal, that of Rushden's Burgess for reacting angrily to Robert Herbert's challenge, but soon enough the game was over. The Town players left the field, only to return for a lap of (dis)honour for the benefit of those long-suffering fans who had bothered to remain.

Halifax Town: Richardson, Heinemann (Midgley 63 mins), Jules, Mitchell, Stoneman, Bushell, Harsley (Smith 84), Redfearn, Farrell, Fitzpatrick, Middleton (Herbert 66).
Rushden & Diamonds: Turley (Pennock 78), Mustafa, Underwood, Butterworth, Peters, Tillson, Hall, Wardley, Partridge (Setchell 89), Lowe (Angel 78), Burgess.
Referee: M.S. Pike (Barrow-in-Furness)
Attendance: 2,699

Match to Remember 49   19 May 2006
Halifax Town 2   Hereford United 3
Conference Play-off Final

There seems a certain degree of irony that Hereford United should have been the team standing between Halifax Town and a return to the Football League. They had, after all, been the side providing the opposition on the season's last day when the Shaymen were relegated to the Conference for the first time in May 1993.

Having suffered a second relegation in 2002, this Play-off Final represented the biggest opportunity for the Shaymen to make a second return to the Football League, a game which was singularly, with so much riding on it, the biggest the club ever played in. A fact not overlooked by the folk of Calderdale, around six thousand of whom made the journey to the Walkers Stadium, home of Leicester City, to cheer the Shaymen on. They returned disappointed, not merely because they had seen their side lose, but more because it seemed at one point that Chris Wilder's Town had had one foot in the door.

Hereford, managed by Graham Turner, had made the Play-off Final having defeated Morecambe over two legs in their semi-final, but having finished runners-up in the Conference to Accrington Stanley, were probably the more fancied of the two sides. Not that the Shaymen seemed concerned, and indeed it was they who took the lead in the 26th minute, Lewis Killeen firing home from 20 yards with the ball swinging away from goalkeeper Wayne Brown into the top corner, a spectacular goal. The lead, however, lasted

Ryan Sugden sees his header hit the arm of Tamika Mkandawire in the Play-off Final at Leicester, but the referee turned away Town's pleas for a penalty.

only seven minutes, as Hereford full-back Ryan Green made his way down the right flank and crossed for Andy Williams to head home at the far post.

In the second half, it was Hereford who had the best of the early exchanges, even having a penalty appeal turned down when Tyrone Thompson nudged Rob Purdie, but the referee waved away the claims, as he had done when Tamika Mkandawire clearly handled the ball from a Ryan Sugden header in the fifth minute.

Town's formation was disrupted when central-defender Greg Young, nursing a troublesome injured shoulder, retired and made way for Steve Bushell, but it was Town's second substitute John Grant, a former Hereford player, who made an impact eight minutes after replacing Ryan Sugden. After making ground down the left, Killeen whipped the ball across for Grant to guide the ball with his right foot beyond Brown. There were 17 minutes remaining.

Could Town hold out? Sadly, no. Bulls' burly substitute Guy Ipoua had been on the field only three minutes when he headed home Simon Travis' cross from the right six yards out. The game was destined to go to extra-time, but not before the ref had turned down another penalty appeal when Chris Senior was impeded by Alex Senior as he went past him.

Both managers offered words of encouragement to two sets of tired players, but it was Hereford who looked the more lively in extra-time, and in the 108th minute they took the lead for the first time when Green curled a lovely shot from just inside the box after the ball had ricocheted to him.

Crestfallen, the Town players had little left to offer, and the only notable piece of action in the second period of injury time was injury to the Hereford goalkeeper, who collided with Martin Foster and required treatment, which held the game up for six minutes.

An Adam Quinn header which cleared the crossbar was the closest Town came to snatching an equaliser which may have taken the game to penalties, but Hereford saw the game out and reclaimed their place back in the Football League after an absence of nine years.

Halifax Town: Kennedy, Haslam, Doughty (Senior 76 mins), Atherton, Quinn, Young (Bushell 61), Thompson, Foster, Sugden (Grant 65), Forrest, Killeen.

Hereford United: Brown, Green, Mkandawire, Beckwith, Jeannin, Travis, Ferrell, Stanley (Pitman 90), Purdie, Stansfield (Fleetwood 94), Williams (Ipoua 75).

Referee: Dean Whitestone (Northampton)
Attendance: 15,499

Match to Remember 50   26 April 2008
Halifax Town 1   Stevenage Borough 2
Blue Square Premier

Not for the first time did Stevenage Borough arrive at The Shay to play a match which would prove hugely significant. In the first instance, it was one that Halifax Town needed to win to avoid relegation to the Blue Square North; in the second it was one which was destined to be the last ever played by the club. Not that many believed either was conceivable, but the docking of 10 points following the club's decision to enter into administration had completely transformed Town's season. Where once they may have settled for mid-table security, now the players found themselves embroiled in a relegation battle following a disastrous set of results which had included a 6–1 mauling at home by Kidderminster Harriers.

Going into this Stevenage game, Town found themselves lying 20th after an unlikely 4–0 win at Crawley Town which left them two points clear of Altrincham, but still in danger of being relegated. The Shaymen knew once again that only victory would ensure safety. A defeat, coupled with an Altrincham win at Weymouth, would mean relegation.

The game, which kicked off at 5.15pm due to television company Setanta's decision to screen live the match at Weymouth, now attracted an above average crowd of 2,229, most spurring on the Shaymen while keeping an ear to radios for news of events at Weymouth, but the match at The Shay was far from a spectacle, with some Town players showing obvious signs of nerves. Still, it was the Shaymen who had the best of the early exchanges, with Danny Forrest failing to capitalise after Jon Shaw had pounced on a loose back pass after 22 minutes, and a couple of shots from on loan Simon Ainge failing to find the target.

But then suddenly Town were rocked when Stevenage took the lead after 27 minutes. Gavin Grant broke down the right and played in Steve Morison, who raced into the box and squeezed the ball between goalkeeper Adam Legzdins and the near post. Town responded with a couple of half chances, only to fall further behind right on the stroke of half-time. Grant, ever a threat down the right flank, broke free and fired home a shot across Legzdins which nestled in the far corner. Still, as the players went in at the break, news came through that Altrincham were losing 2–1, so the advantage was still with the Shaymen.

Andy Campbell tries his luck from the edge of the area in the last match with Stevenage Borough.

But they preferred not to rely on a result 300 miles away and made an all-out effort to change the outcome of the game at The Shay. But the only breakthrough they made was when the referee awarded Town a penalty after 67 minutes when the ball bounced up and hit Morison's arm. Leading scorer Shaw stepped up to score his 20th of the season but nobody reckoned then that it would be the last-ever goal scored for Halifax Town in their present guise.

As the game wore on, Town pushed forward and created a number of opportunities, notably substitute Andy Campbell's 20-yard half volley which was well saved by goalkeeper Clark Masters. The final whistle, though, spelled defeat for the Shaymen who then had an anxious wait for news from the Essex Stadium, Weymouth. There, the game had run into six minutes of injury-time with the scores level at 2–2, but when it ended with no further change, Town players, officials and supporters rejoiced.

For six days at least.

Halifax Town: Legzdins, Griffith, Doughty, Ainge, Quinn, Wright, Killeen (Stamp 79 mins), Kearney (Davies 54), Shaw, Forrest (Campbell 46), Heslop.
Stevenage Borough: Masters, Wilson, Westwood, Henry, Smith, Grant (Berry 89), McMahon, Martin, Moore (Vincenti 72), O'Sullivan (Laird 84).
Referee: P. Quinn (Middlesbrough)
Attendance: 2,229

101 HALIFAX TOWN GREATS

Any such list is always subjective. No two fans would ever, in all probability, pick the same players. The list here represents players who I believe qualify for varying reasons, such as longevity as service, record breakers, or for simply being outstanding. Arguments may rage, but the author has attempted to retain a balance, so players from all eras are represented.

ALLISON, Wayne Anthony

Centre-forward, 6ft 1in, 12st 6lb
Born: Huddersfield, 16 October 1968
Career: Halifax Town, trainee 23 August 1986, professional 6 July 1987; Watford 26 July 1989 (£250,000); Bristol City 9 August 1990 (£300,000); Swindon Town 25 July 1995 (£475,000); Huddersfield Town 10 November 1997 (£800,000); Tranmere Rovers 3 September 1999; Sheffield United July 2002; Chesterfield 25 June 2004, reserve-team coach August 2007 to 7 March 2007; Chester City assistant manager September 2008 to November 2008; Bury coach December 2008 to January 2009; Tranmere Rovers coach October 2009 to cs 2010.
Halifax Town debut: v Rotherham United, Freight Rover Trophy, 5 December 1986

Wayne Allison was an effective and much-sought-after, target-man whose career 20 years and nine clubs after initially making an impact with Halifax Town. Nicknamed 'The Chief', Allison first arrived at The Shay as a schoolboy in 1984, and having signed trainee forms two years later, he played for the Northern Intermediate side under Gerry Brook and as centre-forward, finished top scorer as the youngsters clinched the Northern Intermediate title in 1986–87, a season which saw Allison make his first-team bow under manager Billy Ayre. Allison will probably be best remembered for the part he played in Town's goal fest during the first half of the 1988–89 season when he partnered Terry McPhillips in attack. Between them, they ran up 44 goals, but it was perhaps the two Allison scored in a 3–0 FA Cup win at Altrincham, captured by the television cameras, which put him in the shop window.

    In July 1989 Allison joined Watford in what was then a Halifax Town record deal worth £250,000, but never did himself justice there and when new manager Colin Lee came in Allison was sold to Bristol City. Allison enjoyed some heady nights with the Robins over a five-year period, not least the famous FA Cup third round replay victory at Premier League side Liverpool in January 1994. Allison was top scorer at Ashton Gate in three of his seasons and scored over 50 League and Cup goals. But it was with Swindon Town that he had his most successful spell, finishing top scorer with 17 goals in his first season as his new side clinched the Second Division title. So popular did Allison become at the County Ground that he was voted by supporters as one of Swindon Town's 100 Greats.

    In November 1997 Allison joined Huddersfield Town under Peter Jackson and struck up a lethal partnership with Marcus Stewart. He then enjoyed more glory in the FA Cup with Tranmere Rovers, helping them reach the quarter-finals in consecutive seasons, though he was forced to sit out their appearance in the Final of the Worthington Cup against Leicester City in February 2000 due to being Cup-tied. Allison moved to Neil Warnock's Sheffield United in July

2002, and in what was an unforgettable first season with the club, he figured as the Blades lost agonisingly in the semi-finals of both Worthington and FA Cups to Liverpool and Arsenal respectively, as well as losing the Division One Play-off Final to Wolverhampton Wanderers.

He wound down his career with Chesterfield and later acted as reserve coach, before having moving to Chester City in a coaching role. He briefly coached at Bury, too, then returned to Tranmere Rovers as assistant to Les Parry in October 2009 until the end of that season.

ALLSOP, William Henry

Right-back, 5ft 10in, 11st 8lb
Born: Ripley, 29 January 1912
Died: Halifax, 24 April 1997
Career: Chesterfield district football; Bolton Wanderers 1930; Port Vale August 1931; Halifax Town 2 June 1934 to cs 1947.
Halifax Town debut: v Mansfield Town, Division Three North, 25 August 1934

Had World War Two not intervened, it seems likely that full-back Bill Allsop would have gone on to rack up more League appearances for Halifax Town than any other player. Of his record 509 competitive first-team appearances for the club, 234 were made during wartime, and added to his appearances made in friendlies during this period, Allsop's finally tally of appearances totalled 509, a quite remarkable achievement but one that is testament to his consistency.

Allsop first discovered his love for football when he attended Waingroves School, Ripley, and at the age of 18 he was signed by Second Division Bolton Wanderers, though he was never destined to appear in the first team. After one season with the Burnden Park club, Allsop joined Port Vale in August 1931, though again, he was confined to the reserves for the most part. He made his League debut in a 2-0 victory at Bristol City on 16 January 1932, his only appearance that season, and his extended run in the side towards the end of the following campaign took his total of League appearances for the Valiants to six games. Allsop spent the whole of 1933-34 back in the reserves, and it was to Halifax Town under Alex Raisbeck that he turned for regular first-team football.

Allsop saw more than just regular first-team action; he became an almost permanent fixture in the side over the next 12 seasons, establishing full-back partnerships with Jock Taylor, Alf Pope and Harold Jackson. Adept on either flank, Allsop helped the side to runners'-up spot in his first season at The Shay, missed only eight games in his first five seasons with the club and, under manager Jimmy Thomson, was elected captain at the start of the 1937-38 season, a reward for his splendid level of consistent form.

Despite the outbreak of war in September 1939, Allsop remained in Halifax, and completed a record run of 188 consecutive appearances for the club when he played in the 7-0 defeat at Sheffield Wednesday on 14 April 1945, injury in that match forcing him to sit out the match at Bradford City the following week. His only goal for the club had come during that run, in a 3-2 defeat by Hartlepools United in November 1939.

Allsop spent one more season at The Shay when the Football League recommenced in August 1946 before hanging up his boots. He ran Elite Taxis in Halifax, then joined United Biscuits in Ovenden, retiring as distribution depot manager in 1977. Allsop continued to retain his connections with Halifax Town, being a member of the Old Players' Association and continued to live in Siddal area of the town until his death in April 1997.

ATKINS, William Mark
Centre-forward, 6ft 2in, 12st 7lb
Born: Solihull, 9 May 1939
Career: Birmingham GPO; Aston Villa May 1958; Swindon Town June 1959; Halifax Town 21 August 1965 (player-exchange); Stockport County 16 March 1967; Portsmouth April 1969; Halifax Town 31 October 1969 (£9,000); Rochdale 9 December 1972 (£2,000); Darlington 28 September 1973, coach July 1975; Luddendenfoot player-coach March 1977.
Halifax Town debut: v Tranmere Rovers (h), Division Four, 21 August 1965

Big Bill Atkins twice featured in player-exchange deals involving Halifax Town and was afforded cult status after scoring prolifically in both spells with the club. For despite standing 6ft 3in tall, Atkins was more than just a target man. Quite speedy for a big man, he had nimble feet and was as good on the ground as he was in the air, and on his day was virtually unplayable, as evinced by his performance for Halifax Town against Aston Villa in November 1970 when he scored two senstaional goals. But his crowning moment must surely have been his glancing header which set Town on the way to defeating a star-studded Manchester United side 2–1 at The Shay in a Watney Cup match in July 1971.

Atkins's career took off after being spotted playing for Birmingham GPO and he was signed by Aston Villa manager Eric Houghton in May 1958, but moved to Swindon Town a year later to find first-team football and linked up with future stars Ernie Hunt and Mike Summerbee. He scored handsomely, but when manager Danny Williams sought a new goalkeeper to replace Tony Hicks, Atkins found himself as the makeweight, moving to Halifax Town prior to the start of the 1965–66 season while Peter Downsborough moved to the County Ground. Atkins quickly became a hit with the supporters, top-scoring with 19 League goals as Halifax Town, under Willie Watson, dragged themselves out of re-election uncertainty to mid-table respectability. He continued his rich goalscoring form the following season, and had hit 15 by the time Stockport County came in for him in March 1967. It was an extraordinary deal, for not only was another player involved – in this case Stockport's Dave Shawcross – but both players found themselves playing against their former club the very next day! Though not a scorer in that game Atkins contributed three goals in the end of season run-in, including the 82nd-minute headed goal against Notts County which clinched promotion to the Third Division as Stockport ended the season as champions.

Atkins went on to form a formidable strike partnership in 1967–68 with Jim Fryatt, one which showed no signs of slowing down when Fryatt was sold to Blackburn in October 1968. Atkins, too, was soon on the move again, joining Second Division Portsmouth, though he struggled to impose himself during his time at Fratton Park and desiring a move back north, he jumped at the chance of rejoining Halifax Town in October 1969, who were by now in the Third Division. Atkins carried on from where he had left and finished top scorer in both his first season back at The Shay, and in 1970–71 when Town, now under George Kirby, made a late bid for promotion to the Second Division. But two seasons later, George Mulhall let Atkins go, claiming he wasn't his type of player and he joined Rochdale, staying for less than a year before winding up his career with Darlington, where he scored the last of his 157 League goals. In July 1975 Atkins was appointed coach at Feethams, then in March 1977 he became player-manager of Halifax side Luddendenfoot, who played in the WRCFA, while concentrating on running his own bakery in Keighley.

BARBER, Lewis Frederick

Goalkeeper
Born: Wombwell, 11 April 1906
Died: Halifax, 14 June 1983
Career: Broomhill WMC; Halifax Town trialist October 1925, professional 18 January 1926; Manchester City 3 June 1927, retired 1930.
Halifax Town debut: v Accrington Stanley, Division Three North, 13 February 1926

There is little doubting that Barber was one of the finest goalkeepers to have turned out for Halifax Town, and from the outset he was destined for greater things. Indeed, he was widely tipped for England honours and but for injury would surely have fulfilled that dream. Such were his talents that Barber rose to the first team aged only 19 after spending one season in the reserves aged only 19 and never looked back. Discovered playing for Broomhill WMC, a Barnsley district junior club, Barber was invited to The Shay for trials by manager Joe McClelland in October 1925 and spent a season in the reserves under the tutelage of Bob Suter, though he was called upon for first-team duty twice during 1925–26 due to suspension to Jack Newton, making his League debut in a 1–1 draw with Accrington Stanley despite having a split hand, an injury sustained in a reserve match. The following season Barber ousted Jerry Best from the side and quickly became a Shay idol as Halifax Town made an ultimately unsuccessful challenge for the Division Three North title. Barber played in 33 successive League games until the end of the season, by which time a number of clubs had already cast their eyes over him. In fact, the *Halifax Courier* dated 20 January 1927 ran a story scotching rumours that Barber had been sold to Newcastle United for a 'fabulous transfer fee.' Manager Joe McClelland said such stories were 'groundless' and that as long as the financial position allowed, then the club would not part with their men.

But still not affluent, and with wages to pay during the close season, Halifax Town accepted an offer made by Manchester City – it was believed to be a club record received by the cub of £1,200 – and at the beginning of June 1927 Barber signed for the First Division club, initially as cover for Welsh international Bert Gray. But Barber forced his way into the first team and made the position his own, being ever-present during 1929–30 as City challenged for the title. Sadly, however, despite his growing reputation, tragedy struck in a game at Chelsea in November 1930 when Barber sustained a leg injury which resulted in his premature retirement from top class football. Latterly, Barber worked in Halifax for Pratts Hydraulics and Elliott Wilson engineering firms up until retirement, but remained in the game by acting as a scout for Halifax Town.

BARKAS, Thomas

Inside-left, 5ft 7in, 10st 8lb
Born: South Shields, 27 March 1912
Died: Halifax, 11 June 1991
Career: Bolden Colliery; Hebburn Colliery; Washington Colliery; Bradford City September 1932. Halifax Town 14 December 1934; Rochdale 10 September 1946; Stockport County November 1947; Carlisle United February 1949; Scunthorpe United cs 1949.
Halifax Town debut: v Hartlepools United, Division Three North, 15 December 1934

Tom Barkas was probably the most complete inside-forward seen in a Halifax Town shirt during the 1930s, striking up an effective left-flank partnership with Fred Tunstall after his arrival from Bradford City in December 1934. One of five brothers who all played professional football, Tom followed the most famous of those, Sam, to Bradford City in September 1932 after playing non-League football, latterly with Washington Colliery. But while Sam went on to win five England caps following his move to Manchester City, Tom played in the lower divisions, never destined to appear in the top flight his talents might have suggested he should. Tom joined his brother in the Bradford City side on several occasions before Sam's transfer in April 1934, and before the year was out Tom was on the move, too. Injuries to forwards Albert Valentine and Tom Feeney prompted Halifax Town manager Alex Raisbeck to bring him to The Shay, but having made the switch, Barkas became an automatic selection as Halifax Town made a bold bid for promotion during 1934–35.

Despite being only 22 when he joined the club, Barkas was quickly famed for his craft, powerful shooting, tremendous vision and the ability to play the slide-rule pass, and created many goals for top scorer Valentine while weighing in with plenty himself. During 1936–37 Barkas was second highest scorer with 13 despite being out of the team for two months following an appendix operation. Talks of a move to one of the top clubs were not without foundation, and in fact, only Town's continued run in the FA Cup during 1938–39 prevented a £1,500 move to Newcastle United. An achiever on the field, Barkas was also one off it. He was probably at his peak as a player when the war broke out and in January 1940 he signed up with the RAF and it was while serving with them that he was awarded the B.E.M. for bravery shown during the German raids over Malta in March 1942. Barkas continued to play football with the RAF, and indeed, captained the side to trophy success in a wartime tournament on the island in September 1943 before returning to skipper Halifax Town the following February, helping them lift the Combined Counties Cup after two-legged victory over Huddersfield Town. But despite playing throughout the 1945–46 season, Barkas, upon his return from a Norway FA coaching tour in August 1946, rejected new terms when League football resumed and expressed his desire to find another club.

Barkas settled for Rochdale, and went on to play for Stockport County and Carlisle United before ending his playing days with then non-League side Scunthorpe United, having the misfortune to break his leg following a challenge by Dave Mycock in a reserve match against Halifax in December 1949. Upon retiring from the game, Barkas, who had continued to live in Halifax, took up employment at Holdsworth Mills, then Meredith and Jones, then latterly worked as an assistant at Elland Crematorium and as a lollipop man.

BARR, William Joseph

Defender/Midfielder, 5ft 11in, 10st 8lb
Born: Halifax, 21 January 1969
Career: Halifax Town trainee 23 August 1986, professional 6 July 1987; Crewe Alexandra 17 June 1994, Carlisle United 18 July 1997; Workington Reds October 2001; Carlisle United youth coach, caretaker manager April 2002 to August 2002, youth-team manager; Preston North End coach July 2006 to January 2010; Sheffield Wednesday coach January 2010 to January 2011.
Halifax Town debut: v Bradford City, West Riding Senior Cup, 12 August 1986 (sub)

As a Halifax lad born and bred, nobody felt the pain of Halifax Town's relegation to the Conference in May 1993 more than Billy Barr, particularly as he was by then skipper of the side. Barr had joined Halifax Town as a schoolboy in 1986 and developed under coach Gerry Brook in the Northern

Intermediate side, and though it was younger brother Bobby who made his League debut first, it was Billy who went on to carve out a profitable footballing career for himself before going into coaching. He started out as a forward, a position in which he featured during the side's Northern Intermediate title success of 1986–87, but once promoted to the first team would often appear at full-back, though he would later prove to be something of a jack-of-all-trades.

Restored to the side by Mick Rathbone after largely being overlooked by John McGrath, Barr was made captain and led by example on the field during the relegation season of 1992–93, thumping home a memorable 35-yard effort against Shrewsbury Town and being chosen as the club's Player of the Year, though this was scant consolation for the club's demise. Barr spent one more season with Halifax Town in the Conference before making a clean break in June 1994 and joining Crewe Alexandra. In 1996–97 he helped his new club reach the Division Two Play-offs, but he did not appear in their Wembley Final victory over Brentford. Barr joined Carlisle United in July 1997 and, though injury blighted his time there, he undertook his coaching qualifications and was appointed reserve-team coach following a spell with Workington Reds. He also had a spell as caretaker manager throughout the summer of 2002 during the bitter Michael Knighton-Roddy Collins fiasco, then later served under Paul Simpson, who he followed to Preston North End as coach. Barr then worked under Alan Irvine at Deepdale and followed him to Sheffield Wednesday. Following Irvine's sacking in January 2011, Barr also left the club following the arrival as manager of Gary Megson.

BELL, Derek Martin

Forward, 5ft 8in, 11st 5lb
Born: Wyberton, 30 October 1956
Career: Derby County apprentice, professional October 1974; Halifax Town 29 May 1975; Sheffield Wednesday on loan 11 March 1976; Barnsley 25 October 1978 (£30,000); Lincoln City 22 November 1979 (£33,000); Chesterfield August 1983 (£8,500); Scunthorpe United January 1984; Boston United March 1986; Spalding United; Lincoln United; York City coach; Lincoln City coach January 1999.
Halifax Town debut: v Leeds United, West Riding Senior Cup, 8 August 1975

Derek Bell, nicknamed 'Dinger' by the fans, was one of Halifax Town's most popular in the late 1970s. A livewire forward, he was signed by Johnny Quinn on a free transfer, and though his time at The Shay coincided with a period of struggle, he often put smiles on the long faces of the supporters with some exciting forward play and memorable goals. Who could ever forget his bicycle kick which earned Town a point against Graham Taylor's champions-elect Watford side in April 1978? After completing his apprenticeship, Bell signed professional forms with Dave Mackay's Derby County in October 1974, though he failed to break into the Rams' star-studded first team. But upon the recommendation of Derby assistant manager Des Anderson, Town boss Quinn signed him at end of May 1975 with the offer of regular first-team football. Bell made a significant impact as his goals initially propelled Halifax Town to the top of the Third Division, but the side began to struggle and following Quinn's sacking, his successor Alan Ball Snr immediately dropped Bell to make way for new signings and sent him on a month's loan to relegation rivals Sheffield Wednesday. He returned to The Shay but could not help prevent Town's relegation. Bell struggled to hold down a place in the side under Ball during 1976–77 but was allowed the chance to shine under Jimmy Lawson the following season, and ended as joint-top scorer with Mickey Bullock with nine goals and was voted the supporters' Player of the Year.

In September 1978, Bell became Barnsley manager Allan Clarke's first signing, costing the Tykes £30,000, but so badly did Halifax Town struggle without him that by the following March Bell still headed the side's goalscoring list with the three goals he had scored before he left. Bell immediately helped his new club to promotion, finishing top scorer with 18 League goals, one of which was a penalty against Town on his first return to The Shay in a 2–0 win. In November 1979 Bell became Fourth Division Lincoln City's record transfer, costing £36,000, helping them to promotion as runners-up to Southend United in 1980–81. But the following season, Bell broke his leg and made only fleeting appearances, usually from the bench, and it was not until 1982–83 that he rediscovered his old form, netting a hat-trick in the 9–0 destruction of Bournemouth in December 1982, but the side just missed out on promotion to the Second Division. At the end of that term Bell joined Chesterfield but finished the 1983–84 season with Scunthorpe United, his last League club. Thereafter, he drifted into non-League football, playing for Boston United, Spalding United and Lincoln United, as well as holding coaching positions at York City and Lincoln City.

BETTERIDGE, Frank
Left-winger,
Born: Worksop, 12 January 1911
Died: Halifax, 1972
Career: Manton Colliery; Denaby United; Worksop Town; Halifax Town 4 August 1930; Barrow June 1936; Goole Town July 1937.
Halifax Town debut: v Nelson (a), Division Three North, 17 January 1931

Frank Betteridge could consider himself unlucky. For a while there was mounting excitement at The Shay following the arrival of left-winger Fred Tunstall in February 1933, his signing was at the expense of young Betteridge, who duly found himself confined to the reserves and called up for first-team duty only through Tunstall's unavailability. Yet Betteridge had proved his worth to the side as an exciting winger, even though Halifax Town struggled in his first seasons his early years at The Shay. Betteridge spent his early footballing days turning out for Manton Colliery, Denaby United and Worksop Town, before impressing Halifax Town manager Joe McClelland in the 1930 pre-season trial matches and signing for the club that August. Having been groomed in the reserves, Betteridge was called up for his first-team debut for the match at Nelson in January 1931, combining well with his inside-left partner Sedley Cooper, and though Town lost the game, Betteridge held his place in the side until the end of that season. The following term, Betteridge missed just three matches, all through injury, but Tunstall's arrival saw him relegated to the reserves and first-team opportunities became limited. But over the course of six seasons with Halifax Town, Betteridge did have his moments. Those who witnessed it would remember for many years his audacious shot out of the blue from 20 yards which defeated Accrington Stanley at The Shay in November 1931. Against Hull City in January 1932 he ran half the length of the field to score the equaliser after Town had been two goals down, and it was Betteridge, turning in Valentine's header, who scored the winner over recently crowned champions Doncaster Rovers in the last match of the 1934–35 season to clinch second place, and thus ensure Town's highest-ever finish.

Betteridge's loyalty to Halifax Town never in question, the board of directors awarded him a benefit season in 1935–36, and on 27 April 1936 Halifax Town played out a 2–2 draw with Leeds United in front of 2,000 spectators, but the following Saturday he made what proved to be his last appearance for the club in a 2–1 defeat at Walsall. By a stroke of irony, he lined up alongside

Tunstall for the first and only time – Betteridge featured at inside-left – and while Tunny left to begin a long association with Boston United, Betteridge, given a free transfer, joined Barrow. He spent one season at Holker Road, making 29 League appearances and scoring four goals before finishing his career with Goole Town in the Yorkshire League. Betteridge later returned to Halifax, where he died in 1972.

BREAKS, Edward
Left-back
Born: Halifax, 29 December 1919
Died: Halifax, 9 November 2000
Career: Copley Under-18s; Siddal; Regimental football; Halifax Town amateur August 1947, part-time professional July 1948, reserve coach 1956, first-team coach January 1962 to cs 1962.
Halifax Town debut: v Mansfield Town (h), Division Three North, 13 September 1948

Ted Breaks spent his whole professional career with his home-town club as both player and coach, and though it appeared he was always destined to play for Halifax Town after starring in the local sides with Copley Under-18s and Siddal, conscription in March 1940 meant his first-team debut was delayed until after the end of World War Two. Although even then, he might have considered himself lucky to still be alive, for when serving in Libya with the 7th Queen's Own Hussars, his tank was hit by a German shell. It was while serving with the forces that Breaks developed his footballing skills, being made captain of the regimental team and Halifax Town boss Jimmy Thompson became aware of Breaks' talents after he'd returned home following demobilization in 1946. But though he tried to sign him, Breaks elected to work for Holdsworth Weavers at Shaw Lodge Mills, and it wasn't until Jack Breedon approached him in August 1947 that he committed himself to Halifax Town, signing as an amateur. The period after the war was an austere one for Halifax Town, but Breaks was one of the few leading lights after accepting part-time terms during 1948–49, the player considering himself too old at 27 to make a proper career from football.

Breaks spent two and half years as a regular in the struggling Shay side, but his form led to talk of a move to Southampton after Alf Ramsey had been sold to Tottenham Hotspur. Nothing came of it, and Breaks remained at The Shay, going on to make 186 first-team appearances. Not noted for his scoring prowess, Breaks only managed to find the net once, but it was considered a crucial goal at the time. It came in a match against Crewe Alexandra on 15 April 1950 when he had been switched to the forward line after injuring his knee earlier in the game, and with the scores level at 1–1, he hobbled into the box to crash home the ball from six yards. The goal spurred the side to a 3–1 victory and gave hope of avoiding a re-election application, but ultimately Town were condemned on goal average. With the best of his playing days behind him, manager Harry Hooper offered Breaks the role of reserve coach before he moved up to first-team coach in January 1962, a position he held until the following summer when he went back into the weaving trade with British Furtex at Luddendenfoot. But Breaks remained in the game at local level, first playing and coaching with Hebden Bridge until he was 47, then subsequently with St Mary's as coach.

BROWN, Philip
Right-back, 5ft 11in, 11st 6lb
Born: South Shields, 30 May 1959
Career: St Hilda's Juniors; Hartlepool United 7 July 1978; Halifax Town 30 July 1985; Bolton Wanderers 23 June 1988 (£17,000); Blackpool 25 July 1994; Bolton Wanderers coach cs 1996,

caretaker manager, assistant manager; Derby County manager June 2005 to 30 January 2006; Hull City manager December 2006 to 7 June 2010; Preston North End manager 6 January 2011.
Halifax Town debut: v Bradford City (h), West Riding Senior Cup, 29 July 1985

Phil Brown ended the 1986–87 season as Halifax Town's top scorer with 12 goals, an impressive total considering he played each of his 44 appearances of the 46–game programme that season at right full-back, and even given that six of his goals were penalties. His goal return – he scored 20 in his three seasons at The Shay – suggested Brown liked to join the attack, a dimension that he did indeed add to his game. But Brown was more noted for being an accomplished a defender as Halifax Town had in the 1980s, having arrived in July 1985 with 217 League games with Hartlepool United under his belt. Brown was signed by 'Pool manager Billy Horner from local side St Hilda's Juniors in July 1978 and, turning his back on a career as an electrician, made his League debut in the home defeat by Peterborough United on 1 March 1980. He quickly made the right-back position his own, being ever-present the following season, and thereafter, missed only a handful of games over the course of the next four seasons. It was Mick Jones who brought Brown to The Shay and immediately made him captain. Brown also acted as the club's PFA representative and worked on behalf of his colleagues when the club faced yet another financial crisis in December 1986.

On the field, Brown added authority to the defensive live, playing alongside future internationals Alan Knill and Mick Galloway. But with the club seemingly forever cash-strapped, success was hard to come by, though Brown did play his part in the Sherpa Van Trophy run to the northern semi-final in March 1988, when Town bowed to Burnley on penalties, with Brown scoring the first of Town's allotted five spot kicks. That season saw Brown become the first Halifax Town voted into the PFA Fourth Division side, and a successful season for the player was topped off nicely when he was voted Player of the Year by the Halifax Town supporters. At the end of that season, however, Brown joined Bolton Wanderers, against whom he had starred in three FA Cup meetings between the sides in 1986–87, and helped his new club win the Sherpa Van Trophy in his first season, beating Torquay United 4–1 at Wembley. A move to Blackpool in July 1994 first brought Brown in contact with Sam Allardyce, who was then cutting his teeth in management, and Brown was appointed player-coach. He helped the Seasiders to the Third Division Play-off Final, but they suffered a shock aggregate defeat to Bradford City after holding a two-goal advantage from the first leg.

Retiring from playing in 1996, Brown rejoined Bolton as coach under Colin Todd, taking over as caretaker boss when Todd resigned in September 1999. But Brown renewed acquaintances with Allardyce when he succeeded Todd, though Allardyce was keen to have Brown as his right-hand man, and together they helped shape the club, stabilising them in the Premiership. But Brown had always wanted to try his own luck at management and in June 2005 he took over the reins at Derby County but was sacked after only seven months in charge.

While appeared regularly on television as a football pundit, Brown returned to coaching, joining Hull City under Phil Parkinson on October 2006, then acted as joint manager with Colin Murphy following Parkinson's sacking less than two months later. Having steered the side out of the relegation zone, Brown was appointed full-time manager on 4 January 2007 and Hull City finished 21st, seven points clear of relegation. Astonishingly, the following term, Brown guided the Tigers into the top flight for the first time via the Play-offs following a 1–0 victory over Bristol City. Hull made a terrific start to their first season in the Premier League and Brown was named Manager of the Month for September. But they only just survived, and a series of disappointing results the following term led to Brown being put on 'gardening leave' as Iain Dowie stepped into the breach. Hull City were ultimately relegated and Brown's contract was terminated on 7 June 2010. However, in January 2011 he returned to management with Preston North End in succession to Darren Ferguson.

BURGIN, Andrew
Full-back, 5ft 8in, 9st 8lb
Born: Sheffield, 6 March 1947
Career: Sheffield Wednesday apprentice August 1962, professional March 1964; Rotherham United August 1967, Detroit Cougars (USA) April 1968; Halifax Town on loan 18 December 1968, signed March 1969; Blackburn Rovers 6 September 1974 to January 1977.
Halifax Town debut: v Port Vale (h), Division Four, 21 December 1968

When full-back Mick Buxton broke his leg in the abandoned game at Peterborough United in December 1968, manager Alan Ball immediately turned to Rotherham United to sign Andy Burgin as his replacement, initially on loan for three months. Burgin went straight into the side for Town's next match, started every game until the season's close – his signing had been made permanent in March 1969 – and played his part in the side's promotion from the Fourth Division in the bargain. A steady and reliable full-back, Burgin joined Sheffield Wednesday as an apprentice in August 1962, turning professional in March 1964 and coming into the side as cover for Brian Hill for an FA Cup tie against Everton on 9 January 1965. With the match at Hillsborough ending all-square, Burgin appeared in the replay which Wednesday lost 3–0, though the following Saturday, he made his only League appearance for the Owls in a 3–2 defeat by Liverpool. In August 1967 Burgin moved to Rotherham United, and spent the following summer playing in the North American Soccer League with Detroit Cougars.

Burgin's return to England could not have been more timely, and though he came to The Shay initially to fill the vacancy at left-back created by Buxton's unfortunate injury, it was to his favoured right-flank that he switched before the season was out, a position he made his own over the course of the next five seasons, being ever-present in 1969–70. So assured did Burgin perform that George Kirby was quick to appoint him as skipper for the 1970–71 season, and Kirby's successor Ray Henderson was of similar mind. A player who liked to roam forward, Burgin chipped in with four goals during 1970–71, and two seasons later, his 30-yard winner that completed a fightback against Tranmere Rovers at The Shay proved crucial in the long run as Town avoided relegation on goal average. In September 1974, Burgin joined fellow Third Division side Blackburn Rovers and in a scenario not dissimilar to his first season with Halifax, he helped his new club to instant promotion, featuring in 40 matches as Rovers clinched the title by one point over Plymouth Argyle, and earning the respect of his peers by being named at left-back in the PFA Third Division side.

But a freak accident in September 1975 curtailed Burgin's career, when, in a game at Southampton, he collided with teammate Mike Hickman and received a leg injury that kept him from playing first-team football again. At the end of the 1976–77 season Burgin retired from the game, bowing out with a joint testimonial with Mick Heaton on 16 May 1977 when Blackburn took on First Division runners-up Manchester City at Ewood Park, winning 2–1. After football, Burgin became a publican, and latterly has worked as a school caretaker.

BUSHELL, Stephen Paul

Midfield, 5ft 9in, 11st 6lb
Born: Manchester, 28 December 1972
Career: York City trainee, professional 25 February 1991; Blackpool 22 June 1998; Stalybridge Celtic August 2001; Halifax Town 21 November 2001; Altrincham on loan 24 November 2005; Altrincham July 2006; Halifax Town 15 June 2007; Hyde United 1 January 2008; Bradford Park Avenue October 2008 to February 2009.
Halifax Town debut: v Torquay United, Division Three, 24 November 2001

Combative midfielder Steve Bushell never shirked a tackle during his time with Halifax Town and his performances deservedly earned himself the supporters' Player of the Year award in 2003–04. Having arrived midway through the 2001–02 campaign, Bushell turned out to be one of the few pluses from a season which ended in relegation to the Conference. Bushell started his career as a trainee with York City and broke into the first team in March 1991, a month after turning professional. He went on to make 174 League appearances for the Minstermen and score 10 goals before signing for Blackpool but by the time Halifax Town boss Alan Little brought him to The Shay in November 2001, Bushell had dropped into the Conference with Stalybridge Celtic. Little, of course, knew him well from his own time at York, and doubtless he hoped he would inspire a team already deep in relegation trouble. Despite his best efforts, however, Town could not avoid the drop.

With the club having entered into administration Bushell, a livewire personality, had his contract terminated, but incoming manager Chris Wilder immediately invited him back and made him skipper. But while a return to the Football League remained elusive, it was not for the want of trying on Bushell's behalf. Town lost his services after he broke his leg in a game at Barnet in April 2005, and part of his rehabilitation saw him go out on loan to Altrincham the following November, though he returned to the fold in January 2006 to play his part in Town's push for a Play-off place. Never a prolific scorer, Bushell did contribute several important goals, not least a terrific free-kick in the Play-off semi-final against Grays Athletic at The Shay.

Bushell surprised many with his decision to quit the club once the Play-off Final had been lost and he returned to Altrincham, only to be brought back to The Shay by Wilder in June 2007. But his performances never quite matched those prior to his injury and after taking his tally of first-team appearances to 170 and 10 goals he joined Hyde United in January 2008, then spent a short time with Bradford Park Avenue.

BUTLER, Lee Simon

Goalkeeper, 6ft 2in, 14st 4lb
Born: Sheffield, 30 May 1966
Career: Harworth Colliery August 1985; Lincoln City 16 June 1986; Boston United on loan January 1986; Aston Villa 21 August 1987 (£100,000); Hull City on loan 18 March 1991; Barnsley 22 July 1991 (£165,000); Scunthorpe United on loan 5 February 1996; Wigan Athletic 5 July 1996; Dunfermline Athletic 3 July 1998; Halifax Town 23 September 1999, retired December 2001; Doncaster Rovers 25 January 2002; Halifax Town assistant manager 2 July 2002; Alfreton Town 30 May 2003; Halifax Town coach June 2005; Doncaster Rovers coach 29 January 2008.
Halifax Town debut: v Carlisle United, Division Three, 25 September 1999

Lee Butler was one of the most popular personalities around The Shay, a joker in the changing room, but he will chiefly be remembered for being a top class goalkeeper who answered an emergency call from Mark Lillis and signed for Halifax Town in September 1999 for the first of what proved to be three separate spells with the club. Butler was playing for Harworth Colliery when he was signed by Lincoln City in June 1986 and after being loaned out to Boston United early in his career, he vied with Trevor Swinburne at Sincil Bank. He made his League debut in a 1–1 draw at Cambridge United on 27 September 1986 and eventually made the goalkeeping position his own, though Lincoln would become the first team automatically relegated to the Conference at the end of that 1986–87 season. Yet Butler's performances during a traumatic season had not gone unnoticed, and a £100,000 move to Graham Taylor's First Division Aston Villa side followed, though he would only act as understudy to Nigel Spink and was restricted to just eight first-team appearances in four seasons with the club. After a loan spell at Hull City, Butler was sold to Second Division Barnsley in July 1991, where he spent five seasons before moving to Wigan Athletic in July 1996, immediately helping his new team clinch the Third Division title on goal difference over Fulham, with Butler ever-present.

Butler spent two seasons at Springfield Park but was playing with Scottish Premier Division side Dunfermline Athletic when he answered Lillis's call. He immediately proved a capable custodian, showing a safe pair of hands and being an excellent shot-stopper, and Butler was an overwhelming winner of the club's Player of the Year award at the end of that season. Sadly, Butler's time at The Shay not only coincided with a downward spiral in the club's fortunes, but a recurring knee injury forced his early retirement from playing in December 2001, although he found himself immediately back in the side as substitute for his intended replacement Peter Crookes, who was sent off on his debut against Shrewsbury Town.

Butler moved to Doncaster Rovers, then of the Conference, and returned to action before agreeing to join former Shay teammate Chris Wilder at Alfreton Town, then immediately following him back to The Shay when Wilder took over the reins at Halifax Town, by now also in the Conference. Surprisingly Butler became first-choice keeper once more, making 37 Conference appearances in 2002–03 before returning to Alfreton as coach. But he was soon back to assist Wilder in June 2005 and filled in as emergency 'keeper on three occasions during Town's Play-off season. In January 2008, however, Butler departed for a final time to take up a position as goalkeeping coach at Doncaster Rovers.

CARLIN, William

Inside-forward, 5ft 4in, 9st 5lb
Born: Liverpool, 6 October 1940
Career: Liverpool junior, professional May 1958; Halifax Town 23 August 1962 (fee); Carlisle United 27 October 1964; Sheffield United 19 September 1967 (£40,000); Derby County August 1968 (£63,000); Leicester City 17 October 1970 (£40,000); Notts County September 1971; Cardiff City on loan 23 November 1973.
Halifax Town debut: v Wrexham, Division Three, 25 August 1962

Willie Carlin once stated that signing for Halifax Town was the worst mistake he ever made in football, though in truth it was probably the making of him. For although Town struggled and were relegated in his first season, Carlin did at least get the chance to demonstrate his abilities as a tenacious inside-forward of zeal and craft with a steely resolve that meant he was never afraid to go in where it hurts. How the fans loved him, and he remains in the eyes of many, the best player Halifax Town ever had. Carlin came through the junior ranks at Liverpool, then managed by Phil Taylor, but despite making appearances for England at schoolboy and youth levels he managed only one senior outing with the Reds, a 1–1 draw at Stoke City on 17 October 1959. Seeking first-team football, Carlin made the switch to Third Division Halifax Town in August 1962 and came under the tutelage of coach Don McEvoy. He featured alongside the likes of Alex South, Barry Tait and Dennis Fidler, but despite giving his all to the cause Carlin could not halt the side's slide into the Fourth Division. Never a particularly prolific goalscorer, Carlin, however, proved his class in the League's basement by netting 21 goals during 1963–64 and finishing top scorer.

Frustrated at the lack of success, Carlin handed in a transfer request and finally moved to Carlisle United in October 1964 where he pursued a career which would see him play in all four divisions. Carlisle boss Ron Ashman, who had just sold Hugh McIlmore to Wolves, paid a club record for Carlin's services, saying, '£10,000 well spent, just wait and see,' and Carlin became an instant hit, helping the club to the Third Division Championship within his first year. A broken leg early the following term hindered his and Carlisle's progress, but he recovered to help them consolidate in 14th place, and the following term Carlisle astounded the sceptics by finishing third, just missing out on promotion to the top flight. However, Carlin was not to be denied First Division football, signing for Sheffield United in September 1967, though his one season there ended in relegation. But his talents had grabbed the attention of Derby County manager Brian Clough who was about to shake up the Baseball Ground club. Carlin joined the Rams in August 1968 and along with the legendary Dave Mackay, helped galvanise the club, as Derby won the Second Division Championship in 1968–69. The following season, Carlin played in all but two of Derby's League matches and was also a member of the side which clinched the first ever Watney Cup, beating Manchester United 4–1 in the Final.

More success followed Carlin when he switched to Leicester City under Frank O'Farrell in October 1970, helping them to promotion in his first season. A year later, Third Division Notts County benefitted from his services, and after just missing out on promotion in his first term with the club Carlin recovered from ankle ligament trouble to help steer them to promotion as runners-up to Bolton Wanderers in 1972–73. The following term, he succumbed to injury and having lost his place in the side, was loaned out to Cardiff City that November, making the move permanent the following month and inspiring the side's pull away from the relegation zone. Carlin retired at the end of that season and moved to Majorca, where he ran a bar and restaurant at Cala Bona, before returning to England. He now regularly attends matches at Derby County.

CHADBOURNE, Joe Henry

Centre-forward, 5ft 9in, 12st 7lb
Born: Halifax, 1885
Died: Halifax, 4 August 1958
Career: Halifax Boys' Brigade; Halifax Whitehall 1900; Sowerby Bridge; Elland Ramsdanians; Heckmondwike; Barnsley 1905–06; Bradford City 1906; Burnley 27 November 1908; Mirfield United cs 1910; Halifax Town August 1911; Halifax RFC cs 1912; Hull Kingston Rovers RFC.
Halifax Town debut: v Bradford City Reserves (a), Yorkshire Combination, 9 September 1911

Upon the formation of Halifax Town, manager Joe McClelland's began assembling his first squad of players, with among his first signings that of Joe Chadbourne, a robust centre-forward with Football League experience, but a player who was well known in local sporting circles.

Chadbourne – 'a thorough sportsman' according to Pioneer of the *Halifax Courier* – was born in Halifax in 1885 and made his name with local League sides Halifax Whitehall, Sowerby Bridge and Elland Ramsdanians, before turning out for Heckmondwike in the West Yorkshire League. His reputation grew, and Football League clubs began to take notice, and following trials, he signed professional forms with Barnsley, though he never broke through into the first team. In 1906, Chadbourne moved to Bradford City, though a family bereavement kept him out of the reckoning for a first-team place, but in November 1908 he landed a move to Burnley, making his Football League debut during 1908–09, scoring four goals from nine first-team appearances that term, but by 1910–11 he was playing for Mirfield United.

Chadbourne's signing for the newly formed Halifax Town was a popular one, and so well respected was he by his teammates that he was elected skipper prior to kick-off of the first Yorkshire Combination match against Bradford City at Valley Parade. He led the line well during that inaugural season, and, of course, plundered goals. He scored 15 in all competitions, including a nap hand against Heckmondwike, his former club at Sandhall Lane upon his return from injury in the then record 8–1 victory. At the end of that first season, Chadbourne elected to switch codes and joined Halifax Rugby Club at Thrum Hall but upon the outbreak of World War One, he was enlisted with the Queen's Yorkshire Dragoons and served as a sergeant-major in France. Outside of football, Chadbourne was employed as a taxi proprietor and undertaker at Hope Hall, a business founded by his father.

CHADWICK, David Edwin

Right-wing, 5ft 7in, 9st 10lb
Born: Ooctamund, India, 19 August 1943
Career: Southampton junior, professional October 1960; Middlesbrough July 1966; Halifax Town 22 January 1970 (£7,000); Bournemouth & Boscombe Athletic 24 February 1972 (£12,000); Torquay United on loan 13 December 1972 to 6 March 1973; Gillingham September 1974; Dallas Tornado; Tacota Tides; Fort Lauderdale Strikers; Atlanta Chiefs coach; Georgia Generals; Atlanta Datagraphic; United States Soccer Federation ; AFC Lightning technical director.
Halifax Town debut: v Barrow (h), Division Three, 27 January 1970

Nobody epitomised more the adventurous style of play introduced by manager George Kirby in 1970–71 than flame-haired Dave Chadwick. For although it was Alan Ball Snr who brought him to The Shay, it was under Kirby that he was allowed to express himself. Chadwick joined Ted Bates's Southampton as a junior before signing professional forms in October 1960 and made his first-team debut on 4 November 1961 at home to Bristol Rovers in place of the injured Terry Paine. His six years at The Dell were spent in the shadow of Paine and John Sydenham and as a result he was restricted to just 25 League appearances, his only goal being scored in a 3–1 defeat at Stoke City in September 1962. Chadwick moved to Middlesbrough for regular first-team football in July 1966, missing only two games of their Third Division promotion season of 1966–67. But having lost his place in the side, he joined Halifax Town in January 1970, scoring on his first debut in a 3–0 win over Barrow, the first of four goals he scored that season which helped Town consolidate their Third Division status a year after promotion.

The following season, Chadwick's speedy and tricky wing play was a feature of George Kirby's exciting side which finished third when only two clubs were promoted, and he was voted the club's Player of the Year. A neat executioner of free-kicks, it was from one of his flighted deliveries that

Bill Atkins headed home the first goal in the Watney Cup tie win against Manchester United. But with George Kirby being replaced by Ray Henderson, Chadwick became unsettled and having stated his desire to move south, he left Town for Bournemouth in February 1972. Surprisingly, he failed to make an impact there, and he was loaned to Torquay United. But in the summer of 1974, following what Chadwick described as a phone call 'out of the blue', he spent his first season in the NASL with Dallas Tornado, thus beginning his love affair with life in the States.

Chadwick returned to England for one last season of League football with Gillingham, before rejoining Dallas Tornado in 1975. The following year he signed for the short-lived Tacota Tides of the newly created American Soccer League, then returned to the NASL with the Fort Lauderdale Strikers, where he played for three years before moving into coaching. He joined Atlanta Chiefs in 1980, becoming head coach, and later worked at Georgia Generals in the America Soccer League before returning to Fort Lauderdale in 1983. After coaching stints at Atlanta Datagraphic and for the United States Soccer Federation, Chadwick became technical director and director of coaching at AFC Lightning and led his Under-18s team to become national champions. In 2001 Chadwick was inducted into the Georgia State Soccer Association's Hall of Fame and after 16 years coaching at AFC Lightning, David Chadwick retired in June 2007.

CHAMBERS, William Thomas

Centre-forward, 5ft 8in, 11st 4lb
Born: Wednesbury, 10 August 1906
Died: Sandwell, 1978
Career: Wednesbury; Worcester City; Darlaston; Burnley 7 May 1929 (£250); Darlaston 1931; Halifax Town 27 June 1932; Bolton Wanderers 6 July 1934 (2,600); Oldham Athletic May 1935; Chester 5 June 1936; Bath City July 1938.
Halifax Town debut: v Accrington Stanley, Division Three North, 27 August 1932

Nobody had heard of Bill Chambers when Halifax Town boss Alex Raisbeck signed him from non-League Darlaston, but the new centre-forward with only two League appearances to his name, would leave an indelible mark at The Shay, his prowess in front of goal earning him a record move to Bolton Wanderers. Chambers began his career with his local Wednesbury club before spells at Worcester City and Birmingham Combination side Darlaston attracted the attention of Burnley, and in May 1929 he moved to the Turf Moor club. He spent the most of his time in the reserves, though he was called up for his League debut at outside-right in place of Archie Heslop against Manchester United on 29 March 1930. Chambers helped Burnley to a 4–0 win and he retained his place for the following game against Huddersfield Town, but with the Clarets struggling in the League – they would ultimately be relegated – Chambers was not selected again by manager Bert Pickles.

At the end of the 1930–31 Chambers was put on the open-to-transfer list but, with no immediate takers, returned to Darlaston, from where Town boss Alex Raisbeck picked him up in June 1932. At The Shay, Chambers initially featured in the forward line at inside-left but found goals hard to come by until his switch to centre-forward for the game at Southport on 7 January, where he scored twice – and never looked back. Instrumental in Town's FA Cup run which took them to the fifth round, Chambers ended as top scorer that season with 22 League and Cup goals.

Though not overly mobile, Chambers possessed a crack shot and was devastating in the air, and the following term he smashed the goalscoring record held by Ernie Dixon by netting 30

League goals. Missing the 13–0 debacle at Stockport County through injury, Chambers recorded the first of three hat-tricks that season in the next League game against Chesterfield, and on 7 April 1934 he became the first Town player to net five goals in a League game when he did so in the 6–2 win over Hartlepools United. Chambers's scoring feats attracted the attention of the bigger clubs, but after earlier turning down a £2,000 bid from Everton he made a record £2,600 move to Bolton Wanderers in June 1934. But as at Burnley, Chambers spent the majority of his time in the reserves, though he did net an impressive 18 Central League goals. In May 1935 he joined Oldham Athletic in a swap deal which saw Fred Swift move in the opposite direction, and 10 first-team appearances yielded two goals. In June 1936 he joined Chester for two seasons before finishing his playing career with Bath City.

COLEMAN, Ernest ('Tim')
Inside-forward
Born: Blidworth, 4 January 1908
Died: Nottingham, 20 January 1984
Career: Hucknall Church Boys' Brigade; Hucknall Colliery; Halifax Town 12 July 1926; Grimsby Town 27 February 1929 (£1,250); Arsenal March 1932 (£5,000 plus a player); Middlesbrough August 1934 (£4,000); Norwich City February 1937; Linby Colliery player-manager; Notts County caretaker manager July 1957 to October 1957, in various capacities 1958 to 1966, manager November 1961 to July 1963, April 1965 to March 1966.
Halifax Town debut: v Rochdale, Division Three North, 1 January 1927

Ernest Coleman, nicknamed 'Tim', holds a unique place in the history of Halifax Town. He is the only player to have left the club and gone on to win either a League Championship (or Premier League equivalent) medal, having achieved that feat with Arsenal in 1932–33. Such was his development within the game, Coleman was tipped for international honours, and only injury surely prevented him from being capped for England. Coleman began his road to success by playing for Hucknall Boys Club, but it was Joe McClelland who first spotted his potential, signing him in as a 17-year-old and handing him his League debut against Rochdale on New Year's Day, when he scored the game's only goal. It was during the 1928–29 season that Coleman established himself in the side, initially at outside-right, but it was following his switch to inside-right that he proved most effective, linking up with Ernie Dixon and Tom Bell in the forward line, creating as well as scoring goals, and in March 1929 he secured a big money move to Second Division Grimsby Town.

Coleman made an immediate impact at Blundell Park, contributing seven goals from just eight League appearances that term as Grimsby finished runners-up to Middlesbrough and clinched promotion to the First Division. He was top scorer in two full seasons for the Mariners, racking up a club record 35 Division One in 1930–31. But the following season saw Grimsby were locked in a relegation battle, to which they finally succumbed, their chances of survival rocked by the sale of Coleman in March 1932 to Herbert Chapman's Arsenal. Coleman appeared in six League games for the Gunners towards the end of 1931–32 as Arsenal finished runners-up to Everton, but the following term, appearing in the forward line with the legendary David Jack, Alex James and Cliff Bastin, he scored 24 goals, including two hat-tricks, from 27 League appearances to help Arsenal reclaim their title last won two seasons previously. His form also brought him to the attention of the England selectors, though ultimately full international honours eluded him. The closest he ever got was when he led the line in an international trial match for England against The Rest at Portsmouth on 22 March 1933.

A loss of form during 1933–34, coupled with the signing of Ted Drake, saw Coleman out of the first-team and his eventual signing for Middlesbrough in August 1934. He spent three seasons at Ayresome Park but ended his League career with Norwich City. Coleman went on to take over as player-manager with Linby Colliery but entered League management with Notts County, succeeding Eddie Lowe, initially as caretaker. He remained at Meadow Lane in various capacities, acting as assistant to Frank Hill before taking over as manager between November 1961 and July 1963 and among his discoveries was future England striker Jeff Astle. Coleman returned briefly as manager in April 1963 during a financial crisis, eventually leaving the club in March 1966.

COOPER, Sedley

Inside-forward, 5ft 7in, 10st 7lb
Born: Garforth, 17 August 1911
Died: Leeds, 1q 1981
Career: Carlton Athletic November 1928; Halifax Town trialist April 1929, signed 7 May 1929; Sheffield Wednesday 9 June 1931 (fee); Huddersfield Town June 1936; Notts County March 1937.
Halifax Town debut: v Darlington (h), Division Three North, 6 April 1929

Sedley Cooper arrived at The Shay at a time when the supporters were losing faith with the management. But having seen a crop of youngsters such as George Parkin, Arthur Groves and Tim Coleman all sold to keep the club afloat, the performances of Cooper were a breath of fresh air, belying his inexperience, having joined the club from non-League football with Carlton Athletic aged just 17. Having taken him on as a trialist in April 1929, manager Joe McClelland had no qualms about throwing Cooper into the side for the home game with Darlington as the season went into its final weeks. Town had just come out of a depressing sequence of results, but Cooper was an inspiration to the side, taking over at inside-left and contributing to the 5–1 destruction of the Quakers. 'Cooper is a find,' wrote Pioneer of the *Halifax Courier*, and his place in the side was secure. Cooper appeared in all the final six League games as well as helping Town overcome Huddersfield Town to reach the Final of the West Riding Senior Cup.

Cooper signed professional forms that May and showed consistent form over the next two seasons despite the huge financial crisis hanging over the club. With the sale of Ernie Dixon to Huddersfield Town in September 1929, much responsibility fell on his young shoulders, and though he switched to outside-left to accommodate Ken McDonald late in the season, he finished as top scorer with seven goals. Word was out of other clubs' interest in him during the first half of the 1930–31 season, which intensified when Cooper scored both goals in Town's 2–1 FA Cup first-round replay at Mansfield Town, and again when he scored what was regarded as the fastest goal ever scored by a Town player when netting after just 10 seconds in a 1–1 draw with Lincoln City that April. The club retained his services for the rest of the season, but no one was surprised at his signing for Sheffield Wednesday in June 1931, particularly as the man behind it was former Town boss Joe McClelland, by then installed as assistant secretary to Rob Brown.

Cooper, though, spent two seasons in the reserves at Hillsborough and he did not make his first-team bow until 28 October 1933 when he appeared in the side beaten 6–2 at Wolverhampton Wanderers. Restricted to just 18 senior appearances and four goals during five years there, Cooper joined Huddersfield Town, but his time there was not a success either, and after making just five League starts he left before the season's close and joined Notts

County, where he at last began to blossom. Making a dream start, Cooper scored twice on his debut in a 3–2 win at Swindon Town, a result which, at the time, kept County top of the Third Division South table, though they would ultimately lose out in the title race to Luton Town. Cooper initially partnered the legendary Hughie Gallagher in the attack, and established himself in the side during 1938–39, scoring 10 goals from 33 League appearances, but his career came to a sudden halt with the outbreak of World War Two.

CRAIG, Edward Freeman

Centre-half, 5ft 9½in, 11st
Born: Stewarton, 9 February 1903
Died: 1982
Career: Stewarton Thistle; Fulham December 1924; Bristol City September 1939 (£555); Halifax Town 11 August 1932 to close season 1944.
Halifax Town debut: v Accrington Stanley, Division Three North, 27 August 1932

Two years into his reign as manager of Halifax Town, it was to his former club Bristol City that Alex Raisbeck returned to sign the experienced Ted Craig as he began building his own team at The Shay. Craig proved one of the most reliable defenders of the pre-World War Two era and eventually became skipper, yet Raisbeck's decision to deploy him in the half-back line was surely inspired, for up until signing for the Shaymen Craig had played out his career as an inside-forward. He went on to make a record number of first-team appearances for Halifax Town, though his 11-year association with the club spanned the war years. Craig played Scottish junior football with local side Stewarton Thistle before being signed by Andy Ducat, new manager of Second Division Fulham, in December 1924. He made a scoring debut in a 3–1 win at Middlesbrough on New Year's Day 1925 and spent six seasons at Craven Cottage, featuring in Fulham's run to the quarter-finals of the FA Cup in 1925–26, though it was ironic that his best goal return of 11 coincided with the side's relegation to the Third Division South two years later.

In September 1930, Craig moved to Bristol City, but there was disappointment for him there, too, when the Robins suffered the ignominy of finishing bottom of the Second Division in 1931–32. But with Halifax Town, Craig enjoyed better days, even allowing for the debacles in the 10–0 defeat at Hull City in his first season, and the record 13–0 humiliation at Stockport in his second. Having made the successful switch under Raisbeck to centre-half following the introduction of inside-forward Fred Brown to the side in January 1933, Craig helped Town reach the fifth round of the FA Cup for the first time in 1932–33, and two seasons later, having been appointed skipper, he missed only one match as the side finished runners-up to Doncaster Rovers. Craig made a total of 289 League appearances for the Shaymen and his inclusion in the side for the season's penultimate the game with Oldham Athletic in April 1937 extended to 104 his run of consecutive starts. In 1938–39 Craig was awarded a benefit, and on the evening of FA Cup Final day, 29 April 1939, Halifax Town took on First Division Everton and played out a 3–3 draw.

But for the outbreak of the war, there is little doubt that Craig would have racked up many more League appearances for the club, for though he was fast approaching his fortieth year, he was still an able member of the side and did not play his 433rd and last first-team game until October 1943, a 4–3 defeat at Rochdale.

DAVIES, Edward
Right-winger, 5ft 8in, 10st
Born: Howarden, 11 May 1910
Died: Castleford, 16 October 1982
Career: Castleford Town; Halifax Town 28 May 1929; Chesterfield 13 March 1936; Walsall May 1938; Darlington cs 1939; Halifax Town guest February 1940.
Halifax Town debut: v Accrington Stanley, Division Three North, 28 September 1929

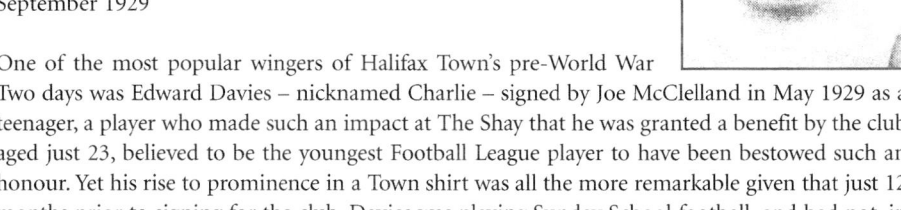

One of the most popular wingers of Halifax Town's pre-World War Two days was Edward Davies – nicknamed Charlie – signed by Joe McClelland in May 1929 as a teenager, a player who made such an impact at The Shay that he was granted a benefit by the club aged just 23, believed to be the youngest Football League player to have been bestowed such an honour. Yet his rise to prominence in a Town shirt was all the more remarkable given that just 12 months prior to signing for the club, Davies was playing Sunday School football, and had not, in fact, kicked a ball in a proper game until he was 16. He had attended evening school, which entered a team in the JOC League, and Davies bought a pair of boots in winning a 'busting' sweep.

Davies moved to the West Riding from his native North Wales and was employed as a surface worker at a Castleford Colliery while weaving his footballing craft on the right wing playing for Castleford Town when he was discovered by McClelland. Davies quickly broke into the first team, but his early seasons with the club were ones of hardship, so it was reckoned Davies's winning goal against Chester in a fourth-round FA Cup replay against Chester was worth hundreds of pounds to the club. But that wasn't his best goal. That surely came at Lincoln City two years later, when he beat man after man before planting the ball past the 'keeper. One of the speediest wingers Town have had, Davies had by then already enjoyed his benefit match when Halifax Town entertained Sheffield Wednesday on 1 October 1934, scoring his side's first goal to inspire a fightback after Wednesday ran up a four-goal lead, but the visitors held on to win an entertaining game 5–3.

Never in a position to hold a player back, nor turn down good money, Halifax Town reluctantly allowed Davies to join Third Division Northern champions-elect Chesterfield in March 1936. On his departure, foreboding *Halifax Courier* reporter Tom Dickinson asked, 'Who else has his sprit and pluck?' But for the player came disappointment. Failing to oust firstly Joe Spence, then Jack Hughes from the first team, Davies made just two League appearances for the Spireites and moved to Walsall in May 1938. Davies' one season at Fellows Park yielded just 12 League appearances and one goal, and his move to Darlington a year later was interrupted by the outbreak of war.

Davies did reappear in a Halifax Town shirt for one last short spell when, in February 1940, he wrote to the *Courier's* Tom Dickinson asking about his chances of getting a game. Dickinson alerted Town manager Jimmy Thomson and Davies duly took his place in the Town side for the wartime meeting with Bradford City on 2 March 1940, helping Town to a 2–2 draw and featured in four more wartime matches that month, scoring one goal, at York City on 16 March. Davies continued to live in Castleford, where he died in October 1982.

DAVISON, Robert
Forward, 5ft 10in, 11st 5lb
Born: South Shields 17 July 1959
Career: Seaham Red Stars; Huddersfield Town 2 July 1980 (£1,000); Halifax Town 7 August 1981 (£20,000); Derby County 2 December 1982 (£98,000); Leeds United 20 November 1987

(£350,000); Derby County on loan 19 September 1991; Leicester City 12 August 1992 (£50,000); Sheffield United on loan 6 March 1993; Sheffield United 4 November 1993; Rotherham United 14 October 1994; Hull City on loan 24 November 1995; Halifax Town 2 July 1996; Guiseley on loan November 1996; Guiseley player-coach May 1997, manager February 1998 to October 2000; Bradford City assistant manager June 2004; Sheffield United coach February 2008; Ferencvaros head coach April 2008 to October 2009; Leeds United assistant youth coach November 2010; England Under-19s assistant coach.

'I am going for potential,' said manager Mickey Bullock as he tried to justify the £20,000 outlay after Halifax Town had completed the signing of a relative unknown striker from Huddersfield Town. But Bullock's judgement was proved wise, and Bobby Davison not only scored goals for fun in his time at The Shay, but his eventual transfer to Derby County probably saved the club from bankruptcy. Davison was playing locally with Seaham Red Stars when signed by Huddersfield Town manager Mick Buxton in July 1980 but his one season at Leeds Road was spent in the reserves, his only first-team start coming as a stand-in for Steve Kindon against Rotherham United on 30 August 1980, with his only other appearance being as a substitute. But seeking a potent striker, it was to Huddersfield that Mickey Bullock turned, and Davison made the switch in August 1981, netting on his debut in a League Cup tie with Preston, a typical predatory strike. Together with his lightning pace, Davison ended his first season at The Shay with 21 League goals, and he continued to score goals the following term, his first hat-trick coming in a Football League Trophy match with Hartlepool on the eve of the season, while his most memorable three-goal haul came in a sensational 4–2 win at Wimbledon in November 1982 in one of his last games for the club.

Having impressed over two legs of a Milk Cup tie against Derby County earlier that season, the Baseball Ground club tabled an offer for the young striker, and after Bullock held out for a more realistic £98,000 Davison thus became new Derby boss manager Peter Taylor's first signing. At the Baseball Ground, Davison became a popular figure, being their leading goalscorer for six consecutive seasons, hitting 26 League and Cup goals in his first season, Derby's best since Ray Straw hit 37 in 1956–57, and he spearheaded two successive promotions as the Rams clinched the Second Division Championship in 1986–87 as well as being named as the supporters' Player of the Year in 1984–85. In November 1987 Davison moved to Second Division Leeds United, scoring 11 goals in their Championship season of 1989–90 as Leeds returned to the old First Division, but two seasons later he found himself behind Lee Chapman and Rod Wallace in the pecking order and was loaned back to Derby in September 1991, where he claimed his 100th goal for the club.

Davison later went on loan to Sheffield United, memorably scoring on his debut in a derby match with Sheffield Wednesday before joining Leicester City in August 1992, but he was never as prolific a goalscorer as before. He later joined Rotherham United and had a loan spell at Hull City, but in 1996 Davison returned to Halifax Town, by now in the Conference, though under John Carroll he failed to command a regular place in the side and scored just one goal. He then went into coaching at Guiseley, became assistant to Colin Todd at Bradford City, then returned as coach at Sheffield United before taking over at Turkish side Ferencvaros, leading the club back to the First Division after an absence of three years. But despite his success there, Davison resigned in October 2009 amid fears for his safety. More recently, he has been assisting Leeds United as youth coach while also acting as assistant manager to Noel Blake's England national Under-19 football team.

DIXON, Ernest

Centre-forward, 5ft 9in, 12st
Born: Pudsey, 10 July 1901
Died: Bradford, 27 April 1941
Career: Calverley; Bradford City August 1921; Halifax Town 10 May 1922; Burnley 11 March 1924 (fee); Halifax Town 23 December 1924; Huddersfield Town 6 September 1929 (£1,000); Nelson 17 October 1929; Tranmere Rovers cs 1930.
Halifax Town debut: v Lincoln City (h), Division Three North, 26 August 1922

Ernie Dixon plundered a record 127 League goals for Halifax Town in two spells with the club, spanning eight years. A dashing and fearless raider, he scored all manner of goals, either marauding down the centre or lashing the ball home from close range. Dixon's overall total was 136 in all competitions, and to many he was a folk hero. But some supporters of that era, while appreciating his obvious prowess in front of goal, would for years talk about the one that got away – undoubtedly the biggest blunder of Dixon's career – the missed penalty in the 41st minute of an FA Cup second round replay with First Division Manchester City in February 1924. But whether put off by the delaying tactics of City 'keeper Jim Mitchell or merely by the sense of occasion, and with the game goalless, Dixon shot straight at Mitchell who gathered easily, and the chance was gone. City won the third match 3–0.

Despite fluffing such a gilt-edged chance, Dixon was still considered one of Halifax Town's prize assets, and when Burnley swooped following the Cup exit he, along with Ben Wheelhouse and George Parkin, was allowed to leave the club to help swell the coffers. But Dixon had only been signed as cover for the prolific George Beal and started just three League games, and when their manager John Haworth signed Tom Roberts, first-team opportunities became even more limited. Town boss Joe McClelland thus brought Dixon back to The Shay two days before Christmas 1924 and the centre-forward took up from where he had left off.

Ernie Dixon had first come to McClelland's attention when scoring two goals for Calverley in their FA Cup defeat by Halifax Town in November 1920. But he arrived at The Shay in May 1922 after a season in Bradford City's reserve side, gaining valuable experience in the Central League, and earning a call-up to the first team, making his one and only League appearance for the Bantams in a goalless draw at Sunderland in a First Division fixture on 25 March 1922. Dixon ended up being top scorer in seven consecutive seasons with Town but several weeks into the 1929–30 season, he became new Huddersfield Town boss Clem Stephenson's first signing when he was sold for £1,000, money which went to pay back-wages to the Halifax players. Dixon had gone to Leeds Road after forward Wilf Lewis broke down in training, but his time there, as it had been at Burnley, was less than fruitful and even shorter. He scored on his debut in a defeat at Birmingham City on 7 September 1929 but had made just five League starts before joining Nelson the very next month.

Dixon ended the 1929–30 season as joint top scorer on nine goals with Tom Carmedy at Nelson but by the start of 1930–31 he had moved again, joining Tranmere Rovers, where he enjoyed a new lease of life, forming a lethal partnership with Jack Kennedy and between them bagging 65 goals in his first season. Dixon spent three seasons at Prenton Park, filling in at centre-half on occasions, and finished with 53 goals from 83 League appearances. Hampered by injuries in 1932–33, Dixon was released at the end of that season, and he later turned out for non-League Gresley Rovers and Mossley while running a fish and chip shop in West Vale, Halifax. He later lived in Bradford but sadly, after a long illness, died in April 1941 aged just 40.

DOWNSBOROUGH, Peter

Goalkeeper, 5ft 10½in, 13st 2lb
Born: Halifax, 13 September 1943
Career: Siddal Junior School; Exley Secondary School; Halifax Boys' Brigade; Halifax Town juniors 4 May 1959, professional 14 September 1960; Swindon Town 21 August 1965 (£3,000 plus a player); Brighton & Hove Albion on loan 23 August 1973; Bradford City on loan 21 November 1973, signed January 1974 (£5,000), retired July 1980.
Halifax Town debut: v Bournemouth & Boscombe Athletic, Division Three, 4 May 1960

Goalkeeper Peter Downsborough gave a Man of the Match display as Third Division Swindon Town pulled off a shock 3–1 victory over Division One side Arsenal in the Final of the League Cup at Wembley in 1969. For while Don Rogers led the Arsenal defence a merry dance, it was Downsborough who performed heroics at the other end to keep the Arsenal forwards at bay. Victory in that match was undoubtedly the highlight of Downsborough's career, though promotion to the Second Division the same season ran it close, yet the unprecedented success Downsborough experienced with Swindon was all a far cry from the time he spent with Halifax Town, his hometown club, whom he joined as a junior in May 1959. Born in the Siddal area, Downsborough was an all round sportsman, excelling at cricket, rugby union, football and won boxing and swimming honours. He began playing football as a centre-forward for Halifax Boys' Brigade but an injury to the regular goalkeeper saw him take his place between the sticks, and so well did he perform that Halifax Town manager Harry Hooper snapped him up. Downsborough turned professional in September 1960, but by then he had already broken through into the first team, appearing in the final game of the season at Bournemouth in May of that year.

The promise he and another local lad David Knowles had shown prompted Hooper to release regular first-choice 'keeper Arthur Johnson, and though it was Knowles who initially got the nod as his successor, the form Downsborough showed in the reserves meant that by the 1961–62 season he had established himself in the first team. But most of Downsborough's time at The Shay was spent battling against the odds, though little blame could be attached to him when Town suffered relegation to the Fourth Division in 1963. Downsborough continued to enhance his reputation over the course of the next two seasons with his agility and fearless approach, he became the club's biggest asset by the mid-1960s, and such was his value by the time he moved to Swindon in August 1965 that he netted Halifax Town £3,000 plus centre-forward Bill Atkins.

Downsborough went on to make 274 League appearances for the Robins, and in September 1969 added an Anglo-Italian Cup-winners' medal to his collection after Swindon defeated AS Roma – their side included future England boss Fabio Capello – over two legs. Following a brief loan spell at Brighton, Downsborough returned to West Yorkshire in November 1973 with Bradford City, where he became something of a folk hero. He was part of the famous FA Cup side which reached the quarter-finals in 1975–75 and the following term missed only one game as the Bantams secured promotion from the Fourth Division. He also endeared himself to the supporters by saving four successive penalties between 19 March and 5 November 1977. Downsborough went on to make 252 League appearances for Bradford City, taking his career total to 650, then a record for a goalkeeper. He retired at the end of the 1979–80 season and was afforded a testimonial against Huddersfield Town upon the season's close. He returned to live in Halifax, and was a school caretaker until his retirement.

DUCKETT, Donald Thwaites

Half-back
Born: Thornton, Bradford, 20 April 1894
Died: Bradford, 1970
Career: Wibsey; Thornton; Queensbury; Bradford City April 1914; Halifax Town 12 December 1924; Bradford 24 November 1927 – retired March 1929.
Halifax Town debut: v Walsall, Division Three North, 13 December 1924

Donald Duckett was the archetypal playmaker and integral part of the side which made a bold bid for the Division Three North title in 1926–27. But while it was marksman Ernie Dixon who grabbed the spotlight with his goalscoring achievements, it was Duckett who made the side tick, the link between defence and attack, yet it was all the more surprising that Duckett should play such a pivotal role in the rise of Halifax Town because by the time he signed for the club from Bradford City in December 1924 he had already turned 30 years old and had recently taken a well-deserved benefit after giving the Bantams 10 years' service.

Duckett, the nephew of Horace Duckett, who was capped twice for England at Rugby Union, came to the fore playing locally with Wibsey, Thornton and Queensbury before signing for First Division Bradford City in April 1914, making his debut in 1–1 draw at Burnley on 8 September 1919, and going on to form an effective half-back line with Charlie Storer and Joe Hargreaves. Short and stocky, Duckett based his game on his ability to cover the ground and play incisive passes but even his best efforts could not prevent the Bantams' relegation in 1921–22, a season in which he was ever-present. Duckett was considered past his best when City allowed him to leave for Halifax Town in December 1924, but he proved a real asset to Town's cause. Inheriting the captaincy from Ellis Hall, he inspired the team to a fifth place finish in 1925–26, and the following term he was instrumental in the side's title challenge, featuring in the half-back line with Alf Dark and Hugh Hubbert.

A disagreement on tactics led to him leaving the club on 24 November 1927, though many questioned whether it was wise to let him go just two days before an important FA Cup tie. Nor were the Halifax Town fans pleased he joined the League leaders Bradford. Duckett signed for the Park Avenue outfit allegedly while in his sickbed suffering with a high temperature and suspected smallpox, and therefore did not make his debut until the end of January, but once recovered went on to make 16 first-team appearances as his new club cantered to the Third Division North title. Duckett, a fine cricketer for the Mountain club, retired in March 1929, and with his footballing days behind him, became a successful businessman in Bradford.

DUNLEAVY, Christopher

Defender, 5ft 10in, 11st 6lb
Born: Liverpool, 30 December 1949
Career: Everton juniors, professional March 1968; Southport July 1969; Washington Darts 1970; Philadelphia Atoms 1973; Chester 21 September 1973; Halifax Town 29 October 1976 (£7,000) to 2 January 1981; Wollongong (Australia) 1981; Blacktown City.
Halifax Town debut: v Doncaster Rovers (h), Division Four, 2 November 1976

Affable Chris Dunleavy enjoyed a four-year career with Halifax Town following his signing from Chester in October 1976. Arriving as a noted centre-back, Dunleavy showed his versatility by playing in all positions across the back four, though it was as a full-back he became mostly recognised. And though his time at The Shay coincided with a period of struggle, Dunleavy was a consistent performer and ever-present in 1978–79. Dunleavy joined Everton as an apprentice but failed to break into the first team, despite turning professional in March 1968. Released by manager Harry Catterick, he joined Southport in July 1969, though he interspersed his time in England with spells in America, playing for Washington Darts in the summer of 1970, and returning in 1973 to turn out for Philadelphia Atoms, appearing in the Final of the League Play-offs on 25 August 1973.

Dunleavy went on to join Chester and finished his first season with the Third Division club as the supporters' Player of the Year. But a broken leg sustained playing against Torquay United in September 1974 meant he missed the rest of Chester's promotion campaign that term. It was in October 1976 that Halifax Town boss Alan Ball Snr paid £7,000 for Dunleavy's services, and he made an immediate impact, scoring the first goal, a powerful header, to set Town on their way to a record-equalling 6–0 League win over Doncaster Rovers on his debut. It was Jimmy Lawson who made Dunleavy skipper for the 1977–78 season, though he had the captaincy taken off him by George Kirby who felt the role was affecting his performances.

During 1979–80 Dunleavy missed just one match due to a family bereavement in April 1980 and, of course, proved an invaluable member of Town's FA Cup team that season which pulled off a shock victory over First Division Manchester City. Dunleavy had intended to leave these shores for Australia at the end of that season, but in the event he delayed it by six months, reappearing in the Town team at the start of the 1980–81 season sporting a bubble-perm. He went on to take his tally to 181 League appearances, and signed off as he had started – with a goal, his 13th for the club, following a typical burst into the box in a 2–2 draw with Port Vale on 20 December 1980 on what was his 400th League appearance. Dunleavy headed off to Australia, playing for Wollongong City, then Blacktown City before embarking upon a highly successful coaching career, latterly with Wests IFC.

EVANS, David Gordon

Centre-back, 5ft 10in, 12st 1lb
Career: West Bromwich Schools Aston Villa apprentice, professional February 1976; Halifax Town 21 June 1979 (£22,500); Bradford City June 1984; Halifax Town 8 August 1990; Brighouse Town August 1992.
Halifax Town debut: v Shrewsbury Town, League Cup, 11 August 1979

David Evans had two spells with Halifax Town, costing £22,500 – not an inconsiderable amount of money for the size of the club – when he first arrived from First Division Aston Villa in June 1979. A cool central-defender with the ability to read the game and with no lack of pace, Evans was worth every penny and gave five years' great service to the club in his first spell. Aged only 21 when he joined the club, such was his maturity that manager George Kirby had little hesitation in naming him as skipper, though he had much more experienced players around him. Evans first signed for Aston Villa in February 1976 after completing his apprenticeship but was restricted to just two League appearances during his time there. However, he made his debut for the club in exceptional circumstances, being called upon because of injuries for a UEFA Cup quarter-final clash with Barcelona in March 1978, with a brief from manager Ron Saunders to contain Johan Cruyff, no less, in front of nearly 50,000 spectators at Villa Park.

Kirby plucked Evans from Villa's reserve side, and at The Shay he quickly became one of the side's prized assets. His finest game was surely in the defeat of First Division Manchester City in the FA Cup in January 1980 but other moments to savour included his headed winner over Bury in February 1983 which gave Town a sixth consecutive League win.

Evans went on to make 238 League appearances in his first spell with the club before being surprisingly given a free transfer in May 1984 as part of a cost-cutting exercise, but Halifax Town's loss was Bradford City's gain. In his first season at Valley Parade he helped the Bantams to the Third Division title, forming a terrific defensive partnership with Peter Jackson, missing only one game of that season and being voted the club's Player of the Year. Evans spent six years at Valley Parade, but he was unable to prevent their slide back to Division Three in 1989–90 and, upon his release by manager John Docherty, he rejoined Halifax Town under Jim McCalliog in August 1990. Packing a crack shot among his many attributes – a blistering free-kick which pierced the Hartlepool United defensive wall in a match in April 1982 being evidence of this – his goal from a free-kick against Manchester United in a Rumbelows Cup tie in September 1990 was more the exquisite type, a delicate chip over 'keeper Jim Leighton that would not have been out of place in the Maracana.

Evans went on to take his tally for Halifax Town to 321 League appearances and 10 goals before he turned down a coaching position at the club offered to him by John McGrath in 1992. He subsequently turned out briefly for Brighouse Town, then of the West Riding County Amateur League, and currently acts as a union rep to the PFA.

FIDLER, Dennis John
Left-winger, 5ft 9in, 11st 7lb
Born: Stockport, 22 June 1938
Career: Manchester United amateur 1954; Manchester City January 1957; Port Vale June 1960; Grimsby Town October 1961; Halifax Town 5 April 1963; Darlington 13 October 1966 (£3,500); Macclesfield Town April 1968; Altrincham 1971; Macclesfield Town 1972; Witton Albion player-coach 1974.
Halifax Town debut: v Coventry City (a), Division Three 6 April 1963

Perhaps Dennis Fidler never quite fulfilled the promise that he showed as a Manchester United junior, where he appeared in their successful FA Youth Cup triumphs in 1955 and 1956, but several years later he became a big hit at Halifax Town, where he showed touches of flair down the left flank and an eye for goal, twice being top scorer. Fidler had first joined United in 1954 but crossed town to join Manchester City two years later, turning professional in January 1957 and making his debut in place of Paddy Fagan, who was away in international duty, in a 2–2 draw with Luton Town the following October. He went on to join Port Vale and scored on his debut in a 3–1 defeat at Bury on 27 August 1960 and played regularly until he was dropped in September 1961.

He was sold to Grimsby Town for £2,000 the following month and contributed three goals from nine League appearances as the Mariners clinched promotion from the Third Division promotion as runners-up. But injury forced him to miss much of that campaign and Fidler was biding his time in the reserves when troubled Halifax Town coach Don McEvoy brought him to The Shay towards the end of the 1962–63 season. Fidler made a scoring debut in an astonishing 5–4 defeat at Coventry City but his arrival could not prevent Town's relegation that season. Nevertheless, he proved his worth to the side over the next few seasons with his exciting wing play, though his time at The Shay was never an easy period for the club. Re-election was necessary in 1964–65 despite Fidler's 11 goals which made him joint top scorer with Brian Westlake, though he topped that figure with 13 goals the following term despite much uncertainty about the future of the club.

Fidler became unsettled and after asking for a transfer he finally moved to Darlington for £3,500 in October 1966, though, as with Halifax, he was joining a club on the verge of relegation. Injuries hampered his time at Feethams and Fidler dropped into the Northern Premier League for the first of two spells with Macclesfield Town, where he became something of a penalty expert and struck up an uncanny understanding with his namesake Brian. In May 1970, he was part of the side which made history by being the first side to lift the FA Trophy after defeating Telford United 2–0 at Wembley. Fidler also had a spell at Altrincham and later became player-manager at Witton Albion. After his playing days were over, Fidler worked in the family wholesale fish business before emigrating to Italy.

FIRTH, Francis Martin
Winger, 5ft 10in, 11st
Born: Dewsbury 27 May 1956
Career: Huddersfield Town apprentice July 1972, professional November 1973; Halifax Town 6 February 1978; Bury August 1982; Witton Albion cs 1984.
Halifax Town debut: v Hartlepool United, Division Four, 7 February 1978

Though not in the same mould perhaps as wingers of previous generations, Franny Firth served Halifax Town well for over four seasons, and though Town often found themselves in the lower reaches of the Fourth Division, he showed flashes of speed and flair, with an eye for goal. It was with Huddersfield Town that Firth began his professional career, being a member of their successful youth side which reached the 1973–74 FA Youth Cup Final only to lose over two legs to Tottenham Hotspur. After signing professional forms, Firth made his League debut as a substitute for former Welsh international Dick Krzywicki in a 5–0 victory over Rochdale in February 1974 but had just started to establish himself in the first team at the start of 1976–77 when he cruelly suffered a broken leg in a match at Barnsley in September 1976 and never appeared in the side again. It was Jimmy Lawson who resurrected his career, bringing him to The Shay in February 1978, and Firth helped spark a revival which would take Halifax Town away from the dreaded re-election zone. But Town were not so fortunate during 1978–79, though with manager George Kirby advocating the use of two flankers Firth thus became a key member of his side.

Injury hampered Firth during the early part of 1979–80, but he returned to volley home the winner against Walsall, the League's last undefeated side that term, and was a member of the side which pulled off a shock win in the FA Cup over First Division Manchester City in January 1980. At the start of 1980–81, Kirby claimed Firth could be the Fourth Division's 'surprise package' and gave him a new role – as an out-and-out striker. He proved how devastating he could be by running in two goals of a memorable 4–2 victory over Bury, and scored seven League and Cup goals in the opening two months of the season. But as Town began to struggle, so his goals dried up, and though he was restored to the wing, he still finished as leading goalscorer in all competitions that season with 10 goals.

Firth's fortunes changed under Mickey Bullock and following a poor start, he was one of four players immediately transfer-listed in September 1981. There were no takers and Firth, to his credit, forced his way back into the side, though his days at The Shay were clearly numbered. Released at the end of the 1981–82 season, he joined Bury, a team which for a good while looked certainties for promotion, but ultimately drifted out of the race. Released after just one season at Gigg Lane, Firth then joined Witton Albion but having retired from the game, he became a postman in the Huddersfield district.

FLEMING, Craig
Centre-half, 6ft, 11st 7lb
Born: Halifax, 6 October 1971
Career: Halifax Town trainee 12 July 1988, professional 21 March 1990; Oldham Athletic 15 August 1991 (£80,000); Norwich City 30 June 1997 (£600,000); Wolverhampton Wanderers on loan January 2007; Rotherham United 31 January 2007; King's Lynn 2007; Lowestoft Town coach 2008.
Halifax Town debut: v Scunthorpe United, Division Four (sub), 2 January 1989

Craig Fleming joined older brother Paul at Halifax Town and made a rapid transition to first-team football, becoming a regular in the side aged just 17, an old head on young shoulders. In fact, so mature was he that new boss Jim McCalliog had little hesitation in playing Craig alongside Dean Martin and Tommy Graham in the heart of the defence in March 1990, the same month he turned professional. Thereafter, Fleming never missed a game for the club, and his £80,000 transfer to Oldham Athletic in August 1991 surprised no one. Craig Fleming's introduction to first-team football had come as an 87th-minute substitute for Colin Blain in a 5–1 defeat of Scunthorpe United on 2 January 1989 when Billy Ayre was manager, but he sprung to prominence a year later when he calmly stroked home the decisive penalty of a Leyland DAF Cup shoot-out against York City at The Shay when extra-time failed to separate the sides. Having played football with Ryburn Juniors, Fleming joined Gerry Brook's Northern Intermediate side in July 1988, and after progressing to the first team he was viewed by McCalliog as an essential part of his side, being paired with the experienced Paul Futcher during the first half of the 1990–91 season. A member of the side which lifted the Yorkshire and Humberside Cup that September, Fleming was also awarded the Young Eagle of the Month award for January 1991, and played all 60 games in differing first-team competitions that season, one of few successes from a miserable campaign.

Having joined Joe Royle's Oldham Athletic, Fleming found himself mixing it with the country's best, the Latics having just secured the old Second Division title. A member of the side which featured in the inaugural Premier League season in 1992–93, Fleming, who had originally been used by Royle at full-back, developed into a sound central-defender, later famously described by Manchester United boss Sir Alex Ferguson as 'the best man-marker in the game,' having seen him at close quarters when Oldham forced United to a replay in the 1994 FA Cup semi-final before bowing out 4–0. Oldham's disappointment that term was compounded when they were relegated.

By the time he had made the last of his 164 League appearances for the Latics, Fleming had been made skipper. But though he may have been readily associated with Oldham, it was with Norwich City, whom he joined in June 1997, that he enjoyed a longer spell. Recovering from injury setbacks, Fleming became a respected member of the side, being voted into the Norwich City Hall of Fame in 1993 and captaining the side to the First Division Championship in 2003–04, and though promotion to the Premiership ended in instant relegation, Fleming was ever-present and spent more time on the pitch that season than any other Premiership player. In 2006–07 Fleming celebrated his testimonial season with a match against Newcastle United at Carrow Road on 26 July 2006.

Fleming went on to make 343 League appearances for the Canaries, scoring 13 goals, and having spent a month's loan period at Wolverhampton Wanderers he signed for Rotherham United in January 2007. The following season he joined King's Lynn but announced his retirement in March 2008 due to persistent ankle injuries. In 2008–09 Fleming joined Ryman League side Lowestoft Town as first-team coach, combining his role there with that of self-employed personal trainer.

FROST, Desmond

Centre-forward, 5ft 11in, 12st 6lb
Born: Congleton, 3 August 1926
Died: Cheshire, June 1993
Career: Civil Defence Messengers; Northamptonshire Regiment; RASC; Congleton Town; Leeds United April 1949 (£5,000); Halifax Town 4 January 1951; Rochdale 3 November 1953; Crewe Alexandra September 1954; Congleton Town.
Halifax Town debut: v Hartlepools United (a), Division Three North, 6 January 1951

Des Frost was the typical robust type of centre-forward that could be found in most sides during the Fifties, and made a notable contribution to Halifax Town's memorable FA Cup run during 1952–53, having joined the club from Leeds United. His signing in January 1951 came at a time when Town were managerless, but while being watched by club officials Frost scored a hat-trick in a Leeds United reserve match against Blackpool, and the Town directors deemed he was the type the side needed to help pull the side clear of the re-election zone. Frost scored on his home debut in the defeat of Chester, and following the arrival of his close pal Jackie Moss, he plundered two hat-tricks before the season's close, including scoring all four goals in the 4–1 victory over Lincoln City on 14 April 1951, as Town avoided the ignominy of re-election by two points.

Frost's path to Leeds, his first League club, had taken in regimental football with the Civil Defence Messengers, Northamptonshire Regiment and RASC, as well as having represented England against Scotland in a services international in Singapore, before turning out for Congleton Town, his hometown club. He arrived at Elland Road in April 1949 and scored two League goals from 10 appearances, though most of his time was spent in the reserves with Moss. Both players were key to Town's survival, however, not only in 1950–51 but also the following term when, with former Leeds teammate Gerry Henry installed as player-manager, Frost finished as top scorer with 23 goals, one of them a sensational 30-yarder that set Town on the way to victory over Grimsby Town on 1 September 1951, probably his best goal in Town's colours.

Injury early in the 1953–54 season saw Frost out of the team, and having failed to rediscover his scoring touch he was transferred to Rochdale in a player-exchange deal which saw Ray Haddington arrive at The Shay. Frost scored on his debut for the Dale and though injury-hit during his first season, his glut of goals early in 1954–55 saw him move to struggling Crewe Alexandra. Frost scored six goals as re-election was staved off, but the following term the side finished bottom of the Third Division North, whereupon Frost was released. He finished with 75 goals from 185 appearances, then rejoined his native Congleton, but a broken leg suffered against Winsford United in September 1959 effectively ended his playing career.

GALLOWAY, Michael

Centre-half, 5ft 11in, 11st 7lb
Born: Oswestry, 30 May 1965
Career: Tynecastle Boys' Club; Elphinstone Primrose; Mansfield Town July 1983; Halifax Town on loan 25 January 1986, signed 21 February 1986 (£1,500); Herat of Midlothian 11 November 1987 (£60,000); Celtic June 1989 (£500,000); Leicester City on loan 3 February 1995; Portsmouth on loan August 1995.
Halifax Town debut: v Colchester United (h), Division Four, 31 January 1986

Was there ever a classier Halifax Town defender in the 1980s than Mick Galloway? Arriving initially on loan from Mansfield Town in January 1986, the flame haired centre-back soon showed why manager Mick Jones wanted to sign him up permanently with his quick reading of situations and tough tackling, as well as his ability to out-jump forwards with his amazing spring and ability to hang in the air. There was never any question that Galloway was destined for bigger and better things, but Halifax Town did get the best part of two years out of him. Born in Oswestry, the son of a soldier, Galloway learnt the rudiments of football playing in Battalion boys' sides and had trials with Berwick Rangers and Leicester City before joining the Tynecastle Boys' Club and turning out for Elphinstone Primrose, winning Scotland Youth and Under-21 international caps before he ventured south to sign for Mansfield Town, managed by Ian Greaves, in July 1983. Galloway broke into the side at Field Mill during 1983–84, but Town boss Mick Jones took up the opportunity to take him on a month's loan, and Galloway proved a fine acquisition after making his debut in a 2–2 draw with Colchester United.

When Galloway's loan period was over, Halifax Town shelled out £1,500 to make the deal a permanent one, and during 1986–87 Galloway missed only three games as he enhanced his growing reputation. Among the eight goals he scored for the club was a memorable powerful header in the middle of a thunderstorm which gave Town victory at Wolverhampton Wanderers in August 1987. The only surprise about his £60,000 move to Hearts in November 1987 was its timing, coming just three days before Town were due to face Billingham Synthonia in a tricky FA Cup first-round tie. Hearts at the time were then leaders of the Scottish Premier Division, and Galloway made his debut as a substitute in a 3–0 win over Dundee United, but despite his impressive performances they were pipped to the title by Celtic. Deployed by manager Alex MacDonald in a ball-winning midfield role, Galloway memorably starred in Hearts' 1987–88 UEFA Cup campaign which saw them reach the quarter-finals before losing to Bayern Munich, and the following season his performances also brought him international recognition, winning the first of his two Scotland Under-21 caps (as an over-age player) against France in March 1989.

When he signed for Hearts, MacDonald had told Galloway, 'You won't be here long,' and true enough, in June 1989, he moved to Celtic, but he was never destined to win a Championship medal, though the fans there well remember his performances in the UEFA Cup, particularly a 30-yard volleyed equaliser against KFC Germinal Ekeren in October 1991 which gave Celtic a 3–1 aggregate win. In November 1989 Galloway won his second Scotland Under-21 international caps, scoring in a 2–0 win over Norway, before making the step-up to the full national side under manager Andy Roxburgh in October 1991 for a European Championship qualifier in Romania. In February 1995 Galloway joined Premier League side Leicester City on loan, but the following term had just joined Portsmouth when he suffered life threatening injuries following a car crash in August 1995 which forced him to quit from playing. On 3 March 1996 Celtic staged a testimonial match with Celtic All Stars, to raise funds for Galloway, but thereafter his life spiralled out of control as depression and drink took hold. Happily, though, Galloway managed to turn things around and in 2008 was back in football in a coaching role at Northern Alliance club Berwick United.

GENNOE, Terence

Goalkeeper, 6ft 2in, 13st 3lb
Born: Shrewsbury, 16 March 1953
Career: Moole Brace Junior School; Wakeman School; Bricklayers Sports, Shrewsbury; Bury May 1973; Blackburn Rovers on loan 15 March; Leeds United on loan 29 March 1975; Halifax Town 25 May 1975 (£3,000); Southampton 23 February 1978 (£35,000); Everton on loan September 1980; Crystal Palace on loan January 1981; Blackburn Rovers August 1981 (£60,000);, retired May 1992; Education Officer and goalkeeping coach; Newcastle United goalkeeping coach May 1997; Celtic coach 1999 to July 2005; Newcastle United coach July 2006 to October 2007.

Halifax Town debut: v Leeds United, West Riding Senior Cup, 8 August 1975

Terry Gennoe arrived at The Shay from Bury faced with the arduous task of trying to oust the consistent Alex Smith from the first team. But so rapid was his development that he found himself in the side at the start of the season, displaying the capabilities that would set him on the road for a long and distinguished career. Gennoe's rise to prominence began while playing local League football in Shrewsbury, and he was signed by Bury as cover for John Forrest. To gain experience he was loaned out to Blackburn Rovers and Leeds United. But it was Johnny Quinn who took a chance on the then 22-year-old and he had no hesitation in throwing him into the first team. But as the team struggled, so Gennoe suffered a loss in confidence and Alex Smith regained his place, but there was no doubting Gennoe was destined for bigger things.

He returned to the side and established himself as first choice, holding off the challenge of the up and coming Mick Leonard and soon other clubs were being alerted to his talents. Tall and commanding in his penalty area, Gennoe possessed quick reflexes and was quick to read developing situations, so it was somewhat ironic that he should move to Lawrie McMenemy's Southampton in February 1978 just days after conceding five goals in a match at Southend. But he put this behind him to oust Peter Wells from the first team and in March 1979 appeared in the League Cup Final defeat to Nottingham Forest at Wembley.

After a loss of form saw him drop down the pecking order, Gennoe had loan spells at Everton and Crystal Palace before he began his long unbroken association with Blackburn, where he set two club records. His total of 289 League games was more than any other goalkeeper in the club's history and he also became the oldest goalkeeper to play for the club when he made his final appearance on the opening day of the 1990–91 season. Gennoe retired from playing at the end of the following season but went on to combine his part-time role as goalkeeper coach with that of the club's education officer and as a qualified teacher, he helped make the club's 'Learning Through Football' programme a particular success. Gennoe later teamed up with Kenny Dalglish as coach at Newcastle United, then followed him to Celtic before returning to Newcastle in July 2006. He retired through injury in October 2007.

GREEN, Horace
Full-back, 5ft 11in, 11st
Born: Barnsley, 23 April 1918
Died: Barnsley, July 2000
Career: Worsborough Bridge Old Boys; Halifax Town amateur 2 November 1936, professional May 1937; Lincoln City 3 February 1949, retired 1955.
Halifax Town debut: v Leeds United (a), West Riding Senior Cup, 20 October 1937

Amid the lean years of the immediate post-war year, one player who performed above his station week in, week out, was Horace Green, skipper who led by example and a player who always gave his best, even when games seemed a lost cause. It could be argued he was deserving of better, but he stayed with the club for over 12 years and the supporters appreciated him for that. Green had been brought to the club by Jimmy Thomson in November 1936, plucked from Barnsley Junior League football where he had been appearing with Worsborough Bridge Old Boys while working in the pit. Initially signed as an amateur, Green turned professional in August 1937 and made his debut in a West Riding Senior Cup match at Leeds United the following October. Before that season was out, he had commanded a regular place in the side, showing his versatility by covering a number of positions, though it was at right-half he was mostly recognised. An accomplished footballer and an obvious choice as skipper – he was first handed the role in 1947–48 under Jack Breedon – Green had made 72 League appearances for the club before the outbreak of World War Two, but manager Thomson was fortunate that he could call on Green throughout the duration of the war years, although the player had been called back to the pit.

The torrid season the club endured upon the re-commencement of League football in 1946–47 was one blessed with few highlights, but a solo goal Green scored in an unexpected 4–1 victory at Hartlepools United was certainly one of them. There, according to the *Halifax Courier*, Green 'took the ball from the edge of his own box, evaded man after man before beating Heywood [the Hartlepools goalkeeper] with a surprise shot from the edge of the penalty area'. Certainly a goal for Green to savour, one of only five he scored for the club in 402 peace and wartime appearances before he moved to Lincoln City in February 1949. There, he succeeded George Stillyards at right-back but he was unable to prevent the Imps' relegation from the Second Division just a year after they had been promoted. But manager Bill Anderson rebuilt the side and at long last, having made the right-back position his own, Green gained his first honour, a Third Division North Championship medal when he appeared in 38 matches as Lincoln edged out Grimsby Town in a thrilling title race in 1951–52. Green went on to rack up 212 League appearances for Lincoln, scoring eight goals, before retiring in 1955.

GROVES, Arthur
Inside-left, 5ft 10in, 11st
Born: Killamarsh, 27 September 1907
Died: Derby, 27 September 1979
Career: Langworth Colliery; Halifax Town 14 May 1927; Blackburn Rovers 31 December 1928 (fee); Derby County July 1933 (£550); Portsmouth January 1936; Stockport County June 1939; Atherstone Town 1945; Heanor Athletic player-coach.
Halifax Town debut: v Durham City, Division Three North, 17 December 1927

It was a measure of the rapid progress that Arthur 'Scroggs' Groves made with Halifax Town that his Shay career was all but brief, for having being signed by Joe McClelland, his flashes of genius quickly had the bigger clubs eyeing him up. Groves arrived at The Shay in May 1927 after making a name for himself with Langworth Colliery, though it was more as a goal creator than a goalscorer that he proved his worth to the side. Starring at inside-left, he linked up well with Ernie Dixon and Tim Coleman and became one of the favourites with the crowds with his fine turn of speed and elusive body shot. With just 30 League appearances to his name, however, Groves's much vaunted move became a reality at the end of December 1928 when, following two fantastic performances against Carlisle United, he joined Blackburn Rovers where, in his first full season, he found his goalscoring touch, contributing 10 goals from just 16 League appearances. But he couldn't match that form the following term and he found himself out of the first team.

In July 1933 Groves moved to Derby County where he provided the openings for Jack Bowers. Nevertheless, he scored 17 goals from 64 League appearances before moving to Portsmouth in January 1936. Groves began the 1938–39 in the side but lost his place to Jimmy McAllinden and with it the chance to appear in the FA Cup triumph over Wolverhampton Wanderers at Wembley in April 1939. When World War Two brought a halt to the 1939–40 season, Groves had become a Stockport County player, but once hostilities had ceased in 1945 he joined Atherstone Town before becoming player-manager at Heanor Athletic.

GWYTHER, David Geoffrey Andrew

Centre-forward, 5ft 11½in, 13st 4lb
Born: Birmingham, 6 December 1948
Career: Farwood Rangers; Swansea Town juniors, professional January 1967; Halifax Town 8 August 1973 (£10,000); Rotherham United 14 February 1976 (£17,000); Newport County 6 December 1979; Crewe Alexandra on loan January 1982; Gloucester City; Port Talbot Town; Briton Ferry; Llanelli.
Halifax Town debut: v Leeds United (a), West Riding Senior Cup, 21 August 1973

Not for nothing did Halifax Town boss Johnny Quinn invite the Wales international selectors to take a look at Dave Gwyther in October 1974. Town's robust centre-forward was in top form, and Quinn reckoned there were players named in the squad for the upcoming European Championships qualifier with Hungary who were not as good as Gwyther. But Gwyther never got the call for the chance to add to his two Wales Under-23 caps he had won in 1972 and instead he carried on plundering goals in the Third Division with Halifax Town, finishing top scorer for the second season running following his move from Swansea City and picking up the supporters' award for Player of the Year.

It was with Swansea Town that Gwyther first came to prominence after his signing from junior side Farwood Rangers. He turned professional in January 1967, and his progress to the first team saw him strike up a deadly strike-force with Herbert Williams. In 1969–70 Gwyther spearheaded Swansea's promotion charge, netting 15 goals, and he was top scorer over the next three seasons, too, netting a total of 58 goals from 213 League appearances. His scoring feats brought him to the attention of the League of Wales FA, and he was included in their tour of Tahiti, New Zealand, Australia and Malaysia in June 1971, and on 5 January 1972 Gwyther won his first Wales Under-23 cap for a match against England at Swindon. His second came three weeks later against Scotland at Aberdeen. Both games ended in 2–0 defeats.

Signed by Halifax Town boss George Mulhall in August 1973 to offset the loss of Alan Waddle, Gwyther scored a trademark header on his debut in the Final of the West Riding Senior Cup against mighty Leeds United, and his haul of 14 goals that season included a headed hat-trick against Frickley Athletic in the FA Cup. But his £17,000 sale to Rotherham United in February 1976 immediately upon Alan Ball Snr's return as manager was the prelude to Halifax Town's relegation to the Fourth Division that season. Gwyther returned to The Shay with the Millers two months later to hammer a nail into Town's coffin by scoring the game's only goal.

With Rotherham, Gwyther was ever present in 1976–77 as the Millers just missed out on promotion on goal difference from Crystal Palace, but three years later, following his signing for Newport County, he was part of the side which not only clinched promotion from the Fourth Division, but also won the Welsh Cup, defeating Shrewsbury Town in the two-legged Final. That success enabled Newport to compete in the 1980–81 European Cup-Winners' Cup, and against all the odds, the side battled through to the quarter-finals, with Gwyther figuring prominently before bowing out to Carl Zeiss Jena.

When he substituted for John Aldridge in a game at Bristol Rovers on 19 February 1983, Gwyther joined an elite band of players (13 to date) to have chalked up 100 League appearances with four different clubs. Gwyther was loaned to Crewe Alexandra in January 1982 and released by Newport manager Colin Addison at the end of 1982–83, before being brought back briefly by the same manager in March 1985. Gwyther ended his professional career with 159 League goals to his name before winding down with Gloucester City, Port Talbot Town, Briton Ferry and Llanelli. In 2010, Gwyther was a partner in Jones & Gwyther Painting & Decorating in Swansea.

HALL, Ellis
Half-back, 5ft 9½in, 12st 7lb
Born: Ecclesfield, 22 June 1889
Died: Ecclesfield, 17 March 1947
Career: Ecclesfield Bible Class FC 1906; Hull City 1906–07; Millwall Athletic 1907; Hastings 1908–09; St Leonard's 1909; Stoke City 3 September 1909; Huddersfield Town May 1910; South Shields June 1912; Goole Town; Hamilton Academical 1919; Halifax Town 9 June 1922; Rochdale on loan November 1925; Consett.
Halifax Town debut: v Lincoln City (h), Division Three North, 26 August 1922

Ellis Hall followed his brother Fretwell to The Shay in June 1922 and was immediately installed as captain, playing a pivotal role in Halifax Town's famous Cup run of 1923–24, scoring at Maine Road to help Town earn a replay against First Division Manchester City. Hall had made a name for himself at a young age and was taken on by Hull City at the age of 16, making eight League appearances in their first season. After spells with non-League Millwall, Hastings, and St Leonard's, he joined Stoke City for one season, then transferred to Huddersfield Town who, like Hull City, were beginning their first season in the Football League and appeared at centre-half in their first-ever League game at Bradford. After making a total of 39 League appearances and two goals, Hall played for non-League South Shields, then Goole Town, before moving to Scotland with Hamilton Academical, where in three seasons he missed only seven games and was made captain.

Ellis Hall signed for Halifax Town following lengthy negotiations, with some papers claiming he had re-signed for Millwall. He was one of a great influx of new players during the 1922 close season as Halifax attempted to put behind them their disappointing first season in the League. In signing the likes of him and other players such as Ernie Dixon, Jack Lees and Lol Burkinshaw, the club were making positive moves (though they nearly crippled themselves financially). Ellis, an authoritative figure, was a model skipper and was ever-present at centre-half, playing all 38 games and scoring his only goal that season in a 3–1 victory over Lincoln City on the opening day.

The following season was one of the most eventful in the club's history as Hall led the side to the second round of the FA Cup, where they played two drawn matches, with Hall netting a coolly lobbed goal in the first match which ended 2–2 at Maine Road. The City programme that day described him as a 'studious player, and good in attack and defence'. In the League he missed only two matches and during 1924–25 he formed a fine half-back partnership with Alf Dark and Andy Martin, before these two became long-term injury casualties. Later, Hall linked up with new signing Donald Duckett, who would succeed him as captain. Once again Ellis Hall was a model of consistency, but in an overall disappointing season, he was forced to miss the last five games of the season through injury and was released at the end of that season. Subsequently, Hall moved to Rochdale, but he never appeared in the first team, before finishing his football career with non-League Consett.

HARRISON, Eric George

Half-back, 5ft 11in, 12st 4lb
Born: Mytholmroyd, 5 February 1938
Career: Mytholmroyd; Halifax Town amateur May 1956, professional 10 July 1957; Hartlepools United 20 August 1964 (£2,000); Barrow July 1966; Southport 27 June 1969; Barrow July 1971; Scarborough cs 1972; Everton assistant coach November 1972, youth coach; Manchester United youth coach June 1981, retired December 1997, Wales assistant manager 1999.
Halifax Town debut: v Gateshead, Division Three North, 9 September 1997

Not all great players turn out to be great coaches. Conversely, great coaches have not always been the greatest of players. Eric Harrison falls into the second bracket, a competitive half-back who plied his trade in the League's basement divisions, yet a player who went on to help develop some of the game's finest talents as youth-team coach at Manchester United. By all accounts, Harrison demanded nothing less than total commitment from his young charges, who numbered among others Ryan Giggs, Gary and Phil Neville, Paul Scholes and David Beckham, and was quick to castigate any player who he felt was slipping standards. It was nothing that he would not have wished upon himself, for though he never hit the dizzy heights Harrison made the most of his talent he was blessed with.

Harrison joined the groundstaff at Halifax Town in May 1956 while serving his apprenticeship as an electrician, and he made his debut as a 17-year-old against Gateshead on 9 September 1957 when the side was being run by the unusual combination of physio Allan Ure and director Vivien Booth, and helped Town to a 4–1 victory. He went on to play 14 matches during 1957–58, contributing much to Town's cause in a season which would see them qualify for the newly created Third Division. Ironically, having established himself in the side the following term and signing as a full-time professional at the end of June 1959, Harrison was then called up for National Service, stationed with the RAF in Stratford, though when allowed, he would join up with the team on matchdays. Memorably on one occasion he needed to be tended to by Ure having arrived with his feet crippled through foot drill. There was no doubting Harrison's dedication to Town's cause. Married on the morning of 6 October 1962, he took his place in the Town side that afternoon and helped Town to a 2–2 draw with Peterborough United. But despite his battling qualities, Harrison could not prevent Town's relegation from the Third Division in 1962–63, nor, despite being ever-present, could he inspire a swift promotion bid the following term.

Though there had been speculation about Harrison's future, the timing of his departure from The Shay was something of a shock, coming just two days before the start of the new season. He joined Hartlepools United and helped them to respectable finishes in his two seasons there. His time at the Victoria Ground coincided with the arrival of manager Brian Clough in October 1965, from whom Harrison later admitted he learnt much about dealing with players. In July 1966, Harrison joined former boss Don McEvoy at perennial strugglers Barrow but helped them to promotion in his first season. He spent three seasons at Holker Road, joining Southport in June 1969, where disappointment was felt with immediate relegation to the Fourth Division. Harrison returned to Barrow where he took his career tally of League appearances to 517 before winding up his playing days with Northern Premier League Scarborough. He moved into coaching at Everton under Harry Catterick before being joining new Manchester United boss Ron Atkinson at Old Trafford in June 1981, where he became youth coach, and his worth was recognised when Alex Ferguson kept him on just over five years later, a decision which benefitted all concerned. When United won the treble in 1998–99 the squad was made up of nine players that had come under the tutelage of Harrison. He later assisted Mark Hughes as manager of Wales, then headed David Beckham's Elite Coaching Academy.

HENDRIE, Paul

Midfield, 5ft 6in, 9st 8lb
Born: Glasgow, 27 March 1954
Career: Kirkintolloch Rob Roy; Birmingham City March 1972; Portland Timbers; Bristol Rovers September 1977; Halifax Town 26 July 1979 (£5,000); Stockport County 8 August 1984 (£1,500); Burton Albion cs 1989; Nuneaton Borough; Bath City; Chelmsley Town player-manager; Redditch manager November 1991; Tamworth manager February 1995 to January 2001.
Halifax Town debut: v Shrewsbury Town (h), League Cup, 11 August 1979

Paul Hendrie wrote his name into Halifax Town folklore with his 75th-minute winner which sank Manchester City in the FA Cup third-round match in the mud at The Shay in January 1980. He rightly savoured the attention afforded him, but five years earlier he went close to even greater glory in the FA Cup, reaching the semi-finals with Birmingham City, the club he had joined in March 1972. The tie with Fulham was settled in the dying seconds of a reply when John Mitchell somewhat fortuitously forced the ball over the line, and the Cottagers went on the meet West Ham in the Final. Hendrie made 23 First Division appearances and scored one goal for the Blues but always cited his most difficult opponent as Pele, whom he came up against in the NASL while playing for Portland Timbers in the summer of 1977. Upon his return, Hendrie joined Bristol Rovers but failing to hold down a regular first-team place, opted for a move to Halifax Town in July 1979.

Pocket-sized Hendrie quickly endeared himself to The Shay supporters with some tigerish performances and never-say-die attitude in the heart of the midfield, and not for nothing was he the only player to have won the supporters' Player of the Year award in consecutive seasons of 1980 and 1981. Hendrie gave Halifax Town five years' service, but doubtless would have remained longer had the club not insisted he take a pay cut in May 1984 in an effort to reduce the wage bill. He moved to Stockport County and remained at Edgeley Park for five years and his total of 121 League appearances and six goals would have been greater but for injury, where he missed much of his last two seasons with the club.

Upon being released in 1989 Hendrie joined Burton Albion, but a stint with Nuneaton Borough was cut short when he suffered a broken leg. He went on to become player manager at

Midland Combination side Chelmsley Town before taking over as manager of Beazer Homes Southern League Midland Division Redditch, helping transform their fortunes, taking them to sixth in 1993–94. Hendrie took over at Tamworth in February 1995 and stayed there until a poor run of results ended with him being dismissed in January 2001. Hendrie is the father of Lee, who carved out a career for himself with Aston Villa, Sheffield United and Derby County, earning one England cap under Kevin Keegan in November 1998.

HILL, Frederick

Inside-forward, 5ft 11in, 12 7lb
Born: Sheffield, 17 January 1940
Career: Bolton Wanderers juniors, professional March 1957; Halifax Town 15 July 1969; Manchester City 4 May 1970 (£12,000); Cape Town City; Peterborough United 10 August 1973 (£6,000); IFK Uppsala (Sweden) cs 1975; Droylsden July 1975; Radcliffe Borough.
Halifax Town debut: v Shrewsbury Town (h), Division Three, 9 August 1969

Freddie Hill's association with Halifax Town was all too brief partly because he was injured half way through his first and only season with the club, but mainly because he was simply too good for Third Division football. Following Town's rise from the Fourth Division in May 1969, manager Alan Ball went to Bolton Wanderers to sign Hill, still aged only 29 and with plenty to offer, for a new club record fee of £6,000. A former raiding inside-forward, noted for ghosting into the penalty area and good enough to be capped twice by England in the last days of the Walter Winterbottom era, Hill, of stooped shoulders, by now performed as a scheming midfielder and was the orchestrator of many of Town's attacking moves.

Halifax Town had adapted well to life in Division Three, and by Christmas were comfortably placed in mid-table. But on 19 January 1970, Hill suffered three broken toes after a challenge by Colin Symm in a friendly with Sunderland at The Shay, and though Ball reckoned he would be out of action for 'a month to six weeks', Hill never appeared in a Town shirt again. But so revered was he that, despite having only 27 first-team appearances and three goals to his name, he was still voted the club's Player of the Year. But no sooner had the season finished than made a shock move back to the First Division when he joined recent European Cup-Winners' Cup holders Manchester City. There he teamed up with former Bolton teammates Wyn Davies and Francis Lee, the barrel-chested striker who was by now an England international and who had brought Hill's name to the attention of coach Malcolm Allison. Hill and Lee had first joined forces at the Burnden Park club when the latter joined the professional ranks at Bolton in May 1961. Hill was already by then an established first-teamer, having joined the club in 1957. He made his League debut in a 1–1 draw with Newcastle United in April 1958, but his real opportunity came with the retirement of Nat Lofthouse, when Dennis Stevens replaced him at centre-forward and Hill coming into the side at inside-forward. He won the first of 10 England Under-23 international caps against West Germany on 15 March 1961 at White Hart Lane, marking the occasion by scoring the third goal in a 4–1 win, and he forced his way to senior selection, making his full debut for England in a 3–1 win over Northern Ireland in Belfast on 20 October 1962. A month later he featured in the 4–0 win over Wales in what was Winterbottom's last game in charge. Hill went on to make 375 League appearances and score 74 goals for the Trotters, though he had frequently asked for a transfer. In 1964, he seemed set to join Liverpool, but the Merseyside club withdrew their offer after Hill failed a medical due to high blood pressure.

Following his move to Manchester City, Hill made 23 League appearances during his first season there, but over the course of the next two years he became more of a fringe player. He moved to Peterborough United in August 1973 and helped them to the Fourth Division title in his first season there, being ever-present, and capping a fine season by being named in the PFA Fourth Division side. Hill had a spell in Sweden playing for IFK Uppsala, managed by his former Halifax Town boss Alan Ball Snr, before returning to the North West, playing for both Droylsden and Radcliffe Borough, and in October 1990 he was granted a belated testimonial when Bolton Wanderers entertained Manchester City.

HOGG, Frederick William

Inside-forward, 5ft 5in, 10st 4lb
Born: Bishop Auckland, 24 April 1918
Died: Halifax 19 August 1991
Career: West Auckland; Luton Town December 1936; Darlington World War Two guest; Halifax Town World War Two guest September 1940; Mansfield Town World War Two guest, signed November 1945 (£350); Notts County World War Two guest; Halifax Town 16 October 1947; Wigan Athletic cs 1950; Nelson; Lancaster City.
Halifax Town debut: v Sheffield Wednesday, North Regional League, 7 September 1940

It was while stationed in Ripponden, near Halifax, as a PE instructor during World War Two that Freddie Hogg, a diminutive and tricky inside-forward, began his association with Halifax Town, turning out as a guest while on the books of Luton Town. Under manager Jimmy Thomson, Hogg made his first Halifax Town start in a 1–1 draw with Sheffield Wednesday at The Shay on 7 September 1940, and appeared regularly for the side over the next three seasons, and proved a popular signing when he returned to play League football for the club in October 1947. Hogg had signed for Luton Town in December 1936, having being scouted while turning out for West Auckland, close to his native County Durham. He was working as a screen operator at the pits and admitted signing as a professional footballer was not a hard decision to make. Having made four League appearances prior to the outbreak of war, Hogg returned north and guested for Darlington before being posted to Yorkshire and turning out for the Shaymen. But Halifax Town lost his services when Hogg was re-stationed in Chesterfield in September 1943 and he went on to guest for Notts County at the request of manager Major Frank Buckley.

In November 1945, Hogg, who was living in Halifax having married in the town, moved to Mansfield Town, for whom he had also guested during the war, and was made skipper. But after making 45 League appearances and scoring eight goals, he jumped at the chance of rejoining Halifax Town in October 1947, though his time there coincided with a period of constant struggle, despite manager Jack Breedon and the board being able to call on the services of the likes of Horace Green, Dave Mycock and Des Collins. However, at the start of the 1949–50 season, Hogg failed to agree terms with the club and found himself out of the team. In the 1950 close season, he joined non-League sides Wigan Athletic, and later played for Nelson and Lancaster City before hanging up his boots in 1957. Employed at Kumficar Sales Ltd, Hogg later took up a position at Webster's brewery until retirement in 1983. Eight years later Hogg was badly injured by a knife attacker.

HOLDEN, Richard William

Winger, 5ft 9in, 12 7lb
Born: Skipton, 9 September 1964
Career: Burnley; Carnegie College; Halifax Town 24 September 1986; Watford 24 March 1988

(£125,000); Oldham Athletic 13 August 1989 (£165,000); Manchester City 10 July 1992 (£900,000); Oldham Athletic 11 October 1993 (£450,000); Blackpool 7 September 1995; Peel player-coach; Barnsley coach 2004, assistant manager May 2005 to November 2006.
Halifax Town debut: v Burnley (a), Division Four, 27 September 1986

Rick Holden was an out-and-out left winger who enjoyed a great rapport with the Shay supporters. Yet he was virtually unheard of when he took his place in the Halifax Town side for their match in September 1986 at Burnley, the club from which he had earlier been rejected. By the time Town boss Mick Jones signed him, Holden was studying for a Sports Science degree at Carnegie College. At The Shay, Holden quickly became a favourite, with his unorthodox running style belying his ability to beat defenders and deliver tantalising crosses into the box. He helped Town recover from a poor start and took them to the fringes of the Play-offs in his first season and was named Play of the Year. During 1887–88 Holden linked up with Neil Matthews and Wayne Allison in the forward line and helped Town to the northern semi-final of the Sherpa Van Trophy against Burnley, of all teams. Town lost the match on penalties, and within three weeks Holden was sold to Watford for a then club record fee of £150,000, a replacement for John Barnes who had moved to Liverpool the previous summer. But Holden could not help prevent Watford's relegation from the old First Division and in 1989 he signed for Second Division Oldham Athletic, managed by Joe Royle.

Holden had his best days in the first of two spells with the Latics, helping them reach the League Cup Final – Oldham lost to Nottingham Forest – and reach the semi-finals of the FA Cup, holding Manchester United to a 3–3 draw only to lose the replay in his first season and the following term he contributed five goals as Oldham won the Second Division title. In July 1992 he made the short trip to Manchester City but never quite hit the heights expected of him and his return to Boundary Park was welcomed by the Oldham fans. The side again reached the semi-finals of the FA Cup in 1993–94, only to be denied a place in the Final itself by a late strike by Manchester United's Mark Hughes and losing heavily in the replay. There was further disappointment for Oldham that season when they were relegated from the Premier League. Holden lost his place in the side following the appointment of Graeme Sharp as manager, and moved to Blackpool, but after making just 22 appearances he was unfortunate to snap his anterior cruciate ligament and retired from the game.

A qualified physiotherapist, Holden took charge of Peel on the Isle of Man, helping them to promotion to the First Division, IOM FA Cup and Charity Shield in 1996–97. He also won international honours as player-coach of the Isle of Man national side. In May 2005 Holden was appointed as Andy Ritchie's right-hand man when the former Oldham striker took over as Barnsley manager, both leaving the club in November 2006 after a poor set of results. In 2010 Holden published his autobiography entitled *Football – It's A Minging Life*.

HOLT, George
Inside-forward, 5ft 4¼in
Born: Halifax, 28 February 1927
Career: RES Gym; Aldershot Reserves; Army; Shaw Lodge; Halifax Town trialist February 1948, amateur April 1949, part-time professional 7 July 1952, retired 1954.
Halifax Town debut: v Mansfield Town (a), Division Three North, 28 February 1948

Inside-forward George Holt was the local lad who made good with his home-town team and who became a key figure in Halifax Town's epic FA Cup run of 1952–53, helping defeat First Division sides Cardiff and Stoke, but cruelly denied a place in the line-up to face Tottenham through injury. Yet Holt's Halifax Town career was unusual in that his second appearance for the club came nearly four years after his first and followed a stint with, of all, clubs, Aldershot. Born in Halifax, Holt was brought up in Southowram and joined crack local side RES Gym. He gained representative honours with Yorkshire Under-16s and Under-18s before embarking on almost three years' national service, during which time he represented the reserve side of Aldershot, playing one game in front of 15,000 at Portsmouth. It was while home on leave that Holt asked Town boss Jack Breedon for a trial and after just two reserve-team outings, he was thrown into the side for a game at Mansfield Town. Town lost the game 3–1 and injury also marred an otherwise memorable 21st birthday for Holt.

Pint-sized Holt returned to the forces and, upon completion of his time, returned home and played for another top local side, Shaw Lodge. It was new Halifax Town boss Billy Wootton who convinced him to play for the club and Holt duly signed as a part-time professional, the status he kept through the remainder of his time with the club. It was his equalising goal against non-League Ashton United that set Town on their way in the FA Cup competition of 1952–53. He also scored in the second round victory over Southport before helping defeat both Cardiff and Stoke in front of huge Shay crowds. But a week before the scheduled match with Spurs, Holt suffered an eye injury in a match with Grimsby which ruled him out of the Spurs match. Missing that match was the biggest regret Holt would have from his time in football. He returned to the side but was unfortunate yet again to suffer injury in the first match of the 1953–54 season. His torn Achilles would keep him out of the side until December and his appearances thereafter were but fleeting ones. Despite being retained by the club for the following season, Holt decided to concentrate on his business – he was a butcher by trade – and never played for another club again.

He went on to establish the firm of George Holt's Pies at Southowram, employing up to 32 staff, before finally retiring in 1989. Holt was a keen bowler and in 1968 reached the last 16 of the Waterloo Championships at Blackpool.

HORSFIELD, Geoffrey Malcolm

Centre-forward
Born: Barnsley, 1 November 1973, 6ft, 11st 7lb
Career: Athersley Recreation FC; Worsborough Bridge; Scarborough 10 July 1992; Halifax Town trialist January 1994; Guiseley cs 1994; Witton Albion cs 1996; Halifax Town 17 October 1996 (£4,000); Fulham 12 October 1998 (£350,000); Birmingham City 10 July 2000 (£2.25 million); Wigan Athletic 5 September 2003 (£1,000,000); West Bromwich Albion 18 December 2003 (£1,000,000); Sheffield United on loan 13 February 2006, signed 24 May 2006 (£1,200,000); Leeds United on loan 3 August 2006 to 2 January 2007; Leicester City on loan 31 January 2007 to 7 May 2007; Scunthorpe United on loan 31 January 2008 to 13 April 2008; Lincoln City player-coach 2 January 2009; Port Vale July 2009 player assistant manager.

Halifax Town debut: v Gateshead (a), Conference, 4 April 1994

Horsfield had two spells with Halifax Town; one rather unproductive, the other quite spectacular, when his goals helped propel the club back into the Football League in 1997–98. Born in Barnsley, he began playing in Barnsley League football before joining Worsborough Bridge, from where he was signed by Neil Warnock for Scarborough in July 1992. Struggling to make an impact there, Horsfield was brought to The Shay by Town boss John Bird in January 1994 but after playing unsuccessfully on the wing was released at the end of that season. It was at Guiseley, his next club, that he began to find the net with consummate regularity – 36 goals in fact during 1994–95 and he continued to score following his move to Witton Albion, though his time there was hit by injuries. Nevertheless, Town boss John Carroll was willing to bring him to the club in October 1996, though he proved to be no automatic first-team choice with Mick Norbury in the side, and it was from off the bench that he scored a crucial goal as Town defeated Stevenage Borough to avoid relegation from the Conference on the last day of the 1996–97 season.

However, when Carroll's successor George Mulhall sold top scorer Norbury in the close season, Horsfield was ready to step into his shoes. Powerfully built, benefitting from the time spent as a hod carrier on building sites, Horsfield developed into a bustling centre-forward in the old-fashioned mould, but with the ability to make goals for himself as well as others and during 1997–98 he topped the Conference goalscoring charts with 30 goals as Town won the Championship and regained Football League status after an absence of five years. Horsfield – nicknamed The Horse – had enhanced his reputation by scoring seven League goals in the Third Division when Kevin Keegan signed him for Fulham in October 1998 for a record £350,000 and he finished as top scorer with 15 goals as the Cottagers won the Second Division Championship in his first season.

In July 2000, Horsfield moved to Steve Bruce's Birmingham City for a club record £2.25 million, helping them reach the Final of the Worthington Cup, only to lose to Liverpool on penalties. He then followed Bruce to Wigan Athletic in September 2003 but was on the move again to West Bromwich Albion the following December, steering them into the Premier League in 2004 and famously scoring one of the goals which staved off relegation on the final day of the 2004–05 season.

Horsfield joined Sheffield United in May 2006 after an initial loan spell, but having failed to nail down a regular place was loaned out in turn to Leeds United, Leicester City and Scunthorpe United. In 2008 it was felt his playing days were over after Horsfield revealed he had testicular cancer, but having fought the disease, he teamed up with former colleague Peter Jackson at Lincoln City as player-coach, grabbing his 78th and last League goal against Gillingham in January 2009. The following July, Port Vale manager Micky Adams appointed Horsfield as his assistant player-manager, though he retired from playing at the end of the 2009–10 season. He later endured an uneasy relationship with Jim Gannon, Mickey Adams's successor, but in 2011 was assistant at Vale Park to caretaker manager Mark Grew.

JACKSON, Harold

Full-back, 5ft 11in, 11st 3lb
Born: Halifax, 20 July 1917
Died: Somerset, June 1996
Career: Halifax Boys' Brigade; Sowerby Bridge West End; Halifax Town trialist cs 1936, professional 20 August 1936, reserve coach February 1946; Stockport County August 1947.
Halifax Town debut: v Hull City, Division Three North, 6 February 1937

A typical pen-picture of full-back Harold Jackson described him as a player 'whose finer touches and general polish, allied to quick and decisive moves have caused several big clubs to say: "How nice he would look in higher company."' Had the war not intervened, that indeed may have been the case, for though Jackson reached his peak as a player, the war robbed him of his best days and he ended up remaining with Halifax Town, the club he had joined from local League football back in 1936. Halifax-born, Jackson learnt to play the game with the Halifax Boys' Brigade before playing local football with Sowerby Bridge West End, and it was under Jimmy Thomson that he came to The Shay as a trialist in the summer of 1936. After impressing, he signed professional forms and made his League debut at left-back in a 1–0 win against Hull City on 6 February 1937 following the sale of Alf Pope to Hearts.

Tall, effective in the air, speedy and with a nice turn of pace, Jackson made the left-back position his own and formed a steady partnership with Bill Allsop. Yet while he became an accomplished defender, he also filled in on the right-wing, and during the war years occasionally acted as an emergency centre-forward. At the beginning of 1937–38 Jackson was entrusted as the side's penalty taker, his three goals for the club all coming from the spot. Later that season, he lost his place in the side to Hugh Campbell, but returned the following term and appeared in 36 games of the 42 match programme. Jackson remained with the club throughout the duration of the war and in 1946 was made coach to the reserves by manager Thomson, though still very much a first-team player. He made 101 wartime appearances, and spent a further season with the club upon the restoration of peacetime football, though sadly it ended with Halifax Town finishing bottom of the Third Division North.

By the time he left The Shay, Jackson had 199 first-team appearances and 14 goals to his credit. He moved to Stockport County in August 1947, but was restricted to just two League appearances. In later life, Jackson moved to Somerset, where he died in June 1996.

JOHNSON, Kevin Peter

Midfield/striker, 5ft 6in, 9st 9lb
Born: Doncaster 29 August 1952
Career: Sheffield Wednesday apprentice, professional July 1970; Southend United September 1972; Gillingham on loan 27 February 1974; Workington 22 July 1974 (£2,500); Hartlepool United 14 February 1975; Huddersfield Town 24 September 1976; Halifax Town 10 August 1978 (£25,000); Hartlepool United 6 January 1981; Gateshead cs 1984.
Halifax Town debut: v Walsall (a), League Cup, 12 August 1978

Midfielder-cum-striker Kevin Johnson became Halifax Town's record buy in August 1978 when manager Jimmy Lawson shelled out £25,000 to Huddersfield Town for his services. Johnson quickly became a crowd favourite, but his silky skills and wicked left foot often had fans wondering why he was playing his trade in the lower reaches of the Football League when as a schoolboy he had kept Kevin Keegan out of the Doncaster Schoolboys' team despite being a year younger than Keegan. Many years later, on BBC1's *Parkinson Show* on 13 October 1979, Keegan afforded Johnson a mention, describing him as the player who, at a young age, appeared to have everything. But while Keegan signed for Fourth Division Scunthorpe United, where through sheer hard work he earned himself a move to Liverpool in 1971 and worldwide fame, Johnson took his chance with First Division Sheffield Wednesday, where first-team opportunities were few. In fact, Johnson made just one solitary first-team appearance for the Owls, and after demanding a pay rise was quickly shown the door.

Johnson resurrected his career with Southend United but moved to struggling Workington in July 1974 at a cost of £2,500, the most the Reds had paid for a player for over 10 years. But within the year, Johnson had moved to Hartlepool, helping the club to respectable finishes in both 1975 and 1976. But having been sold to Huddersfield Town in September 1976, Johnson developed something of a bad boy reputation, though nevertheless he was voted their Player of the Year in 1977–78, and it came as something of a surprise when Huddersfield allowed him to move to Halifax Town.

Johnson was unfortunate to suffer an ankle injury when making his Town debut in a League Cup tie at Walsall, but once he had recovered he proved to be the one shining light in a disastrous season, finishing top scorer, albeit with a meagre seven goals, as the side finished next to bottom of the Fourth Division on goal difference from Crewe. Still, Johnson was a unanimous choice for Player of the Year and the following term he had helped the side to a healthy position in the League until his leg was broken following a crude challenge from Hartlepool's Bob Newton in September 1979. Johnson was out of first-team action for almost a year but once he returned he was never the same player again, and on New Year's Day, he moved back to Hartlepool in a swap deal which saw centre-half Billy Ayre come to The Shay. Johnson took his tally of League appearances for Hartlepool to 148 and scored 11 goals before being released at the end of the 1983–84 season, whereupon he dropped into the Gola League with Gateshead.

JURYEFF, Ian Martin

Forward, 5ft 11in, 12st

Career: Southampton apprentice, professional 28 November 1980; Mansfield Town on loan 22 March 1984; Reading on loan 12 November 1984; Leyton Orient 15 February 1985 (£5,000); Ipswich Town on loan 9 February 1989; Halifax Town 10 August 1989 (£40,000); Hereford United 14 December 1989 (£50,000); Halifax Town 14 September 1990 (£50,000); Darlington on loan 27 August 1992, signed 29 September 1992; Scunthorpe United 20 August 1993; Farnborough Town February 1995; Havant Town July 1996; Weston-Super-Mare; Bashley; Southampton Community Development Officer; Bath City head coach July 2003.

Halifax Town debut: v Hartlepool United (sub), Division Four, 19 August 1989

Though not the most potent of Halifax Town strikers – his record of 24 goals from 113 first-team appearances is evidence of that – Ian Juryeff holds a unique place among the club's record makers. For he became Town's record signing on not one, but two occasions, his time at The Shay separated by a spell at Hereford United, for whom Juryeff also became their record signing. Juryeff began his career with Southampton, serving his apprenticeship before signing professional forms in November 1980. Loaned to Mansfield Town in March 1984, one of Juryeff's career highlights was a hat-trick he scored at Field Mill in a 7–1 win – against Halifax Town. The following term he spent time on loan at Reading before leaving The Saints for Leyton Orient in February 1985. In 1987–88, Juryeff memorably netted 16 goals from just 21 starts to become the side's leading scorer that season, and in total he scored 55 goals from 111 senior appearances.

Second Division Ipswich Town took Juryeff on trial in February 1989, though his time there was not particularly successful, and after turning down the chance to join Gillingham, it was Halifax Town boss Billy Ayre who took him away from Brisbane Road, signing him just nine days prior to the season's opening League game. Short of match practice, Juryeff came off the bench after 76 minutes to head home Town's last goal within five minutes in the record 4–0 first day win over Hartlepool United. Town made a promising start but an infamous 3–0 defeat in the FA Cup at the hands of Conference side Darlington led to a well-publicised spat between Juryeff and Ayre, and on 14 December 1989 the striker made his record £50,000 move to Hereford, though goals did not come easily.

It was on 14 September 1990 that Juryeff made the shock £50,000 return to Halifax Town, now managed by Jim McCalliog, and he became the perfect foil for the prolific Steve Norris. Norris may have claimed the headlines with his 30-goal haul, but during 1990–91 Juryeff also chipped in with nine as the Shaymen avoided the drop to the Conference. But the partnership was broken the following term when John McGrath was installed as McCalliog's successor, with Norris moving to Chesterfield. Two games into the following season, Juryeff, too, was on the move, clearly not part of McGrath's plans. He joined Darlington on a free transfer after an initial month's loan, then made moved to Scunthorpe United just prior to the start of the 1993–94 season. There, Juryeff scored 13 League goals from 44 appearances, taking his tally to 94 from 328.

Thereafter, Juryeff drifted into non-League football, playing for Farnborough Town, Havant Town, Weston-Super-Mare, Bashley and Bath City, where he was head coach. The holder of a UEFA 'A' grade coaching badge, Juryeff also served as Community Development Officer with Southampton, while taking time out in February 2005 to coach with the Global Scouting Network in Long Island, New York.

KENNEDY, Michael Francis Martin

Midfielder, 5ft 10in, 10st 5lb
Born: Salford, 9 April 1961
Career: Salford Schoolboys; Halifax Town apprentice 5 August 1977; professional 11 January 1979; Huddersfield Town 6 August 1980 (£50,000); Middlesbrough August 1982; Portsmouth 19 June 1984 (£100,000); Bradford City 12 January 1988 (£275,000); Leicester City 17 March 1989; Luton Town 18 August 1989; Stoke City 22 August 1990 (£180,000); Chesterfield August 1992; Wigan Athletic July 1993; Lifford coach.
Halifax Town debut: v Bradford City (sub), Division Four, 27 September 1978

Mick Kennedy was living proof of the old adage subscribed to by George Kirby that if you were good enough, you were old enough. Having taken over a club stranded at the foot of the Fourth Division, Kirby was quick to promote Kennedy to the first team, sending him on as substitute for the game at Wimbledon in November 1978, but having witnessed the maturity in such a young player, Kennedy thereafter started every game over the next season and a half, during which time he was never once substituted, so important did Kirby consider him to the engine room of his side. Kennedy, in fact, had already been pressed into action by Kirby's predecessor Jimmy Lawson, when, as a raw 17-year-old, he came on as a 20th-minute sub for Johnny Johnston in a local derby with Bradford City at Valley Parade towards the end of September 1978, in the kind of fiery atmosphere Kennedy would grow to love. His first start followed a few weeks later, but Kennedy was back playing reserve football in the North Midlands League by the time Kirby took over.

Kennedy was a product of the Salford Boys' Club and joined Halifax Town, then under the tutelage of Alan Ball Snr, signing apprentice forms in August 1977. But he did not sign professionally until January 1979, by which time he was already established in the side under Kirby. Kennedy, a player with a crack left foot and a long throw among his armoury, developed a tigerish midfield partnership with Paul Hendrie during 1979-80 as the Shaymen enjoyed better days, and never did he relish a match more than the FA Cup tie with First Division Manchester City in January 1980, when he pitted his wits and came out on top in the dual with Steve Daley, for a short time Britain's most expensive footballer. Kirby saw Kennedy as a vital member of his side which he hoped would challenge for honours and was desperate to keep him at The Shay but in the summer of 1980 after rejecting new terms, the midfielder moved across to Huddersfield Town, newly promoted as champions of Division Four, for a club record £50,000.

Kennedy spent two seasons at the Leeds Road club, helping stabilise them as a Third Division side, before taking his combative qualities to Middlesbrough, where he played under Malcolm Allison. Kennedy had cost £100,000 but the Ayresome Park club recouped all that when he was sold in June 1984 to Portsmouth, where manager Alan Ball recognised his battling qualities as pivotal to the cause. After a near miss in 1985–86, Portsmouth returned to the First Division with Kennedy as skipper in 1986–87. Having won three Republic of Ireland Under-21 caps while a Middlesbrough player, Kennedy won a fourth with Portsmouth, scoring two goals in a match against England in March 1985 and in May 1986 he made the step up to the full national side under Jack Charlton, winning two caps in an international competition against Iceland and Czechoslovakia.

Portsmouth's stay in the top flight was short-lived, but before their relegation was confirmed, Kennedy had returned to Yorkshire in January 1988 to join Bradford City, helping them to the Second Division Play-offs, only to lose to Middlesbrough in the semi-final. Just over a year later he made a transfer-deadline move to Leicester City before spending one season back in the First Division with Luton Town. Two seasons with Stoke City followed before Kennedy wound down his career in the lower divisions with Chesterfield and Wigan Athletic, taking his total of Football League appearances to 536 and 29 goals. Kennedy returned to Clare, Ireland, where his parents originated from, and has been involved coaching successful local side Lifford AFC.

LARGE, Frank

Half-back/centre-forward
Born: Leeds, 26 January 1940
Died: County Mayo, Ireland, 8 August 2003
Career: Leeds Schoolboys; Holbeck Locomotive; British Railways (Halifax); Halifax Town 27 June 1959; Queen's Park Rangers 27 June 1962 (£7,500); Northampton Town 2 March 1963 (£8,000); Swindon Town 6 March 1964 (£10,000); Carlisle United 26 September 1964 (£10,000); Oldham Athletic 24 December 1965 (£7,500); Northampton Town 23 December 1966 ($14,000); Leicester City 10 November 1967 (£20,000); Fulham 12 June 1968; Northampton Town 21 August 1969; Chesterfield 24 November; Baltimore Comets; Kettering Town 1974.
Halifax Town debut: v Leeds United (a), West Riding Senior Cup, 6 April 1959

The awkward, gangly frame of Frank Large charging down the middle cut an ungainly sight, but the converted centre-forward had several key attributes to his game. He was as strong as an ox, would chase lost causes, and above all else he knew how to find the back of the net. And having found his niche up front, Large proved beneficial to Halifax Town in terms of both goals, and in money, when sold to Queen's Park Rangers for the princely sum of £7,500, not bad business for a club which had acquired the player from junior football in Leeds. Large was signed by manager

Harry Hooper after impressing while playing for Holbeck Locomotive and the Halifax branch of British Railways, and joined the groundstaff in June 1959, arriving as a developing half-back, but with his large frame and bustling style, he was soon pressed into action in the forward line. Despite his unorthodox style, goals came easily for Large, and during 1960–61, when he featured in the attack with George Whitelaw, he finished top scorer with 18 goals and soon became hot property. It came as no surprise, then, when Large finally left the club for QPR in June 1962, though his move there was just the start of a somewhat nomadic football career, which included no fewer than three spells with Northampton Town, but he scored goals wherever he went.

Large's stay at Loftus Road lasted just eight months before he joined the Cobblers in March 1963. Northampton were embarking on their meteoric rise through the divisions, having just gone up from the Fourth, and were now heading for the Third Division Championship. Large was the final piece of manager Dave Bowen's jigsaw, and proved an instant hit, contributing 18 goals – he ended as their top scorer – from just 20 League appearances. Large was on his travels again in March 1964, joining Swindon Town, and by the time he returned to Northampton in December 1966 he had scored goals in the colours of Carlisle United and Oldham Athletic. The Cobblers had by now enjoyed their brief flirtation with the First Division and were now fighting against the odds to stay in the Second Division. Large's arrival, plus the eight goals he scored, were not enough to prevent their relegation, but his goals the following term ensured a move to Leicester City in November 1967.

Large found Northampton back in the Fourth Division by the time he rejoined them for a third spell in August 1969, via a spell with Fulham, but he enjoyed his most prolific spell over three seasons, scoring 42 goals from 125 League appearances. Large also featured in Northampton's memorable nine-match FA Cup run which culminated in a 8–2 home defeat by Manchester United, for whom George Best scored six, in February 1970. Best may have made the headlines that day, but quietly Large himself was a scorer of the game's last goal.

Large wound down his League career in England with Chesterfield before enjoying an Indian summer in the NASL with Baltimore Comets and finally ending his playing days with Kettering Town. Upon retirement, he worked as a farmer in County Mayo, Ireland, where he died in August 2003. Northampton Town have since labelled their Supporters' Player of the Year award in his memory.

LEE, Jeffrey Wrenthall
Full-back, 5ft 8in, 9st 13lb
Career: Huddersfield Town amateur; Halifax Town amateur 9 December 1964, professional 2 January 1965; Peterborough United 2 July 1973 (£6,500), Kettering Town 1977, Mansfield Town coach 1979; Bradford City youth-team manager 1982; Rochdale assistant manager 1989 to 1991; Hull City assistant manager 1991; Huddersfield chief scout 1997; Lincoln City scout.
Halifax Town debut: v Brighton & Hove Albion (h), Division Four, 28 December 1964

Jeff Lee served Halifax Town for nine years, and though never a headline-maker he was ever the consummate professional, filling a variety of positions, though chiefly recognised as a left full-back. He served under five managers at The Shay after arriving as an amateur in December 1964 and was offered professional terms the following month by Willie Watson, who allowed him to serve his apprenticeship as a draughtsman. It was an occupation Lee never need turn to, such was his development in the game. An efficient utility player, though not to be confused with Dick Lee who arrived at The

Shay around the same time, Lee played under Watson and his successor Vic Metcalfe, but it was not until the arrival of Alan Ball Snr that he began to establish himself. Appearing in 13 matches of Town's 1968–69 Fourth Division promotion campaign, Lee went on to succeed Mick Buxton at left-back the following term, and made the position his own over the next three seasons. A key member of the side which finished a creditable third in Division Three under George Kirby in 1970–71, he also starred in the shock Watney Cup defeat of Manchester United in July 1971.

Lee's service to the club was recognised with a benefit match on 27 November 1972 when Town defeated a Preston North End side 4–3. But after helping the side avoid relegation after winning their last four matches, he was sold to Peterborough United, immediately helping his new club clinch the Fourth Division title, appearing in all but one match. He remained at London Road until the end of 1976–77 having made 172 League appearances and scored 12 goals for the Posh, taking his career total to 412 League appearances and 10 goals. When teammate Mick Jones left at the end of that season to take over as manager at Kettering Town, Lee followed him there, then served under Jones again as coach at Mansfield Town, whom both joined two years later.

In 1982, both Jones and Lee moved to Bradford City where they worked under Roy McFarland, with Lee acting as youth team manager, guiding his young charges to the Northern Intermediate League title. Lee also worked as assistant manager to Terry Dolan at Rochdale and the pair then worked together for six years at Hull City until 1997 when he joined Huddersfield Town as chief scout, being promoted to the coaching staff in 2002 under Mick Wadsworth. Lee later returned to Huddersfield Town as Chief Scout in August 2003 under Peter Jackson and in 2009 was scouting for Lincoln City.

LEES, John William ('Jack')

Full-back, 5ft 8in, 11st 7lb
Born: Northwich, 26 July 1892
Died: York, 2 April 1983
Career: Northwich Victoria 1919; Preston North End 1919; Halifax Town 6 July 1922, retired March 1930.
Halifax Town debut: v Lincoln City, Division Three North, 26 August 1988

The name of Jack Lees was, for generations, familiar among shoppers in Halifax. The sports shop which adorned his name stood in George Street for many years. But how many of those who frequented it knew anything about the name and the man behind it? For those who watched Halifax Town in the 1920s, Jack Lees was an almost permanent fixture in the side, having joined the club from Preston North End in July 1922. He remained with the club for over eight years, and by the time he hung up his boots he had become Town's record appearance holder. Lees was born in Northwich and began his semi-professional career with Northwich Victoria in 1919 shortly after coming out of the Forces, having served with the Royal Artillery during World War One. But his stay with the Vics was but a short one, for later, he joined First Division Preston North End. But during three seasons at Deepdale, Lees spent much of his time in the reserves, making only 31 League appearances, the wealth of players there eventually forcing him to look elsewhere for first-team football.

Joe McClelland signed Lees in July 1922 as a half-back – his favoured position – and he initially formed the half-back line with Ellis Hall and Tom Langford. But injury to Charlie Treasure forced the Town boss to use Lees as a makeshift right full-back for the away trip to Durham City on 14 October 1922. Town drew the game 2–2, but so comfortably did Lees take to the position, he made it his own. Strong and fearless and quick in recovery, Lees was ever-present in his first season at The Shay, and again in 1925–26, and missed only three games during his first four seasons, forming a terrific full-back partnership with Ben Wheelhouse, both of whom were part of the famous Cup team of 1923–24. His solitary goal for Town was one to savour, a blistering shot from outside the box in a 4–1 win over Wrexham on 24 December 1927.

But by 1928–29 Wheelhouse had a new full-back partner in Frank Thompson, and after spending most of the following term in the reserves, Lees announced his retirement in March 1930 so he could concentrate on his business ventures, having been appointed manager of Beecroft Ltd sports outfitters on Union Street in the town. By then, Lees had established a then club record 248 League appearances.. Beecroft's later moved premises to George Street and in 1949 changed its name to Jack Lees Ltd, and Lees himself remained as manager until retirement in 1963.

A keen cricketer in his day, Lees turned out for Lightcliffe CC while a Halifax Town player. He and his wife later moved to Scarborough, then Strensall, near York, where Lees died in April 1983.

LONSDALE, Joseph Stanley
Left-back/half-back, 5ft 8in, 11st 13lb
Born: Washington, 13 April 1931
Died: Huddersfield, 26 September 2003
Career: Seaham Juniors; Huddersfield Town December 1948; Halifax Town 3 March 1955; Hartlepools United 17 November 1960.
Halifax Town debut: v Gateshead, Division Three North, 5 March 1955

Stan Lonsdale racked up 202 League appearances and 21 goals for Halifax Town, and though he became recognised as an uncompromising left-back he was deployed in a variety of positions, such was his versatility. He arrived at The Shay from neighbouring Huddersfield Town, the club he joined in December 1948 from Seaham Juniors, but despite being at Leeds Road for over six years, Lonsdale failed to break into the first team. It was Willie Watson who brought him to The Shay, initially to fill the left half-back position, though this naturally left-footed player found himself covering on the left wing or at left-back, the position in which he was most accomplished. He linked up with right-back Phil Roscoe during 1957–58 and helped the side not only qualify for the newly created Third Division in 1958 but also compete well over the next few seasons against strong southern competition.

Lonsdale had many fine games at left-back but perhaps his finest hour came against Tranmere Rovers on 27 April 1957 when a goalless first half gave no indication of that goals that would flow in the second. Lonsdale, showing how adaptable he was, switched from the left half-back position to centre-forward and netted twice within six minutes to help Town to a 4–0 win. Two seasons later, he proved to be Town's hero when his third-minute goal in the Final of the West Riding Senior Cup was enough to give the Shaymen the Cup for the first time.

Often in the thick of things, Lonsdale incurred the wrath of opposing supporters, notably during a game at QPR in September 1959 when he had to duck a vicious swing by a home supporter as he went to pick up the ball to take a throw-in. But Lonsdale lost his place in the Town side and elected to join Hartlepools United in November 1960, although having just bought a house at Stump Cross he continued to train at The Shay. Later, Lonsdale moved back to live in Huddersfield, where he lived until his death in September 2003.

LORENSON, Roy Vincent

Centre-half, 6ft 3in, 13st
Born: Liverpool 8 April 1932
Career: St Elizabeth's; Halifax Town trialist December 1951, professional 12 February 1952; Tranmere Rovers October 1960, trainer-coach; Kirkby Town manager July 1975.
Halifax Town debut: v Huddersfield Town, West Riding Senior Cup, 21 April 1952

Not for nothing was Roy Lorenson nicknamed Lofty. At 6ft 3in tall, he cut an imposing figure in the heart of the half-back line for over eight seasons with Halifax Town, commanding in the air and a useful foil at set pieces. Born in Liverpool, Lorenson played amateur football on Merseyside with St Elizabeth's first chancing his luck in the 1951–52 pre-season trials with Halifax Town under Billy Wootton. But it was not until the arrival of Gerry Henry that Lorenson made his first-team debut in a West Riding Senior Cup match with Huddersfield Town in April 1952, two months after turning a full-time professional. He made his mark during 1952–53, a season best remembered for Town's giant-killing exploits in the FA Cup. But after scoring with a shot which came down off the underside of the bar to set the Shaymen on the way to victory in the first-round replay at Ashton United, Lorenson was later overlooked for the defeats of Cardiff and Stoke, and for the fifth round visit of Spurs in front of a record Shay gate.

Lorenson was forced to take a break from full-time football when called up for two years' National Service in 1953, serving in the Far East with the Royal Navy, and following his return in July 1955 bided his time in the reserves until called upon for first-team duty at the end of March 1956. Lorenson became an automatic choice in the side, forming a formidable half-back line with Brian Atkinson and Alex South during 1957–58 as Halifax Town qualified for the newly created Third Division. Not one of the quickest players in the game, Lorenson made up for his lack of pace with solid wholehearted performances, the type of defender which manager Harry Hooper relied upon. And never was his resilience better exemplified than in a stormy encounter at Port Vale in September 1960, where he incurred the wrath of the home supporters following his challenge on Brian Jackson which saw the home player carried off on a stretcher. Lorenson and his defensive partners stood firm to help pull off a remarkable 3–2 victory against a Port Vale side which threw everything at the Town goal.

That game was one of Lorenson's last for the club. A desire to play football closer to his native Liverpool saw him hand in a transfer request in March 1959, and though the board reluctantly agreed to his demands, it wasn't until October 1960 that he left the club, joining Tranmere Rovers in a deal which saw forward Willie Sinclair arrive at The Shay. But Lorenson arrived at the Prenton Park club nursing a thigh injury which blighted his time there, and he managed just 14 League appearances before moving into coaching under manager Ron Yeats. Under his charges were future England international Steve Coppell and future FC Halifax Town assistant manager Trevor Storton. In September 1975 Lorenson took up his position as player-manager of Kirkby Town.

McCARTHY, Philip Paul

Wing-half/outside-left, 5ft 11in
Born: Liverpool 19 February 1943
Died: Liverpool 5 December 1996
Career: Skelmersdale United; Oldham Athletic 20 July 1965; Halifax Town 28 January 1966, released August 1971; Wigan Athletic October 1971.

Halifax Town debut: v Tranmere Rovers, Division Four, 28 January 1966

Phil McCarthy was recognised as an old-fashioned outside-left and was an integral part of the Halifax Town side which clinched promotion from the Fourth Division in 1968–69, making 42 League appearances that season, and supplying the cross from which Les Massie headed home the only goal against Rochdale on the night that promotion was confirmed. Affectionately known to many people as 'Dixie', McCarthy had been spotted while playing for non-League Skelmersdale United and was introduced to League football by Oldham Athletic manager Gordon Hurst, joining the Latics in July 1965. But his time spent there was an unhappy one. Athletic were struggling and before the season was out McCarthy was on the move to The Shay.

Signed by Vic Metcalfe in January 1966 as something of an emergency, McCarthy went straight into the side for that evening's game with Tranmere Rovers but failed to make an instant impression. But during 1966–67 he filled the gap vacated by left-winger Dennis Fidler, and featured prominently in a forward line of Archie Taylor, John Parks and Barry Hutchinson. That season the side memorably reached the third round of the FA Cup, McCarthy a scorer in the 3–1 extra-time victory at Doncaster Rovers in a first-round replay. Metcalfe used him at inside-left during the early part of the 1967–68 season, but Alan Ball Snr's arrival that November saw him revert to the left wing. Massie had arrived from Huddersfield and he owed much of his return of 28 goals to the supply delivered by McCarthy. Ball's side, though, was never prolific, with the emphasis put on fitness and in making life difficult for the opposition, and in that respect, McCarthy's ability to launch throw-ins into the heart of the opposition's penalty area was often put to useful effect. (In 1970–71 McCarthy reached the Final of BBC's long throw competition). During 1968–69 McCarthy's contribution to Town's promotion cause was not overlooked, and he was voted the Supporters' Club Player of the Year.

Under George Kirby in 1970–71 McCarthy lost his place to the patient Barry Holmes, though he returned to the side at left-back, only to suffer a chipped ankle bone in a game against Fulham in March of that season. McCarthy never appeared for Town again, being released from his contract in August 1971 and moving back into non-League soccer with Wigan Athletic. After football, McCarthy became a manager of the well-known Berni Inns before taking on the roles of licensee, shopkeeper and bus driver until his untimely death in December 1996.

McCORMICK, David
Half-back/Goalkeeper
Born: Halifax, 3 November 1920
Died: Cheshire, 1983
Career: St Malachy's, Halifax; Halifax Town trialist September 1947, professional 3 October 1947 to cs 1955; Ashton United February 1956 to 1958; Flint 1958–59.
Halifax Town debut: v Southport (a), Division Three North, 20 September 1947

Many players adapt to various positions throughout the course of their football careers. In the case of Dave McCormick, his switch was more remarkable than most, for after appearing in the first team as a defender – his favoured position was centre-half – he became a recognised goalkeeper, and figured in Town's greatest-ever FA Cup run. McCormick appeared at left back with local Halifax & District League side St Malachy's and didn't join Halifax Town until September 1947, by which time he was nearly 27 years of age. Manager Jack Breedon pitched McCormick into the half-back line and gave him an extended run-out in the side, but he later fell behind Jack France and Horace Green in the pecking order before being recalled in 1949–50. It was injury to reserve goalkeeper Bert Rees that saw McCormick emerge as a genuine custodian in his own right. He took his place between the sticks for the reserves in a Midland League match and having proved more than competent, forged a new career for himself.

McCormick, who was also employed by the Halifax Corporation Transport Division, appeared as goalkeeper in the 1951–52 pre-season trial matches and finally made the transition to the first team in his new position as early as the third match after Ted Elliot dislocated a finger in the home defeat against Accrington Stanley. McCormick took his place in the side at Wrexham on 8 September 1951 and saw off the challenge of not only Elliot, but also Alf Taylor, to become first choice 'keeper until the signing of the exceptional John Savage in March 1952. But a wrist injury sustained by Savage in defeat at Bradford on 27 December 1952 opened the door to the first team for McCormick once again, just as Town were embarking on their historic FA Cup run. McCormick thus found himself heavily involved, and starred in the giant-killing exploits as First Division sides Cardiff City and Stoke City were beaten at The Shay, with his run in the side also coinciding with the fifth-round meeting with Tottenham Hotspur, watched by a record Shay gate on 14 February 1953.

Savage returned to the first team the following month and McCormick's opportunities became limited, though he returned to the first team following Savage's sale to Manchester City in November 1953. During 1954–55 McCormick vied for the goalkeeping jersey with Walter Scott, but the signing of Arthur Johnson in March 1955 saw McCormick relegated to the reserves, playing once again as an outfield player – either at centre-half or full-back – once goalkeeper Harry Mills had also joined the club.

McCormick was awarded a joint benefit with Ted Breaks, with Halifax Town taking on a Football League X1 featuring Savage, then of Manchester City, on 27 April 1955. But seeking first-team football, McCormick joined Lancashire Combination side Ashton United in February 1956 and made his debut at centre-forward in a 2–2 draw with Lancaster City on 11 February. McCormick played in a variety of positions, though ironically never as goalkeeper, and went on to make 78 senior appearances and score nine goals up to the end of 1957–58. The following term, McCormick could be seen playing for Flint, but reappeared one last time for Ashton towards the end of that season when helping out during a spell of fixture congestion. McCormick settled in Cheshire upon retirement and died in 1983.

McHALE, Raymond

Midfielder, 5ft 8in, 12st 6lb

Born: Sheffield, 12 August 1950

Career: Hillsborough Boys' Club; Chesterfield September 1971; Halifax Town October 1974 (£3,000 plus a player); Swindon Town September 1976; Brighton & Hove Albion May 1980 (£100,000); Barnsley March 1981 (£55,000); Sheffield United August 1982 (£20,000); Bury on loan February 1983; Swansea City January 1985; Rochdale August 1986; Scarborough December 1986; Goole Town February 1988; Northwich Victoria cs 1988; Guiseley player-manager October 1988; Scarborough assistant manager January 1989, manager November 1989; Guiseley;

Scarborough manager December 1994, assistant manager March 1996, youth coach September 2001; Oldham Athletic chief scout November 2001 to June 2002.
Halifax Town debut: v Aldershot (a), Division Three, 2 October 1974

Ray McHale was the first signing made by Johnny Quinn after he had been installed as manager following the departure of George Mulhall, arriving in a player-exchange deal which saw Terry Shanahan move to Chesterfield. But the Spireites would soon bemoan his loss, while the Shay supporters began to appreciate his aggressive but skilful play in the heart of the midfield. McHale was a product of the Hillsborough Boys' Club in Sheffield, and came through Chesterfield's junior ranks, appearing on the wing in the side which won the Northern Intermediate League Cup in 1969 but he had moved to a centre-midfield spot by the time he made his League debut at Bournemouth in September 1971.

McHale arrived at The Shay as a noted penalty taker, having missed just one from 12 attempts while at Saltergate. He continued his role with Halifax, and successfully converted penalties in all three rounds of the FA Cup during 1975–76, including one in the third round defeat at First Division Ipswich Town. Sadly, that season saw Town relegated to the Fourth Division, and McHale unsurprisingly sought a move away. His sale to Third Division Swindon Town brought with it the success he deserved, but though the side narrowly missed out on promotion in 1978–79, the following term saw the side make national headlines with their run in the League Cup which carried them to the semi-finals, beating First Division Stoke City and Arsenal en route, only to lose to eventual winners Wolves.

McHale's performances were rewarded with a move to Division One side Brighton but his time there was not a success, and he returned north to play for Barnsley and Sheffield United. After further moves to Swansea City and Rochdale, McHale began his association with Scarborough in December 1986, helping them become the first side automatically promoted from the Conference in his first season under Neil Warnock.

McHale went into management at Guiseley, leading them to success in the FA Vase and Northern Premier League before returning to Scarborough as assistant manager to Colin Morris, succeeding him in November 1989. A dispute with the chairman saw him leave the Seamer Road club, and he rejoined Guiseley, only to return to Scarborough, where he acted in various capacities, acting as joint caretaker manager with Kevin Ratcliffe in January 1999. He left the club in November 2001 to become chief scout at Oldham Athletic, a role he held until June 2002.

MASSIE, Leslie

Inside-forward, 5ft 10in, 11st 4lb
Born: Aberdeen, 20 July 1935
Career: Prowis Youth Club; Banks O'Dee; Huddersfield Town August 1953; Darlington October 1966 (£2,500); Halifax Town 29 June 1967; Bradford 20 August 1969 (£1,750); Workington 11 December 1969; Bradford June 1971; Selby Town 1972.
Halifax Town debut: v Darlington, Division Four, 19 August 1967

Inside-forward Massie famously scored the goal against Rochdale in May 1969 that gave Halifax Town their first promotion as they finished runners-up to Doncaster Rovers in the Fourth Division. After playing Scottish junior football, he was signed by Huddersfield Town manager Andy Beattie in August 1953, though he spent his first three seasons in the reserves. It was Beattie's successor Bill Shankly who gave Massie his League debut in an away fixture at Fulham on 1 September 1956, and he finished his first season with five goals. But he topped the club's goalscoring charts over the next four seasons, going on to score exactly one hundred League goals for the club, and was third only to Jimmy Glazzard and Andy Booth in the club's post-war scoring charts. Massie was part of a forward line that also featured Kevin McHale and a young Denis Law, but towards the end of his time at Leeds Road he was converted to wing-half. In October 1966 Massie moved to Darlington but scored just twice and could not prevent his new side's relegation to the Fourth Division.

It was then that Halifax Town manager Vic Metcalfe stepped in to bring Massie to The Shay and he proved an instant hit, bagging 25 goals in his first season and sharing the Fourth Division goalscoring chart with Port Vale's Roy Chapman. Massie was also the first recipient of the Halifax Town Supporters' Club Player of the Year. With Alan Ball Snr in charge, Massie's goals during 1968–89 were crucial as Halifax Town made a push for their first ever promotion. Feeding off Ian Lawther, he notched 15 goals, including the crucial winner against Rochdale in the penultimate fixture, heading in a cross Phil McCarthy.

At times criticised for his lack of workrate, Massie, nevertheless was a predator in the box, and his record of 41 League goals for the Shaymen from just 86 appearances is testament to that. But once Town had gained promotion, Massie refused the terms of a new contract and found himself out of the team for the season's opening Division Three match with Shrewsbury Town. Despite protests from the fans, Massie was sold to Bradford, but after netting just twice, he was on the move again, joining fellow Fourth Division side Workington and helping them to a respectable 10th-place finish in 1970–71.

Massie returned to Bradford, by now in the Northern Premier Division, and finished his playing days with Selby Town. On leaving football, he became a self-employed haulage driver before taking a job with the Holset Engineering Company in Huddersfield. Later he worked part-time in a car accessory shop.

MONCRIEFF, James Conradi

Centre-forward,
Born: Todmorden, 14 June 1922
Died: Triangle, Halifax, 5 February 1975
Career: Sowerby Bridge Secondary School; Heptonstall; Oxford University; Pegasus; Halifax Town amateur January 1946 to 1955.
Halifax Town debut: v Gateshead (a), North Eastern Cup, 12 January 1946

Jimmy Moncrieff's association with Halifax Town spanned nine years, and though he could never be classed as a regular in the side, his contribution to the cause was a telling one, particularly during 1952–53 when he played an instrumental part in Town's memorable FA Cup run. The family name was well-known in the district. Jimmy Moncrieff's grandfather, James, was the Minister at Warley Congregational Church, while Andrew, Jimmy's father was a well-known sportsman, representing Halifax Town during their first-ever season. Jimmy Moncrieff, born in Todmorden, had attended Sowerby Bridge Secondary School while living at Warley, but he played locally for Heptonstall once the family had moved to the hilltop village.

Moncrieff first appeared for Halifax Town as a centre-forward during the second season of wartime football, and he remained on the books of the club until the end of 1954–55, yet throughout all that time, he was registered solely as an amateur player. Town were able to call upon Moncrieff's services when home on leave from his studies at Oxford University, for whom he also turned out at football, as well as the combined Oxford-Cambridge side, Pegasus, and famously passed up the opportunity to win international amateur honours so that he could assist the Shaymen in their fourth-round FA Cup tie with First Division Stoke City on 31 January 1953. He took his place at centre-forward and had a hand in Derek Priestley's decisive goal which saw them into the fifth round.

It was, indeed, in that Cup run that Moncrieff came to the fore. Having missed the first-round home draw with Ashton United, he came in for the replay and scored the winner, also scoring in the 4–2 second-round victory over Southport, and netted the third goal of the sensational 3–1 win over First Division side Cardiff City in the third. But laid low by flu, Moncrieff was forced to sit out the memorable fifth-round meeting with Tottenham Hotspur.

Aside from football, Moncrieff was also a top local cricketer, noted as a stylish batsman who enjoying two successful spells with Todmorden in the Lancashire League between 1948 and 1957, captaining the first 11 to top four finishes in 1949 and 1950, and in 1954 helping the club to the double of Lancashire League Championship and Worsley Cup. President of Hebden Bridge League Club Heptonstall Slack, he was a popular after-dinner speaker. Moncrieff later played for Bridgeholme CC and Triangle CC, where he was made captain. He died suddenly at his home in Triangle in February 1975.

MOSS, Jack

Inside-forward, 5ft 6in, 11st
Born: Blackrod, 1 September 1923
Died: Bolton, 1975
Career: Horwich Central; Bury December 1943; Rochdale January 1947; Leeds United January 1949 (£7,000); Halifax Town 17 January 1951.
Halifax Town debut: v Shrewsbury Town, Division Three North, 20 January 1951

Halifax Town obtained Jackie Moss in January 1951, so the story goes, on an initial free transfer from Leeds United because they had no money left after the signing of Des Frost from the same club. Town, who struck up the deal with Leeds boss Major Buckley, then forwarded the money once the club's Social Section had made a donation, though at the time, Town chairman Arthur Carter described the arrangement as 'the first practical help that we have had.' But however Moss was obtained, one thing is certain: Halifax Town picked up a real gem.

A blacksmith by trade, Moss began his career with Horwich Central before joining Bury in the last wartime season, making 31 appearances during 1945–46, and had made a further seven first-team appearances once League football returned before he moved to Rochdale in January 1947. Rochdale were enjoying a successful spell and Moss's form caught the attention of Leeds supremo Buckley, who paid Rochdale £7,000 for his services in January 1949, a club record received by the Spotland club. With Leeds, then of the Second Division, Moss broke into the side before the season was out and featured in five matches of the 1949–50 season only to lose his place as Buckley tried to find a winning formula. Thereafter, first-team opportunities became limited, and it was with the reserves that he first teamed up with Des Frost.

Moss followed Frost to The Shay, then managerless, but they found a club in the doldrums and destined for re-election. But fortunes changed slightly following the appointment of Billy Wootton as manager. He installed Moss as skipper for the 1951–52 season, and under his leadership on the field, re-election was averted in the season's final weeks. Wootton was replaced in February 1952 by player-manager Gerry Henry, someone who knew Moss well from his own time at Leeds, and Moss remained a key figure in the side, though he lost the captaincy to Eric

Williams because of injury. But having missed the earlier rounds, Moss returned to the side to play an instrumental role in the FA Cup defeats of First Division Cardiff City and Stoke City during 1952–53 when Town reached the fifth round for only the second time. But following a disastrous season in 1953–54, which ended with the club having to apply for re-election once more, Moss was released by Gerry Henry and retired from the game.

MURPHY, Thomas Edwin
Inside-left
Born: Southbank, 25 March 1921
Died: Middlesbrough, January 2003
Career: Southbank St Peter's; Middlesbrough May 1939; Blackburn Rovers December 1947; Halifax Town 11 March 1949 to June 1954; Redcar Albion September 1955
Halifax Town debut: v Carlisle United (a), Division Three North, 12 March 1949

Eddie Murphy, a tricky inside-forward who inspired players around him, served Halifax Town well over a period of just over five seasons, and was a key member of the side which reached the fifth round of the FA Cup in 1952–53. A product of Southbank St Peters, Murphy came to the attention of Middlesbrough and joined the Ayresome Park club in May 1939, only for the outbreak of war to halt his progress. Yet he remained on their books for eight years before joining Blackburn Rovers in December 1947. Murphy made 20 League appearances and scored three goals in his first season at Ewood Park but could not help Rovers's relegation from the First Division that season and he struggled for form the following term.

It was Jack Breedon who brought Murphy to The Shay in March 1949, a dual signing with Huddersfield Town's former international Ken Willingham, and the pair made their debuts in a goalless draw at Carlisle United. More of a creator than a scorer, Murphy, however, did net some important goals for the Shaymen, not least the second goal in the memorable 3–1 win over Cardiff City in the third round of the FA Cup in January 1953. He figured in each of the Cup matches that term, including the fifth-round match with Spurs in front of a record Shay gate. Earlier, in both 1949–50 and 1950–51 – when he was made skipper – Murphy missed just one match of their League programme, and was sorely missed through injury when Town slipped to FA Cup defeat at non-League Ashington in November 1950. However, when he turned out in the 2–0 victory over Mansfield Town on 2 January 1954, he became the first Town player to complete 200 post-war League appearances and he took his total to 218 before being given a free transfer and joining the all-conquering Teesside Football League side Redcar Albion.

MYCOCK, David
Left Half-back, 5ft 10in, 11st 10lb
Born: Sunderland, 30 August 1921
Died: Halifax, 7 October 1990
Career: Sunderland amateur; Halifax & District Wartime League; Halifax Town 29 May 1946.
Halifax Town debut: v Stockport County, Division Three North, 31 August 1946

Dave Mycock, a fine half-back, served Halifax Town for six seasons, though his time at The Shay coincided with an austere period in the club's history, with Town fighting against the threat of re-election. Nevertheless, he proved a fine acquisition, a reliable man-marker, showing coolness under pressure and an all-round solid defender who was often Town's best player, and one who performed consistently enough to rack up 170 League appearances. Mycock's route to The Shay was an unusual one, for having signed amateur forms with his native Sunderland, he found himself stationed in Halifax during the war, and was playing in the Halifax & District Wartime League when spotted by Town boss Jimmy Thomson. He was building his team for the resumption of peacetime football, and Mycock filled the breach at left-half, thus completing the half-back line with Jack France and Jake Ruecroft.

In the days when players did that sort of thing, Mycock was married on the morning of 12 February 1949 before turning his mind to the game playing in the goalless draw with Crewe that afternoon. Ever a trusty penalty taker – he netted six during his time at The Shay – Mycock was also the scorer of the odd spectacular goal, such as the one he scored in the 5–1 defeat at Darlington in August 1949, when he beat three men before slotting home. During 1948–49, Mycock appeared in all but four League games, and having moved to centre-half following the signing of Billy Morgan, missed just one game of the 1950–51 season. By the end of 1951–52 he had taken his tally to 170 League appearances and 17 goals, but despite not being retained by manager Gerry Henry, he was afforded a testimonial in which Halifax RLFC players took part in one half football, one half rugby on 1 May 1952.

Still, Mycock had one moment of glory still to come. Having moved to Wigan Athletic, he was skipper when they took on the mighty Newcastle United in a third-round FA Cup tie in January 1954. The Magpies included in their side Jimmy Scouler, Ivor Broadis, Bobby Mitchell and the legendary Jackie Milburn but Wigan rose to the challenge and in front of 52,222 spectators, played out an exciting 2–2 draw, only to lose the replay at Springfield Park 4–0. Mycock lived in the Warley district of Halifax up until his death in October 1990.

NICHOLL, Christopher John

Centre-half, 6ft 2in, 12st 7lb
Born: Wilmslow, 12 October 1946
Career: Macclesfield Schools; Handsworth Boys' Club; Burnley apprentice June 1963, professional April 1965; Witton Albion June 1966; Halifax Town trialist June 1968, signed 5 October 1968 (£1,250); Luton Town 27 August 1969 (£30,000); Aston Villa 9 March 1972 (£75,000); Southampton 27 June 1977 (£90,000); Grimsby Town player-assistant manager August 1983, retired as player July 1985; Southampton manager July 1985 to May 1991; Walsall manager September 1994 to June 1997; Northern Ireland coach 1998 – to 2000; Walsall assistant manager November 2001 to January 2002;.
Halifax Town debut: v Newport County, Division Four, 14 September 1968

Centre-half Chris Nicholl enjoyed almost unparalleled success with every club he played for, and was a rising star of Halifax Town's promotion winning side of 1968–69, the only former Town player to appear in the World Cup Finals. But Nicholl's rise to stardom was all the more surprising because of his rejection by First Division Burnley, where, despite being a strapping lad, he was a small fish in a big pool. Nicholl had represented Macclesfield Schools and Handsworth Boys' Club before being taken on as an apprentice by Burnley in June 1963, turning professional in April 1965. It seemed as if Nicholl's progress to the first team would take its natural course, but he failed to break through and was allowed to leave at the end of the 1965–66 season, and was plying his trade with Witton Albion in the Cheshire County League when Alan Ball Snr resurrected his career.

Nicholl initially joined Halifax Town as a trialist, but having impressed, Ball thrust him into first-team action for the away game at Newport County on 14 September and he became an automatic choice in the half-back line alongside John Pickering. He made his signing permanent the following month and went on to make 39 League appearances in that momentous campaign, as well as appearing in each game of the FA Cup which saw Town reach the fourth round and take Stoke City to a replay. Nicholl became hot property, but the only surprise about his transfer to Luton Town in August 1969 was in the manner of it. Hatters' boss Alec Stock tabled an offer for the young centre-half within 30 minutes of the end of the game in August 1969 after Nicholl had starred in a 1–1 draw at Kenilworth Road, and the deal was completed the following day. A year after helping the Shaymen out of the Fourth Division, Nicholl helped Luton out of the Third, as runners-up to Orient, and success followed him. Nicholl moved to Aston Villa in March 1972, replacing the ageing George Curtis at centre-half and played 13 games in Villa's Third Division title run-in. Three seasons later, he missed only one game as Villa returned to the First Division behind Manchester United.

It was Ron Saunders who made Nicholl skipper, and in 1977 he had the honour of lifting the League Cup after a second replay over Everton, having scored an amazing 35-yard goal in that game. It was Nicholl's second success in the competition, for in 1975 he had been part of the side which defeated Norwich City 1–0. Famed for scoring four goals in a 2–2 draw with Leicester in March 1976, Nicholl went on to make 210 League appearances for Villa as well as winning the first of 51 international caps for Northern Ireland, but it was as a player with Southampton, whom he joined in June 1977, that he appeared in the Finals of the World Cup in Spain in 1982.

With Southampton, Nicholl featured in Lawrie McMenemy's exciting side which finished runners-up to Nottingham Forest in the League Cup in 1979, and three years later were second to champions Liverpool in the League. In total, Nicholl made 228 League appearances for the Saints before becoming player-assistant manager under Dave Booth at Grimsby Town in August 1983. Nicholl retired from playing in July 1985 and returned to Southampton as only their sixth manager since the war. He held the post for six years, keeping the Saints in the First Division and unluckily seeing his side defeated by Liverpool in the semi-finals of both FA Cup in 1984 and League Cup the following year. Sacked in May 1991, Nicholl returned to club management with Walsall, guiding them to promotion from Division Three at the first attempt in 1994–95 and after leaving in May 1987, he returned briefly as assistant to Ray Graydon in November 2001, having worked with Lawrie McMenemy coaching the Northern Ireland international side during the interim.

NORRIS, Stephen Mark

Forward, 5ft 9in, 10st 8lb
Born: Coventry, 22 September 1961
Career: Telford United; Scarborough 25 July 1988 (£46,000); Notts County on loan 8 November 1989; Carlisle United on loan 28 December 1989, signed 19 January 1990 (£40,000); Halifax Town 5 October 1990 (player exchange); Chesterfield on loan 16 January 1992, signed 26 February 1992 (£33,000); Scarborough on loan 23 December 1994; VS Rugby 28 March 1995; Worcester City.
Halifax Town debut: v Scunthorpe United (h), Division Four, 6 October 1990

When Halifax Town boss Jim McCalliog traded centre-forward Tony Fyfe for Carlisle United's Steve Norris in September 1990, few could have foreseen the impact he would have during his first season at The Shay. But so prolific was Norris in front of goal, that he went on to become the first player since Bournemouth's Ted MacDougall 30 years earlier to net over half his side's seasonal tally. Norris was something of a late developer, having being signed by Neil Warnock for Scarborough in July 1988 after netting 24 goals in the Conference during 1987–88 with Telford United aged almost 26. He featured in Scarborough's exciting League Cup which saw them see off Chelsea, but Norris was hardly a prolific scorer with the Seasiders, netting just 13 goals before joining Carlisle United in December 1989, initially on loan. Nor did he enjoy a terrific vein of goalscoring form with them. By the time McCalliog came calling, he had scored just five goals from 29 League appearances.

Norris' signing was, on the part of McCalliog, borne out of desperation, for his side had failed to score in any of their opening seven League matches and were stranded at the foot of the Fourth Division. Norris made his Town debut in their eighth goalless game, but when he added the second goal in an improbable 3–0 win, ironically at Carlisle, he never looked back. He went on to score 30 League goals that season and was the player the club had to thank for keeping Halifax Town off the foot of the Fourth Division table, although there was no relegation that season.

Norris became a noted goal-poacher, though he was more than that. Many of his goals were scored with a run-in on the 'keeper, as evinced when the popular football magazine TV programme 'Saint and Greavsie' came to The Shay to focus on Town's top marksman, and 'Nozza' responded by scoring twice by showing defenders a clean pair of heels. With the three goals he had scored for Carlisle prior to his move to Halifax, Norris ensured he ended the season as the Fourth Division's leading scorer with 33 goals, as well as landing the Halifax Town's Player of the Year award. He continued to score goals the following term, too, and quickly became the club's biggest asset, a fact not overlooked by John McGrath, McCalliog's successor. Looking for a quick buck, he sold him to Chesterfield for £33,000 in January 1992, much to the astonishment of the supporters.

Norris proved a hit at Saltergate, netting an impressive 44 goals from 97 League appearances, though manager John Duncan, who arrived as successor to Chris McMenemy in February 1993, questioned his work ethic. Finding himself out of the side, Norris joined struggling Beazer Homes League side VS Rugby in March 1995, netting 10 goals from as many appearances and helping the side avoid relegation. An injury hit spell at Worcester City followed before Norris finally retired and settled back in Chesterfield where he found employment in the brewery distribution industry.

O'REGAN, Kieran Michael
Midfield, 5ft 8in, 10st 12lb
Born: Cork, 9 November 1963
Career: Tramore Athletic; Brighton & Hove Albion 9 April 1983; Swindon Town 12 August 1987; Huddersfield Town 4 August 1988; West Bromwich Albion 8 July 1997 (£25,000); Halifax Town 15 August 1995, temporary assistant manager 20 March 1996, assistant manager 17 February 1997, player-manager 4 August 1998 to 6 April 1999.
Halifax Town debut: v Hednesford Town (a), Conference, 19 August 1995

The signing of Irish midfielder Kieran O'Regan in the summer of 1995 was one of the most significant ever made by Halifax Town. Not because he was the greatest player Halifax Town ever possessed, though O'Regan undoubtedly was a class act, but because John Bird managed to secure his serves at a time when the club was coming out of its latest financial crisis and the Town boss had been instructed by the board to put together a squad on a shoestring budget.

O'Regan was a midfield lynchpin who brought out the best in other players around him. While he had a competitive edge to his game, his main quality was his vision and range of passing, for very rarely did he waste the ball. And so respected was he that twice he was asked to hold the reins with George Mulhall in interim periods until he finally landed the manager's job on a full-time basis, in less-than-satisfactory conditions, it has to be said. Having been a rising star in the League of Ireland side Tramore Athletic, O'Regan was signed in April 1983 by Jimmy Melia for a Brighton side heading for an FA Cup Final with Manchester United. O'Regan made his League debut at full-back in the last League game at Norwich City and put himself on the fringes of the Cup Final squad, but he was overlooked for both the first game which ended 2–2, and the replay.

Back in the Second Division, O'Regan made the right full-back position his own, making 31 League appearances that term and, having already won five Republic of Ireland Under-21 caps, capped a fine season by winning the first of his four full Republic of Ireland caps in an emphatic 8–0 win over Malta in a European Championships qualifying match in November 1983. It was under Chris Cattlin that O'Regan switched to a midfield role, and in August 1987 he moved to Swindon Town, scoring his only goal for the club in a 3–0 win at Huddersfield Town, his next club, whom he joined the following summer, teaming up with former Eire boss Eoin Hand. O'Regan spent five seasons at Leeds Road, being ever-present in 1990–91 when Huddersfield Town just missed out on the Division Three Play-offs, as they did the following term. After making 199 League appearances and scoring 25 goals for the Terriers, O'Regan moved to West Bromwich Albion in July 1993, a club that had just reached the new First Division. Managed by Keith Burkinshaw, the Baggies just avoided immediate relegation on goal difference but did suffer the humiliation of first round FA Cup defeat to Halifax Town in November 1993, with O'Regan a member of that side.

Released in 1995, O'Regan then made the surprise move, however welcome, to Halifax, helping to stabilise the club. A combative and influential midfielder, in the mould of Johnny Giles, O'Regan experienced the highs and lows at The Shay, being part of the side which narrowly avoided relegation from the Conference, then just a season later playing a crucial role as Town cantered to the title. During his time, his experience was drawn upon twice when acting as player-assistant manager to George Mulhall before his hasty full-time appointment in August 1998.
(See also Halifax Town managers).

OWEN, Clifford Lewis

Goalkeeper, 5ft 10in, 11st
Born: Barry, 12 June 1908
Died: Halifax, 11 August 2002
Career: Llanelli 1923; Charlton Athletic cs 1934; Halifax Town 22 May 1935; Chester June 1938; Accrington Stanley; Blackburn Rovers World War Two guest; Manchester City World War Two guest.
Halifax Town debut: v Hartlepools United, Division Three North, 31 August 1935

Cliff Owen was the last of the great Halifax Town pre-World War Two goalkeepers, keeping up a tradition which had seen Charlie Sutcliffe, Herbert Bown, Lewis Barber, Cliff Binns and Watty Shirlaw all pass through the club. He arrived in May 1935, though had manager Alex Raisbeck had his way he would have signed him two years earlier. For without a club in the summer of 1933, Owen's love of the sea saw him sign aboard a South African-bound ship rather than kick his heels at home, but when Raisbeck wanted to sign him he could not pursue Owen's quarry to Capetown, and upon his return to England, Charlton Athletic reached him first.

Born in Barry, South Wales, Owen became prominent in the area before turning professional with Llanelli, a club that were knocking on the door of the Football League, yet following his sojourn to South Africa his time with Charlton was one of frustration, as he found himself behind Alex Wright, Harry Wright and the emerging Sam Bartram in the pecking order. Owen failed to break into the first team but Raisbeck rescued his career and he quickly demonstrated great form with his cat-like agility, safe handling and quick reading of situations. His reputation grew and by 1936–37, top clubs such as Blackpool and Manchester United were casting their eyes over him, and there was talk, not without good reason, of a call-up for international honours, and but for the consistency of Bert Gray, then with Tranmere Rovers, Owen would surely have gained his first Wales cap. How ironic was it, then, that Owen should succeed Gray as Chester custodian in June 1938 when he made the shock departure from the Shay. There were suggestions that Owen and new Town manager Jimmy Thomson never saw eye to eye, and having been placed on Town's open-to-transfer list at the end of the 1937–38 season having made 102 League appearances for the club, Owen cost Chester a small fee. He spent just one year at the Sealand Road club, though doubtless he enjoyed his side's 5–1 victory over Town on 8 October 1938 and the 1–1 return on his first return to The Shay later that season. Owen also featured in Chester's exciting FA Cup run which ended in a fourth-round defeat to Sheffield Wednesday in a second replay at Maine Road. Owen had joined Accrington Stanley when war broke out in September 1939, though he guested for Blackburn Rovers and the reserves of Manchester City before the navy carried him afar to Burma, where he became a prisoner of war. Upon his return, Owen became the landlord of the Fountain Head pub.

PARKIN, George
Half-back, 5ft 7½in, 11st 7lb
Born: Hunslet, 20 August 1903
Died: Agbrigg, 3q 1971
Career: Leeds junior football; Halifax Town August 1920, Burnley 12 March 1924; Chester September 1929; West Ham United; Torquay United 1931; Halifax Town 4 November 1932; Workington cs 1933.
Halifax Town debut: v Scunthorpe United (a), Midland Counties League, 7 May 1921

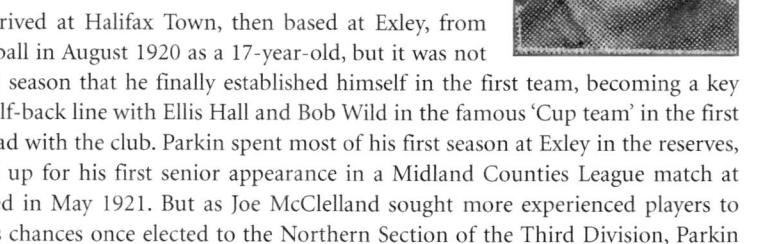

George Parkin arrived at Halifax Town, then based at Exley, from Leeds junior football in August 1920 as a 17-year-old, but it was not until the 1923–24 season that he finally established himself in the first team, becoming a key member of the half-back line with Ellis Hall and Bob Wild in the famous 'Cup team' in the first of two spells he had with the club. Parkin spent most of his first season at Exley in the reserves, but he was called up for his first senior appearance in a Midland Counties League match at Scunthorpe United in May 1921. But as Joe McClelland sought more experienced players to enhance the side's chances once elected to the Northern Section of the Third Division, Parkin found himself back in the reserves honing his craft under Bob Suter.

Parkin made his League debut in October 1921 when he figured in both games against Wigan Borough – his only appearances that term – and he was called upon only eight times the following term. But coming into the side with full-back Ben Wheelhouse and inside-forward Herbert Housley for the trip to Grimsby Town on 15 September 1923, Parkin never looked back, and soon he was showing magnificent form. Described by the *Halifax Courier's* Tom Dickinson as 'neat, dapper and polished', Parkin fully played his part in Town's epic FA Cup run that saw them reach the second round, where they took Manchester City to two replays. But once out of the Cup, Parkin was controversially sold to Burnley in March 1924 along with Ernie Dixon and Ben Wheelhouse, though of the three players, Parkin was the most successful, settling into the first team at Turf Moor and making 125 League appearances and scoring two goals – the only ones he ever managed in League football. At the end of the 1928–29 season he was placed on the open-to-transfer list and had to spend a year out of League football with Chester, and when Burnley's fee was reduced Parkin joined West Ham United, before spending a season with Torquay United.

One of the cleverest players Halifax Town had possessed, Parkin's return to The Shay on 4 November 1932 was welcomed by all, even if, for the player this was his swansong. Looking heavier, nevertheless, he arrived in time for another famous Cup run, and linking up in the half-back line this time with Oliver Thompson and Ted Craig, the Shaymen reached the fifth round for the first time. Parkin played in 25 League and FA Cup matches during 1932–33 to take his tally for the club to 73, but upon being released at the end of that season he joined North Eastern League side Workington. In May 1934 Parkin grabbed two goals in The Reds' record 16–1 demolition of Chopwell Institute.

PATERSON, Jamie Ryan

Midfielder, 5ft 3in, 10st 2lb
Born: Dumfries, 26 April 1973
Career: Halifax Town trainee 14 July 1989, professional 5 July 1991; Falkirk 11 December 1994; Scunthorpe United on loan 12 October 1995, signed 3 November 1995 (£18,000); Halifax Town 30 July 1997; Doncaster Rovers 24 July 2000; Barrow July 2004; Kettering Town 23 October 2004; Mornington Seagulls (Australia) 2006;

It was fitting that Jamie Paterson should fire home one of the goals against Kidderminster Harriers to clinch the Conference title with three games to go in April 1998. Paterson was, after all, the only playing member of the side that had also been with Halifax Town when they were relegated from the Football League five years earlier. He had returned at the beginning of that season after three years away to a club he had first joined as a trainee in July 1989. His brother Toby was already a playing member, having himself followed uncle Russell Black to the club. But while Toby Paterson's association with Town was short and undistinguished, Jamie went on to leave an indelible mark at The Shay and became a real crowd favourite.

Paterson could not have made his debut on a grander stage, coming on as a substitute for Terry McPhillips in a Rumbelows Cup tie against Manchester United at Old Trafford in September 1990, when he famously slipped the ball through the legs of England defender Gary Pallister. But it wasn't until the ill-fated 1992–93 season that he managed to cement a place in the first team, given an extended run-out by manager John McGrath and his successor Mick Rathbone. An attacking and skilful midfield player, pint-sized Paterson flourished the following season, scoring in the memorable 4–2 defeat of Bradford City in the Final of the Yorkshire and Humberside Cup, starring in the FA Cup defeat of West Bromwich Albion, and ending as Town's top scorer in the Conference. He remained with the club he had a great deal of affection for until December 1994 when he made what many considered a dream move to Scottish Premier Division outfit Falkirk. But he struggled to make a real impact though it was with a great sense of pride that he made his only start against Celtic, his boyhood heroes, at Parkhead. However, within the year, Paterson had returned south of the border, joining Scunthorpe United in November 1995 after an initial month's loan spell.

Paterson's return to Halifax Town could not have been timelier, as George Mulhall assembled an exciting and adventurous side that stormed the Conference and made a triumphant return to the Football League. Paterson revelled in the free role afforded him and weighed in with some important goals, not least than when he rounded the goalkeeper to score and put an end to Rushden's challenge at The Shay, and of course firing in Town's second goal when promotion was clinched at Kidderminster. Paterson not only picked up the club's own Player of the Year award, he was also voted Conference Player of the Year that season. Under Kieran O'Regan, Paterson helped fire Town briefly to the top of the Third Division but his love affair with the club was tested following O'Regan's sacking. Paterson fell out of favour during 1999–2000 with boss Mark Lillis, and bade a tearful goodbye to the club following the final home game with Macclesfield Town in May 2000.

Paterson went on to enjoy success with Doncaster Rovers, then of the Conference, and was top scorer in his first two seasons. He also played in the sudden death Play-off Final against Dagenham & Redbridge which saw Rovers regain League status in May 2003, and went onto make eight League appearances and score one goal (a penalty at Darlington) before being released at the end of 2003–04. A brief stint at Barrow followed before Paterson signed for Kettering Town in October 2004, witnessing at first hand the bizarre brief managerial reign of troubled former England star Paul Gascoigne, who took over control of team affairs in October 2005. In 2006, Paterson left these shores for Australia, where he played with Mornington Seagulls, helping them to back-to-back promotions and being top scorer in 2010.

PENTLAND, Frederick Beaconsfield

Inside-forward, 5ft 9in, 12st 5lb
Born: Wolverhampton, 18 September 1883
Died: Poole, 16 March 1962
Career: Willenhall Swifts; Avondale Juniors; Small Heath August 1900; Blackpool June 1903; Blackburn Rovers October 1903; Brentford May 1906; Queen's Park Rangers May 1908; Middlesbrough July 1908; (£350); Halifax Town August 1912; Stoke City February 1913; Halifax Town December 1913 to cs 1914; German Olympic Council 1914–18; France Olympic team coach 1920; Racing de Santander coach 1920; Athletic Bilbao 1921–36; Atletico Madrid; Real Oviedo; Atletico Madrid; Spain coach 1929; Athletic Bilbao; Atletico Madrid; Brentford manager 1936 to 1937, Barrow manager January 1938 to September 1939.
Halifax Town debut: v Doncaster Rovers, Midland Counties League, 7 September 1912

Fred Pentland was one of football's first mavericks, an entertainer who enjoyed a nomadic and colourful career, a personality whose eccentricity belied his astute knowledge of the game. He travelled widely, won five England caps, and went on to achieve immortality-like status in Spain. Yet it was with lowly Halifax Town that he finished his playing career, becoming the club's biggest star in the pre-Football League days when the side played at Sandhall Lane. Born in Wolverhampton, Pentland combined his time as a gun maker's assistant with playing for junior clubs Willenhall Swifts and Avondale Juniors. His first professional club was Small Heath (later to become Birmingham City) whom he joined in August 1900, but in three seasons with them he managed only one first-team appearance.

Pentland came to the fore at Blackpool, whom he joined in June 1903 and where, after a five-goal scoring spree in four consecutive matches, he earned himself a quick-fire move to

First Division Blackburn Rovers just four months later. Pentland responded by netting seven goals from 18 League appearances in his first season, helping Rovers avoid relegation. But he struggled to find the goals thereafter, and in May 1906 he joined Southern League outfit Brentford. It was with fellow Southern League side QPR that Pentland enjoyed his most successful spell after joining them in 1907, helping them clinch the Southern League Championship, and he was also a member of the side which contested the Charity Shield with Manchester United in April 1908.

Pentland ventured north once more to play for Middlesbrough, spending four seasons with them and it was during his time at Ayresome Park that he gained international recognition, winning the first of his England caps in the 2–0 win over Wales in Nottingham on 15 March 1909, though disappointingly for him, Pentland was injured in the first minute of the match and rendered a passenger. Happier times came as a member of the England side which defeated Hungary 8–2 in Budapest and Austria 8–1 in Vienna at the end of that season.

Pentland went on to make 92 League appearances and score 11 goals for Middlesbrough, but he spent 1911–12 with the reserves, averaging over a goal a game as they won the North East League Championship. His signing for Halifax Town which followed in August 1912 was indeed a major coup by Joe McClelland and the directors, who sought players to improve the squad following their election to the Midland Counties League. Pentland scored on his debut in the season's opening home defeat by Doncaster Rovers and went on to find the net regularly, forming an effective combination with Tommy Simons. He played a crucial part in Halifax Town's FA Cup exploits which culminated in a return to his former club QPR, and he chipped in – literally – with a goal to give Town a shock 2–0 lead, but the fairytale return to Park Royal ended in 4–2 defeat.

Despite their achievements, the run in the FA Cup hadn't made Halifax Town a rich club, and Pentland was one of several players sold in February 1913. He joined Southern League side Stoke City for a substantial fee, but returned the following December, his name mentioned in the position of player-manager, though with Joe McClelland still overseeing team affairs, Pentland's role was more of that as a coach. A knee injury sustained in a Bradford Hospitals Charity Cup semi-final replay at Heckmondwike brought an end to his playing days, but while he was forced to sit out the Final, which Town won 5–0 over Scarborough, Pentland was by then planning the next stage of his career.

In May 1914 he secured an important position under the German Olympic Council, and based in Karlsruhe, Baden, was to coach German athletes for the scheduled 1916 Games in Berlin. But the outbreak of war meant he, along with other well known footballers Steve Bloomer and Sam Wolstenholme, was interned for the duration of the war.

When peace was restored, Pentland returned to England, but by the time of the 1920 Amsterdam Olympics, he was coaching France. He then began his long association with Spain, coaching several clubs, including Racing de Santander, and Athletic Bilbao, whom he led to unprecedented success in three spells with the club. A renowned cigar smoker, Pentland wore his bowler hat, even in training, and his players would ritually whip it off his head and stamp on it until it was no more, yet despite his apparent eccentricity he revolutionised their style of play, introducing the short-passing game.

Pentland brought this style of play to the national side, where under manager Jose Maria Mateos, he was appointed coach, and masterminded Spain's 4–3 victory over England in May 1929, thus becoming the first Continental side to defeat England. After a third spell at Athletic Madrid Pentland returned to England at the outbreak of the Spanish Civil War as coach at Brentford, before becoming manager of Barrow in 1938.

PICKERING, John

Centre-half, 5ft 11in, 12st 7lb
Born: Stockton-on-Tees, 7 November 1944
Died: 30 May 2001
Career: Stockton & Durham schoolboy football; Chelsea juniors 1959; non-League football; Newcastle United July 1963; Halifax Town 14 September 1965 (£1,250); Barnsley May 1974; Blackburn Rovers reserve team coach June 1975, assistant manager cs 1978, caretaker manager October 1978, manager February 1979 to May 1979; Carlisle United coach 1980–81; Lincoln City assistant manager and coach 1982, manager July 1985 to December 1985; Newcastle United coach 1988; Lincoln City assistant manager 1990; Middlesbrough coach cs 1991, Academy director
Halifax Town debut: v Colchester United (h), Division Four, 14 September 1965

Central-defender John Pickering made more League appearances than any other player for Halifax Town, and not without good reason. A model of consistency, he became a stalwart in the heart of the Town defence for the best part of a decade and, with Tony Rhodes, forming a Castilian fortress at the back of one of the club's greatest-ever teams. Pickering was a wholehearted defender, a specialist, pure and simple, winning or blocking the ball with head or foot and giving it to those with more creative gifts to use.

Pickering went on to leave an indelible impression at Halifax despite a stuttering start to a career which saw him rejected as a junior at Chelsea in 1959 and treading water in the reserves at Newcastle United. Pickering needed first-team football, but the day he signed for Halifax Town started out for him like any other. He was part of the Newcastle reserve team which travelled to Huddersfield Town for a Central League game on the afternoon of 14 September 1965, but given the option of playing in that match or signing for Halifax Town while in Yorkshire, Pickering chose the latter, and thus the immediate course of his and Halifax Town's fortunes prospered. He made his first-team debut in the half-back line two days in a 1–1 draw with Colchester United at The Shay and didn't miss another game that season. And though injured for the most part of the 1966–67 season, Pickering returned the following term and rarely missed a match until he left the club in 1974. Made skipper by manager Alan Ball, Pickering developed a good understanding with young centre-half Chris Nicholl at the heart of the defence, the rock upon which Ball moulded his promotion-winning side.

Andy Burgin succeeded Pickering as captain in 1970, but nevertheless Pickering was ever-present in three consecutive seasons between 1970 and 1973, instrumental in the side coming close to reaching the Second Division in 1971, and defeating Manchester United in the Watney Cup competition in July 1971. All-told, Pickering served under five managers at Halifax, though it was the last of these, George Mulhall, who reinstalled him as skipper, only to relinquish him of the honour in September 1973, claiming he was too quiet. After making 367 League appearances, Pickering was released by Mulhall in May 1974 and joined Barnsley where he furthered his own coaching career. That had actually begun with local side Elland United, but his first professional coaching position was with the reserves at Blackburn Rovers under new manager (and former teammate) Jim Smith in June 1975. Pickering remained at Ewood Park for five years, becoming assistant to Jim Iley, and succeeding him as manager in February 1979. He broke the Blackburn club record when he shelled out £75,000 for Duncan McKenzie from Chelsea but failed to prevent relegation to the Third Division and consequently he lost his job.

Pickering later held coaching positions at Carlisle United, Lincoln City and Newcastle United before being appointed coach to Lennie Lawrence at Middlesbrough. He spent over 10 years coaching with Middlesbrough, initially with the first team, before moving to Boro's academy in 1998. He was caretaker manager of Middlesbrough for the final game of the 1993–94 season and his service to the club was recognised when manager Bryan Robson gave him the honour of leading the team out at Wembley for the Coca-Cola Cup Final against Chelsea in 1998. After a long illness Pickering died in May 2001.

PRIESTLEY, Derek

Winger
Born: Queensbury, 22 December 1926
Died: Clayton, June 1999
Career: Halifax Town 14 October 1950; Bradford 27 July 1956; Morecambe cs 1957, retired September 1957.
Halifax Town debut: v Carlisle United (a), Division Thee North, 23 August 1951

Derek Priestley was a left-winger who made his name with Halifax Town having started his professional career rather late in the day. He had already turned 23 years of age by the time Town manager Jack Breedon took him out of local football in October 1950, but he went on to become a real crowd favourite. With speed and artistry, and the ability to deliver telling crosses, Priestley delighted The Shay faithful, and was there ever a more popular scorer than when he drove home the ball to knock First Division Stoke City out of the FA Cup to see Town into the fifth round of the FA Cup for only the second – and last – time in 1952–53?

Priestley was, in fact, one of Breedon's last signings, the Town boss resigning in November 1950, and with his successor Billy Wootton favouring George Glaister down the left flank, Priestley was forced to bide his time in the reserves, having to wait until the following season before being handed his debut at Carlisle United on 23 August 1951. But it was under Gerry Henry that he enjoyed his best spell in the Town side, playing his part in the momentous FA Cup run. Having missed Town's first-round tie with non-League Ashton United through injury, Priestley was drafted in for the replay three days later and helped Town to a victory which sparked their run. It is often overlooked that Priestley set up George Holt for the winner against Workington in the second round, or that he was the scorer of the first goal in the thrilling 3–1 victory over Cardiff City in the third. But this all set Priestley up for his crowning moment, firing home from close range in a goalmouth melee to see off Stoke in front of a then record 35,621.

Priestley's performances during that Cup run earned him rave reviews and both Sunderland and Newcastle United showed interest in him, though no offers were made. Still, clearly deserving of a higher grade of football than the Third Division North offered him, Priestley asked to be put on the transfer list in February 1954, and it was probably more than just coincidence that he suddenly lost his place in the team, the directors keen to make a point.

Priestley returned to first-team action, but a knee injury sustained, ironically, at Carlisle's Brunton Park on 2 April 1955, where he had made his League debut, dogged him for the rest of his career. Placed on the open-to-transfer list by Bill Burnikel at the end of 1955–56, Priestley finally made the switch to Bradford that July. But he was never destined to make the first team and by the start of the following season he had signed for Morecambe, finally succumbing to his persistent knee injury and retiring in September 1957.

QUINN, Adam Robert

Centre-half, 6ft 2in, 14st 3lb
Born: Sheffield, 2 June 1983
Career: Sheffield Wednesday trainee; Halifax Town cs 2002; Crawley Town 12 August 2008; Forest Green Rovers on loan November 2010; Darlington 6 January 2011.
Halifax Town debut: v Barnet (a) Conference, 31 August 2002

Adam Quinn was the only player to play the full six seasons for Halifax Town during the reign of Chris Wilder, arriving from virtual obscurity at Sheffield Wednesday to become the bastion of the defence, a solid performer who always gave his all to the cause. Signed by the Owls as a trainee, Quinn failed to break into the first team, but he became part of Wilder's hastily assembled squad, a player perhaps best described then as a raw talent. He made his debut in a goalless draw at Barnet on 31 August 2002 and went on to cement his place in the side towards the end of his second season at The Shay. Among his 14 goals for the club was the headed winner against Farsley Celtic which landed 10-man Halifax Town the West Riding County Cup in April 2004.

During the summer of 2005, Quinn was struck down by a throat infection which meant he missed the opening games of the 2005–06 season, but he returned to the side – albeit two stones lighter – and formed a solid defensive partnership with Greg Young. The Championship was a distinct possibility at one point, but the side had to settle for the Play-offs, only to lose to Hereford in the Final. Nevertheless, Quinn's immense performances that season earned him the supporters' Player of the Year award.

Quinn continued to enhance his reputation and was rewarded with the first of five semi-professional caps when Paul Fairclough selected him for England's European Challenge Trophy match with Holland at Burton on 29 November 2006, a game England won 4–1, some compensation after Quinn had been forced to withdraw from the squad three years earlier due to Town's involvement in the LDV tournament. Occasionally used as an emergency striker, Quinn also found himself between the sticks following the sending off of Mark Cartwright in a game against Aldershot Town in February 2004. When the club went into liquidation in May 2008, Quinn joined Blue Square Premier side Crawley Town, where he joined former teammates Danny Forrest, Jake Wright and Lewis Killeen already at the club, giving the side a 'Halifax' look about it. Under manager Steve Evans, Quinn was handed the captaincy, but he joined Forest Green Rovers on loan in November 2010, then made a permanent switch to Darlington two months later.

RAYNER, Edward

Goalkeeper,
Born: Hemsworth, 28 September 1916
Died: Halifax, 2 May 1988
Career: Doncaster Rovers; Scarborough 1939; Halifax Town guest 1940–41, signed May 1945; Nelson 11 August 1951.
Halifax Town debut: v Hull City (a), North Regional League, 31 August 1940

One person whose name will be forever associated with Halifax Town is that of Ted Rayner, a goalkeeper who arrived at The Shay from

Midland League side Scarborough in May 1945. But his association with the club had begun earlier when he guested for the side during the 1940–41 wartime season, starring in every game throughout the first half of that campaign. Rayner began his career with Doncaster Rovers, but having failed to make the first team he joined Midland League side Scarborough, appearing in the last match played by the club prior to the outbreak of war in September 1939. Having joined the forces, Rayner found himself stationed in Halifax and was immediately signed up by manager Jimmy Thomson, and though he left the area, he returned to make his transfer from Scarborough a permanent one

Tall and commanding in his box, Rayner possessed a powerful and rangy kick, though once peacetime football returned he found himself in competition with Reg Elvy, though it was Rayner's displays that ultimately forced Elvy's move to Blackburn Rovers in March 1947. But disenchanted with the perennial struggle at The Shay, Rayner asked for a transfer in early 1948 – Cyril Hannaby came into the side – but new manager Jack Breedon quickly restored him to the first team and he continued to perform heroically. In a local derby with Bradford City at The Shay in September 1948, Rayner memorably saved a penalty from Jack Murphy in the very first minute.

The arrival of new manager Billy Wootton spelled the end for Rayner once Ted Elliott had been signed but at the end of that season hiss sterling service to the club was rewarded with a benefit on 30 April 1951, when a Ted Rayner X1 beat a Halifax Town side 4–2, with Rayner scoring a 90th-minute penalty, although his last appearance for the club came in the 11–2 Festival of Britain victory over Waterford United on 12 May 1951. Rayner left the club for Nelson in August 1951 but retained his links with Halifax Town for many years, acting as a club official on matchdays for many years. Employed at Crosslee Yarns Ltd., Sowerby Bridge, Rayner was a handy crown green bowls player and a member of his local Ripponden side.

RHODES, John Anthony

Centre-half, 5ft 11in, 11st 6lb
Born: Dover, 17 September 1946
Career: Derby County juniors, professional October 1963; Halifax Town 10 November 1970 (£7,000); Southport 2 August 1976 (£2,000), Burton Albion cs 1977, retired cs 1978.
Halifax Town debut; v Port Vale, Division Three, 28 November 1970

Throughout the first half of the 1970s, Tony Rhodes was a mainstay in the heart of the Halifax Town defence, forming effective centre-back partnerships with firstly John Pickering, then Albert Phelan, having joined the club in November 1970 from First Division Derby County. Just two months earlier, Rhodes had lined up against the Shaymen in a League Cup tie, one of only six senior outings he made for the Rams. Coming through the junior ranks, Rhodes had turned professional in October 1963 but found himself down the pecking order behind Ron Webster and Roy McFarland, and first-team opportunities became even more limited once Derby manager Brian Clough had signed Colin Todd. But when Town boss George Kirby felt in need of a commanding centre-back, it was to the Baseball Ground he turned, paying £7,000 for Rhodes' services and clearly viewing him as an important member of his side.

Rhodes contributed four goals during the colourful 1970–71 campaign, but Town just fell short of promotion, finishing third. But disappointment was tempered by the defeat of Manchester United in the pre-season Watney Cup tournament in July 1971, with Rhodes shadowing Denis Law. A commanding an authoritative figure, he played a key part in Town's great escape in 1972–73 when relegation was avoided on goal average after the side had amazingly won their final four matches under George Mulhall, one of five managers Rhodes played under.

It was Mulhall's successor Johnny Quinn who installed Rhodes as skipper in 1974–75, but while the Shaymen survived another relegation scare that season, their luck ran out the following term. Alan Ball Snr's return as manager in February 1976 did not have the desired effect on the team, and though Rhodes was voted the club's Player of the Year, the Shaymen finished bottom of the Third Division and were thus relegated. Disappointingly, Rhodes then chose to join Southport, but it proved to be a move that ultimately benefitted no one. He played just nine games during 1976–77, a season which ended with Southport ended with a re-election application, and he then spent one final season with Burton Albion.

A keen cricketer, Rhodes played for Halifax side RAFA long after retiring from the game before moving back to Derbyshire where he became a manager in a warehouse.

RICHARDSON, Lee James

Midfielder, 5ft 11in, 11st
Born: Halifax, 12 March 1969
Career: Halifax Town trainee 23 August 1986, professional 6 July 1987; Watford 9 February 1989 (£175,000); Blackburn Rovers 15 August 1990 (£250,000); Aberdeen 16 September 1992 (£150,000); Oldham Athletic 12 August 1994 (£3,000,000); Stockport County on loan 15 August 1997; Huddersfield Town 24 October 1997 (£65,000); Bury on loan August 1999; Livingston 4 February 2000; Chesterfield August 2000, coach, caretaker-manager 22 March 2003 to 12 May 2003, manager 12 March 2007 to 6 May 2009.
Halifax Town debut: v Rochdale, Division Four, 4 May 1987

Lee Richardson came through Gerry Brook's Northern Intermediate side from school and was sold several years later for £175,000, one of several such deals the club did which enabled it to survive. Richardson's signing retained links with Halifax Town that had begun when his own father Colin was a junior with the club in the early Sixties and who later became a staunch supporter of the club. There could have been no prouder father when he saw Lee make his senior bow with his hometown club.

Halifax born, Richardson helped the Under-19s side clinch the Northern Intermediate League title in 1986–87, but by the end of that term he had been handed his first-team debut by manager Billy Ayre, an entertaining affair at Rochdale, won 5–3 by the home side. Richardson, tall and slim, signed professional forms in July 1987 and developed into an energetic midfield player who never shirked a tackle. During 1987–88, he linked up in the midfield with Mick Matthews and Steve Thornber and his first senior goal that season clinched victory in Town's penultimate fixture at Exeter City. His second and last goal the following term, a wicked shot from outside the box, started a 5–0 rout of Peterborough in October 1988, by which time several clubs had been ruling the roost over Town's prodigious starlet.

In February 1989, Richardson made his move to Watford, who were hoping to regain First Division status at the first attempt, though they would ultimately fail in the Play-offs. Richardson proved an able deputy for Tim Sherwood, and in 1989–90 he cemented his place in the side. In August 1990 Richardson moved to Blackburn Rovers and in 1991–92 played his part in the side's promotion to the Premier League via the Play-offs, appearing as a substitute in the 1–0 Final win over Leicester City at Wembley. But he never appeared in the elite division in England, instead joining Scottish Premier League outfit Aberdeen in September 1992, where he had the frustration of finishing runners-up to Rangers in all three major domestic competitions in his first season. Richardson made 29 League appearances as the Dons finished nine points behind champions Rangers, and was also a beaten finalist in the Skol Cup and in the Scottish Cup, despite scoring in their 2–1 defeat.

In August 1994 Richardson moved to Oldham Athletic, a club just relegated from the Premier League, but though he became the resident penalty taker – he was top scorer in 1995–96 – he could not prevent the Latics' relegation to the Second Division in 1996–97. Richardson had a loan spell at Stockport County before spending two and half seasons with Huddersfield Town. Having been loaned to Bury, he headed back to Scotland briefly to play for Livingston, then began a long association with Chesterfield, signing in August 2000 and going on to make 45 League appearances for the Spireites. Following the departure of manager Roy McFarland in March 2003, Richardson took over as caretaker manager before being appointed on a permanent basis the following month. It was an eventful period in charge for Richardson at Saltergate as he saw his side slip out of the Play-off frame two seasons running and memorably going through to the third round of the FA Cup in December 2008 at the expense of Droylsden, who, having beaten Chesterfield after two abandoned matches, were thrown out of the competition for fielding an unregistered player.

Following his sacking, Richardson filled in his time as a drummer with the Weedwackers, a Halifax four-piece combo, while seeking further employment in football. His elder brother Nick Richardson followed Lee to Halifax Town, with the pair briefly being teammates.

ROCHE, Patrick Joseph

Goalkeeper, 6ft 1in, 11st 4lb
Born: Dublin, 4 January 1951
Career: Shelbourne; Manchester United 18 October 1973 (£15,000); Brentford August 1982; Halifax Town 23 August 1984 to cs 1989; Chester City 1989; Northwich Victoria 1989–90.
Halifax Town debut: v Huddersfield Town, West Riding Senior Cup, 11 August 1984

Paddy Roche was a hugely popular goalkeeper with Halifax Town, the club he joined towards the end of his career. His name evoked memories of televised gaffes and ridicule from his time in the First Division with Manchester United, but with Halifax it was hard to see why as Roche brought confidence to a usually shaky defence in a side that struggled for the most part. There is no doubt that Roche had ability. Why else would Manchester United manager Tommy Docherty bring him to Old Trafford in 1973 from Shelbourne, with whom he appeared in the previous season's FAI Cup Final, if not to be looked on as potential successor to long-serving Alex Stepney? Roche bided his time in the reserves, but just when Docherty was about to make him the first choice 'keeper on the eve of the 1976–77 season, Roche had to fly back to Ireland to attend to a family bereavement. Stepney reclaimed the position, and when Roche was at last called upon, a couple of well-publicised errors, notably spilling the ball against Liverpool, rocked his confidence. Under Dave Sexton, he played second fiddle to the emerging Gary Bailey, and his tally of League appearances for the Reds was restricted to just 53.

Nevertheless, Roche was competent enough to earn eight Republic of Ireland international caps, the first coming in a European Nations Cup qualifier in Austria on 10 October 1971 while with Shelbourne, while his last in a 4–0 victory over Turkey under manager Johnny Giles four years later. Released by United in 1982, Roche dropped down the divisions with Brentford, only to produce some erratic form. After two seasons, he joined Halifax Town under boss Mickey

Bullock and went on to defy his critics, for though Town struggled and ended his first season with the club applying for re-election, Roche produced some stunning form and became a hit with the supporters, who voted him their Player of the Year. His finest game was probably in a Milk Cup-tie against Spurs at White Hart Lane, one last chance for Roche to appear on the grander stage, where he performed heroics to keep the score down.

Ever-present in 1985–86 and again two seasons later, Roche played his part in Halifax Town's upturn in fortunes. In 1987–88 he helped them reach the third round of the FA Cup, as well as the northern semi-final of the Sherpa Van Trophy, though sadly Roche will be remembered for his spot-kick miss in the shoot-out at Burnley. Made captain by manager Billy Ayre in 1988–89, injuries restricted Roche and probably swayed Ayre's decision to give him a free-transfer at the end of that campaign with 227 first-team appearances to his name. He then joined Chester City as cover for Billy Stewart and made one appearance for Northwich Victoria in the Conference.

In 1990 Roche returned to Halifax Town to head their Football in the Community programme in succession to former teammate Jim McCalliog, and ran a tuck shop at The Shay on matchdays.

ROSCOE, Philip

Full-back, 6ft 2in, 12 7lb
Born: Barnsley, 3 March 1934
Career: Barnsley junior, professional August 1951; Halifax Town 6 July 1956; Wellington Town July 1964.
Halifax Town debut: v Workington (a), Division Three North, 25 August 1956

Phil Roscoe may not have been the quickest of defenders, but with his sizable frame and crunching tackles he made life difficult for any opposing attacker. One of Harry Hooper's key signings, Roscoe remained a feature of the side over eight seasons with the club. Counting future wrestler and actor Brian Glover among his teammates, Roscoe was a member of the Barnsley Boys' Club which defeated Derby over two legs to win the English Schools Trophy in 1949. He then came through the youth ranks at Second Division Barnsley before signing professional forms in August 1951, though he was never to break into the first team under manager Angus Seed, nor his successor Tim Ward.

Roscoe joined Halifax Town in July 1956 as manager Hooper consciously assembled a side of big players, though he was far from an initial first choice. In fact, it was not until Town had qualified for the newly created Third Division in 1958 that he cemented his place in the side, the Roscoe-Lonsdale full-back partnership becoming most effective. Later, he struck up partnerships with Paddy Stanley and Malcolm Russell, filling both right and left-back positions.

Not a noted goalscorer, Roscoe was, however, a scorer of noteworthy goals. Against Southampton at The Shay in September 1959, a free-kick taken from his own half sailed over the head of goalkeeper Tony Godfrey. Later that season, he repeated the trick from just as far out in Town's 4–3 FA Cup defeat at Gateshead, his free-kick this time deceiving 'keeper Williamson. Roscoe took his tally to 257 League appearances and six goals with the Shaymen, but having spent one season in the Fourth Division, was released by coach Don McEvoy and joined Wellington Town.

RUSSELL, Malcolm

Full-back, 5ft 10in, 11st 10lb
Born: Halifax, 9 November 1945

Career: Celtic Orient; Brighouse Youth; Huddersfield Town 1961; Halifax Town apprentice 18 October 1961, professional March 1963; Southport 16 August 1968 (£7,000); Barrow 17 December 1970 (£6,000); Stockport County 28 July 1972 (£5,000).
Halifax Town debut: v Bradford, Division Three, 4 January 1963

Malcolm Russell made more first-team appearances for Halifax Town than any other home-grown player, taking his total to 210 in six full seasons with the club. Yet his decision to leave for Southport shortly into the historic promotion 1968–69 season was surely one that not only he regretted, but one that disappointed many of the Town fans who had seem him make his debut as a 17-year-old in January 1963. Russell made his name originally as a striker with Southowram side Celtic Orient before signing schoolboy forms with Huddersfield Town. But he was coaxed into joining Halifax Town by coach Eddie Hebblethwaite, becoming their first apprentice in October 1961. His tasks included cleaning the boots of players such as Frank Large and Willie Carlin, but the appointment of Don McEvoy as coach changed the course of his career and he was successfully converted from striker to full-back.

Russell's first-team breakthrough came in the away match at Bradford on 4 January 1963, but despite making 18 League appearances during 1962–63, Halifax Town were relegated. Nevertheless, so assured did Russell perform at right full-back that not only did he make the position his own throughout his time at The Shay, but he also earned a call-up for the England Youth squad in November 1963 and was invited for trials at Lilleshall along with stars in the making such as John Hollins, David Sadler and Howard Kendall under the watchful eye of Wilf McGuinness.

Described as a 'strong and determined defender' Russell was catching the eye of several leading clubs until suffering a pelvic injury which kept him out of the game for a lengthy spell. But he returned to action and reclaimed his first-team position, being ever-present in 1966–67 under Vic Metcalfe. Metcalfe's successor Alan Ball Snr also valued Russell as an important member of the side, and it was under him that he grabbed his only goal for the Shaymen, a deflected shot from 15 yards which was enough to defeat Scunthorpe United in a second-round FA Cup tie in December 1967. But Southport's offer in August 1968 saw Russell depart The Shay where he teamed up once more with manager Don McEvoy. But though the side finished a commendable third in his first season with Russell featuring more prominently in the half-back line, the following term Southport were relegated to the Fourth Division. In December 1970, Russell followed McEvoy to Fourth Division strugglers Barrow, where he was made skipper, and was devastated when, after a second successive re-election application, the Cumbrian side lost their League status to Hereford United in 1972.

Russell then joined Stockport County in July 1972 but a second serious injury curtailed his football career and he retired after just one season with a total of 352 League appearances and four goals to his name. It was in December 1967 that Russell opened up a ladies' hairdressers with his wife, but once his football career was over he ran a newsagent's in Northowram before becoming a director of Worthington Sports, a sports retail outlet based in Brighouse.

SAVAGE, John Alfred
Goalkeeper, 6ft 4in, 13st
Born: Bromley, 14 December 1929
Career: Hull City September 1950; Halifax Town 14 March 1952; Manchester City 17 November 1953 (£4,000); Walsall 17 January 1958; Wigan Athletic cs 1959.
Halifax Town debut: v Scunthorpe United (h), Division Three North, 15 March 1952

Giant goalkeeper John Savage was one of the finest post-war Halifax Town goalkeepers, and he made a telling contribution to Halifax Town's cause following his signing in March 1952. Renowned for his huge kick-outs – he once sent the ball, first bounce, over the crossbar – Savage commanded his own penalty area with authority, and with his reputation growing it was not long before the big clubs came eyeing him. Savage began his career with Hull City, signing professional forms in September 1950, and acted as cover for Joe Robinson. He made his debut against Leicester City on 24 February 1951 but failed to appear in the first team following the signing of Billy Bly, and it was with Halifax Town that he came to prominence. Manager Gerry Henry, concerned at Town's lowly standing in the League, sought to strengthen the defence and having signed Savage on the Friday had no hesitation in throwing him straight into the side at the expense of Dave McCormick for the following day's home clash with Scunthorpe United. Savage went on to play his part as Halifax Town steered clear of the re-election places.

With Savage bringing an air of confidence to the defence, Halifax Town enjoyed better times, and he featured in the early rounds of the FA Cup, but a wrist injury sustained in the home defeat by Bradford on 27 December 1952 meant he was forced to sit out the big Cup ties with Cardiff City, Stoke City and Tottenham Hotspur. But he did write himself into the record books in that game with Bradford, for in the age of no substitutes he was thrust into the forward line and responded with a goal, one of the few occasions of a goalkeeper scoring for the Shaymen. Once fit, Savage reclaimed his position in the first team, and in 1953–54 he continued to impress and it was no surprise when he made a £4,000 move to First Division Manchester City.

At Maine Road, Savage found himself acting as understudy to the legendary Bert Trautmann, and he did not make his first-team debut until December 1954 when City lost 2–0 at Newcastle United. But he was afforded an extended run out at the beginning of the 1956–57 season while Trautmann recovered from a broken neck sustained in the previous season's FA Cup Final victory over Birmingham City, and made 19 League appearances that term before Trautmann reappeared.

Savage was again called upon during 1957–58 but was unfortunate to concede nine goals in a game at West Bromwich Albion on 21 September 1957, and he made the last of his 30 League appearances for City in a 2–0 defeat of Sheffield Wednesday two and a half weeks later. In January 1958 he moved to Walsall as a replacement for Gordon Chilvers and appeared for the Third Division North against the Third Division South in the annual contest shortly after his arrival. Sent-off early in his time there in a game at Swindon Town, Savage put this behind him to make 51 League appearances before being released in May 1959. Savage went on to join Wigan Athletic, then of the Lancashire Combination, and lived in Blackpool in retirement.

SHAWCROSS, Francis David

Wing-half, 5ft 10in, 11st 4lb
Born: Stretford 3 July 1941
Career: Manchester Boys' Club; Manchester City juniors 27 July 1956, professional June 1958; Stockport County 10 June 1965; Halifax Town 16 March 1967 (player exchange), contract cancelled September 1970; Drogheda United February 1971; Altrincham trialist; Macclesfield Town; Droylsden.
Halifax Town debut: v Stockport County, Division Four, 18 March 1967

Dave Shawcross made a most unusual debut for Halifax Town after having made his move from Stockport County on 16 March 1967. For a while he was joining the Shaymen, striker Bill Atkins was making the opposite journey, and both players faced their former club just two days later, though it was Atkins and County who came out on top. The tannoy announcer had a field day that afternoon, announcing the programme team changes: 'Number 10 for Town: Shawcross in place of Atkins. Number 10 for County, Atkins in place of Shawcross!' Just over two years later, Shawcross and Atkins became teammates when the latter rejoined the Shaymen, a team in the ascendency with Shawcross a class act in the heart of the midfield.

Shawcross had been a member of the Manchester Boy's Club before joining the groundstaff of Manchester City in July 1956 and turned professional two years later. He spent nine years at Maine Road, making his debut at left-half in a 4–1 defeat at Arsenal in September 1958, then cementing a place in the side during 1960–61 when he could count on as teammates the likes of Bert Trautmann, Ken Barnes, a young Alan Oakes and Denis Law.

Shawcross showed enough promise to earn himself England youth honours and one England Under-23 cap against West Germany in March 1961, a game in which he lined up against future World Cup-winners George Cohen and Bobby Moore and scored the last goal in a 4–1 win. But a broken leg halted his progress and first-team appearances became limited, and after totalling 47 League appearances and two goals Shawcross was released by the club at the end of the 1964–65 season, whereupon he joined Stockport. In his first season at Edgeley Park, he contributed an impressive nine goals, missing just four League games, and in 1966–67 he had helped County to the top of the Fourth Division and on the way to the Championship when manager Jimmy Meadows elected to swap him for Atkins.

Though Shawcross may have been disappointed not to have seen the job through at Stockport, there was compensation when he featured prominently in Town's Fourth Division promotion drive under Alan Ball Snr in 1968–69. And, having been promoted, Shawcross was the scorer of the first goal back in the Third Division, a delicate chip from a free-kick routine which sealed victory over Shrewsbury Town in the season's opener at The Shay. Shawcross would go on to score 25 League and Cup goals for the Shaymen, his tally bolstered by seven penalties from eight attempts.

Shawcross figured in 41 League and Cup matches during 1969–70, but despite being retained by outgoing manager Alan Ball he would never play under his successor George Kirby, though not by choice. Diagnosed with a nervous complaint in the summer of 1970, Shawcross never trained with the players and was eventually released from his contract in September of that year. He went on to team up with former colleague Mick Meagan, who was manager at League of Ireland side Drogheda United, in February 1971, where he became a favourite among the fans, and he later had spells with non-League clubs Altrincham, Macclesfield Town and Droylsden.

SHIRLAW, Walter Paterson

Goalkeeper, 6ft 1in, 11st 10lb
Born: Wishaw, 23 June 1901
Died: Bradford, 26 October 1981
Career: Larkhall Thistle; Bradford City August 1924; Rochdale August 1927; Bradford City March 1928; Halifax Town 22 June 1932; Workington July 1935; Bradford City scout 1936.
Halifax Town debut: v Accrington Stanley (a), Division Three North, 27 August 1932

The giant frame of goalkeeper 'Watty' Shirlaw arrived at The Shay in June 1932 following the release of Bernard Bilcliff. Vastly experienced, manager Alex Raisbeck made him captain for the 1933–34 season, and he proved a fine last line of defence, even if his goalkeeping was, at times, less than orthodox. Shirlaw, though, had started life as an outfield player, and while attending school in Wishaw, Lanarkshire, he represented Scotland as a winger against England in a schools international at Newcastle in 1913. He developed his goalkeeping skills with junior club side Larkhall Thistle, and it was from there he was signed by Bradford City in August 1924. But Shirlaw was forced to bide his time in the reserves with Jimmy McLaren established as first-team 'keeper and was restricted to just two League appearances during 1925–26, and in August 1927 he joined Rochdale.

Shirlaw found his time at Spotland just as frustrating, failing to oust Harry Moody from the first team, and by the following March he was back at Valley Parade, initially on a month's trial. But with McLaren having moved to Leicester City, Shirlaw ousted Jock Ewart and made the goalkeeping position his own. Ever-present in 1928–29 he helped the Bantams clinch the Division Three North title that season. But by the end of 1931–32 Shirlaw, having made 99 League appearances for City, had lost his place in the side to Jack Gill and Town boss Alex Raisbeck moved swiftly to bring him to The Shay, keen to have the pick of the crop before other clubs snapped them up. Over the next three years, Shirlaw missed only five matches and was a star of Town's FA Cup run in his first season at The Shay. How differently things may have turned out had he not made a fantastic one handed save from Billy Charlton in the second round defeat of Workington when the scores were still goalless but Town went on the reach the fifth round before bowing out in the snow to Luton Town. The following season, Raisbeck elected Shirlaw as captain, helped his side to runners'-up spot.

Years later, folk might have asked him about Town's record 13–0 defeat at Stockport, though Shirlaw could always reply, 'Yes, but I didn't play in that match,' the only one he missed during 1933–34 because of a thigh injury. Released by the club in May 1935, he spent one season with North Eastern League side Workington before returning to work for Bradford City in a scouting capacity. In 1945 he joined the *Telegraph & Argus* newspaper and retired in 1966.

SMITH, Alexander
Goalkeeper, 5ft 9in, 11st
Born: Lancaster, 29 October 1938
Career: Morecambe; Army football; Weymouth cs 1959; Accrington Stanley 8 August 1961; Bolton Wanderers 16 March 1962 (£650); Halifax Town 12 January 1968 (£3,000); Preston North End 11 May 1975, retired cs 1977; Accrington Stanley 1978–79.
Halifax Town debut: v Lincoln City (h), Division Four, 13 January 1968

What goalkeeper Alex Smith lacked in height, he more than made up for it in agility and safe handling, one of the most consistent custodians in the Football League's lower reaches. In his first three and a half years with Halifax Town he missed only three games and but for the emergence of Terry Gennoe, may have stayed with the club longer than he did. Yet, despite being a renowned goalkeeper, the biggest surprise is in the manner in which he became to be a goalkeeper in the first place. For it was not until he was 18 and doing National Service in Weymouth that he was persuaded by Jim Dailey, Weymouth's centre-forward, to be converted from right-winger, where he had played with Morecambe, to goalkeeper, and it was with the south coast club that Smith began to build a fine reputation.

It was Accrington Stanley who gave him his break in League football, signing the promising 'keeper at the beginning of what turned out to be their final season. Smith played in all 33 of Accrington's games played during 1961–62 before the club folded in March 1962. However, he was then quickly snapped up by Bolton Wanderers, but in over five seasons with the Trotters Smith was restricted to just 19 League appearances due to the consistency of England international Eddie Hopkinson.

It was in January 1968 that Smith moved to Halifax Town, being one of Alan Ball's first signings, and he kept 10 clean sheets in almost half the League games he played during the second half of that season. Ever-present during Town's 1968–69 promotion campaign, Smith recovered from the shock of having eight goals put past him by Fulham in September 1969 and being dropped for the first time in his career to rediscover his form. After helping Town to third place in Division Three in 1970–71, Smith's finest hour came in the defeat of Manchester United in the 1971–72 pre-season Watney Cup competition, and not surprisingly did he consider his finest save being that from Willie Morgan's penalty in that game. Smith also played a crucial role in Town's remarkable run that saw them avoid relegation from Division Three, clawing away a looping header in the dying minutes of Town's do-or-die last game at Walsall in May 1973.

Smith continued to hold off the challenge of reserve-team 'keeper Barry White for five seasons, but it was when Alan Ball Snr returned as manager that he lost his place, and at the end of 1975–76 he left the club under something of a cloud following a disagreement with the board over arrangements of a promised benefit match. In total, Smith made 381 first-team appearances in all competitions for Halifax Town, more than any other goalkeeper with the club. He added to his tally by making eight League appearances with Preston before he finally retired from the game. There was just time for Smith to make a poignant return to first-team action with the newly formed Accrington Stanley, turning out once as replacement for injured Mick Finn during the 1978–79 season. During his time with Halifax, Smith had opened a tailor's outfitters with Ian Lawther, but he moved into coaching at the Bolton Wanderers Academy and currently helps out in the family-run business Bolton Bed Centre.

SMITH, William Conway

Inside-forward, 5ft 8in, 11st
Born: Huddersfield, 26 July 1921
Died: Huddersfield, March 1989
Career: Huddersfield Town amateur 1945, professional 18 August 1956; Queen's Park Rangers March 1951; Halifax Town 5 June 1956; Nelson June 1962, retired cs 1963; scout.
Halifax Town debut: v Hull City, Division Three North, 18 August 1956

Inside-forward Conway Smith arrived at Halifax Town having developed a reputation as a fine goal-getter with Queen's Park Rangers, and he continued to score regularly in the Shaymen's colours, helping the side qualify for the newly created Third Division in 1958. Of course, Smith had an advantage when it came to football. His father was speedy left-winger Billy Smith, a Huddersfield Town legend, record appearance holder with the club, a member of the side which claimed the Football League Championship in three successive seasons in the 1920s and winner of three England caps.

Conway, who used his middle name to distinguish himself from his father, followed in his footsteps by joining the then Leeds Road outfit during the war period, turning professional in May 1945. He made his League debut in a First Division fixture at Aston Villa in September 1947 and had become a regular in the side by the time he broke his leg in a game at Sheffield United the following season. Smith recovered to force his way back into the side but, unhappy at the progress made by the club, slapped in a transfer request and eventually joined QPR, managed by his father's former Huddersfield teammate Dave Magnall, in March 1951. Hardly prolific while with Huddersfield – Smith netted only five goals from 37 League appearances – the same cannot be said about his time at Loftus Road, where he was leading marksman in each of his five full seasons with the club. He scored in his first three matches, netted 13 goals despite Rangers' relegation from the Second Division the following term, and went on to record 81 goals from just 174 League outings.

It was in June 1956 that Conway Smith returned north, signing for the Shaymen, then managed by Bill Burnikell, for a four-figure fee. With his thinning hair, Smith cut an instantly recognisable figure, and he quickly became a fans' favourite, forming part of a formidable forward line featuring Andy McCall, Harry Darbyshire and Johnny Kelly. During 1957–58 Smith scored his 100th League goal of his career in a 5–1 defeat at Rochdale on 28 September 1957, thus ensuring that Billy and Conway were the first father and son to reach such a landmark. That season, Conway Smith top-scored with 22 goals as Town finished a creditable ninth to qualify for the newly created Third Division and, ever-present during 1958–59, was again leading scorer as they competed well against their southern counterparts, a real golden period for the side which featured some of the club's finest players.

In 1959–60 Smith formed a useful partnership with the emerging talent of Frank Large, but injuries blighted his final seasons at The Shay, and he appeared only fleetingly. But he did pop up with a couple of important goals. His close-range strike in the relegation battle with Lincoln City, his last in League football on 23 April 1962, settled the issue and staved off relegation, and having already being told of his non-retention by the club he signed off with the headed winner in the West Riding Senior Cup Final against Bradford at Park Avenue on 7 May 1962. Smith moved into non-League football with Nelson, where he joined his former manager Harry Hooper, and upon retiring from football worked in the Rent Office of the Huddersfield Corporation Housing Department until he suffered a fatal heart attack in March 1989.

SOUTH, Alexander William

Centre-half, 5ft 11½in, 11st 4lb
Born: Brighton, 7 July 1931
Career: Whitehawks and Manor Boys' Farm Club; Brighton & Hove Albion juniors, professional March 1949; Liverpool December 1954; Halifax Town October 1956 (£7,000), retired May 1965, trainer 1970–71, pools promoter January 1970.
Halifax Town debut: v Southport, Division Three North, October 1956

Centre-half Alex South became a legendary figure with Halifax Town, racking up a then record number of 302 League appearances following his transfer from Liverpool in October 1956. South began playing football with the Whitehawks and Manor Farm Boys' Club, and joined the groundstaff at his home town club Brighton aged 15 before signing professionally. He became a regular in the side from 1953–54 and made a total of 85 League appearances for the Seagulls before joining his old boss Don Welsh at Liverpool. South spent much of his time at Anfield in the reserves, making only seven first-team outings, but he did have enjoy one real moment of glory, scoring a headed goal in front of the Kop which completed an amazing fightback as the Reds earned a point after visitors Luton Town had taken a four goal lead.

With the assurance of first-team football from manager Bill Burnikell, South joined Halifax Town, scoring on his debut (as well as missing a penalty) in a 3–1 win over Southport at The Shay. South was a rugged no-nonsense defender, strong in the tackle and dominant in the air, and became the mainstay of the team, twice holding the position as captain. During 1957–58 he missed only two games (through suspension) and formed the first of several formidable half-back lines with Brian Atkinson and Roy Lorenson, and later Eric Harrison and Peter Tilley. the Shaymen defied the odds to finish seventh in the table and qualify for the newly created Third Division and South was appointed skipper by Harry Hooper in 1958–59, though he missed the lifting of the West Riding Senior Cup for the first time that season because of damaged knee ligaments.

South was often deployed, to some effect, at centre-forward and set a new club record of 287 League games, bettering Ted Craig's total, in a 3–1 defeat at Aldershot on 19 September 1964, and later that season he became the first Town player to play 300 League games. He reached that milestone at Barrow on 27 February 1965, before making a mad dash back in time to officiate at the opening draw of the Halifax Town Pools, of which South was the first promoter, at the Shay Hotel. By then, South had switched to part-time footballer and retired at the end of the 1964–65 season, whereupon he was appointed commercial manager at the club. A qualified coach, he took charge of several local League sides and was an accomplished cricketer with Warley CC. In January 1970 he became Halifax Town pools promoter, a position he returned to in October 1976, and in 1970–71 he acted as trainer under George Kirby. South has also fitted in other jobs such as milkman and window cleaner, and though now long retired he has retained his passion for football and was still attending matches at The Shay approaching his 80th birthday.

STONEMAN, Paul

Centre-half, 5ft 11in, 12 7lb
Born: Whitley Bay, 26 February 1973
Career: Cramlington Juniors; Blackpool trainee, professional 26 July 1991; Colchester United on loan 23 December 1994; Halifax Town 11 July 1995, youth coach May 2003; Harrogate Town June 2005; Blyth Spartans trialist July 2006; Wakefield AFC trialist July 2006; Bridlington Town player-manager January 2007 to January 2008; Bradford Park Avenue January 2008.
Halifax Town debut: v Hednesford Town, Conference, 19 August 1995

Centre-back Paul Stoneman experienced the high and lows during his 10 seasons with Halifax Town, but he always gave his all to the cause after becoming an instantly popular figure with the supporters by scoring a memorable long-range effort to secure victory over reigning Conference champions Macclesfield Town on his home debut in August 1995. Stoneman came through the system with Cramlington Juniors before joining Blackpool as a trainee, signing professional in July 1991 and making 20 League appearances in 1991–92 under former Halifax boss Billy Ayre as the Seassiders made the Play-offs.

Stoneman was not picked for the Play-off matches but went on to make 43 League appearances for Blackpool, and though he was never on the scoresheet with the Seasiders, he did manage his first League goal when on loan at Colchester United, a 2–2 draw with Hereford United in December 1994. But by the end of that season he was deemed surplus to requirements by Blackpool boss Sam Allardyce and released. Stoneman then became one of Halifax Town boss John Bird's first summer signings in July 1995 as he rebuilt his team on a tight budget following the financial crisis of the previous season. He initially formed a central defensive partnership with Mick Trotter, but under George Mulhall in 1997–98 was part of a three-man back line with Jamie Murphy and Peter Jackson, then following Jackson's departure, the former Coventry City stopper Brian Kilcline. Stoneman went on to play in 38 games in that Conference Championship winning season.

In total, Stoneman amassed 319 first-team appearances in all competitions for Halifax Town, though this total would have been greater but for injury and suspensions, his over-zealousness in the tackle rather than maliciousness seeing him being dismissed 10 times, more than any other Town player. Gaining his coaching qualifications, Stoneman was appointed youth-team coach by Town boss Chris Wilder in May 2003, and in 2004–05 was granted a benefit season.

Ten years after joining Halifax Town, Stoneman joined Harrogate Town, his departure deemed by many as the end of an era, the last of the Conference-winning side to leave the club. Stoneman was made skipper at Harrogate, and after brief spells with Blyth Spartans and Wakefield AFC, he spent a year as player-manager of Bridlington Town. Relieved of his duties in January 2008, he joined Bradford Park Avenue and was a member of their successful Unibond Division One North Championship-winning team of 2007–08.

SUTCLIFFE, Charles Spencer
Goalkeeper
Born: Bradford, 7 October 1890
Died: Bradford, 18 August 1964
Career: Springwood; Liversedge; Heckmondwike 1909; Halifax Town 6 December 1911; York City May 1913; Bradford City guest 1918–19; Leeds City 1919; Rotherham County August 1920; Sheffield United September 1924 (£2,400).
Halifax Town debut: v Knaresborough, Yorkshire Combination, 16 December 1911

During their history, Halifax Town have been renowned for producing top-class goalkeepers. Charlie Sutcliffe was without doubt the club's first, having being signed by Joe McClelland in December 1911. Standing over 6ft tall, Sutcliffe commanded his area and was a terrific shot-stopper. The nephew of former Bolton Wanderers and England international goalkeeper John Sutcliffe, he began his career locally with Springwood, a club in the Bradford and District Junior League, and Liversedge, then of the Heavy Woollen League. By the time he signed for Halifax Town, Sutcliffe had spent two and a half seasons with Heckmondwike and was viewed as the best goalkeeper in the Yorkshire Combination.

Sutcliffe did as much as anyone to help the club reach their first Cup Final, but perhaps his wedding on the morning of the West Riding Junior Cup Final on 13 April 1912 was not the greatest preparation for the match. In the event, Halifax Town lost 2–0 to Mirfield United without ever really posing a threat and Sutcliffe allowed one tame-looking shot to pass by him into the net. Sutcliffe's best game for the club was undoubtedly against Bradford Reserves when, although Town lost 5–1, according to Pioneer of the *Halifax Courier*, 'shots fell like bullets on his citadel. He was that day the agnosure of the crowd.' The following term, Sutcliffe's performances between the sticks were a feature of Town's run to the first round of the FA Cup where, after leading 2–0, the side lost 4–2 at Queen's Park Rangers.

Sutcliffe's name reached wider circles, and in May 1913 he joined York City before the outbreak of war interrupted his career. During 1918–19, he guested for both Bradford City and Leeds City in the Midland Section Subsidiary Competition, and joined the latter club upon the resumption of peacetime football just before they were suspended by the Football League. Though not one of the Leeds City players auctioned off, Sutcliffe nevertheless joined Rotherham County in August 1920, making his debut in a 5–4 home win against South Shields the following

October, his only game that season. After a mid-season spell of three games the following term, he returned to play in the last 11 games. That started an unbroken sequence of 102 League and Cup appearances, his last game coming on 6 September 1924.

It was then that Sutcliffe moved to Sheffield United as replacement for the retiring Ernest Blackwell, and he immediately helped his new club to silverware as the Blades, whose side featured the legendary Billy Gillespie and Fred Tunstall, won the FA Cup by defeating Cardiff City 1–0 at Wembley in May 1925. Sutcliffe spent two seasons at Bramall Lane before retiring having made 51 League and FA Cup appearances. It is believed that just days after getting married, Sutcliffe missed sailing on the *Titanic*'s doomed maiden voyage after catching a cold. The experience may well have affected him, for over the years he was remembered as a bag of nerves in goal, and smoked a pipe prior to kick-off to calm himself down.

SUTER, Ernest Robert

Goalkeeper, 6ft 1in
Born: Epperstone, 10 July 1880
Died: Halifax, 1 December 1945
Career: Southwell; Newark Town; Notts County 1898; Newark Town; Notts County; Goole Town cs 1912; Halifax Town June 1913, trainer July 1921, re-registered as player 20 April 1929, left club cs 1929, rejoined as trainer 10 June 1932 to cs 1933, King Cross CBA groundsman.
Halifax Town debut: v Chesterfield Town, Midland Counties League, 6 September 1913

Bob Suter was all things and more to Halifax Town in an association with the club that spanned 20 years; goalkeeper, trainer, coach, groundsman and general handyman. And though there is no record of him driving the club charabanc, he probably did that, too. But in April 1929, Suter added another feather to his cap when he wrote himself in to the record books as the oldest Englishman to appear in a Football League match. Injuries to regular first-choice 'keepers Howard Mathews and Cliff Binns left the selection committee with a headache for the match at South Shields on 20 April 1929 (pictured here). But without having to turn to one of the regular outfield players, Bob Suter proved a willing hand, and donned the 'keeper's jersey for the first of three first-team outings, despite being in his 49th year.

It was all somewhat ironic that Suter should still find himself playing first-class football at such an age, for he spent the best part of 10 years in the reserves at Notts County while acting as understudy to the legendary Albert Iremonger, who continued to play until he himself was 43 years old. Suter had joined County as an 18-year-old in 1898 but, due to the consistent form of Iremonger, made only 42 League appearances during his time with the club, interspersed with a second spell at Newark Town. Seeking regular first-team football, Suter took over as player-manager of Midland League side Goole Town, and it was only the fact that he could not find employment – he was a driller by trade – in the Yorkshire port that Suter left the club in June 1913.

Suter had been acting as groundsman to Goole Cricket Club, and took up a similar position at Halifax Town, as well as cutting a prominent figure – he was thought to be the tallest 'keeper in the Midland League – between the sticks on matchday. A member of the victorious side which lifted the Hospitals Cup in 1914, Suter spent two full seasons as first-choice 'keeper in the Midland League and throughout the hastily arranged Midland Combination in 1915–16. Upon the return of peacetime football in 1919, Halifax Town were forced to move home, and Suter was among many volunteers who helped shape the ground at Exley into something suitable. Similarly, when Halifax Town applied to join the Football League, Suter was one of many who toiled away to prepare The Shay into a football ground, and acted as groundsman there.

Keeping himself in trim by playing in the reserves, Suter turned out on two occasions during Town's first season in the League but little did he think that seven years later he would be called upon again. By the time he made the last of his three unscheduled appearances at Darlington on 24 April 1929 he became, at 48 years and 288, the oldest Englishman to appear in the Football League (only Welsh international Billy Meredith had been older when he turned out for Manchester City having turned 49). But by the start of the following season, Suter had left the club, his departure coming out of the blue and something of a major shock. He continued to work as a groundsman at King CC, but he returned to The Shay as trainer under Alex Raisbeck in June 1932 and monitored the progress of his son Robert Jnr, who acted as understudy to Watty Shirlaw but who broke into the first team and made three League appearances during 1932–33.

Suter Snr left Halifax Town for a second time at the end of that campaign, returned to King CC and took up employment at tool makers Asquith's. The passing away of this popular fellow in December 1945, aged 65, was deeply felt by many.

TAYLOR, Arthur Matson ('Archie')

Winger, 5ft 10in, 11st
Born: Dunscroft, Doncaster, 7 November 1939
Career: Doncaster Rovers amateur; Bristol City May 1958; Barnsley July 1961; Mansfield Town November 1961; Goole Town 1962; Hull City May 1962; Halifax Town 2 July 1963; Bradford City 1 December 1967; York City October 1968; Gainsborough Trinity July 1971; Goole Town; Frickley Colliery June 1973.
Halifax Town debut: v Carlisle United (a), Division Four, 7 September 1963

If Archie Taylor could have matched the speed with which he used to leave defenders standing with the ability to deliver accurate centres and score more than the 18 goals he managed in his time with Halifax Town, his name may have been bracketed more readily with classy wingers of an earlier age, such as Tunstall and Davies, or those of the future, including Chadwick and Holden. Still, Taylor was blessed with lightning pace and always excited the crowds, and he thus became popular with the fans who, it might be added, also appreciated his willingness to chase lost causes. The supporters always liked a trier.

Taylor's career at The Shay spanned the 'in-between years', joining Town following their relegation to the Fourth Division in 1963, but had departed by the time they elevated themselves back to the Third six years later. Seemingly, he was not part of new manager Alan Ball Snr's plans, preferring the more potent Tony Flower. Taylor started his career with home-town club Doncaster Rovers, whom he joined as an amateur, though he was never destined to break into the first team. However, he made the breakthrough – however short – with Bristol City, whom he joined in May 1958, making a scoring debut in a 4–2 defeat at Oldham Athletic in September 1959. But he failed to hold down a regular first-team place, and three seasons at Ashton Gate yielded just 12 League appearances and two goals.

A short spell at Barnsley followed before Taylor joined Mansfield Town in November 1961, but by the end of that season he had dropped into the Northern Premier League with Goole Town. In May 1962 he tried his luck with Hull City but, having being restricted to just one senior appearance, it was to Don McEvoy's Halifax Town that he turned. Taylor went on to make 173

League appearances and score 16 goals for the Shaymen, his best moments coming when he helped Town establish a club-record seven straight League wins in early 1964, and three seasons later, under Vic Metcalfe, when he featured prominently in the side's impressive run in the FA Cup which saw them reach the third round. Taylor, in fact, had contributed to Town's record Shay score, netting two goals in the 7–0 replay win over Bishop Auckland in the second round.

Following his appointment as manager in November 1967, Alan Ball called time on Taylor's Town career. He was sold to Bradford City, but enjoyed success with York City after joining them in October 1968, appearing in 39 matches as the Minstermen won promotion to the Third Division in 1970–71. Released upon the season's close, Taylor joined Gainsborough Trinity before returning to Goole Town and winding down with Frickley Colliery, who gave him one last chance to play at The Shay when he returned as part of their side beaten 6–1 in a first-round FA Cup tie in November 1973. Taylor left football to become a salesman before setting up his own business supplying hairdressing products.

TILLEY, Peter

Half-back, 6ft 2in, 12st 6lb
Born: Lurgan, 13 January 1930
Died: Bury, 11 August 2008
Career: Newton Heath Locomotive; Mossley 1951; Witton Albion (£420); Arsenal May 1952 (£2,000); Bury November 1953; Halifax Town 12 July 1958; Mossley cs 1963; Ashton United.
Halifax Town debut: v Bournemouth & Boscombe Athletic, Division Three, 27 August 1958

When Halifax Town finished seventh in 1957–58 to qualify for the newly created Third Division, manager Harry Hooper moved to bring the assured half-back Peter Tilley to the club, knowing that he would bring experience required to compete at this new level. His signature was described in the *Halifax Courier* as a 'most important capture' and Hooper was keen to point out why he had signed him. 'We have been concentrating on youngsters, but I do need experience to look after them, and I think that Tilley will be the right man for the job.'

Indeed he was, and appearing in 42 of the 46 game programme Tilley helped the side finish a commendable 9th, featuring mainly in the half-back line alongside the likes of Roy Lorenson, Eric Harrison and Alex South. But when pressed into the forward line, he showed how adept he was. Tilley netted five goals from inside-forward in the last three matches of that 1957–58 season, including a hat-trick in the concluding fixture with Colchester United. Hooper had no qualms about throwing Tilley into the forward line. The jovial, pipe-smoking Irishman had forged a career in that position, initially with Newton Heath Locomotive, Mossley and Witton Albion, to whom Arsenal paid £2,000 for his services in May 1952.

Tilley spent just over a season at Highbury, but was called up for the first team on just one occasion as stand-in for inside-left Doug Lishman in the Gunners' 2–1 home defeat to Chelsea in September 1953. Two months later Tilley returned to the North West when he joined Second Division Bury, spending four and half years at Gigg Lane and proving a wise signing. Virtually ever-present in his first three seasons, Tilley featured in the side which played out an incredible FA Cup tie with Stoke City during 1954–55 which ran to five games, including the abandoned game with just eight minutes of extra-time left in the fourth meeting – the longest-ever clash in the FA Cup proper. Tilley made 36 League appearances and scored 17 goals for Bury, but suffered the disappointment of relegation in 1957. After one further season in the Third Division North he then joined rivals Halifax Town.

Tilley displayed neat and intelligent play which linked defence and attack. But he began the 1959–60 season at centre-forward, showing a willingness to hold up the ball as well as score some memorable goals. Under Don McEvoy, he was elected skipper, but Tilley succumbed to knee ligament trouble and was restricted to just 23 League appearances in 1962–63, his unavailability a contributory factor to the side's relegation that season. Released that May, Tilley rejoined Mossley before finishing his playing career with Ashton United. Later he became a top-class bowls player while acting as senior clerk in Manchester.

TUNSTALL, Fred

Winger, 5ft 7½in, 11st 6lb
Born: Darfield 28 May 1897
Died: 21 July 1971
Career: Darfield St George's; Scunthorpe United August 1920; Sheffield United December 1920 (£1,000); Halifax Town 3 February 1933; Boston United player-manager August 1936, trainer to 1962, manager 1964–65, groundsman.
Halifax Town debut: v Gateshead (Division Three North, 4 February 1933)

For those who saw him play, there is no question that Tunstall was the finest player ever to turn out for Halifax Town. It has often been said that his appearance in the side put an extra 1,000 spectators at the gate, and while the evidence does not necessarily support this, the story does at least indicate how much 'Tunny' was revered at The Shay. His signing by manager Alex Raisbeck in February 1933 was something of a major coup and, though it may be fair to say that his best days were behind him, he still offered much to Town's cause, with crafty wing play and a venomous shot.

Tunstall was widely known in the game well before he signed for Halifax Town. An England international left-winger, with seven caps to his name, he had made his name with Sheffield United after humble beginnings which saw him playing football for church side Darfield St George's before being signed by Scunthorpe United, then of the Midland League, in August 1920. Tunstall had turned 23 by then, but so eye-catching were his performances for The Iron that he was signed by First Division Sheffield United for £1,000 the following December, making his League debut against Spurs several days later. Tunstall quickly endeared himself to the supporters at Bramall Lane, and with the likes of Billy Gillespie and George Green in the side, he became part of one of the Blades' greatest teams.

Tunstall was one of the key players in the Sheffield United side which reached the FA Cup Final in 1925, scoring the goal which defeated Everton in round three and netting a brace in the semi-final against Southampton. But his crowning moment was reserved for the Final itself. Cardiff City provided the opposition, but it was Tunstall who settled the issue, making the most of left-back Harry Wake's hesitancy in dealing with a crossfield ball, nipping in and racing through to beat 'keeper Tom Farquharson for the only goal of the match

Tunstall was awarded his first of his seven England caps in a 2–2 draw with Scotland at Hampden Park on 14 April 1923. His last cap also came at Hampden Park two years later, while in the summer of 1926 Tunstall was part of the English FA touring party which visited Canada. Tunstall went on to make 437 appearances for Sheffield United and scored 129 goals, but by the time he joined Halifax Town he had lost his place in the side following a serious knee injury. He made his debut in a 1–0 win over Gateshead, a game which saw the gate 3,000 up on the previous home match, and he immediately made the outside-left position his own.

It was hoped Tunstall's signing might see Halifax Town into the quarter-final of the FA Cup, but alas, in the blizzard-affected game with Luton Town, the Shaymen slipped to a 2–0 defeat, though four days later he scored his first goal for the club in a 4–2 defeat of Darlington on the way to the first of three hat-tricks he scored for the club. Among his highlights were the scoring of all his side's goals in a 4–2 victory over Stockport County early the following season and helping the side to runners'-up spot in 1934–35 in what was surely Town's greatest side of the pre-World War Two era. Though it has to be said, that while Tunstall was famed for his fearsome shot and all-round great play, he was also a member of the side which crashed 13–0 at Stockport County in January 1934.

By the end of the 1935–36 season Tunstall had scored 40 League goals from 105 appearances but it was then that he took over as player-manager of Boston United, remaining at the club in various capacities until shortly before his death. On 18 September 1937 he scored his side's last goal – a penalty – of a record 10–0 win over Bilsthorpe Colliery in the FA Cup. Tunstall remained as manager through the war years then continued to act as trainer until retiring in 1962, but in 1964–65 he returned as manager for one season while they played in the Boston & District League.

VALENTINE, Albert Finch

Centre-forward, 5ft 7in, 12st
Born: Higher Ince, Wigan, 3 January 1907
Died: Billinge, Wigan, 12 March 1990
Career: Ashton St Thomas'; Southport amateur 9 November 1928, professional 9 January 1929; Cardiff City 20 July 1929; Wigan Borough 18 July 1931; Chester 2 November 1931; Crewe Alexandra 19 August 1932; Macclesfield Town 1933–34; Halifax Town 6 July 1934 (£500); Stockport County 11 June 1937; Accrington Stanley 6 October 1937 (£225); Oldham Athletic 13 August 1938, retired cs 1941.
Halifax Town debut: v Mansfield Town, Division Three North, 25 August 1934

When Halifax Town sold top goalscorer Bill Chambers to Bolton Wanderers in July 1934, manager Alex Raisbeck swiftly moved to sign a replacement, snapping up Albert Valentine from non-League Macclesfield Town. Virtually unheard of when he first arrived, Valentine was soon the talk of the town, and after three seasons at The Shay, enjoyed legendary status, his 33-goal haul in the League in 1934–35 ultimately a record that was never to be broken by any Halifax Town player.

Valentine had first sprung to prominence with Southport, joining as an amateur in September 1928 before turning professional the following January. His 17 goals from just 21 League appearances led to several clubs ruling the roost over this young striker, and in July 1929 he moved to Cardiff City, just relegated from the First Division. But failure to score in his first three games saw Valentine relegated to the reserves, and by the time he joined Wigan Borough two years later he had scored just three goals for the Ninian Park club. Valentine was then unfortunate to join his home-town club when he did. Wigan were cash-strapped, and in October 1931, 12 games into their fixtures, the club was forced to resign from the Football League, though Valentine had the distinction of playing and starting every game and scoring twice, both in the same game in a 4–3 defeat at Crewe Alexandra.

Joining Chester, Valentine struggled to get among the goals, nor was he any more successful once he had moved to Crewe in August 1932. Released after just one season with the Railwaymen, Valentine joined Cheshire League side Macclesfield, where he found a new lease of life, going on to net an incredible 83 League and Cup goals during 1933–34. It was this kind of form which had Halifax Town boss Raisbeck believing Valentine was the natural successor to Chambers, and so he proved. Valentine netted on the opening day victory over Mansfield Town, and went on to score even more prolifically than his predecessor. He equalled and surpassed Chambers's record in 4–0 home success over Gateshead on 6 April 1935 and two more goals meant he finished with 33 League goals as Halifax Town finished runners-up to Doncaster Rovers, with a goal scored in a West Riding Senior Cup match taking his tally for the season to 34.

Of course, Valentine, a dashing and brave leader of the line, was part of arguably the greatest Halifax Town team, which included the likes of Tom Barkas, Arthur Mercer, Fred Tunstall and Charlie Davies, and with such players around him it was no surprise that there was little let-up in the goals the following term. Valentine scored 30 in 1935–36 and was top scorer again in his third and final term in 1936–37.

There was understandable dismay among the supporters when Jimmy Thomson allowed Valentine to leave The Shay in June 1937, and for the player himself, a move to Stockport County was just as disappointing. Valentine failed to break into the side and within four months had been signed by Accrington Stanley as a possible replacement for the recently departed Bob Mortimer. But there he netted just once from seven League appearances and found himself in the reserves. However, he did manage 19 goals in the Lancashire Combination, and three in the Combination Cup, one of which was the only goal of the Final against Clitheroe. In August 1938 he tried to resurrect his career at Oldham Athletic but scored just once from two first-team appearances. Valentine retired from full-time football in 1941 and finished back where he had started, at non-League Ince St Mary's.

WALDEN, Harold

Centre-forward, 5ft 10½in, 11st 10lb
Born: Umballa, India, 10 October 1887
Died: Leeds, 2 December 1955
Career: Regimental football; Linfield; Halifax Town amateur 3 November 1911; Bradford City 15 December 1911; Arsenal December 1920; Bradford cs 1921.
Halifax Town debut: v Bradford Reserves, Yorkshire Combination, 4 November 1911

Centre-forward Harry Walden's time with Halifax Town was short, and though his record was impressive enough – six goals from eight first-team appearances – it was what he went on to achieve in football and beyond that made him particularly noteworthy. Born in Umballa, India when his father was serving with the Cheshire Regiment of the British Army, Walden followed in his father's footsteps, enlisting with Cheshires in 1903 and first began to take football seriously then. When stationed in Belfast, Walden turned out for the Irish Army v English Army, and later played the Army v Navy in 1909–10 and 1910–11.

Walden turned his back on the Army and signed for League of Ireland side Linfield, scoring so prolifically that he was selected to play for the Irish League v Scottish League at Glasgow on 30 October 1911, a game watched by a Halifax Town delegation, and he signed for the club after the match on amateur terms. He made his debut in a Yorkshire Combination victory over unbeaten Bradford Reserves, scoring two second-half goals in a 3–0 win, with Pioneer of the *Halifax Courier* describing his performance in that match as, 'Speedy, quick at snapping up opportunities, a fine and dashing trekker, a dead shot, and a capital receiver of passes, as well as distributor, such are the capabilities which he evinced on Saturday.' Walden went on to score a hat-trick in a 4–0 defeat over a Kirkstall-based Leeds United side and netted a brace in a 4–2 victory over Thornhill Lees Albion in what turned out to be his last appearance for the club, for on 15 December 1911, he signed for First Division Bradford City, making his League debut in a 3–2 home defeat by Notts County the following day.

Walden went on to make 17 League appearances that season, scoring 11 goals, and by retaining amateur status, he was eligible and selected to play for the British Olympic football team at the 1912 Olympic Games held in Stockholm. Walden scored six goals in the first round victory over Hungary, all four goals in the semi-final against Finland, and the opening goal of the Final which saw Britain defeat Denmark 4–2 to claim the gold medal. The outbreak of World War One saw Walden enlist with the Bradford Pals (6th West Yorkshire Regiment) and he rose to second lieutenant, but once peace had been restored he returned to Bradford to play for the Park Avenue club.

Having made 54 League appearances and scored 22 goals for the Bantams, Walden transferred to Arsenal in December 1920, though his time there yielded just two first-team appearances and he returned to Bradford City at the end of that season. But by then he had moved into the entertainment business as a stand up comedian following his first appearance at the Bradford Alhambra in 1919. In 1920 Walden appeared in the first football film *The Winning Goal* and later played himself in the film *Cup Tie Wedding* in 1948. Noted for his 'kiss curl', Walden was engaged in Edgar Warwick's Concert Party which toured the Far East and Australia in 1925, and back home continued to play the northern music halls. Towards the end of his career he became a member of northern impresario Ernest Binns' Arcadian Follies in Morecambe. But he suffered financial problems in later life and was declared bankrupt in 1951. Walden died of a heart attack at Leeds Railway Station in December 1955.

WALLACE, Robert

Half-back, 5ft 9in, 11st

Born: Huddersfield, 14 February 1948

Career: Bradley juniors; Huddersfield Schoolboys; Huddersfield Town apprentice, professional May 1965; Halifax Town 16 March 1967 (£1,000); Chester 8 June 1972 (fee); Aldershot 3 July 1973 to cs 1976.

Halifax Town debut: v Stockport County (sub), Division Four, 18 March 1967

Bob Wallace spent five years with Halifax Town and racked up 234 first-team appearances without ever really getting the credit he deserved. Yet he featured prominently during the successful period of the late Sixties and early Seventies, and famously scored a penalty against Manchester United in the Watney Cup competition which ultimately gave Town victory over Manchester United. Wallace spent his formative years at neighbouring Huddersfield Town, having joined them from Bradley Juniors, and turned professional in May 1965 before making his League debut in a 4–1 win over Charlton Athletic in September 1966. But with only four first-team appearances to his name, Wallace sought regular first-team football and slipped quietly into The Shay in March 1967 when the signing of Bill Atkins was making the headlines. He initially arrived as an inside-forward, but proved his versatility by filling in a variety of positions, including a lengthy stint at right full-back during 1969–70.

Just two months after joining Halifax Town, Wallace found himself in the victorious side which triumphed over Bradford City in the Final of the West Riding Senior Cup, and during the promotion year of 1968–69 he came into the side at the expense of injured Mick Meagan in the half-back line and made 30 appearances, including seven from the bench that term, as well as featuring in that term's gallant FA Cup run, being part of the side which performed heroically when gaining at 1–1 draw at First Division Stoke City. While manager George Kirby put the accent on attack during 1970–71, Wallace's defensive duties were still an essential part of the make-up of the side, so much so that he was ever-present that season. But his finest hour came in the 2–1 defeat of Manchester United in the Watney Cup in July 1971, and a minute after Willie Morgan had seen his penalty saved by Town 'keeper Alex Smith, Wallace showed him how to do it following Dave Sadler's clumsy tackle on Lammie Robertson, calmly stroking the ball past Alex Stepney.

Wallace missed only two games under new manager Ray Henderson during 1971–72 but sought pastures new and joined Chester, where in his only season he scored nine goals, eight of which were penalties. In July 1973 Wallace joined Aldershot, where he spent three seasons, making 76 appearances and scoring just the one goal. In February 1970 Wallace opened a nightclub imaginatively called the Purple People Eater Disco Club and after finishing his playing career remained in the licensing trade by running the Wappy Springs at Outlane for many years.

WARD, Steven Charles
Full-back/Midfielder, 6ft, 12st 5lb
Born: Derby, 21 July 1959
Career: Brighton & Hove Albion apprentice, professional October 1976; Northampton Town August 1979; Halifax Town 18 June 1980; Kettering Town cs 1986.
Halifax Town debut: v Bradford City, West Riding Senior Cup, 5 August 1980

'Tolerate his few deficiencies, which he is working on, but enjoy his pace and ability on the ball.' So wrote Halifax Town manager George Kirby after he had completed the signing of Ward from Northampton Town in August 1980, a suggestion that there was room for improvement. Ward developed his game and became a regular fixture in the side, though after spending six seasons at The Shay, the fans were still left with the feeling that Ward never really fulfilled his potential, a confidence player who very much suffered the 'boo boys' who needed a scapegoat when things were not going well. But Ward, physically strong and with an abundance of pace for a player of his size, still managed to amass over 200 League appearances for the club without ever really holding down a specialist position, being ever-present in 1983–84 when filling a variety of different positions as a jack-of-all trades, the closest Halifax Town had to a Paul Madeley, though nowhere near as gamely or as elegant.

Born in Derby, Ward tried to make it with Brighton & Hove Albion, and signed professional forms in October 1976 after serving his apprenticeship. But without breaking into the first team, he joined Northampton Town in August 1979. George Kirby spotted his potential, and though Ward had his detractors, he often proved a hero. In January 1982, trailing 2–0 at champions-elect Sheffield United, he popped up with a brace to earn Town an unlikely point. And later that season, he crashed an unstoppable shot into the net after a 35–yard running duel with Hartlepool's Alan Sweeney. Ward scored Town's first goal of the 1985–86 season which rescued a point at Chester, but it was also his last. Having played under four managers at The Shay, counting the brief interlude of Billy Ayre, he was released by Mick Jones in May 1986 and finished his playing career with two seasons at Kettering Town.

WATKINSON, William Wainwright

Centre-forward, 5ft 10in, 11st 3lb
Born: Prescot, 16 March 1922
Died: Knowsley, February 2001
Career: Prescot Cables; Liverpool February 1946; Accrington Stanley January 1951 (£3,000); Halifax Town September 1954; Prescot Cables 4 July 1956; Skelmersdale United 1958–59; Prescot BI player-coach August 1959.
Halifax Town debut: v Tranmere Rovers, Division Three North, 18 September 1954

Centre-forward Bill Watkinson arrived at The Shay in September 1954 as something of a 'name' player, as just over three seasons earlier he had been on the books of First Division Liverpool. Though his time at Halifax Town was short, Watkinson made a valuable contribution to the side's cause, helping the club out of the doldrums.

Watkinson had begun his football career with Prescot Cables during the war, and it was in February 1946 that he joined Liverpool under George Kay. Though Watkinson was to spend most of his time playing in the Central League with the reserves – Liverpool's first team did consist of the formidable Billy Liddell, Albert Stubbins and Jack Balmer, after all – Watkinson's brief flirtation with the senior side was quite telling, scoring on his debut in a 2–1 victory at Aston Villa on 26 April 1947 in what was the first of six consecutive appearances he made towards the season's close which ended with Liverpool clinching the 1946–47 First Division title by one point. Thereafter, however, Watkinson found himself for the most part back in the reserves, and by the time he moved to Accrington Stanley in January 1951 he had taken his total with Liverpool to 24 League appearances and two goals.

Accrington paid £3,000 for Watkinson's services, but the fee was justified as he top-scored in his first two full seasons, only to suffer a slipped disc, and his eventual operation sidelined him for much of the 1953–54 season. But the following term Watkinson went down in Accrington folklore when, as a last-minute replacement for Ian Bryden, he netted a hat-trick in an 18-minute spell against Oldham Athletic on 8 September 1954. Before the month was out, Watkinson had become a Halifax Town player, manager Gerry Henry viewing him as a suitable replacement for the departed Des Frost. Watkinson made his debut in a goalless draw with Tranmere Rovers, but he scored a brace in victory at Barrow the following week and, unaffected by Henry's sudden departure, he flourished under Willie Watson and went on to top-score with 15 goals. Watkinson was a fearless leader of the line, a hard-working player who became an essential member of the side, helping Town to a respectable 14th-place finish, a year after their sixth re-election bid.

Though Town struggled for the most part during 1955–56, Watkinson scored some valuable goals early on, not least the header which clinched a 2–0 victory over Workington on 17 December. Injured in that incident, however, Watkinson was sidelined until the new year, and by the time he was available for first-team action Harry Darbyshire had made the centre-forward position his own. Watkinson featured only briefly towards the end of the season and, upon its close, was placed on the open-to-transfer list and in July 1956 he returned to Prescot Cables.

WELLOCK, Maurice

Centre-forward/centre-half, 5ft 9in, 11st 7lb
Born: Bradford, 15 June 1902
Died: Bradford, 3q 1967

Career: Bradford Schoolboys; Bradford City amateur, professional July 1919; Halifax Town December 1919; Blackpool 3 July 1922 (£250); Oldham Athletic 4 February 1927; Torquay United 2 June 1927; Peterborough United 22 June 1928; Darlington 11 June 1929; Halifax Town 10 June 1932, player-trainer 1933, trainer October 1933, released 11 May 1937; Halifax RLFC masseur August 1937.
Halifax Town debut: v Sheffield United Reserves, Midland Counties League, 20 December 1919

Maurice Wellock enjoyed two stints with Halifax Town, appearing in the first team as a teenager, and retaining links with the club long after his playing days were over. He played in Town's first-ever League season, and turned out for clubs the length and breadth of the country, among them Torquay United, for whom he appeared in their first League match following their election to the Third Division South in 1927. Wellock, began his professional career as a centre-forward but later became a noted defender, either at centre-half or right-back, representing Bradford Schoolboys and being a member of their successful side which won the Boys' FA Cup in 1916. Wellock also won two England Schoolboys caps and appeared for Bradford City during the war before signing for the club in July 1919, though he began his association with Halifax Town the following December having failed to make the first team at Valley Parade.

Wellock arrived at the Exley-based club initially on loan and made his debut in a 1–1 draw with Sheffield United Reserves at Exley, playing at centre-forward but having obtained his release from City, he rejoined the Shaymen and was converted to centre-back by Joe McClelland. Following the creation of the Division Three North in 1921, Wellock appeared at centre-half in the first match at Darlington but a thigh injury kept him out of the side for the return match at The Shay the following week. By the end of that first League season, he had established himself at right-back and attracted the attention of several clubs. But the following season was one of sheer frustration, restricted through injury to just two first-team appearances, though he played his part in the reserves' successful campaign where they finished runners-up to Bradford in the Yorkshire League.

Frustrating could also be the term labelling his time at Second Division Blackpool, whom he joined in July 1922, suffering injury and spending much of his four years there time consigned to the reserves there, too, though by the end of 1925–26 he got among the goals during an extended run at centre-forward. Restricted to 26 League appearances and seven goals, Wellock moved to Oldham Athletic, making a triumphant debut by netting four goals on his debut in a 5–2 victory at Grimsby Town on 12 February 1927. The following June he joined newly elected Torquay, and featured in their first League match, a 1–1 draw with local rivals Exeter City. Wellock spent just the one season at Plainmoor then joined non-League Peterborough United before signing for Darlington in June 1929. He enjoyed a prolific first season at Feethams, scoring four in the season's opener in a 5–2 victory over Hartlepools United and recording five hat-tricks in total. His haul of 34 goals in 1929–30 included nine in two games against Rotherham United – four at Millmoor, and five at Feethams two weeks later, and he was top scorer in each of his three seasons with the Quakers.

It was in June 1932 that Wellock made a welcome return to Halifax, by now managed by Alex Raisbeck, initially leading the line but later switching to inside-forward to compensate for his loss of a yard of pace and played his part in the FA Cup run which saw Town reach the fifth round for the first time and which ended in the blizzard against Luton at The Shay. Following Bob Suter's departure in the 1933 close season, Wellock, by now a qualified masseur – he had made the most of his injury lay-off at Blackpool – took on the role as part-time trainer, the position being made official the following October. Wellock continued to play in the first team but hung up his boots at the end of 1933–34.

An ever-willing hand, Wellock helped in the construction of terracing at The Shay ground in June 1936 and remained as trainer until the sudden announcement on 11 May 1937 that his engagement with the club was being terminated. Wellock resurfaced as masseur with Halifax RLFC the following August.

WHALLEY, John William

Winger, 5ft 5in, 11st
Born: Bradford, 17 February 1897
Died: Lancaster, 3q 1972
Career: Crystal Palace; Portsmouth; Sheffield Wednesday; Halifax Town April 1921, retired cs 1926.
Halifax Town debut: v Lincoln City Reserves, Midland Counties League, 16 April 1921

Whalley was an exciting left-winger who featured prominently during Halifax Town's first five seasons in the Football League. Born in Bradford, he made the move down south and began his career with Southern League Crystal Palace before moving to Portsmouth. But following the return of peacetime football in 1919, he returned to Yorkshire and was signed by Sheffield Wednesday, making the first of five League appearances during the 1919–20 season.

With Halifax Town being elected to the newly created Third Division North in March 1921, the board began recruiting new players, and Whalley, by now in the reserves at Wednesday, was one of the first signings, making his debut in place of Tim Helliwell in a 1–0 victory over Lincoln City on 16 April 1921 in the Midland League. Several games later he scored the only goal against Bradford which took Town into the Final of the West Riding Senior Cup for the first time. Omitted from the side when Town played its first Football League match at Darlington, Whalley proved a thorn in their side the following week when Town avenged their opening day loss by defeating the Quakers 5–1 in the first match played at The Shay, and he missed only three more games that season.

Whalley was always a threat down the left flank and supplied many of the crosses from which centre-forward Ernie Dixon benefited. In 1923–24 he played his part in Town's FA Cup run, scoring a memorable solo goal in the 4–2 victory over Northampton Town in the first-round replay which set up a meeting with First Division Manchester City. The match programme for the game at Maine Road described Whalley as 'the midget of the team…a tricky and elusive player,' but a thigh injury hampered his performance in that game, and though Town held out for a draw Whalley was forced to sit out The Shay replay. In 1925–26 Whalley lost his place on the left wing to the newly recruited George Kennie and made only 11 League appearances in a season which proved to be his last. But he was afforded a benefit match, and on 21 April 1926 Halifax Town took on a side selected by Huddersfield Town's George Wilson. Sam Barkas and former Town favourite George Parkin featured in Wilson's side, and they ran out 4–2 winners in a rain affected game which drew in around 2,000 spectators. Having made 141 League appearances, scoring 17 goals, Whalley was released at the end of that season and, despite still being only 29, he never played professional football again.

WHEELHOUSE, Ben

Full-back, 5ft 8in, 11st 4lb
Born: Rothwell, 23 September 1902
Died: Halifax, 20 June 1985

Career: Rothwell Athletic 1920; Leeds Malvern; Halifax Town March 1923; Burnley 11 March 1924; Denaby United cs 1925; Halifax Town September 1926; Rochdale August 1932, retired cs 1934.
Halifax Town debut: v Grimsby Town, Division Three North, 15 September 1923

Ben Wheelhouse was a full-back, adept with either foot, whose service to Halifax Town spanned nine years in two spells. He worked at Beeston Colliery on leaving school, and began playing football with their works' side before joining Rothwell Athletic, helping them to runners'-up spot in the West Riding League in 1920–21. While also assisting Leeds Malvern, Wheelhouse was on the verge of joining Castleford Town until Joe McClelland stepped in and persuaded him to join Halifax Town in March 1923. Wheelhouse developed his game in the reserves before making the breakthrough to the first team, making his debut at right-back for the injured Jack Lees in a 1–1 draw at Grimsby Town on 15 September 1923. But upon Lees's return to the side, Wheelhouse shifted to left-back at the expense of Harry Featherstone and became a regular, as he and Lees struck up a great defensive partnership. Both players featured in Town's famous Cup team of 1923–24, when the side took First Division Manchester City to two replays, but once the run was over, Wheelhouse, who had rapidly become one of the club's starlets, was sold, along with top scorer Ernie Dixon and George Parkin, to Burnley on 11 March 1924, netting Halifax Town a four-figure sum.

Wheelhouse made his Division One debut in a 1–0 home victory over Bolton Wanderers and held his place in the end-of-season run in but the following term was spent largely in the Central League with the reserves. Wheelhouse took his tally of League appearances to 13 before being released in the 1925 close season, whereupon he joined Midland League side Denaby United but it was injury to Ernie Gadsden which prompted Joe McClelland to bring Wheelhouse back to Halifax Town in September 1926. Described by *Halifax Courier* reporter Pioneer as 'fast and absolutely fearless', Wheelhouse quickly renewed acquaintances with Jack Lees and became an automatic choice in the side. During 1929–30, Wheelhouse took on the mantel of the side's penalty taker, and was used occasionally as an emergency centre-forward. It came as a surprise when Wheelhouse was initially given a free transfer by McClelland at the end of that season, but incoming manager Alex Raisbeck elected to retain his services, and he remained with the club for a further two seasons, though both were fraught with financial difficulties.

Wheelhouse was afforded a benefit in 1931–32, and 2,000 spectators turned out to witness Halifax Town play out a 2–2 draw with a strong Huddersfield Town side on 18 April 1932. But at the end of that season, Wheelhouse was given a free transfer and he joined Rochdale, playing for a further two seasons and making 66 League appearances and scoring two goals before retiring from the game. In 1935, Wheelhouse and his wife Irene took over the running of the Punch Bowl Inn, Salterhebble, Halifax, and remained there until 1968. Ben Wheelhouse died at his home in Warley Road in June 1985.

WHITELAW, George
Centre-forward
Born: Paisley, 1 January 1937
Died: Paisley, 8 January 2004
Career: Petershill; St Johnstone 1955; Sunderland 26 February 1958 (£5,000); Queen's Park Rangers 15 March 1959 (£5,000); Halifax Town 27 November 1959 (£5,000); Carlisle United 2 February 1961

(£5,000): Stockport County January 1962; Barrow August 1963; St Johnstone 1964; Stenhousemuir 1964–65.
Halifax Town debut: v Newport County, Division Three, 28 November 1959

Perhaps the most entertaining player ever to wear a Halifax Town shirt, George Whitelaw was the closest thing the club had to its own version of the original 'Clown Prince of Soccer' Len Shackleton of Sunderland, the club Whitelaw joined shortly after Shackleton had been forced to retire. Born in Paisley, Whitelaw played Scottish junior football with Petershill before catching the attention of Sunderland when playing for Scottish Second Division side St Johnstone, whom he had joined in 1955. He signed for the Black Cats in February 1958 but found first-team opportunities rare, and had made only five League starts when he journeyed south in March 1959 to sign for Third Division Queen's Park Rangers, the £5,000 fee part-funded by a £2,000 loan from the QPR Supporters' Club.

Whitelaw proved his worth by scoring five goals in the end of season run-in and thus helping QPR avoided relegation. He was scoring regularly the following term, too, until the appointment of Alec Stock as manager and, having been relegated to the reserves, he became unsettled and longed for a move back north. In stepped Halifax Town manager Harry Hooper, and Whitelaw signed for the club in November 1959, but he did not get off to the best of starts, sent-off on his debut in the away game at Newport for what the referee deemed over zealousness as he charged into Newport 'keeper Len Weare.

With Halifax Town's fixture list giving them successive away matches and Whitelaw's suspension that followed, it was not until 9 January 1960 that The Shay supporters got their chance to see him in action, though Town slipped to defeat at the hands of Norwich City. During his time with Halifax, Whitelaw, who was nicknamed 'Gunlaw' after a TV western of the time, wowed the crowds with his antics, which at any given time may have involved him blowing a 'whistle', stooping down as if to pick the ball up when challenged, then darting away leaving defenders perplexed, or in one moment of hilarity, catching the ball from an opposing 'keeper, immediately tossing it to a nearby opponent and winning Town a free-kick for hand-ball. Even when the side was not winning, he was still a joy to watch, the master of kidology, often worth the admission fee itself. But it could not last, and his failure to settle in Halifax saw Whitelaw ask for a move, citing also the desire to be closer to his invalid mother in Scotland. His 52nd and final League appearance in Town's colours saw him signing off with his 22nd goal, a typical thunderbolt at Reading.

Whitelaw got his wish and signed for Carlisle United on 3 February 1961, and became a crowd favourite with the Brunton Park fans, as he did at his next club, Stockport County, whom he joined in January 1962, making 52 League appearances and scoring 18 goals. He returned north when signing for Barrow in August 1963 but before the season was out had rejoined his first club St Johnstone (though failing to make a first-team appearance) and ended his playing days with Stenhousemuir. While it has often been suggested that Whitelaw was a misguided soul, never close to anyone, with stories of his on-field shenanigans bettered by tales of those off it, it may come as a surprise to learn that Whitelaw was a religious man, always smartly dressed, and had time for strangers. Yet he never found real happiness, and it is suggested he ended living a lonely life in his home country – he declined an invitation to attend a reunion of former Halifax Town players in 1989 – and died in Paisley in January 2004.

WIDDOWFIELD, Edward
Outside-right/Centre-forward, 5ft 10½in, 11st 7lb
Born: Hetton-le-Hole 25 March 1915
Died: Newark, 8 November 1983

Career: Birtley Colliery; Huddersfield Town October 1935; Halifax Town 12 November 1936; Peterborough United 1949; Ransome & Males (Newark).
Halifax Town debut: v Port Vale (h), Division Three North, 14 November 1936

Ted Widdowfield was the last of the great Halifax Town centre-forwards of the pre-war era, filling the void left by Albert Valentine and ending up top scorer in the last peacetime season. Yet manager Jimmy Thomson had originally signed Widdowfield from Huddersfield Town in November 1936 as a right-winger to supply the crosses for Valentine to benefit from, before realising his potential at centre-forward and converting him accordingly.

Widdowfield played for his local side Birtley Colliery and had trials with Crystal Palace and Hartlepools United before signing professional forms with Huddersfield Town in October 1935. But he was called up for the first team on just five occasions, mainly due to injury to Tommy Lang, and when Halifax boss Thomson stepped in to bring him to The Shay Widdowfield jumped at the chance of regular first-team football. Widdowfield had the perfect credentials to be a winger. Extremely fast, he had a number of professional sprinting handicap honours to his name. He had also recently being selected for a Yorkshire League side against the Corinthians, and he went straight into the side against for the home game with Port Vale two days after signing, although his first season was interrupted by a series of niggling injuries.

The 1937 close season saw the departure of Valentine, and though initially Les Copeland succeeded him it was to Widdowfield who Thomson turned to lead the line after the turn of the year, and in only his second game in his new position he netted all Town's goals in a 4–3 success at Accrington Stanley and finished the season as top scorer with 10 goals. The following term, in a forward line which also featured Steve Griffiths, Tom Barkas and Stan Wood, he proved even more prolific. Netting in Town's opening two games of the short-lived 1939–40 League season, Widdowfield continued to score goals for two seasons, despite having joined the Halifax Police Force in February 1940 following the outbreak of war. During 1940–41 he set a club record which was never to be broken when he scored in seven successive matches, including two goals in the astonishing 5–5 draw at Bury on Christmas Day.

Widdowfield joined the RAF in 1941 but returned to The Shay two years later to resume his Town career, taking his tally of goals in all competitions to 94 by the end of the 1944–45 season. After appearing in the first game of the following term, Widdowfield returned to the RAF and thus ended his association with Halifax Town. After the war, Widdowfield was on the books of Peterborough United but, having settled in Newark, turned out for Ransome and Males.

WILD, George Henry 'Judd'
Inside-forward,
Born: Sowerby Bridge, 31 August 1887
Died: Halifax, 3q 1970
Career: Sowerby Bridge Institute; Halifax Town August 1911; Bradford City December 1913; Halifax Town September 1914 to cs 1916; Bradford City 1916 to 1919; Halifax Town August 1919 to cs 1924.
Halifax Town debut: v Bradford City Reserves, Yorkshire Combination, 9 September 1911

Was there ever a more popular player turning out for Halifax Town than George 'Judd' Wild when he took his place in the side for his Football League debut in a 4–3 defeat at Wigan Borough in October 1921? After all, he had only had to wait 10 years for the opportunity, after appearing for the club in the very first match at Bradford City Reserves in the Yorkshire Combination. There were some who reckoned Wild might be too old – he was by then 34 years of age – but he did respond with a goal, and showed that he was far from finished, appearing in 13 games that season and adding a further goal in Town's last win of the season at Accrington Stanley.

Wild played in local League circles for the successful Sowerby Bridge Church Institute, a club who also boasted a cricket side of which Wild also turned out for in the summer. Employed at the Sowerby Bridge Industrial Society, Wild showed promise as a footballer at an early age, and enjoyed a memorable season in 1907–08, helping Sowerby Bridge win the treble of Halifax and District League Championship, the Halifax Charity Cup and Halifax Challenge Cup. Three years later he became a target for Halifax Town manager Joe McClelland who was assembling his first squad of players, and having signed in August 1911, Wild took his place at inside-forward when the side played its first match at Bradford City Reserves.

Diminutive in size but with lightning pace, Wild ended Halifax Town's inaugural season as top scorer with 24 goals, and with the club having transferred to the stronger Midland Counties League for 1912–13, he continued to grab the headlines. Wild figured in that season's remarkable FA Cup run which ended with first round defeat at Queen's Park Rangers, and again the following season, leading the way with four of the club's record 12 goals in the defeat of West Vale Ramblers at the start of their Cup run which ended with defeat at Norwich City in December 1913. But it was once the side had been defeated by the Canaries that the club broke up the side, with Wild one of several sold to Bradford City. But at Valley Parade his first-team duty extended to just two games, for though he scored against Manchester United in his second match on 18 April 1914, Wild was never selected again.

In September 1914 Wild made a welcome return to Sandhall, but the war interrupted his career, and while remaining with the club throughout the season of the quickly assembled Midland Combination in 1915–16 Wild returned to Bradford City when Halifax Town closed down and made 28 wartime appearances, scoring nine goals. When Halifax Town reformed in 1919, with their base at Exley, Wild returned and was top scorer yet again. But during 1920–21, he lost his place in the side to Tom Stott and thus missed out on Town's first West Riding Senior Cup Final appearance. Retained by Joe McClelland, Wild began the 1921–22 season in the reserves as Halifax Town embarked upon their first campaign in the Third Division North. But with results proving disappointing, Wild was called up to the first team and enjoyed something of an Indian summer, even if the side ended having to apply for re-election.

Wild remained on the books of Halifax Town for the next two seasons while helping out trainer Bob Suter and in 1924 was awarded a benefit, with a Halifax Town team taking on a Judd Wild XI on 29 April 1924. Wild continued to play local cricket, turning out for King Cross and then Lightcliffe, being a member of the side which joined the Bradford League in 1924. He had by then moved to that part of Halifax, and was employed as a motor driver or chauffer. In August 1961 Judd Wild and his wife Florence celebrated their 50th wedding anniversary.

HALIFAX TOWN MANAGERS

McCLELLAND, Joseph Bentley

Manager: 23 May 1911 to 1 July 1930
Born: Halifax, 20 April 1885
Died: Lincoln, 2 July 1964
Career: Halifax Trinity; Akroyden League secretary; Halifax & District Association League secretary 1902 to 1912; **Halifax Town secretary-manager May 1911 to July 1930;** *Sheffield Wednesday assistant secretary-manager May 1931, secretary September 1933; Lincoln City secretary-manager June 1936 to July 1947, secretary July 1947 to June 1949; Halifax Town scout September 1957.*

Joe McClelland was the obvious choice as the club's first secretary-manager. He was, after all, one of the most active off-field characters in the district at the time, with a growing reputation and plenty of local contacts. He was also well respected. He had begun playing football at an early age, and in fact, was one of the first to take up the game. In 1906 he was a member of the Halifax Trinity side which played in the Halifax & District Association but at the age of 15, had already taken up interest in the administration side of the game, becoming secretary of the Akroyden League, before taking up a similar position to the Halifax & District AFL. When there was talk of the formation of a town's club, McClelland, with his father Samuel, Dr Howie Muir and Edmund Braginton, was at the forefront, negotiating with the Halifax Corporation for the lease of the Sandhall Lane ground, and it was indeed Joe who announced at the AGM of the Halifax & District FA on 13 June 1911 that 'the formation of a town's club was almost an accomplished fact'.

Assisted in the early days by trainer Joe Midgley and player-coach Charlie Morgan, McClelland made some useful signings, such as the robust centre-forward Joe Chadbourne, nippy inside-forward George 'Judd' Wild and Jock Nixon, and despite defeat in their opening two matches, his side went on to top the League by the turn of the year. Town fell away, but they did go on to reach the Final of the West Riding Junior Cup, if only to lose miserably to Mirfield United. But seeking a move to higher echelons, again McClelland formed part of the Halifax Town delegation which oversaw the club's admission to the Midland Counties League for 1912–13. Having already captured promising 'keeper Charlie Sutcliffe the previous term, McClelland then completed the signing of former England international winger Fred Pentland, and Town enjoyed one of their most memorable FA Cup runs when the first round was reached, with McClelland aware of the sense to switch to Queen's Park Rangers' Park Royal ground when a huge financial offer was made to the club.

At times, McClelland found those early days trying, and on more than one occasion did he press himself into action when short of players, making his debut in a game at Hull City Reserves on 8 February 1913, the first of 14 emergency appearances he made for the club. But amid the struggles came the club's first trophy, the Bradford Hospitals Charity Cup, won in April 1914 with the 5–0 demolition of Scarborough at York. Featuring in the side that was one of

McClelland's other finds, hat-trick hero Percy Roscoe. The outbreak of World War One forced the closure of the club in 1916, but three years later McClelland was helping resurrect Halifax Town at Exley, while later putting forward Town's case for election to the newly created Northern Section of the Third Division, as well as negotiating with the Halifax Corporation the terms of the lease for conversion and use of The Shay as a football ground.

McClelland was at the helm for the first nine years of Town's life in the Football League, ever on the lookout for new players, and with a good eye for potential. He kept tabs on young striker Ernie Dixon, who had scored twice against Town in an FA Cup tie when playing for Calverley and signed him in readiness for the 1922–23 season. Ernie Coleman, Arthur Groves and Lewis Barber were others who passed through the corridors of The Shay, players who established themselves with the club before being sold to keep it afloat. The Bradford Hospitals Cup apart, honours were denied McClelland, although he did enjoy success of sorts in the FA Cup during 1923–24 when he assembled his famous 'Cup-team' which battled through to the second round after three gruelling ties with Northampton Town and then proceeded to take First Division Manchester City to two replays. There were those who hoped the 1926–27 season could have been Town's year, and a strong challenge was made for the title. Lying second behind Stoke at the beginning of March, ultimately Town fell away and finished fourth. Perhaps McClelland realised then that his dream of promotion was never to be realised; lean years followed, and by the end of the 1929–30 season, Town were having to apply for re-election, as they had at the end of the first League season. McClelland felt that the time was right to leave the club, though his resignation was still met with a degree of sadness.

After leaving The Shay, McClelland became assistant secretary-manager to Rob Brown at Sheffield Wednesday in May 1931, then became full-time secretary in September 1933. He left the Hillsborough club in June 1936 to take over as secretary-manager at Lincoln City, where, despite inheriting a skeleton playing squad, the Imps made a strong challenge for the title in his first season, only to lose out to Stockport County in the season's final weeks.

McClelland remained at Lincoln throughout the war years, seeing his side finish second to Blackpool only on goal average in the Football League North (First Championship) in 1941–42, and upon the resumption of League football in 1946–47, remained in charge as Lincoln finished 12th. But during that close season, his role changed slightly, with Bill Anderson promoted from coach to team manager while McClelland concentrated on administrative affairs. He resigned in June 1949 but the following September the club held a benefit match between a Lincoln City XI and Joe McClelland's All Star XI which drew a crowd of 13,000.

McClelland took up office of a local engineering firm Ruston & Hornsby but retained his association with Halifax Town when he was appointed scout for the Lincoln area in September 1958, and in 1962 he was honoured by the WRCFA for 50 years' service to football.

RAISBECK, Alexander Galloway

Manager: 1 July 1930 to 30 May 1936
Born: Wallacestone, Polmont, 26 December 1978
Died: Liverpool, 12 March 1949
Career: Blantyre Boys' Brigade; Larkhall Thistle,; Royal Albert; Hibernian 1896; Stoke City March 1898; Liverpool May 1898 (£350); Partick Thistle 1909 (£500); Hamilton Academical secretary-manager April 1914 to 1917, director 1917; Bristol City manager 28 December 1921, resigned 29 June 2929; **Halifax Town manager 1 July 1930;** *Chester manager 1 June 1936, resigned 12 April 1938; Bath City manager 30 June 1938; Liverpool scout 1939.*

Alex Raisbeck arrived at The Shay from a totally different footballing background to that which Joe McClelland had experienced. For a while McClelland had been heavily involved at local level only before being engaged as manager, Raisbeck had travelled widely and won domestic and international honours, as well as having a wealth of managerial experience behind him. He would draw on that extensively, and his six years with Halifax Town would prove to be as memorable as any the club would witness. Raisbeck's long and distinguished football career first took hold in Scottish junior football before he was signed by Hibernian in 1986. He ventured south to play for Stoke City in March 1898, but after making just four League appearances he moved to Liverpool two months later, commanding a sizeable £350 fee.

During an 11-year association as a player, Raisbeck became one of Liverpool's earliest superstars, first endearing himself to the supporters by famously turning down the chance to win his first Scotland cap in order to concentrate on the Reds' chase for the League and Cup double in his first season. Ultimately, Liverpool missed out, but Raisbeck would not be denied, and he went on to skipper them to two League titles.

Despite standing only 5ft 10in, Raisbeck was a commanding centre-half whose timing and athleticism enabled him to reach the ball before taller opponents. Quick in recovery and smart in the tackle, he was a key player when Liverpool clinched the title for the first time in 1900–01, though he probably did not reach his peak until the 1905–06 season when, despite the shock of relegation two years earlier, he helped steer Liverpool back to the top-flight at the first time of asking and was instrumental when they became the first club to win the Second and First Division titles in successive years. Raisbeck had by then eight Scotland caps to his name, the first coming in a 4–1 win over England on 7 April 1900 at Hampden Park, his last seven years later, also against England in a 1–1 draw at Newcastle.

In 1909 Raisbeck returned to his native country to play out his career with Partick Thistle before being appointed to his first managerial post with Hamilton Academical in April 1914. Later, he became a director of the club before venturing south of the border once more to succeed Joe Palmer as manager of Bristol City in December 1921. The Robins were already struggling in the Second Division and Raisbeck could not prevent their relegation, but he built two fine sides which won the Division Three South Championship in 1922–23 and again four years later.

After a season of struggle in 1928–29 Raisbeck left Bristol City but returned to management with Halifax Town in June 1930, though initially he did not find things easy. His first two seasons were hindered by financial restraints, and there was a time, during 1931–32 when many wondered whether the club would survive at all. But Raisbeck helped turn things around, promoting Maurice Wellock to trainer in succession to John Percy and making some important signings. Ted Craig arrived from Bristol City initially as an inside-forward but converted by Raisbeck into a lynchpin centre-half, Bill Allsop was plucked from Bolton Wanderers' reserves to make the right full-back position his own, Tom Barkas, signed from Bradford City, was one of the craftiest inside-forwards the club ever saw, and then there was Raisbeck's masterstroke signing of former England winger Fred Tunstall in February 1933, just at the height of Town's great FA Cup run when the fifth round was reached for the first time. Raisbeck was also renowned for making good young strikers who were hitherto unknown. Bill Chambers arrived from Darlaston and went on to smash the club record with 30 League goals in 1933–34, alerting the bigger clubs to his talents. When Bolton came in for him, Raisbeck gambled on Witton Albion's Albert Valentine, and he would be repaid handsomely, as he not only broke Chambers's record, but held it 73 years later. Valentine's set his goalscoring record during 1934–35, a season in which Halifax Town finished runners-up to Doncaster Rovers in the Third Division North, the highest position the club ever achieved.

Set against Raisbeck's achievements at The Shay were the darker moments, such as the 10–0 Boxing Day defeat at Hull City, bettered (or worsened) by the 13–0 club record defeat to Stockport County in January 1934. A fluke result, certainly, but one that certainly embarrassed the club.

Raisbeck, a regular church goer, was a popular manager, described by one former player as a 'gentleman' and it was with great disappointment that he left when he did. Town had just finished 17th a year after finishing runners-up and there was a feeling that he had taken them as far as he could. On 13 May 1936 he was appointed the new manager at Chester and took up his new duties at the beginning of the following month.

Raisbeck spent just under two seasons at the Sealand Road club, taking the side close to promotion in his first term after making a blistering start, whereby the side dropped only one point from their opening nine matches, only to finish third. In 1937–38, Chester were among the early season front runners again, but lacked consistency and fell away during the second half. With the side lying ninth, Raisbeck resigned his position on 12 April 1938 after a disagreement with the directors over the club's selection policy.

He resurfaced the following June as manager of Southern League side Bath City, but after just one season he was invited back to Liverpool to act in a scouting capacity, a position he held until his death in March 1949.

THOMSON, James Hunter

Manager: 1 July 1936 to 13 June 1947
Born: Deepdale, Shetland, 9 May 1884
Died: Bury, December 1959
Career: Edinburgh Myrtle; Heart of Midlothian; Leith Athletic; Paisley Abercorn; Leith Athletic; Portsmouth cs 1906; Coventry City 19 June 1911; Bury cs 1913, coach, assistant manager 1921, manager May 1923 to February 1927; Swansea Town manager February 1927 to cs 1934; Wolverhampton Wanderers advisory post; **Halifax Town manager 1 July 1936, resigned 13 June 1947.**

Joe McClelland apart, Jimmy Thomson served Halifax Town longer than any other manager, a total of 11 seasons, though of course, much of that period encompassed the wartime period which hampered the progress he had been making with the club. But for the intervention of the war, there is no telling just what he could have achieved with Halifax Town, but sadly the break-up of the side during that period had a massive effect, and the resumption of League football in 1946–47 saw Town finish bottom of the Third Division North for the first time. Demoralised, Thomson quit his post and never returned to club management. It was all a sad end to what had been a fulfilling football career which had begun at the turn of the century. For Thomson was perhaps the first Shetland Isle football 'star', having been born on the island, though raised in Edinburgh. At an early age, he turned out for Edinburgh Myrtle, then assisted Hearts before the first of two spells with Leith Athletic, while also spending a short time at Paisley Abercorn. In 1905–06 Thomson appeared at right full-back and helped Leith win the Scottish Second Division title, having gone through the whole of the second half of the season unbeaten, finishing three points ahead of Clyde.

With his reputation growing, he ventured south to join Southern League side Portsmouth, where he was noted as a solid full-back. Made skipper by manager Dick Bonney, Thomson went on to make over 158 first-team appearances and score two goals, gaining recognition when selected to play for the Anglo-Scots against the Home Scots in 1909. In June 1911, Thomson moved to Coventry City, then of the Southern League, and made 73 appearances before he joined Second Division Bury, for whom he made 61 League appearances. He retired as a player during the war years but was appointed coach, then assistant manager to William Cameron, succeeding him in May 1923 when Cameron was suspended after a bribery scandal.

Thomson's first season in charge ended successfully when Bury clinched promotion in a tense finish, by 0.02 of a goal over Derby County, and at a time when Huddersfield Town were dominating, Bury finished fifth and fourth in their first two seasons back in the top flight. In February 1927, however, Thomson resigned to take over at managerless Swansea Town, remaining with the club for over six years. But for the most part, Thomson's side battled against relegation to the Third Division South – albeit successfully – though Swansea did have the fillip of lifting the Welsh Cup in 1931–32 after a replay victory over Wrexham. But in 1934, Thomson stood down to take up an advisory post at Wolverhampton Wanderers.

He was enticed back into club management with Halifax Town, however, evidently impressed enough to think that the town was large enough to support a First Division club. His ambition was to gain promotion, and although such an achievement was beyond the Shaymen, initially his side did well. Though the likes of Tunstall and Betteridge had departed, Thomson could still call on the services of Allsop, Craig and Barkas, and a seventh-place finish in 1936–37 was credible enough. But he wanted to build his own team and to that end was not frightened of making tough decisions, evidenced by his releasing of top striker Albert Valentine and goalkeeper Cliff Owen. He also terminated the engagement of trainer Maurice Wellock in favour of Harold Taylor, then moved to bring the likes of Charlie Biggs, Les Copeland and Jabez Foulkes to The Shay. He also brought through a crop of promising youngsters, such as Harold Jackson and Horace Green, and having signed winger Ted Widdowfield from Huddersfield Town converted him with a large degree of success to centre-forward. Thomson had also been famed for attracting young players and selling them to keep the club afloat, so in that respect he was ideally placed at Halifax, among his charges sold for handsome figures being Alf Pope and Ernie Hoyland.

Thomson guided the club through the war years, even lifting some silverware in 1943–44, the Combined Counties Cup after a two-legged aggregate win over Huddersfield Town. But that tough period took its toll on Halifax Town. When peacetime football resumed in 1946, Thomson had lost the services of playmaker Tom Barkas, who moved to Rochdale, and his largely inexperienced squad struggled throughout the campaign. When Town finished bottom Thomson duly resigned his position. He settled in Bury, where he died in December 1959.

BREEDON, John Norman (Jack)

Manager: 26 June 1947 to 30 November 1950
Born: South Hiendley, Barnsley, 29 December 1907
Died: Leeds, 1977
Career: South Hiendley; Barnsley September 1928; Sheffield Wednesday November 1930; Manchester United July 1935; Bolton Wanderers World War Two guest; Manchester City World War Two guest; Burnley October 1945; Cliftonville coach cs 1947; **Halifax Town manager 26 June 1947, resigned 30 November 1950;** *Bradford scout December 1950, manager 2 January 1955, dismissed October 1955; Leeds United scout, retired 1965–66.*

With the directors fully expecting Halifax Town's re-election to the Third Division North, Jack Breedon was appointed Raisbeck's successor on 26 June 1947, his first managerial post. Speaking at the club's AGM shortly afterwards, Breedon reckoned his appointment would be a real stiff test but that he was used to them, but during three years with the club he would not find the going easy. Barnsley born, Breedon had been playing with his local South Hiendley side when signed in 1928 by Second Division Barnsley, where he understudied Tommy Gale. Restricted to just eight League appearances, Breedon showed enough promise to move to First Division Sheffield Wednesday in November 1930 for what was then a record fee for a goalkeeper.

In July 1935, he moved to Manchester United where he played over 300 games over a 10-year period, though most of these were during wartime. A well-built and good shot-stopper, Breedon made his debut for the Reds against Plymouth Argyle on the opening day of the 1935–36 season, but was restricted to just 38 peacetime appearances. However, he became first-choice 'keeper during the war years, only to lose his place in the side to Jack Crompton midway through 1944–45, and having also guested for Bolton Wanderers and Manchester City, he signed for Burnley in October 1945.

Breedon left the Turf Moor club towards the end of the 1946–47 season and having spent a short time coaching at Cliftonville, was offered the managerial post at New Brighton, turning it down due to his wife's reluctance to move from their Leeds home. Instead he turned his attentions to Halifax Town, signing a three-year contract. It would prove to be a tough baptism to football management. Breedon inherited a side which included the likes of Ted Rayner, Horace Green and Dave Mycock, but the size of his task was all too apparent when Town collapsed 6–0 at York City in only his third match in charge, and a run of five consecutive defeats soon followed, setting a trend which Breedon would find hard to buck. Re-election was required at the end of his first season, though he was keen to point out the psychological effect of poverty of the club when he arrived, both from a playing point of view and the state of the ground.

Breedon, in fact, was supportive of the club's attempt to buy The Shay from the Corporation. Such a move was made at the beginning of the 1950–51 season – his letter supporting such a motion appeared in print in the *Halifax Courier* on 20 September 1950 – but the Corporation refused to surrender the ground.

Breedon made a number of important signings for the club such as Oliver Burns, Ted Breaks and Freddie Hogg, and with a view to the future, set about implementing a new scouting system. He was also willing to giving local youngsters a chance, perhaps the most successful being Roy Crossley and Colin Webster. Re-election was avoided in his second season but Breedon and his side endured a torrid time during 1950–51 and had slipped to the foot of the table by the time they hosted Ashington in the first round of the FA Cup. When the North Eastern League side went through on the back of a 3–2 victory, Breedon resigned five days later, claiming he had made his decision before the Cup tie but held it back so as not to affect the players.

Breedon later became chief scout under manager Norman Kirkham at Bradford but was controversially appointed as his successor in January 1955 after both men had been initially relieved of their respective duties. The Park Avenue side finished mid-table that season, but the following term were languishing in 23rd place when Breedon was dismissed in October 1955. His last involvement with football was acting as a scout for Leeds United.

WOOTTON, William (Billy)

Manager: 6 March to 6 February 1952
Born: Longton, 27 August 1904
Died: Stockport, October 2000
Career: Trentham; Stoke City 1923; Congleton Town cs 1924; Port Vale cs 1925; Southend United August 1932; Northwich Victoria player-manager 1935 to cs 1947; Oldham Athletic manager June 1947, resigned September 1950; **Halifax Town manager 5 March 1951, resigned 6 February 1952.**

Following Jack Breedon's departure, the Halifax Town directors were in no rush to appoint a successor. In fact, fully three months had passed by the time they announced Billy Wootton as the club's fifth manager, having been impressed at how he had kept Oldham Athletic afloat and led them to a sixth-place finish on a low budget in 1948–49. Wootton had spent just over three years at the Boundary Park club; at The Shay he would last less than a year having failed to turn around the club's fortunes.

Wootton began his playing career with non-League Trentham before signing for Stoke City in 1923, though he failed to break into the first team. He spent a season with Congleton Town prior to joining Second Division Port Vale in June 1925, but he was never a regular in the side and managed just 56 League appearances during seven years with the club. He made his debut at left-back for injured Jimmy Oakes in a 3–3 draw at Fulham on 12 December 1925, and in 1927–28 appeared at right-back towards the end of the season when the Valiants went through their last six matches without conceding a goal. But his best season coincided with Port Vale's Third Division North Championship success in 1929–30, a year after being relegated, when Wootton appeared in 20 matches. However, the following term, he found himself back in the reserves, with George Shenton and Jack Round the established first-team full-backs.

In August 1932 Wootton made a surprise move to Southend United, but a knee injury restricted him to just two League appearances, and it was soon after his recovery that he took over as player-manager at Northwich Victoria, leading them to success in the Cheshire League Cup and the Cheshire Senior Cup in 1937.

Wootton was a surprise choice as Oldham Athletic manager in June 1947 as successor to Frank Womack. Most supporters had never heard of him, but after a dreadful start in his first season, whereby the side won only one of their opening 17 League fixtures, Wootton lifted the side to 11th, and enjoyed a sixth-place finish the following term. But after another poor start to the 1950–51 season, he resigned after seeing Oldham lose six of their opening eight matches, though he seemingly left the club in better shape than when he took over, having signed a crop of local players such as Ray Haddington and Eric Gemmell, and helping clear a debt of around £15,000.

Wootton, like Jack Breedon before him, would find life at Halifax Town a constant struggle following his arrival on 5 March 1951. In the interim period following Breedon's departure and Wootton's arrival team affairs had been looked after by directors Arthur Carter and Cyril Adams but Wootton took over a team occupying 21st position in the table, despite having a crop of useful players, including Jim Lee, Des Frost and Jackie Moss, at his disposal. Encouraged by his side's performance when gaining a 2–2 draw at Scunthorpe United in his first game in charge, albeit after having thrown away a two goal lead, Wootton saw his new side gain their first victory in six attempts courtesy of George Glaister's last-minute goal against Wrexham. He made Les Horton his first signing, but Town would win only two more matches before the season's close, though re-election was avoided by just two points.

Wootton enjoyed a 3–1 success over League newcomers Workington in what was Town's first opening day win since the war in 1951–52, but thereafter there was little respite for the Town boss, who bemoaned the conditions he was working under. With finances tight Breedon also pointed out other frustrations. 'It is no good talking about coaching,' he said, 'when we have only nine players here, and they do not see the rest until Saturday, just before the match. Even some of those nine players are reserves so we cannot formulate any system for the first team.'

Wootton would also feel fates were stacked against him when chairman Arthur Carter died in office in November 1951. With the side stuck just one place off the bottom of the table, the

Town boss was already considering his position when he appointed Gerry Henry as player-coach in December. A calamitous 8–1 defeat at Grimsby Town did not help matters, and with Town slipping to the foot of the table, Wootton resigned on 6 February 1952, citing not only Town's dismal playing record but also the difficulties he had endured travelling daily from his Stockport home, leaving at 7.45am and returning at 10.00pm. 'It would be better to engage someone who resided in town,' he reckoned. Wootton left the football scene to concentrate on business dealings near Stockport.

HENRY, Gerald Robert

Manager: 27 February 1952 to 15 October 1954
Born: Hemsworth, 5 October 2010
Died: Dewsbury, 3q 1979
Career: Yorkshire Schools; Outwood Stormcocks; Leeds United October 1937; Halifax Town World War Two guest May 1940; Manchester City World War Two guest; Huddersfield Town World War Two guest; Doncaster Rovers World War Two guest; Bradford November 1947; Sheffield United February 1950; **Halifax Town player coach 3 December 1951, player-manager 27 February 1952, manager cs 1953, resigned 15 October 1954**

Gerry Henry may have had designs on becoming a football manager, but even he must have been surprised at his sudden elevation to the Halifax Town hotseat from player-coach in February 1952 to replace Billy Wootton, the man who had brought him to The Shay just over two months earlier. Initially taking up the role as player-manager, Henry retired from playing at the end of that season, acting only as cover, and while League success eluded him, his legacy would be the magnificent FA Cup of 1952–53 when top-flight clubs Cardiff City and Stoke City were beaten on the way to the fifth round meeting with Tottenham Hotspur.

That match with Spurs, of course, was played in front of a record Shay crowd of 36,885, a throwback to the days when Henry appeared regularly in front of such gates during his time in the First Division with Leeds United. Born in Hemsworth, Henry represented Yorkshire Schools in 1934 and joined Leeds as a 17-year-old from local junior side Outwood Stormcocks. Known as a strong shooting inside-forward, he adapted to several roles for United, including an attacking wing-half, right-winger or centre-forward. He made his debut against Manchester United at Old Trafford on 7 April 1939 and spent 10 years with the Elland Road club, though much of his time there was played during the war years. Being a miner by trade meant he was regularly available, and Henry's 186 appearances and 94 goals for Leeds were both wartime club records. In a unique situation, Henry actually turned out against his Leeds colleagues, when, having travelled as a reserve for the game at Manchester City on 12 April 1941, the home side found themselves short of men. The following Saturday Henry found himself assisting Huddersfield Town.

Henry's Leeds career came to an end with the signing of England international Ken Willingham, a high-profile wing-half, and he left for Bradford in November 1947, where he scored 31 goals from 79 games. In February 1950 Henry joined Sheffield Wednesday, making 40 League appearances and scoring seven goals prior to his move to The Shay.

Signed initially as a player, Henry made a scoring debut in a 4–1 win over Darlington, then was immediately made player-coach by Billy Wootton, with responsibilities for the first team in his absence. Soon, however, that role would become full-time following Wootton's resignation, and Henry immediately set about trying to steer the club away from the re-election zone. He brought in goalkeeper John Savage to add confidence to the defence, as well as appointing his old friend Ken Willingham as coach. Henry initially acted as a spur to the rest of his team, leading by example and helping Town pull away from the foot of the table. The Shaymen won four of their last five matches to finish six points clear of the re-election zone.

Henry appeared in 23 League matches that term but felt the need to pick himself only once more during 1952–53 – he would not officially quit from playing until the following close season – as his side managed without him and competed for the most part in the top half of the table for a change. With Henry having brought Allan 'the man with the magic fingers' Ure to the club that close season to help with the fitness work, he relied on Savage, his good friend Albert Cox, Des Frost, Derek Priestley, Jackie Moss, Roy Lorenson and George Holt, and the players gave the long suffering supporters a season to remember through their exploits in the FA Cup. The visits of Cardiff, Stoke and Spurs gripped the town, and Henry enjoyed the exposure the run in the Cup brought.

Town suffered something of a Cup hangover once they returned to League action, however, slipping as low as 19th before rallying to finish 14th, and Henry failed to galvanise his team the following term. Town were long doomed to re-election, that despite appointing the former Northern Ireland international Bobby Browne as coach, as well as adding the likes of George Griffiths and Sid 'Skinner' Normanton to his squad. The Shaymen made a dreadful start, failing to win any of their opening nine matches, and with his side languishing in bottom place, Henry resigned as manager on 15 October 1954, exasperated at his failure to land Hull City forward Sid Gerrie and citing the club's lack of success – the FA Cup run excepted, of course – as his reasons for leaving. 'There has been a run of ill luck against the club through no fault of mine, or the players,' he said, and he slipped out of the game.

BROWNE, Robert James

Caretaker manager: 16 October 1954 to 4 November 1954
Born: Londonderry, 9 February 1912
Died: Leeds, August 1994
Career: Maleven; Clooney Rovers; Derry City; Leeds United October 1935 (£1,500); Derry City World War Two guest; Watford World War Two guest; York City August 1947; Thorne Colliery manager 1949; **Halifax Town coach August 1954, caretaker manager October 1954 to November 1954**.

Bobby Browne's inclusion in the list of official Halifax Town managers is open to debate; his 'reign' lasted all of four games following the resignation of Gerry Henry. Nevertheless, in a season of struggle, his record of one win, two draws and a loss was encouraging and at least gave incoming manager Willie Watson a platform from which to build upon. Browne had been appointed full-time coach to manager Gerry Henry following a trial match on 11 August 1954, with Henry saying, 'We think that if he can impart that determination along with his football ability to our players it will help us a great deal.' He came as successor to Harold Taylor who had left to take charge of Huddersfield Town's Northern Intermediate League side, but little did Browne know then just how fates would give him his brief opportunity to manage the first team, the only League team he found himself in charge of.

Browne drew on his experience from a career which had begun in Ireland, where he served junior clubs Maleven and Clooney Rovers while working as a joiner before coming to prominence as a wing-half with Derry City, being a member of their side which claimed the City Cup in 1934–35, their first major honour. Browne had been groomed for greatness by manager

Billy Gillespie and twice represented the Irish League against the Football League, gaining the attention of English scouts in the process. In October 1935 Browne became one of Leeds United manager Billy Hampson's first signings and he went on to make well over 100 appearances in the Leeds first team. He was never assured of his place at Elland Road but was capped six times during his stay at there, his first international appearance coming just weeks after signing for Leeds, a 5–1 defeat to England in Belfast.

During World War Two Browne continued to make appearances for Leeds when available while also returning to Derry City when he was posted to Ulster, as well as guesting for Watford while stationed as a PT instructor in Colchester. When the Football League resumed in 1946 Browne was by then 34 years old but he played one more season with Leeds before finishing his career with York City. He arrived at The Shay as coach but was thrust into the spotlight following Henry's sudden resignation and found himself preparing the side for the home game with third-placed Gateshead on 16 October 1954. How pleased must he have felt, then, when he saw his side pull off a fine 4–0 win, Town's biggest victory that season.

It was never known whether Browne fancied the role on a full-time basis, but in any case the directors' intention to seek a full-time successor to Henry was fulfilled when Willie Watson arrived as player-manager on 4 November. He was in attendance when Town played out a goalless draw at Crewe Alexandra, Browne's fourth game in charge, and Browne thus reverted to the coaching side. But by the end of that 1954–55 season, Browne had left the club with his position being filled by Les Horsman, and seemingly drifted out of the professional game.

WATSON, Willie

Manager: 5 November 1954 to 4 April 1956, 3 August 1964 to 2 April 1966
Born: Bolton-on-Dearne, 7 March 1920
Died: Johannesburg, 24 April 2004
Career: Paddock; Huddersfield Schools; Huddersfield Town October 1937; Manchester United World War Two guest; Sunderland 12 April 1946 (£8,000); **Halifax Town player manager 5 November 1954 (£4,000), resigned 4 April 1956; Halifax Town manager 3 August 1964;** Bradford City manager 2 April 1966 to January 1968; Wanderers (Johannesburg) manager April 1968 to 1972. Also Yorkshire (1938–58), Leicestershire (1958–62) and England cricketer; Leicestershire coach 1962.

Was there ever a bigger sporting personality in charge at Halifax Town than that of Willie Watson when he first arrived at The Shay in November 1954? Not only was he a former football international, he was also then a current England Test batsman, having gained national acclaim in the summer of 1953 with his heroic performance against the Australians at Lord's, when, with most of the nation tuned in to the BBC's *Test Match Special* and England having been at one point 12–3, Watson and the Essex all-rounder Trevor Bailey raised 163 for the fifth wicket, Watson hanging on for 345 minutes for his 109. The stand saved the match and enabled England to recover the Ashes with a victory at the Oval after four drawn games.

Cricket would supersede Watson's time in football, but it was soccer in which he initially forged a career, following in the footsteps of his father Billy Watson, a member of the Huddersfield Town side which won the League Championship in successive years between 1927 and 1929. Willie Watson, in fact, was so christened in order to differentiate him from his father, but unlike Watson Snr, young Willie went on to become a dual international, thus joining Denis Compton and Arthur Milton in an elite band of those capped by England at cricket and football.

Watson left school at 14 and had a job sweeping the yard at an upholsterers' but showed early promise as a footballer when playing for local League side Paddock. He represented Huddersfield Schoolboys before being signed as an amateur by Huddersfield where his father was in charge of the A team. Watson progressed to the first team and made his debut in a First Division match at Portsmouth on 10 September 1938 at inside-left, though he later became a recognised left-winger. He was also by then developing as a stylish left-handed batsman with Yorkshire with whom he had appeared in the last pre-war summer.

After war was declared, Watson was conscripted into the Army, where he played alongside the likes of Matt Busby, Tommy Lawton, Tom Finney, Frank Swift and Joe Mercer, and his rising status was recognised when he was chosen to play at inside-left for England in a Victory International against Wales at West Bromwich. When he returned to Huddersfield, a disagreement with manager David Steele over where he should play – Watson fancied the inside-forward berth – led to him being transferred to Sunderland in April 1946. At Roker Park, Watson was converted with a great deal of success to right-half by manager Bill Murray, being called up for the national side and winning the first of his four England caps in a 9–2 success over Ireland in November 1949. At the end of that season Watson was a member of the ill-fated squad which went to the 1950 World Cup in Brazil, though he was not called upon to play, and his last cap came against Yugoslavia the following November.

In 1951, Watson was selected for his first Test match against the South Africans at Trent Bridge, but at a time when England was rich in batting talent he rarely commanded a regular place and his 23 Test matches were spread across eight years. But his finest hour came against the Aussies in 1953, and for around 18 months Watson was a prince of England, being voted Wisden's Cricketer of the Year in 1954.

Watson made a total of 211 League appearances and scored 15 goals in his seven seasons with Sunderland before answering the call at The Shay and taking over as player-manager in November 1954. He got off to a dream start, scoring in a 5–3 win over Carlisle United, and immediately helped the side pull away from the re-election zone. Watson, in fact, would not taste defeat with Halifax until his seventh match in charge, and by making some key signings, such as goalkeeper Arthur Johnson and the versatile Stan Lonsdale, Halifax Town enjoyed a 14th-place finish, their highest position since 1938–39.

Watson made more important signings during the 1955 close season, such as Clive Baker, though by failing to win any of their opening six matches Town looked set for a season of struggle. But with Watson returned from touring in South Africa with the England cricket side, Town recovered to move up the table, setting a club record 6–0 defeat of Bradford along the way. In February 1956, Watson's appointment of Bill Burnikell as coach seemed a sound one, yet the manager would come under fire following the FA Cup defeat at non-League Burton Albion, then later when the side managed to win just one of 13 matches, a run which dared to threaten their survival prospects. Perhaps feeling the heat, Watson went on the lookout for new players to improve the side, then claimed he could not devote his time to the club with a new cricket season on the horizon, and on 5 April 1956 he resigned.

Watson went on to score runs prolifically with Yorkshire CC, before leaving in 1958 to become assistant secretary and captain of Leicestershire, for whom he scored heavily and led with much charm until he retired in 1964. He was recalled spasmodically for the England Test side and played his last match against New Zealand in Auckland in March 1959. In all, he scored 25,670 runs at an average of 39.8, though his disappointing Test average of 25.85 hardly reflected his true class.

Watson then went on to act as a Test selector for two years before making a surprise return to football – as manager of Halifax Town, the first to hold the post at The Shay on two separate occasions. But he rejoined a club which was now in the Fourth Division and strapped for cash. Town ended his first season having to apply for re-election but had better fortunes the following term with the arrival of the likes of Bill Atkins, John Pickering and Jim Smith.

Still, tired of the struggles at The Shay and with the club's future uncertain, Watson once again quit before the season's close, taking over as manager at neighbouring Bradford City. He led the Bantams to an 11th-place finish in his first season, then the following term saw his side well in contention for a promotion spot when he resigned in January 1968 to take over as coach and administrator of the Wanderers in Johannesburg. Never a man of many words, it was often suggested Watson was rather the shy introverted type who never enjoyed the limelight. He settled into the way of life in South Africa, becoming a poultry farmer after retiring from the game, and continued to live there until his death in 2004.

BURNIKELL, William Frederick

Manager: 6 April 1956 to 6 December 1956
Born: Southwick-on-Sea, 9 December 1910
Died: 1980
Career: Newcastle junior football; Lincoln City; Bradford City July 1933; Aldershot 1937; Landskrona (Sweden) coach; Helsingborg (Sweden) coach; Sudan coach; Catholic University (Chile) coach; **Halifax Town coach 13 February 1956, caretaker manager 6 April 1956, manager cs 1956, dismissed 6 December 1956**; *Degerfors IF (Sweden).*

To say Bill Burnikell was well-travelled would be something of an understatement. His coaching career took him as far afield as Sweden and Chile, and his experience it was hoped would stand him in good stead when he arrived at The Shay as coach to Willie Watson in February 1956. Within two months, he was given charge of the first team, but despite his wealth of knowledge and different coaching techniques, his lasting legacy was that he became the first Halifax Town manager to be dismissed by the club.

Born in Southwick-on-Sea, Bill Burnikell was spotted playing junior football in Newcastle and was signed by Lincoln City in 1929. He made his career as a half-back, though it was at centre-forward that he made his debut, deputising for Tom Maidment, against Crewe Alexandra on 1 March 1930, his only appearance that term. Burnikell, in fact, had managed only 25 League appearances before his move to Bradford City in July 1933.

At Valley Parade, Burnikell did not establish himself until 1934–35 and made a total of 56 League and Cup appearances, scoring twice, before he journeyed south to play for Aldershot. There he had made 63 League appearances, scoring a further two goals, before the outbreak of war interrupted his playing career. Burnikell served as a PT instructor during the war and also qualified as a coach before he trotted around the globe, coaching both Landskrona and Helsingborg to Championship success in Sweden. He became the official coach in the Sudan for 12 months before spending three years in Chile, where he coached the Catholic University team to the Championship.

Upon returning to England, Willie Watson offered him the opportunity to coach the first team, but with Watson's subsequent resignation just two months later came the opportunity for Burnikell to take over the running of team affairs. Handed the role initially on a caretaker basis, Burnikell took charge for the home game with Rochdale, with the ensuing 1–1 draw halting a run of five successive defeats. He remained in charge for the last six games of the 1955–56 season, and his four-game unbeaten start, including successive wins over promotion-chasing Accrington Stanley and Wrexham, helped the side to a 19th-place finish.

In the close season, Burnikell brought to The Shay several players who would prove to be immensely popular, such as forwards Conway Smith and Andy McCall, and full-back Phil Roscoe. In October, he was also responsible for the signing of centre-half Alex South from Liverpool, and players such as these would take Halifax Town onto better things. But they would do so without Burnikell. Despite an encouraging start to the 1956–57 campaign, a disappointing run going into December saw Burnikell relieved of his duties with immediate effect. The directors cited lack of success on the field – the side was lying twentieth out of 24 clubs – as the main reason, though Burnikell's parting shot suggested there were other problems.' Seven managers [excluding Bobby Browne] cannot all be wrong.'

Burnikell was, however, popular with the players, and on his last day, skipper George Griffiths presented him with an electric shaver as a farewell present, and with that he took leave of the game in England. He returned to Sweden and was coach to Degerfors IF in the early 1960s. It might be interesting to add here, that though he was born Burnikell, throughout his playing career he curiously spelt his name 'Burnicle', a fact that mystified even his own family.

TAYLOR, Harry, BOOTH, Erle Vivian & URE, Allan Richard
Joint managers: 6 December 1956 to 7 October 1957

TAYLOR, Harry
Born: Halifax, 2 January 1897
Died: Mytholmroyd, 23 November 1981

BOOTH, Erle Vivian
Born: 10 May 1906
Died: Ryedale, 1982

URE, Allan Richard
Born: Carlisle, 12 January 1892
Died: Halifax, 11 January 1970

In 1956 footballer Len Shackleton published his autobiography *The Clown Prince Of Soccer* in which one chapter was devoted to 'The Average Director's Knowledge of Football'. The rest of the page was left blank. 'Shack' may have had a point, but at Halifax Town, the collective know-how of chairman Harry Taylor and director Vivian Booth, together with that of trainer Allan Ure, was put to good effect. Directors had, of course, steered the ship in the interim periods in the past while they searched for a team manager, but following the dismissal of Bill Burnikell they were in no rush to appoint a successor and ran team affairs between themselves for around a year. Hence the inclusion of Messrs Taylor, Booth and Ure in this list.

All three men came from varying backgrounds, of course, with Booth, a director of building contractors William Parker & Son Ltd, Sowerby Bridge, first joining the board on 29 March 1950, while Harry Taylor took his seat on the board during the reshuffle in the summer of 1954. He first went into business making poultry appliances in 1922 with his brother Charles but after three years began poultry farming, running a large hatchery for day old chicks at Throstle Nest Farm, Mytholmroyd until retiring in 1971. He became Halifax Town chairman on 24 October 1956, a position he held until standing down in April 1964, though he continued to serve the board until February 1979 when he was made a life president. Taylor died suddenly at his Mytholmroyd home in November 1981.

Allan Ure had a football upbringing; his stepfather was retired army sergeant Bill Norman, who acted as trainer to Barnsley when they won the FA Cup in 1912. He took up the game and was on the books of Blackpool before assisting Millwall and Gillingham. He followed his stepfather to Barnsley where he too acted as trainer, before taking up similar positions at Huddersfield Town, Leeds United and Bradford. Ure arrived at The Shay as trainer on 7 July 1952 and served the club for 10 years before stepping down in January 1962, though he continued to act as masseur.

With Ure given the task of supervising training, the three men took over the running of team affairs, though not getting off to the best of starts with a 4–1 defeat at Shrewsbury Town in a friendly. But with the side lying 20th, they gave themselves the target of avoiding the re-election places and gained their first win with a 4–2 success over Workington on 22 December 1956. They were later heartened by the defeat of League-leaders Derby County and, without significantly adding to the squad, the management team lifted the side to 11th. In fact, so confident were they in the group of players that at the club's AGM on 1 August 1957 Taylor said they were not looking for any new ones because the present crop, which included the likes of Arthur Johnson, George Griffiths, Alex South, Conway Smith and Andy McCall, had done a good job, though the fact that there was, as he put it, 'no money in the kitty', probably had much to do with it.

The board had ambition for the club; not content with a top-half finish, they wanted Second Division football, and though early season results during 1957–58 saw them well off the pace for promotion, the impending formation of the Third and Fourth Division gave them an incentive to be part of the former. To qualify, they needed to finish in the top half, and they were handily placed when events took a dramatic turn.

Vivian Booth had landed himself in hot water with his disparaging remarks to Derby referee Percy Rhodes following the previous season's home defeat to Gateshead on 15 April. On 7 October he was banned by the Football League for 'ungentlemanly conduct', and the following day banned sine-die by the Football Association and forced to stand down from the board with immediate effect – director Jack Rushworth resigned in protest at his treatment – thus bringing to an end the unique management set-up.

The remaining board of directors set about finding a new team manager, though until Harry Hooper took up residence on 4 November, Town won one and drew four of the five matches played, extending an unbeaten run to six matches, and climbed to seventh in the table.

Booth, for his part, was able to rejoin the board in August 1959, becoming vice-chairman the following November after the death of Herbert Child, before resigning through pressure of work on 26 March 1963. Ure, crippled with arthritis in later years, stood down as trainer upon his 70th birthday in January 1962, though he continued to act as part-time masseur. He died at his Northowram home in 1970, three weeks after the death of his wife.

HOOPER, Harry Reed

Manager: 4 November 1957 to 4 May 1962
Born: Nelson, 16 December 1010
Died: Halifax, 24 March 1970
Career: Nelson Schools; Nelson Trades; Nelson November 1928; Sheffield United February 1930; Hartlepools United July 1947; West Ham United trainer 1949; **Halifax Town manager 25 October**

1957, resigned 4 May 1962; Nelson manager May 1962 to December 1962; Huddersfield Town scout January 1963.

Harry Hooper's contribution to Halifax Town's cause should not be understated. For not only did he carry on the impressive work done by Messrs. Taylor, Booth and Ure by ensuring a seventh-place finish in the last season of Division Three North football which qualified the club for the newly formed Third Division, but he also created a side which for several seasons competed above their weight against healthier southern-based sides. An apprentice tailor in his youth, Hooper would later joke that he looked better in vest and shorts than one of his own-made suits! He trod the boards with local works side Nelson Trades and Lancashire Combination side Nelson before joining Sheffield United, where he had a long and distinguished career. A pacy and hard tackling right back, the immaculately styled Hooper secured a first-team berth in 1931–32 and remained with the Blades until 1947. Made skipper by manager Teddy Davison, Hooper led out his team at Wembley for the 1936 FA Cup Final, only for Sheffield United to lose 1–0 to Arsenal. Relegated the season before, the Blades were promoted as runners-up to Blackburn Rovers in 1938–39, with Hooper making 22 League appearances. Hooper had made a total of 269 League appearances and scored 12 goals for the Blades before joining Third Division North outfit Hartlepools United after the war, spending two seasons at the Victoria Ground.

It was at West Ham United that his coaching career took off in 1949, serving under Charlie Paynter and his successor Ted Fenton during eight years at Upton Park, being one of the pioneers of the West Ham 'Academy' that would later spawn dynamic coaches such as Malcolm Allison, Noel Cantwell and John Bond. Hooper also encouraged the fledgling Bobby Moore and Geoff Hurst, as well as his own son, Harry Jnr, who began his own rewarding career with West Ham before enjoying spells with Wolves, Birmingham City and Sunderland, and winning two England Under-23 caps.

Harry Snr's step into management with Halifax Town came about following Vivian Booth's suspension, and he was chosen from a shortlist of six names, among which were Sam Barkas and Dick Duckworth. He took up his duties on 4 November 1957 on the day Town lost 3–1 at Bradford City in a West Riding Senior Cup tie, but got off to a dreadful start with his new side crashing 5–0 at Hartlepools in his first League game and out of the FA Cup at Mansfield Town. But by making some important signings, such as Alan Blackburn, a player Hooper knew well from his time at West Ham, Town regained their form, and pleased the club was moving in the right direction, the directors gave him a contract extension to May 1961 with chairman Harry Taylor saying, 'We are quite happy to give him a contract. We like him and are mutually satisfied.'

And well they should have been. Though Town were stepping somewhat into the unknown in the new Third Division, they competed well with the likes of Brentford, Southampton, Norwich City and Queen's Park Rangers. Purposely packing his side with big, powerful players – South, Lorenson, Tilley, Harrison – Town became a hard side to beat, and their ninth-place finish was the third-highest of the northern teams. A memorable season was also topped off with the winning of the Senior Cup for the first time in the days when there was a certain degree of prestige attached to it.

Hooper would later introduce to the side promising youngsters such as centre-forward Frank Large and goalkeeper Peter Downsborough, as well as signing the mercurial talents of George Whitelaw, one of the most entertaining and popular players the club has ever seen. During 1959–60, the Shaymen were among the early season pace-setters and for a spell led the table, but with little money they could not sustain their challenge. Realising the need for greater finance,

Hooper was at the forefront of the 'new Players Fund Committee' set up that same season, though the following term he seemingly was prepared to play without them when a players' strike threatened the football fixtures. Hooper was ready to throw in a number of local amateurs, and even appealed to anyone who thought they might be suitable to get in touch with him.

When floodlights were erected at The Shay, Hooper wrote personally to Real Madrid in the hope they might provide the opposition when they were officially turned in November 1961, but inevitably Town could not afford the Spanish giants. That was a season in which Town struggled for the first time in a while, and tired of fighting against meagre crowds and the barracking his players were subject to – he claimed that some players had asked to be left out of the side following abuse from the terracing – Hooper jumped at the chance of managing his former club Nelson at the end of that season, while assisting his son in his hairdressing business.

Hooper remained with Nelson until January 1963 when he was appointed chief scout at Huddersfield Town, recommending to the club a 15-year-old Frank Worthington, then on the books at Halifax. He left the post in August 1965 and continued to live in retirement in King Cross, Halifax, until his death in March 1970.

McEVOY, Donald

First-team coach: July 1962 to 14 July 1964
Born: Golcar, 3 September 1928
Died: Huddersfield, 9 October 2004
Career: Kirkheaton Rovers; Bradley Rangers; Huddersfield Town juniors, professional September 1947; Sheffield Wednesday December 1954 (£15,000); Lincoln City January 1959; Barrow player coach July 1960; **Halifax Town first-team coach July 1962**; *Barrow manager August 1964; Grimsby Town manager July 1967 to February 1968; Southport manager March 1968 to January 1970; Barrow manager February 1970 to November 1971.*

Don McEvoy arrived at The Shay in July 1962 having moved into coaching at Barrow, his previous club. He was given the title of first-team coach, but despite some innovative ideas and his willingness to give youth a chance, he failed to wrestle Halifax Town's decline and sadly, was labelled as the man who took the club down into the Fourth Division for the first time.

Born in Golcar, McEvoy played locally with Kirkheaton Rovers and Bradley Rangers before turning professional with Huddersfield Town in September 1947. He made his debut as a centre-forward but under Andy Beattie developed into one of the club's finest defenders, forming a half-back line with Bill McGarry and Len Quested which was a key feature of the club's 1952–53 Second Division promotion success a year after being relegated. McEvoy served the club for over eight years and made 148 League appearances, scoring three goals.

In December 1954, he moved to Sheffield Wednesday, quite ironic given that his last game for Huddersfield had been against the Owls the previous September, when injury in that game opened the door for Ken Taylor. But though Wednesday were relegated at the end of his first season, McEvoy skippered the side to the Second Division title 12 months later. Following a second relegation in 1957–58 McEvoy joined Lincoln City in January 1959 but having lost his place in the side there during 1959–60 he joined Barrow as player-coach in July 1960, making 74 League appearances and helping the side to a respectable ninth place finish in his second season after his first had ended in a re-election application.

McEvoy arrived at The Shay hoping to make his mark in his own right overseeing the first team. Assisting him was Harry Hubbick, one of the game's great characters, but they both joined a club that had just lost star striker Frank Large, sold to QPR, and would struggle to find a suitable replacement.

McEvoy saw his players give much endeavour in gaining a goalless draw at Crystal Palace in his first match in charge, and there was the astonishing 4–3 victory from 3–1 down late on against Swindon Town in September 1962. But Town soon found themselves embroiled in a relegation battle that they were unable to overcome. Not helped, of course, by the terrible winter that term, Town were hit harder than most clubs, and despite the talents of Peter Downsborough, Willie Carlin and Barry Tait at his disposal, McEvoy failed to inspire his team. 'Improve or be dropped' he warned, but it was to no avail. Despite the signing of Dennis Fidler, Town were relegated with four games still to play.

With no money to buy players, McEvoy relied upon youth, and brought through players such as Dave Worthington, Malcolm Russell and Tony Field. He even got himself in shape ready to travel as the side's 12th man in order to release a player to the reserves, though in the event he never called upon himself. But the side made a terrible start to their first campaign in the Fourth Division, slipping into the re-election zone before the season was suddenly transformed with a club record seven consecutive League victories through February and March 1964, and an unbeaten run which was extended to 11 matches. The side finished 10th, but McEvoy felt his future lay away from The Shay. On 14 July 1964 he was appointed manager of Barrow, taking up his position the following month, saying, 'It is one of those opportunities which occur in football and they have to be accepted.'

McEvoy took Dave Worthington with him, but his first season back at Holker Street ended with a re-election application. However, against the odds, he delivered their only promotion in 1966–67 but despite that achievement, he left to take the vacant managerial position at Grimsby Town, though it was a decision he later regretted. With no money for team strengthening, his time there was short, and with a record of just five wins from 24 matches he resigned citing 'differences in opinion concerning policy' between him and the board.

McEvoy later took over at Third Division Southport and led them to eighth place in 1968–69, but he was sacked the following term with the side fighting against relegation. In February 1970, he returned to manage Barrow, now back in the Fourth Division, but there was little joy for him. Re-election was required at the end of his first season back, and with the club lying next to bottom the following term he was sacked in November 1971. Barrow would lose their League status at the end of that term, replaced by Hereford United.

After leaving the game, McEvoy became a publican at the Crown Hotel in Brighouse until 1996, as well as working in local radio. He died in October 2004.

METCALFE, Victor

Tactical advisor: 4 April 1966, manager: 4 July 1966 to 14 November 1967
Born: Barrow-in-Furness, 3 February 1922
Died: Huddersfield, 6 April 2003
Career: Ravensthorpe Albion; Huddersfield Town June 1940, professional December 1945; RAF; Hull City June 1958 (£5,000); Huddersfield Town youth coach 1961 to October 1964; **Halifax Town youth coach 3 November 1964, first-team tactical advisor 4 April 1966, manager 4 July 1966, resigned 14 November 1967;** *Bradford City scout.*

When Vic Metcalfe succeeded Willie Watson in April 1966, he did so as 'tactical advisor', a label that suggested he had not got overall control of the team. When he was 'upgraded' to team manager in the close season, one would have expected a shift in responsibilities. But there lay part of the problem. When chairman Alan Maden suggested the board still had input into team selection, Metcalfe was having none of it and, with actions that suggested he was a man of principles, he cut his ties with the club.

Metcalfe came from a sporting family. His father was a Barrow RL and Skipton RU full-back, but it was the soccer code in which Vic Metcalfe excelled. A product of West Riding Schools football, he joined Huddersfield Town in June 1940 before serving with the RAF during wartime. After hostilities had ceased, he signed professional forms with the Terriers and his position at outside-left went virtually unchallenged over the course of 12 seasons following the resumption of League football.

Huddersfield Town successfully staved off relegation from the First Division during 1950–51, due in no small part to the performances of Metcalfe, and at the end of that season he was rewarded with two England caps when he lined up alongside the likes of Billy Wright, Stan Mortenson, Tom Finney and Jackie Milburn in consecutive wins over Argentina and Portugal.

However, disappointment was to follow in 1951–52 when the Terriers were relegated, but they bounced back at the first attempt under manager Andy Beattie, finishing runners-up to Sheffield United, with Metcalfe, whose 15 goals included two penalties, being one of seven ever-presents. He played his last game for Huddersfield in March 1958 and left for Hull City having amassed 459 League and Cup appearances and 90 goals.

The Tigers clinched promotion from the Third Division in 1958–59, though Metcalfe's contribution was brief, appearing in the opening fixture alone with Plymouth Argyle. He retired in February 1960 on his 38th birthday and took up employment with a radio and electrical firm before being enticed back into football in 1961 as youth coach at Huddersfield Town, a position he held until resigning at the end of October 1964.

Less than a week later, Metcalfe arrived at The Shay to take charge of the development of Town's junior players under the direction of manager Willie Watson, working alongside Clive Baker and Stewart Sutcliffe. But Watson's resignation in April 1966 saw Metcalfe suddenly thrust into the limelight, and he took charge of the first team until the end of the season in a 'tactical advisor' role. Town's future was under real threat and a successive re-election bid looked on the cards until the side pulled clear with three games to go.

Metcalfe was appointed full-time manager with effect from 4 July 1966, with chairman Sid Hitchen's endorsement that 'the board has every confidence in [his] ability. We believe that he has the respect of the players, which is most important'. Metcalfe signed important players such as Barry Hutchinson and Phil McCarthy, and his record was fair, recovering from a poor start to climb the table after hitting a purple patch during November and December. Not only did Town go six matches unbeaten in the League, they were also involved in a memorable FA Cup run which saw them run up a record Shay score in the 7–0 defeat of Bishop Auckland before bowing out to Bristol City in a replay at Ashton Gate. In the League, Town finished a creditable 12th.

But the 1966–67 season would be his only full season in charge, that despite continuing to shape his own team with the signings in the close season of Les Massie, Tony Flower and Ivan Hampton, and in November, of Hugh Ryden, breaking the club's transfer record in the bargain. With the side lying 10th in the table, Metcalfe felt aggrieved at what he felt was unnecessary interference from the board, now headed by Alan Maden, and on 14 November, the day after a board meeting, he resigned his position. Metcalfe withdrew from the game and spent his spare time playing golf, being a member of Crosland Heath Golf Club. He died in April 2003.

BALL, James Alan

Manager: 16 November 1967 to 14 May 1970 and 3 February 1976 to 14 November 1977
Born: Farnworth, Bolton, 23 September 1924
Died: Cyprus, 2 January 1982
Career: Southport amateur 14 October 1945, professional 5 March 1946; Birmingham City 20 May 1947; Southport February 1948 (£500); Oldham Athletic 3 July 1950; Rochdale 2 February 1952; Oswestry Town player-manager 1952–53; Borough United; Ashton United manager 1959–60; Nantwich Town manager; Stoke City coach; Manchester City coach 1967; **Halifax Town manager 16 November 1967;** *Preston North End manager 14 May 1970, dismissed 12 February 1973; Southport manager January 1974, dismissed 28 July 1975; IF Saab (Sweden) temporary coach March 1974, Sirius (Sweden) temporary coach March 1975,* **Halifax Town manager 3 February 1976, dismissed 14 November 1977;** *Blackpool scout 1980–81; IF Saab coach; Sirius coach; Uppsala coach; DjurgÂrdens coach; coaching in Cyprus.*

Of fiery character, Alan Ball Snr nevertheless endeared himself to the Halifax Town supporters by giving the club its first-ever promotion when he guided them to the Fourth Division runners-up spot in 1968–69. And it will be for this achievement he will be mostly remembered rather than that of taking the side back into the Fourth Division, as he did seven years later when he returned for a second stint. Despite success at The Shay, and later at Preston North End, Ball never achieved greatness as a player, unlike his son of the same name who won a League Championship medal with Everton and 72 England caps, as well as being a member of England's victorious World Cup-winning side in 1966. Ball Snr signed professional forms with Southport in March 1946 after serving the club as an amateur and operated at inside-forward before joining Birmingham City in May 1947. However, his time at St Andrew's saw him confined to the reserves as City clinched promotion, and before the season was out he had returned to Southport. Undistinguished spells at Oldham Athletic and Rochdale followed before Ball was appointed player-manager at Oswestry Town of the Birmingham and District League in 1952, where success started to come his way, leading them to the Championship and lifting the Shropshire Senior Cup.

Ball enhanced his coaching reputation with Borough United, Ashton United and Nantwich Town before joining the coaching staff at Stoke City, then under the guidance of Tony Waddington. By November 1967 he was working for Joe Mercer at Manchester City, having left Stoke when it looked as if coach Malcolm Allison was heading to Coventry City, when he got the call to succeed Vic Metcalfe.

Ball believed in his own ability, so much so that he promised Second Division football and 10,000 gates within five years. He put the accent on fitness, sending out his players up the gruelling Beacon Hill and back – 'I want you all back at The Shay within 15 minutes,' he would say – and made some astute signings, such as goalkeeper Alex Smith – he was Ball's first – Andy Burgin and Lammie Robertson, and proved he had an eye for potential by signing teenage Burnley reject centre-half Chris Nicholl from Witton Albion.

Veteran inside-forward Les Massie ended the 1967–68 season as joint leading scorer in the division, and he continued to score important goals as Town led the charge in the second half of the following season to stake their claim for a promotion place. That was duly claimed in their penultimate match against Rochdale at The Shay, and there was glory in the FA Cup as the side made it to the fourth round and forced a replay at First Division Stoke City to make it a memorable season all round.

Ball's signing of former England international Freddie Hill from Bolton was an ingenious one, and Town acquitted themselves well to life back in the Third Division. But when Preston sought a new manager following relegation from the Second Division and the sacking of Bobby Seith, Ball saw it as a too good an opportunity to turn down. He tendered his resignation and moved to Deepdale, where he delivered instant success, leading to Preston to the title at the first attempt with of John Bird, Bobby Ham and Alex Bruce in the side, and Fulham and Halifax Town in hot pursuit.

But by February 1973, Preston were struggling and Ball lost his job. He took over at Southport, though in a somewhat chaotic scenario he divided his time there with that of coaching Swedish club IF Saab, leaving Southport in the hands of, separately, Matt Woods and Jimmy Melia. Despite deploying a ultra-defensive system, Southport finished 1974–75 in a position of mid-table respectability but a subsequent furore over his non-return from Sweden in July saw Ball dismissed at the end of that month.

Ball's reappointment as Halifax Town boss in February 1975 was a controversial one given the manner of Johnny Quinn's sacking, but he proved to be no miracle worker second time around. He went for a quick fix, selling top scorer Dave Gwyther to finance new signings Mickey Bullock and George Jones, but the fact that he brought in too many new faces in too short a space of time in an attempt to halt the slide down the Third Division table probably did more harm than good. Halifax Town finished bottom and were relegated.

Ball was confident Town would make an immediate return and even despite making a poor start – two wins from 13 League games – he was adamant that his side would slip into gear once they had thrashed Doncaster Rovers 6–0. But the result failed to be the prelude to anything remarkable. His side was ever-changing, with new players such as Chris Dunleavy and Tony Loska coming in, and though there was an upturn in fortunes in the New Year, highlighted by another six-goal haul against Workington, Town lost form, winning only one of their last 11 matches and were condemned to re-election when Newport County overhauled them after the Shaymen had completed their fixtures.

Despite scoring six goals in their opening two matches of the 1977–78 campaign, including three at newly elected Wimbledon, Town were soon at the wrong end of the table once more. Ball was skating on thin ice, and he knew it. When defeat at Newport on 12 November left the Shaymen joint bottom with Rochdale, Ball was sacked two days later, despite having earlier been told he had a month to improve results. Ball tried his luck elsewhere, coaching several Swedish clubs including DjurgÂrdens, but he was coaching in Cyprus when he was killed in a car crash on 2 January 1982.

KIRBY, George

Manager: 22 May 1970 to 6 August 1971 and 3 November 1978 to 30 June 1981
Born: Liverpool, 20 December 1933
Died: Elland, 24 March 2000
Career: Everton June 1952; Sheffield Wednesday March 1959; Plymouth Argyle January 1960; Southampton September 1962 (£17,000); Coventry City March 1964 (£12,000); Swansea Town October 1964 (£12,000); Walsall May 1965, New York Generals (NASL) 1957; Brentford October 1968; Worcester City; **Halifax Town coach 18 August 1969, manager 22 May 1970 to 6 August 1971;** *Watford manager 9 August 1971, dismissed 11 May 1973; IA Akranes (Iceland) manager; coaching in Kuwait;* **Halifax Town manager 3 November 1978, dismissed 30 June 1981.**

Like Alan Ball Snr before him, George Kirby experienced mixed fortunes during two spells as Halifax Town manager. His first term in charge saw the side produce probably the most exciting football since the 1930s and come within a whisker of Second Division football. Kirby was also at the helm when the Shaymen pulled off sensational Cup victories over both Manchester United in his first spell, and their neighbours Manchester City in his second, but set against these achievements were the two re-election bids that befell the club upon his return.

George Kirby had moved into coaching towards the end of his playing career which had began with him signing professional forms with Everton, and though his time there was spent mainly in the reserves, he went on to earn himself a fearsome reputation – 'an out-and-out animal' was how one-time Southampton teammate Martin Chivers described him – with his robust style which intimidated defenders and goalkeepers alike. Yet off the field, he was ever the gentleman.

Kirby did net one goal from five first-team appearances at Everton, but it was not until he joined Plymouth Argyle in January 1960 via a short-lived spell at Sheffield Wednesday that his reputation grew, and it was with the Home Park club that he enjoyed his most prolific spell. Forming an effective strike partnership with Wilf Carter, Kirby helped Plymouth to their best-ever finish of fifth place in the Second Division in 1961–62. It was in September 1962 that Kirby moved to Southampton, featuring in their FA Cup run which saw them reach the semi-finals, only to lose to eventual winners Manchester United. Coventry City manager Jimmy Hill then took him to Highfield Road in March 1964 to help re-ignite their Third Division Championship challenge. Kirby responded with a headed hat-trick on his home debut against Oldham Athletic and scored five goals as the Sky Blues won the title butt Kirby did not fit into Hill's long term plans, and the following October he joined Swansea City.

Kirby later played for Walsall and ended his career with Brentford following a stint in the NASL with New York Generals, taking his tally to 110 League goals from 309 appearances. Upon his release from Brentford, Kirby teamed up with Alan Ball Snr as first-team coach at Halifax Town in August 1969, but following Ball's decision to move to Preston in May 1970 Kirby was promoted to manager. It proved a popular move. Putting the emphasis on attack rather than the workmanlike ethos instilled by Ball, Kirby's side proved as exciting as his new kit of tangerine and blue was colourful. With Dave Chadwick weaving down the right flank and Bill Atkins marauding down the middle, for Kirby came the accolade as Division Three Manager of the Month award for February 1971. Town found themselves on the periphery of the promotion race but ultimately, they just missed out in third place. But by scoring 74 goals, Town qualified to take part in the 1971–72 pre-season Watney Cup tournament and on 31 July 1971 they sensationally defeated a First Division Manchester United side featuring the triumvirate George Best, Bobby Charlton and Denis Law. But amid the celebrations, Kirby was contemplating his future, and had accepted the post as Watford manager in succession to Ken Furphy by the time the Shaymen took on, and lost to, West Bromwich Albion in the semi-final.

These were heady days, and memorable, too, in many ways. Who could forget Kirby's innovate idea of playing a recording of the 1970 Wembley FA Cup crowd over the tannoy to try to create more atmosphere among the sparse crowds at The Shay, or his side running out to the theme tune to the hit TV series *Hawaii 5–O*? Then suddenly, Kirby was gone, though his move to Watford was one he would later describe as 'the biggest mistake I ever made'. Hampered by off-field difficulties, Kirby spent two years at Vicarage Road, his association with the club ended following relegation to Division Three in May 1973. But he found success in, of all places, Iceland, taking over at IA Akranes, and leading them to League title success in both 1974 and 1975 and bringing European football to the club.

Midway through a four-year contract, Kirby left Iceland for a coaching post in Kuwait until answering the call of Halifax Town chairman Andrew Delaney to take over once more as manager following the sacking of player-manager Jimmy Lawson. With the side stranded at the foot of the Fourth Division table, Kirby had his work cut out, but he gave it his best shot. Of course the side he inherited was nowhere near the calibre of that which he had left over seven years earlier, although he did have several jewels in his midst. Goalkeeper Mick Leonard would prove his worth by obtaining a move to First Division Notts County less than a year later, there was the skilful Kevin Johnson, and the teenage terrier-like midfielder Mick Kennedy, whom Kirby at once threw into the fray.

Halifax Town's position looked hopeless, but slowly Kirby improved performances, and if re-election became ultimately unavoidable his efforts in lifting the side off the foot of the table was an achievement in itself, even if they were given a huge helping hand by Crewe, who went into freefall. Town overtook them with two games remaining, and despite losing both of those, they kept their noses in front of Crewe on goal average only. Kirby had issues to deal with, not least his sacking of striker Bobby Campbell for what he described as 'conduct in breach of club rules' and the loss of centre-back Arnie Sidebottom once the cricket season had started. But once re-election had been achieved, Kirby set about rebuilding his team.

The prominent signings of Dave Evans and Dave Harris – they formed the central defensive partnership – and midfielder Paul Hendrie immediately galvanised the club, and soon Town were competing at the right end of the table for once. An undefeated run of six games throughout September not only lifted the side to sixth, but also brought Kirby his second Manager of the Month award, and for a short time the side had the fans flocking back to The Shay.

Of course, the 1979–80 season will best remembered for the FA Cup run which included three epic matches with Walsall and culminated in the defeat of First Division Manchester City in January. How Kirby milked the media coverage in the run-up to their fourth round tie at Bolton, though defeat there was the prelude to a less exciting second half of the season.

However, Kirby, who in June 1980 was made chief executive and board member, believed a promotion push was on the cards during 1980–81, but save from some early season sparkle, he found his team battling at the wrong end of the table once more. His dealings in the transfer market led most believing his team was poorer than the previous term. Not helped by poor attendances and lack of finance, Kirby himself may have pointed to the uncertainty at boardroom level, too – he served under four chairmen that season – but Sam Rorke, who had joined the board towards the end of December 1980 and became chairman the following month, felt a parting of the ways was in the best interests of the club once Kirby had failed to steer Town away from the re-election zone. Despite the club comfortably being re-elected to the Fourth Division, Rorke asked for the manager's resignation. When Kirby refused, his sacking on 30 June 1981 was inevitable, and while he was prepared to go to the High Court claiming unfair dismissal, an out of court settlement with Halifax Town suited all concerned.

Kirby never returned to club management, but retained his involvement in football by providing analysis at matches for Pennine Radio and scouting for several clubs, latterly Queen's Park Rangers. But diagnosed with cancer in 1999, Kirby died in Elland Overgate Hospice in March 2000.

HENDERSON, Raymond

Manager: 10 August 1971 to 16 May 1972
Born: Wallsend, 31 March 1937
Career: Wallsend Schools; Wellington Quay; Hendon Boys' Club; Ashington; Middlesbrough May 1957; Hull City June 1961 (£2,000); Reading player coach October 1968; **Halifax Town manager 10 August 1971, dismissed 16 May 1972;** *Everton reserve coach July 1973 to May 1976; Southport manager May 1976 to March 1977.*

George Kirby's sudden departure to Watford at the beginning of August 1971 meant a hasty appointment by the board for his successor with a new League season just over a week away. He turned out to be Ray Henderson, a man who had the unenviable task of trying, if not to emulate Kirby, then at least to match his achievements of the previous season. That he failed was due in part to his break-up of the side – not necessarily by choice – and under mounting criticism, he paid the price after just one season.

Henderson's football career began in his native Wallsend when he was signed by Middlesbrough after a spell with Northern League side Ashington. He developed into a fast-raiding right winger, though he made his League debut as understudy for inside-left Arthur Fitzsimmons in a 3–3 draw at Blackburn Rovers on 30 November 1957. Henderson's four years at Ayresome Park brought just nine League appearances, yet they did yield five goals.

It was with Hull City that he was most revered, being part of a formidable forward line which included Ken Wagstaffe, Chris Chilton, Ken Houghton and Ian Butler, and in 1965–66 Henderson scored 13 goals as the Tigers won the Third Division Championship. He spent seven years at Boothferry Park making 229 League appearances and scoring an impressive 54 goals. In October 1968 he moved into coaching with Reading, working under Roy Bentley, but he was to lose his job as part of an economy drive at the end of the 1970–71 season and was working as a coach with the FA when Halifax Town came calling.

Henderson was appointed with club chairman Arthur Smith claiming, 'We have every confidence in Ray. He is pleasant and personable and we believe capable of bringing us promotion.' Henderson would sign a three-year contract, promising attacking football in much the same vein as that provided by Kirby, but he had little time to prepare his players, meeting them for the first time just two days prior to the opening League match at Mansfield Town.

Henderson enjoyed League Cup victory over Rochdale, and his side performed heroically in the second round at First Division Newcastle United, and other early season highlights included victory over Bournemouth. But FA Cup defeat to non-League Wigan Athletic brought with it mounting pressure, and with the side faltering in the League, the signings of Fred Kemp and Terry Shanahan failed to have any immediate impact, though in the case of another, Frank Brogan, Henderson was particularly unlucky to see him break an ankle in only his third game. The sale of want-away crowd favourite Dave Chadwick to Bournemouth was a blow, and without him Town briefly flirted with relegation. Henderson came up with novel attempts at addressing the situation; in February he accompanied his players to the Yorkshire Television studios to watch a re-run of the previous season's match with Chesterfield. The following week he then agreed to listen to the supporters' views at a meeting in the Shay Club.

During March, the board gave Henderson a vote of confidence – usually an ominous sign – and though a three-match winning streak eased Town's situation and contributed to a 19th-place finish, it was a position that still gave cause for concern. Four days after seeing his side push Leeds United all the way in the Final of the West Riding Senior Cup, Henderson was sacked on 16 May 1972, though there were those, Henderson himself included, who questioned whether he was really given a fair crack of the whip. He was judged, rightly or wrongly, solely on results, though it is often overlooked that it was he who first brought George Mulhall to the club, so for that fact at least he showed he had a degree of foresight.

Henderson resurfaced as coach to the reserves at First Division Everton when Billy Bingham was manager, and returned to club management with struggling Southport, only to lose his job there in March 1977 with the club looking odds on for a re-election application. Henderson later took employment at a printing company, then a medical firm, and lived in Wetherby in retirement.

QUINN, John David

Manager: 18 September 1974 to 2 February 1976
Born: St Helens, 30 May 1938
Career: Prescot Cables; Sheffield Wednesday May 1959; Rotherham United November 1967; **Halifax Town 5 July 1972, player-coach May 1973, player-manager 18 September 1974, manager February 1975, dismissed 2 February 1976;** *Worksop Town player-manager.*

'They could not have sacked a nicer guy' was a *Halifax Courier* headline which would have evoked an element of sympathy for any manager having just lost his job. The manner of Johnny Quinn's sacking, however, also brought with it an angry backlash from the supporters, most resentful of the way the board went behind his back and had lined up the return of Alan Ball Snr, with the national press being privy to the story before Quinn was officially told he was fired.

When they first appointed Quinn, however, the board were mindful of his necessary leadership qualities and that he commanded the respect of his peers after a career which had seen him play top-flight football with Sheffield Wednesday. He had been spotted playing for Prescot Cables in the St Helens Combination League and signed for the Owls upon leaving school in May 1959. Quinn made his debut on the right wing in a 2–0 win over Luton Town on 26 September 1959 but by 1964–65 had established himself as a half-back. The following term he was a member of the Wednesday side which reached the FA Cup Final, only to lose 3–2 to Everton having been two goals up.

In November 1967, having made 173 League appearances (20 goals) for the Owls, Quinn joined Second Division strugglers Rotherham United, but was unable to prevent their relegation. Nevertheless, he was made skipper by manager Tommy Docherty and remained at Millmoor until joining Halifax Town in July 1972, when he was new manager George Mulhall's first signing.

Quinn was made skipper at Halifax, too, and the Shaymen made a promising start to the 1972–73 season, though it was more than coincidence that they began to struggle once Quinn was injured and out of the side. He returned to help the cause towards the end of the campaign, scoring the crucial second goal in victory over Bournemouth – it was his only goal for the club – in the penultimate match as Town won their last four games to avoid relegation on goal average. So impressed were the supporters in Quinn's contribution that he was voted Player of the Year that season.

Having been promoted to player-coach, Quinn missed just one match in 1973–74 to help Town finish ninth, though management at that point must have been the furthest thing from his mind. But when manager George Mulhall suddenly resigned, Quinn was asked to take over in a caretaker capacity, and though his first game ended in defeat at Blackburn Rovers, he was offered the post on a full-time basis. Quinn's reaction was typical humble: 'I am prepared to take the job but if I feel it is too much for me after the next fortnight then I will let [the board] know.' Quinn pledged himself to the cause but immediately came across the problems unique to smaller clubs such as Halifax Town when he found himself with only 12 fit players, two of which were goalkeepers, and with the Football League turning down his plea to postpone a match at Peterborough, Quinn pressed Barry White into what was the first of four outfield appearances.

Quinn would feel the heat with FA Cup defeat at non-League Stafford Rangers just two months into his reign, but by standing down as a player in February 1975 – he had 92 League appearances for the Shaymen to his name – to concentrate on team affairs, he steadied the ship and lifted them away from the relegation zone.

Quinn went into the 1975–76 season with the ringing endorsement by chairman Percy Albon that he was 'as good a manager as we have had in a long time'. Indeed, the Shaymen made a promising start to the 1975–76 season, but the rot set in and Town slid alarmingly down the table to find themselves in 18th place following defeat by Shrewsbury Town on 24 January 1976. In an effort for his players to experience the art of winning, Quinn selected many of his first teamers for a reserve match at Doncaster Rovers, but the plan backfired when Town lost 2–1, though no one then could have predicted that he had picked his last Town team. For while freezing weather putting paid to the next two Third Division fixtures the knives were being sharpened. With 21 games still to play, Quinn may have had enough time to turn things around, but the board were not for giving him the opportunity. Feeling they had to act, Alan Ball Snr was already lined up to replace him and the axe was wielded.

After leaving The Shay, Quinn took over as player-manager at Worksop Town, his last club. At the same time he opened a sports shop with former Wednesday colleague Gerry Young just a stone's throw from the Hillsborough ground and formed 'Johnny Quinn's All Stars', a charity football team featuring former professionals from the South Yorkshire area, which he ran for many years until May 2006.

LAWSON, James Joseph
Manager: 15 November 1977 to 30 October 1978
Born: Middlesbrough, 11 December 1947
Career: South Bank St Peter's; Middlesbrough December 1964; Huddersfield Town May 1968 (£6,000); **Halifax Town May 1976, player-manager October 1977, sacked as manager November 1978, released May 1979.**

Upon Halifax Town's relegation to the Fourth Division in 1976, manager Alan Ball Snr turned to the likes of Jimmy Lawson, whom he signed from Huddersfield Town, in an attempt to deliver instant promotion. How ironic, then, in the wake of Ball's sacking the following year, that the board should turn to Lawson as his successor in the hope he could steer the side away from bottom end of the table. That he was successful in that was no real surprise; as a player he always led by example, but sadly, those who once cheered him were soon berating him when things went from bad to worse the following term, his days as manager numbered with the side anchored at the foot of the Fourth Division. Football, it appeared, could be a cruel game,

As a player, fates too had often been unkind to Lawson, though there were the successes. A scheming midfielder, he signed for Middlesbrough, his home-town club, in December 1964 and appeared in the side towards the 1965–66 run-in but unable to prevent their relegation, the first of several disappointments Lawson suffered in his career. However, the following term Lawson appeared in 19 League games as Boro made a swift return to the Second Division.

Having failed to establish himself under manager Stan Anderson, Lawson joined fellow Second Division side Huddersfield Town in May 1968 and was the midfield tactician of the Terriers' Championship success in 1969–70. But during the first of the two seasons Huddersfield spent in the top flight, Lawson found himself at loggerheads with manager Ian Greaves about his role in the side and was temporarily suspended. Relegation came in 1971–72, and so swift was their descent that by the start of the 1976–77 season, Huddersfield found themselves in the Fourth Division, with Lawson experiencing relegation for the fourth time in his career. Offloaded by then manager Tom Johnston, he left the Leeds Roads club having made 266 League appearances and scoring 46 goals.

Lawson then joined Halifax Town and was immediately installed as skipper by manager Ball, but had little luck with the Shaymen either. They ended their first season back in the Fourth Division having to apply for re-election, though the supporters did at least appreciate his efforts and proved it by voting him their Player of the Year. There was little improvement for the side either at the beginning of the following season and when Ball was sacked, the board felt there was no better candidate to succeed him than Lawson himself.

Lawson's first game in charge was a West Riding Senior Cup tie at against his old club, Huddersfield Town, lost only on penalties, but when it really mattered in the League, he was inspirational in the 2–1 victory over Aldershot. On a shoestring budget, Lawson added the likes of Franny Firth, Peter Burke and Bob Mountford to the squad and saw his side pull away from the re-election zone in the final weeks of the season.

When Bobby Flavell was sold to Chesterfield for £25,000, the board allowed Lawson to use all that money, and the purchase of Huddersfield's Kevin Johnson appeared to be a sound one. But though Town won their second League match, they were soon struggling at the foot of the table as defeat followed defeat. Having had to compensate for the sale of top scorer Derek Bell, Lawson brought in Mick Prendergast, Bobby Campbell and Arnie Sidebottom, and when results still did not improve he even dropped himself so he could see where the problem might lie. But it was all to no avail, and with only one win from their opening 15 League matches, Lawson was sacked as manager on 30 October 1978, although realising his qualities on the pitch, the directors were quick to retain him as a player.

His successor George Kirby was also keen to utilise Lawson and vowed that he was an important member of the side. But Lawson would never feature in the first team under Kirby, nor ever again, the victim of a knee injury. Released at the end of the 1978–79 season, he gave up football and became area manager for fork lift truck makers Coventry Climax. Lawson's son Ian became a professional footballer with Huddersfield Town, Blackpool, Bury and Stockport County.

BULLOCK, Michael Edwin

Manager: 13 July 1981 to 22 October 1984
Born: Stoke, 2 October 1946
Career: North Staffordshire Schools; Stoke Boys; Birmingham City apprentice July 1962; Oxford United June 1967; Orient October 1968 (£10,000); **Halifax Town 19 February 1976 (£5,000), player coach 24 January 1978, coach 1979, manager 13 July 1981, dismissed 22 October 1984;** *Goole Town manager; Ossett Town manager; Hereford United scout; Portsmouth scout; Crystal Palace scout.*

Many supporters questioned the logic of Mickey Bullock as manager in succession to George Kirby in July 1981. He had, after all, been at the club for five years, and been Kirby's right hand man for nearly three of those, and many felt he would be stuck in the old ways when they were calling for a clean break. But Bullock was determined to prove himself in his own right, and to be fair, he did a decent job under often trying circumstances in his first two seasons, only for the club to then go backwards, though the manner of his inevitable sacking smacked of Bullock being made a scapegoat.

His dismissal in October 1984 brought an end to his involvement at Football League level after a career that had spanned 22 years and begun at Birmingham City, for whom he signed apprentice forms in July 1962 before turning professional upon his 17th birthday. He had already made a sensational debut by then, scoring the winner against Manchester United at Old Trafford in January 1964.

Bullock, a fine leader of the line and a terrific header of the ball, moved to Oxford United in June 1967 and was top scorer with 13 goals from 45 League appearances in their Third Division Championship success in his first season before enjoying more success with Orient. Bullock led the way with 19 goals when the O's won the Third Division title in 1969–70 and two seasons later he figured in their FA Cup run to the quarter-finals, scoring in the sensational 3–2 win over Chelsea. In 1973–74 he hit 16 goals when they missed out on promotion to the First Division by one point and in total made 307 first-team appearances for the O's and scored 69 goals.

In February 1976 Bullock became one of Alan Ball Snr's first signings upon his return as Halifax Town manager in an effort to avert relegation from the Third Division. But goals did not come easily and Town were relegated and set for a long period of struggle. When Jimmy Lawson took over as player-manager, he promoted Bullock to player-coach in January 1978, and it was Bullock who briefly took charge of first-team matters following Lawson's sacking.

George Kirby, appointed as manager at the beginning of November 1978, was happy to keep Bullock as his assistant, and though retained as a player, he concentrated solely on coaching before hanging up his boots at the end of that season having made 106 League appearances for the Shaymen, scoring 20 goals. Halifax Town enjoyed a better season in 1979–80, highlighted by the FA Cup victory over First Division Manchester City, but they were condemned to re-election the following term. When Kirby was dismissed, Bullock beat off nearly 40 candidates to succeed him, and the directors immediately backed his judgement by finding £20,000 to buy young untried striker Bobby Davison from Huddersfield Town, a player who would repay Bullock's faith in him.

Bullock appointed Billy Ayre as coach, and Town finished 19th in his first year in charge, but it was an extraordinary season, one in which the club nearly went out of business with Sam Rorke as chairman. Bullock tried to keep his players' minds focussed on the job in hand, but though at times the side played some attractive football, too many late goals conceded meant they were denied the points their play often warranted. The following term it seemed at one point as if Town were re-election certainties when a woeful run left them in 20th place, and that after selling top scorer Bobby Davison for £98,000 to Derby County, money which without Bullock reckoned the club would have gone to the wall. The side was capable of pulling off the odd shock, such as the 4–2 win at Wimbledon, but only 912 bothered to turn out for the visit of Tranmere Rovers on 17 December 1982. Just seven weeks later, however, there were over four thousand present for the visit of Bury after a five-match winning streak had transformed Town's season. Victory in that match made it six, Bullock's finest hour.

Town ended the 1982–83 in a respectable 11th place but had an unhappy time the following season, battling against re-election once more, with FA Cup defeat at the hands of non-League Whitby Town, 12 months after losing to North Shields, singularly the worst experience Bullock surely felt. He promised to put things right, though one wonders how effective his regular calls for Sunday training were as the team succumbed to a bottom-four finish.

Bullock's job was about to become even harder when the board instructed him to curb the wage bill, a policy which led to the departure of the club's best players. Bullock re-appointed Billy Ayre, returning from a spell at Mansfield, and there was one last chance to hobnob with the elite when Town were paired with First Division Tottenham Hotspur in the Milk Cup, but his crop of old heads and young and inexperienced endured a torrid time in the League. Following defeat by Darlington which saw them slip to bottom place, Bullock was sacked on 22 October 1984, though he clearly felt he had been treated unfairly, and rightly said so.

After leaving The Shay, Bullock briefly worked in the media, and was acting as co-commentator with Tony Delahunte of Pennine Radio at Valley Parade in May 1985 when the fire which claimed 56 lives broke out. Bullock later scouted for several clubs, including Portsmouth and Crystal Palace.

JONES, Michael David

Manager: 10 November 1984 to 18 December 1986
Born: Sunderland, 24 March 1947
Career: Derby County juniors, professional November 1964; Notts County 10 July 1969; Peterborough United 10 August 1973 (£6,000); Ottowa Tigers (Canada) player-coach 1976 player-coach; Kettering Town player-manager cs 1979; Mansfield Town manager August 1979 to May 1981; Bradford City coach cs 1981; Derby County coach November 1982 to January 1984; **Halifax Town manager 10 November 1984;** *Notts County trainer 1986; Peterborough United assistant manager 18 December 1986, manager July 1988 to August 1989; Blackpool scout 1989; Notts County coach 1989, assistant manager July 1990 to January 1993; Huddersfield Town assistant manager 1993 to 1995; Plymouth Argyle assistant manager 1995, manager May 1997 to 1998; Brunei national coach 1999 to 2002; Nuneaton Borough assistant manager May 2003; Sheffield United coach July 2004 to May 2007; Crystal Palace assistant manager October 2007; Queen's Park Rangers assistant manager March 2010.*

Mick Jones was appointed as permanent successor to Mickey Bullock on the recommendation of a certain Brian Clough, who knew a thing or two when it came to football. So the story goes, Clough rang the Shay offices to speak with John Crowther, the then chairman, claiming to be the 'the world's greatest manager' and recommending Mick Jones, 'the world's second greatest manager' to the vacant position at Halifax Town. The directors thus appointed Jones, and Crowther has since been left to regale that story to anyone with a passing interest in the club's history.

Jones had first come under Clough's wing as a player when Clough took over as Derby County manager in June 1967. But failing to make the grade at the Baseball Ground, he picked up his career at Notts County, becoming an accomplished centre-half and being a key figure in their 1970–71 Division Four promotion campaign, and again two years later when County went up into the Second Division.

After making 100 League appearances for County, Jones joined Peterborough United in August 1973 and helped the club to the Division Four Championship in his first season. He made 88 League appearances over three seasons, then had a brief spell as player-coach at now defunct Canadian outfit Ottawa Tigers, before he returned to England in 1976 with Kettering Town, initially as player-manager. In a successful spell, he led Kettering to the FA Trophy Final in 1979, only to see his side lose to Stafford Rangers.

In August 1979 Jones had his first taste in League management with Mansfield Town, only for his first season in charge to end in relegation to the Fourth Division, and after being sacked in May 1981, he joined Roy McFarland at Bradford City as assistant manager and stayed there until linking up with Halifax Town.

Jones' appointment as successor to Bullock was not cut and dried. After all, Billy Ayre had made a strong case for the job by losing only one of four games during his caretaker stint. But after the side had won the last of these against Mansfield on 10 November 1984, and following Brian Clough's intervention, Jones was unveiled as Halifax Town's new manager, though he ensured his first task was to make Ayre his right-hand man. The pair worked well together and got off to a terrific start, enjoying victories in the first three matches, including FA Cup success over Goole Town in Jones' first game in charge. But a depressing sequence of results during the second half of the campaign meant that a re-election application became almost inevitable. It was, however, the last time Town would find themselves having to go through this process. The following term, Jones strengthened the side with the signings of Phil Brown and Billy Kellock and snapping up young Nottingham Forest striker David Longhurst. Town may have finished 20th, but the re-election issue had been staved off long before the final whistle.

Jones, of course, was at the helm during the traumatic 1986–87 season, which not only saw Town stranded at the foot of the table early on after losing seven consecutive matches, but also staring possible extension in the face. Under such uncertainty did he continue to work, though not for long. Despite facing the supporters at a public meeting held at the Civic Theatre on 12 December 1986, he never publicly denied his intention to join manager Noel Cantwell at Peterborough United, and six days later he was gone, though no one could have blamed him for securing his own future. He left Halifax Town with a modest record but remained one of the club's most popular managers.

Jones eventually succeeded Cantwell as manager in July 1988, and though he did not enjoy any great success, he did strike up a great working relationship with Neil Warnock, who was on the coaching staff there. Together, the pair would work well at several clubs, with Jones reverting to his role as assistant manager to Warnock at Notts County, Huddersfield Town and Plymouth Argyle. Jones, however, did spend time abroad on his own, enjoying a successful spell coaching the Brunei national team where he performed an amazing feat in getting the tiny Borneo province to their first ever Malaysia Cup Final in 1999, beating Sarawak 2–1 to collect the trophy.

Jones remained with Brunei until 2002, returning to England for spells as assistant manager to Carl Shutt at Nuneaton Borough and as manager of Telford United, where he worked until financial problems led to the collapse of the club, forcing him to leave in April 2004.

The following year, Jones resumed his partnership with Neil Warnock at Sheffield United, helping them to promotion to the Premier League at the end of his first season. When the Blades were relegated 12 months later, Warnock and Jones both resigned. The pair had a short period out of football before joining Crystal Palace in October 2007, with the Eagles turning from relegation battlers to Play-off semi-finalists under their stewardship. With the club in administration, Warnock took over as Queen's Park Rangers manager in March 2010, and Jones in turn followed him to Loftus Road. In May 2011, QPR were crowned Championship champions.

AYRE, William

Caretaker manager 23 October 1984 to 10 November 1984, manager 19 December 1986 to 20 March 1990
Born: Crookhill, 7 May 1952
Died: Ormskirk, 16 April 2002
Career: Crook Town; Bishop Auckland; Scarborough cs 1975; Hartlepool United August 1977; **Halifax Town 1 January 1981, player-coach August 1981;** *Mansfield Town 10 August 1982 (£17,500), acting manager January to February 1983;* **Halifax Town player-coach 17 July 1984, caretaker manager 23 October 1984, assistant player-manager 10 November 1984, manager retired as player 11 December 1986; manager 19 December 1986 to 20 March 1990;** *Blackpool assistant manager May 1990, manager November 1990, dismissed June 1994; Scarborough manager August 1994, resigned December 1994; Southport manager 1995; Swansea City assistant manager March 1996; Cardiff City assistant manager 1998, manager January 2000, assistant manager August 2000 to October 2000; Bury assistant manager November 2001.*

Billy Ayre was granted the manager's job he craved in December 1986 when Mick Jones left for Peterborough, just over two years after feeling the job was rightly his having impressed on a caretaker basis following the dismissal of Mickey Bullock. Ayre worked well as Jones's assistant

… but he was always keen to be his own man, preferably with Halifax. His association with the club had begun when Ayre moved from Hartlepool United in January 1981 in an exchange deal which saw Kevin Johnson move in the opposite direction, with then Town boss George Kirby seeing in Ayre the type of battling qualities he felt would be needed if they were to escape the clutches of the re-election zone, and Ayre quickly showed a steely resolve in the heart of the defence which endeared him to the supporters.

Ayre had begun a career as a teacher while playing part-time football with Crook Town and Bishop Auckland before coming to prominence with Scarborough, whom he joined in the summer of 1975. Under manager Colin Appleton, he helped the side win the FA Trophy in consecutive seasons and was voted player of the year in 1976–77. Having made 116 appearances and scoring 20 goals, Ayre signed as a full-time professional with Hartlepool United when Billy Horner was manager, and though 'Pool were perennial strugglers, the fans quickly appreciated Ayre in the heart of their defence. Ever-present in his first season, he went on to make 141 League appearances and score 27 goals before making his move to The Shay for the first of two spells.

Ayre spent 18 months at The Shay, and though his first season ended in a re-election application, having been appointed player-coach to new manager Mickey Bullock in August 1981, he helped Town to a 19th-place finish, only to then make a shock move to Mansfield Town, where he spent two seasons. It was at Field Mill where Ayre first sampled management, stepping in as caretaker following the sacking of Stuart Boam in January 1983 until the arrival of Ian Greaves.

However, Ayre was brought back to The Shay as player-coach by Bullock in July 1984 though he soon found himself being asked to oversee the first team following Bullock's departure. Ayre was keen to make the manager's position a permanent one and impressed over a four-match period only for the board to appoint Jones.

There was obvious disappointment felt by Ayre, softened somewhat when Jones immediately asked him to be his assistant, and together they worked wonders to keep the club going. When Jones departed on 18 December 1986 with Town's future uncertain, Ayre was the ready-made replacement and he was appointed the club's new manager the following day. Town were lying in 21st position, but there was an immediate upturn in their fortunes and they started to climb the table. They moved up to 11th at the beginning of February and so well were they going that Ayre admitted at one point that he felt his side was good enough to make the Play-offs. Town eventually fell away, but their 15th place finish was still encouraging enough.

Success for Halifax Town was always relative, but with Ayre keen to promote youngsters from the Under-19s Northern Intermediate side, he ensured the club's immediate survival, as the likes of Lee Richardson, Wayne Allison and Phil Whitehead were all sold for princely sums, although the side was worse for their departures. Ayre also had to contend with the sales of other top players such as winger Rick Holden and Mick Galloway, which affected League progress.

With young Terry McPhillips leading the scoring charts, the Shaymen scored a glut of goals during the first half of the 1988–89 season, though once they had dried up, the side in turn began to struggle. Prepared to put his head on the line, Ayre famously dropped three key players in September 1988 after breaking club rules, and in August 1989, having broken the club's transfer record by spending £40,000 on Leyton Orient striker Ian Juryeff, he promptly showed him the door after a dispute between the two. Time, though began to run out for Ayre, as a poor sequence of results left the side perilously close to the foot of the Fourth Division. With a section of supporters demanding his sacking, matters came to a head following the home defeat by Lincoln City on 20 March 1990 and a parting of the ways between manager and club was announced by chairman Jim Brown the following day.

Ayre resurfaced as assistant manager to Graham Carr at Blackpool, succeeding him in November 1990 and transforming their fortunes, taking them from 18th position to the Play-offs having lost only five of their remaining 30 games, only for his side to lose out in the Play-off Final at Wembley after a penalty shoot-out to Torquay United. However, they reached the Play-off Final the following term and had better luck as they defeated Scunthorpe United 4–3 on penalties to reach the Second Division. But after avoiding relegation by a single point in 1993–94, Ayre was sacked that June. He returned as manager at Scarborough, though he lasted only four months in the job and left with the side bottom of the Fourth Division. He took over at Conference side Southport and led them a third-place finish in 1994–95 then went to Swansea City as assistant to Jan Molby, but the pair were both sacked after losing the Third Division Play-off Final to Northampton Town a year after relegation.

Ayre then assisted Frank Burrows at Cardiff City and helped them to promotion to Division Two in 1998–99, before being installed as the Bluebirds' boss in January 2000. Cardiff were relegated that term and Ayre, who reverted to assistant to new manager Bobby Gould, left the club in October 2000. He later served as assistant to Andy Preece at Bury, but in the spring of 2001 he was forced to stand down upon the discovery of lymph node cancer and, though after treatment he appeared to be recovering, he suffered a setback and died in April 2002.

McCALLIOG, James

Manager 21 March 1990 to 2 October 1991
Born: Glasgow 23 September 1946
Career: Glasgow schools; Leeds United amateur May 1963; Chelsea September 1963; Sheffield Wednesday October 1965 (£37,500); Wolverhampton Wanderers 2 August 1969 (£70,000); Manchester United 14 March 1974 (£60,000); Southampton 13 February 1975 (£40,000); Chicago Sting (NASL) April to August 1977; coaching in Nigeria 1977; Lyn Oslo (Norway) coach; Lincoln City player-coach September 1978; Runcorn player-manager 1979; **Halifax Town Football in the Community officer July 1989 to February 1990; Halifax Town manager 21 March 1990, dismissed 2 October 1991.**

Former Scotland international Jim McCalliog had recently stepped down from his role Head of Halifax Town's new initiative Football in the Community scheme when he answered Jim Brown's call to take over in a caretaker capacity following the departure of Billy Ayre. Two games in and seemingly having made a difference, albeit without victory, McCalliog was given the job permanently prior to the match at Rochdale, with his players responding with a 2–0 win. How he had wished his side could respond in similar fashion more often. But the struggles McCalliog would endure at Halifax were a far cry from the successes he enjoyed as a player after initial rejection by Leeds United. He joined Chelsea under Tommy Docherty in September 1963 and made his debut on his 18th birthday in a 3–0 win over Birmingham City, a club who were also on the receiving end when McCalliog scored his only goals for the club, netting twice in a 6–1 victory in November 1964.

His £37,500 move to Sheffield Wednesday was a record fee for a teenager, and his first season saw him help the Owls to the FA Cup Final following semi-final over, ironically, Chelsea, with McCalliog scoring his side's second goal with a header in the last minute. He also scored in the Final at Wembley but Wednesday lost 3–2 to Everton having been two goals to the good. Having won Scotland Youth and two Under-23 caps, McCalliog made the step up to the full national side, winning the first of his five Scotland caps in the unforgettable match with World Champions England at Wembley on 15 April 1967, when his angled drive proved to be the match-winner in the 3–2 success.

McCalliog made 150 League appearances and scored 19 goals for Wednesday before tasting more success with Wolverhampton Wanderers, though he would end up on the losing side, despite being a scorer in the first leg home defeat, of the 1972 all-England UEFA Cup Final against Tottenham Hotspur. The 1973–74 season saw him hampered by injuries but after making a total of 163 League appearances (34 goals) for Wolves, McCalliog re-joined Tommy Docherty at Manchester United on deadline day in March 1974, but they were a club in decline and destined for relegation to the Second Division.

McCalliog appeared in 22 matches of United's matches the following term to earn a Second Division Championship medal but had been sold before the season's end to Southampton, who had been relegated with United. Though Docherty's side would regain First Division status at the first attempt, McCalliog helped heap misery on them when he laid on the winning goal for Bobby Stokes as the Saints defeated United 1–0 to win the FA Cup in May 1976.

McCalliog later played with Chicago Sting in the NASL before a brief spell as player-coach with Lyn Oslo in Norway. He returned to Britain in September 1978, as a player-coach at Lincoln City but soon fell out with manager Colin Murphy and his contract was paid up early in 1979. He briefly moved on to non-League Runcorn as player-manager, before quitting football and taking over a pub in Lytham St Anne's.

It was in July 1989 that McCalliog first became involved with Halifax Town, heading the Football in the Community scheme, and was therefore on hand when Billy Ayre left the club. McCalliog was a purist who believed in football being played on the ground, and shortly into his tenure had to find strong words of motivation when he found his side three goals down at Doncaster Rovers. Somehow, the players turned the game around, one of a series of bizarre matches the side played under him.

McCalliog clearly had an eye for a player, hence his immediate promotion to the first team of youngster Craig Fleming. During the 1990 close season, he would also bring the assured centre-back Paul Futcher to the club, but it was at the other end that he had problems. The run of eight games without a goal from the start of the season was unprecedented, though McCalliog was unwilling to change the team's playing style. In an effort to halt the sequence he broke the club transfer record when bringing back Ian Juryeff from Hereford United, but it was not until the arrival of Carlisle's Steve Norris, traded for Tony Fyfe, that the goals started to come.

Whether it was an inspired signing or a lucky one, no one could say, but even the Town manager could not have foreseen the 30 League goals Norris would score during 1990–91, even though his side failed to rise higher than 22nd all season. There was, however, a tendency to rely on his goalscoring prowess, for once he had lost his form, the side was bound to struggle. Despite McCalliog's signings of Steve Richards (whom he reckoned to be the best centre-half in the Fourth Division) and the experienced Greg Abbott, Town soon found themselves floundering during the 1991–92 season, and with the side having mustered only one win from their opening seven League fixtures and lying next to bottom, McCalliog was sacked following a 3–1 home defeat by Mansfield Town.

After leaving Halifax, he returned to the licensing trade, running the George & Dragon pub at Wetherby, and latterly the King's Arms in Fenwick, Ayrshire, close to his native Glasgow.

McGRATH, John Thomas

Manager: 3 October 1991 to 7 December 1992
Born: Manchester, 23 August 1938
Died: Manchester, 25 December 1998
Career: Bolton Wanderers amateur; Miles Platting Swifts; Bury October 1955; Newcastle United February 1961 (£24,000 plus a player); Southampton February 1968 (£30,000); Brighton & Hove

Albion on loan December 1972; Southampton trainer & youth-team coach 1975–79; Port Vale manager December 1979 to December 1983; Chester City manager January 1984 to May 1985; Preston North End manager May 1986 to February 1990; **Halifax Town manager October 1991, resigned December 1992**.

The appointment of John McGrath as successor to Jim McCalliog, ironically a player he had worked with at Southampton in the 1970s, seemed a sound one at first glance. He had, after all, transformed the fortunes of other ailing clubs such as Port Vale and Preston North End, achieving promotion with the latter a year after a re-election application. McGrath would point out these achievements on the after-dinner circuit, before adding that 'I also managed Halifax Town', indicating in his own jocular fashion how he had found it impossible to do much at The Shay, handicapped by an acute lack of finances, and in turn quality players. His time at Halifax Town would prove to be his last involvement with day-to-day football, as he concentrated on his living made on the after-dinner circuit, regaling stories from an eventful career in professional football which had begun with Bury in the Third Division after treading the boards in Manchester junior soccer.

An uncompromising centre-half, 'Big John' McGrath made his debut for Bury in October 1956 and three seasons later had made 22 League appearances of their ultimate Third Division Championship-winning season when he was sold to Newcastle United in February 1961 in a deal which saw Bob Stokoe move in the opposite direction. He won an England Under-23 cap in an international against West Germany at White Hart Lane, lining up alongside Bobby Moore, shortly after his move to St James's Park and he became a firm favourite with the Toon Army, being ever-present in their 1964–65 Second Division Championship campaign.

Having made 170 League appearances and scoring two goals for the Magpies, McGrath ventured south in February 1968 to play for Ted Bates's Southampton, adding further steel to a side which already contained the likes of Terry Paine, Jimmy Gabriel and Dennis Hollywood. He made 168 League appearances (one goal) for the Saints before retiring from playing at the end of the 1973–74 season and moved into coaching under then manager Lawrie McMenemy.

McGrath, one of the game's most entertaining characters, took his first managerial role at Fourth Division Port Vale in December 1979, but while many felt he was fortunate to keep his job after a poor season in 1980–81 which included an FA Cup defeat by non-League Enfield, he discovered winger Mark Chamberlain and led Port Vale to promotion in 1982–83. However, when the side struggled the following term, McGrath was sacked.

He returned as manager at Chester City, a club rock bottom of the Fourth Division, and though the club successfully sought re-election in 1983–84, McGrath was sacked at the end of the following season despite having led them to a 16th-place finish. In May 1986, he took over at Preston North End with the club having just been re-elected to the Fourth Division after finishing 23rd. With a plastic pitch having been laid, incredibly he transformed the place, leading them to promotion in his first season in charge with the likes of Sam Allardyce, John Thomas and Nigel Jemson in the side, as well as adding Frank Worthington to the squad to aid the run-in. Two years later, Preston made the Play-offs only to lose out in the semi-finals, ironically to Port Vale, one of his former clubs. During 1989–90, however, Preston struggled, and things came to a head when the side entertained Leyton Orient on 13 February. The match was held up for 35 minutes while fans demonstrated on the pitch against Preston's poor record and calling for McGrath's resignation. He duly obliged the following day.

McGrath was installed as Halifax Town's new manager within 24 hours of McCalliog's departure and promised better times ahead, as well as making the club some money. Indeed, he did that, but the selling of leading goalscorer Steve Norris to Chesterfield for what many perceived a knockdown £33,000 was not good business. Without him, Town were short of attacking options and though there was a hint of a revival after Town moved up to 17th, before long the season became an all too familiar one of basement struggle.

McGrath had brought with him former Stockport County full-back Oshor Williams as his assistant, and among his early signings were goalkeeper Lee Bracey and Ronnie Hildersley, whose sensational lobbed effort earned Town a replay in the first round FA Cup tie at Witton Albion. But McGrath went the same way as many Town bosses before him, watching helplessly as they succumbed to the non-League opponents in the replay.

Town's League status was assured long before the season ended only because of the demise of Aldershot, whose resignation meant no team would be relegated. But there would be no reprise the following term and as such McGrath brought in players he had previously worked with, such as strikers John Thomas and Nigel Greenwood, while the signing of former Liverpool midfield ace Jimmy Case, was viewed in some quarters as a potential master-stroke. But Case did not make the desired impact – he was, when all was said and done, 38 years old – and proving an expensive commodity was transferred to Wrexham in February 1993. By which time, McGrath had long since gone, too, with the club's position looking precarious on and off the field.

The opening day 3–2 success at Rochdale and the unexpected 5–2 win at Northampton Town were moments to savour but results such as these proved the exception rather than the rule and with the side heading for the wrong end of the table once more, the last thing the club needed was FA Cup defeat at non-League opposition. The manner in which the Shaymen capitulated at Marine in the first round suggested that McGrath had lost his powers of motivation. When the side slipped to home defeat to Barnet three weeks later, thus extending a winless streak to eight matches, McGrath knew his time was up and tendered his resignation the following day. He never returned to football after that, instead preferring to live off his memories and proving an entertaining and often hilarious orator.

McGrath died suddenly at his Manchester home on Christmas Day 1998.

RATHBONE, Michael

Manager: 8 December 1992 to May 1993
Born: Sheldon, Birmingham 6 November 1958.
Career: Birmingham City apprentice December 1974, professional November 1976; Blackburn Rovers February 1979 (£40,000); Preston North End August 1987 (£20,000); **Halifax Town physio July 1992, manager 8 December 1992 to May 1993, assistant manager and physio June 1993, released March 1995;** *Preston North End physio July 1995; Everton physio September 2002 to May 2010; Preston North End physio January 2011.*

It seems a tad unfair to label Mick 'Baz' Rathbone as the manager who took Halifax Town down into the Conference in May 1993. He had, after all, arrived only as physio but been thrown in at the deep end following John McGrath's resignation. The club had no money, had an uncertain future and were struggling in the League. It was an unenviable position for any manager to come into, not least one as inexperienced as Rathbone, one of football's most likeable personalities.

Rathbone had begun a career which would see him rack up 384 League appearances with three different clubs at First Division Birmingham City, the club he supported as a boy, and made his debut under manager Willie Bell as a substitute in a 1-0 defeat at Tottenham Hotspur on 20 October 1976, a month before he turned professional. Failing to hold down a regular place in the side, however, he moved to Blackburn Rovers in February 1979, where he became the regular first choice at left back until suffering a broken leg in 1983. In 1979-80 he appeared in 28 matches as Rovers, under Howard Kendall, clinched promotion from the Third Division and was a key member of the side which enjoyed a run to the fifth round of the FA Cup the same season.

It was in August 1987 that Rathbone first linked up with John McGrath when he joined Preston North End, though his time there was blighted by injury, forcing his retirement in 1991. He was studying in physiotherapy at Salford University when McGrath, by now manager at Halifax Town, offered him the position of physio at The Shay but he must have been as surprised as anyone when chairman Jim Brown asked him to take control of the first team following McGrath's sudden departure.

Rathbone's first game in charge saw Town slip to a 5-0 defeat at Huddersfield Town in the Autoglass Trophy, and things would not get any easier in the League. With no funds to buy new players, Rathbone brought in players from lower league level such as Curzon Ashton's Dave Ridings, who scored twice in a welcome 3-0 win at Darlington, and Peter Craven from Guiseley. Rathbone stuck with the impressive central defensive pairing of Russell Bradley and Chris Lucketti, but was unfortunate that the club sought fit to sell not only left-back Paul Wilson, but also top scorer Ian Thompstone.

Away form was comparable with many clubs in the division, but their failure to win at home was the root of the problem. Rathbone would see Town claim three points only on one occasion at The Shay, a 2-1 success over Lincoln City in February 1993. As the League position remained ever more critical, he tried to remain upbeat, often claiming his players were fortunate to have so many 'cup finals' to play as relegation to the Conference loomed. In the end, Town's fate came down to the last day, and defeat by Hereford United sealed it.

Rathbone would remain at the club, reverting to assistant manager and physio to Peter Wragg, and in turn, his successor John Bird. He turned out for the team in emergencies and even popped up with a spectacular goal in a 4-0 defeat of Dover Athletic in January 1995. Bird's decision to release Rathbone two months later was one he described as 'the hardest decision I've ever had to make'.

Rathbone then returned to Preston North End as physio, and followed manager David Moyes to Premier League side Everton in September 2002. He spent nearly eight years at Goodison Park, becoming head of sports medicine, a post he left in May 2010 after what the Liverpool Echo described as 'a tumultuous season of injuries' to the Everton players. He went on to establish a business combining sports injury consultancy with motivational and after-dinner speaking. In January 2011, he rejoined Preston North End, now managed by former Halifax player Phil Brown, on a part-time basis, and currently assists the England Under 17s.

WRAGG, Peter

Manager: 2 June 1993 to 13 February 1994
Born: Droylsden, 23 March 1946
Career: New Mills FC; Leek Town, manager 1976, dismissed 1977; Chorley manager; Stalybridge Celtic manager 1979; Hyde United manager June 1983; Macclesfield Town manager March 1986; **Halifax Town manager July 1993, dismissed 13 February 1994;** *Stalybridge Celtic manager March 1994 to 8 September 1996; Southport assistant manager; Hucknall Town assistant manager June 2003; Northwich Victoria assistant manager; Stalybridge Celtic assistant manager 28 September 2004, manager October 2004, resigned 8 January 2005.*

HALIFAX MANAGERS

When Halifax Town dropped into the Conference for the first time in May 1993, the board promised every effort would be made to make an instant return to the Football League. In the first instance, they elected to remain full-time, feeling this would give them an advantage, while in the second they sought an experienced manager, preferably one who knew the Conference well. To that end, the appointment of Peter Wragg seemed a logical one. After all, he had spent his entire footballing career in non-League circles, gaining a vast amount of knowledge as both player and manager. Sadly, things never worked out, and Wragg was, grossly unfairly, almost hounded out of office while his side failed to make an impact in the Conference.

Born in Droylsden, Wragg started out as a player with New Mills FC before becoming a favourite at Leek Town as a fast-raiding right-winger, only for his career to be effectively ended when he suffered a broken leg. He took over as manager at Leek in 1976 but was sacked after just one season and moved to Chorley. In 1979 Wragg became manager at Stalybridge Celtic and led them to the Cheshire County League title for the first and only time. As Hyde United manager, the side reached the Northern Premier League Cup Final, only to lose to South Liverpool.

Much sought after, Wragg began a lengthy spell as manager at Macclesfield Town in March 1986, giving them an unforgettable season in 1986–87 with an unprecedented treble. They clinched the Northern Premier League title with a 3–1 success at Hyde United in front of 1,800 spectators, defeated Marine in a two-legged Final to lift the President's Cup, as well as landing the League Challenge Cup. Macclesfield finished in mid-table in their first Conference season and eliminated two League teams, Carlisle and Rotherham, from the FA Cup. In 1989–90 the club reached the FA Trophy Final for the second time, only to lose 1–0 to Telford United as well as finishing fourth in the League. But Wragg failed to build on it, and following a struggle against relegation in 1992–93 he was sacked and replaced with former Manchester United midfielder Sammy McIlroy.

Having been alerted to his availability by former player and commercial manager Paul Kendall, the Halifax Town board offered Wragg the chance to return to club management, only then to outline the conditions he had to work under. There was little money and previous incumbent Mick Rathbone, who reverted to club physio, was to act as his assistant, a situation Wragg tolerated, though describing it as 'not ideal'. He also found himself taking over a side where several players were already looking for new clubs.

Wragg reckoned that if the club was to compete in the Conference, experienced players were needed to bolster the largely young squad he had inherited. Into the club came the likes of Elfyn Edwards, Colin Lambert and Steve Saunders, who made a scoring debut in the Final of the Yorkshire and Humberside Cup, the performances in the pre-season qualifying matches of that competition having raised expectations among the fans. The 4–2 victory over Bradford City in the Final on a balmy evening in September was a moment to savour, but by then, the purists were already pointing to the fact that Town had already played five matches in the Conference and were still seeking their first win. Four days after landing the Cup, Town then crashed 5–0 at Runcorn.

The longer the run went on, so the pressure on Wragg intensified, and even though the winless streak which had extended to seven Conference matches was broken in sensational fashion with a 6–2 victory at Woking, and followed up by the 6–0 defeat of Stafford Rangers, by then there was simply too much ground to make up on the leaders, and promotion was ruled out long before Christmas, especially as only one team went up in those pre-Conference Play-off days.

Despite failings in the League, Wragg did deliver one of the club's most enjoyable afternoons when West Bromwich Albion, a second-tier club, were beaten 2–1 in front of a live television audience. It was without doubt Town's biggest FA Cup victory since the defeat of Manchester City over 13 years earlier and the national spotlight fell on once more The Shay, while Wragg and the club rightly savoured the moment.

By then the Town boss had made the important capture of centre-back Craig Boardman, and was respected enough to later entice to The Shay Steve Burr, a prolific goalscorer at that level whom Wragg knew well from his time at Macclesfield. But with the side failing to impress in the Conference, question marks arose regarding Wragg's future and Town were lying 12th and had just negotiated a tricky tie at Spennymoor United in the FA Trophy to extend an unbeaten run to eight games when he was summoned to The Shay the very next day by chairman Jim Brown and told that his services were no longer required.

Wragg returned to Bower Fold the following month when Stalybridge were deep in relegation trouble, but with nine wins from 12 games steered them to safety. He left the club in September 1996 and later teamed up with Burr at several clubs, before having a third, brief, spell as manager of Stalybridge, finally resigning in January 2005. For several years Wragg has also been employed by events organisers Arena International.

BIRD, John Charles

Manager: 15 February 1994 to 20 March 1996
Born: Doncaster 9 June 1948
Career: Doncaster United; Doncaster Rovers March 1967; Preston North End 11 March 1971 (£6,000); Newcastle United 28 August 1975 (£60,000 plus a player); Hartlepool United July 1980, coach 1985, manager November 1986 to October 1988; York City manager October 1988 to 23 October 1991; Doncaster Rovers coach 1992; **Halifax Town manager 15 February 1994, resigned 20 March 1996.**

Following the dismissal of Peter Wragg, it was to the experienced manager John Bird that the Halifax Town board turned in the hope of transforming the side's fortunes. Ultimately, Bird failed to deliver, though his record in 1994–95, his one full season in charge, fared favourably against those of any Halifax Town manager, Town's seventh-place finish being their highest in any division since George Kirby took them to third place in the old Third Division 24 seasons earlier.

Bird had turned professional with his home-town club Doncaster Rovers in March 1967 and made his debut in a goalless draw at Workington the following November. He would emerge as a dependable centre-half, though initially he acted as understudy to Stuart Robertson and appeared in only eight matches of Rovers' 1968–69 Fourth Division title success. He became a regular in the side during 1970–71 but before the season was out had moved to Alan Ball Snr's Preston North End to assist their title run-in and appeared in seven matches as the Lilywhites finished as champions, one point ahead of Fulham. Bird missed only game over the course of the next two seasons, and later, under Bobby Charlton, he was made skipper.

It was his controversial sale to First Division Newcastle United in August 1975 which prompted Charlton's resignation, the deal seemingly done without his knowledge or consent. Bird joined a Magpies side destined to reach the Final of the League Cup, though his own earlier involvement in a tie with Blackburn Rovers meant he was Cup-tied and therefore forced to watch their defeat to Manchester City at Wembley from the sidelines.

Bird's time at St James's Park was dogged by injury and disappointment. He appeared in 26 games under Bill McGarry during 1977–78 but was unable to prevent Newcastle's relegation. He remained at the club for a further two years, taking his total to 87 League appearances and five goals before dropping into the Fourth Division with Hartlepool United.

He became mainstay of their defence for three seasons until injuries took hold and he retired from playing in the summer of 1986 with 444 League appearances under his belt and moved into coaching there under Billy Horner before stepping up to replace him as manager in November 1986. In 1987–88 Hartlepool remained on the fringes of the Play-offs but faded in the second half of the season to finish a lowly 16th. The following season, Bird saw his side win five of their opening six matches, then suddenly quit to take over at York City following the resignation of Bobby Saxton. The Minstermen were bottom of the Fourth Division, but Bird turned things around and led them to a respectable 11th-place finish. But over the next two seasons, the side languished in the bottom half of the table and after three years in charge he resigned.

Bird was coaching at Doncaster Rovers when he took up the opportunity to return to management with Halifax Town, though he did not get off to the best of starts, with FA Trophy defeat to Runcorn in his first game. He brought in new players Steve Prindiville and Alex Jones, as well as giving a trial to a raw Geoff Horsfield towards the end of his first season which saw Town finish 13th.

Bird drafted in the experienced George Mulhall to assist him, but in an attempt to achieve promotion from the Conference during 1994–95, the side was put together at much cost – players such as Dave Lancaster and Andy Kiwomya were reputedly on above average wages at the club – and when promotion became an impossibility, the harsh reality of the club's finances hit home and the club nearly went to the wall. Having survived, Bird was forced to operate on a stringent budget, turning to local players such as John Hendrick, Karl Cochrane and Glenn Lee, but all at the expense of success. When Town crashed 7–0 at Stevenage on 9 March 1996, then 6–1 at Macclesfield just two weeks later, Bird feared his time was up, and after discussions with chairman John Stockwell, he left the club.

Bird then turned his back on a career which had stretched 30 years but was far from unoccupied. An accomplished artist, he had opened his own art gallery while a Newcastle player which he successfully ran for eight years, holding several exhibitions, including two in Stavanger, Norway. Now, he devoted to it full-time, selling paintings all over the world, recipients including Prince Edward and the Duchess of Wessex, The Governor of Hong Kong, Lesley Garrett and Russell Crowe, and in 2006 Bird was one of 25 artists selected to take part in the 'Drawings from Turner' project. Based at his gallery in Bawtry, Doncaster, where he exhibits his works, he also busied himself supplying to other galleries nationwide.

CARROLL, John

Manager: 13 April 1996 to 15 February 1997
Born: Liverpool 6 August 1958
Career: Heswall BC; South Liverpool; Weymouth July 1986; Runcorn cs 1987, player-manager August 1991, manager 1992 to November 1995;
Halifax Town manager 13 April 1996 to 15 February 1997;
Gateshead manager November 1997 to cs 1998; Total Network Solutions assistant manager 2002 to 2004; Port Vale academy coach 2007.

John 'Cagsy' Carroll was the surprise, if not controversial, choice of the board as permanent successor to John Bird in April 1996. Having asked George Mulhall and Kieran O'Regan to hold the fort, the board introduced Carroll to the players just minutes after they had earned a 1–1 draw at Telford United, a move that was just as much as a shock to them as it was for the supporters.

Carroll's name was well known in the Conference, as was his style of route-one football which set the supporters against him from the start. Only by delivering on the pitch would he ever win over his fans, but the 6–0 defeat at Stevenage Borough on the opening day of the 1996–97 set a precedence for a season of struggle.

A defeat even worse than that had been the final nail in Carroll's coffin at his previous club

Runcorn, whom he had served as manager since August 1991. The 8–0 loss inflicted by Stevenage Borough on 25 November 1995 led to a parting of the ways, but Halifax Town boss John Stockwell must have thought the Carroll's experience would stand Town in good stead. In the end, his reign at The Shay lasted less than a year.

Born in Liverpool, Carroll made a name for himself in non-League circles as a tough, uncompromising centre-half, starting out with Heswall before joining South Liverpool, being a member of the side which won the FA Amateur trophy in 1984.

Two years later, Carroll moved south to play for Weymouth in the Southern League, spending one season there before returning to the north west and beginning his association with Runcorn, firstly as a player, then player-manager, having been appointed in August 1991. Carroll delivered success of sorts; FA Trophy finalists in 1993 and again the following year, though both matches were lost respectively to Wycombe Wanderers and Woking, and leading Runcorn a seventh-place finish in the Conference in 1993–94. That season saw Carroll retire from playing with 188 Conference appearances and fourteen goals to his name, only for the club then to struggle. A fire at their Canal Street home did not help matters – the side was forced to use neighbouring Witton Albion's ground at Wincham Park – though many reckoned his sacking following the mauling by Stevenage was a kneejerk reaction.

Carroll was not out of work long, answering John Stockwell's call for a new manager. Evidently, he ticked all the right boxes, but despite bringing with him Billy Rodaway as assistant, he found it almost impossible to win over the fans with his direct style of play and failure to get results. He signed enough players in an effort to improve things but it was all to no avail. The side struggled in the Conference, the 4–1 home defeat at the hands of Bishop Auckland in the FA Cup was a disaster, as was the extra-time defeat to Harrogate Railway in the County Cup. When Town crashed at Gloucester City in the FA Trophy, the pressure mounted on Carroll. Seven days later, following a topsy-turvy affair with Bath City at The Shay which saw the visitors ultimately coming out on top 5–4, the board held crisis talks with Carroll, and a mutual agreement was reached, upon which he and Rodaway both left the club.

The John Carroll era was one not looked on with much affection by the fans. But were there any success? Well, the side did lift the West Riding Senior Cup, and Carroll could point to his signings of Mick Norbury, the final day saviour, and Geoff Horsfield and Kevin Hulme, two players who would play a key part in Town's Conference-winning season of 1997–98.

Carroll took over at Gateshead in November 1997 and came up against the Shaymen the following month when they were on the way to the Conference title., denying them victory in a 2–2 draw at the International Stadium on Boxing Day. But he left the club at the end of his first season and later resurfaced at Total Network Solutions as assistant to Ken McKenna before leaving in June 2004. Three years later Carroll was an academy coach at Port Vale.

MULHALL, George

Manager: 27 June 1972 to 18 September 1974, caretaker manager 20 March 1996 to 13 April 1996, manager 17 February 1997 to 4 August 1998.

Born: Falkirk, 8 May 1936

Career: Denny YMCA; Kilsyth Rangers; Aberdeen May 1953; Sunderland September 1962 (£23,000); Cape Town City (SAf) player-coach June 1969; Greenock Morton September 1971; **Halifax Town trainer-coach 18 October 1971, manager 27 June 1972, resigned 18 September 1974;** *Bolton Wanderers assistant manager 18 October 1974; Bradford City manager November 1978 to March 1981; Bolton Wanderers assistant manager March 1981, manager June 1981 to June 1982; Ipswich*

Town scout; Tranmere Rovers assistant manager July 1985 to February 1987; Huddersfield Town chief scout and youth development officer 1990, assistant manager 1992; **Halifax Town youth coach June 1994, assistant manager, caretaker manager 20 March 1996 to 13 April 1996, manager 17 February 1997, director of football 4 August 1998.**

It is arguable which was George Mulhall's greater achievement in his two spells as Halifax Town manager; keeping the club in the old Third Division in the mid-1970s with little or no money, or turning round the club's fortunes by achieving promotion from the Conference a year after narrowly avoiding relegation? But what isn't in dispute is the fact that Mulhall delivered for Halifax Town their only League title and for that reason alone he has become the most revered of all the club's managers. Though of course, nobody could have foreseen the significance of Mulhall's appointment as coach by Ray Henderson back in October 1971, his first such position in England after a lengthy career in both Scotland and England as a dashing winger, good enough to win three Scotland caps.

With two of his elder brothers having forged professional careers with Falkirk and Albion Rovers, George Mulhall's own professional career took off with Aberdeen, signing for the club on his 17th birthday, though he had to wait almost six years to establish himself on the left wing due to the form of Jackie Hather. But he made an immediate impact and his belated meteoric rise continued with selection for the Scotland national side against Northern Ireland in Belfast on 3 October 1959. Mulhall lined up alongside Dave Mackay, John White, Ian St John and Denis Law and made a dream debut, scoring the last goal of a 4–0 win. He helped the Dons to runners-up spot behind Rangers in 1955–56, and made 110 League appearances and scored 30 goals during his time at Pittodrie.

By the time he won his second cap, Mulhall had moved to Second Division Sunderland, where he set a record of 125 consecutive League appearances, making a total of 253 and scoring 66 goals. Initially, he supplied the ammunition for lethal centre-forward Brian Clough, and in 1963–64 he helped Sunderland clinch promotion back to the First Division after an absence of six years. That season was also memorable for two epic FA Cup clashes with Manchester United in which Mulhall starred, only for his side to lose 5–1 in a third meeting. But Mulhall would have his day against United. On the final day of the 1967–68 season, his headed goal denied the Reds the League title and handed it to their bitter rivals Manchester City.

His form with Sunderland earned Mulhall a recall to the Scotland side; he appeared in a 5–1 victory over Northern Ireland, and won his last cap against the same side a year later, then lost his place to Rangers' Davie Wilson. But his consistency and durability were important factors in Sunderland managing to maintain their place in the top flight until tired legs gave way, and Mulhall left the club in 1969. He retreated to South Africa where, in less demanding surroundings, he became player-manager of Durban City, being top scorer in the League and winning a Cup medal. He then appeared for Greenock Morton before pursuing his coaching career following a call from Halifax Town manager Ray Henderson.

Henderson was sacked after just one season in charge at The Shay, but in turn the board promoted Mulhall to manager and against the odds he kept the club in the third tier of English football. The club made headlines in 1972–73 by stopping up on goal average by winning their last four matches, and having made some astute signings, such as centre-forward Dave Gwyther, David Ford, David Pugh and winger Alan Jones, the club finished ninth the following season. The Shaymen had made a modest start to the 1974–75 campaign, but even so Mulhall's resignation following a 3–1 home defeat to Chesterfield came out of the blue. 'Halifax Town is not for me,' he would say, but keen to stay in football he duly joined Ian Greaves as assistant at Bolton Wanderers a month later, helping guide the Trotters to the First Division in 1977–78.

Bradford City tempted him away from Burnden Park in November 1978, and he was unlucky to see his side miss out on promotion from the Fourth Division in his second season in charge. He tamed the wayward Bobby Campbell, whose club record 143 goals included the winner in the first leg of a League Cup tie against League champions Liverpool in August 1980 and by the time Mulhall left the club in March 1981 he had built the nucleus of a side which Roy McFarland would take to promotion in 1981–82.

Mulhall returned to Bolton to assist Stan Anderson, then briefly took over as manager. In July 1985 he was Frank Worthington's right-hand man at Tranmere Rovers before being appointed Huddersfield Town youth development officer. He arrived at The Shay under John Bird in June 1994 to run the youth team there while also assisting Bird as his assistant. When Bird left the club in March 1996, chairman John Stockwell approached Mulhall and Kieran O'Regan to look after the team and, though O'Regan fancied the job, the board made the surprising appointment of John Carroll with two matches of the season to go.

Mulhall reverted to his role as youth-team manager but was called upon again in February 1997 when Carroll left the club. Initially appointed on a caretaker basis, Town won their next three matches, but when their League position looked ever more worrying, Stockwell announced, 'Keep us in the Conference and the job's yours.' Mulhall, with trusted O'Regan at his side, managed to do just that, though it was mightily close with survival assured only with last day victory over Stevenage Borough.

Mulhall's decision to sell top scorer and final-day hat-trick hero Mick Norbury nevertheless astounded the fans, but the canny Scot knew about Geoff Horsfield's potential and assembled possibly the finest ever Halifax Town team with the signings of the likes of Andy Thackeray, Mark Bradshaw and Jamie Murphy, as well as the inspirational centre-back Peter Jackson. Jamie Paterson returned to the fold a better player than when he left, and with marauding midfielder Kevin Hulme acting as skipper, Mulhall's side produced a brand of free-flowing exciting football the supporters hadn't seen in years. He brought the experienced Brian Kilcline out of enforced retirement when Jackson left to take over at Huddersfield, and his side cantered to the Conference title, clinching it with a 2–0 win at Kidderminster Harriers with three games still to play.

Mulhall was by then 62 years old, but he had claimed he wanted to manage in the Football League, and indeed seemed all set to do so having taken his team through a series of friendlies. But four days before the season's opener at Peterborough, he sensationally quit the post, though his reasons for doing so have never been publically declared.

Mulhall was lined up to become director of football at the club 12 months hence, and would in the mean time groom O'Regan as his successor, but there were suggestions that the timing of his decision to step down was to help save Kieran O'Regan's job, with Peter Butler's arrival at the club being viewed as a threat. Other reports stated he felt he needed a rest. Either way, it was a most unsatisfactory end to a marvellous career, one which had left Mulhall achieving cult-like status at The Shay. On 27 July 1999 Halifax Town beat Peter Reid's Sunderland 1–0 in what was a testimonial match for George Mulhall, who is still an occasional visitor to The Shay in retirement.

O'REGAN, Kieran Michael
Manager: 4 August 1998 to 6 April 1999

Kieran O'Regan's transition from player and assistant to Halifax Town manager was always on the cards. The timing and manner of it, however, came 12 months earlier than planned, and as such O'Regan took over without being fully prepared for what lay ahead. Initially set to act as George Mulhall's right hand man for 12 months, the controversial signing of Peter Butler, brother-in-law to chairman Jim Brown, set off a chain of events that led to much political infighting. Out of the blue, Mulhall stepped down leaving O'Regan in charge of the team – with the new football season just four days away.

The new Town boss promoted Andy May, who had arrived as reserve coach, as his assistant, and initially he benefitted from the tide of euphoria which had swept the club to the Conference title. In baking heat, Town got off to the best of starts with a 2–0 victory at Peterborough United and the side suffered only one defeat from their opening seven League games, while also accounting for third-tier Wrexham in the Worthington Cup. But soon questions were being asked of O'Regan, among which were the dilemmas of how to replace top striker Geoff Horsfield, sold to Fulham in October, and of whether to select himself or not. In the first instance, O'Regan threw into the side the Welsh striker Marc Williams, but he was a different type of player and certainly no long-term successor. In the second, as he was clearly a midfield player of class, the supporters were disappointed his name was not the first name on the team sheet more often than it was. Perhaps, though, this management lark brought with it too many pressures to consider playing himself.

Following Horsfield's departure, Town did remarkably well, however, going top of the division following a stormy encounter with Chester City and staying there for nearly three weeks. But when the side lost form O'Regan struggled to turn things round. Seeing his side go seven games without a win through December and January, Town slipped to ninth in the table, and the Play-off places, hitherto Town's realistic hope, became anything but certain, and soon a faction of supporters began to make their voices heard. The sterile goalless draw with Rochdale on Easter Monday was particularly frustrating, though few could have seen that O'Regan would be shown the door just 24 hours later, particularly as he had recently been allowed to bring in striker Justin Jackson.

His sacking brought with it an angry backlash from his supporters, and while Jim Brown cited O'Regan's record of only four wins from the last 19 and a poor disciplinary record as a major reason for the board's actions, most supporters reckoned there was a hidden agenda. To his credit, O'Regan remained silent on the issue and kept involved in the game as an articulate summariser covering Huddersfield Town's matches for Radio Leeds.

WORTHINGTON, David

Manager: 7 April 1999 to May 1999
Born: Halifax, 28 March 1945
Career: **Halifax Town juniors, professional 26 April 1962;** *Barrow 20 July 1964; Grimsby Town June 1966;* **Halifax Town on loan 25 October 1973;** *Southend United 1 December 1973; Cambridge City player-manager July 1976; Bradley Rangers; Halifax Athletic; Boston United 1980 to 1982;* **Halifax Town commercial manager 1995, manager 7 April 1999 to cs 1999, chief scout August 1999, caretaker assistant manager 4 March 2002 to cs 2002;** *Boston United scout; Bolton Wanderers scout 2003.*

Dave Worthington represented Halifax Town in just about every conceivable capacity: player, commercial manager, scout and, for a few short weeks to the end of the 1998–99, manager, where he was given the task of trying to steer the side back into the Play-offs. Ultimately he failed, but he went mightily close. Worthington was Halifax born and came from a footballing family. His father Eric had represented Town during the war, and his two brothers also carved out lengthy careers. Frank Worthington, indeed went on to win eight England caps and forge out a career that took in 11 League clubs, most notably Huddersfield Town, Leicester City and Bolton Wanderers, before assisting John McGrath during Town's relegation season of 1992–93 and turning out for the reserves. Bob Worthington followed Dave into the Halifax Town first team before taking in a career that took in a number of clubs, but best remembered for his lengthy time at Notts County.

Dave was the first to take up a career in football, signing professional forms under Don McEvoy in April 1962, the same month that he made his League debut in a 2–0 home defeat by Coventry City. An inside-forward, he went on to score nine goals from 37 League appearances before following McEvoy to Barrow in July 1964, but his time there was disappointing, with the club being forced to apply for re-election at the end of his first season.

Worthington had his best spell with Grimsby Town, whom he joined in June 1966. Converted successfully to full-back, he was made skipper under Jimmy McGuigan and set a then club record of 224 consecutive appearances (beaten later by Joe Waters), helping the Mariners to the Fourth Division Championship in 1971–72.

Worthington returned for a loan spell at Halifax in October 1973 before making a permanent move to Southend United, and while he was a member of the side which reached the fifth round of the FA Cup in 1975–76 it was a season which also them relegated to the Fourth Division. Released by the club, Worthington took over as player-manager at Cambridge City, a side that had themselves just been relegated from the Southern League Premier Division. He later returned to Halifax and played locally while helping run the family removal business.

In 1995 Worthington was appointed as commercial manager, a position he held for three years, but though a member of the staff he sat out the club's Civic reception following promotion claiming he had never been invited. However, bridges were mended, and in the wake of Kieran O'Regan's sacking in April 1999, he was approached by chairman Jim Brown to oversee the first team until the end of the season. He came in and told the players to put what had gone on behind then set about getting the team back on track. At the time, the Shaymen were lying 11th and three points off the Play-off places, and though Worthington suffered a 4–0 defeat at leaders Cambridge United in his first game in charge, a four-match unbeaten run put them back in contention. But hopes all but vanished with the unexpected defeat to bottom club Scarborough at The Shay in their penultimate match and Worthington found himself taking his side into the last game at Exeter City relying on victory for the Shaymen there and defeat for Swansea City in their game if Town were to make the Play-offs via the back door. In the event, Town lost and Worthington stepped aside to make way for Mark Lillis.

Worthington continued to serve the club as chief scout, stepping in to assist Neil Redfearn in March 2002 following Alan Little's hospitalisation with 10 games remaining of the relegation season, and left the club when it went into administration. He was working for Boston United when he took up the opportunity of scouting abroad for Bolton Wanderers, then managed by Sam Allardyce. Dave Worthington's son Gary also became a professional footballer and, like his father, had two spells with Halifax Town.

LILLIS, Mark Anthony

Manager: 2 June 1999 to 11 September 2000
Born: Manchester, 17 January 1960
Career: Manchester City juniors; Huddersfield Town apprentice 1974, professional 7 July 1977; Manchester City 7 August 1985 (£132,500); Derby County August 1986 (£100,000 plus a player); Aston Villa September 1987 (£130,000); Scunthorpe United September 1989 (£40,000); Stockport County September 1991; Witton Albion August 1992; Macclesfield Town assistant manager cs 1993; Scunthorpe United assistant manager 1996; **Halifax Town manager 2 June 1999, dismissed 11 September 2000;**

Aston Villa scout; Derby County assistant manager ; Northern Ireland coach 2003; Stockport County assistant manager 15 October 2003 to 18 December 2004; Morecambe assistant manager 17 November 2005.

Mark Lillis appeared much sought after by the Town board as the 1998–99 season came to a close. His name had been being linked to the vacant managerial position while he was still involved with Scunthorpe United, who rounded off their campaign with Play-off success at Wembley that May. The following month, Lillis was unveiled as the new Town boss, but having stated how had always wanted to prove himself as a manager, he would find the going tough at The Shay and the club was on a downward spiral by the time he was dismissed in September 2000.

Lillis had been a familiar foe at The Shay as a bustling midfielder-cum-striker in the colours of Scunthorpe, Macclesfield Town and Huddersfield Town, his first club. Manchester born, he joined the Terriers as an apprentice before signing professional forms in July 1977 and made his League debut at Newport County in October 1978 under Mick Buxton. Out of the side when Huddersfield won the Fourth Division Championship in 1979–80, Lillis made up for it three seasons later when, as skipper, he was ever-present and finished top scorer as the side won promotion to the Second Division.

After making 242 first-team appearances for the Terriers and scoring 63 goals, Lillis landed himself his dream move back to Manchester City, his boyhood idols, and became a crowd favourite. He ended his first season as top scorer, his 15 goals including two in the Final of the inaugural Full Members' Cup at Wembley, which City lost 5–4 to Chelsea. Surprisingly sold by Billy McNeill to Derby County in August 1986, a knee injury restricted his appearances, though he recovered to play his part in the Rams' Second Division title success. The following year, Lillis also helped Aston Villa's regain top-flight status under Graham Taylor, finishing as runners-up to Millwall.

But injuries once again took their toll, and Lillis dropped down to the Fourth Division with Scunthorpe United before ending his playing days with Stockport County and at Conference sides Witton Albion and Macclesfield Town, where he became assistant to Sammy McIlroy and became a jack-of-all-trades, even filling in as goalkeeper. Macclesfield clinched the Conference title in 1994–95 but were denied promotion on ground unsuitability.

Lillis joined up with former boss Mick Buxton at Scunthorpe, and continued in his role as assistant manager when Brian Laws came in following Buxton's dismissal in February 1997. Lillis developed a fine reputation as a coach before chancing his luck in his own right as manager at The Shay. He joined a club that for once was full of expectation, and with his blessing, the club forked out a record £150,000 on Scarborough striker Chris Tate and signed up the teenage twins Matthew and Chris Clarke from Wolverhampton Wanderers. Seemingly happy to have Peter Butler as his assistant Lillis initially did quite well, seeing his side maintain Play-off ambitions during the first half of the season, that despite Tate returning to Scarborough after failing to fire the goals he had been bought for.

Lillis pinned his hopes on the likes of Robbie Painter and Lee Potter until the signing of Steve Kerrigan, though his insistence of playing fans' favourite Jamie Paterson on the right flank puzzled many, especially as the player was naturally left-footed. Town faded badly during the second half of the 1999–2000 season, a run of form which did not fuel much hope for better things the following term. Fears were justified, and without a win from their opening six League matches, Lillis paid the price for failure and was sacked two days after a heavy defeat at Mansfield Town had left the side bottom of the table.

After a scouting role at Aston Villa, Lillis returned to coaching as assistant to John Gregory at Derby County, his time there including a spell as caretaker boss when Gregory was suspended. At the same time, Lillis teamed up once again with Sammy McIlroy, who was manager of the Northern Ireland international side squad before the pair took over the reins at Stockport County in October 2003. McIlroy's decision to switch to Morecambe in October 2004 left Lillis in temporary charge at Edgeley Park until the arrival as manager of Chris Turner and in November 2005 he rejoined McIlroy as assistant at Morecambe when Jim Harvey was taken ill, helping transform the club's fortunes as they clinched promotion from the Blue Square Premier following a 2–1 win over Exeter City in the Play-off Final in May 2007.

BUTLER, Peter James and PARKS, Anthony
Joint caretaker managers: 11 September 2000 to 2 October 2000

PETER BUTLER
Born: Halifax, 27 August 1966
Career: Boothtown Juniors; Huddersfield Town apprentice, professional 21 August 1984; Bury 8 July 1986; Cambridge United loan 24 January 1986; Bury 8 July 1986; Cambridge United 10 December 1986; Southend United 12 February 1988 (£75,000); Huddersfield Town on loan 24 March 1992; West Ham United 12 August 1992 (£125,000); Notts County 4 October 1994 (£350,000); Grimsby Town on loan 30 January 1996; West Bromwich Albion on loan 28 March 1996, signed 5 August 1996 (£175,000); **Halifax Town player-coach 1 August 1998, assistant manager June 1999, joint caretaker manager 11 September 2000, dismissed 3 October 2000;** *Sorrento (Aus) player coach 2000; Sabah FA (Malaysia) 2003 to May 2004; Singapore Armed Forces head coach; Persiba Balikpapan (Indonesia); Kelantan FC (West Malaysia) coach; Yangon United FC head coach 2009; BEC Tero Sasana FC head coach September 2010.*

TONY PARKS
Born: Hackney, 26 January 1963
Career: Tottenham Hotspur apprentice, professional 22 September 1980; Oxford United on loan 1 October 1986; Gillingham on loan 1 September 1987; Brentford 24 August 1988 (£60,000); Fulham 27 February 1991; West Ham United 15 August 1991; Stoke City 21 August 1992; Falkirk 14 October 1992; Blackpool 6 September 1996; Burnley 13 August 1997; Doncaster Rovers on loan 13 February 1998; Scarborough 26 February 1999; **Halifax Town player coach cs 1999, joint caretaker manager 11 September 2000, assistant player-manager 2 October 2000, joint caretaker manager 29 August 2001, left club 1 November 2001;** *Crewe Alexandra coach; Football Association coach; Tottenham Hotspur coach November 2008.*

When Mark Lillis was sacked, the temporary managerial appointments of Peter Butler and Tony Parks would have been in ordinary circumstances a logical one. They were, after all, the most experienced professionals on the club's books. Butler was back playing for his home-town club, a former pupil of Halifax Catholic High School and member of Boothtown junior football team, a person self-driven and with the belief that he was going to make it as a professional footballer. That he managed it is testament to his dedication. But never has anyone's arrival at the club sparked off a bigger furore than that of Butler when he joined Halifax Town as player-coach in August 1998, and his refusal to appear on the club's pre-season photo-call with the Conference-winning trophy displayed a touch of arrogance which the fans resented. That despite his performances on the pitch, showing the same battling qualities as a 32-year-old as he did 14 years earlier with Huddersfield Town, his first club. He made his debut as substitute in the season's opening day defeat by Oxford United on 25 August 1984, but though he failed to establish himself at Leeds Road club he still managed to carve out a lengthy playing career. His most successful stints were at Southend United, whom he helped out of the Fourth Division in 1989–90, a year after relegation, and with West Ham, being a key member of the side which finished runners-up in the First Division in 1992–93 and playing in the side's first Premier League campaign under Harry Redknapp.

Defying the medical experts who advised him to retire with a troublesome knee, Butler went on to serve Notts County and West Bromwich Albion before joining Halifax Town in a coaching capacity, though who it was who actually signed him was a matter of some conjecture. Was it then manager George Mulhall, or his brother-in-law Jim Brown, as chairman Chris Holland claimed, who had returned to the board and was soon to take over at the helm once more? Either way, his relationship with Kieran O'Regan was never a smooth one, though it never affected his contribution on the pitch, if one overlooks his sending off on his debut in a Worthington Cup tie at Wrexham.

While Butler never won any major honours during his playing career, the same could not be said of Tony Parks. In fact, he was instrumental in Tottenham Hotspur's 1984 UEFA Cup success, saving Arnor Gudjohnsen's kick in the penalty shoot-out with Anderlecht after the two-legged Final had ended 2–2. In retrospect, however, while only 21 years old, that was the peak of his career.

Parks learnt his craft on Hackney marshes, signing for Spurs after serving his apprenticeship. But during six years at White Hart Lane, he found himself for the most part playing second fiddle to Ray Clemence. But it was after impressing during the latter half of the 1983–84 season that Parks retained his place in the side for both legs of the UEFA Cup Final. Parks later sought regular first-team football at Brentford, before drifting around Fulham, West Ham United and Stoke City before stopping off at Doncaster Rovers after a successful lengthy spell with Falkirk where he helped them win the Scottish First Division title in 1993–94.

Parks was signed as goalkeeping coach in May 1999, though at a time when there was no first-choice 'keeper he was called upon to play in both games of Town's Worthington Cup ties with West Bromwich Albion and occasionally thereafter.

When Lillis was sacked with the side bottom of the table, chairman Bob Walker asked Peter Butler and Tony Parks to man the fort while a successor was sought, and they took charge of four games, gaining four points from a victory at Torquay United and draw at home to Shrewsbury Town in the last two of those to close the gap on a cluster of clubs above them to just one point. A demonstration against Butler following the Shrewsbury game did not deter him from throwing his hat into the ring as manager, but given his unpopularity among the supporters this may just have been devilment on his behalf. If he was serious, it was his final stand, for Paul Bracewell's arrival signalled the end of Butler's association with the club once he had been told he did not figure in the new manager's set up. Butler left claiming, 'I have no regrets about anything that has happened while I have been here and would not change a thing I leave with my pride and dignity intact.'

The irony was that days before Bracewell's arrival, it was Parks who had stated he was worried about his own future, yet he was to remain at the club a further 13 months, even taking up the reins once more jointly with Neil Redfearn in August 2001 following Bracewell's own departure. Yet, once Alan Little had been appointed manager in October 2001, Parks was paid up and left the club at the beginning of the following month and went on to hold various coaching capacities before returning to his spiritual home when he was appointed goalkeeping coach by Tottenham manager Harry Redknapp in November 2008.

As for Butler, his future lay on the other side of the world taking up the role of player-coach at Australian side Sorrento before moving to the Far East where he has held other coaching positions with several clubs. He currently lives in Bali.

BRACEWELL, Paul William

Manager: 2 October 2000 to 29 August 2001
Born: Heswall, 19 July 1962
Career: Stoke City apprentice, professional 6 February 1980; Sunderland 1 July 1983 (£250,000); Everton 25 May 1984 (£425,000); Sunderland 23 August 1989 (£250,000); Newcastle United 16 June 1992 (£250,000); Sunderland player/assistant manager 23 May 1995 (£100,000); Fulham 10 October 1997 (£75,000), player coach, manager 7 May 1999, dismissed 30 March 2000; **Halifax Town manager 2 October 2000, resigned 29 August 2001**; England FA coach.

Paul Bracewell enjoyed the high life during his time as a player with Everton and England, and as a manager at Fulham but, for all that he achieved, he could not translate his experience into success with Halifax Town, his appointment as manager in October 2000 proving to be a costly one and leading many supporters to believe it was one from which the club never recovered.

To assist him at The Shay, Bracewell turned to Richie Barker, his former mentor at Stoke City, where he had begun his career. A midfield player who combined combative qualities with good vision and outstanding passing abilities, Bracewell made his debut in the First Division aged 18 in March 1981 and won 12 England Under-21 caps. He then spent one season with Sunderland before joining Everton, where he achieved unbridled success, winning a League Championships in his first season, as well as being instrumental in Everton's 3–1 European Cup-Winners' Cup Final victory over Rapid Vienna. Seeking an unprecedented treble, Bracewell, however, was on the losing side in the FA Cup Final to Manchester United, the first of four FA Cup Final defeats he would experience.

Everton were runners-up to Liverpool in both League and FA Cup in 1985–86 before injuries began to take their toll on Bracewell. He missed the whole of the next two seasons and was denied the opportunity to add to his three full England caps, having made his international debut in a pre-World Cup tour of Mexico and USA against West Germany on 12 June 1985 when he came on as a 71st-minute substitute for Bryan Robson.

Bracewell returned to action in 1988–89 and was a substitute in the second all-Mersey FA Cup Final which Liverpool won 3–2 in extra-time. He then returned to Second Division Sunderland, immediately helping them reach the Play-off Final which they lost 1–0 to Swindon Town, though uniquely, Sunderland were still promoted when Swindon's promotion was withdrawn due to financial irregularities. This gave Bracewell the chance of playing top flight football once again, only for him to suffer relegation as well being a losing FA Cup finalist for a third time.

In August 1992 Bracewell joined Kevin Keegan's Newcastle United, who were beginning their roller-coaster ride, and he made 25 League appearances during their Championship-winning campaign which saw them take their place in the Premier League. After a further season in which Newcastle finished third, Bracewell went back to Sunderland for a third spell as assistant to Peter Reid, helping them win the Division One title in 1995–96.

In September 1997, Bracewell took a similar role with ambitious Division Two club Fulham, working under head coach Ray Wilkins and director of football Kevin Keegan. When Wilkins was dismissed at the end of the season, Keegan took sole charge of the first team and kept Bracewell as his assistant. When Keegan left to concentrate on his role as England team coach in May 1999, Bracewell succeeded him, but despite Fulham managing to compete in the top half of Division One throughout the campaign he was dismissed on 30 March 2000 in favour of the more experienced Jean Tigana.

Looking for a permanent successor to Mark Lillis, the Halifax Town board were impressed enough by Bracewell's willingness to travel to watch the side in action at Torquay United and unveiled him as manager on 2 October 2000. Bracewell's first act was to show the door to unpopular coach Peter Butler before bringing in Barker, and achieved his immediate objective of retaining the club's League status, having signed the much-travelled Neil Redfearn to help the cause. Though in an otherwise depressing season, people would not forget the FA Cup defeat to non-League Gateshead in a hurry.

Bracewell almost broke the bank with his summer signings of Paul Harsley, Andy Woodward and the injury-prone Dominic Ludden, and though the side won their opening match at Lincoln City, Bracewell would not taste victory again. Following the 2–0 home reversal to Oxford United on 27 August 2001, Bracewell handed in his resignation two days later.

Not many mourned his leaving for, while the purists supporters looked back on his dismal record of just 11 wins from 41 games, even some of the players had grown tired of Bracewell's ideology of sports science and his insistence that they refuel after a match with isotonic drinks and pasta, while others felt betrayed by a man they had signed for just a month earlier. Bracewell picked up his career by joining the England youth set up and currently runs a five-a-side centre in Consett.

LITTLE, Alan

Manager: 12 October 2001 to 12 April 2002
Born: Horden, 5 May 1955
Career: Horden Schools; Durham County Boys; Aston Villa apprentice June 1971, professional January 1973; Southend United 20 December 1974 (£10,000); Barnsley 9 August 1977 (£6,000); Doncaster Rovers 5 December 1979 (£30,000); Torquay United October 1982; Halifax Town 23 November 1983; Hartlepool United July 1985, retired May 1986, coach; York City assistant manager and coach, manager March 1993, dismissed 15 March 1999; Southend United manager 2 April 1999, dismissed 28 September 2000; Hull City scout; **Halifax Town manager 12 October 2001 to 12 April 2002.**

Save for Willie Watson, who initially acted as player-manager before trying his hand at a second stint with the club eight years after leaving, and Dave Worthington, who acted in a caretaker capacity, Alan Little became the first former Town player to take over as manager when he returned to The Shay in October 2001. But his time at the club was shorter than he had wished for, illness forcing him to take time off before the board acted to replace him with Neil Redfearn in April 2002. Just how Little might have changed things around at Halifax will never be known, though there was a feeling his impact would have been negligible given his return of only two wins from 24 League games, a record which contributed to Town's relegation to the Conference at the end of that season.

Alan Little's first association with the club had begun in November 1983, signed by Mickey Bullock on a free transfer from Torquay United after the Gulls had fended off Town's approach the previous summer. But Little's two seasons with the Shaymen were as disappointing as his tenure as a manager would be, both ending with re-election applications. Little had, however, enjoyed success on his travels before arriving at The Shay, despite living in the shadow of his older brother Brian, whom he followed to Aston Villa, signing apprentice forms before turning professional in January 1973. Both appeared for Villa when the side defeated Liverpool to win the FA Youth Cup in 1972, but while Brian, two years his senior, went on to have an illustrious career at Villa and win two England caps, Alan mustered just three League appearances with the club.

He moved to Third Division Southend United in December 1974 and became a regular in the side, though relegation in 1975–76 was tempered only by a magnificent FA Cup run when the Shrimpers reached the fifth round before bowing out to Derby County. Little enjoyed success, however, at Barnsley in 1978–79 under Allan Clarke, making 40 League appearances and scoring seven goals in the Tykes' Fourth Division promotion campaign.

Little moved to Doncaster Rovers, who paid a club-record £25,000 for his services, and in 1980–81 featured in their Fourth Division promotion success under Billy Bremner. In 1981–82 he was named Rovers' Player of the Year award before moving to Torquay United in a deal which saw Clive Wigginton move in the opposite direction and was made captain.

Little, a tough-tackling midfield player, was appointed skipper by Mickey Bullock, too, after his move to The Shay and went on to make 68 League appearances and score six goals, then joined Hartlepool United in July 1985 for one last season before retiring and moving into coaching under manager John Bird. When Bird left for York City in October 1988, Little went with him as his assistant and kept his position when John Ward replaced Bird in October 1991. York were going well during 1992–93 when Ward left to take over at Bristol Rovers that March, but Little took over and the Minstermen went on to finish fourth, gaining promotion via the Play-offs by beating Crewe Alexandra on penalties at Wembley.

The following season, York almost repeated the feat but were beaten in the Division Two Play-off semi-finals by Stockport County, but Little did go on to deliver an unforgettable aggregate victory over Manchester United in the 1995–96 League Cup, and against Everton in 1996. However, York were battling against relegation in March 1999 when Little was sacked.

In April 1999, Little returned to manager his former club Southend United in succession to Alvin Martin and helped them avoid the drop into the Conference. A serious financial crisis saw Little slash the wage bill, yet having recovered from a poor start at the beginning of the 2000–01 season and seen his side rise to 10th in Division Three, Little was sacked towards the end of September.

Alan Little was scouting for his brother Brian when he answered Halifax Town chairman Bob Walker's call on 13 October 2001, faced with the difficult task of keeping them in the League, but his managerial tenure was an unhappy one. The one bright spot was the signing of combative midfielder Steve Bushell, but results failed to improve and there was the uneasiness following an alleged rift with player-coach Neil Redfearn. Then suddenly, Little's rein came to an abrupt when he was forced into hospital on 4 March 2001 with a ruptured appendix. Little recuperated at home but remained as Halifax Town manager in name only until officially being dismissed on 12 April 2002 with relegation to the Conference having already been confirmed. He left saying, 'I feel let down and disappointed but the rest of the people at the club also have to take responsibility. I am the easy one to blame [for relegation] at the moment.'

Once recovered, Little took up employment in Lincoln as a front-line manager for a parcel delivery firm.

REDFEARN, Neil

Joint caretaker manager: 29 August 2001 to 12 October 2001, manager 4 March 2002 to 25 April 2002.
Born: Dewsbury, 20 June 1965
Career: Nottingham Forest juniors; Bolton Wanderers 23 June 1982; Lincoln City 23 March 1984 (£8,500); Doncaster Rovers 22 August 1986 (£17,500); Crystal Palace 31 July 1987 (£100,000); Watford 21

November 1988 ((£150,000); Oldham Athletic 12 January 1990 (£150,000); Barnsley 5 September 1991 (£150,000); Charlton Athletic 1 July 1998 (£1,000,000); Bradford City 31 July 1999 (£250,000); Wigan Athletic 17 March 2000 (£112,500); **Halifax Town player-coach 16 March 2001, joint caretaker manager 29 August 2001 to 12 October 2001, manager 4 March 2002 to 25 April 2002**; *Boston United s 2002, assistant manager March 2004; Rochdale 18 March 2004; Scarborough assistant player-manager 16 June 2004, manager October 2005; Bradford Park Avenue; Stocksbridge Park Steels March 2007; Northwich Victoria manager 19 June 2007 to 17 September 2007; Frickley Athletic September 2007; Bridlington Town 5 November 2007; York City youth team coach February 2008; Emley July 2008; Salford City October 2008; York City caretaker manager November 2008, assistant manager; Leeds United Academy coach 1 January 2009.*

Neil Redfearn enjoyed a long and varied football career, making a total of 790 League appearances and scoring 157 goals with 11 clubs. He arrived at The Shay in March 2001 28 years after his father Brian, a left-winger, had last played for the club, and had two shots as manager during 2001–02. Neil Redfearn courted controversy in his time with Halifax and come the close of the season was at the helm when the side was relegated to the Conference for a second time. He, of course, could never have foreseen any of that when he began his career playing in Nottingham Forests' youth team. He sought first-team football at Bolton Wanderers, making his League debut in a 1–1 draw at Rotherham United on 19 February 1983 and earned a reputation as a bustling goalscoring midfielder in the colours of Lincoln City and Doncaster Rovers. In 1987 he joined Crystal Palace and was employed by manager Steve Coppell to supply crosses for Ian Wright and Mark Bright, but he became unsettled and after asking for a transfer, moved to Second Division Watford, helping them reach the Play-offs in his first season, only to lose on the away goals rule to Blackburn Rovers in the semi-finals, despite scoring.

After a move to Oldham Athletic in January 1990, Redfearn wrote himself into Latics' folklore by scoring an injury-time penalty for a 3–2 win (after being two goals down) against Sheffield Wednesday in May 1991 that returned them to the top flight after a gap of 68 years. But he never played in the top flight with Oldham, reserving that honour for Barnsley, with whom he probably had his best years. In his seven seasons at Oakwell, he hardly missed a single game and was named club captain and in 1996–97 scored 17 goals as the Tykes won promotion to the Premier League for the first time in the club's history. Redfearn missed only one game top-scored with 10 League goals in the 1997–98 season, though it was not enough to save them from relegation after just one season.

Redfearn made 338 first-team appearances and scored 84 goals for Barnsley and his performances earned him a club record £1 million move to Charlton Athletic in July 1998, though his one season at The Valley also ended in relegation from the Premiership.

Redfearn then moved to Bradford City, though nine months later he was on the move again, joining Wigan Athletic, his 10th club, but fell out of favour with manager Bruce Rioch and was placed on the transfer list.

Nevertheless, with his background, Neil Redfearn became a high-profile signing in March 2001 when he joined Halifax Town as player-coach to Paul Bracewell, and he helped the club stave off relegation, but he would be unable to prevent their slide into the Conference the following season despite having two stints as manager.

His first came after Bracewell's sudden departure five games into the League programme, when the board asked him and Tony Parks to take charge of the side. The pair initially did well enough, picking up eight points from their first five matches, that chairman Bob Walker offered them the positions on a permanent basis, only for talks to stall over the length of contract on offer. When it was clear that no agreement could be reached, Walker turned instead to Alan Little.

Though still part of the backroom staff, if Redfearn's weekly column for the *Daily Telegraph* is to be believed, Little banished him from training with the first team and refused to pick him. But with Town continuing to struggle it was with a certain degree of irony that the board should turn to Redfearn as manager when Little was hospitalised in March 2002. With Parks having by this time left the club, Redfearn turned to chief scout Dave Worthington to assist him, though the situation the pair found themselves in was a hopeless one. Defeat at Leyton Orient had left the Shaymen 10 points adrift at the foot of the table, and only 10 games left, in the words of Redfearn 'to work a miracle'.

Among the three victories Redfearn achieved in his second spell as manager was the highest of the season, a 4–1 success over Cheltenham Town, but relegation was confirmed with a 5–0 defeat at Darlington with three games still to play. There was no happy send off either for Redfearn. With the administrator set to take over the club, Town not only lost 4–2 to Rushden & Diamonds in the last match of the season, but Redfearn was also sent off and forced to watch the final 36 minutes from the unfinished East Stand wearing a hard-hat.

Redfearn was among the players released by administrator Peter O'Hara, and though it was expected that he would be contracted as the club's new manager, tired of waiting for terms to be discussed, he opted for a move to Boston United, where he spent nearly two years. He finished his Football League career at Rochdale in the spring of 2004, his 790th and last appearance, which made him fifth in the all-time list of most Football League appearances, coming in the penultimate match against Southend United on 1 May 2004.

Redfearn went on to become player-coach at Scarborough under former Oldham teammate Nick Henry before taking over as manager following Henry's sacking in October 2005. He resigned and subsequently turned out for Bradford Park Avenue, making his 1,000th competitive appearance on 4 November 2006 against Solihull Borough in the second qualifying round of the FA Trophy.

Redfearn joined Stocksbridge Park Steels in March 2007, then drifted around a host of different clubs in various capacities, and latterly has been coaching at the Leeds United Academy.

WILDER, Christopher John

Manager: 2 July 2002 to May 2008
Born: Stocksbridge, 23 September 1967
Career: Southampton apprentice, professional 26 September 1985; Sheffield United 20 August 1986; Walsall on loan 2 November 1989; Charlton Athletic on loan 12 October 1990, on loan 28 November 1991; Leyton Orient on loan 27 February 1992; Rotherham United 30 July 1992 (£50,000); Notts County 2 January 1996 (£150,000); Bradford City 27 March 1997 (£150,000); Sheffield United 25 March 1998 (£150,000); Northampton Town on loan 6 November 1998; Lincoln City on loan 25 March 1999; Brighton & Hove Albion 1 August 1999; Halifax Town 22 October 1999, retired 19 July 2001; Alfreton Town September
2001, player-manager October 2001; **Halifax Town manager 2 July 2002 to cs 2008**; *Bury assistant manager 30 June 2008; Oxford United manager 21 December 2008.*

Just a year after leaving Halifax Town, Chris Wilder was back at The Shay as manager following the club's relegation to the Conference and having entered into administration. In trying times, he would remain at the helm for six seasons, all the while hindered by the restraints of a CVA, yet he remained a loyal servant to the club and came within a whisker of taking Town back into the Football League in 2006.

Wilder had begun his career as a trainee at Southampton but despite not making the first team at The Dell, enjoyed a lengthy career which saw him play for 11 League clubs, notably at Sheffield United, whom he joined from the Saints in August 1986 and appeared in the old First Division, and at Rotherham United.

At the Bramall Lane club, Wilder became a dependable right-back, but injury meant he appeared in only eight games of United's promotion season of 1989–90 when the Blades returned to the top flight under manager Dave Bassett after an absence of 14 years. Loaned out to Walsall, Charlton and Leyton Orient, Wilder then joined Second Division Rotherham United in July 1992, making 132 League appearances (11 goals) before continuing on his travels with Notts County and Bradford City before rejoining Sheffield United. Further loan spells at Northampton Town and Lincoln City were followed by a permanent move to Brighton & Hove Albion in August 1999, but having made only 11 League appearances, he moved north once again to join Halifax Town, then managed by Mark Lillis, in October 1999 as the club looked for a suitable replacement for Andy Thackeray, who had been released at the end of the previous season.

Halifax Town, however, were already on a downward spiral by the time Wilder joined the club, but he proved a sturdy and reliable full-back only for a back injury sustained at Blackpool in December 2000 to curtail his career. He never played League football again, being forced to retire in July 2001, aged 33. But Wilder remained in football by taking over as player-manager of Alfreton Town in September 2001, leading them to an unprecedented level of success, immediately landing the Northern Counties (East) League Premier Division Championship, League Cup, President's Cup and Derbyshire Senior Cup.

Having noted Wilder's success at Alfreton, the new Town board installed him as manager. Despite all the problems, he put together a useful squad, and assisted by Shaun McAuley, almost took Town into the Play-offs in his first season back – the side were lying third in February only to finish eighth. Hopes were high for the 2003–04, but Wilder would not only suffer the pain of seeing his side lost a club record 10 consecutive Conference matches, but also from that of a blow struck allegedly by Staines' Kezie Ibe at the end of an FA Trophy replay. The Shaymen flirted with relegation but regrouped the following season, with players such as Adam Quinn, Lewis Killeen, Steve Bushell and Craig Midgley featuring prominently, just missing out on the Play-offs once more.

When McAuley left the club in 2005, Wilder brought in turn Wayne Jacobs and his good friend Lee Butler to assist him as he looked long term. He even signed a contract extension, a shrewd move by chairman Geoff Ralph, who saw Wilder finally take the Shaymen into the Play-offs in 2005–06 after finishing fourth. But after two pulsating games with Grays Athletic in the semi-finals, they lost out in the Final to Hereford United after extra-time at the Walker's Stadium, Leicester. Wilder would not go as close again with Halifax.

Though he never enjoyed an easy relationship with the fans, or the press for that matter – he refused to talk to the *Halifax Courier* in August 2006 – Wilder resisted a move to Hartlepool United during the close season, but in September 2006 he seemed set to take over at Cambridge United in response to what he claimed were false promises made by chairman Ralph. However, he stayed put, but the club began to struggle on and off the pitch. With no money to buy players, he relied heavily on the loan system, with Neil Trotman and Simon Heslop being particularly successful, though he did well to land striker Jon Shaw on the eve of the 2007–08 season, and he responded by scoring 27 goals in all competitions. But it was a troublesome season, highlighted by the club entering into administration and being docked 10 points which saw the Shaymen dragged into the relegation mire. They survived on the season's last day, only for the club to go into liquidation a week later and Wilder, like all the staff at the club, was released from his contract and forced to find alternative employment.

Often criticised for being a negative tactician, Wilder was still respected in the game and soon was back in work at Bury as assistant to new boss Alan Knill. But ever wanting to return to being a manager, the following December he replaced Darren Paterson at Conference side Oxford United. Wilder had always said that given a level playing field he would show his real capabilities as a manager, and after just failing to make the Play-offs in his first season at the Kassam Stadium, Wilder's side finally clinched promotion back to the Football League via the Play-offs after finishing third, defeating York City 3–1 at Wembley in May 2010.

VINCE, James William

Manager 1 July 2008 to 7 April 2009
Born: Altrincham, 24 April 1967
Career: Manchester United trainee; Stoke City; Crewe Alexandra; Linotype; Altrincham; Witton Albion August 1987; Altrincham; Winsford United; Altrincham youth team manager; Styal player manager; Abbey Hey manager 2003; Witton Albion reserve manager, manager October 2005, resigned 26 May 2010; Crewe Alexandra Academy coach; FC Halifax Town manager 1 July 2008, dismissed April 2009; Woodley Sports manager 16 October 2010, resigned October 2010.

The formation of the new club, plying its trade in the Unibond First Division North, was a whole new experience, but with the size of the club in comparison with others came the weight of expectation, and in Jim Vince the board hoped they had appointed the right man to meet it. He had been a manager at Witton Albion for two and a half years and had delivered success of sorts, just twice missed out on promotion from the Unibond Premier League Division via the Play-offs. The sceptics, however, were quick to point out how Witton had slipped up in the final run-in from strong positions, even surrendering a fourteen point lead to Fleetwood Town in 2007–08.

The manner in which Vince cut his ties with Witton was another issue, turning his back on the club after claiming he needed a rest following an Achilles heel operation, only for him then to be unveiled as FC Halifax Town's first manager. Vince would claim that the opportunity was too great to turn down, and in a career which never hit any notable heights, it was perhaps understandable move.

A youth-team player with Manchester United, Vince failed to make the grade and, though later on the books of Stoke City and Crewe Alexandra, he spent all his playing days in the lower reaches of non-League football. A central-defender which he himself described as 'one you wouldn't like to play against', Vince turned out for Linotype and Altrincham reserves before beginning his association with Witton Albion in August 1987. He soon returned to Altrincham and had a spell at Winsford United, where he made 12 first-team appearances, before returning once more to Altrincham as manager of the youth team.

It was indeed as a coach that Vince, a likeable and approachable man, excelled, and he later turned his hand to managing at Cheshire and Altrincham League level with Styal and Abbey Hey before returning to Witton Albion as reserve-team manager before succeeding Gary Finley with the first team in October 2005.

Vince combined his time at Witton with that of coaching at the Crewe Alexandra Academy under Dario Gradi and had excellent credentials when FC Halifax Town came calling. Appointed from a short-list of four, Town chairman David Bosomworth described Vince as 'the outstanding choice', but he would have his work cut out signing suitable players as most were already taken by other clubs. Vince appointed former Nottingham Forest striker Nigel Jemson as his assistant, though it was one he would live to regret. But to his credit, by bringing in the likes of Steve Payne, Junior Brown, Scott Phelan and Tom Baker, Vince showed he knew the type of players needed at this level. He took the side to the top of the table where they remained for some time, though other clubs soon caught up with them, and during a troubled second half of the season Vince had few answers, his efforts not helped by alleged internal wranglings. With the side faultering in the race for the Play-offs, Vince was sacked on 7 April 2009 and slipped silently away from The Shay.

He briefly resurfaced as manager at Woodley Sports – he resigned after just two weeks – but elected to concentrate on coaching and in 2010 headed Crewe's Pro Academy training week in Adelaide, returning the following year.

JEMSON, Nigel Bradley

Caretaker manager 7 April 2009 to cs 2009
Born: Hutton, Preston, 10 August 1969
Career: Preston North End trainee, professional 6 July 1987; Nottingham Forest 24 March 1988 (£150,000); Bolton Wanderers on loan 23 December 1988; Preston North End on loan 15 March 1989; Sheffield Wednesday 17 September 1991 (£800,000); Grimsby Town on loan 10 September 1993; Notts County 8 September 1994 (£300,000), Watford on loan 12 January 1995; Coventry City on loan 23 March 1995; Rotherham United on loan 15 February 1996; Oxford United 23 July 1996 (£60,000); Bury 5 February 1998 (£100,000); Ayr United 10 September 1999; Oxford United 27 January 2000; Shrewsbury Town 19 July 2000; Ballymena United cs 2003; Ilkeston Town 2004, player-manager 2006, dismissed May 2008; FC Halifax Town player-assistant manager July 2008, caretaker manager April 2009; Arnold Town cs 2009; Rainworth Miners Welfare October 2009 to January 2010.

In the wake of Jim Vince's departure, Nigel Jemson was handed the reins on a caretaker basis, though the fact that he was unable to inspire his side to victory in the four remaining games of the season probably surprised no one more than Jemson himself, given his endless belief he had in his own ability. After all, was not it Brian Clough, one of his former managers, who once said of Jemson that he was the only person with a bigger ego than himself?

Therein seemingly lay the problem, for Jemson had arrived as assistant to Vince from Ilkeston Town where he had been a player-manager. The cracks soon appeared but, once Vince had gone, Jemson was always likely to be a stop-gap at The Shay.

Nevertheless, Jemson publicly stated he wanted the job permanently, confident in his own ability, as he had been throughout his career, which had begun with Preston, his hometown club. Within a year of signing professional terms, Jemson was bought by Brian Clough for Nottingham Forest on the recommendation, by all accounts, of a local greengrocer, but though he may have had a high opinion of himself, as well as winning his solitary England Under-21 cap against Wales in December 1990 (when he lined up alongside Alan Shearer), Jemson did at least deliver, scoring the only goal against Oldham Athletic in the Final of the Littlewoods Cup in April 1990.

That was probably the highlight of his career, though he would later score again at Wembley, grabbing both goals for Rotherham United in a 2–1 success over Shrewsbury Town in the Final of the Auto Windscreen Shield six years later.

Prior to joining the Millers, Jemson had played for five other clubs, including a loan spell back at Preston, seemingly find it difficult to settle down. In all, he played for 12 League clubs, finishing with Shrewsbury Town for whom he unforgettably glanced in a last-minute winner against Premier League side Everton in the third round of the FA Cup in January 2003. Jemson had earlier scored a League hat-trick in the space of eight minutes in a 4–3 defeat at Bury, but he was unable to preserve the Shrews' League status.

Jemson made a surprise move to Ballymena, where he spent one season, before joining Ilkeston, succeeding Phil Stant as player-manager in October 2005. But having been dismissed at the end of 2007–08, he immediately resurfaced as Jim Vine's right-hand man. Clearly carrying a few pounds, Jemson, nevertheless, proved he still had an eye for goal, and his return of eight goals during 2008–09 was impressive enough. But he split the fans, if not the dressing room, and was a surprise choice to lead the team once Vince had gone.

Jemson had but four games to try and save Town's season. He won none, and by the end of the season the board were looking elsewhere. But clearly feeling he still had something to offer and, feeling his playing days were not over, Jemson proved it by turning out for Arnold Town before finishing with Rainworth MW. He later became a fireman based in Bingham, Nottinghamshire.

ASPIN, Neil

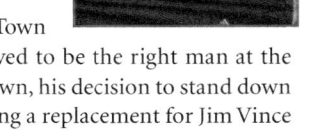

Manager April 28 2009 -
Born: Gateshead, 12 April 1965
Career: Leeds United apprentice, professional 6 October 1982; Port Vale 28 July 1989 (£200,000); Darlington 1999; Hartlepool United 24 January 2001; Harrogate Town player-coach cs 2001, manager 19 January 2005; FC Halifax Town manager 28 April 2010.

In light of what he achieved in his first two seasons at FC Halifax Town – back-to-back promotions – quite simply put, Neil Aspin proved to be the right man at the right time. After four and a half years as manager at Harrogate Town, his decision to stand down coincided with that of David Bosomworth and his board in seeking a replacement for Jim Vince and Nigel Jemson, and his appointment could not have worked out better for Aspin, or the club.

Totally focussed on the job in hand, Aspin showed the same steely resolve which had made him a respected full-back, having come through the youth ranks at Leeds United. Aspin was one of a crop of youngsters handed his League debut by Allan Clarke during 1981–82, and he went on to cement his place in the side. Silverware eluded the club, though how painful it must have been for Aspin and Leeds to not only lose an FA Cup semi-final to Coventry City in April 1987, but also miss out in the Division Two Play-offs following a third match with Charlton Athletic the following month.

Aspin fell out of favour with manager Howard Wilkinson and moved to Port Vale in July 1989, where he spent the majority of his career. The winner of the club's Player of the Year award in his first season, he helped the side win the Autoglass Trophy in May 1993, beating Stockport 2–1 in the Final, and the following term, he played 40 games as Port Vale won promotion from the Second Division, a successful season for Aspin topped off by being voted by his peers in the PFA divisional team of the year.

Aspin played in the 1996 Anglo-Italian Cup Final which Vale lost 5–2 to Genoa and went on to make 348 League appearances for the Valiants, enjoying a testimonial in which singer Robbie Williams appeared.

In the 1999 close season Aspin joined Third Division Darlington, where he experienced once more the pain of Play-off defeat as the Quakers lost 1–0 to Peterborough United at Wembley, and he played out his League career the following season with Hartlepool United, taking his League tally to a staggering 615 appearances and eight goals.

Aspin began his association with Harrogate Town as player-coach under John Reed in 2001–02, retiring in 2004. But he returned to Wetherby Road as manager in January 2005 in succession to Reed and, despite operating on a low budget, he consistently kept the North

Yorkshire side in the top half of the Conference North and came close to reaching the Conference National in 2005–06 when the side qualified for the end of season Play-offs, only to lose to Stafford Rangers in the semi-finals, and in 2007–08 Harrogate Town lifted the West Riding County Cup.

But feeling he could not operate on the budget on offer, Aspin tendered his resignation before accepting the position as manager at FC Halifax Town. Bringing with him Trevor Storton as his trusted assistant, he then raided his former club to sign several players, 'keeper Jonathan Hedge, Nick Gray and Richard Marshall among them, as well as signing centre-forward James Dean, who repaid him faithfully with goals aplenty, and in an unforgettable season Town won the chase with Lancaster City to clinch the Unibond First Division North title, totalling 100 points and scoring 108 goals.

The following term, the Shaymen won the Evo-Stik Premier in even more emphatic style, Aspin having strengthened his side with the signing of players such as Mark Bower, Liam Hogan, Danny Holland and Jamie Vardy. Town proved far and away superior to anyone else in the League and clinched the title at Retford United on 9 April with five games still to play.

But the season was not without tragedy. His assistant Trevor Storton lost his battle with cancer, in March, and Aspin was quick to pay tribute to a colleague who had offered much.

There is a feeling that Aspin will prove to be a great manager at a higher level, though whether that will be with FC Halifax Town nobody can be sure. But after two seasons at The Shay his record speaks for itself, and nobody could ask for anything more.

1911-12

Yorkshire Combination

Manager: Joe McClelland

Did you know that?

- The inaugural meeting of Halifax Town was held at home of Samuel McClelland, where 14 people responded to 50 invitations.

- Joe Chadbourne was elected the first Halifax Town captain in a poll held among the players prior to the first match against Bradford City Reserves, 9 September 1911. He received five votes, as opposed to Jock Nixon (four) and Bert Firth and Charlie Morgan (one each).

- Clem Garforth, who played his only game in the first match, went on to make 232 appearances and score 451 points for Halifax RLFC. He later became licensee of the West Hill Hotel, Hanson Lane, which was badly damaged during a German bombing raid on 22 November 1940.

- Halifax Town's colours were black-and-white striped shirts and white shorts.

- Their first nicknames were either the Magpies or Sandhallites.

- The first goal by a Halifax Town player at Sandhall Lane was scored by Andy McGill in the 2–1 Bradford Hospitals Cup win over Knaresborough.

- Admission to the ground for adults was 6d.

- Highest League win: 8–1 v Heckmondwike (h), 16 March.

- Heaviest League defeat: 2–6 v Bradford City Reserves (a), 9 September.

Match No.	Date	Venue	Opponents	Result		Scorers	Attendance
1	Sep 9	A	Bradford City Reserves	L	2-6	Redding 2	2,000
2	16	H	Scarborough	L	0-1		3,000
3	30	H	York City	W	3-1	Nixon, Culpan, Chadbourne	
4	Oct 7	A	Thornhill Lees Albion	W	5-2	Taylor, Wild 3 (1 pen), Robertson	
5	14	H	Fryston Colliery	W	2-0	Chadbourne, Houldsworth	2,000
6	Nov 4	H	Bradford Reserves	W	3-0	Culpan, Walden 2	
7	11	A	York City	W	7-0	Wild 3, Culpan, Chadbourne, Leyland, Walden
8	18	H	West Vale Ramblers	L	1-2	Wild	4,000
9	Dec 9	H	Thornhill Lees Albion	W	4-2	Walden 2, Culpan, Potter	
10	16	A	Knaresborough	W	6-2	Nixon, Wild 3, Longworth 2	
11	23	H	Stourton United	W	4-0	Potter, Wild 2 (1 pen), Farrar	
12	25	H	Mirfield United	W	1-0	Wild	5,000
13	26	A	Mirfield United	L	0-3		
14	30	A	Stourton United	W	4-1	(unknown)	
15	Jan 1	A	Bradford Reserves	L	1-5	Chadbourne	
16	Feb 10	A	Morley	W	3-0	Fyfe, Wild 2	
17	17	H	Morley	L	1-2	Farrar	
18	24	A	Heckmondwike	W	5-0	Wild 3, Fyfe, Leyland	
19	Mar 16	H	Heckmondwike	W	8-1	Chadbourne 5, Wild 2, Fyfe	
20	23	A	Fryston Colliery	L	1-2	Chadbourne	
21	Apr 5	H	Bradford City Reserves	L	2-3	Fyfe 2	
22	6	H	Goole Town	D	1-1	Fyfe	
23	11	A	West Vale Ramblers	L	1-2	Chadbourne	
24	20	H	Knaresborough	W	2-0	Wild, Farrar	
25	24	A	Scarborough	L	2-4	Roscoe, Wild	
26	27	A	Goole Town	D	0-0		

Final League Position: 7th in Yorkshire Combination

EXPUNGED MATCHES

							Apps
							Gls
Oct 28	H	Leeds United	W	3-0	Wild, Culpan, Chadbourne		
Nov 25	A	Leeds United	W	4-0	Walden 3, Wild		50

Player Appearances

	Finch,H	Firth,EB	Houldsworth,GE	Street,H	Gorforth,C	Morgan,C	Nixon,J	McGill,A	Chadbourne,JH	Reading,WL	Wild,GH	Potter,H	Orr,E	Leyland,S	Culpan,S	Groves	Robertson	Taylor,P	Boden	Marsland,F	Frith,H	Baxter,R	Walden,HA	Goodall,F	Royston	Farren,FW	Farrar,W	Sutcliffe,CS	Longworth,J	Barraclough,AJ	Sutcliffe,CH	Pritchard	Green,H	Fyfe,G	Wroe	Harrreau,A	Roscoe,P	Fowler,E	Spencer,J	Roper,J	Taylor,E
	1	2	3	4	5	6	7	8	9	10	11																														
	1	2	3	4		6	7	4	9	10	8	5	11																												
	1	2	3			6	7	10	9		8	4		5	11																										
	1		2			6	7				8	4		5	11	3	9	10																							
	1		2			6	7	9	10		8	4		5						3	11																				
	1	3				6	7		10		8	2		5	11								4	9																	
	1	3				6	7		10		8	4		5	11								9	2																	
	1	3				6	7		10		8	4		5	11								9	2																	
						6	7					4		5	11					1	8	9			2	3	10														
						6	7				8	4		5					11						2	3	9	1	10												
						6	7				8	4		5	11											3	9	1		2	10											
						6	7				8	4		5	11											3	9	1		2	10											
														5	11											3	9	1													
						6	7				8			5	11						4		2			3	9	1			10										
						6	7		10		8			5							4		2			3	9	1			11										
							7				8	4		5					11		6					3	9	1					2	10							
							7				8	4		5					11		6						9	1					2	10	3						
							7				8	4		5					11		6					3	9	1					2	10							
							7		9	6	8	4		5					11							3		1					2	10							
		3					7		9	6	8	4		5					11									1					2	10							
														5														1					2	10							
														5														1					2	10							
		3		6					9										11	1										7	5		2			4	8	10			
										6	9																10	1			5	4				7	11	2	3		
		3					7				10	11									6						9	1			5	4				8			2		
		2					7				10	6	4						11								9	1			5	8							3		
8	10	5	3	1		14	21	3	12	8	21	16	1	20	10	1	1	1	1	9	2	8	4	4	2	10	13	16	2	3	2	2	11	10	1	1	3	2	1	3		
		1						2		11	2	22	2		2	4		1	1					5			3	2					6			1					

| | | | | | | 6 | 7 | | 9 | | 8 | 2 | | 5 | 10 | | | | | 11 | 1 | 4 | | | | | | | | | | | | | | | | | 3 | | |
| | | | | | | 6 | 7 | | 10 | | 8 | 2 | | 5 | | | | | | 11 | 1 | 4 | 9 | | | | | 3 | | | | | | | | | | | | | |

* Note there is a degree of uncertainty regarding the line ups of some matches between 1911-12 and 1918-19, due to poor newspaper reports, hence there may be some discrepancies about some of the appearance and goal totals.

League Table

	P	W	D	L	F	A	Pts
Bradford City Reserves	26	20	3	3	98	25	43
Bradford Reserves	26	18	4	4	102	31	40
Goole Town	26	16	4	6	75	36	36
Scarborough	26	16	4	6	68	46	36
Morley	26	16	4	6	58	39	36
Mirfield United	26	14	6	6	55	32	34
Halifax Town	26	14	2	10	66	40	30
York City	26	8	4	14	37	70	20
Fryston Colliery	26	9	1	16	50	61	19
Knaresborough	26	6	6	14	43	66	16
West Vale Ramblers	26	7	2	17	36	91	16
Thornhill Lees Albion	26	6	3	17	35	81	15
Stourton United	26	4	4	18	32	77	12
Heckmondwike	26	2	5	19	23	90	9

Leeds United resigned from League

1912-13

Midland Counties League
Manager: Joe McClelland

Did you know that?

- Captain was Fred Farren.
- Halifax Town put out their first team for a Yorkshire Combination match with Bradford Reserves on 21 September 1912, only to lose 2–1.
- The charabanc which took the players to Horsforth on 28 September 1912 for their first-ever FA Cup match was called Pioneer.
- Aubrey Temple Sharpe was a former county cricketer with Leicestershire and Derbyshire.
- Prior to their FA Cup tie at Queen's Park Rangers, the Halifax Town players and officials spent the night at the Grafton Hotel, Tottenham Court Road.
- For four games, admission fees at Sandhall Lane were reduced to 4s to try and entice more spectators
- The first Halifax Town player to be sent off in a match was Jock Nixon, for retaliation shortly before half-time in the match with Rotherham Town on 19 April 1913.
- Biggest League win: 6–1 v Rotherham Town (h), 19 April.
- Heaviest League defeat: 1–6 v Lincoln City Reserves (a), 9 November.

Match No.	Date		Venue	Opponents	Result		Scorers	Attendance
1	Sep	7	H	Doncaster Rovers	L	1-2	Pentland	1,500
2		14	A	Chesterfield Town	D	3-3	Simons, Pentland, Wild	3,500
3	Oct	5	H	Grimsby Town Reserves	W	1-0	Pentland	3,000
4		19	H	Goole Town	L	1-2	Woodward	
5		24	A	Notts County Reserves	W	3-2	Simons, Woodward, Nixon	
6		26	A	Sheffield United Reserves	D	2-2	Simons, Pentland	
7	Nov	9	A	Lincoln City Reserves	L	1-6	Simons	
8		14	H	Worksop Town	W	5-1	Wild 2, Nixon, Simons 2	
9		23	A	Castleford Town	L	1-2	Pentland	
10	Dec	21	H	Chesterfield Town	D	0-0		3,000
11		25	A	Scunthorpe United	L	0-3		
12		28	H	Scunthorpe United	W	4-1	Whyte, Pentland 2, Wild	
13	Jan	1	H	Lincoln City Reserves	W	5-1	Whyte 2, Wild, Nixon, Roscoe	
14		4	A	Leeds City Reserves	L	2-3	Wild 2	
15		18	H	Castleford Town	W	2-0	Marsh 2	
16		23	H	York City	W	2-1	Pentland 2	
17		25	A	Grimsby Town Reserves	L	2-3	Pentland, Whyte	
18	Feb	1	H	Leeds City Reserves	W	6-3	Nixon 2, Whyte 2 (2 scorers unknown)	
19		4	A	Rotherham Town	L	0-4		
20		8	A	Hull City Reserves	D	0-0		
21		15	H	Sheffield Wednesday Reserves	L	2-3	Whyte 2	
22		20	H	Rotherham County	L	1-2	Wild	
23		22	A	Goole Town	D	0-0		2,000
24		27	H	Denaby United	L	1-2	Whyte	
25	Mar	1	H	Mexborough Town	W	5-0	Green 2, Whyte 2, (1 scorer unknown)	
26		8	A	Denaby United	L	0-3		
27		13	A	Sheffield United Reserves	W	1-0	Nixon (pen)	300
28		15	H	Hull City Reserves	W	2-0	(unknown)	
29		21	A	Gainsborough Trinity	L	0-3		
30		22	A	Doncaster Rovers	L	0-2		
31		24	H	Gainsborough Trinity	D	2-2	Whyte, Nixon	
32		29	H	Notts County Reserves	W	2-1	Whyte, Roscoe	
33		31	A	Mexborough Town	W	2-1	Wild 2	
34	Apr	5	A	Rotherham County	D	2-2	Whyte, Roscoe	
35		9	A	York City	L	0-2		
36		12	A	Sheffield Wednesday Reserves	L	1-2	Wild	4,000
37		17	A	Worksop Town	L	0-1		500
38		19	H	Rotherham Town	W	6-1	McGovern, Wild 2, Whyte, Green, Roscoe	

Final League Position: 14th in Midland Counties League

Apps
Gls

FA CUP

P	Sep	28	A	Horsforth	W	4-2	Pentland 3, Wild	
Q1	Oct	12	A	Hebden Bridge	W	3-2	Simons 2, Pentland (pen)	4,000
Q2	Nov	2	H	Knaresborough	W	6-0	McGovern, Pentland 3, Simons, Woodward	
Q3		16	H	South Kirkby Colliery	W	6-4	Nixon, Simons 3, Wild, Pentland	
Q4		30	H	Nelson	D	3-3	Roscoe, Pentland, Nixon	4,000
R	Dec	3	A	Nelson	W	3-2	McGovern, Whyte, Pentland	3,000
Q5		14	A	Walsall	D	0-0		6,027
R		19	H	Walsall	W	1-0	Whyte	3,000
1	Jan	11	A*	Queen's Park Rangers	L	2-4	Roscoe, Pentland	9,000

*Home tie switched to Park Royal, Queen's Park Rangers

Apps
Gls

League Table

	P	W	D	L	F	A	Pts
Rotherham County	38	28	5	5	111	37	61
Chesterfield Town	38	20	11	7	78	41	51
Gainsborough Trinity	38	22	6	10	84	40	50
Doncaster Rovers	38	21	7	10	67	43	49
Leeds City Reserves	38	18	7	13	68	52	45
Goole Town	38	14	14	10	52	49	42
Sheffield Wednesday Reserves	38	16	7	15	78	69	39
Grimsby Town Reserves	38	15	9	14	65	67	39
Sheffield United Reserves	38	15	8	15	68	57	38
York City	38	16	6	16	69	80	38
Rotherham Town	38	17	4	17	55	67	38
Hull City Reserves	38	17	3	18	65	73	37
Lincoln City Reserves	38	16	3	19	81	73	35
Halifax Town	38	14	7	17	68	67	35
Scunthorpe United	38	13	8	17	55	78	34
Castleford Town	38	12	9	17	55	56	33
Worksop Town	38	12	5	21	47	91	29
Notts County Reserves	38	10	6	22	67	85	26
Mexborough Town	38	11	3	24	42	77	25
Denaby United	38	7	4	27	39	112	18

1913-14

Midland Counties League
Manager: Joe McClelland

Did you know that?

- Trainer Bright Heyhirst went on to serve Halifax RLFC and in 1926–27 was trainer to the touring All Blacks. A former dentist, he later became masseur to Yorkshire CC.
- Captain was Tom Splitt.
- Halifax Town scored six goals in each half to set up a scoring record of 12–0 over West Vale Ramblers.
- Bob Suter was understudy to the great Albert Iremonger at Notts County.
- Following Halifax Town's 2–0 victory over Mirfield United on 15 November 1913, centre-forward Joe Linford was driven away to sign professional forms in the presence of William Black, Dr Muir and Joe McClelland at his Bingley home.
- Prior to their FA Cup tie in Norwich, the players stopped at the Great Eastern Hotel, Norwich.
- Reigning champions Rotherham County were beaten 1–0 courtesy of Harry Farren's penalty on 31 January 1913. New signing Frank Cannon made his third appearance against County, and in each case a penalty had been awarded to his side.
- Frank Cannon was killed in France while serving with the 11th Essex Regt. in February 1916.
- Biggest League victory: 4–0 v Mexborough Town (h), 26 March.
- Heaviest League defeat: 0–7 v Grimsby Town Reserves (a), 17 January.
- Ever-present: Bob Suter.

Match No.	Date		Venue	Opponents	Result		Scorers	Attendance
1	Sep	6	H	Chesterfield Town	D	0-0		
2		13	A	Worksop Town	W	1-0	Roscoe	
3		20	H	Leeds City Reserves	W	2-1	W.J. Hughes, Brearley	
4		27	H	Grimsby Town Reserves	D	1-1	W.J. Hughes (pen)	3,000
5	Oct	4	H	Sheffield Wednesday Reserves	L	2-3	Wild, Longbottom	
6		25	A	Gainsbrough Trinity	L	1-5	Longbottom	
7	Nov	8	A	Doncaster Rovers	W	3-0	Linford 2, Child	
8		22	A	Leeds City Reserves	W	2-1	Linford 2	2,500
9	Dec	6	H	Lincoln City Reserves	D	1-1	W.J. Hughes (pen)	
10		20	H	Sheffield United Reserves	D	1-1	Pentland	
11		25	H	York City	W	1-0	W.J. Hughes	
12		26	A	York City	L	0-2		
13		27	H	Hull City Reserves	L	0-1		
14	Jan	1	H	Doncaster Rovers	W	3-1	Adams, W.J. Hughes 2	
15		3	A	Sheffield United Reserves	W	2-0	McCreadie, Adams	
16		10	H	Scunthorpe United	L	1-3	Pentland	
17		17	A	Grimsby Town Reserves	L	0-7		
18		24	H	Gainsbrough Trinity	L	0-1		
19		31	A	Rotherham County	W	1-0	Farren (pen)	
20	Feb	7	H	Rotherham County	L	1-2	Cannon	
21		9	A	Mexborough Town	L	0-1		
22		14	A	Chesterfield Town	L	1-2	Cannon	
23		21	H	Worksop Town	W	1-0	Cannon	
24		28	A	Scunthorpe United	L	1-2	Cannon	
25	Mar	14	A	Hull City Reserves	L	0-2		
26		21	A	Rotherham Town	D	0-0		
27		26	H	Mexborough Town	W	4-0	Pentland 2, Beevers, Cannon	
28		28	A	Lincoln City Reserves	D	2-2	McCreadie, Cannon	
29	Apr	4	A	Sheffield Wednesday Reserves	L	0-2		
30		10	H	Goole Town	L	0-2		
31		11	A	Goole Town	L	1-2	Adams	
32		13	A	Castleford Town	L	0-3		
33		23	H	Castleford Town	L	1-2	Adams	
34		25	H	Rotherham Town	W	3-0	Adams 2, McCreadie	

Final League Position: 14th in Midland Counties League

Apps
Gls

FA CUP

Q1	Oct	11	H*	West Vale Ramblers	W	12-0	Wild 4, Blackburn 3, W.J. Hughes 2, Longbottom 2, Roscoe	
Q2	Nov	1	A**	Rothwell	D	1-1	Wild	
R		6	H	Rothwell	W	6-0	W.J. Hughes 2, Linford, 3 unknown	
Q3		15	H	Mirfield United	W	2-0	Wild 2	
Q4		29	A	Rotherham County	D	1-1	Longbottom	6,685
R	Dec	4	H	Rotherham County	W	5-2	W.J. Hughes 2 (1 pen), Wild, Linford, Roscoe	
Q5		13	A	Norwich City	L	0-2		6,284

* Away tie switched to Sandhall Lane
** Home tie switched to Rothwell

Apps
Gls

Solar, ER	Farren, H	Spirt, T	Martin, J	Thompson, AH	Child, J	Smith, R	Wild, GH	Hughes, WJ	Longbottom, C	Roscoe, P	Jordon, H	Brearley, A	Wheathead, G	Blackburn, T	Linford, J	Brumitte, T	Beevers	Pentland, FB	Hughes, TJ	McCreadie, W	McAllister, T	Marsh, J	Maddison	Adams, H	Haseby, T	Lawrence, F	Wishart, J	Cannon, F	Scruton, J	Buinand, W	Carter, J	Sharp, AT
1	2	3	4	5	6	7	8	9	10	11																						
1	3	2	4	5	6		8	9	7	11	10																					
1	2	3	4	5	6		8	9	7			10	11																			
1	2	3	4		6		8	10	7		9	5	11																			
1	2	3	4		6		8	5	10	7			11	9																		
1	2	3	4		6		8	5	10	7			11	9																		
1	2	3	4		6		8	5		7		10	11	9																		
1	2	3	4	11	6		8	5		7			10	9																		
1	2		4	3	6		8	5	10	7			11	9																		
1		3	4		6			5	10	7			11		2	8	9															
1	2		4		6			5	7			10			3	8	9	11														
1	2		5												3		9															
1	2		5		6				8		10				3		9		7	4	11											
1	2		4		6			5		7					3		8	11				9	10									
1	2		4		6			5		7					3		8	11		10	9											
1	2		4					5		7					3		8	11		10	9	6										
1	10	2	4		6										3		8	11			9	5	7									
1	2		4		6				7						3	10	8							5	9							
1	2		4		6					9					3	10	7			8				5	11							
1	2		4		6					11					3	8	7			9				5	10							
1	2		4							11					3	8	7			9	6			5	10							
1		2			6					11					3	4	8	7		9				5	10							
1		3			6					11		4			2		8	7		9				5	10							
1		3										6			2	8	7	11		9				5	10							
1		3			6					11		4			2	8	10	7						5	9							
1		3			6					11		4			2	8	10	7						5	9							
1		3	6							11		4			2	8	10	7						5	9							
1		3	5		6							4			2	8	10	7		11					9							
1		3													2		10															
1		3													2		10															
1		3			4					6	11				2			7		9				5	10	8						
1			4		6						11				3			7		9	5					8	2	10				
1		3	4		2					6						10		7		9				5	8							
1		3	4		2					6								7		9				5	10	8						
34	20	22	26	5	28	1	9	14	11	20	2	14	10	3	2	23	13	21	2	16	1	1	3	15	4	1	3	14	3	1	1	
					1				1	6	2	1			1			4		4	3			6				6				

1	2	3	4		6		8	5	10	7			11	9																		
1	2	3	4		6		8		10	7			11	9										5								
1	2	3	4		6		8	5		7			11	10	9																	
1	2	3	4		6		8	5		7	10	11		9																		
1	2	3	4		6		8	5	10	7			11	9																		
1	2	3	4		6		8	5	10	7			11	9																		
1	2	3	4		6		8	5	10	7			11	9																		
7	7	7	7		7		7	6	5	7	1	1	7	3	5									1								
							8	6	3	2			3	2																		

League Table

	P	W	D	L	F	A	Pts
Rotherham County	34	25	2	7	92	38	52
Gainsborough Trinity Reserves	34	22	6	6	75	36	50
Chesterfield Town	34	19	4	11	80	43	42
Sheffield Wednesday Reserves	34	17	6	11	63	50	40
Goole Town	34	16	6	12	52	39	38
Grimsby Town Reserves	34	16	6	12	68	56	38
Scunthorpe United	34	16	4	14	55	55	36
Castleford Town	34	15	4	15	54	51	34
Rotherham Town	34	13	8	13	46	62	34
Sheffield United Reserves	34	11	10	13	60	62	32
Lincoln City Reserves	34	11	9	14	49	60	31
York City	34	13	5	16	48	60	31
Worksop Town	34	13	3	18	51	61	29
Halifax Town	34	11	6	17	38	51	28
Hull City Reserves	34	11	5	18	37	55	27
Doncaster Rovers	34	12	2	20	30	51	26
Mexborough Town	34	10	4	20	41	85	24
Leeds City Reserves	34	8	4	22	45	75	20

1914-15

Midland Counties League
Manager: Joe McClelland

Did you know that?

- Captain was Jimmy Wishart.
- Halifax Town went 14 matches unbeaten in the League between 19 September and 26 December.
- In December, the players agreed to take a pay cut to help the club in difficulties caused by the war.
- Halifax Town won 2-1 at Goole Town on 30 January 1915, playing with only 10 men and manager Joe McClelland at inside-left. Jack Hughes scored both Town's goals, though a local reporter credited them to Wishart, and claimed Nixon 'did striking things in the wing', even though Nixon was not playing!
- Biggest League win: 6-1 v Mexborough Town (h), 26 December 1914.
- Heaviest League defeat: 0-5 v Grimsby Town Reserves (a), 22 April 1915.
- Town's biggest victories and worst defeats were against the same opposition as the previous season.

Match No.	Date	Venue	Opponents	Result		Scorers	Attendance
1	Sep 5	H	Heckmondwike	D	1-1	Crowther (pen)	
2	12	A	Chesterfield Town	L	1-5	Crowther (pen)	
3	19	H	Chesterfield Town	D	1-1	Nixon	
4	28	H	Rotherham Town	W	3-2	Wild, Crowther, Scrutton	
5	Oct 3	H	Hull City Reserves	W	1-0	Wild (pen)	
6	10	A	Bradford Reserves	W	2-0	Kirby, Scrutton	
7	29	H	Doncaster Rovers	W	4-1	Scrutton 3 (1 pen), Wild	
8	Nov 7	A	Castleford Town	D	1-1	Kirby	
9	14	H	Bradford Reserves	W	1-0	Nixon	
10	21	A	Hull City Reserves	W	1-0	Crowther	
11	28	H	York City Reserves	W	2-0	Wild, Crowther	
12	Dec 5	A	Lincoln City Reserves	W	1-0	Crowther	
13	12	H	Grimsby Town Reserves	W	2-0	Wild, Armitage	
14	19	A	York City Reserves	W	1-0	Armitage	
15	25	A	Sheffield United Reserves	D	0-0		
16	26	H	Mexborough Town	W	6-1	Scrutton 2, Armitage 3, Wild	
17	Jan 1	A	Leeds City Reserves	L	0-3		
18	2	A	Rotherham County	L	0-4		
19	9	H	Sheffield Wednesday Reserves	D	1-1	Armitage	
20	14	H	Scunthorpe United	W	2-1	Armitage, Nixon	
21	16	A	Doncaster Rovers	L	1-2	Roscoe	
22	23	H	Lincoln City Reserves	W	1-0	Wild	
23	30	A	Goole Town*	W	2-1	Hughes 2	
24	Feb 6	H	Castleford Town	W	3-1	Hughes, Wishart, Wild	
25	16	H	Leeds City Reserves	L	0-4		
26	20	H	Gainsborough Trinity Reserves	W	3-1	Hughes 2 (2 pens), Wild	
27	27	A	Sheffield Wednesday Reserves	L	0-2		
28	Mar 6	H	Goole Town	D	3-3	Wild, Linford 2	
29	13	A	Heckmondwike	W	1-0	Hughes (pen)	
30	20	H	Rotherham County	L	0-2		
31	27	A	Gainsborough Trinity Reserves	L	0-1		
32	Apr 2	A	Rotherham Town	L	0-2		
33	3	H	Sheffield United Reserves	L	1-3	Mulholland	
34	5	A	Mexborough Town	D	2-2	Mulholland, Scrutton	
35	10	A	Scunthorpe United	L	1-2	Mulholland	
36	15	H	Worksop Town	D	0-0		
37	17	A	Worksop Town	L	0-4		
38	22	A	Grimsby Town Reserves	L	0-5		

Final League Position: 10th in Midland Counties League
* Halifax Town played with only 10 men

Apps
Gls

FA CUP

Q1	Sep 26	A	Castleford Town	L	1-2	Roscoe	

Apps
Gls

League Table

	P	W	D	L	F	A	Pts
Rotherham County	38	23	8	7	104	42	54
Leeds City Reserves	38	24	5	9	99	42	53
Chesterfield Town	38	20	10	8	76	41	50
Goole Town	38	20	7	11	103	58	47
Sheffield Wednesday Reserves	38	20	7	11	92	56	47
Gainsborough Trinity Reserves	38	19	8	11	78	46	46
Grimsby Town Reserves	38	21	3	14	73	54	45
Worksop Town	38	17	11	10	70	55	45
Rotherham Town	38	20	4	14	112	65	44
Halifax Town	38	16	9	13	49	37	41
Bradford Reserves	38	16	6	16	83	86	38
Sheffield United Reserves	38	15	6	17	57	46	36
Scunthorpe United	38	13	9	16	70	79	35
Lincoln City Reserves	38	12	9	17	76	74	33
Doncaster Rovers	38	14	3	2	58	82	31
York City	38	12	7	19	45	72	31
Mexborough Town	38	10	8	20	37	89	28
Castleford Town	38	9	9	20	50	103	27
Hull City Reserves	38	8	2	28	39	105	18
Heckmondwike	38	5	1	32	30	169	11

1915-16 Midland Counties League

Manager: Joe McClelland

Did you know that?

- Admission at Sandhall Lane was 6d for adults, 3d under 18s, 1d schoolboys, ladies free and half-price for soldiers.
- Captain was goalkeeper Bob Suter.
- A spectator at the home match with Rotherham County on 23 October was Billy Martin, injured in the Army before reaching the firing line in France.
- At their friendly match with 1st Lincolnshire Garrison Regt. on 6 November, a collection raised £21 for the *Halifax Courier's* 'Comforts Fund'.
- Trainer Stansfield turned out for the home match with Mexborough Town on 27 November.
- Biggest League victory: 2–0 v Sheffield United Reserves (h), 11 September, v Chesterfield Town (h), 20 November.
- Heaviest League defeat: 2–7 v Doncaster Rovers (a), 22 April.

Match No.	Date	Venue	Opponents	Result		Scorers	Attendance
1	Sep 11	H	Sheffield United	W	2-0	Wild 2	
2	18	A	Goole Town	D	0-0		
3	Oct 9	A	Silverwood Colliery	L	1-3	Wild	
4	23	H	Rotherham County	D	2-2	Wild 2 (1 pen)	
5	30	A	Rotherham County	L	0-4		
6	Nov 13	H	Silverwood Colliery	W	1-0	Wild (pen)	
7	20	H	Chesterfield Town	W	2-0	Longbottom, Billings	
8	27	H	Mexborough Town	W	2-1	Longbottom, Roscoe	
9	Dec 4	A	Chesterfield Town	L	0-4		
10	11	A	Sheffield United	L	1-5	Longbottom (pen)	
11	Jan 8	H	Goole Town	W	2-1	Wild 2	
12	29	A	Mexborough Town	D	0-0		
13	Feb 5	H	Doncaster Rovers	W	2-1	Roscoe, Beevers	
14	Apr 22	A	Doncaster Rovers	L	2-7	Wild, Beevers	

Final League Position: 4th in Midland Counties League

Apps
Gls

Sutor, ER	Birkwhistle, T	Parton, J	Hibbert, H	Walsart, J	Brearley, A	Lounds, H	Wild, GH	Brookbank, C	Longbottom, C	Roscoe, P	Heath, W	Barker	McClelland, JB	Marsland, F	Needham	Mexhi, Wh	Bennett	Ackroyd, J	Billings	Stansfield, S	Plant	Smith	Barron	Nurns	Clayton	Islip, E	Beevers, T
1	2	3	4	5	6	7	8	9	10	11																	
1	2	3	4	5	6	7		9	10	11	8																
1	2		4	5		7	8	9	10	11		3	6														
1	2	3	4	5	6	7	8		10		9			11													
1	2	3			6	7	8		10	11			4	5	9												
1	2	3	5				8		10	11			4				9	6	7								
1	2	3	5			7	8		10	11			4					6	8								
1	2	3	5			7	8	9	10				4	6		11											
1	2	3	5			7				11	6		4				8	9	10								
		5						9	7		6	11	2		8		3			1	4	10					
1	2	3	5			7	8	10	11				4	6													9
1	2	3	5			7	8	10	11				6				4										9
1	2	3	5			7	8	10	11				6				4										9
12	12	11	12	4	4	11	11	3	14	12	2	1	3	2	6	6	3	2	2	4	1	1	1	1	1	1	4
								9	3	2									1								2

League Table

	P	W	D	L	F	A	Pts
Chesterfield Town	16	12	2	3	44	16	26
Rotherham County	16	8	3	5	23	34	19
Goole Town	16	7	4	5	23?	31	18
Halifax Town	14	6	3	5	17	28	15
Sheffield United Reserves	16	5	4	7	33	28	14
Worksop Town	14	6	2	6	16	16	14
Doncaster Rovers	16	5	3	9	38	28?	12
Mexborough Town	16	3	6	7	20	34?	12
Silverwood Colliery	16	5	1	0	23	49	11

Games against Worksop Town (home and away) not played

1919-20 Midland Counties League
Manager: Joe McClelland

Did you know that?

- Halifax Town discarded their black-and-white-striped shirts in favour of royal blue with white 'knickers'. Their nickname was the 'Royal Blues' or 'Exleyites'.
- Captain was Jock Nixon.
- John Pagan was a local sprint champion.
- The cost to send 12 players, one trainer and manager to Scunthorpe United on 8 November was a princely sum of £10 3s 6d.
- Ernest Smith originally played under the name of A.W. Inger.
- Halifax Town's 7–0 defeat of Apperley Bridge in the FA Cup on 27 September was a record score at Exley.
- Biggest League win: 5–2 v Silverwood Colliery (h), 1 November.
- Heaviest League defeat: 1–6 v Hull City Reserves (a), 29 April.

Match No.	Date		Venue	Opponents	Result		Scorers	Attendance
1	Sep	6	A	Mexborough Town	L	0-3		3,000
2		13	H	Scunthorpe United	W	2-1	Wild (pen), Kirby	
3		20	A	Rotherham Town	L	2-5	Robinson, Pagan	
4	Oct	4	A	Sheffield Wednesday Reserves	W	1-0	S. Smith	
5		25	A	Silverwood Colliery	L	1-3	Robinson	
6	Nov	1	H	Silverwood Colliery	W	5-2	Wild 2, W. Smith 2, Wishart	
7		8	A	Scunthorpe United	L	1-4	Cook	2,100
8		22	H	Chesterfield Municipal	L	0-4		
9		29	A	Sheffield United Reserves	L	2-4	Turnbull, S. Smith	
10	Dec	6	A	Notts County Reserves	L	0-1		
11		13	H	Grimsby Town Reserves	L	2-3	Cook, S. Smith	
12		20	H	Sheffield United Reserves	D	1-1	E. Smith	
13		25	A	Leeds United	D	3-3	Wellock, Clarkson, Birtwhistle (pen)	
14		26	H	Hull City Reserves	W	3-1	E. Smith 2, Wild	
15		27	A	Grimsby Town Reserves	L	0-5		
16	Jan	10	H	Sheffield Wednesday Reserves	W	4-2	Wellock 2, Cook 2	
17		17	H	Lincoln City Reserves	W	3-0	Cook, Wild, E. Smith	
18		24	A	Gainsborough Trinity	W	2-1	Wellock, Birtwhistle (pen)	4,000
19		31	H	Worksop Town	L	1-2	Wild	
20	Feb	7	A	Notts County Reserves	W	3-1	Wild, O'Rourke, Lowe	
21		14	H	Leeds United	D	0-0		
22		28	H	Barnsley Reserves	W	3-1	Cook 2, Wild	
23	Mar	4	H	Rotherham Town	D	0-0		
24		6	A	Chesterfield Municipal	L	0-3		
25		13	A	Barnsley Reserves	W	1-0	Wellock	
26		20	H	Gainsborough Trinity	W	2-0	Robinson, Wild	
27		27	A	Lincoln City Reserves	L	1-2	Lawrence	
28	Apr	2	A	Castleford Town	W	2-1	Wild, Brown	
29		5	H	Castleford Town	W	3-2	Wellock, Wild, Birtwhistle	2,000
30		6	A	Worksop Town	L	1-2	Wellock	
31		15	H	Mexborough Town	L	1-3	Robinson	
32		17	A	Rotherham County	L	0-2		
33		24	H	Rotherham County	L	1-2	Wild	
34		29	A	Hull City Reserves	L	1-6	Cook	

Final League Position: 14th in Midland Counties League

FA CUP

Q1	Sep	27	H	Apperley Bridge	W	7-0	Wild 2, Pagan, McCreadie, Cook, Robinson 2	
Q2	Oct	11	A	Castleford Town	L	0-3		3,000

League Table

	P	W	D	L	F	A	Pts
Chesterfield Municipal	34	24	5	5	73	35	53
Sheffield United Reserves	34	20	11	3	73	28	51
Scunthorpe United	34	18	7	9	71	39	43
Worksop Town	34	20	3	11	71	52	43
Mexborough Town	34	18	6	10	63	45	42
Sheffield Wednesday Reserves	34	16	6	12	53	44	38
Rotherham Town	34	14	8	12	83	71	36
Castleford Town	34	14	8	12	53	46	36
Hull City Reserves	34	16	2	16	74	59	34
Grimsby Town	34	14	5	15	66	64	33
Rotherham County Reserves	34	13	5	16	60	57	31
Leeds United	34	11	9	14	56	56	31
Notts County Reserves	34	10	11	13	50	56	31
Halifax Town	34	13	4	17	52	70	30
Lincoln City Reserves	34	8	7	19	43	83	23
Barnsley Reserves	34	6	9	19	46	72	21
Silverwood Colliery	34	6	7	21	38	89	19
Gainsborough Trinity	34	7	3	24	37	95	17

1920-21

Midland Counties League
Manager: Joe McClelland

Did you know that?

- Halifax Town won their last 13 League and cup matches at Exley.
- Tom Jenkinson was the son of the famous John Jenkinson of Bradford and Yorkshire County Rugby fame.
- In Town's FA Cup match with Allerton Bywater on 9 October, the referee blew for time five minutes early, then called the players back out to complete the match.
- Initial plans for The Shay, drawn up in November 1920, included two playing fields for school children, three or four hard tennis courts and a bowling green.
- Halifax Town appeared in blue-and-white-striped shirts for the first time in the game with Castleford Town on 8 January 1921.
- Skipper Ernie Whiteside scored two own goals in the 5–0 defeat at Notts County on 13 January 1921.
- Clem Longbottom refused to play in Town's game with Nottingham Forest Reserves on 15 January 1921 because he wanted to watch the local Stainland v West Vale derby.
- Tempestuous Jack Scull was sent off twice, in the games with Rotherham County Reserves on 30 October 1920 and in the West Riding Senior Cup semi-final replay with Bradford on 9 May 1921.
- New signings Jimmy Haldane and Jock Jamieson originally played under the names 'Jackson' and 'Thompson' respectively.
- Biggest League win: 4–0 v Barnsley Reserves (h), 11 December 1920.
- Heaviest League defeat: 0–5 v Rotherham County Reserves (a), 25 October, v Notts County Reserves (a), 13 January, v Scunthorpe United (a), 7 May.
- Ever-present: Ernie Smith.

Match No.	Date		Venue	Opponents	Result		Scorers	Attendance
1	Aug	28	H	Denaby United	W	3-1	Stott, Anderson, Jenkinson	
2	Sep	4	H	Worksop Town	W	3-0	Jenkinson, Stott, Smith	
3		18	H	Sheffield United Reserves	L	1-3	Anderson	
4	Oct	16	H	Doncaster Rovers	W	2-0	Woolgar, Anderson	
5		25	A	Rotherham County Reserves	L	0-5		8,000
6		30	H	Rotherham County Reserves	L	0-2		2,000
7	Nov	13	H	Mexborough Town	D	0-0		
8		27	H	Rotherham Town	D	1-1	Jones	
9	Dec	4	A	Barnsley Reserves	D	2-2	Jones 2	
10		11	H	Barnsley Reserves	W	4-0	Smith, Jones, Wild, Robinson	
11		18	A	Castleford Town	L	2-4	Jones, Jenkinson	
12		25	H	Leeds United	W	2-0	Smith (pen), Clark	5,000
13		27	A	Leeds United	L	0-3		4,000
14		28	A	Doncaster Rovers	L	0-1		6,000
15	Jan	1	A	Hull City Reserves	L	1-2	Jones	
16		8	H	Castleford Town	W	4-3	Woolgar, Rogers (pen), Smith, Stott	
17		13	A	Notts County Reserves	L	0-5		2,000
18		15	H	Nottingham Forest Reserves	W	3-2	Whiteside, Wild, Stott	
19		22	H	Chesterfield Municipal	W	2-0	Whiteside, Stott	
20		24	H	Sheffield United Reserves	D	1-1	Robinson	
21		29	A	Gainsborough Trinity	L	0-2		
22	Feb	5	H	Gainsborough Trinity	W	4-1	Stott 2, Wild 2	
23		12	A	Chesterfield Municipal	L	1-2	Wild	4,300
24		17	A	Nottingham Forest Reserves	L	0-1		3,000
25		19	H	Scunthorpe United	W	1-0	Betts (og)	3,500
26		26	A	Grimsby Town Reserves	L	0-1		6,000
27	Mar	5	H	Notts County Reserves	W	3-1	Helliwell, Wild, Smith	
28		12	H	Mexborough Town	D	1-1	Whiteside	
29		19	H	Grimsby Town Reserves	W	2-1	Whiteside, Wild	
30		25	A	Lincoln City Reserves	L	1-5	Whiteside	9,000
31		26	H	Denaby United	W	3-0	Helliwell, Smith 2	
32		29	H	Hull City Reserves	W	2-0	Stott, Anderson	3,000
33	Apr	7	A	Rotherham Town	L	0-2		3,000
34		9	A	Worksop Town	L	1-3	Whiteside	
35		16	H	Lincoln City Reserves	W	1-0	Whiteside	4,000
36		23	H	Sheffield Wednesday Reserves	W	2-1	Stott, Jamieson	
37		30	A	Sheffield Wednesday Reserves	W	1-0	Smith	
38	May	7	A	Scunthorpe United	L	0-5		

Final League Position: 11th in Midland Counties League

1 own-goal

Apps
Gls

FA CUP

	Date		Venue	Opponents	Result		Scorers	Attendance
Q1	Sep	11	H	Rowntrees	W	5-3	Stott 3, Robinson, Jenkinson	
Q2		25	H	Liversedge	W	3-1	Wild, Anderson, Robinson	3,000
Q3	Oct	9	H	Allerton Bywater	W	4-1	Wild, Smith 2, Jenkinson	
Q4		23	H	Harrogate	W	1-0	Jenkinson (pen)	
Q5	Nov	6	A	Calverley	W	4-2	Wild, Jenkinson, Whiteside, Anderson	
Q6		20	A	Castleford Town	L	1-3	Robinson	

Apps
Gls

414

League Table

	P	W	D	L	F	A	Pts
Lincoln City Reserves	38	27	3	8	95	40	57
Notts County Reserves	38	22	9	7	80	45	53
Chesterfield Town	38	18	11	9	70	46	47
Scunthorpe United	38	18	9	11	64	43	45
Rotherham Town	38	18	8	12	68	48	44
Sheffield United Reserves	38	16	10	12	73	63	42
Rotherham County	38	16	9	13	57	37	41
Castleford Town	38	17	6	15	61	56	40
Sheffield Wednesday Reserves	38	16	7	15	66	50	39
Worksop Town	38	16	7	15	62	55	39
Halifax Town	38	17	5	16	54	62	39
Leeds United Reserves	38	15	8	15	49	51	38
Gainsborough Trinity	38	14	8	16	58	60	36
Nottingham Forest Reserves	38	13	10	15	69	77	36
Hull City Reserves	38	12	9	17	52	68	33
Doncaster Rovers	38	11	10	17	38	54	32
Mexborough Town	38	10	11	17	39	61	31
Grimsby Town Reserves	38	11	6	21	45	72	28
Barnsley Reserves	38	9	8	21	55	86	26
Denaby United	38	4	6	28	37	118	14

1921-22

Division Three (North)
Manager: Joe McClelland

Did you know that?

- Halifax Town's first League goal was scored by John Woods after 15 minutes of their second match, the first game at The Shay.
- Captain was Sam Challinor.
- David Anderson was licensee of the Pineapple Hotel at North Bridge, Halifax.
- Abe Waddington played in two Test matches for England in 1920 and 1921.
- Jock Jamieson joined the police force and became known as 'Mr Murder' of Scotland Yard, after working on more cases than any other officer in 33 years. Halifax Town conceded their first League goal in the first minute of their opening match at Darlington.
- Admission at The Shay was 1s for adults, 6d for ladies and youths, and 3d for schoolboys.
- Revd P.M. Weston, vicar of St. Marks', Siddal, was elected club chaplain on 16 December 1921.
- Town adopted a black kitten, found in the Shay Pavilion, as mascot.
- Halifax Town failed to win back-to-back matches.
- Johnny Whalley's hat-trick in the 5–5 draw with Crewe Alexandra on 29 April was the first in the League by a Halifax Town player.
- Biggest League win: 5–1 v Darlington (h), 3 September.
- Heaviest League defeat: 1–5 v Wrexham (a), 18 March.
- Tommy Birtwhistle became an unofficial knur and spell world champion.

Match No.	Date	Venue	Opponents	Result		Scorers	Attendance
1	Aug 27	A	Darlington	L	0-2		8,532
2	Sep 3	H	Darlington	W	5-1	Woods 2, Dent 2, Hetherington	10,143
3	10	A	Rochdale	D	3-3	Woods 2, Hetherington	8,000
4	17	H	Rochdale	D	1-1	Challinor	10,754
5	24	A	Tranmere Rovers	D	2-2	Woods 2	8,000
6	Oct 1	H	Tranmere Rovers	L	0-2		8,189
7	8	H	Stalybridge Celtic	L	2-3	Dent, Wellock	8,358
8	15	A	Stalybridge Celtic	L	1-2	Woods	4,000
9	22	A	Wigan Borough	L	3-4	Wild, Dent 2	3,000
10	29	H	Wigan Borough	L	1-2	Woods	7,000
11	Nov 5	H	Hartlepools United	W	3-0	Dent, Hetherington 2	6,500
12	12	A	Hartlepools United	L	0-4		7,000
13	19	A	Southport	L	0-3		5,000
14	26	H	Southport	D	1-1	Whalley	3,000
15	Dec 10	H	Accrington Stanley	W	2-1	Challinor, Anderson	8,000
16	17	A	Crewe Alexandra	L	1-2	Jamieson	6,000
17	24	A	Grimsby Town	L	1-4	Hetherington	5,000
18	26	A	Stockport County	D	0-0		
19	27	H	Stockport County	W	1-0	Woods	
20	31	H	Walsall	L	1-3	Anderson	4,000
21	Jan 14	A	Walsall	L	1-4	Hetherington	4,667
22	16	H	Grimsby Town	W	2-0	Hetherington 2	
23	21	A	Lincoln City	L	1-3	Jamieson	
24	Feb 4	A	Ashington	L	1-3	Humpish	
25	11	H	Ashington	W	2-0	Pinkney 2	
26	16	H	Lincoln City	L	1-2	Hetherington	
27	18	A	Barrow	D	1-1	Hetherington	5,000
28	25	H	Barrow	W	3-2	Whalley, Smith, Hetherington	8,000
29	Mar 4	A	Durham City	L	1-3	Wellock (pen)	2,000
30	11	H	Durham City	W	3-2	Woods 2, Linley	
31	18	A	Wrexham	L	1-5	Woods	4,000
32	25	H	Wrexham	D	0-0		4,000
33	Apr 1	A	Nelson	D	0-0		7,000
34	8	H	Nelson	W	3-1	Jamieson 2, Dent	
35	15	H	Chesterfield	L	1-2	Wellock (pen)	
36	17	A	Accrington Stanley	W	2-1	Wild, Whalley	6,000
37	22	A	Chesterfield	L	0-2		4,000
38	29	H	Crewe Alexandra	D	5-5	Whalley 3, Dent 2	

Final League Position: 18th in Division Three (North)

Apps
Gls

FA CUP
Did not enter

League Table

	P	W	D	L	F	A	Pts
Stockport County	38	24	8	6	60	21	56
Darlington	38	22	6	10	81	37	50
Grimsby Town	38	21	8	9	72	47	50
Hartlepools United	38	17	8	13	52	39	42
Accrington Stanley	38	19	3	16	73	57	41
Crewe Alexandra	38	18	5	15	60	56	41
Stalybridge Celtic	38	18	5	15	62	63	41
Walsall	38	18	3	17	66	65	39
Southport	38	14	10	14	55	44	38
Ashington	38	17	4	17	59	66	38
Durham City	38	17	3	18	68	67	37
Wrexham	38	14	9	15	51	56	37
Chesterfield	38	16	3	19	48	67	35
Lincoln City	38	14	6	18	48	59	34
Barrow	38	14	5	19	42	54	33
Nelson	38	13	7	18	48	66	33
Wigan Borough	38	11	9	18	46	72	31
Tranmere Rovers	38	9	11	18	51	61	29
Halifax Town	38	10	9	19	56	76	29
Rochdale	38	11	4	23	52	77	26

1922-23

Division Three (North)
Manager: Joe McClelland

Did you know that?

- Halifax Town's 100th League goal was scored by Cliff Price, Town's second goal in the 3–2 defeat at Ashington on 31 March 1923.
- Captain was Ellis Hall.
- The 6–1 FA Cup victory over Rotherham County on 18 November was a Shay record.
- Matt Ellson was a schoolmaster.
- Ernie Dixon scored 22 goals in all competitions
- Town's run of three consecutive League victories between 3–17 March was a club record
- The attendance (estimated) of 18,000 for the visit of Nelson on Christmas Day was a Shay record.
- Goalkeeper Herbert Bown scored a penalty in Town's 2–1 victory over Stalybridge Celtic in the last match of the season, having scored one in Sid Hetherington's benefit match two days earlier.
- Halifax Town reached the Final of the West Riding Senior Cup for the first time, only to lose 1–0 to Leeds United.
- Biggest League win: 3–0 v Bradford (h), 16 September, v Hartlepools United 21 October, v Barrow (h), 17 March.
- Heaviest League defeat: 1–4 v Accrington Stanley (a), 30 December.
- Ever-presents: Herbert Bown, Jack Lees, Ellis Hall.

Match No.	Date		Venue	Opponents	Result		Scorers	Attendance
1	Aug	26	H	Lincoln City	W	3-1	Price, E. Hall, Ellson	15,000
2	Sep	2	A	Lincoln City	D	0-0		
3		9	A	Bradford	D	2-2	Dixon, Ellson	14,000
4		12	A	Nelson	L	0-2		5,000
5		16	H	Bradford	W	3-0	Dixon 3 (1 pen)	16,500
6		23	H	Tranmere Rovers	W	3-1	Dixon 2, Price	10,000
7		30	A	Tranmere Rovers	L	1-2	Dixon	5,000
8	Oct	7	H	Durham City	L	1-3	Burkinshaw	9,000
9		14	A	Durham City	D	2-2	Dixon, Whalley	3,000
10		21	H	Hartlepools United	W	3-0	Whalley, Dixon, Price	10,000
11		28	A	Hartlepools United	L	2-3	Price 2	4,502
12	Nov	4	H	Wigan Borough	W	1-0	Dixon	10,000
13		11	H	Wigan Borough	L	0-1		10,500
14		25	H	Chesterfield	W	2-0	Dixon, Whalley	10,000
15	Dec	9	H	Crewe Alexandra	W	1-0	Price	8,000
16		23	A	Grimsby Town	W	1-0	Price	
17		25	H	Nelson	D	2-2	Price, F. Hall	18,000
18		30	A	Accrington Stanley	L	1-4	Vallis	5,000
19	Jan	6	H	Accrington Stanley	D	0-0		18,000
20		20	H	Walsall	L	1-2	Price	8,000
21		22	H	Grimsby Town	W	1-0	F. Hall	4,000
22		27	A	Walsall	L	1-2	Price	7,068
23	Feb	3	H	Darlington	W	2-1	Price, Ellson	10,000
24		10	A	Darlington	W	1-0	Ellson	1,830
25		17	H	Wrexham	D	1-1	Ellson	
26		24	A	Wrexham	L	1-2	Dixon	4,000
27	Mar	3	H	Rochdale	W	1-0	Dent	8,000
28		10	A	Rochdale	W	1-0	Dixon	6,000
29		17	H	Barrow	W	3-0	Dent, Dixon 2	9,000
30		21	A	Chesterfield	L	0-3		6,000
31		24	A	Barrow	W	1-0	Burkinshaw	4,000
32		31	A	Ashington	L	2-3	Dixon, Price	4,000
33	Apr	2	A	Crewe Alexandra	L	1-2	Dixon	3,633
34		7	H	Ashington	D	0-0		4,000
35		14	A	Southport	W	3-1	Whalley, Price, Dent	4,000
36		21	H	Southport	L	0-1		8,000
37		28	A	Stalybridge Celtic	L	3-4	Dixon 2, Price	3,000
38	May	5	H	Stalybridge Celtic	W	2-1	Bown (pen), Price	6,000

Final League Position: 7th in Division Three (North)

Apps
Gls

FA CUP

*Q4	Nov	18	H	Rotherham Town	W	6-1	Dixon (pen), Price 3, Crawshaw, Whalley	5,000
Q5	Dec	2	A	Accrington Stanley	D	1-1	Page (og)	
R		4	H	Accrington Stanley	W	1-0	Dent	4,000
Q6		16	A	Mansfield Town	W	2-0	Price, Dixon	5,766
1	Jan	13	A	South Shields	L	1-3	Price	10,374

*Away tie switched to The Shay

Apps
Gls

1 own-goal

League Table

	P	W	D	L	F	A	Pts
Nelson	38	24	3	11	61	41	51
Bradford	38	19	9	10	67	38	47
Walsall	38	19	8	11	51	44	46
Chesterfield	38	19	7	12	68	52	45
Wigan Borough	38	18	8	12	64	39	44
Crewe Alexandra	38	17	9	12	48	38	43
Halifax Town	38	17	7	14	53	46	41
Accrington Stanley	38	17	7	14	59	65	41
Darlington	38	15	10	13	59	46	40
Wrexham	38	14	10	14	38	48	38
Stalybridge Celtic	38	15	6	17	42	47	36
Rochdale	38	13	10	15	42	53	36
Lincoln City	38	13	10	15	39	55	36
Grimsby Town	38	14	5	19	55	52	33
Hartlepools United	38	10	12	16	48	54	32
Tranmere Rovers	38	12	8	18	49	59	32
Southport	38	12	7	19	32	46	31
Barrow	38	13	4	21	50	60	30
Ashington	38	11	8	19	51	77	30
Durham City	38	9	10	19	43	59	28

1923-24

Division Three (North)

Manager: Joe McClelland

Did you know that?

- Fred Fayers was initially appointed captain, before Ellis Hall was reinstated in September.
- Jimmy Moore was an FA Cup-winner with Barnsley in 1912.
- Centre-forward for non-League Peterborough & Fletton United in the FA Cup match was former Town player Andy Lincoln.
- Town found themselves 2–0 down after only four minutes of their match at Crewe Alexandra on 22 December.
- Halifax Town set a then club record of eight unbeaten League matches between 24 November and 5 January. Victories over Peterborough United and Rotherham County took the unbeaten run to 10 matches.
- Halifax Town made £2,397 from their eight FA Cup ties.
- Ben Wheelhouse, Ernie Dixon and George Parkin were all transferred to Burnley within a two-day period.
- Joe Lees and Herbert Lounds were team mates at Rotherham County.
- Biggest League win: 3–0 v Walsall (h) 27 October, v Ashington (h), 10 November, v Accrington Stanley, 29 December
- Heaviest League defeat: 0–7 v Doncaster Rovers (a), 22 March, a then club record.
- Halifax Town were celebrated in musical tomes with a song written by Tom and Ella Newsome. Entitled, Hurrah! Hurroo! Hurray! it told the story of Billy Bray who took his uncle John to a match at The Shay and was performed by Fred Hutchings at the Great Halifax Town Night at the Palace and Hippodrome on 5 October. Its rip-roaring chorus went:

'We don't care who we're meeting, The Shay Brigade will take some beating.

We're here – to cheer – the team we love so dear,

So shout with might and main,

We play the game boys we do, we're here again.'

- Ever-present: Herbert Bown.

Match No.	Date		Venue	Opponents	Result		Scorers	Attendance
1	Aug	25	A	Lincoln City	D	1-1	Featherstone (pen)	
2		27	H	Tranmere Rovers	D	0-0		10,000
3	Sep	1	H	Lincoln City	W	1-0	Dixon	
4		6	A	Tranmere Rovers	L	0-3		7,000
5		8	H	Grimsby Town	L	1-3	Dixon	8,000
6		15	A	Grimsby Town	D	1-1	Housley	
7		22	H	New Brighton	W	2-1	Featherstone, Moore	8,000
8		29	A	New Brighton	L	0-2		6,000
9	Oct	6	H	Wolverhampton Wanderers	D	2-2	Housley, Ellson	5,140
10		13	A	Wolverhampton Wanderers	L	0-4		15,000
11		20	A	Walsall	L	0-2		6,307
12		27	H	Walsall	W	3-0	Housley, Moore, Dixon	6,000
13	Nov	3	A	Ashington	L	0-4		4,700
14		10	H	Ashington	W	3-0	Housley, Dixon 2	
15		17	H	Wigan Borough	L	1-2	Dixon	1,000
16		24	A	Wigan Borough	W	1-0	Foster	10,000
17	Dec	8	A	Durham City	D	2-2	Whalley, Dixon	4,000
18		22	A	Crewe Alexandra	D	2-2	Turner (og), Moore	
19		25	H	Hartlepools United	W	1-0	Foster	10,000
20		26	A	Hartlepools United	W	3-1	Housley, Dixon, Moore	3,200
21		29	H	Accrington Stanley	W	3-0	Moore, Housley, Whalley	
22	Jan	1	H	Crewe Alexandra	W	2-0	Whalley, Dixon	4,000
23		5	A	Accrington Stanley	W	2-1	Dixon 2	
24		19	A	Bradford	L	0-1		14,000
25		26	H	Bradford	D	0-0		10,000
26	Feb	9	H	Chesterfield	W	2-0	Housley, Oldacre	4,000
27		16	A	Rotherham County	L	2-3	Dixon, Hodgson	8,000
28		23	H	Rotherham County	L	0-2		
29	Mar	1	A	Wrexham	W	1-0	Housley	4,000
30		8	H	Wrexham	D	0-0		6,000
31		10	H	Durham City	W	2-1	Dixon 2	1,000
32		15	H	Doncaster Rovers	L	0-1		4,000
33		22	A	Doncaster Rovers	L	0-7		7,000
34		26	A	Chesterfield	D	1-1	Housley	4,000
35		29	H	Rochdale	L	0-1		4,000
36	Apr	5	A	Rochdale	L	0-3		6,000
37		12	H	Southport	W	1-0	JWD Lees	3,000
38		18	A	Barrow	L	0-1		3,000
39		19	A	Southport	L	0-3		6,000
40		21	H	Barrow	W	1-0	Whalley	3,000
41		26	H	Darlington	L	1-4	Moore	3,000
42	May	3	A	Darlington	D	0-0		3,000

Final League Position: 14th in Division Three (North)

1 own-goal

Apps
Gls

FA Cup

Q5	Dec	1	A	Peterborough & Fletton United	W	1-0	Foster	6,129
Q6		15	H	Rotherham County	W	1-0	Moore	11,340
1	Jan	12	A	Northampton Town	D	1-1	Dixon	12,110
R		17	H	Northampton Town	D	1-1*	Housley	12,000
2R		21	N	Northampton Town	W	4-2*	Moore, Dixon, Whalley, Wild	7,500
2	Feb	2	A	Manchester City	D	2-2	Moore, Whalley	30,970
R		6	N**	Manchester City	D	0-0*		21,590
2R		11	N***	Manchester City	L	0-3		28,128

* After extra-time. ** Played at Bramall Lane, Sheffield United.
*** Played at Old Trafford, Manchester United.

Apps
Gls

League Table

	P	W	D	L	F	A	Pts
Wolverhampton Wanderers	42	24	15	3	76	27	63
Rochdale	42	25	12	5	60	26	62
Chesterfield	42	22	10	0	70	39	54
Rotherham County	42	23	6	3	70	43	52
Bradford	42	21	10	1	69	43	52
Darlington	42	20	8	4	70	53	48
Southport	42	16	14	2	44	42	46
Ashington	42	18	8	6	59	61	44
Doncaster Rovers	42	15	12	5	59	53	42
Wigan Borough	42	14	14	4	55	53	42
Grimsby Town	42	14	13	5	49	47	41
Tranmere Rovers	42	13	15	4	51	60	41
Accrington Stanley	42	16	8	8	48	61	40
Halifax Town	42	15	10	7	42	59	40
Durham City	42	15	9	8	59	60	39
Wrexham	42	10	18	4	37	44	38
Walsall	42	14	8	10	44	59	36
New Brighton	42	11	13	8	40	53	35
Lincoln City	42	10	12	20	43	59	32
Crewe Alexandra	42	7	13	22	32	58	27
Hartlepools United	42	7	11	24	33	70	25
Barrow	42	8	9	25	35	80	25

1924-25

Division Three (North)
Manager: Joe McClelland

Did you know that?

- Halifax Town were founder members of the Midland Combination League for reserve sides.
- Halifax Town wore blue shirts with gold shoulders.
- Captain was Alf Dark.
- Tommy Duncan and his brother John were the first pair of brothers to be transferred together when they joined Leicester City from Raith Rovers in 1922.
- Halifax Town provided the opposition against Rosendale United for ex-Town player Jimmy Wishart's benefit match on 22 September
- Town's home game with Crewe Alexandra on 12 March kicked off at 4.15pm after the ceremonies of the visit of Princess Mary opening the Linford Moore Kitchenman Ward at Halifax Infirmary had been concluded.
- Biggest League win: 4–0 v Rotherham County (h), 3 January
- Biggest League defeat: 0–3 v Darlington (a), 2 January.
- Town's biggest win of the season came the day after the heaviest defeat.
- Ever-present: Jimmy Lodge.

Match No.	Date		Venue	Opponents	Result		Scorers	Attendance
1	Aug	30	H	Wrexham	W	3-1	Seabrook 2, King	10,000
2	Sep	6	A	Rotherham County	D	0-0		4,000
3		13	H	Chesterfield	W	1-0	Howson	7,000
4		20	A	Accrington Stanley	L	0-2		8,000
5		27	H	Barrow	W	2-0	Martin, Howson	10,000
6	Oct	4	H	New Brighton	L	1-2	King	12,000
7		11	A	Grimsby Town	D	1-1	King	8,000
8		18	H	Hartlepools United	W	2-0	Duncan, Martin (pen)	
9		25	A	Nelson	L	1-2	Whalley	10,000
10	Nov	1	H	Ashington	D	0-0		5,000
11		8	A	Southport	L	1-3	King	5,000
12		15	A	Bradford	L	1-2	Shankly	14,000
13		22	A	Durham City	W	2-1	Shankly, King	2,000
14	Dec	6	A	Wigan Borough	L	0-2		8,000
15		13	H	Walsall	D	1-1	Howson	3,000
16		20	H	Tranmere Rovers	L	1-3	Whalley	4,000
17		25	H	Lincoln City	W	1-0	Seabrook	10,000
18		26	A	Lincoln City	D	1-1	Seabrook	8,000
19		27	A	Wrexham	D	0-0		3,000
20	Jan	2	A	Darlington	L	0-3		
21		3	H	Rotherham County	W	4-0	Seabrook 2, Whalley, Dixon	5,000
22		17	A	Chesterfield	W	3-1	Dixon 3	5,000
23		24	H	Accrington Stanley	D	2-2	Howson 2	5,000
24		26	A	Doncaster Rovers	W	2-0	Horsman (og), Dixon	
25		31	A	Barrow	L	1-2	Dixon	3,000
26	Feb	7	A	New Brighton	L	1-3	Duncan	5,000
27		14	H	Grimsby Town	W	1-0	Seabrook	3,000
28		21	A	Hartlepools United	D	1-1	Dixon	5,000
29		28	H	Nelson	L	2-4	Seabrook (pen), Hall	10,000
30	Mar	7	A	Ashington	L	0-2		
31		12	H	Crewe Alexandra	D	2-2	Seabrook, Dixon	3,000
32		14	H	Southport	W	2-0	Duncan, Howson	4,000
33		21	A	Doncaster Rovers	W	1-0	Duncan	4,000
34		28	H	Durham City	W	3-0	Seabrook 2, Howson	5,000
35	Apr	4	A	Crewe Alexandra	D	1-1	Dixon	4,000
36		10	A	Rochdale	L	1-3	Howson	3,000
37		11	A	Wigan Borough	L	1-2	Howson	4,000
38		13	H	Rochdale	W	3-1	Dixon 2, Howson	6,000
39		14	H	Darlington	D	1-1	Howson	11,000
40		18	A	Walsall	W	2-0	Duncan, Martin	2,583
41		25	A	Tranmere Rovers	W	2-0	Seabrook, Howson	4,000
42	May	2	H	Bradford	L	1-3	Dixon	8,000

Final League Position: 9th in Division Three (North)

1 own-goal

Apps
Gls

FA CUP

1	Nov	29	H	Rochdale	L	0-1		12,000

Apps
Gls

	Fryer, HC	Lees, JW	Lodge, JW	Dirk, AJ	Hall, E	Martin, AF	Lounds, H	Howson, W	Seabrook, A	King, J	Foster, JTF	Duncan, TG	Whaley, JW	Shankly, J	Walsh, C	McEachran, G	McGriffin, G	Haywood, JW	Newton, F	Dutchet, DT	Dixon, E	Price, GL
	1	2	3	4	5	6	7	8	9	10	11											
	1	2	3	4	5	6	7	8	9	10	11											
	1	2	3	4	5	6	7	8	9	10	11											
	1	2	3	4	5	6		8	9	10	11	7										
	1	2	3	4	5	6			9	10		7	8	11								
	1	2	3	4	5	6			9	10		7	8	11								
	1	2	3	4	5	6				10		7	8	11	9							
	1	2	3	4	5	6				10		7	8	11	9							
	1	2	3	4	5	6				10		7	8	11	9							
	1	2	3	4	5	6			9	10	7	8	11									
	1	2	3	4	5	6				10	7	8		11	6							
	1		3		5	6			10		7	8	11	9	4	3						
	1	2	3		5	6				10	7	8	11	9	4							
	1	2	3	5	4			8			7	11		6		9	10					
	1	2	3		5			10		7		11		9		8		4	6			
	1	2	3		5			10		7		11		9		8		4	6			
	1	2	3		5			10	8		7	11		4				6	9			
	1	2	3		5			10	8		7	11		4				6	9			
	1	2	3		5		7	10	8			11		4				6	9			
	1	2	3		5			10	8		7	11		4				6	9			
	1	2	3		5			10	8		7	11		4				6	9			
	1	2	3		5			10	8		7	11		4				6	9			
	1	2	3		5			10	8		7	11		4				6	9			
	1	2	3		5			10	8		7	11		4				6	9			
	1	2	3		5				8		7	10	11	4				6	9			
	1	2	3		5				8		7	10	11	4				6	9			
	1	2	3		5				8		7	10	11	4				6	9			
	1	2	3		5				8		7	10	11	4				6	9			
	1	2	3		5	6		10	8		7		11					4	9			
	1	2	3		5	6		10	8		7		11					4	9			
		2	3		5	6		10	7		11	8						4	9	1		
		2	3		5	6		10	7		11	8	9					4		1		
		2	3		5	6		10	7		11	8						4	9	1		
		2	3		5	6		10	7		11	8						4	9	1		
		2	3		5	6		10	7		11	8						4	9	1		
		2	3		5	6		10	7		11	8						4	9	1		
		2	3	5		6		10	7			8	11					4	9	1		
		2	3	5		6		10	7			8	11					4	9	1		
		2	3	5		6		10	7			8	11					4	9	1		
		2	3	5		6		10	7			8	11					4	9	1		
		2	3	5		6		10	7			8	11					4	9	1		
	31	41	42	17	37	26	4	30	33	12	35	26	31	7	19	1	2	28	25	11		
				1	3			12	12	5		5	3	2					12			

	Fryer, HC	Lees, JW	Lodge, JW	Dirk, AJ	Hall, E	Martin, AF	Lounds, H	Howson, W	Seabrook, A	King, J	Foster, JTF	Duncan, TG	Whaley, JW	Shankly, J	Walsh, C
	1	2	3		5	6				10	7	8	11	9	4
	1	1	1		1	1				1	1	1	1	1	1

League Table

	P	W	D	L	F	A	Pts
Darlington	42	24	10	8	78	33	58
Nelson	42	23	7	12	79	50	53
New Brighton	42	23	7	12	75	50	53
Southport	42	22	7	13	59	37	51
Bradford	42	19	12	11	84	42	50
Rochdale	42	21	7	14	75	53	49
Chesterfield	42	17	11	14	60	44	45
Lincoln City	42	18	8	16	53	58	44
Halifax Town	42	16	11	15	56	52	43
Ashington	42	16	10	16	68	76	42
Wigan Borough	42	15	11	16	62	65	41
Grimsby Town	42	15	9	18	60	60	39
Durham City	42	13	13	16	50	68	39
Barrow	42	16	7	19	51	74	39
Crewe Alexandra	42	13	13	16	53	78	39
Wrexham	42	15	8	19	53	61	38
Accrington Stanley	42	15	8	19	60	72	38
Doncaster Rovers	42	14	10	18	54	65	38
Walsall	42	13	11	18	44	53	37
Hartlepools United	42	12	11	19	45	63	35
Tranmere Rovers	42	14	4	24	59	78	32
Rotherham County	42	7	7	28	42	88	21

1925-26 Division Three (North)

Manager: Joe McClelland

Did you know that?

- Captain was Donald Duckett.
- Ernie Dixon scored in four consecutive matches between 15 September and 3 October.
- Ernie Dixon became the first Town player to score four goals in a League match, in the 5–1 defeat of Rotherham United on 19 September.
- Andy Martin scored from 40 yards in the 2–1 win over Durham City on 10 October.
- Ernie Dixon top scored with 21 League goals, a then club record.
- Biggest League win: 5–0 v Walsall (h), 26 December.
- Heaviest League defeat: 1–4 v Coventry City, 26 September.
- Ever-present: Jack Lees.
- Town's return of 45 points was a new club record.

Match No.	Date	Venue	Opponents	Result		Scorers	Attendance
1	Aug 29	A	Chesterfield	L	0-1		6,907
2	Sep 1	H	Rochdale	D	1-1	Howson	7,362
3	5	H	Bradford	L	1-2	Howson	11,229
4	7	H	Hartlepools United	W	2-1	Dixon, Martin	4,169
5	12	A	Grimsby Town	L	0-1		7,722
6	15	A	Rochdale	L	1-2	Dixon	6,528
7	19	H	Rotherham United	W	5-1	Dixon 4, Martin	2,537
8	26	A	Coventry City	L	1-4	Dixon	8,799
9	Oct 3	A	Accrington Stanley	W	1-0	Dixon	4,798
10	10	H	Durham City	W	2-1	Martin, Kennie	4,491
11	17	A	Wrexham	W	2-1	Kennie, Dixon	4,859
12	24	A	Doncaster Rovers	D	2-2	Howson, Waites	7,066
13	31	H	Barrow	W	3-2	Dixon 2, Dark	4,726
14	Nov 7	A	Nelson	D	1-1	Dixon	4,538
15	14	H	Crewe Alexandra	W	1-0	Smeaton	8,189
16	21	A	New Brighton	L	1-2	Waites	4,086
17	Dec 5	A	Ashington	W	1-0	Dixon	2,847
18	12	H	Nelson	D	1-1	Dixon	7,204
19	19	A	Lincoln City	W	1-0	Seabrook	4,444
20	26	H	Walsall	W	5-0	Howson 3, Seabrook, Waites	8,139
21	Jan 1	A	Hartlepools United	D	1-1	Waites	5,036
22	2	H	Chesterfield	W	2-0	Waites, Martin (pen)	10,940
23	9	H	Ashington	D	0-0		9,397
24	16	A	Bradford	D	2-2	Martin, Dixon	22,180
25	23	H	Grimsby Town	L	0-2		7,896
26	25	A	Walsall	L	1-3	Smeaton	1,073
27	30	A	Rotherham United	D	1-1	Dixon	5,314
28	Feb 6	H	Coventry City	W	1-0	Dixon	6,047
29	13	H	Accrington Stanley	D	1-1	Dixon	5,110
30	20	A	Durham City	L	0-2		2,354
31	27	A	Wrexham	L	0-2		4,539
32	Mar 6	H	Doncaster Rovers	L	0-3		5,086
33	13	A	Barrow	W	2-1	Dixon, Waites	1,894
34	18	H	Southport	W	3-0	Seabrook 2, Dixon	2,203
35	27	H	Crewe Alexandra	W	1-0	Cotton	4,861
36	Apr 2	A	Tranmere Rovers	L	1-3	Waites	11,797
37	3	H	New Brighton	W	1-0	Cotton (pen)	6,394
38	6	H	Tranmere Rovers	D	1-1	Cotton	4,850
39	10	A	Wigan Borough	D	0-0		6,348
40	15	H	Wigan Borough	W	2-0	Dixon, Low	2,859
41	24	A	Southport	L	1-3	Seabrook	2,956
42	May 1	H	Lincoln City	L	0-2		1,958

Final League Position: 5th in Division Three (North)

Apps
Gls

FA CUP

	Date	Venue	Opponents	Result			Attendance
1	Nov 28	H	Rotherham United	L	0-3		9,468

Apps
Gls

	Newton, J	Lees, JW	Gadsden, E	Ducklett, DT	Dark, AJ	Martin, AF	Seabrook, A	Smeeton, AR	Dixon, E	Howson, W	Kennie, G	Duncan, TG	Whalley, JW	McGinn, A	Reproc, HA	Wares, SH	Moughton, W	Barber, LF	Campbell, A	Cotton, WC	Low, J	McCaffery, J
	1	2	3	4	5	6	7	8	9	10	11											
	1	2	3	4	5	6	7		9	10		8	11									
	1	2	3	4	5	6	7		9	10		8	11									
	1	2	3		5	6	7		9			8	11	4	10							
	1	2	3	4	5	6		10	9			8	11			7						
	1	2	3	5		6		8	9	10		7	11	4								
	1	2	3	4	5	6		10	9	8	11					7						
	1	2	3	4	5	6		10	9	8	11					7						
	1	2	3	4	5	6		10	9	8	11					7						
	1	2	3	4	5			10	9	8	11			6		7						
	1	2	3	4	5	6		10	9	8	11					7						
	1	2	3	4	5	6		10	9	8	11					7						
	1	2	3	4	5	6		10	9	8	11					7						
	1	2	3	4	5	6		10	9	8	11					7						
	1	2	3	4	5	6	8	10	9		11					7						
	1	2	3	4	5	6	8	10	9		11					7						
	1	2	3	4	5	6	8	10		9	11					7						
	1	2	3	4	5	6	8	10	9		11					7						
	1	2	3	4	5	6	8	10		9	11					7						
	1	2	3	4	5	6	8	10	9		11					7						
	1	2	3	4	5	6	8	10	9		11					7						
	1	2	3	4		6	8	10	9		11					7	5					
	1	2	3	4		6	8	10	9		11					7	5					
		2	3	4		6	8	10	9		11					7	5	1				
		2	3	4		6	8			9		10	11			7		1				
	1	2	3	4	5	6	8		100	9	11					7						
	1	2	3	4	5	6	8		10	9	11					7						
	1	2		4	5	6	8		10	9			11			7			3			
	1	2		4	5	6	8		10	9			11			7			3			
	1	2		4	5	6	8		10				11			7			3	9		
	1	2		4	5	6	8		10				11			7			3	9		
	1	2		4	5	6			10	9			11			7			3	8		
	1	2		4	5	6	7	10	9					5					3	8	11	
	1	2			6	8	10	7						5					3	9	11	
	1	2		4		6	7	10	9		11					4			3	8		
	1	2		4		6	7	10	9		11			5					3	8		
	1	2			5	6	8		9							7	4		3		10	11
	40	42	32	40	34	41	30	36	36	18	28	6	11	6	1	34	4	2	10	5	5	1
				1	5	5	2	21	6	2			7						3	1		

| | 1 | 2 | 3 | 4 | 5 | 6 | | 10 | 9 | 8 | 11 | | | | | 7 | | | | | | |
| | 1 | 1 | 1 | 1 | 1 | 1 | | 1 | 1 | 1 | 1 | | | | | 1 | | | | | | |

League Table

	P	W	D	L	F	A	Pts
Grimsby Town	42	26	9	7	91	40	61
Bradford	42	26	8	3	101	43	60
Rochdale	42	27	5	10	104	58	59
Chesterfield	42	25	5	12	100	54	55
Halifax Town	42	17	11	14	53	50	45
Hartlepools United	42	18	8	16	82	73	44
Tranmere Rovers	42	19	6	17	73	83	44
Nelson	42	16	11	15	89	71	43
Ashington	42	16	11	15	70	62	43
Doncaster Rovers	42	16	11	15	80	72	43
Crewe Alexandra	42	17	9	16	63	61	43
New Brighton	42	17	8	17	69	67	42
Durham City	42	18	6	18	63	70	42
Rotherham United	42	17	7	13	69	92	41
Lincoln City	42	17	5	20	66	82	39
Coventry City	42	16	6	20	73	82	38
Wigan Borough	42	13	11	13	68	74	37
Accrington Stanley	42	17	3	22	81	105	37
Wrexham	42	11	10	21	63	92	32
Southport	42	11	10	21	62	92	32
Walsall	42	10	6	26	58	107	26
Barrow	42	7	4	31	50	98	18

1926-27

Division Three (North)
Manager: Joe McClelland

Did you know that?

- Captain was Donald Duckett.
- A then record Shay crowd of 18,866 watched Town's 2–0 defeat of Bradford on 23 October.
- The *Halifax Courier* organised mass singing prior to Town's home game with Barrow on 5 February.
- Town moved into second place following their 1–0 win at Walsall on 12 February, four points behind leaders Stoke City.
- Halifax Town set a club record of 13 unbeaten League matches between 20 November and 12 February.
- Town drew five consecutive League matches between 20 November and 27 December.
- Town won a then club record six consecutive matches between 8 January and 12 February.
- Biggest League victory: 5–1 v Barrow, 5 February.
- Heaviest League defeat: 1–5 v Stoke City, 7 May.
- Ernie Dixon beat his own record haul by scoring 22 League goals.
- Ever-presents: Alf Dark, Ernie Dixon.

Match No.	Date		Venue	Opponents	Result		Scorers	Attendance
1	Aug	28	H	Stockport County	W	4-1	Williams (og), Dixon 2, Waites	8,269
2		30	H	Durham City	L	1-2	Martin	5,664
3	Sep	4	A	Hartlepools United	W	1-0	Dixon	3,371
4		8	A	Durham City	W	1-0	Smith	1,780
5		11	H	Crewe Alexandra	W	3-1	Dixon, Smith, Housley	7,685
6		18	A	Barrow	D	1-1	McCafferty	6,689
7		25	H	Walsall	D	1-1	Dixon	6,051
8	Oct	2	H	Lincoln City	W	2-1	McCafferty, Martin	7,825
9		9	A	Accrington Stanley	L	2-4	Smith, Housley	3,914
10		16	A	Rotherham United	W	4-2	Dixon, Martin (pen), Housley, Smith	4,597
11		23	H	Bradford	W	2-0	McCafferty 2	18,866
12		30	A	Nelson	D	0-0		7,316
13	Nov	6	H	Chesterfield	W	3-1	Smith, Dixon 2	7,089
14		13	A	Ashington	L	0-3		1,459
15		20	H	New Brighton	D	2-2	Dixon 2	5,581
16	Dec	4	H	Wigan Borough	D	0-0		6,986
17		18	H	Stoke City	D	2-2	Housley, McCafferty	10,965
18		25	H	Southport	D	1-1	Housley (pen)	8,793
19		27	A	Southport	D	0-0		7,176
20	Jan	1	H	Rochdale	W	1-0	Coleman	10,846
21		3	A	Wigan Borough	D	1-1	Martin (pen)	5,431
22		8	A	Wrexham	W	2-1	Seabrook, Smith	3,707
23		15	H	Stockport County	W	3-1	Dixon 2, Seabrook	9,784
24		22	H	Hartlepools United	W	2-1	Martin (pen), Seabrook	5,930
25		29	A	Crewe Alexandra	W	2-1	Dixon 2	13,915
26	Feb	5	H	Barrow	W	5-1	Seabrook, Dixon 2, Waites, Martin	10,231
27		12	A	Walsall	W	1-0	Seabrook	3,867
28		19	A	Lincoln City	L	1-3	Waites	4,344
29		26	H	Accrington Stanley	W	4-3	Waites, Dixon 2, Seabrook	7,547
30	Mar	5	H	Rotherham United	W	4-2	Seabrook, Dixon, Smith, Martin (pen)	6,220
31		12	A	Bradford	L	1-2	Martin	28,286
32		19	H	Nelson	W	4-1	Dixon 2, Smith 2	13,602
33		26	A	Chesterfield	L	0-2		3,607
34	Apr	2	H	Ashington	D	1-1	Smeaton	6,253
35		4	A	Doncaster Rovers	L	0-2		3,964
36		9	H	New Brighton	W	3-0	Martin, Coleman 2	2,446
37		15	A	Tranmere Rovers	D	0-0		11,171
38		16	H	Wrexham	L	0-1		7,284
39		18	A	Rochdale	L	0-2		8,501
40		19	H	Tranmere Rovers	W	2-0	Dixon, McCafferty	4,514
41		30	H	Doncaster Rovers	W	2-1	J Barber, Dixon	4,299
42	May	7	A	Stoke City	L	1-5	Housley	10,319

Final League Position: 4th in Division Three (North)

1 own-goal

Apps
Gls

FA CUP

1	Nov	27	A	Grimsby Town	L	2-3	McCafferty, Dixon	8,700

Apps
Gls

League Table

	P	W	D	L	F	A	Pts
Stoke City	42	27	9	6	92	40	63
Rochdale	42	26	6	10	105	65	58
Bradford	42	24	7	11	101	59	55
Halifax Town	42	21	11	10	70	53	53
Nelson	42	22	7	13	104	75	51
Stockport County	42	22	7	13	93	69	49
Chesterfield	42	21	5	16	92	68	47
Doncaster Rovers	42	18	11	13	81	65	47
Tranmere Rovers	42	19	8	15	85	67	46
New Brighton	42	18	10	14	79	67	46
Lincoln City	42	15	12	15	90	78	42
Southport	42	15	9	18	80	85	39
Wrexham	42	14	10	18	65	73	38
Walsall	42	14	10	18	68	81	38
Crewe Alexandra	42	14	9	19	71	81	37
Ashington	42	12	12	18	60	90	36
Hartlepools United	42	14	6	22	66	81	34
Wigan Borough	42	11	10	21	66	83	32
Rotherham United	42	10	12	20	70	92	32
Durham City	42	12	6	24	58	105	30
Accrington Stanley	42	10	7	25	62	98	27
Barrow	42	7	8	27	54	117	22

1927-28

Division Three (North)
Manager: Joe McClelland

Did you know that?

- Goalkeeper Lewis Barber was transferred to Manchester City for a record fee for a Halifax Town player.
- Fred Fox won one England cap against France in Paris in May 1925 when a Gillingham player.
- Captain was Donald Duckett, then Alf Dark from November.
- Goalkeeper Jack Pennington kept goal for Sale water-polo team. Town won the first five matches in which he played.
- Donald Duckett was sold to leaders Bradford on 24 November, two days before Town's FA Cup tie with Hartlepools United.
- Andy Martin missed a penalty in the cup tie with Hartlepools awarded when a defender fisted the ball into the net!
- A new record Shay gate of 19,935 saw Town's 2–1 victory over Bradford City on 10 September.
- Former Town 'keeper Horace Firth was one of 24 people to share a £6,000 *Sunday Chronicle* jackpot for correctly forecasting the results of 21 League matches in January.
- Biggest League victory: 6–1 v Ashington, 5 September.
- Highest League defeat: 2–6 v Barrow, 24 March.
- Ever-present: Andy Martin.

Match No.	Date		Venue	Opponents	Result		Scorers	Attendance
1	Aug	27	A	Crewe Alexandra	D	1-1	Martin	5,174
2		29	H	Barrow	W	5-2	Seabrook, Housley 3, Hubbert	7,769
3	Sep	3	H	Chesterfield	L	1-2	Martin	9,464
4		5	H	Ashington	W	6-1	Proctor 2, Seabrook 2, Dixon 2	4,944
5		10	H	Bradford City	W	2-1	Dixon, Seabrook	19,935
6		12	A	Ashington	D	3-3	Dixon 2, Housley	1,655
7		17	A	New Brighton	L	1-3	Martin	5,700
8		19	H	Darlington	W	2-1	Dixon, Martin	4,101
9		24	H	Lincoln City	W	3-1	Dixon, Seabrook, Martin	9,615
10	Oct	1	A	Hartlepools United	W	1-0	Seabrook	4,571
11		8	H	Accrington Stanley	W	3-1	Housley, Martin (pen), Dixon	7,173
12		15	A	Wigan Borough	W	3-1	Martin, Housley, Dixon	4,989
13		22	A	Stockport County	L	0-3		9,291
14		29	H	Tranmere Rovers	D	2-2	Dixon, Seabrook	9,503
15	Nov	5	A	Bradford	L	2-3	Seabrook 2	17,747
16		19	A	Nelson	L	2-3	Bell, Hubbert	3,862
17	Dec	3	A	Rotherham United	D	0-0		4,965
18		17	A	Durham City	D	1-1	Smeaton	1,164
19		24	H	Wrexham	W	4-1	Martin 2, Bell, Lees	3,032
20		26	A	Doncaster Rovers	D	1-1	Bell	11,380
21		27	H	Doncaster Rovers	L	0-1		12,909
22		31	H	Crewe Alexandra	D	0-0		4,266
23	Jan	7	A	Chesterfield	L	0-3		3,437
24		14	H	Nelson	W	5-1	Martin 2, Dixon 2, Waites	3,119
25		21	A	Bradford City	D	0-0		18,747
26	Feb	4	A	Lincoln City	L	2-5	Dixon, Groves	5,515
27		11	H	Hartlepools United	W	4-1	Smeaton, Dixon 2, Martin	2,424
28		18	A	Accrington Stanley	L	2-3	Dixon, Groves	3,241
29		25	H	Wigan Borough	D	2-2	Bell, Waites	2,678
30	Mar	3	H	Stockport County	L	1-3	Dixon	4,770
31		10	A	Tranmere Rovers	D	2-2	Martin, Bell	5,858
32		17	H	Bradford	D	1-1	Seabrook	15,842
33		24	A	Barrow	L	2-6	Dixon, Seabrook	4,470
34		25	H	Southport	W	1-0	Bell	1,792
35	Apr	6	A	Darlington	L	0-2		6,187
36		7	A	Southport	L	1-3	Groves	5,324
37		10	H	Rochdale	D	1-1	Waites	3,595
38		14	H	Rotherham United	D	0-0		3,171
39		21	A	Rochdale	D	2-2	Coleman, Dixon	2,099
40		23	H	New Brighton	D	1-1	Martin	1,761
41		28	H	Durham City	W	3-1	Coleman, Smeaton, Bell	2,553
42	May	5	A	Wrexham	L	0-2		1,726

Final League Position: 12th in Division Three (North)

Apps
Gls

FA CUP

1	Nov	26	H	Hartlepools United	W	3-0	Proctor, Seabrook, Coleman	10,341
2	Dec	10	A	Tranmere Rovers	L	1-3	Seabrook	8,554

Apps
Gls

League Table

	P	W	D	L	F	A	Pts
Bradford	42	27	9	6	101	45	63
Lincoln City	42	24	7	11	91	64	55
Stockport County	42	23	8	11	89	51	54
Doncaster Rovers	42	23	7	12	80	44	53
Tranmere Rovers	42	22	9	11	105	72	53
Bradford City	42	18	12	12	85	60	48
Darlington	42	21	5	16	89	74	47
Southport	42	20	5	17	79	70	45
Accrington Stanley	42	18	8	16	76	67	44
New Brighton	42	14	14	14	72	62	42
Wrexham	42	18	6	18	64	67	42
Halifax Town	42	13	15	14	73	71	41
Rochdale	42	17	7	18	74	77	41
Rotherham United	42	14	11	17	65	69	39
Hartlepools United	42	16	6	20	69	81	38
Chesterfield	42	13	10	19	71	78	36
Crewe Alexandra	42	12	10	20	77	86	34
Ashington	42	11	11	20	77	103	33
Barrow	42	10	11	21	54	102	31
Wigan Borough	42	10	10	22	56	97	30
Durham City	42	11	7	24	53	100	29
Nelson	42	10	6	26	76	136	26

1928-29

Division Three (North)

Manager: Joe McClelland

Did you know that?

- In 1919–20, Sam Taylor scored both Huddersfield Town's goals in the FA Cup final semi-final victory over Bristol City and was a member of the side beaten by Aston Villa in the final at played Stamford Bridge. He was a greyhound breeder based in Lincolnshire.

- Harry Green was the holder of a Royal Humane Society certificate for life saving when he pulled a boy out of the River Trent.

- Captain was Fred McLachlan.

- Arthur Groves was sold to Blackburn Rovers on 31 December.

- Ernest 'Tim' Coleman was transferred to Grimsby Town on 27 February. He would become the only player to leave Halifax Town and win a League championship medal as a member of Arsenal's victorious side in 1932–33.

- Bob Suter was aged 48 years and 288 days when he turned out for Town at Darlington on 24 April. It was his third game in five days.

- Halifax Town provided the opposition for Ashington's last League game at their Portland Park home on 27 April. Ashington were voted out of the League in the close season.

- Ernie Dixon was top scorer in seven consecutive seasons with Halifax Town.

- Biggest League win: 5–1 v Hartlepools United, 6 April

- Heaviest League defeat: 0–3 v Lincoln City, 22 September, v Crewe Alexandra, 29 December, v Stockport County, 19 January,

- Ever-present: Fred McLachlan

Match No.	Date	Venue	Opponents	Result		Scorers	Attendance
1	Aug 25	H	Crewe Alexandra	D	2-2	Dixon, Coleman	8,088
2	29	A	Wigan Borough	D	1-1	Bell	8,820
3	Sep 1	A	Tranmere Rovers	L	1-2	S. Taylor	6,193
4	8	H	Stockport County	D	1-1	Dixon	7,542
5	15	A	Barrow	W	3-1	Dixon 2, Beynon	8,037
6	17 H	H	Wigan Borough	W	1-0	S. Taylor	5,170
7	22	A	Lincoln City	L	0-3		6,322
8	29	H	Bradford City	D	1-1	Coleman	14,609
9	Oct 6	A	Accrington Stanley	D	1-1	Coleman	4,480
10	13	H	Hartlepools United	W	2-0	Dixon, Bell	3,746
11	20	H	Chesterfield	D	1-1	Bell	5,351
12	27	A	Wrexham	D	2-2	Bell, Dixon (pen)	5,943
13	Nov 3	H	New Brighton	D	1-1	Bell	5,725
14	10	A	Rochdale	D	2-2	Coleman, Bell	2,038
15	17	H	Southport	W	2-1	Bell, S. Taylor	5,934
16	Dec 1	H	Nelson	L	1-2	Coleman	5,988
17	8	A	South Shields	L	1-2	Bell	4,172
18	15	H	Ashington	W	1-0	Groves	3,422
19	22	A	Doncaster Rovers	L	0-1		3,574
20	25	A	Carlisle United	L	1-2	Groves	10,394
21	26	H	Carlisle United	W	5-2	Dixon, Coleman, Bell 2, Beynon	8,599
22	29	A	Crewe Alexandra	L	0-3		5,794
23	Jan 5	H	Tranmere Rovers	W	2-0	Beynon, C. Taylor	3,238
24	19	A	Stockport County	L	0-3		11,799
25	26	H	Barrow	W	2-0	Coleman, Bell	4,380
26	Feb 2	H	Lincoln City	W	4-2	Dixon 2, Hubbert, Coleman	3,927
27	9	A	Bradford City	D	2-2	Dixon, Hubbert	19,957
28	16	H	Accrington Stanley	W	4-2	Coleman, Dixon 2, Bell	3,768
29	23	A	Hartlepools United	L	1-3	Coleman	2,867
30	Mar 2	A	Chesterfield	L	2-3	Dixon, Bell	3,212
31	9	H	Wrexham	L	1-2	Dixon	4,240
32	16	A	New Brighton	L	0-1		2,959
33	23	H	Rochdale	D	1-1	Bell	3,787
34	30	A	Southport	L	0-1		3,294
35	Apr 1	A	Rotherham United	D	0-0		2,679
36	2	H	Rotherham United	W	3-1	Dixon, Bell, Beynon	3,112
37	6	H	Darlington	W	5-1	Foster 2 (1 pen), Hickman 2, Watson (og)	4,171
38	13	A	Nelson	L	1-3	Cooper	3,182
39	20	H	South Shields	L	0-2		3,604
40	24	A	Darlington	L	0-2		1,411
41	27	A	Ashington	W	3-0	Foster, Cooper, Dixon	706
42	May 4	H	Doncaster Rovers	D	2-2	Morgan (og), Dixon	2,862

Final League Position: 13th in Division Three (North)

Apps
2 own-goals Gls

FA CUP

| 1 | Nov 24 | A | Stockport County | L | 0-1 | | 8,748 |

Apps
Gls

Appearances

Matthews, WH	Lees, JW	Thompson, F	Lowson, EB	Green, H	McLachlan, F	Coleman, E	Bell, T	Dixon, E	Taylor, SJT	Wilbourn, H	Proctor, N	Beynon, JA	Hubbert, H	Gluthen, WS	Wheelhouse, B	Lawrrick, W	Groves, A	Binns, CH	Taylor, C	Hickman, G	Asstrop, S	Foster, CL	Stockdale, TW	Cooper, S	Sutter, ER
1	2	3	4	5	6	7	8	9	10	11															
1	2	3	4		5	7	8	9	10		6	11													
1	2	3	4		5	7	8	9	10		6	11													
1	2	3	4		5	7	8	9	10		6	11													
1	2		4		5	7		9	10		6	11	3	8											
1	2		4		5	7		9	10		6	11	3	8											
1			4		5	7		9	10		6		3	8	2	11									
1			4		5	7	8		9		6		3		2	11	10								
1			4		5	7	8	9			6	11	3		2		10								
1			4		5	7	8	9		11	6		3		2		10								
1			4		5	7	8	9		11	6		3		2		10								
1			4		5	7		9	8	10	11	6			3		2								
1			4		5	7		9	8	10	11	6			3		2								
1			4		5	7		9	8	10	11	6			3		2								
1			4		5	7		9	8	10	11	6			3		2								
1			4		5	7		9	8			6	11		3		2		10						
			4		5	7		9	8	10		6	11		3		2	1							
1			4		5	7		9	8			6	11		3		2		10						
1			4		5	7	8	9				6	11		3		2		10						
1	2		4		5	7	8	9				6	11		3				10						
1	2		4		5	7	8	9				6	11		3				10						
1	2		4		5	7	8	9				6	11		3				10						
1	2	3	4		5	7	10	9				6	11						8						
1	2	3	4		5	7	10	9				6	11						8						
1		3	4		5	8	10	9				6	11		2					7					
1		3	4		5	8	10	9				6		11	2					7					
1		3	4		5	8	10	9				6		11	2					7					
1		3	4		5	8	10	9				6		11	2					7					
1		3	4		5	8	10	9				6		11	2					7					
1		3	4		5		10	9				6		11	2				7	8					
			4		5		8	9				6		3	2			1	10	7	11				
			4		5		8	9				6		3	2			1	10	7	11				
		3	4		5		10	9				8	11		2			1		7		6			
		3	4		5		8	9				10	11		2			1		7		6			
		3	4		5		8	9				10	11		2			1		7		6			
		3	4		5		8	9							2			1		7		11	6	10	
1		3	4		5		8	9							2					7		11	6	10	
		3	4		5		8	9			6				2					7		11		10	1
		3			5		2	9			6								8	7		11	4	10	1
1			4		5		2	9			6				3					7		11	4	10	
1			4		5		2	9			6	7			3							11	4	10	
33	11	19	41	1	42	29	39	41	13	7	39	20	23	3	33	2	10	7	6	17	2	8	8	6	2
						10	15	17	3			4	2				2		1	2		3		2	

| | | | 4 | | 5 | 7 | 9 | 8 | 10 | 11 | 6 | | | | 3 | | 2 | | | | 1 | | | | |
| 1 | | 1 | | 1 | 1 | 1 | 1 | 1 | 1 | | 1 | 1 | | | | | 1 | | | | | | | | |

League Table

	P	W	D	L	F	A	Pts
Bradford City	42	27	9	6	128	43	63
Stockport County	42	28	6	8	111	58	62
Wrexham	42	21	10	11	91	69	52
Wigan Borough	42	21	9	12	82	49	51
Doncaster Rovers	42	20	10	12	76	66	50
Lincoln City	42	21	6	15	91	67	48
Tranmere Rovers	42	22	3	17	79	77	47
Carlisle United	42	19	8	15	86	77	46
Crewe Alexandra	42	18	8	16	80	68	44
South Shields	42	18	8	16	83	74	44
Chesterfield	42	18	5	19	71	77	41
Southport	42	16	8	18	75	85	40
Halifax Town	42	13	13	16	63	62	39
New Brighton	42	15	9	18	64	71	39
Nelson	42	17	5	20	77	90	39
Rotherham United	42	15	9	18	60	77	39
Rochdale	42	13	10	19	79	96	36
Accrington Stanley	42	13	8	21	68	82	34
Darlington	42	13	7	22	64	88	33
Barrow	42	10	8	24	64	93	28
Hartlepools United	42	10	6	26	59	112	26
Ashington	42	8	7	27	45	115	23

1929-30

Division Three (North)
Manager: Joe McClelland

Did you know that?

- Captain was Fred McLachlan.
- George Hickman played county cricket for Warwickshire.
- Scotsman John Percy, appointed trainer in August 1929, served in a similar capacity with Aberdare, Grimsby Town and South Shields.
- Bernard Foster's father was Jack Foster, ex-Huddersfield Town player.
- Chairman William Blair once played football for Staffordshire club Langley.
- Clifford Binns's £1,500 transfer to Blackburn Rovers was a record for a Third Division goalkeeper.
- Halifax Town's 'Save Our Shay' Fund, set up at the end of October 1929, realised almost £500 by the following March.
- Halifax Town lost five consecutive League matches between 22 February and 22 March.
- Ken McDonald scored 137 goals in 148 games for Bradford.
- Biggest League win: 4–0 v New Brighton, 19 October, 1929, v Barrow, 21 December 1929.
- Heaviest League defeat: 1–7 v Accrington Stanley, 1 February 1930.

Match No.	Date		Venue	Opponents	Result		Scorers	Attendance
1	Aug	31	H	Port Vale	L	1-2	Dixon	8,101
2	Sep	2	A	Tranmere Rovers	D	3-3	Hickman, Dixon 2	5,154
3		7	A	Rotherham United	L	0-2		6,524
4		9	H	Tranmere Rovers	L	0-1		4,093
5		14	H	Rochdale	L	2-3	Hickman 2	4,982
6		16	H	Doncaster Rovers	W	1-0	Foster	2,668
7		21	A	South Shields	L	0-1		2,883
8		23	A	Doncaster Rovers	L	0-1		1,921
9		28	H	Accrington Stanley	D	1-1	Wheelhouse	4,763
10	Oct	5	A	Darlington	L	2-3	Martin 2	4,393
11		12	H	Hartlepools United	D	0-0		4,138
12		19	H	New Brighton	W	4-0	Foster 2, Martin, Cowper (og)	2,756
13		26	A	Stockport County	L	0-6		7,586
14	Nov	2	H	York City	D	2-2	Wheelhouse (pen), Hickman	4,656
15		9	A	Crewe Alexandra	L	1-4	Howlett	4,656
16		16	H	Southport	D	1-1	Bell	2,899
17		23	A	Nelson	L	0-1		2,568
18	Dec	7	A	Wigan Borough	L	1-2	Gilchrist	1,359
19		19	H	Wrexham	W	2-0	Cooper, Gilchrist	1,539
20		21	A	Barrow	W	4-0	Foster, Cooper, Hickman, Wheelhouse (pen)	3,843
21		25	H	Lincoln City	D	1-1	Strang	4,618
22		26	A	Lincoln City	W	1-0	Gilchrist	10,304
23		28	A	Port Vale	L	0-3		4,519
24	Jan	4	H	Rotherham United	D	1-1	Wheelhouse (pen)	4,501
25		11	H	Barrow	L	0-1		4,156
26		18	A	Rochdale	W	3-0	Cooper 2, Proctor	2,759
27		25	H	South Shields	L	0-2		4,564
28	Feb	1	A	Accrington Stanley	L	1-7	Stockdale (pen)	3,467
29		8	H	Darlington	W	3-1	Bell, Moore, Cooper	3,007
30		15	A	Hartlepools United	L	0-3		3,022
31		20	H	Carlisle United	W	1-0	Roberts	1,709
32		22	A	New Brighton	L	0-4		4,338
33	Mar	1	H	Stockport County	L	0-3		4,118
34		8	A	York City	L	0-3		5,000
35		15	H	Crewe Alexandra	L	1-3	Bell	2,467
36		22	A	Southport	L	0-4		3,148
37		29	H	Nelson	D	1-1	Cooper	4,185
38	Apr	5	A	Carlisle United	L	0-2		3,833
39		12	H	Wigan Borough	W	2-1	McDonald, Martin	2,847
40		18	A	Chesterfield	L	0-2		5,363
41		19	H	Wrexham	L	1-2	Bell	1,777
42		21	H	Chesterfield	W	3-2	Gilchrist, Cooper, Hickman	2,942

Final League Position: 21st in Division Three (North)

1 own-goal

Apps
Gls

FA CUP

| 1 | Nov | 30 | A | Carlisle United | L | 0-2 | | 8,190 |

Apps
Gls

	Binns, CH	Lees, JW	Wheelhouse, B	McLachlan, F	Strang, R	Proctor, N	Hickman, G	Gilchrist, AE	Dixon, E	Martin, JC	Partridge, E	Childs, H	Foster, BD	Cooper, S	Stonhdale, TW	Bell, T	Roberts, J	Lowson, EB	Davies, E	Schofield, R	Howlett, CE	Julian, S	Kellett, CA	Matthews, WH	Moore, F	Ramsbottom, E	Wilson, JE	McDonald, K
	1	2	3	4	5	6	7	8	2	10	11																	
	1		2	6	5		7		2	8	11	3	4	10														
	1		2	5			7			8	11	3	4	10	6	9												
	1		2	5			7			8	3	4	10	6	9	11												
	1		2	6	5		7		8	10	3	4			9	11												
	1		2		5	6	7		8	10	3	9				11	4											
	1		2		5	6	7		8	10	3	9				11	4											
	1		2		5	6	7			10	3	9			8	11	4											
	1	2	9	5		6				10	3				8		4	7	11									
	1		2	5		6	7		9	11	3		10		8		4											
	1		2		5	6	7		9	11	3		10		8		4											
	1		2		5	6	7		9	11	3	8					4		10									
	1		2		5	6	7		9		3	8				11	4		10									
	1		2		5	6	7			11	3	8					4		10	9								
	1		2		5	6	7	8		11	3						4		10	9								
	1		2		5	6	7			11		8	10		9		4				3							
	1		2		5	6	7	8					10		9	11	4				3							
	1		2		5	10	7	9				8	6			11	4				3							
	1		2	4	5	6	7	8					9	10			11				3							
	1		2	4	5	6	7	8					9	10			11				3							
	1		2	4	5	6	7	8					9	10			11				3							
	1		2	4	5	6	7	8						10			11	9			3							
	1		2	4	5	6	7	8						10			11	9			3							
	1		2	4	5	6	7	8						10			11				3	9						
	1		2	4	5	6	7	8						10			11				3	9						
	1		2	4	5	6			8			9	10			11		7			3							
			2	4	5	6			8			9	10			11		7			3		1					
			2	4	5				8			9	10	6		11		7			3		1					
		2	9	4	5							10		8			6	7			3		1	11				
		2	9	4	5							10		8			6	7			3		1	11				
		2	9		5	6	7					4	10		8	11					3		1					
		2			5	6	7	9				4	10		8	11					3		1					
		2	9		5	6						4	10		8	11	7				3		1					
		2		4	5	6							9		8	11	7	10			3			1				
		2	4	5	6		11					10	8				7				3				1	9		
		2		4	5	6	7		10			11	8								3				1	9		
		2		4	5	6	7		10			11	8								3				1	9		
			2	4	5	6	7		10			11	8			6					3				1	9		
			2	4	5	6	7		10			11	8								3				1	9		
			2	4	5	6	7		10			11	8								3				1	9		
				4	5		7	10			2	6	11								3				1	9		
				4	5		7	11			2	6	10		8						3				1	9		
	26	10	36	28	38	32	33	15	2	18	15	16	23	4	23	22	18	9	6	2	27	2	7	2	1	8	8	
			4			1	1	6	4	3	4			4	7	1	4	1			1				1			

| | 1 | | 2 | | 5 | 6 | 7 | | 8 | | | | | 10 | | 9 | 11 | 4 | | | 3 | | | | | | | |
| | 1 | | 1 | | 1 | 1 | 1 | | 1 | | | | | 1 | | 1 | 1 | 1 | | | 1 | | | | | | | |

League Table

	P	W	D	L	F	A	Pts
Port Vale	42	30	7	5	103	37	67
Stockport County	42	28	7	7	106	44	63
Darlington	42	22	6	14	108	73	50
Chesterfield	42	22	6	14	76	56	50
Lincoln City	42	17	14	11	83	61	48
York City	42	15	16	11	77	64	46
South Shields	42	18	10	14	77	74	46
Hartlepools United	42	17	11	14	81	74	45
Southport	42	15	13	14	81	74	43
Rochdale	42	18	7	17	89	91	43
Crewe Alexandra	42	17	8	17	82	71	42
Tranmere Rovers	42	16	9	17	83	86	41
New Brighton	42	16	8	18	69	79	40
Doncaster Rovers	42	15	9	18	62	69	39
Carlisle United	42	16	7	19	90	101	39
Accrington Stanley	42	14	9	19	84	81	37
Wrexham	42	13	8	21	67	88	34
Wigan Borough	42	13	7	22	60	88	33
Nelson	42	13	7	22	51	80	33
Rotherham United	42	11	8	23	67	113	30
Halifax Town	42	10	8	24	44	79	28
Barrow	42	11	5	26	41	98	27

1930-31

Division Three (North)
Manager: Alex Raisbeck

Did you know that?

- Captain was Dick Strang.
- Halifax Town reverted to blue-and-white-striped shirts.
- Bright Heyhirst acted as masseur to the England Test players during the Headingley Test against the Australians which began on 11 July 1930.
- James Barrie played for Bethlehem City and Fall River in the United States before joining Halifax Town.
- The Halifax Town Social Section came up with the idea of 'One Mile Of Pennies' (the equivalent of £220) to be laid around the pitch.
- On 13 February 1931 captain Dick Strang kicked-off a football match on bicycles performed by the Aston Brothers when the players attended a 'Footballers' Night' at the invitation of Palace Theatre manager Wally Stephenson, where Cosgrove and Westwood sang special football numbers. The following day, Halifax Town defeated Stockport County 3–0.
- Sedley Cooper scored a goal within 10 seconds in the 1–1 draw at Accrington Stanley on 11 April 1931.
- Halifax Town conceded double figures for the first time when losing 10–0 at Hull City on Boxing Day.
- Biggest League win: 4–0 v Crewe Alexandra, 25 October 1930.
- Heaviest League defeat: 0–10 v Hull City, 26 December 1930.
- Albert Pape once figured in one of the more unusual soccer transfers when he travelled with his Clapton Orient side for the game at Manchester United on 7 February 1925, only to sign for the Reds prior to kick-off and turn out against his former colleagues minutes later.
- Ever-presents: Sedly Cooper, John McFarlane.

Match No.	Date	Venue	Opponents	Result		Scorers	Attendance
1	Aug 30	H	Hartlepools United	W	3-1	Pape, Davies, Cooper	8,056
2	Sep 1	H	Gateshead	W	3-0	Cooper 2, Pape	8,189
3	6	A	Wigan Borough	L	0-3		8,379
4	8	H	Doncaster Rovers	L	0-2		7,764
5	13	H	Nelson	W	1-0	Pape (pen)	5,433
6	18	A	Doncaster Rovers	D	3-3	Woodhouse, Pape, Hopkins	2,079
7	20	A	Darlington	L	1-4	McFarlane	3,523
8	27	H	Wrexham	D	0-0		6,239
9	Oct 4	H	New Brighton	W	1-0	Pape	5,944
10	11	A	Stockport County	L	0-3		7,137
11	18	A	Tranmere Rovers	D	2-2	Cooper, Hopkins	7,272
12	25	H	Crewe Alexandra	W	4-0	Pape 3 (2 pens), Hopkins	5,882
13	Nov 1	A	York City	L	1-4	Cooper	3,830
14	8	H	Rotherham United	L	0-1		6,045
15	15	A	Chesterfield	L	0-7		3,991
16	22	H	Barrow	W	4-0	Pape 3, McFarlane	2,539
17	Dec 6	H	Accrington Stanley	D	1-1	Donaldson	4,330
18	20	A	Carlisle United	L	1-5	Woodhouse	3,869
19	25	H	Hull City	D	1-1	Cooper	7,496
20	26	A	Hull City	L	0-10		4,022
21	27	A	Hartlepools United	L	1-2	Pape	4,419
22	Jan 3	H	Wigan Borough	L	0-1		4,148
23	13	A	Southport	L	2-5	Donaldson, Pape	2,532
24	17	A	Nelson	L	2-3	McFarlane, Pape (pen)	2,452
25	24	H	Darlington	W	1-0	McFarlane	3,202
26	31	A	Wrexham	L	2-3	Betteridge, Davies	1,213
27	Feb 7	A	New Brighton	L	0-3		2,845
28	14	H	Stockport County	W	3-0	Cooper, McFarlane, Bain	4,580
29	16	A	Rochdale	W	3-2	Betteridge, Bain 2	1,118
30	21	H	Tranmere Rovers	W	2-1	Betteridge (pen), Cooper	7,174
31	Mar 7	H	York City	D	0-0		2,429
32	14	A	Rotherham United	L	1-2	Betteridge	4,045
33	21	H	Chesterfield	D	1-1	McFarlane	5,312
34	25	A	Crewe Alexandra	W	1-0	McFarlane	1,507
35	28	A	Barrow	L	1-3	Cooper	4,898
36	Apr 3	A	Lincoln City	L	1-4	Pape	10,728
37	4	H	Southport	D	0-0		4,987
38	6	H	Lincoln City	W	3-2	Bain 2, Davies	4,616
39	11	A	Accrington Stanley	D	1-1	Cooper	2,658
40	18	H	Rochdale	W	1-0	McFarlane	2,875
41	25	A	Carlisle United	L	2-6	Strang, McFarlane	2,160
42	May 2	A	Gateshead	L	1-3	Donaldson	3,165

Final League Position: 17th in Division Three (North)

Apps
Gls

FA Cup

1	Nov 29	H	Mansfield Town	D	2-2	Cooper, Pape (pen)	5,968
R	Dec 3	A	Mansfield Town	W	2-1	Cooper 2	4,770
2	13	A	Fulham	L	0-4		9,563

Apps
Gls

Bilcliff, B	Wheelhouse, B	Barrie, JW	Bain, D	Strang, R	Proctor, N	Davies, E	McFarlane, J	Pape, A	Woodhouse, RT	Cooper, S	Crowther, J	Hopkins, WT	Hudson, JE	Graham, RH	Chadwick, W	Donaldson, TA	Julian, S	Betteridge, F	McLachlan, F
1	2	3	4	5	6	7	8	9	10	11									
1	2	3	4	5	6	7	8	9	10	11									
1	2	3	4	5	6	7	9		10	11	8								
1	2	3	4	5	6	7	8	9	10	11									
1	2	3	4	5	6	7	8	9	10	11									
1	2	3	4	5	6		8	9	10	11		7							
		2	4	5	6		8	9	10	11		7	1	3					
1		2	4	5	6	7	8	9	10	11				3					
1		2	4	5	6	7	8	9	10	11				3					
1		2	4	5	6	7	8	9	10	11				3					
1		2	4	5	6		8	9		11		7		3	10				
1		2	4	5	6		8	9		11		7		3	10				
1		2	4	5	6		8	9		11		7		3	10				
1		2	4	5	6		8	9		11		7		3	10				
1		2	4	5	6		8	9		11		7		3	10				
1	2	3	4	5	6		8	9		11		7				10			
1	2	3	4	5	6		8		10	11		7				9			
1	2	3	4	5			8	9	10	11		7		6					
1		2	4		6		8	9		11		7		5		10	3		
1		2	4		6		8	9		11		7		5		10	3		
1	2		4	5	6		8	9	10	11		7					3		
1	2	4	9	5	6		8			11		7				10	3		
1	2		4	5	6		10	9		11		7				8	3		
1	2		4	5	6		8	9		10				3		7		11	
1	2	3	4	5	6	7	8	9		10								11	
1	2	3	4	5	6	7	8	9		10								11	
1	2		4	5	6	7	8	9		10				3				11	
1	2	3	9	5	6	7	8			10								11	4
1	2	3	9	5	6	7	8			10								11	4
1	2	3	9	5	6	7	8			10								11	4
1	2	3	9	5		7	8			10				6				11	4
1	2	3	9	5	6	7	8			10								11	4
1	2	3	9	5			8			10		7		6				11	4
1	2	3	9	5			8			10		7		6				11	4
1	2	3	9	5			8			10		7		6				11	4
1	2	3		5			8	9		10				6		7		11	4
1		2	10	5	6	7	8	9		11				3					4
1	2	3	9	5		7	8			10				6				11	4
1		3	9	5	6	7	8			10				2				11	4
1	2	3	9	5		7	8			10				6				11	4
1	2	3	9	5		7	8			10				6				11	4
1	2	3		5	6	7	8			10						9		11	4
41	29	38	40	40	33	22	42	26	13	42	1	18	1	24	5	9	5	18	15
	4		5	1		3	9	15	2	10		3				3		4	

Bilcliff, B	Wheelhouse, B	Barrie, JW	Bain, D	Strang, R	Proctor, N	Davies, E	McFarlane, J	Pape, A	Woodhouse, RT	Cooper, S	Crowther, J	Hopkins, WT	Hudson, JE	Graham, RH	Chadwick, W	Donaldson, TA	Julian, S	Betteridge, F	McLachlan, F
1	2		4	5	6		8	9	10	11		7		3					1
1	2		4	5	6		8	9	10	11		7		3					
1	2		4	5	6		8		10	11		7		3	9				1
3	3		3	3	3		3	2	3	3		3		3	1				
								1		3									

League Table

	P	W	D	L	F	A	Pts
Chesterfield	42	26	6	10	102	57	58
Lincoln City	42	25	7	10	102	59	57
Wrexham	42	21	12	9	94	62	54
Tranmere Rovers	42	24	6	12	111	74	54
Southport	42	22	9	11	88	56	53
Hull City	42	20	10	12	99	55	50
Stockport County	42	20	9	13	77	61	49
Carlisle United	42	20	5	17	98	81	45
Gateshead	42	16	13	13	71	73	45
Wigan Borough	42	19	5	18	75	86	43
Darlington	42	16	10	16	71	59	42
York City	42	18	6	18	85	82	42
Accrington Stanley	42	15	9	18	84	108	39
Rotherham United	42	13	12	17	81	83	38
Doncaster Rovers	42	13	11	18	65	65	37
Barrow	42	15	7	20	68	89	37
Halifax Town	42	13	9	20	55	89	35
Crewe Alexandra	42	14	6	22	66	93	34
New Brighton	42	13	7	22	49	76	33
Hartlepools United	42	12	6	24	67	86	30
Rochdale	42	12	6	24	62	107	30
Nelson	42	6	7	29	43	113	19

1931-32

Division Three (North)
Manager: Alex Raisbeck

Did you know that?

- Billy Hopkins made his debut at Doncaster Rovers on 10 October 1931 after getting married in the morning.
- A second 'Mile of Pennies' was stopped in October 1931 after differences between the Social Section, who wanted to use the money for terracing under the stand, and the club's directors, who wanted it to help meet running costs.
- Captain was Dick Strang.
- Halifax Town played a 2–2 draw with Huddersfield Town in Ben Wheelhouse's Benefit match on 18 April 1932.
- Charlie Davies bought his first pair of football boots after winning a 'busting sweep'.
- Prior to signing for Halifax Town, Ted Crawford scored 150 goals in two seasons in the East Riding football with Filey Town.
- Unemployed people were allowed into The Shay at half price for a friendly with Rhyl Athletic on 6 February 1932.
- Former and future Halifax Town players Sam Julian and Albert Valentine were both members of the Wigan Borough side which resigned from the Football League in October 1931.
- Halifax Town's 9–1 defeat at Lincoln City on 16 January became their heaviest. But up until then, incredibly, the Shaymen had been the only side to have prevented Lincoln from scoring in the League when they defeated the Imps 3–0 on 5 September.
- Biggest League win: 4–0 v Doncaster Rovers, 20 February 1932.
- Heaviest League defeat: 1–9 v Lincoln City, 16 January 1932.

Match No.	Date	Venue	Opponents	Result		Scorers	Attendance
1	Aug 29	A	Hull City	L	0-1		8,503
2	31	H	New Brighton	D	0-0		6,008
3	Sep 5	H	Lincoln City	W	3-0	Davies, Hanks, Mays	4,109
4	7	A	Barrow	L	1-3	Mays	8,534
5	12	A	Chester	L	1-3	McLachlan	6,824
6	14	H	Barrow	W	1-0	Crawford	3,431
7	19	H	Hartlepools United	W	2-0	Mays, Crawford	4,396
8	Oct 3	H	Darlington	L	0-3		5,732
9	10	A	Doncaster Rovers	L	1-3	Mays (pen)	3,930
10	17	H	Rochdale	W	3-2	Crawford 2, Betteridge	4,082
11	24	A	Crewe Alexandra	L	3-4	Betteridge, Crawford 2	5,526
12	31	H	Carlisle United	D	1-1	Betteridge	4,379
13	Nov 7	A	Wrexham	W	3-2	Crawford, Davies, Mays	7,061
14	14	H	Accrington Stanley	W	1-0	Betteridge	5,015
15	21	A	Stockport County	L	1-2	Mays	4,416
16	Dec 5	A	Tranmere Rovers	L	2-5	Johnson, Crawford	4,012
17	19	A	Southport	D	2-2	Crawford, Vincent (og)	3,129
18	25	H	Gateshead	L	1-2	Davies	11,649
19	26	A	Gateshead	D	1-1	Mays	11,655
20	Jan 2	H	Hull City	D	2-2	Mays, Betteridge	4,163
21	11	H	Rotherham United	D	1-1	Johnson	1,430
22	16	A	Lincoln City	L	1-9	Johnson	7,086
23	23	H	Chester	W	2-1	McFarlane, Davies	3,703
24	30	A	Hartlepools United	L	1-4	Mays	2,961
25	Feb 13	A	Darlington	L	0-3		1,807
26	20	H	Doncaster Rovers	W	4-0	Crawford 3, Bain	2,977
27	27	A	Rochdale	W	4-1	Johnson, Betteridge, Crawford, Read	3,154
28	Mar 5	H	Crewe Alexandra	W	4-1	Davies, Crawford, Johnson 2	4,090
29	12	A	Carlisle United	L	0-4		3,453
30	19	H	Wrexham	W	1-0	Crawford	3,068
31	26	A	Accrington Stanley	L	0-4		2,591
32	28	H	Walsall	L	1-2	Betteridge	3,624
33	29	A	Walsall	L	2-4	McFarlane 2	2,627
34	Apr 2	H	Stockport County	D	2-2	Betteridge, Crawford	4,117
35	9	A	Rotherham United	L	0-5		2,951
36	16	H	Tranmere Rovers	D	0-0		2,997
37	23	H	York City	L	2-7	McFarlane, Crawford	2,154
38	28	H	York City	W	4-1	McFarlane 2, Crawford, Betteridge	1,618
39	30	H	Southport	W	3-0	Crawford 2, Davies	3,303
40	May 7	A	New Brighton	L	0-2		1,974

Final League Position: 17th in Division Three (North)

1 own-goal

Apps
Gls

Expunged Match

	Sep 26	A	Wigan Borough	W	1-0	Crawford	1,976

FA Cup

1	Nov 28	A	Newark Town	D	1-1	Mays	2,525
R	Dec 2	H	Newark Town	W	2-1	Crawford, Mays	3,500
2	12	H	Accrington Stanley	W	3-0	McFarlane, Mays, Betteridge	11,648
3	Jan 9	H	Bournemouth & Bosc. Ath.	L	1-3	Betteridge	18,288

Apps
Gls

	Blissit, B	Wheelhouse, B	Barrie, JW	Bain, D	Strang, R	McGrae, J	Davies, E	McFarlane, J	Mays, AW	Johnson, WJ	Betteridge, F	Crawford, EC	McLachlan, F	Hinks, A	Read, E	Graham, RH	Hatch, NJ	March, W	Taylor, GE	Hopkins, WT	Langhorn, AE	Armitage, JW	Helliwell, C	Roberts, L	Donaldson, TA
1	2	3	4	5	6	7	8	9	10	11															
1	2	3	4	5	6	7		8	10	11	9														
1	2	3	8	5	6	7		9		11		4	10												
1	2	3	8	5	6	7		9		11			10	4											
1	2				6	7	8	9	10	11		4		5	3										
1	2		8		6	7		10			9	4		5	3	11									
1	2				6	7		10			9	4		5	3	11	8								
1	2				6	7		10			9	4		5	3	11	8								
	2		4		6			9	10	11				5	3		8	1	7						
	2		4		6	7		8	10	11	9			5	3			1							
	2		4		6	7		8	10	11	9			5	3			1							
1		2	4		6	7		8	10	11	9			5	3										
1		2	4		6	7		8	10	11	9			5	3										
1		2	4		6	7		8	10	11	9			5	3										
1		2	4		6	7		9	10	11				5	3		8								
1	2	3		5	6	7		8	10	11	9			4											
1	2	3		5	6	7	8	10		11	9			4											
1	2	3	4	5	6	7	8	10		11	9														
1	2	3		5	6	7		8	10	11	9			4											
1	2	3		5	6	7	8	9	10	11				4											
1	2		4	5		7	8	9	10	11				6	3										
1	2			5	6	7	8	9	10	11				4	3										
	2			5	6	7	8	9	10	11				4	3		1								
	2			5	6	7	8	9	10	11				4	3		1								
	2		4	5		7		8	10	11	9									1	3	6			
	2		4		6	7	8		10	11	9			5						1	3				
	2		4		6	7	8		10	11	9			5		1					3				
	2		4		6	7	8		10	11	9			5						1	3				
		2	4		6	7	8		10	11	9			5						1	3				
	2		4		6	7	8		10	11	9			5						1	3				
	2			5	6	7	8		10	11	9			4						1	3				
	2				6		8		10	11	9	4		5				7		1	3				
1	2			5	6		8		10	11	9			4							3		7		
	2			5	6	7	8			11	9		10	4							3				
	2			5		7	8			11	9		10	4						1	3	6			
1	2					7			10	11	9	4	8	5							3	6			
	2						7			11	9	4	8	5			1		10		3	6			
1		3		5		7	8			11	9	10	4								2	6			
1	2	3		5		7	8			11	9		10	4								6			
1	2	3		5			7	8		11	9	4	10									6			
25	34	17	20	21	32	36	23	25	27	37	29	9	9	34	15	3	7	2	2	8	14	7	1		
			1		6	6	9	6	9	20	1	1	1												

| 1 | 2 | | | | 6 | 7 | | 10 | | | 9 | 4 | | 5 | 3 | 11 | 8 | | | | | | | | |

	2			5	6	7		8	10	11	9			4	3										
1	2	3		5	6	7		8	10	11	9			4											
1	2	3	4	5	6	7	8	10		11	9														
1	2	3	4	5	6	7		8	10	11	9														
4	3	4	2	4	4	4	1	4	3	4	4			2	1										

League Table

	P	W	D	L	F	A	Pts
Lincoln City	40	26	5	9	106	47	57
Gateshead	40	25	7	8	94	48	57
Chester	40	21	8	11	78	60	50
Tranmere Rovers	40	19	11	10	107	58	49
Barrow	40	24	1	15	86	59	49
Crewe Alexandra	40	21	6	13	95	66	48
Southport	40	18	10	12	58	53	46
Hull City	40	20	5	15	82	53	45
York City	40	18	7	15	76	81	43
Wrexham	40	18	7	15	64	69	43
Darlington	40	17	4	19	66	69	38
Stockport County	40	13	11	16	55	53	37
Hartlepools United	40	16	5	19	78	100	37
Accrington Stanley	40	15	6	19	75	80	36
Doncaster Rovers	40	16	4	20	59	80	36
Walsall	40	16	3	21	57	85	35
Halifax Town	40	13	8	19	61	87	34
Carlisle United	40	11	11	18	64	79	33
Rotherham United	40	14	4	22	63	72	32
New Brighton	40	8	8	24	38	76	24
Rochdale	40	4	3	33	48	135	11

*Wigan Borough resigned from League

1932-33

Division Three (North)
Manager: Alex Raisbeck

Did you know that?

- Following Town's FA Cup victory over Barnsley on 25 November, the players went for long weekend stay at Elms Hotel, Morecambe, at the generosity of the club's directors.
- Captain was Oliver Thompson.
- Hughie Flack won one cap for Ireland while a Burnley player.
- Maurice Wellock scored his 100th League goal in the 5–3 defeat at York City on 19 November 1932.
- Director Charles Mattock weaned the Halifax Town players on his famous butter drops.
- Despite losing 5–1 at home to Crewe Alexandra on 18 January 1933, the Halifax Town players were entertained to a complimentary dinner by G.P. Wilkinson, at the Crown and Anchor Hotel, Bull Green.
- When Halifax Town played their fourth round FA Cup match at Chester on 28 January, the players wore red jerseys borrowed from Huddersfield Town.
- A Shay record attendance was set when 29,235 turned out for the visit of Luton Town in the fifth round of the FA Cup on 18 February 1933.
- Halifax Town players and officials were compelled to travel to Doncaster Rovers for a scheduled match on 25 February despite the ground being under sixteen inches of snow following the worst snowstorm for forty years. Football League regulations decreed that the referee had to be the one to call the game off.
- Fred Tunstall scored the only goal of the game in Sheffield United's FA Cup Final success over Cardiff City in 1925.
- Former Town player Tim Coleman was selected to play centre-forward in an international trial match for England against The Rest on 22 March 1933.
- Following Town's FA Cup fourth-round replay with Chester at The Shay on 2 February 1933, Halifax pubs were allowed to stay open till 5.30pm.
- When Oliver Thompson missed the home game with York City on 1 April 1933 he ended a run of 112 consecutive appearances.
- Biggest League win: 5–1 v Mansfield Town, 29 April 1932.
- Heaviest League defeat: 0–6 v Stockport County, 11 February 1932.

Match No.	Date		Venue	Opponents	Result		Scorers	Attendance
1	Aug	27	A	Accrington Stanley	L	1-4	Betteridge	5,082
2		31	H	Hartlepools United	W	4-0	Betteridge, Davies, Wellock, Craig	5,663
3	Sep	3	H	Tranmere Rovers	W	4-1	Betteridge, Chambers, Wellock, Craig	7,338
4		7	A	Hartlepools United	D	1-1	Wellock	4,587
5		10	A	Wrexham	L	2-5	Wellock, Davies	6,539
6		17	H	Walsall	W	4-0	Wellock 2, Chambers, Thompson	8,688
7		24	A	Gateshead	L	0-3		5,467
8	Oct	1	H	Stockport County	L	1-3	Betteridge	6,754
9		8	A	Darlington	L	1-2	Betteridge	1,440
10		15	H	Doncaster Rovers	D	0-0		6,238
11		22	A	New Brighton	W	3-0	Betteridge 3	2,578
12		29	H	Chester	L	0-2		4,906
13	Nov	5	A	Barrow	D	3-3	Betteridge, Chambers, Wellock	5,354
14		12	H	Carlisle United	L	0-1		4,890
15		19	A	York City	L	3-5	Wellock 2 (1 pen), Craig	3,642
16	Dec	3	A	Rochdale	L	0-1		3,608
17		12	H	Southport	W	1-0	Chambers	1,420
18		17	A	Mansfield Town	D	2-2	Helliwell, Chambers (pen)	4,668
19		24	H	Rotherham United	W	2-1	Chambers, Wellock	5,332
20		26	A	Hull City	L	1-3	Wellock	15,199
21		27	H	Hull City	L	1-3	Wellock	9,311
22		31	H	Accrington Stanley	D	0-0		5,585
23	Jan	2	A	Southport	W	2-1	Davies 2	3,204
24		7	A	Tranmere Rovers	W	3-2	Davies, Chambers 2	3,877
25		18	H	Crewe Alexandra	L	1-5	Chambers	2,008
26		21	A	Wrexham	D	0-0		4,854
27	Feb	4	H	Gateshead	W	1-0	Wellock	7,477
28		9	A	Walsall	L	0-4		3,215
29		11	A	Stockport County	L	0-6		4,198
30		22	H	Darlington	W	4-2	Chambers, Tunstall 3	1,376
31	Mar	4	H	New Brighton	D	3-3	Hanks, Tunstall, Brown	3,864
32		11	A	Chester	L	3-6	Brown, Wellock 2	7,287
33		18	H	Barrow	W	2-0	Brown, Chambers (pen)	3,968
34		25	A	Carlisle United	L	3-5	Chambers 2, Davies	4,605
35		30	A	Doncaster Rovers	L	1-5	L Roberts	3,118
36	Apr	1	H	York City	W	2-0	Tunstall, Chambers	2,845
37		8	A	Crewe Alexandra	L	1-2	Chambers	3,030
38		15	H	Rochdale	W	2-0	Brown, Chambers (pen)	4,032
39		17	H	Barnsley	D	1-1	Wellock	4,413
40		18	A	Barnsley	W	2-1	Brown, Davies	5,183
41		29	H	Mansfield Town	W	5-1	Chambers 3, Brown, Davies	2,305
42	May	6	A	Rotherham United	L	1-6	Chambers	1,588

Final League Position: 15th in Division Three (North)

Apps
Gls

FA Cup

	Date		Venue	Opponents	Result		Scorers	Attendance
1	Nov	26	H	Darwen	W	2-0	Wellock 2	10,400
2	Dec	10	H	Workington	W	2-1	Davies, Wilson (og)	9,849
3	Jan	14	A	Doncaster Rovers	W	3-0	Brown, Chambers 2	11,730
4		28	A	Chester	D	0-0		10,529
R	Feb	2	H	Chester	W	3-2*	Wellock 2, Davies	14,224
5		18	H	Luton Town	L	0-2		29,235

*After extra-time

Apps
Gls

Shaw, WP	Midgley, J	Barrie, JW	Thompson, O	Cooke, A	Roberts, L	Davies, E	Craig, EF	Wollick, M	Chambers, WT	Bewsridge, F	Hallowell, C	Read, E	Flack, H	Spier, FH	Hebden, JT	Pavitt, C	Hanks, A	Brown, FW	Harker, SJ	Roberts, S	Hutchinson, W	Tunsall, F
1	2	3	4	5	6	7	8	9	10	11												
1		3	4		6	7	8	9	10	11	2	5										
1		3	4		6	7	8	9	10	11	2	5										
1		3	4		6	7	8	9	10	11	2	5										
1		3	4		6	7	8	9	10	11	2	5										
1		3	4		6	7	8	9	10	11	2	5										
1		3	4	5	6	7	8	9	10	11	2											
1		3	4	5	6	7	8	9	10	11	2											
1		3	4		6	7	8	9	10	11	2	5										
1		3	4		6	7	8	9	10	11		5	2									
		3	4	6		7	8	9	10	11		5	2	1								
1		3	4	6		7	8	9	10	11		5	2									
1		3	4	6		7	8	9	10	11		5	2									
1			4	6		7	8	9	10	11		3		2	5							
1		3	4	5		7	8	9		11			2		6	10						
1		3	4			7	8	9				5	2		6		10	11				
1		3	4			7	11	9	10			5	2		6		8					
1		3	4			7	8		10		9	5	2		6				11			
1		3	4			7	8	9	10			5	2		6				11			
1		3	4	9		7	8	5	10				2		6				11			
1		3	4			7	8	9	10			5	2		6				11			
1			4		6	7	5	9	10		3		2				8		11			
1			4			7	5	10	9		3		2		6		8		11			
1		3	4			7	5	10	9				2		6		8	11				
1		3	4			7	5	10	9				2		6		8	11				
		3	4			7	5	10			9		2	1	6		8		11			
		3	4				9	5	10				2	1			8	8		7		11
1		3	4	6				9					2		5	10	8		7		11	
1		3	4			7	5	10	9				2			6		8			11	
1		3	4	5		7		9			2					6	10	8			11	
1		3	4			7	5	9					2			6	10	8			11	
1			4			7	5	10	9		3		2			6		8			11	
1			4			7	5	10	9		3		2			6		8			11	
1			4		6	7	10	8	9		3	5	2								11	
1		3		6		7	5	10	9			4	2				8				11	
1		3	4	6		7	5	10	9				2				8				11	
1		3	4	6		7	5	10	9				2				8				11	
1		3	4	6		7	5	10	9				2				8				11	
1		3	4	6		7	5	10	9				2				8				11	
1		3	4	6		7	5	10	9				2				8				11	
1		3	4	6				5	10	9			2				8		7		11	
39	1	36	41	18	12	40	40	41	35	15	16	18	32	3	1	19	5	21	2	9	2	16
			1			1	8	3	16	20	9	1				1	6				5	

Shaw, WP	Midgley, J	Barrie, JW	Thompson, O	Cooke, A	Roberts, L	Davies, E	Craig, EF	Wollick, M	Chambers, WT	Bewsridge, F	Hallowell, C	Read, E	Flack, H	Spier, FH	Hebden, JT	Pavitt, C	Hanks, A	Brown, FW	Harker, SJ	Roberts, S	Hutchinson, W	Tunsall, F
1		3	4			7	8	9		11		5	2			6	10					
1		3	4			7	8	9	10			5	2		6				11			
1		3	4			7	5	10	9				2			6	8	11				
1		3	4			7	5	10	9	11			2			6	8					
		3	4			7	5	10	9	11			2	1		6	8					
1		3	4			7	5	10	9				2			6	8		11			
5		6	6			6	6	6	5	3		2	6	1		6	1	4	2		1	
						2		4	2								1					

League Table

	P	W	D	L	F	A	Pts
Hull City	42	26	7	9	100	45	59
Wrexham	42	24	9	9	106	51	57
Stockport County	42	21	12	9	99	58	54
Chester	42	22	8	12	94	66	52
Walsall	42	19	10	13	75	58	48
Doncaster Rovers	42	17	14	11	77	79	48
Gateshead	42	19	9	14	78	67	47
Barnsley	42	19	8	15	92	80	46
Barrow	42	18	7	17	60	60	43
Crewe Alexandra	42	20	3	19	80	84	43
Tranmere Rovers	42	17	8	17	70	66	42
Southport	42	17	7	18	70	67	41
Accrington Stanley	42	15	10	17	78	76	40
Hartlepools United	42	16	7	19	87	116	39
Halifax Town	42	15	8	19	71	90	38
Mansfield Town	42	14	7	21	84	100	35
Rotherham United	42	14	6	22	60	84	34
Rochdale	42	13	7	22	58	80	33
Carlisle United	42	13	7	22	51	75	33
York City	42	13	6	23	72	92	32
New Brighton	42	11	10	21	63	88	32
Darlington	42	10	8	24	66	109	28

1933-34
Division Three (North)
Manager: Alex Raisbeck

Did you know that?

- Halifax Town adopted Maurice Wellock's Alsatian dog as mascot.
- Captain was goalkeeper Watty Shirlaw.
- Samuel McClelland, father of Joseph, the club's first manager, died on 27 December 1933 aged 70.
- Stockport's 13–0 defeat of Town on 6 January set a FL record, matched only by Newcastle United's 13–0 win v Newport County. Bob Suter conceded a record score on his debut.
- Bill Chambers became the first Town player to score five League goals in a match in Town 6–2 victory over Hartlepools United, 7 April 1934.
- Bill Chambers became the first Town player to score 30 goals in a season.
- Famed for his record as a penalty taker, Tunstall missed his first penalty for seven years in 2–1 defeat at Walsall on 17 Feb 1934.
- Biggest League win: 5–0 v Chesterfield, 20 January 1934.
- Heaviest League defeat: 0–13 v Stockport County, 6 January 1934.
- Ever-presents: Ted Craig and Hugh Flack.

Match No.	Date		Venue	Opponents	Result		Scorers	Attendance
1	Aug	26	A	Carlisle United	L	0-1		7,198
2		30	H	Chester	W	1-0	Chambers	8,517
3	Sep	2	H	Stockport County	W	4-2	Tunstall 4 (1 pen)	9,517
4		6	A	Chester	W	2-1	Chambers, Tunstall	8,747
5		9	A	Chesterfield	L	2-4	Tunstall 2	10,884
6		16	A	Crewe Alexandra	D	1-1	Chambers	6,094
7		23	H	New Brighton	D	1-1	Davies	9,890
8		30	A	Rotherham United	W	2-1	Chambers 2	3,122
9	Oct	7	H	Walsall	W	2-0	Chambers 2	6,952
10		14	A	York City	L	0-1		5,555
11		21	H	Accrington Stanley	W	2-1	Brown, Betteridge	7,334
12		28	A	Gateshead	L	0-4		3,239
13	Nov	4	H	Darlington	W	2-0	Chambers, Pescod	7,157
14		11	A	Southport	W	4-1	Wellock, Mercer, Chambers 2	2,032
15		18	H	Wrexham	L	1-3	Brown	6,456
16	Dec	2	H	Mansfield Town	W	4-2	Davies, Wellock, Tunstall, Brown	5,781
17		16	H	Tranmere Rovers	L	0-2		7,533
18		23	A	Rochdale	W	2-1	Davies, Chambers	3,258
19		25	H	Barrow	W	4-1	Chambers, Davies, Tunstall 2	11,870
20		26	A	Barrow	L	2-5	Tunstall (pen), Betteridge	4,828
21		30	H	Carlisle United	W	3-2	Wellock, Chambers, Chambers	5,697
22	Jan	1	A	Hartlepools United	L	0-5		2,408
23		6	A	Stockport County	L	0-13		7,807
24		20	H	Chesterfield	W	5-0	Chambers 3, Tunstall, Mercer	10,237
25		27	H	Crewe Alexandra	W	3-2	Davies, Tunstall 2 (1 pen)	8,524
26	Feb	3	A	New Brighton	L	0-3		2,568
27		10	H	Rotherham United	W	3-2	Wellock, Brown, Chambers	5,218
28		17	A	Walsall	L	0-2		5,741
29		19	A	Barnsley	L	0-1		7,028
30		24	H	York City	W	3-0	Davies, Tunstall 2	5,400
31	Mar	3	A	Accrington Stanley	D	1-1	Tunstall	1,934
32		10	H	Gateshead	L	2-4	Mercer 2	1,874
33		17	A	Darlington	L	2-4	Brown 2	2,742
34		24	H	Southport	W	6-2	Betteridge, Chambers 3, Brown, Presgrave	4,303
35		30	A	Doncaster Rovers	L	0-3		11,386
36		31	A	Wrexham	W	2-0	Presgrave, Chambers	6,050
37	Apr	2	H	Doncaster Rovers	L	0-1		5,807
38		7	H	Hartlepools United	W	6-2	Chambers 5, Wellock	4,849
39		14	A	Mansfield Town	L	1-6	Betteridge	3,262
40		21	H	Barnsley	D	1-1	Chambers	13,850
41		28	A	Tranmere Rovers	L	2-3	Chambers 2 (1 pen)	1,903
42	May	5	H	Rochdale	W	4-2	Chambers, Hall, Tunstall 2	3,434

Final League Position: 9th in Division Three (North)   Apps / Gls

FA Cup

1	Nov	25	H	Barnsley	W	3-2	Brown, Ferguson, Chambers	14,726
2	Dec	9	H	Hartlepools United	D	1-1	Brown	13,400
R		13	A	Hartlepools United	W	2-1*	Brown, Cooke	9,500
3	Jan	13	A	Bolton Wanderers	L	1-3	Tunstall	24,885

* After extra-time   Apps / Gls

League Table

	P	W	D	L	F	A	Pts
Hull City	42	26	7	9	100	45	59
Wrexham	42	24	9	9	106	51	57
Stockport County	42	21	12	9	99	58	54
Chester	42	22	8	12	94	66	52
Walsall	42	19	10	13	75	58	48
Doncaster Rovers	42	17	14	11	77	79	48
Gateshead	42	19	9	14	78	67	47
Barnsley	42	19	8	15	92	80	46
Barrow	42	18	7	17	60	60	43
Crewe Alexandra	42	20	3	19	80	84	43
Tranmere Rovers	42	17	8	17	70	66	42
Southport	42	17	7	18	70	67	41
Accrington Stanley	42	15	10	17	78	76	40
Hartlepools United	42	16	7	19	87	116	39
Halifax Town	42	15	8	19	71	90	38
Mansfield Town	42	14	7	21	84	100	35
Rotherham United	42	14	6	22	60	84	34
Rochdale	42	13	7	22	58	80	33
Carlisle United	42	13	7	22	51	75	33
York City	42	13	6	23	72	92	32
New Brighton	42	11	10	21	63	88	32
Darlington	42	10	8	24	66	109	28

1934-35

Division Three (North)
Manager: Alex Raisbeck

Did you know that?

- Bill Chambers's £2,600 transfer to Bolton Wanderers on 6 July 1934 was a record fee received by Halifax Town.
- Halifax Town broke with tradition and held their first practice match of the season on 9 August 1934, seven days before the traditional start of the Wakes week holiday so that more supporters could attend.
- Captain was Ted Craig.
- Charlie Davies was awarded a benefit while still aged only 23 and only into his sixth season with Halifax Town. Halifax Town lost 5–3 to Sheffield Wednesday on 1 October 1934.
- Jackie Foster became licensee of Royal Hotel in Barrow.
- Albert Valentine's five-goal haul in the 6–2 victory over New Brighton on 9 March 1935 was the last time a Halifax Town player achieved this feat.
- Halifax Town played a friendly at Macclesfield Town on 15 April to help with Macclesfield's finances.
- Halifax Town's reserve side defeated South Kirkby Colliery 4–0 in the Yorkshire Cup final on 30 April 1935.
- Albert Valentine set a club record when he scored 33 League goals during the season.
- Halifax Town's runners'-up spot was their highest-ever placing in the Football League.
- Biggest League win: 6–2 v New Brighton (h), 9 March 1935.
- Heaviest League defeat: 0–5 v Wrexham (a), 16 February 1935, v Chester, 2 March 1935.
- Ever-present: Albert Cooke.

Match No.	Date		Venue	Opponents	Result		Scorers	Attendance
1	Aug	25	H	Mansfield Town	W	2-1	Mercer, Valentine	9,386
2		27	A	Rotherham United	D	2-2	Valentine, Cooke	7,090
3	Sep	1	A	Barrow	L	0-2		7,766
4		3	H	Rotherham United	W	2-1	Valentine, Ferguson	7,710
5		8	H	Carlisle United	W	4-0	Valentine 2, Mercer, Tunstall (pen)	7,808
6		15	A	Rochdale	W	4-2	Tunstall 3, Valentine	7,830
7		17	H	Walsall	D	1-1	Tunstall (pen)	6,655
8		22	H	Lincoln City	W	2-1	Valentine 2	8,382
9		29	A	Tranmere Rovers	L	0-1		5,241
10	Oct	6	H	Wrexham	W	3-2	Valentine 2, Tunstall (pen)	8,638
11		13	A	Southport	W	2-1	Mercer, Valentine	3,630
12		20	H	Chester	W	1-0	Davies	14,488
13		27	A	New Brighton	D	0-0		3,233
14	Nov	3	H	York City	W	5-3	Cooke 2, Valentine 2 (1 pen), Tunstall	9,013
15		10	A	Darlington	W	1-0	Valentine	4,277
16		17	H	Accrington Stanley	W	2-1	Valentine 2	10,899
17	Dec	1	H	Stockport County	W	2-1	Valentine, Tunstall	10,024
18		8	A	Crewe Alexandra	L	1-3	Craig	4,190
19		15	H	Hartlepools United	W	4-1	Atherton 2, Tunstall, Park (og)	8,526
20		25	H	Chesterfield	L	0-2		12,655
21		29	A	Mansfield Town	L	0-4		8,144
22	Jan	1	A	Chesterfield	L	0-4		7,347
23		5	H	Barrow	W	2-1	Davies, Tunstall (pen)	8,285
24		12	A	Gateshead	L	1-3	Tunstall (pen)	2,729
25		19	A	Carlisle United	W	4-2	Barkas, Tunstall 2, Valentine	4,657
26		26	H	Rochdale	D	1-1	Tunstall (pen)	7,133
27	Feb	2	A	Lincoln City	W	3-2	Davies, Feeney, Valentine	5,021
28		9	H	Tranmere Rovers	L	1-2	Valentine	17,363
29		16	A	Wrexham	L	0-5		2,576
30		23	H	Southport	W	4-3	Valentine 2, Barkas, Feeney	6,350
31	Mar	2	A	Chester	L	0-5		5,770
32		9	H	New Brighton	W	6-2	Barkas, Valentine 5	4,673
33		16	A	York City	W	1-0	Betteridge	4,322
34		23	H	Darlington	W	2-1	Betteridge, Valentine	4,245
35		30	A	Accrington Stanley	D	1-1	Valentine (pen)	3,155
36	Apr	6	H	Gateshead	W	4-0	Barkas, Valentine 2, Tunstall	7,630
37		13	A	Stockport County	L	1-2	Barkas	7,257
38		20	H	Crewe Alexandra	W	1-0	Cooke	8,004
39		22	A	Walsall	L	1-4	Davies	5,957
40		27	A	Hartlepools United	W	3-0	Mercer, Valentine, Betteridge	2,404
41	May	2	A	Doncaster Rovers	W	1-0	Valentine	8,113
42		4	A	Doncaster Rovers	W	1-0	Betteridge	8,653

Final League Position: 2nd in Division Three (North)

1 own-goal

Apps
Gls

FA Cup

1	Nov	24	H	Hartlepools United	D	1-1	Atherton	12,439
R		28	A	Hartlepools United	L	0-2		8,787

Apps
Gls

League Table

	P	W	D	L	F	A	Pts
Doncaster Rovers	42	26	5	11	87	44	57
Halifax Town	42	25	5	12	73	67	55
Chester	42	20	14	8	91	58	54
Lincoln City	42	22	7	13	87	58	51
Darlington	42	21	9	12	83	59	51
Tranmere Rovers	42	20	11	11	74	55	51
Stockport County	42	22	3	17	93	72	47
Mansfield Town	42	19	9	14	75	62	47
Rotherham United	42	19	7	16	83	73	45
Chesterfield	42	17	10	15	71	52	44
Wrexham	42	16	11	15	73	69	43
Hartlepools United	42	17	7	18	83	78	41
Crewe Alexandra	42	14	11	17	63	86	39
Walsall	42	13	10	19	81	72	36
York City	42	15	6	21	73	82	36
New Brighton	42	14	8	20	53	76	36
Barrow	42	13	9	20	53	87	35
Accrington Stanley	42	12	10	20	63	89	34
Gateshead	42	13	8	21	53	96	34
Rochdale	42	11	11	20	53	71	33
Southport	42	10	12	20	55	85	32
Carlisle United	42	8	7	27	51	102	23

1935-36
Division Three (North)
Manager: Alex Raisbeck

Did you know that?

- Captain was Ted Craig.
- Halifax Town played in hoops for FA Cup tie with Rochdale, 30 November 1935.
- Wilf Feeney returned from injury for game v Wrexham on 21 September 1935 and scored within 45 seconds.
- Bill Merry, signed from Manchester United in November, was a team mate of Valentine at Cardiff City.
- Hebden Bridge youth William Joyce scored on his debut against Southport on 7 December but never played in first team again.
- Crowd favourite Charlie Davies joined champions-elect Chesterfield on 13 March 1936.
- Biggest League win: 4–1 v Wrexham (h), 21 September 1935, v New Brighton (a) 2 November 1936.
- Heaviest League defeat: 0–3 v Oldham Athletic (a), 28 September 1935.
- Ever-present: Ted Craig.

Match No.	Date		Venue	Opponents	Result		Scorers	Attendance
1	Aug	31	A	Hartlepools United	L	0-1		5,615
2	Sep	2	H	Carlisle United	W	1-0	Smith	8,709
3		7	H	Mansfield Town	W	1-0	Valentine	11,090
4		12	A	Carlisle United	D	0-0		9,563
5		14	A	Rotherham United	L	0-2		7,300
6		16	H	Walsall	D	1-1	Bennett (og)	6,155
7		21	H	Wrexham	W	4-1	Feeney, Valentine 2, Presgrave	9,988
8		28	A	Oldham Athletic	L	0-3		8,605
9	Oct	5	H	Rochdale	W	2-0	Barkas, Valentine	7,396
10		12	H	Darlington	L	0-1		8,403
11		19	A	York City	D	2-2	Feeney, Valentine	3,213
12		26	H	Barrow	W	3-2	Valentine 2, Davies	5,651
13	Nov	2	A	New Brighton	W	4-1	Barkas, Betteridge 2, Valentine	3,006
14		9	H	Chesterfield	L	2-3	Valentine 2	9,560
15		16	A	Stockport County	L	0-1		6,611
16		23	H	Crewe Alexandra	L	2-4	Valentine 2	7,196
17	Dec	7	H	Southport	L	1-2	Joyce	5,340
18		21	H	Lincoln City	W	2-1	Barkas 2	5,002
19		25	A	Gateshead	D	2-2	Inskip (og), Valentine	2,718
20		26	H	Gateshead	D	1-1	Barkas	4,414
21		28	H	Hartlepools United	L	0-1		4,624
22	Jan	4	A	Mansfield Town	L	2-3	Smethurst, Valentine	3,756
23		11	A	Accrington Stanley	L	0-2		2,306
24		18	H	Rotherham United	W	1-0	Barkas	4,103
25	Feb	1	A	Oldham Athletic	W	4-2	Valentine 4	6,731
26		8	A	Rochdale	L	0-2		4,309
27		15	A	Darlington	L	2-3	Barkas, Valentine	2,856
28		22	H	York City	W	2-0	Valentine, Barkas	3,690
29		29	A	Chesterfield	L	1-3	Presgrave	3,341
30	Mar	7	H	New Brighton	W	3-0	Davies, Valentine, Smith	3,374
31		11	A	Wrexham	W	3-1	Barkas, Valentine 2	946
32		14	A	Barrow	D	0-0		2,390
33		21	H	Stockport County	D	0-0		5,167
34		28	A	Crewe Alexandra	L	2-3	Valentine 2	3,958
35	Apr	4	H	Accrington Stanley	W	1-0	Presgrave	4,229
36		10	A	Tranmere Rovers	W	2-0	Valentine 2	12,629
37		11	A	Southport	L	0-2		2,424
38		13	H	Tranmere Rovers	W	1-0	Merry	6,451
39		18	H	Chester	L	2-3	Smith, Smethurst	5,932
40		25	A	Lincoln City	L	1-3	Valentine	2,189
41		29	A	Chester	L	1-3	Valentine	3,973
42	May	2	A	Walsall	L	1-2	Valentine	3,282

Final League Position: 17th in Division Three (North)

2 own-goals

Apps
Gls

FA Cup

1	Nov	30	H	Rochdale	W	4-0	Barkas 2, Betteridge 2	7,341
2	Dec	14	H	Hartlepools United	D	1-1	Valentine (pen)	7,698
R		18	A	Hartlepools United	D	0-0*		7,713
2R		23	N**	Hartlepools United	L	1-4*	Cooke	4,900

* After extra-time
**Played at St James' Park, Newcastle.

Apps
Gls

League Table

	P	W	D	L	F	A	Pts
Chesterfield	42	24	12	6	92	39	60
Chester	42	22	11	9	100	45	55
Tranmere Rovers	42	22	11	9	93	58	55
Lincoln City	42	22	9	1	91	51	53
Stockport County	42	20	8	14	65	49	48
Crewe Alexandra	42	19	9	14	80	76	47
Oldham Athletic	42	18	9	15	86	73	45
Hartlepools United	42	15	12	15	57	61	42
Accrington Stanley	42	17	8	17	63	72	42
Walsall	42	16	9	17	79	59	41
Rotherham United	42	16	9	17	69	66	41
Darlington	42	17	6	19	74	79	40
Carlisle United	42	14	12	16	56	62	40
Gateshead	42	13	14	15	56	76	40
Barrow	42	13	12	17	58	65	38
York City	42	13	12	17	62	95	38
Halifax Town	42	15	7	20	57	61	37
Wrexham	42	15	7	20	66	75	37
Mansfield Town	42	14	9	19	80	91	37
Rochdale	42	10	13	19	58	88	33
Southport	42	11	9	22	48	90	31
New Brighton	42	9	6	27	43	102	24

1936-37

Division Three (North)
Manager: Jimmy Thomson

Did you know that?

- Jimmy Thomson beat off competition from among others former Town boss Joe McClelland for the manager's job at Shay.
- Captain was Albert Watson.
- Ted Craig played his 100th consecutive League match for Town in the 2–1 home defeat by Wrexham on 10 April.
- In the last game with Crewe Alexandra on 1 May, Crewe took lead after five minutes, missed an open goal and hit the bar before Town equalised with the last kick of the first half – a Valentine penalty. Town won 4–1.
- Albert Valentine's total of 25 League goals included six penalties.
- Biggest League win: 6–1 v Carlisle United (h), 2 January 1937.
- Heaviest League defeat: 0–6 v Rotherham United (a), 21 November 1936.
- Ever-present: Bill Allsop.

Match No.	Date		Venue	Opponents	Result		Scorers	Attendance
1	Aug	29	H	York City	L	1-2	Smith	8,955
2		31	A	Barrow	W	2-1	Valentine 2	4,344
3	Sep	5	A	Carlisle United	W	2-1	Watson, Valentine	5,864
4		7	H	Barrow	W	2-1	Goodall, Valentine (pen)	4,576
5		12	H	Hartlepools United	W	2-0	Barkas 2	5,798
6		16	A	Crewe Alexandra	W	1-0	Valentine (pen)	3,710
7		19	A	Southport	L	1-2	Smith	5,696
8		26	H	Tranmere Rovers	W	2-1	Murphy, Valentine	10,833
9	Oct	3	A	Hull City	D	0-0		9,642
10		10	A	Mansfield Town	L	0-3		7,731
11		17	H	New Brighton	D	0-0		5,174
12		24	A	Lincoln City	L	1-4	Barkas	6,062
13		31	H	Accrington Stanley	W	3-0	Valentine, Smith, Murphy	7,252
14	Nov	7	A	Oldham Athletic	L	0-1		5,677
15		14	H	Port Vale	L	0-1		7,443
16		21	A	Rotherham United	L	0-6		5,918
17	Dec	5	A	Wrexham	W	2-0	Valentine 2	4,330
18		19	A	Gateshead	W	2-0	Smith, Valentine	2,135
19		25	A	Chester	D	1-1	Valentine	11,241
20		26	A	York City	L	0-4		6,418
21		28	H	Chester	W	1-0	Smith	6,290
22	Jan	2	H	Carlisle United	W	6-1	Smith 2, Evans, Valentine 2, Widdowfield	4,946
23		9	A	Hartlepools United	L	3-5	Valentine 3 (1 pen)	6,154
24		16	H	Stockport County	D	1-1	Valentine (pen)	8,918
25		23	H	Southport	D	1-1	Barkas	4,718
26		30	A	Tranmere Rovers	L	1-2	Barkas	4,216
27	Feb	6	H	Hull City	W	1-0	Barkas	8,251
28		13	H	Mansfield Town	D	0-0		4,970
29		20	A	New Brighton	D	1-1	Barkas	2,677
30		27	H	Lincoln City	L	2-3	Valentine (pen), Feeney	4,303
31	Mar	6	A	Accrington Stanley	L	2-3	Widdowfield, Feeney	3,338
32		20	A	Port Vale	L	1-3	Valentine	5,732
33		26	A	Rochdale	W	5-3	Hoyland 2, Barkas 2, Widdowfield	5,000
34		27	H	Rotherham United	W	4-1	Valentine 4	5,820
35		29	H	Rochdale	W	3-2	Barkas, Hoyland 2	5,898
36	Apr	3	A	Stockport County	D	0-0		14,048
37		10	H	Wrexham	L	1-2	Smith	4,683
38		17	A	Darlington	D	3-3	Feeney 2, Barkas	2,419
39		19	H	Darlington	W	4-1	Feeney 3, Smith	2,615
40		24	H	Gateshead	W	2-1	Barkas, Robinson	4,689
41		26	H	Oldham Athletic	L	0-1		3,243
42	May	1	H	Crewe Alexandra	W	4-1	Valentine 2 (1 pen), Barkas, Watson	2,412

Final League Position: 7th in Division Three (North)

Apps
Gls

FA Cup

| 1 | Nov | 28 | A | Darlington | L | 1-2 | Valentine | 11,331 |

Apps
Gls

League Table

	P	W	D	L	F	A	Pts
Stockport County	42	23	14	5	84	39	60
Lincoln City	42	25	7	10	103	57	57
Chester	42	22	9	11	87	57	53
Oldham Athletic	42	20	11	11	77	59	51
Hull City	42	17	12	13	63	69	46
Hartlepools United	42	19	7	16	75	69	45
Halifax Town	42	18	9	15	63	63	45
Wrexham	42	16	12	14	71	57	44
Mansfield Town	42	18	8	16	91	76	44
Carlisle United	42	18	8	16	65	68	44
Port Vale	42	17	10	15	53	64	44
York City	42	16	11	15	73	70	43
Accrington Stanley	42	16	9	17	73	69	41
Southport	42	12	13	17	73	87	37
New Brighton	42	13	11	18	55	70	37
Barrow	42	13	10	19	70	86	36
Rotherham United	42	14	7	21	73	91	35
Rochdale	42	13	9	20	63	86	35
Tranmere Rovers	42	12	9	21	71	88	33
Crewe Alexandra	42	10	12	20	55	83	32
Gateshead	42	11	10	21	63	98	32
Darlington	42	8	14	20	66	96	30

1937-38

Division Three (North)
Manager: Jimmy Thomson

Did you know that?

- Harold Taylor was appointed trainer from 75 applicants.
- Les Copeland understudied the great Hughie Gallacher at Chelsea.
- Captain was Bill Allsop.
- Tom T. Dickinson's Halifax Town written history *Milestones* went on sale on 18 December 1937.
- Halifax Town drew 1–1 with First Division Everton in a Shay friendly on 12 February.
- Goalkeeper Charlie Briggs signed for Halifax Town in the press-room at Leeds Road after watching the Huddersfield Town v York City FA Cup replay on 9 March.
- Biggest League win: 2–0 v Gateshead (h), 23 October, v Port Vale (a), 13 November, v New Brighton, 26 February, v Lincoln City (h), 25 April.
- Town lost 2–0 to Yorkshire League side Selby Town in the final of the Wes
- Heaviest League defeat: 0–4 v Crewe Alexandra (a), 2 April.
- Ever-present: Bill Allsop.

Match No.	Date		Venue	Opponents	Result		Scorers	Attendance
1	Aug	28	A	Chester	D	1-1	Barkas	8,328
2		30	H	Rotherham United	L	1-3	Copeland	7,666
3	Sep	4	H	Accrington Stanley	L	1-2	Jackson (pen)	7,085
4		6	A	Rotherham United	L	1-4	Courts (og)	6,010
5		11	A	Carlisle United	L	2-5	Barkas 2	5,974
6		13	H	Rochdale	L	2-3	Jackson (pen), Hoyland	2,409
7		18	H	Hull City	W	1-0	Copeland	6,142
8		25	H	Tranmere Rovers	W	1-0	Hoyland	7,607
9	Oct	2	A	York City	D	1-1	Hoyland	6,278
10		9	H	Bradford City	L	0-2		13,306
11		16	A	New Brighton	L	0-2		4,092
12		23	H	Gateshead	W	2-0	Barkas, Griffiths	4,075
13		30	A	Oldham Athletic	L	1-2	Griffiths	6,288
14	Nov	6	H	Darlington	W	1-0	Hoyland	5,570
15		13	A	Port Vale	W	2-0	Copeland, Barkas	6,579
16		20	H	Crewe Alexandra	W	2-1	Copeland, Barkas	6,474
17	Dec	4	H	Wrexham	D	0-0		3,782
18		25	A	Southport	D	2-2	Scott 2	5,642
19		27	H	Southport	D	1-1	Griffiths	4,901
20	Jan	1	H	Chester	D	1-1	Campbell	6,594
21		8	A	Barrow	L	1-2	Widdowfield	4,542
22		15	A	Accrington Stanley	W	4-3	Widdowfield 4	2,081
23		22	H	Carlisle United	D	0-0		6,228
24		29	A	Hull City	W	1-0	Widdowfield	7,588
25	Feb	5	A	Tranmere Rovers	L	0-2		8,919
26		14	H	York City	D	2-2	Robinson, Widdowfield	1,785
27		19	A	Bradford City	L	0-3		9,198
28		26	H	New Brighton	W	2-0	Widdowfield, Clark	4,551
29	Mar	5	A	Gateshead	L	1-4	Pritchard	12,276
30		12	H	Oldham Athletic	W	2-1	Copeland 2	6,550
31		19	A	Darlington	L	0-3		3,856
32		26	H	Port Vale	W	2-1	Widdowfield 2	4,363
33	Apr	2	A	Crewe Alexandra	L	0-4		3,545
34		9	H	Barrow	D	1-1	Pritchard	3,025
35		15	A	Doncaster Rovers	D	2-2	Craig, Griffiths	19,356
36		16	A	Wrexham	L	0-2		3,291
37		18	H	Doncaster Rovers	L	0-1		6,571
38		23	H	Hartlepools United	D	0-0		2,821
39		25	H	Lincoln City	W	2-0	Clark (pen), Widdowfield	1,772
40		30	A	Lincoln City	L	0-2		3,108
41	May	4	A	Hartlepools United	L	0-2		4,940
42		7	A	Rochdale	D	1-1	Griffiths	2,065

Final League Position: 18th in Division Three (North)

1 own-goal

Apps
Gls

FA Cup

1	Nov	27	A	York City	D	1-1	Barkas	7,063
R	Dec	1	H	York City	L	0-1		6,244

Apps
Gls

League Table

	P	W	D	L	F	A	Pts
Tranmere Rovers	42	23	10	9	81	41	56
Doncaster Rovers	42	21	12	9	74	49	54
Hull City	42	20	13	9	80	43	53
Oldham Athletic	42	19	13	10	67	46	51
Gateshead	42	20	11	11	84	59	51
Rotherham United	42	20	10	12	68	56	50
Lincoln City	42	19	8	15	66	50	46
Crewe Alexandra	42	18	9	15	71	53	45
Chester	42	16	12	14	77	72	44
Wrexham	42	16	11	15	58	63	43
York City	42	16	10	16	70	68	42
Carlisle United	42	15	9	18	57	67	39
New Brighton	42	15	8	19	60	61	38
Bradford City	42	14	10	18	66	69	38
Port Vale	42	12	14	16	65	73	38
Southport	42	12	14	16	53	82	38
Rochdale	42	13	11	18	67	78	37
Halifax Town	42	12	12	18	44	66	36
Darlington	42	11	10	2	54	79	32
Hartlepools United	42	10	12	20	53	80	32
Barrow	42	11	10	2	41	71	32
Accrington Stanley	42	11	7	24	45	75	29

1938-39

Division Three (North)

Manager: Jimmy Thomson

Did you know that?

- Stan Wood was a member of the West Brom side which clinched promotion from Division Two and won the FA Cup in 1930–31.
- Jabez Foulkes was a scorer for Stockport County in their record 13–0 victory over Halifax Town in January 1934.
- Halifax Town and Rochdale had to play a second game at Spotland in the Jubilee Fund after the first match at The Shay failed to net £500.
- Fred Mason scored with a header in the first minute of his League debut against Barrow on 1 October 1938. It was the only goal of the game.
- Manager Jimmy Thomson tried to sign Tranmere Rovers's former England international Pongo Waring, but the fee was too high.
- Town defeated Rochdale 7–3 in the first round of the FA Cup to set a Shay record of goals scored.
- Ernest Ferneyhough became the first of three goalkeepers to be on the winning side on their only League appearance for the club when he played in Town's 5–4 victory at Rochdale on 18 February.
- Biggest League win: 5–1 v Carlisle United (h), 25 March 1939.
- Heaviest League defeat: 1–5 v Chester (a), 8 October.
- Ever-presents: Ted Craig, Horace Green.

Match No.	Date		Venue	Opponents	Result		Scorers	Attendance
1	Aug	27	H	Accrington Stanley	W	2-0	Widdowfield, Randle (og)	7,153
2		29	H	Bradford City	D	2-2	Griffiths, Foulkes	8,340
3	Sep	3	A	Barnsley	L	0-1		8,216
4		5	H	Stockport County	D	3-3	Widdowfield 2, Barkas	6,822
5		10	H	Oldham Athletic	D	0-0		11,295
6		12	A	Bradford City	L	0-1		6,762
7		17	A	York City	L	0-3		6,018
8		24	A	New Brighton	L	0-1		5,375
9	Oct	1	H	Barrow	W	1-0	Mason	6,113
10		8	A	Chester	L	1-5	Foulkes	6,792
11		15	H	Rochdale	W	2-1	Widdowfield, Barkas	5,626
12		22	A	Rotherham United	W	1-0	Barkas	7,611
13		29	H	Doncaster Rovers	D	0-0		8,619
14	Nov	5	A	Southport	L	0-1		7,723
15		12	H	Crewe Alexandra	D	0-0		6,680
16		19	A	Carlisle United	W	2-1	Widdowfield, Griffiths	4,606
17	Dec	3	A	Hartlepools United	L	0-1		4,603
18		17	A	Wrexham	L	2-3	Griffiths, Widdowfield	2,878
19		24	A	Accrington Stanley	W	2-1	Widdowfield, Ruecroft	2,663
20		26	H	Lincoln City	W	2-0	Graham 2	7,793
21		27	A	Lincoln City	D	0-0		8,391
22		31	H	Barnsley	L	1-4	Widdowfield	12,636
23	Jan	9	A	Darlington	D	1-1	Widdowfield	1,445
24		14	A	Oldham Athletic	L	0-1		5,603
25		21	H	York City	W	2-1	Wood, Widdowfield	3,393
26		28	H	New Brighton	W	3-1	Widdowfield, Griffiths, H Jackson (pen)	4,090
27	Feb	4	A	Barrow	D	0-0		6,385
28		11	H	Chester	D	1-1	Widdowfield	5,217
29		18	A	Rochdale	W	5-4	Widdowfield 2, Griffiths, Wood, Atack	6,521
30		25	H	Rotherham United	D	1-1	Widdowfield	4,950
31	Mar	4	A	Doncaster Rovers	D	0-0		6,552
32		11	H	Southport	D	1-1	Widdowfield	3,163
33		18	A	Crewe Alexandra	D	2-2	Griffiths, Widdowfield	4,241
34		25	H	Carlisle United	W	5-1	Graham, Widdowfield 2, Griffiths, Wood	3,772
35	Apr	1	A	Darlington	L	0-1		3,645
36		7	A	Hull City	D	1-1	Green	10,613
37		8	H	Hartlepools United	W	2-0	Widdowfield, Wood	3,379
38		10	H	Hull City	W	1-0	Griffiths	4,229
39		15	A	Gateshead	L	0-2		3,149
40		22	H	Wrexham	L	0-2		3,389
41		24	H	Gateshead	D	3-3	Wood, Widdowfield 2	1,574
42	May	6	A	Stockport County	D	3-3	Widdowfield, Wood, Green	3,351

Final League Position: 12th in Division Three (North)

1 own-goal

Apps
Gls

FA Cup

1	Nov	26	H	Rochdale	W	7-3	Widdowfield 4, H Jackson (pen), Wood 2	10,921
2	Dec	10	H	Mansfield Town	D	1-1	Griffiths	14,208
R		14	A	Mansfield Town	D	3-3*	Griffiths, Widdowfield, Wood	6,083
2R		19	N**	Mansfield Town	D	0-0*		2,431
3R		21	N***	Mansfield Town	W	2-1*	Widdowfield, Bungay (og)	1,219
3	Jan	7	A	Birmingham City	L	0-2		23,522

* After extra-time ** Played at Belle View, Doncaster.
*** Played at Old Trafford, Manchester.

1 own-goal

Apps
Gls

Biggs, CE	Allsop, WH	Dirk, SJH	Green, H	Craig, EF	Brookes, AG	Foulkes, JB	Griffiths, JS	Widdowfield, E	Barkas, T	Wood, S	Jackson, H	Ruecroft, J	Scott, H	Wintle, W	Jackson, AG	Graham, A	Mason, FC	Massey, KBW	Hutton, H	Atack, S	Fenneyhough, E	Ashbridge, K	Cooper, WGE
1	2	3	4	5	6	7	8	9	10	11													
1	2		4	5		7	8	9	10	11	3	6											
1	2		4	5	6	7	8	9	10	11	3												
1	2		4	5	6		8	9	10	11	3		7										
1	2		4	5	6		8	9	10	11	3		7										
1	2		4	5			8	9	10		3	6		7	11								
1	2		4	5		7	8	9	10	11	3	6											
1	2	3		5	6	7	11	9	10				4			8							
1	2	3		5	6	7			10	11			4			8	9						
1	2	3		5	6	7	8		10				4		11	9							
1	2		4	5	6	7	8	9	10	11	3				11								
1	2		4	5	6	7	8	9	10	11	3												
1	2		4	5		7	8	9	10	11	3	6											
1	2		4	5		7	8	9	10	11	3	6											
1	2		4	5		7	8	9	10	11	3	6											
1	2		4	5			8	9		11	3	6	7		10								
1	2		4	5		7		9		11	3	6			10	8							
1	2		4	5		7	8	9			3	6			10		11						
1	2		4	5			7	9	8		3	6			10		11						
1		2	5				8	9	10		3	6	7				11	4					
1	2		4	5		7	8	9		11	3	6			10								
1	2		4	5		7	10	9		11	3	6				8							
1	2		4	5		7	8	9	10	11	3	6											
1	2		4	5		7	8	9		10	3	6					11						
1	2		4	5		7	8	9		10	3	6					11						
1	2		4	5		7	8	9		10	3	6					11						
	2	3	5			7	8	9	10	11		6						4	1				
1	2		3	5		7	8	9	10	11		6						4					
1	2		4	5		7	8	9	10	11	3	6											
1	2		4	5		7		9	10	11	3	6				8							
	2		4	5			7	9	10	11	3	6				8				1			
1	2		4	5			7	9	10	11	3	6				8							
1	2		4	5			7	9	10	11	3	6				8							
1	2		4	5			7	9	10	11	3	6				8							
1	2		4	5			8	9	10	11	3	6				7							
1	2		4	5			8	9	10	11	3	6				7							
1	2		4	5			8	9	10	11	3	6									7		
1	2		4	5				9	10	11	3	6			8						7		
1	2		4	5			8	9	10	11	3	6							7				
1	2		4	5		7	8	9	10	11	3	6											
40	41	1	42	42	10	27	38	40	34	35	36	35	3	2	3	14	2	3	7	3	1	1	2
				2		2	8	23	3	6	1	1			3	1			1				
1	2		4	5		7	8	9	10	11	3	6											
1	2		4	5		7	8	9	10	11	3	6											
1	2		4	5		7	8	9	10	11	3	6											
1	2		4	5		7	8	9	10	11	3	6											
1	2		4	5			8	9	10	11	3	6	7										
6	6		6	6		5	6	6	6	6	6	1											
						2	6		2	1													

League Table

	P	W	D	L	F	A	Pts
Barnsley	42	30	7	5	94	34	67
Doncaster Rovers	42	21	14	7	87	47	56
Bradford City	42	22	8	12	89	56	52
Southport	42	20	10	12	75	54	50
Oldham Athletic	42	22	5	15	73	59	49
Chester	42	20	9	13	83	70	49
Hull City	42	18	10	14	83	74	46
Crewe Alexandra	42	19	6	17	82	70	44
Stockport County	42	17	9	16	91	77	43
Gateshead	42	14	14	14	74	67	42
Rotherham United	42	17	8	17	64	64	42
Halifax Town	42	13	16	13	52	54	42
Barrow	42	16	9	17	63	65	41
Wrexham	42	17	7	18	63	79	41
Rochdale	42	15	9	18	92	82	39
New Brighton	42	15	9	18	63	73	39
Lincoln City	42	12	9	21	65	92	33
Darlington	42	13	7	22	62	92	33
Carlisle United	42	13	7	22	65	111	33
York City	42	12	8	22	64	92	32
Hartlepools United	42	12	7	23	55	94	31
Accrington Stanley	42	7	6	29	43	103	20

1939-40

Division Three (North)
Manager: Jimmy Thomson

Did you know that?

- Halifax Town replaced their solid wood goalposts with new oval-shaped ones.
- Sam Hanna was a baseball star.
- All players received 30s per match.
- Eric Worthington was father to footballing brothers, Dave, Bob and Frank.
- The friendly with Chesterfield on 4 November was ended early by referee Arthur Ellis so that the visiting players could get away before dark!
- Sam Doran was the first professional footballer to land in France with the British Expeditionary Force.
- Halifax Town scored three goals in eight minutes against Leeds United on 25 May to turn a 2–0 deficit into a 3–2 win.
- Captain was Tom Barkas.
- Biggest win: 3–0 v Stockport County (a), 26 August.
- Heaviest defeat: 1–6 v Newcastle United (a), 29 May.
- Ever-present: Bill Allsop.
- Goalkeeper Hugh Turner won two caps for England in May 1931.
- Guest players: Charlie Davies (Darlington), Gerry Henry (Leeds United), John Hargreaves (Leeds United), J. Hodgson (Darlington), Alex Lee (Leeds United), John Mahon (Huddersfield Town), Eddie Ruecroft (Wellington Juniors), John Short (Leeds United), Leslie Thompson (Leeds United), Hugh Turner (Huddersfield Town).

Match No.	Date		Venue	Opponents	Result		Scorers	Attendance
1	Aug	26	A	Stockport County	W	3-0	Doran, Widdowfield, Wood	7,853
2		28	H	Oldham Athletic	W	2-0	Widdowfield, Bruce	6,361
3	Sep	2	H	Wrexham	D	1-1	Baines	6,417

Position at time of abandonment of League: 3rd in Division Three (North)

Apps
Gls

North Eastern League

Match No.	Date		Venue	Opponents	Result		Scorers	Attendance
1	Oct	21	A	Bradford City	L	1-5	Widdowfield (pen)	3,105
2		28	H	Darlington	L	2-4	Baines, Widdowfield (pen)	3,000
3	Nov	11	A	Hartlepools United	L	2-3	Baines, Allsop	2,000
4		18	H	York City	L	1-4	Hutton	3,000
5		25	H	Huddersfield Town	W	2-1	Barkas, Mahon	1,856
6	Dec	9	A	Middlesbrough	L	1-3	Wood	1,000
7		23	H	Newcastle United	L	3-4	Widdowfield 2, Baines	5,000
8		25	H	Bradford	L	2-3	Widdowfield 2	5,000
9		26	A	Bradford	L	0-3		5,490
10	Jan	6	A	Hull City	L	0-2		1,500
11	Mar	2	H	Bradford City	D	2-2	Baines, Wood	1,000
12		9	A	Hartlepools United	W	3-1	Widdowfield 2, Baines	2,000
13		16	A	York City	L	1-3	Davies	2,000
14		23	H	Huddersfield Town	L	2-3	J. Ruecroft, Baines	4,250
15		26	A	Darlington	L	1-2	Wood	896
16	Apr	6	A	Middlesbrough	D	1-1	Wood (pen)	3,000
17	May	18	H	Hull City	L	0-1		500
18		25	H	Leeds United	W	3-2	Wood (pen), Griffiths, Graham	600
19		29	A	Newcastle United	L	1-6	Hargreaves	1,279

Away match v Leeds United not played
Halifax Town finished 11th in North Eastern League

Apps
Gls

League War Cup

Match No.	Date		Venue	Opponents	Result		Scorers	Attendance
1	Apr	13	A	Hartlepools United	L	1-2	Baines	1,941

Apps
Gls

Biggs, CE	Adova, WH	Jackson, H	Green, H	Craig, EF	Ruecroft, J	Doran, S	Bruce, W	Widowfield, E	Barkas, T	Wood, S	Baines, R	Clark, SJH	Worthington, E	Hutton, H	Mahon, J	Ruecroft, EJ	Griffin, JS	Johnstone, R	Brown, AW	Kaye, G	Chapman, W	Adams, EF	Davies, E	Wesley, JC	Turner, H	Chester, TH	Graham, W	Wigglesworth, JL	France, J	Lee, AH	Hodgson, J	Thompson, L	Henry, GR	Short, JD	Hargreaves, J	Kaye	Chapman	Adams	Davies	Wesley	Turner	Chester	Graham	Wigglesworth	France	Lee	Hodgson	Thompson	Henry	Short	Hargreaves
1	2	3	4	5	6	7	8	9	10	11																																									
1	2	3	4	5	6	7	10	8		11	9																																								
1	2	3	4	5	6		8	7	10	11	9																																								
3	3	3	3	3	3	2	3	3	2	3	2																																								
						1	1	2		1	1																																								
1	2		4	5	6		8	10	11	9	3	7																																							
1	2	3	4	5	6		8	10	11	9		7																																							
1	2		5	4			8	10	6	9	3	7	11																																						
1	2		4	5	6		9	10		8	3		11	7																																					
1	2		4		5		8	10	6	9	3		11	7																																					
1	2		4	5	6		8	10	11	9	3	7																																							
1	2		4	5	6		9	10	11	8	3					7																																			
1	2		4	5	6		9	10	11		3					7	8																																		
1	2		4	5	6		9	10	11		3					7	8																																		
1	2		4				9	10	11							8	3	5	6	7																6	7														
	2		4	5	6		8		11	9							3				1	7	10																	1	7	10									
	2		4	5	6		8		10	9		11									7		1	3													7		1	3											
	2		4	5	6		8		10	9		11									7		1	3													7		1	3											
3	2		4	5	6		8	10	11	9											7		1														7		1												
3	2		4	5	6		8	10	11	9											7		1														7		1												
3			4	5	6			8	11	9			7										1	2	10														1	2	10										
3			4	5	6				11	9							8						1	2	10	7													1	2	10	7									
3		4		6			7		11	9							8						1	2	10		5												1	2	10		5								
3				5	4				11	9																			1	2	6	7	8	10											1	2	6	7	8	10
10	19	3	17	16	18		16	13	18	16	8	4	6	2	3	5	21	1	1	1	5	1	7	5	3	1	1	1	1	1	1	1	1	1	1	5	1	7	5	3	1	1	1	1	1					1	1
	1				1		8	1	5	6		1	1					1					1														1														1
	3			4	5	6				11	9			7				8			10			1	2											10				1	2										
	1		1	1	1				1	1			1			1					1			1	1											1			1	1										
																		1																																	

League Table

	P	W	D	L	F	A	Pts
Huddersfield Town	20	15	4	1	54	22	34
Newcastle United	20	12	0	8	53	39	24
Bradford	19	10	2	7	44	38	22
Middlesbrough	20	9	4	7	49	42	22
Leeds United	18	9	3	6	36	27	21
Bradford City	19	9	3	7	41	36	21
Hull City	20	8	1	11	35	41	17
York City	20	8	1	11	36	51	17
Darlington	19	6	3	10	44	56	15
Hartlepools United	20	6	1	13	27	47	13
Halifax Town	19	3	2	14	28	53	8

1940-41

North Regional League
Manager: Jimmy Thomson

Did you know that?

- Proceeds from Town's friendly with an Army X1 on 24 August went to the Halifax Infirmary.
- Captain was Tom Barkas.
- Tom Barkas missed Town's home game with Oldham Athletic on 23 November as he was selected to play for the RAF against The Army at Hull.
- Bojor, a Polish airman who had travelled with the RAF for a friendly at The Shay on 7 December, played for Halifax Town at right-back.
- Bobby Davidson was a member of the Arsenal side which won the League championship in 1937–38.
- Ted Widdowfield scored in seven consecutive matches between 30 November and 18 January – a club record.
- Biggest win: 8–1 v Doncaster Rovers (h), 12 April.
- Heaviest defeat: 1–4 v Huddersfield Town (h), 18 January.
- Ever-presents: Bill Allsop, Horace Green.
- Guest players: Cliff Binns (Barnsley), Tom Chester (Notts County), Robert Connor (Bradford), A. Dempsey (Leeds United), Ted Gilbert (Spurs), George Greaves (Aldershot), G. Hamilton (Queen's Park), P. Hastings (Clyde), Fred Hogg (Luton Town), Stan Hunter (Norton Woodseats), Lawrence Kelly (Aldershot), John Laidler (Barrow), Sam Malpass (Fulham), Vic Orton (York City), Alf Pope (Herts), Frank Pollard (Bury), Fred Prior (Bradford), Walter Palmer (Bradford), Jimmy Stephen (Bradford), Clem Smith (Stoke City), George Wardle (Exeter City), T. Wilson (RAF).

Match No.	Date	Venue	Opponents	Result		Scorers	Attendance
1	Aug 31	A	Hull City	L	2-4	Pope 2	1,500
2	Sep 7	H	Sheffield Wednesday	D	1-1	Widdowfield	2,000
3	14	A	Bradford	D	0-0		
4	21	A	Bradford City	W	2-1	Barkas, Wardle	2,000
5	28	H	Huddersfield Town	D	1-1	Barkas	5,000
6	Oct 5	H	Bradford	L	2-3	Wardle, Barkas	2,000
7	12	H	Bradford City	W	5-1	Wardle, Widdowfield 3, Hogg	3,000
8	19	A	Sheffield Wednesday	L	2-4	Fallaize, Wardle	3,000
9	26	H	York City	W	2-1	Fallaize, Wardle	3,000
10	Nov 2	H	Blackburn Rovers	D	1-1	Barkas	1,000
11	9	H	Hull City	W	3-0	Widdowfield 3 (1 pen)	1,000
12	16	A	Oldham Athletic	W	2-1	Widdowfield, Wardle	2,800
13	23	H	Oldham Athletic	L	0-1		3,000
14	30	A	York City	D	2-2	Widdowfield 2	1,500
15	Dec 14	A	Huddersfield Town	D	1-1	Widdowfield	637
16	21	H	Leeds United	D	2-2	Widdowfield (pen), Wood	3,000
17	25	A	Bury	D	5-5	Wardle, Hogg, Watson (og), Widdowfield 2	2,915
18	Jan 4	H	Huddersfield Town	L	1-2	Widdowfield	3,000
19	11	A	Huddersfield Town	W	2-1*	Widdowfield (pen), Wardle	2,088
20	18	H	Huddersfield Town	L	1-4	Widdowfield	1,846
21	Feb 8	A	Blackburn Rovers	W	1-0	Wardle	1,500
22	Mar 8	H	Huddersfield Town	W	4-0	Barkas 3, Widdowfield	1,000
23	15	H	Bradford	D	2-2	Barkas, Wardle	1,500
24	22	H	Burnley	D	2-2	Barkas, Widdowfield	2,500
25	Apr 5	H	Chesterfield	D	0-0		2,000
26	12	H	Doncaster Rovers	W	8-1	Widdowfield 3, Wardle 3, Wood, Hogg	2,000
27	14	H	Blackburn Rovers	D	3-3	Wardle 3	
28	19	A	Burnley	L	1-3	Fallaize	2,000
29	26	A	Doncaster Rovers	D	2-2	Smith, Widdowfield	1,164
30	May 3	H	Middlesbrough	W	4-2	Wardle, Widdowfield, Barkas 2	1,000

Final League Position: 7th in North Regional League

* After extra-time.

Matches 18, 19, 20 were in the West Riding Cup.

League War Cup

R1/1	Feb 15	H	Leeds United	L	1-3	Widdowfield		4,000
R1/2	Mar 1	A	Leeds United	D	2-2	Holley (og), Wood		5,000

Apps
1 own-goal   Gls

Apps
1 own-goal   Gls

Rayner, E	Hastings, P	Alsop, WH	Green, H	Craig, EF	Ruscroft, J	Orton, V	Barkas, T	Pope, AL	McDiarmid, W	Wood, S	Chester, TH	Wardle, G	Hogg, F	Widdowfield, E	Wilson, T	Luffe, JH	Elliot, WG	Fallaize, RA	Kelly, L	Dempsey, AG	Dennis, J	Jackson, H	Poland, F	Connor, R	Hunter, S	Doran, S	Gilbert, EH	Binns, CH	Hamilton, C	Greaves, G	Malpass, ST	Palmer, W	Prior, FE	Stephen, JF	Harris, S	Moncrieff, JC	Smith, C
1	2	3	4	5	6	7	8	9	10	11																											
1		3	4	5			10			6	2	7	8	9	11																						
1		3	4	5			10			6	2	7		9	11	8																					
1		3	4		5		10			11	2	7	8	9			6																				
1		3	4		5		10			11	2	7	8				6	9																			
1		3	2	6	5	7	10			11		9	8						4																		
1		3	4	5	6		10			11		7	8	9						2																	
1		3	4	5	6		10			11		7	8					9		2																	
1		3	4	5	6					11	2	7	8					9			10																
1		3	2	5	6		10			11		7	8	4				9																			
1		3	4	5	6		10	2		11		7	8	9																							
1		3	4	5	6		10	2		11		7	8	9																							
1		3	4	5	6					11		7	8	10				9				2															
1		3	4	5	6	11	10	2				7	8	9																							
1		3	2	5	4	7	10			6		11	8	9																							
1		3	4	5	6		10			11		7	8	9						2																	
1		3	4	5			10			6		7	8	9						2	11																
		3	4	5	6		10			11		7	8	9						2		1															
		3	4	5	6					11		7	8	9						2			1	10													
		3	4	5	6		10			11		7	8	9						2					1												
		3	4	5	6					11		7	8	9						2						1	10										
		3	4	5	6		10			11		7	8	9														1	2								
		3	4	5	6		10			11		7		9														1		2	8						
		3	4	5	6		10			11		7	8	9														1				2					
		3	4	5	6		10			11		7	8	9														1					2				
		3	4	5	6		10			11	2	7	8	9														1									
		3	4	5	6		10			11	2	7	8	9														1									
		3	4	5	6					11			8					9										1						2	7	10	
		3	4	5	6					11		7	8	9														1						2		10	
		3	4	5	6		10			11	2	7	8	9														1									
17	1	30	30	28	27	4	24	4	1	29	8	28	27	24	2	1	2	6	1	2	1	7	1	1	1	1	1	9	1	1	1	1	3	1	2		
							11	2		2		17	3	24			3																		1		

		3	4		5		11			6	2	7	8	9								1		10													
		3	4	5	6		10			11		7	8	9						2								1									
		2	2	1	2		2			2	1	2	2	2						1		1		1				1									
							1					1																									

1941-42

North Regional League

Manager: Jimmy Thomson

Did you know that?

- Hit hard by the restrictions caused by the war, in November 1941 Halifax Town appealed for the supporters to give the club clothing coupons to help buy a new kit.
- Captain was Ted Craig.
- Reg Fallaize was a Channel Islander evacuated from Guernsey.
- Tom Finney and Bill Shankly appeared at The Shay with Preston North End on 25 October. Stanley Matthews played at The Shay for Blackpool on 15 November.
- A collection at the Rotherham United match at The Shay on 17 January raised £6 16s 7d for Churchill's 'Aid To Russia' fund.
- A young Nat Lofthouse scored Bolton Wanderers' second goal in the 2–2 draw at The Shay on 4 April.
- Geoff Walker was still only 15 years of age when he played for Town against Leeds United on 6 April. He scored twice in a 6–1 win.
- Willie Waddell, who guested for the club against Bolton Wanderers on 4 April went on to win 17 Scotland caps as a Rangers player and was their manager between 1969 and 1972.
- Willie McFadyen was a prolific goalscorer with Motherwell and helped them win the Scottish title in 1931–32. He won two Scotland caps and scored in each of his appearances.
- Guest players: Tom Chester (Notts County), Bobby Davidson (Coventry City), Reg Dann (Bradford), George Davies (Bury), George Greaves (Aldershot), Archie Hastie (Bradford City), Fred Hogg (Luton Town), James Isaacs (Huddersfield Town), Herbert Knott (Hull City), Willie McFadyen (Clapton Orient), Bill McKellor (Huddersfield Town), Tom McGarry (Bradford), J. Manning (Huddersfield Town), S. Offord (Bradford), Clem Smith (Stoke City), Bob Shotton (Barnsley), Jack Wesley (Bradford), Geoff Walker (Bradford), Willie Waddell (Aberdeen), George Wardle (Exeter City).
- Biggest victory: 6–1 v Leeds United (h), 6 April.
- Heaviest defeat: 0–6 v Barnsley (a), 28 March.
- Ever-present: Bill Allsop.

Match No.	Date		Venue	Opponents	Result		Scorers	Attendance
1	Aug	30	H	Burnley	L	2-3	Smith, Wardle	3,000
2	Sep	6	A	Burnley	W	1-0	Jackson	3,000
3		13	A	Bolton Wanderers	D	1-1	Wood	2,000
4		20	H	Bolton Wanderers	W	2-0	Hogg, Wood	4,000
5		27	H	Rochdale	W	4-2	Jackson, Hogg, Wood, Davidson	4,000
6	Oct	4	A	Rochdale	D	2-2	Wood, Hogg	2,000
7		11	A	Blackburn Rovers	L	0-2		1,000
8		18	H	Blackburn Rovers	D	0-0		1,500
9		25	H	Preston North End	L	0-1		5,000
10	Nov	1	A	Preston North End	L	2-6	Gallimore (og), Wood (pen)	5,000
11		8	A	Blackpool	L	1-9	Doran	4,000
12		15	H	Blackpool	L	1-2	Wood (pen)	6,000
13		22	A	Southport	W	3-2	Wardle 2, Hanna	1,000
14		29	H	Southport	W	2-1	L. Green, Wood	3,000
15	Dec	6	A	Oldham Athletic	L	2-6	L. Green, Davidson	479
16		13	H	Oldham Athletic	W	3-0	L. Green, Wardle, H. Green	2,000
17		20	A	Bury	L	1-3	Ruecroft	600
18		25	H	Bury	W	2-0	Wood, Wardle	

1 own-goal

Apps
Gls

North Regional League (Second Championship)

1	Dec	27	H	Huddersfield Town	D	2-2	Wood, Hogg	5,000
2	Jan	3	A	Rotherham United	W	1-0	Wardle	3,000
3		10	A	Doncaster Rovers	L	1-2	Wood (pen)	2,208
4		17	H	Rotherham United	L	0-2		2,000
5	Feb	21	A	Huddersfield Town	L	0-1		1,150
6		28	H	Grimsby Town	D	2-2	Hogg, Doran	3,000
7	Mar	14	H	Barnsley	L	2-4	Wood 2 (1 pen)	3,000
8		21	A**	Grimsby Town	W	3-1	McKellor, Wardle 2	2,000
9		28	A	Barnsley	L	0-6		2,500
10	Apr	4	H	Bolton Wanderers	D	2-2	Waddell, Parker	2,000
11		6	H	Leeds United	W	6-1	McGarry 2, Manning, McKellor, Walker 2	2,000
12		11	A	Leeds United	L	1-3	Wood	2,500
13		18	H	York City	D	1-1	McGarry	1,500
14		25	A	Chesterfield	L	1-4	Knott	1,500
15	May	2	H	Huddersfield Town	D	1-1	Wardle	2,000
16		9	A	Huddersfield Town	W	2-1*	Kershaw 2	1,605
17		16	H	Chesterfield	W	5-2*	McGarry 2, Davies 2, Davidson (pen)	2,000
18		23	A	York City#	L	0-2		4,710
19		30	H	York City#	W	4-3	McGarry, Davies, Davidson (pen), H. Green	4,311

* After extra-time   ** Played at Old Show Ground, Scunthorpe
\# Combined Counties Cup Final

Apps
Gls

Matches 1 – 9 were in the Football League War Cup qualifying competition. Halifax Town failed to qualify for the knockout stage.
Matches 11 – 19 were in the Combined Counties Cup.
Halifax Town finished 20th in the First Championship and 19th in the Second Championship

Greaves,G	Jackson,H	Allison,WH	Green,H	Craig,EF	Ruecroft,J	Wardle,G	Hogg,F	Smith,C	Barkas,T	Wood,S	Chester,TH	Hanna,S	Davidson,RT	Booth,PM	Doran,S	McKelvyen,W	Nicholls,JH	Green,L	Robinson,G	Dann,RW	McKellor,WH	Otford,SJ	Elliott,WG	Wedowfield,E	Wesley,JC	Waddell,W	Parker,RW	Kershaw,G	Walker,RG	Whitehouse,J	McGarry,T	Manning,J	Nicholson,S	Knott,H	Worthington,E	Hastie,A	Isaac,J	Fitzsimmons,DJ	Davies,G	Stanton,R	Smith,G
1	2	3	4	5	6	7	8	9	10	11																															
1	9	3	4	5	6	7	8		10	11	2																														
1	9	3	4	5	6	7	8			11	2	10																													
1	9	3	4	5	6	7	8			11	2	10																													
1	9	3	4	5	6	7	8			11	2		10																												
1	9	3	4	5	6	7	8			11	2		10																												
1	9	3	4	5	6		8			11	2	10		7																											
1		3	4	5	6	7	8			11	2		10		9																										
1	2	3	4	5	6	7	8			11			10		9																										
		3	4	5	6	7	8			11	2		10		9	1																									
		3	4	5	6		8			11	2	10		7	9	1																									
		3	4	5	6	7	8			11	2	9	10			1																									
		3	4	5	6	7	8			11	2	9	10			1																									
		3	4	5	6	7	8			11	2		10			1	9																								
		3	4	5	6	7	8			11	2			8	1	9																									
1		3	4	5	6	7	8			11	2		10				9																								
1		3	4	5	6	7	8			11	2		10				9																								
1		3	4	5	6	7	8			11	2		10				9																								
12	8	18	18	18	18	16	17	1	2	18	16	6	12	1	2	4	6	5																							
	2		1		1	5	3	1			8		1	2		1		3																							
1		3	4	5	6	7	8			11	2		10					9																							
1		3	4	5		7	8			11		2	10					9																							
1		3	4	5	6					11	2	7	10					9	8																						
1		3	4	5	6	7	8			11	2		10					9																							
1		3	4	5		9	8			11	2	10											6	7																	
1		3	4				8			6	2				10	9				5	7	11																			
1		3	4			7	8			11	2					10				5			6	9																	
1		3	2	5			11	8		6			10			4		9		7																					
1		3	4	5						6	2					8		9		7						11															
1		3	4	5						6	2									7							8	9	10	11											
1		3	4	5																7							8	6	11	2	9	10									
1		3	4	5	6					11	2									7							8	10		9											
1		3	4	5	6	7				10	2															11	8	9													
1		3	4	5	6	7				10	2									11								8	9												
1	2	4	5	6	7	8				3																11							9	0							
1	2	4	5	6						3				9						7									10						8	11					
1	2	4	5	6	7	8				3					10													9									11				
1				5	6	11	4			3					10					7								8										9			
1		2	4	5	6					11					10													8										9	3	7	
19	19	18	17	12	11	10				18	11	3	8	1	1	4			6	1	3	9	1	1	1		3	4	5	2	6	1	1	1	1	1	1	3	1	1	
			1			4	2			5				2		1				2							1	1	2	2		6	1		1			3			

1942-43

North Regional League
Manager: Jimmy Thomson

Did you know that?

- Halifax Town received £209 for participating in the previous season's War Cup, enough for manager Jimmy Thomson to buy two sets of jerseys, pants and stockings.
- Captain was Bill Allsop.
- Town scored three goals in a two-minute period in the 5-0 defeat of Rotherham United on 13 February.
- Former Halifax Town skipper Fred McLachlan, now aged 46 and not having kicked a ball for ten years, appeared twice for the Halifax Defence League in February.
- Keeper Charlie Briggs assisted Tottenham Hotspur.
- Town's War Cup second leg match at Chesterfield on 13 March lasted 111 minutes.
- Halifax Town didn't lose a game in which Alan Niblo scored (won seven and drew one).
- Guest players: W. Brown (Hibernian), Jack Bell (Albion Rovers), Peter Cabrelli (Raith Rovers), Sam Doran (Bradford), Bobby Davidson (Coventry City), William Findlay (Albion Rovers), George Greaves (Aldershot), Sam Hall (Clapton Orient), Fred Hogg (Luton Town), George Highmoor (Newcastle United), David Jones (Bury), Tom McGarry (Bradford), David Millar (East Fife), John Trodden (Bradford City), Leslie Taylor (Leeds United), Jack Wesley (Bradford), Bob Wilson (Airdrie), Wally Wildman (Torquay United), D. Williams (Rochdale).
- Biggest victory: 5-0 v Rotherham United (h) 13 February.
- Heaviest defeat: 3-7 v Middlesbrough (a), 24 April.
- Ever-present: Bill Allsop.

Match No.	Date		Venue	Opponents	Result		Scorers	Attendance
1	Aug	29	A	Sheffield United	L	1-3	Davidson	5,000
2	Sep	5	H	Sheffield United	W	3-2	Wood, McGarry 2	2,000
3		12	A	Rochdale	W	3-1	Wood 2, E. Ruecroft	
4		19	H	Rochdale	W	3-0	Trodden 2, E. Ruecroft	3,000
5		26	A	Chester	L	1-4	McNeil (og)	2,500
6	Oct	3	H	Chester	W	3-1	Davidson, Wood, Wesley	4,000
7		10	A	Oldham Athletic	L	0-3		2,000
8		17	H	Oldham Athletic	W	4-1	Niblo 2, E. Ruecroft, Hogg	2,000
9		24	H	Rotherham United	W	4-0	Davidson 2, Hogg, Niblo	2,000
10		31	A	Rotherham United	W	4-1	Niblo 2, Hogg, Wood	1,500
11	Nov	7	A	Doncaster Rovers	W	2-1	Niblo, Wood	2,451
12		14	H	Doncaster Rovers	L	1-2	Wood	4,000
13		21	H	Huddersfield Town	W	2-1	Wilson, Davidson	4,000
14		28	A	Huddersfield Town	L	1-4	Davidson	3,033
15	Dec	5	H	Leeds United	D	1-1	Niblo	1,500
16		12	H	Leeds United	W	5-1	Niblo 2, Hogg, Davidson, E. Ruecroft	4,000
17		19	H	Burnley	D	0-0		2,500
18		25	A	Burnley	D	1-1	Wood	

1 own-goal

Apps
Gls

	Dec	26	A	Bradford City	D	1-1*	Millman (og)	2,000
2	Jan	2	H	Bradford City	w	3-2	Davidson 2, Niblo	2,000
3		9	A	Bradford	L	1-5	Wilson	2,773
4		16	H	Bradford	L	0-2		3,000
5		23	H	Oldham Athletic	W	4-3	Wesley 2, E. Ruecroft, Wildman	1,500
6		30	A	Oldham Athletic	W	1-0	Davidson	2,000
7	Feb	6	A	Rotherham United	W	3-2	Millar, Hogg, Davidson	2,000
8		13	H	Rotherham United	W	5-0	Hogg 2, E. Ruecroft, Wood, Jackson (pen)	2,000
9		20	A	Bury	L	0-4		4,000
10		27	H	Bury	D	2-2	Davidson, Jackson (pen)	2,000
11	Mar	6	H	Chesterfield	W	2-1	Niblo, Davidson	5,000
12		13	A	Chesterfield	L	0-2**		6,500
13		20	A	Bradford City	L	0-1		2,000
14		27	H	Bradford City	W	3-1	Hogg 2, Williams	2,000
15	Apr	3	A	Huddersfield Town	L	0-1		3,430
16		10	H	Huddersfield Town	L	0-2		3,000
17		17	H	Middlesbrough	L	2-4	Davidson, Hogg	3,000
18		24	A	Middlesbrough	L	3-7	Martin (og), Jackson, Wood	2,000

2 own-goals

Apps
Gls

* Abandoned after 67 minutes. Football League ordered the result to stand.
** After extra-time. 90 minutes 0-1. Extra-time consisted of 20-minute halves, until Chesterfield scored sudden death winner after 111 minutes.

Matches 1 – 10 were in the Football League War Cup qualifying competition.
Halifax Town finished 21st and qualified for the knockout stage.
Matches 11 & 12 were in the Football League War Cup First Round.
Matches 15 & 16 were in the Combined Counties Cup competition.
Halifax Town finished 12th in First Championship and 35th in Second Championship

	Greaves, G	Green, H	Alsop, WH	Crowther, K	Craig, EF	Ruecroft, J	Ruecroft, EJ	Hogg, F	Trouden, JJ	Davidson, RT	Wood, S	McGarry, T	Wesley, JC	Jackson, H	Cabralli, P	Brown, W	Naki, A	Brigiis, CE	Wilson, R	Wildman, WR	Millar, D	Bell, JG	Taylor, LT	Findlay, W	Williams, D	Kershaw, G	Jones, D	Highmoor, GW	Widowfield, E	Hall, SR	little, WA
	1	2	3	4	5	6	7	8	9	10	11																				
	1	2	3		5	6	7	8	4	10	11	9																			
	1	2	3	4	5	6	7	8	9	10	11																				
	1	2	3	4	5	6	7		9	10	11		8																		
	1	2	3	4	5	6	7	8	9		11		10																		
	1	4	2		5		7			10	11		8	3	6	9															
	1	4	2		5	6	7			10	11		8	3		9															
	1	4	2		5		7	8		10	11			3	6		9														
		4	2		5	6	7	8		10	11			3			9	1													
		4	2		5	6	7	8		10	11			3			9	1													
		4	2		5	6	7	8		10	11			3			9	1													
		4	2		5	6	7	8		10	11			3			9	1													
		4	2		5	6	9	8		10	11			3				1	7												
		4	2		5	6	9	8		10	11			3				1	7												
	1	4	2		5	6	7	8		10	11			3		9															
	1	4	2		5	6	7	8		10	11			3		9															
	1	4	2		5	6	7	8		10	11			3		9															
	12	18	18	4	18	16	18	15	5	17	18	1	4	13	2	2	9	6	2												
					4	4	2	7	8	2	1		9						1												
	1	4	2		5	6	7	8		10	11			3		9															
	1		2		5	6	7	8		10	11			3		9	4														
	1	4	2		5	6	7	8		10	11			3			9														
	1	4	2	9	5	6	7	8	11	10				3																	
	1	4	2		5	6	7	8			11		10	3						9											
		4	2		5	6		8		10	11	7		3		9	1														
		4	2		5	6		8		10	11	7		3			1		9												
		4	2		5	6	7	8		10	11	9		3			1														
		4	2		5	6	7	8		10	11	9		3			1														
		4	2		5	6				10	11	7		3		9	1														
		4	2			5		8		10	6	7		3		9	1			11											
		4	2			5		8		10	6	7		3		9	1			11											
		4	2	6		5		8		10	11	9		3			1				7										
		4	2			5		8		10	6	11		3			1				7	9									
		4	2			5		8		10	11			3			1					9	6	7							
		4	2			5		8		10	11			3			1						6	7	9						
		4	2			5		8		10	6			3										7	9	1	11				
	1	4	2		5	6		8			9			3							10			7			11				
	6	17	18	2	11	18	7	18	1	16	17	10	18		6	11	2	1	2	1	2	2	1	2	3	2	1	2			
	30				2	6		7	2		2	3		2			1	1	1			1									

1943-44

North Regional League
Manager: Jimmy Thomson

Did you know that?

- After losing 5–1 at Oldham Athletic on 23 October, Town scored three goals in a four-minute spell in the return at The Shay seven days later and cantered to a 5–0 win.
- Captain was A. Johnstone, then Tom Barkas from 26 February.
- Town's game with Burnley at The Shay on 18 December lasted only 80 minutes after the visitors turned up late.
- William Bell and Jock Wallace featured in a Corps. Troops X1 against the Scottish Infantry Division, whose side included Arsenal's Les Compton, in a Northern Command Cup tie at The Shay on 11 December.
- Robinson travelled with his Bury team mates for the match at The Shay on 8 January, but was loaned to Halifax Town shortly before kick-off. He scored both Town's goals in a 2–0 win!
- Because of military call-ups, manager Jimmy Thomson had to find five replacements for the match with Oldham Athletic on 12 February.
- Future England international Frank Swift kept goal for Manchester City in the match at The Shay on 19 February.
- Harry Strike was killed in action leading his section in Normandy in June 1944.
- Guest players: William Bell (Kilmarnock), George Boothroyd (Huddersfield Town), George Bratley (Crystal Palace), Oliver Burns (Burnley), Bobby Davidson (Coventry City), J. Edington (Arsenal), Fred Fisher (Millwall), Albert Flatley (Port Vale), Eddie Fleetwood (Barnsley), Jimmy Grummett (Lincoln City), G. Hamilton (Queen's Park), S. Hicks (Arsenal), Percy Humphries (Fulham), Gordon Jackson (Bradford City), A Johnston (Partick Thistle), Harry McMenemy (Dundee), J. Miller (Bradford), M Morrison (East Stirling), W. Poxton (Doncaster Rovers), L. Robinson (Bury), George Rymer (Barnsley), Fred Smith (Bradford), J. Stewart (Falkirk), Sid Storey (Huddersfield Town), Joe Taylor (Oldham Athletic), Henry Topping (Bristol Rovers), Jock Wallace (Partick Thistle), J. Walmsley (Preston North End), Jack Wesley (Bradford), K. Wilkinson (Huddersfield Town), Dick Woffinden (Barnsley), D. Woodhead (Huddersfield Town).
- Biggest win: 5–0 v Oldham Athletic (h), 30 October.
- Heaviest defeat: 2–6 v Manchester United (a), 27 December.
- As well as medals for the winning of the Combined Counties Cup, the Halifax Town players also received three war savings certificates.
- Ever-presents: Bill Allsop, Jake Ruecroft.

Match No.	Date	Venue	Opponents	Result		Scorers	Attendance
1	Aug 28	A	Rotherham United	L	0-3		2,500
2	Sep 4	H	Rotherham United	W	2-1	Ford (og), Humphries	3,000
3	11	H	Sheffield Wednesday	D	2-2	Davidson, Taylor	1,500
4	18	A	Sheffield Wednesday	L	0-2		7,000
5	25	H	Chester	L	1-4	Jackson	3,000
6	Oct 2	A	Chester	L	1-3	Jones	3,500
7	9	H	Rochdale	D	2-2	Morrison 2	4,000
8	16	A	Rochdale	L	3-4	Davidson 3	3,000
9	23	H	Oldham Athletic	L	1-5	Widdowfield	2,737
10	30	A	Oldham Athletic	W	5-0	Wallace 3, Storey, Jones	3,620
11	Nov 6	H	Doncaster Rovers	W	1-0	Widdowfield	4,000
12	13	A	Doncaster Rovers	L	1-3	Wallace	7,257
13	20	A	Huddersfield Town	D	0-0		3,416
14	27	H	Huddersfield Town	W	4-1	Wallace 3, Jones	4,000
15	Dec 4	H	Leeds United	W	2-1	Jones 2	3,000
16	11	A	Leeds United	L	0-4		4,000
17	18	H	Burnley	D	1-1	Widdowfield	2,000
18	25	A	Burnley	W	1-0	Wallace	4,194

Final League Position: 18th in Division Three

1 own-goal

Apps
Gls

	Dec 27	A	Manchester United	L	2-6	Wallace, Flatley	13,500
1	Dec 27	A	Manchester United	L	2-6	Wallace, Flatley	13,500
2	Jan 1	H	Manchester United	D	1-1	Porter (og)	4,000
3	8	H	Bury	W	2-0	Robinson 2	4,000
4	15	A	Bury	D	0-0		1,900
5	22	H	Stockport County	L	0-1		2,000
6	29	A	Stockport County	L	3-4	Davidson 2 (1 pen), Wallace	6,000
7	Feb 5	A	Oldham Athletic	W	3-1	Wallace 3	4,900
8	12	H	Oldham Athletic	L	0-3		4,000
9	19	H	Manchester City	L	3-5	Smith 2, Fisher	4,000
10	26	A	Manchester City	L	0-4		3,000
11	Mar 4	H	Bradford City	W	4-2	Smith 4	2,000
12	11	A	Bradford City	W	3-1	Jones 3	1,737
13	18	A	Huddersfield Town	L	1-2	Jones	3,001
14	25	H	Huddersfield Town	W	4-1	Jones 2, Flatley, Bailey (og)	3,000
15	Apr 1	H	York City	W	4-1	Jones, Barkas 2 (1 pen)	4,000
16	8	A	York City	D	1-1	Smith	5,110
17	15	A	Leeds United	D	2-2	Barkas, Smith	6,000
18	22	H	Leeds United	W	5-2	Jones 2, Green, Butterworth (og), Barkas	4,000
19	29	A	Huddersfield Town*	W	4-1	Clegg (og), Jones 2, Fleetwood	4,293
20	May 6	H	Huddersfield Town*	L	2-4	Taylor, Jones	5,537

Apps
Gls

4 own-goals

Matches 1 – 10 were in the Football War Cup qualifying competition. Halifax Town failed to qualify for the knockout stage.
Matches 11 – 20 were in the Combined Counties Cup competition.
* Combined Counties Cup Final
Halifax Town finished 32nd in the First Championship and 26th in the Second Championship

Briggs, CE	Alison, WH	Jackson, H	Green, H	Sykes, H	Rencroft, J	Taylor, G	Hogg, F	Nolo, H	Davidson, RT	Hille, WA	Craig, EF	Humphreys, PR	Jones, WR	Wood, S	Trodden, JJ	Hitchen, T	Wesley, JC	Jones, WM	Walmsley, J	Waldonfield, E	Garner, GG	Bell, W	Burns, GH	Morrison, M	Wallace, J	Gruemmett, J	Elington, J	Dunn, L	Coyle, O	Johnston, ACM	Storey, S	Fatley, AA	Proctor, W	Woodhead, D	Topping, H	McMenemy, H	Hamilton, GB	Stake, H	Brient, E	Banns, CP	Barrett, J	Robinson, L	Duffy, AC	Boothroyd, G	Stewart, J	Wilkinson, K	Wolfendon, RS	Fraser, FW	Smith, FH	Bradley, GW	Barlas, T	Hicks, S	Heavey, JW	Eloy, R	Jackson, Ab	Millar, JW	Rymer, GH	Fleetwood, ED
1	2	3	4	5	6	7	8	9	10	11																																																	
1	2	3	4		6	9	8		10	11	5	7																																														
1	2	3	4		6	7	8		10		5		9	11																																												
1	2	3	4		6		8		10		5				7	9	11																																									
1	2	3	4		6				10		5				7	9	11	8																																								
	3		2		6			9	4		5							10	8	1	7	11																																					
	2	3	4		5				10	11											7		1	6	8	9																																	
	2	3	4		6				10		5							11			7		1			9	8																																
	2		4		5				10												7		1			9	8	3	6	11																													
	2	3	4		6															8	7		1			9	10				5	11																											
	2	3	4		6									11							7		1			9	10				5		8																										
	3		2		6															4	7					9	10				5		8	1	11																								
	2		4		6							7								8			1			9	10				5		11			3																						
	2		4		5								11							8	7		1			9	10				5					3	6																						
	2		4		6															8	7		1			9	10				5		11			3																						
	2		4		5										11					9							10						7			3		1	6	8																		
	2		4		5															8	7		1			9	10						11			3			6																			
	2		4		6															7			1				9				5		11						3		8	10																
5	18	9	18	1	18	3	4	2	9	2	7	3	1	3	2	2	4	10	1	10	1	10	1	1	1	11	10	1	1	1	6	1	7	1	1	5	1	3	1	1																		
		1			1						4		1					6		3					2	8								1																									

	2		4		6																		1			9					5		7			3	10		11	8																		
	2		4		5							11						8		7			1			9							10			3	6																					
	2		4		5				10				7													9					5		11			3	6				8																	
	2		4		6				10				7										1			9					5					3			11			g																
	2		4		6				10									8					1			9	11				5		7			3					1																	
	2		4		6				10											7		9				8					5		11			3							10															
	2				6				8											7		1				9							11			3	6	1							9													
	2		4		5				8			7										1					10						11			3									10	6	7	9									
	2				5				4								11					1				9	10						7													6			3	8							
	2				5															8													11			3		4								6	9		10	1	7						
	2		8		5													9				1					11						7			3		4								6			10		1						
	2				5													9				1				8							7			3		4								6			10			11						
	2		4		5													9				1				8							7			3										6			10		1	1					
	2		4		5										11			9				1				8							7			3										6			10								
	2		4		5													8				1											7			3		11								6	9		10								
	2		4		5													8															7			3										6	9		10					1			
	2		4		5													9															7			3										6			10						1	8	
	2		4		5													9															7			3										6			10						1	8	
	2		4		5													9															7			3										6			10						1	8	
20		15		20					8		3	2		1	12	1	5		10		7	8			5	19			19	4	1	7		1		1	1	2	1	12	1	4	1	11	1	1	2	1	1	4	3						
									1			2			13				5			2												2			1	8			4									1								

G. Taylor played number 11 in matches 18, 19 and 20 of the Combined Counties Cup.

1944-45

North Regional League

Manager: Jimmy Thomson

Did you know that?

- Captain was Tom Barkas.
- Tom Barkas received his BEM on 16 February for heroism during the German bombing raids in Malta.
- Wally Ardron went on to set the Nottingham Forest record for most goals in a season when he scored 36 in 1950–51.
- The second half of the War Cup match with Chesterfield at The Shay on 24 March was broadcast in the General Forces programme, with commentary courtesy of Ivan Sharpe.
- Bill Allsop ended a run of 188 consecutive appearances when he missed the game with Bradford City on 21 April.
- Former Town guest George Wardle scored for Chelsea against Millwall in the South Cup Final at Wembley on 7 April.
- Guest players: Wally Ardron (Rotherham United), Bobby Barclay (Huddersfield Town), George Boothroyd (Huddersfield Town), John Battye (Huddersfield Town), Harry Baird (Huddersfield Town), A. Clarke (Bradford), Albert Flatley (Bradford), Jimmy Grummett (Lincoln City), Bill Gorman (Brentford), Ray Haddington (Bradford), Gerry Henry (Leeds United), Fred Hogg (Luton Town), Joe Lodge (Huddersfield Town), H. Riddell (Huddersfield Town), Clem Smith (Stoke City), Harry Topping (Bristol Rovers), George Thompson (Huddersfield Town), Dick Woffinden (Barnsley), Alf Young (Huddersfield Town).
- Biggest win: 5–1 v Oldham Athletic (h), 28 October.
- Heaviest defeat: 0–7 v Sheffield Wednesday (a), 14 April.
- Ever-present: Jake Ruecroft.

Match No.	Date		Venue	Opponents	Result		Scorers	Attendance
1	Aug	26	A	Bolton Wanderers	D	0-0		6,504
2	Sep	2	H	Bolton Wanderers	W	2-0	Rigby (og), Riddell	4,000
3		9	H	Hull City	D	1-1	Smith	5,000
4		16	A*	Hull City	L	0-2		8,000
5		23	A	Preston North End	L	0-1		4,500
6		30	H	Preston North End	D	1-1	Grummett	5,000
7	Oct	7	H	Southport	D	2-2	Widdowfield 2	3,000
8		14	A	Southport	D	2-2	Smith, Widdowfield	
9		21	A	Oldham Athletic	W	1-0	Smith	3,909
10		28	H	Oldham Athletic	W	5-1	Smith 2, Grummett, Widdowfield 2	4,000
11	Nov	4	H	Burnley	W	2-1	Widdowfield 2	3,000
12		11	A	Burnley	W	2-1	Widdowfield 2	2,000
13		18	H	Blackpool	W	4-3	Smith 2, Barkas, Widdowfield	7,000
14		25	A	Blackpool	L	2-4	Grummett 2	6,000
15	Dec	2	A	Blackburn Rovers	L	0-4		2,000
16		9	H	Blackburn Rovers	W	2-1	Smith 2	3,000
17		16	H	Rochdale	W	4-2	Smith, Worthington 2, Senior	2,000
18		23	A	Rochdale	L	0-3		4,000

* Played at The Boulevard, Hull.

1 own-goal

Apps / Gls

Match No.	Date		Venue	Opponents	Result		Scorers	Attendance
1	Dec	25	A	Huddersfield Town	D	0-0		11,589
2		30	H	Huddersfield Town	W	4-2	Widdowfield 3, Barkas (pen)	10,500
3	Jan	6	H	Manchester City	D	1-1	Wood	10,000
4		13	A	Manchester City	W	3-2	Worthington, Flatley, Widdowfield	11,000
5	Feb	3	A	Bury	L	1-2	Tate	3,706
6		10	H	Bury	D	2-2	Worthington, Jackson (pen)	6,000
7		17	H	Oldham Athletic	L	0-2		4,000
8		24	A	Oldham Athletic	W	2-1	Flatley, Haddington	4,971
9	Mar	3	A	Preston North End	L	0-2		3,500
10		10	H	Manchester United	W	1-0	Ardron	6,000
11		17	A	Manchester United	L	0-2		12,000
12		24	H	Chesterfield	D	1-1	Harvey	8,000
13		31	A	Chesterfield	L	1-3**	Barkas (pen)	12,700
14	Apr	2	A	Crewe Alexandra	L	1-4	Harvey	6,000
15		7	H	Sheffield Wednesday	W	3-2	Worthington 2, Barkas	4,000
16		14	A	Sheffield Wednesday	L	0-7		4,000
17		21	A	Bradford City	L	0-4		2,894
18		28	H	Bradford City	W	2-0	Worthington, Flatley	1,000

Apps / Gls

Matches 1 – 8, 10 & 11 were in the Football League War Cup qualifying competition.
Halifax Town finished 29th and qualified for the knockout stage.
Matches 12 & 13 were in the Football League War Cup First Round.
Halifax Town finished 18th in the First Championship and 45th in the Second Championship.

Eby, R	Allsop, WH	Topping, H	Green, H	Ruecroft, J	Wolfenden, RS	Tate, W	Smith, C	Niblo, A	Grummett, J	Worboys, RT	Riddell, H	Barclay, R	Thurlow, ACE	Bartas, T	Widdowfield, F	Fraser, JT	Thompson, GH	Jackson, H	Birch, NJJ	Boothroyd, G	Briggs, CE	Stewart, A	Battye, JE	Senior, CRA	Ratley, AAA	Worthington, E	Young, A	Wood, S	Harvey, W	Waddington, WR	France, J	Gorman, WC	Ashton, W	Baird, HHC	Henry, GH	Ruecroft, EJ	Hogg, F	Clarke, A	Istt, D
1	2	3	4	5	6	7	8	9	10	11																													
1	2	3	4	5	6	7	8		10		9	11																											
	2	3	4	5	6	7	8		11		9		1	10																									
1	2	3	4	5	6		8		10		9				7	11																							
1	2	3	4	5	6	7	8		10		9					11																							
	2		4	5			8		11		9			10	7		1	3	6																				
	2		4	5	6		8		7					10	9	11		3		1																			
	2		4	5	6		8		7					10	9	11		3		1																			
	2		4	5	6		8		11					10	9			3		1	7																		
	2		4	5	6		7		11					10	9			3		1	8																		
	2		4	5	6		7		11			1		10	9			3			8																		
	2		4	5	6	11	7							10	9			3		1	8																		
	2		4	5	6		7		11			1		10	9			3			8																		
	2		4	5	6		7		11					10	9			3		1	8																		
	2		4	5	6	7	8		11					10	9			3		1																			
	2		4	5		7	8							10	9			3		1		6	11																
	2		4	5			8							10				3		1		6	11	7	9														
	2		4	6	3		8		11					10	9					1				7		5													
4	18	5	18	18	15	7	18	1	15	1	5	1	3	14	13	4	1	12	1	2	8	6	2	2	2	1	1												
									10		4		1		1	10								1		2													
	2		4	5	6		8		11					10	9			3	1				7																
	2		4	5	6		8		11					10	9			3	1				7																
	2		4	5	6		8							10	9			3	1				7		11														
	2		4	5	6		8							10	9			3	1				11	7															
	2		4	5	6	11	8							10	9			3	1					7															
	2		4	5	6		8		11					10				3	1				7	9															
	2		4	5	6	7	8		11					10				3	1					9															
	2		4	5	6	7								10				3	1				11				8	5											
	3		2	5	6	7			11					10				1				8					9		4										
	2		4	5	6				10										1					7			8		11	3	9								
	2		3	5	6		8							10				1					7	9		11			4										
	2		3	5	6				11					10				1					7				9		4			8							
	2		3	5	6		8							10				1					11			7		4					9						
	2		3	5	6				10									1					11	9			8		4					7					
	2		3	5	6									10				1					8	9		11			4					7					
	2		3	5	6	11												1					8	9					4					7	10				
			2	5					10									1					11	9		3	6		4					7	8				
	2		3	5					10														11	9					4					7	8	1	6		
	17		18	18	16	5	7		11					14	5			8	14	3		1	14	11	4	6	5	10	1	1	1	1	5	3	1	1			
						1								3	4			1					3	5	1	2	1		1										

1945-46

North Regional League

Manager: Jimmy Thomson

Did you know that?

- Captain was Tom Barkas.
- David Millar started in goal and Town kicked-off with only 10 men following Charlie Briggs's delay in reaching Darlington on 20 October. When Briggs arrived after 20 minutes, Millar went up front and later grabbed the winning goal.
- The 6–5 victory for Halifax Town over Darlington on 27 October represented the most goals scored (since bettered) in a match at The Shay. At one point, three goals were scored in a three-minute period.
- Clem Smith scored four goals in the 6–5 victory over Darlington, including three goals in nine minutes.
- Clem Smith became the only Halifax Town player to score successive hat-tricks when, a week after getting four goals against Darlington, he scored three in the 6–2 home victory over Lincoln City.
- Walter Tate became a town councillor.
- Halifax Town were unbeaten in nine games from 29 September to 8 December.
- Former Town guest Wally Ardron scored all Rotherham United's goals in their 4–1 win at The Shay on Christmas Day.
- Guest players: Lewis Brook (Huddersfield Town), Albert Burrows (Huddersfield Town), Albert Flatley (Bradford), Louis Gordon (Clyde), Billy Graham (Norwich City), William Harvey (Grimsby Town), David Millar (East Fife), Alex Shirley (Dundee United), Clem Smith (Stoke City), Fred Smith (Bradford).
- Biggest win: 6–2 v Lincoln City (h), 3 November 1945.
- Heaviest defeat: 1–5 v Bradford City (a), 1 September.
- Ever-present: Jack France.

Match No.	Date		Venue	Opponents	Result		Scorers	Attendance
1	Aug	25	H	Bradford City	D	0-0		3,000
2	Sep	1	A	Bradford City	L	1-5	Jackson (pen)	5,011
3		8	H	Carlisle United	W	5-2	Millar 2, C. Smith 3	5,000
4		15	A	Carlisle United	L	1-4	Doran	5,000
5		22	H	Gateshead	L	1-4	C. Smith	3,000
6		29	A	Gateshead	D	3-3	Brook 2, Oliver	3,000
7	Oct	6	A	York City	D	0-0		5,000
8		13	H	York City	W	3-1	C. Smith 2, Gledhill (og)	5,000
9		20	A	Darlington	W	2-1	Gordon, Millar	7,568
10		27	H	Darlington	W	6-5	Barkas, C. Smith 4, Oliver	4,000
11	Nov	3	H	Lincoln City	W	6-2	Green, C. Smith 3, J Ruecroft, Gordon	3,000
12		10	A	Lincoln City	W	2-1	Gordon, Hazeldine	6,426
13	Dec	1	H	Hartlepools United	W	3-2	Gordon 2, C. Smith	3,000
14		8	A	Hartlepools United	D	0-0		3,564
15		15	A	Doncaster Rovers	L	0-3		4,301
16		22	H	Doncaster Rovers	L	2-3	Gordon 2	2,190
17		25	H	Rotherham United	L	1-4	France	
18		26	A	Rotherham United	L	3-6	Harvey 2, Chapman	11,546

Final position: 6th in Division Three North (East)

Apps
1 own-goal   Gls

Division Three North (East) Cup

1	Jan	5	H	Hartlepools United	L	2-5	Barkas 2	3,000
2		12	A	Gateshead	D	2-2	Gordon, Barkas	3,000
3		19	H	Gateshead	L	0-1		2,000
4		26	H	Lincoln City	L	1-3	France	3,000
5	Feb	2	A	Lincoln City	W	3-2	C. Smith, Oliver, Barkas	5,705
6		9	H	Doncaster Rovers	W	4-1	Hazeldine 2, Barkas, Gordon	4,139
7		16	A	Doncaster Rovers	D	1-1	Gordon	9,070
8		23	H	York City	L	0-1		2,000
9	Mar	2	A	York City	D	1-1	Oliver	4,000
10		9	A	Hartlepools United	D	1-1	Moncrieff	5,874

Halifax Town finished 9th but failed to qualify for knockout stage.

Apps
Gls

Division Three North Second Championship

11		23	A	Lincoln City	D	1-1	Gordon	4,500
12		30	H	Lincoln City	L	2-3	Merron, Hazeldine	3,000
13	Apr	6	H	Oldham Athletic	W	1-0	Boothman (og)	4,000
14		13	A	Oldham Athletic	D	1-1	Gordon	5,190
15		20	H	Stockport County	L	0-1		2,000
16		22	A	Wrexham	D	1-1	Hazeldine	2,500
17		27	A	Stockport County	L	2-3	Jackson 2 (1 pen)	2,000

Final position: 17th in Division Three North Second Championship

Apps
1 own-goal   Gls

FA Cup

R1/1	Nov	17	H	York City	W	1-0	Gordon	5,849
R1/2		24	A	York City	L	2-4	Barkas 2	7,573

Apps
Gls

	Rayner,E	Allison,WH	Jackson,H	Green,H	Rowcroft,J	France,J	Doran,S	Smith,C	Widdowfield,E	Millar,D	Rowcroft,EJ	Barkas,T	Wild,J	Worthington,E	Wood,S	Haughey,F	Graham,W	Oliver,G	Briggs,CE	Brook,L	Wettenden,RS	Flatley,AA	Burrows,A	Gordon,L	Shelley,AG	Hazeldine,AV	Harvey,W	Chapman,L	Mounzieff,JC	Merron,J	Turner,E	Smith,FH	England,FW	Killarney,A	Binns,E	Morsfield,WJT	Butler,A	Taylor,C
	1	2	3	4	5	6	7	8	9	10	11																											
	1	2	3	4	5	6	7	8		9		10	11																									
	1	2	3	4	5	6		8		9		10		7	11																							
	1	2		4	5	6	9	8		10				7	11	3																						
	1	2	3	4	5	6		8		9				7				10	11																			
		2		3	5	6	4	8				10		7					11	1	9																	
		2		3	5	6	4	8		9		10		7					11	1																		
		2		3	5	4	9	8				10							11	1				6	7													
		2	3		5	6	4	8		10									11	1							7	9										
		2	3	4	5	6		8				10							11	1							9	7										
	1	2	3	4	5	6	7	8				10							11								9		11									
	1	2	3	4	5	6		8				10															9	7	11									
	1	2		3	5	6	4	8				10															9	7	11									
	1	2		3	5	6	4	8				10															9	7	11									
	1	2		3	5	6	4	8				10															9	7	11									
	1	2	3	4	5	6				10																	7	11	8	9								
	1	2	3	4	5	6				10																	7	11	8	9								
	12	18	11	17	18	18	11	16	1	7	1	14	1	5	2	1		7	6	1	1	1		8	7	8	2	2										
		1		1	1	1		13		7				2		2			7					1	2	1												
		2	3	4	5	6		8		10									1					9	7	11												
		2		3	5	6		8		10									1					9		11	7	4										
		2		3	5	6		8							10				1					9	11	7		4										
		2	3	4	5	6		8							10	11	1							9		7												
		2		3	5	6		8		10									11	1				9		7		4										
		2		3	5	6	7	8		10										1				9		11			4									
		2		3	5	6	7	8							10					1				9		11			4									
		2		3	5	6	7	8		10										1				9		11			4									
		2		3	5	6		8											11	1				10		7		9	4									
		2		3	5	6		8											11	1				10		7		9	4									
	10	2	10	10	10	3	10			5				3	4	10			10	2	10		1	5	5													
				1			1			6					2				3		2			1														
		2		3	5	6				10									11	1				8		7			9	4								
		2		3	5	6				10									11	1				8		7			9	4								
		2	7		5	3													11	1				8				4	6	9	10							
		2	7	3	5	6				10									11	1				8				4		9								
		2	7	3	5	6				10										1						11		4				8	9					
			7	3		6				10										1						11	5		4			8	9	2				
			7	3	5	6														1						11			4		8		9	2	10			
	5	5	6	6	7					5					4	7			4		5			3	5	3	2	2	2	3	2	1						
		2																		2		2			1													
	1	2	3	4	5		7		9	10		6			11			8									9	4										
	1	2	3	4	5		7			10		6			11			8																9				
	2	2	2	2	2		2		1	2		2			2			2									1	1										
										2								1																				

1946-47

Division Three (North)

Manager: Jimmy Thomson

Did you know that?

- Minimum admission price was 1s 3d.
- Needing ready cash at the gates, Halifax Town didn't offer any season tickets during 1946–47.
- Captain was Horace Green.
- The surprise victory over leaders Doncaster Rovers on 18 January ended a run of eight consecutive defeats, and a run of 11 matches without a win.
- During Town's home game with York City on 19 April 1947 a collection was taken for the family of Halifax RLFC player Hudson Irving, who died in a game at Thrum Hall versus Dewsbury. A total of £30 was raised.
- Halifax Town dropped to bottom place on 1 February following the 1–0 home defeat to New Brighton and remained there until the end of the season.
- Town finished bottom for the first time.
- Biggest League win: 4–1 v Hartlepools United (a), 2 November.
- Heaviest League defeat: 1–6 v Oldham Athletic (a), 1 January, v Rotherham United (a), 13 January, v Southport (a), 29 March, v Gateshead (a), 3 May.

Match No.	Date	Venue	Opponents	Result		Scorers	Attendance
1	Aug 31	A	Stockport County	L	1-4	Quinn	8,193
2	Sep 2	H	Oldham Athletic	D	1-1	Binns	6,503
3	7	H	Wrexham	D	0-0		6,000
4	12	A	Barrow	L	0-3		6,917
5	14	A	Doncaster Rovers	L	0-2		13,765
6	16	H	Barrow	W	3-2	Walshaw, Moncrieff, Mycock	4,784
7	21	H	Rochdale	W	3-0	Quinn, Hazeldine, Mycock	4,119
8	28	A	New Brighton	D	1-1	Moncrieff	9,798
9	Oct 5	H	Darlington	L	0-2		5,592
10	12	H	Carlisle United	L	0-1		3,420
11	19	A	Hull City	L	0-3		23,289
12	26	H	Gateshead	W	2-1	Humphreys, Ruecroft (pen)	3,372
13	Nov 2	A	Hartlepools United	W	4-1	Waters 2, Green, Quinn	6,709
14	9	H	Crewe Alexandra	L	1-2	Wrigglesworth	4,491
15	16	A	Lincoln City	L	1-3	Waters	7,944
16	23	H	Southport	D	1-1	Waters	2,599
17	Dec 7	H	Chester	L	1-2	Quinn	3,830
18	21	H	Tranmere Rovers	L	1-3	Burgess	3,610
19	25	H	Bradford City	L	1-2	Burgess	5,032
20	26	A	Bradford City	L	1-3	Quinn	13,060
21	28	H	Stockport County	L	1-2	Hazeldine	5,820
22	Jan 1	A	Oldham Athletic	L	1-6	Dooley	11,964
23	4	A	Wrexham	L	0-2		7,099
24	13	A	Rotherham United	L	1-6	Moncrieff	8,001
25	18	H	Doncaster Rovers	W	4-2	Massey, England, Waters 2	8,814
26	25	A	Rochdale	L	0-1		7,504
27	Feb 1	H	New Brighton	L	0-1		3,842
28	15	A	Carlisle United	L	0-1		8,449
29	Mar 15	A	Crewe Alexandra	L	0-2		3,731
30	29	A	Southport	L	1-6	Fisher	2,607
31	Apr 4	A	Accrington Stanley	D	1-1	Dooley	4,769
32	5	A	Rotherham United	L	2-3	Fisher, Green	4,355
33	7	H	Accrington Stanley	W	2-1	Fisher 2	2,747
34	12	A	Chester	L	0-2		4,627
35	19	H	York City	L	0-3		3,804
36	26	A	Tranmere Rovers	D	1-1	Green	4,755
37	May 3	A	Gateshead	L	1-6	Collins	1,292
38	10	A	Darlington	W	1-0	Fisher	5,474
39	17	H	Hull City	W	2-0	Quinn, Fisher	4,888
40	24	H	Hartlepools United	L	1-4	Waters	3,949
41	26	A	York City	L	0-2		5,745
42	Jun 7	H	Lincoln City	L	2-3	Waters 2	2,513

Final League Position: 22nd in Division Three (North)

Apps
Gls

FA Cup

1	Nov 30	A	Barrow	D	0-0		4,776
R	Dec 4	H	Barrow*	W	1-0	Waters	6,000
2	14	H	Stockport County	D	1-1	Waters	6,000
R	18	A	Stockport County	L	1-2	Massey	7,500

*After extra-time

Apps
Gls

League Table

	P	W	D	L	F	A	Pts
Doncaster Rovers	42	33	6	3	123	40	72
Rotherham United	42	29	6	7	114	53	64
Chester	42	25	6	11	95	51	56
Stockport County	42	24	2	16	78	53	50
Bradford City	42	20	10	12	62	47	50
Rochdale	42	19	10	13	80	64	48
Wrexham	42	17	12	13	65	51	46
Crewe Alexandra	42	17	9	16	70	74	43
Barrow	42	17	7	18	54	62	41
Tranmere Rovers	42	17	7	18	66	77	41
Hull City	42	16	8	18	49	53	40
Lincoln City	42	17	5	20	86	87	39
Hartlepools United	42	15	9	18	64	73	39
Gateshead	42	16	6	20	62	72	38
York City	42	14	9	19	67	81	37
Carlisle United	42	14	9	19	70	93	37
Darlington	42	15	6	21	68	80	36
New Brighton	42	14	8	20	57	77	36
Oldham Athletic	42	12	8	22	55	80	32
Accrington Stanley	42	14	4	24	56	92	32
Southport	42	7	11	24	53	85	25
Halifax Town	42	8	6	28	43	92	22

1947-48

Division Three (North)
Manager: Jack Breedon

Did you know that?

- Captain was Horace Green
- Don Stretton scored after four minutes on his League debut in a 2–1 victory at Hull City on 11 September.
- Accrington Stanley ended a four-match run without a goal by defeating Town 2–0 at Peel Park on 4 October.
- As part of their preparation for the FA Cup match at Wrexham, the players went on a 10-mile country walk around Elland.
- Jim Mills was known as 'Smiler'.
- Halifax Town went seventeen League and Cup games without a win between 15 November and 6 March.
- Halifax Town's first win in 18 matches came at Crewe Alexandra on 13 March and coincided with the Halifax Centenary Celebrations.
- Hugh O'Donnell won an FA Cup-winners' medal with Preston North End in 1938.
- Biggest League win; 4–0 v Stockport County (h), 1 September.
- Heaviest League defeat: 0–6 v York City (a), 30 August.
- Town's biggest win came two days after their heaviest defeat.

Match No.	Date		Venue	Opponents	Result		Scorers	Attendance
1	Aug	23	H	Wrexham	L	0-1		9,266
2		25	A	Stockport County	L	1-2	Jowett	15,087
3		30	A	York City	L	0-6		9,515
4	Sep	1	H	Stockport County	W	4-0	Collins 2, Roberts, Massey	8,664
5		6	A	Rochdale	L	1-2	Fisher	10,868
6		11	A	Hull City	W	2-1	Stretton, Burns	21,642
7		13	H	New Brighton	L	1-2	Collins	8,057
8		15	H	Hull City	L	0-2		8,565
9		20	A	Southport	L	0-2		6,871
10		27	H	Lincoln City	L	0-1		7,162
11	Oct	4	A	Accrington Stanley	L	0-2		6,969
12		11	H	Mansfield Town	D	1-1	Collins	6,713
13		18	A	Chester	D	0-0		6,402
14		25	H	Crewe Alexandra	W	4-1	Collins (pen), Stretton, Hogg, Burns	8,185
15	Nov	1	A	Carlisle United	L	2-5	Collins, Stretton	11,784
16		8	H	Rotherham United	W	2-1	Stretton 2	12,078
17		15	A	Hartlepools United	D	1-1	Mycock	5,461
18		22	H	Gateshead	D	0-0		5,277
19	Dec	6	H	Tranmere Rovers	D	2-2	Collins (pen), Lewis	5,625
20		20	A	Wrexham	L	3-6	Burns 2, France (pen)	7,910
21		25	H	Barrow	D	1-1	Booth	10,097
22		26	A	Barrow	L	1-2	Booth	9,987
23	Jan	3	H	York City	L	0-1		7,696
24		10	A	Darlington	L	1-4	Collins	4,288
25		17	H	Rochdale	L	2-3	Collins, Burns	7,310
26		24	A	Oldham Athletic	D	1-1	Lewis	8,778
27		31	A	New Brighton	L	0-1		3,958
28	Feb	7	H	Southport	D	0-0		3,679
29		14	A	Lincoln City	L	1-3	Lewis	12,552
30		21	H	Accrington Stanley	D	3-3	Priestley 2, Jowett	4,055
31		28	A	Mansfield Town	L	1-3	Priestley	10,664
32	Mar	6	H	Chester	D	1-1	Cockroft	7,256
33		13	A	Crewe Alexandra	W	1-0	Priestley	5,425
34		20	H	Carlisle United	W	2-1	Lewis, Priestley	9,802
35		27	A	Rotherham United	L	0-3		15,792
36		29	H	Bradford City	D	0-0		10,241
37		30	A	Bradford City	L	1-2	Massey	12,756
38	Apr	3	H	Hartlepools United	D	0-0		5,920
39		10	A	Gateshead	L	0-3		4,826
40		17	H	Darlington	D	1-1	Priestley	7,414
41		24	A	Tranmere Rovers	W	1-0	Massey	3,184
42	May	1	H	Oldham Athletic	L	1-5	Priestley	4,598

Final League Position: 21st in Division Three (North)

Apps
Gls

FA Cup

1	Nov	29	A	Wrexham	L	0-5		10,032

Apps
Gls

League Table

	P	W	D	L	F	A	Pts
Lincoln City	42	26	8	8	81	40	60
Rotherham United	42	25	9	8	95	49	59
Wrexham	42	21	8	13	74	54	50
Gateshead	42	19	11	12	75	57	49
Hull City	42	18	11	13	59	48	47
Accrington Stanley	42	20	6	16	62	59	46
Barrow	42	16	13	13	49	40	45
Mansfield Town	42	17	11	14	57	51	45
Carlisle United	42	18	7	17	88	77	43
Crewe Alexandra	42	18	7	17	61	63	43
Oldham Athletic	42	14	13	15	63	64	41
Rochdale	42	15	11	16	48	72	41
York City	42	13	14	15	65	60	40
Bradford City	42	15	10	17	65	66	40
Southport	42	14	11	17	60	63	39
Darlington	42	13	13	16	54	70	39
Stockport County	42	13	12	17	63	67	38
Tranmere Rovers	42	16	4	22	54	72	36
Hartlepools United	42	14	8	20	51	73	36
Chester	42	13	9	20	64	67	35
Halifax Town	42	7	13	22	43	76	27
New Brighton	42	8	9	25	38	81	25

1948-49

Division Three (North)

Manager: Jack Breedon

Did you know that?

- Captain was Stan Scrimshaw.
- Eddie Hodgkinson ran a youth club in Mansfield.
- Derek Taylor was the twin son of trainer Harold Taylor.
- Jimmy Dougal scored on his one and only outing for Scotland in a 2–1 defeat by England at Hampden Park on 15 April 1939 while a Preston North End player.
- The game at Hull City on 5 February was watched by a crowd of 37,114, the highest attendance Halifax Town ever played before.
- Scunthorpe United became the first non-League side to knock Halifax Town out of the FA Cup while members of the Football League. The attendance at the Old Show Ground on 6 December was a then record for Scunthorpe.
- Horace Green made a surprise move to Lincoln City on 3 February.
- Harry Fearnley was one of two League goalkeepers with the same name. The other played for Huddersfield Town and Oxford United.
- Biggest League win: 2–0 v Hartlepools United (h), 30 October, v Wrexham (h), 18 December, v Rotherham United (h), 19 February.
- Heaviest League defeat: 0–6 v Hull City (a), 5 February.

Match No.	Date		Venue	Opponents	Result		Scorers	Attendance
1	Aug	21	A	Wrexham	L	1-2	Howsam	11,257
2		23	H	Barrow	W	1-0	O'Donnell	10,519
3		28	H	York City	L	1-2	Moore (pen)	10,749
4		31	A	Barrow	D	0-0		6,023
5	Sep	4	H	Bradford City	D	1-1	Moore (pen)	10,995
6		6	A	Mansfield Town	L	1-2	Crossley	11,763
7		11	H	Doncaster Rovers	W	1-0	Morgan	8,884
8		13	H	Mansfield Town	D	2-2	Crossley, Massey	8,900
9		18	H	Hull City	L	2-4	Crossley, Hogg	18,563
10		25	A	Rotherham United	L	0-4		16,023
11	Oct	2	H	Accrington Stanley	W	1-0	Lavery	10,976
12		9	A	Stockport County	L	1-3	Crossley	12,904
13		16	H	Carlisle United	L	3-4	Mycock (pen), Crossley, Maguire	11,544
14		23	A	Gateshead	W	2-1	Gilmour, Maguire	6,026
15		30	H	Hartlepools United	W	2-0	Massey, Mycock (pen)	9,735
16	Nov	6	A	Darlington	L	1-2	Crossley	9,613
17		13	H	Rochdale	W	2-1	Mycock, Hodgkinson	7,743
18		20	A	New Brighton	L	0-2		5,607
19	Dec	18	H	Wrexham	W	2-0	Howsam, Gilmour	4,647
20		25	H	Tranmere Rovers	L	0-1		11,493
21		27	A	Tranmere Rovers	D	2-2	Mycock (pen), Maguire	6,854
22	Jan	1	A	York City	D	2-2	Birch, Howsam	9,175
23		15	A	Bradford City	L	1-2	Mycock	8,619
24		22	A	Doncaster Rovers	W	2-1	Howsam, Dougal	14,374
25		29	H	Chester	L	1-2	Howsam	9,160
26	Feb	5	A	Hull City	L	0-6		37,114
27		12	H	Crewe Alexandra	D	0-0		5,511
28		19	H	Rotherham United	W	2-0	Crossley, Priestley	9,286
29		26	A	Accrington Stanley	L	0-1		3,951
30	Mar	5	H	Stockport County	L	0-1		2,944
31		12	A	Carlisle United	D	0-0		9,734
32		19	H	Gateshead	D	2-2	Whittingham 2	7,692
33		26	A	Hartlepools United	D	0-0		4,756
34	Apr	2	H	Darlington	L	0-3		5,637
35		9	A	Rochdale	L	0-1		6,885
36		15	A	Oldham Athletic	D	2-2	Crossley, Hodgkinson	23,607
37		16	H	New Brighton	L	0-2		8,928
38		18	H	Oldham Athletic	W	3-1	Murphy, Crossley, Whittingham	7,305
39		23	A	Chester	W	1-0	Dougal	3,858
40		26	A	Southport	W	3-2	Crossley 2, Murphy	7,031
41		30	H	Southport	L	0-1		5,977
42	May	7	A	Crewe Alexandra	D	0-0		4,247

Final League Position: 19th in Division Three (North)

Apps
Gls

FA Cup

1	Dec	4	H	Scunthorpe United	D	0-0*		16,000
R		6	A	Scunthorpe United	L	0-1		12,736

* After extra-time.

Apps
Gls

League Table

	P	W	D	L	F	A	Pts
Hull City	42	27	11	4	93	28	65
Rotherham United	42	28	6	8	90	46	62
Doncaster Rovers	42	20	10	12	53	40	50
Darlington	42	20	6	16	83	74	46
Gateshead	42	16	13	13	69	58	45
Oldham Athletic	42	18	9	15	75	67	45
Rochdale	42	18	9	15	55	53	45
Stockport County	42	16	11	15	6	56	43
Wrexham	42	17	9	16	56	62	43
Mansfield Town	42	14	14	14	52	48	42
Tranmere Rovers	42	13	15	14	46	57	41
Crewe Alexandra	42	16	9	17	52	74	41
Barrow	42	14	12	16	4	48	40
York City	42	15	9	18	74	74	39
Carlisle United	42	14	11	17	60	77	39
Hartlepools United	42	14	10	13	45	58	38
New Brighton	42	14	8	20	46	58	36
Chester	42	11	13	13	57	56	35
Halifax Town	42	12	11	13	45	62	35
Accrington Stanley	42	12	10	20	55	64	34
Southport	42	11	9	22	45	64	31
Bradford City	42	10	9	23	45	77	29

1949-50

Division Three (North)

Manager: Jack Breedon

Did you know that?

- Adult season tickets cost 35s.
- Captain was George Hinsley.
- Town's home match with Mansfield Town on 19 November was played in thick fog and many supporters had not realised that the visitors had won 3–0!
- Rippondon-born John Core was a student at Leeds University.
- Dave McCormick first appeared in goal for Halifax Town during the match at Bradford City on 4 February when he temporarily replaced injured Pat Egglestone. Town won the match 3–1.
- Prior to their 4–1 victory over Halifax Town at The Shay on 4 March, Accrington Stanley had only scored eight away goals. John Core and George Holt represented the Northern Counties against Lancashire in the Final of the Amateur Championships Final at Morecambe on 22 April.
- Biggest League win: 5–2 v Gateshead (h), 29 August.
- Heaviest League defeat: 1–7 v Gateshead (a), 22 August.

Match No.	Date		Venue	Opponents	Result		Scorers	Attendance
1	Aug	20	H	Hartlepools United	L	1-2	Mycock (pen)	9,002
2		22	A	Gateshead	L	1-7	Whittingham	9,740
3		27	A	Darlington	L	1-5	Mycock	8,827
4		29	H	Gateshead	W	5-2	Crossley, Whittingam 2, Mycock (pen)	5,923
5	Sep	3	H	New Brighton	W	3-0	Scott, Crossley, Whittingham	8,503
6		5	A	Southport	D	1-1	Scott	7,879
7		10	A	York City	L	1-3	Mycock	8,776
8		12	H	Southport	D	0-0		7,003
9		17	A	Rochdale	L	0-1		8,755
10		24	H	Bradford City	W	3-1	Scott 2, Hindle	11,714
11	Oct	1	A	Chester	L	1-5	Scott	5,451
12		8	H	Tranmere Rovers	L	0-1		7,209
13		15	A	Crewe Alexandra	L	3-6	Crossley, Dale, Whittingham	10,095
14		22	H	Barrow	W	1-0	Dale	5,296
15		29	A	Lincoln City	L	0-1		12,498
16	Nov	5	H	Rotherham United	W	4-3	Murphy, Hindle, Whittingham, Dale	6,760
17		12	A	Carlisle United	W	2-0	Hindle, Dale	7,347
18		19	H	Mansfield Town	L	0-3		7,213
19	Dec	3	H	Wrexham	D	0-0		4,418
20		17	A	Hartlepools United	D	3-3	Morgan, Maguire, Murphy	3,896
21		24	H	Darlington	L	1-3	Murphy	6,170
22		26	A	Stockport County	L	0-2		15,223
23		27	H	Stockport County	W	3-1	Hindle 2, Core	8,851
24		31	A	New Brighton	D	1-1	Murphy	4,729
25	Jan	14	H	York City	L	1-2	Hindle (pen)	6,286
26		21	A	Rochdale	W	3-2	Core, Watson (og), Bennett	10,398
27		28	A	Accrington Stanley	L	0-1		4,244
28	Feb	4	A	Bradford City	W	3-1	Murphy, Maguire, Core	15,787
29		11	A	Oldham Athletic	L	1-2	Core	10,923
30		18	H	Chester	W	2-1	Hindle, Core	6,009
31		25	A	Mansfield Town	L	0-1		5,746
32	Mar	4	H	Accrington Stanley	L	1-4	Core	5,726
33		11	A	Barrow	L	0-4		5,640
34		18	H	Lincoln City	L	0-1		5,461
35		25	A	Rotherham United	L	1-2	Core	7,549
36	Apr	1	H	Carlisle United	D	1-1	Core	4,179
37		7	A	Doncaster Rovers	L	0-4		20,981
38		8	A	Tranmere Rovers	L	1-2	Maguire	6,787
39		10	H	Doncaster Rovers	D	2-2	Dale, Core	8,709
40		15	H	Crewe Alexandra	W	3-1	Dale 2, Breaks	6,713
41		22	A	Wrexham	W	3-2	Massey, Dale, Maguire	6,044
42		29	H	Oldham Athletic	D	1-1	Murphy	4,222

Final League Position: 21st in Division Three (North)

1 own-goal

Apps
Gls

FA Cup

| 1 | Nov | 26 | A | Tranmere Rovers | L | 1-2 | Hindle | 9,664 |

Apps
Gls

League Table

	P	W	D	L	F	A	Pts
Doncaster Rovers	42	19	17	6	66	38	55
Gateshead	42	23	7	12	87	54	53
Rochdale	42	21	9	12	68	41	51
Lincoln City	42	21	9	12	60	39	51
Tranmere Rovers	42	19	11	12	51	48	49
Rotherham United	42	19	10	13	80	59	48
Crewe Alexandra	42	17	14	11	66	55	48
Mansfield Town	42	18	12	12	66	54	48
Carlisle United	42	16	15	11	68	51	47
Stockport County	42	19	7	16	55	52	45
Oldham Athletic	42	16	11	15	58	63	43
Chester	42	17	6	19	70	79	40
Accrington Stanley	42	16	7	19	57	62	39
New Brighton	42	14	10	18	45	63	38
Barrow	42	14	9	19	47	53	37
Southport	42	12	13	17	51	71	37
Darlington	42	11	13	18	56	69	35
Hartlepools United	42	14	5	23	52	79	33
Bradford City	42	12	8	22	61	76	32
Wrexham	42	10	12	20	39	54	32
Halifax Town	42	12	8	22	58	85	32
York City	42	9	13	20	52	70	31

1950-51

Division Three (North)

Manager: August–November 1950 Jack Breedon; March–May 1951 Billy Wootton

Did you know that?

- Captain was Eddie Murphy.
- Halifax Town wore claret shirts with light blue sleeves.
- John Core scored Town's first goal of the season in the 39th minute of the 1–1 draw with Rochdale in the fifth match.
- Over 1,000 Halifax Town fans made the trip to Bradford for the first derby in 22 years on 14 October on overcrowded trains.
- Des Frost became Town's record signing when joining from Leeds United on 5 January.
- The fees for Frost and Jackie Moss were paid for in part by £900 from the Climb the League Fund and £600 from the Social Section.
- Des Frost scored all his side's goals in the 4–1 victory over Lincoln City on 3 February, the first Town player to score all four goals in a League game since Ted Widdowfield in January 1938.
- A white ball was used for the second half of Town's goalless draw at Rochdale on 10 April.
- Following the last game of the season, the Town players and officials were entertained to dinner by York City chairman W.H. Sessions.
- Biggest League win: 4–0 v Southport (h), 14 April.
- Heaviest League defeat: 0–5 v Gateshead 4 September.
- Ever-present: Billy Morgan.

Match No.	Date		Venue	Opponents	Result		Scorers	Attendance
1	Aug	19	H	New Brighton	L	0-2		7,680
2		24	A	Barrow	L	0-2		6,407
3		26	A	Bradford City	L	0-2		14,959
4		28	H	Barrow	D	0-0		5,228
5	Sep	2	H	Rochdale	D	1-1	Core	10,219
6		4	A	Gateshead	L	0-5		13,035
7		9	A	Chester	L	1-2	Hindle	7,720
8		11	H	Gateshead	W	1-0	Core	6,468
9		16	H	Shrewsbury Town	W	3-1	Jowett, Hindle, Core	7,473
10		23	A	Lincoln City	L	1-3	Mycock (pen)	11,358
11		30	A	Darlington	D	2-2	Webster, Muphy	5,919
12	Oct	7	H	Oldham Athletic	W	3-0	Core, Hindle, Mycock	7,929
13		14	A	Bradford	L	1-2	Core	14,621
14		21	H	Scunthorpe United	D	3-3	Core, Tomlinson 2	9,512
15		28	A	Wrexham	D	2-2	Core, Glaister	7,972
16	Nov	4	H	Rotherham United	L	1-2	Morgan	9,175
17		11	A	Mansfield Town	L	1-3	Tomlinson	9,744
18		18	H	Tranmere Rovers	L	0-1		6,854
19	Dec	2	H	Accrington Stanley	D	2-2	Tomlinson, Dale	4,883
20		16	A	New Brighton	L	0-1		2,124
21		23	H	Bradford City	L	1-2	Glaister	5,778
22		25	A	Crewe Alexandra	D	0-0		5,853
23		26	H	Crewe Alexandra	W	1-0	Dale	8,042
24	Jan	6	A	Hartlepools United	L	2-5	Glaister, Willetts (og)	2,987
25		13	H	Chester	W	3-1	Glaister 2, Frost	5,421
26		20	H	Shrewsbury Town	L	0-2		8,360
27		27	H	Hartlepools United	W	1-0	Frost	6,674
28	Feb	3	H	Lincoln City	W	4-1	Frost 4	8,760
29		10	H	York City	L	1-3	Dale	8,299
30		17	A	Darlington	L	0-2		4,428
31		24	A	Oldham Athletic	L	0-2		15,500
32	Mar	3	H	Bradford	D	2-2	Murphy, Moss	10,533
33		10	A	Scunthorpe United	D	2-2	Murphy, Frost	8,447
34		17	H	Wrexham	W	1-0	Glaister	5,702
35		24	A	Rotherham United	L	0-2		14,195
36		26	A	Stockport County	L	1-2	Frost	6,308
37		27	H	Stockport County	W	1-0	Dale	8,272
38		31	H	Mansfield Town	L	0-1		5,537
39	Apr	7	A	Tranmere Rovers	L	2-3	Dale, Glaister	6,170
40		10	A	Rochdale	D	0-0		3,342
41		14	H	Southport	W	4-0	Frost 3, Hindle	6,509
42		17	A	Southport	D	1-1	Hindle	3,707
43		21	A	Accrington Stanley	L	0-1		4,550
44		26	A	Carlisle United	L	0-1		7,954
45		28	H	Carlisle United	W	1-0	Frost	4720
46	May	5	A	York City	D	0-0		2,791

Final League Position: 22nd in Division Three (North)

1 own-goal

Apps
Gls

FA Cup

1	Nov	25	H	Ashington	L	2-3	Glaister, Core	7,546

Apps
Gls

Rayner, E	Westlake, FA	Breaks, E	Crossley, R	McCock, D	Morgan, WA	Massey, KBW	Core, J	Dale, RV	Murphy, TE	Hindle, T	Drake, KL	Smyth, HR	Glaister, G	Webster, C	Jowett, HH	Trice, Y	Fraser, R	Tomlinson, F	Elliott, E	Morris, E	Moncrieff, JC	Frost, D	Moss, J	Seddon, FO	Lee, J	Horton, L
1	2	3	4	5	6	7	8	9	10	11																
1		3	9	5	6	7		8	10	11	2	4														
1		3	9	5	6	7		8	10		2	4	11													
		3		5	6		9	8	10		2		11	4	7											
1		3		5	6		9	8	10		2		11	4	7											
1		3		5	6		9		10	8	2		11	4	7											
		3		5	6				10	8	9		11	4	7	1	2									
		3		5	6		9		10	8	2		11	4	7	1										
		3		5	6		9		10	8	2		11	4	7	1										
		3		5	6		9		10	8			11	4	7	1	2									
		3		5	6		9		10	8	2		11	4	7	1										
1		3		5	6		9		10	8	2		11	4	7											
1		3		5	6		9		10	8	2		11	4				7								
1		3		5	6		9		10	8	2		11	4				7								
1		3		5	6		9		10	8	2		11	4				7								
1	3			5	6			9	10	8	2		11	4				7								
1		3		5	6		9		10	8	2		11	4				7								
		3		5	6	11	9		10	8	2			4				7	1							
		3		5	6		9		10	8	2		11					7	1	4						
		3		5	6		9		10	8	2		11					7	1		4					
		3		5	6		9		10	8	2		11					7	1		4					
		3		5	6		9		10	8	2		11					7	1		4					
		3		5	6		8		10	4	2		11					7	1			9				
		3		5	6		7		10	8	4		11			2		1				9				
		3		5	6		7		10	11	4					2		1				9	8			
		3			6		7		10		2		11					1				4	9	8	5	
1		3		5	6		7		10		2		11									4	9	8		
		3		5	6	11	7		10		2							1				4	9	8		
		3		5	6		7		10	11	2							1				4	9	8		
		3		5	6		7		10		2		11					1				4	9	8		
		3		5	6		7		10		4		11					1					9	8	2	
		3		5	6		7		10		4		11					1					9	8	2	
		3		5	6		7		10		4		11					1					9	8	2	
		3		5	6		7				4		11					1					9	8	2	10
		3		5	6		7		10		4		11					1					9	8	2	
1		3		5	6		7		10		4		11										9	8	2	
1		3		5	6		7		10		4		11										9	8	2	
		3		5	6		7		10		4		11				1						9	8	2	
		3		5	6		7		10	11							1						9	8	2	4
		3		5	6		7		10	11							1						9	8	2	4
		3		5	6				10	11							7	1					9	8	2	4
		3		5	6				10	11							7	1					9	8	2	4
		3		5	6				10	7			11					1					9	8	2	4
		3		5	6	7			10	11								1					9	8	2	4
		3		5	6	7		8	10	11														9	2	4
16	2	45	3	45	46	7	14	30	45	31	37	2	34	16	9	5	4	14	25	1	8	23	20	1	15	8
				2	1		7	5	3	5			7	1	1			4				12	1			

		3		5	6		9	8		10	2		11	4				7								
1		1		1	1		1	1		1	1		1	1				1								
								1			1															

League Table

	P	W	D	L	F	A	Pts
Rotherham United	46	31	9	6	103	41	71
Mansfield Town	46	26	12	8	73	48	64
Carlisle United	46	25	12	9	79	50	62
Tranmere Rovers	46	24	11	11	83	62	59
Lincoln City	46	25	8	13	81	58	58
Bradford Park Avenue	46	23	8	15	90	72	54
Bradford City	46	21	10	15	90	63	52
Gateshead	46	21	8	17	84	62	50
Crewe Alexandra	46	19	10	17	6	60	48
Stockport County	46	20	8	13	63	63	48
Rochdale	46	17	11	13	69	62	45
Scunthorpe United	46	13	18	15	55	57	44
Chester	46	17	9	20	62	64	43
Wrexham	46	15	12	19	55	71	42
Oldham Athletic	46	16	8	22	73	73	40
Hartlepools United	46	16	7	23	64	66	39
York City	46	12	15	19	66	77	39
Darlington	46	13	13	20	59	77	39
Barrow	46	16	6	24	57	76	38
Shrewsbury Town	46	15	7	24	40	74	37
Southport	46	13	10	23	56	72	36
Halifax Town	46	11	12	23	50	69	34
Accrington Stanley	46	11	10	25	43	101	32
New Brighton	46	11	8	27	40	90	30

1951-52

Division Three (North)

Manager: August 1951–February 1952 Billy Wootton; February–April 1952 Gerald Henry

Did you know that?

- Captain was Jackie Moss.
- Town's 3–1 victory over Workington on 18 August was their first opening-day success since the war.
- Dave McCormick started his first game as goalkeeper in the first team in the 2–1 defeat at Wrexham on 8 September due to injury to Ted Elliott.
- Des Frost, Jackie Moss and Les Horton arrived just in time for kick-off for the game at Accrington Stanley on 25 September after their car broke down on the way.
- Jimmy Lee signed for Chelsea on 4 October, netting Town a club record £2,500.
- Chairman Arthur Carter died on 21 November.
- Coach Ken Willingham won twelve caps for England at right half-back as a Huddersfield Town player.
- Town's 2–0 victory at Rochdale on 23 February ended a run of 40 consecutive away League matches without a win.
- Biggest League win: 4–1 v Darlington (h), 1 December, v Chester (h), 1 March.
- Heaviest League defeat: 1–8 v Grimsby Town (a), 29 December.
- Ever-present: Des Frost.

Match No.	Date		Venue	Opponents	Result		Scorers	Attendance
1	Aug	18	H	Workington	W	3-1	Moss, Hindle, Frost	9,511
2		23	A	Carlisle United	D	2-2	Frost 2	14,545
3		25	A	Barrow	D	0-0		8,019
4		27	A	Gateshead	L	0-3		5,674
5	Sep	1	H	Grimsby Town	W	3-0	Frost, Brown (og), Moss	9,879
6		3	H	Accrington Stanley	L	0-4		7,163
7		8	A	Wrexham	L	1-2	Moss	7,130
8		10	H	Carlisle United	L	1-2	Moss	8,287
9		15	H	Chesterfield	D	0-0		7,104
10		22	A	Bradford	L	1-6	Horton	16,068
11		25	A	Accrington Stanley	D	2-2	Frost, Hindle	5,977
12		29	A	Hartlepools United	L	1-6	Frost	8,979
13	Oct	6	H	York City	D	1-1	Frost	6,087
14		13	A	Chester	L	1-5	Mycock	4,569
15		20	H	Lincoln City	L	1-3	Frost	6,328
16		27	A	Scunthorpe United	L	1-2	Frost	8,729
17	Nov	3	H	Tranmere Rovers	W	1-0	Dale (pen)	4,649
18		10	A	Southport	L	2-3	Dale, Frost	6,353
19		17	H	Crewe Alexandra	L	2-3	Frost 2	5,902
20	Dec	1	H	Darlington	W	4-1	Davison (og), Henry, Moss, Hindle	6,079
21		8	A	Oldham Athletic	L	0-2		8,772
22		22	H	Barrow	L	0-1		5,126
23		25	A	Bradford City	L	2-3	Frost, Moss	15,142
24		26	H	Bradford City	D	1-1	Holt	8,914
25		29	A	Grimsby Town	L	1-8	Hindle (pen)	13,548
26	Jan	1	A	Workington	L	1-2	Swain	4,872
27		5	H	Wrexham	W	2-0	Frost, Hindle	5,924
28		12	A	Stockport County	L	2-6	Moss, McCaig	10,004
29		19	A	Chesterfield	L	1-3	Moss	7,615
30	Feb	9	H	Hartlepools United	W	2-0	Mycock, Murphy	5,503
31		16	A	York City	L	2-6	Mycock, Moss	7,902
32		23	A	Rochdale	W	2-0	Frost, McCaig	5,703
33	Mar	1	H	Chester	W	4-1	Frost 2, Henry (pen), Murphy	6,922
34		8	A	Lincoln City	L	1-4	Frost	15,439
35		10	H	Bradford	D	0-0		6,429
36		15	H	Scunthorpe United	W	2-1	White (og), Frost	8,418
37		22	A	Tranmere Rovers	W	2-1	Murphy, Frost	6,960
38		24	H	Stockport County	L	1-2	Priestley	5,318
39		29	A	Southport	L	0-1		3,760
40	Apr	5	A	Crewe Alexandra	L	1-4	Henry	2,818
41		12	H	Gateshead	L	0-1		7,553
42		14	H	Mansfield Town	W	1-0	Murphy	5,962
43		15	A	Mansfield Town	L	2-4	Priestley, Frost	8,214
44		19	A	Darlington	W	2-0	Murphy, Holt	5,963
45		26	H	Oldham Athletic	W	1-0	Frost	8733
46		28	H	Rochdale	W	1-0	Frost	5,962

Final League Position: 20th in Division Three (North)

3 own-goals

Apps
Gls

FA Cup

1	Nov	24	A	Wrexham	L	0-1		9,187

Apps
Gls

League Table

	P	W	D	L	F	A	Pts
Lincoln City	46	30	9	7	121	52	69
Grimsby Town	46	29	8	9	96	45	66
Stockport County	46	23	13	10	74	40	59
Oldham Athletic	46	24	9	13	90	61	57
Gateshead	46	21	11	14	66	49	53
Mansfield Town	46	22	8	16	73	60	52
Carlisle United	46	19	13	14	62	57	51
Bradford Park Avenue	46	19	12	15	74	64	50
Hartlepools United	46	21	8	17	71	65	50
York City	46	18	13	15	73	52	49
Tranmere Rovers	46	21	6	19	76	71	48
Barrow	46	17	12	17	57	61	46
Chesterfield	46	17	11	18	65	66	45
Scunthorpe United	46	14	16	16	65	74	44
Bradford City	46	16	10	20	61	68	42
Crewe Alexandra	46	17	8	21	63	82	42
Southport	46	15	11	20	53	71	41
Wrexham	46	15	9	22	63	73	39
Chester	46	15	9	22	72	85	39
Halifax Town	46	14	7	25	61	97	35
Rochdale	46	11	13	22	47	79	35
Accrington Stanley	46	10	12	24	61	92	32
Darlington	46	11	9	26	64	103	31
Workington	46	11	7	28	50	91	29

1952-53

Division Three (North)

Manager: Gerald Henry

Did you know that?

- Captain was Eric Williams.
- The directors donated £50 to the Lynmouth Flood Relief Fund in Halifax in September.
- Halifax Town wore navy blue shirts and white shorts.
- Halifax Town were drawn at home in each of their five FA Cup ties.
- Former Halifax Town players John Core and Bob Tomlinson were members of the Ashton United which side which took the Shaymen to a replay in the first round of the FA Cup.
- Halifax Town players wore special sponge pads which were inserted into their boots when they played their first round replay at Ashton United, at the suggestion of trainer Allen Ure.
- Town wore unaccustomed white shirts and black shorts against Cardiff City's red shirts and white shorts in their FA Cup match at The Shay on 10 January.
- A total of 126,490 people watched Halifax Town's six FA Cup ties.
- Biggest League win: 5–2 v Workington (h), 20 December.
- Heaviest League defeat: 0–5 v Bradford City (a), 18

Match No.	Date		Venue	Opponents	Result		Scorers	Attendance
1	Aug	23	A	Workington	L	0-2		9,714
2		25	H	Hartlepools United	W	3-2	Frost, Priestley 2	9,246
3		30	H	Chesterfield	W	3-1	Frost, Murphy, Priestley	8,746
4	Sep	1	A	Hartlepools United	D	0-0		10,826
5		6	A	Tranmere Rovers	D	0-0		9,116
6		10	A	Accrington Stanley	D	1-1	Geddes	6,867
7		13	H	York City	D	0-0		9,970
8		15	H	Accrington Stanley	W	3-0	Murphy, Wilkinson, Frost	8,883
9		20	A	Grimsby Town	L	0-2		17,852
10		22	A	Stockport County	D	1-1	Frost	5,914
11		27	H	Barrow	W	1-0	Darbyshire	8,770
12		29	H	Oldham Athletic	D	2-2	Cox, Holt	8,999
13	Oct	4	A	Wrexham	L	1-2	Darbyshire	12,320
14		11	A	Carlisle United	W	2-1	Frost, Wilkinson	7,213
15		18	H	Southport	W	4-1	Frost 2, Holt, Murphy	10,610
16		25	A	Crewe Alexandra	D	1-1	Holt	8,348
17	Nov	1	H	Port Vale	L	1-2	Holt (pen)	11,693
18		8	A	Chester	L	1-2	Holt (pen)	5,235
19		15	H	Scunthorpe United	W	2-1	Lorenson, Frost	7,247
20		29	H	Bradford City	D	1-1	Geddes (pen)	8,209
21	Dec	13	H	Darlington	W	3-2	Moncrieff, Murphy, Priestley	7,984
22		20	H	Workington	W	5-2	Moncrieff 3, Hampson, Holt	4,805
23		26	A	Bradford	W	2-1	Moncrieff, Holt	22,252
24		27	H	Bradford	L	2-4	Savage, Murphy	19,693
25	Jan	3	A	Chesterfield	L	1-2	Frost	9,295
26		12	H	Gateshead	L	1-3	Frost	4,000
27		17	H	Tranmere Rovers	D	0-0		8,448
28		24	A	York City	D	2-2	Lorenson, Frost	9,604
29	Feb	4	A	Gateshead	L	1-3	Frost	4,020
30		7	H	Grimsby Town	W	3-2	Darbyshire, Frost, Hampson	9,038
31		19	A	Barrow	L	1-5	Priestley	2,524
32		21	H	Wrexham	D	0-0		6,227
33		28	H	Carlisle United	W	2-1	Twentyman (og), Hampson	7,635
34	Mar	7	A	Southport	D	1-1	Hampson	5,463
35		14	A	Crewe Alexandra	L	1-3	Frost	6,509
36		21	A	Port Vale	D	1-1	Murphy	17,945
37		28	H	Chester	W	3-1	Murphy, Hampson, Holt	3,296
38	Apr	4	A	Scunthorpe United	D	1-1	Holt	6,451
39		6	H	Mansfield Town	L	1-2	Frost	5,794
40		7	A	Mansfield Town	L	1-2	Darbyshire	7,953
41		11	H	Stockport County	W	3-0	Hampson 2, Holt	5,853
42		14	A	Rochdale	D	1-1	Moss	3,429
43		18	A	Bradford City	L	0-5		13,283
44		21	A	Oldham Athletic	L	0-1		23,679
45		25	H	Rochdale	W	3-1	Frost 2, Watson (og)	4,826
46		29	A	Darlington	W	2-0	Rutherford (og), Murphy	3,223

Final League Position: 14th in Division Three (North)

3 own-goals

Apps
Gls

FA Cup

1	Nov	22	H	Ashton United	D	1-1	Holt	12,101
R		25	A	Ashton United	W	2-1	Lorenson, Moncrieff	7,849
2	Dec	6	H	Southport	W	4-2	Hampson, Moncrieff 2, Holt	10,872
3	Jan	10	H	Cardiff City	W	3-1	Priestley, Murphy, Moncrieff	23,162
4		31	H	Stoke City	W	1-0	Priestley	35,621
5	Feb	14	H	Tottenham Hotspur	L	0-3		36,885

Apps
Gls

Player Appearances

McCormick, D	Williams, E	Cox, AEH	Geddes, A	Packard, JE	Moss, J	Holt, G	Morgan, WA	Frost, D	Murphy, TE	Priestley, D	Lorenson, RV	Savage, JA	Wilkinson, A	Bickerstaffe, J	Darbyshire, H	Henry, BR	Hampson, A	Mouncrieff, JC	Mulvaney, J	Breaks, E	Schofield, T	Senior, AG
1	2	3	4	5	6	7	8	9	10	11												
1	2	3	8	5	4	7		9	10	11	6											
	2	3	8	5	4	7	6	9	10	11		1										
	2	3	8	5	4	7	6	9	10	11		1										
	2	3	8	5	4		6	9	10	11		1	7									
	2	3	8	5	4			9	10	11	6	1	7									
	2	3	8	5	4			9	10	11	6	1	7									
	2	3	4	5		8		9	10	11		1	7	6								
	2	3	4	5		8		9	10	11		1	7	6								
	2	3	4	5			8	10	11			1	7	6	9							
	2	3	4	5		7	8	10	11			1		6	9							
	2	3	8	5	4	7			10	11		1		6	9							
	2	3	8	5	4	7			10	11		1		6	9							
	2	3	4	5	6	7	8	10				1	11		9							
	2	3	4	5	6	7	8	10				1	11		9							
	2	3		5		8		9	10	11	6	1	7	4								
	2	3		5		8		9	10	11	6	1			7	4						
	2	3		5		8		9	10	11	6	1	7	4								
	2	3				8		9	10		6	1	11	5	4		7					
	2	3	4	5		8			10		6	1	11		9		7					
	2	3	4	5		8			10	11	6	1					7	9				
	2	3	4	5		8			10	11	6	1					7	9				
	2	3	4	5	6	8		7	10	11		1						9				
	2	3	4	5	6	8			10	11		1					7	9				
1			4		10		8			11	6			5	7			9	2	3		
1	2	3	4	5	6	8		9	10	11							7					
1	2	3		5	4	8			10	11	6		7					9				
1	2	3		5	6		8	10	11	4				7			9					
1	2		4	5		8		9		11	6			10	7		3					
1	2	3	4	5	6	8		9		11				10	7							
1		3	4		6		8	10	11		5	9			7		2					
	3		5	4		8	10	11	6			9			7		2	1				
1		3		5	4	8		10	11	6			9		7		2					
	2	3		5	4	8		9	10	11	6	1			7							
	2	3		5	4	8		9	10	11	6	1			7							
	2	3		5	4	7		9	10	11	6	1			8							
	2	3		5		8		9	10		6	1	11	4	7							
	2	3		5		8		9	10	11		1		4	7							
	2	3		5	6	8		9	10	11		1		4	7							
	2	3		5	4	8			10	11	6	1			9	7						
	2			5	4	8			10	11	6	1			9	7	3					
	2		4	5	6	8			10	11		1			9	7	3					
	2			5	4	8		9	10	11	6	1				7	3					
	2			5		8		9	10	11	6	1		4		7	3					
	2			5		8		9	10	11	6	1				7	3	4				
	2			5		8		4	9	10	11	6	1				7	3				
10	42	38	26	43	33	35	5	35	43	41	26	55	14	9	25	1	24	7	1	11	1	1
	1	2		1		10		17	8	5	2		1	2		4	7	5				

Cup

	2	3	8	5		7		9	10		6	1	11		4							
	2	3	4	5		8			10	11	6	1		7			9					
	2	3	4	5		8			10	11	6	1				7	9					
1	2	3	4	5	6	8			10	11						7	9					
1	2	3	4	5		8		7	10	11							9					
1	2	3	4	5	6			9	10	11					8	7						
3	6	6	6	6	3	5		3	6	5	3	3	1		3	3	4					
						2			1	2	1					1	4					

League Table

	P	W	D	L	F	A	Pts
Oldham Athletic	46	22	15	9	77	45	59
Port Vale	46	20	18	8	67	35	58
Wrexham	46	24	8	14	86	66	56
York City	46	20	13	13	60	45	53
Grimsby Town	46	21	10	15	75	59	52
Southport	46	20	11	15	63	60	51
Bradford Park Avenue	46	19	12	15	75	61	50
Gateshead	46	17	15	14	76	60	49
Carlisle United	46	18	13	15	82	68	49
Crewe Alexandra	46	20	8	18	70	68	48
Stockport County	46	17	13	16	82	69	47
Chesterfield	46	18	11	17	65	63	47
Tranmere Rovers	46	21	5	20	65	63	47
Halifax Town	46	16	15	15	68	68	47
Scunthorpe United	46	16	14	16	62	56	46
Bradford City	46	14	18	14	75	80	46
Hartlepools United	46	16	14	16	57	61	46
Mansfield Town	46	16	14	16	55	62	46
Barrow	46	16	12	13	66	71	44
Chester	46	11	15	20	64	85	37
Darlington	46	14	6	26	58	96	34
Rochdale	46	14	5	27	62	83	33
Workington	46	11	10	25	55	91	32
Accrington Stanley	46	8	11	27	39	89	27

1953-54

Division Three (North)
Manager: Gerald Henry

Did you know that?

- Walter Rickett was an England B international who was a member of Blackpool's side which lost the FA Cup Final to Manchester United in 1948.
- Halifax Town had nine players out either injured or ill prior to their home game with Barrow on 5 September. Des Frost sustained injury during the match and played on with a shoulder strap – and Town won 2–0!
- After their two FA Cup ties during 1952–53 Halifax Town were invited to play Ashton United when they switched on their floodlights at the Hurst Cross ground on 20 October 1953. Town won the game 3–0.
- Norman Hallam was a Methodist minister based in Rossington.
- Goalkeeper John Savage was transferred to Manchester City on 17 November for a then club record fee of £4,000.
- Walter Rickett, Edgar Packard and Albert Cox were involved in a motor accident at Edgerton on 22 December.
- Biggest League win: 3–0 v Workington (h), 5 December.
- Heaviest League defeat: 0–5 v Wrexham (a), 19 December, v Carlisle United (a), 16 April.

Match No.	Date		Venue	Opponents	Result		Scorers	Attendance
1	Aug	19	H	Gateshead	D	0-0		9,696
2		22	H	Wrexham	L	0-2		8,941
3		24	A	Stockport County	D	1-1	Priestley	8,822
4		29	A	Mansfield Town	L	1-3	Frost	6,888
5		31	H	Stockport County	L	0-1		3,211
6	Sep	5	H	Barrow	W	2-0	Moncrieff, Murphy	7,552
7		8	A	Rochdale	W	1-0	Horsman	6,105
8		12	A	Bradford City	L	0-2		14,958
9		14	H	Rochdale	D	1-1	Priestley	6,186
10		19	H	Chesterfield	W	2-1	Horsman, Frost	6,327
11		23	A	Grimsby Town	L	1-2	Horsman	7,552
12		26	A	Tranmere Rovers	L	0-1		6,220
13		28	H	Grimsby Town	W	2-0	Horsman 2 (1 pen)	3,710
14	Oct	3	A	Hartlepools United	L	0-2		8,255
15		10	H	Barnsley	L	1-2	Murphy	9,354
16		17	A	Bradford	L	2-4	Hampson, Horsman	14,261
17		24	H	Port Vale	L	0-1		10,361
18		31	A	Crewe Alexandra	L	1-3	Horsman	6,529
19	Nov	7	H	Chester	D	1-1	Hampson	3,335
20		14	A	Southport	L	0-1		2,551
21		28	A	Scunthorpe United	L	2-3	Priestley, Moncrieff	8,151
22	Dec	5	H	Workington	W	3-0	Murphy, Moncrieff, Rickett (pen)	3,704
23		12	A	Gateshead	L	0-4		4,758
24		19	A	Wrexham	L	0-5		6,265
25		25	H	Accrington Stanley	W	2-0	Moncrieff, Hampson	5,517
26		26	A	Accrington Stanley	L	0-3		8,717
27	Jan	2	H	Mansfield Town	W	2-0	Moncrieff, Geddes	4,965
28		9	H	Darlington	D	0-0		4,535
29		16	A	Barrow	D	1-1	Hampson	3,437
30		23	H	Bradford City	L	0-1		7,969
31		30	A	Darlington	D	1-1	Rickett	2,942
32	Feb	6	A	Chesterfield	W	2-1	Wood 2	6,574
33		20	H	Hartlepools United	W	1-0	Hampson	4,861
34		27	A	Barnsley	W	2-1	Haddington, Hampson	9,123
35	Mar	6	H	Bradford	D	2-2	Suddards (og), Wood	5,308
36		15	A	Port Vale	L	0-2		10,533
37		20	H	Crewe Alexandra	W	1-0	Murphy	5,209
38		27	A	Chester	L	1-3	Clarke	3,207
39	Apr	3	H	Southport	L	1-2	Murphy	3,636
40		10	A	York City	D	1-1	Clarke	3,860
41		16	A	Carlisle United	L	0-5		5,188
42		17	H	Scunthorpe United	L	0-3		4,674
43		19	H	Carlisle United	W	2-0	Shadbolt, Clarke	3,514
44		24	A	Workington	L	1-3	Hampson	6,863
45		27	H	York City	L	2-3	Priestley, Clarke	3792
46		29	H	Tranmere Rovers	D	1-1	Pennington	1,338

Final League Position: 23rd in Division Three (North)

1 own-goal

Apps
Gls

FA Cup

1	Nov	21	H	Rhyl Athletic	D	0-0		10,322
R		26	A	Rhyl Athletic	L	3-4*	Priestley, Murphy, Haddington	7,000

* After extra-time

Apps
Gls

League Table

	P	W	D	L	F	A	Pts
Port Vale	46	26	17	3	74	21	69
Barnsley	46	24	10	12	77	57	58
Scunthorpe United	46	21	15	10	77	56	57
Gateshead	46	21	13	12	74	55	55
Bradford City	46	22	9	15	60	55	53
Chesterfield	46	19	14	13	76	64	52
Mansfield Town	46	20	11	15	88	67	51
Wrexham	46	21	9	16	81	68	51
Bradford Park Avenue	46	18	14	14	77	68	50
Stockport County	46	18	11	17	77	67	47
Southport	46	17	12	17	63	60	46
Barrow	46	16	12	18	72	71	44
Carlisle United	46	14	15	17	83	71	43
Tranmere Rovers	46	18	7	21	59	70	43
Accrington Stanley	46	16	10	20	66	74	42
Crewe Alexandra	46	14	13	19	49	67	41
Grimsby Town	46	16	9	21	51	77	41
Hartlepools United	46	13	14	19	59	65	40
Rochdale	46	15	10	21	59	77	40
Workington	46	13	14	19	59	80	40
Darlington	46	12	14	20	50	71	38
York City	46	12	13	21	64	86	37
Halifax Town	46	12	10	24	44	73	34
Chester	46	11	10	25	48	67	32

1954-55

Division Three (North)

Manager: August–October 1954 Gerald Henry; October–November 1954 Bobby Browne (caretaker); November 1954–May 1955 Willie Watson

Did you know that?

- New Halifax Town player-manager Willie Watson was also a Test cricketer and was voted Wisden Player of the Year for 1954.
- Ian Crawford was known as 'John'.
- Captain was Les Horsman.
- Bill Watkinson's transfer to Halifax Town was temporarily put on hold after he scored a hat-trick for Accrington Stanley in a 4–0 defeat of Oldham Athletic on 8 September. He eventually joined the Shaymen for a record fee nine days later.
- Town's game at Chesterfield on 19 March was interrupted by a heavy snowstorm which necessitated the brushing of the pitch markings once it had subsided.
- Biggest League win: 4–0 v Gateshead (h), 16 October.
- Heaviest League defeat: 0–4 v Southport (a), 19 February, v Gateshead (a), 5 March, v Carlisle United (a), 2 April.
- Ever-present: George Griffiths.

Match No.	Date		Venue	Opponents	Result		Scorers	Attendance
1	Aug	21	A	Scunthorpe United	D	2-2	Priestley, Crawford	10,388
2		25	H	Stockport County	L	1-2	Clarke	8,332
3		28	H	Barnsley	D	1-1	Priestley	10,247
4		30	A	Stockport County	L	1-2	Pennington	9,865
5	Sep	4	A	Bradford City	L	0-2		14,184
6		8	H	Mansfield Town	L	1-2	Horsman	5,899
7		11	H	Oldham Athletic	D	0-0		6,371
8		13	A	Mansfield Town	L	1-2	Griffiths (pen)	9,567
9		18	H	Tranmere Rovers	D	0-0		7,287
10		20	A	Barrow	W	3-1	Watkinson 2, Geddes	3,129
11		25	A	York City	L	1-2	Phillips (og)	6,233
12		29	H	Barrow	L	1-2	Watkinson	4,191
13	Oct	2	H	Southport	L	0-1		6,214
14		9	A	Hartlepools United	L	0-1		7,422
15		16	H	Gateshead	W	4-0	Clarke 2, Priestley, Griffiths (pen)	7,025
16		23	A	Darlington	L	0-1		10,721
17		30	H	Chesterfield	W	2-0	Clarke, Griffiths	6,416
18	Nov	6	A	Crewe Alexandra	D	0-0		3,707
19		13	H	Carlisle United	W	5-3	Dubois, Hampson, Watson, Priestley 2	6,930
20		27	H	Grimsby Town	W	3-2	Clarke, Watkinson 2	8,589
21	Dec	4	A	Bradford	W	1-0	Dubois	10,330
22		11	H	Chester	W	3-1	Darbyshire, Hampson, Priestley	3,712
23		18	A	Scunthorpe United	W	3-1	Clarke, Griffiths (pen), Priestley	11,281
24		25	H	Accrington Stanley	D	1-1	Dubois	13,740
25		27	A	Accrington Stanley	L	1-3	Watkinson	12,390
26	Jan	1	A	Barnsley	L	0-3		13,128
27		29	H	Workington	D	2-2	Bell, Dubois	8,639
28	Feb	5	A	Tranmere Rovers	W	2-1	Clarke, Lamont (og)	4,968
29		12	H	York City	D	3-3	Hampson, Priestley, Clarke	6,202
30		19	A	Southport	L	0-4		2,502
31	Mar	5	A	Gateshead	L	0-4		4,322
32		12	H	Darlington	W	4-1	Dubois, Watkinson 2, Hampson	5,606
33		16	H	Rochdale	L	1-2	Hampson	2,836
34		19	A	Chesterfield	L	1-2	Newton	6,006
35		26	H	Crewe Alexandra	D	3-3	Briggs (og), Watkinson 2	3,530
36		28	H	Hartlepools United	W	1-0	Hampson	3,693
37	Apr	2	A	Carlisle United	L	0-4		4,134
38		8	A	Wrexham	D	1-1	Newton	7,147
39		9	H	Chester	W	3-1	Watkinson 3	6,980
40		11	H	Wrexham	W	2-0	Clarke, Watkinson	6,902
41		16	A	Grimsby Town	W	1-0	Newton	5,916
42		18	H	Bradford City	D	0-0		6,646
43		23	H	Bradford	D	0-0		6,875
44		30	A	Rochdale	D	2-2	Watkinson, Dubois	4,850
45	May	2	H	Oldham Athletic	W	2-1	Crawford, Clarke	4,332
46		4	A	Workington	L	0-1		2,660

Final League Position: 14th in Division Three (North)

3 own-goals

Apps
Gls

FA Cup

| 1 | Nov | 20 | A | Grimsby Town | L | 1-2 | Watkinson | 10,174 |

Apps
Gls

League Table

	P	W	D	L	F	A	Pts
Barnsley	46	30	5	11	86	46	65
Accrington Stanley	46	25	11	10	96	67	61
Scunthorpe United	46	23	12	11	81	53	58
York City	46	24	10	12	92	63	58
Hartlepools United	46	25	5	16	64	49	55
Chesterfield	46	24	6	16	81	70	54
Gateshead	46	20	12	14	65	69	52
Workington	46	18	14	14	68	55	50
Stockport County	46	18	12	16	84	70	48
Oldham Athletic	46	19	10	17	74	68	48
Southport	46	16	16	14	47	44	48
Rochdale	46	17	14	15	69	66	48
Mansfield Town	46	18	9	19	65	71	45
Halifax Town	46	15	13	18	63	67	43
Darlington	46	14	14	18	62	73	42
Bradford	46	15	11	20	56	70	41
Barrow	46	17	6	23	70	89	40
Wrexham	46	13	12	21	65	77	38
Tranmere Rovers	46	13	11	22	55	70	37
Carlisle United	46	15	6	25	78	89	36
Bradford City	46	13	10	23	47	55	36
Crewe Alexandra	46	10	14	22	68	91	34
Grimsby Town	46	13	8	25	47	78	34
Chester	46	12	9	25	44	77	33

1955-56

Division Three (North)

Managers: August 1955–April 1956 Willie Watson; April–May 1956 Bill Burnikell

Did you know that?

- Captain was George Griffiths.
- Striker Alf Clarke played in goal at Mansfield Town on 1 October after Arthur Johnson missed his train at Liverpool and arrived too late.
- Halifax Town deployed the deep-lying forward 'Revie Plan' for the home games with Darlington and Southport, with indifferent results.
- Town followed up their record 6–0 victory over Bradford on 3 December by failing to score in two FA Cup matches with non-League Burton Albion.
- Manager Willie Watson saw his side win for the last time on 14 January at Crewe Alexandra. Though Town won once more at Darlington on 3 March prior to him resigning a month later, Watson was away on a scouting mission and had left coach Bill Burnikell in charge of the team.
- Tommy Capel came up against his brother Fred when Town played at Chesterfield on 17 March.
- Biggest League win: 6–0 v Bradford (h), 3 December.
- Heaviest League defeat: 0–5 v York City (a), 24 December.
- Ever-present: George Griffiths.

Match No.	Date		Venue	Opponents	Result		Scorers	Attendance
1	Aug	20	A	Workington	L	0-2		6,731
2		22	H	Carlisle United	D	2-2	Clarke, Watkinson	7,741
3		27	H	York City	L	2-4	Watkinson, Dubois	8,603
4		30	A	Carlisle United	D	2-2	Clarke, Rodger	10,553
5	Sep	3	A	Derby County	L	1-4	Rodger	18,767
6		7	A	Bradford City	L	0-2		12,547
7		10	H	Crewe Alexandra	W	2-0	Lonsdale 2	5,436
8		12	H	Bradford City	W	3-2	Clarke, Hampson, Watkinson	8,808
9		17	A	Hartlepools United	L	2-3	Lonsdale, Watkinson	7,348
10		21	A	Scunthorpe United	L	0-1		8,834
11		24	H	Stockport County	W	1-0	Watkinson	6,839
12		26	H	Wrexham	D	1-1	Baker	4,111
13	Oct	1	A	Mansfield Town	L	1-3	Griffiths (pen)	5,683
14		8	H	Barrow	W	1-0	Rodger	5,718
15		15	A	Grimsby Town	L	0-4		13,092
16		22	H	Darlington	W	3-0	Baker 2, Watkinson	5,010
17		29	A	Gateshead	D	1-1	Capel	2,569
18	Nov	5	H	Southport	L	0-1		6,618
19		12	A	Tranmere Rovers	L	1-2	Baker	5,541
20		26	A	Rochdale	L	1-2	Lonsdale	4,354
21	Dec	3	H	Bradford	W	6-0	Baker 3, Hampson 2, Watkinson	8,421
22		17	H	Workington	W	2-0	Clarke, Watkinson	5,018
23		24	A	York City	L	0-5		9,623
24		26	H	Oldham Athletic	W	5-1	Lonsdale, Hampson 2, Darbyshire, Dubois	5,276
25		27	A	Oldham Athletic	W	3-1	Griffiths (pen), Clarke, Darbyshire	5,097
26		31	H	Derby County	D	2-2	Darbyshire, Hampson	9,596
27	Jan	7	H	Chesterfield	W	3-0	Dubois, Hampson, Lonsdale	7,939
28		14	A	Crewe Alexandra	W	4-1	Lonsdale, Clarke 2, Hampson	3,633
29		21	A	Hartlepools United	L	0-2		7,361
30		28	A	Accrington Stanley	D	2-2	Hampson, Lonsdale	9,383
31	Feb	4	A	Stockport County	L	1-3	Hampson	5,552
32		11	H	Mansfield Town	D	1-1	Dubois	5,350
33		18	A	Barrow	D	2-2	Lonsdale, Griffiths (pen)	6,221
34	Mar	3	A	Darlington	W	2-1	Watkinson, Darbyshire	4,509
35		10	H	Gateshead	D	3-3	Lonsdale 2, Darbyshire	7,429
36		17	A	Chesterfield	L	0-3		7,364
37		24	H	Tranmere Rovers	L	0-2		4,364
38		30	A	Chester	L	0-1		6,031
39		31	A	Southport	L	0-2		5,499
40	Apr	2	H	Chester	L	0-1		4,445
41		7	H	Rochdale	D	1-1	Griffiths (pen)	3,212
42		14	A	Bradford	D	1-1	Baker	5,775
43		21	H	Accrington Stanley	W	2-0	Darbyshire, Hampson	4,691
44		25	A	Wrexham	W	2-1	Hampson, Clarke	3,977
45		28	H	Scunthorpe United	L	0-3		2,839
46		30	H	Grimsby Town	L	0-1		4,315

Final League Position: 19th in Division Three (North)

Apps
Gls

FA Cup

1	Nov	19	A	Goole Town	W	2-1	Lonsdale, Watson	4,300
2	Dec	12	H	Burton Albion	D	0-0		7,886
R		14	A	Burton Albion	L	0-1		5,217

Apps
Gls

League Table

	P	W	D	L	F	A	Pts
Grimsby Town	46	31	6	9	76	29	68
Derby County	46	28	7	11	110	55	63
Accrington Stanley	46	25	9	12	92	57	59
Hartlepools United	46	26	5	15	81	60	57
Southport	46	23	11	12	66	53	57
Chesterfield	46	25	4	17	94	66	54
Stockport County	46	21	9	16	90	61	51
Bradford City	46	18	13	15	78	64	49
Scunthorpe United	46	20	8	18	75	63	48
Workington	46	19	9	18	75	63	47
York City	46	19	9	18	85	72	47
Rochdale	46	17	13	16	66	84	47
Gateshead	46	17	11	18	77	84	45
Wrexham	46	16	10	20	66	73	42
Darlington	46	16	9	21	60	73	41
Tranmere Rovers	46	16	9	21	59	84	41
Chester	46	13	14	19	52	82	40
Mansfield Town	46	14	11	21	84	81	39
Halifax Town	46	14	11	21	66	76	39
Oldham Athletic	46	10	18	18	76	86	38
Carlisle United	46	15	8	23	71	95	38
Barrow	46	12	9	25	61	83	33
Bradford	46	13	7	26	61	122	33
Crewe Alexandra	46	9	10	27	50	105	28

1956-57

Division Three (North)

Managers: August–December 1956 Bill Burnikell; December 1956–April 1957 Harry Taylor & E. Vivian Booth (caretakers)

Did you know that?

- A famous face in the Hull City side at The Shay on 18 August was ex-Blackpool and England forward Stan Mortenson.
- Andy McCall is the father of future Bradford City, Everton and Rangers Scotland international Stuart McCall.
- Hooliganism reared its ugly head at The Shay as early as 10 September when a spectator through a stone at a linesman over an offside decision during Town's 3–2 victory over Barrow, The police were called.
- After 100 consecutive League appearances for the Shaymen, skipper George Griffiths missed the 6–1 defeat at Scunthorpe United on 15 September.
- Despite being handicapped by an injured ankle, Harry Darbyshire was forced to play at Derby County on 29 September after Bert Ferguson rang to say his train from Sheffield was late. Darbyshire played, Ferguson arrived in a taxi too late, and Town suffered a 6–0 defeat.
- Alex South scored and missed a penalty on his Town debut against Southport on 13 October following his move from Liverpool.
- Halifax Town ended Hartlepools United's record of 14 consecutive home wins with victory at the Victoria Ground on 3 November.
- Having defeated Hartlepools at The Shay on 16 March, Town could claim to have beaten three of the top four teams.
- Biggest League win: 4–0 v Tranmere Rovers (h), 27 April.
- Town's win at Hartlepools United on 3 November brought an end to the Pools' record of 14 consecutive home wins.
- Heaviest League defeat: 0–6 v Derby County (a), 29 September.

Match No.	Date		Venue	Opponents	Result		Scorers	Attendance
1	Aug	18	H	Hull City	W	1-0	Darbyshire	8,402
2		21	A	Oldham Athletic	L	3-4	Smith, Darbyshire 2	13,306
3		25	A	Workington	L	1-3	Hutchinson	8,353
4		27	H	Oldham Athletic	D	1-1	McCall	4,529
5	Sep	1	H	York City	D	0-0		8,192
6		3	A	Barrow	L	0-1		6,178
7		8	H	Rochdale	W	2-1	Darbyshire 2	8,137
8		10	H	Barrow	W	3-2	Smith, Darbyshire 2	5,738
9		15	A	Scunthorpe United	L	1-6	Smith	7,143
10		19	A	Wrexham	L	2-3	Darbyshire, Smith	9,241
11		22	H	Crewe Alexandra	W	1-0	Hutchinson	6,744
12		24	H	Wrexham	L	1-2	Hutchinson	4,633
13		29	A	Derby County	L	0-6		16,340
14	Oct	6	A	Mansfield Town	L	0-2		9,039
15		13	H	Southport	W	3-1	Darbyshire, South, Smith	5,938
16		20	A	Accrington Stanley	L	0-4		8,079
17		27	H	Chester	W	2-1	Shore, Lonsdale	4,982
18	Nov	3	A	Hartlepools United	W	1-0	Hutchinson	10,273
19		10	H	Bradford City	L	0-2		9,703
20		24	H	Carlisle United	L	1-3	Waters (og)	4,515
21	Dec	1	A	Chesterfield	L	1-2	Capel (og)	8,261
22		15	A	Hull City	L	1-3	Darbyshire	9,837
23		22	H	Workington	W	4-2	McCall, Hutchinson, Griffiths (pen), Smith	3,176
24		25	A	Gateshead	L	1-2	Darbyshire	2,653
25		29	A	York City	W	2-1	Hutchinson, Darbyshire	8,102
26	Jan	5	A	Bradford	L	1-2	Darbyshire	6,796
27		12	A	Rochdale	D	1-1	Lonsdale	5,527
28		19	H	Scunthorpe United	W	1-0	Heward (og)	4,496
29		26	H	Bradford	W	3-1	Smith, Darbyshire 2	6,405
30	Feb	2	A	Crewe Alexandra	W	3-1	Smith, Darbyshire 2	4,451
31		9	H	Derby County	W	1-0	Darbyshire	8,535
32		16	H	Mansfield Town	W	2-1	Sharp 2	5,433
33		23	A	Southport	D	1-1	Hutchinson	2,928
34	Mar	2	H	Accrington Stanley	L	0-1		8,149
35		9	A	Chester	D	1-1	Lorenson	5,098
36		16	H	Hartlepools United	W	2-0	Sharp, Lonsdale	5,652
37		23	A	Bradford City	L	0-1		16,047
38		30	H	Stockport County	W	3-2	Kelly, McCall, Darbyshire	7,452
39	Apr	6	A	Carlisle United	D	0-0		5,845
40		13	H	Chesterfield	W	2-1	Smith, Lonsdale	4,752
41		15	H	Gateshead	L	0-1		3,717
42		19	A	Darlington	W	1-0	Darbyshire	5,988
43		20	A	Tranmere Rovers	W	2-0	McCall, Darbyshire	6,641
44		22	H	Darlington	W	3-2	Baker 2, Fowler	5,694
45		27	H	Tranmere Rovers	W	4-0	Lonsdale 2, Smith 2	5,741
46		29	A	Stockport County	D	2-2	Baker 2	6,049

Final League Position: 11th in Division Three (North)

Apps
3 own-goals Gls

FA Cup

1	Nov 17	H	Oldham Athletic	L	2-3	Hutchinson, Smith	9,736

Apps
Gls

League Table

	P	W	D	L	F	A	Pts
Derby County	46	26	11	9	111	53	63
Hartlepools United	46	25	9	12	90	63	59
Accrington Stanley	46	25	8	13	95	64	58
Workington	46	24	10	12	93	63	58
Stockport County	46	23	8	15	91	75	54
Chesterfield	46	22	9	15	96	79	53
York City	46	21	10	15	75	61	52
Hull City	46	21	10	15	84	69	52
Bradford City	46	22	8	16	78	68	52
Barrow	46	21	9	16	76	62	51
Halifax Town	46	21	7	18	65	70	49
Wrexham	46	19	10	17	97	74	48
Rochdale	46	18	12	16	65	65	48
Scunthorpe United	46	15	15	16	71	69	45
Carlisle United	46	16	13	17	76	85	45
Mansfield Town	46	17	10	19	91	90	44
Gateshead	46	17	10	19	72	90	44
Darlington	46	17	8	21	82	95	42
Oldham Athletic	46	12	15	19	66	74	39
Bradford	46	16	3	27	66	93	35
Chester	46	10	13	23	55	84	33
Southport	46	10	12	24	52	94	32
Tranmere Rovers	46	7	13	26	51	91	27
Crewe Alexandra	46	6	9	31	43	110	21

1957-58

Division Three (North)

Managers: August–November 1957 Harry Taylor and E. Vivian Booth (caretakers); November 1957–April 1958 Harry Hooper

Did you know that?

- Captain was George Griffiths.
- The eight goals shared with Workington on 24 August was the highest tally Halifax Town had been involved in on the season's opening day.
- The referee of the previous season's FA Cup Final between Aston Villa and Manchester United, Frank Coultas of Hull, lasted only 12 minutes of Town's home game with Bury on 26 August before pulling a leg muscle.
- Former Town player Andy Geddes died in New Cumnock, Ayrshire, on 11 February aged just 33.
- A scheduled visit of boxer Floyd Patterson to the town on 29 March 1958 was cancelled after Harry Hooper claimed it would affect the attendance for the home game with Bradford.
- One of Halifax Town's most faithful supporters, Walter Smith, who had followed the club since their formation in 1911 until Boxing Day 1957, died on 3 April. Known to all as 'Boaty Walt', he was famous for his shout of 'Now the Town'.
- Phil Roscoe missed Town's game at Mansfield Town on 7 April, because he was getting married.
- By finishing seventh, Halifax Town qualified for the newly created Third Division. It was Town's highest League position since 1937.
- Biggest League win: 5–0 v Carlisle United (h), 22 February.
- Heaviest League defeat: 0–5 v Hartlepools United (a), 9 November.
- Ever-present: Arthur Johnson.

Match No.	Date		Venue	Opponents	Result	Scorers	Attendance
1	Aug	24	A	Workington	D 4-4	Baker, Sharp 2, Griffiths (pen)	7,640
2		26	H	Bury	L 1-2	Sharp	10,190
3		31	H	Bradford City	W 3-2	McQuade, Griffiths (pen), Baker	10,445
4	Sep	2	A	Bury	L 0-1		16,181
5		7	A	Hull City	L 2-5	Griffiths, Neilson (og)	11,593
6		9	H	Gateshead	W 4-1	McCall 2, South, Shore	3,753
7		14	H	Stockport County	D 0-0		7,687
8		16	A	Gateshead	D 0-0		3,169
9		21	H	Oldham Athletic	W 4-0	Fowler, Smith 2, Lonsdale	5,311
10		23	H	Darlington	W 1-0	McQuade	3,746
11		28	A	Rochdale	L 1-5	Smith	5,309
12	Oct	2	A	Darlington	L 0-5		3,735
13		5	H	Crewe Alexandra	W 2-0	Fowler, Smith	4,235
14		12	A	York City	D 1-1	Sharp	6,878
15		19	H	Chester	W 2-1	Sharp, Harrison	5,042
16		26	A	Chesterfield	D 1-1	Lorenson	9,375
17		31	A	Scunthorpe United	D 1-1	Griffiths	9,373
18	Nov	2	H	Tranmere Rovers	D 1-1	Mulholland	6,289
19		9	A	Hartlepools United	L 0-5		6,195
20		23	A	Carlisle United	L 1-2	Shore	8,134
21		30	H	Southport	W 4-1	Smith 2, Griffiths, Sharp	5,757
22	Dec	7	A	Bradford	W 2-0	Blackburn, Smith	8,516
23		14	H	Barrow	W 3-1	Kelly, Smith, Simpson (og)	6,193
24		21	H	Workington	D 2-2	Blackburn, Sharp	6,299
25		26	H	Scunthorpe United	L 0-1		9,942
26		28	A	Bradford City	L 0-3		17,203
27	Jan	4	A	Wrexham	L 1-2	Baker	6,500
28		11	H	Hull City	D 2-2	Smith 2	5,858
29		18	A	Stockport County	L 2-4	Priest, Smith	8,108
30	Feb	1	H	Oldham Athletic	W 4-2	Blackburn 2, Smith 2	7,750
31		15	A	Crewe Alexandra	W 2-1	Smith 2	4,068
32		22	H	Carlisle United	W 5-0	Blackburn, Priest, Smith 2, Sharp	5,059
33	Mar	1	A	Chester	D 1-1	Priest	6,304
34		8	H	Chesterfield	W 3-2	Blackburn, McCall 2	5,586
35		15	A	Tranmere Rovers	L 0-2		12,638
36		22	H	York City	W 2-1	Smith, Blackburn	5,813
37		29	H	Bradford	W 2-0	Blackburn, Hutchinson	6,358
38	Apr	5	H	Accrington Stanley	L 0-2		7,160
39		7	A	Mansfield Town	L 1-2	Priest	8,325
40		8	H	Mansfield Town	W 4-0	Smith (pen), Keery (og), Baker 2	6,116
41		12	H	Southport	W 3-0	McCall, Smith, Hutchinson	2,609
42		14	A	Accrington Stanley	L 1-2	Hutchinson	4,458
43		19	A	Hartlepools United	W 3-0	Blackburn, Smith (pen), Hutchinson	7,368
44		21	H	Wrexham	D 0-0		7,527
45		26	A	Barrow	W 3-0	Baker 2, Sharp	3,586
46		29	H	Rochdale	W 4-1	Lorenson, Blackburn, Smith (pen), Baker	7,419

Final League Position: 7th in Division Three (North)

3 own-goals

Apps
Goals

FA Cup

1	Nov	16	A	Mansfield Town	L 0-2		9,697

Apps

League Table

	P	W	D	L	F	A	Pts
Scunthorpe United	46	29	8	9	88	50	66
Accrington Stanley	46	25	9	12	83	61	59
Bradford City	46	21	15	10	73	49	57
Bury	46	23	10	13	94	62	56
Hull City	46	19	15	12	78	67	53
Mansfield Town	46	22	8	16	100	92	52
Halifax Town	46	20	11	15	83	69	51
Chesterfield	46	18	15	13	71	69	51
Stockport County	46	18	11	17	74	67	47
Rochdale	46	19	8	19	79	67	46
Tranmere Rovers	46	18	10	18	82	76	46
Wrexham	46	17	12	17	61	63	46
York City	46	17	12	17	68	76	46
Gateshead	46	15	15	16	68	76	45
Oldham Athletic	46	14	17	15	72	84	45
Carlisle United	46	19	6	21	80	78	44
Hartlepools United	46	16	12	18	73	76	44
Barrow	46	13	15	18	66	74	41
Workington	46	14	13	19	72	81	41
Darlington	46	17	7	22	78	89	41
Chester	46	13	13	20	73	81	39
Bradford	46	13	11	22	68	95	37
Southport	46	11	6	29	52	88	28
Crewe Alexandra	46	8	7	3	47	93	23

1958-59

Division Three

Manager: Harry Hooper

Did you know that?

- Groundsman Arthur Evans prepared the pitch for the new season with 600lb of seed harmone weed killer.
- Harry Hooper introduced hula-hoops for training, claiming they helped loosen body muscles.
- Captain was Andy McCall.
- Jackie Sharp broke his leg in a pre-season practice match on 14 August.
- Kevin Verity went on to become manager of the Trinidad and Tobago national side between November 1972 and December 1973, then became a coach under England manager Ron Greenwood.
- Unable to prevent Town putting thee goals past him at The Shay on 20 December was future England World Cup-winning goalkeeper Gordon Banks, a member of the Chesterfield side beaten 3-2.
- In March, former Halifax Town amateur Frank Core was appointed Education Officer with the government of Uganda in East Central Africa.
- Pressed into the forward line for the last three games, half-back Peter Tilley scored in each, including a hat-trick in the last match with Colchester United.
- Halifax Town won the West Riding Senior Cup for the first time, defeating Bradford City 1-0 in the final at Valley Parade.
- Biggest League win: 5-1 v Doncaster Rovers (h), 28 March.
- Heaviest League defeat: 0-5 v Southampton (a), 17 September.
- Ever-presents: Stan Lonsdale, Conway Smith.

Match No.	Date		Venue	Opponents	Result		Scorers	Attendance
1	Aug	23	A	Chesterfield	W	3-2	Priest 3	10,685
2		27	A	Bournemouth & Bosc. Ath.	L	0-3		12,217
3		30	H	Notts County	D	1-1	Lorenson	9,789
4	Sep	1	H	Bournemouth & Bosc. Ath.	L	0-1		9,520
5		6	A	Mansfield Town	L	3-4	Smith, Rose, South	9,763
6		8	H	Southampton	W	2-0	Priest, Smith	6,364
7		13	H	Swindon Town	W	1-0	McCall	7,998
8		17	A	Southampton	L	0-5		16,493
9		20	A	Brentford	L	0-2		12,643
10		22	H	Newport County	W	3-1	Smith, Tilley, Lonsdale	4,373
11		27	H	Hull City	L	1-2	Priest	7,730
12	Oct	2	A	Newport County	W	2-0	Verity 2	6,939
13		4	A	Bradford City	W	3-1	Verity, Smith 2	13,577
14		11	A	Southend United	L	2-3	South, Smith	12,307
15		18	H	Bury	W	4-2	Baker 2, South, Verity	8,595
16		25	A	Queen's Park Rangers	L	1-3	South	9,607
17	Nov	1	H	Rochdale	W	2-1	Smith, South	7,129
18		8	A	Doncaster Rovers	W	2-1	Blackburn, Priest	6,796
19		22	A	Reading	L	0-3		12,518
20		29	H	Stockport County	W	4-3	Smith (pen), Verity 2, South	4,127
21	Dec	20	H	Chesterfield	W	3-2	Tilley, Blackburn, Smith (pen)	5,172
22		26	A	Accrington Stanley	L	2-4	Blackburn, Roscoe	9,980
23		27	H	Accrington Stanley	L	0-2		7,285
24	Jan	3	A	Notts County	D	4-4	Blackburn, Kilford (og), Smith 2	8,909
25		17	H	Mansfield Town	D	0-0		3,403
26		24	H	Tranmere Rovers	W	2-1	Smith, McCall	9,665
27		31	A	Swindon Town	W	2-0	Smith, Blackburn	9,568
28	Feb	7	H	Brentford	D	0-0		4,654
29		14	A	Hull City	L	0-4		13,233
30		21	H	Bradford City	D	3-3	Smith, Sharp, Priest	8,581
31		28	H	Southend United	W	1-0	Smith (pen)	7,114
32	Mar	7	A	Bury	L	1-3	Smith	7,278
33		14	H	Queen's Park Rangers	W	2-1	Priest, South	5,586
34		21	A	Rochdale	L	0-1		3,544
35		28	H	Doncaster Rovers	W	5-1	McCall 2, South, Blackburn 2	5,110
36		30	A	Norwich City	L	1-3	Thomas	29,976
37		31	H	Norwich City	D	1-1	Smith	11,938
38	Apr	4	A	Plymouth Argyle	D	1-1	Smith (pen)	19,590
39		11	H	Reading	W	4-1	Smith (pen), Harrison, Fagan, Sharp	5,608
40		15	H	Wrexham	W	4-1	Sharp 2, Thomas, Fagan	4,217
41		18	A	Stockport County	W	1-0	Thomas	7,134
42		20	H	Plymouth Argyle	L	0-1		8,966
43		22	A	Wrexham	D	1-1	Thomas	7,948
44		25	H	Tranmere Rovers	W	3-0	Tilley 2, Smith	4,235
45		27	A	Colchester United	L	1-3	Tilley	5,769
46		30	H	Colchester United	W	4-1	Tilley 3, Smith	5,981

Final League Position: 9th in Division Three

1 own-goal

Apps
Gls

FA Cup

	Date		Venue	Opponents	Result		Scorers	Attendance
1	Nov	15	A	Southport	W	2-0	Tilley, South	6,331
2	Dec	6	H	Darlington	D	1-1	Harrison	11,153
R		10	A	Darlington	L	0-3		7,400

Apps
Gls

League Table

	P	W	D	L	F	A	Pts
Plymouth Argyle	46	23	16	7	83	59	62
Hull City	46	26	9	11	90	55	61
Brentford	46	21	15	10	76	49	57
Norwich City	46	22	13	11	83	62	57
Colchester United	46	21	10	15	71	67	52
Reading	46	21	8	17	73	63	50
Tranmere Rovers	46	21	8	17	82	67	50
Southend United	46	21	8	17	85	80	50
Halifax Town	46	21	8	17	80	77	50
Bury	46	17	14	15	63	58	48
Bradford City	46	18	11	17	84	76	47
Bournemouth & Bosc. Ath.	46	17	12	17	69	69	46
Queen's Park Rangers	46	19	8	19	74	77	46
Southampton	46	17	11	18	83	80	45
Swindon Town	46	16	13	17	59	57	45
Chesterfield	46	17	10	19	67	64	44
Newport County	46	17	9	20	69	68	43
Wrexham	46	14	14	18	63	77	42
Accrington Stanley	46	15	12	19	71	87	42
Mansfield Town	46	14	13	19	73	98	41
Stockport County	46	13	10	23	65	78	36
Doncaster Rovers	46	14	5	27	50	90	33
Notts County	46	8	13	25	55	96	29
Rochdale	46	8	12	26	37	79	28

1959-60

Division Three

Manager: Harry Hooper

Did you know that?

- Captain was Peter Tilley.
- Queen's Park Rangers brought the kick-off time forward on 17 October from 3.15pm to 3.00 so that Halifax Town players and officials could catch a suitable train home.
- George Whitelaw signed for Halifax Town on 27 November but did not appear at The Shay until 9 January due to suspension and postponements.
- Dr. Mackay injected all the players with a new anti-flu vaccine on 4 February.
- Alec Shirley, who appeared for Town during the war, appeared on a TV quiz on 13 February, with his specialist knowledge being boxing.
- Former player Lance Wrigglesworth was given a FA permit to return to local amateur football with Rhodes Street.
- Town set a club record away victory when they won 5–0 at Accrington Stanley on 9 April. The result was also Accrington's heaviest defeat of the season, and Town's first win at Peel Park for 14 seasons.
- Biggest League win: 5–0 v Accrington Stanley (a), 9 April.
- Heaviest League defeat: 0–7 v Port Vale (a) 28 December.

Match No.	Date		Venue	Opponents	Result		Scorers	Attendance
1	Aug	22	H	Southend United	W	2-1	Smith, Blackburn	8,014
2		24	A	Coventry City	W	1-0	Smith	20,007
3		29	A	Mansfield Town	D	1-1	Blackburn	8,947
4		31	H	Coventry City	D	2-2	Fletcher, Smith	9,131
5	Sep	5	A	York City	W	2-1	Tilley, Smith	8,649
6		7	A	Colchester United	L	0-1		8,350
7		12	H	Bury	W	1-0	Smith	10,842
8		14	H	Colchester United	W	3-2	Large 2, Smith	6,254
9		19	A	Barnsley	W	2-1	Tilley, Smith (pen)	13,577
10		22	A	Brentford	D	1-1	Thomas	15,744
11		26	H	Southampton	W	3-1	Smith, Roscoe, McCall	12,550
12		28	H	Brentford	W	1-0	Smith	8,243
13	Oct	3	A	Reading	D	1-1	Dunn	13,254
14		5	H	Shrewsbury Town	L	1-2	Smith	4,864
15		10	H	Bradford City	W	4-0	Blackburn, Flockett (og), Smith 2	14,482
16		17	A	Queen's Park Rangers	L	0-3		13,789
17		24	H	Grimsby Town	L	1-2	Tilley	6,334
18		31	A	Swindon Town	D	1-1	McCall	11,312
19	Nov	7	H	Tranmere Rovers	L	0-3		5,605
20		21	H	Accrington Stanley	L	0-2		5,901
21		28	A	Newport County	L	1-5	Holmes (pen)	7,558
22	Dec	12	A	Wrexham	L	1-2	Large	8,800
23		19	A	Southend United	L	0-3		5,817
24		26	H	Port Vale	D	1-1	Large	6,175
25		28	A	Port Vale	L	0-7		9,664
26	Jan	2	H	Mansfield Town	W	4-2	Holmes 2, Lonsdale, Large	4,773
27		9	A	Norwich City	L	0-1		5,008
28		16	H	York City	L	1-2	Whitelaw	3,812
29		23	A	Bury	D	2-2	Blackburn 2	10,401
30	Feb	6	H	Barnsley	W	5-0	Holmes 2, Large 3	5,157
31		13	A	Southampton	L	2-3	Blackburn, Large	11,515
32		27	H	Bradford City	W	2-1	Large 2	14,954
33	Mar	5	H	Queen's Park Rangers	W	3-1	Fletcher, Tilley, Holmes (pen)	6,731
34		12	A	Grimsby Town	L	2-3	Lonsdale, Large	7,312
35		19	H	Newport County	W	2-1	Whitelaw, Large	4,409
36		28	A	Tranmere Rovers	D	1-1	Holmes	9,436
37	Apr	2	H	Bournemouth & Bosc. Ath.	W	1-0	Large	5,442
38		9	A	Accrington Stanley	W	5-0	Whitelaw, Holmes 3 (1 pen), Large	2,650
39		11	H	Reading	D	2-2	Fletcher, Whitelaw	6,192
40		16	H	Swindon Town	W	3-1	Whitelaw, Large, Fletcher	6,524
41		18	A	Norwich City	L	0-3		33,232
42		23	A	Chesterfield	L	1-2	Large	6,775
43		25	A	Shrewsbury Town	D	2-2	Smith, Fagan	7,514
44		28	H	Chesterfield	L	0-1		5,393
45		30	H	Wrexham	W	2-0	Whitelaw 2	4,540
46	May	4	A	Bournemouth & Bosc. Ath.	L	0-1		6,349

Final League Position: 15th in Division Three

1 own-goal

Apps
Gls

FA Cup

1	Nov	14	A	Gateshead	W	4-3	Smith, Roscoe, Tilley 2	4,570
2	Dec	5	A	Workington	L	0-1		8,577

Apps
Gls

League Table

	P	W	D	L	F	A	Pts
Southampton	46	26	9	11	106	75	61
Norwich City	46	24	11	11	82	54	59
Shrewsbury Town	46	18	16	12	97	75	52
Grimsby Town	46	18	16	12	87	70	52
Coventry City	46	21	10	15	78	63	52
Brentford	46	21	9	16	78	61	51
Bury	46	21	9	16	64	51	51
Queen's Park Rangers	46	18	13	15	73	54	49
Colchester United	46	18	11	17	83	74	47
Bournemouth & Bosc. Ath.	46	17	13	16	72	72	47
Reading	46	18	10	18	84	77	46
Southend United	46	19	8	19	76	74	46
Newport County	46	20	6	20	80	79	46
Port Vale	46	19	8	19	80	79	46
Halifax Town	46	18	10	18	70	72	46
Swindon Town	46	19	8	19	69	78	46
Barnsley	46	15	14	17	65	66	44
Chesterfield	46	18	7	21	71	84	43
Bradford City	46	15	12	19	66	74	42
Tranmere Rovers	46	14	13	19	72	75	41
York City	46	13	12	21	57	73	38
Mansfield Town	46	15	6	25	81	112	36
Wrexham	46	14	8	24	68	101	36
Accrington Stanley	46	11	5	30	57	123	27

1960-61

Division Three
Manager: Harry Hooper

Did you know that?

- Captain was Peter Tilley.
- In July 1960 manager Harry Hooper's New Players Fund was merged with the Halifax Town Social Section to form the Halifax Town Supporters' Club, with L.K. Holloway its first chairman.
- Winger Gerry Priestley was an accomplished clarinet player.
- Striker Rodney Green was a teacher at Guiseley Green.
- There were nasty scenes when Halifax Town held out for a 3–2 win at Port Vale on 20 September after home player Brian Jackson went off on a stretcher. The Town players were pelted with stones and orange peel by irate home supporters, the visitors' dressing room window was smashed and the team bus was escorted from the ground by police.
- Halifax Town played their first-ever match in the League Cup in a second round tie at Nottingham Forest, played on a Thursday afternoon, 6 October. The attendance of 4,445 was Forest's lowest since the war.
- Halifax Town set a club record of scoring in 18 consecutive matches in a season between 12 September and 26 December.
- After defeating Southend United 6–2 on 24 December, Town did not win again for three months, 14 matches later.
- Biggest League win: 5–0 v Tranmere Rovers (h), 10 September.
- Heaviest League defeat: 1–6 v Grimsby Town (a), 22 October.

Match No.	Date		Venue	Opponents	Result		Scorers	Attendance
1	Aug	20	A	Swindon Town	D	1-1	Smith	13,109
2		22	H	Torquay United	W	3-2	Priestley 2, Whitelaw	5,516
3		27	H	Brentford	W	1-0	Whitelaw	6,379
4	Sep	1	A	Torquay United	D	1-1	Blackburn	7,574
5		3	A	Watford	L	3-4	Blackburn, Priestley, Whitelaw	13,853
6		5	A	Chesterfield	L	0-3		5,355
7		10	H	Tranmere Rovers	W	5-0	Blackburn, Holmes, Billington (og), Large, Priestley	5,222
8		12	H	Chesterfield	W	2-1	Whitelaw, Large	6,478
9		17	H	Bradford City	W	3-2	Holmes, Large 2	9,678
10		19	A	Port Vale	W	3-2	Whitelaw, Large, Blackburn	10,251
11		24	A	Shrewsbury Town	D	1-1	Blackburn	7,205
12		26	H	Port Vale	D	3-3	Whitelaw 2, Large	5,967
13	Oct	1	H	Walsall	W	1-0	Whitelaw	7,481
14		4	A	Bury	L	1-4	Whitelaw	13,352
15		8	A	Newport County	D	1-1	Whitelaw	3,698
16		15	H	Colchester United	W	2-1	Lorenson, Large	6,461
17		22	A	Grimsby Town	L	1-6	Large	10,423
18		29	H	Hull City	W	3-0	Large, Priestley, Sinclair (pen)	6,734
19	Nov	12	H	Coventry City	D	2-2	Priestley 2	7,057
20		19	A	Bristol City	L	2-3	Large, Blackburn	10,910
21	Dec	10	H	Bournemouth & Bosc. Ath.	W	2-1	Whitelaw, Tilley	4,623
22		17	H	Swindon Town	D	1-1	Whitelaw	4,512
23		24	H	Southend United	W	6-2	Blackburn 2, Large 2, Whitelaw, Sinclair	6,330
24		26	A	Southend United	D	2-2	Whitelaw, Sinclair (pen)	8,597
25		31	A	Brentford	L	0-2		6,983
26	Jan	14	H	Watford	D	0-0		5,517
27		21	A	Tranmere Rovers	L	2-6	Blackburn, Tilley	6,433
28		28	A	Reading	D	1-1	Whitelaw	5,688
29	Feb	4	A	Bradford City	D	2-2	Large, Priestley	8,142
30		11	H	Shrewsbury Town	D	1-1	Large	3,203
31		18	A	Walsall	D	0-0		12,567
32		25	H	Notts County	L	0-1		4,242
33	Mar	4	A	Colchester United	L	1-3	Blackburn	4,710
34		11	H	Grimsby Town	D	0-0		4,089
35		18	A	Hull City	L	2-4	Large, South	4,997
36		23	A	Notts County	D	1-1	Tilley	8,346
37		25	H	Reading	W	1-0	Large	3,971
38	Apr	1	A	Coventry City	L	0-2		8,756
39		3	A	Barnsley	D	1-1	Holmes	8,995
40		8	H	Bristol City	W	2-1	Holmes 2	4,883
41		10	H	Barnsley	W	1-0	Smith	4,683
42		15	A	Queen's Park Rangers	L	1-5	Allan	9,069
43		17	H	Queen's Park Rangers	D	1-1	Holmes (pen)	4,194
44		22	H	Newport County	W	2-1	Green, Blackburn	3,713
45		24	H	Bury	L	0-2		6,995
46		29	A	Bournemouth & Bosc. Ath.	W	2-1	Large 2	7,394

Final League Position: 9th in Division Three

1 own-goal

Apps
Gls

FA Cup

1	Nov	5	H	Hartlepools United	W	5-1	Priestley, Whitelaw, Large, Sinclair (pen), Blackburn	6,431
2		29	H	Crewe Alexandra	D	2-2	Large, Sinclair	4,556
R	Dec	5	A	Crewe Alexandra	L	0-3		7,125

Apps
Gls

League Cup

2	Oct	6	A	Nottingham Forest	L	0-2		4,445

Apps
Gls

League Table

	P	W	D	L	F	A	Pts
Bury	46	30	8	3	108	45	68
Walsall	46	28	6	12	98	60	62
Queen's Park Rangers	46	25	10	11	93	60	60
Watford	46	20	12	14	85	72	52
Notts County	46	21	9	16	82	77	51
Grimsby Town	46	20	10	16	77	69	50
Port Vale	46	17	15	14	96	79	49
Barnsley	46	21	7	18	83	80	49
Halifax Town	46	16	17	13	7	78	49
Shrewsbury Town	46	15	16	15	83	75	46
Hull City	46	17	12	17	73	73	46
Torquay United	46	14	17	15	75	83	45
Newport County	46	17	11	18	8	90	45
Bristol City	46	17	10	19	70	68	44
Coventry City	46	16	12	13	80	83	44
Swindon Town	46	14	15	17	62	55	43
Brentford	46	13	17	16	56	70	43
Reading	46	14	12	20	72	83	40
Bournemouth & Bosc. Ath.	46	15	10	21	58	76	40
Southend United	46	14	11	21	60	76	39
Tranmere Rovers	46	15	8	23	79	115	38
Bradford City	46	11	14	21	65	87	36
Chesterfield	46	10	12	24	67	87	32
Colchester United	46	10	12	24	65	100	32

1961-62

Division Three

Manager: Harry Hooper

Did you know that?

- Captain was Peter Tilley.
- Halifax Town's 2,000th League goal was scored by Conway Smith, the side's second in the 47th minute of the 6–2 defeat at Queen's Park Rangers on 25 September.
- John Follows, 17, from Blackpool, became Halifax Town's first apprentice in October 1961. Malcolm Russell later signed as an apprentice, with his father offering to pay him 10s a goal.
- Halifax Town's floodlights were switched on for the first time in the 37th minute of the first half of Town's 2–1 victory over Peterborough United on 11 November, to the applause of 5,000 wet and bedraggled supporters.
- Wakefield Trinity hooker Milan Kosanovic tipped off Town officials as to where they could get hold of a Yugoslav flag and anthem for the visit OFK Belgrade on 16 November.
- The attendance of 4,778 was the lowest for the League game at Southend United on 2 December.
- On 12 January, trainer Allan Ure was presented with a cake decorated with two teams, goalposts and a football pitch for his 70th birthday.
- On his last Town appearance, Conway Smith scored the game's only goal against Bradford in the Final of the West Riding Senior Cup. He was also booked.
- Biggest League win: 3–1 v Bournemouth (h), 20 January.
- Heaviest League defeat: 0–6 v Swindon Town (a), 16 April.
- Ever-present: Frank Large.

Match No.	Date	Venue	Opponents	Result		Scorers	Attendance
1	Aug 19	H	Barnsley	W	3-1	Barnett, Large, Priestley	6,114
2	22	A	Brentford	W	2-0	Barnett, Burgess	7,509
3	26	A	Portsmouth	D	1-1	Tilley	16,322
4	28	H	Brentford	W	1-0	Large	7,759
5	Sep 2	H	Crystal Palace	D	1-1	Large	9,583
6	4	A	Coventry City	L	1-3	Priestley	13,158
7	9	A	Bournemouth & Bosc. Ath.	L	1-2	Redfearn	9,672
8	16	H	Watford	W	2-0	Large, Barnett	5,922
9	23	A	Hull City	W	2-1	Priestley, Harrison	13,611
10	25	A	Queen's Park Rangers	L	2-6	Green, WC Smith	11,907
11	30	H	Northampton Town	L	1-3	WC Smith (pen)	5,737
12	Oct 6	A	Reading	L	2-3	Roscoe, Large	11,365
13	11	A	Torquay United	W	3-2	Barnett, Large 2	4,665
14	14	H	Newport County	D	0-0		5,402
15	21	H	Bradford	L	0-2		11,996
16	28	H	Grimsby Town	D	3-3	Priestley, Large, Barnett	5,032
17	Nov 11	H	Peterborough United	W	2-1	K Smith, Giles	5,256
18	18	A	Port Vale	D	1-1	Large	9,374
19	Dec 2	A	Southend United	L	1-2	Redfearn	4,778
20	23	H	Portsmouth	L	0-1		4,378
21	Jan 13	A	Crystal Palace	L	3-4	Hopper, Barnett 2	17,696
22	20	H	Bournemouth & Bosc. Ath.	W	3-1	Barnett, Hopper, Large	4,453
23	27	H	Bristol City	L	3-4	Redfearn 2, Hopper	5,777
24	Feb 3	A	Watford	D	0-0		7,237
25	10	H	Hull City	W	2-1	K Smith, Barnett	4,124
26	17	A	Northampton Town	L	1-3	K Smith	7,900
27	19	H	Torquay United	W	1-0	Hopper	4,274
28	23	H	Reading	W	2-1	Large, K Smith	2,868
29	Mar 5	A	Newport County	W	1-0	Priestley	2,963
30	14	A	Shrewsbury Town	D	0-0		4,702
31	17	A	Grimsby Town	L	0-3		8,191
32	19	H	Swindon Town	W	2-0	Priestley, K Smith	4,255
33	24	H	Shrewsbury Town	L	1-2	Large	4,146
34	27	A	Barnsley	W	2-1	Large, Priestley	5,080
35	31	A	Peterborough United	L	1-5	Hopper	7,738
36	Apr 7	H	Port Vale	D	3-3	Hopper, Large, K Smith	2,938
37	9	A	Notts County	L	1-2	Priestley	3,293
38	14	A	Bristol City	L	3-4	K Smith, Large, Redfearn	6,807
39	16	A	Swindon Town	L	0-6		6,937
40	18	H	Bradford	L	2-3	Barnett, Hopper	4,196
41	21	H	Southend United	L	0-2		1,813
42	23	A	Lincoln City	W	1-0	WC Smith	5,355
43	24	H	Lincoln City	L	0-3		4,160
44	28	A	Notts County	D	0-0		4,822
45	30	H	Coventry City	L	0-2		2,607
46	May 3	H	Queen's Park Rangers	D	1-1	Roscoe (pen)	2,316

Final League Position: 18th in Division Three

FA Cup

							Apps
							Gls
1	Nov 4	A	Rochdale	L	0-2		6,838

League Cup

							Apps
							Gls
1	Sep 11	A	Watford	L	0-3		6,298

Downsborough, P	Stanley, PJ	Roccie, P	Tilley, P	South, AV	Fagan, G	Priestley, G	Barnet, G	Burgess, MR	Large, F	Redburn, B	Hanson, FG	Green, HR	Smith, WC	Knowles, JD	Smith, K	Gillet, TR	Hopper, W	Stradder, CJ	Brier, JD	Worthington, D	Lovell, T
1	2	3	4	5	6	7	8	9	10	11											
1	2	3	4	5	6	7	8	9	10	11											
1	2	3	4	5	6	7	8	9	10	11											
1	2	3	4	5	6	7	8	9	10	11											
1	2	3	4	5	6	7	8	9	10	11											
1	2	3	4	5	6	7	8	9	10	11											
1	2	3	4	5		7	8		10	11	6	9									
1	2	3	4	5		7			10	11	6	9	8								
1	2	3	4	5		7			10	11	6	9	8								
1	2	3	4	5		7			10	11	6	9	8								
1	2	3		5	6	7	8	9	10	11	4										
	2	3		5	6	7	8	9	10	11	4			1							
	2	3		5	6	7	8	9	10	11	4			1							
	2	3		5	6	7	8		10	11	4		9	1							
	2	3		5	6	7	8		10	11	4			1	9						
	2	3		5		7	8	6	10		4			1	9	11					
	2	3		5		7	8	6	10	11	4			1	9						
	2	3		5		7	8	6	10	11	4			1	9						
	2	3		5		7	8		6	11	4			1	10	9					
	2	3		5		7	8		6	11	4			1	10	9					
	2	3		5		7	8		6	11	4			1	10	9					
	2	3		5		7	8		6	11	4			1	10	9					
1	2	3	5			7	8		6	11	4				10	9					
1	2	3	5			7	8		6	11	4				10	9					
1	2	3	5			7	8		6	11	4				10	9					
1	2	3	5			7	8		6	11	4				10	9					
1	2	3	5			7	8		6	11	4				10	9					
1	2	3	5			7	8		6	11	4				10	9					
1	2	3	5			7	8		6	11	4				10	9					
1		3	4	5	2	7			10	11	6	9			8						
1		3	4	5	2	7			10	11	6	9			8						
1		3	4	5	2	7			10	11	6				8	9					
1		3	4	5	2	7			10	11	6				8	9					
1	2		4	5	3	7			10	11	6				8	9					
1	2	3			5		7	4	10	11	6		8			9					
1	2			5	3	7	8	6	9	11	4				10						
1		2	4		3	7	8	5	10	11	6					9					
	2	3	4	5	11		8	6	10				1	9		7					
1	2	3	4	5	11		7	9	10		6				8						
1	2	3	5	6				9	11	4		8			10		7				
1	2	3	5	6				9		4		8			10		7	11			
1	2	3	4	5				6		10		8					9	7	11		
1	2	3	4	5				6				10					9	7	11	8	
1	2	3	8	5	11			9	6		4				10						7
34	41	44	32	37	22	39	32	19	46	39	37	6	9	12	27	1	20	4	3	1	1
	2	1			8	10	1		15	5		1	1	3			7	1	7		

| | 2 | 3 | | 5 | | 7 | 8 | 6 | 10 | 11 | 4 | | | | 1 | 9 | | | | | |
| 1 | 1 | | 1 | | 1 | 1 | 1 | 1 | 1 | | | | | | 1 | 1 | | | | | |

| 1 | 2 | 3 | 4 | 5 | 6 | 7 | 8 | | 10 | 11 | | 9 | | | | | | | | | |
| 1 | 1 | 1 | 1 | 1 | 1 | 1 | 1 | | 1 | 1 | | 1 | | | | | | | | | |

League Table

	P	W	D	L	F	A	Pts
Portsmouth	46	27	11	8	87	47	65
Grimsby Town	46	28	6	12	80	56	62
Bournemouth & Bosc. Ath.	46	21	17	8	69	45	59
Queen's Park Rangers	46	24	11	11	111	73	59
Peterborough United	46	26	6	14	107	82	58
Bristol City	46	23	8	15	94	72	54
Reading	46	22	9	15	77	66	53
Northampton Town	46	20	11	15	85	57	51
Swindon Town	46	17	15	14	78	71	49
Hull City	46	20	8	18	67	54	48
Bradford	46	20	7	19	80	78	47
Port Vale	46	17	11	18	65	58	45
Notts County	46	17	9	20	67	74	43
Coventry City	46	16	11	19	64	71	43
Crystal Palace	46	14	14	18	83	80	42
Southend United	46	13	16	17	57	69	42
Watford	46	14	13	19	63	74	41
Halifax Town	46	15	10	21	62	84	40
Shrewsbury Town	46	13	12	21	73	84	38
Barnsley	46	13	12	21	71	95	38
Torquay United	46	15	6	25	76	100	36
Lincoln City	46	9	17	20	57	87	35
Brentford	46	13	8	25	53	93	34
Newport County	46	7	8	31	46	102	22

1962-63

Division Three

Manager: Don McEvoy (chief coach)

Did you know that?

- Frank Large was sold to Queen's Park Rangers for a club record £7,500 on 27 June 1962.
- Alex South missed Town's friendly with Barnsley on 13 August as he playing in the Parish Cup Final with Warley CC, for whom former Town player Roy Crossley was captain.
- Captain was Alex South.
- Dave Worthington scored Town's first goal in the League Cup in the 64th minute of the 3–2 home defeat by Mansfield Town.
- The game with Peterborough United on 8 October was brought forward to a 7.15pm kick-off to allow a group of supporters from Keighley to leave early and catch a bus back.
- Garbutt Richardson was a member of the Accrington Stanley side which resigned from the League in March 1962.
- Peter Foxley successfully 'Beat The Clock' with his wife on ABC's *Sunday Night At The London Palladium* on 9 December.
- Town's game at Brighton on 3 February was one of only four games played that day. It was covered by the BBC 1 for the *Saturday Sport* programme at 9.55pm..
- The Arctic blast put paid to eight scheduled Town matches, including six at The Shay.
- Town wore a new strip of royal blue shirts, white crew neck and long sleeves with white cuff for the first time in their home match with Colchester United on 15 March.
- Trainer Harry Hubbick had his own camp bed at The Shay.
- Biggest League win: 3–0 v Millwall (h), 21 May.
- Heaviest League defeat: 1–7 v Northampton Town (a), 17 September.

Match No.	Date	Venue	Opponents	Result		Scorers	Attendance
1	Aug 18	A	Crystal Palace	D	0-0		17,598
2	20	A	Queen's Park Rangers	L	0-5		11,143
3	25	H	Wrexham	W	2-0	Priestley, Tait	4,744
4	27	H	Queen's Park Rangers	L	1-4	Tait	7,353
5	31	A	Reading	L	2-4	Holden, Priestley (pen)	6,677
6	Sep 4	A	Barnsley	L	0-1		7,848
7	8	A	Bristol Rovers	L	2-5	Holden, Tait	9,501
8	11	H	Barnsley	W	2-0	Tait 2	3,772
9	15	H	Brighton & Hove Albion	W	2-1	Tait, Worthington	3,897
10	17	A	Northampton Town	L	1-7	Worthington	13,975
11	22	A	Carlisle United	L	0-1		4,895
12	24	H	Northampton Town	L	1-3	Priestley	4,202
13	29	H	Swindon Town	W	4-3	Tait 3, Redfearn	3,354
14	Oct 1	A	Peterborough United	D	1-1	Burgess	10,474
15	6	H	Shrewsbury Town	D	2-2	Tait 2 (1 pen)	4,666
16	8	H	Peterborough United	W	2-0	Tait 2 (1 pen)	4,878
17	13	A	Millwall	D	1-1	Tait	14,400
18	19	H	Southend United	L	0-1		5,953
19	27	A	Colchester United	D	1-1	Priestley	4,576
20	Nov 10	A	Bournemouth & Bosc. Ath.	D	1-1	Tait	8,804
21	17	H	Coventry City	L	2-4	Holden 2	3,956
22	Dec 1	H	Watford	L	1-3	Holden	3,296
23	8	A	Bristol City	D	2-2	Priestley, Tait	6,244
24	15	H	Crystal Palace	D	2-2	Richardson, Tait (pen)	2,055
25	Jan 4	A	Bradford	D	1-1	Redfearn	3,806
26	Feb 2	A	Brighton & Hove Albion	W	1-0	Holden	6,526
27	23	A	Shrewsbury Town	L	2-4	Tait, Worthington	4,320
28	Mar 9	A	Southend United	D	1-1	Worthington	6,858
29	15	H	Colchester United	L	1-2	Tait (pen)	5,269
30	23	A	Notts County	L	0-5		5,076
31	26	H	Carlisle United	L	2-4	McConnell (og), Hopper	2,925
32	30	H	Bournemouth & Bosc. Ath.	W	3-1	Priestley (pen), Carlin, Hopper	1,803
33	Apr 3	H	Port Vale	L	0-4		2,808
34	6	A	Coventry City	L	4-5	Carlin, Tilley, Fidler, Tait (pen)	19,656
35	12	A	Hull City	L	0-2		9,831
36	13	H	Bradford	D	4-4	Harrison, Priestley, Holden 2	4,470
37	15	H	Hull City	L	0-2		3,633
38	20	A	Watford	L	1-2	Harrison	3,688
39	22	A	Port Vale	L	0-2		5,968
40	27	H	Bristol City	L	2-5	Tait, Holden	2,297
41	May 1	A	Wrexham	L	1-3	Redfearn	4,337
42	4	A	Swindon Town	D	1-1	Holden	14,343
43	7	H	Notts County	W	2-1	Redfearn, Roscoe (pen)	1,781
44	11	H	Reading	L	1-2	Holden	1,202
45	18	H	Bristol Rovers	L	2-3	Stanley, Fidler	2,297
46	21	H	Millwall	W	3-0	Tait, Roscoe, Worthington	1,353

Final League Position: 24th in Division Three

1 own-goal

Apps
Gls

FA Cup

1	Nov 3	H	Bradford	W	1-0	Redfearn	12,086
2	24	A	Lincoln City	L	0-1		7,009

Apps
Gls

League Cup

1	Sep 13	H	Mansfield Town	L	2-3	Worthington, Tait	3,871

Apps
Gls

Player appearances grid

Column headers (left to right):
Downsborough, P; Stanley, PJ; Roscoe, P; Burgess, MR; South, AW; Harrison, EG; Priestley, G; Hollett, W; Hopper, W; Tait, BS; Redfearn, B; Carlin, W; Strodder, CJ; Brier, JD; Giles, TR; Worthington, D; Kneivett, JJ; Lovell, T; Tilley, P; Reed, G; Richardson, G; Russell, M; Finlet, DJ

Do	St	Ro	Bu	So	Ha	Pr	Ho	Hp	Ta	Re	Ca	St	Br	Gi	Wo	Kn	Lo	Ti	Rd	Ri	Ru	Fi
1	2	3	4	5	6	7	8	9	10	11												
1	2	3	4	5	6	7	10	9	8	11												
1	2	3	4	5	6	7	9		8	11	10											
1	2	3	4	5	6	7	9		8	11	10											
1	3		6	5	4	7	9		8	11	10	2										
	3	4	5			10	9	7	11	8	2	6										
1	3	4	5		7	9	8		10	2	6	11										
1	2	3	4	5	6	7		10	11	8				9								
1	2	3	4	5	6	7		8	11		10		9									
1		3	4	5	6	7		8	11	10	2		9									
	3	4	5	6		8			10	2		11	9	1	7							
1		3	5	4	11		8		10	2	6		9		7							
	3	4	5	6			8	11	10	2	9		7	1								
	2	3	9	5	6	7	10		8	11				1		4						
	2	3		5	6	7	10		8	9				1	11	4						
	2	3		5	6	7	9		8	11	10			1		4						
	2	3		5	6	7	9		8	11	10			1		4						
	2	3			6	7	9		8	11	10			1		4	5					
	2	3			6	8	10		11				9	1	7	4	5					
	2	3		5	6	7	9		8	11	10			1		4						
	2	3		5	6	7	9		8	11	10			1		4						
1		3	9	5	6	7	11		8		10	2				4						
1	2	3		5	6	7	11		8		10					4	9					
1	2	3		5	6	7	11		8		10					4	9					
1		3		5	4	8	9			11	10		7			6			2			
1		3		5	6	7	9		8	11	10	4							2			
1		3		5	6		9		8	11	10	4	7						2			
		3		5	6		9		8	11	10	4		7	1				2			
		3		5	6			8	11	10		4		9	1				2			
			3	6	7	9		8	11	10	3	4		1					2			
1			5	6	7	11	9	8		10	3					4			2			
1			5	8	7	11	9			10	3	6				4			2			
1			5	8	7	11	9			10	3	6				4			2			
	5	3		9	8			7		10	2	6			1	4					11	
		3		5	9	7			8		10		6		1	4			2	11		
	2	3		5	6	7	8	9		10				1		4				11		
1	2	3		5	6	7	8	9		10						4				11		
1		3		5	6		8	9	7		10					4			2	11		
1		3		5	6		8	9		10	7					4			2	11		
1		3		5	6			9	8		10	7				4			2	11		
1		3	6	4				8	9	10				7		5			2	11		
1		3		5	4		8	9		10			6	7					2	11		
1		3		5	4		8	9		10			6	7					2	11		
1		3		5	4		8	9		10			6	7					2	11		
1	5	3			4	7	10	9			8		6						2	11		
1	5	3		4		7		8		10	2	6		9						11		
30	22	40	15	42	44	31	37	15	34	28	37	16	19	2	16	16	4	23	2	2	18	13
	1	2	1		2	7	11	2	22	4	2			5		1		1			2	

Cup appearances
	2	3		5	6	7	9		8	11	10					1		4				
	2	3		5	6	7	9		8	11	10					1		4				
	2	2		2	2	2	2		2	2	2					2		2				
							1															

1	2	3	4	5	6	7			10	11	8				9							
1	1	1	1	1	1	1			1	1	1				1							
										1					1							

League Table

	P	W	D	L	F	A	Pts
Northampton Town	46	26	10	10	109	60	62
Swindon Town	46	22	14	10	87	56	58
Port Vale	46	23	8	15	72	58	54
Coventry City	46	18	17	11	83	69	53
Bournemouth & Bosc. Ath.	46	18	16	12	63	46	52
Peterborough United	46	20	11	15	93	75	51
Notts County	46	19	13	14	73	74	51
Southend United	46	19	12	15	75	77	50
Wrexham	46	20	9	17	84	83	49
Hull City	46	19	10	17	74	69	48
Crystal Palace	46	17	13	16	68	58	47
Colchester United	46	18	11	17	73	93	47
Queen's Park Rangers	46	17	11	13	85	76	45
Bristol City	46	16	13	17	100	92	45
Shrewsbury Town	46	16	12	13	83	81	44
Millwall	46	15	13	13	82	87	43
Watford	46	17	8	21	82	85	42
Barnsley	46	15	11	20	63	74	41
Bristol Rovers	46	15	11	20	70	88	41
Reading	46	16	8	22	74	78	40
Bradford	46	14	12	20	79	97	40
Brighton & Hove Albion	46	12	12	22	58	84	36
Carlisle United	46	13	9	24	61	89	35
Halifax Town	46	9	12	25	64	106	30

1963-64

Division Four
Manager: Don McEvoy (chief coach)

Did you know that?

- Bound for New Zealand, Paddy Stanley signed for Kettering Town in June 1963 after his sailing date had been delayed.
- When David Jackson signed for the Shaymen, it was the first time he had been separated from his twin brother Peter. They had played together at Wrexham, Bradford City and Tranmere Rovers, and would later be reunited at Frickley Athletic, Altrincham and Hyde United.
- Captain was Willie Carlin.
- Only four supporters made the trip for Town's game at Carlisle United on 7 September.
- Malcolm Russell rushed back from Lilleshall, where he had been attending FA trials, to play in the League Cup tie with Rochdale on 25 September.
- In November, Town gave a trial to Spanish player Jose Roman, who was in the third week of a month's holiday.
- Goalkeeper Mick Granger broke a finger in the FA Cup tie with Workington on 16 November, and having being pressed into the forward line, scored Town's consolation goal in a 4–1 defeat.
- Halifax Town reached the fourth round of the League Cup for the only time, but suffered what was then their biggest-ever home defeat when they crashed 7–1 to Norwich City.
- Oxford United had just reached the quarter-finalists of the FA Cup when they lost 3-1 at The Shay on 21 February.
- Town's 4–2 victory at Workington on 28 February was their first win away from home in 17 attempts.
- Tony Field and partner Barry Walker competed in the national freestyle hairdressing competition in York in March.
- Town set a club record of seven consecutive League victories between 21 February and 21 March.
- Town's 4–1 victory over Hartlepools United on 30 March was a club record 11th consecutive League game without defeat.
- Biggest League win: 5–1 v Torquay United (h), 31 August.
- Heaviest League defeat: 2–5 v Chester (a), 25 January.
- Ever-present: Eric Harrison.

Match No.	Date		Venue	Opponents	Result		Scorers	Attendance
1	Aug	24	A	Barrow	D	0-0		5,269
2		26	H	Darlington	D	2-2	Carlin, Arnell	4,050
3		31	H	Torquay United	W	5-1	Arnell, Carlin 2, Harrison, Bartlett	4,008
4	Sep	7	A	Carlisle United	L	0-3		5,224
5		9	A	Darlington	D	0-0		4,512
6		14	H	Aldershot	D	3-3	Worthington 2, Carlin	3,866
7		16	H	Tranmere Rovers	W	2-0	Bartlett, Worthington	4,513
8		21	A	Bradford City	D	0-0		6,058
9		28	H	Lincoln City	L	0-2		4,470
10		30	A	Tranmere Rovers	D	2-2	Arnell 2	8,414
11	Oct	5	A	Gillingham	L	1-2	Harrison	11,376
12		9	A	Exeter City	D	0-0		7,317
13		12	A	Oxford United	D	2-2	Twist, Carlin	6,437
14		14	H	Exeter City	W	2-0	Jackson, Carlin	3,971
15		19	H	Workington	L	1-3	Harrison	5,423
16		22	A	Southport	L	1-3	Carlin	3,052
17		26	A	Newport County	L	2-4	Bartlett, Arnell	3,182
18		28	H	Southport	W	4-1	Fidler 2, Carlin, Bartlett	3,570
19	Nov	2	H	Stockport County	W	4-2	Harrison, Fidler 2, Taylor	3,972
20		9	A	Bradford	D	4-4	Arnell, Carlin, Worthington, Taylor	8,060
21		23	A	Doncaster Rovers	L	1-3	Twist	5,119
22		30	H	Brighton & Hove Albion	D	2-2	Fidler, Carlin	2,835
23	Dec	14	H	Barrow	W	1-0	Harrison	2,241
24		21	A	Torquay United	L	2-3	Carlin 2	3,648
25		28	A	Rochdale	L	1-4	Twist	3,678
26	Jan	11	H	Carlisle United	L	1-2	Twist	3,389
27		18	A	Aldershot	D	0-0		8,449
28		25	A	Chester	L	2-5	Carlin, Westlake	6,353
29	Feb	1	H	Bradford City	L	0-1		4,783
30		8	A	Lincoln City	L	0-4		5,936
31		15	H	Gillingham	D	0-0		2,080
32		22	H	Oxford United	W	3-1	Fidler, Twist, Westlake	3,117
33		28	A	Workington	W	4-2	Fidler, Westlake, Carlin, Taylor	4,483
34	Mar	4	H	Chesterfield	W	3-2	Carlin 2, Westlake	2,807
35		7	H	Newport County	W	2-0	Carlin, Westlake	2,996
36		11	H	Rochdale	W	3-2	Westlake 2, Taylor	3,911
37		14	A	Stockport County	W	2-1	Taylor, Fidler	1,935
38		21	H	Bradford	W	2-1	Bingley, Westlake	5,135
39		27	A	Hartlepools United	D	1-1	Carlin (pen)	4,841
40		28	A	York City	W	3-1	Carlin 2, Woods (og)	3,546
41		30	H	Hartlepools United	W	4-1	Westlake, Taylor 2, Carlin	4,860
42	Apr	4	H	Doncaster Rovers	L	0-2		5,255
43		11	A	Brighton & Hove Albion	L	0-3		7,088
44		18	H	Chester	W	1-0	Fidler	3,227
45		20	H	York City	W	2-0	Taylor, Field	2,910
46		25	A	Chesterfield	D	2-2	Westlake 2	3,045

Final League Position: 10th in Division Four

1 own-goal

Apps
Gls

FA Cup

| 1 | Nov | 16 | A | Workington | L | 1-4 | Granger | 5,967 |

Apps
Gls

League Cup

1	Sep	4	A	Chesterfield	W	1-0	Fidler	5,622
2		25	H	Rochdale	W	4-2	Carlin 2, Harrison, Fidler	4,744
3	Oct	16	H	Walsall	W	2-0	Taylor 2	4,617
4	Nov	27	H	Norwich City	L	1-7	Bartlett	4,822

Apps
Gls

Players (columns): Downsborough, P | Russell, M | Bingley, W | Bartlett, F | South, AW | Harrison, EG | Tweed, F | Tait, BS | Arnall, AJ | Carlin, W | Fidler, DJ | Roscoe, P | Jackson, D | Taylor, AM | Worthington, D | Richardson, G | Brier, JD | Wilkinson, SJ | Granger, M | Ivers, M | Kelly, J | Westlake, B | Field, A

1	2	3	4	5	6	7	8	9	10	11												
1		2	4	5	6	7	8	9	10	11	3											
1		2	8	5	6	7		9	10	11	3	4										
1		2	8	5	6	7		9		10	3	4	11									
1	2	3	8	5	6	7			10		4	11	9									
1	2		8	5	6	7			10	11	3	4		9								
1	2		8		6	7			10	11	3	4		9	5							
1	2		8		6	7			10	11	3	4		9	5							
1	2				6	7		8	10	3	4	11	9	5								
1	2	3			6	7		9	10	11			8	5								
1	2	3			6	7			10		4	11	8	5								
1	2				6	7		9	10		3	4	11	8	5							
1	2		4		6	7		9	10		3		11	8	5							
1		2	8		6	11			10		3	4	7	9	5							
1	2	3	8		6	7		9	10			4	11		5							
1	2	3	8		6	7			10			4	11	9	5							
1	2		8		4	7		9	10		3		11		5	6						
	2	8		5	4			9	10	11	3		7			6	1					
1		2	8	5	4			9	10	11	3		7			6						
	2			5	6			9	10	11	3	4	7	8			1					
	2	4	5	6	7			10	11	3	9		8		1							
	2	8		4	7			9	10	11	3			5	6			1				
1	2		8		6	7			10	11	3			9	5				4			
1	2				6	7			10	11	3	8		9	5				4			
1	2				6	7			10	11	3	8		9	5				4			
1	2		8	6	4	7			10	11	3			9		5						
1	2		8	6	4	7			10	11	3				5				9			
1	2			6	4	7			10	11	3		8	5					9			
1		2		5	6	7			10	11	3	4		8					9			
1		2		5	6				10	11	3	4		8					9			
1		2		5	6				10	11	3	4	7	8					9			
1		2		5	6	8			10	11	3	4	7						9			
1		2		5	6	8			10	11	3	4	7						9			
1		2		5	6	8			10	11	3	4	7						9			
1		2		5	6	8			10	11	3	4	7						9			
1		2	8		6				10	11	3	4	7						9			
1		2		5	6	8			10	11	3	4	7						9			
1		2		5	6	8			10	11	3	4	7						9			
1		2		5	6	8			10	11	3	4	7						9			
1		2		5	6	8			10	11	3	4	7						9			
1		2		5	6	8			10		3	4	7						9	11		
1		2		5	6	8				11	3	4	7						9	10		
1		2		5	6	8				11	3	4	7						9	10		
1		2		5	6	8				11	3	4	7						9	10		
42	20	32	21	31	46	40	2	14	41	38	40	35	31	20	18	4	2	1	1	3	20	4
	1	4		5	5		6	21	10			1	7	4							11	1

FA Cup / other:

	2			5	6	7		9	10	11	3	4		8			1		1		1	
1			1	1	1	1		1	1	1	1	1		1			1					
																						1

	2	8	5	6	7			9	10	11	3	4										
1	2		8		6	7			10	11	3	4		9	5							
1	2	3	8		6	7		9	10		4	11		5								
	2		8		4	7			9	10	11	3			5	6	1					
3	3	2	4	1	4	4		3	4	3	3	3	1	1	3	1	1					
			1		1				2	2		2										

League Table

	P	W	D	L	F	A	Pts
Gillingham	46	23	14	9	59	30	60
Carlisle United	46	25	10	11	113	58	60
Workington	46	24	11	11	76	52	59
Exeter City	46	20	18	8	62	37	58
Bradford City	46	25	6	15	76	62	56
Torquay United	46	20	11	15	80	54	51
Tranmere Rovers	46	20	11	15	85	73	51
Brighton & Hove Albion	46	19	12	15	71	52	50
Aldershot	46	19	10	17	83	78	48
Halifax Town	46	17	14	15	77	77	48
Lincoln City	46	19	9	18	67	75	47
Chester	46	19	8	19	65	60	46
Bradford	46	18	9	19	75	81	45
Doncaster Rovers	46	15	12	19	70	75	42
Newport County	46	17	8	21	64	73	42
Chesterfield	46	15	12	19	57	71	42
Stockport County	46	15	12	19	50	68	42
Oxford United	46	14	13	19	59	63	41
Darlington	46	14	12	20	66	93	40
Rochdale	46	12	15	19	56	59	39
Southport	46	15	9	22	63	88	39
York City	46	14	7	25	52	66	35
Hartlepools United	46	12	9	25	54	93	33
Barrow	46	6	18	22	51	93	30

1964-65

Division Four
Manager: Willie Watson

Did you know that?

- Willie Watson beat off competition from among other former Town player Bill Holden for the vacant managerial position at The Shay.
- Halifax Town lost 14–6 to Bradford City in the first round of a six-a-side competition at Roundhay Park Gala Sports Club on 4 August.
- Halifax Town conceded five goals in each of their first three away matches.
- John Brier, sent off at Doncaster on 26 September, was suspended by the Football League for 'persistently tackling in a dangerous manner'.
- Prior to pulling off a shock FA Cup replay over the Shaymen, South Liverpool lost 2–0 at home to Netherfield in a Lancashire Combination League match.
- Halifax Town chartered a plane for the first time when they played at Brighton on 26 December. They flew from Leeds-Bradford Airport at 8am, then took a coach from London to Brighton. They returned home on the 8pm flight.
- Elaine Hartley was runner-up to Miss Oldham Athletic in the National Federation of Football Supporters' Clubs Northern Queen Final at the Spa Ballroom, Scarborough on 22 May 1965.
- Biggest League win: 4–0 v Darlington (h), 25 August.
- Heaviest League defeat: 1–5 v Darlington (a), 31 August, v Bradford (a), 5 December.
- Ever-present: Archie Taylor.

Match No.	Date		Venue	Opponents	Result		Scorers	Attendance
1	Aug	22	A	Tranmere Rovers	L	2-5	Fidler, Twist	7,800
2		25	H	Darlington	W	4-0	Twist, Fidler, Westlake, Carlin (pen)	3,971
3		29	H	Wrexham	W	2-1	Westlake, Fidler	4,377
4		31	A	Darlington	L	1-5	Carlin	4,844
5	Sep	5	A	Southport	L	2-5	Frear 2	3,374
6		8	A	Crewe Alexandra	D	2-2	Westlake, Twist	3,436
7		12	H	Bradford	L	2-3	Westlake, Fidler	7,319
8		15	H	Crewe Alexandra	W	2-0	Westlake 2	3,743
9		19	A	Aldershot	L	0-2		4,531
10		26	H	Doncaster Rovers	L	2-4	Frear, Carlin (pen)	4,917
11		30	A	Lincoln City	W	3-2	Westlake, Carlin 2 (1 pen)	6,578
12	Oct	3	A	Chesterfield	L	0-3		6,506
13		6	H	Lincoln City	W	2-1	Drysdale (og), Fidler	2,608
14		10	A	Oxford United	L	0-1		8,172
15		12	A	Newport County	W	2-0	Carlin 2	5,320
16		17	H	Barrow	W	3-2	Carlin, Field, Jackson	3,154
17		19	H	Newport County	W	2-0	Carlin (pen), Westlake	3,355
18		24	A	Hartlepools United	L	0-4		4,525
19		27	H	York City	D	1-1	Field	2,933
20		31	H	Rochdale	L	1-2	Frear	4,089
21	Nov	7	A	Millwall	L	1-5	Howard	7,990
22		21	A	Chester	L	0-1		6,028
23		28	H	Torquay United	L	0-1		1,959
24	Dec	5	A	Bradford	L	1-5	Fidler	6,042
25		12	H	Tranmere Rovers	L	0-1		1,693
26		19	A	Wrexham	D	1-1	Frear	3,526
27		26	A	Brighton & Hove Albion	L	1-2	Frear	19,341
28		28	H	Brighton & Hove Albion	D	1-1	Taylor	3,299
29	Jan	2	H	Southport	W	2-1	Frear (pen), Fidler	2,577
30		23	A	Aldershot	D	3-3	Fidler 2, Wooler	2,398
31		30	H	Bradford City	L	0-3		3,725
32	Feb	6	A	Doncaster Rovers	L	0-4		6,034
33		13	H	Chesterfield	W	2-1	South, Lee	1,738
34		20	H	Oxford United	L	1-3	Wooler	1,887
35		27	A	Barrow	L	0-1		2,841
36	Mar	13	A	Rochdale	L	0-3		4,829
37		16	H	Hartlepools United	W	2-1	Westlake, Twist	1,916
38		20	H	Millwall	L	1-2	Fidler	1,240
39		22	A	Stockport County	L	0-2		6,515
40		27	A	Bradford City	L	1-3	Taylor	3,892
41	Apr	3	H	Chester	L	3-4	Westlake 2, Fidler	1,945
42		10	A	Torquay United	L	0-2		3,245
43		17	H	Stockport County	L	0-1		2,371
44		19	H	Notts County	D	1-1	Twist	1,913
45		20	A	Notts County	L	0-4		4,080
46		24	A	York City	L	0-4		12,719

Final League Position: 23rd in Division Four

1 own-goal

Apps
Gls

FA Cup

1	Nov	14	H	South Liverpool	D	2-2	South, Westlake	3,912
R		18	A	South Liverpool	L	2-4	Frear, Westlake	5,500

Apps
Gls

League Cup

1	Sep	2	H	Darlington	L	1-3	Westlake	2,690

Apps
Gls

League Table

	P	W	D	L	F	A	Pts
Brighton & Hove Albion	46	26	11	3	102	57	63
Millwall	46	23	16	7	78	45	62
York City	46	28	6	12	91	56	62
Oxford United	46	23	15	3	87	44	61
Tranmere Rovers	46	27	6	13	99	56	60
Rochdale	46	22	14	10	74	53	58
Bradford	46	20	17	9	86	62	57
Chester	46	25	6	15	119	81	56
Doncaster Rovers	46	20	11	15	84	72	51
Crewe Alexandra	46	18	13	15	90	81	49
Torquay United	46	21	7	13	70	70	49
Chesterfield	46	20	8	13	58	70	48
Notts County	46	15	14	17	67	73	44
Wrexham	46	17	9	20	84	92	43
Hartlepools United	46	15	13	13	67	85	43
Newport County	46	17	8	21	85	81	42
Darlington	46	18	6	22	84	87	42
Aldershot	46	15	7	24	64	84	37
Bradford City	46	12	8	23	70	88	32
Southport	46	8	16	22	58	89	32
Barrow	46	12	6	23	59	105	30
Lincoln City	46	11	6	23	58	99	28
Halifax Town	46	11	6	23	54	103	28
Stockport County	46	10	7	23	44	87	27

1965-66

Division Four

Manager: August 1965– April 1966 Willie Watson; April–May 1966 Vic Metcalfe (tactical advisor)

Did you know that?

- Halifax Town intended playing only three games on a Saturday, but reviewed this in the new year due to poor attendances.
- Captain was Eric McMillan.
- Keith Bambridge became Halifax Town's first-ever substitute used in a League game when he replaced injured Jeff Lee in the 37th minute of the third match at Stockport County on 27 August.
- Halifax Town did not win until their ninth match on 1 October, the last team in the League to record victory.
- Halifax Town ended a League record of 37 matches without a clean sheet on 1 October 1965 when they defeated Bradford 1–0.
- Charlie Mitten was the son of the former Manchester United and Fulham player.
- Former player Ben Wheelhouse, licensee of the Punch Bowl, Salterhebble, offered to hand over £50 in February if local businesses raised £30,000 in funds for cash-strapped Halifax Town.
- The Mayor of Halifax, Councillor Harry Ludlum launched the 'Save Halifax Town Fund' on 8 March. It realised over £8,000, £100 of which was donated by brewers Tetley.
- Long before the advent of the Goalometer, Mr J. Buckley of Castlefields, Rastrick, offered to pay a shilling for every Town goal.
- The attendance of 1,403 for the visit of Hartlepools United on 15 April was the lowest in the entire Football League that season.
- Archie Taylor ended a run of 121 first-team appearances when he missed the game at Rochdale on 19 April.
- Jim Smith went on to become manager of eight League clubs and was affectionately nicknamed 'Bald Eagle'.
- Willie Watson was set to take charge of Halifax Town for the last time for a game against Luton Town on 1 April, only for the match to be postponed due to snow.
- Biggest League win: 4–0 v Wrexham (h), 10 December.
- Heaviest League defeat: 2–5 v Tranmere Rovers (a), 28 January.

Match No.	Date		Venue	Opponents	Result		Scorers	Attendance
1	Aug	21	H	Tranmere Rovers	D	2-2	Atkins 2	2,888
2		23	A	Colchester United	L	0-1		4,473
3		27	A	Stockport County	L	0-3		9,889
4	Sep	3	H	Darlington	D	2-2	Wooler, Bambridge	2,017
5		11	A	Lincoln City	D	3-3	Fidler, Wooler, Smith	4,454
6		14	H	Colchester United	D	1-1	Smith	2,903
7		18	H	Notts County	L	0-1		2,523
8		25	A	Chester	L	0-1		6,907
9	Oct	1	H	Bradford	W	1-0	Westlake	3,960
10		5	H	Bradford City	W	3-2	McMillan, Fidler, Atkins	3,676
11		9	A	Newport County	L	1-3	Fidler (pen)	3,195
12		16	H	Torquay United	L	0-2		2,627
13		23	A	Chesterfield	L	2-3	Atkins, Balmer	8,695
14		29	H	Rochdale	W	4-1	Smith, McMillan, Fidler 2	2,786
15	Nov	6	A	Luton Town	L	1-4	Balmer	7,879
16		20	A	Hartlepools United	W	2-1	Fidler, Atkins	4,282
17	Dec	10	H	Wrexham	W	4-0	Atkins 2, Balmer, Fidler (pen)	1,884
18		27	A	Barnsley	W	2-1	Atkins, Fidler (pen)	8,834
19		28	H	Barnsley	D	2-2	Balmer, Fidler	5,410
20		31	H	Newport County	D	4-4	Balmer, Atkins 2, Westlake	2,570
21	Jan	8	A	Barrow	L	0-3		4,922
22		22	H	Barrow	W	2-1	McMillan, Atkins	1,554
23		28	A	Tranmere Rovers	L	2-5	Taylor 2	5,949
24	Feb	5	H	Stockport County	L	0-1		2,870
25		12	H	Chesterfield	W	4-1	Fidler 2, Atkins, McCarthy	1,554
26		23	A	Crewe Alexandra	L	0-3		2,990
27		26	H	Lincoln City	D	2-2	Atkins 2	2,984
28	Mar	5	H	Crewe Alexandra	W	1-0	Balmer	2,886
29		8	A	Doncaster Rovers	L	2-3	Clarke, Atkins	6,849
30		12	A	Notts County	D	1-1	Balmer	3,961
31		16	A	Bradford City	W	1-0	McMillan	4,993
32		18	H	Chester	W	2-0	Balmer, Butler (og)	5,117
33		26	A	Bradford	L	1-2	Taylor	4,598
34		28	A	Darlington	L	0-2		7,614
35	Apr	8	A	Aldershot	D	0-0		3,974
36		9	A	Southport	L	0-1		3,376
37		12	H	Aldershot	L	3-4	Westlake, McMillan, Atkins	2,998
38		15	H	Hartlepools United	W	1-0	Atkins	1,533
39		19	A	Rochdale	W	1-0	Balmer	2,186
40		22	A	Doncaster Rovers	D	2-2	Smith, Atkins	16,999
41		27	A	Port Vale	L	0-2		4,824
42		29	H	Southport	L	1-2	McMillan	3,497
43	May	2	A	Torquay United	L	0-1		7,623
44		7	A	Wrexham	D	2-2	Atkins, McMillan	3,431
45		10	H	Port Vale	W	2-0	Fidler 2 (1 pen)	2,494
46		16	H	Luton Town	W	3-0	Westlake, McMillan, Lee	3,002

Final League Position: 15th in Division Four

Apps
Sub Apps
1 own-goal Gls

FA Cup

1	Nov 13	A	Southport	L	0-2		4,694

Apps
Sub Apps
Gls

League Cup

1	Sep 1	A	Bradford	L	0-1		3,423

Apps
Sub Apps
Gls

League Table

	P	W	D	L	F	A	Pts
Doncaster Rovers	46	24	11	11	85	54	59
Darlington	46	25	9	12	72	53	59
Torquay United	46	24	10	12	72	49	58
Colchester United	46	23	10	13	70	47	56
Tranmere Rovers	46	24	8	14	93	66	56
Luton Town	46	24	8	14	90	70	56
Chester	46	20	12	14	79	70	52
Notts County	46	19	12	15	61	53	50
Newport County	46	18	12	16	75	75	48
Southport	46	18	12	16	68	69	48
Bradford	46	21	5	20	102	92	47
Barrow	46	16	15	15	72	76	47
Stockport County	46	18	6	22	71	70	42
Crewe Alexandra	46	16	9	21	61	63	41
Halifax Town	46	15	11	20	67	75	41
Barnsley	46	15	10	21	74	78	40
Aldershot	46	15	10	21	75	84	40
Hartlepools United	46	16	8	22	63	75	40
Port Vale	46	15	9	22	48	59	39
Chesterfield	46	13	13	20	62	78	39
Rochdale	46	16	5	25	71	87	37
Lincoln City	46	13	11	22	57	82	37
Bradford City	46	12	13	2	63	94	37
Wrexham	46	13	9	24	72	104	35

1966-67

Division Four
Managers: Vic Metcalfe

Did you know that?

- Captain was Malcolm Russell.
- Halifax Town's 2–2 draw with Aldershot on 27 August was one of eight predicted correctly by Percy Harrison of Gainsborough when he scooped £338,356 on the pools.
- Waiting to sign Chester's Bryn Jones at Wakefield railway station, manager Vic Metcalfe and chairman Alan Maden were informed he was not coming following an announcement made over the tannoy system!
- On 6 November the Halifax Town players and officials went to the Odeon cinema to watch Goal!, the official FIFA film of the 1966 World Cup.
- Halifax Town finished runners-up to Wigan Athletic in the Northern Floodlit League.
- Town's 7–0 win over Bishop Auckland in the second round of the FA Cup was a record victory at The Shay.
- The directors invited 19 fans to fly on a chartered plane for the match at Newport County scheduled for 18 November, but abandoned the idea when only eight took up the offer. Town travelled by coach only for the game to be postponed.
- In February, fans donated £100 to help by the club a short-wave radiant heat machine.
- Town's Bill Atkins and Stockport's Dave Shawcross were involved in a player-exchange deal on 17 March, then found themselves on opposite sides with their new clubs the very next day.
- Biggest League win: 5–2 v Notts County (h), 12 November.
- Heaviest League defeat: 0–4 v Wrexham (a), 3 September.
- Ever-present: Malcolm Russell.

Match No.	Date		Venue	Opponents	Result		Scorers	Attendance
1	Aug	20	A	Luton Town	L	0-2		6,149
2		27	H	Aldershot	D	2-2	Atkins 2	2,052
3	Sep	3	A	Wrexham	L	0-4		5,251
4		5	A	York City	L	3-4	Westlake, Atkins 2	4,206
5		9	H	Southend United	D	2-2	Atkins, May (og)	2,835
6		16	A	Tranmere Rovers	L	0-1		5,907
7		23	H	Bradford City	D	2-2	Atkins, Fidler	5,046
8		27	H	York City	W	2-1	Atkins, Taylor	2,869
9	Oct	1	A	Exeter City	L	2-3	Atkins, Fidler (pen)	4,559
10		7	A	Lincoln City	D	3-3	Parks, Atkins, Fidler	3,956
11		15	H	Chesterfield	W	1-0	Atkins	2,264
12		18	A	Brentford	L	0-1		6,093
13		21	A	Stockport County	L	1-2	Smith	11,100
14		29	H	Rochdale	D	1-1	Parks	2,771
15	Nov	5	A	Southport	L	0-2		4,474
16		12	H	Notts County	W	5-2	Hutchinson 2 (1 pen), Atkins, Parks 2	2,461
17		15	H	Brentford	W	3-2	Atkins, Hutchinson, J Lee	2,671
18		19	A	Chester	W	2-0	Hutchinson, Atkins	5,265
19	Dec	3	A	Port Vale	W	1-0	Atkins	4,002
20		10	H	Crewe Alexandra	W	1-0	Atkins	4,716
21		17	H	Luton Town	D	1-1	Parks	3,622
22		26	H	Barrow	L	1-4	Hutchinson	8,082
23		31	A	Aldershot	W	1-0	Parks	4,640
24	Jan	2	A	Barrow	L	0-1		8,262
25		14	A	Southend United	L	0-1		6,905
26		21	H	Tranmere Rovers	W	2-1	Hutchinson 2	5,999
27	Feb	4	A	Bradford City	W	2-1	Hutchinson 2	8,143
28		11	H	Exeter City	D	0-0		6,351
29		25	H	Lincoln City	D	0-0		4,531
30	Mar	4	A	Chesterfield	D	1-1	Hutchinson	5,909
31		11	H	Newport County	D	2-2	Parks, Hutchinson	3,625
32		18	H	Stockport County	L	0-1		6,335
33		25	A	Bradford	L	0-1		5,623
34		27	A	Barnsley	L	1-4	Hutchinson	5,354
35		28	H	Barnsley	D	1-1	Hutchinson	4,348
36	Apr	1	H	Southport	W	2-0	Parks 2	3,590
37		8	A	Notts County	L	1-2	Wooler	3,024
38		11	H	Hartlepools United	W	2-1	McCarthy, Hutchinson	3,252
39		15	H	Chester	W	2-1	Shawcross 2	3,506
40		22	H	Rochdale	L	0-3		2,416
41		24	A	Hartlepools United	W	3-1	Parks 3	3,479
42		29	H	Port Vale	D	2-2	Wallace, Holmes	3,562
43	May	1	A	Newport County	L	0-3		1,620
44		6	A	Crewe Alexandra	D	1-1	Wallace	4,146
45		13	H	Bradford	D	0-0		2,829
46		16	H	Wrexham	W	3-1	Wooler, McCarthy 2 (1 pen)	2,050

Final League Position: 12th in Division Four

Apps
Sub Apps
1 own-goal Gls

FA Cup

1	Nov	26	H	Doncaster Rovers	D	2-2	Hutchinson 2	8,336
R		29	A	Doncaster Rovers	W	3-1*	Parks, McCarthy, Atkins	9,191
2	Jan	7	A	Bishop Auckland	D	0-0		4,234
R		10	H	Bishop Auckland	W	7-0	Hutchinson 2, Atkins, Taylor 2, Parks 2	14,297
3		28	H	Bristol City	D	1-1	Parks	15,591
R		31	A	Bristol City	L	1-4	Hutchinson	23,188

* After extra-time

Apps
Sub Apps
Gls

League Cup

1	Aug	23	H	Darlington	D	0-0		2,963
R		29	A	Darlington	L	0-4		5,321

Apps
Sub Apps
Gls

White, M	Russell, M	Clarke, M	Smith, JM	Pickering, J	Holt, R	Cliff, JG	Lee, R	Wooler, MG	Atkins, WM	Taylor, AM	Raynor, R	Westlake, B	Lee, JW	Balmer, JM	McCarthy, P	McMahon, E	Fidler, DJ	Park, >A	Bodell, N	Holmes, B	Hutchinson, JB	Snowcross, FD	Wallace, RA	Birth, JW
1	2	3	4	5	6	7	8	9	10	11														
	2	3	4	5			8	10		1	6	7	9	11										
1	2	3	4	5				10	8		6		9			7	11							
1	2		4	5	3		6	10	7		9					8	11							
1	2		4	5	3		6	10	7		9					8	11							
1	2		4	5	3		6	10	7		9					8	11							
1	2			5	3		6	10	7		4			8	11	9								
1	2		4	5	3			10	8		6					7	11	9						
1	2		4	5	3		12	10	8		6					7	11*	9						
1	2	3	4	5				10	8		6					7	11	9						
1	2		4		5			10	8		6			11	7			9	3					
1	2		4		5			10	8		6			11	7			9	3					
1	2*	12	4		5			10	8		6			11	7			9	3					
1	2		4		5			10	8		6			11				9	3	7				
1	2		4		5			10	8		6			11				9	3	7				
1	2		4		5			10	7		6			11				9	3		8			
1	2		4		5			10	7		6			11				9	3		8			
1	2	3	4		5			10	7		6			11				9			8			
1	2		4		5			10	7		6			11				9	3		8			
1	2		4		5			10	7		6			11				9	3		8			
1	2		4		5			10	7		6							9	3	11	8			
1	2		4		5			10	7		6			11				9	3		8			
1	2	3	4		5			10	7		6			11				9			8			
1	2	3	4		5			10	7		6			11				9			8			
1	2		4		5			10	7		6			11				9	3		8			
1	2		4		5			10	7		6			11				9	3		8			
1	2		4		5			10	7		6			11				9	3		8			
1	2		4		5			10	7		6			11				9	3		8			
1	2		4		5			10	7		6			11				9	3		8			
1	2		4		5		9	10	7		6			11					3		8			
1	2		4		5			10	7		6			11				9	3		8			
1	2		4		5				7		6			11				9	3		8*	10	12	
1	2		4		5						6			11				9	3		8	10	7	
1	2		4		5		9		7		6								3		8	10	7	
1	2		4		5	6								11				9	3		8	10	7	
1	2		4		5	6								11				9	3		8	10	7	
1	2		4		5	6	12							11				9*	3		8	10	7	
1	2		4		5	6	9		7					11					3		8	10		
1	2		4		5	6	9		7					11					3		8	10		
1	2		4		5			8						11				9	3	7		6	10	
1	2		4		5			8						11				9	3	7		6	10	
1	2		4	12	5			8						11				9*	3	7		6	10	
1	2		4	6	5				9	11									3	7		10	8	
1	2		4	3	5			9		7				11							6	8	10	
1	2		4	3	5			9		7					6							10	8	
45	46	7	45	13	43	1	11	13	31	38	1	5	30	2	35	11	8	32	31	7	25	15	10	1
				1		1		2													1			
		1						2	15	1		1	1		3		3	12		1	14	2	2	

1	2		4		5			10	7		6			11				9	3		8			
1	2		4		5			10	7		6			11				9	3		8			
1	2		4		5			10	7		6			11				9	3		8			
1	2		4		5			10	7		6			11				9	3		8			
1	2		4		5			10	7		6			11				9	3		8			
1	2		4		5			10	7		6			11				9	3		8			
6	6		6		6			6	6		6			6				6	6		6			
								2	2					1			4				5			

1	2	3	4	5				9	10	8		6	7					11						
	2	3	4	5					10	8	1	6	7	9				11						
1	2	2	2	2				1	2	2	1	2	2	1				2						

League Table

	P	W	D	L	F	A	Pts
Stockport County	46	26	12	8	69	42	64
Southport	46	23	13	10	69	42	59
Barrow	46	24	11	11	76	54	59
Tranmere Rovers	46	22	14	10	66	43	58
Crewe Alexandra	46	21	12	13	70	55	54
Southend United	46	22	9	15	70	49	53
Wrexham	46	16	20	10	76	62	52
Hartlepools United	46	22	7	17	66	64	51
Brentford	46	18	13	15	58	56	49
Aldershot	46	18	12	16	72	57	48
Bradford City	46	19	10	17	74	62	48
Halifax Town	46	15	14	17	59	68	44
Port Vale	46	14	15	17	55	58	43
Exeter City	46	14	15	17	50	60	43
Chesterfield	46	17	8	21	60	63	42
Barnsley	46	13	15	18	60	64	41
Luton Town	46	16	9	21	59	73	41
Newport County	46	12	16	13	56	63	40
Chester	46	15	10	21	54	78	40
Notts County	46	13	11	22	53	72	37
Rochdale	46	13	11	22	53	75	37
York City	46	12	11	23	65	79	35
Bradford	46	11	13	22	52	79	35
Lincoln City	46	9	13	24	58	82	31

1967-68

Division Four

Managers: August–November 1967 Vic Metcalfe; November 1967–May 1968 Alan Ball Snr

Did you know that?

- Town gave out free season tickets to the over 90s, though Mark Turner also got one despite only being 89!
- Captain was Norman Bodell, then Hugh Ryden.
- Halifax Town and 18 supporters took a chartered plane from Leeds-Bradford airport for the match at Swansea Town on 28 October.
- After negotiations spanning 30 hours, Hugh Ryden signed for Town from Chester on 3 November for a club record £5,000.
- Halifax Town needed a good run in the FA Cup to pay off a £540 fine incurred by Shay Club licensee Alec Walton for selling drinks to non-members.
- Town introduced new minimum admission fee of 5s, up from 4s, at the home game with Aldershot on 23 December.
- The crowd limit for the Birmingham City FA Cup tie on 27 January was set at 28,000. 76 police officers were on duty.
- On 5 March, manager Alan Ball refereed a match between Halifax Town staff and a Showbiz team. The match ended 4-4.
- New signing Mark Pearson, ex-Manchester United and Fulham, made his debut for Town in the abandoned match with Swansea Town on 23 March. Due to injury and illness, he would not start another game for the club until the following March.
- Halifax Town lost 5–2 to Lincoln City in the final of the Daily Express 5-a-side soccer championships at Mecca Rolarena, Kirkstall Road, Leeds.
- Les Massie became the first Town player to top the divisional goalscoring lists, sharing the honour with Port Vale's Roy Chapman with 25 goals apiece.
- Biggest League win: 4–1 v Newport County (h), 2 March.
- Heaviest League defeat: 1–5 v Crewe Alexandra (a), 30 September.
- Ever-present: John Pickering.

Match No.	Date		Venue	Opponents	Result		Scorers	Attendance
1	Aug	19	H	Darlington	W	2-0	Wooler, Flower	4,382
2		26	A	Aldershot	D	1-1	Massie	4,065
3	Sep	2	H	Workington	W	2-1	Shawcross (pen), Massie	4,384
4		4	H	Exeter City	D	1-1	Massie	5,009
5		9	A	Lincoln City	L	0-1		6,200
6		16	A	Brentford	D	0-0		6,892
7		23	H	Bradford City	W	1-0	Taylor	6,697
8		27	A	Exeter City	D	0-0		3,958
9		30	A	Crewe Alexandra	L	1-5	Parks	6,006
10	Oct	7	H	York City	W	2-1	Massie, Shawcross (pen)	4,480
11		14	A	Newport County	W	1-0	Flower	2,658
12		21	H	Hartlepools United	W	3-0	Parks, Taylor, Shawcross (pen)	4,865
13		25	A	Chester	L	2-3	Massie, Taylor	3,419
14		28	A	Swansea Town	L	1-2	Massie	6,285
15		31	H	Chester	D	2-2	Butler (og), Smith	4,105
16	Nov	4	H	Barnsley	D	1-1	Massie	6,762
17		11	A	Wrexham	L	0-2		7,691
18		15	A	Workington	D	1-1	Massie	1,756
19		18	H	Southend United	L	1-2	Smith	4,884
20		25	A	Luton Town	L	0-2		11,572
21	Dec	2	H	Doncaster Rovers	L	2-3	Massie 2	4,359
22		16	A	Darlington	D	0-0		3,546
23		23	H	Aldershot	D	2-2	Flower, Massie	3,761
24		26	A	Port Vale	L	1-2	Flower	6,946
25		30	H	Port Vale	L	0-1		3,956
26	Jan	13	H	Lincoln City	W	1-0	Shawcross	5,028
27		20	H	Brentford	W	3-0	Massie 2, Ryden	4,610
28	Feb	3	A	Bradford City	W	1-0	Massie	9,498
29		17	H	Notts County	W	3-1	Needham (og), Flower, Ryden	5,880
30		24	A	Southend United	D	2-2	Massie, Flower	6,973
31	Mar	2	H	Newport County	W	4-1	Massie 3, Hampton	4,336
32		5	A	Crewe Alexandra	L	0-1		5,889
33		9	H	Rochdale	W	2-0	Massie, McCarthy	4,933
34		15	A	Hartlepools United	D	0-0		5,158
35		30	A	Barnsley	D	0-0		11,586
36	Apr	2	H	Swansea Town	D	2-2	Massie 2	2,534
37		6	H	Wrexham	D	2-2	Massie, Shawcross	4,088
38		13	A	York City	W	2-1	Massie 2	5,837
39		15	H	Chesterfield	L	0-2		4,749
40		16	A	Chesterfield	D	0-0		7,746
41		20	H	Luton Town	L	0-1		5,091
42		22	A	Bradford	W	1-0	Morris	3,224
43		26	A	Doncaster Rovers	D	0-0		7,917
44		29	A	Rochdale	L	1-2	Morris	1,928
45	May	4	H	Bradford	W	1-0	Massie	2,827
46		10	H	Notts County	L	0-1		1,802

Final League Position: 11th in Division Four

	Apps
	Sub Apps
2 own-goals	Gls

FA Cup

1	Dec	13	H	Crewe Alexandra	W	3-2	Ryden 2, Wallace	6,816
2	Jan	6	H	Scunthorpe United	W	1-0	Russell	7,804
3		27	H	Birmingham City	L	2-4	Ryden, Holt	18,117

	Apps
	Sub Apps
	Gls

League Cup

1	Aug	23	H	Bradford	W	5-0	Massie 2, Wooler, Shawcross (pen) Taylor	4,810
R	Sep	13	A	Sunderland	L	2-3	Massie, Flower	13,322

	Apps
	Sub Apps
	Gls

	White, M	Russell, M	Pickering, J	Smith, JM	Holt, R	Showcross, FD	Taylor, AM	Massie, L	Wooler, MG	Wallace, RA	Flower, AJ	Hampen, IK	Farks, JA	Lee, JW	McCarthy, P	Ryden, HJ	Bonell, N	Lee, R	Sneddon, JD	Smith, A	Morris, E	Blyth, JW	Holmes, B	Cullen, PJ
	1	2	3	4	5	6	7	8	9	10	11													
	1		3	4	5	6	7	8	9	10	11	2												
	1	2	3	4	5	6	7	8	9*	10	11	12												
	1	2	3	4	5	6	7	8		10	11		9											
	1	2	3	4	5	6	7*	8		9	12		10	11										
	1	2	3	4	5	6	7	8	9		11		10											
	1	2	3	4	5	6	7	8			11		10											
	1	2	3	4	5	6	7		9		11	8	10											
	1	2	3	4	5	6	7		9		11	8	10											
	1	2	3	4	5	6	7	8	12		11		9*	10										
	1	2	3	4	5	6	11	8	12		7		9*	10										
	1	2	3	4	5	6	11	8			7		9	10										
	1	2	3	4	5	6	11	8			7		9	10										
	1	2	3	4	5	6	11	8	9		7			10										
	1	2	3	4	5	6	11	8	9		7			10										
	1	2	3	4	5	6	11*	8		12	7			10	9									
	1		3	4	5			8		10	7			11	9	2	6							
	1	2	3	4	5			8	9		12	7		6*	11	10								
	1	2	3	4	5*	6	8	9		12	7			11	10									
	1	3	12	4			7	8			11	2	9*		6	10		5						
	1	3		6	4	5			10	7	9		2		11	8								
	1	3		6	4			8		10	7	2			11	9		5						
	1	3		6	4			8		10	7	2			11	9		5						
	1		3		6	4		8		10	7	2			11	9		5						
	1		3	12	4		6	8		10	7	2			11	9*		5						
		2	5		4	6		8		10	7	3			11	9			1					
		2	5		4	6		8		10	7	3			11	9			1					
		2	4		5	6		8		10	7	3			11	9			1					
		3	4		5	6		8		10	7	2			11	9			1					
		3	4		5	6		8		10	7	2			11	9			1					
		2	4		5	6		8		10	7	3			11	9			1					
		2	4		5	6		8		10	7	3			11	9			1					
		2	4		5	6		8		10	7	3			11	9			1					
		2	4		5	6		8		10	7	3			11	9			1					
		2	4		5	6		8		10	7	3			11	9			1					
		2	4		5	6		8		10	7	3			11	9			1					
		2	4		5	6		8		10	7	3			11	9			1					
		2	4		5	6		8		10	7	3			11	9			1					
		2	4		5			8	12	10	7				11	6*	3		1	9				
		2	4		5			8		6	7	3			11	10			1	9				
		2	4		5			8	12	6	7	3			11	10*			1	9				
		2	4		5			8		10	7				11	9	3		1		6			
	2*	4			5			8	9	10	7		12			3			1	11	6			
	12	6			5			8		10	7			2		9*	3		1	11	4			
			4		5			8		10			9*			2	3		1	11	6	7	12	
	25	40	45	23	43	33	19	44	11	31	44	23	8	4	39	29	5	3	5	21	6	4	1	
		1	1	1			4	3			2		1									1		
			2		5	3	25	1		6	1	2		1	2				2					

	1	3	6	4			8		10	7	2			11	9		5							
	1	2	5			6		8		10	7	3			11	9		4						
		2	5	12	4	6*		8		10	7	3			11	9			1					
	2	3	3	1	1	2		3		3	3	3			3	3		2	1					
				1																				
		1		1				1							3									

	1	2	3	4	5	6	7	8	9*	10	11			12										
	1	2	3	4	5	6	7	8	9		11			10										
	2	2	2	2	2	2	2	2	1	2				1										
														1										
				1	1	3	1		1															

League Table

	P	W	D	L	F	A	Pts
Luton Town	46	27	12	7	87	44	66
Barnsley	46	24	13	9	68	46	61
Hartlepools United	46	25	10	11	60	46	60
Crewe Alexandra	46	20	18	8	74	49	58
Bradford City	46	23	11	12	72	51	57
Southend United	46	20	14	12	77	58	54
Chesterfield	46	21	11	14	71	50	53
Wrexham	46	20	13	13	72	53	53
Aldershot	46	18	17	11	70	55	53
Doncaster Rovers	46	18	15	13	66	56	51
Halifax Town	46	15	16	15	52	49	46
Newport County	46	16	13	17	58	63	45
Lincoln City	46	17	9	20	71	68	43
Brentford	46	18	7	21	61	64	43
Swansea Town	46	16	10	20	63	77	42
Darlington	46	12	17	17	47	53	41
Notts County	46	15	11	20	53	79	41
Port Vale	46	12	15	19	61	72	39
Rochdale	46	12	14	20	51	72	38
Exeter City	46	11	16	19	45	65	38
York City	46	11	14	21	65	68	36
Chester	46	9	14	23	57	78	32
Workington	46	10	11	25	54	87	31
Bradford	46	4	15	27	30	82	23

1968-69

Division Four

Manager: Alan Ball Snr

Did you know that?

- Captain was Mick Meagan.
- Mick Meagan won 16 Republic of Ireland caps before joining Town, and won another after leaving the club, but didn't win any while a Halifax Town player.
- Ian Lawther won four Northern Ireland caps before joining Town.
- In September, Town received a third £100 cheque from an anonymous supporter, who reckoned he would stop sending the club money if his identity was revealed.
- On his first return to Brentford, his former club, Ian Lawther was sent off.
- In January, chairman Alan Maden accepted the position of president of the recently formed Halifax Sunday Football League.
- In January, Halifax Town fans were voted the best behaved in Division Four by a panel headed by Football League secretary Alan Hardaker for the John White Award.
- The 30,109 who watched Town's game at Stoke City in the fourth round of FA Cup was largest away crowd the Shaymen had played before since their tie with Manchester City in 1924.
- For match practice during the bad weather, Town used a training ground at Squires Gate, Blackpool in March after Stan Mortenson had agreed to Alan Ball's request.
- Referee Roy Harper collapsed after eight minutes of Town's game at York City on 5 May, and later died.
- Halifax Town finished runners-up to Doncaster Rovers – as they had done in 1934-35.
- Town gained 22 points away from home – a club record, and their final total of 57 points was also a club record..
- Biggest League win: 4–1 v Doncaster Rovers (h), 26 October.
- Heaviest League defeat: 0-4 v Darlington (h), 7 September, v York City (h), 11 January.
- Ever-presents: John Pickering, David Shawcross, Alex Smith.

Match No.	Date		Venue	Opponents	Result		Scorers	Attendance
1	Aug	10	A	Southend United	L	1-2	Shawcross	10,530
2		17	H	Lincoln City	L	0-1		4,536
3		24	A	Aldershot	W	2-0	Ryden 2	4,449
4		28	A	Notts County	W	2-1	Massie, Lawther	4,980
5		31	H	Bradford	W	3-0	Shawcross 2 (1 pen), Wallace	4,876
6	Sep	7	H	Darlington	L	0-4		5,058
7		14	A	Newport County	L	0-2		1,564
8		18	A	Workington	D	1-1	Massie	4,292
9		21	H	Wrexham	W	2-0	Lawther 2	2,674
10		28	A	Swansea Town	L	0-1		7,431
11	Oct	4	A	Scunthorpe United	W	1-0	Lawther	3,942
12		8	H	Notts County	W	3-1	McCarthy 2, Massie	3,630
13		12	H	Peterborough United	W	2-1	Nicholl, Massie	4,175
14		19	A	Port Vale	D	1-1	Lawther	4,493
15		26	H	Doncaster Rovers	W	4-1	Shawcross, McCarthy 2, Massie	6,634
16	Nov	4	A	Chesterfield	L	0-2		4,673
17		9	H	Bradford City	D	1-1	Lawther	7,429
18		23	H	Exeter City	W	2-1	Shawcross, Massie	3,186
19		30	A	Brentford	D	1-1	Hampton	6,002
20	Dec	21	H	Port Vale	W	2-1	Nicholl, Massie	3,806
21		26	H	Scunthorpe United	W	2-0	Lawther, Shawcross	7,268
22	Jan	11	H	York City	L	0-4		5,512
23		14	A	Doncaster Rovers	D	0-0		8,656
24		18	A	Bradford City	D	1-1	Flower	7,971
25	Feb	1	H	Chester	D	0-0		4,181
26		5	A	Peterborough United	D	0-0		5,618
27	Mar	1	H	Southend United	D	1-1	Nicholl	3,522
28		4	H	Colchester United	W	2-1	Pearson, Massie	3,400
29		8	A	Lincoln City	D	0-0		6,974
30		12	A	Chester	D	2-2	Lawther, Massie	4,452
31		25	H	Chesterfield	D	0-0		4,377
32		29	A	Darlington	W	1-0	Flower	5,081
33	Apr	4	A	Grimsby Town	W	1-0	Massie	7,844
34		5	A	Swansea Town	W	2-1	Massie, Lawther	6,155
35		7	H	Workington	W	3-0	Shawcross, Flower, Lawther	6,965
36		12	A	Wrexham	D	2-2	Lawther 2	3,591
37		15	H	Grimsby Town	D	0-0		6,492
38		19	H	Newport County	W	3-0	Massie 3	6,445
39		21	A	Colchester United	D	0-0		7,429
40		24	A	Exeter City	L	1-2	Flower	6,432
41		28	H	Brentford	W	2-0	Flower, Lawther	6,948
42		30	A	Rochdale	L	0-1		13,266
43	May	3	H	Aldershot	W	1-0	Lawther	6,596
44		5	A	York City	D	0-0		4,012
45		8	H	Rochdale	W	1-0	Massie	17,186
46		12	A	Bradford	D	0-0		6,112

Final League Position: 2nd in Division Four

Apps
Sub Apps
Gls

FA Cup

1	Nov	16	A	Bilston	W	3-1	Massie, Flower, Lawther	4,300
2	Dec	7	H	Crewe Alexandra	D	1-1	Wallace	6,636
R		11	A	Crewe Alexandra	W	3-1	Shawcross 2 (1 pen), Massie	7,625
3	Jan	4	A	Swansea Town	W	1-0	Massie	9,726
4		25	A	Stoke City	D	1-1	Massie	30,109
R		28	H	Stoke City	L	0-3		24,891

Apps
Sub Apps
Gls

League Cup

1	Aug	14	H	Hull City	L	0-3		4,493

Apps
Sub Apps
Gls

League Table

	P	W	D	L	F	A	Pts
Doncaster Rovers	46	21	17	8	65	38	59
Halifax Town	46	20	17	9	53	37	57
Rochdale	46	18	20	8	68	35	56
Bradford City	46	18	20	8	65	46	56
Darlington	46	17	18	11	62	45	52
Colchester United	46	20	12	14	57	53	52
Southend United	46	19	13	14	78	61	51
Lincoln City	46	17	17	12	54	52	51
Wrexham	46	18	14	14	61	52	50
Swansea Town	46	19	11	16	58	54	49
Brentford	46	18	12	16	64	65	48
Workington	46	15	17	14	40	43	47
Port Vale	46	16	14	16	46	46	46
Chester	46	16	13	17	76	66	45
Aldershot	46	19	7	20	66	66	45
Scunthorpe United	46	18	8	20	61	60	44
Exeter City	46	16	11	19	66	65	43
Peterborough United	46	13	16	17	60	57	42
Notts County	46	12	18	16	48	57	42
Chesterfield	46	13	15	18	43	50	41
York City	46	14	11	21	53	75	39
Newport County	46	11	14	21	49	74	36
Grimsby Town	46	9	15	22	47	69	33
Bradford	46	5	10	31	32	106	20

1969-70

Division Three

Manager: Alan Ball Snr

Did you know that?

- Following promotion, season ticket sales topped a record £900.
- Captain was John Pickering.
- Luton Town manager Alec Stock tabled an offer for centre-half Chris Nicholl within 30 minutes of the end of Town's match at Kenilworth Road on 26 August. Nicholl signed the following day for a record £30,000.
- The 8–0 defeat by Fulham on 16 September was Town's worst-ever home defeat.
- Bill Atkins returned to The Shay in a record £9,000 move from Portsmouth on 31 October.
- After receiving a letter saying he would be killed by a cyanide-tipped dart, manager Alan Ball watched the match at Barnsley on 1 November from the directors' box flanked by plain clothes police officers.
- On loan Roy Vernon was a League Championship winner with Everton in 1963–64 and won 32 caps for Wales.
- Freddie Hill won the supporters' Player of the Year award despite missing almost half the season after breaking three toes in a friendly with Sunderland on 19 January.
- Dave Shawcross's only penalty miss from eight attempts with the Shaymen came in a 2–0 home defeat by Barnsley on 28 February 1970.
- Halifax Town had 19 players booked.
- Biggest League win: 4–1 v Bournemouth (h), 17 January.
- Heaviest League defeat: 0–8 v Fulham (h), 16 September.
- Ever-present: Andy Burgin.

Match No.	Date		Venue	Opponents	Result		Scorers	Attendance
1	Aug	9	H	Shrewsbury Town	W	1-0	Shawcross	5,926
2		16	A	Orient	L	0-1		6,027
3		23	H	Bradford City	D	0-0		10,274
4		26	A	Luton Town	D	1-1	Hill	13,759
5		30	A	Bristol Rovers	L	0-2		11,768
6	Sep	6	H	Stockport County	W	1-0	Burgin	4,927
7		13	A	Plymouth Argyle	L	0-1		9,070
8		16	H	Fulham	L	0-8		5,809
9		20	H	Doncaster Rovers	D	1-1	Lawther	5,875
10		27	A	Bournemouth & Bosc. Ath.	D	0-0		5,727
11		29	A	Barrow	W	1-0	Shawcross	3,512
12	Oct	4	H	Bury	W	2-0	Robertson, Ryden	4,934
13		7	H	Orient	D	1-1	Lawther	4,367
14		11	A	Walsall	L	1-2	Lawther	6,328
15		18	A	Torquay United	W	1-0	Ryden	7,732
16		25	H	Mansfield Town	L	1-2	Shawcross	3,625
17	Nov	1	A	Barnsley	L	0-2		13,229
18		8	H	Rochdale	W	3-1	Lennard 2, Hill	6,557
19		22	H	Tranmere Rovers	D	2-2	Hill, Atkins	3,727
20	Dec	6	H	Southport	W	1-0	Atkins	3,028
21		13	H	Plymouth Argyle	W	2-0	Holmes, Lawther	3,619
22		26	A	Bradford City	L	1-2	Atkins	14,295
23		27	H	Bristol Rovers	D	1-1	Shawcross	5,388
24	Jan	10	A	Doncaster Rovers	W	1-0	Shawcross	6,365
25		17	H	Bournemouth & Bosc. Ath.	W	4-1	Atkins 2, Lawther, Pickering	3,093
26		27	A	Barrow	W	3-0	Chadwick, Lawther, Atkins	4,345
27		31	A	Bury	D	1-1	Verity	4,788
28	Feb	2	A	Stockport County	W	1-0	Verity	3,428
29		11	A	Reading	L	1-4	Shawcross (pen)	15,160
30		14	A	Shrewsbury Town	L	1-3	Robertson	3,824
31		21	A	Mansfield Town	D	3-3	Lawther, Atkins, Chadwick	6,052
32		28	H	Barnsley	L	0-2		6,562
33	Mar	3	H	Rotherham United	W	4-2	Verity, McCarthy 2, Robertson	4,429
34		6	A	Tranmere Rovers	D	1-1	McCarthy	3,009
35		11	A	Brighton & Hove Albion	L	0-4		16,759
36		14	H	Reading	D	1-1	Shawcross	3,917
37		17	H	Gillingham	D	1-1	McCarthy	3,173
38		21	A	Rotherham United	D	1-1	Chadwick	7,244
39		28	H	Brighton & Hove Albion	W	1-0	Chadwick	4,006
40		30	A	Rochdale	L	0-5		5,345
41		31	H	Torquay United	D	1-1	McCarthy	3,493
42	Apr	4	H	Luton Town	D	0-0		3,482
43		7	A	Southport	L	0-1		3,158
44		15	H	Fulham	L	1-2	McCarthy	7,072
45		22	A	Gillingham	L	0-2		4,568
46		24	H	Walsall	L	0-1		1,812

Final League Position: 18th in Division Three

Apps
Sub Apps
Gls

FA Cup

1	Nov	15	H	Chester	D	3-3	Atkins, Lawther, Hill	5,032
R		19	A	Chester	L	0-1		8,352

Apps
Sub Apps
Gls

League Cup

1	Aug	13	A	Barnsley	W	1-0	Flower	9,546
2	Sep	3	A	West Ham United	L	2-4	Lawther, Wallace	20,717

Apps
Sub Apps
Gls

Players

Smith, A; Wallace, RA; Bugin, A; Leonard, D; Pickering, J; Robertson, AL; Rowe, AJ; Shawcross, FD; Lawther, WI; Hill, F; McGarthy, P; Nichol, CJ; Ryden, JW; Lee, JW; Cullen, TJ; Turnbull, F; Connaughton, PJ; Verity, DA; Atkins, WM; Holmes, B; Chadwick, DE; Vernon, TR; Graham, P; Brearley, K; Buxton, MJ

League Table

	P	W	D	L	F	A	Pts
Orient	46	25	12	9	67	36	62
Luton Town	46	23	14	9	77	43	60
Bristol Rovers	46	20	16	10	80	59	56
Fulham	46	20	15	11	81	55	55
Brighton & Hove Albion	46	23	9	14	57	43	55
Mansfield Town	46	21	11	14	70	49	53
Barnsley	46	19	15	12	68	59	53
Reading	46	21	11	14	87	77	53
Rochdale	46	18	10	18	69	60	46
Bradford City	46	17	12	17	57	50	46
Doncaster Rovers	46	17	12	17	52	54	46
Walsall	46	17	12	17	54	67	46
Torquay United	46	14	17	15	62	59	45
Rotherham United	46	15	14	17	62	54	44
Shrewsbury Town	46	13	18	15	62	63	44
Tranmere Rovers	46	14	16	16	56	72	44
Plymouth Argyle	46	16	11	19	56	64	43
Halifax Town	46	14	15	17	47	63	43
Bury	46	15	11	20	75	80	41
Gillingham	46	13	13	20	52	64	39
Bournemouth & Bosc. Ath.	46	12	15	19	48	71	39
Southport	46	14	10	22	48	66	38
Barrow	46	8	14	24	46	81	30
Stockport County	46	6	11	29	27	71	23

1970-71

Division Three
Manager: George Kirby

Did you know that?

- George Kirby introduced a new playing strip, tangerine shirts with light blue shorts.
- Captain was Andy Burgin.
- The referee stopped the game against Wrexham on 22 August so groundsman Dennis Greenway could refit one of the portable corners of the pitch which had become elevated during play.
- After 16-year-old John Goldstraw applied for the vacant managerial position in the summer, he was invited to be manager for the day by George Kirby for the home game with Walsall on 5 September.
- The 2,078 gate for the game at Bury on 20 October was then the lowest in their history.
- To create more atmosphere at The Shay, manager George Kirby planned to play a recording of the Wembley crowd at last season's FA Cup Final over the tannoy system. But Bristol Rovers would not agree to the idea, and the Football League poured scorn on it.
- Local group The Talismen recorded a single entitled *Halifax Town* penned by band member and former Town player Cedric Thomas. It was released in February.
- At half-time in the match with Bristol Rovers on 6 February, supporter Brian Barrand won a competition to take three penalties against reserve 'keeper Barry White. He scored with his first, put the second over the bar, and saw White save his third.
- With a record of two wins and two draws, George Kirby was named Bell's Third Division Manager of the Month.
- With 74 goals, Town were the Third Division's leading scorers.
- Halifax Town used just 16 players all season – the fewest in their history.
- Biggest League win: 4–0 v Doncaster Rovers (h), 12 December, v Reading (h), 23 January.
- Heaviest League defeat: 0–5 v Chesterfield (a), 10 October.
- Ever-presents: Dave Chadwick, Dave Lennard, John Pickering, Alex Smith.

Match No.	Date		Venue	Opponents	Result		Scorers	Attendance
1	Aug	15	A	Preston North End	D	1-1	McCarthy	9,646
2		22	H	Wrexham	W	2-0	Atkins, Robertson (pen)	3,789
3		29	A	Gillingham	L	1-2	Lennard	5,240
4	Sep	5	H	Walsall	W	2-1	Atkins, Pickering	3,515
5		11	A	Doncaster Rovers	W	2-1	Brierley 2	4,570
6		19	H	Brighton & Hove Albion	L	0-1		3,424
7		22	H	Plymouth Argyle	W	4-1	Burgin, Chadwick, Brierley, Atkins	3,112
8		26	A	Barnsley	D	2-2	Brierley 2	9,439
9		29	H	Rotherham United	L	1-3	Atkins	5,891
10	Oct	3	H	Shrewsbury Town	W	2-0	Atkins, McCarthy	3,322
11		10	A	Chesterfield	L	0-5		8,251
12		17	H	Preston North End	W	1-0	Atkins	5,922
13		20	A	Bury	D	1-1	Brierley	2,708
14		24	A	Fulham	L	1-3	Brierley	10,749
15		31	H	Bradford City	L	1-2	Atkins	5,615
16	Nov	7	A	Mansfield Town	L	2-3	Lennard, Atkins	5,549
17		9	A	Tranmere Rovers	W	1-0	Robertson	3,638
18		14	H	Aston Villa	W	2-1	Atkins 2	5,845
19		28	H	Port Vale	W	2-0	Burgin, Chadwick	3,404
20	Dec	5	A	Bristol Rovers	L	0-1		12,289
21		12	H	Doncaster Rovers	W	4-0	Lennard, Rhodes, Atkins, Brierley	3,175
22		19	A	Wrexham	D	2-2	Atkins, Burgin	6,021
23		26	H	Rochdale	L	1-4	Brierley	5,584
24	Jan	2	A	Plymouth Argyle	D	1-1	Atkins	6,218
25		9	A	Rotherham United	D	2-2	Atkins, Wallace	7,446
26		11	H	Torquay United	W	2-0	Lawther, Pickering	4,022
27		16	H	Bury	W	3-0	Holmes, Lennard 2	5,089
28		23	H	Reading	W	4-0	Wallace, Atkins, Lennard, Chadwick	4,617
29		30	A	Port Vale	W	1-0	Burgin	4,059
30	Feb	6	H	Bristol Rovers	D	0-0		7,716
31		13	A	Reading	D	1-1	Lennard	5,210
32		20	H	Tranmere Rovers	W	4-3	Wallace (pen), Rhodes, McCarthy (pen), Lawther	4,243
33		27	A	Bradford City	W	1-0	Lawther	9,420
34	Mar	6	H	Fulham	W	2-1	Wallace, Holmes	8,019
35		13	A	Aston Villa	D	1-1	Chadwick	33,522
36		16	H	Swansea City	D	2-2	Chadwick, Lennard	8,153
37		20	H	Mansfield Town	L	0-1		6,667
38		27	A	Walsall	D	0-0		3,824
39	Apr	3	H	Gillingham	W	2-1	Pickering, Wallace (pen)	4,026
40		10	A	Rochdale	W	3-0	Rhodes, Lennard, Atkins	5,756
41		14	A	Shrewsbury Town	D	2-2	Atkins, Lennard	5,046
42		17	H	Chesterfield	W	1-0	Lennard	6,609
43		24	H	Brighton & Hove Albion	W	2-0	Chadwick, Robertson	10,671
44		28	A	Torquay United	L	0-2		3,244
45	May	1	H	Barnsley	W	4-1	Chadwick, Atkins, Holmes, Wallace (pen)	6,332
46		4	A	Swansea City	L	1-3	Rhodes	3,789

Final League Position: 3rd in Division Three

Apps
Sub Apps
Gls

FA Cup

1	Nov	21	A	Chesterfield	L	0-2		11,596

Apps
Sub Apps
Gls

League Cup

1	Aug	19	H	Bradford City	W	3-2	Brierley, Burgin, Atkins	6,146
2	Sep	8	A	Derby County	L	1-3	McCarthy	20,029

Apps
Sub Apps
Gls

Smith, A	Burgin, A	Buxton, MJ	Robertson, AL	Pickering, J	Wallace, RA	Chadwick, DE	Atkins, WM	Brierley, K	Leonard, D	McCarthy, P	Lawrie, WI	Holmes, B	Lee, JW	Rhodes, JA	Verity, DA
1	2	3	4	5	6	7	8	9*	10	11	12				
1	2	3	4	5	6	7	8	9	10	11*	12				
1	2	3	4	5	6	7	8	9	11*		12				
1	2	3	4	5	6	7	8	9	10	11					
1	2	3	4	5	6	7	8	9	10	11					
1	2	3*	4	5	6	7	8	9	10	11	12				
1	2	3	4	5	6	7	8	9	10	11					
1	2	3	4	5	6	7	8	9	10	11*	12				
1	2	3	4	5	6	7	8	9	10	11*	12				
1	2		4	5	6	7	8	9	10	11		3			
1	2		4	5	6	7*	8	9	10	11	12	3			
1	2	3	4	5	6	7	8	9	10	11					
1	2	3	4*	5	6	7	8	9	10	11	12				
1	2	3	4	5	6	7	8	9	10	11					
1	2	3	4	5	6	7	8	9	10	11*	12				
1	2		4	5	6	7	8	9	10	11		3			
1	2		4	5	6	7	8	9	10	11		3			
1	2		4	5	6	7	8	9	10	11		3			
1	2			5	4	7	8	9*	10		12	11	3	6	
1	2			5	4	7	8	9	10		12	11	3	6*	
1	2			5	4	7	8	9	10			11	3	6	
1	2			5	4	7	8	9	10			11	3	6	
1	2			5	4	7	8	9	10	11*	12		3	6	
1	2		12	5	4	7	8	9*	10	11			3	6	
1	2			5	4	7	8	9	10			11	3	6	
1	2			5	4	7	8		10		9	11	3	6	
1	2			5	4	7	8		10		9	11	3	6	
1	2			5	4	7	8		10		9	11	3	6	
1	2			5	4	7	8		10		9	11	3	6	
1	2			5	4	7	8	12	10		9	11*	3	6	
1	2			5	4	7	8*		10	12	9	11	3	6	
1	2			5	4	7			9	10	3	8	11	6	
1	2		12	5	4	7	8*		10	3	9	11		6	
1	3			5	4	7	8		10		9	11	2	6	
1	2		12	5*	4	7	8		10		9	11	3	6	
1	2			5	4	7	8		10		9	11	3	6	
1	2			5	4	7	8	9	10			11	3	6	
1	2			5	4	7	8*	9	10		12	11	3	6	
1	2		9	5	4	7	8		10			11	3	6	
1	2		9	5	4	7	8		10			11	3	6	
1	2		9	5	4	7	8		10			11	3	6	
1	2		9	5	4	7	8		10			11	3	6	
1			9	5	4	7	8*		10		12	11	3	6	2
1			9	5	4	7	8		10			11	3	6	2
1	2		9	5	4	7	8		10		12	11	3*	6	
46	43	14	25	46	46	46	45	28	46	23	12	25	31	28	2
			3				1			1	12	1	2		
	4		3	3	6	7	18	9	11	3	3	3		4	

1	2	12	4		6*	7	8	9	10	11	5		3		
1	1		1		1	1	1	1	1	1			1		
	1														

1	2	3	4	5	6	7	8	9	10	11					
1	2	3	4	5	6	7	8	9	10	11*	12				
1	1	1	1	1	1	1	1	1	1						
										1					
	1					1	1		1						

League Table

	P	W	D	L	F	A	Pts
Preston North End	46	22	17	7	63	39	61
Fulham	46	24	12	10	68	41	60
Halifax Town	46	22	12	12	74	55	56
Aston Villa	46	19	15	12	54	46	53
Chesterfield	46	17	17	12	66	38	51
Bristol Rovers	46	19	13	14	69	50	51
Mansfield Town	46	18	15	13	64	62	51
Rotherham United	46	17	16	13	64	60	50
Wrexham	46	18	13	15	72	65	49
Torquay United	46	19	11	16	54	57	49
Swansea City	46	15	16	15	59	56	46
Barnsley	46	17	11	13	49	52	45
Shrewsbury Town	46	16	13	17	58	62	45
Brighton & Hove Albion	46	14	16	13	50	47	44
Plymouth Argyle	46	12	19	15	63	63	43
Rochdale	46	14	15	17	61	68	43
Port Vale	46	15	12	13	52	59	42
Tranmere Rovers	46	10	22	14	45	55	42
Bradford City	46	13	14	13	49	62	40
Walsall	46	14	11	21	51	57	39
Reading	46	14	11	21	48	85	39
Bury	46	12	13	21	52	60	37
Doncaster Rovers	46	13	9	24	45	66	35
Gillingham	46	10	13	23	42	67	33

1971-72
Division Three
Manager: Ray Henderson

Did you know that?

- Halifax Town wore numbers on the front of their shirts for the Watney Cup ties.
- Had Town made the final of the Watney Cup, it would have been played at The Shay.
- The club made 3,717 from the two matches in the Watney Cup, plus £4,000 for qualifying.
- Captain was Andy Burgin.
- Revd David Thomas, vicar of St Mary's Church of England, Luddendenfoot, became club chaplain in July 1971.
- Both Halifax Town and Newcastle United played friendlies at North Shields to celebrate the completion of social amenities. Newcastle boss Joe Harvey officially opened them.
- Dave Lennard signed for Blackpool on 7 October, netting Town a record £30,500.
- The game at Swansea City on 27 November was delayed by 16 minutes while the waterlogged pitch was prepared.
- Blackpool's Fred Kemp joined Town on 30 November in a record £13,500 deal.
- The players enjoyed a mid-season break in Majorca.
- With Town struggling, manager Ray Henderson took his players to the Yorkshire Television Studios on 7 February to watch a re-run of the previous season's match with Chesterfield.
- In the Final of the West Riding Senior Cup on 12 May, Leeds' Scotland international Peter Lorimer beat Alex Smith from the halfway line for the winner.
- Biggest League win: 4–1 v Wrexham (h), 19 February.
- Heaviest League defeat: 0–5 v Brighton & Hove Albion (h), 4 March.
- Ever-present: John Pickering.

Match No.	Date		Venue	Opponents	Result	Scorers	Attendance
1	Aug	14	A	Mansfield Town	D 0-0		5,801
2		21	H	York City	W 3-1	Lennard 2, Atkins	4,930
3		28	A	Bradford City	L 1-2	Robertson	6,053
4	Sep	4	H	AFC Bournemouth	W 1-0	Wallace	4,778
5		11	A	Barnsley	W 2-1	Lennard, Robertson	5,992
6		18	H	Aston Villa	L 0-1		7,462
7		25	A	Port Vale	L 0-1		3,724
8		29	A	Bolton Wanderers	D 1-1	Atkins	9,588
9	Oct	2	H	Tranmere Rovers	W 3-2	Farley 2, Brierley	4,234
10		9	A	Oldham Athletic	D 0-0		9,536
11		16	H	Mansfield Town	D 1-1	Wallace (pen)	3,864
12		19	H	Rochdale	D 2-2	Brierely, Farley	3,288
13		23	H	Chesterfield	W 2-0	Pickering, Johnston	4,667
14		30	A	Wrexham	L 0-2		7,426
15	Nov	6	H	Rotherham United	D 1-1	Brogan	5,409
16		13	A	Brighton & Hove Albion	L 1-2	Brogan	9,896
17		15	H	Plymouth Argyle	L 0-1		2,832
18		27	A	Swansea City	L 0-3		5,285
19	Dec	4	H	Walsall	W 3-1	Chadwick, Shanahan, Wallace (pen)	3,421
20		18	A	AFC Bournemouth	L 1-3	Chadwick	10,853
21		27	H	Blackburn Rovers	L 0-1		7,218
22	Jan	1	A	Aston Villa	L 0-1		32,749
23		8	H	Bradford City	W 2-1	Robertson, Shanahan	4,867
24		22	H	Bolton Wanderers	L 0-1		3,919
25		29	A	Rochdale	L 2-3	Atkins, Wallace	3,124
26	Feb	5	H	Bristol Rovers	W 2-1	Kemp, Chadwick	2,021
27		12	A	Chesterfield	L 1-2	Wallace (pen)	6,477
28		19	H	Wrexham	W 4-1	Robertson, Kemp, Atkins, Chadwick	2,478
29		26	A	Rotherham United	L 2-3	Robertson 2	7,869
30	Mar	4	H	Brighton & Hove Albion	L 0-5		2,432
31		11	A	Oldham Athletic	D 0-0		3,404
32		14	H	Torquay United	D 0-0		2,080
33		18	A	York City	D 1-1	Kemp	4,361
34		22	A	Torquay United	L 0-2		4,226
35		25	H	Barnsley	W 2-0	Wallace (pen), Atkins	2,702
36		31	A	Tranmere Rovers	W 3-2	Waddle, Atkins, Shanahan	5,125
37	Apr	4	H	Port Vale	W 2-0	Holmes, Kemp	3,629
38		8	A	Bristol Rovers	L 0-1		5,642
39		12	A	Notts County	L 1-3	Atkins	14,979
40		15	H	Swansea City	L 0-1		2,620
41		18	H	Notts County	W 3-1	Atkins, Holmes, Wallace	3,943
42		21	A	Walsall	D 0-0		6,096
43		25	A	Plymouth Argyle	D 1-1	Atkins	7,756
44		29	H	Shrewsbury Town	D 0-0		2,405
45	May	3	H	Shrewsbury Town	L 0-3		2,329
46		8	A	Blackburn Rovers	L 0-2		6,499

Final League Position: 17th in Division Three

Apps
Sub Apps
Gls

FA Cup

1	Nov	20	A	Wigan Athletic	L 1-2	Burgin	8,814

Apps
Sub Apps
Gls

League Cup

1	Aug	18	H	Rochdale	D 1-1	Lennard	5,195
R		24	A	Rochdale	D 2-2*	Chadwick, Atkins	6,061
2R		31	H	Rochdale	W 2-0	Wallace, Brierley	5,718
2	Sep	8	A	Newcastle United	L 1-2	Lennard	19,930

*After extra-time

Apps
Sub Apps
Gls

League Table

	P	W	D	L	F	A	Pts
Aston Villa	46	32	6	8	85	32	70
Brighton & Hove Albion	46	27	11	8	82	47	65
Bournemouth	46	23	16	7	73	37	62
Notts County	46	25	12	9	74	44	62
Rotherham United	46	20	15	11	69	52	55
Bristol Rovers	46	21	12	13	75	56	54
Bolton Wanderers	46	17	16	13	51	41	50
Plymouth Argyle	46	20	10	16	74	64	50
Walsall	46	15	18	13	62	57	48
Blackburn Rovers	46	19	9	18	54	57	47
Oldham Athletic	46	17	11	18	59	63	45
Shrewsbury Town	46	17	10	19	73	65	44
Chesterfield	46	18	8	20	57	57	44
Swansea City	46	17	10	19	46	59	44
Port Vale	46	13	15	18	43	59	41
Wrexham	46	16	8	22	59	63	40
Halifax Town	46	13	12	21	48	61	38
Rochdale	46	12	13	21	57	83	37
York City	46	12	12	22	57	66	36
Tranmere Rovers	46	10	16	20	50	71	36
Mansfield Town	46	8	20	18	41	63	36
Barnsley	46	9	18	19	32	64	36
Torquay United	46	10	12	24	41	69	32
Bradford City	46	11	10	25	45	77	32

1972-73

Division Three
Manager: George Mulhall

Did you know that?

- Halifax Town wore an all-white strip with tangerine and blue trim.
- Captain was Johnny Quinn.
- Goalkeeper Alex played his 200th League game for Town in the 1–0 home defeat to Chesterfield on 2 September.
- On 29 September, the *Daily Mirror* reported that Alan Waddle had been transferred to Preston – it was a hoax.
- Halifax Town took part in the annual festivities in the town of St Just, Cornwall, whose invitation was sent out to the club playing Plymouth during the holidays.
- On 6 November, Halifax Town played a friendly at Blyth Spartans designed to boost morale. Town lost the game 4–2.
- Bookies William Hill gave odds of 6-1 on former Town boss Alan Ball succeeding sacked Frank O'Farrell as Manchester United boss.
- Halifax Town went 15 League games without a win between 23 September and 13 January.
- On 2 April, Halifax Town announced they would not be charging the newly introduced VAT on the rest of the home fixtures.
- The attendance of 970 for home match with Brentford on 4 April was the lowest in the Football League during the season.
- After scoring the goal which preserved Town's Third Division status, Alan Waddle signed for Liverpool on 22 June 1973 for a club record £45,000. His next goal would be the winner in the Merseyside derby, and in 1977 he would win a winners' medal as a non-playing substitute when Liverpool defeated Borussia Monchengladbach to win the European Cup in Rome.
- Biggest League win: 3–0 v Bristol Rovers (h), 19 August, v Scunthorpe United (a), 7 September.
- Heaviest League defeat: 1–4 v Bristol Rovers (a), 30 December.
- Ever-presents: John Pickering, Tony Rhodes.

Match No.	Date		Venue	Opponents	Result		Scorers	Attendance
1	Aug	12	A	Brentford	W	1-0	Atkins	10,160
2		19	H	Bristol Rovers	W	3-0	Burgin, Brogan, Atkins	2,812
3		22	H	Wrexham	D	2-2	Burgin, Brogan (pen)	3,759
4		25	A	Shrewsbury Town	D	0-0		3,458
5		29	A	AFC Bournemouth	L	0-1		11,456
6	Sep	2	H	Chesterfield	L	0-1		3,784
7		8	A	Scunthorpe United	W	3-0	Brogan (pen), Robertson 2	4,848
8		16	H	Walsall	L	0-1		2,923
9		18	A	Port Vale	L	1-2	Verity	5,715
10		23	A	Rotherham United	W	1-0	Robertson	6,568
11		30	H	Bolton Wanderers	D	1-1	Robertson	4,664
12	Oct	7	H	Notts County	L	0-1		3,233
13		9	A	Rochdale	D	0-0		5,425
14		13	A	Tranmere Rovers	D	1-1	Atkins	4,131
15		21	H	Grimsby Town	D	1-1	Campbell (og)	3,068
16		24	H	Watford	D	1-1	Robertson	2,046
17		28	A	Plymouth Argyle	L	1-2	Robertson (pen)	6,910
18	Nov	4	A	Wrexham	D	0-0		4,038
19		11	H	Port Vale	D	2-2	Robertson 2	2,026
20		25	H	Swansea City	D	1-1	Atkins	1,815
21	Dec	2	A	Blackburn Rovers	L	0-3		7,402
22		22	A	Southend United	D	1-1	Brogan	4,154
23		26	H	Rotherham United	L	0-1		3,327
24		30	A	Bristol Rovers	L	1-4	Kemp	8,468
25	Jan	13	H	Oldham Athletic	L	0-3		4,829
26		27	H	Scunthorpe United	W	1-0	Irvine	1,607
27	Feb	3	H	Rochdale	D	0-0		2,411
28		7	A	Chesterfield	L	0-2		4,978
29		24	A	York City	L	1-2	Verity	3,483
30		27	H	Shrewsbury Town	L	0-1		1,474
31	Mar	3	A	Notts County	L	0-3		9,820
32		6	A	Charlton Athletic	L	0-1		3,001
33		10	H	Tranmere Rovers	w	2-1	Kemp, Burgin	1,687
34		13	H	York City	W	1-0	Shanahan	1,918
35		17	A	Grimsby Town	D	0-0		10,836
36		24	H	Plymouth Argyle	W	2-1	Burgin, Wilkie	1,839
37		28	A	Watford	L	1-2	Waddle	5,184
38		31	A	Swansea City	L	0-2		2,499
39	Apr	4	H	Brentford	W	3-2	Shanahan 3	970
40		7	A	Blackburn Rovers	D	2-2	Womble, Hale	4,838
41		14	A	Oldham Athletic	D	1-1	Wilkie	8,071
42		16	A	Bolton Wanderers	L	0-3		20,062
43		21	H	Charlton Athletic	W	3-0	Waddle, Wilkie, Shanahan	1,573
44		24	H	Southend United	W	2-1	Womble, Shanahan	2,887
45		28	H	AFC Bournemouth	W	2-0	Hale (pen), Quinn	3,380
46	May	1	A	Walsall	W	1-0	Waddle	3,989

Final League Position: 20th in Division Three

								Apps
								Sub Apps
							1 own-goal	Gls

FA Cup

1	Nov	18	A	Barnsley	D	1-1	Shanahan	4,330
R		21	H	Barnsley	W	2-1	Robertson, Kemp	2,461
2	Dec	9	A	Scunthorpe United	L	2-3	Robertson 2	4,037

								Apps
								Sub Apps
								Gls

League Cup

1	Aug	15	H	Bury	L	1-2	Atkins	3,309

								Apps
								Sub Apps
								Gls

League Table

	P	W	D	L	F	A	Pts
Bolton Wanderers	46	25	11	10	73	39	61
Notts County	46	23	11	12	65	47	57
Blackburn Rovers	46	20	15	11	57	47	55
Oldham Athletic	46	19	16	11	72	54	54
Bristol Rovers	46	20	13	13	72	56	53
Port Vale	46	21	11	14	56	69	53
Bournemouth	46	17	16	13	68	44	50
Plymouth Argyle	46	20	10	16	74	66	50
Grimsby Town	46	20	8	18	63	61	48
Tranmere Rovers	46	15	16	15	56	52	46
Charlton Athletic	46	17	11	18	65	67	45
Wrexham	46	14	17	15	55	54	45
Rochdale	46	14	17	15	48	54	45
Southend United	46	17	10	19	67	54	44
Shrewsbury Town	46	15	14	17	46	54	44
Chesterfield	46	17	9	20	57	61	43
Walsall	46	18	7	21	56	66	43
York City	46	13	15	13	42	46	41
Watford	46	12	17	17	40	48	41
Halifax Town	46	13	15	13	40	53	41
Rotherham United	46	17	7	22	57	65	41
Brentford	46	15	7	24	57	69	37
Swansea City	46	14	9	23	57	73	37
Scunthorpe United	46	10	10	26	33	72	30

1973-74

Division Three

Manager: George Mulhall

Did you know that?

- Manager George Mulhall drove back from Scotland at 5am to sign Huddersfield Town's Alan Jones on 23 August.
- Captain was John Pickering.
- Town's League Cup conquerors Wolves went on to win the Cup, defeating Manchester City 2–1 in the Final.
- Town fan and future Commercial Manager Tony Thwaites's book *The Shaymen* went on sale in October.
- Dave Gwyther scored a headed hat-trick in the 6–1 FA Cup win over Frickley Colliery. It was his third such hat-trick, and his fourth FA Cup hat-trick.
- Halifax Town played their 200th League game at Chesterfield on 23 February, drawing the match 1–1.
- John Pickering ended a run of 190 consecutive League starts when he missed the match at Port Vale on 13 April with a thigh strain.
- Halifax Town finished above Huddersfield Town for the first time.
- George Mulhall played in a benefit match on 6 May for Leeds United's Billy Bremner.
- Biggest League win: 3–1 v Walsall (h), 3 February.
- Biggest League defeat: 0–4 v Huddersfield Town (a), 26 December.
- Ever-present: David Pugh.

Match No.	Date		Venue	Opponents	Result		Scorers	Attendance
1	Aug	25	H	Oldham Athletic	D	0-0		4,883
2	Sep	1	A	York City	D	1-1	Jones	3,960
3		8	H	Southend United	D	0-0		2,604
4		11	A	Grimsby Town	L	1-4	Gwyther	7,860
5		15	A	Bristol Rovers	L	0-2		7,485
6		18	H	Charlton Athletic	W	2-1	Wilkie 2	2,160
7		22	H	Hereford United	D	1-1	Gwyther	2,538
8		28	A	Tranmere Rovers	W	1-0	Gwyther	5,840
9	Oct	2	A	Charlton Athletic	L	2-5	Wilkie, Gwyther	5,131
10		6	H	Chesterfield	W	2-0	Gwyther, Jones	2,728
11		13	A	Brighton & Hove Albion	W	1-0	Gwyther	6,228
12		20	H	Wrexham	L	1-2	Rhodes	2,299
13		27	A	Cambridge United	W	1-0	Gwyther	4,630
14	Nov	3	H	AFC Bournemouth	D	1-1	Gwyther	2,324
15		10	A	Plymouth Argyle	D	1-1	Jones	8,014
16		12	A	Watford	D	0-0		5,358
17		17	H	Port Vale	W	1-0	Pugh	2,094
18	Dec	8	A	Aldershot	L	1-2	Ford	3,019
19		22	H	Tranmere Rovers	W	2-1	Pugh, Shanahan	1,844
20		26	A	Huddersfield Town	L	0-4		11,514
21		29	A	Southend United	W	2-1	Shanahan 2	6,387
22	Jan	5	A	Shrewsbury Town	W	2-0	Hale (pen), Shanahan	2,542
23		12	H	Bristol Rovers	D	0-0		4,507
24		19	A	Oldham Athletic	L	2-3	Kemp, Shanahan	8,461
25		27	H	Southport	D	1-1	Gwyther	4,178
26	Feb	3	H	Walsall	W	3-1	Jones, Shanahan 2	3,543
27		16	H	Brighton & Hove Albion	D	2-2	Shanahan 2	2,767
28		23	A	Chesterfield	D	1-1	Pugh	6,538
29	Mar	2	H	Huddersfield Town	D	0-0		8,126
30		10	H	Cambridge United	L	0-1		2,346
31		13	A	Hereford United	L	1-3	Wilkie	6,170
32		16	A	Wrexham	L	1-2	D. Smith	4,672
33		19	A	Walsall	D	2-2	D. Smith, Gwyther	3,960
34		23	H	Plymouth Argyle	W	1-0	Saxton (og)	1,715
35		26	H	Shrewsbury Town	W	1-0	Shanahan	1,346
36	Apr	1	A	Southport	D	1-1	Kemp	1,083
37		6	H	Watford	D	0-0		1,886
38		9	H	Grimsby Town	L	1-2	D. Smith (pen)	1,624
39		13	A	Port Vale	D	1-1	Kemp	2,707
40		15	A	Blackburn Rovers	D	1-1	Shanahan	4,788
41		16	H	Blackburn Rovers	D	1-1	Wilkie	2,446
42		20	H	Aldershot	D	0-0		1,552
43		22	H	Rochdale	W	1-0	Shanahan	1,431
44		24	A	AFC Bournemouth	D	1-1	D. Smith	4,475
45		27	A	Rochdale	D	1-1	D. Smith	1,320
46		30	H	York City	W	2-1	Hale, Shanahan	4,275

Final League Position: 9th in Division Three

Apps
Sub Apps
1 own-goal
Gls

FA Cup

	Date		Venue	Opponents	Result		Scorers	Attendance
1	Nov	24	H	Frickley Colliery	W	6-1	Gwyther 3, Ford, Hale (pen), Rhodes	3,560
R	Dec	15	H	Oldham Athletic	L	0-1		4,687

Apps
Sub Apps
Gls

League Cup

	Date		Venue	Opponents	Result		Scorers	Attendance
1	Aug	28	H	Barnsley	D	1-1	Rhodes	2,768
R	Sep	4	A	Barnsley	W	1-0	Rhodes	4,168
2	Oct	8	H	Wolverhampton Wanderers	L	0-3		8,222

Apps
Sub Apps
Gls

Smith, A	Burgin, A	Dunn, JD	Kemp, FG	Pickering, J	Rhodes, JA	Jones, A	Pugh, DG	Shanahan, TC	Ford, D	Hale, KO	Cullen, PJ	Gwyther, DGA	Wilkie, JC	Worthington, D	McDonald, G	Smith, DA	White, BJ
1	2	3	4*	5	6	7	8	9	10	11	12						
1	2	3	10	5	6	7	8		4	11		9					
1	2	3	4*	5		7	6	8*	9	11		10	12				
1	2	3		5	6	7	4	12	9	11		10	8*				
1	2	3	4	5	6	7	11		8			10	9				
1	2	3	4	5	6	7	11	12	8*			10	9				
1	2	3	4	5	6	7	11		8			10	9				
1	2	3	4*	5	6	7	11	12	8			10	9				
1	2	3	4	5	6	7	11		8			10	9				
1	3*		12	5	6	7	11		7	8	4						
1		3	12	5	6	7	11	7*	8	4		10	9				
1		3		5	6	7	11	9	8	4		10		2			
1		3	12	5	6	7	11	9	8*	4		10		2			
1		3	12	5	6*	7	11	9	8	4		10		2			
1		3	11	5		7	6	9	8	4		10		2			
1	2	3	11	5		7	6	9	8	4		10					
1	2	3	9	5	6	7	11	12	8	4*		10					
1	2	3	9	5	6	7	4	11	8			10					
1	2	3	9	5	6		7	4	11	8		10					
1	2	3	9	5*	6		11	7	8	4		10					12
1	2	3	9	5	6		11	7	8	4		10					
1	2	3	9	5	6	7	11	10	8*	4			12				
1	2	3	9	5	6	7	11	10		4			8				
1	2	3	9	5	6		11	8	7	4		10					
1	2	3	9	5	6	7	4	8	11			10	7				
1	2	3	9	5	6		7	8	11	4		10*	12				
1	2	3	9	5	6		7	8	11	4		10					
1	2	3	9	5	6		7	8*	11	4		10	12				
1	2	3	9	5			6	8	11*	4		10	12				7
1	2	3	9	5	6			8	11	4		10					7
1	2	3	9				6	5	8	4		10			11	7	
1	2	3	9				6	5	8	4		10	7		11		
	2	3	9				6	5	8	4		10	7		11		1
	2	3	9				6	5	8	4*		10	7		11	12	1
1	2	3	9				6	5	8	4		10			11	3	
	2	3	9				6	5	8	4		10			11	7	1
	2	3	9				6	5	8	4		10			11	7	1
	2	3	9				6	5	8	4		10			11	7	1
41	41	45	40	38	41	23	46	35	34	34		42	14	5	10	12	5
		4				4				1		7		3	1		
		3		1	4	3	13	1	2			10	5		5		

1	2	3	8	5	6	7	11		9	4		10					
1	2	3	9	5	6	7	11		8	4		10					
2	2	2	2	2	2	2		2	2			2					
												3					
				1				1	1								

1	2	3	4	5	6	7	8	9	10	11							
1	2	3	4	5	6	7	8		9	11		10					
1	2	3	4*	5	6	7	11	12	8			10	9				
3	3	3	3	3	3	3		1	3	2		2	1				
							2										

League Table

	P	W	D	L	F	A	Pts
Oldham Athletic	46	25	12	9	83	47	62
Bristol Rovers	46	22	17	7	65	33	61
York City	46	21	19	6	67	38	61
Wrexham	46	22	12	12	63	43	56
Chesterfield	46	21	14	11	55	42	56
Grimsby Town	46	18	15	13	67	50	51
Watford	46	19	12	15	64	56	50
Aldershot	46	19	11	16	65	52	49
Halifax Town	46	14	21	11	48	51	49
Huddersfield Town	46	17	13	16	56	55	47
Bournemouth	46	16	15	15	54	58	47
Southend United	46	16	14	16	62	62	46
Blackburn Rovers	46	18	10	18	62	64	46
Charlton Athletic	46	19	8	19	66	73	46
Walsall	46	16	13	17	57	48	45
Tranmere Rovers	46	15	15	16	50	44	45
Plymouth Argyle	46	17	10	19	59	54	44
Hereford United	46	14	15	17	53	57	43
Brighton & Hove Albion	46	16	11	19	52	58	43
Port Vale	46	14	14	18	52	58	42
Cambridge United	46	13	9	24	48	81	35
Shrewsbury Town	46	10	11	25	41	62	31
Southport	46	6	16	24	35	82	28
Rochdale	46	2	17	27	38	94	21

1974-75

Division Three

Managers: August–September 1974 George Mulhall; September 1974–April 1975 Johnny Quinn

Did you know that?

- Halifax Town had four Under-23 internationals on their books: David Ford (England), and John Collins, Dave Gwyther, David Pugh (all Wales).
- Minimum ground admission was 45p.
- Captain was Tony Rhodes.
- Town's playing strip was all-blue with tangerine trim.
- Hat-trick hero for Stoke City in the 3–0 League Cup win over Town was only playing because Alan Hudson was injured in a car crash the previous weekend.
- Former Elland Grammar School pupil became the first black player to turn out for Town when he made his debut against Chesterfield on 17 September.
- Town had to pay Tranmere a £500 fee after registering their former coach as a player.
- Goalkeeper Barry White's four first-team appearances were all as an outfield player.
- Halifax Town had two players on their books called Alex Smith.
- The first meeting of Halifax Town past and present players was held on 29 May 1975 and included John Mulroy, who played in their Exley days.
- Biggest League win: 3–0 v Preston North End (h), 2 November.
- Heaviest League defeat: 0–4 v Southend United (a), 2 September, v Gillingham (a), 9 November, v Wrexham (a), 4 February.
- Halifax Town recorded identical attendance – 2,063 – for consecutive home games with Plymouth Argyle and Grimsby Town.
- Ever-present: Goalkeeper Alex Smith.

Match No.	Date	Venue	Opponents	Result		Scorers	Attendance
1	Aug 17	H	Charlton Athletic	D	2-2	Downes 2	2,513
2	24	A	Walsall	D	1-1	Shanahan (pen)	3,280
3	31	H	Crystal Palace	W	3-1	Downes 2, Gwyther	3,295
4	Sep 2	A	Southend United	L	0-4		7,973
5	7	A	Watford	D	2-2	Moir, Collins	6,078
6	14	H	Bury	L	0-1		3,167
7	17	H	Chesterfield	L	1-3	Gwyther	1,906
8	21	A	Blackburn Rovers	L	0-1		7,884
9	25	A	Peterborough United	D	1-1	Ford	8,156
10	28	H	Port Vale	D	1-1	Ford	1,897
11	Oct 2	A	Aldershot	L	1-3	Jones	2,464
12	4	A	Tranmere Rovers	L	1-3	Moir	2,584
13	12	H	Swindon Town	D	0-0		1,730
14	15	H	Southend United	W	3-1	Gwyther, Moir 2	1,210
15	19	A	Hereford United	D	0-0		6,833
16	26	H	Colchester United	D	1-1	Blair	1,935
17	Nov 2	H	Preston North End	W	3-0	Moir, McHale, Blair	4,878
18	9	A	Gillingham	L	0-4		5,809
19	16	H	Huddersfield Town	W	2-1	Blair, Gwyther	6,827
20	30	H	Brighton & Hove Albion	W	1-0	Gwyther	1,961
21	Dec 7	A	Grimsby Town	L	1-2	Gwyther	4,331
22	21	H	AFC Bournemouth	W	3-2	McHale, Downes, Gwyther	1,523
23	26	A	Bury	L	1-4	Downes	6,260
24	28	H	Plymouth Argyle	D	1-1	Blair	2,063
25	Jan 11	H	Grimsby Town	D	1-1	Gwyther	2,063
26	Feb 1	H	Gillingham	D	1-1	McHale	1,742
27	4	A	Wrexham	L	0-4		2,532
28	8	A	Preston North End	L	0-1		9,786
29	15	H	Wrexham	W	1-0	Gwyther	2,039
30	19	A	Chesterfield	D	1-1	Ford	4,385
31	22	A	Huddersfield Town	W	2-1	Gwyther, Scaife	7,931
32	28	A	Crystal Palace	D	1-1	Gwyther	18,024
33	Mar 8	H	Peterborough United	W	2-1	Phelan, McHale	2,322
34	15	A	Port Vale	L	1-2	Downes	3,334
35	18	A	Charlton Athletic	L	1-3	Downes	9,561
36	22	H	Watford	W	2-0	Jones, A. Smith (2)	1,872
37	28	A	Plymouth Argyle	L	0-2		19,580
38	29	A	AFC Bournemouth	W	1-0	Rhodes	5,247
39	Apr 1	H	Blackburn Rovers	D	1-1	McHale	8,689
40	4	A	Colchester United	L	0-2		3,501
41	8	H	Aldershot	W	1-0	McHale	1,835
42	12	H	Tranmere Rovers	D	0-0		2,201
43	16	A	Brighton & Hove Albion	D	0-0		10,309
44	19	A	Swindon Town	L	1-3	Downes	6,615
45	22	H	Walsall	W	1-0	Gwyther	2,030
46	26	H	Hereford United	D	2-2	McHale (pen), Harrold	1,893

Final League Position: 17th in Division Three

Apps
Sub Apps
Gls

FA Cup

| 1 | Nov 23 | A | Barnsley | W | 2-1 | Jones 2 | 5,314 |
| 2 | Dec 14 | A | Stafford Rangers | L | 1-2 | Gwyther | 5,534 |

Apps
Sub Apps
Gls

League Cup

| 1 | Aug 20 | A | Barnsley | W | 1-0 | Gwyther | 5,139 |
| 2 | Sep 11 | A | Stoke City | L | 0-3 | | 17,805 |

Apps
Sub Apps
Gls

League Table

	P	W	D	L	F	A	Pts
Blackburn Rovers	46	22	16	8	68	45	60
Plymouth Argyle	46	24	11	11	79	58	59
Charlton Athletic	46	22	11	13	76	61	55
Swindon Town	46	21	11	14	64	58	53
Crystal Palace	46	18	15	13	66	57	51
Port Vale	46	18	15	13	61	54	51
Peterborough United	46	19	12	15	75	53	50
Walsall	46	18	13	15	67	52	49
Preston North End	46	19	11	16	63	56	49
Gillingham	46	17	14	15	65	60	48
Colchester United	46	17	13	16	70	63	47
Hereford United	46	16	14	16	64	66	46
Wrexham	46	15	15	16	65	55	45
Bury	46	16	12	18	53	50	44
Chesterfield	46	16	12	18	62	66	44
Grimsby Town	46	15	13	18	55	64	43
Halifax Town	46	13	17	16	49	63	43
Southend United	46	13	16	17	46	51	42
Brighton & Hove Albion	46	16	10	20	56	64	42
Aldershot*	46	14	11	21	53	63	38
Bournemouth	46	13	12	21	44	58	38
Tranmere Rovers	46	14	9	23	55	57	37
Watford	46	10	17	19	52	75	37
Huddersfield Town	46	11	10	25	47	76	32

+ Aldershot were deducted one point for fielding an unregistered player.

1975-76 Division Three

Managers: August 1975–February 1976 Johnny Quinn; February–April 1976 Alan Ball Snr

Did you know that?

- Halifax Town wore a new strip of blue shirts with white trim and white shorts, provided by the Supporters' Club.
- Captain was David Pugh, then Tony Rhodes.
- Sky-divers dropped onto the pitch before Town's opening match with Millwall.
- On the way back from Colchester on 6 September, Town players and officials were involved in a bomb alert and were among hundreds of travellers evacuated from King's Cross station.
- The second half of the League Cup tie with Sheffield United on 10 September was delayed because of thunder and lightning.
- Bobby Flavell's signing from Burnley on 12 March was completed with just 10 minutes to spare so he could play in the following day's game with Swindon Town.
- Dave Gwyther scored the winner for Town against Rotherham United on 27 December, and the winner for Rotherham against Town on 19 April.
- The attendance of 856 for the last match with Colchester United on 26 April remained the lowest-ever for a League match at The Shay.
- Biggest League win: 5–2 v Chester (h), 27 September.
- Heaviest League defeat: 1–4 v Southend United (a), 20 October.
- Ever-present: Ray McHale.

Match No.	Date		Venue	Opponents	Result		Scorers	Attendance
1	Aug	16	H	Millwall	L	1-2	Downes	2,460
2		23	A	Aldershot	W	2-1	McHale, Gwyther	3,221
3		30	H	Walsall	W	2-1	Ford, Gwyther	2,076
4	Sep	6	A	Colchester United	W	1-0	McHale (pen)	2,819
5		13	H	Shrewsbury Town	D	0-0		2,501
6		20	A	Cardiff City	D	0-0		8,035
7		23	A	Grimsby Town	D	2-2	Bell 2	6,353
8		27	H	Chester	W	5-2	Bell, Rhodes 2, McHale, Phelan	2,240
9	Oct	4	A	Gillingham	D	1-1	Bell	5,934
10		11	A	Swindon Town	L	1-3	McHale	6,214
11		18	H	Hereford United	L	0-1		2,667
12		20	A	Southend United	L	1-4	McHale	3,089
13		25	A	Bury	D	0-0		7,516
14	Nov	1	H	Crystal Palace	L	1-3	McHale	3,282
15		4	H	Preston North End	W	2-1	Bell, Rhodes	3,366
16		8	A	Mansfield Town	D	1-1	McHale	5,288
17		15	H	Brighton & Hove Albion	L	1-3	Ford	2,201
18		29	A	Wrexham	D	1-1	McHale	3,063
19	Dec	6	H	Peterborough United	L	0-1		2,289
20		20	A	Chesterfield	W	2-1	Bell, Gwyther	3,703
21		26	H	Port Vale	L	1-3	Bell	2,959
22		27	A	Rotherham United	W	1-0	Gwyther	7,614
23	Jan	10	A	Walsall	L	0-2		7,167
24		17	H	Cardiff City	D	1-1	Phelan	2,399
25		24	A	Shrewsbury Town	L	0-2		3,398
26	Feb	7	A	Preston North End	L	1-2	McHale	5,480
27		14	H	Mansfield Town	L	1-2	Downes	2,378
28		21	A	Brighton & Hove Albion	L	0-1		13,686
29		24	H	Grimsby Town	W	2-1	Downes, McHale (pen)	2,229
30		28	A	Bury	L	0-2		3,606
31	Mar	2	H	Sheffield Wednesday	D	0-0		5,876
32		9	H	Gillingham	D	1-1	G. Jones	1,886
33		13	H	Swindon Town	L	0-2		1,846
34		17	A	Hereford United	W	2-1	G. Jones, Overton	7,395
35		20	H	Wrexham	L	0-1		2,970
36		23	H	Southend United	W	1-0	McHale	1,450
37		27	A	Peterborough United	L	0-1		4,933
38		30	H	Chesterfield	W	1-0	Overton	1,975
39	Apr	3	A	Millwall	L	0-1		7,237
40		7	A	Chester	L	1-2	Overton	3,369
41		13	A	Crystal Palace	D	1-1	McHale	19,175
42		17	A	Port Vale	D	1-1	Phelan	3,169
43		19	H	Rotherham United	L	0-1		2,614
44		20	A	Sheffield Wednesday	L	0-1		13,143
45		24	H	Aldershot	L	1-3	Harris	1,608
46		26	H	Colchester United	D	1-1	Smith (og)	856

Final League Position: 24th in Division Three

Apps
Sub Apps
1 own-goal Gls

FA Cup

1	Nov	22	H	Altrincham	W	3-1	McHale 2 (1 pen), Rhodes	4,077
2	Dec	13	A	Stafford Rangers	W	3-1	McHale (pen), Downes, Gwyther	4,650
3	Jan	3	A	Ipswich Town	L	1-3	McHale (pen)	23,488

Apps
Sub Apps
Gls

League Cup

1,1L	Aug	19	H	Hartlepool	W	4-1	Phelan, Albeson (og), Bell 2	1,476
1,2L		25	A	Hartlepool	L	1-2	Downes	1,726
2	Sep	10	H	Sheffield United	L	2-4	Rhodes, Downes	7,925

Apps
Sub Apps
1 own-goal Gls

League Table

	P	W	D	L	F	A	Pts
Hereford United	46	26	11	3	86	55	63
Cardiff City	46	22	13	11	69	48	57
Millwall	46	20	16	10	54	43	56
Brighton & Hove Albion	46	22	9	15	78	53	53
Crystal Palace	46	18	17	11	61	46	53
Wrexham	46	20	12	14	66	55	52
Walsall	46	18	14	14	74	61	50
Preston North End	46	19	10	17	62	57	48
Shrewsbury Town	46	19	10	17	61	59	48
Peterborough United	46	15	18	13	63	63	48
Mansfield Town	46	16	15	15	58	52	47
Port Vale	46	15	16	15	55	54	46
Bury	46	14	16	16	51	46	44
Chesterfield	46	17	9	20	65	69	43
Gillingham	46	12	19	15	58	68	43
Rotherham United	46	15	12	19	54	65	42
Chester	46	15	12	19	43	62	42
Grimsby Town	46	15	10	21	62	74	40
Swindon Town	46	16	8	22	62	75	40
Sheffield Wednesday	46	12	16	18	48	59	40
Aldershot	46	13	13	20	59	75	39
Colchester United	46	12	14	20	41	65	38
Southend United	46	12	13	2	65	75	37
Halifax Town	46	11	13	22	41	61	35

1976-77

Division Four
Manager: Alan Ball Snr

Did you know that?

- Seven players were booked in the League Cup replay with Darlington on 30 August.
- By failing to win any of their opening League six matches, Town made their worst start since 1966.
- Town's 6–0 victory over Doncaster Rovers on 2 November equalled the League record set in 1955 when Bradford were beaten by the same score.
- In an effort to cut costs, Halifax Town put up for sale all their 21 professional players on 26 January.
- Halifax Town scored six goals twice in a League season for the first time since 1933–34.
- Town did not arrive for their match at Hartlepool on 5 March until 2.30pm after getting lost en route in Middlesbrough town centre.
- Biggest League win: 6–0 v Doncaster Rovers (h), 2 November.
- Heaviest League defeat: 0–4 v Cambridge United (a), 1 April.
- An interested spectator at Town's FA Cup tie with Luton Town on 8 January was England manager Don Revie, checking out the form of the Hatters' central-defender Paul Futcher.

Match No.	Date	Venue	Opponents	Result		Scorers	Attendance
1	Aug 21	H	AFC Bournemouth	L	2-3	G. Jones, McHale	1,711
2	24	A	Colchester United	L	0-3		2,489
3	28	A	Workington	D	1-1	McHale	2,081
4	Sep 4	H	Rochdale	D	0-0		2,003
5	10	A	Southend United	D	1-1	Bell	5,143
6	18	H	Exeter City	L	1-2	Lawson (pen)	1,424
7	24	H	Hartlepool	W	1-0	Bullock	1,393
8	Oct 2	A	Watford	D	0-0		4,353
9	9	H	Scunthorpe United	L	0-1		1,854
10	16	A	Crewe Alexandra	L	1-3	McCann	2,363
11	23	H	Cambridge United	L	0-2		1,523
12	27	A	Bradford City	L	0-3		7,271
13	30	H	Bradford City	W	2-1	Johnston, Bullock	2,149
14	Nov 2	H	Doncaster Rovers	W	6-0	Dunleavy, Hoy 2, Carroll, Bullock, Lawson	2,350
15	6	A	Darlington	D	0-0		3,392
16	9	H	Swansea City	W	1-0	Hoy	2,244
17	27	A	Newport County	D	1-1	Lawson	2,901
18	Dec 18	A	Southport	D	0-0		1,164
19	27	H	Huddersfield Town	D	0-0		8,720
20	29	A	Barnsley	L	0-1		5,528
21	Jan 22	A	AFC Bournemouth	L	0-3		3,888
22	29	A	Brentford	L	1-2	Hoy	4,520
23	31	A	Stockport County	D	1-1	Flavell	3,004
24	Feb 5	H	Workington	W	6-1	Johnston 2, Lawson, Carroll 2, Flavell	1,580
25	8	H	Torquay United	W	2-0	Hoy, Flavell	2,124
26	12	A	Rochdale	L	1-4	Bullock	2,255
27	14	H	Darlington	W	2-1	Bullock, Johnston	1,720
28	19	H	Southend United	W	3-1	Hoy, Johnston, Bradley	1,994
29	26	A	Exeter City	L	0-1		5,995
30	Mar 5	A	Hartlepool	L	0-1		1,651
31	8	H	Colchester United	L	1-2	Lawson (pen)	2,079
32	12	H	Watford	D	1-1	Bullock	1,902
33	19	A	Scunthorpe United	L	1-2	Dunleavy	2,902
34	22	H	Aldershot	W	2-0	Bullock 2	1,341
35	26	H	Crewe Alexandra	W	3-0	Carroll, Hoy, Dunleavy	1,589
36	Apr 1	A	Cambridge United	L	0-4		4,376
37	5	A	Huddersfield Town	L	0-1		7,591
38	9	H	Barnsley	L	0-1		3,529
39	12	A	Doncaster Rovers	L	0-3		4,840
40	16	H	Bradford City	W	2-1	Johnston, Bell	6,402
41	19	H	Brentford	D	0-0		1,464
42	23	A	Swansea City	L	1-2	Carroll	7,344
43	30	H	Newport County	D	0-0		1,299
44	May 4	A	Aldershot	D	0-0		2,359
45	7	A	Torquay United	L	2-3	Trainer, Bullock	2,574
46	14	H	Southport	D	1-1	Dunleavy	1,364

Final League Position: 21st in Division Four

Apps
Sub Apps
Gls

FA Cup

1	Nov 20	A	Stafford Rangers	D	0-0		4,482
R	23	H	Stafford Rangers	W	1-0	Phelan	3,877
2	Dec 14	H	Preston North End	W	1-0	Lawson	5,219
3	Jan 8	H	Luton Town	L	0-1		5,519

Apps
Sub Apps
Gls

League Cup

1, 1L	Aug 14	H	Darlington	D	0-0		1,750
1, 2L	18	A	Darlington	D	1-1	G. Jones	2,911
R	30	H	Darlington	L	1-2*	Lawson	1,818

* After extra-time

Apps
Sub Apps
Gls

526

League Table

	P	W	D	L	F	A	Pts
Cambridge United	46	26	13	7	87	40	65
Exeter City	46	25	12	9	70	46	62
Colchester United	46	25	9	2	77	43	59
Bradford City	46	23	13	0	78	51	59
Swansea City	46	25	8	3	92	68	58
Barnsley	46	23	9	4	62	39	55
Watford	46	18	15	3	67	50	51
Doncaster Rovers	46	21	9	6	71	65	51
Huddersfield Town	46	19	12	5	60	49	50
Southend United	46	15	19	2	52	45	49
Darlington	46	18	13	5	59	64	49
Crewe Alexandra	46	19	11	6	47	60	49
Bournemouth	46	15	18	3	54	44	48
Stockport County	46	13	19	4	53	57	45
Brentford	46	18	7	21	77	76	43
Torquay United	46	17	9	20	59	67	43
Aldershot	46	16	11	9	49	59	43
Rochdale	46	13	12	21	50	59	38
Newport County	46	14	10	22	42	58	38
Scunthorpe United	46	13	11	22	49	73	37
Halifax Town	46	11	14	21	47	58	36
Hartlepool	46	10	12	24	47	73	32
Southport	46	3	19	24	33	77	25
Workington	46	4	11	21	41	102	19

1977-78

Division Four

Managers: August–October 1977 Alan Ball Snr; October 1977–April 1978 Jimmy Lawson

Did you know that?

- Captain was Chris Dunleavy.
- Halifax Town introduced a new away kit of yellow-and-blue stripes.
- The Shaymen were Wimbledon's first opponents in the League after the Dons had replaced Workington. Halifax Town had been Workington's first opponents in August 1951.
- Halifax Town were involved in their first-ever penalty shoot-out after drawing 1–1 with Huddersfield Town in a West Riding Senior Cup match on 15 November. Huddersfield won 5–4 on penalties.
- Bobby Hoy supplemented his football income by performing as a Country and Western singer.
- Goalkeeper Terry Gennoe made a £30,000 move to Southampton, despite conceding five goals at Southend on 17 February on his last Town appearance.
- Town fan George Jones won a competition in April when he named the club's new money-making scheme the 'Shaymaker Lottery'.
- Pop star Elton John flew in from Paris to watch Watford, of whom he was chairman, earn a 1–1 draw at The Shay on 22 April.
- Despite going up as champions, Watford failed to beat Halifax Town during the season, both games ending in 1–1 draws.
- Halifax Town racked up 185 penalty points, 10 more than the maximum.
- Biggest League win: 3–0 v Hartlepool United (h), 23 August.
- Heaviest League defeat: 0–5 v Southend United (a), 17 February.

Match No.	Date	Venue	Opponents	Result		Scorers	Attendance
1	Aug 20	A	Wimbledon	D	3-3	Carroll 2, Bell	4,616
2	23	H	Hartlepool United	W	3-0	Carroll, Bullock 2	1,614
3	27	H	Northampton Town	L	0-1		1,869
4	Sep 3	A	Reading	L	1-2	Carroll	3,242
5	10	H	Crewe Alexandra	D	1-1	Flavell	1,128
6	13	A	Darlington	L	1-2	Bullock	1,863
7	17	A	AFC Bournemouth	D	0-0		3,282
8	24	H	Southend United	L	0-1		1,537
9	27	H	Barnsley	D	1-1	Carroll	2,728
10	Oct 1	A	Brentford	L	1-4	Bullock	6,240
11	4	A	Rochdale	L	1-3	Alcock	1,201
12	8	H	Huddersfield Town	D	0-0		4,956
13	15	H	Torquay United	D	0-0		1,077
14	21	A	Southport	W	2-1	Horsfall, Powell	2,225
15	29	A	Scunthorpe United	L	0-2		2,420
16	Nov 5	H	Doncaster Rovers	L	0-1		1,757
17	12	A	Newport County	L	0-2		3,992
18	19	H	Aldershot	W	2-1	Trainer, Flavell	1,093
19	Dec 3	A	Watford	D	1-1	Smith	9,429
20	10	H	Swansea City	W	3-1	Carroll, Bullock, May (og)	1,722
21	17	H	Rochdale	W	3-1	Bullock, Flavell, Johnston	1,918
22	26	A	Grimsby Town	D	0-0		6,051
23	27	H	Stockport County	D	1-1	Horsfall	4,036
24	31	A	Doncaster Rovers	D	1-1	Carroll	3,918
25	Jan 2	H	York City	W	2-0	Bullock, Bell	3,774
26	14	H	Wimbledon	L	1-2	Bullock	2,770
27	Feb 7	A	Hartlepool United	D	1-1	Alcock	3,475
28	17	A	Southend United	L	0-5		6,128
29	22	A	Crewe Alexandra	D	0-0		1,462
30	25	H	Brentford	D	1-1	Smith	1,764
31	28	H	AFC Bournemouth	D	0-0		1,632
32	Mar 4	A	Huddersfield Town	D	2-2	Trainer, Dunleavy	6,571
33	7	H	Darlington	L	0-2		1,619
34	11	A	Torquay United	D	2-2	Carroll, Mountford	2,948
35	14	A	Northampton Town	W	2-1	Mountford, Bell	2,279
36	18	H	Southport	W	2-1	Flavell, Smith	1,680
37	25	A	Stockport County	W	3-1	Bell 2, Mountford	2,168
38	27	H	Grimsby Town	D	0-0		2,481
39	28	H	Scunthorpe United	D	2-2	Burke, Bell	2,215
40	31	A	York City	D	1-1	Bell	1,526
41	Apr 4	A	Barnsley	L	2-3	Lawson (pen), Bullock	6,150
42	8	H	Newport County	W	3-1	Lawson 2, Dunleavy	1,653
43	15	A	Aldershot	D	0-0		3,727
44	18	H	Reading	L	2-4	Smith, Bell	1,632
45	22	H	Watford	D	1-1	Bell	3,542
46	29	A	Swansea City	L	0-2		16,130

Final League Position: 20th in Division Four

Apps
Sub Apps
1 own-goal
Gls

FA Cup

1	Nov 26	A	Chesterfield	L	0-1		4,948

Apps
Sub Apps
Gls

League Cup

1,1L	Aug 13	A	Rochdale	D	1-1	Horsfall	1,512
1,2L	16	H	Rochdale	L	1-2	Lawson	1,784

Apps
Sub Apps
Gls

Gennoe, TW	Flavell, RW	Loska, ASP	Smith, S	Dunberry, CP	Bradley, LH	Carroll, J	Johnston, J	Bullock, ME	Bell, DM	Horsfall, TW	Lawson, JJ	Gregoire, RB	Alcock, T	Trainer, J	Leonard, MC	Powell, M	Frith, FM	Burke, P	Mountford, RW
1	2	3	4	5	6	7	8	9	10	11									
1	2	3	4	5	6	7		9	10	11	8								
1	2	3	4	5	6	7		9	8	11	10								
1	2	3	4	5	6	7		9	8		10	11							
1	3	2	4	5	6	7		12	8	11*	10	9							
1	3	2	4	6		7		8	9		10	11*	5	12					
1	3	2*	4	6		7		8	9	11	10		5	12					
1	2	3	4	6		7	12	9	8	11*	10		5						
	3	2	4	6		7	11	9	8		10		5		1				
	2	3	4	6		7		9	8*	12	10		5	11	1				
1	2		4	6	3	7		9			10	8	5	11					
1	2		4	6	3	7	11	9	12		10*	8	5						
1	2		4	6	3	7	11	9	8	10			5						
1	2		4	6*	3	7	11	12	8	10			5			9			
1	2		4	6	3	7	11	12	8	10*			5			9			
1	2		4	6	3		11	9	8	10			5			7			
1	2		4	6	3		7		8	11	10*		5	12		9			
1	2	3	4	6		8	7	9	11		10		5						
1	2	3	7	5		8	4	9	11		10		6						
1	2	3	7	5		8	4	9	11		10		6						
1	2	3	7	5	12	8	4*	9	11		10		6						
1	2	3	4	5	12	8		9	11	7	10*		6						
1	2	3	4	5		8		9	11	7	10		6						
1	2	3	4	5	12	8		9	11	7	10*		6						
1	2	3	4	5	12	8		9	11	7*	10		6						
1	2	3		5		8	4	9	11		10	6			7				
1	2	3	12	5		8	4	9	11*		10	6			7				
	2	3	8	5			4	9	11		10		6	1	7				
	2	3	8	5		12	4	9	11		10*		6	1	7				
	2	3		5		8	4	9	11		10		6	1	7				
	2	3		5		8	4	9	11		10		6	1	7				
	7	3		5	2	8	4	9	11		10*		6	1		12			
	10	3		6		11	8	4				2	1			7	5	9	
	10	3	7	6	2	8	4		11				1				5	9	
	10	3	7	6	2	8	4		11				1				5	9	
		4	6	3		8			11		10		2	1		7	5	9	
		4	6	3		8			11		10		2	1		7	5	9	
	8		4	6	3				11		10		2	1		7	5	9	
	8	3	4	6	2				11		10			1		7	5	9	
	8	3	4		2			9	11		10		6	1		7	5		
	8	3	4	6				9	11		10		2	1		7	5		
	8	3	4	6				9	11		10		2	1		7	5		
	8	3	4	6*					12	11	10		2	1		7	5	9	
	8	3	4		2*				12	11	10		6	1		7	5	9	
	8	3	4		2				11		10		6	1		7	5	9	
26	44	36	40	43	23	32	25	32	43	15	38	5	14	26	20	4	17	13	10
			1		4	1	1	5	1	1			3		1				
4		4	2		8	1	9	9	2	3		2	2			1		1	3

| 1 | 2 | 3 | 7 | 5 | | 8 | 4 | 9 | 11 | | 10 | | 6 | | | | | | |
| 1 | 1 | 1 | 1 | | 1 | 1 | 1 | 1 | | 1 | | | 1 | | | | | | |

	8	3		5	4	9	6	10		11	7			2	1				
	7	3		5	4*	9	6	10	12	11	8			2	1				
	2	2		2	2	2	2	2		2	2			2	2				
									1										
											1			1	1				

League Table

	P	W	D	L	F	A	Pts
Watford	46	30	11	5	85	38	71
Southend United	46	25	10	11	66	39	60
Swansea City	46	23	10	13	87	47	56
Brentford	46	21	14	11	86	54	56
Aldershot	46	19	16	11	67	47	54
Grimsby Town	46	21	11	14	57	51	53
Barnsley	46	18	14	14	61	49	50
Reading	46	18	14	14	55	52	50
Torquay United	46	16	15	15	57	56	47
Northampton Town	46	17	13	16	63	68	47
Huddersfield Town	46	15	15	16	63	55	45
Doncaster Rovers	46	14	17	15	52	65	45
Wimbledon	46	14	16	16	66	67	44
Scunthorpe United	46	14	16	16	50	55	44
Crewe Alexandra	46	15	14	17	50	69	44
Newport County	46	16	11	19	65	73	43
Bournemouth	46	14	15	17	41	51	43
Stockport County	46	16	10	20	56	56	42
Darlington	46	14	13	19	52	59	41
Halifax Town	46	10	21	15	52	62	41
Hartlepool United	46	15	7	24	51	84	37
York City	46	12	12	22	50	69	36
Southport	46	6	19	21	52	76	31
Rochdale	46	8	8	30	43	85	24

1978-79

Division Four

Managers: August–November 1978 Jimmy Lawson; November 1978–May 1979 George Kirby

Did you know that?

- Player-manager Jimmy Lawson introduced an all-white playing strip.
- Captain was Chris Dunleavy, then Steve Smith from April.
- Kevin Johnson signed for Halifax Town from Huddersfield Town on 9 August for a then club record £25,000.
- After winning their second match of the season, Halifax Town went 22 League games without victory – a club record.
- At one point, Halifax Town had eight former Huddersfield Town players in their squad; Lawson, Hutt, Mountford, Johnson, Smith, Sidebottom, Firth and Campbell.
- Scottish clubland singer Tommy Degnan, based in Grimsby, composed and recorded a single *The Shaymen of Halifax*, coupled with a catchy B-side *The Shaymen Song*. He sang of Halifax Town being 'the best team in Yorkshire' but days after the record hit the shops in October, Town dropped to the bottom of the Fourth Division.
- Arnie Sidebottom was a medium-pace bowler for Yorkshire and won one England Test cap against Australia in July 1985. His son Ryan also played for Test cricket England.
- Halifax Town's home game with Scunthorpe United was postponed four times. In total 14 home and away original and rearranged matches involving Halifax Town fell foul of the weather.
- Despite being 'sacked' by manager George Kirby in May for breaches of club discipline, striker Bobby Campbell went on to break Bradford City's goalscoring record and won two Northern Ireland international caps.
- Biggest League win: 2–0 v Portsmouth (h), 3 March, v Bradford City (h), 26 April.
- Heaviest League defeat: 0–3 v Port Vale (h), 14 October.
- Ever-present: Chris Dunleavy.

Match No.	Date	Venue	Opponents	Result		Scorers	Attendance
1	Aug 19	A	Barnsley	L	2-4	Burke, Bell	5,634
2	22	H	Stockport County	W	2-1	Bell, Bullock	2,253
3	26	H	Grimsby Town	L	1-2	Bullock	2,055
4	Sep 2	A	Aldershot	L	0-1		2,884
5	9	A	Torquay United	L	0-2		2,048
6	12	H	York City	L	0-1		1,701
7	16	H	Darlington	L	0-2		1,203
8	23	A	Hartlepool United	L	1-3	Lawson	3,947
9	27	A	Bradford City	L	0-3		4,115
10	30	H	Crewe Alexandra	D	0-0		985
11	Oct 7	A	Rochdale	D	1-1	Bell	1,579
12	14	H	Port Vale	L	0-3		1,591
13	18	A	Wigan Athletic	L	0-1		5,216
14	21	A	Portsmouth	L	1-3	Firth	12,365
15	28	H	AFC Bournemouth	L	0-2		1,184
16	Nov 4	A	Hereford United	D	2-2	Mountford, Dunleavy	3,616
17	11	H	Aldershot	D	1-1	Mountford	1,438
18	18	A	Grimsby Town	L	1-2	Prendergast	4,128
19	Dec 2	A	Wimbledon	L	1-2	Campbell	2,374
20	9	H	Reading	D	0-0		1,401
21	16	H	Wigan Athletic	L	1-2	Carroll	2,437
22	26	A	Huddersfield Town	L	0-2		5,341
23	30	A	Northampton Town	L	1-2	Nixon	2,208
24	Feb 10	A	Crewe Alexandra	L	0-1		1,594
25	24	A	Port Vale	W	1-0	Bentley (og)	3,117
26	27	A	Darlington	L	1-2	Mountford	1,403
27	Mar 3	H	Portsmouth	W	2-0	Ellis (og), Johnson	1,741
28	6	H	Doncaster Rovers	D	0-0		1,658
29	10	A	AFC Bournemouth	L	0-1		3,078
30	13	A	York City	L	0-2		2,196
31	23	A	Stockport County	W	2-1	Johnson, Campbell	3,033
32	27	H	Barnsley	L	0-2		5,654
33	31	A	Newport County	L	0-2		3,927
34	Apr 3	H	Torquay United	W	1-0	Trainer	1,112
35	7	H	Wimbledon	W	2-1	Trainer, Johnson	1,576
36	14	H	Huddersfield Town	L	2-3	Mountford, Sidebottom	4,027
37	16	A	Scunthorpe United	L	0-1		1,624
38	17	A	Doncaster Rovers	D	1-1	Sidebottom	2,227
39	21	H	Northampton Town	D	2-2	Geidmintis (og), Johnson	1,172
40	26	H	Bradford City	W	2-0	Campbell, Dunleavy	2,343
41	28	A	Reading	L	0-1		7,408
42	May 5	H	Newport County	L	1-2	Burke	1,007
43	7	H	Rochdale	W	2-1	Johnson (pen), Bradley	2,150
44	9	H	Hereford United	W	1-0	Johnson	1,036
45	14	H	Hartlepool United	L	2-4	Firth, Johnson (pen)	1,012
46	18	H	Scunthorpe United	L	2-3	Bradley 2	1,037

Final League Position: 23rd in Division Four

							Apps
							Sub Apps
						3 own-goals	Gls

FA Cup

1	Nov 25	A	Carlisle United	L	0-1		5,238
							Apps
							Sub Apps
							Gls

League Cup

1,1L	Aug 12	A	Walsall	L	1-2	Bullock	4,589
1,2l	15	H	Walsall	L	0-2		2,276
							Apps
							Sub Apps
							Gls

League Table

	P	W	D	L	F	A	Pts
Reading	46	26	13	7	76	35	65
Grimsby Town	46	26	9	11	82	49	61
Wimbledon	46	25	11	10	78	46	61
Barnsley	46	24	13	9	72	42	61
Aldershot	46	20	17	9	62	47	57
Wigan Athletic	46	21	13	12	63	48	55
Portsmouth	46	20	12	14	62	48	52
Newport County	46	21	10	15	66	55	52
Huddersfield Town	46	18	11	17	57	53	47
York City	46	18	11	17	51	55	47
Torquay United	46	19	8	19	58	65	46
Scunthorpe United	46	17	11	13	54	60	45
Hartlepool United	46	13	18	15	51	66	44
Hereford United	46	15	13	13	50	53	43
Bradford City	46	17	9	20	62	68	43
Port Vale	46	14	14	13	51	70	42
Stockport County	46	14	12	20	58	60	40
Bournemouth	46	14	11	21	47	48	39
Northampton Town	46	15	9	22	64	76	39
Rochdale	46	15	9	22	47	64	39
Darlington	46	11	15	20	49	66	37
Doncaster Rovers	46	13	11	22	50	73	37
Halifax Town	46	9	8	23	39	72	26
Crewe Alexandra	46	6	14	23	40	90	26

1979-80

Division Four

Manager: George Kirby

Did you know that?

- Captain was Dave Evans.
- At half-time between the home match with Doncaster Rovers on 21 August, future Commonwealth gold medallist Peter Elliott won an 800m race around the speedway track.
- Local League goalkeeper John Hough was forced to play in the home match with Hereford United on 15 September because Mickey Bullocks' car broke down on the way to Football League HQ at Lytham with John Kilner's registration form.
- Walsall were the last team in the Football League to lose when they did so at The Shay on 20 October.
- The 10,061 attendance figure for the Boxing Day clash with Huddersfield Town was the last time a League game attracted a five-figure gate at The Shay.
- Halifax Town's unusually high attendance of 3,639 for the visit of Peterborough United on 29 December was due in part to the club's decision to hand out vouchers which could be exchanged for tickets for the forthcoming FA Cup tie with Manchester City.
- Halifax Town were only Yorkshire club in the fourth round of the FA Cup.
- Halifax Town's 3,000th League goal was scored by John Smith in the 60th minute of their 3–1 defeat at Wigan Athletic on 12 April.
- Halifax Town conceded only nine goals from their first 18 home matches, and 11 from their last five.
- Biggest League win: 3–1 v Crewe Alexandra (h), 1 September.
- Heaviest League defeat: 0–5 v Huddersfield Town (a), 5 April.
- Ever-present: Mick Kennedy.

Match No.	Date		Venue	Opponents	Result		Scorers	Attendance
1	Aug	18	A	Tranmere Rovers	L	0-2		2,650
2		21	H	Doncaster Rovers	D	1-1	Harris	2,501
3		25	A	Peterborough United	L	1-2	Johnson	4,014
4	Sep	1	H	Crewe Alexandra	W	3-1	Burke, Johnson 2 (1 pen)	1,418
5		7	A	Northampton Town	D	0-0		2,759
6		15	H	Hereford United	W	1-0	Mountford	1,500
7		18	H	Rochdale	W	1-0	Stafford	2,390
8		22	A	AFC Bournemouth	W	1-0	Moore (og)	3,233
9		29	H	Hartlepool United	W	2-1	Mountford, Dunleavy	2,293
10	Oct	2	A	Rochdale	D	2-2	Hendrie, Burke	2,359
11		6	H	Newport County	W	2-1	Mountford (pen), Dunleavy	2,540
12		9	A	Doncaster Rovers	L	1-2	Whiteley	3,551
13		13	A	Darlington	D	1-1	Burke	1,670
14		20	H	Walsall	W	2-1	Kennedy, Firth	3,184
15		23	H	Bradford City	L	0-1		7,012
16		27	A	Torquay United	L	0-3		3,340
17	Nov	3	H	Tranmere Rovers	D	0-0		2,181
18		7	A	Bradford City	L	0-2		4,439
19		10	H	Port Vale	D	0-0		1,798
20		17	A	Aldershot	L	1-3	Burke	3,352
21	Dec	1	A	Portsmouth	L	1-3	Firth	14,087
22		8	H	Lincoln City	W	1-0	Hendrie	1,991
23		21	A	Scunthorpe United	L	0-1		1,473
24		26	H	Huddersfield Town	W	2-1	Kennedy, Burke	10,061
25		29	H	Peterborough United	D	0-0		3,639
26	Jan	12	A	Crewe Alexandra	L	1-2	Firth	2,579
27	Feb	2	A	Hereford United	L	0-2		2,814
28		9	H	AFC Bournemouth	W	2-0	Smith, Dunleavy	1,939
29		12	A	York City	D	2-2	Harris, Evans	2,124
30		16	A	Hartlepool United	W	2-1	Harris, Firth	3,392
31		23	H	Darlington	D	1-1	Evans (pen)	2,129
32	Mar	1	A	Walsall	L	0-2		5,859
33		4	A	Northampton Town	W	2-1	Smith 2	1,377
34		14	A	Newport County	L	2-5	Smith 2	4,777
35		19	H	Wigan Athletic	D	0-0		1,406
36		22	A	Port Vale	L	0-1		2,993
37		29	H	Aldershot	W	1-0	Kennedy	1,202
38	Apr	5	A	Huddersfield Town	L	0-5		10,580
39		7	H	York City	D	1-1	Firth	1,778
40		8	H	Scunthorpe United	D	2-2	Burke, Mountford	1,660
41		12	A	Wigan Athletic	L	1-3	Smith	5,076
42		19	H	Portsmouth	L	1-2	Hendrie	2,950
43		22	H	Stockport County	L	1-3	Firth	1,233
44		25	H	Lincoln City	L	0-4		2,696
45		29	H	Torquay United	D	3-3	Firth 2, Evans	1,022
46	May	2	A	Stockport County	L	1-4	Kennedy	1,979

Final League Position: 18th in Division Four

								Apps
								Sub Apps
							1 own-goal	Gls

FA Cup

	Date		Venue	Opponents	Result		Scorers	Attendance
1	Nov	24	H	Scarborough	W	2-0	Burke, Stafford	3,778
2	Dec	15	A	Walsall	D	1-1	Kennedy	4,651
R		18	H	Walsall	D	1-1*	Harris	3,641
2R		24	H	Walsall	W	2-0*	Burke, Smith	6,530
3	Jan	5	H	Manchester City	W	1-0	Hendrie	12,599
4		26	A	Bolton Wanderers	L	0-2		21,085

* After extra-time

								Apps
								Sub Apps
								Gls

League Cup

	Date		Venue	Opponents	Result		Scorers	Attendance
1,1L	Aug	11	H	Shrewsbury Town	D	2-2	Johnson, Mountford	1,904
1,2L		14	A	Shrewsbury Town	L	0-1		4,820

								Apps
								Sub Apps
								Gls

League Table

	P	W	D	L	F	A	Pts
Huddersfield Town	46	27	12	7	101	48	66
Walsall	46	23	18	5	75	47	64
Newport County	46	27	7	12	83	50	61
Portsmouth	46	24	12	10	91	49	60
Bradford City	46	24	12	10	77	50	60
Wigan Athletic	46	21	13	12	76	61	55
Lincoln City	46	18	17	11	64	42	53
Peterborough United	46	21	10	15	58	47	52
Torquay United	46	15	17	14	70	69	47
Aldershot	46	16	13	17	62	53	45
Bournemouth	46	13	18	15	52	51	44
Doncaster Rovers	46	15	14	17	62	63	44
Northampton Town	46	16	12	18	51	66	44
Scunthorpe United	46	14	15	17	58	75	43
Tranmere Rovers	46	14	13	19	50	56	41
Stockport County	46	14	12	20	48	72	40
York City	46	14	11	21	65	82	39
Halifax Town	46	13	13	20	46	72	39
Hartlepool United	46	14	10	22	59	64	38
Port Vale	46	12	12	22	56	70	36
Hereford United	46	11	14	21	38	52	36
Darlington	46	9	17	20	50	74	35
Crewe Alexandra	46	11	13	22	35	68	35
Rochdale	46	7	13	26	33	79	27

1980-81

Division Four
Manager: George Kirby

Did you know that?

- Mick Kennedy moved to Huddersfield Town on 6 August for a club record £50,000.
- Minimum ground admission for adults was £1.30.
- Halifax Town reverted to blue shirts with white trim and white shorts.
- Captain was Dave Evans.
- Halifax Town reverted to blue shirts and white shorts.
- Halifax Town operated under four different chairmen throughout the course of the season.
- Everton striker Imre Varadi turned down a move to The Shay, yet so sure of signing him were Halifax Town that his pen-picture featured in the match programme for the game at Peterborough United on 20 August.
- 'Keeper Ian Turner, on loan from Walsall, was an FA Cup-winner with Southampton in 1976.
- Biggest League win: 4–2 v Bury (h), 23 August.
- Heaviest League defeat: 1–5 v Southend United (a), 13 March.

Match No.	Date		Venue	Opponents	Result		Scorers	Attendance
1	Aug	16	H	Mansfield Town	L	0-2		1,682
2		20	A	Peterborough United	D	2-2	Ward, Firth	3,885
3		23	H	Bury	W	4-2	Firth 2, Dunleavy, Allatt	1,861
4		29	A	Stockport County	D	1-1	Firth	2,487
5	Sep	6	A	Lincoln City	L	0-3		3,720
6		13	H	Scunthorpe United	W	1-0	Firth	1,226
7		16	H	Wigan Athletic	L	0-1		2,052
8		20	A	Crewe Alexandra	L	1-2	Nattress	2,102
9		27	H	Wimbledon	L	0-1		1,407
10	Oct	1	A	Wigan Athletic	L	1-4	Firth	4,247
11		4	A	Torquay United	L	0-1		1,849
12		7	H	York City	W	3-1	Nattress, Hendrie, O'Neil	1,088
13		11	H	Southend United	L	1-5	O'Neil	1,609
14		18	A	Doncaster Rovers	D	0-0		4,044
15		20	A	Tranmere Rovers	L	0-2		2,314
16		25	H	Hereford United	D	0-0		1,288
17		28	H	Bradford City	W	2-0	Graham, Hendrie	2,365
18		31	A	Northampton Town	L	1-2	McIlwraith (pen)	2,226
19	Nov	4	A	York City	D	1-1	Evans	1,837
20		8	H	Hartlepool United	L	1-2	Goodman	1,692
21		11	H	Peterborough United	L	2-3	Nattress, McIlwraith (pen)	1,151
22		15	A	Mansfield Town	W	1-0	McIlwraith (pen)	2,561
23		29	H	AFC Bournemouth	L	1-2	Bullock	987
24	Dec	6	A	Aldershot	L	1-2	Burton	2,335
25		20	H	Port Vale	D	2-2	Dunleavy, Nattress	1,215
26		26	A	Rochdale	D	1-1	Nattress	2,623
27		27	H	Darlington	L	1-2	Graham	1,805
28	Jan	10	H	Tranmere Rovers	D	1-1	Graham	1,268
29		17	A	AFC Bournemouth	L	1-2	Firth (pen)	2,413
30		24	H	Stockport County	W	2-0	Allatt, Graham	3,286
31		31	A	Bury	D	0-0		3,144
32	Feb	7	A	Scunthorpe United	D	2-2	Ayre, Hendrie	2,073
33		11	A	Bradford City	D	0-0		3,056
34		14	H	Lincoln City	L	1-3	Firth (pen)	4,444
35		21	A	Wimbledon	L	0-3		2,501
36	Mar	7	H	Torquay United	W	2-1	Graham 2	2,008
37		13	A	Southend United	L	1-5	Graham	5,542
38		21	H	Doncaster Rovers	L	0-3		3,762
39		24	A	Crewe Alexandra	W	1-0	McIlwraith (pen)	2,266
40		28	A	Hereford United	W	1-0	Allatt	2,588
41	Apr	4	H	Northampton Town	L	0-1		1,996
42		11	A	Hartlepool United	L	0-3		1,576
43		18	A	Darlington	L	1-3	McIlwraith (pen)	2,015
44		20	H	Rochdale	W	2-0	Graham 2	2,278
45		26	A	Port Vale	D	0-0		2,301
46	May	2	H	Aldershot	W	1-0	Jopling (og)	1,587

Final League Position: 23rd in Division Four

Apps
Sub Apps
1 own-goal   Gls

FA Cup

| 1 | Nov | 22 | A | Hull City | L | 1-2 | Firth | 4,024 |

Apps
Sub Apps
Gls

League Cup

| 1,1L | Aug | 9 | A | Bury | D | 2-2 | Firth, Evans | 3,029 |
| 1,2L | | 12 | H | Bury | L | 0-1 | | 2,268 |

Apps
Sub Apps
Gls

League Table

	P	W	D	L	F	A	Pts
Southend United	46	30	7	9	79	31	67
Lincoln City	46	25	15	6	66	25	65
Doncaster Rovers	46	22	12	12	59	49	56
Wimbledon	46	23	9	14	64	46	55
Peterborough United	46	17	18	11	68	54	52
Aldershot	46	18	14	14	43	41	50
Mansfield Town	46	20	9	17	58	44	49
Darlington	46	19	11	16	65	59	49
Hartlepool United	46	20	9	17	64	61	49
Northampton Town	46	18	13	15	65	67	49
Wigan Athletic	46	18	11	17	51	55	47
Bury	46	17	11	13	70	62	45
Bournemouth	46	16	13	17	47	48	45
Bradford City	46	14	16	16	53	60	44
Rochdale	46	14	15	17	60	70	43
Scunthorpe United	46	11	20	15	60	69	42
Torquay United	46	18	5	23	55	63	41
Crewe Alexandra	46	13	14	19	48	61	40
Port Vale	46	12	15	13	57	70	39
Stockport County	46	16	7	23	44	57	39
Tranmere Rovers	46	13	10	23	59	73	36
Hereford United	46	11	13	22	38	62	35
Halifax Town	46	11	12	23	44	71	34
York City	46	12	9	25	47	66	33

1981-82

Division Four

Manager: Mickey Bullock

Did you know that?

- Captain was Dave Evans.
- 17-year-old Steve Walker's League career extended to just 19 minutes when he replaced Glyn Chamberlain in the match at Stockport County on 13 November.
- Town's run of nine unbeaten matches between 2 January and 20 February was their longest in 11 seasons.
- 62 free-kicks were awarded in the game at Bournemouth on 30 January.
- Halifax Town drew a 22 League games, equalling the record set by Aldershot in 1971-72. Their run included seven successive draws between 22 January and 20 February.
- Having taken exception to a story run by reporter Ian Rushworth about his plans to hold stock car racing at The Shay, Town chairman Sam Rorke banned the *Halifax Courier* from travelling with the team for the match at Peterborough on 26 January. Rushworth made his own way there.
- Sam Rorke allows the fans to 'pay what you can afford' for the home game with Crewe Alexandra on 20 March.
- Town lost seven matches after they had been in front.
- Bobby Davison is the first Town player to net 20 goals since Les Massie in 1967-68.
- Biggest League win: 4-1 v Stockport County (h), 2 April.
- Heaviest League defeat: 1-7 v Blackpool (a), 30 September.
- Ever-presents: Bobby Davison, Dave Evans.

Match No.	Date		Venue	Opponents	Result		Scorers	Attendance
1	Aug	29	A	Port Vale	D	0-0		3,883
2	Sep	5	H	Peterborough United	D	1-1	Davison	1,805
3		12	A	Aldershot	L	1-3	Graham	1,733
4		19	H	AFC Bournemouth	D	1-1	Davison	1,588
5		22	H	Tranmere Rovers	L	0-2		1,943
6		26	A	Hartlepool United	L	2-3	Davison, McIlwraith	1,800
7		30	A	Blackpool	L	1-7	Davison	5,084
8	Oct	3	H	Bury	W	2-1	Allatt, Graham	2,420
9		10	A	Hereford United	D	2-2	Davison, Graham	2,359
10		17	H	Rochdale	D	0-0		2,140
11		20	A	Darlington	D	1-1	Graham	1,642
12		24	H	Colchester United	L	0-2		1,374
13		31	A	Crewe Alexandra	W	1-0	Allatt	2,291
14	Nov	3	H	Torquay United	L	1-2	Graham	1,523
15		7	H	Mansfield Town	W	2-1	Evans, Allatt	1,447
16		13	A	Stockport County	L	1-2	Allatt	2,493
17		28	H	Scunthorpe United	L	1-2	Graham	1,396
18	Dec	5	A	Wigan Athletic	L	0-2		4,022
19	Jan	2	H	Sheffield United	D	2-2	Ward 2	11,623
20		13	A	Rochdale	W	1-0	Davison	1,122
21		22	H	Port Vale	D	1-1	Ward	2,965
22		26	A	Peterborough United	D	0-0		3,016
23		30	A	AFC Bournemouth	D	1-1	Ward	4,690
24	Feb	6	H	Aldershot	D	2-2	Ayre, Davison	1,754
25		9	A	Tranmere Rovers	D	1-1	Ayre	1,454
26		13	A	Bury	D	1-1	Ward	3,590
27		20	H	Blackpool	D	0-0		2,245
28		27	H	Hereford United	L	1-2	Davison	2,098
29	Mar	2	A	Hull City	L	0-2		6,952
30		9	A	Darlington	D	3-3	Davison 2, Ayre	1,508
31		12	A	Colchester United	D	1-1	Ayre	2,464
32		20	H	Crewe Alexandra	W	2-1	Spooner, Ward	2,128
33		23	H	Bradford City	D	0-0		5,926
34		27	A	Mansfield Town	L	2-3	Davison 2	2,197
35	Apr	2	H	Stockport County	W	4-1	Firth, Davison 2, Spooner	2,135
36		10	A	Bradford City	L	2-5	Davison, Graham	5,179
37		12	H	Sheffield United	L	1-5	Hendrie	8,077
38		17	H	Wigan Athletic	D	0-0		3,660
39		20	A	Northampton Town	W	1-0	Graham (pen)	1,935
40		24	A	Scunthorpe United	D	0-0		1,643
41		27	A	Torquay United	D	2-2	Davison 2	1,331
42	May	1	H	Hartlepool United	W	2-0	Evans, Ward	1,305
43		4	H	Northampton Town	W	2-1	Davison 2	1,730
44		7	A	York City	L	0-4		2,423
45		11	H	York City	D	0-0		1,903
46		14	H	Hull City	D	2-2	Davison, Hendrie	2,293

Final League Position: 19th in Division Four

Apps
Sub Apps
Gls

FA Cup

1	Nov	21	H	Peterborough United	L	0-3		2,614

Apps
Sub Apps
Gls

League Cup

1,1L	Sep	1	H	Preston North End	L	1-2	Davison	2,719
R		15	A	Preston North End	D	0-0		4,090

Apps
Sub Apps
Gls

League Table

	P	W	D	L	F	A	Pts
Sheffield United	46	27	15	4	94	41	96
Bradford City	46	26	13	7	88	45	91
Wigan Athletic	46	26	13	7	80	46	91
Bournemouth	46	23	19	4	62	30	88
Peterborough United	46	24	10	12	71	57	82
Colchester United	46	20	12	14	82	57	72
Port Vale	46	18	16	14	56	49	70
Hull City	46	19	12	15	70	61	69
Bury	46	17	17	12	80	59	68
Hereford United	46	16	19	11	64	58	67
Tranmere Rovers	46	14	18	14	51	56	60
Blackpool	46	15	13	18	66	60	58
Darlington	46	15	13	18	61	62	58
Hartlepool United	46	13	16	17	73	84	55
Torquay United	46	14	13	19	47	59	55
Aldershot	46	13	15	18	57	68	54
York City	46	14	8	24	69	91	50
Stockport County	46	12	13	21	48	67	49
Halifax Town	46	9	22	15	51	72	49
Mansfield Town*	46	13	10	23	63	81	47
Rochdale	46	10	16	20	50	62	46
Northampton Town	46	11	9	26	57	84	42
Scunthorpe United	46	9	15	22	43	79	42
Crewe Alexandra	46	6	9	31	29	84	27

* Two points deducted for fielding an ineligible player

1982-83

Division Four
Manager: Mickey Bullock

Did you know that?

- Kitchen manufacturers Macdee became the club's first sponsors.
- Captain was Paul Hendrie.
- Bobby Davison netted a hat-trick at Wimbledon on 13 November, the first by a Town player away from home since John Parks scored all three goals against Hartlepool in April 1967. It's the first League hat-trick by a Town player since Shanahan's three goals against Brentford in April 1973.
- Bobby Davison moved to Derby County on 2 December for a record £98,000.
- Town won 2–1 at Mansfield Town on 8 January despite not having arrived at the ground until 2.30pm for a 3pm kick-off.
- Halifax Town won six consecutive matches between 3 January and 5 February to move from 20th to 8th in the League table.
- Steve Spooner scored an astonishing goal in the win at Tranmere Rovers on 23 April. On a bone-hard ground, his daisy-cutter hit a divot and the ball flew into the roof of the net.
- Barry Gallagher's first-ever League goal was the winner against Town on his League debut for Bradford City in October 1979.
- Biggest League win: 4–0 v Colchester United (h), 14 January.
- Heaviest League defeat: 1–6 v Aldershot (a), 7 May.
- Ever-present: Keith Nobbs.

Match No.	Date		Venue	Opponents	Result		Scorers	Attendance
1	Aug	28	A	Colchester United	L	0-1		2,610
2	Sep	3	H	Mansfield Town	D	0-0		2,225
3		7	H	Darlington	W	2-0	Hendrie, Spooner	1,891
4		11	A	Swindon Town	W	1-0	Davison	3,450
5		18	H	Aldershot	L	1-3	Davison	2,243
6		25	A	Bury	L	0-2		2,244
7		28	A	York City	L	2-3	Davison 2	1,772
8	Oct	1	H	Chester	D	0-0		1,925
9		9	A	Blackpool	D	0-0		4,150
10		15	H	Port Vale	L	0-2		2,009
11		19	H	Bristol City	D	2-2	Davison 2	1,465
12		23	A	Rochdale	D	2-2	Spooner, Keenan (og)	1,765
13		29	H	Crewe Alexandra	L	0-3		1,726
14	Nov	3	A	Peterborough United	L	1-2	Nobbs	2,038
15		5	H	Hereford United	D	2-2	Spooner, Smith	1,065
16		13	A	Wimbledon	W	4-2	Davison 3, Allatt	2,104
17		27	A	Hartlepool United	W	2-1	Wood, Staniforth	1,367
18	Dec	17	H	Tranmere Rovers	L	1-2	Hamilton (og)	912
19		27	A	Hull City	D	1-1	Staniforth	10,042
20		28	H	Scunthorpe United	W	3-1	Spooner, Staniforth, Nuttall	2,270
21	Jan	1	A	Stockport County	L	2-4	Allatt, Spooner (pen)	2,871
22		3	H	Torquay United	W	3-0	Spooner (pen), Nuttall, Allatt	1,776
23		8	A	Mansfield Town	W	2-1	Nuttall 2	2,398
24		14	H	Colchester United	W	4-0	Nuttall, Staniforth 3	1,863
25		22	A	Darlington	W	2-1	Staniforth 2	1,175
26	Feb	1	H	Northampton Town	W	2-0	Ward, Staniforth	1,927
27		5	H	Bury	W	1-0	Evans	4,021
28		12	A	Chester	L	0-2		1,907
29		15	A	Bristol City	L	0-3		3,169
30		18	H	Blackpool	W	2-0	Spooner (pen), Allatt	2,366
31		26	A	Port Vale	L	1-2	Spooner	5,163
32	Mar	1	H	Peterborough United	L	1-2	Staniforth	2,002
33		4	H	Rochdale	D	0-0		2,128
34		11	A	Crewe Alexandra	D	1-1	Staniforth	2,518
35		15	H	Swindon Town	W	1-0	Nuttall	1,806
36		19	A	Hereford United	L	0-2		2,006
37	Apr	1	A	Scunthorpe United	L	0-2		3,775
38		4	H	Hull City	L	1-2	Nuttall	5,011
39		10	A	Northampton Town	L	1-3	Staniforth	2,208
40		15	H	York City	D	2-2	Allatt 2	2,117
41		23	A	Tranmere Rovers	W	2-1	Spooner 2 (1 pen)	1,401
42		29	H	Hartlepool United	D	1-1	Staniforth	1,245
43	May	2	A	Torquay United	W	3-1	Wood, Allatt, Smith	1,558
44		7	A	Aldershot	L	1-6	Staniforth	1,701
45		10	H	Wimbledon	D	1-1	Spooner	1,233
46		13	H	Stockport County	W	1-0	Staniforth	1,522

Final League Position: 11th in Division Four

Apps
Sub Apps
2 own-goals   Gls

FA Cup

1	Nov	20	H	North Shields	L	0-1		2,277

Apps
Sub Apps
Gls

Milk Cup

1,1L	Aug	31	H	Derby County	W	2-1	Davison, Staniforth	2,820
1,2L	Sep	15	A	Derby County	L	2-5*	Davison 2	8,534

* After extra-time

Apps
Sub Apps
Gls

League Table

	P	W	D	L	F	A	Pts
Wimbledon	46	29	11	6	96	45	98
Hull City	46	25	15	6	75	34	90
Port Vale	46	26	10	10	67	34	88
Scunthorpe United	46	23	14	9	71	42	83
Bury	46	23	12	11	74	46	81
Colchester United	46	24	9	13	75	55	81
York City	46	22	13	11	88	58	79
Swindon Town	46	19	11	16	61	54	68
Peterborough United	46	17	13	16	58	52	64
Mansfield Town	46	16	13	17	61	70	61
Halifax Town	46	16	12	18	59	66	60
Torquay United	46	17	7	22	56	65	58
Chester	46	15	11	20	55	60	56
Bristol City	46	13	17	16	59	70	56
Northampton Town	46	14	12	20	65	75	54
Stockport County	46	14	12	20	60	79	54
Darlington	46	13	13	20	61	71	52
Aldershot	46	12	15	19	61	82	51
Tranmere Rovers	46	13	11	22	49	71	50
Rochdale	46	11	16	19	55	73	49
Blackpool*	46	13	12	21	55	74	49
Hartlepool United	46	13	9	24	46	76	48
Crewe Alexandra	46	11	8	27	53	71	41
Hereford United	46	11	8	27	42	79	41

* Two points deducted for fielding an ineligible player

1983-84

Division Four
Manager: Mickey Bullock

Did you know that?

- Captain was Paul Hendrie.
- Joe Gallagher was an England B international.
- Steve Thornber made his League debut as a 69th substitute in the home match with Chester on 14 February, and scored Town's equaliser in a 2–2 draw within five minutes from 25 yards with his first touch of the ball.
- After production problems, only 350 of the intended 1,200 match programmes were printed for the home game with Bristol City on 17 March.
- Barry Gallagher became only the eighth Town player to net four goals in a game when he did so against Rochdale on 23 April. It was the first four-goal haul by a Town player since Des Frost in February 1951.
- Goalkeeper Lee Smelt published a booklet entitled *Practice Keeping*.
- Biggest League win: 5–0 v Rochdale (h), 23 April.
- Heaviest League defeat: 1–7 v Mansfield Town (a), 10 April.
- Ever-presents: Dave Evans, Steve Ward.

Match No.	Date		Venue	Opponents	Result		Scorers	Attendance
1	Aug	27	H	Torquay United	D	2-2	Cook, Hendrie	1,448
2	Sep	3	A	Hereford United	D	0-0		3,188
3		6	A	Swindon Town	W	3-2	Kendall, Staniforth, Cook	3,635
4		9	H	Mansfield Town	D	0-0		1,725
5		18	A	Bury	L	0-3		3,258
6		23	H	Hartlepool United	W	3-2	Mell 2, Staniforth	1,418
7		27	H	Northampton Town	D	2-2	Staniforth, Mell	1,519
8	Oct	1	A	Wrexham	L	0-1		5,472
9		8	A	Bristol City	L	0-3		6,739
10		15	H	Peterborough United	W	2-1	Mell, Nuttall	1,079
11		18	H	Crewe Alexandra	W	1-0	Ward	1,352
12		21	A	Doncaster Rovers	L	2-3	Staniforth, Cook (pen)	3,299
13		29	H	Aldershot	W	1-0	B. Gallagher	1,242
14	Nov	2	A	Chester City	D	1-1	Cook (pen)	1,211
15		4	H	Tranmere Rovers	L	1-2	Hendrie	1,735
16		11	A	Stockport County	L	0-4		2,034
17		25	H	Darlington	L	0-2		1,018
18	Dec	2	A	Reading	L	0-1		3,930
19		17	A	Colchester United	L	1-4	Greenway	1,866
20		26	H	York City	L	1-2	Little	2,457
21		27	A	Rochdale	D	1-1	Cook	1,898
22		31	H	Blackpool	W	1-0	Little (pen)	1,958
23	Jan	2	A	Chesterfield	D	0-0		2,298
24		7	H	Hereford United	W	2-1	Cooper, Little	1,037
25		14	A	Torquay United	D	1-1	Nuttall	1,369
26		21	H	Bury	D	0-0		1,728
27	Feb	4	H	Wrexham	D	1-1	Smith	1,184
28		11	A	Hartlepool United	L	0-3		1,658
29		14	H	Chester City	D	2-2	B. Gallagher, Thornber	911
30		18	A	Aldershot	L	2-5	Staniforth, B. Gallagher (pen)	2,382
31		25	H	Doncaster Rovers	L	1-2	Harle (og)	2,408
32	Mar	3	A	Crewe Alexandra	L	1-6	B. Gallagher (pen)	2,050
33		5	A	Tranmere Rovers	L	2-3	Staniforth, Cook	1,486
34		9	H	Stockport County	W	2-0	B. Gallagher 2	1,261
35		17	H	Bristol City	L	1-2	Evans	1,204
36		24	A	Peterborough United	L	0-4		2,304
37		30	H	Swindon Town	W	2-1	Kendall, B. Gallagher	1,008
38	Apr	7	A	Northampton Town	D	1-1	Evans	1,356
39		10	A	Mansfield Town	L	1-7	Foster (og)	1,696
40		13	H	Reading	L	0-1		1,113
41		20	H	York City	L	1-4	Mell	7,123
42		23	H	Rochdale	W	5-0	Mell, B. Gallagher 4	1,422
43		28	A	Darlington	L	2-3	Ward, Nuttall	1,161
44	May	4	H	Chesterfield	W	2-1	Mell, B. Gallagher (pen)	1,001
45		7	A	Blackpool	L	0-4		2,324
46		11	H	Colchester United	W	4-1	Ward, B. Gallagher 2, Mell	1,248

Final League Position: 21st in Division Four

Apps
Sub Apps
2 own-goals Gls

FA Cup

1	Nov	19	H	Whitby Town	L	2-3	Ward, Evans	2,588

Apps
Sub Apps
Gls

Milk Cup

1,1L	Aug	30	H	Darlington	L	0-1		1,331
1,2L	Sep	13	A	Darlington	L	2-3	Kendall, Staniforth	1,793

Apps
Sub Apps
Gls

Player	Smelt, LA	Nobbs, AK	Wood, MJ	Evans, DG	Smith, A	Hendrie, PF	Ward, SC	Cook, JW	Mel, SA	Hanson, N	Staniforth, DA	Kendall, PS	Gallagher, BP	Nuttall, M	Gallagher, JA	Vasey, KG	Little, A	Greenwey, M	Cooper, SB	Thornber, SJ
1	2	3	4	5	6	7	8	9*	10	11	12									
1	2	3	4	5	6	9	8			11	10	7								
1	2	3	4	5	6	9	8	12		11	10	7*								
1	2	3	4	5	6	9*	8	12		11	10	7								
1	2	3	4	5	6	9	8*			11	10	7	12							
1	2	3	4	5	6	11	8			9	10	7								
1	2	3	4	5	6	11	8			9	10	7								
1	2	3	4	5	6	11*	12	8		9	10	7								
1	2	3	4*	5	6	11	12	8		9	10		7							
1	2	3	4	5	6	11	9	8		10*	12	7								
1	2	3	4	5	6	11	9	8			10	12	7*							
1	2	3	4	5	6	11	9	8		12	10		7*							
1	2	3	4		6	11	10	8		9		7		5						
1	2	3	4		6	11	10	8*		9		7	12	5						
	2	3	4	10*	6	11	9	8				7	12	5	1					
1		3	4	2	6	11		8			10	7	9	5						
1	2	3	4	5	6	11	9		12		10	7*				8				
1	2	3	4	5	6	7	9*	10			12					8	1			
1	2	3	4	5	6	11	12				10		9			8	-*			
1	2	3	4	5	6	11	12				10					8	-*	9		
1	2	3	4	5	6	11	10				7					8	2	9*		
1	2		4	5*	6	11			10	12		7				8	3	9		
1	2		4		6	11			10	5		7				8	3	9		
1	2		4		6	11			10	5		7				8	3	9		
1	2	12	4	5	6	11			10	8		7					3	9*		
1	2	6	4			11		12	10	5	8	7					3	9*		
1	2	6	4	12		11		9	10	5	8	7*					3			
1	2	3	4	5		11*		9	10	6	7	12				8				
1	2	10	4		6	11*			9	5	7					8	3		12	
1	2	3	4		6	11			9	5	7					8			10	
1	2	3	4	12	6	11	9*			5	7					8			10	
1	2	3	4	5	6	11	12		9		7					8			10*	
1		3	4	5	6	11	10	12	9*	2	7					8				
1		3	4	5	6	11	10	9*	12	2	7					8				
1		3	4	5	6	11	10*	12	9	2	7					8				
1	2	3	4	5	6	11			9	10	7					8				
1	6	3	4	5		11	10	12	9	4	7*					8				
1	6	3	4	5		11*	10	12	9	4	7					8				
	6	3	4	5		11	10*	12	9	4	7			1		8				
1	10	3	4	5	6	11			9	4	12	7				8*				
1	7	3	4	5	6	11		10		4	9					8				
1	2	3	4	5	6	11	7*	10				9	12			8				
1	2	3	4	5	6	11	7	10*				9	12			8				
1	2	3	4	5	6	11	7	10				9				8				
1		3	4	5	6	11	7*	10		2	9	12				8				
1	7	3	4	5	6	11		10		2	9*	12				8				
44	41	42	46	37	40	46	25	22	1	28	36	32	13	4	2	27	0	7	3	
		1		2			5	8	1	2	3	3	8			1		1		
		2	1	2	3	6	8		6	2	14	3				3	1	1	1	

1	2	3	4		6	11	8	12			10	7	9*	5						
1	1	1	1		1	1	1				1	1	1	1						
				1																
		1				1														

1	2	3	4	5	6		8	9*	10	11		7	12							
1	2	3	4	5	6	9	8*	12		11	10	7								
2	2	2	2	2	2	1	2	1	1	2	1	2								
								1				1								
						1	1													

League Table

	P	W	D	L	F	A	Pts
York City	46	31	8	7	96	39	101
Doncaster Rovers	46	24	13	9	82	54	85
Reading	46	22	16	8	84	56	82
Bristol City	46	24	10	12	70	44	82
Aldershot	46	22	9	15	76	69	75
Blackpool	46	21	9	16	70	52	72
Peterborough United	46	18	14	14	72	48	68
Colchester United	46	17	16	13	69	53	67
Torquay United	46	18	13	15	59	64	67
Tranmere Rovers	46	17	15	14	53	53	66
Hereford United	46	16	15	15	54	53	63
Stockport County	46	17	11	18	60	64	62
Chesterfield	46	15	15	16	59	61	60
Darlington	46	17	8	21	49	50	59
Bury	46	15	14	17	61	64	59
Crewe Alexandra	46	16	11	19	56	67	59
Swindon Town	46	15	13	18	58	56	58
Northampton Town	46	13	14	19	53	78	53
Mansfield Town	46	13	13	20	66	70	52
Wrexham	46	11	15	20	59	74	48
Halifax Town	46	12	12	22	55	89	48
Rochdale	46	11	13	22	52	80	46
Hartlepool United	46	10	10	26	47	85	40
Chester City	46	7	13	26	45	82	34

1984-85

Division Four

Managers: August–November 1984 Mickey Bullock; October–November 1984 Billy Ayre (caretaker); November 1984–May 1985 Mick Jones

Did you know that?

- DIY firm Madeley's were the club's sponsors.
- Captain was Alan Little.
- Cec Podd holds the record for most League appearances for Bradford City – 502.
- Garry Watson had his jaw broken after a flare-up with former Town player Vernon Allatt in the match at Crewe on 23 November.
- Alan Knill's equaliser prevented Blackpool from recording a club record eighth consecutive win in the League on 5 January.
- Halifax Town won their 2,500th League game in style, defeating League-leaders Bury 4–1 on 12 January.
- Town ended the game at Darlington on 8 March with eight men following injuries to Kendall and 'keeper Roche, and dismissals of Knill and Podd.
- Halifax Town's late season victory over Hereford United guaranteed promotion for Bury, which spawned a fanzine at Gigg Lane entitled *Where Were You At The Shay?*
- Biggest League win: 4–1 v Bury (h), 12 January.
- Heaviest League defeat: 0–4 v Scunthorpe United (a), 28 September, v Chester (h), 22 March.

Match No.	Date		Venue	Opponents	Result		Scorers	Attendance
1	Aug	25	H	Blackpool	L	0-2		1,870
2	Sep	1	A	Bury	L	0-3		1,717
3		8	H	Aldershot	L	1-2	Little	1,004
4		15	A	Northampton Town	W	1-0	Thornber	1,437
5		17	A	Tranmere Rovers	L	0-1		1,432
6		21	H	Southend United	W	1-0	Gallagher	1,120
7		28	A	Scunthorpe United	L	0-4		1,929
8	Oct	6	A	Chester City	L	0-2		1,412
9		13	H	Chesterfield	L	1-3	Gallagher	1,592
10		19	H	Darlington	L	0-1		1,224
11		24	A	Peterborough United	L	0-2		3,770
12		26	A	Colchester United	W	3-1	Lowe, Ayre, Gallagher	2,295
13	Nov	6	A	Torquay United	D	1-1	Lowe	1,153
14		10	H	Mansfield Town	W	1-0	Cook	1,237
15		23	A	Crewe Alexandra	W	1-0	Ward	1,920
16		30	H	Port Vale	W	2-1	Lowe 2	1,688
17	Dec	15	A	Hereford United	L	0-3		5,148
18		22	A	Swindon Town	L	1-2	Ward	2,414
19		26	H	Hartlepool United	L	2-3	Ayre, Gallagher	1,409
20	Jan	1	A	Rochdale	L	0-2		1,671
21		5	A	Blackpool	D	1-1	Knill	5,184
22		12	H	Bury	W	4-1	Lowe 3, Gallagher	2,584
23	Feb	1	A	Scunthorpe United	L	1-2	Lowe	1,317
24		8	A	Southend United	L	1-2	Ward	1,362
25		12	H	Tranmere Rovers	W	2-1	Lowe, Cook	914
26		16	H	Wrexham	L	1-2	Thornber	1,119
27		23	A	Exeter City	L	0-1		2,549
28		26	H	Northampton Town	W	1-0	Little (pen)	1,009
29	Mar	1	H	Colchester United	D	0-0		1,022
30		5	H	Peterborough United	D	0-0		1,071
31		9	A	Darlington	L	0-2		3,690
32		12	A	Wrexham	W	1-0	Thornber	1,025
33		16	A	Chesterfield	L	0-3		2,870
34		22	H	Chester City	L	0-4		1,014
35		26	H	Exeter City	L	2-3	McNiven, Gallagher	1,011
36		30	H	Torquay United	L	0-1		890
37	Apr	2	A	Aldershot	L	0-2		1,523
38		6	A	Hartlepool United	W	1-0	McNiven	1,640
39		8	H	Rochdale	L	0-2		1,706
40		13	A	Mansfield Town	L	1-2	Little	1,928
41		19	H	Crewe Alexandra	D	1-1	Gallagher	1,416
42		23	H	Stockport County	W	2-1	Lowe, Ward	1,291
43		27	A	Port Vale	L	1-3	McNiven	2,029
44	May	3	H	Hereford United	W	2-1	McNiven, Lowe	1,629
45		6	A	Stockport County	W	3-0	Lowe, Gallagher, Shaw	1,480
46		10	H	Swindon Town	W	2-1	Cook, Sanderson	2,307

Final League Position: 21st in Division Four

Apps
Sub Apps
Gls

FA Cup

	Date		Venue	Opponents	Result		Scorers	Attendance
1	Nov	17	H	Goole Town	W	2-0	Gallagher, Cook	1,847
2	Dec	8	A	Burnley	L	1-3	Gallagher	5,548

Apps
Sub Apps
Gls

Milk Cup

	Date		Venue	Opponents	Result		Scorers	Attendance
1,1L	Aug	28	H	Chesterfield	D	1-1	Lowe	1,174
1,2L	Sep	4	A	Chesterfield	W	2-1	Little, Lowe	2,976
2,1L		26	H	Tottenham Hotspur	L	1-5	Gallagher	7,027
2,2L	Oct	9	A	Tottenham Hotspur	L	0-4		14,802

Apps
Sub Apps
Gls

League Table

	P	W	D	L	F	A	Pts
Chesterfield	46	26	13	7	64	35	91
Blackpool	46	24	14	8	73	39	86
Darlington	46	24	13	9	66	49	85
Bury	46	24	12	10	76	50	84
Hereford United	46	22	11	13	65	47	77
Tranmere Rovers	46	24	3	19	83	66	75
Colchester United	46	20	14	12	87	65	74
Swindon Town	46	21	9	16	62	58	72
Scunthorpe United	46	19	14	13	83	62	71
Crewe Alexandra	46	18	12	16	65	69	66
Peterborough United	46	16	14	16	54	53	62
Port Vale	46	14	18	14	61	59	60
Aldershot	46	17	8	21	56	63	59
Mansfield Town	46	13	18	15	41	38	57
Wrexham	46	15	9	22	67	70	54
Chester City	46	15	9	22	60	72	54
Rochdale	46	13	14	19	55	69	53
Exeter City	46	13	14	19	57	79	53
Hartlepool United	46	14	10	22	54	67	52
Southend United	46	13	11	22	58	83	50
Halifax Town	46	15	5	26	42	69	50
Stockport County	46	13	8	25	58	79	47
Northampton Town	46	14	5	27	53	74	47
Torquay United	46	9	14	23	38	63	41

1985-86

Division Four
Manager: Mick Jones

Did you know that?

- Halifax Town wore blue-and-white-striped shirts for the first time since 1950.
- Captain was Phil Brown.
- Full-back Phil Brown's chemistry teacher at secondary school was future Olympic 10,000m bronze medallist Brendan Foster.
- Town's Boxing Day match with Rochdale at The Shay was an 11.00am kick-off.
- The attendance of 1,006 for Town's game at Southend United on 5 March became an all-time low at Roots Hall.
- Biggest League win: 5–2 v Wrexham (h), 14 March.
- Heaviest League defeat: 0–4 v Cambridge United (a), 8 April.
- Ever-present: Paddy Roche.

Match No.	Date		Venue	Opponents	Result		Scorers	Attendance
1	Aug	17	A	Chester City	D	1-1	Ward	1,750
2		23	H	Scunthorpe United	W	2-1	Graham (og), Lowe	1,094
3		27	A	Mansfield Town	L	0-2		3,299
4		30	H	Preston North End	W	2-1	Longhurst 2	2,011
5	Sep	6	A	Colchester United	L	1-3	Gallagher	2,023
6		13	H	Orient	W	2-1	Nicholson, Longhurst	1,243
7		17	H	Southend United	L	2-3	Longhurst, Kendall	1,514
8		21	A	Port Vale	L	2-3	Kellock 2	2,754
9		27	H	Cambridge United	D	1-1	Kellock	1,409
10	Oct	1	A	Torquay United	L	0-2		1,131
11		5	H	Aldershot	D	1-1	Kellock (pen)	1,066
12		12	A	Wrexham	L	1-2	Gallagher	1,609
13		18	H	Tranmere Rovers	L	1-2	Gallagher	1,412
14		23	A	Exeter City	L	0-1		1,719
15		26	H	Burnley	D	2-2	Kellock, Lowe	2,334
16	Nov	2	A	Crewe Alexandra	D	2-2	Longhurst 2	1,493
17		4	A	Stockport County	L	1-2	Gallagher	1,673
18		9	H	Peterborough United	D	1-1	Gallagher (pen)	1,007
19		23	A	Northampton Town	L	0-4		1,514
20	Dec	3	H	Hereford United	W	1-0	Lowe	1,015
21		14	A	Swindon Town	L	2-3	Coleman (og), Kellock	4,516
22		22	A	Scunthorpe United	D	3-3	Brown 2, Kendall	2,285
23		26	H	Rochdale	D	1-1	Kellock	2,253
24	Jan	1	A	Hartlepool United	L	0-3		3,392
25		4	H	Crewe Alexandra	W	1-0	Lowe	1,031
26		11	A	Preston North End	W	1-0	Kellock	3,184
27		17	H	Chester City	L	1-2	Kellock (pen)	1,473
28		31	H	Colchester United	D	2-2	Sanderson, Kellock	989
29	Feb	4	H	Exeter City	W	1-0	Longhurst	1,004
30		7	A	Tranmere Rovers	W	3-0	Diamond 2, Nicholson	1,357
31	Mar	5	A	Southend United	L	1-2	Diamond	1,006
32		8	A	Aldershot	W	2-1	Kellock, Longhurst	1,314
33		14	H	Wrexham	W	5-2	Kellock 3 (1 pen), Knill, Sanderson	1,268
34		22	A	Burnley	W	3-1	Nicholson, Lowe, Longhurst	3,321
35		28	H	Hartlepool United	W	3-2	Longhurst, Kellock (pen), Lowe	2,064
36		31	A	Rochdale	L	0-1		1,931
37	Apr	4	H	Stockport County	D	0-0		1,836
38		8	A	Cambridge United	L	0-4		1,909
39		12	A	Peterborough United	D	1-1	Knill	2,260
40		14	H	Torquay United	D	0-0		1,062
41		18	H	Northampton Town	W	2-0	Longhurst 2	1,105
42		22	A	Orient	L	0-1		1,443
43		26	A	Hereford United	L	1-2	Kellock	2,212
44		29	H	Port Vale	W	2-0	Longhurst, Kellock (pen)	1,389
45	May	2	A	Swindon Town	L	1-3	Lowe	1,626
46		5	H	Mansfield Town	L	1-2	Longhurst	1,414

Final League Position: 20th in Division Four

Apps
Sub Apps
2 own-goals   Gls

FA Cup

1	Nov	16	H	Scunthorpe United	L	1-3	Kendall	1,501

Apps
Sub Apps
Gls

League Cup

1,1L	Aug	20	H	Hull City	D	1-1	Shaw	820
1,2l	Sep	3	A	Hull City	L	0-3		3,299

Apps
Sub Apps
Gls

League Table

	P	W	D	L	F	A	Pts
Swindon Town	46	32	6	8	82	43	102
Chester City	46	23	15	8	83	50	84
Mansfield Town	46	23	12	11	74	47	81
Port Vale	46	21	16	9	67	37	79
Orient	46	20	12	14	79	64	72
Colchester United	46	19	13	14	88	63	70
Hartlepool United	46	20	10	16	68	67	70
Northampton Town	46	18	10	18	79	58	64
Southend United	46	18	10	18	69	67	64
Hereford United	46	18	10	18	74	73	64
Stockport County	46	17	13	16	63	71	64
Crewe Alexandra	46	18	9	19	54	61	63
Wrexham	46	17	9	20	68	80	60
Burnley	46	16	11	19	60	65	59
Scunthorpe United	46	15	14	17	50	55	59
Aldershot	46	17	7	22	66	74	58
Peterborough United	46	13	17	16	52	64	56
Rochdale	46	14	13	19	57	77	55
Tranmere Rovers	46	15	9	22	74	73	54
Halifax Town	46	14	12	20	60	71	54
Exeter City	46	13	15	18	47	59	54
Cambridge United	46	15	9	22	65	80	54
Preston North End	46	11	10	25	54	89	43
Torquay United	46	9	10	27	43	88	37

1986-87

Division Four

Managers: August–December 1986 Mick Jones; December 1986–May 1987 Billy Ayre

Did you know that?

- Barry Diamond had a penalty 'goal' disallowed by referee Trevor Simpson in a pre-season West Riding Senior Cup tie with Huddersfield Town at The Shay on 16 August after the ball escaped through a 'hole' in the net. The ref believed he must have shot wide.
- Town's victory over Aldershot was their first opening-day success since 1972.
- Phil Whitehead became Halifax Town's then-youngest player in the Football League when he played at Burnley on 27 September aged 16 years and 284 days.
- Former Halifax Town junior and England international Frank Worthington made his 800th League appearance for Tranmere Rovers in the goalless draw at The Shay on 17 October.
- Wayne Allison had not netted for five games with Town's Under-19s side, but took only two minutes to register a goal when he came on as a 66th-minute substitute to score the game's only goal against Hartlepool on 20 April.
- Phil Brown marked his 300th League appearance by scoring a penalty in the 1–1 draw with Scunthorpe United on 3 April.
- The attendance of 911 for the home match with Colchester United on 29 April was the lowest in the League that season.
- Town were drawn at home in the first round of the FA Cup for the sixth successive season.
- Biggest League win: 4–0 v Leyton Orient (h), 21 November.
- Heaviest League defeat: 3–6 v Northampton Town (h), 30 September.
- Ever-present: Phil Brown.

Match No.	Date		Venue	Opponents	Result		Scorers	Attendance
1	Aug	23	H	Aldershot	W	1-0	Black	1,020
2		30	A	Cambridge United	L	0-1		2,261
3	Sep	5	H	Southend United	L	0-1		1,060
4		12	A	Wrexham	L	1-3	Brown (pen)	2,250
5		16	A	Preston North End	L	2-3	Knill, Longhurst	5,259
6		19	H	Stockport County	L	0-2		1,071
7		27	A	Burnley	L	0-3		3,240
8		30	H	Northampton Town	L	3-6	Brown, Holden, Longhurst	1,034
9	Oct	4	H	Swansea City	W	1-0	Galloway	1,003
10		11	A	Torquay United	L	0-1		1,571
11		17	H	Tranmere Rovers	D	0-0		1,245
12		21	A	Wolverhampton Wanderers	W	2-1	N. Matthews, M. Matthews	4,380
13		25	A	Crewe Alexandra	D	2-2	Brown (pen), Black	1,666
14		31	H	Cardiff City	D	1-1	Brown (pen)	1,640
15	Nov	4	H	Exeter City	W	2-0	N. Matthews, Knill	1,390
16		9	A	Scunthorpe United	L	1-2	Knill	2,059
17		21	H	Orient	W	4-0	Brown (pen), Longhurst 2, Foster (og)	1,405
18		28	A	Colchester United	L	1-3	Longhurst	2,567
19	Dec	13	A	Peterborough United	L	0-2		3,135
20		19	H	Hereford United	W	2-1	M. Matthews, Longhurst	1,005
21		26	A	Hartlepool United	D	0-0		1,696
22		27	H	Rochdale	W	3-1	Brown, M. Matthews, Black	1,667
23	Jan	3	A	Orient	W	3-1	Longhurst 2, Black	2,207
24		31	H	Wrexham	W	2-1	Longhurst, Brown	1,532
25	Feb	3	A	Southend United	W	3-2	Galloway, Westley (og), Brown (pen)	2,047
26		7	H	Preston North End	L	1-3	Farnaby	2,968
27		14	A	Stockport County	L	0-2		1,835
28		21	H	Burnley	D	2-2	Nicholson, Sword	1,735
29		24	H	Lincoln City	L	1-2	Black	1,088
30		27	A	Northampton Town	L	0-1		6,351
31	Mar	3	A	Cardiff City	D	0-0		1,785
32		7	H	Crewe Alexandra	L	0-3		994
33		13	A	Tranmere Rovers	W	4-3	Martin, M. Matthews, Brown, Sword	1,653
34		17	H	Wolverhampton Wanderers	L	3-4	Longhurst, Allison, Sanderson	2,079
35		21	H	Torquay United	L	2-4	Galloway, Allison	1,246
36		24	A	Aldershot	L	1-4	Allison	1,911
37		29	A	Swansea City	W	2-0	Black, Sanderson	3,972
38	Apr	3	H	Scunthorpe United	D	1-1	Brown (pen)	1,232
39		11	A	Exeter City	D	2-2	Black, Brown (pen)	1,698
40		14	H	Cambridge United	W	1-0	Black	1,194
41		18	A	Lincoln City	D	0-0		1,673
42		20	H	Hartlepool United	W	1-0	Allison	1,115
43		26	A	Hereford United	L	0-1		2,061
44		29	H	Colchester United	D	0-0		911
45	May	4	A	Rochdale	L	3-5	Black, Seasman (og), Brown (pen)	2,992
46		9	H	Peterborough United	W	1-0	Holden	1,004

Final League Position: 15th in Division Four

3 own-goals

Apps
Sub Apps
Gls

FA Cup

1	Nov	15	H	Bolton Wanderers	D	1-1	Longhurst	3,370
R		18	A	Bolton Wanderers	D	1-1*	Brown	4,652
2R		24	H	Bolton Wanderers	L	1-3	Galloway	3,338

*After extra-time

Apps
Sub Apps
Gls

League Cup

1,1L	Aug	26	A	Huddersfield Town	L	1-3	Brown	2,363
1,2L	Sep	2	H	Huddersfield Town	D	2-2*	Galloway, Thornber	1,353

*After extra-time

Apps
Sub Apps
Gls

League Table

	P	W	D	L	F	A	Pts
Northampton Town	46	30	9	7	103	53	99
Preston North End	46	26	12	8	72	47	90
Southend United	46	25	5	16	68	55	80
Wolverhampton Wanderers	46	24	7	15	69	50	79
Colchester United	46	21	7	18	64	56	70
Aldershot	46	20	10	16	64	57	70
Orient	46	20	9	17	64	61	69
Scunthorpe United	46	18	12	16	73	57	66
Wrexham	46	15	20	11	70	51	65
Peterborough United	46	17	14	15	57	50	65
Cambridge United	46	17	11	18	60	62	62
Swansea City	46	17	11	18	56	61	62
Cardiff City	46	15	16	15	48	50	61
Exeter City	46	11	23	12	53	49	56
Halifax Town	46	15	10	21	59	74	55
Hereford United	46	14	11	21	60	61	53
Crewe Alexandra	46	13	14	19	70	72	53
Hartlepool United	46	11	18	17	44	65	51
Stockport County	46	13	12	21	40	69	51
Tranmere Rovers	46	11	17	18	54	72	50
Rochdale	46	11	17	18	54	73	50
Burnley	46	12	13	21	53	74	49
Torquay United	46	10	18	13	56	72	48
Lincoln City	46	12	12	22	45	65	48

1987-88

Division Four

Manager: Billy Ayre

Did you know that?

- Club sponsors were curtain and soft furnishing retailers G.H. Moody & Son.
- Captain was Phil Brown.
- With the Football League allowing the use of two substitutes for the first time, Halifax Town created history when Neil Matthews and Wayne Allison became the first pair of subs to score when they did so on the season's opening day 2–2 draw with Darlington. Town later had a point taken off them when it was discovered that Matthews hadn't been registered.
- Scarborough included five former Halifax Town players when the two sides met at Seamer Road on 21 November – Paul Kendall, Tommy Graham, Ray McHale, Simon Lowe and sub Stewart Mell.
- Rick Holden was sold to Watford on 24 March 1988 for a then club record £125,000.
- The attendance of 866 for the visit of Hartlepool United on 23 April is the second lowest in the club's history.
- Halifax Town completed a League double over champions Wolves, winning both games 2–1.
- Biggest League win: 3–1 v Newport County (h), 5 September, Swansea City (h), 16 September, v Hartlepool United (h), 23 April.
- Heaviest League defeat: 1–4 v Leyton Orient (a), 31 October, Darlington (a), 20 February.
- Ever-present: Phil Brown.

Match No.	Date		Venue	Opponents	Result		Scorers	Attendance
1	Aug	15	H	Darlington	D	2-2	Allison, N. Matthews	1,342
2		22	A	Wolverhampton Wanderers	W	1-0	Galloway	7,223
3		28	H	Rochdale	L	1-2	Holden	2,275
4		31	A	Wrexham	D	2-2	Brown (pen), Black	1,661
5	Sep	5	H	Newport County	W	3-1	Holden, N. Matthews 2	1,095
6		12	A	Bolton Wanderers	L	0-2		4,445
7		16	H	Swansea City	W	3-1	M. Matthews, Holden, N. Matthews	1,236
8		18	H	Tranmere Rovers	W	2-1	N. Matthews, Brown	1,754
9		26	A	Cambridge United	L	1-2	Holden	1,805
10		29	A	Cardiff City	D	0-0		3,666
11	Oct	3	H	Hereford United	W	2-1	N. Matthews, Holden	1,414
12		10	A	Scunthorpe United	L	0-1		2,105
13		16	H	Stockport County	W	2-0	Martin 2	1,696
14		21	A	Hartlepool United	L	1-2	M. Matthews	2,768
15		24	H	Peterborough United	D	0-0		1,615
16		31	A	Leyton Orient	L	1-4	Holden	3,208
17	Nov	3	H	Burnley	W	2-1	Martin, N. Matthews	3,419
18		6	H	Colchester United	L	1-2	Galloway	1,432
19		21	A	Scarborough	D	1-1	Black	2,892
20		27	H	Crewe Alexandra	L	1-2	McPhillips	1,416
21	Dec	12	A	Torquay United	W	2-1	N. Matthews, Holden	2,422
22		18	H	Exeter City	W	2-0	Collins (og), Heathcote	1,302
23		26	H	Cambridge United	D	1-1	Black	1,667
24	Jan	1	A	Rochdale	D	0-0		2,050
25		12	H	Bolton Wanderers	D	0-0		2,689
26		15	A	Tranmere Rovers	L	0-2		3,317
27		23	A	Swansea City	D	1-1	Allison	5,064
28	Feb	5	A	Newport County	L	0-1		1,509
29		16	H	Wolverhampton Wanderers	W	2-1	Holden, Brown	2,281
30		20	A	Darlington	L	1-4	Allison	1,824
31		23	H	Wrexham	W	2-0	M. Matthews, Holden	1,284
32		27	A	Hereford United	L	1-2	Holden	1,905
33	Mar	1	H	Cardiff City	L	0-1		1,128
34		4	A	Stockport County	L	0-1		2,171
35		12	H	Scunthorpe United	D	2-2	Duffield 2	1,807
36		26	A	Peterborough United	L	0-1		2,308
37	Apr	1	A	Colchester United	L	1-2	Duffield	1,992
38		4	H	Scarborough	D	2-2	Duffield, N. Matthews	1,747
39		8	A	Burnley	L	1-3	Allison	5,766
40		14	H	Leyton Orient	W	1-0	Black	1,006
41		19	A	Carlisle United	D	1-1	McPhillips	1,517
42		23	H	Hartlepool United	W	3-1	Black, Brown, Duffield	866
43		26	H	Carlisle United	D	1-1	McPhillips	1,002
44		29	A	Crewe Alexandra	D	0-0		1,403
45	May	2	H	Torquay United	L	2-3	Duffield, Brown (pen)	1,218
46		7	A	Exeter City	W	2-1	Duffield, Richardson	1,602

Final League Position: 18th in Division Four

								Apps
								Sub Apps
							1 own-goal	Gls

FA Cup

1	Nov	14	A*	Billingham Sythonia	W	4-2	Black 2, Robinson, N. Matthews	1,153
2	Dec	5	A	Grimsby Town	D	0-0		3,239
R		8	H	Grimsby Town	W	2-0	M. Matthews, Thornber	2,633
3	Jan	9	H	Nottingham Forest	L	0-4		4,013

* Played at The Victoria Ground, Hartlepool

								Apps
								Sub Apps
								Gls

League Cup

1,1L	Aug	18	H	York City	D	1-1	Allison	1,359
1,2L		25	A	York City	L	0-1		2,382

								Apps
								Sub Apps
								Gls

Roche, PJC	Barr, WJ	Harrison, FN	Matthews, M	Robinson, DA	Galloway, M	Richardson, LJ	Thornber, S	Ferebee, SR	Black, RP	Holden, RW	Allison, WA	Matthews, N	Brown, P	Martin, DS	Shaw, A	McPhillips, TP	Rieming, P	Heathcote, M	Bain, CA	Duffield, P	Kendall, PS	Willis, PE
1	2	3	4	5	6	7	8	9*	10+	11	12	13										
1		3	4	5	6	7	8		12	11	10*	9	2									
1		3	4	5	6	7*	8	13	12	11	10	9+	2									
1		3	4	5	6	7+	8		10	11	12	9*	2	13								
1		3	4		6		8	9*		11	10	12	2	7+	5	13						
1		3	4		6	7*	8		12	11	10	9	2		5							
1		3	4			7	8			11	10*	9	2	5	6	12						
1		3	4		6	7*	8		12	11	10+	9	2		5	13						
1		3	4*		6	7	8		9+	11	10		2	12	5	13						
1		3	4	7	6		8		9*	11			2	10	5	12						
1	13	3	4+	7	6		8			11		9*	2	10	5	12						
1	13	3	4	7	6		8			11		9*	2	10+	5	12						
1	12	3	4	5	6		8	9		11			2	7		10*						
1		3	4	5	6		8	9*		11	10		2	7		12						
1		3	4	5	6		8	9*		11	10		2	7		12						
1		3	4	5	6		8	13		11	10*	9+		7	2	12						
1		3	4		6		8	12		11	10*	9	2	7	5							
1		3*	4		6		8	10		11	12	9	2	7	5							
1	12		4	5			8	13	10	11		9	2	7+	6		3*					
1			4	6			8	12	10*	11		9	2	7	5	3						
1	3		4			13	8	12	10	11		9	2	7*	6		5+					
1	3		4	5			13	8+		10*	11	12	9	2		6		7				
1	3		4+	5			13	8		10*	11	12	9	2	7			6				
1	3		4*	5			12	8		10+	11	13	9	2	7			6				
1	3		4	5			8			11	10	9	2	7				6				
1	3		4				8			11	10+	9*	2	7			12	13	6			
1	3		4			6	8			11	10	9	2	7				5				
1	3		4			6*	8		10+	11		9	2	7			13	12	5			
1	3		4	5			8			11	10	9	2	7				6				
1	3		4	5		8*	8			12	11	10	9	2	7			12	6			
1	3		4	5			8			11	10*	9	2	7				12	6			
1	3		4+	5			13	8		12	11		9	2	7			10*	6			
1	3		4	5			13	8*		10	11+		9	2	7			12	6			
1	3		4	5			6	8			11	10	9	2	7							
1	3		4	5				6			11	10		2	7	5			8	9		
1	3*		4	5			11	8			10	13	2	7	12			9+	6			
1			4	5			11	8			10	3	2	7*	6			9	12			
1	3		4	5			11			12	10*	8	2	7	6			9				
1	12			5+			11*			13		10	2	7	6	8		3	9	4		
1	3		4				11				10		2	7	6	8		9*	5	12		
1	3		4*				12			11	10		2	7	6	8		9+	5	13		
1	3		4	5						11	10		2	7	12	8		9	6*			
1	3		4*	5			12			11	10		2	7		8		9	6			
1	3		4	5*			12+	13		11	10		2	7		8		9	6			
1	3		4				8			11*	10		2	7				9	6		12	
1	3+		4	5			12	8		11			2	7*	13	8		9	6			
46	25	18	45	32	17	20	34	6	19	35	29	29	44	38	21	11	7	7	2	12	9	
	5					10	1	6	8		6	3		2	3	14	2		1		1	2
		3		2	1			5	10	4	9	5	3		3		1	7				

			4	6			8	12	10	11*		9	2	7	5	3						
1	3		4				8			10	11		9	2	7	6		5				
1	3		4		12	8			10	11		9	2	7	6	5*						
1	3		4+	5			14	8		10*	11	12	9	2	7			6				
4	3		4	2			4			4	4		4	4	4	3		1				
							2		1			1										
	1		1					1		2			1									

1		3	4	5	6	7*	8	13	12	11	10+	9	2									
1	12	3	4		6	7			13	10+	11		9	2	5	8*						
2		2	2	1	2	2	1		1	2	1	2	2	2	1	1						
	1										2	1										
												1										

League Table

	P	W	D	L	F	A	Pts
Wolverhampton Wanderers	46	27	9	10	82	43	90
Cardiff City	46	24	13	9	66	41	85
Bolton Wanderers	46	22	12	12	66	42	78
Scunthorpe United	46	20	17	9	76	51	77
Torquay United	46	21	14	11	66	41	77
Swansea City	46	20	10	16	62	56	70
Peterborough United	46	20	10	16	52	53	70
Leyton Orient	46	19	12	15	85	63	69
Colchester United	46	19	10	17	47	51	67
Burnley	46	20	7	19	57	62	67
Wrexham	46	20	6	20	69	58	66
Scarborough	46	17	14	15	56	48	65
Darlington	46	18	11	17	71	69	65
Tranmere Rovers**	46	19	9	18	61	53	64
Cambridge United	46	16	13	17	50	52	61
Hartlepool United	46	15	14	17	50	57	59
Crewe Alexandra	46	13	19	14	57	53	58
Halifax Town*	46	14	14	18	54	59	55
Hereford United	46	14	12	20	41	59	54
Stockport County	46	12	15	19	44	58	51
Rochdale	46	11	15	20	47	76	48
Exeter City	46	11	13	22	53	68	46
Carlisle United	46	12	8	26	57	86	44
Newport County	46	6	7	33	35	105	25

* Deducted one point for fielding unregistered player
** Deducted two points for failing to fulfil a fixture

1988-89

Division Four

Manager: Billy Ayre

Did you know that?

- Captain was Paddy Roche.
- Club sponsors were Fee.
- John Bramhall went on to become assistant chief executive of the PFA.
- Halifax Town bowed out of the Littlewoods Cup on the away goals rule after two drawn matches with Scarborough. Only Cup-winners Luton Town would remain unbeaten.
- Halifax Town won away on the season's opening day for the first time since 1972.
- Halifax Town scored in 20 consecutive League and Cup matches from the start of the season.
- Commercial manager Tony Thwaites published his updated club history, entitled *From Sandhall to The Shay*, which went on sale in February.
- Town's four goals scored in the 4–1 win at Doncaster Rovers on 21 October were all scored within the first 14 minutes of kick-off.
- Lee Richardson joined Rick Holden at Watford on 9 February in a new club record deal worth £175,000.
- Dean Martin was sent off four times during the season.
- Halifax Town held a reunion of former (and present) players at South Ward WMC on 8 May.
- Biggest League win: 5–0 v Peterborough United (h), 25 October.
- Heaviest League defeat: 1–4 v Exeter City (a), 10 September.

Match No.	Date		Venue	Opponents	Result		Scorers	Attendance
1	Aug	27	A	Torquay United	W	2-0	Bramhall, Allison	2,769
2	Sep	3	H	Burnley	L	1-2	McPhillips	3,371
3		10	A	Exeter City	L	1-4	A. Whitehead	1,725
4		16	H	Carlisle United	D	3-3	McPhillips 3 (1 pen)	1,546
5		19	A	Stockport County	D	1-1	Martin (pen)	2,202
6		23	H	Tranmere Rovers	L	2-3	W. Barr, McPhillips	1,662
7	Oct	1	A	York City	L	3-5	Allison 2, Horner	2,238
8		4	H	Wrexham	W	4-0	N. Matthews, Allison, McPhillips, Horner	1,199
9		8	A	Cambridge United	L	1-2	McPhillips	1,800
10		14	H	Rochdale	W	4-1	McPhillips 2 (1 pen), W. Barr, N. Matthews	2,553
11		21	A	Doncaster Rovers	W	4-1	McPhillips 2, Watson, N. Matthews	3,038
12		25	H	Peterborough United	W	5-0	Richardson, McPhillips, Watson, N. Matthews 2	2,248
13		29	A	Grimsby Town	L	2-3	Bramhall, M. Matthews	3,260
14	Nov	4	H	Hartlepool United	W	1-0	Allison	2,182
15		8	H	Colchester United	W	3-2	Martin, McPhillips 2 (1 pen)	2,176
16		12	A	Hereford United	L	1-3	Horner	1,929
17		26	A	Lincoln City	L	1-2	Allison	3,479
18	Dec	2	H	Crewe Alexandra	L	0-1		2,026
19		17	H	Scarborough	L	0-2		1,890
20		26	A	Darlington	W	2-0	McPhillips 2	2,131
21		31	A	Rotherham United	L	0-2		5,258
22	Jan	2	H	Scunthorpe United	W	5-1	Allison 2, Watson, N. Matthews, Robinson	2,650
23		14	A	Burnley	L	1-2	Allison	8,297
24		20	H	Torquay United	W	2-0	Allison 2	1,830
25		28	A	Carlisle United	L	1-3	Bramhall	3,007
26	Feb	4	H	Stockport County	D	2-2	Watson, McPhillips	1,938
27		10	A	Tranmere Rovers	L	0-2		4,674
28		14	H	Leyton Orient	D	2-2	N. Matthews, Allison	1,477
29		17	H	Cambridge United	D	0-0		1,531
30	Mar	1	A	Peterborough United	L	1-2	Pullan	2,159
31		3	H	Doncaster Rovers	W	2-0	Watson, Broadbent	1,675
32		11	A	Hartlepool United	L	0-2		1,786
33		14	H	Grimsby Town	W	2-1	Allison, McPhillips	1,609
34		17	H	Exeter City	L	0-3		1,473
35		25	A	Scunthorpe United	D	0-0		4,591
36		27	H	Darlington	W	1-0	W. Barr	1,849
37	Apr	1	A	Scarborough	L	1-3	McPhillips	2,365
38		4	A	Leyton Orient	L	0-2		3,288
39		7	H	Rotherham United	D	1-1	McPhillips (pen)	2,947
40		14	H	York City	D	0-0		1,875
41		21	A	Wrexham	L	0-3		1,782
42		25	A	Rochdale	D	1-1	W. Barr	1,388
43		29	A	Lincoln City	L	0-1		1,261
44	May	1	A	Colchester United	L	2-3	Hill (og), McPhillips	5,065
45		5	A	Crewe Alexandra	D	2-2	Broadbent, Allison	3,476
46		13	H	Hereford United	D	2-2	McPhillips 2 (1 pen)	1,082

Final League Position: 21st in Division Four

1 own-goal

Apps
Sub Apps
Gls

FA Cup

	Date		Venue	Opponents	Result		Scorers	Attendance
1	Nov	19	H	York City	W	1-0	McPhillips	2,894
2	Dec	10	A	Altrincham	W	3-0	W. Barr, Allison 2	3,967
3	Jan	7	A	Kettering Town	D	1-1	Watson	5,800
R		10	H	Kettering Town	L	2-3	Bramhall, W. Barr	5,632

Apps
Sub Apps
Gls

League Cup

	Date		Venue	Opponents	Result		Scorers	Attendance
1,1L	Aug	31	A	Scarborough	D	1-1	Watson	2,196
1,2L	Sep	6	H	Scarborough	D	2-2	Allison, McPhillips	1,713

Apps
Sub Apps
Gls

League Table

	P	W	D	L	F	A	Pts
Rotherham United	46	22	16	8	76	35	82
Tranmere Rovers	46	21	17	8	62	43	80
Crewe Alexandra	46	21	15	10	67	48	78
Scunthorpe United	46	21	14	11	77	57	77
Scarborough	46	21	14	11	67	52	77
Leyton Orient	46	21	12	13	86	50	75
Wrexham	46	19	14	13	77	63	71
Cambridge United	46	18	14	14	71	62	68
Grimsby Town	46	17	15	14	65	59	66
Lincoln City	46	18	10	18	64	60	64
York City	46	17	13	16	62	63	64
Carlisle United	46	15	15	16	53	52	60
Exeter City	46	18	6	22	65	68	60
Torquay United	46	17	8	21	45	60	59
Hereford United	46	14	16	16	66	72	58
Burnley	46	14	13	19	52	61	55
Peterborough United	46	14	12	20	52	74	54
Rochdale	46	13	14	19	56	82	53
Hartlepool United	46	14	10	22	50	78	52
Stockport County	46	10	21	15	54	52	51
Halifax Town	46	13	11	22	69	75	50
Colchester United	46	12	14	20	60	78	50
Doncaster Rovers	46	13	10	23	49	78	49
Darlington	46	8	18	20	53	76	42

1989-90

Division Four

Managers: August 1989–April 1990 Billy Ayre; April–May 1990 Jim McCalliog

Did you know that?

- Former player Paul Kendall became the club's new commercial manager in succession to Tony Thwaites. Kendall was at the time a player with Macclesfield Town.

- Wayne Allison was sold for a club record £250,000 when he went to Watford on 6 July 1989 – the third time a player had been sold to Watford breaking the club's transfer record.

- Captain was John Bramhall, then Mitch Cook from January.

- Former Town defender Alan Knill won his only Wales cap in the 1–0 defeat by Holland on 14 September 1989.

- Ian Juryeff became Halifax Town's most expensive player when he joined from Leyton Orient on 10 August for £40,000. He became Hereford United's record but when he joined them on 14 December for £50,000.

- The first goal of the season, scored by Andy Watson in the 37th minute of the 4–0 opening day win over Hartlepool United was Town's 3,500th in the League.

- Former player Paddy Roche succeeded Jim McCalliog as head of the Football in the Community scheme in February.

- Halifax Town were awarded penalties in consecutive home games against Hereford, Southend and Maidstone. Each was missed by three different players – McPhillips, Bramhall and Butler.

- Town's 4–0 win over Hartlepool was their record opening day League win.

- Halifax Town won more games away (7) than they did at home (5).

- Biggest League win: 4–0 v Hartlepool United) h), 19 August.

- Heaviest League defeat: 0–3 v Peterborough United (a), 14 April.

Match No.	Date	Venue	Opponents	Result		Scorers	Attendance
1	Aug 19	H	Hartlepool United	W	4-0	Watson 2, Hall, Juryeff	1,524
2	26	A	Colchester United	D	2-2	Hicks (og), Watson	2,404
3	Sep 2	H	Torquay United	W	3-1	Watson, Matthews 2	1,893
4	9	A	Wrexham	L	1-2	Hall	1,700
5	15	H	Carlisle United	D	1-1	Juryeff	2,121
6	22	A	Cambridge United	L	0-1		2,220
7	27	A	Scarborough	W	3-2	Watson 2, Juryeff	3,147
8	30	H	Exeter City	L	1-2	Matthews	1,720
9	Oct 6	H	Gillingham	L	0-1		1,776
10	14	A	Lincoln City	L	1-2	Juryeff	4,071
11	17	H	Chesterfield	L	3-4	Bramhall, Matthews, Hall	2,998
12	21	H	Rochdale	W	1-0	Juryeff	1,864
13	28	A	Grimsby Town	D	1-1	Bramhall	4,021
14	31	H	Hereford United	D	1-1	Matthews	1,235
15	Nov 3	H	Stockport County	W	1-0	Horner	5,490
16	10	H	Southend United	L	1-2	Juryeff	1,908
17	25	H	Maidstone United	L	1-2	Juryeff	1,353
18	Dec 2	A	Aldershot	L	0-2		1,749
19	15	H	Doncaster Rovers	L	0-2		1,233
20	26	A	York City	W	2-0	Richardson 2	3,665
21	30	A	Burnley	L	0-1		9,105
22	Jan 1	H	Peterborough United	D	2-2	Naylor, McPhillips	1,578
23	6	A	Scunthorpe United	D	1-1	Cowling (og)	3,051
24	12	H	Colchester United	D	1-1	Hall	1,397
25	20	A	Hartlepool United	L	0-2		2,444
26	26	H	Wrexham	W	4-2	Matthews 2, Watson, Richardson	1,436
27	Feb 2	A	Cambridge United	D	0-0		1,526
28	10	A	Carlisle United	D	1-1	Matthews	4,844
29	17	H	Aldershot	W	4-1	Cook, Graham, Matthews, Richardson	1,275
30	24	A	Maidstone United	W	2-1	McPhillips, Richardson	2,182
31	Mar 3	H	Scunthorpe United	L	0-1		1,793
32	7	A	Exeter City	L	0-2		5,528
33	10	H	Scarborough	L	1-2	Matthews	1,490
34	16	A	Gillingham	L	1-3	Matthews	3,825
35	20	H	Lincoln City	L	0-1		1,423
36	24	H	Chesterfield	D	1-1	Watson	2,363
37	27	A	Torquay United	L	0-1		1,911
38	31	H	Rochdale	W	2-0	McPhillips, Watson	2,494
39	Apr 7	H	Grimsby Town	D	2-2	Watson, Butler	3,620
40	11	A	Hereford United	W	1-0	Barr	1,817
41	14	A	Peterborough United	L	0-3		4,570
42	16	H	York City	D	2-2	Butler, P. Fleming (pen)	1,605
43	21	A	Doncaster Rovers	W	4-3	Cook, Barr, Richardson, Butler	2,212
44	24	H	Burnley	D	0-0		2,556
45	27	A	Southend United	L	0-2		3,656
46	May 5	H	Stockport County	L	1-2	Matthews	4,744

Final League Position: 23rd in Division Four

2 own-goals

Apps
Sub Apps
Gls

FA Cup

	Date	Venue	Opponents	Result		Scorers	Attendance
1	Nov 18	A	Stafford Rangers	W	3-2	P. Fleming, Horner 2	2,508
2	Dec 9	A	Darlington	L	0-3		4,041

Apps
Sub Apps
Gls

League Cup

	Date	Venue	Opponents	Result		Scorers	Attendance
1,1L	Aug 22	H	Carlisle United	W	3-1	Cook, Hall, Watson	1,604
1,2L	29	A	Carlisle United	L	0-1		3,045
2,1L	Sep 20	A	Middlesbrough	L	0-4		10,613
3	Oct 3	H	Middlesbrough	L	0-1		1,641

Apps
Sub Apps
Gls

League Table

	P	W	D	L	F	A	Pts
Exeter City	46	28	5	13	83	48	89
Grimsby Town	46	22	13	11	70	47	79
Southend United	46	22	9	15	61	48	75
Stockport County	46	21	11	14	68	62	74
Maidstone United	46	22	7	17	77	61	73
Cambridge United	46	21	10	15	76	66	73
Chesterfield	46	19	14	13	63	50	71
Carlisle United	46	21	8	17	61	60	71
Peterborough United	46	17	17	12	59	46	68
Lincoln City	46	18	14	14	48	48	68
Scunthorpe United	46	17	15	14	69	54	66
Rochdale	46	20	6	20	52	55	66
York City	46	16	16	14	55	53	64
Gillingham	46	17	11	18	46	48	62
Torquay United	46	15	12	19	53	66	57
Burnley	46	14	14	18	45	55	56
Hereford United	46	15	10	21	56	62	55
Scarborough	46	15	10	21	60	73	55
Hartlepool United	46	15	10	21	66	88	55
Doncaster Rovers	46	14	9	23	53	60	51
Wrexham	46	13	12	21	51	67	51
Aldershot	46	12	14	20	49	69	50
Halifax Town	46	12	13	21	57	65	49
Colchester United	46	11	10	25	48	75	43

1990-91

Division Four
Manager: Jim McCalliog

Did you know that?

- Captain was Dave Evans.
- Halifax Town won the Yorkshire & Electricity Cup, their first honour since winning the West Riding Senior Cup in 1967.
- The team wore Argentina-style light-blue-and-white-striped shirts.
- Ian Juryeff broke his own record as Halifax Town's most expensive player when he rejoined from Hereford United on 14 September for £50,000.
- Halifax Town's failure to score in their opening eight League games was a Football League record.
- Town's 5–3 victory over Blackpool on 27 October was the side's first League win at The Shay in 15 attempts.
- Dean Martin scored within ten seconds after coming on as a 67th-minute substitute in the home game with Rochdale on 21 December.
- Kick-off for Town's game at Maidstone on 27 February was delayed for half an hour because of fog.
- Jonathan Gould is the son of former Arsenal and West Ham forward Bobby Gould. He went on to play for Celtic, winning the Scottish title in 1997–98 and earning two Scotland international caps.
- Graham Cooper represented Halifax Town in the Rumbelows Sprint Challenge. He failed to qualify for the Final. Former Town player Paul Fleming, then of Mansfield Town, finished seventh of eight runners in the Final held prior to the Rumbelows Cup Final at Wembley.
- Steve Norris became the first Town player to score 30 goals in a season since Albert Valentine in 1934–35. He also became the first player since Bournemouth's Ted MacDougall in 1971–72 to score more than half the club's final tally of League goals.
- Craig Fleming played every minute of all 60 competitive games.
- Biggest League win: 5–2 v Walsall (h), 2 March.
- Heaviest League defeat: 1–5 v Stockport County (a), 18 January.
- Ever-present: Craig Fleming.

Match No.	Date		Venue	Opponents	Result		Scorers	Attendance
1	Aug	25	H	Stockport County	D	0-0		2,362
2	Sep	1	A	Lincoln City	L	0-1		2,947
3		8	H	Doncaster Rovers	L	0-1		2,394
4		15	A	Darlington	L	0-3		2,993
5		18	A	Peterborough United	L	0-2		3,082
6		21	H	Torquay United	L	0-1		1,447
7		29	A	Northampton Town	L	0-1		2,977
8	Oct	6	H	Scunthorpe United	D	0-0		1,468
9		13	A	Carlisle United	W	3-0	Barr, Norris, Graham	3,697
10		20	A	York City	D	3-3	Norris 2, Graham	2,601
11		23	H	Hereford United	L	0-4		1,762
12		27	H	Blackpool	W	5-3	Norris (pen), Ellis, Graham, Gregory, Juryeff	1,945
13	Nov	2	A	Aldershot	D	2-2	Norris 2	2,686
14		9	H	Gillingham	L	1-2	Dobson	1,708
15		24	A	Burnley	L	1-2	Juryeff	6,620
16	Dec	1	A	Walsall	L	1-3	Norris	4,153
17		15	H	Chesterfield	W	2-1	Norris (pen), Ellis	1,415
18		21	H	Rochdale	W	2-0	Butler, Martin	1,831
19		26	A	Scarborough	L	1-4	Norris	1,327
20		29	A	Cardiff City	L	0-1		2,903
21	Jan	1	H	Hartlepool United	L	1-2	Norris	1,707
22		12	H	Lincoln City	D	1-1	Broadbent	1,447
23		18	A	Stockport County	L	1-5	Norris	4,030
24		26	H	Darlington	D	0-0		1,658
25	Feb	1	H	Peterborough United	D	1-1	Richardson	1,133
26		5	A	Torquay United	L	1-3	Norris	2,233
27		16	H	Burnley	L	1-2	Norris	4,755
28		22	A	Gillingham	L	0-1		2,800
29		27	A	Maidstone United	L	1-5	Norris (pen)	1,020
30	Mar	2	H	Walsall	W	5-2	Norris 3 (2 pens), Juryeff 2	1,464
31		9	A	Chesterfield	L	1-2	Norris	3,565
32		12	A	Wrexham	W	2-1	Juryeff, Norris	1,263
33		15	H	Northampton Town	W	2-1	Norris 2	1,348
34		19	H	Carlisle United	D	1-1	Juryeff	1,004
35		23	A	Scunthorpe United	D	4-4	Richardson, Norris 2 (1 pen), Ellis	3,134
36		26	H	Wrexham	W	2-0	Norris 2	1,429
37		30	H	Scarborough	L	1-2	Norris	1,623
38	Apr	1	A	Rochdale	D	1-1	Juryeff	2,040
39		6	H	Cardiff City	L	1-2	Juryeff	1,364
40		13	A	Hartlepool United	L	1-2	Norris (pen)	3,185
41		16	H	Maidstone United	W	3-2	Ellis, Richardson, Juryeff	1,002
42		19	H	York City	W	2-1	Norris, Evans	1,421
43		23	A	Doncaster Rovers	W	2-1	Cooper, Norris	2,360
44		27	A	Hereford United	L	0-1		1,820
45		30	A	Blackpool	L	0-2		5,883
46	May	11	H	Aldershot	W	3-0	Paterson, Flower (og), Norris	1,428

Final League Position: 22nd in Division Four

Apps
Sub Apps
1 own-goal Gls

FA Cup

1	Nov	17	H	Wrexham	W	3-2	Norris, Graham, Juryeff	2,002
2	Dec	11	A	Rotherham United	D	1-1	Juryeff	2,906
R		17	H	Rotherham United	L	1-2	Norris	2,132

Apps
Sub Apps
Gls

League Cup

1,1L	Aug	28	H	Lincoln City	W	2-0	Fyfe, Richardson	1,239
1,2L	Sep	5	A	Lincoln City	L	0-1		2,376
2,1L		26	H	Manchester United	L	1-3	Evans	7,500
2,2L	Oct	10	A	Manchester United	L	1-2	Gregory	22,295

Apps
Sub Apps
Gls

League Table

	P	W	D	L	F	A	Pts
Darlington	46	22	17	7	68	38	83
Stockport County	46	23	13	10	84	47	82
Hartlepool United	46	24	10	12	67	48	82
Peterborough United	46	21	17	8	67	45	80
Blackpool	46	23	10	13	78	47	79
Burnley	46	23	10	13	70	51	79
Torquay United	46	18	18	10	64	47	72
Scunthorpe United	46	20	11	15	71	62	71
Scarborough	46	19	12	15	59	56	69
Northampton Town	46	18	13	15	57	58	67
Doncaster Rovers	46	17	14	15	56	46	65
Rochdale	46	15	17	14	50	53	62
Cardiff City	46	15	15	16	43	54	60
Lincoln City	46	14	17	15	50	61	59
Gillingham	46	12	18	16	57	60	54
Walsall	46	12	17	17	48	51	53
Hereford United	46	13	14	19	53	58	53
Chesterfield	46	13	14	19	47	62	53
Maidstone United	46	13	12	21	66	71	51
Carlisle United	46	13	9	24	47	89	48
York City	46	11	13	22	45	57	46
Halifax Town	46	12	10	24	59	79	46
Aldershot	46	10	11	25	61	101	41
Wrexham	46	10	10	26	48	74	40

1991-92

Division Four

Managers: August–October 1991 Jim McCalliog; October 1991–May 1992 John McGrath

Did you know that?

- Club sponsors were Paraglas.
- Captain was Dave Evans.
- Town's home strip was sky blue shirts and shorts.
- Town's 2–0 win at Hereford United on 6 November ended their 100 per cent home record.
- The attendance of 881 for the match with Wrexham on 13 December was the lowest in the Football League that season.
- Dave Evans made his 500th League appearance in the 4–0 defeat at Northampton Town on Boxing Day.
- Juryeff's goal in the 57th minute in Town's 3–2 defeat at Mansfield Town on 21 April ended a run of 523 minutes without an away goal.
- Biggest League win: 2–0 v Chesterfield (h), 19 October, v Doncaster Rovers (a), 11 January.
- Heaviest League defeat: 0–4 v Rotherham United (h), 13 September, v Northampton Town (a), 26 December, v Chesterfield (a), 7 April, v Cardiff City (a), 11 April.

Match No.	Date		Venue	Opponents	Result		Scorers	Attendance
1	Aug	17	H	Northampton Town	L	0-1		1,834
2		24	A	Maidstone United	W	1-0	Juryeff	1,216
3		30	H	York City	D	0-0		2,167
4	Sep	7	A	Walsall	L	0-3		2,981
5		13	H	Rotherham United	L	0-4		2,653
6		17	H	Cardiff City	D	1-1	Bradley	1,041
7		27	H	Mansfield Town	L	1-3	Norris	2,026
8	Oct	5	A	Lincoln City	D	0-0		2,092
9		12	H	Gillingham	L	0-3		1,435
10		19	H	Chesterfield	W	2-0	Norris 2 (1 pen)	1,506
11		26	A	Rochdale	L	0-1		2,323
12	Nov	2	H	Burnley	L	0-2		4,491
13		6	A	Hereford United	W	2-0	Juryeff, Norris	2,207
14		9	A	Barnet	L	0-3		4,837
15		22	H	Scarborough	W	1-0	Richardson	1,395
16		30	A	Blackpool	L	0-3		3,118
17	Dec	13	H	Wrexham	W	4-3	Paterson, Richardson 2, Juryeff	881
18		21	H	Maidstone United	D	1-1	Cooper	1,040
19		26	A	Northampton Town	L	0-4		3,147
20		28	A	York City	D	1-1	Wilson	2,396
21	Jan	11	A	Doncaster Rovers	W	2-0	Norris, Hutchinson	2,067
22		18	H	Scunthorpe United	L	1-4	Paterson	1,232
23		25	A	Carlisle United	D	1-1	Richardson	2,091
24	Feb	8	H	Rochdale	D	1-1	Cooper	2,213
25		12	H	Blackpool	L	1-2	Barr (pen)	2,158
26		15	A	Wrexham	L	0-2		2,076
27		22	H	Doncaster Rovers	D	0-0		1,285
28		28	A	Crewe Alexandra	L	2-3	Wilson, Richardson	3,514
29	Mar	3	A	Scunthorpe United	L	0-1		2,448
30		6	A	Carlisle United	W	3-2	Bradley, Cooper, Wilson	1,015
31		11	H	Hereford United	L	0-2		918
32		14	A	Burnley	L	0-1		10,903
33		21	H	Barnet	W	3-1	Richardson 2, Wilson (pen)	1,756
34		28	A	Scarborough	L	0-3		1,363
35		31	A	Rotherham United	L	0-1		4,517
36	Apr	3	H	Walsall	W	1-0	Wilson	1,006
37		7	A	Chesterfield	L	0-4		1,802
38		11	A	Cardiff City	L	0-4		5,261
39		14	H	Crewe Alexandra	W	2-1	Barr 2	1,022
40		21	A	Mansfield Town	L	2-3	Juryeff, Abbott	3,936
41		25	H	Lincoln City	L	1-4	Richardson	1,296
42	May	2	A	Gillingham	L	0-2		2,413

Final League Position: 20th in Division Four

Apps
Sub Apps
Gls

Expunged Match

	Sep	20	A	Aldershot	W	3-1	Bradley, Norris 2 (1 pen)	2,695

FA Cup

	Date		Venue	Opponents	Result		Scorers	Attendance
1	Nov	16	A	Witton Albion	D	1-1	Hildersley	2,002
R		27	H	Witton Albion	L	1-2*	Richardson	2,172

* After extra-time

Apps
Sub Apps
Gls

League Cup

	Date		Venue	Opponents	Result		Scorers	Attendance
R1/1	Aug	20	H	Tranmere Rovers	L	3-4	Norris (pen), Richardson, Juryeff	1,910
R1/2		27	A	Tranmere Rovers	L	3-4*	Barr 2, Cooper	4,285

* After extra-time

Apps
Sub Apps
Gls

League Table

	P	W	D	L	F	A	Pts
Burnley	42	25	8	9	79	43	83
Rotherham United	42	22	11	9	70	37	77
Mansfield Town	42	23	8	11	75	53	77
Blackpool	42	22	10	10	71	45	76
Scunthorpe United	42	21	9	12	64	59	72
Crewe Alexandra	42	20	10	12	66	51	70
Barnet	42	21	6	15	81	61	69
Rochdale	42	18	13	11	57	53	67
Cardiff City	42	17	15	10	66	53	66
Lincoln City	42	17	11	14	50	44	62
Gillingham	42	15	12	15	63	53	57
Scarborough	42	15	12	15	64	68	57
Chesterfield	42	14	11	17	49	61	53
Wrexham	42	14	9	19	52	73	51
Walsall	42	12	13	17	48	58	49
Northampton Town	42	11	13	18	46	57	46
Hereford United	42	12	8	22	44	57	44
Maidstone United	42	8	18	16	45	56	42
York City	42	8	16	18	42	58	40
Halifax Town	42	10	8	24	34	75	38
Doncaster Rovers	42	9	8	25	40	65	35
Carlisle United	42	7	13	22	41	67	34

1992-93

Division Three

Managers: August–December 1992 John McGrath; December 1992–May 1993 Mick Rathbone

Did you know that?

- Captain was Russell Bradley, then Billy Barr.

- During his time as a Liverpool player, Jimmy Case won four League titles, three European Cups, one UEFA Cup and the League Cup. He was also on the losing side twice to Manchester United in the FA Cup Final, with Liverpool in 1977 (when he scored) and Brighton in 1983.

- Jason Peake was awarded the Young Eagle of the Month for October.

- Barry Fry, just sacked as Barnet boss, attended the game at The Shay on 5 December after their travelling supporters gave him a ticket for the match.

- Jason Hardy, Dave Ridings and Jimmy Case all scored in consecutive matches, but never again that season.

- A carnival atmosphere ensued for the home match with Shrewsbury Town on 20 March as the *Halifax Courier* launched their 'Staying Alive' campaign. Children were given balloons, there was a pre-match children's five-a-side tournament, music from the Friendly Brass Band, and firework display provided by Standard Fireworks, Huddersfield.

- The attendance of 7,451 for the final match with Hereford United was the highest in the League since the 8,077 for the visit of Sheffield United in April 1982.

- Halifax Town's total of just three home wins was their lowest-ever return.

- Biggest League win: 5–2 v Northampton Town (a), 26 September.

- Heaviest League defeat: 0–4 v Walsall (h), 24 April.

- Ever-present: Chris Lucketti.

Match No.	Date		Venue	Opponents	Result		Scorers	Attendance
1	Aug	15	A	Rochdale	W	3-2	Hildersley 2, Wilson (pen)	2,497
2		22	H	Scunthorpe United	D	0-0		1,793
3		29	A	Cardiff City	L	1-2	Thompstone	7,692
4	Sep	1	A	Crewe Alexandra	L	1-2	G. Wilson (og)	3,228
5		12	A	Lincoln City	L	1-2	Lucketti	2,689
6		15	H	Darlington	W	1-0	Greenwood	1,287
7		19	H	Scarborough	L	3-4	Greenwood, Wilson (pen), Hirst (og)	1,230
8		26	A	Northampton Town	W	5-2	Thompstone 3, Lucketti, Greenwood	2,021
9	Oct	3	A	Carlisle United	D	1-1	Bradley	3,824
10		10	H	Colchester United	L	2-4	Matthews, German	2,445
11		17	A	Walsall	W	2-1	Smith (og), Peake	3,867
12		24	H	Gillingham	W	2-0	Matthews, Thompstone	1,218
13		31	A	Hereford United	L	0-3		1,936
14	Nov	3	A	Shrewsbury Town	L	0-1		2,704
15		7	H	Torquay United	L	0-2		1,651
16		21	A	Wrexham	D	1-1	Hardy	1,873
17		28	H	Chesterfield	D	1-1	Hardy	1,432
18	Dec	5	H	Barnet	L	1-2	Greenwood	1,253
19		19	H	Bury	L	0-1		1,760
20		26	H	Doncaster Rovers	D	2-2	Megson, Thompstone	1,854
21		29	A	York City	D	1-1	Williams	4,068
22	Jan	9	A	Darlington	W	3-0	Ridings 2, Thompstone	1,984
23		16	H	Northampton Town	D	2-2	Ridings 2	1,323
24		23	A	Scarborough	L	0-2		1,552
25		26	H	Cardiff City	L	0-1		1,339
26		30	A	Scunthorpe United	L	1-4	Paterson	2,460
27	Feb	6	H	Rochdale	L	2-3	Jones (og), Barr (pen)	1,906
28		16	H	Lincoln City	W	2-1	Case, Greenwood	1,260
29		20	H	Crewe Alexandra	L	1-2	Case	1,604
30		26	A	Colchester United	L	1-2	Thompstone	3,007
31	Mar	6	H	Carlisle United	L	0-2		1,309
32		13	A	Torquay United	L	0-2		3,345
33		20	H	Shrewsbury Town	D	1-1	Barr	3,872
34		23	A	Chesterfield	L	1-2	Thompstone	2,382
35		26	H	Wrexham	L	0-1		3,970
36	Apr	3	A	Barnet	D	0-0		3,042
37		10	A	Doncaster Rovers	W	1-0	Barr	2,160
38		12	H	York City	L	0-1		3,983
39		17	A	Bury	W	2-1	Paterson, German	3,069
40		24	H	Walsall	L	0-4		2,829
41	May	1	A	Gillingham	L	0-2		7,151
42		8	H	Hereford United	L	0-1		7,451

Final League Position: 22nd in Division Three

Apps
Sub Apps
4 own-goals   Gls

FA Cup

1	Nov 14	A	Marine	L	1-4	German	1,892

Apps
Sub Apps
Gls

League Cup

1/1L	Aug 18	H	Hartlepool United	L	1-2	Megson	1,370
1/2L	25	A	Hartlepool United	L	2-3	Thomas, Lucketti	2,191

Apps
Sub Apps
Gls

League Table

	P	W	D	L	F	A	Pts
Cardiff City	42	25	8	9	77	47	83
Wrexham	42	23	11	8	75	52	80
Barnet	42	23	10	9	66	48	79
York City	42	21	12	9	72	45	75
Walsall	42	22	7	13	76	61	73
Crewe Alexandra	42	21	7	14	75	56	70
Bury	42	18	9	15	63	55	63
Lincoln City	42	18	9	15	57	53	63
Shrewsbury Town	42	17	11	14	57	52	62
Colchester United	42	18	5	19	67	76	59
Rochdale	42	16	10	16	70	70	58
Chesterfield	42	15	11	16	59	63	56
Scarborough	42	15	9	18	66	71	54
Scunthorpe United	42	14	12	16	57	54	54
Darlington	42	12	14	16	48	53	50
Doncaster Rovers	42	11	14	17	42	57	47
Hereford United	42	10	15	17	47	60	45
Carlisle United	42	11	11	20	57	65	44
Torquay United	42	12	7	23	45	67	43
Northampton Town	42	11	8	23	48	74	41
Gillingham	42	9	13	20	48	64	40
Halifax Town	42	9	9	24	45	68	36

1993-94

GM Vauxhall Conference

Managers: August 1993–February 1994 Peter Wragg; February–May 1994 John Bird

Did you know that?

- Club colours were navy-blue-with-white-striped shirts, and navy blue shorts.
- Captain was Billy Barr.
- Halifax Town's first goal in the Conference was scored in the 60th minute of the second match, away at Southport.
- Scorer of Town's first Conference goal at The Shay was Jamie Paterson, in the 20th minute of the 1–1 draw with Stafford Rangers on 30 August in the second home match.
- Town successfully defended the winning of the Yorkshire and Humberside Cup by defeating Bradford City in the Final on 7 September. They had not played for it since winning the competition in 1990.
- The first substitute used by Town in the Conference was Shaun Constable, who replaced Dave Ridings in the 62nd minute of the 2–2 draw at Southport on 24 August.
- Town won their first match in the Conference in their 8th match with a 6–2 victory at Woking on 25 September. It was the first time they had scored as many goals away from home since defeating Knaresborough in the Yorkshire Combination in December 1911.
- Jamie Paterson became the first Town player to score a hat-trick in the Conference in the 6–0 defeat of Telford on 2 October.
- When Halifax Town won at Spennymoor United in the FA Trophy game on 12 February they ended the Northern Premier League outfit's unbeaten run of 23 League and Cup matches.
- Town played two games in two days v Dagenham (29 April) and Altrincham (30 April), the first time since April 1980.
- Excerpts from the home game with Kidderminster Harriers on 2 May later featured in an episode of *A Touch Of Frost* starring David Jason.
- Biggest Conference win: 6–0 v Telford (h), 21 October.
- Heaviest Conference defeat: 0–5 v Runcorn (a), 11 September.
- Ever-present: Jamie Paterson.

Match No.	Date		Venue	Opponents	Result		Scorers	Attendance
1	Aug	21	H	Kettering Town	D	0-0		1,810
2		24	A	Southport	D	2-2	Lucketti, Harvey (og)	2,423
3		28	A	Slough Town	L	0-2		1,170
4		30	H	Stafford Rangers	D	1-1	Paterson	1,228
5	Sep	4	H	Yeovil Town	D	1-1	Filson	1,152
6		11	A	Runcorn	L	0-5		732
7		17	H	Witton Albion	D	0-0		1,099
8		25	A	Woking	W	6-2	Paterson 2, Saunders 2, Hanson, Peake	1,848
9	Oct	2	H	Telford United	W	6-0	Peake, Paterson 3 (1 pen), Saunders 2	1,118
10		5	A	Stalybridge Celtic	D	1-1	Megson	1,233
11		9	A	Merthyr Tydfil	L	1-2	Lambert	911
12		16	A	Dagenham & Redbridge	L	0-3		1,303
13		23	H	Woking	L	2-3	Lambert, Paterson	1,201
14		30	A	Bath City	D	2-2	Paterson, Peake	712
15	Nov	6	H	Bromsgrove Rovers	W	3-0	Saunders 2, Megson	1,003
16		20	H	Welling United	D	1-1	Lambert	1,035
17		26	A	Witton Albion	D	2-2	Lambert 2	848
18	Dec	18	A	Dover Athletic	W	2-1	Paterson, Peake	1,348
19	Jan	4	A	Kidderminster Harriers	L	1-2	Peake	2,016
20		8	A	Kettering Town	W	1-0	Ridings	2,409
21		11	H	Stalybridge Celtic	W	2-1	Ridings 2	1,012
22		15	H	Runcorn	D	1-1	Lambert	1,196
23		29	A	Welling United	W	2-0	Megson, Ridings	1,121
24	Feb	2	H	Southport	D	2-2	Lambert, Barr	1,310
25		5	A	Stafford Rangers	D	1-1	Hemming (og)	1,082
26		19	A	Telford United	L	2-3	Edwards, Lormor	1,072
27	Mar	12	H	Dover Athletic	L	0-1		760
28		19	A	Macclesfield Town	W	1-0	Peake	1,115
29		26	H	Bath City	D	0-0		1,008
30		29	H	Merthyr Tydfil	W	2-1	Hanson 2	771
31	Apr	2	A	Northwich Victoria	W	2-0	Hanson, Barr	927
32		4	A	Gateshead	L	1-2	Paterson	659
33		7	A	Altrincham	D	0-0		1,019
34		16	A	Yeovil Town	D	0-0		1,823
35		19	H	Northwich Victoria	L	1-2	Smith	803
36		23	H	Gateshead	W	3-1	Paterson 2, Barr	760
37		26	H	Macclesfield Town	L	1-2	Smith	732
38		29	H	Dagenham & Redbridge	L	0-1		643
39		30	A	Altrincham	D	0-0		799
40	May	2	H	Kidderminster Harriers	W	1-0	Barr	1,141
41		5	A	Bromsgrove Rovers	L	0-1		1,050
42		7	H	Slough Town	W	1-0	Paterson	935

Final League Position: 13th in GM Vauxhall Conference

Apps
Sub Apps
2 own-goals   Gls

FA Cup

1	Nov	14	H	West Bromwich Albion	W	2-1	Peake, Saunders	4,250
2	Dec	4	A	Stockport County	L	1-5	Barr	5,498

Apps
Sub Apps
Gls

FA Trophy

1	Jan	22	H	Emley	W	2-1	Paterson, Baker (og)	1,579
2	Feb	12	A	Spennymoor United	W	2-1	Paterson, Peake	1,426
3	Mar	5	A	Runcorn	D	1-1	Brabin (og)	1,302
R		8	H	Runcorn	L	0-2		1,406

Apps
Sub Apps
2 own-goals   Gls

League Table

	P	W	D	L	F	A	Pts
Kidderminster Harriers	42	22	9	11	63	35	75
Kettering Town	42	19	15	8	46	24	72
Woking	42	18	13	11	58	58	67
Southport	42	18	12	12	57	51	66
Runcorn	42	14	19	9	63	57	61
Dagenham & Redbridge	42	15	14	13	62	54	59
Macclesfield Town	42	16	11	15	48	49	59
Dover Athletic	42	17	7	18	48	49	58
Stafford Rangers	42	14	15	13	56	52	57
Altrincham	42	16	9	17	41	42	57
Gateshead	42	15	12	15	45	53	57
Bath City	42	13	17	12	47	38	56
Halifax Town	42	13	16	13	55	49	55
Stalybridge Celtic	42	14	12	16	54	55	54
Northwich Victoria	42	11	19	12	44	45	52
Welling United	42	13	12	17	47	49	51
Telford United	42	13	12	17	41	49	51
Bromsgrove Rovers	42	12	15	15	54	66	51
Yeovil Town	42	14	9	19	49	62	51
Merthyr Tydfil	42	12	15	15	60	61	49
Slough Town	42	11	14	17	44	58	47
Witton Albion	42	7	13	22	37	63	34

1994-95

GM Vauxhall Conference
Manager: John Bird

Did you know that?

- Club sponsors were Westgrove.
- Captain was Alex Jones.
- Club colours were blue shirts with red trim and white shorts.
- Gary Worthington became the third generation of the family to play for Halifax Town after grandfather Eric and father Dave.
- Kevin Langley played in the first 16 matches of Everton's 1986–87 League Championship winning season.
- Town set a club record of six unbeaten games since the start of the season with their 2–0 victory over Southport at The Shay on 6 September.
- Richard Wilmot became the first substitute goalkeeper used by Halifax Town when he replaced Darren Heyes in the match at Macclesfield Town on 24 September.
- Town did not reach Dagenham until five minutes after the scheduled kick-off time on 1 October, then won 4–1.
- The home game with Stafford Rangers on 5 November was an 11am kick-off.
- At 36 years and 62 days, Mick Rathbone became Halifax Town's oldest-ever scorer when he fired home from 20 yards in the 4–0 defeat of Dover on 7 January.
- Halifax Town used a club record 38 players in the Conference.
- Biggest Conference win: 6–0 v Stafford Rangers (h), 5 November.
- Heaviest Conference defeat: 1–5 v Kettering Town (a), 11 March.

Match No.	Date		Venue	Opponents	Result		Scorers	Attendance
1	Aug	20	A	Woking	W	3-1	Prindiville, German, Jones	1,760
2		24	H	Northwich Victoria	D	0-0		994
3		27	H	Bromsgrove Rovers	W	4-2	Prindiville, Jones, Worthington, Power (og)	1,047
4		29	A	Stalybridge Celtic	D	1-1	Flounders	1,337
5	Sep	3	A	Dover Athletic	D	1-1	Kiwomya	1,654
6		6	H	Southport	W	2-0	Paterson 2	1,308
7		10	H	Farnborough Town	L	0-1		1,143
8		17	A	Kidderminster Harriers	L	0-3		2,062
9		24	A	Macclesfield Town	D	1-1	Lancaster	1,010
10	Oct	1	A	Dagenham & Redbridge	W	4-1	Paterson, Worthington, Kiwomya, Lancaster	952
11		8	H	Altrincham	D	1-1	Worthington	1,175
12		11	A	Southport	L	0-4		1,236
13		15	H	Bath City	W	4-2	Kiwomya 2, Lancaster, Worthington	775
14		29	A	Farnborough Town	L	0-2		815
15	Nov	5	H	Stafford Rangers	W	6-0	Lancaster, Prindiville, Kiwomya 2, Lambert, Worthington	750
16		19	A	Yeovil Town	L	1-3	Paterson	1,801
17		26	H	Kettering Town	W	2-1	Lambert, Paterson	1,021
18	Dec	10	A	Welling United	D	1-1	Kiwomya	712
19		20	H	Runcorn	W	4-0	Lancaster, Leitch, Worthington, Kiwomya	733
20		26	A	Gateshead	W	2-1	Kiwomya, Worthington (pen)	932
21		31	A	Altrincham	L	1-3	Hanson	1,058
22	Jan	2	H	Gateshead	W	3-2	Kiwomya, Worthington (pen), Hanson	1,099
23		7	H	Dover Athletic	W	4-0	Hanson, Rathbone, Lancaster, Kiwomya	1,017
24	Feb	4	A	Woking	W	4-0	Hanson 2, Lancaster, Worthington	1,038
25		7	A	Stafford Rangers	W	1-0	Hanson	844
26		14	A	Dagenham & Redbridge	D	1-1	Kiwomya	927
27		25	H	Merthyr Tydfil	D	2-2	Hanson, Kiwomya (pen)	910
28		28	A	Northwich Victoria	L	0-3		831
29	Mar	7	H	Macclesfield Town	L	0-1		1,002
30		11	A	Kettering Town	L	1-5	Beddard	1,330
31		18	H	Welling United	W	4-0	Hutchinson, Kiwomya, Fleming, German	783
32		20	A	Stevenage Borough	L	0-1		1,293
33		25	H	Yeovil Town	W	2-1	German, Lambert	816
34		27	A	Bath City	D	0-0		475
35	Apr	1	H	Stevenage Borough	L	0-2		753
36		8	H	Stalybridge Celtic	D	1-1	Beddard	802
37		11	A	Merthyr Tydfil	L	0-2		403
38		15	H	Telford United	D	1-1	Prindiville	609
39		17	A	Telford United	D	1-1	Johnson	829
40		22	A	Bromsgrove Rovers	W	1-0	Hanson	897
41		29	H	Kidderminster Harriers	L	1-2	Bancroft (og)	1,754
42	May	6	A	Runcorn	W	3-0	Hanson 3	985

Final League Position: 8th in GM Vauxhall Conference

Apps
Sub Apps
2 own-goals Gls

FA Cup

Q4	Oct	22	H	Lancaster City	W	3-1	Worthington 2, Lancaster	779
1	Nov	12	H	Runcorn	D	1-1	Kiwomya	1,286
R		21	A	Runcorn	W	3-1*	Lancaster 2, Lambert	1,288
2	Dec	3	H	Mansfield Town	D	0-0		2,396
R		13	A	Mansfield Town	L	1-2	Lancaster	2,648

* After extra-time

Apps
Sub Apps
Gls

FA Trophy

1	Jan	24	A	Bamber Bridge	L	0-1		1,058

Apps
Sub Apps
Gls

League Table

	P	W	D	L	F	A	Pts
Macclesfield Town	42	24	8	10	70	40	80
Woking	42	21	12	9	76	54	75
Southport	42	21	9	12	68	50	72
Altrincham	42	20	8	14	77	60	68
Stevenage Borough	42	20	7	15	68	49	67
Kettering Town	42	19	10	13	73	56	67
Gateshead	42	19	10	13	61	53	67
Halifax Town	42	17	12	13	68	54	63
Runcorn	42	16	10	16	59	71	58
Northwich Victoria	42	14	15	13	77	66	57
Kidderminster Harriers	42	16	9	17	63	61	57
Bath City	42	15	12	15	55	56	57
Bromsgrove Rovers	42	14	13	15	66	69	55
Farnborough Town	42	15	10	17	45	64	55
Dagenham & Redbridge	42	13	13	16	56	69	52
Dover Athletic	42	11	16	15	48	55	49
Welling United	42	13	10	19	57	74	49
Stalybridge Celtic	42	11	14	17	52	72	47
Telford United	42	10	16	16	53	62	46
Merthyr Tydfil	42	11	11	20	53	63	44
Stafford Rangers	42	9	11	22	53	79	38
Yeovil Town*	42	8	14	20	50	71	37

* Deducted one point

1995-96

GM Vauxhall Conference

Managers: August 1995–March 1996 John Bird; March–April 1996 George Mulhall & Kieran O'Regan (joint); April 1996 John Carroll

Did you know that?

- Club colours were blue-and-white-striped shirts with black trim and white shorts.
- Kieran O'Regan was captain.
- Club sponsors were Holland Decorators.
- John Hendrick was lead singer with local Irish/Indie band Belt of the Celts.
- After signing for Dagenham on 17 December, Steve Prindiville was not allowed to play in the game between the sides the following day.
- The attendance of 509 for the visit of Stalybridge Celtic on 5 March was Town's lowest-ever for a Conference match.
- The 7–0 loss at Macclesfield Town on 9 March was Halifax Town's worst-ever Conference defeat.
- Halifax Town's fox mascot – without a name – made its first appearance at the home game with Altrincham on 16 March. The club decided to use a fox a mascot after a real one had been visiting The Shay and digging up parts of the pitch.
- George Mulhall took charge of Halifax Town for the match with Southport on 26 March, almost 22 years after he was last manager here.
- Biggest Conference win: 3–0 v Dagenham & Redbridge (h), 6 January.
- Heaviest Conference defeat: 0–7 v Macclesfield Town (a), 9 March.

Match No.	Date		Venue	Opponents	Result		Scorers	Attendance
1	Aug	19	A	Hednesford Town	L	0-3		1,594
2		22	H	Macclesfield Town	W	1-0	Stoneman	1,169
3		26	H	Slough Town	L	1-2	Johnson	917
4		29	A	Stalybridge Celtic	L	0-1		905
5	Sep	2	H	Welling United	W	2-1	O'Regan, Johnson	766
6		5	H	Gateshead	W	2-0	Beddard, Midwood	743
7		9	A	Woking	L	0-2		2,065
8		12	H	Northwich Victoria	W	2-0	Stoneman, Simpson (og)	829
9		16	H	Kidderminster Harriers	L	0-2		1,008
10		20	A	Gateshead	L	2-3	Worthington, Midwood	559
11		23	A	Altrincham	L	2-3	Trotter, Worthington	1,085
12		26	H	Morecambe	D	1-1	Midwood	910
13		30	H	Dover Athletic	W	1-0	Hendrick	905
14	Oct	7	A	Runcorn	W	1-0	Midwood	637
15		14	H	Stevenage Borough	L	2-3	Brown, Johnson	858
16		28	A	Farnborough Town	D	0-0		908
17	Nov	4	H	Bath City	W	3-1	Midwood 2, Cochrane	811
18		11	H	Kettering Town	W	2-0	Worthington 2	929
19		18	A	Dagenham & Redbridge	D	1-1	Midwood	701
20		25	A	Welling United	D	0-0		666
21	Dec	2	H	Bromsgrove Rovers	D	1-1	Worthington	843
22		9	A	Slough Town	W	3-2	Beddard 2, Midwood	862
23		16	H	Runcorn	L	1-3	Johnson	834
24	Jan	1	A	Southport	D	0-0		1,318
25		6	H	Dagenham & Redbridge	W	3-0	Cochrane, Johnson, O'Regan	729
26		20	A	Stevenage Borough	L	0-2		1,841
27	Feb	3	H	Hednesford Town	L	1-3	Brook	859
28		17	A	Northwich Victoria	D	1-1	Brook	879
29		24	H	Bath City	L	1-2	Sansam	547
30	Mar	2	A	Dover Athletic	L	2-3	Lee, Midwood	895
31		5	H	Stalybridge Celtic	L	2-3	Trotter, O'Regan	509
32		9	A	Macclesfield Town	L	0-7		1,348
33		12	A	Morecambe	W	1-0	Cochrane	645
34		16	H	Altrincham	D	1-1	Stoneman	755
35		18	A	Kidderminster Harriers	L	1-6	Johnson	1,168
36		26	H	Southport	D	2-2	Horner, O'Regan	694
37		30	H	Farnborough Town	D	0-0		697
38	Apr	6	H	Telford United	D	0-0		771
39		8	A	Kettering Town	W	2-1	Daws, Hendrick	1,317
40		13	A	Telford United	D	1-1	Trotter	708
41		20	H	Woking	D	2-2	Brook 2	1,064
42	May	3	A	Bromsgrove Rovers	W	1-0	Midwood	887

Final League Position: 15th in GM Vauxhall Conference

1 own-goal

Apps
Sub Apps
Gls

FA Cup

Q4	Oct	21	A	Runcorn	L	1-2	Worthington	901

Apps
Sub Apps
Gls

FA Trophy

1	Jan	20	H	Southport	W	2-1	Johnson, Cochrane	966
2	Feb	10	H	Bromsgrove Rovers	L	0-1		887

Apps
Sub Apps
Gls

League Table

	P	W	D	L	F	A	Pts
Stevenage Borough	42	27	10	5	101	44	91
Woking	42	25	8	9	83	54	83
Hednesford Town	42	23	7	12	71	46	76
Macclesfield Town	42	22	9	11	66	49	75
Gateshead	42	18	13	11	58	46	67
Southport	42	18	12	12	77	64	66
Kidderminster Harriers	42	18	10	14	78	66	64
Northwich Victoria	42	16	12	14	72	64	60
Morecambe	42	17	8	17	78	72	59
Farnborough Town	42	15	14	13	63	58	59
Bromsgrove Rovers	42	15	14	13	59	57	59
Altrincham	42	15	13	14	59	64	58
Telford United	42	15	10	17	51	56	55
Stalybridge Celtic	42	16	7	19	59	68	55
Halifax Town	42	13	13	16	49	63	52
Kettering Town	42	13	9	20	68	84	48
Slough Town	42	13	8	21	63	76	47
Bath City	42	13	7	22	45	66	46
Welling United	42	10	15	17	42	53	45
Dover Athletic	42	11	7	24	51	74	40
Runcorn	42	9	8	25	48	87	35
Dagenham & Redbridge	42	7	12	23	43	73	33

1996-97

GM Vauxhall Conference

Managers: August 1996–February 1997 John Carroll;
February–May 1997 George Mulhall & Kieran O'Regan (joint)

Did you know that?

- Captain was Kieran O'Regan.
- Club colours were blue-and-white-striped shirts with white and blue collars, and white shorts.
- Town's 6–0 loss at Stevenage Borough was their worst-ever opening-day defeat.
- The winning goal for Harrogate Railway in the West Riding County Cup match November was scored by 'keeper Mark Fenton, a punt downfield which bounced over opposite number Andy Woods, the only instance of such a goal being scored in this fashion at The Shay.
- At half-time in the home match with Northwich Victoria on Boxing Day, fitness conditioner Tommy Gildert broke the World Superstars record by doing 144 press-ups in 60 seconds.
- Only relegated Bromsgrove Rovers scored fewer goals away from home than Town's 16.
- Biggest Conference win: 4–1 v Slough Town (h), 24 August, v Stalybridge Celtic (h), 17 September.
- Heaviest Conference defeat: 0–6 v Stevenage Borough (a), 17 August.

Match No.	Date		Venue	Opponents	Result		Scorers	Attendance
1	Aug	17	A	Stevenage Borough	L	0-6		2,117
2		20	H	Altrincham	D	1-1	Brook	842
3		24	H	Slough Town	W	4-1	Worthington, Horner, Jm Brown, Midwood	793
4		26	A	Southport	L	1-2	Horner	1,543
5		31	A	Kettering Town	L	1-4	Norbury	1,541
6	Sep	3	H	Gateshead	W	2-0	Norbury, Brook	679
7		7	H	Rushden & Diamonds	L	1-3	Norbury	948
8		10	A	Altrincham	L	1-2	Brook	673
9		17	H	Stalybridge Celtic	W	4-1	Ellison, Norbury 2, Trotter	664
10		21	A	Hayes	D	0-0		521
11		24	H	Telford United	L	0-3		663
12	Oct	1	A	Macclesfield Town	L	0-1		951
13		5	H	Kidderminster Harriers	L	2-3	Norbury, Horner	786
14		19	H	Woking	L	0-4		807
15	Nov	2	H	Dover Athletic	D	2-2	McInerney, Hulme	1,038
16		9	A	Bath City	D	0-0		567
17		23	H	Welling United	D	1-1	Brook	608
18		30	H	Kettering Town	W	2-1	Horsfield, Davison	790
19	Dec	7	A	Stalybridge Celtic	W	3-2	Stoneman 2 (1 pen), Horsfield	814
20		14	H	Morecambe	D	1-1	Brook	883
21		21	A	Woking	D	2-2	Horsfield, Lyons (pen)	2,331
22		26	H	Northwich Victoria	L	0-3		1,078
23		28	A	Gateshead	W	1-0	Norbury	466
24	Jan	28	H	Bromsgrove Rovers	W	1-0	Norbury (pen)	608
25	Feb	1	A	Bromsgrove Rovers	L	0-3		686
26		15	H	Bath City	L	4-5	Horsfield 2, Lyons, Martin	655
27		22	H	Farnborough Town	W	3-0	Brook, Horsfield, Day (og)	694
28	Mar	1	A	Welling United	W	1-0	Brook	688
29		4	H	Hednesford Town	W	1-0	Brook	623
30		8	A	Kidderminster Harriers	L	0-3		2,523
31		15	H	Dover Athletic	L	1-3	Stoneman	703
32		17	A	Northwich Victoria	D	2-2	Norbury (pen), Horsfield	911
33		28	H	Southport	W	2-0	Murphy, Martin	792
34		31	A	Farnborough Town	L	0-3		675
35	Apr	5	A	Slough Town	L	0-1		760
36		7	A	Hednesford Town	D	1-1	Lyons	1,017
37		12	A	Telford United	D	1-1	Norbury	759
38		16	A	Morecambe	L	0-1		711
39		19	H	Hayes	D	2-2	Norbury, Lyons	684
40		26	A	Rushden & Diamonds	L	0-1		2,629
41		30	H	Macclesfield Town	D	3-3	Murphy, Horsfield, Hulme	2,191
42	May	3	H	Stevenage Borough	W	4-2	Norbury 3, Horsfield	1,191

Final League Position: 19th in GM Vauxhall Conference

Apps
Sub Apps
1 own-goal   Gls

FA Cup

Q1	Sep	14	A	Oldham Town	W	3-2	Hendrick, Brook 2	445
Q2		28	H	Bishop Auckland	L	1-4	Brook	628

Apps
Sub Apps
Gls

FA Trophy

1	Jan	18	A	Stalybridge Celtic	W	1-0	Brook	973
2	Feb	8	A	Gloucester City	L	0-3		1,118

Apps
Sub Apps
Gls

League Table

	P	W	D	L	F	A	Pts
Macclesfield Town	42	27	9	6	80	30	90
Kidderminster Harriers	42	26	7	9	84	42	85
Stevenage Borough	42	24	10	8	87	53	82
Morecambe	42	19	9	14	69	56	66
Woking	42	18	10	14	71	63	64
Northwich Victoria	42	17	12	13	61	54	63
Farnborough Town	42	16	13	13	58	53	61
Hednesford Town	42	16	12	14	52	50	60
Telford United	42	16	10	16	46	56	58
Gateshead	42	15	11	16	59	63	56
Southport	42	15	10	17	51	61	55
Rushden & Diamonds	42	14	11	17	61	63	53
Stalybridge Celtic	42	14	10	13	53	58	52
Kettering Town	42	14	9	19	53	62	51
Hayes	42	12	14	16	54	55	50
Slough Town	42	12	14	16	62	65	50
Dover Athletic	42	12	14	16	57	68	50
Welling United	42	13	9	20	50	60	48
Halifax Town	42	12	12	18	55	74	48
Bath City	42	12	11	19	53	80	47
Bromsgrove Rovers	42	12	5	25	47	67	41
Altrincham	42	9	12	21	49	73	39

1997-98

GM Vauxhall Conference
Manager: George Mulhall

Did you know that?

- Captain was Kevin Hulme.
- After just avoiding relegation, the bookies were offering odds of 66-1 for Halifax Town to win the Conference at the start of the season.
- Halifax Town went 12 League and Cup games unbeaten from the start of the season – a club record.
- Halifax Town wore an all-blue strip with white trim.
- Town were unbeaten in their first 12 Conference matches.
- Peter Jackson was Newcastle United's Player of the Year in 1986–87, ahead of Peter Beardsley and Paul Gascoigne.
- The first defeat was suffered in a Spalding Cup match at Stalybridge Celtic on 7 October.
- Brian Kilcline was skipper of Coventry City when they defeated Spurs 3–2 to win the FA Cup in May 1987.
- Halifax Town's second goal in the final day 6–2 defeat at Welling was the club's 301st in the Conference.
- Halifax Town went through the full season unbeaten at home – 42 Conference matches and five Cup matches.
- Geoff Horsfield finished as the top scorer in the Conference with 30 goals, one ahead of Rushden's Darren Collins.
- Jamie Paterson was named Conference Player of the Year.
- Biggest Conference win: 6–1 v Telford United (h), 16 September.
- Heaviest Conference defeat: 2–6 v Welling (a), 2 May.
- Ever-present: Mark Bradshaw.

Match No.	Date	Venue	Opponents	Result		Scorers	Attendance
1	Aug 16	A	Hayes	W	2-1	Horsfield, Lyons	907
2	23	A	Slough Town	D	1-1	Paterson (pen)	740
3	25	A	Southport	D	0-0		1,889
4	30	H	Welling United	W	1-0	Paterson	1,011
5	Sep 2	A	Telford United	W	3-0	Brook, Horsfield 2	805
6	5	H	Yeovil Town	W	3-1	Horsfield 3	1,515
7	16	H	Telford United	W	6-1	Horsfield 3, O'Regan, Stoneman, Hulme	1,119
8	20	A	Farnborough United	W	2-1	Horsfield, Brook	919
9	30	H	Leek Town	W	2-1	Paterson, Bradshaw	1,329
10	Oct 4	H	Kettering Town	W	3-0	Hulme, Bradshaw, Thackeray	1,836
11	18	H	Stevenage Borough	W	4-0	Horsfield 2, Hulme, Bradshaw (pen)	2,139
12	28	A	Morecambe	D	1-1	Horsfield	3,940
13	Nov 1	A	Cheltenham Town	L	0-4		2,508
14	8	A	Kidderminster Harriers	W	2-1	Paterson, Kilcline	1,799
15	15	H	Stalybridge Celtic	W	1-0	Stoneman	1,421
16	22	H	Hereford United	W	3-0	Horsfield 3	2,214
17	29	A	Woking	D	2-2	Horsfield, Paterson (pen)	3,319
18	Dec 5	H	Stalybridge Celtic	W	3-1	Lyons, Horsfield 2	2,453
19	9	H	Northwich Victoria	W	4-2	Lyons, Bradshaw, Paterson 2	2,165
20	13	A	Leek Town	L	0-2		1,282
21	20	H	Hednesford Town	D	1-1	Horsfield	3,338
22	26	A	Gateshead	D	2-2	Paterson, Horsfield	1,239
23	29	A	Kettering Town	D	1-1	Philliskirk	2,278
24	Jan 1	H	Gateshead	W	2-0	Horsfield 2	3,149
25	17	A	Stevenage Borough	W	2-1	Hulme, Philliskirk	2,946
26	24	H	Slough Town	W	1-0	Horsfield	2,098
27	Feb 7	A	Rushden & Diamonds	L	0-4		3,675
28	14	A	Dover Athletic	W	1-0	Paterson	1,316
29	21	A	Yeovil Town	W	1-0	Paterson (pen)	2,584
30	28	H	Farnborough United	W	1-0	Horsfield	2,352
31	Mar 7	A	Dover Athletic	D	1-1	Hulme	1,949
32	14	A	Hednesford Town	D	0-0		1,856
33	17	H	Morecambe	W	5-1	Bradshaw, Thackeray, Paterson, Kilcline, Horsfield	2,507
34	21	H	Rushden & Diamonds	W	2-0	Wooding (og), Paterson	3,951
35	28	H	Hayes	D	1-1	Horsfield	2,506
36	Apr 4	H	Woking	W	1-0	Hulme	2,826
37	11	A	Hereford United	D	0-0		3,304
38	13	H	Southport	W	4-3	Paterson, Hulme, Hanson 2	4,701
39	18	A	Kidderminster Harriers	W	2-0	Horsfield, Paterson	3,151
40	20	A	Northwich Victoria	L	0-2		2,106
41	25	H	Cheltenham Town	D	1-1	Horsfield	6,357
42	May 2	A	Welling United	L	2-6	Horsfield, Brook	1,344

Final League Position: 1st in GM Vauxhall Conference

Apps
Sub Apps
1 own-goal Gls

FA Cup

Q1	Sep 13	H	Droylsden	W	4-1	Brook 2, Paterson, Horsfield	799
Q2	27	H	Leigh RMI	W	4-0	Paterson 2 (1 pen), Brook, Horsfield	1,103
Q3	Oct 11	H	Ossett Town	W	5-0	Horsfield, Hulme 2, Brook (2)	1,060
Q4	25	A	Gainsborough Trinity	L	1-2	Horsfield	1,730

Apps
Sub Apps
Gls

FA Trophy

1	Jan 10	H	Blyth Spartans	W	2-1	Brook, Lyons	1,712
2	31	H	Slough Town	D	1-1	Paterson	1,633
R	Feb 3	A	Slough Town	L	0-2		876

Apps
Sub Apps
Gls

League Table

	P	W	D	L	F	A	Pts
Halifax Town	42	25	12	5	74	43	87
Cheltenham Town	42	23	9	10	63	43	78
Woking	42	22	8	12	72	46	74
Rushden & Diamonds	42	23	5	14	79	57	74
Morecambe	42	21	10	11	77	64	73
Hereford United	42	18	13	11	56	49	67
Hednesford Town	42	18	12	12	59	50	66
Slough Town	42	18	10	14	58	49	64
Northwich Victoria	42	15	15	12	63	59	60
Welling United	42	17	9	16	64	62	60
Yeovil Town	42	17	8	17	73	63	59
Hayes	42	16	10	16	62	52	58
Dover Athletic	42	15	10	17	60	70	55
Kettering Town	42	13	13	16	53	60	52
Stevenage Borough	42	13	12	17	59	63	51
Southport	42	13	11	18	56	58	50
Kidderminster Harriers	42	11	14	17	56	63	47
Farnborough Town	42	12	8	22	56	70	44
Leek Town	42	10	14	18	52	67	44
Telford United	42	10	12	20	53	76	42
Gateshead	42	8	11	23	51	87	35
Stalybridge Celtic	42	7	8	27	48	93	29

1998-99

Division Three

Manager: August 1998–March 1999 Kieran O'Regan; March–May 1999 Dave Worthington (caretaker)

Did you know that?

- Halifax Town wore blue shirts with a dash of white. Their away strip was of similar design in lime green, with yellow shorts.
- To celebrate Halifax Town's Conference success, comic entertainers The Grumbleweeds, whose member Tony Jo was a Town fan, recorded a CD entitled *We're Coming Back*.
- Captain was Kevin Hulme.
- Club sponsors were Nationwide Building Society.
- Halifax Town's first League goal following promotion was scored by Dave Hanson in the 48th minute of the opening game at Peterborough United.
- Tim Carter made his debut as a substitute for injured Lee Martin in a 4–0 win at Scunthorpe United on 3 October. When he made his first start at Carlisle on 7 November, he came off injured at half-time and was replaced by Kevin Hulme.
- Mark Sertori acted as masseur to the England World Cup team under Fabio Capello in 2010.
- Geoff Horsfield made a club record £350,000 move to Fulham on 12 October.
- A week after taking charge of the Worthington Cup Final between Spurs and Leicester, referee Terry Heilbron officiated in Town's game with Leyton Orient on 26 March.
- Halifax Town's total of 66 points (three points for a win) beat the club record of 60 set in 1982–83.
- Biggest League win: 4–0 v Scunthorpe United (a), 3 October.
- Heaviest League defeat: 0–4 v Torquay United (a), 6 March, v Cambridge United (a), 10 April.

Match No.	Date		Venue	Opponents	Result		Scorers	Attendance
1	Aug	8	A	Peterborough United	W	2-0	Hanson, Horsfield	5,746
2		15	H	Brentford	W	1-0	Horsfield	3,876
3		22	A	Darlington	D	2-2	Horsfield 2	4,200
4		28	H	Shrewsbury Town	W	2-0	Hulme, Horsfield	3,424
5		31	A	Plymouth Argyle	L	0-1		6,544
6	Sep	4	H	Hartlepool United	W	2-1	Hulme, Horsfield	3,820
7		8	A	Southend United	D	0-0		3,620
8		11	H	Cardiff City	L	1-2	O'Regan	2,814
9		19	A	Hull City	W	2-1	Horsfield, Hanson	4,719
10		26	H	Torquay United	D	1-1	Paterson	2,753
11	Oct	3	A	Scunthorpe United	W	4-0	Paterson 2, Williams 2	4,989
12		11	A	Rochdale	L	0-1		3,628
13		16	H	Barnet	D	1-1	Guinan	2,223
14		20	H	Cambridge United	D	3-3	Stoneman, Thackeray, Paterson	1,906
15		24	A	Leyton Orient	L	0-1		3,655
16		31	H	Swansea City	W	2-0	Hulme, Paterson	2,383
17	Nov	7	A	Carlisle United	W	1-0	Stoneman	3,636
18		10	H	Chester City	W	3-2	Paterson, Thackeray 2	2,427
19		21	A	Brighton & Hove Albion	W	1-0	Paterson	3,305
20		27	H	Mansfield Town	D	2-2	Thackeray, Paterson (pen)	3,227
21	Dec	12	A	Scarborough	L	0-1		2,251
22		19	H	Exeter City	D	1-1	Williams	2,342
23		26	H	Darlington	D	0-0		3,557
24		28	A	Rotherham United	L	1-3	Guinan	4,728
25	Jan	2	A	Shrewsbury Town	D	2-2	Power, O'Regan	2,806
26		9	H	Peterborough United	D	2-2	Stoneman (pen), Williams	2,784
27		23	A	Plymouth Argyle	W	2-0	Williams 2	2,762
28		30	H	Rotherham United	L	2-4	Stoneman, Power	4,251
29	Feb	6	A	Hartlepool United	L	0-2		2,374
30		13	H	Southend United	W	3-1	Hulme, Power 2	2,302
31		19	A	Cardiff City	D	1-1	Bradshaw	8,570
32		27	H	Hull City	L	0-1		4,455
33	Mar	6	A	Torquay United	L	0-4		1,715
34		13	H	Carlisle United	W	1-0	Bradshaw	2,432
35		16	A	Brentford	D	1-1	Stansfield	3,713
36		20	A	Swansea City	W	2-1	J Murphy, Paterson	4,974
37		26	H	Leyton Orient	L	1-2	Butler	2,978
38	Apr	3	A	Barnet	D	2-2	Paterson, Bradshaw	2,055
39		5	H	Rochdale	D	0-0		2,759
40		10	A	Cambridge United	L	0-4		4,838
41		13	A	Mansfield Town	W	1-0	Thackeray	2,471
42		17	H	Brighton & Hove Albion	W	1-0	Jackson	2,773
43		24	A	Chester City	D	2-2	Newton, Bradshaw	2,461
44		27	H	Scunthorpe United	W	1-0	Stoneman	3,486
45	May	1	H	Scarborough	L	1-2	Jackson	3,308
46		8	A	Exeter City	L	1-2	Jackson	3,180

Final League Position: 10th in Division Three

FA Cup

1	Nov	13	A	Manchester City	L	0-3		11,106

League Cup

1,1L	Aug	11	A	Wrexham	W	2-0	Horsfield, Hanson	2,655
1, 2L		18	H	Wrexham	L	0-2*		2,692
2,1L	Sep	15	H	Bradford City	L	1-2	Hanson	5,716
2,2L		22	A	Bradford City	L	1-3	Paterson	6,237

* After extra-time. Halifax Town won 4–2 on penalties (sequence: Stoneman scored (1–0), Lucas scored (2–1), Brown scored (3–2), Sertori scored (4–2))

Players

Martin, LB | Thackeray, AJ | Bradshaw, M | Lucas, R | Stoneman, P | Murphy, S | Duerden, IC | Hulme, KP | Hanson, DP | Horsfield, GM | Brown, J | Senior, MA | Butler, RJF | O'Regan, KM | Murphy, JA | Williams, ML | Paterson, JS | Carter, TD | Quinlan, SA | Newton, CJ | Power, LM | Stainsfield, JE | Ebbrington, C | Jackson, JJ | Grant, GM | Overson, VD

1	2	3	4	5	6	7	8	9	10	11															
1	2	3	7	6	5	12	8	9	10*	11	4														
1	2	3	5	6			8	9	10	11*	4	7	12												
1	2	3	4	6			8	9	10	11	5	7													
1	2	3	5	6			8	9	10	11	4	7													
1	2	3	5	6			8*	9	10	11	4		7	12											
1	2	3	5	6			8	9*	10	11	4	7	13		12+										
1	2	3	5	6			8	9	10	11	4	7*	12												
1	2	3	5*	6			8	9	10	11	4		7			12									
1	2*	3	13	6			8	9+	10		4	5	11		12	7									
1+		3	11	6			8			12	4	10	2*		5	9	7	13							
1	2	3	11	6			8*			12	4	10			5	9	7								
1	2	3	11	6						12	4	10			5	9*	7		8						
1	2	3		6						4	10	11		5	9	7		8							
1	2	3		6						4	10	11		5	9	7		8							
1	2	3		6			8*			12	4		11	5	9	7		10							
	2	3	12	6			8			11	4			5	9	7	1*	10							
1	2	3	12	6			8			11	4			5	9*	7		10							
1	2	3	4	6	12					11		8		5	9*	7		10							
1	2	3	4		6*					11		8		5	9	7		10	12						
1	2	3	4	6						11*		8		5	9	7	10+	13	12						
1	2	3+	5	6				12		11	4	8			5	9	7	10*	13						
1	2	3*	8	6				10		11	4			5	9			7	12						
	2	3	12	6				9+		11	4	8*		5	13		1	10	7						
	2	3		6				9		11	4		7	5*	12		1	10	8						
	2		3	6			8	10*			4	5	7		9		1	12	11						
	2	3		6			8			12	4	11	7*		9		1		10	5					
	2	3		6			8	12		7	4	11		5*	9		1		10						
	2	3		6	8*			12			4	11			9		1		10	5	7				
1	2		3	6			8			12	4*				9			11	5	7+	10	13			
1	2	11	3	6			8*	13		12	4				14			9+	5	7	10#				
1	2	11*	3				8	10		6	4				13			5	7	9+	12				
1	2		3	6			8*	10		12	4	11	7+					5		9	13				
	1	3	13	6	8+			12		4			7	2				11*	10	5	9				
1		3		6						8	4	11	7	2					10	5	9				
1		3	13				8		9		6	4	11	7+	2		12		10	5*					
1		3					8			12	2	4	11	6*	5		7		10		9				
	3	8+					13			12	2	4	11		5	7	1		10*	6	9				
	3						8			2+	4	11	12	5		7	1*	13	10	6	9				
1		3	4	6	8			10		2*		11				12			7	5	9				
1	2	3	4	6	10*		8+	14		5	12	11							7	13	9#				
1	2	3	10	6			8*	14		5	4	11		13		12			7#		9+				
1	2	3	10	6			8	13		5	4	11+				12			7		9*				
1	2		3	6	5		8*	12			4	11				7			10		9				
1	12	3	14	6	5			10		2*	4	11				7+		8#	13		9				
1	2		3	6	5		8*	12		10+	4	11				7		13			9				
37	37	41	29	40	12	1	28	19	10	32	39	33	15	21	18	29	9	12	8	14	12	4	16		
			1		7		2	1			12		8	1			4	2	6	5	1		6	4		3
	5	4		5				4	2	7				1	2	1	6	10		2	1	4	1		3

1	2	3	8*	6	12			11	4	10		5	9	7											
1	1	1		1				1	1	1		1	1	1											
			1																						

1	2	3	7	5	6	13	8	9+	10*	11	4									12					
1	2		3	6	7		8	9	10*	11	5	4	12												
1	2	3	5	6			8	9	10	11	4		7*			12									
1	2	3		6			8	9	10		4	5	11*		12	7									
4	4	3	3	4	2		4	4	4	3	4	2	2			1									
					1								1		1	1					1				
								2	1																

League Table

	P	W	D	L	F	A	Pts
Brentford	46	26	7	13	79	56	85
Cambridge United	46	23	12	11	78	48	81
Cardiff City	46	22	14	10	60	39	80
Scunthorpe United	46	22	8	16	69	58	74
Rotherham United	46	20	13	13	79	61	73
Leyton Orient	46	19	15	12	68	59	72
Swansea City	46	19	14	13	56	48	71
Mansfield Town	46	19	10	17	60	58	67
Peterborough United	46	18	12	16	72	56	66
Halifax Town	46	17	15	14	56	56	66
Darlington	46	18	11	17	65	58	65
Exeter City	46	17	12	17	47	50	63
Plymouth Argyle	46	17	10	19	56	54	61
Chester City	46	13	18	15	57	66	57
Shrewsbury Town	46	14	14	18	52	63	56
Barnet	46	14	13	19	54	71	55
Brighton & Hove Albion	46	16	7	23	49	66	55
Southend United	46	14	12	20	52	58	54
Rochdale	46	13	15	18	42	55	54
Torquay United	46	12	17	17	47	58	53
Hull City	46	14	11	21	44	62	53
Hartlepool United	46	13	12	21	52	65	51
Carlisle United	46	11	16	19	43	53	49
Scarborough	46	14	6	26	50	77	48

1999-2000

Division Three
Manager: Mark Lillis

Did you know that?

- Halifax Town wore blue-and-white-striped shirts and blue shorts.
- Club sponsors were Nationwide Building Society.
- Captain was Graham Mitchell.
- Sarah Scott became the club's first female physio.
- Rochdale mascot Desmond the Dragon was sacked by the club after getting into a spat with Town's Freddie Fox during half-time at the match at Spotland on 3 September.
- James Stansfield played cricket for Brighouse CC.
- Robert Herbert became Halifax Town's youngest-ever player when he replaced Robbie Painter in the match with Brighton at The Shay on 11 September. He was aged 16 years and 13 days.
- Paul Stoneman made his 200th first-team appearance in all competitions in the 4–0 defeat at Torquay United on 5 February.
- Halifax Town had three players sent off in the match at York City on 29 April.
- Biggest League win: 5–2 v Carlisle United (h), 25 September.
- Heaviest League defeat: 0–4 v Darlington (a), 4 December, v Torquay United (a), 5 February.

Match No.	Date		Venue	Opponents	Result		Scorers	Attendance
1	Aug	7	H	Darlington	L	0-1		3,721
2		14	A	Hartlepool United	W	2-0	Stoneman, S. Murphy	2,719
3		21	H	Plymouth Argyle	L	0-1		2,431
4		28	A	Leyton Orient	L	0-1		3,703
5		31	H	Torquay United	W	2-0	Tate, Power	1,981
6	Sep	3	H	Rochdale	W	1-0	Mitchell	4,198
7		11	H	Brighton & Hove Albion	W	2-1	Paterson, Tate	2,532
8		18	A	Southend United	L	1-4	Stoneman	4,532
9		25	H	Carlisle United	W	5-2	Paterson 3 (2 pens), Painter, Stoneman	2,545
10	Oct	2	A	Shrewsbury Town	D	0-0		2,307
11		9	A	Macclesfield Town	W	2-0	Rowe, Paterson	2,185
12		16	H	Peterborough United	W	2-1	Tate, Paterson (pen)	3,292
13		19	H	York City	L	0-2		2,963
14		23	A	Carlisle United	D	1-1	Rowe	2,593
15	Nov	2	H	Cheltenham Town	D	1-1	Painter	1,956
16		5	A	Swansea City	L	1-3	Tate	3,357
17		12	H	Exeter City	W	1-0	Bradshaw	2,440
18		23	A	Hull City	W	1-0	Painter	6,067
19		27	H	Mansfield Town	L	0-1		2,322
20	Dec	4	A	Darlington	L	0-4		4,581
21		11	H	Rotherham United	D	0-0		2,538
22		18	A	Chester City	L	1-2	Potter	2,037
23		26	H	Lincoln City	W	3-0	Cullen, Mitchell, Painter	2,371
24		28	A	Barnet	W	1-0	Cullen	2,450
25	Jan	3	H	Northampton Town	D	2-2	Paterson (pen), Hendon (og)	3,001
26		8	A	Rotherham United	W	1-0	Potter	4,450
27		15	H	Hartlepool United	D	1-1	Cullen (pen)	3,548
28		22	A	Plymouth Argyle	D	1-1	Painter	4,841
29		29	H	Leyton Orient	L	0-2		2,655
30	Feb	5	A	Torquay United	L	0-4		1,856
31		12	H	Rochdale	L	0-2		3,504
32		19	A	Mansfield Town	W	2-0	Painter, Cullen	2,476
33		26	H	Southend United	D	0-0		2,068
34	Mar	4	A	Brighton & Hove Albion	L	1-2	Wilder	5,311
35		7	H	Swansea City	L	0-1		1,657
36		11	A	Cheltenham Town	L	0-3		3,478
37		18	H	Hull City	L	0-1		2,519
38		21	A	Exeter City	L	0-1		1,652
39		25	A	Lincoln City	D	1-1	Jones	3,028
40	Apr	1	H	Chester City	L	0-1		2,431
41		8	A	Northampton Town	W	4-3	Painter, Stoneman, Middleton, Kerrigan	5,207
42		15	H	Barnet	L	1-2	Painter	1,734
43		22	A	Peterborough United	L	1-2	Kerrigan	7,194
44		24	H	Shrewsbury Town	W	2-1	Tretton (og), Kerrigan	2,123
45		29	A	York City	L	0-2		3,079
46	May	6	H	Macclesfield Town	L	0-1		2,007

Final League Position: 18th in Division Three

Apps
Sub Apps
2 own-goals
Gls

FA Cup

1	Oct	30	A	Doncaster Rovers	W	2-0	Tate, Paterson	5,588
2	Nov	20	A	Reading	D	1-1	Mitchell	5,918
R		30	H	Reading	L	0-1		2,156

Apps
Sub Apps
Gls

League Cup

1,1L	Aug	10	H	West Bromwich Albion	D	0-0		2,451
1,2L		24	A	West Bromwich Albion	L	1-5	Tate	8,316

Apps
Sub Apps
Gls

League Table

	P	W	D	L	F	A	Pts
Swansea City	46	24	13	9	51	30	85
Rotherham United	46	24	12	10	72	36	84
Northampton Town	46	25	7	14	63	45	82
Darlington	46	21	16	9	66	36	79
Peterborough United	46	22	12	12	63	54	78
Barnet	46	21	12	13	59	53	75
Hartlepool United	46	21	9	16	60	49	72
Cheltenham Town	46	20	10	16	50	42	70
Torquay United	46	19	12	15	62	52	69
Rochdale	46	18	14	14	57	54	68
Brighton & Hove Albion	46	17	16	13	64	46	67
Plymouth Argyle	46	16	18	12	55	51	66
Macclesfield Town	46	18	11	17	66	61	65
Hull City	46	15	14	17	43	43	59
Lincoln City	46	15	14	17	67	69	59
Southend United	46	15	11	20	53	61	56
Mansfield Town	46	16	8	22	50	65	56
Halifax Town	46	15	9	22	44	58	54
Leyton Orient	46	13	13	20	47	52	52
York City	46	12	16	18	39	53	52
Exeter City	46	11	11	24	46	72	44
Shrewsbury Town	46	9	13	24	40	67	40
Carlisle United	46	9	12	25	42	75	39
Chester City	46	10	9	27	44	79	39

2000-01

Division Three

Managers: August 2000–September 2000 Mark Lillis; September 2000–October 2000 Peter Butler & Tony Parks (joint caretakers); October 2000–April 2001 Paul Bracewell

Did you know that?

- Captain was Graham Mitchell.
- The attendance of 612 for Town's 'home' match with Tranmere Rovers in the League Cup at Valley Parade on 6 September was a record low for the competition.
- Steve Thompson was twice voted Player of the Year at Leicester City.
- Gregg Shannon and made his only appearance for Town in the Worthington Cup tie with Tranmere Rovers on 6 September, played at Valley Parade, Bradford. Grant Holt scored his only Town goal from three appearances, none of which were at The Shay.
- The new floodlights at The Shay were used for the first time for the visit of Cheltenham Town on 17 October.
- Chris Brass, who joined the club on loan from Burnley in September, went on to become the youngest manager in the Football League since Ivor Broadis in 1946 when he was appointed York City manager in June 2003, aged 27.
- Biggest League win: 3–0 v Southend United (a), 17 February, v Barnet (h), 24 March, v Macclesfield Town (h), 16 April.
- Heaviest League defeat: 1–5 v Mansfield Town (a), 9 September.

Match No.	Date		Venue	Opponents	Result		Scorers	Attendance
1	Aug	12	A	Carlisle United	D	2-2	Bradshaw, Kerrigan	4,491
2		29	H	Lincoln City	D	1-1	Kerrigan	2,013
3		26	A	Kidderminster Harriers	L	1-2	Gaughan	2,956
4		28	H	Rochdale	L	1-2	Bradshaw	2,783
5	Sep	2	H	Leyton Orient	D	2-2	Harrison, Kerrigan	1,592
6		9	A	Mansfield Town	L	1-5	Fitzpatrick	2,397
7		12	A	Cardiff City	L	2-4	Middleton, Jones	5,087
8		16	H	Southend United	L	0-1		1,447
9		23	A	Torquay United	W	2-1	Kerrigan, Fitzpatrick	1,921
10		30	H	Shrewsbury Town	D	0-0		1,606
11	Oct	7	A	Scunthorpe United	L	0-1		2,635
12		14	H	Hull City	L	0-2		3,003
13		17	H	Cheltenham Town	L	1-2	Rezai	1,382
14		21	A	Barnet	L	0-1		1,580
15		24	H	York City	L	1-3	Stoneman (pen)	1,984
16		28	A	Macclesfield Town	D	0-0		1,734
17	Nov	4	H	Exeter City	W	3-1	Kerrigan 2, Jones	1,836
18		11	A	Darlington	W	1-0	Jones	3,488
19		25	H	Chesterfield	D	2-2	Thompson, Kerrigan	2,769
20	Dec	2	A	Brighton & Hove Albion	L	1-2	Kerrigan	6,595
21		16	H	Hartlepool United	L	0-1		2,042
22		23	H	Plymouth Argyle	W	2-0	Stoneman, Kerrigan	1,670
23		26	A	Blackpool	W	1-0	Jones	5,044
24	Jan	6	H	Kidderminster Harriers	W	3-2	Thompson, Murphy, Kerrigan	1,824
25		13	A	Rochdale	W	1-0	Kerrigan	4,123
26		27	A	Plymouth Argyle	L	0-1		4,176
27	Feb	3	A	Leyton Orient	L	0-3		3,849
28		10	H	Mansfield Town	L	3-4	Mitchell, Asher (og), Kerrigan	1,857
29		17	A	Southend United	W	3-0	M. Clarke, Matthews, Kerrigan	3,746
30		20	H	Cardiff City	L	1-2	Middleton	1,991
31		24	H	Torquay United	W	2-1	Jones, Kerrigan	1,783
32	Mar	3	A	Shrewsbury Town	L	1-2	Reilly	2,604
33		6	A	Hull City	L	0-1		6,167
34		10	H	Scunthorpe United	L	3-4	Kerrigan 2, Reilly	2,352
35		17	A	Cheltenham Town	L	2-4	Matthews, Proctor	3,134
36		24	H	Barnet	W	3-0	C. Clarke, Kerrigan, Proctor	1,639
37		27	H	Carlisle United	D	0-0		4,111
38		31	A	Hartlepool United	D	1-1	Proctor	4,198
39	Apr	10	H	Blackpool	L	1-2	Jules	3,311
40		14	A	York City	L	1-2	Proctor	3,465
41		16	H	Macclesfield Town	W	3-0	Middleton, Kerrigan 2	1,945
42		21	A	Exeter City	D	0-0		4,235
43		28	H	Darlington	W	1-0	Middleton	2,287
44		30	A	Lincoln City	D	1-1	Middleton	3,701
45	May	3	H	Brighton & Hove Albion	D	0-0		3,979
46		5	A	Chesterfield	L	0-3		5,750

Final League Position: 23rd in Division Three

1 own-goal

								Apps
								Sub Apps
								Gls

FA Cup

1	Nov	18	H	Gateshead	L	0-2		1,902

								Apps
								Sub Apps
								Gls

League Cup

1,1L	Aug	22	A	Tranmere Rovers	L	0-3		4,405
1,2L	Sep	6	H*	Tranmere Rovers	L	1-2	Holt	612

*Played at Valley Parade, Bradford

								Apps
								Sub Apps
								Gls

League Table

	P	W	D	L	F	A	Pts
Brighton & Hove Albion	46	28	8	0	73	35	92
Cardiff City	46	23	13	0	95	58	82
Chesterfield	46	25	14	7	79	42	80
Hartlepool United	46	21	14	1	71	54	77
Leyton Orient	46	20	15	1	59	51	75
Hull City	46	19	17	0	47	39	74
Blackpool	46	22	6	8	74	58	72
Rochdale	46	18	17	1	59	48	71
Cheltenham Town	46	18	14	4	59	52	68
Scunthorpe United	46	18	11	7	62	52	65
Southend United	46	15	18	3	55	53	63
Plymouth Argyle	46	15	13	8	54	61	58
Mansfield Town	46	15	13	8	64	72	58
Macclesfield Town	46	14	14	8	51	62	56
Shrewsbury Town	46	15	10	21	49	65	55
Kidderminster Harriers	46	13	14	9	47	61	53
York City	46	13	13	20	42	63	52
Lincoln City	46	12	15	9	58	66	51
Exeter City	46	12	14	20	40	58	50
Darlington	46	12	13	21	44	56	49
Torquay United	46	12	13	21	52	77	49
Carlisle United	46	11	15	20	42	65	48
Halifax Town	46	12	11	23	54	68	47
Barnet	46	12	9	25	67	81	45

2001-02

Division Three

Managers: August 2001 Paul Bracewell; September–October 2001 Neil Redfearn & Tony Parks (joint caretaker); October 2001–March 2002 Alan Little; March–April 2002 Neil Redfearn

Did you know that?

- Captain was Paul Stoneman.
- Former Manchester United trainee Jamie Wood was an international with the Cayman Islands.
- After finishing top scorer with 19 in 2000–01, Steve Kerrigan failed to register a goal this term.
- Halifax Town's 3,889th and last-ever League goal was scored by Ian Fitzpatrick in the 86th minute in the last game against Rushden & Diamonds at The Shay.
- Halifax Town became the first club to be relegated twice to the Conference.
- The club had four different managerial teams throughout the course of the season.
- Biggest League win: 4–1 v Cheltenham Town (h), 16 March.
- Heaviest League defeat: 1–6 v Oxford United (a), 29 December.

Match No.	Date	Venue	Opponents	Result		Scorers	Attendance
1	Aug 11	A	Lincoln City	W	2-1	Midgley, Harsley	3,753
2	28	H	Exeter City	D	1-1	Swales	1,937
3	25	A	Southend United	L	1-4	Redfearn (pen)	3,525
4	27	H	Oxford United	L	0-2		2,271
5	Sep 1	A	York City	L	0-1		2,646
6	8	H	Macclesfield Town	D	0-0		1,714
7	15	A	Swansea City	W	2-0	Harsley 2	3,794
8	18	H	Mansfield Town	W	1-0	Jones	1,880
9	22	H	Leyton Orient	D	0-0		2,021
10	25	A	Rochdale	L	0-2		3,410
11	29	A	Hull City	L	0-3		9,572
12	Oct 5	H	Scunthorpe United	D	0-0		2,603
13	13	A	Plymouth Argyle	L	0-3		5,065
14	20	H	Bristol Rovers	D	0-0		1,898
15	23	H	Luton Town	L	2-4	Harsley, Fitzpatrick	2,140
16	27	A	Carlisle United	D	0-0		3,157
17	Nov 3	H	Darlington	D	2-2	Redfearn, Fitzpatrick	2,192
18	10	A	Rushden & Diamonds	L	1-2	Redfearn	3,883
19	20	A	Hartlepool United	L	0-3		2,963
20	24	H	Torquay United	W	2-0	Middleton, Fitzpatrick	1,681
21	Dec 1	A	Cheltenham Town	L	1-2	Harsley	3,304
22	15	H	Shrewsbury Town	L	1-2	Harsley	1,703
23	26	A	Macclesfield Town	D	1-1	Bushell	2,421
24	29	A	Oxford United	L	1-6	Harsley	6,046
25	Jan 12	A	Exeter City	D	0-0		2,763
26	19	H	Lincoln City	W	3-0	Jones 2, Fitzpatrick	2,007
27	22	A	Kidderminster Harriers	L	0-2		2,295
28	26	A	Scunthorpe L	L	0-4		3,465
29	29	H	Southend United	D	1-1	Jones	1,251
30	Feb 2	H	Hull City	L	0-1		3,400
31	9	A	Bristol Rovers	L	0-2		6,921
32	12	H	York City	D	1-1	Fitzpatrick	2,818
33	16	H	Plymouth Argyle	L	0-2		2,330
34	23	A	Swansea City	L	0-1		1,601
35	26	A	Mansfield Town	L	1-2	Fitzpatrick	4,513
36	Mar 2	A	Leyton Orient	L	1-3	Redfearn	4,748
37	5	H	Rochdale	L	1-2	Redfearn	2,825
38	9	A	Shrewsbury Town	L	0-3		3,729
39	12	H	Kidderminster Harriers	W	1-0	Midgley	1,227
40	16	H	Cheltenham Town	W	4-1	Midgley, Fitzpatrick, Harsley 2 (1 pen)	1,870
41	23	A	Luton Town	L	0-5		6,830
42	29	H	Carlisle United	D	2-2	Woodward, Redfearn	2,728
43	Apr 1	A	Darlington	L	0-5		3,401
44	6	H	Hartlepool United	L	0-2		1,838
45	13	A	Torquay United	W	4-2	Stoneman, Harsley, Middleton, M. Clarke	2,692
46	20	H	Rushden & Diamonds	L	2-4	Harsley (pen), Fitzpatrick	2,699

Final League Position: 24th in Division Three

Apps
Sub Apps
Gls

FA Cup

1	Nov 17	H	Farnborough Town	W	2-1	Middleton, Wood	1,914
2	Dec 8	H	Stoke City	D	1-1	Harsley	3,335
R	12	A	Stoke City	L	0-3		4,356

Apps
Sub Apps
Gls

Worthington Cup

1	Aug 21	A	Barnsley	L	0-2		5,418

Apps
Sub Apps
Gls

League Table

	P	W	D	L	F	A	Pts
Plymouth Argyle	46	31	9	6	71	28	102
Luton Town	46	30	7	9	96	48	97
Mansfield Town	46	24	7	15	72	60	79
Cheltenham Town	46	21	15	10	66	49	78
Rochdale	46	21	15	10	65	52	78
Rushden & Diamonds	46	20	13	13	69	53	73
Hartlepool United	46	20	11	15	74	48	71
Scunthorpe United	46	19	14	13	74	56	71
Shrewsbury Town	46	20	10	16	64	53	70
Kidderminster Harriers	46	19	9	18	56	47	66
Hull City	46	16	13	17	57	51	61
Southend United	46	15	13	18	51	54	58
Macclesfield Town	46	15	13	18	41	52	58
York City	46	16	9	21	54	67	57
Darlington	46	15	11	20	60	71	56
Exeter City	46	14	13	19	48	73	55
Carlisle United	46	12	16	18	49	56	52
Leyton Orient	46	13	13	20	55	71	52
Torquay United	46	12	15	19	46	63	51
Swansea City	46	13	12	21	53	77	51
Oxford United	46	11	14	21	53	62	47
Lincoln City	46	10	16	20	44	62	46
Bristol Rovers	46	11	12	23	40	60	45
Halifax Town	46	8	12	26	39	84	36

* Chesterfield deducted 9 points for financial irregularities

2002-03

Nationwide Conference
Manager: Chris Wilder

Did you know that?

- Captain was Steve Bushell.
- Steve Kerrigan ended a personal 16-month goal draught when he scored the opening goal against Telford United in the 27th minute of the first match of the season.
- Halifax Town supporters were used as extras for another episode of *Frost*, and were filmed following Town's match with Kettering Town.
- Charlie Hartfield became the only player to make two appearances for the club and score in both games, netting against Stevenage on 23 November and Dagenham the following week.
- Chris Wilder was named Nationwide Manager of the Month for January.
- In February, supporters named a beer after Halifax Town at the nearby Three Pigeons public house.
- By winning at Scarborough on 15 February, Halifax Town equalled a club record of four successive away wins, last achieved in 1926–27. they also equalled a club record of eight away wins in a League season, matching the feats of the class of 1926–27, 1934–35, 1997–98 and 1999–2000.
- Biggest League win: 4–0 v Kettering Town (h), 8 October.
- Heaviest League defeat: 0–5 v Northwich Victoria (h), 26 August.

Match No.	Date	Venue	Opponents	Result		Scorers	Attendance
1	Aug 17	H	Telford United	W	2-0	Kerrigan, Midgley (pen)	1,616
2	20	A	Morecambe	L	0-2		1,524
3	24	A	Farnborough Town	L	0-3		626
4	26	H	Northwich Victoria	L	0-5		1,491
5	31	A	Barnet	D	0-0		1,316
6	Sep 2	H	Scarborough	W	2-1	Parke, Mallon	1,557
7	7	A	Burton Albion	D	2-2	Mallon, Parke	1,636
8	10	H	Doncaster Rovers	W	2-1	Clarkson, Ryan (og)	3,082
9	17	H	Chester City	D	0-0		2,178
10	21	A*	Yeovil Town	L	0-3		2,126
11	24	A	Southport	L	0-2		1,008
12	28	H	Nuneaton Borough	W	3-1	Stoneman, Farrell, Fitzpatrick	1,402
13	Oct 5	A	Stevenage Borough	W	1-0	Midgley	1,722
14	8	H	Kettering Town	W	4-0	Mallon 3 (1 pen), Stoneman	1,639
15	12	H	Margate	D	2-2	Sanders (og), Fitzpatrick	1,519
16	19	A	Hereford United	D	1-1	Mallon	1,699
17	Nov 2	H	Gravesend & Northfleet	W	2-1	Mallon, Farrell	1,529
18	9	A	Forest Green Rovers	W	2-0	Quailey, Mallon	753
19	23	H	Stevenage Borough	W	1-0	Hartfield	1,517
20	30	H	Dagenham & Redbridge	D	3-3	Killeen, Fitzpatrick, Hartfield	1,630
21	Dec 7	A	Woking	L	1-2	Killeen	1,734
22	14	H	Burton Albion	L	0-1		1,469
23	20	A	Doncaster Rovers	D	0-0		3,201
24	26	A	Leigh RMI	W	2-0	Fitzpatrick, Parke	817
25	28	H	Morecambe	W	1-0	Farrell	2,122
26	Jan 1	H	Leigh RMI	W	1-0	Clarkson	2,050
27	4	A	Telford United	W	2-1	Quailey 2	880
28	18	H	Farnborough Town	W	1-0	Monington	1,894
29	25	A	Northwich Victoria	W	2-0	Quailey, Clarkson	1,014
30	Feb 8	H	Barnet	L	2-4	Killeen 2	2,119
31	15	A	Scarborough	W	1-0	Sandwith	1,835
32	Mar 1	A	Chester City	L	0-2		2,928
33	4	H	Yeovil Town	L	2-3	Parke 2	2,222
34	8	H	Southport	L	3-4	Parke, Fitzpatrick, Garnett	1,544
35	15	A	Nuneaton Borough	L	0-2		1,231
36	22	A	Dagenham & Redbridge	D	0-0		1,766
37	29	H	Woking	D	1-1	Midgley	1,558
38	Apr 5	H	Margate	L	1-2	Midgley	509
39	12	H	Hereford United	W	1-0	Quailey	1,299
40	19	A	Kettering Town	W	1-0	Clarkson	713
41	21	H	Forest Green Rovers	D	1-1	Farrell	1,366
42	26	A	Gravesend & Northfleet	L	0-1		1,950

Final League Position: 8th in Nationwide Conference

2 own-goals

Apps
Sub Apps
Gls

FA Cup

Q4	Oct 26	A	Burton Albion	L	1-2	Quailey	1,990

Apps
Sub Apps
Gls

FA Trophy

3	Jan 14	H	Doncaster Rovers	W	4-1	Killeen 2, Quailey, Fitzpatrick	1,770
4	Feb 1	H	Grays Athletic	W	3-2	Quailey, Clarkson, Midgley (pen)	1,653
5	22	A	Farnborough Town	L	0-2		863

Apps
Sub Apps
Gls

League Table

	P	W	D	L	F	A	Pts
Yeovil Town	42	28	11	3	100	37	95
Morecambe	42	23	9	10	86	42	78
Doncaster Rovers	42	22	12	8	73	47	78
Chester City	42	21	12	9	59	31	75
Dagenham & Redbridge	42	21	9	12	7'	59	72
Hereford United	42	19	7	16	64	51	64
Scarborough	42	18	10	14	63	54	64
Halifax Town	42	18	10	14	50	51	64
Forest Green Rovers	42	17	8	17	6'	62	59
Margate	42	15	11	13	60	66	56
Barnet	42	13	14	15	65	68	53
Stevenage Borough	42	14	10	13	6'	55	52
Farnborough Town	42	13	12	17	57	56	51
Northwich Victoria	42	13	12	17	66	72	51
Telford United	42	14	7	21	54	69	49
Burton Albion	42	13	10	19	52	77	49
Gravesend & Northfleet	42	12	12	13	62	73	48
Leigh RMI	42	14	6	22	44	71	48
Woking	42	11	14	17	52	81	47
Nuneaton Borough	42	13	7	22	5'	78	46
Southport	42	11	12	19	54	69	45
Kettering Town	42	8	7	27	3?	73	31

2003-04

Nationwide Conference
Manager: Chris Wilder

Did you know that?

- Captain was Steve Bushell.
- Lee Elam signed for Halifax Town on 14 May 2003, then represented England's National Game XI, but was never chosen once the new season had started.
- Halifax Town provided the opposition on the season's opening day for relegated Exeter City's first match in the Conference at St James Park.
- Jake Sagare's plane flight from America was funded by the Halifax Town Supporters' Trust.
- Manager Chris Wilder made a shock return to action when he played the full 90 minutes of Town's County Cup match at Yorkshire Amateur on 2 December.
- Halifax Town's 1–0 victory over Lincoln City in the quarter-finals of the LDV Vans Trophy earned them the Performance of the Round award.
- Ben Thornley, who made three first-team appearances, had nine Premiership outings to his name with Manchester United.
- Halifax Town lost 10 consecutive Conference matches between 3 January and 3 April.
- During Town's disastrous run of form, the club brought in psychic Peter Leckie to untangle energy lines which he felt may have been hampering the team.
- Biggest League win: 3–0 v Dagenham (h), 1 November.
- Heaviest League defeat: 1–7 v Hereford United (a), 25 November.

Match No.	Date		Venue	Opponents	Result		Scorers	Attendance
1	Aug	9	A	Exeter City	D	1-1	Killeen	3,722
2		12	H	Morecambe	W	1-0	Cameron	2,160
3		16	H	Gravesend & Northfleet	W	1-0	Mallon	1,675
4		23	A	Leigh RMI	D	1-1	Midgley	849
5		25	H	Tamworth	L	1-2	Midgley	1,849
6		30	A	Barnet	L	1-4	Midgley	1,341
7	Sep	6	H	Northwich Victoria	W	5-3	Killeen 2, Elam, Lee, Midgley (pen)	1,440
8		13	A	Chester City	L	0-2		2,628
9		20	H	Margate	L	0-1		1,452
10		23	A	Shrewsbury Town	L	0-2		3,807
11		27	A	Forest Green Rovers	W	2-1	Elam, Farrell	722
12	Oct	4	H	Stevenage Borough	W	2-1	Farrell, Lee	1,437
13		7	H	Accrington Stanley	D	1-1	Lee	2,116
14		11	A	Aldershot Town	L	1-3	Monington	2,882
15		18	A	Woking	D	2-2	Mallon, Bushell	1,917
16	Nov	1	H	Dagenham & Redbridge	W	3-0	Lee, Sandwith, McCombe	1,379
17		11	H	Telford United	D	1-1	Lee	1,332
18		14	A	Burton Albion	D	2-2	Killeen, Midgley (pen)	1,541
19		22	H	Farnborough Town	W	2-0	Midgley (2 pens)	1,250
20		25	A	Hereford United	L	1-7	Killeen	1,875
21		29	A	Northwich Victoria	W	1-0	Bushell	757
22	Dec	6	H	Chester City	L	0-3		1,928
23		13	H	Exeter City	W	2-0	Sagare, Midgley (pen)	1,267
24		20	A	Morecambe	L	0-2		1,603
25		26	H	Scarborough	W	1-0	Lee	2,136
26	Jan	3	H	Barnet	L	1-2	Killeen	1,517
27		17	A	Gravesend & Northfleet	L	0-1		985
28		24	H	Shrewsbury Town	D	0-0		1,830
29	Feb	8	A	Margate	L	0-2		391
30		21	A	Stevenage Borough	L	0-1		1,715
31		24	H	Aldershot Town	L	1-2	Mallon	843
32	Mar	6	A	Accrington Stanley	L	1-2	Kempron (og)	1,717
33		9	H	Forest Green Rovers	L	0-1		883
34		13	A	Telford United	L	1-2	Killeen	1,337
35		25	A	Scarborough	L	0-1		1,220
36		27	A	Farnborough Town	L	0-1		644
37		30	H	Burton Albion	L	1-4	Little	1,228
38	Apr	3	H	Hereford United	L	1-2	Midgley (pen)	1,389
39		9	H	Leigh RMI	W	2-1	Allan, Bushell	1,415
40		12	A	Tamworth	L	0-2		1,095
41		17	A	Dagenham & Redbridge	W	1-0	Midgley (pen)	1,344
42		24	H	Woking	D	2-2	Little (pen), Midgley	1,191

Final League Position: 19th in Nationwide Conference

Apps
Sub Apps
1 own-goal Gls

FA Cup

1	Oct	26	A	Northwich Victoria	L	0-1		1,111

Apps
Sub Apps
Gls

FA Trophy

3	Jan	10	A	Chester City	W	2-1	Killeen, Farrell	1,561
4	Feb	10	H	Staines Town	D	1-1	Battams (og)	1,020
R		12	A	Staines Town	W	3-2*	Quinn, Farrell, Midgley (pen)	728
5		14	H	Maidenhead United	L	0-2		1,345

*After extra-time

Apps
Sub Apps
1 own-goal Gls

League Table

	P	W	D	L	F	A	Pts
Chester City	42	27	11	4	85	34	92
Hereford United	42	28	7	7	103	44	91
Shrewsbury Town	42	20	14	8	67	42	74
Barnet	42	19	14	9	60	46	71
Aldershot Town	42	20	10	12	80	67	70
Exeter City	42	19	12	11	71	57	69
Morecambe	42	20	7	15	66	66	67
Stevenage Borough	42	18	9	15	58	52	63
Woking	42	15	16	11	65	52	61
Accrington Stanley	42	15	13	14	68	61	58
Gravesend & Northfleet	42	14	15	13	69	66	57
Telford United	42	15	10	17	49	51	55
Dagenham & Redbridge	42	15	9	18	59	64	54
Burton Albion*	42	15	7	20	57	59	51
Scarborough	42	12	15	15	51	54	51
Margate	42	14	9	19	56	64	51
Tamworth	42	13	10	19	49	68	49
Forest Green Rovers	42	12	12	18	58	80	48
Halifax Town	42	12	8	22	43	65	44
Farnborough Town	42	10	9	23	53	74	39
Leigh RMI	42	7	8	27	46	97	29
Northwich Victoria	42	4	11	27	30	80	23

* Burton Albion deducted one point for fielding an inligible player

2004-05

Nationwide Conference National

Manager: Chris Wilder

Did you know that?

- Captain was Steve Bushell.
- Club sponsors were Warm Shield.
- Steve Haslam made 25 Premiership appearances with Sheffield Wednesday.
- Mark Monington scored in four successive matches between 17 and 31 August.
- Scott Willis was the nephew of entertainer Cilla Black.
- Chairman Geoff Ralph interrupted a holiday in Florida to attend Halifax Town's FA Cup second-round tie with Chester City on 4 December.
- Geoff Ralph had part-ownership of a race horse called Shaydreambeliever.
- Biggest League win: 5–1 v Leigh RMI (h), 2 April.
- Heaviest League defeat: 2–4 v Dagenham (a), 25 September.

Match No.	Date		Venue	Opponents	Result		Scorers	Attendance
1	Aug	14	A	Tamworth	L	1-2	Foster	1,325
2		17	H	Scarborough	W	2-1	Monington, Midgley (pen)	1,887
3		21	H	Barnet	L	2-3	Howell, Monington	1,382
4		28	A	Leigh RMI	W	3-0	Monington, Killeen, Midgley	578
5		31	H	Carlisle United	D	2-2	Monington, Bushell	2,696
6	Sep	4	A	Hereford United	W	3-2	Killeen, Sugden, Bushell	3,022
7		11	H	Forest Green Rovers	W	4-0	Mansaram, Sugden 2, Killeen	1,418
8		18	A	Canvey Island	W	1-0	Mansaram	789
9		21	H	Morecambe	L	1-3	Stoneman	1,667
10		25	A	Dagenham & Redbridge	L	2-4	Killeen 2	1,122
11	Oct	2	H	Exeter City	W	2-1	Mansaram, Howell (pen)	1,438
12		8	A	Woking	L	1-2	Quinn	1,864
13		12	A	Burton Albion	D	2-2	Howell, Mallon	1,194
14		16	H	Farnborough Town	W	2-0	Quinn, Mansaram	1,288
15		23	H	Gravesend & Northfleet	W	1-0	Mallon	1,410
16	Nov	6	A	Stevenage Borough	L	1-2	Sugden	1,820
17		20	H	Aldershot Town	W	2-0	Sugden, Killeen	1,724
18		27	A	Northwich Victoria	W	2-1	Quinn, Killeen	1,272
19	Dec	7	A	York City	D	1-1	Killeen	2,394
20		11	H	Canvey Island	W	4-1	Midgley 2, Ross, Foster	1,522
21		18	A	Forest Green Rovers	D	0-0		613
22		28	H	Dagenham & Redbridge	D	2-2	Midgley (pen), Ross	1,934
23	Jan	3	H	Accrington Stanley	L	1-2	Howell	2,472
24		11	A	Crawley Town	W	1-0	Ross (pen)	1,267
25		25	H	Burton Albion	W	2-0	Mansaram, Sugden	1,256
26		29	A	Morecambe	L	1-2	Midgley (pen)	1,910
27	Feb	12	H	Stevenage Borough	W	2-1	Midgley, Howell	1,497
28		19	A	Aldershot Town	D	0-0		2,903
29		22	A	Accrington Stanley	D	1-1	Sugden	1,402
30		26	H	Northwich Victoria	D	2-2	Midgley, Mansaram	1,636
31	Mar	5	A	Crawley Town	W	2-1	Foster, Midgley (pen)	1,957
32		8	A	Gravesend & Northfleet	W	3-0	Midgley, Howell, Killeen	716
33		14	H	York City	W	2-0	Groves (og), Meechan	2,165
34		19	A	Scarborough	L	1-3	Ross (pen)	2,109
35		25	H	Tamworth	D	3-3	Young, Sugden, Midgley	1,998
36		28	A	Carlisle United	L	0-1		5,474
37	Apr	2	H	Leigh RMI	W	5-1	Sugden, Midgley, Killeen, Chin, Ingram	1,704
38		5	A	Exeter City	L	1-2	Killeen	3,568
39		9	A	Barnet	L	1-3	Killeen	3,924
40		16	H	Hereford United	L	0-1		2,343
41		19	A	Farnborough Town	L	2-3	Young, Grant	469
42		23	H	Woking	W	3-1	Blunt, Sugden 2	1,398

Final League Position: 9th in Nationwide Conference National

1 own-goal

Apps
Sub Apps
Gls

FA Cup

Q4	Oct	30	H	Leek Town	D	2-2	Midgley 2 (1 pen)	1,544
R	Nov	1	A	Leek Town	W	1-0*	Bushell	1,244
1		13	H	Cambridge United	W	3-1	Foster, Midgley, Ross	2,368
2	Dec	4	A	Chester City	L	1-3	Ross	4,497

* After extra-time

Apps
Sub Apps
Gls

FA Trophy

3	Jan	15	H	Northwich Victoria	L	0-1		1,345

Apps
Sub Apps
Gls

League Table

	P	W	D	L	F	A	Pts
Barnet	42	26	8	8	90	44	86
Hereford United	42	21	11	10	68	41	74
Carlisle United	42	20	13	9	74	37	73
Aldershot Town	42	21	10	11	68	52	73
Stevenage Borough	42	22	6	14	65	52	72
Exeter City	42	20	11	11	71	50	71
Morecambe	42	19	14	9	69	50	71
Woking	42	18	14	10	58	45	68
Halifax Town	42	19	9	14	74	56	66
Accrington Stanley	42	18	11	13	72	58	65
Dagenham & Redbridge	42	19	8	15	68	60	65
Crawley Town	42	16	9	17	50	50	57
Scarborough	42	14	14	14	60	46	56
Gravesend & Northfleet	42	13	11	18	58	64	50
Tamworth*	42	14	11	17	53	63	50
Burton Albion	42	13	11	18	50	66	50
York City	42	11	10	21	39	66	43
Canvey Island	42	9	15	18	53	65	42
Northwich Victoria**	42	14	10	18	58	72	42
Forest Green Rovers	42	6	15	21	41	81	33
Farnborough Town	42	6	11	25	35	89	29
Leigh RMI	42	4	6	32	31	98	18

* 3 points deducted for fielding inilegible player
** 10 points deducted for entering into administration and voluntarily demoted

2005-06

Nationwide Conference
Manager: Chris Wilder

Did you know that?

- Captain was Steve Bushell, then Martin Foster.
- Halifax Town played in blue-and-white-striped shirts and white shorts.
- Peter Atherton played 318 Premier League matches with Coventry City, Sheffield Wednesday and Bradford City.
- Halifax Town's FA Cup tie with Rushden at The Shay on 6 November was played on a Sunday.
- Halifax Town launched their Academy in conjunction with Calderdale College at The Shay on 24 November.
- Danny Forrest's goal in the 1–1 draw at Accrington on 2 January was Halifax Town's 500th in the Conference.
- Supporters' team AFC Halifax played their first match, losing 7–1 to Kidderminster Harriers on 4 February on Savile Park, prior to the first-team match between the two clubs at The Shay which ended goalless.
- Ryan Sugden was married the day before Halifax Town's Play-off Final match with Hereford United.
- Biggest League win: 4–0 v Tamworth (h), 10 September.
- Heaviest League defeat: 0–4 v Gravesend & Northfleet (a), 17 September.
- Town's biggest win came a week before their heaviest defeat.

Match No.	Date	Venue	Opponents	Result		Scorers	Attendance
1	Aug 13	A	Morecambe	L	0-1		2,150
2	16	H	Burton Albion	W	1-0	Brabin	1,681
3	20	H	Aldershot Town	D	1-1	Grant	1,571
4	27	A	Forest Green Rovers	D	2-2	Midgley (pen), Senior	905
5	29	H	York City	W	1-0	Midgley (pen)	2,078
6	Sep 3	A	Stevenage Borough	L	0-1		1,682
7	10	H	Tamworth	W	4-0	Midgley, Forrest, Grant, Senior	1,453
8	17	A	Gravesend & Northfleet	L	0-4		918
9	20	A	Kidderminster Harriers	W	1-0	Killeen	1,566
10	24	H	Hereford United	W	2-1	Grant, Senior	1,559
11	27	H	Altrincham	W	2-0	Midgley (pen), Grant	1,453
12	Oct 1	A	Grays Athletic	D	1-1	Grant	1,807
13	8	A	Exeter City	L	2-4	Grant, Killeen	3,154
14	15	H	Cambridge United	W	1-0	Senior	1,621
15	29	A	Woking	D	2-2	Killeen, Quinn	2,054
16	Nov 12	H	Dagenham & Redbridge	W	3-0	Mansaram 2, Killeen	1,532
17	19	A	Southport	W	2-0	Foster, Forrest	1,402
18	26	H	Scarborough	L	0-2		1,843
19	Dec 3	H	Crawley Town	D	2-2	Forrest, Grant	1,616
20	10	A	Canvey Island	W	1-0	Quinn	664
21	26	H	Accrington Stanley	D	2-2	Killeen, Grant	2,688
22	30	H	Scarborough	W	1-0	Foster	1,682
23	Jan 2	A	Accrington Stanley	D	1-1	Forrest	3,014
24	9	H	Morecambe	D	0-0		1,962
25	21	A	Aldershot Town	L	1-3	Killeen	2,417
26	24	H	Burton Albion	W	2-1	Grant, Foster (pen)	1,540
27	28	H	Forest Green Rovers	W	1-0	Quinn	1,284
28	Feb 4	H	Kidderminster Harriers	D	0-0		1,544
29	11	A	Hereford United	L	0-1		2,555
30	18	H	Grays Athletic	W	2-1	Thompson, Grant	1,666
31	21	A	Altrincham	W	2-1	Killeen, Sugden	1,139
32	25	A	Tamworth	W	2-1	Killeen, Senior	1,672
33	Mar 11	H	Exeter City	W	2-0	Sugden 2	2,104
34	18	A	Cambridge United	D	1-1	Grant	2,288
35	28	H	Woking	W	1-0	Bushell	1,465
36	Apr 1	A	Dagenham & Redbridge	L	0-1		1,078
37	8	H	Southport	W	2-1	Forrest, Sugden	1,791
38	14	H	Stevenage Borough	D	1-1	Young	2,253
39	17	A	York City	W	2-0	Grant, Bushell	4,084
40	22	A	Crawley Town	D	2-2	Senior, Killeen	1,285
41	25	A	Gravesend & Northfleet	W	2-0	Sugden 2	1,680
42	29	H	Canvey Island	L	0-2		2,049

Final League Position: 4th in Nationwide Conference

Play-Offs

	Date	Venue	Opponents	Result		Scorers	Attendance
SF1	May 6	H	Grays Athletic	W	3-2	Bushell, Sugden, Killeen	3,848
SF2	10	A	Grays Athletic	D	2-2	Foster 2 (1 pen)	2,886
F	19	N	Hereford United*	L	2-3	Killeen, Grant	15,499

* After extra-time. Played at Walker Stadium, Leicester

FA Cup

	Date	Venue	Opponents	Result		Scorers	Attendance
Q4	Oct 22	H	Farsley Celtic	W	2-0	Senior 2	1,469
1	Nov 6	H	Rushden & Diamonds	D	1-1	Senior	2,303
R	15	A	Rushden & Diamonds	D	0-0*		2,133

* After extra time. Rushden won 5-4 on penalties (Midgley scored (1-1), Senior scored (2-2), Forrest scored (3-3), Foster scored (4-4), Ingram missed (4-4), Thompson missed (4-5)

FA Trophy

	Date	Venue	Opponents	Result		Scorers	Attendance
1	Dec 17	H	Southport	D	0-0		1,101
R	20	A	Southport	W	1-0	Forrest	589
2	Jan 14	H	Hereford United	L	0-1		1,220

League Table

	P	W	D	L	F	A	Pts
Accrington Stanley	42	28	7	7	76	45	91
Hereford United	42	22	14	6	59	33	80
Grays Athletic	42	21	13	8	94	55	76
Halifax Town	42	21	12	9	55	40	75
Morecambe	42	22	8	12	68	41	74
Stevenage Borough	42	19	12	11	62	47	69
Exeter City	42	18	9	15	65	48	63
York City	42	17	12	13	63	48	63
Burton Albion	42	16	12	14	50	52	60
Dagenham & Redbridge	42	16	10	16	63	59	58
Woking	42	14	14	14	58	47	56
Cambridge United	42	15	10	17	51	57	55
Aldershot Town	42	16	6	20	61	74	54
Canvey Island	42	13	12	17	47	58	51
Kidderminster Harriers	42	13	11	18	39	55	50
Gravesend & Northfleet	42	13	10	19	45	57	49
Crawley Town**	42	12	11	19	48	55	44
Southport	42	10	10	22	36	68	40
Forest Green Rovers	42	8	14	20	49	62	38
Tamworth	42	8	14	20	32	63	38
Scarborough	42	9	10	23	40	66	37
Altrincham*	42	10	11	21	40	71	23

* Altrincham deducted 18 points for fielding ineligible player
** Crawley Town deducted 3 points for exceeding agreed annual player budget

2006-07

Nationwide Conference National
Manager: Chris Wilder

Did you know that?

- Captain was Tom Kearney.
- Manager Chris Wilder made an offer upon the final whistle for FC United of Manchester's Steve Torpey after the winger had impressed and scored in a friendly at The Shay on 1 August.
- Halifax Town played in blue shirts with a waist band.
- Shane Smeltz arrived at The Shay with 12 New Zealand international caps to his name and won a further 25 after leaving the club. In June 2010 he famously scored New Zealand's goal in a 1–1 draw with holders Italy in the World Cup in South Africa.
- Nick Gray is the son of former Leeds United and Scotland winger Eddie Gray.
- Halifax Town provided the opposition at the Kassam Stadium when Oxford United played their first game in the Conference.
- Andy Campbell won four England Under-21 caps between March and August 2000 when a Middlesbrough player. He scored on his debut against Yugoslavia in a 3–0 victory, lining up alongside Rio Ferdinand, Frank Lampard and Gareth Barry.
- Halifax Town ran up a record score in their 14–3 success over Pontefract Collieries on 28 November. The 17 goals scored was also a Shay record.
- Felix Bastians was a German Under-19 international.
- Biggest League win: 4–1 v St Albans City (h), 9 December, v Weymouth (h), 20 February.
- Heaviest League defeat: 0–4 v Morecambe (a), 9 April.
- Ever-present: Craig Mawson.

Match No.	Date	Venue	Opponents	Result	Scorers	Attendance
1	Aug 12	A	Oxford United	L 0-2		5,785
2	15	H	Southport	D 1-1	Smeltz	2,002
3	19	H	Grays Athletic	L 0-2		1,589
4	26	A	Cambridge United	W 2-1	Roberts, Quinn	2,056
5	28	H	Morecambe	D 1-1	Torpey	1,909
6	Sep 2	A	Aldershot Town	L 0-1		2,330
7	9	H	Gravesend & Northfleet	D 1-1	Sugden	1,435
8	12	A	Altrincham	L 0-1		1,036
9	16	A	Weymouth	L 0-1		1,910
10	19	H	Dagenham & Redbridge	W 3-1	Wright, Sugden, Forrest	1,268
11	23	H	Forest Green Rovers	D 2-2	Sugden, Forrest	1,561
12	30	A	Stevenage Borough	L 1-2	Sugden	1,904
13	Oct 3	H	Kidderminster Harriers	W 2-0	Campbell, Wright	1,438
14	7	A	Exeter City	L 1-4	Killeen	3,114
15	10	A	Rushden & Diamonds	W 1-0	Torpey	1,839
16	14	H	Tamworth	W 3-1	Torpey 2, Sugden	1,646
17	21	H	Burton Albion	L 1-2	Torpey	1,844
18	Nov 4	A	Northwich Victoria	L 2-3	Forrest, Torpey	1,150
19	18	H	Stafford Rangers	W 3-1	Joynes, Killeen 2	1,681
20	25	A	Crawley Town	L 0-2		1,062
21	Dec 2	H	Woking	W 3-0	Uhlenbeek, Joynes, Forrest	1,536
22	9	H	St Albans City	W 4-1	Atkinson 2, Smeltz, Senior	1,617
23	23	A	York City	L 0-2		3,588
24	30	A	Dagenham & Redbridge	L 0-1		1,261
25	Jan 1	H	Altrincham	D 1-1	Joynes	1,791
26	23	H	York City	D 1-1	Ainsworth	2,308
27	27	A	St Albans City	L 2-3	Bastians, Stamp	1,009
28	Feb 17	A	Stafford Rangers	W 3-2	Stamp, Bastians, Trotman	1,062
29	20	H	Weymouth	W 4-1	Bastians, Trotman, Uhlenbeek 2	1,277
30	27	H	Northwich Victoria	L 0-2		1,221
31	Mar 3	A	Woking	D 2-2	Bastians, Hutchinson (og)	1,419
32	6	A	Kidderminster Harriers	L 0-1		1,203
33	10	H	Exeter City	W 2-1	Strong, Forrest	1,591
34	13	H	Rushden & Diamonds	D 0-0		1,314
35	17	A	Tamworth	L 0-1		1,337
36	21	H	Oxford United	D 1-1	Forrest	1,473
37	27	A	Southport	D 1-1	Stamp	936
38	31	A	Grays Athletic	L 0-1		801
39	Apr 3	A	Gravesend & Northfleet	L 0-2		946
40	7	H	Cambridge United	W 1-0	Torpey	1,942
41	9	A	Morecambe	L 0-4		2,412
42	14	H	Aldershot Town	W 2-0	Campbell, Forrest	1,611
43	17	A	Burton Albion	L 0-1		1,436
44	21	A	Forest Green Rovers	L 0-2		1,664
45	24	H	Crawley Town	W 2-1	Stamp, Quinn	1,561
46	28	H	Stevenage Borough	W 2-1	Campbell 2	2,515

Final League Position: 16th in Nationwide Conference National

1 own-goal

Apps
Sub Apps
Gls

FA Cup

Q4	Oct 28	A	Burton Albion	L 0-1		1,938

Apps
Sub Apps
Gls

FA Trophy

1	Dec 16	H	Hyde United	W 3-1	Senior, Atkinson, Smeltz	1,180
2	Jan 13	A	Oxford United	D 2-2	Foster (pen), Stamp	2,631
R	16	H	Oxford United	W 2-1	Smeltz, Joynes	1,330
3	Feb 3	H	Redditch United	W 3-1	Uhlenbeek, Stamp, Killeen	1,592
4	24	A	Kidderminster Harriers	L 1-3	Trotman	1,580

Apps
Sub Apps
Gls

League Table

	P	W	D	L	F	A	Pts
Dagenham & Redbridge	46	28	11	7	93	48	95
Oxford United	46	22	15	9	66	33	81
Morecambe	46	23	12	11	64	46	81
York City	46	23	11	12	65	45	80
Exeter City	46	22	12	12	67	48	78
Burton Albion	46	22	9	15	52	47	75
Gravesend & Northfleet	46	21	11	14	63	56	74
Stevenage Borough	46	20	10	16	76	66	70
Aldershot Town	46	18	11	17	64	62	65
Kidderminster Harriers	46	17	12	17	43	50	63
Weymouth	46	18	9	19	56	73	63
Rushden & Diamonds	46	17	11	18	58	54	62
Northwich Victoria	46	18	4	24	51	69	58
Forest Green Rovers	46	13	18	15	59	64	57
Woking	46	15	12	19	56	61	57
Halifax Town	46	15	10	21	55	62	55
Cambridge United	46	15	10	21	57	66	55
Crawley Town*	46	17	12	17	52	52	53
Grays Athletic	46	13	13	20	56	55	52
Stafford Rangers	46	14	10	22	49	71	52
Altrincham	46	13	12	21	53	67	51
Tamworth	46	13	9	24	43	61	48
Southport	46	11	14	21	57	67	47
St Albans City	46	10	10	26	57	89	40

* 10 points deducted for entering administration

2007-08

Blue Square Premier
Manager: Chris Wilder

Did you know that?

- Captain was Tom Kearney.
- Evoking memories of fund-raising in the 1930s, the Supporters' Club launched their 'mile of pennies' around the Shay pitch (about 360 yards) in August.
- Despite loan players not being able to play in County Cup matches, manager Chris Wilder named five on the bench for the clash with Ossett Albion – and the club was promptly thrown out of the competition.
- Halifax Town used a record nine loan players.
- Town's 6–1 defeat by Kidderminster Harriers on 8 April was their worst at home since Fulham won 8–0 in September 1969.
- Halifax Town's last-ever goal was Jon Shaw's 64th-minute penalty in the final match of the season against Stevenage Borough at The Shay. It was the 639th goal scored by the club in the Conference.
- Biggest League win: 4–0 v Crawley Town (a), 22 April.
- Heaviest League defeat: 1–6 v Kidderminster Harriers (h), 8 April.

Match No.	Date		Venue	Opponents	Result		Scorers	Attendance
1	Aug	11	A	Weymouth	L	1-2	Kearney	1,612
2		14	H	Altrincham	D	2-2	Campbell 2	1,401
3		18	H	Histon	D	0-0		1,280
4		25	A	Ebbsfleet United	L	0-1		931
5		27	H	Droylsden	W	3-0	Campbell 3 (1 pen)	1,302
6	Sep	1	A	Oxford United	D	1-1	Torpey (pen)	4,926
7		6	A	Stafford Rangers	W	3-2	Killeen, Shaw 2	927
8		11	H	Woking	W	1-0	Griffith	1,304
9		14	A	Torquay United	L	1-3	Shaw (pen)	2,727
10		18	H	Northwich Victoria	W	3-1	Shaw 2, Killeen	1,256
11		22	H	Rushden & Diamonds	D	1-1	Torpey	1,384
12		27	A	York City	L	2-3	Griffith, Forrest	2,134
13	Oct	2	H	Burton Albion	D	2-2	Shaw, Stride (og)	1,206
14		6	A	Cambridge United	D	2-2	Shaw (pen), Belle	3,027
15		9	H	Kidderminster Harriers	L	0-1		1,365
16		16	H	Grays Athletic	D	0-0		1,104
17		20	A	Aldershot Town	L	0-1		2,389
18	Nov	3	H	Crawley Town	W	3-0	Heslop, Shaw, Griffith	1,197
19		17	A	Stevenage Borough	W	3-2	Stamp, Heslop, Shaw	2,421
20		24	H	Salisbury City	D	1-1	Belle	1,237
21	Dec	8	H	Exeter City	L	0-3		1,160
22		26	A	Farsley Celtic	L	0-3		1,501
23		29	A	Salisbury City	L	0-1		1,212
24	Jan	1	H	Farsley Celtic	W	2-0	Jackson (og), Shaw	1,538
25		5	A	Woking	L	0-1		1,299
26		26	A	Northwich Victoria	D	2-2	Nelthorpe, Shaw	1,024
27	Feb	9	A	Rushden & Diamonds	D	2-2	Nelthorpe, Campbell	1,472
28		12	H	York City	D	2-2	Joynes, Whitehouse	2,875
29		16	H	Cambridge United	L	1-2	Heslop	1,402
30		23	H	Stafford Rangers	D	0-0		1,103
31	Mar	1	H	Weymouth	W	2-1	Campbell, Heslop	971
32		4	A	Altrincham	D	3-3	Shaw 2 (1 pen), Campbell (pen)	903
33		8	A	Histon	W	3-1	Clarke, Davies, Griffith	622
34		11	H	Torquay United	W	3-2	Shaw 2, Ellis (og)	894
35		15	A	Forest Green Rovers	L	0-2		690
36		22	H	Oxford United	L	0-3		1,369
37		24	A	Droylsden	L	0-2		887
38		29	A	Exeter City	L	0-1		3,096
39	Apr	5	H	Forest Green Rovers	D	1-1	Stamp	1,094
40		8	H	Kidderminster Harriers	L	1-6	Shaw (pen)	1,097
41		10	H	Ebbsfleet United	W	1-0	Heslop	1,063
42		12	H	Grays Athletic	D	3-3	Taylor, Forrest, Shaw (pen)	1,204
43		15	A	Burton Albion	L	1-2	Stamp	1,607
44		19	H	Aldershot Town	D	0-0		1,545
45		22	A	Crawley Town	W	4-0	Killen, Shaw 2, Murphy (og)	817
46		26	H	Stevenage Borough	L	1-2	Shaw (pen)	2,229

Final League Position: 20th in Blue Square Premier

4 own-goals

Apps
Sub Apps
Gls

FA Cup

Q4	Oct	27	A	Evesham United	D	0-0		652
R		30	H	Evesham United	W	2-1	Shaw, Heslop	1,025
1	Nov	10	H	Burton Albion	L	0-4		1,936

Apps
Sub Apps
Gls

FA Trophy

1	Jan	8	H	Leamington	W	2-1	Shaw (pen), Heslop	805
2		12	A	Bishop's Stortford	D	2-2	Shaw 2	731
R		29	H	Bishop's Stortford	W	4-1	Quinn, Nelthorpe, Shaw, Sharpe	728
3	Feb	2	H	Rushden & Diamonds	L	0-2		1,052

Apps
Sub Apps
Gls

League Table

	P	W	D	L	F	A	Pts
Aldershot Town	46	31	8	7	82	48	101
Cambridge United	46	25	11	10	66	41	86
Torquay United	46	26	8	12	83	57	86
Exeter City	46	22	17	7	83	58	83
Burton Albion	46	23	12	11	79	56	81
Stevenage Borough	46	24	7	15	82	55	79
Histon	46	20	12	14	76	67	72
Forest Green Rovers	46	19	14	13	76	59	71
Oxford United	46	20	11	15	56	48	71
Grays Athletic	46	19	13	14	58	47	70
Ebbsfleet United	46	19	12	15	65	61	69
Salisbury City	46	18	14	14	70	60	68
Kidderminster Harriers	46	19	10	17	74	57	67
York City	46	17	11	18	71	74	62
Crawley Town*	46	19	9	18	73	67	60
Rushden & Diamonds	46	15	14	17	55	55	59
Woking	46	12	17	17	53	61	53
Weymouth	46	11	13	22	53	73	46
Northwich Victoria	46	11	11	24	52	78	44
Halifax Town**	46	12	16	18	61	70	42
Altrincham	46	9	14	22	56	82	41
Farsley Celtic	46	10	9	27	48	86	39
Stafford Rangers	46	5	10	31	42	99	25
Droylsden	46	5	9	32	46	103	24

* 6 points deducted due to financial irregularities
** 10 points deducted for entering administration

2008-09

Unibond First Division North

Managers: August 2008–April 2009 Jim Vince; April 2009 Nigel Jemson

Did you know that?

- Adult admission at The Shay was £10.
- Prior to the start of the season, Nigel Jemson, Steve Payne and Tony Barras had racked up a total of 995 League appearances between them.
- Captain was Steve Payne, then Tony Barras from October.
- The first goal for the new club was scored by Steve Payne in the 26th minute of the 2–1 victory at Trafford in Town's second game.
- Tony Barras was a scorer for York City in a shock 3–0 win over Manchester United in the Coca-Cola Cup in September 2005.
- The President's Cup match at The Shay on 11 November was billed as the newest club (FC Halifax Town) versus the oldest club (Sheffield FC). Town won 3–1 after extra-time.
- Halifax Town played in a spare all-blue kit until the arrival of their pre-ordered regular kit, which they wore for the first time in the home game with Chorley on 15 November.
- Instead of the FC Halifax Town players being listed, the match programme for the game at Newcastle Blue Star on 21 March mistakenly featured line-up, pen pics and photograph of AFC Halifax, the supporters team, who sponsored the match.
- Biggest League win: 7–1 v Salford City (h), 7 September.
- Heaviest League defeat: 0–3 v Bamber Bridge (h), 16 August, v Newcastle Blue Star (a), 21 March.

Match No.	Date		Venue	Opponents	Result		Scorers	Attendance
1	Aug	16	H	Bamber Bridge	L	0-3		1,549
2		19	A	Trafford	W	2-1	Payne, Jemson	497
3		23	A	Lancaster City	L	0-2		564
4		25	H	Durham City	D	0-0		1,130
5	Sep	9	A	Mossley	L	1-3	Morning	507
6		16	H	Warrington Town	W	1-0	Gedman	778
7		20	H	Salford City	W	7-1	King, Gedman 2, Stott 2, Adams, Jemson	1,102
8	Oct	7	A	Garforth Town	D	2-2	J. Brown, King	431
9		11	H	Skelmersdale United	W	3-0	J. Brown, Coo, Stott	1,107
10		21	A	Bamber Bridge	W	5-2	J. Brown 2, Stott, Daniel, McAllister (og)	315
11		25	H	Clitheroe	W	4-0	Daniel 3, Stott	1,228
12	Nov	1	A	Curzon Ashton	W	1-0	J. Brown	601
13		4	H	Mossley	W	2-0	J. Smith (pen), J. Brown	1,124
14		8	A	Woodley Sports	W	3-2	Stott 2 (1 pen), Kennedy (og)	433
15		15	H	Chorley	W	3-1	Stott (pen), Gedman, Barras	1,346
16		22	A	Rossendale United	L	0-1		648
17		29	H	Newcastle Blue Star	D	3-3	Gedman, Baker, Ellis	1,290
18	Dec	13	H	Rossendale United	L	1-2	Jemson	954
19		20	A	Radcliffe Borough	W	4-1	Baker, Collins, Stott (pen), Gedman	480
20		26	H	Ossett Albion	D	1-1	Jemson	1,675
21	Jan	1	A	Harrogate Railway Athletic	L	0-2		704
22		3	H	Wakefield FC	W	3-2	Jemson 2, Baker	1,150
23		10	H	Radcliffe Borough	D	1-1	Adams	1,172
24		17	A	Salford City	W	1-0	Stott	520
25		24	H	Garforth Town	W	5-1	Barnes, Meadowcroft, Stott, Ross (pen), Phelan	1,183
26		31	A	Wakefield FC	W	4-1	Sutton, Stott 2, D. Brown	570
27	Feb	14	A	Warrington Town	D	1-1	Stott	452
28		21	A	Colwyn Bay	L	1-3	J. Brown	750
29		28	H	Colwyn Bay	D	1-1	J. Brown	1,224
30	Mar	7	A	Durham City	D	1-1	Meadowcroft	744
31		10	H	Harrogate Railway Athletic	W	2-1	Adams, Barnes	866
32		14	H	Woodley Sports	L	0-1		1,101
33		21	A	Newcastle Blue Star	L	0-3		512
34		24	A	Clitheroe	W	2-1	Joynes, Sutton	488
35		28	H	Lancaster City	D	0-0		1,116
36	Apr	4	A	Skelmersdale United	L	1-2	Peers	588
37		10	A	Ossett Albion	D	2-2	Stott, Joynes	860
38		13	H	Curzon Ashton	L	1-2	Jemson (pen)	1,325
39		18	H	Trafford	D	2-2	Jemson (pen), Barnes	969
40		25	A	Chorley	D	0-0		561

Final League Position: 8th in Unibond First Division North

Apps
Sub Apps
2 own-goals   Gls

FA Cup

P	Aug	30	H	Silsden	D	0-0		833
R	Sep	3	A	Silsden	W	3-1	Stott 2 (1 pen), J. Smith	442
Q1		13	A	Ryton	W	4-0	Stott, Morning, Gedman 2	385
Q2		27	A	Nantwich Town	L	1-4	Moore	1,091

Apps
Sub Apps
Gls

FA Trophy

Prel	Oct	4	A	Harrogate Railway Athletic	L	1-2	Daniel	373

Apps
Sub Apps
Gls

League Table

	P	W	D	L	F	A	Pts
Durham City (C) (P)	40	25	12	3	93	41	87
Skelmersdale United	40	26	8	6	96	51	86
Newcastle Blue Star (P)	40	21	10	9	93	54	73
Colwyn Bay	40	23	7	10	72	49	73
Curzon Ashton	40	20	8	12	66	44	68
Ossett Albion	40	19	9	12	76	61	66
Lancaster City	40	19	8	13	69	64	65
FC Halifax Town	40	17	12	11	7	52	63
Wakefield	40	16	8	16	65	62	56
Mossley	40	16	6	18	63	70	54
Bamber Bridge	40	16	5	19	69	78	53
Clitheroe	40	15	7	13	64	76	52
Woodley Sports	40	16	3	21	57	74	51
Chorley	40	13	8	19	56	66	47
Trafford	40	13	7	20	72	83	46
Garforth Town	40	13	5	22	77	99	44
Radcliffe Borough	40	12	6	22	5	66	42
Harrogate Railway Athletic	40	13	3	24	59	82	42
Warrington Town	40	11	8	21	50	73	41
Salford City	40	10	6	24	59	107	36
Rossendale United	40	8	10	22	53	83	34

2009-10

Unibond First Division North
Manager: Neil Aspin

Did you know that?

- Captain was Ryan Crossley, then Steve Payne from March.
- Club sponsors were Doodson Broking Group.
- Assistant manager Trevor Storton made his Liverpool debut as a stand-in for Tommy Smith in a 2–1 win at Leeds United on 30 September 1972.
- Halifax Town wore blue shirts with white sleeves and blue shorts.
- Town's 100th League goal of the season was scored by Richard Marshall in the 9th minute of the 2–1 victory over Radcliffe Borough at The Shay on 15 April.
- FC Halifax Town were unbeaten in their last 17 League matches.
- James Dean scored a total of 40 League and Cup goals.
- Town failed to score in only one of their League matches – at Prescot Cables on 7 November.
- Biggest League win: 6–1 v Salford City (h), 12 December.
- Heaviest League defeat: 2–3 v Radcliffe Borough (a), 27 February.

Match No.	Date		Venue	Opponents	Result		Scorers	Attendance
1	Aug	15	A	Colwyn Bay	W	3-0	J. Dean 2, Marshall	854
2		18	H	Warrington Town	W	4-1	Gray, Baker, Crossley, Peers	1,253
3		22	H	Trafford	W	2-0	J. Dean, Marshall	1,359
4		25	A	Chorley	D	3-3	J. Dean, Peers, Gray	675
5		31	H	Garforth Town	W	1-0	Gray	1,554
6	Sep	5	A	Lancaster City	W	1-0	Peers	698
7		15	A	Salford City	W	3-0	Marshall 2, Payne	544
8		19	H	Leigh Genesis	W	3-1	Gray, J. Dean, Marshall	1,293
9		29	H	Curzon Ashton	W	1-0	Payne (pen)	1,504
10	Oct	19	A	Harrogate Railway Athletic	W	2-1	Gray, J. Dean	638
11	Nov	7	A	Prescot Cables	L	0-1		614
12		10	H	AFC Fylde	W	3-0	Payne, J. Dean 2	1,045
13		14	A	Skelmersdale United	D	2-2	Payne (pen), J. Dean	927
14		28	H	Woodley Sports	W	2-1	J. Dean, Marshall	1,249
15	Dec	5	A	Leigh Genesis	D	1-1	Marshall	619
16		12	H	Salford City	W	6-1	J. Dean 3, Gray 2, Marshall	1,242
17		15	H	Wakefield FC	D	1-1	Lowe	966
18	Jan	19	H	Bamber Bridge	W	4-1	J. Dean 3, Gray	917
19		23	A	Bamber Bridge	W	2-0	Marshall, J. Dean	486
20	Feb	2	A	Mossley	D	3-3	Lowe, J. Dean, Marshall (pen)	419
21		6	A	Wakefield FC	D	1-1	J. Dean	659
22		13	H	Harrogate Railway Athletic	W	3-0	Marshall, Gray, Peers	1,271
23		20	H	Mossley	W	4-2	Crossley, Marshall, Gray, Winter	1,267
24		23	H	Rossendale United	W	2-0	J. Dean (pen), Peers	801
25		27	A	Radcliffe Borough	L	2-3	Phelan, Winter	568
26	Mar	2	H	Ossett Albion	W	5-0	Gray 3, Winter 2	935
27		6	H	Prescot Cables	W	3-0	Winter, Marshall, Lowe	1,322
28		9	A	Warrington Town	W	3-1	Gray 2, J. Dean	505
29		13	H	Colwyn Bay	W	3-0	Lowe, J. Dean, Phelan	1,388
30		16	A	Clitheroe	W	2-1	Hardy (pen), J. Dean	653
31		20	A	AFC Fylde	D	2-2	Wilde, Gray	741
32		27	A	Trafford	W	3-0	Wilde, Peers, Gray	512
33		30	A	Woodley Sports	D	2-2	Gregory, J. Dean	514
34	Apr	2	H	Chorley	W	1-0	Payne	1,508
35		5	A	Rossendale United	W	3-0	Sykes, Wilde, Gray	745
36		7	A	Garforth Town	W	4-3	Wilde, Marshall 2, Gray	642
37		10	H	Lancaster City	W	4-0	Gregory 2, Payne, J. Dean	3,152
38		12	A	Curzon Ashton	W	5-0	Gray, Payne, Gregory, J. Dean, Marshall	803
39		15	H	Radcliffe Borough	W	2-1	Payne, Marshall	1,589
40		17	A	Ossett Albion	W	4-2	J. Dean, Gregory, Marshall, Ryan (og)	1,170
41		20	H	Clitheroe	D	2-2	Wilde, Baker	1,932
42		24	H	Skelmersdale United	D	1-1	Marshall	2,939

Final League Position: 1st in Unibond First Division North

1 own-goal

Apps
Sub Apps
Gls

FA Cup

	Date		Venue	Opponents	Result		Scorers	Attendance
P	Aug	29	A	Brandon United	W	6-0	Marshall 3, J. Dean, Payne, Gray	217
Q1	Sep	12	A	Norton & Stockton Ancients	W	4-0	Gray, Marshall, Baker, Phelan	390
Q2		26	A	Droylsden	W	2-0	Payne, J. Dean	901
Q3	Oct	10	H	Burscough	W	1-0	Gray	1,459
Q4		24	H	Wrexham	L	0-1		2,843

Apps
Sub Apps
Gls

FA Trophy

	Date		Venue	Opponents	Result		Scorers	Attendance
P	Oct	3	A	Trafford	W	4-3	J. Dean 3, Harrison	298
Q1		17	H	Romulus	W	2-0	Payne, Crossley	938
Q2		31	A	Shepshed Charterhouse	W	5-0	J. Dean 2, Payne, Gray, Sanasy	481
Q3	Nov	21	A	Guiseley	L	1-3	Gray	919

Apps
Sub Apps
Gls

592

League Table

	P	W	D	L	F	A	Pts
FC Halifax Town	42	30	10	2	108	38	100
Lancaster City	42	31	3	8	95	45	96
Curzon Ashton	42	23	12	7	93	50	75
Colwyn Bay	42	23	6	13	77	57	75
Skelmersdale United	42	22	8	12	80	56	74
Leigh Genesis	42	21	8	13	81	51	71
Mossley	42	18	11	13	73	67	65
Clitheroe	42	18	8	16	72	66	62
Warrington Town	42	18	6	18	65	69	60
Radcliffe Borough	42	17	6	19	65	78	57
Salford City	42	16	8	18	63	74	56
Trafford	42	15	8	19	79	73	53
AFC Fylde	42	15	8	19	67	79	53
Bamber Bridge	42	14	10	18	58	67	52
Prescot Cables	42	13	11	18	51	68	50
Chorley	42	13	10	19	56	76	49
Harrogate Railway Athletic	42	15	7	20	58	79	49
Wakefield	42	12	12	18	49	58	48
Woodley Sports	42	10	15	17	53	67	45
Garforth Town	42	11	7	24	64	94	40
Ossett Albion	42	7	7	28	52	91	28
Rossendale United	42	6	7	29	38	94	25

2010-11

Evo-Stick Premier
Manager: Neil Aspin

Did you know that?

- Admission was £11.
- Captain was Mark Bower.
- Halifax Town wore blue shirts with a vertical white stripe down the right-hand side and blue shorts.
- Before skippering FC Halifax Town to the Evo-Stik Premier title, Mark Bower had experienced relegation with Bradford City, Luton Town and Darlington.
- Tom Baker became the first FC Halifax Town player to play 100 League and Cup games, reaching the milestone in the 2–1 win at Matlock Town on 16 November.
- Liam and Scott Hogan became the latest pair of brothers to have turned out for either old or new club. Others since 1911 were; Fred & Harry Farren, Jake & Eddie Ruecroft, Kevin & Dave Verity, Dave & Bob Worthington, Billy and Bobby Barr, Paul & Craig Fleming, Lee & Nick Richardson, Paul & Jimmy Willis, Dean & Lee Martin, Matt and Chris Clarke.
- Jamie Vardy became the first player to net hat-tricks in successive matches since Clem Smith during the war season of 1945–56.
- Danny Holland's 34th-minute goal in the 5–1 win at Whitby Town on 11 April was the club's 100th in the League.
- Tom Baker scored 14 League and Cup goals, of which 10 were penalties – a club record.
- Players to have played for both Halifax Town and FC Halifax Town are; Paul Gedman, Nick Gray, Tom Harban, Jonathan Hedge, Nathan Joynes, Jon Kennedy, Craig Mawson, Neil Ross, Kevin Sanasy, Ryan Sugden, Mark Whitehouse and Simon Wood.
- Biggest League win: 8–1 v Ossett Town (h), 18 January.
- Heaviest League defeat: 0–2 v North Ferriby United (h), 20 November.
- Ever-present: Tom Baker.

Match No.	Date		Venue	Opponents	Result		Scorers	Attendance
1	Aug	21	H	Buxton	W	2-1	Holland, Vardy	1,756
2		24	A	Frickley Athletic	D	0-0		748
3		28	A	Chasetown	L	1-2	Taylor	611
4		30	H	Colwyn Bay	D	1-1	Marshall	1,561
5	Sep	4	A	Mickleover Sports	W	3-2	Holland, Vardy 2	678
6		7	H	Northwich Victoria	D	1-1	Holland	1,166
7		18	H	Whitby Town	W	5-1	Dean 3, Holland 2	1,271
8		21	A	Stocksbridge Park Steels	W	5-3	Holland 2, Dean, Metcalfe, Garner	658
9		28	H	Hucknall Town	W	4-0	Dean 2, Baker (pen), Garner	1,191
10	Oct	2	A	Ashton United	W	3-0	Holland, Dean, Baker (pen)	543
11		5	A	Burscough	W	2-0	Bayliss (og), Garner	494
12		19	H	Bradford Park Avenue	W	1-0	Holland	2,011
13		26	H	Burscough	W	3-2	Marshall, Baker (pen), Dean	1,264
14	Nov	6	A	Marine	W	6-0	Holland, Dean 2, Baker, Vardy 2	728
15		13	H	Retford United	W	3-0	Vardy 2, Bower	1,589
16		16	A	Matlock Town	W	2-1	Dean 2	549
17		20	H	North Ferriby United	L	0-2		1,605
18	Dec	11	A	FC United of Manchester	W	1-0	Garner	2,805
19	Jan	1	H	FC United of Manchester	W	4-1	Vardy, Gregory, Marshall, Taylor	4,023
20		3	A	Colwyn Bay	L	1-2	Phelan	827
21		8	A	Northwich Victoria	W	3-0	Dean, Gregory, Baker	678
22		22	H	Ossett Town	W	8-1	Dean 2, Gregory 2, Vardy 2, Phelan, Marshall	1,284
23		24	A	Bradford Park Avenue	W	3-1	Vardy, Gregory, Baker (pen)	1,328
24		29	A	North Ferriby United	W	3-0	Vardy 2, Gregory	743
25	Feb	12	A	Worksop Town	D	1-1	Baker (pen)	766
26		15	H	Kendal Town	W	3-0	Baker (pen), Gregory 2	1,232
27		22	A	Nantwich Town	W	6-0	Baker, Gregory 3, McDonald (og), Marshall	529
28	Mar	1	H	Worksop Town	D	0-0		1,318
29		5	H	Ashton United	W	1-0	Vardy	1,648
30		12	A	Buxton	L	1-2	Baker (pen)	803
31		15	H	Stocksbridge Park Steels	W	5-1	Holland 3, Baker (pen), Vardy	1,073
32		19	A	Hucknall Town	W	2-1	Gregory 2	567
33		22	H	Chasetown	W	3-2	Vardy 3	1,343
34		26	A	Kendal Town	W	4-2	Lowe, Vardy 3	891
35		29	H	Nantwich Town	W	3-1	Vardy 2, L. Hogan	1,347
36	Apr	2	H	Matlock Town	D	2-2	Gregory 2	2,132
37		9	A	Retford United	W	2-0	Holland, L. Hogan	842
38		13	A	Whitby Town	W	5-1	Gregory, Holland, Phelan 2, Baker (pen)	491
39		16	H	Marine	W	1-0	Holland	1,844
40		19	H	Frickley Athletic	W	3-1	Gregory, Holland, Baker	1,106
41		23	H	Mickleover Sports	D	1-1	Holland	2,404
42		25	A	Ossett Town	D	0-0		890

Final League Position: 1st in Evo-Stik Premier

2 own-goals

Apps
Sub Apps
Gls

FA Cup

Q1	Sep	11	H	Whitby Town	D	2-0	Metcalfe, Dean	978
Q2		25	A	Ashton United	W	2-1	Taylor 2	526
Q3	Oct	9	H	Harrogate Town	W	4-0	Baker (pen), Vardy, Taylor, Holland	1,834
Q4		23	H	Mansfield Town	L	0-1		2,986

Apps
Sub Apps
Gls

FA Trophy

Q1	Oct	16	A	Durham City	W	2-0	Gray, Dean	282
Q2		30	A	Curzon Ashton	L	1-2	Vardy	392

Apps
Sub Apps
Gls

League Table

	P	W	D	L	F	A	Pts
FC Halifax Town	42	30	8	4	108	36	98
Colwyn Bay	42	24	7	11	67	56	79
Bradford Park Avenue	42	23	8	11	84	55	77
FC United of Manchester	42	24	4	14	76	53	76
North Ferriby United	42	22	7	13	78	51	73
Buxton	42	20	10	12	71	52	70
Kendal Town	42	21	5	16	80	77	68
Marine	42	20	7	15	74	64	67
Worksop Town	42	21	6	15	72	54	66
Chasetown	42	20	6	16	76	59	66
Matlock Town	42	20	6	16	74	59	66
Northwich Victoria	42	18	9	15	66	55	63
Stocksbridge Park Steels	42	17	6	19	75	75	57
Ashton United	42	16	5	21	57	62	53
Mickleover Sports	42	15	7	20	70	76	52
Whitby Town	42	14	9	19	58	77	51
Nantwich Town	42	13	7	22	68	90	46
Frickley Athletic	42	11	11	20	43	68	44
Burscough	42	12	7	23	56	73	43
Hucknall Town	42	11	10	21	57	80	43
Ossett Town	42	9	5	28	45	103	32
Retford United	42	5	2	35	31	111	17

AGAINST LEAGUE CLUBS

	P	Home W	D	L	F	A	Away W	D	L	F	A	Total W	D	L	F	A
Accrington Stanley	64	16	9	7	50	38	6	8	18	39	70	22	17	25	89	108
Aldershot	44	10	8	4	37	28	4	6	12	19	40	14	14	16	56	68
Ashington	16	4	4	0	13	2	2	1	5	10	18	6	5	5	23	20
Aston Villa	4	1	0	1	2	2	0	1	1	1	2	1	1	2	3	4
Barnet	10	2	1	2	9	6	1	2	2	3	6	3	3	4	12	12
Barnsley	36	7	6	5	28	21	5	4	9	19	29	12	10	14	47	50
Barrow	70	28	3	4	71	30	8	10	17	37	58	36	13	21	108	88
Blackburn Rovers	8	0	3	1	4	5	0	1	3	1	7	0	4	4	5	12
Blackpool	14	3	1	3	10	9	1	2	4	3	17	4	3	7	13	26
Bolton Wanderers	6	0	2	1	1	2	0	1	2	1	6	0	3	3	2	8
Bournemouth	32	9	3	4	26	16	3	5	8	10	20	12	8	12	36	36
Bradford City	66	12	12	9	45	40	7	6	20	28	60	19	18	29	73	100
Bradford	44	9	8	5	40	26	4	6	12	27	43	13	14	17	67	69
Brentford	22	8	3	0	16	5	2	4	5	8	14	10	7	5	24	19
Brighton & Hove Albion	24	5	4	3	13	16	4	1	7	9	16	9	5	10	22	32
Bristol City	10	1	1	3	10	14	0	1	4	7	15	1	2	7	17	29
Bristol Rovers	14	2	4	1	8	5	0	0	7	3	17	2	4	8	11	22
Burnley	14	1	3	3	8	11	1	0	6	6	13	2	3	9	14	24
Bury	28	8	1	5	22	14	1	6	7	10	26	9	7	12	32	40
Cambridge United	16	1	5	2	6	8	1	0	7	3	18	2	5	9	9	26
Cardiff City	16	0	3	5	6	11	0	4	4	4	12	0	7	9	10	23
Carlisle United	70	16	10	9	72	51	7	12	16	39	66	23	22	25	111	117
Charlton Athletic	6	2	1	0	7	3	0	0	3	3	9	2	1	3	10	12
Cheltenham Town	6	1	1	1	6	4	0	0	3	3	9	1	1	4	9	13
Chester City	66	16	8	9	53	42	4	9	20	35	72	20	17	29	88	114
Chesterfield	84	26	7	9	72	42	4	8	30	35	98	30	15	39	107	140
Colchester United	38	7	7	5	33	26	2	4	13	17	36	9	11	18	50	62
Coventry City	10	1	2	2	7	10	1	0	4	7	14	2	2	6	14	24
Crewe Alexandra	98	27	10	12	80	57	10	17	22	58	91	37	27	34	138	148
Crystal Palace	8	1	2	1	7	7	0	3	1	5	6	1	5	2	12	13
Darlington	100	24	13	13	82	63	12	9	29	45	96	36	22	42	127	159
Derby County	4	1	1	0	3	2	0	0	2	1	10	1	1	2	4	12
Doncaster Rovers	72	12	9	15	51	43	11	11	14	40	63	23	20	29	91	106
Durham City	14	5	0	2	15	10	2	3	2	9	11	7	3	4	24	21
Exeter City	30	7	4	4	20	15	1	5	9	9	20	8	9	13	29	35
Fulham	4	1	0	1	2	9	0	0	2	2	5	1	0	3	4	14
Gateshead	46	10	6	7	41	29	2	4	17	16	64	12	10	24	57	93
Gillingham	18	2	4	3	8	10	0	1	8	4	19	2	5	11	12	29
Grimsby Town	44	9	7	6	30	25	3	6	13	19	49	12	13	19	49	74
Hartlepool United	108	39	5	10	104	4	12	12	30	53	104	51	17	40	157	148
Hereford United	36	7	6	5	20	22	4	4	10	14	27	11	10	15	34	49
Huddersfield Town	12	2	3	1	6	5	1	1	4	4	15	3	4	5	10	20
Hull City	42	7	4	10	23	28	5	3	13	16	52	12	7	23	39	80
Kidderminster Harriers	4	2	0	0	4	2	0	0	2	1	4	2	0	2	5	6

AGAINST LEAGUE CLUBS

	P	Home W	D	L	F	A	Away W	D	L	F	A	Total W	D	L	F	A
Leyton Orient	18	3	4	2	13	10	1	0	8	5	17	4	4	10	18	27
Lincoln City	78	19	5	15	58	49	6	11	22	36	84	25	16	37	94	133
Luton Town	10	1	2	2	6	6	0	1	4	2	14	1	3	6	8	20
Macclesfield Town	6	1	1	1	3	1	1	2	0	3	1	2	3	1	6	2
Maidstone United	6	1	1	1	5	5	2	0	1	4	6	3	1	2	9	11
Mansfield Town	66	12	9	12	45	40	4	5	24	39	82	16	14	36	84	122
Millwall	6	1	0	2	5	4	0	1	2	2	7	1	1	4	7	11
Nelson	18	4	3	2	20	13	0	3	6	7	15	4	6	8	27	28
New Brighton	42	9	7	5	35	21	3	4	14	16	34	12	11	19	51	55
Newport County	30	10	4	1	33	15	4	2	9	14	29	14	6	10	47	44
Northampton Town	32	6	4	6	24	26	5	2	9	19	34	11	6	15	43	60
Norwich City	4	0	1	1	1	2	0	0	2	1	6	0	1	3	2	8
Notts County	22	4	2	5	16	13	2	4	5	13	25	6	6	10	29	38
Oldham Athletic	36	7	8	3	28	19	3	4	11	21	35	10	12	14	49	54
Oxford United	6	1	0	2	4	6	0	1	2	3	9	1	1	4	7	15
Peterborough United	38	8	8	3	28	18	1	6	12	12	33	9	14	15	40	51
Plymouth Argyle	22	6	1	4	14	8	0	5	6	6	15	6	6	10	20	23
Port Vale	52	8	9	9	33	37	5	7	14	21	42	13	16	23	54	79
Portsmouth	6	1	0	2	3	3	0	1	2	3	7	1	1	4	6	10
Preston North End	10	4	0	1	9	5	1	1	3	5	7	5	1	4	14	12
Queen's Park Rangers	10	2	2	1	8	8	0	0	5	4	22	2	2	6	12	30
Reading	20	4	3	3	17	12	0	3	7	9	21	4	6	10	26	33
Rochdale	126	33	17	13	106	67	17	18	28	78	103	50	35	41	184	170
Rotherham United	60	13	7	10	52	44	6	7	17	26	65	19	14	27	78	109
Rushden &Diamonds	2	0	0	1	2	4	0	0	1	1	2	0	0	2	3	6
Scarborough	14	1	1	5	9	14	1	1	5	6	16	2	2	10	15	30
Scunthorpe United	58	11	8	10	41	40	3	10	16	31	53	14	18	16	72	93
Sheffield United	2	0	0	1	1	5	0	1	0	2	2	0	1	1	3	7
Sheffield Wednesday	2	0	1	0	0	0	0	0	1	0	1	0	1	1	0	1
Shrewsbury Town	32	6	6	4	18	13	1	7	8	13	27	7	13	12	31	40
Southampton	4	2	0	0	5	1	0	0	2	2	8	2	0	2	7	9
Southend United	46	9	5	9	31	29	3	6	14	25	53	12	11	23	56	82
Southport	76	18	12	8	61	32	7	9	22	40	76	25	21	30	101	108
Stalybridge Celtic	4	1	0	1	4	4	0	0	2	4	6	1	0	3	8	10
Stockport County	92	22	10	14	72	53	8	9	29	45	112	30	19	43	117	165
Stoke City	2	0	1	0	2	2	0	0	1	1	5	0	1	1	3	7
Swansea City	24	6	3	3	17	11	3	1	8	11	20	9	4	11	28	31
Swindon Town	22	7	2	2	17	12	3	3	5	14	22	10	5	7	31	34
Torquay United	56	13	7	8	42	29	7	5	16	29	50	20	12	24	71	79
Tranmere Rovers	104	20	15	17	69	59	14	13	25	69	94	34	28	42	138	153
Walsall	46	13	4	6	41	24	4	5	14	18	43	17	9	20	59	67
Watford	16	2	5	1	8	6	0	5	3	8	11	2	10	4	16	17
Wigan Athletic	8	0	2	2	1	3	0	0	4	2	10	0	2	6	3	13
Wigan Borough	20	3	2	5	10	11	3	3	4	11	14	6	5	9	21	25
Wimbledon	8	1	1	2	4	5	1	1	2	8	10	2	2	4	12	15
Wolverhampton W.	6	1	1	1	7	7	2	0	1	3	5	3	1	2	10	12
Workington	22	8	2	1	33	14	1	4	6	14	22	9	6	7	47	36
Wrexham	108	28	14	12	88	46	10	13	31	62	112	38	27	43	150	158
York City	92	16	15	15	65	62	6	16	24	53	108	22	31	39	118	170

AGAINST CONFERENCE CLUBS

	P	W	D	L	F	A	W	D	L	F	A	W	D	L	F	A
		Home					**Away**					**Total**				
Accrington Stanley	6	0	2	1	4	5	0	2	1	3	4	0	4	2	7	9
Aldershot Town	10	2	2	1	6	3	0	1	4	2	8	2	3	5	8	11
Altrincham	14	1	6	0	8	6	1	2	4	9	13	2	8	4	17	19
Barnet	6	0	0	3	5	9	0	1	2	2	7	0	1	5	7	16
Bath City	8	2	1	1	11	8	0	3	1	3	4	2	4	2	14	12
Bromsgrove Rovers	8	3	1	0	9	3	2	0	2	2	4	5	1	2	11	7
Burton Albion	12	2	1	3	7	9	1	3	2	9	10	3	4	5	16	19
Cambridge United	6	2	0	1	3	2	1	2	0	5	4	3	2	1	8	6
Canvey Island	4	1	0	1	4	3	2	0	0	2	0	3	0	1	6	3
Carlisle United	2	0	1	0	2	2	0	0	1	0	1	0	1	1	2	3
Cheltenham Town	2	0	1	0	1	1	0	0	1	0	4	0	1	1	1	5
Chester City	4	0	1	1	0	3	0	0	2	0	4	0	1	3	0	7
Crawley Town	8	3	1	0	8	3	2	1	1	8	5	5	2	1	16	8
Dagenham & Redbridge	16	4	3	1	18	8	2	2	4	8	11	6	5	5	26	19
Doncaster Rovers	2	1	0	0	2	1	0	1	0	0	0	1	1	0	2	1
Dover Athletic	10	2	1	2	7	5	2	2	1	8	7	4	3	3	15	12
Droylsden	2	1	0	0	3	0	0	0	1	0	2	1	0	1	3	2
Ebbsfleet United*	12	5	1	0	8	2	1	0	5	3	9	6	1	5	11	11
Exeter City	10	4	0	1	8	5	0	1	4	5	12	4	1	5	13	17
Farnborough Town	14	5	1	1	9	1	1	1	5	4	13	6	2	6	13	14
Farsley Celtic	2	1	0	0	2	0	0	0	1	0	3	1	0	1	2	3
Forest Green Rovers	12	2	3	1	9	5	2	2	2	6	7	4	5	3	15	12
Gateshead	10	5	0	0	12	3	2	1	2	8	8	7	1	2	20	11
Grays Athletic	6	1	1	1	2	1	0	2	1	4	5	1	3	2	6	6
Hayes	4	0	2	0	3	3	1	1	0	2	1	1	3	0	5	4
Hednesford Town	6	1	1	1	3	4	0	2	1	1	4	1	3	2	4	8
Hereford United	10	3	0	2	6	5	1	2	2	5	11	4	2	4	11	16
Histon	2	0	1	0	0	0	1	0	0	3	1	1	1	0	3	1
Kettering Town	12	5	1	0	13	2	3	1	2	7	11	8	2	2	20	13
Kidderminster Harriers	16	3	4	1	9	14	2	0	6	5	16	5	4	7	14	30
Leek Town	2	1	0	0	2	1	0	0	1	0	2	1	0	1	2	3
Leigh RMI	6	3	0	0	8	2	2	1	0	6	1	5	1	0	14	3
Macclesfield Town	8	1	1	2	5	6	1	1	2	2	9	2	2	4	7	15
Margate	4	0	1	1	2	3	0	0	2	1	4	0	1	3	3	7
Merthyr Tydfil	4	1	1	0	4	3	0	0	2	1	4	1	1	2	5	7
Morecambe	16	3	4	1	11	7	1	1	6	3	13	4	5	7	14	20

AGAINST CONFERENCE CLUBS

		Home					Away					Total			
	P	W	D	L	F	A	W	D	L	F	A	W	D	L	F	A
Northwich Victoria	20	4	2	4	17	20	4	3	3	14	14	8	5	7	31	34
Nuneaton Borough	2	1	0	0	3	1	0	0	1	0	2	1	0	1	3	3
Oxford United	4	0	1	1	1	4	0	1	1	1	3	0	2	2	2	7
Runcorn	6	1	1	1	6	4	2	0	1	4	5	3	1	2	10	9
Rushden & Diamonds	8	1	2	1	4	4	1	1	2	3	7	2	3	3	7	11
St. Albans City	2	1	0	0	4	1	0	0	1	2	3	1	0	1	6	4
Salisbury City	2	0	1	0	1	1	0	0	1	0	1	0	1	1	1	2
Scarborough	8	4	0	0	6	2	1	0	3	2	6	5	0	3	8	8
Shrewsbury Town	2	0	1	0	0	0	0	0	1	0	2	0	1	1	0	2
Slough Town	8	3	0	1	7	3	1	1	2	4	6	4	1	3	11	9
Southport	16	4	3	1	17	12	1	4	3	6	11	5	7	4	23	23
Stafford Rangers	8	2	2	0	10	2	3	1	0	8	5	5	3	0	18	7
Stalybridge Celtic	10	3	1	1	12	7	2	2	1	6	5	5	3	2	18	12
Stevenage Borough	20	6	1	3	19	13	3	0	7	8	18	9	1	10	27	31
Tamworth	8	2	1	1	11	6	1	0	3	3	6	3	1	4	14	12
Telford United	14	3	3	1	16	6	2	3	2	11	9	5	6	3	27	15
Torquay United	2	1	0	0	3	2	0	0	1	1	3	1	0	1	4	5
Welling United	10	3	2	0	9	3	2	2	1	6	7	5	4	1	15	10
Weymouth	4	2	0	0	6	2	0	0	2	1	3	2	0	2	7	5
Witton Albion	2	0	1	0	0	0	0	1	0	2	2	0	2	0	2	2
Woking	22	6	3	2	20	13	2	5	4	21	20	8	8	6	41	33
Yeovil Town	8	2	1	1	8	6	1	1	2	2	6	3	2	3	10	12
York City	8	2	2	0	6	3	1	1	2	5	6	3	3	2	11	9

* includes results v Gravesend & Northfleet

Abandoned Matches

December 1912 v Scunthorpe United Reserves (h), Midland Counties League, 2–2
Nixon, Pentland
Shuttleworth, F. Farren, H. Farren, Sharpe, McGovern, T. McAllister, Nixon, Wild, Pentland, Whyte, Roscoe
Att: 1,200
Abandoned 82 mins – bad light

5 March 1914 v Castleford Town (h), Midland Counties League, 1–1
Cannon
Suter, Birtwhistle, Splitt, Child, Wishart, Brearley, McCreadie, Beevers, Cannon, Pentland, Roscoe
Abandoned 70 mins – waterlogged pitch

31 October 1914 v Worksop Town (h), Midland Counties League, 3–1
Kirby Roscoe, Scrutton
Suter, Birtwhistle, Parton, Hibbert, Wishart, Brearley, Nixon, Wild, Kirby, Scrutton, Roscoe
Abandoned 82 mins – bad light

13 February 1915 v Grimsby Town Reserves (a), Midland Counties League, 0–5
Suter, Birtwhistle, Parton, Hibbert, Wishart, Green, Bartlett, Wild, J. Hughes, Mulholland, Roscoe
Abandoned half–time – Halifax Town refused to play (snow)

5 February 1920 v Mexborough Town (a), Midland Counties League, 0–1
Suter, Birtwhistle, Scull, Lowe, Marrison, Brook, E. Smith, Wild, Wellock, S. Smith, Robinson
Abandoned half-time – fog

22 December 1934 v Doncaster Rovers (a), Division Three North, 1–2
Davies
Shirlaw, Allsop, Taylor, Ferguson, Craig, Cooke, Davies, Mercer, Atherton, Barkas, Tunstall
Abandoned 57 mins – fog

26 December 1942 v Bradford City (a), League War Cup, 1–1
Millman (og)
Greaves, Allsop, Jackson, Green, Craig, J. Ruecroft, E. Ruecroft, Hogg, Niblo, Davidson, Wood
Abandoned 67 mins – bad light

26 January 1952 v Bradford (h), Division Three North, 0–1
McCormick, Williams, Breaks, Henry, Mycock, Bickerstaffe, McCaig, Moss, Frost, Murphy, Hindle
Att: 9,757
Abandoned 53 mins – frozen pitch

3 December 1960 v Notts County (a), Division Three, 2–0
Whitelaw, Blackburn
Knowles, Stanley, Hudson, Tilley, South, Fagan, Priestley, Blackburn, Whitelaw, Large, Evans
Abandoned half-time – waterlogged pitch

7 January 1961 v Queen's Park Rangers (h), Division Three, 0–1
Knowles, Stanley, Hudson, Tilley, South, Fagan, Dunn, Sinclair, Whitelaw, Large, Blackburn
Abandoned half-time – frozen pitch

22 December 1962 v Wrexham (a), Division Three, 1–1
Redfearn
Downsborough, Russell, Roscoe, Harrison, South, Tilley, Priestley, Tait, Holden, Carlin, Redfearn
Att: 9,000
Abandoned 29 mins – fog

23 March 1968 v Swansea Town (h), Division Four, 0–0
Smith, Russell, Hampton, Pickering, Holt, Shawcross, Flower, Massie, Ryden, Pearson, McCarthy
Att: 4,253
Abandoned 59 mins – waterlogged pitch

14 December 1968 v Peterborough United (a), Division Four, 0–0
Smith, Hampton, Buxton, Pickering, Nicholl, Wallace, Flower, Massie, Lawther, Shawcross, Lee
Attendance: 3,000
Abandoned half–time – frozen pitch

3 December 1982 v Northampton Town (h), Division Four, 3–2
Spooner 2, Allatt
Smelt, Nobbs, Goodman, Evans, Smith, Hendrie, Ward, Spooner, Allatt, Staniforth, Wood
Att: 1,229
Abandoned 78 mins – fog

6 January 2007 v Gravesend & Northfleet (a), Nationwide Conference, 2–1
Forrest, Killeen
Mawson, Toulson, Doughty, Kearney, Quinn, Trotman, Gray, Foster, Joynes, Forrest, Killeen
Att: 1,026
Abandoned 61 mins – waterlogged pitch

Players of the Year

Inaugurated in 1967–68.

1967–68	Les Massie	1989–90	Brian Butler
1968–69	Phil McCarthy	1990–91	Steve Norris
1969–70	Freddie Hill	1991–92	Lee Bracey
1970–71	Dave Chadwick	1992–93	Billy Barr
1971–72	John Pickering	1993–94	Craig Boardman
1972–73	Alex Smith	1994–95	Steve Prindiville
1973–74	Johnny Quinn	1995–96	Kieran O'Regan
1974–75	Dave Gwyther	1996–97	Andy Woods
1975–76	Tony Rhodes	1997–98	Jamie Paterson
1976–77	Jimmy Lawson	1998–99	Paul Stoneman
1977–78	Derek Bell	1999–00	Lee Butler
1978–79	Kevin Johnson	2000–01	Steve Kerrigan
1979–80	Paul Hendrie	2001–02	Paul Harsley
1980–81	Paul Hendrie	2002–03	Craig Midgley
1981–82	Bobby Davison	2003–04	Steve Bushell
1982–83	Dave Staniforth	2004–05	Ryan Sugden
1983–84	Barry Gallagher	2005–06	Adam Quinn
1984–85	Paddy Roche	2006–07	Lewis Killeen
1985–86	Dave Longhurst	2007–08	Jon Shaw
1986–87	Rick Holden	2008–09	Tom Baker
1987–88	Phil Brown	2009–10	James Dean
1988–89	John Bramhall	2010–11	Jamie Vardy

Sendings Off

Halifax Town players sent off during a match

Jock Nixon v Rotherham Town (h), Midland League, 19 April 1913 – retaliation just before half-time
Arthur Brearley v Mirfield United (h), Midland League, 15 November 1913 – fighting
Harry Farren v Lincoln City Reserves (h), Midland League, 6 December 1913 – bad foul
Jimmy Wishart v Rotherham Town (h), Midland League, 28 September 1914 – retaliation
Jock Nixon v Bradford Reserves (a), Midland League, 10 October 1914 – retaliation
Jack Hughes v Goole Town (a), Midland League, 6 March 1915 – retaliation second half
George Wild v York City (a), friendly, 16 October 1915 – fighting
Clem Longbottom v Rotherham County (a), Midland Combination, 30 October 1915 – fighting
Jack Scull v Rotherham County Reserves (h), Midland League, 30 October 1920 – retaliation
Jack Scull v Bradford (h), WRSC, 9 May 1921 – retaliation 55 mins
Sam Challinor v Stockport County (a), Division 3 (N), 26 December 1921 – retaliation 88 mins
Maurice Wellock v Chesterfield (a), Division 3 (N), 22 April 1922 – bad foul near end
Matt Ellson v Tranmere Rovers (a), Division 3 (N), 30 September 1922 – retaliation
Jack Newton v Bradford (a), Division 3 (N), 16 January 1926 – retaliation 35 mins

SENDINGS OFF

Webster Swift v Doncaster Rovers (a), Division 3 (N), 26 December 1927 – bad foul 55 mins
George McGrae v Stockport County (a), Division 3 (N), 21 November 1931 – violent conduct 80 mins
Dan Ferguson v Chesterfield (h) Division 3 (N), 25 December 1934 – bad foul 80 mins
Jake Ruecroft v Doncaster Rovers (a), War Cup, 10 January 1942 – fighting 79 mins
Bobby Davidson v Huddersfield Town (a), Northern Regional, 28 November 1942 – fighting second half
Jock Wallace v Doncaster Rovers (h), Northern Regional, 6 November 1943 – bad foul 89 mins
Stan Wood v Carlisle United (a), Division 3 (NE), 15 September 1945 – dissent early in second half
Eddie Murphy v Mansfield Town (a), Division 3 (N), 29 August 1953 – fighting in second half
Andy Geddes v Accrington Stanley (a), Division 3 (N), 26 December 1953 – retaliation 72 mins
Alex South v Bury (a), Division 3 (N), 2 September 1957 – fighting 43 mins
Paddy Stanley v Bradford City (a), WRSC Final, 8 May 1959 – fighting 67 mins
George Whitelaw v Newport County (a), Division 3, 28 November 1959 – bad foul 64 mins
Frank Large v Torquay United (h), Division 3, 22 August 1960 – fighting near end of game
Paddy Stanley v Newport County (a), Division 3, 5 March 1962 – retaliation 70 mins
Willie Carlin v Barnsley (h), Division 3, 11 September 1962 – retaliation just after half-time
Alex South v Bradford (h), Division 3, 13 April 1963 – second bookable offense 42 mins
Walt Bingley v Newport County (a), Division 4, 26 October 1963 – retaliation 88 mins
John Brier v Doncaster Rovers (h), Division 4, 26 September 1964 – second bookable offense 85 mins
Walt Bingley v Barrow (a), Division 4, 27 February 1965 – retaliation 70 mins
Eric McMillan v Bradford (a), WRSC, 5 May 1966 – fighting 68 mins
Phil McCarthy v Chester (a), Division 4, 19 November 1966 – retaliation 50 mins
Barry Hutchinson v Rochdale (a), Division 4, 22 April 1967 – fighting 44 mins
Phil McCarthy v Barnsley (a), Division 4, 30 March 1968 – retaliation 57 mins
Ian Lawther v Brentford (a), Division 4, 30 November 1968 – foul language 33 mins
Tony Flower v Jeunnesse (a), friendly, 26 May 1969 – retaliation 80 mins
Jeff Lee v Bradford City (a), Division 3, 26 December 1969 – bad foul 88 mins
Lammie Robertson v Rochdale (h), Division 3, 19 October 1971 – fighting 81 mins
David Ford v Southend United (a), Division 3, 1 September 1974 – bad foul 60 mins
Kenny Blair v Wrexham (a), Division 3, 4 February 1975 – dissent 70 mins
Steve Downes v Plymouth Argyle (a), Division 3, 28 March 1975 – retaliation 50 mins
Dave Gwyther v Swindon Town (a), Division 3, 11 October 1975 – retaliation 71 mins
Bobby Flavell v Exeter City (a), Division 4, 26 February 1977 – bad foul 36 mins
Jimmy Lawson v Exeter City (a), Division 4, 26 February 1977 – fighting 68 mins
Jimmy Lawson v Rochdale (a), League Cup, 13 August 1977 – fighting 33 mins
Jack Trainer v Scunthorpe United (h), Division 4, 29 March 1978 – second bookable offense 64 mins
Derek Bell v Hartlepool United (a), Division 4, 23 September 1978 – second bookable offense 60 mins
Dave Harris v Bradford City (a), Division 4, 7 November 1979 – retaliation 78 mins
Steve Ward v Stockport County (a), Division 4, 29 August 1980 – bad foul 40 mins
Brian Chambers v Rochdale (h), Division 4, 20 April 1981 – retaliation 90 mins
Paul Hendrie v Aldershot (a), Division 4, 12 September 1981 – second bookable offense 45 mins
Steve Ward v Northampton Town (a), Division 4, 20 April 1982 – second bookable offense 87 mins
Dave Evans v Stockport County (a), Division 4, 1 January 1983 – dissent 86 mins
Tony Smith v Bristol City (a), Division 4, 8 October 1983 – professional foul 54 mins
Alan Little v York City (h), Division 4, 26 December 1983 – second bookable offense 84 mins
Alan Knill v Darlington (a), Division 4, 9 March 1985 – second bookable offense 65 mins
Cec Podd v Darlington (a), Division 4, 9 March 1985 – retaliation 75 mins
Steve Brookes v Port Vale (a), Division 4, 27 April 1985 – second bookable offense 67 mins
Cec Podd v Hartlepool United (a), Division 4, 1 January 1986 – bad foul 59 mins
Barry Diamond v Aldershot (a), Division 4, 8 March 1986 – fighting half-time
Phil Brown v Stockport County (h), Division 4, 16 October 1987 – second bookable offense 80 mins
Russell Black v Exeter City (a), Division 4, 7 May 1988 – bad foul 61 mins

Dean Martin v Brandon United (a), friendly, 6 August 1988
Dean Martin v Hartlepool United (h), Division 4, 4 November 1988 – dissent 41 mins
Dean Martin v Stockport County (h), Division 4, 4 February 1989 – retaliation 79 mins
Dean Martin v Leyton Orient (a), Division 4, 4 April 1989 – bad foul 52 mins
Neil Matthews v Hull City (h), Yorks & Humberside Cup, 8 August 1989 – ungentlemanly conduct 27 mins
Dean Martin v Torquay United (a), Division 4, 27 March 1990 – bad foul 80 mins
Dave Evans v Stockport County (a), Division 4, 18 January 1991 – professional foul 41 mins
Ian Juryeff v Chesterfield (a), Division 4, 9 March 1991 – violent conduct 34 mins
Shaun Gore v Carlisle United (h), Division 4, 19 March 1991 – retaliation 86 mins
Ian Juryeff v Rotherham United (h), Division 4, 13 September 1991 – second bookable offense 74 mins
Russell Bradley v Lincoln City (a), Division 4, 5 October 1991 – deliberate handball 27 mins
Chris Lucketti v Burnley (h), Division 4, 2 November 1991 – professional foul 55 mins
Tommy Graham v Burnley (h), Division 4, 2 November 1991 – bad foul second half
Russell Bradley v Cardiff City (a), Division 4, 11 April 1992 – bad foul 72 mins
Jamie Paterson v Cardiff City (a), Division 4, 11 April 1992 – violent conduct 78 mins
Ronnie Hildersley v Northampton Town (h), Division 3, 16 January 1993 – fighting 90 mins
Billy Barr v Scunthorpe United (a), Division 3, 30 January 1993 – retaliation 57 mins
Martin Filson v Slough Town (a), GMVC, 28 August 1993 – second bookable offense 54 mins
Billy Barr v Slough Town (a), GMVC, 28 August 1993 – dissent 62 mins
Peter Costello v Bath City (a), GMVC, 23 October 1993 – foul language 44 mins
Kevin Megson v Bath City (a), GMVC, 23 October 1993 – fighting 60 mins
David German v Woking (a), GMVC, 20 August 1994 – violent conduct 45 mins
Alex Jones v Northwich Victoria (h), GMVC, 24 August 1994 – second bookable offense 66 mins
Lee Fowler v Northwich Victoria (h), Bob Lord Trophy, 20 September 1994 – professional foul 7 mins
Alex Jones v Runcorn (h), GMVC, 20 December 1994 – second bookable offense 73 mins
Mick Trotter v North Ferriby (a), Friendly, 1 August 1995 – foul language
Elliot Beddard v Northwich Victoria (h), GMVC, 12 September 1995 – retaliation 58 mins
Jon Brown v Runcorn (a), FA Cup, 21 October 1995 – violent conduct 87 mins
Elliot Beddard v Runcorn (a), FA Cup, 21 October 1995 – dissent 89 mins
Jon Brown v Farnborough Town (a), GMVC, 28 October 1995 – professional foul 64 mins
Mick Trotter v Runcorn (h), GMVC, 16 December 1995 – professional foul 43 mins
Michael Midwood v Telford United (h), GMVC, 6 April 1996 – second bookable offense 87 mins
Simon Johnson v Woking(h), GMVC, 20 April 1996 – second bookable offense 16 mins
Paul Stoneman v Stevenage Borough (a), GMVC, 17 August 1996 – violent conduct 47 mins
Mark Cameron v Southport (a), GMVC, 26 August 1996 – violent conduct 88 mins
Noel Horner v Kettering Town (a), GMVC, 31 August 1996 – second bookable offense 42 mins
John Francis v Woking (h), GMVC, 19 October 1996 – bad foul 35 mins
Paul Stoneman v Woking (h), GMVC, 19 October 1996 – second bookable offense 50 mins
Mick Norbury v Woking (a), GMVC, 21 December 1996 – second bookable offense 63 mins
Paul Stoneman v Bromsgrove Rovers (a), GMVC, 1 February 1997 – bad foul 43 mins
Paul Cox v Dover Athletic (h), GMVC, 15 March 1997 – second bookable offense 60 mins
Paul Cox v Morecambe (a), GMVC, 16 April 1997 – bad foul 58 mins
Paul Cox v Hayes (h), GMVC, 19 April 1997 – use of elbow 42 mins
Darren Lyons v Welling (h), GMVC, 30 August 1997 – retaliation 45 mins
Kieran O'Regan v Kidderminster Harriers (h), GMVC, 8 November 1997 – professional foul 88 mins
Noel Horner v Leek Town (a), GMVC, 13 December 1997 – bad foul 76 mins
Gary Brook v Blyth Spartans (h), FA Trophy, 10 January 1998 – violent conduct 83 mins
Paul Stoneman v Rushden & Diamonds (a), GMVC, 7 February 1998 – use of elbow 86 mins
Kieran O'Regan v Southport (h), GMVC, 13 April 1998 – retaliation 60 mins
Stephen Murphy v Wrexham (a), Worthington Cup, 11 August 1998 – bad foul 28 mins
Peter Butler v Wrexham (h), Worthington Cup, 18 August 1998 – second bookable offense 44 mins
Richard Lucas v Southend United (a), Division 3, 8 September 1998 – second bookable offense 90 mins

SENDINGS OFF

Mark Sertori v Swansea City (h), Division 3, 31 October 1998 – violent conduct 87 mins
Kevin Hulme v Chester City (a), Division 3, 10 November 1998 – retaliation 55 mins
Paul Stoneman v Torquay United (a), Division 3, 6 March 1999 – violent conduct 90 mins
Peter Butler v West Bromwich Albion (a), Worthington Cup, 24 August 1999 – bad foul 41 mins
Darryn Stamp v Brighton and Hove Albion (a), Division 3, 4 March 2000 – second bookable offense 55 mins
Peter Butler v Brighton and Hove Albion (a), Division 3, 4 Match 2000 – second bookable offense 89 mins
Paul Stoneman v York City (a), Division 3, 29 April 2000 – second bookable offense 63 mins
Alan Reilly v York City (a), Division 3, 29 April 2000 – violent conduct 77 mins
Craig Middleton v York City (a), Division 3, 29 April 2000 – second bookable offense 79 mins
Steven Hawe v Gateshead (h), FA Cup, 18 November 2000 – second bookable offense 66 mins
Neil Redfearn v Scunthorpe United (h), Division 3, 5 October 2001 – second bookable offense 57 mins
Craig Middleton v Hartlepool United (a), Division 3, 20 November 2001 – retaliation 22 mins
Peter Wright v Stoke City (a), FA Cup, 12 December 2001 – bad foul 90 mins
Peter Crookes v Shrewsbury Town (h), Division 3, 15 December 2001 – professional foul 85 mins
Andy Woodward v Macclesfield Town (a), Division 3, 26 December 2001 – retaliation 56 mins
Jamie Wood v Oxford United (a), Division 3, 29 December 2001 – violent conduct 23 mins
Paul Stoneman v Oxford United (a), Division 3, 29 December 2001 – bad foul 64 mins
Paul Stoneman v Southend United (h), Division 3, 29 January 2002 – second bookable offense 87 mins
Paul Stoneman v Rochdale (h), Division 3, 6 March 2002 – second bookable offense 39 mins
Gary Jones v Luton Town (a), Division 3, 23 March 2002 – bad foul 33 mins
Matt Clarke v Darlington (a), Division 3, 1 April 2002 – deliberate handball 15 mins
Neil Redfearn v Rushden & Diamonds (h), Division 3, 20 April 2002 – retaliation 54 mins
Steve Bushell v Northwich Victoria (h), NC, 26 August 2002 – violent conduct 24 mins
Paul Stoneman v Northwich Victoria, NC, 26 August 2002 – second bookable offense 55 mins
Lee Butler v Yeovil Town (a), NC, 21 September 2002 – professional foul 68 mins
Shaun Garnett v Stevenage Borough (a), NC, 5 October 2002 – deliberate handball 32 mins
Andy Farrell v Chesterfield (a), LDV Vans, 22 October 2002 – bad foul 43 mins
Steve Bushell v Burton Albion (a), FA Cup, 26 October 2002 – second bookable offense 39 mins
Phil Clarkson v Gravesend & Northfleet (h), NC, 2 November 2002 – violent conduct 32 mins
Adam Quinn v Forest Green Rovers (a), NC, 9 November 2002 – second bookable offense 86 mins
Shaun Garnett v Doncaster Rovers (a), NC, 20 December 2002 – bad foul 30 mins
Phil Clarkson v Morecambe (h), NC, 28 December 2002 – second bookable offense 77 mins
Mark Monington v Yeovil Town (h), NC, 3 March 2003 – second bookable offense 85 mins
Kevin Sandwith v Nuneaton Borough (a), NC, 15 March 2003 – violent conduct 43 mins
James Dudgeon v York City (h), LDV, 14 October 2003 – foul 68 mins
Kevin Sandwith v Morecambe (a), NC, 20 December 2003 – second bookable offense 71 mins
Adam Yates v Scarborough (h), NC, 26 December 2003 – violent conduct 35 mins
James Dudgeon v Scarborough (h), NC, 26 December 2003 – violent conduct 35 mins
Jonny Allan v Gravesend & Northfleet (a), 17 January 2004 – violent conduct 20 mins
Mark Cartwright v Aldershot Town (h), NC, 24 February 2004 – bad foul 81 mins
Craig Midgley v Accrington Stanley (a), NC, 6 March 2004 – retaliation 38 mins
Michael Senior v Farsley Celtic (n), WRCC Final, 14 April 2004 – second bookable offense 40 mins
Steve Haslam v Tamworth (a), NC National, 14 August 2004 – professional foul 53 mins
Adam Quinn v Morecambe (h), NC National, 21 September 2004 – professional foul 39 mins
Lewis Killeen v Woking (a), NC National, 8 October 2004 – second bookable offense 45 mins
Denny Ingram v Stevenage Borough (a), NC National, 6 November 2004 – retaliation 28 mins
Denny Ingram v Scarborough (a), NC National, 19 March 2005 – second bookable offense 90 mins
John Grant v Barnet (a), NC National, 9 April 2005 – foul language 61 mins
Matt Doughty v Tamworth (h), NC National, 10 September 2005 – violent conduct 81 mins
Martin Foster v Altrincham (h), NC National, 27 September 2005 – violent conduct 90 mins
Denny Ingram v Exeter City (a), NC National, 8 October 2005 – foul and abusive language half-time
Steve Haslam v Rushden & Diamonds (a), FA Cup, 14 November 2005 – second bookable offense 114 mins

Danny Forrest v York City (a), NC, 23 December 2006 – dissent 69 mins
Tyrone Thompson v Weymouth (h), NC, 20 February 2007 – retaliation 90 mins
Andy Campbell v Burton Albion (a), NC, 17 April 2007 – dissent 41 mins
Shane Smeltz v Forest Green Rovers (a), 21 April 2007 – fighting half-time
Jon Shaw v Cambridge United (a), 6 October 2007, Blue Square Premier – violent conduct 45 mins
Anthony Griffith v Kidderminster Harriers (a), 9 October 2007, Blue Square Premier – second bookable offense 12 mins
Jake Wright v Aldershot Town (a), 20 October 2007, Blue Square Premier – dissent 54 mins
Ryan Toulson v Crawley Town (h), 3 November 2007, Blue Square Premier – second bookable offense 61 mins
Anthony Griffith v Burton Albion (h), FA Cup, 10 November 2007 – professional foul 27 mins
Tom Kearney v Stevenage Borough (a), Blue Square Premier, 17 November 2007 – violent conduct 55 mins
Anthony Griffith v Farsley Celtic (h), Blue Square Premier, 1 January 2008 – dangerous play 29 mins
Nathan Joynes v Northwich Victoria (a), Blue Square Premier, 26 January 2008 – dangerous play 46 mins
Simon Ainge v Burton Albion (a), Blue Square Premier, 15 April 2008 – second bookable offense 72 mins
Paul Collins v Ossett Albion (h), Unibond 1N, 26 December 2008 – spitting 62 mins
Tom Baker v Colwyn Bay (a), Unibond 1N, 21 February 2009 – second bookable offense 90 mins
Paul Evans v Ossett Albion (a), Unibond 1N, 10 April 2009 – bad foul 76 mins
Damian Allen v Ossett Albion (a), Unibond 1N, 10 April 2009 – second bookable offense 80 mins
Scott Phelan v Stamford (a), President's Cup, 8 December 2009 – retaliation 70 mins
Paul Sykes v Salford City (h), Unibond 1N, 12 December 2009 – violent conduct 89 mins
Tom Baker v Prescot Cables (h), Unibond 1N, 6 March 2010 – bad foul 60 mins
Aaron Hardy v Clitheroe (a), Unibond 1N, 16 March 2010 – second bookable offense 68 mins
Bradley Barnes v Trafford (a), Unibond 1N, 27 March 2010 retaliation 86 mins
Scott Phelan v Bradford PA (a), Evo-Stik Prem, 24 January 2011 – retaliation 76 mins
Liam Hogan v Worksop Town (h), Evo-Stik Prem, 1 March 2011 – second bookable offense 52 mins

Internationals

No player has ever been selected to play a full international while a Halifax Town player, but the following have all represented England at semi-professional level.

Mark Bradshaw — England Semi-Professional v Holland, at Crawley, 3 March 1998 (won 2–1, one goal).
Lee Elam — England National Game XI v Republic of Ireland, at Merthyr Tydfil, 20 May 2003 (won 4–0), v Wales, at Merthyr Tydfil, 22 May 2003 (won 2–0), v Scotland, at Carmarthen, 25 May 2003 (won 1–0).
Steve Haslam — England National Game XI v Ireland, at Cork, 24 May 2005 (sub) (won 1–0), v Wales, Cork, 26 May 2005 (won 1–0), v Scotland, at Cork, 28 May 2005 (won 3–2).
Adam Quinn — England National Game XI v Holland, at Burton, 29 November, 2006 (won 4–1).
Jon Shaw — England C v Gibraltar, at Colwyn Bay, 20 May 2008 (sub) (won 1–0), v Scotland, Colwyn Bay, 22 May 2008 (won 1–0), v Grenada, at St George's, 31 May 2008 (drew 1–1), v Barbados, at Bridgetown, 2 June 2008 (won 4–1, one goal).

FC Halifax Town
Jonathan Hedge — National Game X1 v Poland, at Grodzisk Wielkopolski, 17 November 2009 (sub) (won 2–1).

HALIFAX TOWN ON TV

- Brighton & Hove Albion 0 Halifax Town 1, Div 3, 2 February 1963 – highlights shown on *Saturday Sport* the same evening. (BBC)
- Bradford City 1 Halifax Town 1, Div 4, 18 January 1969 – highlights shown on *Sunday Soccer* (YTV) the following day.
- Barnsley 2 Halifax Town 2, Div 3, 26 September 1970 – highlights shown on *Sunday Soccer* (YTV) the following day.
- Halifax Town 1 Chesterfield 0, 17 April 1971 – highlights shown on *Sunday Soccer* (YTV) the following day.
- Halifax Town 2 Manchester United 1, Watney Cup, 31 July 1971 – highlights shown on *Match of the Day* (BBC1) the same evening.
- Halifax Town 0 West Bromwich Albion 2, Watney Cup, 4 August 1971 – highlights shown on Sportsnight the same evening.
- Halifax Town 3 York City 1, Div 3, 21 August 1971 – highlights shown on *Sunday Soccer* (YTV) the following day.
- Walsall 1 Halifax Town 1, Div 3, 24 August 1974 – highlights shown on *Star Soccer* (ATV) the following day.
- Halifax Town 0 Bury 1, Div 3, 14 September 1974 – highlights shown on *Sunday Soccer* (YTV) the following day.
- Colchester United 0 Halifax Town 1, 6 September 1975 – highlights shown on *Match of the Week* (Anglia TV) the following day.
- Portsmouth 3 Halifax Town 1, Div 4, 1 December 1979 – highlights shown on *Sunday Soccer* (Southern TV) the following day.
- Halifax Town 1 Manchester City 0, FA Cup 3rd Round, 5 January 1980 – highlights shown on *Football Special* (YTV) the following day.
- Bolton Wanderers 2 Halifax Town 0, FA Cup 4th Round, 26 January 1980 – highlights shown on *Sunday Soccer* (YTV) the following day.
- Halifax Town 1 Scunthorpe United 2, Div 4, 28 November 1981 – highlights shown on *Match of the Day* (BBC1) the same evening.
- Halifax Town 1 Tottenham Hotspur 5, Milk Cup 2nd Round 1st Leg, 26 September 1984 – highlights shown on *Sportsnight* (BBC1) the same evening.
- Altrincham 0 Halifax Town 3, FA Cup 2nd Round, 10 December 1988 – highlights shown on *Match of the Day* (BBC1) the same evening.
- Halifax Town 0 Hereford United 1, Div 3, 8 May 1993 – highlights shown on *Football Special* (YTV) the following day.
- Halifax Town 2 West Bromwich Albion 1, FA Cup 1st Round, 14 November 1993 – match shown live on Sky Sports.
- Halifax Town 1 Macclesfield Town 2, GMVC, 26 April 1994 – match screened live on Wire TV.
- Southport 4 Halifax Town 0, GMVC, 11 October 1994 – match screened live on Wire TV.
- Stafford Rangers 0 Halifax Town 1, GMVC, 7 February 1995 – match screened live on Wire TV.
- Merthyr Tydfil 2 Halifax Town 0, GMVC, 11 April 1995 – match screened live on L!VE TV.
- Halifax Town 1 Farnborough Town, GMVC, 28 February 1998 – match shown live on L!VE TV.
- Halifax Town 2 Hartlepool United 1, GMVC, 4 September 1998 – match shown live on Sky Sports.

- Manchester City 3 Halifax Town 0, FA Cup 1st Round, 13 November 1998 – match shown live on Sky Sports.
- Doncaster Rovers 0 Halifax Town 2, FA Cup 1st Round, 30 October 1999 – highlights shown on *Match of the Day* (BBC1) the same evening.
- Halifax Town 1 Accrington Stanley 2, Conference National, 3 January 2005 – match shown live on Sky Sports.
- Halifax Town 2 York City 0, Conference National, 14 March 2005 – match shown live on Sky Sports.
- Carlisle United 1 Halifax Town 0, Conference National, 28 March 2005 – match shown live on Sky Sports.
- Halifax Town 1 York City 0, Conference National, 29 August 2005 – match shown live on Sky Sports.
- Halifax Town 0 Morecambe 0, Conference National, 9 January 2006 – match shown live on Sky Sports.
- Grays Athletic 2 Halifax Town 2, Conference Play-offs, 10 May 2006 – match shown live on Sky Sports.
- Hereford United 3 Halifax Town 2, Play-off Final, 20 May 2006 – match shown live on Sky Sports.
- Halifax Town 1 Oxford United 1, Conference, 21 March 2007 – match shown live on Sky Sports.
- Stafford Rangers 2 Halifax Town 3, Blue Square Premier, 6 September 2007 – match shown live on Setanta 1.
- York City 3 Halifax Town 2, Blue Square Premier, 27 September 2007 – match shown live on Setanta 1.
- Halifax Town 1 Ebbsfleet United 0, Blue Square Premier, 10 April 2008 – match shown live on Setanta 1.

Chairmen

Dr Alan Howie Muir, 1 June 1 1911 – 20 August 1913
William R. Black, 20 August 1913 – 18 August 1916
Dr Alan Howie Muir, 5 June 1919 – 4 November 1929
William Blair, 20 December 1929 – 24 July 1931
David Brook, 29 July 1931 – 23 June 1933
Charles Edgar Mattock, 27 June 1933 – 11 July 1947
Arthur Bowman Carter (died in office), 11 July 1947 – 21 November 1951
Cyril Granville Adams, 26 November 1951 – 22 July 1954
James Mitchell, July 1954 – 24 October 1956
Harry Taylor, 24 October 24 1956 – 14 April 1965
Sidney Hitchen, 14 April 1965 – 6 September 1966
Alan Knowles Maden, 20 September 1966 – 28 June 1971
Arthur Smith, 28 June 1971 – 16 November 1972
Percy Albon, 16 November 1972 – 31 October 1977
Andrew Delaney, 31 October 1977 – 26 August 1980
John S. Crowther, 26 August 1980 – 20 November 1980

John Goldthorpe, 20 November 1980 – 19 January 1981
Samuel John Rorke, 19 January 1981 – 2 June 1982
Jack Turner, 2 June 1982 – 20 April 1984
John S. Crowther, 20 April 1984 – April 1986
John Madeley, 11 June 1986 – 18 August 1987
John Rodney Thomas, August 1987 – 31 October 1988
Douglas Moody, November 1988 – 25 February 1989
Stuart James Brown, 27 February 1989 – 27 February 1995
John C. Stockwell, 6 March 1995 – 7 June 1998
Christopher Holland, 7 June 1998 – 12 August 1998
Stuart James Brown, 12 August 1998 – 3 October 2000
Robert F. Walker, 3 October 2000 – 17 May 2002
Douglas Tait, 24 May 2002 – 31 July 2002
David Cairns, 1 August 2002 – 19 November 2003
Raymond Moreland, 19 November 2003 – 3 March 2004
Geoffrey Ralph, 20 August 2004 – 16 March 2007

SECRETARIES

Trevor Noble, August 1952–June 1956
Fred Stow, June 1956–July 1958
Norman Howe, August 1958–January 1967
Alan Vidler, February 1967–May 1968
Pauline Hicks, June 1968–September 1969
Michael Cosway, September 1969–August 1971
Cyril Rennison, August 1971–January 1972
Brian Lawless, February 1972–February 1973
Nick Fletcher, March 1973–August 1976
David Holland, August 1976–August 1979
Mike Walker, October 1979–January 1980
Martyn Firth, January 1980–October 1980
Carol Bell, October 1980–September 1987
Anne Pettifor, September 1987–1991
Bev Fielding, 1991–November 1991
Angela Harrison November 1991–June 1993
Bev Fielding June 1993–July 1994
Derek Newiss, July 1994–June 1998
Hilary Molyneux-Horrocks, June 1998–2000
Mike Riley, August 2000–October 2001
Richard Groves, July 2002–December 2005
Angela Firth, December 2005–June 2009
Hayley Horne, June 2009–

Minor Cups

Northern Section Cup

This competition was introduced, along with its Southern Section equivalent, during the 1933–34, and competed for by clubs up until the outbreak of World War Two, although Halifax Town abstained in 1938–39.

1933–34
First round: 29 January 1934 v Accrington Stanley (a) 2–2
Chambers, Tunstall
Shirlaw, Flack, Bell, Ferguson, Craig, Cooke, Brown, Mercer, Chambers, Betteridge, Tunstall

Replay: 5 February 1934 v Accrington Stanley (h) 0–3
Shirlaw, Flack, Johnman, Ferguson, Craig, Cooke, Higgins, Mercer, Chambers, Betteridge, Tunstall
Att: 2,500

1934–35
First round: 21 January 1935 v Barrow (h) 3–1
Cooke, Tunstall, Feeney
Milton, Allsop, Banner, Ferguson, Craig, Cooke, Davies, Mercer, Feeney, Barkas, Tunstall
Att: 1,958

Second round: 12 March 1935 v Stockport County (h) 0–0
Shirlaw, Allsop, Banner, Millington, Craig, Cooke, Presgrave, Feeney, Valentine, Barkas, Tunstall
Att: 1,500

Replay: 20 March 1935 v Stockport County (a) 1–3
Betteridge
Shirlaw, Allsop, Banner, Millington, Craig, Cooke, Davies, Hollingworth, Valentine, Barkas, Betteridge
Att: 2,225

1935–36
First round: 2 October 1935 v Accrington Stanley (h) 1–3
Presgrave
Owen Allsop, Williams, Hale, Craig, Cooke, Presgrave, Feeney, Valentine, Pope, Barkas

1936–37
First round: 2 November 1936 v Rotherham United (a) 0–1
Owen, Allsop, Pope, Watson, Craig, Thomas, Goodall, Smith, Valentine, Robinson, Murphy
Att: 1,592

1937–38
First round: 20 September 1937 v York City (h) 4–1
Pritchard, Barkas, Hoyland, Dawson
Owen, Allsop, Jackson, Pritchard, Craig, Brookes, Rose, Dawson, Copeland, Barkas, Hoyland
Att: 2,000

Second round: 17 January 1938 v Doncaster Rovers (a) 1–4
Jackson (pen)
Collier, Barkas, Jackson, Green, Craig, Brookes, Hoyland, Griffiths, Widdowfield, Barkas, Campbell
Att: 1,072

Football League Trophy

This competition was introduced in 1982–83, with competing teams divided into groups, with winners of each going through to the knockout stages.

1982–83
Group: 14 August 1982 v Bradford City (a) 0–1
Smelt, Nobbs, Carr, Evans, Smith, Hendrie, Hallybone, Davison, Staniforth, Spooner, Ward (Nuttall)
Att: 2,420

MINOR CUPS

Group: 17 August 1982 v Hull City (h) 1–0
Davison
Smelt, Nobbs, Carr, Evans, Smith, Hendrie, Hallybone, Davison, Staniforth, Spooner, Ward
Att: 1,323

Group: 21 August 1982 v Hartlepool United (h) 3–0
Davison 3
Smelt, Nobbs, Carr, Evans (Goodman), Smith, Hendrie, Hallybone, Davison, Staniforth, Spooner, Ward
Att: 938

	P	W	D	L	F	A	BPts
1 Bradford City	3	2	1	0	5	0	1 8
2 Halifax Town	3	2	0	1	4	1	1 7
3 Hull City	3	1	1	1	2	2	0 4
4 Hartlepool Utd	3	0	0	3	1	9	0 0

LDV VANS TROPHY

The current LDV Vans Trophy was launched in the 1983–84 for teams in the old Third and Fourth Divisions (the Associate Members of the Football League), and split into two regions, North and South, with the winners of each region meeting in the final. In 1985–86, teams were organised into qualifying groups, with the winners going through to the knockout stages. From 1986–87, the top two teams qualified for the knockout stages. In 1996–97 the competition became a straight knockout, and in 2000–01 clubs from the Nationwide Conference were also allowed to take part.

Over the years, the competition has had various sponsors, as such;
Associate Members' Cup – 1983–84
Freight Rover Trophy – 1984–87
Sherpa Van Trophy – 1987–89
Leyland DAF Cup – 1989–91
Autoglass Trophy – 1991–94
Auto Windscreens Shield – 1994–2000
LDV Vans Trophy – 2000–

ASSOCIATE MEMBERS' CUP
1983–84
Northern Area
First round: 20 February 1984 v Tranmere Rovers (a) 0–2
Smelt, Nobbs, Wood, Evans, Kendall, Hendrie, B Gallagher, Little, Cook, Thornber (Mell), Ward
Att: 937

FREIGHT ROVER TROPHY
1984–85
Northern Area
First round, first leg: 14 February 1985 v Darlington (h) 4–1
Shaw, Francis, Greenway, Martin
Hunt, Watson, Thornber, Moyses, Kendall, Knill (Martin), Fleming, Shaw, Sanderson, Francis, Greenway
Att: 403

First round, second leg: 3 March 1985 v Darlington (a) 0–7
Hunt, Podd, Watson, Kendall, Moyses, Martin, Cook, Fleming (Ward), Sanderson, Francis, Greenway
Att: 765

1985–86
Preliminary group: 21 January 1986 v Scunthorpe United (a) 2–3
Longhurst, Gallagher
Roche, Brown, Ward, Thornber, Knill, Kendall, Gallagher, Kellock, Lowe (Fleming), Longhurst, Nicholson
Att: 1,244

Preliminary group: 11 February 1986 v Lincoln City (h) 1–1
Shaw
Hunt, Podd, Brown, Shaw (Diamond), Knill, Galloway, Fleming (Longhurst), Martin, Lowe, Sharpe, Sanderson
Att: 150

	P	W	D	L	F	A	Pts
1 Scunthorpe Utd	2	2	0	0	6	3	6
2 Halifax Town	2	0	1	1	3	4	1
3 Lincoln City	2	0	1	1	2	4	1

1986–87
Northern Area
Preliminary group: 2 December 1986 v Mansfield Town (a) 2–2
Longhurst 2
Roche, Brown, Farnaby, M Matthews, Knill, Galloway, Sanderson, Thornber, Black, Longhurst, Holden
Att: 1,944

Preliminary group: 5 December 1986 v Rotherham United (h) 0–0
Roche, Brown, Farnaby, M. Matthews, Knill, Galloway, Sanderson, Thornber, Allison, Longhurst, Holden
Att: 1,017

	P	W	D	L	F	A	Pts
1 Halifax Town	2	0	2	0	2	2	3
2 Mansfield Town	2	0	2	0	3	3	3
3 Rotherham Utd	2	0	2	0	1	1	3

First round: 21 January 1987 v Middlesbrough (h) 1–2
Galloway
Roche, Brown, Shaw, M. Matthews, Knill, Galloway, Sanderson, Thornber, Black, Longhurst, Holden
Att: 1,411

SHERPA VAN TROPHY
1987–88
Northern Area
Preliminary group: 27 October 1987 v Grimsby Town (a) 1–2
Robinson
Roche, W. Barr (Shaw), Harrison, M. Matthews, Robinson, Galloway, Martin, Thornber, Ferebee (McPhillips), Allison, Holden

Preliminary group: 24 November 1987 v Scunthorpe United (h) 3–0
M. Matthews, N. Matthews, Martin
Roche, Brown, Ferebee (W. Barr), M. Matthews, Robinson, Shaw, Martin, Thornber (McPhillips), N. Matthews, Black, Holden
Att: 686

	P	W	D	L	F	A	Pts
1 Halifax Town	2	1	0	1	4	2	3
2 Grimsby Town	2	1	0	1	2	3	3
3 Scunthorpe Utd	2	1	0	1	2	3	3

First round: 19 January 1988 v Chesterfield (h) 2–1
Allison, Black
Roche, Brown, W. Barr, M. Matthews, Fleming, Richardson, Martin, Thornber (Black), N. Matthews, McPhillips (Allison), Holden
Att: 1,001

Second round: 18 February 1988 v Darlington (a) 2–1
M. Matthews, N. Matthews
Roche, Brown, W. Barr, M. Matthews, Richardson, Fleming, Martin, Thornber, N. Matthews, Allison, Holden
Att: 1,510

Semi–final: 8 March 1988 v Burnley (a) 0–0 aet
Roche, Brown, W. Barr, M. Matthews, Fleming (N. Matthews), Richardson, Martin, Thornber (McPhillips), Duffield, Allison, Holden
Att: 10,222
Burnley won 5–3 on penalties
Penalty sequence: Brown scored (1–1), Martin scored (2–2), M Matthews scored (3–3), Roche missed (3–4)

1988–89
Northern Area
Preliminary group: 6 December 1988 v Scunthorpe United (a) 2–1
N. Matthews, Allison
Roche, Hedworth, Horner, L. Richardson, Robinson, Bramhall, W. Barr, Watson, Willis (Blain), Allison, N. Matthews
Att: 1,547

Preliminary group: 20 December 1988 v Huddersfield Town (h) 1–0
Watson
P. Whitehead, Hedworth, Horner, L. Richardson, Robinson, Bramhall, Martin, Watson, W. Barr, Allison, N. Matthews
Att: 2,437

	P	W	D	L	F	A	Pts
1 Halifax Town	2	2	0	0	3	1	6
2 Huddersfield T	2	1	0	1	1	1	3
3 Scunthorpe Utd	2	0	0	2	1	3	0

First round: 17 January 1989 v Darlington (h) 3–0
Allison, N. Matthews, Martin
P. Whitehead, W. Barr, Horner, L. Richardson, Robinson, Bramhall, Martin, Watson, Fleming, Allison, N. Matthews
Att: 1,421

MINOR CUPS

Second round: 21 February 1989 v Blackpool (h) 0–2
Sinclair, W. Barr, Horner, Pullan, Robinson (A. Whitehead), Bramhall, Fleming (Broadbent), Watson, McPhillips, Allison, Blain
Att: 3,281

LEYLAND DAF CUP
1989–90
Northern Area
Preliminary group: 7 November 1989 v Lincoln City (h) 3–0
Cook, Juryeff, Martin
Whitehead, P. Fleming, Cook (Butler), Hedworth, Bramhall, Horner, Martin, Watson, Broadbent, Juryeff, Hall
Att: 824

Preliminary group: 12 December 1989 v Chesterfield (a) 1–2
Richardson
Brown, P. Fleming, Smith, Barr (Matthews), Bramhall, Horner, Martin, Watson (Broadbent) Richardson, Harrison, Hall
Att: 1,275

	P	W	D	L	F	A	Pts
1 Halifax Town	2	1	0	1	4	2	3
2 Lincoln City	2	1	0	1	3	3	3
3 Chesterfield	2	1	0	1	2	4	3

First round: 9 January 1990 v York City (h) 1–1
Horner
Brown, P Fleming, Harrison, Hedworth, Bramhall, Horner, Hall (C. Fleming), Broadbent, Richardson, Butler (Barr), Matthews
Att: 1,063
Halifax Town won 7–6 on penalties
Penalty sequence: Barr scored (1–0), P. Fleming scored (2–1), Hedworth scored (3–2), Bramhall scored (4–3), Richardson missed (4–4), Horner missed (4–4), Broadbent scored (5–5), Matthews scored (6–6), C Fleming scored (7–6)

Second round: 30 January 1990 v Stockport County (h) 3–1 aet
Matthews 2, Hall
Brown, P. Fleming, Cook, Hedworth, Harrison, Horner, Hall, Martin, Richardson, Butler (Naylor), Matthews
Att: 1,779

Semi-final: 20 February 1990 v Doncaster Rovers (a) 0–3
Brown, P. Fleming, Cook, Hedworth, Naylor, Martin, Hall, Watson, Richardson, Butler (C. Fleming), Matthews
Att: 5,754

1990–91
Northern Area
Preliminary group: 5 November 1990 v Rotherham United (h) 1–1
Norris (pen)
Gould, Barr, Ellis, Evans, C. Fleming, Graham (P. Fleming), Gregory, Norris, Juryeff, Dobson, Donnelly
Att: 956

Preliminary group: 9 January 1991 v Scarborough (a) 2–1
Broadbent, Cook
Gould, P. Fleming, Barr, Evans, C. Fleming, Graham, Butler, Norris, Broadbent, Cook, Ellis
Att: 641

	P	W	D	L	F	A	Pts
1 Halifax Town	2	1	1	0	3	2	4
2 Rotherham Utd	2	0	2	0	2	2	2
3 Scarborough	2	0	1	1	2	3	1

First round: 22 January 1991 v Blackpool (h) 0–1
Gould, P. Fleming, Cook, Evans, C. Fleming, Graham, Butler, Norris, Juryeff, Martin, Ellis (Broadbent)
Att: 1,267

AUTOGLASS TROPHY
1991–92
Northern Area
Preliminary group: 19 November 1991 v Bury (a) 2–2
Cooper 2
Gould, Barr, Bradley, Lucketti, Richards (Evans), Lewis, Abbott, Cooper (Hildersley), Juryeff, Richardson, Ellis
Att: 788

Preliminary group: 7 January 1992 v Scunthorpe United (h) 0–2
Gould, Barr, Hutchinson, Lucketti, Bradley, Lewis, Abbott, Kamara, Juryeff (Griffiths), Richardson, Hildersley (Donnelly)
Att: 646

	P	W	D	L	F	A	Pts
1 Bury	2	1	1	0	5	3	4
2 Scunthorpe Utd	2	1	0	1	3	3	3
3 Halifax Town	2	0	1	1	2	4	1

1992–93
Northern Area
Preliminary group: 1 December 1992 v Bradford City (h) 0–4
Bracey, Megson, Wilson, Lucketti, Thompstone, Bradley, Matthews, German, Paterson, Lancashire (Barr), Hardy
Att: 1,434

Preliminary group: 15 December 1992 v Huddersfield Town (a) 0–5
Bracey, Barr, Wilson, German, Lucketti, Bradley (Lancashire), Paterson, Peake, Thompstone, Greenwood, Hildersley
Att: 1,236

	P	W	D	L	F	A	Pts
1 Huddersfield Town	2	1	1	0	5	0	3
2 Bradford City	2	1	1	0	4	0	3
3 Halifax Town	2	0	0	2	0	9	0

AUTO WINDSCREEN SHIELD
1998–99
Northern Area
Second round: 5 January 1999 v York City (h) 4–2
Lucas, Williams 2, Hanson
Carter, Wills, Lucas, Sertori, J. Murphy, Stansfield, O'Regan, Hulme (S. Murphy), Williams, Hanson, Butler
Att: 1,446

Third round: 23 February 1999 v Rochdale (h) 1–2
Bradshaw (pen)
Martin, Thackeray, Lucas (Grant), Sertori, Stansfield (Newton), Stoneman (Brown), Etherington, Hulme, Williams, Hanson, Bradshaw
Att: 2,327
Rochdale won on Golden Goal
Away tie switched to The Shay

1999–00
Northern Area
First round: 7 December 1999 v Hartlepool United (a) 0–1
L. Butler, Wilder, Jules (Herbert), Stansfield, Stoneman, Holt (Lucas), Williams, Gaughan, M. Clarke, Painter, Reilly
Att: 1,482

LDV TROPHY
2000–01
Northern Area
First round: 9 December 2000 v Wrexham (a) 1–0
Jones
Butler, Wainwright, Murphy, G. Mitchell, Stoneman, Wilder, Thompson, Rezai, Jones (Reilly), Kerrigan (M. Clarke), Middleton
Att: 1,545

Second round: 9 January 2001 v Stoke City (h) 2–3
Kerrigan, Jones
Butler, Wainwright (Painter), Murphy, G. Mitchell, C. Clarke, Howe, Thompson, Stoneman (Reilly), Jones, Kerrigan (M. Clarke), Middleton
Att: 1,917

2001–02
Northern Area
First round: 16 October 2001 v Huddersfield Town (a) 0–0
Butler, Harsley (Midgley), Jules (Swales), Mitchell, Stoneman, M. Clarke, Middleton, Redfearn, Kerrigan (Wood), Jones, Smith
Att: 3,570
Huddersfield Town won 4–3 on penalties
Penalty sequence: Mitchell scored (1–0), Stoneman missed (1–1), Redfearn scored (2–2), Wood scored (3–3), Smith missed (3–4)

2002–03
Northern Area
First round: 22 October 2002 v Chesterfield (a) 0–2
Morgan, Asher (Ibbotson), Grayston (Heinemann), Herbert, Garnett, Haigh, Mallon, Senior, Farrell, Ryan (Parke), Fitzpatrick
Att: 1,382

MINOR CUPS

2003–04
Northern Area
First round: 14 October 2003 v York City (h) 2–1
Mallon, Quinn
Cartwright, Hockenhull, Sandwith, Bushell, Quinn, Dudgeon, Mallon, Hudson, Sagare (Tozer), Killeen (Senior), Elam (Midgley)
Att: 1,148

Second round: 4 November 2003 v Scarborough (a) 1–0
Midgley (pen)
Cartwright, Hockenhull, Sandwith, Bushell, Dudgeon, Quinn, Mallon, Hudson, Lee, Sagare (Killeen), Midgley
Att: 899

Third round: 16 December 2003 v Lincoln City (h) 1–0
Sandwith
Cartwright, Yates, Sandwith, Bushell (Hudson), Colley, Dudgeon, Mallon, Owen, Farrell, Sagare (Allan), Midgley (Hockenhull)
Att: 1,162

Semi-final: 20 January 2004 v Blackpool (a) 2–3
Killeen, Owen
Cartwright, Hockenhull, Sandwith, Bushell, Monington, Colley, Mallon (Lee), Owen, Sagare (Farrell), Killeen, Midgley (Quinn)
Att: 4,764

2005–06
Northern Area
First round: 18 October 2005 v Bury 6–1
Midgley (pen), Mansaram 2, Haslam, Killeen, Parrish (og)
Butler, Haslam, Doughty, Leister, Quinn, Young, Midgley (Wright), Foster (Thompson), Mansaram, Killeen, Bowler (Forrest)
Att: 1,191

Second round: 13 Dec 2005 v Scunthorpe United (h) 1–3
Doughty
Butler, Ingram, Doughty, Jacobs (Thompson), Young, Atherton, Midgley, Foster, Forrest, Senior (Mansaram), Bowler (Killeen)
Att: 1,124

WATNEY INVITATION CUP
One of the first sponsored Cup competitions of the early 1970s, this competition was competed for by the previous season's highest-scoring clubs in each of the Football League's four divisions not qualifying for Europe or gaining promotion. Halifax Town were the Third Division's highest scorers in 1970–71.

1971–72
First round: 31 July 1971 v Manchester United (h) 2–1
Atkins, Wallace (pen)
Smith, Burgin, Lee, Wallace, Pickering, Rhodes, Chadwick, Atkins, Robertson, Lennard Holmes
Att: 19,765

Semi-final: 4 August 1971 v West Bromwich Albion (a) 0–2
Smith, Burgin, Lee, Wallace, Pickering, Rhodes, Chadwick, Atkins, Robertson, Lennard. Holmes
Att: 12,069

CONFERENCE LEAGUE CUPS
A knockout tournament which has been contested for in various guises by clubs in the Conference.

DRINKWISE CUP
1993–94
Second round: 2 November 1993 v Gateshead (h) 3–0
Costello, Paterson, Ridings
Heyes, German, Craven, Barr, Filson, Cunningham (Megson), Peake, Costello, Ridings, Paterson, Saunders
Att: 749

Third round: 21 December 1993 v Macclesfield Town (h) 1–2
Saunders
Heyes, German, Craven, Barr, Filson, Megson, Peake, Ridings, Constable, Saunders, Cunningham (Cameron)
Att: 621

Bob Lord Trophy
1994–95
First round, first leg: 20 September 1994 v Northwich Victoria (h) 0–1
Wilmot, Sunley, Prindiville, Jones, Fowler, Stoker (Paterson), Leitch, Grayson (Lancaster), Lambert, Worthington, Kiwomya
Att: 476

First round, second leg: 10 October 1994 v Northwich Victoria (a) 1–1 aet
Lambert
Wilmot, Sunley, Prindiville, Jones, Hall, Langley (Flounders), Paterson, Lambert, Lancaster (Grayson), Worthington, Kiwomya
Att: 780

Spalding Cup
1995–96
Second round: 10 January 1996 v Gateshead (a) 0–4
Woods, Smith, Annan, O'Regan, Stoneman, Brown, Hendrick, Scaife (Horner), Midwood (Johnson), Trotter, Cochrane
Att: 327

1996–97
First round: 8 October 1996 v Altrincham (h) 0–1 aet
Heyes, Horner (James Brown), Mudd, O'Regan, Trotter, Stoneman, Midwood, Beckford, Norbury, Brook (Worthington), McInerney (Cameron)
Att: 379

1997–98
First round: 7 October 1997 v Stalybridge Celtic (a) 1–3
Boardman
Martin, Thackeray, Griffiths, Horner, Boardman, Stoneman, Paterson, Hulme (Place), Brook, Lyons, Brown
Att: 489

GLS Cup
2004–05
Third round: 3 March 2005 v Stalybridge Celtic (a) 3–7
Hoyle 2, Corby
Parry, Salm, Cockerill, Kerridge (Walker), O'Brien, Ellis (Small), Tuck, Maslak, Hoyle, Toulson, Wdowckz (Corby)
Att: 250

JC Thompson Shield
Played annually between the reigning Conference champions and the winners of the FA Trophy.

1998–99
6 October 1998 v Cheltenham Town (a) 1–0
Williams
Carter, Thackeray, Bradshaw, Sertori, J. Murphy, Stansfield, Lucas, Hulme (Place), Williams (Paterson), S. Murphy, Brown
Att: 1,337

Bradford Hospitals Charity Cup
1911–12
First round: 23 September 1911 v Knaresborough (h) 2–1
McGill, Chadbourne
Finch, E. Firth, Houldsworth, Potter, Leyland, Morgan, Nixon, McGill, Chadbourne, Redding, Wild
Att: 4,000

Second round: 21 October 1911 v Heckmondwike (h) 4–1
Wild 2, Chadbourne, Redding (pen)
Finch, E. Firth, Houldsworth, Potter, Leyland, Morgan, Nixon, Wild, Chadbourne, Redding, Marsland

Semi-final: 2 December 1911 v Bradford City Reserves (h) 0–2
H. Firth, Barraclough, Farren, Potter, Leyland, Morgan, Nixon, Wild, Walden, Chadbourne, Marsland
Att 4,500

MINOR CUPS

1912–13
First round: 4 November 1912 v Bradford City (a) 0–3
Sutcliffe, F. Farren, Green, Sharp, McGovern, T. McAllister, Nixon, Woodward, Simons, Whyte, Marsh

1913–14
Second round: 24 February 1914 v Marsden United (h) 4–2
Beevers, Roscoe 2, Cannon
Suter, Hauxby, Splitt, Brearley, Wishart, Child, McCreadie, Beevers, Cannon, Pentland, Roscoe.

Semi-final: 14 April 1914 v Heckmondwike (h) 1–1
Adams (pen)
Suter, Child, Splitt, Martin, Wishart, Brearley, McCreadie, Beevers, Adams, Cannon, Roscoe

Replay: 16 April 1914 v Heckmondwike (a) 1–0
Cannon
Suter, Child, Splitt, Martin, Wishart, Brearley, McCreadie, Cannon, Adams, Pentland, Roscoe

Final: 18 April 1914 v Scarborough 5–0
Adams, Cannon, Roscoe 3
Suter, Child, Splitt, Martin, Wishart, Brearley, McCreadie, Cannon, Adams, Beevers, Roscoe
Played at Holgate Road, York

WEST RIDING JUNIOR CUP

1911–12
Third round: 13 January 1912 v Stourton United (h) 1–1
Farrar
C. Sutcliffe, Goodall, Farren, Potter, Leyland, Fyfe, Nixon, Wild, Chadbourne, Farrar, Eccles

Replay: 27 January 1912 v Stourton United (a) 1–0
Chadbourne
C. Sutcliffe, Potter, Farren, Fyfe, Leyland, Morgan, Nixon, Wild, Chadbourne, Farrar, Eccles

Fourth round: 3 February 1912 v Thornhill Lees Albion (h) 2–0
Farrar 2
C. Sutcliffe, Wroe, Farren, Potter, Leyland, Baxter, Nixon, Wild, Farrar, Fyfe, Marsland

Fifth round: 2 March 1912 v Knaresborough (h) 1–1
Fyfe
C. Sutcliffe, Potter, Farren, Redding, Leyland, Baxter, Nixon, Wild, Farrar, Fyfe, Chadbourne

Replay: 9 March 1912 v Knaresborough (a) 2–2 aet
Scorers unknown
C. Sutcliffe, Potter, Farren, Morgan, Leyland, Baxter, Nixon, Wild, Farrar, Fyfe, Longworth

Second Replay: 19 March 1912 v Knaresborough 1–0
Nixon
C. Sutcliffe, Moncrieff, Farren, Potter, Leyland, Redding, Nixon, Wild, Chadbourne, Fyfe, Marsland
Played at Valley Parade, Bradford

Semi-final: 30 March 1912 v Barnoldswick United 2–1
Nixon, Longworth
C. Sutcliffe, E Firth, Houldsworth, Redding, Leyland, Fyfe, Nixon, Wild, Chadbourne, Longworth, Culpan
Played at Park Avenue, Bradford

Final: 13 April 1912 v Mirfield United 0–2
C. Sutcliffe, E Firth, Baxter, Potter, Leyland, Redding, Nixon, Wild, Chadbourne, Fyfe, Culpan.
Played at Dewsbury and Savile Ground

WEST RIDING SENIOR CUP

Apart from the early seasons and the period just after World War Two, this competition was competed for by the clubs in the West Riding, later West Yorkshire, which were members of the Football League. It was held on a straight knockout basis until 1983. Then, a round-robin system was introduced, with clubs playing each other in a pre-season tournament, with points awarded for goals scored in each half and bonus points for high scorers. The competition floundered in the late 1980s and was superseded by the Yorkshire and Humberside Cup, only to be revived briefly in 1991. Thereafter, with Leeds United and Huddersfield unwilling to take part, Halifax Town and Bradford met in one-off Finals in 1996–97 and 1999–2000, with Halifax Town winning on both occasions. The trophy has not been played for since.

1912–13
First round: 19 September 1912 v Goole Town (a) 1–2
Simons
Sutcliffe, H. Farren, Green, McGovern, Wagstaffe, T. McAllister, Nixon, Wild, Pentland, Simons, Whyte

1913–14
First round: bye

Second round: 18 September 1913 v Huddersfield Town (h) 0–2
Suter, Splitt, Farren, Martin, Thompson, Child, Longbottom, Wild, T. Hughes, McDevitt, Roscoe

1914–15
First round: bye

Second round: 4 February 1915 v Goole Town (a) 2–4
Hughes 2
Suter, Birtwhistle, Parton, Hibbert, Wishart, Armitage, Milner, Wild, Hughes, Scrutton, Roscoe

1919–20
First round: 17 March 1920 v Castleford Town (a) 1–2
Cook
Suter, Birtwhistle, Scull, Lowe, Heath, Slater, E. Smith, Wild, Wellock, Cook, Robinson

1920–21
Semi-final: 18 April 1921 v Bradford (a) 2–2
Stott, Whiteside
Haldane, Birtwhistle, Scull, Anderson, Wellock, Jones, Smith, Stott, Whiteside, Jamieson, Whalley

Replay: 9 May 1921 v Bradford (h) 1–0
Whalley
Haldane, Birtwhistle, Scull, Anderson, Wellock, Jones, Smith, Stott, Whiteside, Jamieson, Whalley
Att: 4,000.

Final: 14 May 1921 v Bradford City (a) 1–4
Whalley
Haldane, Birtwhistle, Scull, Anderson, Wellock, Jones, Smith, Stott, Whiteside, Jamieson, Whalley
Att: 11,500

1921–22
First round: 29 March 1922 v Bradford (a) 0–1
Waddington, Watson, Mackrill, Howson, Wellock, Linley, Pinkney, Wild, Woods, Dent, Whalley
Att: 1,000

1922–23
First round: 27 September 1922 v Castleford Town (a) 0–0
Bown, Treasure, Mackrill, Lees, E. Hall, Langford, Vallis, Ellson, Dixon, Price, Hardaker
Att: 2,000

Replay: 5 October 1922 v Castleford Town (h) 5–1
Dixon, Price, Crawshaw 2, Waddington (og)
Bown, Treasure, Mackrill, Lees, E. Hall, Wild, Burkinshaw, Crawshaw, Dixon, Price, Whalley

Semi-final: 19 October 1922 v Huddersfield Town (h) 3–1
Whalley, Burkinshaw 2
Bown, Lees, Mackrill, F. Hall, E. Hall, Langford, Burkinshaw, Crawshaw, Dixon, Price, Whalley
Att: 3,000

Final: 25 October 1922 v Leeds United (a) 0–1
Bown, Lees, Mackrill, F. Hall, E. Hall, Langford, Burkinshaw, Crawshaw, Dixon, Price, Whalley
Att: 6,000

1923–24
Semi-final: 30 April 1924 v Leeds United (a) 1–3
Housley
Bown, J.W. Lees, Featherstone, Wild, E. Hall, Howson, Foster, J.W.D. Lees, Housley, Moore, Whalley

MINOR CUPS

1924–25
Semi-final: 3 November 1924 v Bradford City (h) 1–2
Martin
Fryer, Lees, Lodge, Walsh, Hall, Martin, Foster, Duncan, Dark, King, Shankly.
Att: 4,000

1925–26
First round: 19 April 1926 v Bradford (h) 2–0
Seabrook, Martin (pen)
Newton, Lees, Campbell, Duckett, Dark, Martin, Seabrook, Low, Dixon, Smeaton, Kennie

Semi-final: 26 April 1926 v Huddersfield Town (a) 1–4
Dixon
Newton, Lees, Campbell, Duckett, Dark, Martin, Seabrook, Low, Dixon, Smeaton, McCafferty
Att: 2,000

1926–27
First round: 14 February 1927 v Bradford (h) 2–3
Martin 2
L. Barber, Wheelhouse, Gadsden, Duckett, Dark, Smeaton, Waites, Seabrook, Dixon, Smith, Martin
Att: 2,000

1927–28
Semi-final: 20 February 1928 v Bradford (a) 0–3
Fox, Smeaton, Wheelhouse, Thompson, Dark, Brannigan, Waites, Bell, Dixon, Groves, Martin
Att: 4,048

1928–29
Semi-final: 22 April 1929 v Huddersfield Town (h) 3–3
Cooper, Dixon, Foster
Suter, Bell, Wheelhouse, Stockdale, McLachlan, Proctor, Hickman, C. Taylor, Dixon, Cooper, Foster

Replay: 29 April 1929 v Huddersfield Town (a) 1–0
Dixon
Matthews, Bell, Wheelhouse, Stockdale, McLachlan, Proctor, Hickman, Lowson, Dixon, Cooper, Foster
Att: 4,000

Final: 11 May 1929 v Leeds United 0–4
Matthews, Lees, Wheelhouse, Stockdale, McLachlan, Proctor, Hickman, Bell, Dixon, Cooper, Foster
Played at Valley Parade, Bradford

1929–30
Semi-final: 20 November 1929 v Huddersfield Town (a) 0–4
Binns, Wheelhouse, Julian, Lowson, Strang, Proctor, Hickman, Foster, Bell, Cooper, Partridge
Att: 1,000

1930–31
Semi-final: 22 September 1930 v Huddersfield Town (h) 0–2
Hardcastle, Barrie, Graham, Bain, Strang, Proctor, Davies, McFarlane, Pape, Woodhouse, Cooper
Att: 2,000

1931–32
Semi-final: 26 October 1931 v Bradford (h) 1–2
Davies
Taylor, Barrie, Graham, Bain, Strang, Read, Davies, McFarlane, Crawford, Johnson, Betteridge

1932–33
Semi-final: 28 September 1932 v Huddersfield Town (a) 1–4
Roberts
Shirlaw, Helliwell, Barrie, Thompson, Cooke, L. Roberts, Davies, Craig, Wellock, Chambers, Betteridge
Att: 1,000

1933–34
First round: 25 September 1933 v Leeds United (h) 3–1
Brown, Chambers, Betteridge
Shirlaw, Rawlinson, Johnman, Ferguson, Craig, Cooke, Davies, Brown, Chambers, Wellock, Betteridge
Att: 3,000

Semi-final: 2 October 1933 v Huddersfield Town (h) 1–5
Chambers (pen)
Shirlaw, Flack, Johnman, Ferguson, Craig, Cooke, Davies, Brown, Chambers, Wellock, Betteridge
Att: 4,350

1934–35
Semi-final: 29 October 1934 v Bradford (a) 1–3
Valentine
Shirlaw, Allsop, Taylor, Ferguson, Craig, Cooke, Presgrave, Mercer, Valentine, Atherton, Tunstall
Att: 1,381

1935–36
Semi-final: 26 February 1936 v Huddersfield Town (a) 2–3
Barkas, Presgrave
Owen, Allsop, Pope, Coode, Craig, Cooke, Presgrave, Merry, Valentine, Barkas, Tunstall
Att: 1,194

1936–37
Semi-final: 5 October 1936 v Leeds United (a) 1–3
Valentine
Collier, Allsop, Pope, Watson, Craig, Thomas, Goodall, Smith, Valentine, Barkas, Hill

1937–38
First round: 20 October 1937 v Leeds United (a) 1–1
Barkas
Owen, Allsop, Jackson, Rose, Craig, Green, Widdowfield, Griffiths, Thomas, Barkas, Hoyland

Replay: 1 November 1937 v Leeds United (h) 3–0
Barkas 2, Thomas
Owen, Allsop, Willis, Birks, Craig, Brookes, Rose, Griffiths, Thomas, Barkas, Hoyland
Att: 1,000

Semi-final: 28 March 1938 v Goole Town (h) 4–0
Brookes, Widdowfield 3
Owen, Allsop, Clark, Green, Craig, Brookes, Rose, Griffiths, Widdowfield, Barkas, Campbell
Att: 500

Final: 12 May 1938 v Selby Town 0–2
Collier, Allsop, Clark, Green, Craig, Brookes, Rose, Griffiths, Widdowfield, Barkas, Campbell
Att: 3,000
Played at Goole Town

1938–39
First round: 17 April 1939 v Selby Town (a) 2–0
Widdowfield, Cooper
Briggs, Allsop, Jackson, Green, Craig, Ruecroft, Cooper, Griffiths, Widdowfield, Barkas, Wood

Semi-final: 26 April 1939 v Huddersfield Town (a) 0–1
Briggs, Allsop, Jackson, Green, Craig, Ruecroft, Hutton, Griffiths, Widdowfield, Barkas, Wood
Att: 500

1939–1949: Competition suspended

1949–50
Semi-final: 18 April 1950 v Bradford City (h) 2–3
Scott, Core
Egglestone, Drake, O'Grady, Crossley, McCormick, Morgan, Massey, Hindle, Core, Murphy, Scott

1950–51
Semi-final: 4 April 1951 v Bradford (a) 1–4
Core
Rayner, Drake, Breaks, Moncrieff, Mycock, Horton, Tomlinson, Moss, Core, Hindle, Glaister
Att: 2,191

1951–52
First round: 21 April 1952 v Huddersfield Town (a) 1–1
Morgan
Savage, Williams, Mycock, Hunter, Bickerstaffe, Lorenson, Dale, Morgan, Frost, Murphy, Priestley
Att: 2,855

Replay: 30 April 1952 v Huddersfield Town (h) 1–0
Priestley
Savage, Williams, Mycock, Hunter, Bickerstaffe, Lorenson, Holt, Morgan, Frost, Murphy, Priestley
Att: 4,366

Semi-final: 5 May 1952 v Bradford City (h) 2–1
Murphy, Frost
McCormick, Williams, Mycock, Hunter, Lorenson, Moss, Holt, Morgan, Frost, Murphy, Priestley
Att: 3,762

Final: 8 October 1952 v Leeds United (a) 1–2
Frost
Savage, Williams, Cox, Geddes, Packard, Moss, Frost, Holt, Darbyshire, Murphy, Priestley
Att: 3,500
Final held over from previous season

1952–53
First round: 16 March 1953 v Bradford City (h) 1–2
Murphy
Savage, Williams, Cox, Moss, Packard, Morgan, Wilkinson, Holt, Frost, Murphy, Priestley
Att: 3,000

1953–54
Semi-final: 14 December 1953 v Huddersfield Town (a) 0–3
McCormick, Horsman, Bell, Geddes, Packard, Moss, Rickett, Wood, Pennington, Murphy, Priestley
Att: 6,988

1954–55
Semi-final: 9 February 1955 v Bradford (a) 2–4
Hampson, Newton
Scott, Griffiths, Ferguson, Geddes, Horsman, Bell, Dubois, Newton, Watkinson, Hampson, Sharp
Att: 4,162

1955–56
Semi-final: 3 October 1955 v Leeds United (a) 2–2
Sharp, Clarke
Johnson, Griffiths, Lonsdale, Darbyshire, Horsman, Bell, Dubois, Rodger, Clarke, Baker, Sharp
Att: 6,500

Replay: 17 October 1955 v Leeds United (h) 0–1
Johnson, Horsman, Lonsdale, Darbyshire, Harris, Bell, Dubois, Baker, Watkinson, Clarke, Rodger
Att: 4,000

1956–57
Semi-final: 10 October 1956 v Huddersfield Town 2–1
Smith, Shore
Mills, Griffiths, Ferguson, Baker, Lorenson, Lonsdale, Hutchinson, Smith, Shore, McCall, Kelly
Played at Valley Parade, Bradford

Final: 26 November 1956 v Leeds United (a) 1–3
Smith
Mills, Griffiths, Ferguson, Darbyshire, South, Lorenson, Hutchinson, Smith, Shore, McCall, Lonsdale
Att: 3,500

1957–58
Semi-final: 4 November 1957 v Bradford City (a) 1–3
Griffiths (pen)
Johnson, Griffiths, Lonsdale, Atkinson, South, Lorenson, Sharp, Smith, Mulholland, McQuade, Kelly
Att: 4,688

1958–59
Semi-final: 6 April 1959 v Leeds United (a) 0–0
Knowles, Roscoe, Stanley, Harrison, Lorenson, Large, Sharp, Tilley, Fagan, McCall, Lonsdale
Att: 3,000

Replay: 4 May 1959 v Leeds United (h) 3–0
Smith 2, Lonsdale
Johnson, Roscoe, Stanley, Harrison, Lorenson, Large, Thomas, Smith, Tilley, McCall, Lonsdale
Att: 5873

Final: 8 May 1959 v Bradford City (a) 1–0
Lonsdale
Johnson, Roscoe, Stanley, Harrison, Lorenson, Large, Thomas, Smith, Fagan, McCall, Lonsdale
Att: 8,258

1959–60
Semi-final: 13 October 1959 v Leeds United (a) 0–3
Johnson, Roscoe, Stanley, Harrison, Lorenson, Large, McCall, Smith, South, Tilley, Blackburn
Att: 5,000

1960–61
First round: 27 March 1961 v Huddersfield Town (a) 1–3
Allan
Knowles, Stanley, Hudson, Harrison, South, Fagan, Priestley, Smith, Allan, Sinclair, Blackburn

1961–62
Semi-final: 12 March 1962 v Leeds United (h) 3–0
Redfearn 3
Downsborough, Stanley, Roscoe, Harrison, Tilley, Large, Priestley, Barnett, Hopper, K. Smith, Redfearn
Att: 2,316

Final: 7 May 1962 v Bradford (a) 1–0
W.C. Smith
Downsborough, Stanley, Roscoe, Harrison, South, Large, Lovell, W.C. Smith, Burgess, K. Smith, Fagan
Att: 5945

1962–63
Semi-final: 29 May 1963 v Leeds United (h) 5–0
Wainwright, Tait 2 (1 pen), Brier, Madeley (og)
Downsborough, Russell, Roscoe, Harrison, South, Brier, Wainwright, Carlin, Worthington, Tait, Fidler
Att: 1,069

Final: 31 May 1963 v Bradford (a) 0–3
Downsborough, Roscoe, Russell, Harrison, South, Brier, Wainwright, Carlin, Worthington, Tait, Fidler
Att: 3870

1963–64
First round: 22 January 1964 v Bradford (h) 1–2
Westlake
Downsborough, Russell, Roscoe, Harrison, Richardson, South, Twist, Bartlett, Westlake, Carlin, Fidler
Att: 3,186

1964–65
Semi-final: 6 March 1965 v Huddersfield Town (h) 1–4
Taylor (pen)
Downsborough, Bingley, Brier, Goodall, South, Lee, Westlake, Twist, Wooler, Jackson, Taylor
Att: 2,882

1965–66
Semi-final: 5 May 1966 v Bradford (a) 2–5
Atkins, Fidler
White, Russell, Clarke, Smith, Pickering, McMillan, Field, Westlake, Wooler, Atkins, Fidler
Att: 724

1966–67
Semi-final: 10 May 1967 v Leeds United (h) 2–0
Taylor 2
White, Russell, Pickering, Blyth, Holt, J. Lee, Holmes, Wallace, Wooler, Shawcross, Taylor
Att: 4,411

Final: 18 May 1967 v Bradford City (h) 3–0
Smith 2, McCarthy
White, Russell, Pickering, Smith, Holt, J. Lee, Taylor, Wallace, Wooler, Shawcross, McCarthy
Att: 5,667

1967–68
Semi-final: 24 April 1968 v Bradford (h) 1–2
Wooler
A Smith, Hampton (McCarthy), R. Lee, Pickering, Holt, Blyth, Flower, Massie, Wooler, Wallace, Morris
Att: 2163

1968–69
Semi-final: 14 May 1969 v Leeds United (h) 0–5
Smith, Hampton, Burgin, Pickering, Shawcross, J. Lee, Flower, Pearson (Verity), Lawther, Wallace, McCarthy
Att: 11,085

1969–70
Semi-final: 20 April 1970 v Leeds United (h) 3–0
Shawcross, Buxton, Atkins
Smith, Burgin, Buxton, Lee, Shawcross, Wallace, Chadwick, Atkins, Lawther, Lennard (Verity), Holmes
Att: 1,649

Final: 15 September 1970 v Huddersfield Town (h) 1–3
Atkins
Smith, Holmes, Lee, Robertson, Lawther, Wallace, Chadwick, Atkins, Brierley, Lennard, McCarthy
Att: 5,900
Final held over from previous season

1970–71
Semi-final: 22 December 1970 v Leeds United (h) 3–0
Atkins 2, Lennard
Smith, Burgin (Lawther), Lee, Wallace, Pickering, Rhodes, Chadwick, Atkins, Brierley, Lennard, McCarthy
Att: 3,885

Final: 10 May 1971 v Huddersfield Town (a) 0–1
White, Burgin, Lee, Wallace, Pickering, Rhodes, Chadwick, Atkins (Verity), Lawther, Lennard, Holmes
Att: 8,219

1971–72
Semi-final: 11 December 1971 v Bradford City (a) 4–3
Brierley, Wallace (pen), Kemp, Atkins
White, Burgin, Lee, Wallace, Pickering, Rhodes, Chadwick, Atkins, Brierley, Kemp, Verity (Robertson)
Att: 3,434

Final: 12 May 1972 v Leeds United (a) 3–4
Atkins 2, Robertson
Smith, Burgin, Lee, Wallace, Pickering, Rhodes, Holmes, Kemp, Robertson, Atkins, Waddle
Att: 6,256

1972–73
Semi-final: 21 February 1973 v Bradford City (h) 3–1
Irvine, Brierley 2
Smith, Burgin, Lee, Hale, Pickering, Rhodes, Brogan, Verity, Irvine (Shanahan), Kemp, Brierley
Att: 1,812

Final: 21 August 1973 v Leeds United (a) 1–2
Gwyther
Smith, Burgin, Quinn, Kemp, Pickering, Rhodes, Irvine, Pugh, Shanahan, Gwyther (Ford), Hale
Att: 4,650
Final held over from previous season

1973–74
Semi-final: 10 May 1974 v Bradford City (h) 1–2
Wilkie
White, Burgin, Quinn, Hale, Pugh (Wilkie), Rhodes, D. Smith, Shanahan, Kemp, Gwyther, McDonald
Att: 1,709

1974–75
Semi-final: 1 January 1975 v Bradford City (a) 2–3
Ford, Jones
White, Quinn, Farrimond, McHale, Rhodes, Phelan, Jones, Blair, Downes, Ford, Harrold
Att: 3,694

1975–76
Semi-final: 8 August 1975 v Leeds United (a) 2–4
Gwyther, McHale
Gennoe, Smith, Collins, McHale (Harrold), Rhodes, Phelan, A. Jones, Pugh, Bell, Gwyther, Luckett
Att: 2,099

1976–77
Semi-final: 29 March 1977 v Leeds United (h) 3–4
Carroll, Bullock, Gethin
Leonard, Trainer, Loska, Flavell, Dunleavy, Bradley, Bell (Gethin), Carroll, Bullock, Lawson, Gregoire, McGill
Att: 3,442

1977–78
Semi-final: 15 November 1977 v Huddersfield Town (h) 1–1
Johnston
Huddersfield Town won 5–4 on penalties
Leonard, Flavell, Bradley (Loska), Smith, Dunleavy, Trainer, Johnston, Bell, Bullock, Lawson, Carroll (Horsfall)
Att: 1,123
Penalty sequence: (Huddersfield kicked first) Lawson scored (1–1), Trainer scored (2–2), Johnston scored (3–3), Horsfall scored (4–4), Smith missed (4–4), Loska missed (4–5).

1978–79
Semi-final: 18 December 1978 v Bradford City (a) 1–2
Campbell
Hough, Bradley, O'Hare, Johnston, Burke, Sykes, Firth, Johnson (Smith), Campbell, Kennedy, Stafford. Other used subs: Carroll, Hutt
Att: 842

1979–80
Semi-final: 19 February 1980 v Bradford City (h) 0–1
Hough, Dunleavy, Goodman (Rowe), Evans, Harris, Hendrie, Whiteley, Kennedy, Dryhurst, Smith, Stafford
Att: 1,248

1980–81
Semi-final: 5 August 1980 v Bradford City (h) 0–1
Kilner, Nattress, Burton, Evans, Goodman (Harris), Dunleavy, Firth, Hendrie (Stafford), Allatt, Dryhurst, Ward
Att: 851

1981–82
Semi-final: 16 January 1982 v Bradford City (a) 1–0
Firth
Smelt, Chamberlain, Whiteley, Evans, Ayre, Hendrie, Ward, Firth, Allatt, Spooner, Graham
Att: 1,295

Final: 23 August 1982 v Leeds United (a) 2–3 aet
Hallybone, Davison
Smelt, Kendall (Wood), Carr, Evans, Smith, Hendrie, Hallybone, Davison, Staniforth, Spooner, Ward
Att: 1,228
Final held over from previous season

1982–83
No competition

1983–84
12 August 1983 v Bradford City (h) 0–2
Smelt, Nobbs, Greenway (Kendall), Evans, Smith, Hendrie, B. Gallagher (Staniforth), Cook (Nuttall), Mell, Ward, Hanson
Att: 1,080

16 August 1983 v Leeds United (h) 2–0
Staniforth, Mell
Smelt, Nobbs, Greenway, Evans, Smith, Hendrie, Ward, Cook, Mell, Hanson, Staniforth (Nuttall)
Att: 1,402

MINOR CUPS

23 August 1983 v Huddersfield Town (a) 0–2
Smelt, Nobbs, Wood, Evans, Smith, Hendrie, Ward, Cook (Nuttall), Mell, Hanson, Staniforth
Att: 1,531

1984–85
11 August 1984 v Huddersfield Town (h) 1–4
Ward
Roche, Kendall, Greenway, Moyses (Thornber), Ayre, Knill, Cook, Little, Lowe, Gallagher, Ward
Att: 1,095

15 August 1984 v Leeds United (a) 1–3
Gallagher
Roche, Podd, Watson, Moyses, Kendall, Knill, Cook, Little, Lowe, Gallagher, Ward
Att: 1,469

18 August 1984 v Bradford City (a) 1–3
Knill
Roche, Podd, Watson, Moyses, Kendall, Knill, Greenway, Little, Lowe, Gallagher, Ward (Ayre)
Att: 1,592

1985–86
29 July 1985 v Bradford City (h) 2–5
Gallagher 2
Hunt, Podd, Ward, Knill, Brown, Shaw, Gallagher, Kellock, Lowe, Longhurst, Nicholson
Att: 1,502

7 August 1985 v Leeds United (h) 0–6
Hunt, Podd, Ward, Thornber, Knill (Kendall), Brown, Gallagher (Fleming), Kellock, Lowe, Longhurst, Nicholson

10 August v Huddersfield Town (a) 1–5
Kellock (pen)
Roche, Brown, Ward, Shaw, Kendall, Ayre (Thornber), Gallagher, Kellock, Lowe, Longhurst (Fleming), Nicholson
Att: 933

1986–87
9 August 1986 v Leeds United (a) 0–3
Roche, Fleming (Black), Brown, Shaw, Knill, Galloway, Sanderson (Martin), Thornber, Diamond, Longhurst, Robinson
Att: 2,303

12 August 1986 v Bradford City (h) 0–1
Roche, Fleming, Brown, Shaw, Knill, Galloway, Sanderson, Thornber, Diamond (Martin), Longhurst (W. Barr), Black
Att: 1,104

16 August 1986 v Huddersfield Town (h) 0–2
Roche (Whitehead), Brown, Fleming, Shaw (Martin), Knill, Galloway (Willis), Sanderson, Thornber, Diamond, Longhurst (W. Barr), Black (Nicholson)
Att: 559

1987–88
1 August 1987 v Leeds United (a) 0–1
Fenton, Brown, Harrison, M. Matthews, Robinson, Galloway, Richardson (Shaw), Thornber (Martin), Ferebee, Black (Allison), Holden
Att: 2,808

7 August 1987 v Huddersfield Town (a) 1–0
Thornber
Fenton, Martin (Blain), Harrison, M. Matthews, Robinson, Shaw, Richardson (Barr), Thornber, Ferebee (Allison), Black, Holden
Att: 894

9 August 1987 v Bradford City (a) 0–3
Patterson, Martin, Harrison (J. Willis), M. Matthews, Robinson, Shaw, Richardson, Thornber, Ferebee, Black (Allison), Holden
Att: 2,589

1991–92
3 August 1991 v Huddersfield Town (h) 1–2
Richardson
Gould, Evans, Kamara, Abbott, Lucketti, Graham (Barr), Megson (Paterson), Norris, Juryeff, Richardson, Cooper
Att: 1,237

7 August 1991 v Leeds United (a) 2–0
Paterson, Cooper
Gould, Evans (Barr), Kamara, Abbott (Cooper), Lucketti, Richards, Paterson (Megson), Norris, Juryeff, Richardson, Ellis
Att: 2,174

10 August 1991 v Bradford City (h) 1–4
Norris
Gould, Barr, Kamara, Graham, Richards, Lucketti, Megson (Paterson), Norris, Juryeff, Richardson, Cooper
Att: 1,145

1992–93

1 August 1992 v Bradford City (a) 0–3
Bracey, Megson, Wilson, Abbott, Lucketti, Bradley (Kamara), German, Thompstone, Juryeff, Greenwood, Hardy (Case)
Att: 1,105

5 August 1992 v Huddersfield Town (h) 0–0
Bracey, Megson, Wilson, Thompstone, Lucketti, Bradley, Matthews, Case, Thomas (Greenwood), Juryeff, Ridings (Hildersley)
Att: 1,073

1996–97

Final: 10 December 1996 v Bradford City (h) 2–1 aet
Norbury, Worthington
Woods, Jon Brown, Mudd, O'Regan, Cox (Norbury), Stoneman, Horner, Worthington, Horsfield (Midwood), Davison (Brook), McInerney
Att: 482

1999–00

Final: 24 July 1999 v Bradford City (h) 1–0
Paterson (pen)
Adamson, Russell, Jules, Sertori, Stoneman, Mitchell, Paterson, Gaughan, Tate, Painter (Power), Murphy (P. Butler)
Att: 2,050

YORKSHIRE AND HUMBERSIDE CUP

Competing teams were divided into two groups, but each team only played three matches. The winners of each group went through to the Final.

1988–89

Group: 13 August 1988 v Grimsby Town (a) 1–0
M. Matthews
Roche, Blain, W. Barr, M. Matthews, Bramhall, R. Barr, Martin, Horner, N. Matthews (Watson), Allison, L. Richardson
Att: 1,100

Group: 16 August 1988 v Rotherham United (a) 0–1
P. Whitehead, Blain, W. Barr, M. Matthews, Bramhall, R. Barr, Martin, Horner, N. Matthews (Watson), Allison, L. Richardson (Willis)
Att: 1,416

Group: 22 August 1988 v Sheffield United 0–1
Roche, Blain, W. Barr, M. Matthews, Bramhall, A. Whitehead, Willis (McPhillips), Horner, N. Matthews, Allison (Watson), L. Richardson
Played behind closed doors at Leeds Road, Huddersfield

Group B	P	W	D	L	F	A	Pts
Sheffield United	3	2	1	0	2	0	7
Bradford City	3	1	1	1	4	3	4
Grimsby Town	3	1	1	1	2	2	4
Rotherham United	3	1	1	1	2	2	4
Halifax Town	3	1	0	2	1	2	3
Doncaster Rovers	3	0	2	1	2	4	2

1989–90

Group: 8 August 1989 v Hull City (h) 0–3
Whitehead, Hedworth, Barr, Hall (Richardson), Bramhall, Horner, Martin, Watson, McPhillips (Broadbent), Cook, Matthews
Att: 684

Group: 11 August 1989 v Leeds United (h) 2–1
Hall, Watson
Whitehead, P. Fleming, Cook, Hedworth, Bramhall, Horner, Martin, Watson, McPhillips, Butler (Richardson), Hall (Barr)
Played behind closed doors

Group: 14 August 1989 v Sheffield United (h) 1–0
Cook (pen)
Brown, P. Fleming, Cook, Hedworth, Bramhall, Horner (Richardson), Martin, Watson (Broadbent), Matthews, Butler, Hall

Group A	P	W	D	L	F	A	Pts
Hull City	3	3	0	0	7	1	9
Halifax Town	3	2	0	1	3	4	6
Rotherham United	3	1	2	0	4	3	5
Leeds United	3	1	1	1	4	3	4
Sheffield United	3	1	1	1	4	3	4
Scarborough	3	1	0	2	3	5	3
Doncaster Rovers	3	1	0	2	2	4	3
Scunthorpe United	3	0	0	3	2	6	0

1990–91

Group: 11 August 1990 v Grimsby Town (a) 1–0
McPhillips
Brown, P. Fleming, Cook, Evans, C. Fleming, Futcher, Barr, Butler, McPhillips, Fyfe, Graham
Att: 1,326

Group: 14 August 1990 v Bradford City (a) 1–0
Evans
Brown, P. Fleming, Cook, Evans, C Fleming, Futcher, Barr, Butler, McPhillips (Richardson), Fyfe, Graham
Att: 3,242

Group: 18 August 1990 v Hull City (a) 2–2
McPhillips, C. Fleming
Brown, P. Fleming, Cook, Evans, C. Fleming, Futcher, Hall, Butler (Richardson), McPhillips, Fyfe, Graham
Att: 1,288

Final: 11 September 1990 v Rotherham United (a) 3–2 aet
P. Fleming, Richardson, Broadbent
Brown, P. Fleming, Cook, Evans, C. Fleming, Futcher, Butler, Richardson, McPhillips (Broadbent), Fyfe (Hall), Graham
Att: 4,095

Group B	P	W	D	L	F	A	Pts
Halifax Town	3	2	1	0	4	2	7
Leeds United	3	2	0	1	7	2	6
Hull City	3	1	2	0	5	4	5
Bradford City	3	1	1	1	2	2	4
Lincoln City	3	1	1	1	5	6	4
Grimsby Town	3	0	2	1	1	2	2
Whitby Town	3	0	2	1	3	6	2
Scarborough	3	0	1	2	2	5	1

1993–94

Group: 31 July 1993 v Grimsby Town (a) 0–0
Bracey, German, Hardy, Barr, Lucketti, Rathbone, Peake, Ridings (Hook), Filson, Paterson, Craven
Att: 491

Group: 3 August 1993 v Scarborough (h) 3–1
Peake, Ridings, Barr
Bracey, Barr, Hardy, Edwards, Filson, Lucketti, Peake (Circuit), Ridings, Constable, Paterson, Timmons (Cameron)
Att: 680

Group: 7 August 1993 v Hull City (h) 2–1
Cameron, Constable
Bracey, Barr, Craven, Edwards, Filson (German), Lucketti, Peake, Constable (Circuit), Ridings, Paterson, Cameron
Att: 873

Final: 7 September 1993 v Bradford City (a) 4–2
Constable, Blake (og), Saunders, Paterson
Heyes, Megson (Ridings), Barr, Edwards, Lucketti, Constable, Peake, Saunders, Hanson, Paterson, Craven (Hardy)
Att: 1,993

Group A	P	W	D	L	F	A	Pts
Halifax Town	3	2	1	0	5	2	7
Hull City	3	1	1	1	3	3	4
Grimsby Town	3	0	2	1	0	1	2
Scarborough	3	0	2	1	2	4	2

1994–95

Group: 30 July 1994 v Barnsley (a) 0–4
Wilmot, Fleming, Prindiville, Jones, Boardman, Langley, Leitch (Paterson), Lambert, Grayson (Hanson), Flounders, Kiwomya
Att: 1,250

Group: 2 August 1994 v Doncaster Rovers (h) 0–0
Heyes, German, Prindiville, Jones, Boardman, Langley, Leitch (Sunley), Lambert, Grayson (Hanson), Flounders, Paterson
Att: 597

Group: 5 August 1994 v Hull City (a) 1–2
Hanson
Heyes, German, Prindiville, Hook, Boardman (Fowler), Langley, Paterson, Lambert, Hanson, Flounders, Kiwomya (Leitch)
Att: 1,501

Group A	P	W	D	L	F	A	Pts
Hull City	3	2	1	0	8	4	7
Barnsley	3	1	2	0	8	4	5
Doncaster Rovers	3	0	2	1	1	4	2
Halifax Town	3	0	1	2	1	6	1

WEST RIDING COUNTY CUP
1995–96
Second Round: 5 December 1995 v Ossett Town (h) 5–1
O'Regan, Midwood 3, Johnson
Woods, Smith, Annan, O'Regan, Stoneman, Trotter, Hendrick (Brown), Cochrane (Johnson), Midwood, Worthington, Thompson (Brook)
Att: 250

Third round: 14 February 1996 v Farsley Celtic (a) 0–1
Heyes, Smith, Annan, O'Regan, Stoneman, Trotter, Lee, Hendrick, Midwood (Benn), Brook, Cochrane (Beddard)
Att: 211

1996–97
First round: 4 November v Harrogate Railway (h) 1–2 aet
Trotter
Gibson (Woods), Hand, Mudd, O'Regan, Cox, Trotter, Horsfield, Worthington (Place), Norbury (Griffiths), Brook, McInerney
Att: 187

1997–98
First round: 11 November 1997 v Guiseley (a) 0–1
Woods, Hand, Bradshaw (Griffiths), Rosser, Kilcline, Boardman, Place, Horner, Midwood, Paterson (Hamlet), Hurst
Att: 580

2002–03
First round: 5 November 2002 v Ossett Albion (h) 3–0
Fitzpatrick 2, Haigh
Morgan Wood, Grayston, Bushell, Heinemann, Haigh, Herbert, Senior, Ryan, Clamp (Summerscales), Fitzpatrick (Agar)
Att: 335

Second round: 10 December 2002 v Ossett Town (a) 2–1
Quinn, Parke
Poole, Grayston, Heinemann, Senior, Kerrigan, Quinn, Herbert, Clarkson, Ryan (Toulson), Parke, Golden (Summerscales)
Att: 320

Third round: 11 February 2003 v Harrogate Town (h) 1–2
Monington
Morgan, Asher (Fitzpatrick), Grayston, Senior, Quinn, Monington, Shaw (Midgley), McAuley, Ryan (Sandwith), Farrell, Beresford
Att: 430

2003–04
Second round: 2 December 2003 v Yorkshire Amateur (a) 4–1
McSweeney, Farrell 2, Dudgeon
Parry, Wilder, McAuley, Senior, Mierswinski, Dudgeon, McSweeney (Agar), Hockenhull, Farrell, Allan (Clamp), Sagare (Golden)
Att: 96

Third round: 18 February 2004 v Bradford Park Avenue (a) 3–1
Quinn, Donaldson, Mallon
Parry, McAuley, Senior, Colley, Quinn, Hockenhull, Hudson, Donaldson (Hoyle), Allan (Naylor), Mallon
Att: 382

Semi–final: 16 March 2004 v Goole AFC (a) 1–0
Allan
Parry, Yates, Naylor, Senior (Maslak), Lee, Hockenhull, Mallon, Hudson, Allan, Farrell (Golden), Midgley
Att: 317

Final: 14 April 2004 v Farsley Celtic 2–1
Allan, Quinn
Parry, Yates, Naylor, Senior, Quinn, Stoneman, Mallon, Hudson, Allan, Farrell (Toulson), Midgley (Hockenhull)
Att: 537
Played at Woodlesford, Leeds

2004–05
Second round: 30 November 2004 v Goole AFC (a) 2–1
Naylor, Small
Parry, Toulson, Naylor, Maslak, Stoneman, Clarke (O'Brien), Chin (Kerridge), Tuck, Hoyle, Mallon (Small), Golden
Att: 205

Third round: 2 February 2005 v Silsden (a) 5–0
Midgley 2, Meechan 2, Tuck
Parry, Toulson, Naylor, Maslak, Stoneman, Monington (O'Brien), Midgley, Blunt, Meechan (Tuck), Ross (Hoyle), Golden
Att: 763

Semi–final: 10 March 2005 v Ossett Albion (a) 3–0
Meechan, Toulson, Ross
Parry, O'Brien, Cockerill, Blunt, Stoneman, Monington (Hoyle), Chin, Toulson, Tuck, Meechan, Ross
Att: 200

Final: 13 April 2005 v Guiseley 0–1
Gawthorne, O'Brien (Tuck), Cockerill, Toulson, Stoneman, Clarke, Meechan, Chin, Ross, Mansaram, Howell
Att: 465
Played at Woodlesford, Leeds

2005–06
Second round: 6 December 2005 v Tadcaster Albion (a) 5–1
Senior 4, Tuck
Butler, Salm, Doughty (Wdowczyk), Jacobs (Stevens), Toulson, Young, Tuck, Leister, Senior, Midgley, Bowler (Swann)
Att: 270

Third round: 31 January 2006 v Harrogate Town (a) 1–4 aet
Tuck
Gawthorne, Salm, Wdowczyk, Bushell (O'Hare), Yates, Young (Howes), Tuck, Jacobs, Toulson, Midgley (Stevens), Bowler
Att: 310

2006–07
First round: 31 October 2006 v Tadcaster Albion (h) 7–2
Smeltz 3, Senior 2, Torpey, Gray
Hedge, Toulson, Doughty (Haslam), Gray, Quinn, Wright, Forrest (Uhlenbeek), Jacobs, Smeltz, Senior, Torpey
Scorers:
Att: 183

Second round: 28 November 2006 v Pontefract Collieries (h) 14–3
Sugden 4, Senior 3, Jacobs, Foster 2 (1 pen), Smeltz 3, Rawnsley
Butler, Haslam, Doughty (Rawnsley), Jacobs, Toulson, Bleau, Uhlenbeek (Sherrife), Foster, Sugden, Forest (Smeltz), Senior
Att: 231
Halifax Town expelled from competition for fielding ineligible player

2007–08
Second round : 2 December 2007 v Farsley Celtic (a) 1–0
Killeen
Mawson, Scott, Wright, Heslop (Bushell), Atherton, Young, Gray, Griffith, Toulson, Killeen, Torpey
Att: 472

Third round: 6 February 2008 v Ossett Albion (h) 4–1
Campbell, Gray, Stamp, Killeen
Mawson, Harban, Bailey (Sharpe), Kearney, O'Callaghan (Ainge), Atherton, Killeen, Gray, Stamp, Campbell (Griffith), Torpey
Att: 174
Halifax Town expelled from competition for fielding ineligible players

FC HALIFAX TOWN

West Riding County Cup
2008–09
First round: 28 October 2008 v Wakefield FC (a) 0–1
Ellison, King, Jemson, Meadowcroft, Adams, J. Smith, J. Brown (Barras), Phelan, Stott, Daniel, Hinsley
Att: 140

2009–10
First round: 2 November 2009 v Harrogate Railway Athletic (a) 1–0
Sanasy
Hedge, Hotte, Codman, Aspin, Riley, Richardson, Peers, Phelan, Sanasy, Harrison, Marshall
Att: 87

Second round: 9 December 2009 v Farsley Celtic (a) 1–2
Sanasy
Senior, Carney, Richardson, Hotte, Aspin (J. Smith), Sykes, Peers, Keris, Heffernan, Fry, Sanasy
Att: 139

2010–11
First round: 2 November 2010 v Ossett Town (a) 5–0
Metcalfe 3, Gray, Taylor
Senior (Dean), Riley, Lowe, Garner, Bower, Plummer, Gray, Phelan (Hedge), Taylor, Marshall, Metcalfe
Att: 90

Second round: 14 December 2010 v Barnoldswick United (a) 5–0
Marshall 3, S. Hogan, Phelan
Senior, Hardy, Heffernan, Garner (Hedge), Riley, Lowe, Taylor, Phelan, S. Hogan, Marshall, Metcalfe
Att: 100

Third round: 1 February 2011 v Harrogate Railway Athletic (a) 3–2
Holland, Phelan, S. Hogan
Senior, Eastwood, Heffernan, Milne, Riley, Aspin (Phelan), Marshall, Nogan S. Hogan, Holland, Jones
Att: 118

Semi-final: 8 March 2011 v Guiseley (a*) 1–3
Phelan (pen)
Senior, Eastwood, Heffernan, Milne, Riley, Jones, Coduri, Phelan (Mead), S. Hogan, Gregory (Keris), Metcalfe
Att: 235
* Home tie switched to Nethermoor, Guiseley

President's Cup
2008–09
First round: 23 September 2008 v Ossett Albion (a) 4–3
Ellis, Jemson, Davidson 2
Senior, Hinsley, C. Smith, Payne, Adams, Morning (Moore), Hilton (M. Smith), Phelan, Sugden (Davidson), Jemson, Ellis
Att: 248

Second round: 11 November 2008 v Sheffield FC (h) 3–1
J. Brown, Ellis, Stott
Ellison, Coo, King (J. Brown), Adams, Barras, Hinsley, Gill (Phelan), Baker, Stott, J. Smith (Gedman), Ellis
Att: 382

Third round: 16 December 2008 v Retford Town (h) 0–2
Kennedy, Coo, Collins, Sutton, Meadowcroft, Adams, Baker (Stott), Phelan, Ellis, Gedman, Allen
Att: 295

2009–10
Preliminary round: 8 September 2009 v Wakefield FC (h) 1–0 aet
J. Dean
Senior, Wood (Hardy), Lowe, Hotte, Riley, Codman, Roberts (Baker), Phelan, J. Dean, Jerome (Stringer), Marshall
Att: 422

First round: 13 October 2009 v Ossett Albion (h) 3–1
J. Dean, Marshall 2
Senior, Hardy, Codman, Hotte, Riley, Penford (Marshall), Peers, Sanasy (Gray), J. Dean, Baker (Phelan), Harrison
Att: 439

MINOR CUPS

Second round: 17 November 2009 v Mossley (h) 2–1
Peers, J. Dean
Senior, Gray, Richardson, Hotte, Crossley (Riley), Lowe, Peers, Phelan (Harrison), J. Dean, Baker, Sanasy (J. Smith)
Att: 410

Third round: 8 December 2009 v Stamford (a) 1–2 aet
Marshall
Hedge, Hardy, Lowe, Payne, Riley, Sykes (Peers), Gray, Phelan, J. Dean (Sanasy), Baker, Marshall
Att: 168

CHAIRMAN'S CUP
2009–10

Semi-final v Mickleover Sports (h) 2–2
Marshall, Hedge
Senior, Hotte, Richardson, Hardy, Riley (Gray), Sykes, Peers, Phelan, J. Dean (Hedge), Marshall, Lowe
Att: 427

Mickleover Sports won 3–1 on penalties
Penalty sequence: Sykes missed (0–0), Hotte missed (0–1), Hedge scored (1–2), Senior missed (1–3)

UNIBOND LEAGUE CHALLENGE CUP
2008–09

First round: 30 September 2008 v Wakefield FC (h) 2–1
Stott 2
Kennedy, Coo, C. Smith, Adams, Barras (Hinsley), Morning, J. Smith, Phelan, Stott, Davidson, Ellis (Moore)
Att: 335

Second round: 18 October 2008 v Curzon Ashton (h) 1–2
Phelan
Kennedy, Moore, King (Hinsley), Adams, Meadowcroft, Jemson, Phelan, Baker, Stott, Daniel, J. Smith (Ellis)
Att: 697

2009–10

First round: 22 September 2009 v Garforth Town (a) 1–0
Whitehouse
Senior, Wood, Codman, Hotte, Riley, Hardy, Peers (Gray), Phelan, Marshall (Smith), Harrison (Ross), Whitehouse
Att: 152

Second round: 27 October 2009 v Ossett Albion (h) 2–0
J. Dean 2
Senior, Wood, Richardson, Hotte, Riley, Penford (Hardy), Gray, Phelan, Sanasy (J. Dean), Marshall, Harrison
Att: 401

Third round: 24 November 2009 v Durham City (a) 4–2
Riley 2, Sanasy, J. Smith
Hedge, Peers, Codman, Hotte, Riley, Sykes, Richardson (Gray), Phelan, J. Smith, Baker, Marshall (Sanasy)
Att: 125

Fourth round: 26 January 2010 v North Ferriby United (h) 1–1 aet
Richardson
Senior, Hardy, Codman, Hotte, Crossley, Lowe, Peers (Carney), Richardson, Heffernan (Kerris), Fry, Marshall (Gray)
FC Halifax Town won 3–1 on penalties
Att: 387

Semi-final: 9 February 2010 v Boston United (a) 2–5
J. Dean, Parker (og)
Hedge, Carney (J. Dean), Codman, Hotte, Riley, Lowe, Peers, Phelan, Gray (Winter), Fry (Hardy), Richardson
Att: 559

EVO-STIK LEAGUE CHALLENGE CUP
2010–11

Third round: 3 January 2011 v Bradford Park Avenue (a) 3–0
Holland, Gregory, Phelan
Hedge, Hardy, Lowe, Garner (Phelan), Riley, Milne, Taylor, Marshall, Gregory (Dean), Holland, S. Hogan
Att: 245
Halifax Town expelled for fielding ineligible player

FRIENDLIES

1911–12
20 February 1912   v Huddersfield Town (h) 2–0
Farrar, Fyfe

1912–13
3 September 1912   v Bradford City (h) 2–3
Simons 2
Att: 500

1913–14
18 October 1913   v Huddersfield Town Reserves (h) 2–3
Blackburn, Wild (pen)

7 March 1914   v Hebden Bridge (a) 6–2
Pentland (pen), Cannon 4, Beevers

1914–15
17 October 1914   v Port Vale (a) 2–1
Crowther 2
24 October 1914   v Bradford City (h) 0–0

1915–16
25 September 1915   v Bradford City Reserves (h) 2–0
Potter (og), Brooksbank
2 October 1915   v York City (h) 3–0
Wild (pen), Brooksbank, Roscoe
16 October 1915   v York City (a) 1–0
Longbottom
6 November 1915   v 1st Lincolnshire Garrison Regiment (h) 3–0
Lounds 2, Wild
22 January 1916   v York City (h) 5–1
Wild, Islip, Beevers 2, Marsland
19 February 1916   v Great Harwood (h) 2–2
Barron, Marsland
5 March 1916   v 5th Reserve Cavalry Regiment (h) 3–1
Wild 2, Marsland
26 March 1916   v Royal Engineers (h) 2–1
Roscoe, Barraclough

1919–20
3 January 1920   v Yorkshire Amateur (h) 3–1
Birtwhistle (pen), Wild, E. Smith
10 April 1920   v Leeds United (h) 1–1
Robinson
Att: 1,500

1920–21
2 October 1920   v Harrogate (h) 6–0
Jenkinson 3, Woolgar 3
28 March 1921   v Harrogate (a) 0–3

1921–22
3 December 1921   v Barnsley (h) 1–3
Linley
Att: 2,000
4 May 1922   v Doncaster Rovers (a) 4–2
Wild, Wellock (pen), Hillam 2

1924–25
3 September 1924   v Leeds United 1–0
Scorer: Shankly
Att: 2,000
Played at Altofts, Leeds

1925–26
20 March 1926   v Carlisle United (a) 0–1
Att: 4,578
17 April 1926   v Motherwell (h) 0–2

1926–27
27 April 1927   v Bury (h) 2–2
Dixon, Seabrook
(Bob Suter Benefit match)

1930–31
11 September 1930   v Boothtown (a) 1–3
Betteridge

1931–32
6 February 1932   v Rhyl Athletic (h) 2–1
Davies 2
Att: 2,000
20 April 1932   v Scarborough (a) 1–1
Mays

FRIENDLIES

1934–35
15 April 1935   v Macclesfield Town (a) 2–4
Mercer 2
Att: 2,549

1937–38
12 February 1938   v Everton (h) 1–1
Griffiths
Att: 6,594

1938–39
Both matches in aid of the Jubilee Fund
20 August 1938   v Rochdale (h) 4–1
Widdowfield 2, Foulkes 2
Att: 4,000
23 August 1938   v Rochdale (a) 1–5
Mason

1939–40
19 August 1939   v Rochdale (a) 1–3
Barkas
Match in aid of the Jubilee Fund
16 September 1939   v Leeds United (h) 3–2
Barkas, Widdowfield, Green
Att: 750
23 September 1939   v Bradford City (h) 3–3
Barkas, Widdowfield 2 (1 pen)
30 September 1939   v Sheffield United (h) 1–1
Baines
Att: 4,000
7 October 1939   v Oldham Athletic (h) 1–1
Worthington
14 October 1939   v Barnsley (a) 2–1
Widdowfield, Baines
4 November 1939   v Chesterfield (h) 0–2
16 December 1939   v Chesterfield (a) 1–1
Barkas
30 December 1939   v Sheffield Wednesday (h) 0–0
22 March 1940   v Accrington Stanley (a) 2–5
Scorers unknown
25 March 1940   v Bradford (L) 2–1
Wood, Barkas
30 March 1940   v Accrington Stanley (h) 3–1
Baines 2, Widdowfield
27 April 1940   v Stockport County (h) 4–0
Wrigglesworth, Baines, Wood (pen), Topping (og)

1940–41
24 August 1940   v Army X1 (h) 2–2
Widdowfield, Hogg
7 December 1940   v Royal Air Force X1 (h) 1–3
Hogg
28 December 1940   v Bolton Wanderers (h) 4–1
Widdowfield, Wood, Barkas 2

1948–49
8 January 1949   v Rochdale (h) 2–1
Scott 2

1949–50
10 December 1949   v Bristol City (h) 1–1
Whittingham
7 January 1950   v Bristol City (a) 0–4

1950–51
9 December 1950   v Bradford City (h) 5–0
Murphy, Massey, Dale, Tomlinson, Young
Att: 2,000
12 May 1951   v Waterford United (h) 11–2
Dale 3, Priestley 3, Moss 2, Hughes 2, Mycock
Att: 3,500
Festival of Britain match

1951–52
15 December 1951   v Bournemouth & Boscombe Athletic (a) 2–2
Hindle, Priestley
Att: 5,151

1953–54
20 October 1953   v Ashton United (a) 3–0
Rickett, Murphy, Horsman
Att: 2,000

1956–57
8 December 1956   v Shrewsbury Town (a) 1–4
Shore

1961–62
5 August 1961   v Huddersfield Town (h) 3–4
Redfearn 2, Burgess
12 August 1961   v Huddersfield Town (a) 1–4
Burgess
16 November 1961   v Belgrade SV 1–1
Large
Att: 10,005
24 November 1961   v Darlington (h) 3–2
Hopper 2, Barnett

1962–63

7 August 1962	v Huddersfield Town (h) 5–2 Holden, Tait 2, Hopper 2 Att: 2,530
13 August 1962	v Barnsley (a) 2–6 Tait, Roscoe (pen) Att: 3,697

1963–64

20 August 1963	v Scarborough (a) 3–1 Bingley (pen), Field, Taylor

1964–65

11 August 1964	v Goole Town (a) 4–1 Twist, Carlin 2 (1 pen), Howard
15 August 1964	v Scarborough (a) 5–2 Westlake 3, Field, Carlin

1965–66

7 August 1965	v Oldham Athletic (h) 3–5 Bambridge, Fidler 2 (1 pen) Att: 1,000
10 August 1965	v Bury (h) 1–2 Fidler (pen) Att: 1,000
16 Aug	v Scarborough (a) 1–0 Bambridge Att: 868

1966–67

8 August 1966	v Bradford (h) 2–0 Wooler, Atkins Att: 1,332
10 August 1966	v Huddersfield Town (h) 1–0 Wooler Played behind closed doors
12 August 1966	v Bradford (a) 0–2 Att: 2,039

1967–68

7 August 1967	v Barrow (a) 1–2 Shawcross (pen)
9 August 1967	v Ipswich Town (h) 2–0 Wooler 2
14 August 1967	v Goole Town (a) 5–1 McCarthy, Wallace, Wooler 3
9 April 1968	v Go-Ahead Deventer (Holland) 0–1 Att: 3,592

1968–69

31 July 1968	v Scarborough (a) 0–2
3 August 1968	v Ayr United (a) 2–2 Scorers: Massie, Ryden
20 May 1969	v US Namur (Belgium) (a) 1–1 Flower
24 May 1969	v Havange (France) (a) 3–0 Flower, Wallace, Robertson
26 May 1969	v Jeunesse (Luxembourg) (a) 2–1 Massie, Lawther

1969–70

27 July 1969	v Drogheda (a) 2–1 Wallace, Massie
29 July 1969	v Drumcondra (a) 3–0 Lawther 2, Robertson
31 July 1969	v Derry City (a) 4–1 Flower 4
2 August 1969	v Stranraer (a) 2–2 Wallace, Massie
3 January 1970	v Port Vale (a) 1–1 Verity
19 January 1970	v Sunderland (h) 4–0 Shawcross 3, Flower Att: 2,481
24 January 1970	v Bolton Wanderers (h) 0–2 Att: 3,520
5 May 1970	v Ross County (a) 3–0 Lawther 3
7 May 1970	v Elgin City (a) 3–1 McBeth (pen), Atkins, Chadwick
8 May 1970	v Inverness Thistle (a) 3–2 Atkins, Chadwick, Lawther

1970–71

1 August 1970	v Morton (h) 2–1 McCarthy (pen), Roberston Att: 2,048
3 August 1970	v Montrose (h) 2–0 McCarthy, Atkins Att: 979
8 August 1970	v Altrincham (a) 1–0 Brierley Att: 1,542
10 August 1970	v Hyde United (a) 3–1 Lawther, Riordon, Swain (pen) Att: 450

1971–72

25 July 1971	v Drogheda (a) 1–1 Atkins

FRIENDLIES

27 July 1971	v Dundalk (a) 3–3 Lennard 2, Chadwick
20 September 1971	v North Shields (a) 4–0 Wallace, Robertson, Lennard, Verity

1972–73

26 July 1972	v Barnsley (a) 0–0 Played behind closed doors
29 July 1972	v Arbroath (h) 2–0 Kemp, Waddle
31 July 1972	v Crook Town (a) 1–3 Mulhall
2 August 1972	v Arbroath (a) 1–0 Waddle
5 August 1972	v Cowdenbeath (a) 2–0 Kemp 2 Att: 800
30 October 1972	v St Just (a) 7–1 Robertson 2, Lee, Atkins, Pickering, Quinn, Smith
6 November 1972	v Blyth Spartans (a) 2–4 Swaine, Ewart (og)
10 January 1973	v Sheffield Wednesday (a) 0–2 Played behind closed doors

1973–74

8 August 1973	v Bury (a) 3–2 Kemp, Irvine, AN Other Played behind closed doors
13 August 1973	v Exeter City (a) 2–2 Gwyther, Kemp
15 Aug	v Newport County (a) 0–1
17 August 1973	v Bradford City (h) 1–2 Kemp Att: 1,427

1974–75

3 August 1974	v Rotherham Town (a) 1–0 Downes Att: 926
5 August 1974	v Bath City (a) 4–2 Ford, Shanahan 2 (1 pen), Gover (og)
7 August 1974	v Yeovil Town (a) 0–1
12 August 1974	v Doncaster Rovers (h) 4–0 Rhodes, Downes 2, Gwther

1975–76

2 August 1975	v Rochdale (h) 3–0 Gwyther 2, Harris Att: 891
5 August 1975	v Darlington (h) 1–1 Downes Att: 583
6 March 1976	v Orgryte IS (Norway) 2–0 G. Jones, Bullock Att: 736

1976–77

2 August 1976	v Forres Mechanics (a) 2–1 McHale, Bullock
4 August 1976	v Inverness Caledonians (a) 1–1 Harris
5 August 1976	v Elgin City (a) 1–4 Bell
7 August 1976	v Dunfermline Athletic (a) 1–2 A Jones
8 August 1976	v Hamilton Academical (a) 1–4 Bell Att: 1,000

1977–78

2 August 1977	v Oldham Athletic (h) 0–5 Att: 846
6 August 1977	v Altrincham (a) 3–2 Carroll, Johnston, Brooke (og)
8 August 1977	v Bridlington Trinity (a) 2–0 Carroll, Lawson (pen)
9 August 1977	v Radcliffe Borough (a) 2–3 Bell, Carroll

1978–79

29 July 1978	v Bridlington Trinity (a) 5–1 Smith, Trainer, Carroll, Lawson, Johnston
6 August 1978	v Leeds United (a) 1–1 Carroll Played behind closed doors

1979–80

28 July 1979	v Bridlington Trinity (a) 2–1 Mountford 2
3 August 1979	v Alloa Athletic (h) 3–1 Harris, Mountford, Hendrie Att: 556
6 August 1979	v Boston United (h) 0–1 Att: 502
7 August 1979	v Nelson (a) 3–3 Johnson 2, Firth (pen)

1980–81

26 July 1980	v Scarborough (a) 1–2 Burton

28 July 1980 v Accrington Stanley (a) 1–1
Dryhurst
30 July 1980 v Nelson (a) 2–0
O'Brien (og), Evans
2 August 1980 v Macclesfield Town (a) 1–0
Allatt
14 August 1980 v Bradley Rangers (a) 0–9

1981–82
1 August 1981 v Bridlington Trinity (a) 2–0
Hendrie, Carr
5 August 1981 v Nelson (a) 3–0
Bullock 2, Allatt
10 August 1981 v Cliftonville (h) 4–0
Graham, Hendrie, Allatt,
Bullock
Att: 2,000
15 August 1981 v Huddersfield Town (h) 0–3
Att: 2,906
18 August 1981 v Bradley Rangers (a) 5–0
Allatt 3, Graham (pen),
Bullock

1982–83
2 August 1982 v Mossley (a) 2–1
Davison, Evans
Att: 300
4 August 1982 v Nelson (a) 0–0
6 August 1982 v Bradley Rangers 5–1
Davison 2, Hallybone 2,
Staniforth
Att: 300
Played at Old Earth, Elland
10 August 1982 v Harrogate Town (a) 0–0
10 December 1982 v Manchester United (h) 2–3
Staniforth, Allatt
Att: 1,090

1983–84
26 July 1983 v Nelson (a) 4–0
Mell 2, Staniforth, Evans
28 July 1983 v Morecambe (a) 2–0
Smith, Ward
1 August 1983 v Bradley Rangers (a) 2–0
Ward, B. Gallagher
3 August 1983 v Harrogate Town (a) 4–0
Cook 2, Kendall, Hanson
Att: 150
5 August 1983 v Mossley (a) 2–3
Mell, Cook
8 August 1983 v Newcastle Town (a) 1–0
B. Gallagher
20 August 1983 v Phoenix Park (a)
Result not known

1984–85
1 August 1984 v Harrogate Town (a) 6–3
Lowe 2, Cook, Ayre, Kendall,
Little
6 August 1984 v Mossley (a) 1–3
Sanderson
8 August 1984 v Newcastle Blue Star (a) 2–1
Cook, Gallagher
17 December 1984 v Emley (a) 3–1
Ward, Chippendale,
Gallagher

1985–86
25 July 1985 v Oxford United (h) 1–5
Kellock
Att: 627

1986–87
30 July 1986 v Berwick Rangers (a) 0–0
1 August 1986 v Peterlee Town (a) 2–0
Longhurst, Sanderson
4 August 1986 v Shepshed Charterhouse (a) 2–0
Longhurst 2
5 August 1986 v Northwich Victoria (a) 1–1
Robinson
6 August 1986 v Farsley Celtic (a) 2–4
W. Barr 2
18 August 1986 v Farsley Celtic (a) 1–1
Scorer: Longhurst
27 January 1987 v Frickley Athletic (a) 1–3
Longhurst
9 March 1987 v Whitby Town (a) 2–1
Martin, Diamond

1987–88
21 July 1987 v Army X1 (a) 5–1
N. Matthews 2, Ferebee,
Holden, Martin
22 July 1987 v Aldershot (a) 3–1
M. Matthews 2, Robinson
24 July 1987 v Liversedge (a) 2–1
Cunningham, Allison
29 July 1987 v Harrogate Town (a) 3–1
McPhillips 2, Simpson
30 July 1987 v Whitby Town (a) 4–1
Black 3, Martin
3 August 1987 v Ferryhill (a) 5–1
Black 3 (1 pen), Brown
(pen), Thornber

FRIENDLIES

4 August 1987	v Peterlee Town (a) 3–1 Robinson, Ferebee, Brown	24 July 1991	v Garforth Town (a) 5–0 Ellis, Norris 2 (1 pen), Graham, Paterson
1988–89		29 July 1991	v Annbank (a) 7–2 Megson, Norris 4 (1 pen), Hutchinson, Juryeff
1 August 1988	v Harrogate Town (a) 1–1 Mead		
4 August 1988	v Durham City (a) 2–1 Allison, M. Matthews	30 July 1991	v Cumnock Juniors (a) 3–1 Norris 3
6 August 1988	v Brandon United (a) 0–1	1 August 1991	v Pollock Juniors (a) 5–3 Norris 2, Juryeff 2, Richardson
7 August 1988	v Newcastle Blue Star (a) 1–1 Martin		
8 August 1988	v Hartlepool United 0–1 Played at Durham University	**1992–93**	
		27 July 1992	v Bacup Borough (a) 1–2 Richardson
1989–90		29 July 1992	v Eccleshill United (a) 5–1 Richardson, Greenwood, Kenton, Lucketti, Bradley
24 July 1989	v Harrogate Town (a) 4–0 Gardner (og), McPhillips, Richardson, Broadbent		
		3 August 1992	v Brighouse Town (a) 2–0 Evans (og), Thomas
25 July 1989	v Whitley Bay (a) 2–0 McPhillips, Matthews	8 August 1992	v Hyde United (a) 1–1 Greenwood
26 July 1989	v Newcastle Blue Star (a) 2–1 Cook, Butler	11 August 1992	v Frickley Athletic (a) 2–2 Juryeff 2
2 August 1989	v Lancaster City (a) 1–0 McPhillips (pen)	12 August 1992	v Radcliffe Borough (a) 0–2
		12 August 1992	v Bolton Wanderers (a) 0–1
3 August 1989	v Barrow (a) 0–0	12 October 1992	v Oldham Athletic (h) 1–1 Paterson Att: 1,412
10 August 1989	v Watford (a) 1–1 Wilkinson (og)		
1990–91		**1993–94**	
20 July 1990	v Tadcaster Albion (a) Result not known	26 July 1993	v Truro City (a) 1–0 Filson
28 July 1990	v Selby Town (a) 3–2 Broadbent, Martin, Fyfe Att: 212	28 July 1993	v Tavistock (a) 2–0 Cameron, Hook
		4 August 1993	v Guiseley (a) 1–2 Constable
31 July 1990	v Pollock Juniors (a) 2–1 Fyfe, Barr	10 August 1993	v Accrington Stanley (a) 3–1 Peake, Gregory, Megson
2 August 1990	v Cumnock Juniors (a) 0–0	12 August 1993	v Bamber Bridge (a) 0–1
4 August 1990	v Hamilton Academical (a) 2–0 Fyfe 2	14 August 1993	v Boston United (a) 1–0 Paterson
6 August 1990	v Bradley Rangers (a) 2–2 Scorers unknown	16 August 1993	v Curzon Ashton (a) 2–1 Hook, McLeish
7 August 1990	v Oldham Athletic (h) 0–3	28 February 1994	v Lincoln City (a) 3–0 Peake 2, Craven
20 August 1990	v Bradley Rangers (a) Result not known		
21 August 1990	v Blackburn Rovers (h) 0–1 Att: 836	14 March 1994	v Doncaster Rovers (a) 2–1 Craven, Paterson
		1994–95	
1991–92		19 July 1994	v Tavistock (a) 1–1 Fowler
20 July 1991	v Tadcaster Albion (a) 1–1 Scorer unknown	23 July 1994	v North Ferriby United (a) 1–1 Flounders

26 July 1994	v Farsley Celtic (a) 3–2 Flounders 2 (1 pen), Leitch	**1997–98**	
9 August 1994	v Harrogate Town (a) 2–0 Jones, Flounders	16 July 1997	v Lancaster City (a) 2–1 Lyons 2 (1 pen)
13 August 1994	v Gainsborough Trinity (a) 1–1 Grayson	19 July 1997	v Brighouse Town (a) 6–0 Brown, Brook 2, Griffiths, Hamlet, Bradshaw
16 August 1994	v Leeds United (a) 1–1 Flounders	23 July 1997	v Huddersfield Town (h) 2–1 Bradshaw, Midwood Att: 1,500
15 December 1994	v Tranmere Rovers (h) 0–2		
5 April 1995	v Buxton (h) 3–0 Dunphy, Johnson 2	29 July 1997	v Frickley Athletic (a) 2–3 Lyons, Brook
		1 August 1997	v Doncaster Rovers (h) 0–1
		6 August 1997	v Leeds United (h) 0–1
1995–96		11 August 1997	v Ossett Town (a) 5–1 Paterson 2, Hulme, O'Regan, Lyons
22 July 1995	v Liversedge (a) 2–5 Worthington, Prindiville		
25 July 1995	v Barnsley (h) 0–4		
29 July 1995	v Buxton (a) 4–0 Ludlow 2, Johnson, Wright	**1998–99**	
1 August 1995	v North Ferriby United (a) 2–1 O'Regan, Johnson	14 July 1998	v Brighouse Town (a) 7–0 Delaney (og), Nicholson (og), Hulme, Thackeray, Paterson, Starbuck, Duerden Att: 450
4 August 1995	v Guiseley 1–1 Ludlow Played at Otley Town	22 July 1998	v Hyde United (a) 3–1 Starbuck, Daley (og), Paterson
8 August 1995	v Harrogate Town (a) 0–0		
11 August 1995	v Leeds United (h) 0–2 Att: 1,139	25 July 1998	v Burnley (h) 3–3 Horsfield, Stoneman, Sertori Att: 2,962
1996–97		29 July 1998	v Huddersfield Town (h) 1–0 Paterson Att: 2,863
20 July 1996	v Bishop Auckland 0–0 Played at Bishop Auckland College		
27 July 1996	v Rochdale (h) 1–2 Midwood	1 August 1998	v Bradford City (a) 1–2 J. Murphy (pen) Att: 2,498
30 July 1996	v Harrogate Town (a) 4–1 Bryant (og), Davison 2, Kerr		
2 August 1996	v Bury (h) 0–1	**1999–00**	
7 August 1996	v Mossley (a) 3–1 Cochrane, Critchley (og), Kerr (pen)	13 July 1999	v Brighouse Town (a) 1–3 Jackson
10 August 1996	v Guiseley (a) 2–1 Norbury, Horner	16 July 1999	v Grimsby Town (h) 3–0 Painter, Jackson, Power, Att: 1,106
12 August 1996	v Stockport County (h) 0–1	21 July 1999	v Manchester City (h) 0–2
24 October 1996	v Sheffield Wednesday Reserves (h) 2–1 O'Regan, Norbury (pen)	26 July 1999	v Grantham Town (a) 3–0 Power 3
25 January 1997	v Chester City (h) 2–0 Hulme, Davison	27 July 1999	v Sunderland (h) 1–0 Tate George Mulhall Testimonial
Mar 12 1997	v Brighouse Town (h) 4–1 Lyons 2, Hamlet, Worthington (pen)	29 July 1999	v Emley (a) 3–0 Jackson, M. Clarke, Tate
21 March 1997	v Derby County Reserves (h) 2–1 Worthington 2	31 July 1999	v Ossett Town (a) 2–0 M. Clarke, Power

FRIENDLIES

3 August 1999	v Morecambe (a) 3–2 Hulme, Jackson, Gaughan
3 May 2000	v Sheffield Wednesday (a) 1–0 M. Clarke

2000–01

13 July 2000	v Brighouse Town (a) 6–0 M. Clarke 2, Fitzpatrick (pen), Jules, Bradshaw, Herbert
15 July 2000	v Ripon City (a) 9–0 Painter, Kerrigan 3, Reilly (pen), M. Clarke, Underwood 2, Holt
18 July 2000	v Guiseley (a) 0–0
19 July 2000	v Whitby Town (a) 2–2 Fitzpatrick, Kerrigan
21 July 2000	v North Ferriby United (a) 3–2 Jones 3
24 July 2000	v Longford Town 3–0 Bradshaw, Stansfield, Jones Played at Shelbourne
26 July 2000	v Waterford United (a) 1–0 Kerrigan
28 July 2000	v Kilkenny City (a) 0 6–1 Kerrigan 4, Jones, Potter
31 July 2000	v Worksop Town (a) 2–5 Stoneman, Herbert
1 August 2000	v Emley 0–0 Played at Belle Vue, Wakefield
7 August 2000	v Bradford Park Avenue (a) 1–0 Holt
22 November 2000	v Huddersfield Town (a) 1–2 Armstrong (og) Played behind closed doors
20 January 2001	v Huddersfield Town (a) 1–1 Rezai Played behind closed doors
11 April 2001	v Huddersfield Town (a) 2–1 Potter, Fitzpatrick Played behind closed doors

2001–02

21 July 2001	v Manchester City (h) 1–2 Roberts Att: 3,041
24 July 2001	v Huddersfield Town (h) 0–2 Att: 1,717
28 July 2001	v Raith Rovers (a) 0–1 Att: 869
31 July 2001	v Bolton Wanderers (h) 0–1 Att: 1,150
4 August 2001	v Northwich Victoria (a) 1–1 Midgley
7 August 2001	v Brighouse Town (a) 0–1
15 August 2001	v Middlesbrough (a) 1–0 Wood Played behind closed doors
26 November 2001	v Sheffield Wednesday (a) 2–1 Midgley, Jones

2002–03

16 July 2002	v Bradford City 1–2 Ward Played at Apperley Bridge
18 July 2002	v Huddersfield Town 0–2 Played at Storthes Hall
24 July 2002	v York City 1–2 Ward Played at Durham City
1 August 2002	v Barnsley (a) 0–0 Played behind closed doors
3 August 2002	v Sheffield United (h) 2–0 Midgley, Ward Att: 651
6 August 2002	v Mansfield Town (h) 0–1 Played behind closed doors
13 August 2002	v Leeds United (h) 2–3 Midgley, Fitzpatrick Att: 3,248
26 September 2002	v Doncaster Rovers (a) 1–1 Smith Played behind closed doors
12 November 2002	v Oldham Athletic (h) 0–2 Played behind closed doors

2003–04

12 July 2003	v Farsley Celtic (a) 2–1 Midgley, Killeen Att: 500
19 July 2003	v Huddersfield Town (h) 2–3 Mallon, Hudson Att: 2,183
24 July 2003	v Bolton Wanderers (h) 2–1 Farrell, Cullen Att: 959
30 Jul 2003	v Stockport County (h) 1–3 Parke Att: 653
2 August 2003	v Staveley Miners Welfare (a) 6–0 Farrell, Cullen 2 (1 pen), Parke, Hindley (pen), Killeen
6 August 2003	v Middlesbrough (h) 0–3 Att: 1,221

2004–05

14 July 2004	v Brighouse Town (a) 1–1
	Mallon
16 July 2004	v Bellingham (a) 4–2
	Lee 4
21 July 2004	v Wakefield & Emley (a) 4–3
	Killeen 3, Midgley
24 July 2004	v Farsley Celtic (a) 1–1
	Midgley (pen)
27 July 2004	v Wigan Athletic (h) 0–3
	Att: 686
31 July 2004	v Scunthorpe United (h) 0–3
	Att: 576
2 August 2004	v Grimsby Town (h) 1–1
	Midgley
	Att: 485
4 August 2004	v Frickley Athletic (a) 3–3
	Hoyle 2, Golden
7 August 2004	v Garforth Town (a) 2–3
	Ingram, Hoyle
11 August 2004	v Liversedge (a) 4–1
	Stoneman, Toulson, Hoyle, Adam
25 October 2004	v Sheffield Wednesday Reserves (a) 2–2
	Mansaram, Midgley
	Played behind closed doors

2005–06

13 July 2005	v Brighouse Town (a) 4–2
	Sugden, Mansaram, Midgley (pen), Tamm
16 July 2005	v Bradford City (h) 1–2
	Midgley
	Att: 1,421
21 July 2005	v Leeds United (h) 0–2
	Att: 1,424
30 July 2005	v Chesterfield (h) 2–2
	Atherton, Sugden (pen)
	Att: 593
5 August 2005	v Stocksbridge Park Steels (a) 2–1
	Midgley, Leister

2006–07

19 July 2006	v Brighouse Town (a) 5–2
	Senior, Melo, Thompson, Killeen, Forrest
	Att: 400
22 July 2006	v Wakefield FC (a) 4–1
	Smeltz, Foster, Sugden, Killeen
29 July 2006	v Barnsley (h) 0–1
1 August 2006	v FC United of Manchester (h) 2–4
	Prince, Forrest
4 August 2006	v Wigan Athletic (h) 1–2
	Campbell
	Att: 1,330
25 September 2006	v Wigan Athletic (a) 1–5
	Senior
	Played behind closed doors
21 November 2006	v Doncaster Rovers (a) 0–1
	Played behind closed doors
29 January 2007	v Sheffield Wednesday (a) 3–1
	Stamp, Forrest, Vickers
	Played behind closed doors

2007–08

14 July 2007	v Sheffield Wednesday (h) 0–3
	Att: 2,227
17 July 2007	v Rotherham United 1–0
	Stamp
	Played behind closed doors at Hooton Lodge
21 July 2007	v Livingston (a) 0–3
24 July 2007	v Hamilton Academical (a) 3–2
	Winters, Stamp, Torpey
28 July 2007	v Wigan Athletic (h) 0–4
	Att: 1,166
1 August 2007	v Bradford Park Avenue (a) 0–0
4 August 2007	v Bradford City (h) 0–1
	Att: 1,449

2008–09

19 July 2008	v Tamworth (a) 0–2
	Att: 618
22 July 2008	v Bury (h) 0–1
	Att: 1,063
26 July 2008	v Alsager Town (a) 2–0
	Hunter, Buckley
29 July 2008	v Alfreton Town (a) 1–6
	Ross
	Att: 204
2 August 2008	v Ashton United (a) 0–1
7 August 2008	v Guiseley (a) 0–1
9 August 2008	v Ossett Albion (a) 2–0
	Payne, Stott

FRIENDLIES

2009–10

11 July 2009	v Brighouse Town (a) 5–1	
	Gray, J. Dean, Baker, Phelan (pen), N. McDonald	
	Att: 500	
16 July 2009	v Oldham Athletic (h) 2–1	
	Peers, M. McDonald	
	Att: 836	
18 July 2009	v Accrington Stanley (h) 1–3	
	J. Dean	
	Att: 617	
21 July 2009	v Farsley Celtic (a) 3–1	
	J. Dean, Marshall, Sykes	
25 July 2009	v Stalybridge Celtic (a) 0–0	
1 August 2009	v York City (h) 3–1	
	Marshall, Dean, Crossley	
	Att: 854	
8 August 2009	v North Ferriby United (a) 1–3	
	Peers	

2010–11

17 July 2010	v Brighouse Town (a) 5–0
	Holland, Taylor 4
24 July 2010	v Droylsden (h) 0–0
	Att: 646
31 July 2010	v Hyde United (a) 1–1
	Holland (pen)
	Att: 401
3 August 2010	v Gateshead (h) 0–0
	Att: 474
7 August 2010	v Grimsby Town (h) 1–2
	Taylor. Att: 777
10 August 2010	v Clitheroe (a) 3–2
	Taylor, Phelan, Gray
14 August 2010	v Trafford (a) 2–0
	Vardy, Garner

BENEFITS AND TESTIMONIALS

Sid Hetherington
3 May 1923, Halifax Town 3 Football League X1 2, Att: 2,000

George Wild
29 April 1924, Halifax Town 0 George Wild X1 3

Johnny Whalley
21 April 1926, Halifax Town 2

Bob Suter
27 April 1927, Halifax Town 2 Bury 2

Ben Wheelhouse
18 April 1932, Halifax Town 2 Huddersfield Town 2, Att: 2,000

Edward Davies
1 October 1934, Halifax Town 3 Sheffield Wednesday 5, Att: 3,000 (£104)

Frank Betteridge
27 April 1936, Halifax Town 2 Leeds United 2, Att: 2,000 (£83 19s 6d)

Ted Craig
29 April 1939, Halifax Town 3 Everton 3, Att: 4,000

Ted Rayner
30 April 1951, Halifax Town 2 Ted Rayner X1 4, Att: 1,000

Dave Mycock
1 May 1952, Halifax Town v Halifax RLFC (first-half football 1–1, second-half rugby 15–15), Att: 6,000

Dave McCormick & Ted Breaks
27 April 1955, Halifax Town 4 Football League X1 10, Att: 2,000

Arthur Johnson & Stan Lonsdale
5 May 1960, Halifax Town 3 International X1 6, Att: 3,000

Jeff Lee
27 November 1972, Halifax Town 4 Preston North End 3, Att: 849

Tony Geidmintis
12 May 1981, Halifax Town X1 0 Everton 0

Billy Ayre
5 August 1987, Halifax Town v Halifax RLFC (first-half football 3–1, second-half rugby 20–32), Att: 445

George Mulhall
27 July 1999, Halifax Town 1 Sunderland 0

Paul Stoneman
7 May 2005, Halifax Town 4 Paul Stoneman X1 5

Tommy Gildert (physio)
19 March 2006, Halifax Town X1 11 Celebrity X1 4

Halifax Town Players

Surname	Forenames	Born	Died	From
Abbott	Gregory Stephen	Coventry 14/12/1963		Bradford City Jul 1991
Ackroyd	John			Norland Apr 1915
Adams	Edward Fairclough	Anfield 30/11/1906	28/11/1991	Burnley guest Feb 1940
Adams	Harold			Wath Athletic Dec 1913
Adamson	Christopher	Ashington 4/11/1978		West Brom loan Jul 1999
Adekola	David Adeolu	Nigeria 18/5/1968		Hereford Utd Mar 1995 trialist
Agar	Sam	Pontefract 4/9/1985		Trainee Aug 2002
Ainge	Simon Christopher	Shipley 18/2/1988		Bradford City loan Jan 2008
Ainsworth	Lionel Glenn Robert	Nottingham 1/10/1987		Derby Co loan Jan 2007
Aistrup	Sidney Roy	Sheffield 7/5/1909	1/1996	
Alcock	Terence	Hanley 9/12/1946		Port Vale Sep 1977
Allan	John	Stirling 22/3/1931		Bradford Mar 1961
Allan	Jonathon	Penrith 24/5/1983		Northwich Vic Dec 2003
Allatt	Vernon	Hednesford 28/5/1959		Hednesford Town Nov 1979 Bolton Wand Nov 1982
Allison	Wayne Anthony	Huddersfield 16/10/1968		Trainee Jul 1987
Allsop	William Henry	Ripley 29/1/1912	24/4/1997	Port Vale Jun 1934
Anderson	David Robert	Shettleston 1881	1966	Roswell Aug 1920
Annan	Richard Amondo	Leeds 4/12/1968		Guiseley Oct 1995
Ardron	Walter	Swinton-on-Dearne 19/9/1918	1978	Rotherham Utd guest Mar 1945
Armitage	John W			Feb 1931
Armitage	Richard			Heckmondwike Dec 1914
Arnell	Alan Jack	Chichester 25/11/1933		Tranmere Rov Jul 1963
Ashbridge	Kenneth	Burnley 12/11/1916	1/2002	Burnley Sep 1938 Oct 1935
Asher	Alistair Andrew	Leicester 14/10/1980		Mansfield Town Aug 2002
Atack	Sidney	Methley 10/5/1918	1983	Bradford May 1937
Atherton	Peter	Orrell 6/4/1970		Bradford City Jul 2005 Wigan Ath coach Jun 2007
Atherton	William Jackson	Manchester 4/5/1905	1976	Doncaster Rov Jun 1934
Atkins	William Mark	Solihull 9/5/1939		Swindon Town Aug 1965 Portsmouth Oct 1969
Atkinson	Brian	Rotherham 16/11/1934		Sheffield Utd Jun 1956
Atkinson	Robert	Beverley 29/4/1987		Barnsley loan Nov 2006
Austick	John	Bradford 1897		Bradford City Dec 1919
Ayre	William	Crookhill 7/5/1952	16/4/2002	Hartlepool Utd Jan 1981 Mansfield Town Jul 1984
Bailey	Alexander Christopher	Newham 21/9/1983		Chesterfield Oct 2007
Bain	David	Rutherglen 5/8/1900		Bristol City Aug 1930
Bainbridge	HP			Wallsend Nov 1920
Baines	Cecil Peter	Manchester 11/9/1919	1997	Wrexham guest Dec 1943
Baines	Reginald	York 3/6/1906	1974	York City Aug 1939
Baird	Henry HC	Belfast 17/8/1913	27/5/1973	Huddersfield Town guest Mar 1945
Baker				Ollerton Colliery Apr 1920
Baker	Clive	Adwick-le-Street 5/7/1934		Doncaster Rov Aug 1952
Baker	Henry	Sheffield 23/1/1897		St John's Inst Jun 1921
Ballantyne	John Thomas	Durham 1903	1965	Bradford City Aug 1922
Balmer	John Michael	Hexham 25/5/1946		Rugby Town May 1965
Bambridge	Keith Graham	Rawmarsh 1/9/1935		Darlington Mar 1965
Banner	William Arthur	Warrington 20/5/1907	1974	Manchester NE May 1934
Barber	Bernard	Wombwell 1905		Wombwell Ath May 1927
Barber	John	Salford 8/1/1901	30/3/1961	Southport Aug 1926
Barber	Lewis Frederick	Wombwell 11/4/1906	14/6/1983	Broomhill WMC Oct 1925
Barclay	Robert	Scotswood 27/10/1906	1969	Huddersfield Town guest Sep 1944
Barkas	Thomas	South Shields 27/3/1912	11/6/1991	Bradford City Dec 1934
Barker				Heckmondwike Aug 1915
Barker				Apr 1920
Barnett	Graham	Stoke 17/5/1936		Tranmere Rov Aug 1961
Barr	Robert Andrew	Halifax 5/12/1969		Trainee Jul 1988
Barr	William Joseph	Halifax 21/1/1969		Trainee Jul 1987
Barraclough	Alfred J			Sowerby Bridge Aug 1911
Barrett	Jack	Halifax 23/4/1926	23/10/2006	Dec 1943
Barrie	James William	Old Kilpatrick 21/10/1902		Fall River (USA) Jul 1930
Barron				Dec 1915
Bartlett	Albert B	Morpeth 3/1884		Heckmondwike Feb 1915
Bartlett	Frank	Chester-le-Street 8/11/1930		Barnsley Jul 1963
Bastians	Felix	Bochum, Germany 9/5/1988		Nottingham For loan Jan 2007
Bates	Keith	Huddersfield 1/9/1933		Melsham Nov 1956
Bateson	Arthur			local Feb 1921
Batty	Harold	Castleford 1895		Goole Town May 1914
Battye	John E			Dec 1944

THE HISTORY OF HALIFAX TOWN

1911–2008

To	League A	S	G	CONF A	S	G	FA Cup A	S	G	FL Cup A	S	G
Guiseley Sep 1992	24	5	1				2	0	0	2	0	0
cs 1915												
cs 1914												
	7	0	0				0	0	0	0	0	0
Mar 1995				2	0	0	0	0	0			
Ossett Albion Jan 2004				11	1	0	0	0	0			
				2	0	1	0	0	0			
	2	0	0				0	0	0	0	0	0
Lancaster City cs 1978	14	0	2				0	0	0	0	0	0
Weymouh Jul 1961	10	0	1				0	0	0	0	0	0
Northwich Vic Aug 2004				9	5	1	0	0	0			
Bolton Wand Aug 1982	93	5	14									
Rochdale Aug 1983							2	0	0	3	0	0
Watford Jul 1989	74	10	22				4	1	2	3	0	2
Ret cs 1947	239	0	0				20	0	0	0	0	0
Ret cs 1922	10	0	2				6	0	2	0	0	0
Morecambe cs 1996				20	1	0	0	0	0			
cc Sep 1932	8	0	0				0	0	0	0	0	0
cs 1915												
Runcorn Jul 1964	14	0	6				1	0	0	3	0	0
cs 1939	1	0	0				0	0	0	0	0	0
Hucknall Town Jul 2003				34	1	0	1	0	0			
cs 1939	4	0	1				0	0	0	0	0	0
cs 2006				15	3	0	0	0	0			
cs 2008												
Preston NE cs 1935	15	0	2				2	0	1	0	0	0
Stockport Co Mar 1967	197	2	71				13	0	3	10	0	3
Rochdale Dec 1972												
Burton Albion Aug 1959	67	0	0				1	0	0	0	0	0
				4	0	2	0	0	0			
cs 1920												
Mansfield Town Aug 1982	95	0	7				3	0	0	6	0	0
Manager Dec 1986												
cs				2	2	0	0	1	0			
Rochdale cs 1932	60	0	5				5	0	0	0	0	0
cs 1921												
May 1940												
cs 1920												
Southport Jul 1959	58	0	22				5	0	0	0	0	0
Brighton & HA cs 1922	20	0	0				0	0	0	0	0	0
cs 1923	2	0	0				0	0	0	0	0	0
Derry City cs 1967	28	0	9				1	0	0	1	0	0
cs 1966	8	1	1				0	0	0	1	0	0
cs 1935	9	0	0				0	0	0	0	0	0
cs 1928	1	0	0				0	0	0	0	0	0
Rochdale cs 1927	12	0	1				0	0	0	0	0	0
Manchester City Jun 1927	35	0	0				0	1	0	0	0	0
Rochdale Sep 1946	169	0	36				14	0	5	0	0	0
cs 1916												
cs 1920												
Macclesfield Town cs 1962	32	0	10				1	0	0	1	0	0
Chorley cs 1989	4	1	0				0	0	0	1	0	0
Crewe Alex Jun 1994	179	18	13	39	0	4	13	1	3	8	1	2
cs 1912												
cs 1944												
Worcester City cs 1933	91	0	0				10	0	0	0	0	0
cs 1916												
Castleford Town 1919												
Goole Town cs 1964	21	0	4				0	0	0	4	0	1
				8	1	4	0	0	0			
Melsham 1956	1	0	0				0	0	0	0	0	0
cs 1921												
cs 1915												

Surname	Forenames	Born	Died	From
Baxter	Reginald			Oct 1911
Beckford	Jason Neil	Manchester 14/2/1970		Burnley loan Sep 1996
Beddard	Elliott James	Leeds 15/6/1976		Farsley Celtic Feb 1995
Beevers				Doncaster Rov Dec 1915
Beevers	Thomas			Manchester football Dec 1913
Bell	Derek Martin	Wyberton 30/10/1956		Derby Co May 1975
Bell	Jack G			Albion Rov guest Mar 1943
Bell	Joseph G	Wednesbury 1912		Walsall May 1933
Bell	Thomas	Seaham 9/11/1906	1983	Merthyr Town Jul 1927
Bell	Thomas Anthony P	Crompton 30/12/1923	11/1988	Stockport Co Jul 1953
Bell	William			Trainer Nov 1912
Bell	William	Kilmarnock		Kilmarnock guest Oct 1943
Belle	Cortez Marvin	Coventry 27/8/1983		Llanelli Jul 2007
Benn	Wayne	Pontefract 7/8/1976		Bradford PA Jan 1996
Bennett	'Bandsman'			Dec 1919
Bennett	Walter H	Mexborough 15/12/1918		Doncaster Rov Jan 1950
Beresford	John	Sheffield 4/9/1966		Alfreton Town nc Jan 2003
Best	Jeremiah	Newcastle 22/8/1897		Coventry City Aug 1926
Betteridge	Frank	Worksop 12/1/1911	1972	Worksop Town Aug 1930
Beynon	John Alfred	Cardiff 1902	26/6/1937	West Brom Jul 1928
Bickerstaffe	John	St Helens 8/11/1918	1982	Lincoln City Sep 1951
Bilcliff	Bernard	Chapeltown 6/6/1904	1955	Chesterfield May 1930
Billings				Nov 1915
Billy	Christopher Anthony	Huddersfield 2/1/1973		Carlisle Utd Jan 2007
Bingley	Walter	Sheffield 17/4/1930		York City Jul 1963
Binns	Clifford Herman	Cowling 9/3/1907	1/1977	Portsmouth Rov Apr 1928
				Barnsley guest Feb 1941
Binns	Eric	Halifax 13/8/1924	9/2007	Huddersfield Town May 1946
Birch	James Victor Tomlinson	Ashover 25/10/1927		Huddersfield Town Aug 1948
Birch	Neville JJ	Rugby 17/9/1917	1979	Sep 1944
Birkett	Ernest			Dec 1943
Birks	Clifford	Hanley 13/12/1910	1998	Torquay Utd Jun 1936
Birtwhistle	Thomas	Great Harwood 1/2/1890	11/1970	Hebden Bridge loan Feb 1913
				Hebden Bridge Dec 1913
Black	Russell Palmer	Dumfries 29/7/1960		Mansfield Town Aug 1986
Blackburn	Alan	Pleasley 4/8/1935		West Ham Utd Nov 1957
Blackburn	Thomas			Feb 1913
Blackham	Samuel	Edmonton 19/8/1890	1956	Bradford May 1922
Blackwell	Ernest	Sheffield 1899		Heeley Friends Jan 1920
Blain	Colin Anthony	Urmston 7/3/1970		Trainee Jul 1988
Blair	Kenneth George	Portadown 28/9/1952		Derby Co Oct 1974
Bleau	MicahJoel	Bradford 8/11/1987		Academy Nov 2006
Blunt	Jason John	Penzance 16/8/1977		Tamworth Sep 2004
Blyth	John William (Ian)	Edinburgh 26/5/1947		Rotherham Utd May 1967
Boardman	Craig George	Barnsley 30/11/1970		Peterborough United Nov 1993
				Stalybridge Celtic Aug 1997
Bodell	Norman	Manchester 29/1/1938		Crewe Alex Oct 1966
Boden				Calverley Oct 1911
Booth	Philip			Oct 1941
Booth	Wilfred	Mapplewell 26/12/1918		Wombwell Ath Dec 1947
Boothroyd	George	Huddersfield 4/1/1919	3/1992	Huddersfield Town guest Jan 1944
Bowler	Justin Michael	Leeds 26/6/1986		Leeds United Aug 2005
Bown	Herbert Arthur	East Ham 3/5/1893	1959	Leicester City May 1922
Brabin	Gary	Liverpool 9/12/1970		Witton Alb Jul 2005
Bracey	Lee Michael Ian	Ashford 11/9/1968		Swansea City Oct 1991
Bradley	Lee Herbert	Manchester 27/5/1957		Stockport Co Oct 1976
Bradley	Russell	Birmingham 28/3/1966		Hereford Utd Sep 1991
Bradshaw	Mark	Ashton-under-Lyme 7/6/1969		Macclesfield Town May 1997
Bramhall	John	Warrington 20/11/1956		Rochdale Aug 1988
Branch	Paul Michael	Liverpool 18/10/1978		Chester City Oct 2007
Brannigan	Daniel McKay	Dunasken 22/12/1902	8/1990	Glenburn Rov Jun 1927
Brass	Christopher Paul	Easington 24/7/1975		Burnley loan Sep 2000
Bratley	George William	Rotherham 17/1/1909	1978	Crystal Pal guest Feb 1944
Brayshaw	Charles H	Seccunderbrad 1898		Army May 1921
Breaks	Edward	Halifax 29/12/1919	9/11/2000	Regmnt football Aug 1947
Brearley	Arthur			Rochdale Aug 1913
Brennand	W			Apr 1914
Brier	John David	Halifax 3/4/1941		Burnley Aug 1961
Brierley	Keith	Dewsbury 14/12/1951		Dec 1969
Briggs	Charles Edward	Newtown 4/4/1911		Bradford Sep 1938
Broadbent	Graham	Halifax 20/12/1958		Emley Sep 1988
Brobbin	Sydney	Salford 29/12/1911	1979	Altrincham Jun 1934
Brogan	Frank Anthony	Glasgow 3/8/1942		Ipswich Town Nov 1971
Brook	Charles	Huddersfield 1898		Huddersfield Town Dec 1919
Brook	Gary	Dewsbury 9/5/1964		Boston Utd Sep 1995
Brook	Lewis	Halifax 27/7/1918	10/6/1996	Huddersfield Town guest Sep 1945
Brookes	Arthur Goodreid	Moxley 24/3/1914	10/2001	West Brom Jun 1937

HALIFAX TOWN PLAYERS 1911-2008

To	League A	S	G	CONF A	S	G	FA Cup A	S	G	FL Cup A	S	G
cs 1912												
				3	0	0	0	0	0			
Guiseley cs 1996				14	16	5	0	1	0			
cs 1915												
cs 1914												
Barnsley Oct 1978	104	8	21				4	0	0	4	3	2
cs 1934												
Chesterfield cs 1930	89	0	26				2	0	0	0	0	0
Mossley cs 1956	117	0	1				6	0	0	0	0	0
Brentford trainer Aug 1913												
Northwich Vic Jan 2008				16	3	2	1	0	0			
Bradford PA Feb 1996				1	0	0	0	0	0			
cs 1920												
South Normanton cs 1950	7	0	1				0	0	0	0	0	0
Alfreton Town Feb 2003												
Rotherham Utd Oct 1926	9	0	0				0	0	0	0	0	0
Barrow Jun 1936	109	0	33				11	0	4	0	0	0
Rotherham United cs 1929	20	0	4				0	0	0	0	0	0
cs 1953	37	0	0				1	0	0	0	0	0
Shelbourne cs 1932	67	0	0				7	0	0	0	0	0
cs 1916												
Farsley Celtic Aug 2007				10	3	0	0	0	0			
cs 1965	64	0	1				2	0	0	3	0	0
Blackburn Rov Jan 1930	34	0	0				1	0	0	0	0	0
Goole Town cs 1947	6	0	1				0	0	0	0	0	0
Kippax Legion Nov 1950	3	0	1				0	0	0	0	0	0
cs 1945												
cs 1944												
cs 1938	2	0	0				0	0	0	0	0	0
cs 1922	2	0	0				7	0	0	0	0	0
Eastern Pride (Aus) cs 1988	63	9	14				7	0	3	3	1	0
Margate cs 1961	124	0	34				3	0	1	1	0	0
cs 1913												
Bradford cs 1923	6	0	0				0	0	0	0	0	0
cs 1920												
Northwich Vic cs 1989	18	5	0				0	0	0	0	0	0
Southport cs 1976	42	1	4				3	0	0	0	1	0
Alfreton Town Aug 2005				22	4	1	2	1	0			
Hyde Utd cs 1968	5	0	0				0	0	0	0	0	0
Scarborough Aug 1995				64	2	0	7	2	0			
Sheffield FC cs 1998												
Altrincham cs 1968	36	0	0				6	0	0	0	0	0
Calverley Oct 1911												
cs 1942												
cs 1948	6	0	2				0	0	0	0	0	0
Altrincham Jul 2006				5	14	0	2	1	0			
Hull City Jan 1925	80	0	1				13	0	0	0	0	0
Southport Jan 2006				4	0	1	0	0	0			
Bury Aug 1993	73	0	0	1	0	0	1	0	0	2	0	0
Northwich Vic cs 1979	62	10	4				2	0	0	2	2	0
Scunthorpe Utd Jun 1993	55	2	4				3	0	0	2	0	0
Droylsden cs 2001	73	10	7	42	0	5	6	1	0	5	0	0
Scunthorpe Utd Jan 1990	62	0	5				6	0	1	5	0	0
Oct 2007				0	0	0	0	2	0			
Peterborough Utd cs 1928	15	0	0				0	0	0	0	0	0
	6	0	0				0	0	0	0	0	0
cs 1921	1	0	0				0	0	0	0	0	0
ret cs 1956	179	0	1				5	0	0	0	0	0
cs 1920												
cs 1914												
Goole Town cs 1966	78	2	0				3	0	0	3	0	0
Bradford Jul 1973	51	4	11				1	1	0	3	1	2
Clyde cs 1946	53	0	0				6	0	0	0	0	0
Emley Jan 1991	13	19	3				1	1	0	1	1	0
cc May 1935	1	0	0				0	0	0	0	0	0
cs 1973	25	2	6				3	0	0	1	0	0
cs 1920												
Ossett Town cs 1998				63	11	15	6	0	7			
cs 1939	47	0	0				2	0	0	0	0	0

Surname	Forenames	Born	Died	From
Brookes	Stephen Michael	Norris Green 18/6/1955		Barrow Mar 1985
Brooksbank	Clifford	Halifax 1889	1955	Bristol City Aug 1915
Broskom	George Richard	Rotherham 4/12/1896	3/1984	Reading Jun 1921
Brown				Mar 1920
Brown	Allan Winston	Consett 26/8/1914	1996	Huddersfield Town guest Jan 1940
Brown	David James	Hartlepool 28/1/1957		Preston NE Jul 1989
Brown	Frederick Walter	Sutton Coldfield 1911		Rochdale Jul 1932
Brown	George A	Whittam Park 1913		Hartlepools Utd May 1936
Brown	James	Liverpool		Lancaster City Aug 1996
Brown	Jonathan	Barnsley 8/9/1966		Exeter City Jul 1995
Brown	Linton James	Driffield 12/4/1968		Guiseley Dec 1992
Brown	Nicholas James	Northampton 25/1/1973		Norwich City Jul 1991
Brown	Philip	South Shields 30/5/1959		Hartlepool Utd Jul 1985
Brown	W			Hibernian guest Oct 1942
Bruce	Walter			Belfast Celtic Jun 1939
Bullock	Michael Edwin	Stoke 2/10/1946		Orient Feb 1976
Bullock	Simon John	Stoke 28/9/1962		Stoke City Sep 1980
Burgess	Michael Ralph	Montreal, Canada 17/4/1932		Bournemouth Jun 1961
Burgess	Walter	Golborne 19/6/1921	6/1988	Coleraine Aug 1946
Burgin	Andrew	Sheffield 6/3/1947		Rotherham Utd Dec 1968
Burke	Peter	Rotherham 26/4/1957		Barnsley Mar 1978
Burkinshaw	Laurence	Kilnhurst 2/12/1893	1969	Birmingham City Jun 1922
Burns	Oliver Houston	Larkhall 16/5/1914	12/1989	Oldham Ath guest Oct 1943
				Oldham Ath Oct 1946
Burr	Steven	Aberdeen 12/1/1961		Stafford Rangers Dec 1993
Burrows	Albert			Huddersfield Town guest Oct 1945
Burton	Kenneth Owen	Sheffield 11/2/1950		Chestefield Aug 1980
Bushell	Stephen Paul	Manchester 28/12/1972		Stalybridge Celtic Nov 2001
				Altrincham Jun 2007
Butcher	John Melvin	Newcastle 27/5/1956		Oxford Utd loan Sep 1982
Butler	Arthur			Feb 1946
Butler	Brian Francis	Salford 4/7/1966		Stockport Co Aug 1989
Butler	Lee Simon	Sheffield 30/5/1966		Dunfermline Sep 1999
				Alfreton Town Jul 2002
				Alfreton Town Jun 2005
Butler	Peter James F	Halifax 27/8/1966		West Brom Aug 1998
Butterworth	William			Aug 1920
Buxton	Michael James	Corbridge 29/5/1943		Burnley Jun 1968
Buxton	Nicholas Gareth	Doncaster 6/9/1976		Eastwood Town loan Dec 1995
Cabrelli	Peter	Dundee 23/10/1910		Raith Rov guest Oct 1942
Cameron	David	Bangor, Wales 24/8/1975		Chester City loan Aug 2003
Cameron	James Ray	Manchester		Winsford Utd Aug 1993
Cameron	Mark			Liverpool Aug 1996
Campbell	Alexander	Ayr		Glenburn Rov Sep 1925
Campbell	Andrew Paul	Middlesbrough 18/4/1979		Dunfermline Ath Aug 2006
Campbell	Hugh	Glasgow		Distillery Jul 1937
Campbell	Robert McFaul	Belfast 13/9/1956		Aston Villa loan Feb 1975
				Huddersfield Town Sep 1978
Cannon	George Frank	Hammersmith 8/11/1885	2/1916	Castleford Town Jan 1914
Capel	Thomas A	Chorlton 27/6/1922		Coventry City Oct 1955
Carlin	William	Liverpool 6/10/1940		Liverpool Aug 1962
Carney	David Raymond	Camden, Australia 16/8/1983		Oldham Ath Mar 2004
Carr	Everton Dale	Antigua 11/1/1961		Leicester City Jul 1981
Carroll	Joseph	Radcliffe 6/1/1957		Oldham Ath Sep 1976
Carter	A			Mytholmroyd Apr 1915
Carter	J			Arpr 1914
Carter	Timothy Douglas	Bristol 5/10/1967	19/6/2008	Millwall Jul 1998
Cartwright	Mark Neville	Chester 13/1/1973		Shrewsbury Town Sep 2003
Case	James Robert	Liverpool 18/5/1954		Bournemouth May 1992
Chadbourne	Joe Henry	Halifax 1885	4/8/1958	Mirfield Utd Aug 1911
Chadwick	David Edwin	Ooctamund, India 19/8/1943		Middlesbrough Jan 1970
Chadwick	Wilfred	Bury 7/10/1900	2/1975	Stoke City Oct 1930
Challinor	Samuel	Middlewich 2/4/1900		Brentford Jul 1921
Chamberlain	Glyn	Chesterfield 29/7/1957		Chesterfield Jul 1981
Chambers	Brian Mark	Newcastle 31/10/1949		Bournemouth Mar 1981
Chambers	William Thomas	Wednesbury 10/8/1906	1978	Darlaston Jun 1932
Chapman	Leonard			Nov 1945
Chapman	W			Jan 1940
Charles	Frederick	High Garrett 10/5/1889	1976	Castleford Town Sep 1919
Chester	Thomas Holland	Glasgow 7/11/1907	1979	Notts County guest Mar 1940
Child	James Frederick	Leeds 1893		Castleford Town Dec 1912
Childs	Henry	Acomb 7/11/1908	1977	Notts County Jul 1929
Chin	Gordon Robert	Burnaby, British Colombia 26/3/1983		
Chippendale	Brian Albert	Bradford 29/10/1964		York City loan Nov 1984
Chmilowskyj	Roman	Bradford19/4/1959		Assoc school Apr 1977
Christie	David	Salford 26/2/1973		Preston NE Jan 1993
Christie	Gilbert David	Dundee 18/11/1891	1973	Huddersfield Town May 1914

HALIFAX TOWN PLAYERS 1911-2008

To	League A	S	G	CONF A	S	G	FA Cup A	S	G	FL Cup A	S	G
Morecambe cs 1985	16	0	0				0	0	0	0	0	0
cs 1916												
cs 1922	1	0	0				0	0	0	0	0	0
cs 1920												
cs May 1991	38	0	0				0	0	0	6	0	0
Accrington Stan Jul 1934	54	0	13				7	0	4	0	0	0
cs 1937	10	0	0				1	0	0	0	0	0
Barrow Oct 1996				7	2	1	2	0	0			
Nuneaton Bor Jun 1999	32	8	0	101	3	1	8	0	0	3	0	0
Hull City Jan 1993	3	0	0				0	0	0	0	0	0
cc 1994	2	0	0	3	0	0	0	0	0	0	0	0
Bolton Wan Jun 1988	135	0	19				8	0	1	6	0	1
cs 1940												
Manager Jul 1981	98	8	20				5	0	0	6	1	1
cs 1982	15	2	1				1	0	0	0	0	0
Gillingham Mar 1963	34	2	1				0	0	0	1	0	0
cs 1947	13	0	2				4	0	0	0	0	0
Blackburn Rov Sep 1974	243	0	9				12	0	1	13	0	1
Rochdale Jul 1980	79	6	9				6	0	2	2	1	0
Mexborough Town Aug 1923	26	0	2				5	0	0	0	0	0
	25	0	5				1	0	0	0	0	0
Nelson 1949												
Hednesford Town Mar 1994				8	0	0	0	0	0			
Worksop Town cs 1981	26	1	1				1	0	0	1	0	0
Altrincham Jul 2006	25	0	1	111	15	8	6	2	1	0	0	0
Hyde Utd Jan 2008												
	5	0	0				0	0	0	0	0	0
cs 1946												
Northwich Vic cs 1991	44	12	4				5	0	0	7	1	0
Doncaster Rov Jan 2002	92	1	0	40	0	0	10	0	0	1	0	0
Alfreton Town May 2003												
Doncaster Rov coach Jan 2008												
Sorrento (Aus) 2000	63	0	1				4	0	0	4	0	0
Stoke City Oct 1925												
Coach Mar 1971	36	0	0				4	0	0	2	1	0
				6	3	1	0	0	0			
Winsford Utd Mar 1994				2	1	0	0	1	0			
Sep 1996				0	2	0	0	0	0			
cs 1926	10	0	0				0	0	0	0	0	0
Farsley Celtic Jul 2008				27	25	12	0	0	0			
cs 1938	25	0	1				0	0	0	0	0	0
	33	4	3				1	0	0	0	0	0
Brisbane City May 1979												
Fulham cs 1914												
Heanor Town Jul 1956	7	0	1				1	0	0	0	0	0
Carlisle Utd Oct 1964	95	0	32				3	0	0	6	0	2
Hamilton Acad Nov 2004				2	1	0	0	0	0			
Rochdale Mar 1983	49	4	0				1	0	0	4	0	0
Barrow cs 1979	76	6	14				5	1	0	3	0	0
cs 1915												
cs 1914												
Sunderland coach cs 1999	9	1	0				0	0	0	0	0	0
Runcorn FC Hylton cs 2004				32	0	0	1	0	0			
Wrexham Feb 1993	17	4	2				1	0	0	1	0	0
Halifax RFC cs 1912												
Bournemouth Feb 1972	95	0	15				2	0	0	6	0	1
cs 1931	5	0	0				1	0	0	0	0	0
Accrington Stan Jun 1922	23	0	2				0	0	0	0	0	0
Kettering Town cs 1982	35	0	0				1	0	0	2	0	0
Poole Town cs 1981	10	0	0				0	0	0	0	0	0
Bolton Wanderers Jul 1934	70	0	50				7	0	3	0	0	0
cs 1946												
cs 1941												
cs 1920												
Army Sep 1914												
cs 1930	16	0	0				0	0	0	0	0	0
St Johnstone Nov 2004 (rel Apr 2005)	2	7	1	0	0	0						
	1	1	0				0	0	0	0	0	0
cs 1977	1	0	0				0	0	0	0	0	0
Rossendale Utd 1993	6	3	0				0	0	0	0	0	0
cc Nov 1914												

Surname	Forenames	Born	Died	From
Circuit	Steven	Sheffield 11/4/1972		Stafford Rangers Jun 1992
				Boston Utd trial Oct 1994
Clamp	James	York 14/9/1984		Nottingham For cs 2002
Clark	Herbert	c. 1896		Abertillery Aug 1920
Clark	Samuel James Hughes	Coatbridge 15/11/1912	3/1987	Blackburn Rov May 1937
Clarke	Albert			Bradford guest May 1945
Clarke	Alfred	Hollinwood 23/8/1926		Oldham Ath Mar 1954
Clarke	Christopher E	Leeds 18/12/1980		Wolves Jul 1999
				York City Oct 2004
Clarke	Matthew P	Leeds 18/12/1980		Wolves Jul 1999
Clarke	Michael	Sheffield 28/11/1944		Aldershot Jul 1965
Clarke	Sidney	Swansea		Shrewsbury Town Oct 1936
Clarke	Thomas	Halifax 21/12/1987		Huddersfield Town loan Feb 2008
Clarkson				Dec 1919
Clarkson	Philip Ian	Garstang 13/11/1968		Blackpool Jul 2002
Clayton				Dec 1915
Cliff	John George	Middlesbrough 7/11/1946		Middlesbrough Jul 1966
Cobain	Sydney Percival	Newtonards 6/8/1896	1971	Nov 1921
Cochrane	Karl	Halifax 25/1/1970		Brighouse Town Oct 1995
Cockerill	David Matthew	Mansfield 7/6/1987		Sheffield Wed Feb 2005
Cockroft	Hubert	Barnsley 21/11/1918	1979	Bradford City Jul 1947
Coleman	Ernest	Blidworth 4/1/1908	20/1/1984	Hucknall Colliery Jul 1926
Colley	Karl Peter	Sheffield 13/10/1983		Frickley Ath Dec 2003
Collier	Austin	Dewsbury 24/7/1914	5/1991	Rochdale Nov 1947
Collier	Thomas			Barnsley jun football Aug 1936
Collins	Albert Desmond	Chesterfield 15/4/1923		Chesterfield Nov 1946
Collins	John Lindsay	Bedwelty 21/1/1949		Portsmouth Aug 1974
Collins	Simon Jonathan	Pontefract 16/12/1973		Huddersfield Town loan Jan 1994
Connaughton	Patrick John	Wigan 23/9/1949		Manchester Utd loan Oct 1969
Connor	Robert	Bradford 13/10/1925		Bradford guest Jan 1941
Constable	Shaun David	Maidstone 21/3/1968		Scunthorpe Utd Aug 1993
				Altrincham Sep 1995
Coode	Jack	Oldham 8/3/1910	1972	Manchester Utd Mar 1935
Cook	Herbert			RAF Sep 1919
Cook	Jeffrey William	Hartlepool 14/3/1953		Plymouth Arg Aug 1983
Cook	Mitchell Christopher	Scarborough 15/10/1961		Scarborough Aug 1989
Cooke	Albert	Royston 11/4/1908	4/1988	Hull City Jul 1932
Cooper	Graham	Huddersfield 22/5/1962		Wrexham Jan 1991
Cooper	Sedley	Garforth 17/8/1911	1981	Carlton Ath May 1929
Cooper	Stephen Brian	Birmingham 22/6/1964	14/2/2004	Birmingham City loan Dec 1983
Cooper	William George Edward	York 2/11/1917	1978	Chesterfield Mar 1939
Copeland	James Leslie	Chorlton-cum-Hardy 1/10/1909	7/1991	Chelsea Aug 1937
Corby	Declan Finbar	Bradford 15/1/1987		Thackley Mar 2005
Core	Frank	Halifax 5/9/1932		Local Nov 1953
Core	John	Ripponden 29/3/1929		Local 1949
Costello	Peter	Halifax 31/10/1969		Lincoln City loan Oct 1993
Cotton	William Charles	Liverpool 10/4/1894	1971	Buckley Utd Mar 1926
Cox	Albert Edward Harrison	Treeton 24/6/1917	4/2003	Sheffield Utd Jun 1952
Cox	Paul Richard	Nottingham 6/1/1972		Gresley Rov Oct 1996
Coyle	O			Oct 1943
Coyne	Cyril	Barnsley 2/5/1924	1981	Leeds Utd Jun 1951
Craig	Edward Freeman	Stewarton 9/2/1903	1982	Bristol City Aug 1932
Craven	Peter A	Hanover, Germany 30/6/1968		Guiseley Mar 1993
Crawford	Edmund Charles	Filey 31/10/1906	1977	Filey Town Jun 1931
Crawford	John Campbell (Ian)	Falkirk 27/6/1922	1996	Oldham Ath Jul 1954
Crawshaw	Richard Leigh	Manchester 21/9/1898	1965	Manchester City Jul 1922
Cresswell	Ryan Anthony	Rotherham 22/12/1987		Sheffield Utd loan Jan 2007
Crofts				Retford Town Apr 1920
Crookes	Peter	Liverpool 5/7/1982		Liverpool Mar 2001
Crosby	Andrew Keith	Rotherham 3/3/1973		Doncaster Rov loan Oct 1993
Crossley	Roy	Hebden Bridge 16/10/1923	2003	Huddersfield Town Aug 1948
Crowther	George Lisle	Bishop Middleham 1892	1957	Rotherham Town Jun 1914
Crowther	John	Walsden		Mar 1930
Crowther	Kenneth	Halifax 17/12/1924	6/1994	Luddenden FC Aug 1942
Cruise	James Arthur	Bradford 1895	1968	Apr 1920
				Yorkshire Amateur Jan 1922
Cullen	David Jonathan (Jon)	Durham City 10/1/1973		Sheffield Utd loan Dec 1999
				USA Jul 2003
Cullen	Patrick Joseph	Mexborough 9/8/1949		Mexborough Town May 1968
Culpan	Sutcliffe	Halifax 10/5/1888	1969	West Vale Ramblers Sep 1911
Cunningham	Daniel Harvey	Manchester 11/9/1968		Witton Alb Nov 1993
Dadson	Sammy Junior T	Enfield 3/11/1988		Blackburn Rov Sep 2007
Dale	Frederick William	Balby 26/10/1925		Scunthorpe Utd Aug 1949
Dann	Reginald Walter	Maidstone 6/6/1916	1948	Bradford guest Feb 1942
Darbyshire	Harold	Leeds 22/10/1931	6/1991	Leeds Utd Jul 1952
Dark	Alfred James	Bristol 21/8/1893	3/8/1964	Port Vale Jun 1924
Davidson	Robert Trimming	Lochgelly 27/4/1913	10/1988	Coventry City guest Sep 1941

HALIFAX TOWN PLAYERS 1911-2008

To	League A	S	G	CONF A	S	G	FA Cup A	S	G	FL Cup A	S	G
Boston Utd Sep 1993	0	1	0	0	1	0	0	0	0	0	0	0
Boston Utd Oct 1994												
cs 2004												
Rochdale cs 1921												
cs 1940	20	0	2				0	0	0	0	0	0
cs 1956	71	0	22				2	0	0	0	0	0
Blackpool Feb 2002	50	1	1	3	1	0	3	1	0	2	0	0
Guiseley cs 2005												
Darlington Jul 2002	42	27	2				5	1	0	0	0	0
Heanor Town	50	1	1				0	0	0	3	0	0
cs 1937	2	0	0				0	0	0	0	0	0
				7	0	1	0	0	0			
cs 1920												
Lancaster City Jul 2003				38	0	4	1	0	0			
cs 1916												
cc Sep 1966	1	0	0				0	0	0	0	0	0
cs 1922	1	0	0				0	0	0	0	0	0
Eccleshill Utd 2006				18	8	3	0	0	0			
cs 2005												
Peterborough Utd cs 1948	10	0	1				0	0	0	0	0	0
Grimsby Town Feb 1929	48	0	15				2	0	1	0	0	0
Hucknall Town Mar 2004				6	1	0	0	0	0			
Goole Town Aug 1948	1	0	0				0	0	0	0	0	0
cs 1939	5	0	0				0	0	0	0	0	0
Carlisle Utd Mar 1948	44	0	10				5	0	0	0	0	0
Sheffield Wed Jul 1976	82	0	1				5	0	0	5	0	0
				1	2	0	0	0	0			
	3	0	0				0	0	0	0	0	0
Altrincham Jun 1994				24	10	0	0	2	0			
Emley 1995												
cs 1936	19	0	0				1	0	0	0	0	0
cs 1920												
Worksop Town cs 1985	49	7	9				3	0	1	4	1	0
Darlington May 1991	52	2	2				0	0	0	7	0	1
cs 1933	135	0	4				10	0	2	0	0	0
Emley cs 1992	33	7	4				0	0	0	2	0	1
Sheffield Wed Jun 1931	79	0	19				4	0	3	0	0	0
	7	0	1				0	0	0	0	0	0
Bradford City Sep 1946	2	0	0				0	0	0	0	0	0
cs 1938	22	0	6				2	0	0	0	0	0
cs 2005												
cs 1954	1	0	0				0	0	0	0	0	0
Ashton Utd cs 1952	28	0	15				1	0	1	0	0	0
	5	0	3				0	0	0	0	0	0
Crewe Alex cs 1926	54	0	1				8	0	0	0	0	0
Sheffield Utd youth coach												
cs 1997				22	1	0	0	0	0			
cs 1944												
cs 1952	4	0	0				0	0	0	0	0	0
cs 1944	287	0	5				25	0	0	0	0	0
Preston NE Mar 1994	7	0	0				2	0	0	0	0	0
Liverpool May 1932	30	0	21				4	0	1	0	0	0
Macclesfield Town cs 1955	11	0	2				0	0	0	0	0	0
Nelson Feb 1923	7	0	0				1	0	1	0	0	0
				14	1	0	0	0	0			
cs 1920												
Hyde Utd cs 2002	1	0	0				0	0	0	0	0	0
				0	1	0	0	0	0			
Buxton cs 1951	41	0	15				2	0	0	0	0	0
Hirst Dec 1914												
Rochdale cs 1931	1	0	0				0	0	0	0	0	0
cs 1943												
Yorkshire Amateur cs 1920	1	0	0				0	0	0	0	0	0
cs 1922												
	11	0	4	7	0	0	0	0	0	0	0	0
Spennymoor Utd Oct 2003												
cs 1973	1	5	0				0	0	0	0	0	0
Boothtown cs 1912												
Southport Apr 1994												
cs 2008				0	2	0	0	0	0			
Southport Jul 1952	70	0	16				2	0	0	0	0	0
Bury Aug 1957	162	0	32				7	0	0	0	0	0
Barrow May 1928	129		1				4	0	0	0	0	0

Surname	Forenames	Born	Died	From
Davies	Clint Aaron	Perth, Australia 24/4/1983		Bradford City loan Jul 2003
Davies	Edward	Howarden 11/5/1910	16/10/1982	Castleford Town May 1929
				Darlington guest Feb 1940
Davies	Gareth Michael John	Chesterfield 4/2/1983		Chesterfied Feb 2008
Davies	George	Earlestown 1916		Bury guest May 1942
Davison	Robert	South Shields 17/7/1959		Huddersfield Town Aug 1981
				Rotherham Utd Jul 1996
Daws	Anthony	Sheffield 10/9/1966		Lincoln City Mar 1996
Dawson	Adam	Craster 23/12/1912	5/2004	Torquay Utd Sep 1937
Dempsey	AG			Leeds Utd guest Oct 1940
Dennis	John (Jack)			Navy Oct 1940
Dent	Frederick	Sheffield 24/1/1896	1983	Sheffield Wed Jun 1921
Diamond	Barry	Dumbarton 20/2/1960		Rochdale Feb 1986
Dingwall	William Norman	Gateshead 29/7/1923		Sheffield Utd Jul 1947
Dixon				Apr 1915
Dixon	Ernest	Pudsey 10/7/1901	27/4/1941	Bradford City May 1922
				Burnley Dec 1924
Dobson	Paul	Hartlepool 17/12/1962		Scarborough loan Oct 1990
Doggart	Frank	1888		Mirfield Utd May 1912
Donaldson	Clayton Andrew	Bradford 7/2/1984		Hull City loan Feb 2004
Donaldson	Thomas	Selby 18/4/1906	1989	Selby Town Jul 1930
Donnelly	Paul Anthony	Liverpool 23/12/1971		Trainee Jul 1988
Donovan	Kevin	Halifax 17/12/1971		Huddersfield Town loan Feb 1992
Dooley	George W	Chesterfield 29/12/1922	4/2004	Chesterfield Dec 1946
Doran	Sam	Bradford 22/12/1912	10/1995	Reading Aug 1939
Dougal	James	Denny 3/10/1913	17/10/1999	Carlisle Utd Oct 1948
Dougal	John	Falkirk 7/8/1934		Pegasus May 1956
Doughty	Matthew Liam	Warrington 2/11/1981		Rochdale Jul 2004
Downes	Steve Fleming	Leeds 2/12/1949		Chesterfield Jun 1974
Downey	Alfred Francis (Sam)	Dublin 20/8/1898	9/1985	Bradford City May 1922
Downsborough	Peter	Halifax 13/9/1943		Juniors May 1959
Doxford				Nov 1912
Drake	Kenneth Lawrence	Skipton 17/2/1922		Nov 1946
Dryhurst	Carl David	Sutton Coldfield 8/11/1960		Sutton Town Nov 1979
Dubois	Joseph Martin	Monkstown 27/12/1927	7/1987	Grimsby Town Jul 1954
Duckett	Donald Thwaites	Thornton 20/4/1894	1970	Bradford City Dec 1924
Duckworth	Ronald	Halifax 7/12/1901	1974	Stainland Feb 1921
Dudgeon	James Fleming	Newcastle 19/3/1981		Scarborough loan Sep 2003
Duerden	Ian Christopher	Burnley 27/3/1978		Telford Utd Jul 1998
Duffield	Peter	Middlesbrough 4/2/1969		Sheffield Utd loan Mar 1988
Duffy	A			Dec 1943
Dunbavin	Ian Stuart	Knowsley 27/5/1980		Shrewsbury Town Jul 2004
Duncan	Thomas Kerr	Lochgelly 1/9/1897	9/2/1940	Leicester City Sep 1924
Dunleavy	Christopher	Liverpool 30/12/1949		Chester Oct 1976
Dunn	Barry	Middlesbrough 17/12/1939		Doncaster Rov Sep 1959
Dunn	Leslie			Guest 1941
Dunphy	Sean	Rotherham 5/11/1970		Kettering Town Mar 1995
Eccles	G			Millwall Ath Dec 1911
Edington	J			Oct 1943
Edmonds	Darren	Watford 12/4/1971		Mossley Nov 1992
Edmondson	H			Hebden Bridge Apr 1915
Edwards	James Elfyn	Aberystwyth 4/5/1960		Macclesfield Town Aug 1993
Egan	John	Kilsyth 19/8/1937		Stenhousemuir Nov 1959
Egglestone	Patrick	Penrith 17/3/1927		Bradford City Sep 1949
Elam	Lee Patrick G	Bradford 24/9/1976		Morecambe May 2003
Elliott	Edward	Carlisle 24/5/1919	1984	Chester Nov 1950
Elliott	Stuart	Hendon 27/8/1977		Exeter City Jul 2002
Elliott	William G			Sep 1940
Ellis	David			Bury Jan 1948
Ellis	Mark Edward	Bradford 6/1/1962		Bradford City Oct 1990
Ellis	Simon Anthony	Dewsbury 16/2/1988		Trainee Mar 2005
Ellison	Anthony Lee	Bishop Auckland 13/1/1973		Crewe Alexandra Sep 1996
Ellson	Merton Frederick	Northampton 10/7/1890	1958	Leeds United May 1922
Elvy	Reginald	Churwell, Leeds 25/11/1920	13/7/1991	RAF Mar 1944
Embrey	Sydney	Bolton 16/02/1903	1981	Mar 1924
England	Frederick Watson	Holmfirth 11/7/1923	12/2002	Huddersfield Town Apr 1946
Etherington	Craig	Basildon 16/9/1979		West Ham Utd loan Feb 1999
Evans	David Gordon	West Bromwich 20/5/1958		West Brom Jun 1979
				Bradford City Aug 1990
Evans	Denzil Ralph	Hungerford 9/10/1915	2/1996	Bury Jul 1936
Evans	John Royston	Lampeter 9/2/1939		Chester Nov 1960
Everingham	Nicholas	Hull 11/2/1973		Odham Ath Feb 1993
Fagan	George	Dundee 27/9/1934		Leeds Utd Jun 1958
Fallaize	Reginald A			Sep 1940
Farley	John Dennis	Middlesbrough 21/9/1951		Watford loan Sep 1971
Farnaby	Craig	Hartlepool 8/8/1967		Middlesbrough Sep 1986
Farrar	Thomas Briggs	Northowram 1889	26/2/1942	West Vale Ramblers Dec 1911Sep 1911

HALIFAX TOWN PLAYERS 1911-2008

To	League			CONF			FA Cup			FL Cup		
	A	S	G	A	S	G	A	S	G	A	S	G
				8	0	0	0	0	0			
Chesterfield Mar 1936	196	0	29				19	0	2	0	0	0
Gainsborough Trin Jul 2008				10	1	1	0	0	0			
Derby Co Dec 1982	63	0	29	11	14	1	3	1	0	4	0	4
Guiseley May 1997												
Scarborough Aug 1996				5	0	1	0	0	0			
Rochdale Jan 1938	6	0	0				0	0	0	0	0	0
cs 1941												
Chesterfield Aug 1923	38	0	12				1	0	1	0	0	0
Gainsborough Trin cs 1987	17	5	3				3	0	0	1	1	0
Boston Utd cs 1948	9	0	0				0	0	0	0	0	0
cs 1915												
Burnley Mar 1924	237	0	127				16	0	5	0	0	0
Huddersfield Town Sep 1929												
	1	0	1				0	0	0	0	0	0
cs 1913												
				2	2	0	0	0	0			
Bridlington Town cs 1932	10	0	3				0	0	0	0	0	0
Northwich Vic cs 1992	9	4	0				0	0	0	0	1	0
	6	0	0				0	0	0	0	0	0
Chesterfield Jun 1947	11	0	2				0	0	0	0	0	0
cs 1946												
Chorley Jul 1949	21	0	2				2	0	0	0	0	0
Kettering Town cs	3	0	0				0	0	0	0	0	0
Altrincham cs 2008				122	12	0	8	0	0			
Scarborough cs 1976	38	12	12				4	1	1	4	1	2
Blackpool Feb 1923	1	0	0				0	0	0	0	0	0
Swindon Town Aug 1965	148	0	0				2	0	0	5	0	0
cs 1913												
cs 1952	134	0	0				5	0	0	0	0	0
Corby Town cs 1981	4	4	0				0	0	0	0	0	0
cs 1957	78	0	10				1	0	0	0	0	0
Bradford Nov 1927	119	0	0				2	0	0	0	0	0
cs 1921												
				9	1	0	0	1	0			
Doncaster Rov Oct 1998	1	1	0				0	0	0	0	1	0
	12	0	7				0	0	0	0	0	0
cs 1944												
Scarborough Nov 2005				53	0	0	5	0	0			
Bristol Rov cs 1926	32	0	5				1	0	0	0	0	0
Wollongong (Aus) Jan 1981	181	0	13				12	0	0	8	0	0
cs 1961												
Scarborough cs 1961												
Gainsborough Trin cs 1995				2	0	0	0	0	0			
cs 1912												
Gainsborough Trin 1993	0	2	0				0	0	0	0	0	0
cs 1915												
Southport Apr 1994				25	1	1	2	0	0			
Accrington Stan Aug 1960	5	0	0				0	0	0	0	0	0
Shrewsbury Town Aug 1950	20	0	0				0	0	0	0	0	0
Yeovil Town Oct 2003				14	1	2	1	0	0			
cs 1951	33	0	0				0	0	0	0	0	0
Harrogate Town Mar 2003				9	3	0	0	0	0			
cs 1941												
Barrow Oct 1948	2	0	0				0	0	0	0	0	0
Tadcaster Alb Mar 1992	33	4	4				5	0	0	0	0	0
cs 2005												
Hereford Utd Oct 1996				1	1	1	0	0	0			
cs 1924	23	0	6				4	0	0	0	0	0
Bolton Wan Mar 1947	21	0	0				4	0	0	0	0	0
cs 1924	3	0	0				0	0	0	0	0	0
cs 1947	18	0	1				2	0	0	0	0	0
	4	0	0				0	0	0	0	0	0
Bradford City Jun 1984	286	5	10				15	0	1	15	0	2
Brighouse Town Aug 1992												
Watford cs 1937	21	0	1				0	0	0	0	0	0
Witton Alb Jul 1961	7	0	0				1	0	0	0	0	0
cs 1993	2	0	0				0	0	0	0	0	0
	67	0	3				3	0	0	2	0	0
cs 1941												
	6	0	3				0	0	0	0	0	0
Shotton Comrades cs 1987	7	3	1				0	2	0	0	0	0
cs 1912												

Surname	Forenames	Born	Died	From
Farrar	W			Dec 1912
Farrell	Andrew	Easington 21/12/1983		Trainee Mar 2002
				Harrogate Town Oct 2004
Farren	Frederick William	Kettering 1885	2/11/1959	Bradford City loan Nov 1911
				Bradford City cs 1912
Farren	Harry	Kettering 1890	1949	Hull City cs 1912
Farrimond	Sydney	Hindley 17/7/1940		Coach Nov 1974
Fayers	Frederick	King's Lynn 29/1/1890	4/2/1954	Manchester City May 1923
Fearnley	Harrison Lockhead	Morley 27/5/1923		Leeds Utd Jan 1949
Featherstone	Harold W	Wallsend 20/6/1898		Ashington Aug 1923
Feeney	Wilfred Thomas	Grangetown 26/8/1910	1973	Stockport Co Aug 1934
Fenton	Mark			Harrogate Town Aug 1987
Ferebee	Stewart Raymond	Carshalton 6/9/1960		Darlington Jul 1987
Ferguson	Archibald Daniel	Flint 25/1/1906		Chester Jul 1933
Ferguson	Hubert	Belfast 23/5/1926	1994	Frickley Col Sep 1954
Ferguson	Michael Kevin	Burnley 9/3/1943		Al Akraanes Dec 1976
Ferneyhough	Ernest	Barnsley 5/7/1918	4/1999	Great Houghton Feb 1939
Fidler	Dennis John	Stockport 22/6/1938		Grimsby Town Apr 1963
Field	Anthony	Halifax 6/7/1946		Illingworth Utd Jul 1963
Filson	Robert Martin	St Helens 25/6/1968		Stalybridge Cel Jul 1993
Finch	Henry	Preston		Clitheroe Central Aug 1911
Findlay	William	Motherwell 1921	9/1/2001	Albion Rov guest Mar 1943
Firth				March 1921
Firth	Edwin Bertram	Dewsbury 1885	1950	Mirfield Utd Aug 1911
Firth	Francis Martin	Dewsbury 27/5/1956		Huddersfield Town Feb 1978
Firth	Horace	1889	1956	Aug 1911
Fisher	Frederick William	Barnsley 11/4/1910	1944	Millwall guest Feb 1944
Fisher	Ronald	Sheffield 9/3/1923	1/1987	Sheffield FC Aug 1950
Fisher	Stanley	Barnsley 29/9/1924	10/2003	Barnsley Jan 1947
Fitzpatrick	Ian Matthew	Manchester 22/9/1980		Manchester Utd Mar 2000
Fitzsimmons	DJ			May 1942
Fitzsimmons	Stephen	Scotland 1901		West Calder Nov 1921
Flack	Hugh David	Belfast 26/4/1903		Distillery Oct 1932
Flatley	Albert Austin	Bradford 5/9/1919	9/4/1987	Port Vale guest Nov 1943
Flavell	Robert William	Berwick 7/3/1956		Burnley Mar 1976
				Barnsley Dec 1980
Fleetwood	Edric Denton	Barnsley 1910	1969	Barnsley guest Apr 1944
Fleming	Craig	Halifax 6/10/1971		Trainee Mar 1990
Fleming	Paul	Halifax 6/9/1967		Appren Sep 1985
				Guiseley Nov 1994
Fletcher	Douglas	Sheffield 17/9/1930		Darlington Jun 1959
Flounders	Andrew John	Hull 13/12/1963		Rochdale cs 1994
Flower	Anthony John	Nottingham 2/1/1945		Notts Co Jun 1967
Ford	David	Sheffield 2/3/1945		Sheffield Utd Aug 1973
Ford	Stuart Trevor	Sheffield 20/7/1971		Scarborough loan Mar 1995
Forrest	Daniel Paul Halafihi	Keighley 23/10/1984		Bradford City loan Aug 2005
				Bradford City cs 2006
Foster	Bernard Osborne	Watford 10/12/1907	4/1993	Arsenal May 1929
Foster	Clifford Lake	Rotherham 1/4/1904	1959	Oldham Ath Mar 1929
Foster	John Thomas	Southwick 21/3/1903		Ashington Sep 1923
Foster	Martin	Sheffield 19/101977		Forest Green Rov Jul 2004
Foulkes	Jabez	Fryston 28/8/1913	7/2004	Bradford Jun 1938
Fowler	E			Apr 1912
Fowler	John Barry (Jack)	Rotherham 13/4/1935		Sheffield Utd May 1956
Fowler	Lee Edward	Nottingham 26/1/1970		Doncaster Rov Dec 1993
Fox	Frederick Samuel	Highworth, Swindon 22/11/1898	15/5/1968	Millwall Ath Jun 1927
Foxley	Peter	Middlesbrough 28/1/1939		Jul 1960
France	Darren Brian	Hull 8/8/1967		Doncaster Rov loan Oct 1993
France	John (Jack)	Stalybridge 30/11/1913	12/1995	Bath City Jun 1939
Francis	John Andrew	Dewsbury 21/11/1963		Emley Feb 1985
				Burnley Oct 1996
Frear	Bryan	Cleckheaton 8/7/1933	1997	Chesterfield Jul 1964
Frost	Desmond	Congleton 3/8/1926	6/1993	Leeds Utd Jan 1951
Fry	Russell Harok	Hull 4/12/1985		Hull City loan Aug 2006
Fryer	Henry Charles	Luton 26/9/1897	1975	Torquay Utd
Futcher	Paul	Chester 25/9/1956		Barnsley Jul 1990
Fyfe	George	Govan		Hibernian Jan 1912
Fyfe	Tony	Carlisle 23/2/1962		Carlisle Utd Jan 1990
Gadsden	Ernest	Bulwell 22/12/1895	1966	Blackpool May 1925
Gaia	Marcio dos Santos	Sao-Matens-Es, Brazil 8/9/1978		Grays Ath Mar 2008
Gallagher	Barry Patrick	Bradford 7/4/1961		Bradford City Mar 1983
Gallagher	Joseph Anthony	Liverpool 11/1/1955		Burnley loan Oct 1983
Galloway	Herbert			Barnsley junior football Jan 1926
Galloway	Michael	Oswestry 30/5/1965		Mansfield Town Jan 1986
Gannon	James Paul	Southwark, Ireland 7/9/1968		Sheffield Utd loan Feb 1990
Garforth	Clement	Halifax 1889	25/12/1947	Local Sep 1911
Garner	G			Oct 1943

HALIFAX TOWN PLAYERS 1911-2008

To	League A	S	G	CONF A	S	G	FA Cup A	S	G	FL Cup A	S	G
cs 1913												
Harrogate Town cs 2004	7	2	0	19	30	6	0	0	0	0	0	0
Leek Town Nov 2004												
Kettering Town May 1913												
banned Feb 1914												
cs 1976												
retired cs 1924	8	0	0				0	0	0	0	0	0
Newport County Jul 1949	3	0	0				0	0	0	0	0	0
cs 1924	20	0	2				0	0	0	0	0	0
Chester cs 1937	52	0	11				2	0	0	0	0	0
Harrogate Town Aug 1987												
Harrogate Town Aug 1988	6	6	0				0	1	0	0	2	0
Stockport Co Jul 1935	69	0	1				6	0	1	0	0	0
retired 1958	95	0	0				5	0	0	0	0	0
Rochdale Mar 1977	2	0	0				0	0	0	0	0	0
cs 1939	1	0	0				0	0	0	0	0	0
Darlington Oct 1966	142	1	39				4	0	0	7	0	2
Barrow Aug 1966	21	0	3				1	0	0	0	0	0
Dagenham & Red cs 1994				10	3	1	0	0	0			
cs 1912												
cs 1921												
West Vale Ramblers cs 1912												
Bury Aug 1982	157	11	19				7	0	1	6	0	1
cs 1913												
cs 1951	4	0	0				0	0	0	0	0	0
cs 1948	26	0	7				0	0	0	0	0	0
Shrewsbury Town Jul 2003	37	12	10	29	9	5	3	1	0	1	1	0
May 1942												
cs 1922	1	0	0				0	0	0	0	0	0
Crewe Alex cs 1934	74	0	0				10	0	0	0	0	0
Chesterfield Aug 1978	92	0	7				1	0	0	5	0	0
Vastar Haninge (Swe) 1981												
Oldham Ath Aug 1991	56	1	0				3	0	0	4	0	0
Mansfield Town Jul 1991	135	4	1	23	0	1	7	0	1	7	1	0
Chorley Jul 1995												
Bath City cs 1960	20	0	4				1	0	0	0	0	0
Northampton Town Dec 1994				9	2	1	2	2	0			
Boston Utd 1970	78	1	11				9	0	1	4	0	2
cs 1976	83	2	6				5	0	1	8	0	0
				5	0	0	0	0	0			
				95	12	14	4	0	0			
Crawley Town May 2008												
cs 1930	23	0	4				0	0	0	0	0	0
cs 1930	8	0	3				0	0	0	0	0	0
Grimsby Town cs 1925	73	0	2				9	0	1	0	0	0
Rushden & D Jun 2007				91	6	8	6	0	1			
Crewe Alex Jun 1939	27	0	2				5	0	0	0	0	0
cs 1912												
cs 1959	19	0	3				0	0	0	0	0	0
Telford Utd Mar 1995				12	3	0	5	0	0			
Brentford Mar 1928	13	0	0				0	0	0	0	0	0
Weymouth Jul 1963	0	0	0				0	0	0	1	0	0
				0	2	0	0	0	0			
Torquay Utd cs 1948	51	0	1				5	0	0	0	0	0
Emley cs 1985	1	3	0	2	0	0	0	0	0	0	0	0
Emley Nov 1996												
cs 1965	35	0	7				2	0	1	1	0	0
Rochdale Nov 1953	116	0	54				4	0	0	0	0	0
				2	2	0	0	0	0			
cs 1925	31	0	0				1	0	0	0	0	0
Grimsby Town Jan 1991	15	0	0				3	0	0	4	0	0
cs 1912												
Carlisle Utd Oct 1990	13	3	0				0	0	0	2	0	1
cs 1928	82	0	0				3	0	0	0	0	0
Weymouth May 2008				6	3	0	0	0	0			
Scarborough cs 1986	110	5	27				4	0	2	8	0	1
	4	0	0				1	0	0	0	0	0
cs 1928	1	0	0				0	0	0	0	0	0
Hearts Nov 1987	79	0	5				3	0	1	4	0	1
	2	0	0				0	0	0	0	0	0
Local Sep 1911												
cs 1944												

Surname	Forenames	Born	Died	From
Garnett	Shaun Maurice	Wallasey 22/11/1969		Oldham Ath Sep 2002
Garside	M			Local Apr 1915
Gaughan	Steven Edward	Doncaster 14/4/1970		Darlington Jul 1999
Gawthorpe	Adrian	Halifax 13/2/1988		Trainee Apr 2005
Gayle	Howard Anthony	Liverpool 18/5/1958		Blackburn Rov Aug 1992
Geddes	Andrew	Craigbank 6/9/1922	11/2/1958	Mansfield Town Jul 1952
Gedman	Paul Jonathan	Wigan 14/6/1981		Bradford City Sep 2002
Geidmintis	Anthony	Stepney 30/7/1949	17/4/1993	Northampton Town Jul 1979
Gennoe	Terence William	Shrewsbury 16/3/1953		Bury May 1975
German	David	Sheffield 16/10/1973		Sheffield Wed Jul 1990
Gethin	Paul			Bolton Wan Jul 1976
Gibson	Paul Richard	Sheffield 1/11/1976		Manchester Utd loan Oct 1996
Gilbert	Edward H			Tottenham Hotspur guest Jan 1941
Gilchrist	Albert Edward	Sheffield		Arsenal Jul 1929
Giles	Terence R	Halifax 25/3/1943		Huddersfield Town Sep 1961
Gilmour	George Reynolds	Barrhead 7/5/1919	1987	Edinburgh City Sep 1948
Glaister	George	Bywell 18/5/1918		Stockport Co Aug 1950
Glidden	W Sydney	Coxlodge 30/1/1908		West Brom Jun 1928
Golden	Ryan John	Dewsbury 28/9/1985		Trainee Aug 2002
Goodall	Bernard	Islington 4/10/1937	9/1/2005	Carlisle Utd Nov 1964
Goodall	F			York City Nov 1911
Goodall	Richard			Ashton National Aug 1936
Goodman	Malcolm John	Solihull 6/5/1961		Bromsgrove Rov Sep 1979
Gordon	Louis			Clyde guest Oct 1945
Gore	Shaun Michael	London 21/9/1968		Fulham loan Feb 1991
Gorman	William Charles	Sligo 13/7/1911	1978	Brentford guest Mar 1945
Gould	Jonathan Alan	Paddington 18/7/1968		Clevedon Town Oct 1990
Goulding	Derek A	Liverpool 6/5/1963		Southport Nov 1996
Graham	Alexander	Coatbridge		Brentford Sep 1938
Graham	Deiniol William	Cannock 4/10/1969		Scunthorpe Utd Sep 1995
Graham	Peter	Worsborough Common 19/4/1947		Barnsley loan Mar 1970
Graham	Robert Henry	Middlesbrough 12/10/1900	1965	Wrexham Aug 1930
Graham	Thomas	Glasgow 31/3/1958		Barnsley Oct 1980 Scarborough Jan 1990
Graham	William	Hetton-le-Hole 3/10/1914	1996	Norwich City guest Mar 1940
Granger	Michael	Leeds 7/10/1931		Hull City Jul 1963
Grant	Gareth Michael	Leeds 6/9/1980		Bradford City loan Feb 1999
Grant	John Anthony Carlton	Manchester 9/8/1981		Shrewsbury Town Mar 2005
Gray	Nicholas James	Harrogate 17/10/1985		Leeds Utd Sep 2006
Gray	Ryan Paul	Dewsbury 28/8/1974		Barnsley Apr 1994
Grayson	Simon Darrell	Sheffield 21/10/1968		Gainsborough Trin Jun 1994
Grayston	Neil James	Keighley 25/11/1975		Southport Jul 2002
Greaves	George	Darfield		Aldershot guest Mar 1941
Green	Harold	Sedgley 3/8/1904		Nottingham For Jul 1928
Green	Harold Rodney (Rod)	Halifax 24/6/1939		Elland Utd Aug 1960
Green	Herbert			Heckmondwike Jan 1912 Heckmondwike May 1914 Jan 1912 Croft Steel Works Sep 1919
Green	Horace	Barnsley 23/4/1918	7/2000	Worsborough Bridge Nov 193
Green	Lawrence			Denaby Utd guest Nov 1941
Greenway	Mark	Halifax 19/4/1966		Appren Jun 1982
Greenwood	Nigel Patrick	Preston 27/11/1966		Preston NE Jul 1992
Gregoire	Roland Barry	Liverpool 23/11/1958		Appren Aug 1976
Gregory	Anthony Gerard	Doncaster 21/3/1968		Sheffield Wed Aug 1990 cs 1993
Gregory	Ernest W			Rotherham Town Sep 1914
Gregory	Paul Gordon	Sheffield 26/7/1961		Scunthorpe Utd loan Sep 1986
Griffith	Anthony James	Huddersfield 28/10/1986		Doncaster Rov Aug 2007
Griffiths	George	Earlestown 23/6/1924	1/2004	Bury Jun 1954
Griffiths	James Stephen	Stairfoot, Barnsley 23/2/1914	10/6/1998	Chesterfield Jul 1937 Portsmouth guest Dec 1939
Griffiths	Neil	Halifax 4/9/1972		Trainee Jul 1989
Griffiths	William	Manchester 20/5/1979		Trainee May 1997
Groves				Oct 1911
Groves	Arthur	Killamarsh 27/9/1907	27/9/1979	Langworth Col May 1927
Grummett	James	Hoyland 31/7/1918	11/5/1996	Lincoln City guest Oct 1943
Guinan	Stephen Anthony	Birmingham 24/12/1975		Nottingham For loan Oct 1998
Gwyther	David Geoffrey Andrew	Birmingham 6/12/1948		Swansea City Aug 1973
Haddington	William Raymond (Ray)	Bradford 18/11/1923	1994	Bradford guest Feb 1944 Rochdale Nov 1953
Haigh	Graham	Huddersfield 16/9/1946		Apprent Sep 1963
Haigh	Philip	Boston 27/9/1982		Nottingham For Jul 2002
Haldane	James	Edinburgh 17/9/1898		Penicuik Jnrs Apr 1921
Hale	Alfred	Kiveton Park 24/1/1906	1972	Llanelly Oct 1934
Hale	Kenneth Oliver	Blyth 13/9/1939		Darlington Jul 1972
Hall				Feb 1913
Hall	David	Manchester 19/10/1973		Oldham Ath Sep 1994

HALIFAX TOWN PLAYERS 1911-2008

To	League A	League S	League G	CONF A	CONF S	CONF G	FA Cup A	FA Cup S	FA Cup G	FL Cup A	FL Cup S	FL Cup G
Morecambe Nov 2003				40	0	1	0	0	0			
cs 1915												
Barrow Aug 2001	35	12	1				2	0	0	2	1	0
cs 2005												
Carlisle Utd Oct 1992	2	3	0				0	0	0	0	0	0
cs 1955	50	0	4				6	0	0	0	0	0
Wrexham Nov 2002				0	2	0	0	0	0			
Cheltenham Town cs 1980	10	2	0				0	0	0	0	0	0
Southampton Feb 1978	78	0	0				8	0	0	6	0	0
Sheffield Wed Jun 1995	30	9	2	42	14	3	6	1	1	1	0	0
cs 1977												
				3	0	0	0	0	0			
Denaby Utd cs 1930	15	0	4				1	0	0	0	0	0
Nelson cs 1963	3	0	1				0	0	0	0	0	0
East Fife cs 1950	36	0	2				2	0	0	0	0	0
Accrington Stan Sep 1951	34	0	7				1	0	1	0	0	0
Worcester City cs 1929	3	0	0				0	0	0	0	0	0
cs 2003				0	1	0	0	0	0			
Hillingdon Bor Jul 1965	23	0	0				0	0	0	0	0	0
cs 1912												
cs 1937	5	0	1				0	0	0	0	0	0
Alvechurch cs 1982	70	16	1				3	0	0	2	0	0
	15	0	0				0	0	0	0	0	0
West Brom Jan 1992	33	0	0				5	0	0	2	0	0
Chorley cs 1997				8	1	0	0	0	0			
cs 1939	14	0	3				0	0	0	0	0	0
Dagenham & Red Sep 1995				1	0	0	0	0	0			
	6	0	0				0	0	0	0	0	0
Workington cs 1932	40	0	0				4	0	0	0	0	0
Doncaster Rov Aug 1982	124	5	21				5	0	1	5	0	0
Frickley Ath cs 1991												
Scarborough Jul 1965	2	0	0				1	0	1	1	0	0
	0	3	0				0	0	0	0	0	0
Aldershot Town Jul 2006				36	14	14	2	1	0			
Harrogate Town Aug 2008				2	12	0	0	0	0			
Gainsborough Trin Feb 1995				0	3	0	0	0	0			
Gainsborough Trin Aug 1994												
Alfreton Town Jul 2003				23	9	0	1	0	0			
Castleford Town cs 1929	1	0	0				0	0	0	0	0	0
Bradford Jun 1962	9	0	2				0	0	0	1	0	0
Heckmondwike May 1913												
Heckmondwike Mar 1915												
cs 1920												
Lincoln City Feb 1949	155	0	5				15	0	0	0	0	0
Oswestry Town cs 1985	15	1	1				1	0	0	1	0	0
Bamber Bridge cs 1993	21	4	5	3	0	0	0	0	0	1	1	0
Sunderland Nov 1977	5	0	0				0	0	0	0	0	0
Buxton Jan 1992	16	1	1	5	1	0	0	0	0	2	1	1
rel Oct 1993	16	1	1									
cs 1915												
	6	0	0				0	0	0	0	0	0
Port Vale Aug 2008				35	2	4	1	0	0			
Earlestown Jul 1958	166	0	14				6	0	0	0	0	0
Portsmouth Jun 1939	76	0	14				8	0	2	0	0	0
Emley cs 1993	2	2	0				0	0	0	0	0	0
Hyde Utd Oct 1999				0	2	0	0	2	0			
cs 1912												
Blackburn Rov Dec 1928	30	0	5				0	0	0	0	0	0
	12	0	2				0	0	0	0	0	0
Rotherham Utd Feb 1976	104	0	26				7	0	5	6	0	1
	8	0	1				2	0	1	0	0	0
Bedford Town cs												
cc Nov 1964	1	0	0				0	0	0	0	0	0
rel Nov 2002				9	2	0	1	0	0			
cs 1922	8	0	0				0	0	0	0	0	0
Dinnington Ath cs 1936	27	0	0				4	0	0	0	0	0
Hartlepool Utd man Jun 1974	52	0	4				2	0	1	2	0	0
cs 1913												
Stalybridge Cel Feb 1995				4	1	0	1	1	0			

Surname	Forenames	Born	Died	From
Hall	Derek Robert	Ashton-under-Lyme 5/1/1965		Southend Utd Jul 1989
Hall	Ellis	Ecclesfield 22/6/1889	17/3/1947	Hamilton Acad Jun 1922
Hall	Fretwell	Ecclesfield 1/7/1892	1937	Brighton & HA Jun 1921
Hall	James			Mar 1934
Hall	Jeffrey			Mar 1924
Hall	Samuel Ronald			Luton Town guest Apr 1943
Hallam	Norman Henry	Stoke 23/10/1920	1997	Barnsley Oct 1953
Hallybone	James Michael	Leytonstone 15/5/1962		Orient Jul 1982
Hamilton	GB			Queen's Park guest Dec 1943
Hamilton	George			Rangers guest Feb 1941
Hamlet	Gareth	Huddersfield 10/1/1980		Trainee Nov 1997
Hampson	Alan	Prescot 31/12/1927	8/1989	Everton Nov 1952
Hampton	Ivan Keith	Kimberley 15/10/1942		Notts Co Jun 1967
Hand	Paul	Halifax 18/7/1979		Trainee May 1997
Hanks	Albert	Doncaster 26/4/1908	1979	Brodsworth Main Mar 1931
Hanna	Samuel			1940–41
Hannaby	Cyril	Doncaster 11/10/1923		Hull City Feb 1948
Hanson	David Paul	Huddersfield 19/11/1968		Bury Sep 1993
				Leyton Orient Jan 1998
Hanson	Neil	Blackburn 16/6/1964		Preston NE Aug 1983
Harban	Thomas John	Barnsley 12/11/1985		Barnsley Jan 2008
Hardaker				Thirsk Oct 1919
Hardaker	James	1901		Calverley Aug 1922
Hardcastle	William			Sep 1930
Hardy	Jason Paul	Burnley 14/12/1969		Burnley loan Jan 1992
				Burnley Jul 1992
Hargreaves	John	Rotherham 1/5/1915	1978	Leeds Utd guest May 1940
Harker	Stanley Jefferson	Bradford 1 Oct 1909	1973	Wyke Aug 1931
Harold	Ian Brian	Liverpool 165/1/1969		Barrow Aug 1996
Harris	David	Stoke 19/11/1953		Port Vale Jul 1979
Harris	Geoffrey Robert	Manchester 1/2/1956		Oldham Ath Jul 1978
Harris	Thomas John	Swansea 18/5/1934		Leeds Utd Oct 1955
Harrison	A			Apr 1912
Harrison	Eric George	Halifax 5/2/1938		Mytholmroyd May 1956
Harrison	Francis Nicholas	Middlesbrough 19/9/1963		Guiseley Mar 1987
Harrison	Fred Parker	Bradford 21/6/1911	1986	Bradford Jun 1936
Harrison	Gerald Randall	Lambeth 15/4/1972		Sunderland Aug 2000
Harrold	Mark Anthony	Halifax 29/1/1957		Apprent Aug 1974
Harsley	Paul	Scunthorpe 29/5/1978		Scunthorpe Utd May 2001
Hart	Ian			Sep 1995
Hartfield	Charles Joseph	Lambeth 4/9/1971		Caernarfon Town Nov 2002
Harvey				Mar 1920
Harvey	William	Grimsby		Grimsby Town guest Feb 1945
Haslam	Steven Robert	Sheffield 6/9/1979		Sheffield Wed Aug 2004
				Northampton Town Sep 2004
Hastie	Archibald	Shotts		Bradford City guest May 1942
Hastings	P			Aug 1940
Haughey	Frederick	Conisborough 12/05/1921		Sep 1945
Hauxby	Thomas			Abertillery Jan 1914
Hawe	Steven John	Machbrafelt 23/12/1980		Blackburn Rov loan Nov 2000
Hawley	William	Sheffield 1894		Blackpool Jun 1921
Hayes	Lawrence	Hemsworth 6/3/1916	2/1990	South Kirkby Col Sep 1935
Haywood	Johnson William (Johnny)	Eckington 11/4/1899	1977	Chelsea May 1924
Hazeldine	Albert Victor	Royton 28/7/1918		West Ham Utd Nov 1945
Heath	Harold	Sheffield		Feb 1920
Heath	Westby	Ribblesdale 22/2/1891	11/2/1961	Luton Town Oct 1915
Heathcote	Michael	Kelloe 10/9/1965		Sunderland loan Dec 1987
Heavey	J			Mar 1944
Hebden	John T	Castleford 12/11/1900	1956	Clapton Orient Oct 1932
Hedge	Jonathan	Rotherham 19/7/1988		Rotherham United Jul 2006
Hedworth	Christopher	Newcastle 5/1/1964		Barnsley Aug 1988
Heinemann	Nicholas	Bradford 4/1/1985		Trainee Mar 2002
Helliwell	Charles	Barnsley		May 1931
Helliwell	Sidney	Sheffield 30/1/1904	11/1939	Hednesford Town Mar 1934
Helliwell	Timothy	1896		Mythomroyd Feb 1921
Hendrick	John	Halifax 5/11/1964		Liversedge Sep 1995
Hendrie	Paul	Glasgow 27/3/1954		Bristol Rov Jul 1979
Henry	Gerald Robert	Barnsley 5/10/1920	1979	Leeds Utd guest May 1940
				Sheffield Wed Nov 1951
Henry	Liburd Algernon	Roseau, Dominica 29/8/1967		Watford loan Sep 1988
Herbert	Robert	Durham 29/8/1983		Trainee Oct 2000
Heslop	Simon James	York 1/5/1987		Barnsley loan Oct 2007
Hetherington	Sidney	Monkwearmouth 24/8/1896	1974	Southwick Aug 1921
Heyes	Darren Lee	Swansea 11/1/1967		Rochester Aug 1993
Heyhirst	Brighton	Hebden Bridge 1880	4/1962	Trainer Apr 1915
Heys	Michael	Preston 23/6/1938		Workington Nov 1963
Hibbert	Henry Crookes	Sheffield 1888		Sheffield Wed Jul 1914

HALIFAX TOWN PLAYERS 1911-2008

To	League A	S	G	CONF A	S	G	FA Cup A	S	G	FL Cup A	S	G
Hereford Utd Jul 1991	48	1	4				2	0	0	5	0	1
Consett cs 1926	115	0	2				14	0	1	0	0	0
cs 1923	52	0	2				5	0	0	0	0	0
cs 1934	2	0	1				0	0	0	0	0	0
cs 1924	2	0	0				0	0	0	0	0	0
Goole Town Jan 1954	3	0	0				1	0	0	0	0	0
Dagenham Aug 1983	11	5	0				0	0	0	2	0	0
Barrow cs 1999												
Bradford City Jul 1956	121	0	32				8	0	1	0	0	0
Peterborough Utd Jul 1969	57	2	2				7	0	0	1	0	0
Bradford PA cs 1999												
cs 1931	14	0	2				1	0	0	0	0	0
Scarborough cs 1848	2	0	0				0	0	0	0	0	0
Hednesford Town Jul 1995	19	12	2	44	9	17	0	0	0	4	0	2
Nuneaton Bor cs 1999												
Chorley Jan 1994	1	1	0				0	0	0	1	0	0
FC Halifax Town Aug 2008				4	2	0	0	0	0			
cs 1920												
cs 1923	3	0	0				0	0	0	0	0	0
cs 1931												
	20	6	2	5	3	0	0	0	0	0	0	0
Prestwich Heyes cs 1994												
cs 1932	6	0	0				2	0	0	0	0	0
Sep 1996				4	0	0	0	0	0			
Stafford Rangers cs 1981	69	2	3				5	0	1	3	1	0
cc Dec 1976	10	5	1				0	0	0	0	0	0
Tunbridge Wells	9	0	0				3	0	0	0	0	0
cs 1912												
Hartlepools Utd Aug 1964	199	0	10				9	0	1	6	0	1
cs 1990	48	6	0				0	1	0	2	0	0
cs	3	0	0				0	0	0	0	0	0
Prestwich Heyes cs Oct 2000	7	2	1				0	0	0	2	0	0
Rossendale Utd cs 1976	8	6	1				1	0	0	0	0	0
Northampton Town Jul 2002	45	0	11				3	0	1	1	0	0
Darlington Oct 1995				0	1	0	0	0	0			
Ilkeston Town Dec 2002				2	0	2	0	0	0			
cs 1920												
Northampton Town Aug 2004				95	0	0	7	0	0			
Bury Jun 2007												
Bradford City Aug 1946												
cs 1914												
	6	2	0				1	0	0	0	0	0
cs 1922	7	0	0				0	0	0	0	0	0
cs 1936	1	0	0				0	0	0	0	0	0
Yeovil Town cs 1925	1	0	0				0	0	0	0	0	0
cs 1947	10	0	2				0	0	0	0	0	0
cs 1920												
Stockport Co 1919												
	7	0	1				1	0	0	0	0	0
cs 1944												
Chesterfield 1933	1	0	0				0	0	0	0	0	0
Harrogate Town cs 2008												
Blackpool Sep 1990	38	0	0				3	0	0	3	0	0
Liversedge Nov 2003	3	0	0				0	0	0	0	0	0
cs 1933	30	0	1				0	0	0	0	0	0
Goole Town 1935	1	0	0				0	0	0	0	0	0
cs 1921												
Bradford PA Dec 1996				33	6	2	2	0	1			
Stockport Co Aug 1984	187	0	11				10	0	1	10	0	0
	24	0	3				0	0	0	0	0	0
Manager Feb 1952												
	1	4	0				0	0	0	0	0	0
Durham City Aug 2003	15	10	0	0	3	0	0	0	0	0	1	0
				28	2	5	3	0	1			
rel Mar 1922	27	0	11				0	0	0	0	0	0
VS Rugby Oct 1996				64	0	0	7	0	0			
Halifax RLFC 1915												
cs 1963	1	0	0				0	0	0	0	0	0
cs 1915												

Surname	Forenames	Born	Died	From
Hickman	George	Lanchester 17/1/1909	26/8/1978	West Brom Jul 1928
Hicks	S			Arsenal guest Mar 1944
Hiftle	William Adam	Byker 16/1/1917		Doncaster Rov guest Apr 1943
Higgins	David Kenneth	Halifax 9/10/1974		Sowerby Utd Mar 1994
Higgins	George	Batley 12/9/1932		Huddersfield T Jul 1957
Higgins	William	Scotland 1913		Kilmarnock jun football Dec 1933
Highmoor	George Wilfred	Clara Vale 1924		Newcastle Utd guest Apr 1943
Hildersley	Ronald C	Kirkaldy 6/4/1965		Montreal Sprint Nov 1991
Hill	David			Trial Sep 1936
Hill	Frederick	Sheffield 17/1/1940		Bolton Wan Jul 1969
Hindle	Thomas	Keighley 22/2/1921		York City Sep 1949
Hinsley	George	Sheffield 19/7/1914	1989	Bradford City Jul 1949
Hird				Mar 1920
Hitchen	Trevor	Sowerby Bridge 25/9/1926		Aug 1943
Hockenhull	Darren	Knowsley 5/9/1982		Blackburn Rov Jul 2003
Hodgkinson	Edwin Slack	Ilkeston 27/11/1920	10/2004	Leeds Utd Jul 1948
Hodgson	George			Dec 1923
Hodgson	Joseph	South Moor		Darlington guest 1940
Hogg	Frederick William	Bishop Auckland 24/4/1918	19/8/2001	Luton Town guest Sep 1940
				Mansfield Town Oct 1947
Holden	Richard William	Skipton 9/9/1964		Carnegie Col Sep 1986
Holden	William	Bolton 1/4/1928	25/1/2011	Bury May 1962
Hollingworth	James W	Manchester 1911		Manchester NE May 1934
Holmes	Barry	Bradford 4/10/1942		Ossett Alb Jul 1966
Holmes	Thomas	Hemsworth 14/12/1934		Barnsley Jul 1959
Holt	George	Halifax 28/2/1927		Army Feb 1948
				Shaw Lodge 1947
Holt	Grant	Carlisle 12/4/1981		Workington Reds Sep 1999
Holt	Raymond	Thorne 29/10/1939		Oldham Ath Jul 1966
Hook	Steven Jack	Todmorden 1/11/1974		Trainee Jul 1991
Hopkins	William John	Queensferry 1913		Chester Aug 1930
Hopper	William	Bishop Auckland 20/2/1938		West Auckland Dec 1961
Horner	Noel	Halifax 18/2/1978		Trainee 1996
Horner	Philip Matthew	Leeds 10/11/1966		Leicester City Aug 1988
Horsfall	Thomas William	Hamilton 7/1/1951		Cambridge Utd Jul 1977
Horsfield	Geoffrey Malcolm	Barnsley 1/11/1973		Scarborough Jan 1994
				Witton Alb Oct 1996
Horsman	Leslie	Burley-in-Wharfedale 26/5/1920	1996	Bradford Jul 1953
Horton	Leslie	Salford 12/7/1921		York City Mar 1951
Horwood	Neil Kenneth	Peterhead 4/8/1964		Grimsby Town loan Dec 1986
Hotte	Timothy Alwin	Bradford 4/10/1963		Harrogate Town Aug 1985
Hough	John	Halifax 9/6/1954	3/7/2009	Halifax IDC Dec 1978
Houghton	Scott Aaron	Hitchin 22/10/1971		Leyton Orient Jan 2002
Houldsworth	George Evelyn	Huddersfield 1887	1960	Aug 1911
Housley	Herbert	Worsnop 1897		Loughborough Corin Jul 1923
				Shirebrook May 1926
Howard	Stanley	Chorley 1/7/1934	19/6/2004	Barrow Jul 1964
Howatt				Dec 1912
Howell	Dean	Burton-on-Trent 29/11/1980		Morecambe Jul 2004
				Carlisle Utd Feb 2006
Howes	Kieran	Brighton 24/11/1988		Under 19s Jan 2006
Howlett	Charles Edward	Auckland 26/9/1906	1990	Evenwood Aug 1929
Howsam	Alfred Dennis	Sheffield 21/10/1922	1981	Chesterfield Jun 1948
Howson	Horace	Hunslet 2/2/1899	1972	Careau Aug 1921
Howson	William	Garforth 2/10/1893	1959	Oldham Ath Aug 1924
Hoy	Robert	Halifax 10/1/1950		Blackburn Rov May 1976
Hoyland	Ernest	Thurnscoe 17/1/1914		Firbeck Jan 1937
Hoyle	Matthew James	Halifax 15/11/1986		Trainee Aug 2003
Hubbert	Hugh	Bradford 12/10/1899	1966	Bradford Jul 1927
Hudson	Daniel Robert	Doncaster 25/6/1979		Doncaster Rov Jul 2003
Hudson	Geoffrey Alan	Leeds 14/10/1931		Bradford City Aug 1959
Hudson	John E	Barnsley		Feb 1930
Hughes	Thomas J			Rhyl Ath Jun 1913
Hughes	William Jack	Rhyl 1889	1955	Norwich City Jun 1913
				Barrow Dec 1914
Hulme	Kevin	Farnworth 2/12/1967		Macclesfield Town Oct 1996
Humphreys	Percy Ronald	Bradford 28/10/1924	1999	Boothtown Sep 1943
Humpish	Albert Edward (Ted)	Newcastle 3/4/1902	1986	Jan 1922
Hunt	Robert	Newcastle 20/9/1966		Barnsley Jan 1985
Hunt-Brown	Peter Barry	Halifax 19/2/1937		Elland Utd Dec 1958
Hunter	Donald	Thorne 10/3/1927		Huddersfield Town Aug 1951
Hunter	Stanley			guest Jan 1941
Hurst	Christopher Mark	Barnsley 3/10/1973		Huddersfield Town loan Nov 1997
Hutchinson	George Henry	Allerton Bywater 31/10/1929	30/7/1996	Leeds Utd Jul 1956
Hutchinson	Ian Nicholas	Stockton-on-Tees 7/11/1972		Trainee Jul 1991
				Gillingham Mar 1995
Hutchinson	James Barry	Sheffield 27/1/1936	12/7/2005	Darlington Nov 1966

HALIFAX TOWN PLAYERS 1911-2008

To	League A	S	G	CONF A	S	G	FA Cup A	S	G	FL Cup A	S	G
Scarborough cs 1930	50	0	8				1	0	0	0	0	0
rel Jun 1995				2	3	0	0	0	0			
cs 1958	5	0	0				0	0	0	0	0	0
cs 1934												
Raith Rov Mar 1993	21	10	2				0	2	1	2	0	0
cs 1937												
Manchester City May 1970	25	0	3				2	0	1	2	0	0
Rochdale Mar 1952	85	0	17				3	0	1	0	0	0
Nelson Sep 1950	32	0	0				1	0	0	0	0	0
cs 1920												
Notts Co May 1945												
Stalybridge Cel Aug 2005				32	6	0	1	0	0			
cs 1950	13	0	2				1	0	0	0	0	0
cs 1925	3	0	1				0	0	0	0	0	0
	49	0	2				2	0	0	0	0	0
Wigan Ath cs 1950												
Watford Mar 1988	66	1	12				7	0	0	2	0	0
Hereford Utd cs 1963	37	0	11				2	0	0	0	0	0
cs 1935	6	0	0				0	0	0	0	0	0
Thackley cs 1973	82	8	8				2	1	0	5	1	0
Chesterfield Jul 1961	50	0	16				2	0	0	0	0	0
Aldershot Mar 1948	57	0	12				5	0	2	0	0	0
ret cs 1954												
Barrow Aug 2001	0	6	0				0	0	0	1	0	1
Scaunthorpe Utd Jul 1968	86	0	0				7	0	1	2	0	0
Bury 1994				1	1	0	0	0	0			
cc Apr 1932	20	0	3				3	0	0	0	0	0
Workington Jul 1963	35	0	9				0	0	0	0	0	0
Bangor City Aug 1998				55	25	4	3	2	0			
Blackpool Sep 1990	70	2	4				6	0	2	6	0	0
Dover Ath Mar 1978	15	1	2				0	0	0	2	0	1
Worsborough Br cs 1994	10	0	7	65	8	39	4	0	4	4	0	1
Fulham Oct 1998												
Coach Jul 1955	120	0	8				3	0	0	0	0	0
Ashton Utd Oct 1952	35	0	1				1	0	0	0	0	0
	3	0	0				0	0	0	0	0	0
Frickley Ath 1985	2	2	0				0	0	0	0	0	0
Halifax IDC cs 1980	1	0	0				0	0	0	0	0	0
Stevenage Bor Mar 2002	7	0	0				0	0	0	0	0	0
ret Oct 1911												
Loughborough Corin cs 1924	71	0	21				11	0	1	0	0	0
cs 1928												
Chorley cs 1965	21	0	1				2	0	0	1	0	0
cs 1913												
Colchester Utd Aug 2005				27	8	6	3	1	0			
Weymouth Jun 2006												
cs 2006												
Shildon cs 1930	2	0	1				0	0	0	0	0	0
Gainsborough Trin cs 1949	20	0	5				0	0	0	0	0	0
Selby Town cs 1922	35	0	0				1	0	0	0	0	0
ret Mar 1926	48	0	18				1	0	0	0	0	0
York City Aug 1977	30	0	7				4	0	0	0	0	0
Blackpool Jan 1938	30	0	8				2	0	0	0	0	0
Liversedge cs 2004				0	1	0	0	0	0			
cs 1929	59	0	4				2	0	0	0	0	0
Belper Town May 2004				21	7	0	1	0	0			
Exeter City Jul 1961	52	0	0				3	0	0	0	0	0
cs 1950	1	0	0				0	0	0	0	0	0
cs 1914												
Bradford City Jan 1914												
cs 1920												
York City Sep 1999	30	1	4	51	0	9	4	0	0	4	1	0
cs 1948	3	0	1				0	0	0	0	0	0
Walker Celtic cs 1922	8	0	1				0	0	0	0	0	0
Goole Town cs 1986	3	0	0				0	0	0	0	0	0
cs 1959	1	0	0				0	0	0	0	0	0
Southport Aug 1952	11	0	0				0	0	0	0	0	0
				2	1	0	0	0	0			
Bradford City Jul 1958	44	0	11				1	0	1	0	0	0
Berwick Ran cs 1992	7	1	1	9	2	1	0	0	0	0	0	0
Weymouth cs 1995												
Rochdale Jul 1967	25	0	14				6	0	5	0	0	0

Surname	Forenames	Born	Died	From
Hutchinson	William L	Chester-le-Street		Darlington Dec 1932
Hutt	Geoffrey	Hazelwood 28/9/1949		York City Apr 1978
Hutton	Harold	Bolton		Hebble Motors Nov 1938
Ibbotson	Luke			
Ingledow	Jamie Graeme	Barnsley 23/8/1980		Stocksbridge PS Sep 2002
Ingram	Stuart Denevan	Sunderland 27/6/1976		Forest Green Rov Mar 2004
Irvine	William John	Carrickfergus 18/6/1943		Brighton &HA Dec 1972
Isaac	James	Cramlington 23/10/1916	1993	Huddersfield Town guest May 1942
Isitt	Derek	Bradford 1927		Apr 1945
Islip	Ernest	Parkwood Springs 1892	1941	Huddersfield Town Dec 1915
Jackson	Alfred Gordon	Bradford 30/01/1920	2000	Sep 1938
Jackson	David	Stoke 23/1/1937		Tranmere Rov Jul 1963
Jackson	Harold	Halifax 20/7/1917	1996	Sowerby Br WE Aug 1936
Jackson	Justin Jonathan	Nottingham 10/12/1974		Notts Co Feb 1999
Jackson	Peter Allan	Bradford 6/4/1961		Chester City Jul 1997
Jacobs	Wayne Graham	Sheffield 3/2/1969		Bradford City Jul 2005
Jamieson	John Pretsel (Jock)	Newton Grange 9/12/1898	1974	Lochgelly Utd Apr 1921
Jeffrey	Harold	1894		Leeds Utd Oct 1920
Jenkinson	Thomas Henry	Bradford 15/5/1895	1974	Bradford City Jul 1920
Johnman	John	Newmains 1905		Stockport Co Jul 1933
Johnson	Arthur	Liverpool 23/1/1933		Blackburn Rov Mar 1955
Johnson	Kevin Peter	Doncaster 29/8/1952		Huddersfield Town Aug 1978
Johnson	Howard Simon (Simon)	Doncaster 27/6/1971		Armthorpe Welf Mar 1995
Johnson	William Joseph (Joe)	Wednesbury 23/6/1899		Wigan Bor Jul 1931
Johnston	A			Partick Thist guest Oct 1943
Johnston	John	Belfast 2/5/1947		Blackpool loan Oct 1971 Southport Jul 1976
Johnstone	Robert	Coldstream 18/9/1908		Bradford guest Dec 1039
Jones				Dec 1919
Jones	Alan	Grimethorpe 21/1/1951		Huddersfield Town Aug 1973
Jones	Alexander	Blackburn 27/11/1964		Rochdale Mar 1994
Jones	David	Hodthorpe 9/4/1914		Bury Apr 1943
Jones	Gary	Huddersfield 6/4/1969		Hartlepool Utd Mar 2000
Jones	George Alexander	Radcliffe 21/4/1945		Oldham Ath Feb 1976
Jones	John (Darkie)			Byker WE Aug 1920
Jones	William M			1943/44
Jones	William R			Port Vale guest Sep 1943
Jordon	H			Huddersfield Town Sep 1913
Jowett	Harold Uttley	Halifax 15/11/1923	2005	Elland Utd Jul 1950
Jowett	Kenneth Stuart	Bradford 9/3/1927	1993	Fryston Col cs 1946
Joyce	William	Hebden Bridge		Aug 1935
Joynes	Nathan	Hoyland 7/8/1985		Barnsley loan Nov 2006 Barnsley Jan 2008
Jules	Mark Anthony	Bradford 5/9/1971		Chesterfield Jun 1999
Julian	Samuel	Eastwood 31/10/1901	1972	Heanor Town Jun 1929
Juryeff	Ian Martin	Gosport 24/11/1962		Leyton Orient Aug 1989 Hereford Utd Sep 1990
Kamara	Alan	Sheffield 15/7/1958		Scarborough Aug 1991
Kaye	George	Huddersfield		Bradford guest Dec 1939
Kearney	Thomas James	Liverpool 7/10/1981		Bradford City Sep 2006
Kellett	Charles Arthur	Chesterfield 26/12/1908	2/1990	Dec 1929
Kellock	William	Glasgow 7/2/1954		Port Vale Jul 1985
Kelly	Anthony Gerald	Prescot 1/10/1964		Knowsley Dec 1996
Kelly	James	Bradford 1/7/1938		Queensbury Utd Sep 1962
Kelly	John Carmichael	Paisley 21/2/1921	2/1/2001	Greenock Morton Jul 1956
Kelly	Lawrence	Bellshill 1/6/1905		Aldershot guest Oct 1940
Kemp	Frederick George	Salerno, Italy 27/2/1946		Blackpool Nov 1971
Kendall	Paul Scott	Halifax 19/10/1964		Apprentice Jun 1981 Scarborough Mar 1988
Kennedy	Jon	Rotherham 30/11/1980		Witton Alb Jan 2006
Kennedy	Michael Francis Martin	Salford 9/4/1961		Appren Jan 1979
Kennie	George	Bradford 17/5/1904	11/4/1994	Mansfield Town May 1925
Kent	Paul	Rotherham 23/2/1954		Norwich City Aug 1976
Kerridge	Matthew David	Halifax 17/11/1986		Under 19s Nov 2004
Kerrigan	Steven John	Baillieston 19/10/1972		Shrewsbury Town Mar 2000
Kershaw	Geoffrey			guest Apr 1942
Keys	Paul A	Ipswich 4/9/1962		Luton Town loan Mar 1982
Kilcline	Brian	Nottingham 7/5/1962		Mansfield Town Oct 1997
Killarney	Arthur	Huddersfield 26/2/1921		Feb 1939
Killeen	Lewis Keith	Peterborough 23/9/1982		Sheffield Utd loan Nov 2002 Sheffield Utd Jun 2003
Kilner	John Ian	Bolton 3/10/1959		Preston NE loan Feb 1979 Preston NE Sep 1979
King	John	Birmingham 1901		Leicester City Jul 1924
Kirby	Frederick	Co Durham		Middlesbrough Sep 1914 Buishop Auckland Sep 1919

HALIFAX TOWN PLAYERS 1911-2008

To	League			CONF			FA Cup			FL Cup		
	A	S	G	A	S	G	A	S	G	A	S	G
cs 1933	2	0	0				0	0	0	0	0	0
ret cs 1980	75	1	0				7	0	0	2	0	0
cs 1939	7	0	0				0	0	0	0	0	0
rel Sep 2002				0	1	0	0	0	0			
Scarborough Jan 2006				62	2	1	6	0	0			
Great Harwood Dec 1973	9	1	1				0	0	0	0	0	0
cs 1945												
Birmingham City Nov 1923												
cs 1944	3	0	0				0	0	0	0	0	0
Frickley Col cs 1965	66	0	2				3	0	0	4	0	0
Stockport Co Aug 1947	83	0	3				12	0	1	0	0	0
Morecambe Aug 1999	16	1	3				0	0	0	0	0	0
Huddersfield Town man Oct 1997				8	0	0	2	0	0			
Bradford City ass/man Jun 2007				8	3	0	0	0	0			
cs 1922	17	0	4				0	0	0	0	0	0
cs 1921												
cs 1921												
Dunfermline Ath cs 1934	36	0	0				4	0	0	0	0	0
Wrexham May 1960	215	0	0				9	0	0	0	0	0
Hartlepool United Jan 1981	51	6	10				1	0	0	3	0	1
Eastwood Town cs 1996				18	3	7	1	0	0			
Accrington Stan Jun 1932	27	0	6				3	0	0	0	0	0
	70	7	8				5	0	0	5	0	0
Fleetwood Town cs 1979												
cs 1920												
Chesterfield Sep 1976	109	0	6				5	1	2	11	0	0
Stalybridge Cel Jun 1995				51	0	2	5	0	0			
Nuneaton Bor Jul 2002	58	18	11				2	2	0	2	1	0
Southport Jan 1977	18	1	4				0	1	0	3	0	1
cs 1921												
cs 1914												
Goole Town cs 1951	9	0	1				0	0	0	0	0	0
cs 1949	29	0	2				1	0	0	0	0	0
Southport cs 1936	1	0	1				0	0	0	0	0	0
				10	2	4	0	0	0			
Stalybridge Cel Jul 2008												
Alfreton Town Jun 2002	88	9	1				3	1	0	4	0	0
Wigan Borough Jul 1931	32	0	0				1	0	0	0	0	0
Hereford Utd Dec 1989	88	2	20				7	0	2	6	0	1
Darlington Aug 1992												
cs 1992	35	2	0				0	0	0	2	0	0
Wrexham Jun 2008				66	5	1	3	1	0			
cs 1930	2	0	0				0	0	0	0	0	0
Kettering Town cs 1986	41	2	17				0	0	0	2	0	0
Sligo Rov 1997				0	1	0	0	0	0			
cs 1963	3	0	0				0	0	0	0	0	0
Portadown cs 1958	35	0	2				1	0	0	0	0	0
Hereford Utd Jun 1974	106	5	9				5	0	0	3	0	1
Scarborough Jul 1986	100	16	4				3	0	1	7	0	1
Macclesfield Town cs 1988												
Witton Alb cs 2006				18	0	0	0	0	0			
Huddersfield Town Aug 1980	74	2	4				6	0	1	2	0	0
cs 1926	28	0	2				1	0	0	0	0	0
cc Jan 1977	12	0	0				0	0	0	3	0	0
cs 2005												
Stirling Alb Jan 2003	70	8	21	4	5	1	3	0	0	2	1	0
	1	1	0				0	0	0	0	0	0
Altrincham May 1998				23	1	2	1	0	0			
cs 1947	2	0	0				0	0	0	0	0	0
				178	29	40	9	1	0			
Crawley Town Jun 2008												
	114	0	0				7	0	0	4	0	0
Bangor City cs 1982												
Nuneaton Town cs 1925	12	0	5				1	0	0	0	0	0
cs 1915												
cs 1920												

Surname	Forenames	Born	Died	From
Kiwomya	Andrew Derek	Huddersfield 1/10/1967		Rotherham Utd Jul 1994
				Notts Co Feb 1998
Knill	Alan Richard	Slough 8/10/1964		Southampton Jul 1984
Knott	Herbert	Goole 5/12/1914	1986	Hull City guest Apr 1942
Knowles	John David	Halifax 11/4/1941		Juniors Dec 1958
Laidler	John Ralph	Windermere 5/1/1919		Forces Sep 1940
Lambert	Colin A	Manchester 21/9/1963		Macclesfield Town Aug 1993
Lancashire	Graham	Blackpool 19/10/1972		Burley loan Nov 1992
Lancaster	David	Preston 8/9/1961		Rochdale Jul 1994
Lang	James	Larkhall		Jan 1936
Langford	Thomas Sidney	Wolverhampton 4/10/1892	1960	Swindon Town Jul 1922
Langley	Kevin James	St Helens 24/5/1964		Wigan Ath Jul 1994
Langthorn	Albert Edward	Leeds 29/8/1910	12/1985	Carlton Ath May 1931
Large	Frank	Leeds 26/1/1940	8/8/2003	British Railways Jun 1959
Laverick	William	Pelton Fell		Ashington Sep 1928
Lavery	John	Belfast 24/11/1919		Bradford City Sep 1948
Law				Apr 1913
Lawrence				Mar 1920
Lawrence	F			Jan 1914
Lawson	James Joseph	Middlesbrough 11/12/1947		Huddersfield Town May 1976
Lawther	William Ian	Belfast 20/10/1939	26/4/2010	Brentford Aug 1968
Lee	Alexander H			Leeds Utd guest May 1940
Lee	Andrew G	Liverpool 14/9/1962		Runcorn Jul 1996
Lee	Christian Earl	Aylesbury 8/10/1976		Farnborough Town May 2003
Lee	Glen Paul	Halifax 4/3/1972		Brighouse Town Dec 1995
Lee	James	Rotherham 26/1/1926	2001	Hull City Feb 1951
Lee	Jeffrey Wrenhall	Countesthorpe 3/10/1945		Huddersfield Town Dec 1964
Lee	Richard	Sheffield 11/9/1944		Mansfield Town Jul 1966
Lees	John William	Northwich 26/7/1892	1984	Preston NE Jul 1922
Lees	Joseph WD	Coalville 1894	1933	Guildford Town Mar 1924
Legzdins	Adam Richard	Stafford 28/11/1986		Birmingham City loan Nov 2005
				Brimingham City loan Oct 2007
Leister	Brenton Ross	Leeds 3/9/1985		Leeds Utd Aug 2005
Leitch	Grant	South Africa 31/10/1972		Blackpool Jul 1994
Lennard	David	Manchester 31/12/1944		Bolton Wan Jun 1969
Leonard	Michael Christopher	Carshalton 9/5/1959		Epsom & Ewell Jul 1976
				Chesterfield loan Nov 1990
Lewis	Charles Reginald	Liverpool 11/5/1921	8/1999	South Liverpool Oct 1947
Lewis	Dudley Keith	Swansea 17/11/1962		Huddersfield Town loan 1991
				Wrexham Aug 1992
Leyland	Samuel			Chorley Sep 1911
Lincoln	Andrew	Seaham Harbour 17/5/1902	1977	Glen Ross Aug 1921
Linford	Joseph	Keighley 1895	1967	Keighley Celtic Oct 1913
				Goole Town Feb 1914
Linley	Harold			Huddersfield Town Nov 1921
Little	Alan	Harden, Newcastle 5/2/1955		Torquay United Nov 1983
Little	Colin Campbell	Wythenshawe 4/11/1972		Macclesfield Town Mar 2004
Livingstone	WE			Rotherham Co Aug 1919
Lodge	James William	Felling 11/1/1895	1971	Hull City Jun 1924
Lodge	Thomas Joseph	Huddersfield 16/4/1921	7/2002	Huddersfield Town guest Sep 1944
Logan	David	Middlesbrough 5/12/1963		Northampton Town Aug 1988
Longbottom	Clement	Halifax 1889	30/10/1959	Castleford Town May 1913
Longbottom	Ernest	Halifax 10/2/1898	12/1999	Stainland Jan 1921
Longhurst	David John	Northampton 15/1/1965	8/9/1990	Nottingham For Jul 1985
Longley	Scott Edward	Wakefield 16/7/1973		Trainee Jul 1992
Longworth	John William	Halifax 1888		Dec 1911
Lonsdale	Joseph Stanley	Washington 13/4/1931	26/9/2003	Huddersfield Town Mar 1955
Lorenson	Roy Vincent	Liverpool 8/4/1932		St Elizabeth's De 1951
Lormor	Anthony	Ashington 29/10/1970		Lincoln City loan Feb 1994
Loska	Anthony Stephen Patrick	Chesterton 11/2/1950		Chester Oct 1976
Lounds	Herbert Ernest	Masborough 1889	1964	Gainsborough Trin Sep 1915
				Rotherham Co May 1923
Lovell	Trevor	Halifax 19/1/1940		Juniors Aug 1960
Low	John			Dunfermline Ath Mar 1926
Lowe	Edward			Doncaster Rov Sep 191
Lowe	Nicholas Paul	Headington 28/10/1952		Oxford Utd loan Aug 1974
Lowe	Scott	Sheffield 16/09/1984		Sheffield Wed Mar 2004
Lowe	Simon John	Westminster 26/12/1962		Barnsley Jul 1984
Lowson	Edmund Benjamin	Evenwood 21/3/1903	7/1955	Durham City May 1928
Lucas	Richard	Chapletown 22/9/1970		Hartlepool Utd Aug 1998
Luckett	Paul	Coventry 21/1/1957		Coventry City Aug 1974
Lucketti	Christopher James	Littleborough 28/9/1971		Stockport Co Jul 1991
Ludden	Dominic James	Basildon 30/3/1974		Preston NE Jun 2001
Ludlow	Lee	Newcastle 14/3/1976		Notts Co Jul 1995
Lumb				Apr 1915
Lyons	Darren Peter	Manchester 9/11/1964		Winsford Utd Dec 1996
McAllister	S			Dec 1912

HALIFAX TOWN PLAYERS 1911-2008

To	League A	S	G	CONF A	S	G	FA Cup A	S	G	FL Cup A	S	G
Scunthorpe Utd Mar 1995				29	6	13	4	0	1			
Cambridge City cs 1998												
Swansea City Aug 1987	118	0	6				6	0	0	7	0	0
Bury Jul 1963	72	0	0				6	0	0	1	0	0
cs 1941												
Hednesford Town cs 1995				58	1	10	6	0	1			
	2	0	0				0	0	0	0	0	0
Rochdale Feb 1996				21	3	7	5	0	4			
cc Feb 1936	1	0	0				0	0	0	0	0	0
cs 1923	27	0	0				2	0	0	0	0	0
rel Oct 1994				13	1	0	1	0	0			
cs 1933	2	0	0				0	0	0	0	0	0
Queen's Park Ran Jun 1962	134	0	50				6	0	2	1	0	0
cc Oct 1928	2	0	0				0	0	0	0	0	0
cs 1949	3	0	1				0	0	0	0	0	0
cs 1913												
cs 1920												
cs 1914												
cs 1979	93	0	9				5	0	1	7	0	2
Stockport Co Jul 1971	87	14	24				9	0	2	2	0	1
Knowsley Utd Oct 1996				8	0	0	2	0	0			
ret 2004				17	9	6	1	0	0			
Brighouse Town Feb 1996				4	1	1	0	0	0			
Chelsea Oct 1951	26	0	0				0	0	0	0	0	0
Peterborough Utd Jul 1973	233	9	3				14	0	0	7	0	0
Buxton 1973	14	0	0				0	0	0	0	0	0
ret Mar 1930	248	0	1				18	0	0	0	0	0
Scunthorpe Utd cs 1924	5	0	1				0	0	0			
				40	0	0	3	0	0			
St Patrick's Ath Jul 2006				2	7	0	0	0	0			
Chorley Jun 1995				11	0	1	1	0	0			
Blackpool Oct 1971	97	0	16				3	0	0	8	0	2
Notts Co Sep 1979	72	0	0				1	0	0	6	0	0
cs 1949	24	0	4				1	0	0	0	0	0
	21	3	0				2	0	0	1	0	0
Torquay Utd Dec 1992												
cs 1912												
Boldon Villa 1922	1	0	0				0	0	0	0	0	0
Bradford City Dec 1913												
Goole Town cs 1914												
cs 1922	22	0	1				0	0	0	0	0	0
Hartlepool Utd Jul 1985	68	0	6				1	0	0	4	0	1
Altrincham Jul 2004				8	0	2	0	0	0			
cs 1920												
Nuneaton Town cs 1925	42	0	0				1	0	0	0	0	0
Stockport Co Oct 1988	3	0	0				0	0	0	2	0	0
Bradford City Jan 1914												
Stainland Jan 1921												
Northampton Town Jul 1987	85	0	24				4	0	1	4	0	0
Mossley 1993	1	0	0				0	0	0	0	0	0
cs 1912												
Hartlepools Utd Nov 1960	202	0	21				10	0	1	0	0	0
Tranmere Rov Oct 1960	216	0	7				10	0	1	0	0	0
				7	0	1	0	0	0			
Stafford Ran Jul 1979	101	1	0				5	0	0	4	0	0
Gainsborough Trin 1919												
cs 1925												
Bedford Town cs 1963	8	0	0				0	0	0	0	0	0
cs 1926	5	0	1				0	0	0	0	0	0
cs 1920												
	9	0	0				0	0	0	1	0	0
Buxton cs 2004				2	0	0	0	0	0			
Hartlepool Utd Aug 1986	74	3	19				2	1	0	5	0	2
cs 1930	59	0	0				2	0	0	0	0	0
Boston Utd Jul 2000	39	9	0				2	1	0	3	0	0
Hartlepool Utd Mar 1976	26	1	0				2	0	0	0	0	0
Bury Oct 1993	73	5	2	8	0	1	2	0	0	2	0	1
Leigh RMI Aug 2002	2	0	0				1	0	0	0	0	0
Spennymoor Utd Sep 1995				0	2	0	0	0	0			
cs 1915												
Altrincham May 1998				27	14	7	1	2	0			
cs 1913												

Surname	Forenames	Born	Died	From
McAllister	Thomas	Scotland 1882		Castleford Town May 1912 Dec 1913
McAuley	Sean	Sheffield 23/6/1972		Portland Timbers (USA) Aug 2002
McCafferty	Joseph	Steventon 1902		Motherwell Apr 1926
McCaig	Robert Alexander Marshall	Dumfries 15/8/1923	1/1986	Stockport Co Jan 1952
McCall	Andrew	Hamilton 15/3/1925		Lovells Ath Jul 1956
McCann	James	Dundee 20/5/1954		Nottingham For loan Oct 1976
McCarthy	Philip Paul	Liverpool 19/2/1943		Oldham Ath Jan 1966
McClare	Sean Patrick	Rotherham 12/1/1978		Drogheda Utd Feb 2005
McClelland	Joseph Bentley	Halifax 20/4/1885	3/7/1964	Manager Feb 1913
McCombe	James Paul	Pontefract 1/1/1983		Scunthorpe Utd loan Oct 2003
McCormick	David	Halifax 3/11/1920		St Malachy's Sep 1947
McCreadie	William	Scotland 1886		Haslingdden Dec 1913 Bradford City Jun 1919
McDermaid	W			Aug 1940
McDevitt	Daniel	Scotland		Abercorn Jun 1913
McDonald	Gerard	Milnthorpe 3/12/1952	10/4/2005	Blackburn Rov Aug 1973
McDonald	Kenneth	Llanwrst 24/4/1898		Hull City Mar 1930
McEachran	Grant	Barrow 1894	1966	Doncaster Rov Aug 1924
McFadyen	William	Overton 23/6/1904	1971	Clapton Orient guest Oct 1941
McFarlane	John	Shettleston 1905		Liverpool Jul 1930
McGarry	Thomas	Heworth 28/9/1918	1953	Bradford guest Apr 1942
McGill	Andrew			Mirfield Utd Aug 1911
McGill	James Morrison	Glasgow 27/11/1946		Hull City Feb 1976
McGinn	Alexander	New Cumnock 10/10/1893		Blackpool Jun 1925
McGovern	Thomas			Leith Ath Jun 1912
McGrae	Joseph Russell	Kirkdale, Liverpool 24/10/1903	1975	Clapton Orient Jul 1931
McGraffin	George			Mar 1924
McHale	Raymond	Sheffield 12/8/1950		Chesterfield Oct 1974
McHale	William	Kelty, East Fife 9/8/1929		Carlisle Utd Mar 1955
McIlwraith	James McLean	Troon 17/4/1954		Bury Oct 1980
McInerney	Ian Dominic	Liverpool 26/1/1964		Runcorn Sep 1996
McKellor	William Henry			Huddersfield Town guest Feb 1942
McKernan	James M	Halifax 21/2/1954		Appren Oct 1969
McLachlan	Dugald	Falkirk 10/9/1953		Preston NE loan Oct 1972
McLachlan	Frederick	Kirkudbright 21/8/1899		Bury Jul 1928
McMenemy	Harold	Glasgow 26/3/1912		Dundee guest Dec 1943
McMillan	Eric	Beverley 2/11/1936		Hull City Jul 1965
McNiven	David Scott	Stonehouse 9/9/1955		Pittsburgh Spirit (Can) Mar 1985
McPhillips	Terence Peter	Manchester 1/10/1968		Trainee Oct 1987
McQuade	James	Barrhead 14/10/1933		Dumbarton Aug 1957
McStay	Henry	Co. Armagh 6/3/1985		Leeds Utd loan Sep 2004 Leeds Utd Mar 2005
McSweeney	Leon	Cork 19/2/1983		Scarborough Nov 2003
Mackrill	Percy A	Wynburg, South Africa 19/10/1894	1949	Ponypridd Jul 1921
Maddison				Northampton Town Dec 1913
Maguire	James Edward	Meadowfield 23/7/1917	9/2000	Swindon Town Oct 1948
Mahon	John	Gillingham 28/12/1911	1993	West Brom guest Nov 1939
Mallinson	Trevor	Huddersfield 25/4/1945		Huddersfield Town Dec 1964
Mallon	Ryan	Sheffield 22/3/1983		Sheffield Utd loan Jul 2002 Sheffield Utd Jun 2003
Malpass	Samuel Thomas	Consett 12/9/1918	1993	Fulham Mar 1941
Manning	J			Huddersfield Town guest Apr 1942
Mansaram	Darren Timothy D	Doncaster 25/6/1984		Grimsby Town loan Sep 2004 Grimsby Town Jan 2005
Marrison				Jan 1920
Marsh	Joseph	Stocksbridge 1887		Bailiff Bridge Sep 1912 Bailiff Bridge loan Dec 1913
Marsh	Wiliam	Brodsworth 1911		Brodsworth Main May 1931
Marsland	Frederick			Bradford City Oct 1911 Hebden Bridge Apr 151
Martin	Andrew Fitzsimmons	Wigtown 22/9/1896	1978	Blackpool May 1924
Martin	Dean Stacey	Halifax 9/9/1967		Appren Sep 1985 Scunthorpe Utd loan Oct 1994 Rochdale loan Dec 1996 Rochdale loan Feb 1997
Martin	James Colin	Stoke-on-Trent 2/12/1898	27/6/1969	Southend Utd Jul 1929
Martin	Lee Brandon	Huddersfield 9/9/1968		Rochdale Aug 1997
Martin	William Henry			Merthyr Town cs 1913 Aug 1919
Maslak	Matthew Peter	Halifax 2/4/1987		Trainee Mar 2004
Mason	Frederick C	Leeds		Aug 1938
Massey	Kendrick Bernard Woolley	Ripley 5/11/1920		Peterborough Utd Aug 1938
Massie	Leslie	Aberdeen 20/7/1935		Darlington Jun 1967
Matthews	Michael	Hull 25/9/1960		North Ferriby Utd Sep 1986 Hull City Aug 1992

HALIFAX TOWN PLAYERS 1911-2008

To	League			CONF			FA Cup			FL Cup		
	A	S	G	A	S	G	A	S	G	A	S	G
cs 1913												
cs 1914												
Sheffield Wed coach Jul 2005				17	8	0	1	0	0			
Brentford 1927	20	0	5				1	0	1	0	0	0
Crewe Alex Jul 1952	17	0	2				0	0	0	0	0	0
cs 1960	139	0	15				7	0	0	0	0	0
	2	0	1				0	0	0	0	0	0
Wigan Ath Oct 1971	179	1	18				17	0	1	6	1	1
Bradford PA Mar 2005				1	0	0	0	0	0			
cs 1920												
				7	0	1	0	0	0			
Ashton Utd Feb 1956	118	0	0				9	0	0	0	0	0
Goole Town cs 1914												
cs 1920												
cs 1941												
cs 1914												
cs 1974	10	3	0				0	0	0	0	0	0
Coleraine cs 1930	8	0	1				0	0	0	0	0	0
cs 1925	1	0	0				0	0	0	0	0	0
Northampton Town Jul 1932	65	0	15				3	0	1	0	0	0
West Vale Ramblers Sep 1912												
cc Apr 1977	31	1	0				3	0	0	1	0	0
Great Harwood cs 1927	7	0	0				0	0	0	0	0	0
Brentford Aug 1913												
Macclesfield Town cs 1932	33	0	0				4	0	0	0	0	0
cc Feb 1925	3	0	0				0	0	0	0	0	0
Swindon Town Sep 1976	86	0	21				5	0	4	6	0	0
Berwick Ran cs 1955	3	0	0				0	0	0	0	0	0
Highlands Pk (SAf)	33	3	6				0	0	0	1	0	0
Leigh RMI Jun 1997				7	0	1	0	0	0			
Mossley cs 1972	0	0	0				0	1	0	0	0	0
	1	1	0				0	0	0	0	0	0
cs 1930	95	0	1				1	0	0	0	0	0
Scarborough cs 1967	49	1	8				1	0	0	1	0	0
Morecambe cs 1985	12	0	4				0	0	0	0	0	0
Crewe Alex Aug 1991	61	32	29				3	0	1	5	3	1
cs 1958	9	0	2				0	0	0	0	0	0
				7	1	0	2	0	0			
cs 2005												
Hucknall Town Dec 2003												
Pontypridd cs 1923	57	0	0				5	0	0	0	0	0
cs 1914												
cs 1949	55	0	7				3	0	0	0	0	0
cs 1965	3	0	0				0	0	0	0	0	0
				y	20	13	2	0	1			
York City Aug 2005												
				13	8	8	1	0	0			
Sligo Rov Feb 2006												
cs 1920												
Bailiff Bridge cs 1913												
cs 1932	4	0	0				0	0	0	0	0	0
Hebden Bridge Aug 1912												
cs 1915												
Rochdale Aug 1928	149		31				5	0	0	0	0	0
Scunthorpe Utd Jul 1991	149	4	7	22	1	2	11	0	0	7	0	0
Congleton Town Aug 1930	18	0	4				0	0	0	0	0	0
Macclesfield Town Aug 1999	37	0	0	32	0	0	5	0	0	4	0	0
South Liverpool Jun 1914												
cs 1920												
Brighouse Town												
cs 1939	2	0	1				0	0	0	0	0	0
Scarborough cs 1951	83	0	7				4	0	1	0	0	0
Bradford Aug 1969	89	0	40				9	0	4	3	0	3
Scarborough Dec 1988	121	1	10				6	0	1	5	0	0
Boston Utd cs 1993												

Surname	Forenames	Born	Died	From
Matthews	Neil	Grimsby 19/9/1966		Grimsby Town loan Oct 1986 Grimsby Town Aug 1987 Stockport Co loan Sep 1991
Matthews	Robert David	Slough 14/10/1970		Stockport Co loan Feb 2001
Matthews	Thomas	25/09/1960		Hull City loan Aug 2006
Matthews	William Howard	Roadend 29/11/1884	9/2/1963	Port Vale Aug 1928
Mawson	Craig John	Keighley 16/5/1979		Burnley Feb 2001 Hereford Utd Jun 2006
May	Rory Joseph	Birmingham 25/11/1984		Lincoln City loan Mar 2004
Mays	Albert William (Billy)	Yryshir, Merthyr 12/3/1902	1959	Walsall Jun 1931
Meagan	Michael Kevin	Dublin 29/5/1934		Huddersfield Town Jul 1968
Meechan	Alexander Thomas	Plymouth 29/1/1980		Leigh RMI Nov 2004
Meechan	M			cs 1912
Megson	Kevin Craig	Halifax 1/7/1971		Bradford City Mar 1991
Mell	Stewart Albert	Doncaster 15/10/1957		Doncaster Rov Jul 1983
Mercer	Arthur Stanley	St Helens 1/1/1903	1994	Chester Nov 1933
Merron	John			Feb 1946
Merry	William	Fishguard 14/12/1910	1983	Manchester Utd Nov 1935
Middleton	Craig Dean	Nuneaton 10/9/1970		Cardiff City Mar 2000
Midgley	Craig Steven	Bradford 24/5/1976		Hartlepool Utd Jun 2001
Midgley	John Robinson (Jack)	Bradford 1910		Bradford City Jul 1932
Midwood	Michael Adrian	Huddersfield 19/4/1976		Huddersfield Town Jun 1995 Happy Valley (Hong Kong) Jan 1997 Glentoran Oct 1997
Mierzwinski	Mark Francis	York 8/2/1985		Trainee Dec 2003
Mike	Leon Jonathan	Manchester 4/9/1981		Manchester City loan Feb 2001
Millar	David	Paisley		East Fife guest Feb 1943
Miller				Mar 1920
Miller	JW			Mar 1944
Millington	George Edward	Aston 1/11/1911	10/2000	Manchester NE Jul 1934
Mills	Henry Owen (Harry)	Blyth 23/8/1922	1990	Huddersfield Town Dec 1955
Mills	James	Dalton 30/9/1915	14/1/1994	Hull City Dec 1947
Mills	Joseph	Wigan		Clitheroe Jul 1935
Milner	Clifford			Feb 1915
Milnes	Charles	Manchester 1885	6/11/1956	Rochdale Jun 1914
Milton	Stanley	Ravensthorpe 23/2/1913	6/1993	Oct 1932
Mitchell	Graham Lee	Shipley 16/2/1968		Cardiff City Jul 1999
Mitchell	HG			Sourton Utd cs 1912
Mitchell	Paul Alexander	Stalybridge 26/8/1981		Wigan Ath loan Mar 2001
Mitten	Charles	Altrincham 14/12/1943		Altrincham Oct 1965
Moir	Richard John	Glasgow 22/10/1945		Shrewsbury Town Jul 1974
Molloy	John Thomas	Middlewich 1907		Mossley May 1936
Moncrieff	Andrew Mason	Halifax 1893	1957	March 1912
Moncrieff	James Conradi	Todmorden 14/6/1922	5/2/1975	Pegasus Jan 1946
Monington	Mark David	Bilsthorpe 21/10/1970		Boston Utd Nov 2002
Monoghan	William	Scotland		Oct 1925
Mooney	Ernest			Shipley Nov 1919
Moore	Frederick	Worksop		Worksop Town Feb 1930
Moore	James	Felling 1/9/1891	1972	Brighton & HA Aug 1923
Moore	Kenneth	Bradford 13/9/1921	6/2004	Nov 1947
Morefield	William John T (Jack)	Barnwood 26/10/1922	12/1997	May 1946
Morgan	Charles	Bootle 1882		Bradford Aug 1911
Morgan	Philip Jonathan	Stoke 18/12/1974		Stoke City loan Mar 1998
Morgan	Stephen Alphonso	Oldham 19/9/1968		Hull City Sep 2000
Morgan	Thomas	Leeds 29/3/1983		Guiseley cs 2002
Morgan	William Alfred	Rotherham 26/9/1926		Sheffield Utd Aug 1948
Morris				Mar 1920
Morris	Elfred	Colwyn Bay 9/6/1942		Chester Mar 1968
Morris	Ernest	Stocksbridge 11/5/1921		Grantham Nov 1950
Morrison	M			East Stirling guest Oct 1943
Moss	Jack	Blackrod 1/9/1923	1975	Leeds Utd Jan 1951
Mountford	Robert William	Stoke 23/2/1952	26/8/2008	Huddersfield Town Mar 1978
Moyses	Christopher Raymond	Lincoln 1/11/1965		Lincoln City Jul 1984
Mudd	Paul Andrew	Hull 13/11/1970		Lincoln City loan Apr 1996 Lincoln City Jul 1996
Mulholland	John Anthony	Dumbarton 2/1/1932	7/2000	Chester Jun 1957
Mulholland	Thomas S	Ireland 1888		West Stanley Feb 1915
Mulroy	James Gerald	Halifax 1/2/1900	1982	Standard Screw Co Sep 1919
Mulvaney	James	Airdrie 27/4/1921	6/1993	Bath City Nov 1952
Munroe	Karl Augustus	Manchester 23/9/1979		Macclesfield Town Aug 2004
Murphy	James Anthony	Manchester 25/2/1973		Doncaster Rov Mar 1997 Cambridge Utd Nov 1997
Murphy	James Joseph	Hulme 9/9/1907	1974	Stalybridge Celtic May 1936
Murphy	Peter	Dublin 27/10/1980		Blackburn Rov loan Oct 2000
Murphy	Stephen	Dublin 5/4/1978		Huddersfield Town Jul 1998
Murphy	Thomas Edward (Eddie)	Southbank 25/3/1921	2/2003	Blackburn Rov Mar 1949
Mycock	David	Sunderland 30/8/1921	7/10/2000	May 1946

HALIFAX TOWN PLAYERS 1911-2008

To	League A	S	G	CONF A	S	G	FA Cup A	S	G	FL Cup A	S	G
	111	6	30				10	0	1	4	0	0
Stockport Co Jul 1990												
	8	0	2				0	0	0	0	0	0
				3	0	0	0	0	0			
Chester Nov 1930	40	0	0				1	0	0	0	0	0
Morecambe Aug 2001	9	0	0	62	0	0	1	0	0	0	0	0
FC Halifax Town Jul 2008												
				2	1	0	0	0	0			
Margate cs 1932	26	0	9				4	0	3	0	0	0
Drogheda Utd Jul 1969	23	0	0				5	0	0	1	0	0
Forest Green Rov Jul 2005				4	5	1	0	0	0			
cs 1913												
Stalybridge Cel cs 1994	37	4	1	29	3	3	1	1	0	3	1	0
Burton Alb cs 1984	22	8	8				0	1	0	1	1	0
Dartford cs 1935	39	0	8				5	0	0	0	0	0
cs 1946												
St James Gate 1936	11	0	1				2	0	0	0	0	0
Bedworth Utd Aug 2002	66	10	8				1	1	1	2	1	0
Farsley Celtic Jul 2006	12	12	3	107	32	31	7	4	3	1	0	0
Bedlington Town cs 1933	1	0	0				0	0	0	0	0	0
Happy Valley (Hong Kong) Jan 1997				43	6	11	1	2	0			
Happy Valley (Hong Kong) 1998												
Ossett Alb Aug 2004												
	2	5	0				0	0	0	0	0	0
cs 1920												
cs 1944												
Runcorn cs 1935	11	0	0				0	0	0	0	0	0
Blyth Spartans cs 1957	27	0	0				1	0	0	0	0	0
Gainsborough Trin cs 1948	19	0	0				0	0	0	0	0	0
cs 1936	3	0	0				0	0	0	0	0	0
cs 1915												
Rochdale Oct 1914												
York City Aug 1936	8	0	0				0	0	0	0	0	0
Bradford PA Jul 2002	128	2	3				6	0	1	4	0	0
cs 1913												
	11	0	0				0	0	0	0	0	0
Yeovil Town cs 1966	1	0	0				0	0	0	0	0	0
cs 1975	16	3	5				0	2	0	2	0	0
Macclesfield Town May 1937	6	0	0				0	0	0	0	0	0
cs 1912	42	0	13				4	0	4	0	0	0
cs 1955												
Woodley Sports Sep Sep 2005				47	6	6	1	0	0			
cs 1926	4	0	0				0	0	0	0	0	0
cs 1920												
cs 1930	2	0	1				0	0	0	0	0	0
Queen's Park Ran cs 1924	40	0	6				8	0	3	0	0	0
cs 1950	31	0	2				0	0	0	0	0	0
cs 1949	65	0	0				1	0	0	0	0	0
ret Mar 1912												
				1	0	0	0	0	0			
Total Network Solutions Oct 2000	1	0	0				0	0	0	0	0	0
cs 2003				5	0	0	0	0	0			
Rochdale Jul 1953	108	0	3				3	0	0	0	0	0
cs 1920												
Carnarvon Town Nov 1968	9	0	2				0	0	0	1	0	0
cs 1951	1	0	0				0	0	0	0	0	0
cs 1954	124	0	11				6	0	0	0	0	0
Crewe Alex Aug 1980	56	6	11				2	1	0	2	0	1
Boston Utd cs 1985	21	4	0				1	0	0	1	0	0
				42	1	0	1	0	0			
cs 1997												
Lovell's Ath Jul 1958	8	0	1				0	0	0	0	0	0
cs 1915												
cs 1920												
rel Jan 1953	1	0	0				0	0	0	0	0	0
Northwich Vic Mar 2005				5	1	0	0	0	0			
cs 1997	21	2	1	37	1	2	1	0	0	0	0	0
Morecambe 1999												
Hyde Utd cs 1937	13	0	2				1	0	0	0	0	0
	18	3	1				1	0	0	0	0	0
Glenavon cs 1999	22	7	1				0	1	0	4	0	0
cs 1954	218	0	29				10	0	2	0	0	0
cs 1952	170	0	17				5	0	0	0	0	0

Surname	Forenames	Born	Died	From
Myers	Peter William	Sheffield 15/9/1982		Trainee Mar 2001
Nattress	Clive	Durham 24/5/1951		Darlington Jun 1980
Naylor	Dominic John	Watford 12/8/1970		Watford Dec 1989
Naylor	Edward Arnold	Bradford 24/12/1921	12/2000	Bradford Aug 1948
Naylor	Peter Gordon	Bradford 22/8/1985		Trainee Aug 2003
Needham				Oct 1915
Nelthorpe	Craig Robert	Doncaster 10/6/1987		Doncaster Rov loan Jan 2008
Newman	Frank	Nuneaton 1898		Exeter City Aug 1923
Newton	Christopher John	Leeds 5/11/1979		Trainee Jul 1998
Newton	Eric David	Worrall 21/6/1932		Norton Woodseats Dec 1954
Newton	Frank	Menston 12/11/1902		Northampton Town May 1924
Newton	James (Jack)	Horsforth		Bradford City May 1925
Niblo	Alan			guest Oct 1942
Nicholl	Christopher John	Wilmslow 12/10/1946		Witton Alb Jun 1968
Nicholls	James Henry	Coseley 27/11/1919		guest Nov 1941
Nicholson	Gary Anthony	Newcastle 4/11/1960		York City Jul 1985
Nicholson	Sidney			Aberdeen guest Apr 1942
Nixon	John (Jock)	Edinburgh		Stockport Co Aug 1911
				Belfast Celtic May 1914
				Aug 1919
Nixon	Jonathan Charles	Preston 20/1/1948		Barnsley Jun 1978
Nobbs	Alan Keith	Bishop Auckland 19/9/1961		Middlesbrough Aug 1982
Norbury	Michael Shaun	Hemsworth 22/1/1969		Stafford Rangers Jul 1996
Normanton	Sidney	Barnsley 20/8/1926	24/4/1995	Barnsley Jul 1954
Norris	Stephen Mark	Coventry 22/9/1961		Carlisle Utd Oct 1990
North	Eric	Halifax 6/10/1923	1992	Lee Mount Aug 1948
Nunns				Dec 1915
Nuttall	Martin	Oldham 12/9/1961		Oldham Ath Aug 1982
O'Brien	Eamonn Niall	Clitheroe 19/9/1985		Trainee Nov 2004
O'Callaghan	Brian Patrick	Limerick 24/2/1981		Cork City Jan 2008
O'Donnell	Hugh	Buckhaven 15/2/1913	1965	Rochdale Mar 1948
O'Grady	Gerald M			Limerick Apr 1950
O'Hare	Christopher John	Melbourne, Australia 27/12/1986		Trainee Jan 2006
O'Hare	Eamon Brian	Belfast 5/11/1951		Stump Cross Dec 1978
O'Neil	Thomas Patrick	St Helens 25/10/1952	1/5/2006	Tranmere Rov Aug 1980
O'Regan	Kieran Michael	Cork 9/11/1963		West Bromwich Alb Aug 1995
O'Rourke	Michael	Harrogate 1898		Dec 1919
O'Toole	Christopher Patrick	Dublin 2/1/1965		Bridgnorth Town Mar 1994
Obebo	Godfrey	Lagos 16/4/1966		Bury Mar 1993
Offord	Stanley J	Bradford		Bradford guest Feb 1942
Oldacre	Percy	Stoke-on-Trent 25/10/1892	1970	Sheffield Utd Aug 1923
Oleksewycz	Steven Michael	Halifax 24/2/1983		Trainee Oct 2000
Oliver	Dean Colin	Derby 4/12/1987		Sheffield Utd loan Oct 2007
Oliver	George	Houghton-le-Spring 22/1/1919	1981	Oct 1945
Ord	Michael	Huddersfield 22/5/1981		Ripon City Sep 2000
Ormandy	John	Liverpool 25/1/1912	1/1997	Oldham Ath Jul 1947
Orr	Edwin			Sowerby Bridge Inst Sep 1911
Orton	Victor			York City guest Aug 1940
Overson	Vincent David	Kettering 15/5/1962		Burnley Aug 1998
Overton	John	Rotherham 2/5/1956		Aston Villa loan Mar 1976
Owen	Clifford Lewis	Barry 12/6/1908	11/8/2002	Charlton Ath May 1935
Owen	Valentine	Manchester 11/7/1972		Northwich Vic Dec 2003
Packard	Edgar	Mansfield 7/3/1919	2/1996	Sheffield Wed Aug 1952
Pagan	John W	Halifax 1894	1963	Siddal RUFC Aug 1919
Painter	Peter Robert (Robbie)	Wigan 26/1/1971		Rochdale Jul 1999
Palfreyman	George Barry	Sheffield 13/3/1933		Sheffield FC Jan 1954
Palmer	Walter			Bradford guest Mar 1941
Pape	Albert Arthur	Elsecar 13/7/1897	18/11/1955	Hartlepools Utd Jul 1930
Parke	Simon Anthony	Bradford 17/3/1972		Southport Jul 2002
				Bradford Feb 2007
Parker	Reginald W			Apr 1942
Parkin	George	Hunslet 20/8/1903	1971	Aug 1920
				Torquay Utd Nov 1932
Parks	Anthony	Hackney 28/1/1963		Scarborough May 1999
Parks	John Alfred	Wath 14/9/1943		Sheffield Utd Sep 1966
Parnaby	Stuart	Durham 19/7/1982		Middlesbrough loan Oct 2000
Parry	Craig John	Barnsley 15/3/1984		Barnsley Dec 2003
Parry	David Edward	Southport 11/2/1948		Tranmere Rov Sep 1968
Parton	Jack	Oxford 1888		Coventry City Sep 1914
Partridge	Edward Wooldridge	Lye 13/2/1891	1970	Manchester Utd Jul 1929
Paterson	Jamie Ryan	Dumfries 26/4/1973		Trainee Jul 1989
				Scunthorpe Utd Jul 1997
Paterson	Toby Lee	Dumfries 15/5/1971		Trainee 1988
Patterson	Kelvin			Trainee 1986
Peake	Jason William	Leicester 29/9/1971		Leicester City Aug 1992
Pearson	Mark	Sheffield 28/10/1939		Fulham Mar 1968
Peel	Nathan James	Blackburn 17/5/1972		Sheffield Utd loan Feb 1993

HALIFAX TOWN PLAYERS 1911-2008

To	League A	S	G	CONF A	S	G	FA Cup A	S	G	FL Cup A	S	G
Frickley Ath cs 2002	0	1	0				0	0	0	0	0	0
Bishop Auckland cs 1981	37	0	5				1	0	0	2	0	0
Hong Kong Oct 1990	5	1	1				0	0	0	0	0	0
cs 1949	7	0	0				0	0	0	0	0	0
Bradford PA 2005				0	2	0	0	0	0			
cs 1916												
				6	1	2	0	0	0			
Exeter City Jun 1924	4	0	0				0	0	0			
Doncaster Rov Jul 2000	12	10	0				0	1	0	0	0	0
cs 1955	10	0	3				0	0	0	0	0	0
cs 1925	2	0	0				0	0	0	0	0	0
Coventry City Jun 1926	40	0	0				1	0	0	0	0	0
Luton Town Aug 1969	42	0	3				6	0	0	1	0	0
Blyth Spartans cs 1987	54	6	4				1	2	0	4	0	0
Belfast Celtic May 1913 banned Feb 1915												
cs 1920												
Burton Alb cs 1979	12	7	1				0	0	0	2	0	0
Bishop Auckland Oct 1984	87	0	1				2	0	0	4	0	0
Hednesford Town May 1997				30	1	14	2	0	1			
cs 1955	13	0	0				0	0	0	0	0	0
Chesterfield Jan 1992	57	0	37				5	0	2	2	0	1
cs 1949	1	0	0				0	0	0	0	0	0
cs 1916												
Barrow cs 1984	39	11	10				1	0	0	0	1	0
Bradford PA 2005												
rel Feb 2008				1	0	0	0	0	0			
cs 1949	13	0	1				1	0	0	0	0	0
cs 1950												
cs 2006												
Stump Cross 1979												
Southport cs 1982	39	1	2				0	1	0	0	0	0
Apr 1999	15	4	2	115	1	5	7	0	0	2	1	0
cs 1920												
Cobh Ramblers cs 1994				5	2	0	0	0	0			
cs 1993	0	3	0				0	0	0	0	0	0
Crewe Alex cs 1924	8	0	1				0	0	0	0	0	0
Ossett Town cs 2002	0	5	0				0	0	0	0	0	0
				2	0	0	0	0	0			
Gateshead Oct 1946												
Harrogate Town Mar 2001	0	0	0				0	0	0	0	1	0
cs 1948	7	0	0				0	0	0	0	0	0
cs 1912												
rel Sep 1998	0	0	0				0	0	0	0	1	0
	14	0	2				0	0	0	0	0	0
Chester cs 1938	102	0	0				7	0	0	0	0	0
Altrincham 2004				15	2	0	0	0	0			
Sutton Town cs 1954	85	0	0				8	0	0	0	0	0
Halifax RUFC Oct 1919												
Gateshead 2001	46	12	8				3	0	0	2	0	0
cs 1954	1	0	0				0	0	0	0	0	0
Burscough Rang cs 1931	26	0	15				3	0	1	0	0	0
Harrogate Town Sep 2003				18	24	6	0	1	0			
cs 2007												
cs 1942												
Burnley Mar 1924	55	0	0				7	0	0	0	0	0
Workington cs 1933												
Crewe Alex coach Nov 2001	5	1	0				0	0	0	3	0	0
Weymouth Feb 1968	40	0	14				6	0	4	0	0	0
	6	0	0				0	0	0	0	0	0
Bradford PA Apr 2005				3	1	0	0	0	0			
Wigan Ath Oct 1968	2	0	0				0	0	0	0	0	0
cs 1920												
Manchester Central Dec 1929	15	0	0				0	0	0	0	0	0
Falkirk Dec 1994	91	18	22	91	2	32	13	1	4	3	1	1
Doncaster Rov Jul 2000												
cc Mar 1990	0	1	0				0	0	0	0	0	0
cs 1987												
Rochdale Mar 1994	32	1	1	27	0	6	3	0	1	0	0	0
Bacup Borough cs 1969	2	3	1				0	1	0	0	0	0
	3	0	0				0	0	0	0	0	0

HALIFAX TOWN: THE COMPLETE RECORD

Surname	Forenames	Born	Died	From
Pennington	John	Bolton 1906		Middlewich Jul 1927
Pennington	John (Jack)	Marsden 12/9/1928	1987	Marsden Nov 1953
Pentland	Frederick Beaconsfield	Wolverhampton 19/8/1883	16/3/1962	Middlesbrough Aug 1912 Stoke City Dec 1913
Pescod	George	Sunderland 31/10/1909	1978	Liverpool Jul 1933
Pettinger	Paul Allen	Sheffield 1/10/1975		Lees Utd loan Feb 1995
Phelan	Albert	Sheffield 27/4/1945		Chesterfield Oct 1974
Philliskirk	Anthony	Sunderland 10/2/1965		Cardiff City loan Dec 1997
Phipps	Cecil Harry	Leicester 25/10/1896	1968	Leicester City Aug 1921
Pickering	John	Stockton 7/11/1944	30/5/2001	Newcastle Utd Sep 1965
Pinkney	Ernest	Glasgow 23/11/1888	1975	Tranmere Rov Jul 1921
Place	Damian James	Halifax 31/12/1978		Trainee May 1997
Plant				Dec 1915
Podd	Cyril Casey Marcel	St Kitts, West Indies 7/8/1952		Bradford City Aug 1984
Pollard	Frank			Bury guest Dec 1940
Poole	Ryan Philip	Leicester 30/4/1985		Sheffield Utd cs 2002
Pope	Alfred Leslie	Lofthouse 8/1/1913	8/1987	Leeds Utd Jul 1935 Hearts guest
Potter	Harry	Bradford 1885		Bradford City Sep 1911
Potter	Lee	Salford 3/9/1978		Bolton Wan Dec 1999
Powell	Wayne	Caerphilly 25/10/1956		Bristol Rov loan Oct 1977
Power	Lee Michael	Lewisham 30/6/1972		Plymouth Arg Dec 1998
Poxton	W			Doncaster Rov guest Nov 1943
Prendergast	Michael John	Denaby 24/11/1950		Barnsley loan Mar 1978
Prendergast	Rory	Pontefract 6/4/1978		Blackpool loan Nov 2005
Presgrave	Gordon Edwin	Whitwell 15/1/1915	1976	Worksop Town Mar 1933
Price	Ernest Clifford	Market Bosworth 13/6/1900		Leicester City Jun 1922
Price	George L	Cudworth		Frystol Col cs 1924
Price	James Richard	Normanton 27/10/1981		Doncaster Rov loan Aug 2003
Priest	Harold (Mick)	Clay Cross 26/10/1935		Sheffield Utd Jan 1958
Priestley	Derek	Queensbury 22/12/1926	31/5/1999	Oct 1950
Priestley	Gerald	Halifax 2/3/1931		Crystal Pal Jul 1960
Priestley	Maurice	Bradford 27/10/1922	1986	Bradford Jan 1948
Prindiville	Steven	Harlow 26/12/1968		Wycombe Wan Feb 1994
Prior	Frederick E			Bradford guest Mar 1941
Pritchard				Dec 1911
Pritchard	Andrew Smart	Airdrie 23/6/1912		Ards Jul 1937
Procter	Michael Anthony	Sunderland 3/10/1980		Sunderland loan Mar 2001
Proctor	Norman	Alnwick 11/5/1896	27/2/1947	Tranmere Rov Jul 1927
Pugh	David George	Markham 22/1/1947		Chesterfield Aug 1973
Pullan	Christopher John	Durham 14/12/1967		Watford loan Feb 1989
Quailey	Brian Sullivan	Leicester 21/3/1978		Doncaster Rov Sep 2002
Quinn	Adam Robert	Sheffield 2/6/1983		Sheffield Wed Jul 2002
Quinn	John David	St Helens 30/5/1938		Rotherham Utd Jul 1972
Quinn	Patrick Anthony	Croy 21/6/1918	15/5/1979	Ashfield Juniors Jul 1946
Rathbone	Michael John	Sheldon, Birmingham 6/11/1958		Physio Jul 1993
Rawlinson	Norris	Manchester 1906	1968	Aug 1933
Rawnsley	Simon Daniel	Bradford 18/11/1987		Academy Nov 2006
Rayner	Edward	Hemsworth 28/9/1916	2/5/1988	Scarborough Aug 1945
Raynor	Harold A	Hipperholme 1903		Selby Town May 1925
Raynor	Robert	Nottingham 30/8/1940	3/2007	Nottingham For Aug 1965
Read	Edward	Rhos-on-Sea 16/6/1903	4/1997	Aug 1931
Redding	William Leach	Woolwich 1882	1968	Colne Aug 1911
Redfearn	Brian	Bradford 20/2/1935		Darlington Jun 1961
Redfearn	Neil David	Dewsbury 20/6/1965		Wigan Ath Mar 2001
Reed	George	Normanton 16/7/1938		Swillington Feb 1961
Reilly	Alan	Dublin 22/8/1970		Manchester City Dec 1999
Rezai	Carl Sarbaz	Manchester 16/10/1982		Trainee Oct 2000
Rhodes	Andrew Charles	Askern 23/8/1964		Airdrie Mar 1998
Rhodes	John Anthony (Tony)	Dover 17/9/1946		Derby Co Nov 1970
Richards	Ian	Barnsley 5/10/1979		Blackburn Rov Aug 1999
Richards	Marc John	Wolverhampton 8/7/1982		Blackburn Rov loan Feb 2002
Richards	Stephen C	Dundee 24/10/1961		Scarborough Jul 1991
Richardson	Barry	Wallsend 5/8/1969		Doncaster Rov Dec 2001
Richardson	Garbutt	Newcastle 24/10/1938		Carlisle Utd Nov 1962
Richardson	Lee James	Halifax 12/3/1969		Trainee Aug 1986
Richardson	Nicholas John	Halifax 11/4/1967		Emley Nov 1988
Rickett	Walter	Sheffield 20/3/1917	7/1991	Rotherham Utd Aug 1953
Riddell	H			Sep 1944
Ridings	David John	Farnworth 27/2/1970		Curzon Ashton Aug 1992 Curzon Ashton Jan 1993
Riley				Nov 1919
Riley				Apr 1921
Ringer	Walter Albert	Stanley 4/10/1941		Dec 1959
Roberts	Eric	Batley 16/1/1921	1985	Altofts Col Aug 1947
Roberts	Joseph	Tranmere 2/10/1900	1984	York City Jun 1929
Roberts	Leonard	Rotherham		Mar 1931

HALIFAX TOWN PLAYERS 1911-2008

To	League A	S	G	CONF A	S	G	FA Cup A	S	G	FL Cup A	S	G
Stockport Co cs 1928	28	0	0				2	0	0	0	0	0
cs 1954	7	0	2				0	0	0	0	0	0
Stoke City Feb 1913												
cs 1914												
cs 1934	8	0	1				1	0	0	0	0	0
				7	0	0	0	0	0			
Boston Utd cs 1977	118	0	4				9	0	1	5	0	1
				4	0	2	0	0	0			
cs 1922	5	0	0				0	0	0	0	0	0
Barnsley May 1974	364	3	5				18	0	0	15	0	0
Accrington Stan Jun 1922	30	0	2				0	0	0	0	0	0
Harrogate Railway cs 1999				0	3	0	0	1	0			
cs 1916												
Scarborough Jul 1986	52	5	0				2	0	0	4	1	0
Nuneaton Bor Oct 2003												
Hearts Feb 1937	53	0	0				3	0	0	0	0	0
Goole Town cs 1913												
Brdaford PA cs 2001	13	9	2				0	0	0	0	0	0
	4	0	1				0	0	0	0	0	0
Boston Utd Nov 1999	17	8	5				0	0	0	0	2	0
	4	0	1				1	0	0	0	0	0
				6	0	0	0	0	0			
Carlisle Utd cs 1936	21	0	5				0	0	0	0	0	0
Southampton cs 1923	44	0	15				5	0	5	0	0	0
cc Jun 1926	11	0	0				0	0	0	0	0	0
				5	0	0	0	0	0			
Sutton Town 1960	30	0	12				2	0	0	0	0	0
Bradford Jul 1956	145	0	19				9	0	3	0	0	0
cs 1963	105	0	23				6	0	1	3	0	0
cs 1949	24	0	8				0	0	0	0	0	0
Dagenham & Red Nov 1995				73	0	5	5	0	0			
cs 1912												
Clapton Orient Aug 1938	15	0	2				2	0	0	0	0	0
	11	1	4				0	0	0	0	0	0
Workington Jul 1931	126	0	3				7	0	1	0	0	0
Rotherham Utd Jul 1976	91	5	3				5	0	0	7	0	0
	5	0	1				0	0	0	0	0	0
Nuneaton Bor May 2003				26	8	5	1	0	1			
Crawley Town Aug 2008				181	13	8	12	0	0			
Manager Sep 1974	88	4	1				5	0	0	6	0	0
Macclesfield Town cs 1947	25	0	6				4	0	0	0	0	0
rel Mar 1995				7	1	1	0	0	0			
Macclsfield Town May 1934	4	0	0				0	0	0	0	0	0
cs 2007												
Nelson Aug 1951	138	0	0				7	0	0	0	0	0
Huddersfield Town Nov 1925	1	0	0				0	0	0	0	0	0
cc May 1967	17	0	0				1	0	0	2	0	0
Bellfield St Anne's cs 1935	53	0	1				4	0	0	0	0	0
cs 1912												
Bradford City Jul 1963	67	0	9				3	0	1	2	0	0
Boston Utd cs 2002	39	3	6				3	0	0	1	0	0
cs 1962	2	0	0				0	0	0	0	0	0
Bohemians 2002	30	15	2				0	0	0	1	0	0
Salford City 2001	8	3	1				1	0	0	0	0	0
Emley Jul 1998				8	0	0	0	0	0			
Southport Aug 1976	233	0	9				8	0	2	13	0	3
Burton Alb cs 2001	13	11	0				1	0	0	1	0	0
	5	0	0				0	0	0	0	0	0
Doncaster Rov May 1992	25	1	0				2	0	0	2	0	0
Gainsborough Trin cs 2002	24	0	0				0	0	0	0	0	0
Barrow Jul 1964	20	0	1				0	0	0	3	0	0
Watford Feb 1989	43	13	2				4	2	0	4	0	0
Cardiff City Aug 1992	90	12	17				2	1	1	6	4	2
Sittingbourne cs 1954	31	0	2				0	0	0	0	0	0
cs 1945												
Curzon Ashton Aug 1992	21	0	4	15	1	4	2	0	0	0	0	0
Lincoln City Feb 1994												
cs 1920												
cs 1921												
cs 1961	6	0	0				0	0	0	0	0	0
cs 1848	5	0	1				0	0	0	0	0	0
Southport Mar 1930	22	0	1				1	0	0	0	0	0
cs 1934	23	0	1				0	0	0	0	0	0

Surname	Forenames	Born	Died	From
Roberts	Mark Alan	Northwich 16/10/1983		Crewe Alex loan Aug 2006
Roberts	Samuel	Connah's Quay 26/7/1911	3/1991	Rhyl Ath Dec 1932
Robertson				Oct 1911
Robertson	Archibald Lamond (Lammie)	Paisley 27/9/1947		Bury Feb 1969
Robinson				Apr 1915
Robinson	David Alan	Cleveland 14/1/1965		Hartlepool Utd Jul 1986
Robinson	Gladney	Settle 14/10/1915	5/1991	Settle Aug 1936
Robinson	L			Bury guest Jan 1944
Robinson	Peter	Ashington 4/9/1957		Darlington loan Dec 1985
Robinson	Samuel			Bradford Sep 1919
Roche	Patrick Joseph Christopher	Dublin 4/1/1951		Brentford Aug 1984
Rodger	Richard John	Hemsworth 1/7/1936		Ryburn Utd Aug 1954
Rogers	Arthur	Leeds 1896		Leeds Utd Aug 1920
Rollins	Kevin	Halifax 2/1/1947		Appren Jul 1963
Roper				Mar 1921
Roper	J			Goole Town Apr 1912
Roscoe	Percy			Apr 1912
Roscoe	Philip	Barnsley 3/3/1934		Barnsley Jul 1956
Rose	Gordon	Sheffield 22/3/1935		Sheffield Utd Jul 1958
Rose	James	Leeds		Bradford City Aug 1937
Ross	Neil James	West Bromwich 10/8/1982		Macclesfield Town Nov 2004
Rosser	Michael James	Keighley 9/12/1977		Trainee Jun 1994
Rotherforth	Edmund	Fryston 1906	1968	Pontefract Town Jul 1929
Rowe	Anthony			cs 1979
Rowe	Rodney Carl	Huddersfield 30/7/1975		York City loan Sep 1999
Royston				Morley Dec 1911
Ruecroft	Edward Joseph	Pontefract 20/2/1917	2002	Dec 1939
Ruecroft	Jacob	Lanchester 1/5/1915	2005	Goole Town May 1938
Russell	Malcolm	Halifax 9/11/1945		Appren Oct 1961
Russell	Matthew Lee	Dewsbury 17/1/1978		Scarborough Jul 1999
Ryan	Leon	Sunderland 8/11/1982		Scunthorpe Utd Oct 2002
Ryden	Hugh Johnston	Renton 7/4/1943		Chester Nov 1967
Rylands	David Robert	Liverpool 7/3/1953		Hereford Utd Jun 1976
Rymer	George Herbert	Barnsley 6/10/1923		Barnsley guest Apr 1944
Sagare	Jake	USA 5/4/1980		Portland Timbers (USA) Sep 2003
Salisbury	James Arron	Preston 10/3/1984		Wigan Ath loan Mar 2005
Salm	Andrew Paul	Huddersfield 8/12/1987		Cof Ex 2004
Sanasy	Kevin Roy	Leeds 2/11/1984		Bradford City loan Sep 2004
Sanderson	Paul David	Blackpool 16/12/1966		Chester City Aug 1984
Sandwith	Kevin	Workington 30/4/1978		Doncaster Rov Nov 2002
Sansam	Christian	Hull 26/12/1975		Scunthorpe Utd Feb 1996
Saunders	Stephen John Peter	Warrington 21/9/1964		Altrincham Sep 1993
Savage	John Alfred	Bromley 14/12/1929		Hull City Mar 1952
Scaife	Nicholas	Middlesbrough 14/5/1975		York City loan Dec 1995
Scaife	Robert Henry	Northallerton 12/10/1955		Middlesbrough loan Jan 1975
Schofield	Robert	Rochdale 7/11/1904	1978	Newton Heath May 1929
Schofield	Thomas	Halifax 22/6/1926		Boothtown Aug 1952
Scott	Donald	Elland 20/10/1922		Sep 1948
Scott	Harold	Crofton 2/5/1920	12/1995	Horbury Nov 1937
Scott	Robert	Epsom 15/8/1973		Macclesfield Town Jun 2007
Scott	Walter	Douglas 23/6/1932		Dumbarton Aug 1954
Scrimshaw	Stanley	Hartlepool 7/8/1915	1988	Frickley Col Oct 1947
Scrutton	John	Leeds 1896		Hunslett Carr Apr 1914
Scull	John Alfred	Saltaire 15/9/1897	1977	Idle Jan 1920
Seabrook	Arthur	Luton 2/10/1895	10/1981	Northampton Town May 1924
Seddon	Frank Owen	Stockton 1/5/1928		Hull City Jan 1951
Senior	Allan Gordon	Dewsbury 29/9/1930		Aug 1952
Senior	Charles RA			Dec 1944
Senior	Christopher Marc	Huddersfield 18/11/1981		Scarborough Aug 2005
Senior	Michael Graham	Huddersfield 3/3/1981		Huddersfield Town Sep 2002
Sertori	Mark Anthony	Manchester 1/9/1967		Scunthorpe Utd Jul 1998
Shadbolt	William Henry	Shrewsbury 4/8/1932	1980	Sheffield Wed Mar 1954
Shanahan	Terence Christopher	Paddington 5/12/1951		Ipswich Town Nov 1971
Shankly	James	Glenbuck 19/6/1902	1972	Guildford Town Jun 1924
Shannon	Gregg Zachary	Maghreafelt 15/2/1981		Sunderland cs 2000
Sharp				Chesterfield Dec 1919
Sharp	Aubrey Temple	Whitwick 23/3/1889	15/2/1973	Old Reptonians Sep 1912
Sharp	John (Jack)	Castleford 25/4/1937		Fryston Col Dec 1954
Sharpe	Philip	Leeds 12/1/1968		Trainee Aug 1986
Sharpe	Thomas Robert	Nottingham 12/10/1988		Nottingham For loan Jan 2008
Shaw	Adrian	Easington 13/4/1966		Nottingham For Dec 1984
Shaw	Jonathan Steven	Sheffield 11/10/1983		Burton Alb Aug 2007
Shaw	Mark			Academy Feb 2003
Shawcross	Francis David	Stretford 3/7/1941		Stockport Co Mar 1967
Sheriffe	Jess Jo	Hebden Bridge 2/1/1990		Academy Nov 2006
Shirlaw	Walter Paterson	Wishaw 23/6/1901	26/10/1981	Bradford City Jun 1932
Shirley	Alexander Gordon	Milngavie 31/10/1918	1990	Dundee Utd guest Oct 1945

HALIFAX TOWN PLAYERS 1911-2008

To	League A	S	G	CONF A	S	G	FA Cup A	S	G	FL Cup A	S	G
				12	1	1	0	0	0			
Newry Town cs 1933	9	0	0				0	0	0	0	0	0
Oct 1911												
Brighton & HA Dec 1972	142	8	20				5	0	3	8	0	0
cs 1915												
Peterborough Utd Jul 1989	72	0	1				6	0	1	3	0	0
Lancaster City cs 1938	23	0	2				1	0	0	0	0	0
	3	2	0				0	0	0	0	0	0
cs 1920												
Chester City cs 1989	184	0	0				12	0	0	12	0	0
Rochdale cs 1957	15	0	3				0	0	0	0	0	0
cs 1921												
cs 1965	1	0	0				0	0	0	0	0	0
cs 1921												
cs 1912												
Rotherham Co 1916												
Wellington Town Jul 1964	257	0	6				9	0	1	6	0	0
cs 1959	8	0	1				0	0	0	0	0	0
cs 1938	6	0	0				0	0	0	0	0	0
Alfreton Town Jul 2005				4	9	4	0	2	2			
Silsden cs 1998												
cs 1930	1	0	0				0	0	0	0	0	0
cs 1980												
	7	2	2				1	0	0	0	0	0
cs 1912												
cs 1946												
Scarborough cs 1947	60	0	2				12	0	0	0	0	0
Southport Aug 1968	183	1	0				11	0	1	9	0	0
Scarborough Oct 1999	3	4	0				0	0	0	0	1	0
Koo Tee Pee (Fin) 2003				0	5	0	1	0	0			
Stockport Co Dec 1969	54	1	6				5	0	3	2	0	0
Bangor City cs 1977	5	0	0				0	0	0	1	0	0
Vancouver Whitecaps 2004				11	14	1	0	1	0			
				2	0	0	0	0	0			
cs 2005												
				0	2	0	0	0	0			
Vcardiff City Jul 1987	88	16	5				4	0	0	4	0	0
Lincoln City Mar 2004				51	0	2	1	0	0			
Scarborough Mar 1996				5	0	1	0	0	0			
ret cs 1994				14	0	6	2	0	1			
Manchester City Nov 1953	61	0	1				3	0	0	0	0	0
				2	0	0	0	0	0			
	5	1	1				0	0	0	0	0	0
Rochdale cs 1930	6	0	0				0	0	0	0	0	0
cs 1953	1	0	0				0	0	0	0	0	0
cs 1950	20	0	5				0	0	0	0	0	0
cs 1939	11	0	2				1	0	0	0	0	0
cs 2008				11	1	0	1	0	0			
cs 1955	13	0	0				0	0	0	0	0	0
Shrewsbury Town Nov 1949	52	0	0				1	0	0	0	0	0
cs 1920												
cs 1922	8	0	0				6	0	0	0	0	0
Crewe Alex cs 1927	104	0	35				2	0	2	0	0	0
Stockton Jan 1952	4	0	0				0	0	0	0	0	0
Macclesfield Town cs 1953	1	0	0				0	0	0	0	0	0
Altrincham Jul 2007				14	36	7	2	1	3			
Ossett Alb Oct 2004				12	9	0	0	1	0			
York City Sep 1999	44	1	0				1	0	0	6	0	0
cc Aug 1954	3	0	1				0	0	0	0	0	0
Chesterfield Oct 1974	88	8	23				2	1	1	2	2	0
Nuneaton Town Jul 1925	7	0	2				1	0	0	0	0	0
Dungannon Swifs Feb 2001	0	0	0				0	0	0	1	0	0
cs 1920												
cs 1914												
Goole Town cs 1959	92	0	16				1	0	0	0	0	0
Eendracht Wervick (Bel) Feb 1988	0	1	0				0	0	0	0	0	0
				1	0	0	0	0	0			
Bridlington Town cs 1988	95	5	1				7	1	0	4	1	1
Rochdale Jul 2008				36	1	20	3	0	1			
cs 2003												
Altrincham Sep 1970	126	6	21				8	0	2	5	0	1
cs 2007												
Workington Jul 1935	121	0	0				11	0	0	0	0	0

673

Surname	Forenames	Born	Died	From
Shore	Brian	Huddersfield 1/2/1935		Oct 1956
Short	John David	Gateshead 25/1/1921	1986	Leeds Utd guest May 1940
Shotton	Robert	Witton Gilbert 17/10/1910	36161	Barnsley guest May 1942
Shuttleworth	LP			Leeds City Oct 1912
Sidebottom	Arnold	Barnsley 1/4/1954		Huddersfield Town Oct 1978
Simms	Robert	Horsforth 13/5/1902		Castleford Town Sep 1923
Simons	Henry Thomas	Hackney 26/11/1887	26/8/1956	Sheffield Utd cs 1912
Sinclair	Ronald McDonald	Stirling 19/11/1964		Leeds Utd loan Mar 1987
				Leeds Utd loan Dec 1988
Sinclair	William Mearns	Blairhall 14/10/1934		Tranmere Rov Oct 1960
Skivington	Glenn	Barrow 19/1/1962		Derby Co loan Mar 1983
Slater		Halifax 1892		Army Dec 1919
Small	Benjamin Michael	Leeds 24/6/1988		Academy Nov 2004
Smeaton	Arthur Richardson (Alec)	South Shields 27/9/1900	1956	Bristol Rov Jul 1926
Smelt	Lee Adrian	Edmonton 13/3/1958		Nottingham For Oct 1981
Smeltz	Shane	Goppingen, New Zealand 29/2/1980		AFC Wimbledon Jul 2006
Smethurst	Charles Freeman Vincent	Bolsover 30/12/1913	2/1985	Bolsover Col May 1934
Smikle	Brian Junior	Dudley 3/11/1985		West Brom Feb 2006
Smith				Dec 1915
Smith	Alexander	Lancaster 29/10/1938		Bolton Wan Jan 1968
Smith	Alexander	Dewsbury 11/5/1947		Colchester Utd Feb 1975
Smith	Anthony	Sunderland 20/2/1957		Peterborough Utd Aug 1982
Smith	C			Apr 1941
Smith	Clement	Wath-on-Dearne 28/7/1910	1/1970	South Kirkby Col May 1935
				War
Smith	Craig Mark	Bradford 8/6/1984		Trainee Sep 2001
Smith	David Bryan	Sheffield 11/12/1950		Huddersfield Town loan Mar 1974
Smith	Ernest	Bradford 1900		Bradford Nov 1919
				Wakefield City Jan 1922
Smith	Frederick Gregg	West Sleekburn 25/12/1942		American football Sep 1974
Smith	Frederick H			Bradford guest Feb 1944
Smith	Gareth Shaun	Leeds 9/4/1971		Trainee Aug 1987
Smith	Gavin	Cambuslang 25/9/1917	1992	Barnsley guest May 1942
Smith	Grant Gordon	Irvine 5/5/1980		Sheffield Utd loan Sep 2001
Smith	James Michael	Sheffield 17/10/1940		Aldershot Jul 1965
Smith	John	Coatbridge 27/11/1956		Los Angeles Sky Hawks Nov 1979
Smith	Kenneth	South Shields 21/5/1932		Toronto Italia Oct 1961
Smith	Nigel	Leeds 21/12/1969		Farsley Celtic Mar 1994
Smith	Paul Michael	Rotherham 9/11/1964		Licoln City Oct 1995
Smith	R			Stockport County Aug 1913
Smith	Stanley	Halifax 1896		Asquith's Oct 1919
Smith	Stephen	Huddersfield 28/4/1946		Huddersfield Town Aug 1977
Smith	William	Denby 1890		Southampton Jun 1914
Smith	William			Hebden Bridge Oct 1919
Smith	William Conway	Huddersfield 13/7/1926	3/1989	Queen's Park Rang Jun 1956
Smith	William E	Sheffield 1911/1900		Rochdale Aug 1926
Smyth	Herbert Robert	Manchester 28/2/1921	8/1998	Ipswich Town Aug 1950
Snedden	John Duncan	Bonnybridge 3/2/1942		Leyton Orient loan Nov 1967
Snell	Albert Edward	Dunscroft 7/2/1931		Sunderland Nov 1955
South	Alexander William	Brighton 7/7/1931		Liverpool Oct 1956
Spencer	J			West Vale Ramblers Apr 1912
Splitt	Thomas	Lochgelly 1886	1954	Burnley Jul 1913
Spooner	Stephen Alan	Sutton 25/1/1961		Derby Co Dec 1981
Stafford	Andrew Grant	Littleborough 28/10/1960		Blackburn Rov Dec 1978
Stamp	Darryn Michael	Beverley 21/9/1978		Scunthorpe Utd loan Feb 2000
				Stevenage Bor Jan 2007
Staniforth	David Albry	Chesterfield 6/10/1950		Bradford City Jul 1982
Stanley	Patrick Joseph	Dublin 9/3/1938		Leeds Utd May 1958
Stansfield	James Edward	Dewsbury 18/9/1978		Huddersfield Town Jul 1998
Stansfield	Samuel			Trainer Nov 1915
Stephen	James Findlay	Fethercairn 23/8/1922		Bradford guest Mar 1941
Stevens	Neil James	Pudsey 23/2/1989		Cof Ex Dec 2005
Stewart	Alexander			Oct 1944
Stewart	J			Falkirk guest Feb 1944
Stockdale	Thomas William	Frickley 3/4/1903	1977	Manchester Utd Aug 1928
Stoker	Gareth	Bishop Auckland 22/2/1973		Sep 1994
Stonehouse	Basil Henry	Guisborough 27/10/1952		Middlesbrough loan Oct 1972
Stoneman	Paul	Whitley Bay 26/2/1973		Blackpool Jul 1995
Storey	S			Huddersfield Town guest Oct 1943
Stott	Thomas	1889		Ebbw Vale Aug 1920
Strang	Richard	Rutherglen 19/3/1900	15/2/1971	Poole Town Jul 1929
Street	H			Reading Aug 1911
Stretton	Donald	Clowne 4/9/1920	1978	Thorne Col Jun 1947
Strike	Henry	Ayrshire	30/6/1944	Dec 1943
Strodder	Colin John	Hessle 23/12/1941		Huddersfield Town Jun 1961
Strong	Gregory	Bolton 5/9/1975		Dundee Mar 2007
Sugden	Ryan Stephen	Bradford 26/12/1980		Morecambe Jul 2004

HALIFAX TOWN PLAYERS 1911-2008

To	League A	S	G	CONF A	S	G	FA Cup A	S	G	FL Cup A	S	G
cs 1957	9	0	3				0	0	0	0	0	0
cs 1913												
cs 1979	21	0	2				1	0	0	0	0	0
cs 1924	2	0	0				0	0	0	0	0	0
Merthyr Town Nov 1912												
	14	0	0				0	0	0	0	0	0
Sirling Alb cs 1961	21	0	3				2	0	2	0	0	0
	4	0	0				0	0	0	0	0	0
cs 1920												
cs 1005												
Torquay Utd cs 1928	77	0	6				3	0	0	0	0	0
Cardiff City Aug 1984	119	0	0				3	0	0	4	0	0
Wellington Phoenix Jun 2007				13	18	2	0	1	0			
Gillingham Aug 1936	16	0	2				3	0	0	0	0	0
Kidderminster Har Jul 2006				11	1	0	0	0	0			
cs 1916												
Preston NE May 1975	341	0	0				15	0	0	15	0	0
cs 1976	46	0	1				2	0	0	3	0	0
Hartlepool Utd Aug 1984	81	2	3				1	0	0	4	0	0
cs 1941												
Chester Jul 1937	55	0	12				1	0	0	0	0	0
Bradford PA Jan 2003	0	2	0				0	0	0	0	0	0
	12	1	5				0	0	0	0	0	0
Wakefield City cs 1921	4	0	1				6	0	2	0	0	0
cs 1922												
rel Oct 1974	3	0	0				0	0	0	0	1	0
Emley May 1991	6	1	0				0	0	0	0	0	0
	11	0	0				0	0	0	0	0	0
Lincoln City Mar 1968	113	1	7				8	1	0	5	0	0
Workington cs 1980	26	2	6				6	0	1	0	0	0
Trowbridge Town Jul 1962	27	0	7				1	0	0	0	0	0
Farsley Celtic cs 1994				7	1	2	0	0	0			
cs 1996				27	0	0	1	0	0			
cs 1914												
cs 1920												
cs 1979	78	3	4				2	0	0	2	0	0
cs 1915												
cs 1920												
Nelson Jun 1962	179	0	72				7	0	2	0	0	0
Barrow Jun 1927	33	0	10				1	0	0	0	0	0
Rochdale Sep 1950	2	0	0				0	0	0	0	0	0
	5	0	0				2	0	0	0	0	0
cs 1957	25	0	0				0	0	0	0	0	0
ret cs 1965	302	0	12				14	0	2	5	0	0
cs 1912												
Nelson Jun 1914												
Chesterfield Jul 1983	71	1	13				1	0	0	2	0	0
Stockport Co Aug 1981	33	8	1				7	0	1	4	0	0
	5	0	0	27	14	7	2	0	0	0	0	0
Northwich Vic Mar 2008												
Burton Alb Jun 1984	66	3	21				1	0	0	4	0	2
Kettering Town Jun 1963	119	0	1				6	0	0	2	0	0
Ossett Town Oct 2000	24	2	1				1	0	0	0	0	0
cs 1916												
cs 2006												
cs 1945												
Scarborough cs 1930	12	0	1				0	0	0	0	0	0
Hereford Utd Mar 1995												
	1	1	0				0	0	0	0	0	0
Harrogate Town Jun 2005	137	2	12	128	9	11	11	1	0	8	0	0
cs 1921												
Northampton Town Jul 1932	99	0	2				8	0	0	0	0	0
cs 1913												
cs 1948	10	0	5				1	0	0	0	0	0
Boston Utd cs 1963	20	0	0				0	0	0	0	0	0
Alfreton Town Aug 2007				7	1	1	0	0	0			
Farsley Celtic Jan 2007				69	18	23	5	0	0			

Surname	Forenames	Born	Died	From
Summerscales	Benn Julian	Ossett 1985		Trainee Nov 2002
Sunderland	William			Henden Bridge Mar 1915
Sunley	Mark	Guisborough 11/8/1972		Darlington Jun 1994
Sutcliffe	CH			Norwich City Dec 1911
Sutcliffe	Charles Spencer	Bradford 7/10/1890	18/8/1964	Heckmondwike Dec 1911
Suter	Ernest Robert	Epperstone 10/7/1880	1/12/1945	Goole Town Jun 1913
Suter	Francis Robert	Nottingham 11/4/1911	4/1987	Bradford Jul 1932
Swain	Sidney	Liverpool 14/10/1927		Jul 1951
Swales	Stephen Colin	Whitby 26/12/1973		Hull City Jul 2001
Swann	Scott	Bradford 4/10/1988		Cof Ex 2005
Swift	Webster	Wombwell 1902	1967	Wombwell Ath Jul 1927
Sword	Thomas William	Newcastle 12/11/1957		Hartlepool Utd loan Feb 1987
Sykes	Graham			Luddendenfoot Dec 1978
Sykes	H			Aug 1943
Tait	Barry Stuart	York 30/6/1938		Bradford City Jul 1962
Tate	Christopher Douglas	York 27/12/1977		Scarborough Jul 1999
Tate	Walter	Halifax 25/4/1927	12/1991	Aug 1944
Tattersall	John Garner			Warley Circuit Oct 1936
Taylor	Albert Herbert	Worksop 2/5/1924		Sheffield Utd Jul 1951
Taylor	Arthur Matson (Archie)	Doncaster 7/11/1939		Hull City Jul 1963
Taylor	Charles	Sheffield		Manchester Utd Aug 1928
Taylor	Charles			Nov 1945
Taylor	Daryl Shea	Birmingham 14/11/1984		Tamworth Jun 2007
Taylor	Derek Milton	Bradford 6/6/1927	1984	Bradford Aug 1948
Taylor	E			Oct 1911
Taylor	G			Aug 1943
Taylor	George E			Worksop Town Aug 1931
Taylor	John Swinley	Cowdenbeath 17/8/1909	1964	Bristol City May 1934
Taylor	Joseph Thomas	West Bromwich 23/7/1909	11/1/1977	Oldham Ath guest Apr 1944
Taylor	Leslie T			Bury guest Mar 1943
Taylor	P			Chester Oct 1911
Taylor	Samuel James	Darnall 17/9/1893	1/1973	Southampton May 1928
Thackeray	Andrew John	Huddersfield 13/2/1968		Rochdale Jul 1997
Thomas	Cedric David	Heptonstall 19/9/1936		Heptonstall Jul 1957
Thomas	John William	Wednesbury 5/8/1958		Everton loan Oct 1979
				Hartlepool Utd Jul 1992
Thomas	Wynford Glyn	Swansea 12/4/1915	1987	Swansea Town Jul 1936
Thompson	AH			Carlisle Utd Jul 1913
Thompson	Charles			Feb 1928
Thompson	Frank	Egerton 16/5/1901		Swindon Town Aug 1928
Thompson	George Herbert	Maltby 15/9/1926		Huddersfield Town guest Sep 1944
Thompson	Leslie			Leeds Utd May 1940
Thompson	Oliver	Wheatley Hill 11/5/1900	24/7/1975	York City Jun 1932
Thompson	Simon Lee	Sheffield 27/2/1970		Scarborough Jul 1995
Thompson	Steven James	Oldham 2/11/1964		Rotherham Utd Jun 2000
Thompson	Tyrone I'yungo B	Sheffield 8/5/1982		Scarborough Aug 2000
Thompstone	Ian Philip	Manchester 17/1/1971		Exeter City Jul 1992
Thornber	Stephen John	Dewsbury 11/10/1965		Juniors Jan 1983
				Scunthorpe Utd Mar 1996
Thornley	Benjamin Lindsay	Bury 21/4/1975		Mar 2004
Threlfall	Joseph Richard	Ashton 5/3/1916	1994	Mossley Oct 1947
Thurlow	Alexander Charles Edward	Depwade 24/2/1922	1956	Huddersfield Town guest Sep 1944
Thwaites	Peter	Batley 21/8/1936		Swillington Feb 1961
Tilley	Peter	Lurgan 13/1/1930	11/8/2008	Bury Jul 1958
Timmons	John	Manchester 1/7/1960		Macclesfield Town Aug 1993
Timons	Christopher Bryan	Longworth 8/12/1974		Mansfield Town loan Aug 1995
Tolson	Neil	Walsall 25/10/1973		Kettering Town Mar 2003
Tomlinson	Francis	Manchester 5/1/1926		Stalybridge Celtic May 1950
Tomlinson	Robert Windle	Blackburn 4/6/1924	1996	Mossley Jun 1951
Topping	Harry (Henry)	Kearsley 21/9/1913	2001	Bristol Rov guest Nov 1943
Torpey	Stephen Robert	Liverpool 16/9/1981		FC United of Manchester Aug 2006
Toulson	Ryan	Dewsbury 18/11/1985		Trainee 2002
Toze	Edward	Manchester 6/3/1923	1987	Aug 1950
Tozer	Lewis Michael	Greenwich 12/8/1984		Leicester City loan Sep 2003
Trainer	John (Jack)	Glasgow 14/7/1952		Cork Hibernians Aug 1976
Treasure	Charles James	Farrington Gurney 1/9/1896	1985	Bristol City Jun 1922
Trodden	John Joseph	Sheffield 1/11/1912	1995	Preston NE guest Aug 1942
Trotman	Neal Anthony	Levenshulme 26/4/1987		Oldham Ath loan Jan 2007
				Oldham Ath loan Apr 2007
Trotter	Michael	Hartlepool 27/10/1969		Buxton Dec 1994
Tuck	Lee Andrew	Halifax 30/6/1988		Trainee Nov 2004
Tunstall	Fred	Darfield 28/5/1897	21/7/1971	Sheffield Utd Feb 1933
Turnbull	Alexander	1889		Nov 1919
Turnbull	Frederick	Wallsend 28/8/1946		Aston Villa loan Oct 1969
Turner	Alan	Sheffield 22/9/1935		Sheffield Utd Jun 1958
Turner	Eric	Huddersfield 13/1/1921	1993	Wooldale May 1946
Turner	Hugh	Wigan 6/8/1904	1997	Fulham guest Mar 1940

HALIFAX TOWN PLAYERS 1911-2008

To	League A	S	G	CONF A	S	G	FA Cup A	S	G	FL Cup A	S	G
cs 2003												
cs 1915												
Stalybridge Cel Nov 1994				7	1	0	0	0	0			
West Vale Ramblers Dec 1911												
York City May 1913												
cs 1929	4	0	0				15	0	0	0	0	0
cs	3	0	0				1	0	0	0	0	0
cs 1952	8	0	1				0	0	0	0	0	0
Whitby Town Aug 2002	20	4	1				1	0	0	1	0	0
cs 2006												
Barnsley Jul 1928	14	0	0				0	0	0	0	0	0
	8	0	2				0	0	0	0	0	0
cs 1979												
Crewe Alex Sep 1963	36	0	22				2	0	0	1	0	1
Scarborough Dec 1999	18	0	4				2	0	1	2	0	1
cs 1945												
cs 1937	4	0	0				0	0	0	0	0	0
cc Dec 1951	8	0	0				0	0	0	0	0	0
Bradford City Dec 1967	173	0	16				9	0	2	7	0	3
cs 1929	6	0	1				0	0	0	0	0	0
cs 1946							1	0	0			
Kettering Town Jul 2008				10	14	1	1	1	0			
cs 1949	2	0	0				0	0	0	0	0	0
Nov 1911												
cs 1932	7	0	0				0	0	0	0	0	0
Clapton Orient Jul 1935	32	0	0				2	0	0	0	0	0
West Vale Ramblers Dec 1911												
Grantham Feb 1929	13	0	3				1	0	0	0	0	0
Nuneaton Bor Jun 1999	37	1	5	41	0	2	5	0	0	4	0	0
Southport Jul 1960	20	0	5				0	0	0	0	0	0
	15	2	0				1	0	0	2	0	1
Bamber Bridge cs 1993												
Runcorn cs 1938	50	0	0				0	0	0	0	0	0
cs 1914												
cs 1928												
cs 1929	19	0	0				0	0	0	0	0	0
Chesterfield trainer cs 1933	41	0	1				6	0	0	0	0	0
Dagenham & Red Dec 1995				19	1	0	1	0	0			
Leigh RMI Jul 2000	35	1	2				1	0	0	1	0	0
Crawley Town Jun 2007				72	6	1	4	0	0			
Scunthorpe Utd Mar 1993	31	0	9				1	0	0	1	1	0
Swansea City Aug 1988	94	10	4	1	0	0	9	1	1	3	1	1
cs 1996												
Mar 2004				1	2	0	0	0	0			
Wellington Town cs 1948	30	0	0				1	0	0	0	0	0
ret Nov 1961	2	0	0				0	0	0	0	0	0
Mossley cs 1963	183	0	17				9	0	3	2	0	0
Witton Alb Aug 1993				14	0	0	0	0	0			
Hyde Utd Jul 2003				2	1	0	0	0	0			
cs 1951	14	0	4				1	0	0	0	0	0
Ashton Utd Aug 1952	8	0	0				0	0	0	0	0	0
Stalybridge Celtic Feb 2008				33	16	9	4	0	0			
Altrincham Dec 2007				28	9	0	2	2	0			
cs 1951	5		0				0	0	0	0	0	0
				2	1	0	0	0	0			
cs 1979	101	4	5				5	0	0	7	0	0
Taunton Utd 1923	8	0	0				0	0	0	0	0	0
				11	0	2	0	0	0			
VS Rugby Nov 1996				62	3	4	2	0	0			
Bradford PA 2005												
Boston Utd Aug 1936	105	0	40				7	0	1	0	0	0
Dec 1919												
	7	0	0				0	0	0	0	0	0
cs 1959	7	0	0				0	0	0	0	0	0
Mossley cs 1947	7	0	0				0	0	0	0	0	0

HALIFAX TOWN: THE COMPLETE RECORD

Surname	Forenames	Born	Died	From
Turner	Ian	Middlesbrough 17/1/1953		Walsall loan Jan 1981
Twist	Franklin	Liverpool 2/11/1940		Bury Jul 1963
Uhlenbeek	Gustav Reinier	Paramaribo 20/8/1970		Mansfield Town Aug 2006
Valentine	Albert Finch	Higher Ince, Wigan 3/6/1907	12/3/1990	Macclesfield Town Jul 1934
Vallis	Gilbert Arthur	Bristol 1/1/1898	1962	Bridgend Town Jun 1922
Veitch	Thomas	Edinburgh 16/10/1949	1987	Denver (NASL) Aug 1975
Verity	David Anthony	Halifax 21/9/1949		Scunthorpe Utd Sep 1968
Verity	Kevin Patrick	Halifax 16/3/1940		Juniors Aug 1958
Vernon	Thomas Royston	Holywell 14/4/1937	5/12/1993	Stoke City loan Jan 1970
Vesey	Kieron Gerard	Manchester 24/11/1966		Trainee Feb 1983
Waddell	William	Forth 7/3/1921	13/10/1992	Rangers guest Apr 1942
Waddington	Abraham	Clayton 4/2/1893	28/10/1959	Bradford City Mar 1922
Waddle	Alan Robert	Wallsend 9/6/1954		Wallsend BC Oct 1971
Wagstaffe	Edward Herbert	Bethnal Green 1885		Sheffield Utd cs 1912
Wainwright	Derek	Bradford 26/9/1944		Lightcliffe Oct 1962
Wainwright	Neil	Warrington 4/11/1977		Sunderland loan Oct 2000
Waites	Sydney Hastings	Gateshead 20/9/1901		Newark Town Sep 1925
Walden	Harold Adrian	Umballa, India 10/10/1887	2/12/1955	Army Nov 1911
Walker				May 1921
Walker	Adam	Beverley 16/7/1988		CofEx Mar 2005
Walker	Harold	Leeds		Feb 1924
Walker	Robert Geoffrey	Bradford 29/9/1926	1997	Bradford guest Apr 1942
Walker	Steven	Ilkeston 25/12/1963		Oct 1981
Wallace	John			Partick Thist guest Oct 1943
Wallace	Robert	Huddersfield 14/2/1948		Huddersfield Town Mar 1967
Walmsley	J			Preston NE guest Oct 1943
Walsh	Charles	Glossop 1/11/1899		Stalybridge Cel Aug 1924
Walshaw	Philip Desmond	Leeds 16/4/1929		Sep 1946
Ward	Stephen Charles	Derby 21/7/1959		Nortahmpton Town Jun 1980
Wardle	George	Kibblesworth 24/9/1919	1991	Exeter City loan Sep 1940
Waring	Thomas Allen	Preston 3/8/1929	1972	Burnley Jul 1954
Waters	Samuel	Croy 31/5/1917	1975	Third Lanark Jul 1946
Watkinson	William Wainwright	Prescot 16/3/1922	2/2001	Accrington Stanley Aug 1954
Watmough				Idle Apr 1920
Watson	Albert	Felling-on-Tyne 19/8/1902		Blackpool Jul 1936
Watson	Alexander	Stirling 2/8/1889		Pontypridd Dec 1921
Watson	Andrew Anthony	Leeds 1/4/1967		Harrogate Town Aug 1988
Watson	Garry	Bradford 7/10/1955		Bradford City Jul 1984
Watson	George William	Tyneside 1907		Partick Thist Oct 1933
Watson	Willie	Bolton-on-Dearne 7/3/1920	24/4/2004	Sunderland Nov 1954
Wdowczyk	Christopher Stefan	Huddersfield 2/8/1989		Trainee Mar 2005
Webster	Colin	Halifax 5/3/1930		May 1950
Wellock	Maurice	Bradford 16/6/1902	1967	Bradford City Dec 1919
				Darlington Jun 1932
Wesley	John Crawshey	Cheltenham 19/1/1908		Bradford guest Feb 1940
Westlake	Brian	Newcastle-under-Lyme 19/9/1943		Doncaster Rov Jan 1964
Westlake	Francis Arthur	Bramborough 11/8/1915		Sheffield Wed Jun 1950
Whalley	John William	Bradford 17/2/1897	1972	Sheffield Wed Apr 1921
Wheelhouse	Ben	Rothwell 23/9/1902	20/6/1985	Rothwell Ath Mar 1923
				Denaby Utd Sep 1926
White	Barry James	Beverley 30/7/1950		Hull City Jun 1970
White	Malcolm	Wolverhampton 24/4/1941		Bradford City Nov 1965
Whitehead	Alan	Bury 20/11/1956		York City Aug 1988
Whitehead	George			Barnoldswick Utd Aug 1913
				Hebden Bridge Apr 1914
Whitehead	Philip Matthew	Halifax 17/12/1969		Trainee Aug 1986
				Barnsley loan Mar 1991
Whitehouse	James			guest 1942
Whitehouse	Mark Stephen	Pontefract 6/9/1984		Ossett Alb Feb 2008
Whitelaw	George	Paisley 1/1/1937	8/1/2004	Queen's Park Rang Nov 1959
Whiteley	Andrew Mark	Sowerby Bridge 1/8/1961		Aug 1979
Whiteside	Ernest	Lytham 1/2/1890		Shelbourne Aug 1920
Whiting				Apr 1920
Whittingham	Alfred	Altofts 19/6/1914	1993	Huddersfield Town Mar 1949
Whyte	James			Leith Ath cs 1912
Widdowfield	Edward	Hetton-le-Hole 25/3/1915	8/11/1983	Huddersfield Town Nov 1936
				War
Wilbourn	Henry	Eckington 10/2/1905	1991	Watford Jul 1928
Wild	George Henry	Sowerby Bridge 31/8/1887	1970	Sowerby Br Inst Aug 1911
				Bradford City Sep 1914
Wild	James			guest Sep 1945
Wild	Robert Durham	Shipley 13/9/1895	1/12/1939	Nelson Jun Sep 1922
Wilder	Christopher John	Stocksbridge 23/9/1967		Brighton & HA Oct 1999
Wildman	Walter Ross	Wombwell 22/4/1919	1972	Torquay Utd guest Jan 1943
Wilkes	David Allan	Barnsley 10/3/1964		Barnsley loan Mar 1983
Wilkie	John Carlin	Dundee 1/7/1947		Ross County Jan 1973
Wilkinson	Albert	Barnsley 3/11/1928		Denaby Utd Jul 1952

HALIFAX TOWN PLAYERS 1911-2008

To	League A	League S	League G	CONF A	CONF S	CONF G	FA Cup A	FA Cup S	FA Cup G	FL Cup A	FL Cup S	FL Cup G
	5	0	0				0	0	0	0	0	0
Tranmere Rov Jul 1965	64	0	10				2	0	0	4	0	0
cs 2007				23	7	3	0	0	0			
Stockport Co Jun 1937	114	0	88				6	0	2	0	0	0
cs 1923	12	0	1				0	0	0	0	0	0
Hartlepool Utd Aug 1976	20	2	0				2	0	0	0	0	0
Yeovil Town cs 1973	64	14	5				4	0	0	2	1	0
Ilkeston Town cs 1960	13	0	6				1	0	0	0	0	0
	4	0	0				0	0	0	0	0	0
cs 1984	2	0	0				0	0	0	0	0	0
Bradford City cs 1923	7	0	0				0	0	0	0	0	0
Liverpool Jun 1973	33	6	4				1	0	0	0	0	0
Scunthorpe Utd Nov 1912												
cs 1963												
	13	0	0				1	0	0	0	0	0
Stockport Co cs 1928	96	0	14				2	0	0	0	0	0
Bradford City Dec 1911												
cs 1921												
cs 2005												
cs 1924	5	0	0				0	0	0	0	0	0
cs 1982	0	1	0				0	0	0	0	0	0
Chester Jun 1972	190	11	16				10	1	2	9	1	2
Preston NE cs 1925	19	0	0				1	0	0	0	0	0
cs 1947	6	0	1				0	0	0	0	0	0
Kettering Town cs 1986	233	13	17				6	1	1	12	0	0
cs 1955	12	0	0				0	0	0	0	0	0
	25	0	9				4	0	2	0	0	0
Prescot Cables Jul 1956	60	0	24				4	0	1	0	0	0
cs 1920												
Gateshead cs 1937	29	0	2				1	0	0	0	0	0
cs 1922	8	0	0				0	0	0	0	0	0
Swansea City Jul 1990	78	8	15				6	0	1	5	1	2
Whitby Town cs 1985	21	0	0				1	0	0	3	1	0
rel Nov 1933	2	0	0				0	0	0	0	0	0
Apr 1956	33	0	1				4	0	1	0	0	0
cs 2006												
Rochdale Sep 1951	16	0	1				1	0	0	0	0	0
Blackpool Jul 1922	115	0	24				11	0	4	0	0	0
Trainer Oct 1933												
Tranmere Rov Sep 1966	100	0	27				2	0	2	4	0	1
cs 1951	2	0	0				0	0	0	0	0	0
cs 1926	141	0	17				13	0	2	0	0	0
Burnley Mar 1924	190	0	4				18	0	0	0	0	0
Rochdale Aug 1932												
Goole Town 1975	23	0	0				3	0	0	0	0	0
Los Angeles Wolves Mar 1968	100	0	0				8	0	0	3	0	0
cc Apr 1989	10	1	1				0	0	0	2	0	0
Mytholmroyd Dec 1913												
cs 1915												
Barnsley Mar 1990	51	0	0				4	0	0	2	0	0
Guiseley cs 2008				0	4	1	0	0	0			
Carlisle Utd Feb 1961	52	0	22				3	0	1	1	0	0
cs 1982	30	16	1				1	0	0	0	0	0
Rochdale cs 1921												
cs 1920												
cs 1949	39	0	9				1	0	0	0	0	0
cs 1913												
cs 1939	40	0	23				6	0	6	0	0	0
cs 1929	7	0	0				1	0	0	0	0	0
Bradford City Dec 1913	13	0	2				22	0	15	0	0	0
cc 1922												
cs 1924	51	0	0				7	0	1	0	0	0
ret Jul 2001	51	0	1				4	0	0	1	0	0
	4	0	0				0	0	0	0	0	0
Ross County May 1974	29	8	8				0	0	0	1	0	0
Rotherham Utd Jul 1953	14	0	2				1	0	0	0	0	0

Surname	Forenames	Born	Died	From
Wilkinson	K			guest Feb 1944
Wilkinson	Stephen J	Halifax 6/8/1946		St Mary's Aug 1963
Williams	D			Bury guest Mar 1943
Williams	Eric	Manchester 10/7/1921		Mossley Oct 1951
Williams	Frank (Tiny)	Halifax 23/5/1921	1999	Boothtown Aug 1952
Williams	Idris			Burton Town Jun 1935
Williams	Marc Lloyd	Bangor 8/2/1973		Bangor City Jul 1998
Williams	Michael Anthony	Bradford 21/11/1969		Sheffield Wed loan Dec 1992
				Oxford Utd Nov 1999
Willis	James Anthony	Liverpool 12/7/1968		Trainee Jul 1986
Willis	John	Sheffield 1916		St Vincent (Sheffield) cs 1937
Willis	Paul Edward	Liverpool 24/1/1970		Trainee Aug 1987
Willis	Robert Smith	Tynemouth 31/1/1901		Rochdale Aug 1926
Willis	Scott Leon	Liverpool 20/2/1982		Lincoln City Jun 2004
Wills	David John	Ashton-under-Lyme 9/3/1979		Manchester City Dec 1998
Wilmot	Richard Gary	Matlock 29/8/1969		Scunthorpe Utd Dec 1993
Wilson				Army guest Jan 1943
Wilson	James E	Garforth 1/1/1909		Leeds Utd Mar 1930
Wilson	Owen Lee	Mansfield 23/5/1972		Telford Utd Aug 1995
Wilson	Paul Anthony	Bradford 2/8/1968		Northampton Town Dec 1991
Wilson	R			Airdrie guest Nov 1942
Wilson	T			Barnsley guest Sep 1940
Winder	Nathan James	Barnsley 17/2/1983		Trainee 2001
Winter	Wallace	Todmorden 25/5/1918	8/1999	Aug 1938
Wishart	James	Darvel 1886		Haslingden Jan 1914
Woffinden	Richard Shaw	Rotherham 20/2/1917	1987	Barnsley guest Feb 1944
Womble	Trevor	Durham 7/6/1951		Rotherham Utd loan Mar 1973
Wood	Graham	Doncaster 10/2/1933		Wolverhampton Wand Jun 1953
Wood	Jamie	Salford 21/9/1978		Hull City Aug 2001
Wood	Michael James	Bury 3/7/1952		Bradford City Aug 1982
Wood	Simon	Halifax 2/7/1985		Trainee 2002
Wood	Stanley	Winsford 1/7/1905	17/2/1967	West Brom Alb Jun 1938
Woodhead	D			guest Nov 1943
Woodhouse	Roland Thomas	Leyland 15/1/1897	1969	Wrexham Jun 1930
Woods	Andrew	Colchester 15/1/1976		Oldham Ath Aug 1995
Woods	John	1896		Stalybridge Cel Aug 1921
Woodward	Andrew Stephen	Stockport 23/9/1973		Sheffield Utd Jun 2001
Woodward	William Robinson	Knaresborough 1892		Bradford City Sep 1912
Wooler	Michael Graham	Huddersfield 23/10/1944		Huddersfield Town Dec 1964
Woolgar				West Riding Regt Aug 1920
Worboys	Ronald Tudor	Halifax 1/8/1923	1/1993	Aug 1944
Worthington	David	Halifax 28/3/1945		Juniors Apr 1962
				Grimsby Town loan Oct 1973
Worthington	Eric	Manchester 1/7/1919	11/1971	Manchester NE Aug 1939
Worthington	Gary Lee	Cleethorpes 10/11/1966		Exeter City Aug 1994
				Dagenham & Red Aug 1996
Worthington	Peter Robert (Bob)	Halifax 22/4/1947		Appren May 1965
Wray	John Gordon	Mytholmroyd 7/7/1941		Stainland Utd Sep 1964
Wrigglesworth	John Lancelot	Halifax 4/7/1924		Watford Mar 1940
Wright	Albert			Mar 1923
Wright	Jake Maxwell	Keighley 11/3/1986		Bradford City loan Aug 2005
				Bradford City Jun 2006
Wright	Paul Antony	Barking 29 7 1969		Oct 1992
Wright	Peter David	Preston 15/8/1982		Newcastle Utd Aug 2001
Wroe				Jan 1912
Wynn	George Arthur	Treflach 28/10 1886	28/10 1966	Llandudno Town Jan 1922
Yates	Adam	Stoke 28/5/1983		Crewe Alex loan Nov 2003
Yates	Stephen	Bristol 29/1/1970		Scarborough Jan 2006
Young	Alfred	Sunderland 4/11/1905	30/8/1977	Huddersfield Town guest Dec 1944
Young	Gregory James	Doncaster 25/4/1983		Grimsby Town Feb 2005
Young	Kenneth	Halifax 11/6/1930		Ovenden Nov 1949

KEY: cc contract cancelled, cs close season. rel released. ret retired

HALIFAX TOWN PLAYERS 1911-2008

To	League A	S	G	CONF A	S	G	FA Cup A	S	G	FL Cup A	S	G
Hallam cs 1964	2	0	0				0	0	0	1	0	0
Mossley cs 1954	111	0	0				6	0	0	0	0	0
Bacup Borough cs 1948	4	0	0				0	0	0	0	0	0
Rochdale May 1937	14	0	0				0	0	0	0	0	0
York City Mar 1999	18	6	6				1	0	0	0	1	0
	11	1	1				1	0	0	0	0	0
Worksop Town 2000												
Stockport Co Dec 1987												
cs 1938												
Darlington Mar 1989	1	5	0				0	0	0	1	0	0
Rochdale cs 1927	2	0	0				0	0	0	0	0	0
Runcorn FC Halton Jan 2005				2	0	0	0	0	0			
Altrincham 1999												
Hitchin Town Feb 1995				22	1	0	1	0	0			
Shrewsbury Town Aug 1930	8	0	0				0	0	0	0	0	0
Dagenham & Red Oct 1995				2	3	0	0	0	0			
Burnley Feb 1993	45	0	7				1	0	0	2	0	0
Chesterfield 2002	0	1	0				0	0	0	0	0	0
cs 1939	2	0	0				0	0	0	0	0	0
ret Dec 1919												
	9	1	2				0	0	0	0	0	0
Scarborough Apr 1955	19	0	3				0	0	0	0	0	0
Swansea City Jul 2002	10	6	0				1	0	1	1	0	0
Dudley Hill Ath cs 1984	80	1	2				2	0	0	2	2	0
Liversedge cs 2005												
cs 1946	35	0	6				6	0	3	0	0	0
Chorley cs 1931	13	0	2				3	0	0	0	0	0
Doncaster Rov Aug 1998				64	0	0	1	0	0			
cs 1922	21	0	12				0	0	0	0	0	0
Northwich Vic cs 2002	29	1	1				2	0	0	1	0	0
Castleford Town Nov 1912												
Gainsborough Trin cs 1968	51	7	7				0	0	0	3	0	0
cs 1921												
cs 1945												
Barrow Jul 1964	42	0	9				1	0	0	2	0	1
cs 1946												
Dagenham & Red Dec 1995				65	11	15	5	1	3			
cs 1997												
Middlesbrough Aug 1966	12	0	0				0	0	0	0	0	0
cs 1965	7	0	0				0	0	0	0	0	0
Rochdale cs 1947	10	0	1				0	0	0	0	0	0
Blackburn Rov cs 1923	1	0	0				0	0	0	0	0	0
				66	9	2	4	1	0			
Crawley Town Jun 2008												
Oct 1992	1	0	0				0	0	0	0	0	0
Burscough cs 2002	3	11	0				0	2	0	0	1	0
cs 1912												
Mansfield Town Feb 1922	1	0	0				0	0	0	0	0	0
				12	0	0	0	0	0			
Morecambe Aug 2006				0	3	0	0	0	0			
Altrincham Jan 2008				58	9	3	3	0	0			
Sep 1953	1	0	0				0	0	0	0	0	0

FC Halifax Town Players

Surname	Forenames	Born	From
Adams	Lincoln Levi S	Huddersfield 19/9/1979	Bradford PA Jul 2008
Allen	Damien Samuel	Cheadle 1/8/1986	Morecambe Oct 2008
Aspin	Neil	Gateshead 12/4/1965	Harrogate Town Jun 2009
Baker	Thomas	Salford 28/3/1985	Bradford PA Oct 2008
Barnes	Bradley Andrew	Trafford 12/12/1988	Southport 19/3/2010 loan
Barnes	Michael Thomas	Chorley 24/6/1988	Southport Jan 2009
Barras	Anthony	Billingham 29/3/1971	Witton Albion Jul 2008
Bower	Mark James	Bradford 23/1/1980	Darlington 21 June 2010
Brown	David	Tadcaster 29/5/1989	Guiseley Jan 2009
Brown	Junior	Crewe 7/5/1989	Crewe Alexandra Jul 2008
Carney	Kevin Jason	Halifax 21/9/1991	Under 19s
Clegg	Ross Thomas	Manchester 30/5/1981	Bradford Park Avenue Jul 2008
Codman	Daniel	Halifax 1/6/1990	Huddersfield Town Jul 2009
Collins	Paul Joesph	Manchester 19/7/1986	Woodley Sports Dec 2008
Coo	Cavelle Stefan	Manchester 7/8/1987	Droylsden Sep 2008
Coduri	Jordan James	Huddersfield 13/12/1992	Under 19s Mar 2011
Crossley	Ryan Stuart	Halifax 12/11/1980	Guiseley Jul 2009
Daniel	Colin Alan	Nottingham 15/2/1988	Crewe Alex on loan Oct 2008
Davidson	Daniel David	Halifax 18/7/1984	Harrogate Railway Sep 2008
Dean	James	Blackburn 12/5/1985	Bury Jul 2009
Dean	Luke James	Leeds 14/5/1991	Bradford City loan 15 Dec 2009
Eastwood	Scott	Halifax 30/11/1992	Under 19s Feb 2011
Ellington	Lee Simon	Bradford 3/7/1980	Harrogate Town loan Mar 2011
Ellis	Daniel James	Stockport 18/11/1988	Droylsden Aug 2008
Ellison	Craig	Manchester 23/10/1987	Alsager Town Oct 2008
Evans	Paul Simon	Oswestry 1/9/1974	Oxford United Jan 2009
Fry	George Christy	Halifax 12/3/1993	Under 19s Dec 2009
Garner	Simon	Blackburn 15/8/1982	Clitheroe May 2010
Gedman	Paul Jonathan	Wigan 14/6/1981	Droylsden Sep 2008
Gill	Kurtis	Liverpool 16/2/1989	Alsager Town Nov 2008
Gray	Nicholas	Harrogate 17/10/1985	Harrogate Town Jul 2009
Gregory	Brett Lee	Sheffield 26/8/1988	Mansfield Town loan Mar 2010
			Mansfield Town Dec 2010
Harban	Thomas John	Barnsley 12/11/1985	Halifax Town Jul 2008
Hardy	Aaron	South Elmsall 26/5/1986	Harrogate Town Jul 2009
Harrison	Paul	01/01/1985	Leeds Carnegie Sep 2009
Hedge	Jonathan Trevor	Rotherham 19/7/1988	Harrogate Town cs 2009
Heffernan	Sanchez Saxon	Bradford 23/9/1991	Under 19s 2009
Hilton	Anthony	Leeds 1/11/1989	Leeds Carnegie Sep 2008
Hinsley	Luke	Doncaster 12/5/1990	Yorkshire Main Aug 2008
Hogan	Liam Anthony	Salford 8/2/1989	Woodley Sports May 2010
Hogan	Scott Andrew	Salford 13/4/1992	Woodley Sports Nov 2010
Holland	Daniel	Mansfield 18/2/1983	Eastwood Town Jul 2008
Horne	Louis Peter	Bradford 28/5/1991	Bradford City loan 26 Nov 2010
Hotte	Mark Stephen	Bradford 27/9/1978	Bradford PA Mar 2009
Jemson	Nigel Bradley	Preston 10/10/1969	Alfreton Town Jul 2008
Jerome	Samuel Benjamin R	Huddersfield 31/8/1991	Lincoln City Aug 2009
Jones	Kingsley Benjamin	Bradford 2/10/1982	Harrogate Railway Ath Jul 2008
Jones	Matthew	Halifax 12/3/1992	Under 19s Feb 2011
Joynes	Nathan	Hoyland 7/8/1985	Stalybridge Celtic 20/03/2009
Kennedy	Jon	Rotherham 30/11/1980	Droylsden Aug 2008
Keris	Hayden James	Halifax 5/1/1992	Under 19s Dec 2009
King	Kristofer Keith	Littleborough 1/9/1989	Wigan Athletic Jul 2008
Lee	Andrew	Bradford 18/8/1982	Ossett Town loan Feb 2010
Leitch-Smith	Ajay	Crewe 6/3/1990	Crewe Alex loan Nov 2008
Lowe	Daniel	Pontefract 03/07/1985	Harrogate Railway Jul 2009
Marshall	Richard James	Dewsbury 01/05/1986	Harrogate Town 2009
Mawson	Craig John	Skipton 16/5/1979	Halifax Town Jul 2008
Meadowcroft	Daniel Brian	Manchester 22/5/1985	Droylsden Oct 2008
Metcalfe	Scott	Manchester 28/3/1988	Trafford June 2010
Milne	Andrew	York 30/9/1990	Barrow 11 Jan 2011

FC HALIFAX TOWN PLAYERS 2008-2011

2008-11

To	League A	S	G	FA Cup A	S	G	FL Cup A	S	G
Hyde United cs 2009	33	3	3	4	0	0	1	0	0
Bury Jul 2009	24	6	0	0	0	0			
	106	0	18	9	0	2	3	1	0
	3	0	0	0	0	0			
AFC Fylde Aug 2009	9	5	3	0	0	0			
ret cs 2009	20	0	1	1	1	0			
Guiseley May 2011	41	0	1	4	0	0	2	0	0
Eastwood Town Jun 2009	5	10	1	0	0	0			
Northwich Victoria cs 2009	29	4	8	2	0	0	0	1	0
	3	0	0	0	0	0			
Wakefield FC Mar 2010	13	0	0	3	1	0	3	0	0
New Mills 2009	9	0	1	0	0	0			
Curzon Ashton cs 2009	32	0	1	2	0	0	1	0	0
ret Sep 2010	20	0	2	5	0	0	1	2	1
	5	0	4	0	0	0	1	0	1
Brighouse Town 2009	0	1	0	0	0	0			
	59	4	42	7	1	3	4	2	6
	1	0	0	0	0	0			
	1	3	0	0	0	0			
Salford City Jan 2009	1	8	1	0	1	0	0	1	0
Garforth Town cs 2009	2	0	0	0	0	0			
Farsley Celtic Aug 2009	9	4	0	0	0	0			
	32	6	4	3	0	0	2	0	0
Salford City Sep 2009	14	6	6	2	0	2			
Alsager Town Nov 2008									
	45	8	20	6	2	3	5	0	3
	31	2	22	0	0	0			
Ossett Albion 2009	4	0	0	2	0	0			
	75	0	1	7	0	0	5	0	0
Harrogate Railway Nov 2009	0	1	0	0	2	0	1	2	1
	77	0	0	7	0	0	6	0	0
	0	1	0	0	0	0			
Wakefield FC Aug 2009	2	6	0	1	1	0	1	0	0
	41	0	2	4	0	0	1	0	0
	6	8	0	0	0	0			
	34	6	18	4	0	1	1	0	0
	1	0	0	0	0	0			
Ossett Town Jul 2010	6	14	0	0	2	0	3	1	0
Arnold Town cs 2009	17	8	8	0	4	0	0	1	0
	0	1	0	0	0	0			
Harrogate Railway Aug 2008	0	1	0	0	0	0			
Matlock Town	8	0	2	0	0	0			
Worksop Town Jun 2009	33	0	0	4	0	0	1	0	0
Leigh Genesis Jan 2009	6	4	2	4	0	0			
	3	3	0	0	0	0			
	4	0	0	0	0	0			
	59	0	5	3	0	0	3	0	0
Harrogate Town Mar 2011	43	18	24	6	1	4	5	0	0
Droylsden Aug 2008	1	0	0	0	0	0			
Northwich Victoria 13/3/09	21	0	2	0	0	0	1	0	0
	7	11	1	2	2	1	1	1	0
	7	2	0	0	0	0			

Surname	Forenames	Born	From
Moore	Peter Francis	Liverpool 13/8/1988	Wigan Ath Aug 2008
Morning	Adam Mark	Oldham 7/12/1986	New Mills Jul 2008
Nogan	Lee Martin	Cardiff 21/5/1969	Whitby Town Jan 2011
Payne	Stephen John	Castleford 1/8/1975	Stalybridge Celtic Jul 2008
Peers	Mark	St Helens 14/5/1984	Fleetwood Town Feb 2009
Penford	Thomas James	Leeds 5/1/1985	Farsley Celtic Oct 2009
Phelan	Scott Richard	Liverpool 13/3/1988	Bradford City Sep 2008
Plummer	Matthew Robert	Hull 18/1/1989	North Ferriby Utd May 2010
Proffitt	Dorryl Sefton	Hanley 2/5/1982	Alsager Town Aug 2008
Richardson	Luke	Bingley 11/7/1986	Harrogate Railway Nov 2009
Riley	James Michael	Keighley 02/05/1985	Harrogate Railway 23/3/09
Roberts	Joseph	09/09/1989	Blackburn Rovers Sep 2009
Ross	Neil James	West Bromwich 10/8/1982	Buxton Jul 2008
Sanasy	Kevin Roy	Leeds 2/11/1984	Worksop Town Oct 2009
Senior	Philip Anthony	Huddersfield 30/10/1982	Ilkeston Town Jul 2008
Smith	Craig Colin	Wigan 20/12/1984	Manchester City Aug 2008
Smith	Jamie	Sheffield 19/11/1983	Harrogate Town Oct 2009
Smith	Jonathan Robert	Wigan 31/10/1988	Aberdeen Aug 2008
Smith	Luke	24/11/1981	Aug 2009
Smith	Miles Richard J	Bradford 1/2/1990	Scunthorpe Utd Sep 2008
Stott	Ashley	Withington 14/6/1988	Bangor City Aug 2008
Stringer	Luke James	Halifax 14/11/1989	Huddersfield Town Under 19s 2009
Sutton	Ritchie Aidan	Stoke 29/4/1986	Northwich Victoria Dec 2008
Sykes	Paul Kevin	Pontefract 13/1/1977	Stalybridge Celtic Jun 2009
Sugden	Ryan Stephen	Bradford 26/12/1980	Bradford PA Aug 2008
Taylor	Nathan Anthony James	Rochdale 2/4/1990	Clitheroe 2010
Vardy	Jamie	Sheffield 11/1/1987	Stocksbridge Pk Steels May 2010
Villermann	Andrew Sean	Bradford 23/9/1991	Bradford City 20/3/2009 loan
Walker	Justin	Nottingham 6/9/1975	Ilkeston Town Jul 2008
Whitehouse	Mark Stephen	Pontefract 6/9/1984	Bradford PA Aug 2009
Wilde	Michael	Birkenhead 27/8/1983	Fleetwood Town loan Mar 2010
Winter	Harry John Joel	Trafford 16/6/1989	Northwich Victoria loan Jan 2010
			Northwich Victoria Jul 2010
Wood	Simon James	Halifax 2/7/1985	Brighouse Town loan Sep 2009
Woods	Stephen John	Davenham 15/12/1976	Northwich Victoria loan Mar 2011

FC HALIFAX TOWN PLAYERS 2008-2011

To	League			FA Cup			FL Cup		
	A	S	G	A	S	G	A	S	G
Warrington Town Jan 2009	5	3	0	4	0	1	1	0	0
New Mills Oct 2008	1	2	1	2	1	1			
ret Apr 2010	45	2	9	9	0	2	4	0	2
Chester Jul 2010	18	22	7	3	0	0	3	1	0
Guiseley Jul 2010									
Kidderminster Harriers	72	11	6	7	1	1	6	0	0
Bridlington Town 25 Oct 2010	6	1	0	2	0	0			
Witton Albion Aug 2008	1	3	0	0	0	0			
Thackley Sep 2010	5	5	0	0	0	0			
Bradford PA Mar 2011	45	9	0	5	1	0	4	1	0
Clitheroe 2010									
ret 2010	5	4	1	0	1	0			
Bradford PA Dec 2009	0	1	0	0	0	0	1	1	1
	11	0	0	2	0	0			
Harrogate Railway	3	0	0	0	1	0			
AFC Emley Jul 2010	1	3	0	0	0	0	0	1	0
Peterhead Aug 2009	11	8	1	4	0	1	1	0	0
	0	2	0	0	1	0			
Bangor City Jun 2009	29	7	15	4	0	3	1	0	0
Nantwich Town Jun 2009	20	0	2	0	0	0			
Ossett Town Jul 2010	10	4	1	1	0	0			
Northwich Victoria Jan 2011	6	10	2	1	3	3	1	1	0
	32	1	22	2	1	1	1	0	1
	1	0	0	0	0	0			
	7	1	0	4	0	0	1	0	0
North Ferriby Oct 2009	0	5	0	0	2	0	1	0	0
	6	5	5	0	0	0			
	16	1	5	1	0	0			
	6	3	0	0	0	0